W9-BYD-981

EASTERN HEMISPHERE

Prentice Hall

Needham, Massachusetts
Upper Saddle River, New Jersey
Glenview, Illinois

Program Consultants

Heidi Hayes Jacobs

Heidi Hayes Jacobs has served as an educational consultant to more than 1,000 schools across the nation and abroad. Dr. Jacobs served as an adjunct professor in the Department of Curriculum on Teaching at Teachers College, Columbia University. She has written a best-selling book and numerous articles on curriculum reform. She completed her undergraduate studies at the University of Utah in her hometown of Salt Lake City. She received an M.A. from the University of Massachusetts, Amherst, and completed her doctoral work at Columbia University's Teachers College in 1981.

The backbone of Dr. Jacobs' experience comes from her years as a teacher of high school, middle school, and elementary school students. As an educational consultant, she works with K–12 schools and districts on curriculum reform and strategic planning.

Brenda Randolph

Brenda Randolph is the former Director of the Outreach Resource Center at the African Studies Program at Howard University, Washington, D.C. She is the Founder and Director of Africa Access, a bibliographic service on Africa for schools. She received her B.A. in history with high honors from North Carolina Central University, Durham, and her M.A. in African studies with honors from Howard University. She completed further graduate studies at the University of Maryland, College Park, where she was awarded a Graduate Fellowship.

Brenda Randolph has published numerous articles in professional journals and bulletins. She currently serves as library media specialist in Montgomery County Public Schools, Maryland.

Michal L. LeVasseur

Michal LeVasseur is an educational consultant in the field of geography. She is an adjunct professor of geography at the University of Alabama, Birmingham, and serves with the Alabama Geographic Alliance. Her undergraduate and graduate work is in the fields of anthropology (B.A.), geography (M.A.), and science education (Ph.D.).

Dr. LeVasseur's specialization has moved increasingly into the area of geography education. In 1996, she served as Director of the National Geographic Society's Summer Geography Workshop. As an educational consultant, she has worked with the National Geographic Society as well as with schools to develop programs and curricula for geography.

Special Program Consultant

Yvonne S. Gentzler, Ph.D.
Iowa State University
College of Family and Consumer Sciences
Ames, Iowa

ISBN 0-13-063007-1

1 2 3 4 5 6 7 8 9 10 06 05 04 03 02

Content Consultants for the World Explorer Program

Africa
Barbara Brown
African Studies Center
Boston University
Boston, Massachusetts

Ancient World
Maud Gleason
Department of Classics
Stanford University
Stanford, California

East Asia
Leslie Swartz
Vice President for Program Development and Harvard East Asian Outreach Program at The Children's Museum, Boston
Boston, Massachusetts

Latin America
Daniel Mugan
Center for Latin American Studies
University of Florida
Gainesville, Florida

Middle East
Elizabeth Barlow
Center for Middle Eastern and North African Studies
University of Michigan
Ann Arbor, Michigan

North Africa
Laurence Michalak
Center for Middle East Studies
University of California
Berkeley, California

Religion
Michael Sells
Department of Religion
Haverford College
Haverford, Pennsylvania

Russia, Eastern Europe, Central Asia
Janet Vaillant
Davis Center for Russian Studies
Harvard University
Cambridge, Massachusetts

South Asia
Robert Young
Department of History
West Chester University
West Chester, Pennsylvania

Western Europe
Ruth Mitchell-Pitts
Center for West European Studies
University of North Carolina
Chapel Hill, North Carolina

Teacher Advisory Board

Jerome Balin
Lincoln Junior High School
Naperville, Illinois

Elizabeth Barrett
Tates Creek Middle School
Lexington, Kentucky

Tricia Creasey
Brown Middle School
Thomasville, North Carolina

Patricia H. Guillory
Fulton County Schools
Atlanta, Georgia

Stephanie Hawkins
Oklahoma City Public Schools
Oklahoma City, Oklahoma

Fred Hitz
Wilson Middle School
Muncie, Indiana

Kristi Karis
West Ottawa Public Schools
Holland, Michigan

Peggy Lehman
Carmel Junior High/Carmel-Clay Schools
Carmel, Indiana

Peggy McCarthy
Beulah School
Beulah, Colorado

Cindy McCurdy
Hefner Middle School
Oklahoma City, Oklahoma

Deborah J. Miller
Detroit Public Schools
Detroit, Michigan

Lawrence Peglow
Pittsburgh Public Schools
Pittsburgh, Pennsylvania

Paula Rardin
Riverview Gardens Schools
St. Louis, Missouri

Kent E. Riley
Perry Meridian Middle School
Indianapolis, Indiana

Christy Sarver
Brown Middle School
Thomasville, North Carolina

Lyn Shiver
Northwestern Middle School
Alpharetta, Georgia

Mark Stahl
Longfellow Middle School
Norman, Oklahoma

Table of Contents

GEOGRAPHY Tools and Concepts 1

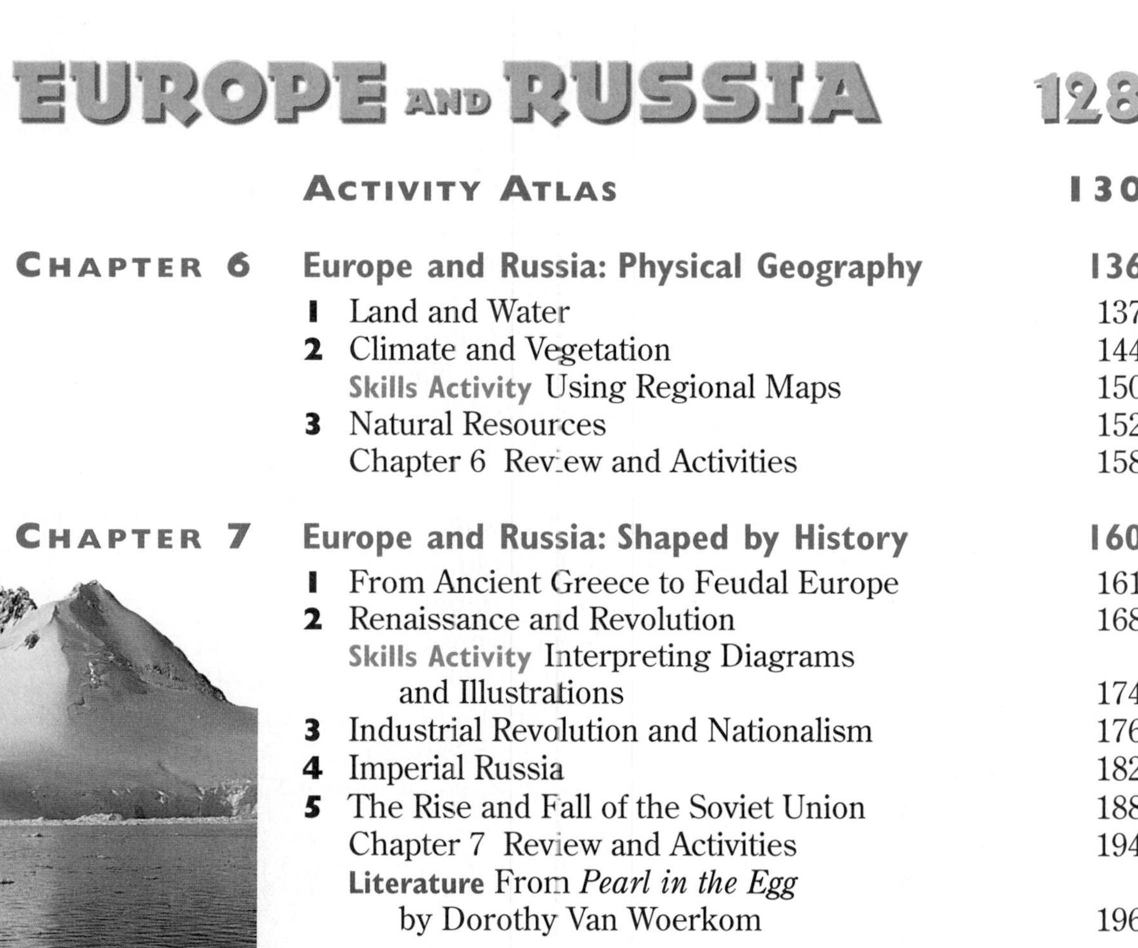

10
EURO CENT
5 EURO
1 EURO
2 EURO
5 EURO CENT
50
EURO CENT

AFRICA 304

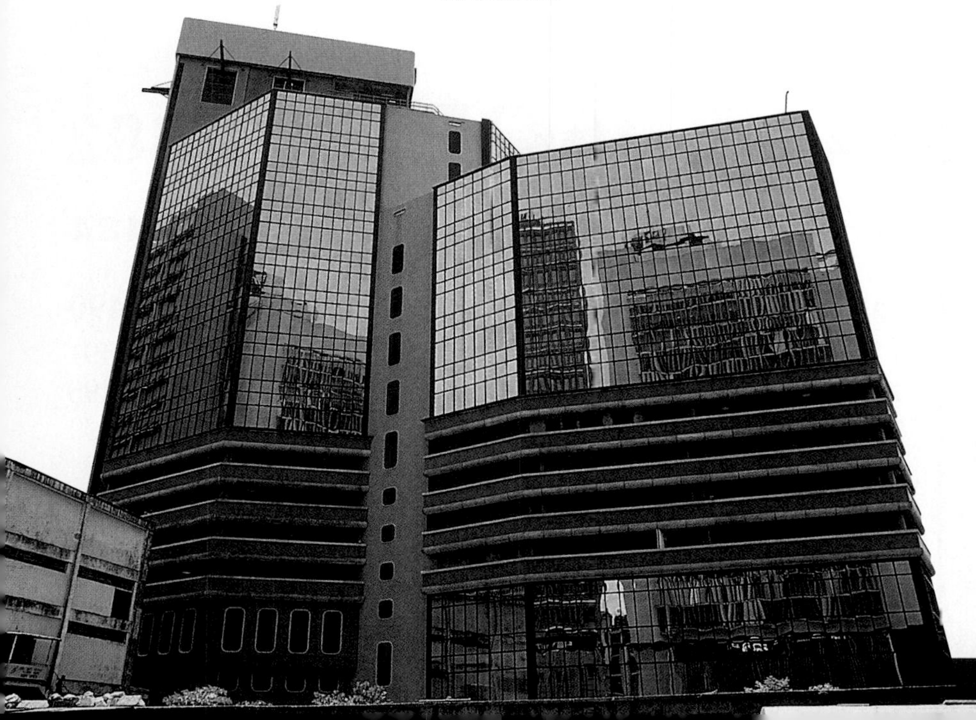

OF SPECIAL INTEREST

A hands-on approach to learning and applying key social studies skills

Step-by-step activities for exploring important topics in the Eastern Hemisphere

Map and statistics for every nation in the Eastern Hemisphere

Profiles of people who made a difference in their countries

Literature selections written by authors from the Eastern Hemisphere

Maps and charts providing a closer look at countries

Detailed drawings show how the use of technology makes countries unique

Views of countries through the eyes of student artists

MAPS

MAPS

CHARTS, GRAPHS, AND TABLES

How can I get the most out of my social studies book? How does my reading relate to my world? Answering questions like these means that you are an active reader, an involved reader. As an active reader, you are in charge of the reading situation!

The following strategies tell how to think and read as an active reader. You don't need to use all of these strategies all the time. Feel free to choose the ones that work best in each reading situation. You might use several at a time, or you might go back and forth among them. They can be used in any order.

Give yourself a purpose

The sections in this book begin with a list called "Questions to Explore." These questions focus on key ideas presented in the section. They give you a purpose for reading. You can create your own purpose by asking questions like these: How does the topic relate to my life? How might I use what I learn at school or at home?

Preview

To preview a reading selection, first read its title. Then look at the pictures and read the captions. Also read any headings in the selection. Then ask yourself: What is the reading selection about? What do the pictures and headings tell about the selection?

Reach into your background

What do you already know about the topic of the selection? How can you use what you know to help you understand what you are going to read?

Ask questions

Suppose you are reading about the continent of South America. Some questions you might ask are: Where is South America? What countries are found there? Why are some of the countries large and others small? Asking questions like these can help you gather evidence and gain knowledge.

Predict

As you read, make a prediction about what will happen and why. Or predict how one fact might affect another fact. Suppose you are reading about South America's climate. You might make a prediction about how the climate affects where people live. You can change your mind as you gain new information.

Connect

Connect your reading to your own life. Are the people discussed in the selection like you or someone you know? What would you do in similar situations? Connect your reading to something you have already read. Suppose you have already read about the ancient Greeks. Now you are reading about the ancient Romans. How are they alike? How are they different?

Visualize

What would places, people, and events look like in a movie or a picture? As you read about India, you could visualize the country's heavy rains. What do they look like? How do they sound? As you read about geography, you could visualize a volcanic eruption.

Respond

Talk about what you have read. What did you think? Share your ideas with your classmates.

Assess yourself

What did you find out? Were your predictions on target? Did you find answers to your questions?

Follow up

Show what you know. Use what you have learned to do a project. When you do projects, you continue to learn.

GEOGRAPHY
TOOLS AND CONCEPTS

Are you curious about our Earth? Do you want to know why some places in the world are cold and some are hot? Have you wondered why more people live in cities and fewer people live in other places? If you answered *yes* to any of these questions, you want to know more about geography.

GUIDING QUESTIONS

The readings and activities in this book will help you discover answers to these Guiding Questions.

1. **GEOGRAPHY** What is the Earth's geography like?
2. **HISTORY** How has the world's population changed over time?
3. **CULTURE** What is a culture?
4. **GOVERNMENT** What types of government exist in the world today?
5. **ECONOMICS** How do people use the world's resources?

PROJECT PREVIEW

You can also discover answers to the Guiding Questions by working on projects. You can find several project possibilities on pages 126–127.

1 What is the Earth's geography like?
2 How has the world's population changed over time?
3 What is a culture?
4 What types of government exist in the world today?
5 How do people use the world's resources?

EXPLORER'S JOURNAL

A journal can be your personal book of discovery. As you explore geography, you can use your journal to keep track of the things you learn and do. You can also record thoughts about your explorations. For your first entry, write about how you can use maps to find your way around.

Discovery Activities About

Geography

Learning about geography tools and concepts means being an explorer, and no explorer would start out without first checking some facts. Use the activities on the following pages to begin exploring the world of geography. They will help you learn what geography is and how it can help you.

▲ Why do people in this place wear this type of clothing?

▼ Why dc relatively few people live in this area?

World: Physical

PLACE

1. Explore the Meaning of Geography Think about the word *geography*. The word part *geo* comes from a Greek word meaning "earth." *Graphy* means "science of," from an earlier word that meant "to write." How would you define *geography*?

People who are interested in geography are very curious about our world. They often ask questions such as "Where are things?" and "Why are they where they are?"

Look at the pictures on these two pages. The question that accompanies each picture is the type of question that geographers ask. For each picture, write another question a geographer might ask.

▲ Why did ancient people in this area become expert sailors?

▶ Why do visitors to this area become short of breath easily?

EUROPE
ITALY
SAHARA
AFRICA
ASIA
AUSTRALIA
ANTARCTICA
Arctic Circle
Tropic of Cancer
Equator
Tropic of Capricorn
Antarctic Circle

0 1,500 3,000 mi
0 1,500 3,000 km

KEY

Elevation

Feet	Meters
Over 13,000	Over 3,960
6,500–13,000	1,980–3,960
1,600–6,500	480–1,980
650–1,600	200–480
0–650	0–200
Below sea level	Below sea level

Robinson Projection

LOCATION

2. What Kinds of Maps Does Geo Leo Need?

Geographers do more than ask questions about the Earth. They also gather, organize, and analyze geographic information. Geographers use many different types of maps to do this work.

Examine the map below and the maps on the next page. Be sure to read the title of each map so you know what the map is about. Then help Geo Leo plan a trip to South Asia, an area that includes the countries of Afghanistan, India, Pakistan, and Bangladesh.

A. *"If I wanted to find out how many people live in the city of Mumbai, India, which map would I use?"*

B. *"On my trip to South Asia, I want to search for gigantic insects that live in tropical rain forests. Which map do I use to find the tropical rain forests?"*

C. *"South Asia is a region that has many different types of climate. Which map will help me bring the right gear for Pakistan's arid climate?"*

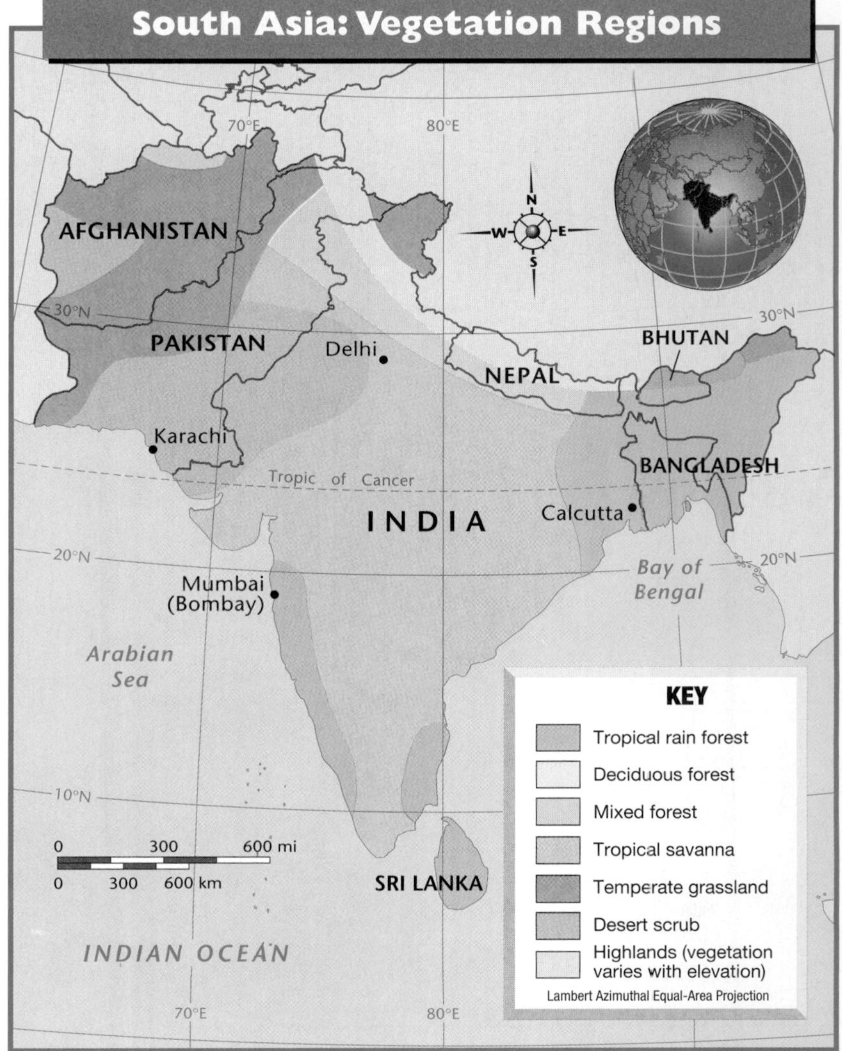

BONUS

Which type of vegetation grows in only one South Asian country?

South Asia: Climate Regions

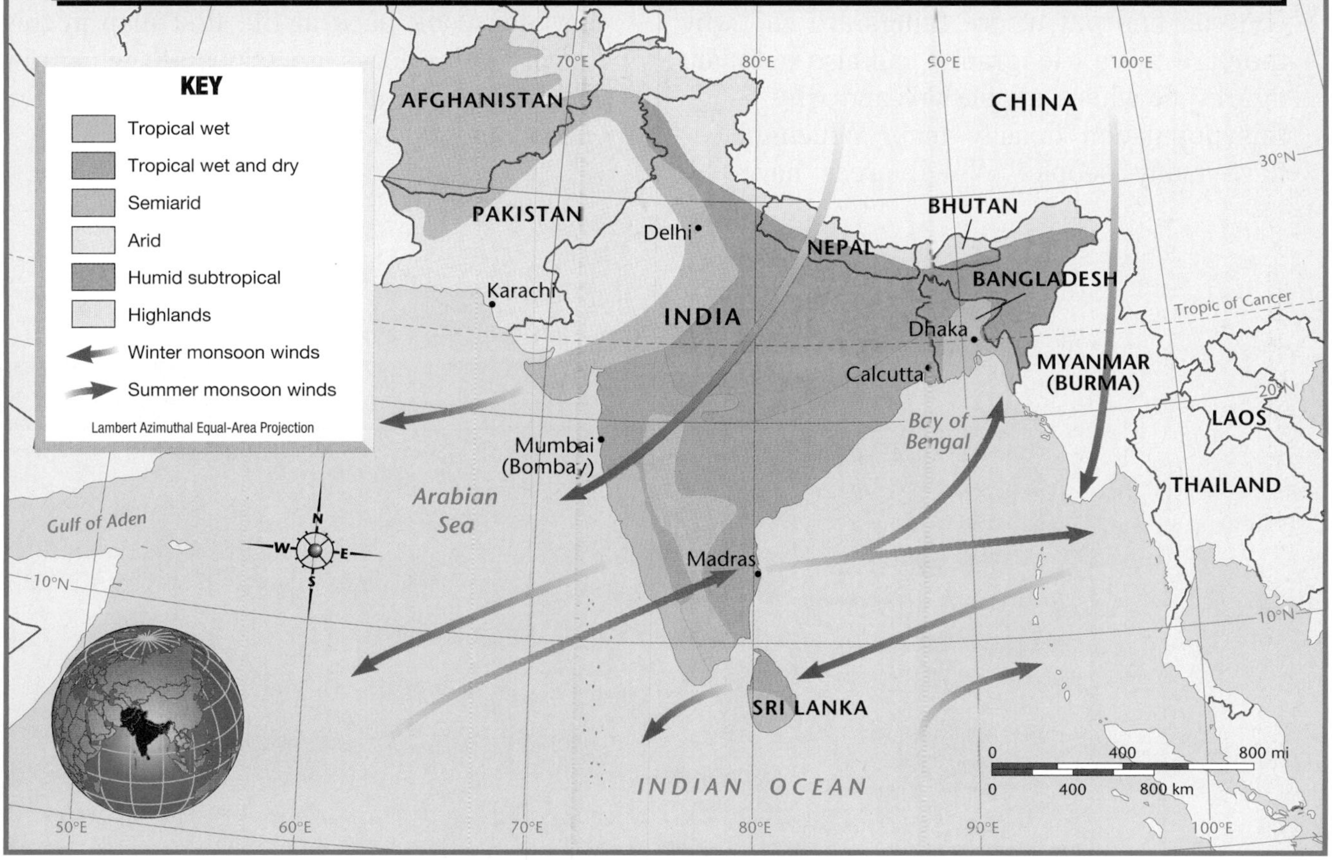

South Asia: Population Density

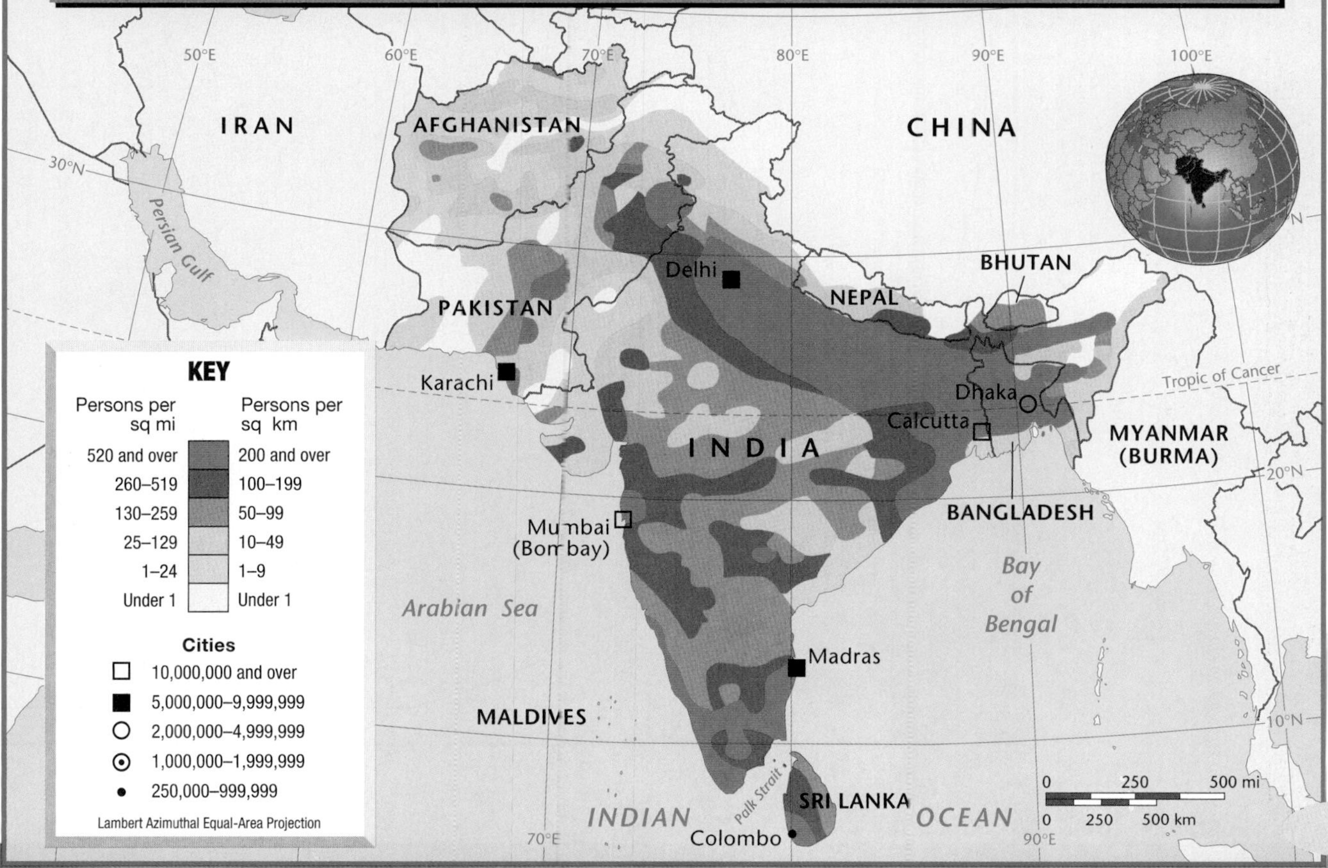

REGIONS

3. Analyze Density As you explore geography, you can find out where things are and why they are there. Geography can also help you figure out where people are and why. Study this population density map. Which places have many people? Which areas have the fewest? Why do you think people live where they do? Look back at the first map in this Activity Atlas for some clues. Try to draw conclusions about how physical features influence where cities are located.

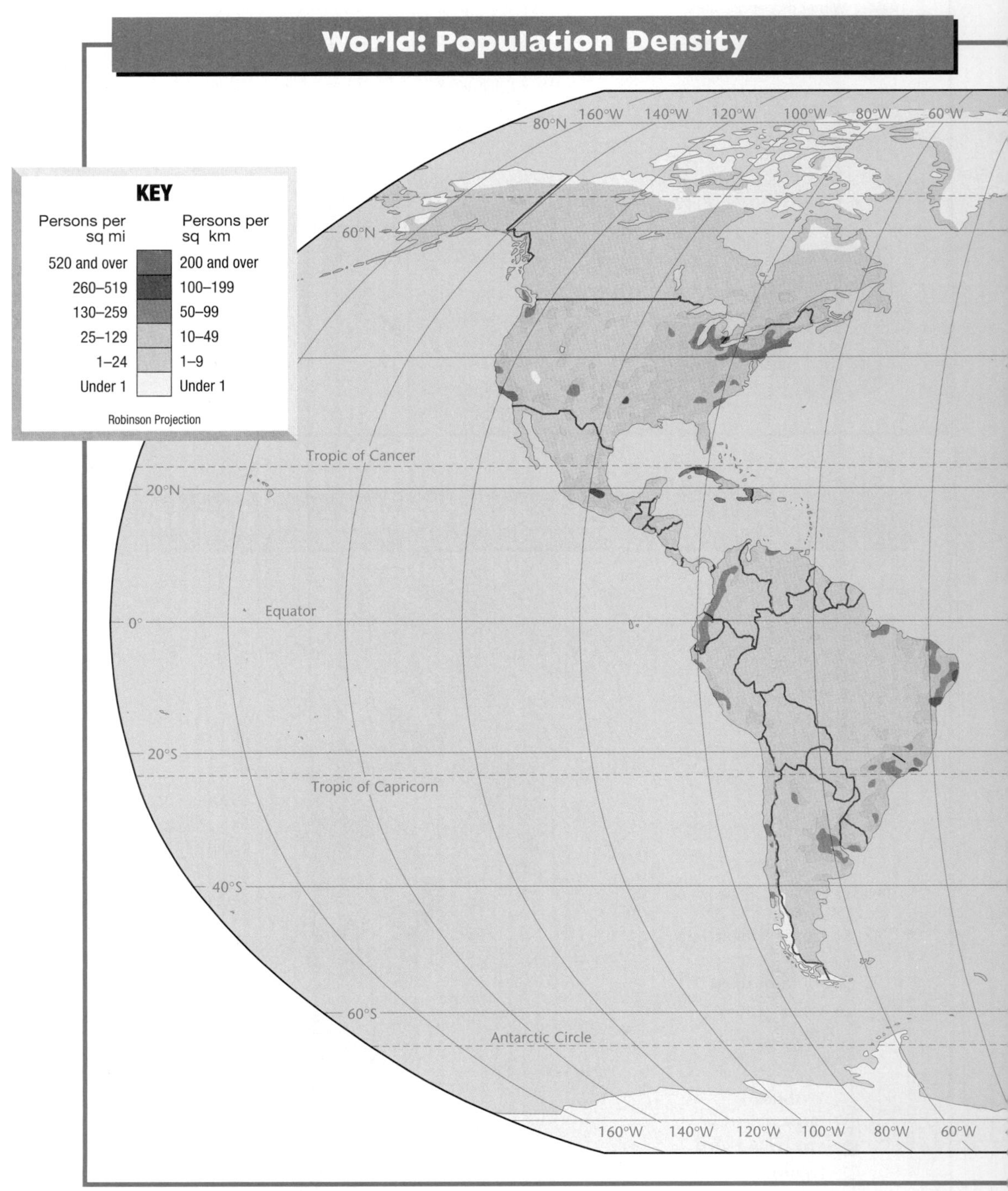

MOVEMENT

4. Create a "Mental Map" Mental maps exist in people's minds, not on paper. Each of us has a file of mental maps, which show the routes to and around places such as school, home, or the mall. To put a mental map on paper, simply choose somewhere you like to go, and draw a map of how you get there. Include as many details as you can—landmarks, streets, buildings, and other details. Then, test the map by giving it to another person to follow. Is it clear? If not, make corrections. Finally, compare it with the maps on the previous pages. What is different? What is the same?

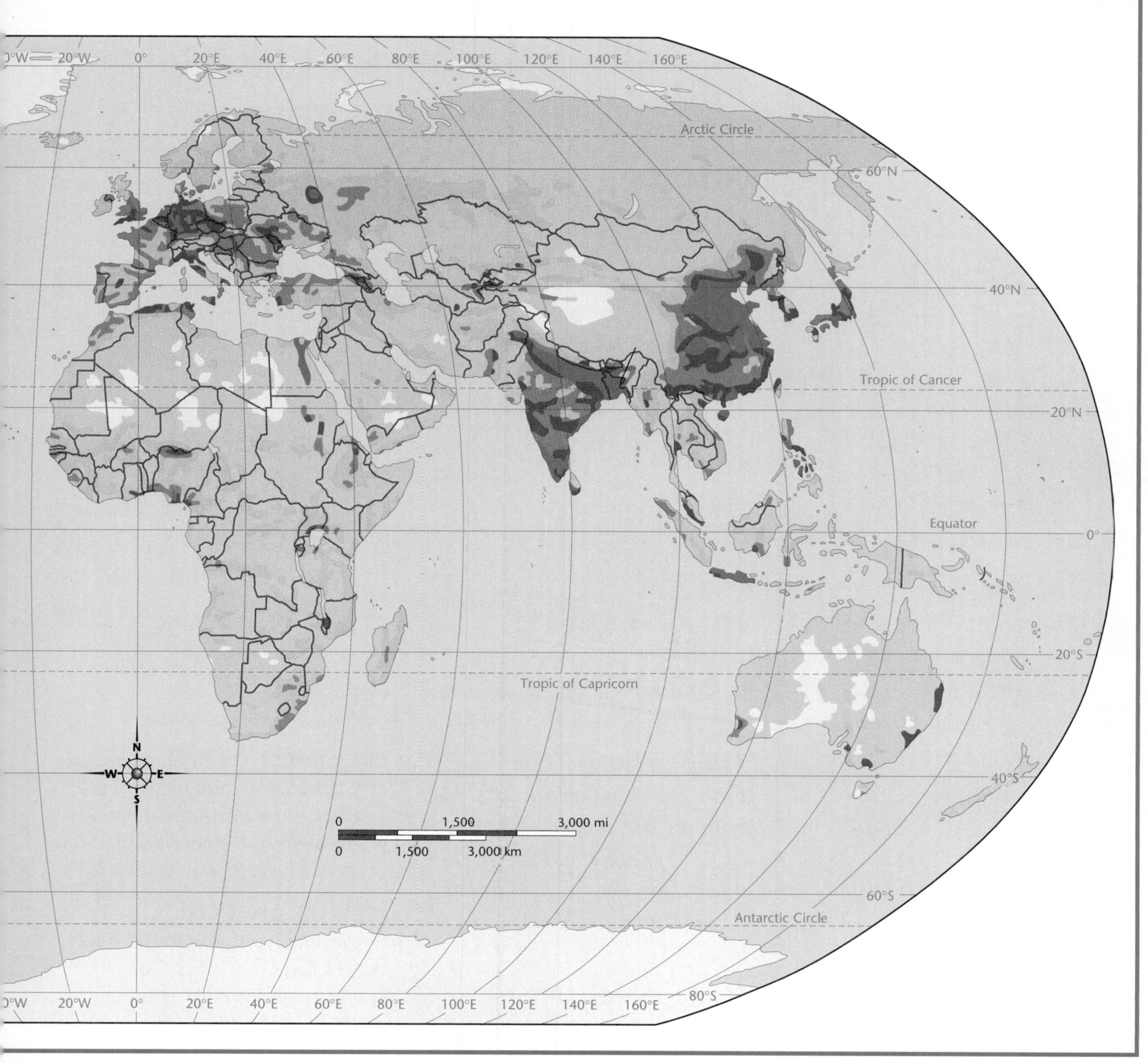

The World of Geography

SECTION 1
The Five Themes of Geography

SECTION 2
The Geographer's Tools

PICTURE ACTIVITIES

This photograph of San Francisco, California, was taken from the air. Pictures like this tell something about the world of geography. The following activities will help you understand how.

Study the picture

Find several natural features such as forests, hills, or oceans. Notice things that people have made such as roads, towns, and industries. If someone in a plane took a photograph of your region, what do you think the picture would show?

Make a prediction

In this picture, dense fog all but covers San Francisco's Golden Gate Bridge. How do you think the fog might affect traffic across the bridge and ships in the water?

The Five Themes of Geography

Reach Into Your Background

If you were going to tell someone how to get to your school from where you live, what would you say? You might say something like "Go six blocks north and one block east." Or you might say your school is next to a local park or shopping center. These directions are examples of geography at work in your everyday life.

Questions to Explore

1. What is geography?
2. How can the five themes of geography help you understand the world?

Key Terms

geography
latitude
parallel
degree
Equator
longitude
meridian
Prime Meridian
plain

What would it be like to look at the Earth from a spaceship? Michael Collins, an astronaut who went to the moon, did just that. In his book *Carrying the Fire,* Collins described what he saw in July 1969 from his space capsule, 200 miles above the Earth. Even that far away, Collins could see natural features of the planet and evidence of the Earth's people.

> "The Indian Ocean flashes incredible colors of emerald jade and opal in the shallow water surrounding the Maldive Islands; then on to the Burma [Myanmar] coast and nondescript green jungle, followed by mountains, coastline, and Hanoi. We can see fires burning off to the southeast, and we scramble for our one remaining still camera to record them. Now the sun glints in unusual fashion off the ocean near Formosa [Taiwan]. There are intersecting surface ripples just south of the island, patterns which are clearly visible and which, I think, must be useful to fishermen who need to know about these currents. The island itself is verdant—glistening green the color and shape of a shiny, well-fertilized gardenia leaf."

▼ From hundreds of miles in space, huge clouds drifting over the Indian Ocean look like haze. What features can you see on the land?

The Study of the Earth

From his high perch, Michael Collins described the colors of the ocean and the plant life on the land. He wrote about how land and water looked. He saw fires set by human beings. Collins was looking at the world as a geographer does.

Geography is the study of the Earth, our home. Geographers analyze the Earth from many points of view. They may discuss how far one place is from another. You do this when you tell someone directions. But they also study such things as oceans, plant life, landforms, and people. Geographers study how the Earth and its people affect each other.

Predict What do you think each of the five geographic themes means?

The Themes of Geography: Five Ways to Look at the Earth

In their work, geographers are guided by two basic questions: (1) Where are things located? and (2) Why are they there? To find the answers, geographers use five themes to organize information. These themes are location, place, human-environment interaction, movement, and regions.

Location Geographers begin to study a place by finding where it is, or its location. There are two ways to talk about location—its absolute location and its relative location. Absolute location describes a place's exact position on the Earth. You might call absolute location a geographic address. Geographers identify the absolute location by

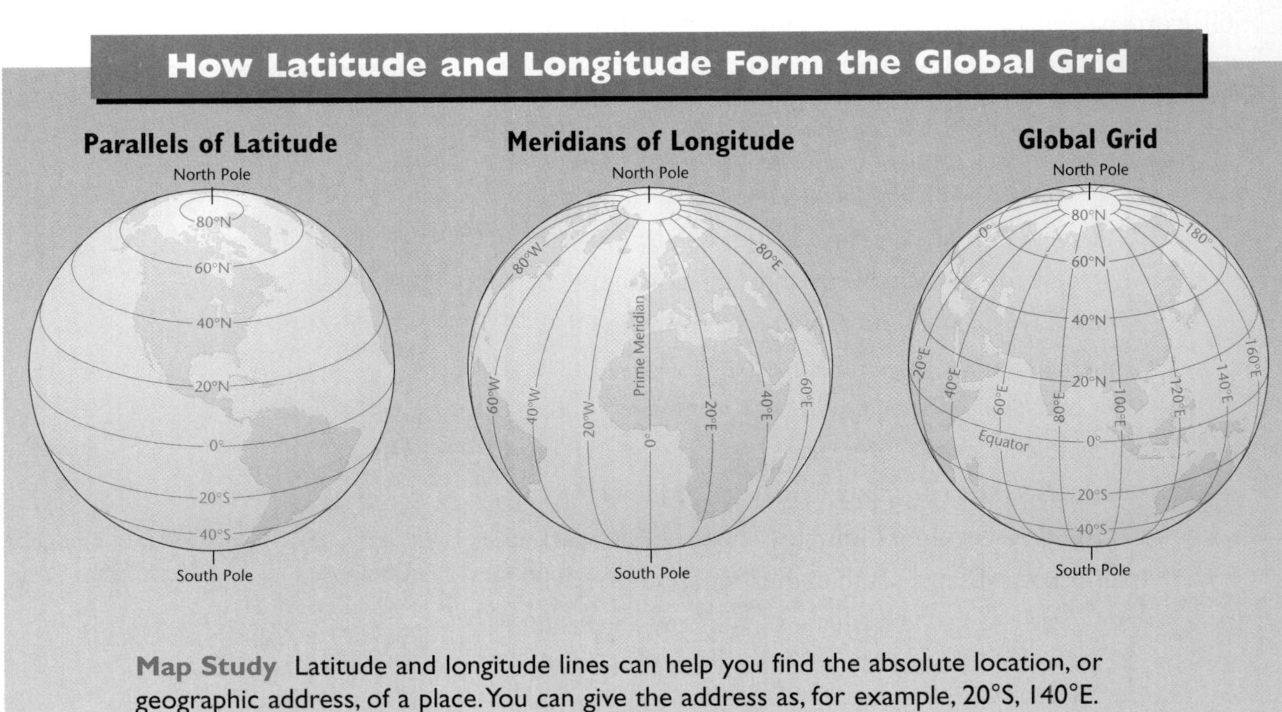

Map Study Latitude and longitude lines can help you find the absolute location, or geographic address, of a place. You can give the address as, for example, 20°S, 140°E. **Location** Find 20°S, 140°E on the Global Grid. What continent is found at this address?

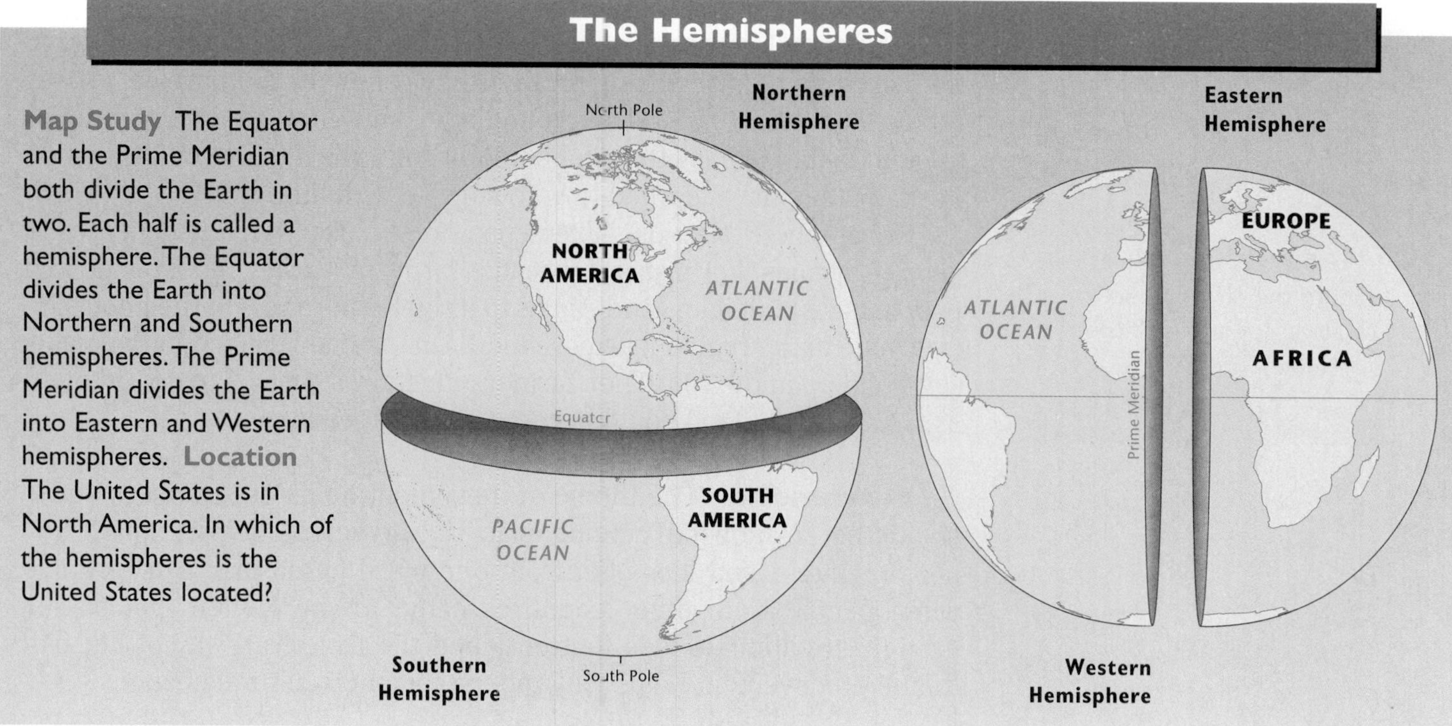

Map Study The Equator and the Prime Meridian both divide the Earth in two. Each half is called a hemisphere. The Equator divides the Earth into Northern and Southern hemispheres. The Prime Meridian divides the Earth into Eastern and Western hemispheres. **Location** The United States is in North America. In which of the hemispheres is the United States located?

using two kinds of imaginary lines around the Earth: latitude and longitude. With these lines, they can pinpoint any spot on the Earth.

Lines of **latitude** are east-west circles around the globe. They are also called **parallels,** because they are parallel to one another. They never meet. These circles divide the globe into units called **degrees.** In the middle of the globe is the parallel called the **Equator,** which is 0 degrees latitude. Geographers measure locations either north or south of the Equator. The farthest latitude north of the Equator is 90° north, the location of the North Pole. The farthest latitude south of the Equator is 90° south, the location of the South Pole.

Geographers also must pinpoint a place from east to west. For this they use lines of **longitude.** These lines, also called **meridians,** circle the globe from north to south. All meridians run through the North and South poles. The **Prime Meridian,** which runs through Greenwich, England, is 0 degrees longitude. Geographers describe locations as east or west of the Prime Meridian. The maximum longitude is 180°, which is halfway around the world from the Prime Meridian.

Geographers also discuss relative location. This explains where a place is by describing places near it. Suppose you live in Newburg, Indiana. You might give Newburg's relative location by saying: "I live in Newburg, Indiana. It's about 180 miles southwest of Indianapolis."

Place Geographers also study place. This includes a location's physical and human features. To describe physical features, you might say the climate is hot or cold. Or you might say that the land is hilly. To emphasize human features, you might talk about how many people live in a place and the kinds of work they do.

Using Latitude
Latitude can be used to measure distance north or south. One degree of latitude is equal to about 69 miles. For example, Fort Wayne, Indiana, is located 6 degrees north of Chattanooga, Tennessee. Therefore, we can determine that Fort Wayne is located about 414 miles north of Chattanooga ($6 \times 69 = 414$).

Predict What two things about the environment of a place do you think the theme of interaction stresses?

Human-Environment Interaction The theme of interaction stresses how people affect their environment, the physical characteristics of their natural surroundings, and how their environment affects them. Perhaps they deliberately cut trails into the mountainside. Perhaps they have learned how to survive with little water.

Geographers also use interaction to discuss the consequences of people's actions. For instance, because farms in Turkey receive little rain, people have built dams and canals to irrigate the land. On the good side, everyone in the region has more food. On the bad side, irrigation makes salt build up in the soil. Then farmers must treat the soil to get rid of the salt. As a result, food could become more expensive.

Movement The theme of movement helps geographers understand the relationship among places. Movement helps explain how people, goods, and ideas get from one place to another. For example, when people from other countries came to the United States, they brought traditional foods that enriched the American way of life. The theme of movement helps you understand such cultural changes.

Regions Geographers use the theme of regions to make comparisons. A region has a unifying characteristic such as climate, land, population, or history. For instance, the Nile Valley region is a snake-shaped region on either side of the Nile River. The region runs through several countries. Life in the valley is much different from life in the regions alongside the valley. There the landscape is mostly desert.

The Rift Valley—Lake Naivasha

Edwin Rioba
Age 16
Kenya
The Great Rift Valley of East Africa was formed over millions of years by earthquakes and volcanic eruptions. Running from Syria in Asia to Mozambique in Africa, it stretches some 4,500 miles (7,200 km). **Place** Based on this picture, what landforms do you think are commonly found in the Great Rift Valley?

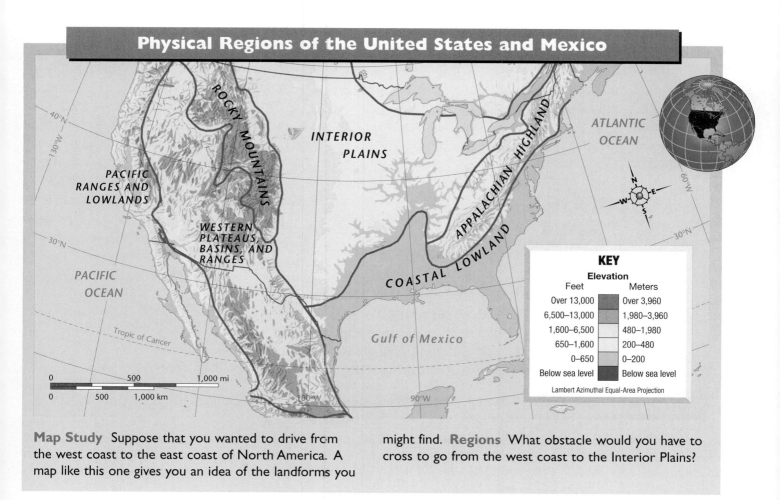

Physical Regions of the United States and Mexico

ROCKY MOUNTAINS
INTERIOR PLAINS
PACIFIC RANGES AND LOWLANDS
WESTERN PLATEAUS, BASINS, AND RANGES
APPALACHIAN HIGHLAND
COASTAL LOWLAND
ATLANTIC OCEAN
PACIFIC OCEAN
Gulf of Mexico
Tropic of Cancer
40°N
30°N
130°W
100°W
90°W
60°W
0 500 1,000 mi
0 500 1,000 km

KEY

Elevation

Feet	Meters
Over 13,000	Over 3,960
6,500–13,000	1,980–3,960
1,600–6,500	480–1,980
650–1,600	200–480
0–650	0–200
Below sea level	Below sea level

Lambert Azimuthal Equal-Area Projection

Map Study Suppose that you wanted to drive from the west coast to the east coast of North America. A map like this one gives you an idea of the landforms you might find. **Regions** What obstacle would you have to cross to go from the west coast to the Interior Plains?

On maps, geographers use color and shape or special symbols to show regions. One map may show a **plain,** a region of flat land. The map above shows different regions of elevation, to show the height of land above sea level. A place can be part of several regions at the same time. For example, Houston, Texas, is in both a plains region and an oil-producing region.

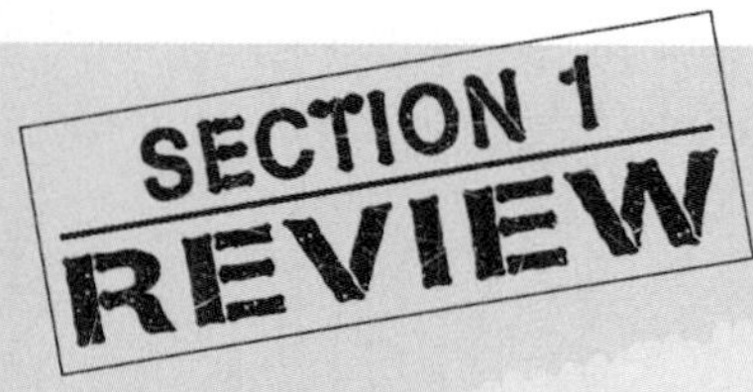

1. **Define** (a) geography, (b) latitude, (c) parallel, (d) degree, (e) Equator, (f) longitude, (g) meridian, (h) Prime Meridian, (i) plain.
2. What are two questions geographers ask when they study the Earth?
3. List the five themes of geography.
4. Give an example of how each theme can be used.

Critical Thinking

5. **Identifying Central Issues** You decide to start a geography club. When you invite a friend to join, she tells you she thinks geography is boring. She would rather learn about people, not just places. What could you say to change her mind?

Activity

6. **Writing to Learn** Make a chart listing the five geography themes. Find the location of your town or city on a map. Write down a relative location that tells where your city or town is. Then, take a walk around your neighborhood and think about the other four themes. Complete the chart by adding descriptions of your neighborhood that relate to each theme.

The Geographer's Tools

Reach Into Your Background

Skulls-and-crossbones. Ships with black sails. Cannons. Swords. Treasure maps. That's right, MAPS. These things are all tools in great pirate tales. Maps are also one of the most important tools geographers use. Geographers and movie pirates aren't the only ones who use them. You do too!

Questions to Explore

1. What are some of the different ways of showing the Earth's surface and why do geographers use them?
2. What are the advantages and disadvantages of different kinds of maps and globes?

Key Terms

globe
scale
distortion
projection
compass rose
cardinal direction
key

Key People

Gerardus Mercator
Arthur Robinson

You might expect a map to be printed on a piece of paper. But hundreds of years ago, people made maps out of whatever was available. The Inuit (IN oo it) people carved detailed, accurate maps on pieces of wood. The Inuits were once called Eskimos. These Native Americans have lived in northern regions of the world for centuries. They needed maps that were portable, durable, and waterproof. Carved maps remind us that making maps is not just an exercise in school. People rely on maps, sometimes for their very survival.

▼ The Marshall Islanders made wood maps of the southwest Pacific Ocean. Curved palm sticks show ocean currents and shells show islands.

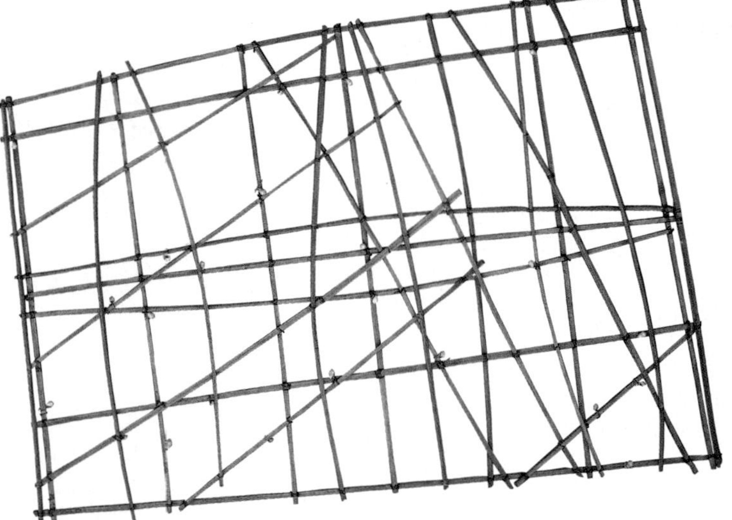

Globes and Maps

Hundreds of years ago, people knew very little about the land and water beyond their own homes. Their maps showed only the areas they traveled. Other places either were left out or were only an empty space on their maps. Sometimes they filled the empty spaces with drawings of lands, creatures, and people from myths and stories.

As people explored the Earth, they collected information about the shapes and sizes of islands, continents, and bodies of water. Mapmakers wanted to present this information accurately. The best way was to put it on a **globe,** a round ball like the Earth itself. By using the same shape, mapmakers could show the continents and oceans of the Earth much as they really are. The only difference would be the **scale,** or size.

But there is a problem with globes. Try putting a globe in your pocket every morning. Try making a globe large enough to show the details of your state or community. A globe just cannot be complete enough to be useful and at the same time be small enough to be convenient. People, therefore, invented flat maps.

Flat maps, however, present another problem. The Earth is round. A map is flat. Can you flatten an orange peel without tearing it? There will be wrinkled and folded sections. The same thing happens when mapmakers create flat maps. It is impossible to show the Earth on a flat surface without some **distortion,** or change in the accuracy of its shapes and distances. Something is going to look larger or smaller than it is.

Predict Why do you think it would be hard to make an accurate map of the world on a flat sheet of paper?

An Orange Peel Map

Chart Study It is almost impossible to flatten an orange peel. The peel tears, wrinkles, and stretches. Mapmakers can make a flat map of an orange—or of the Earth—by using mathematics. But even a map laid out to look like this flattened orange peel is not accurate. **Critical Thinking** Look carefully at the photographs. As the orange peel is flattened, what distortions do you think might occur?

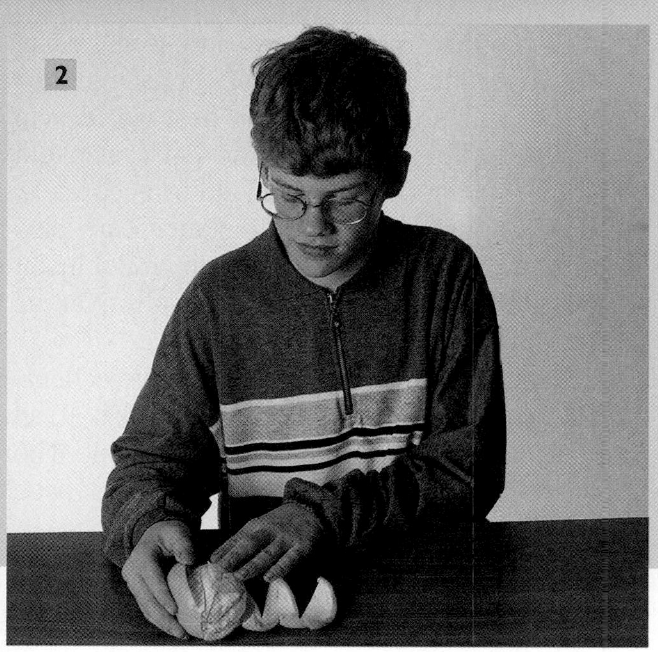

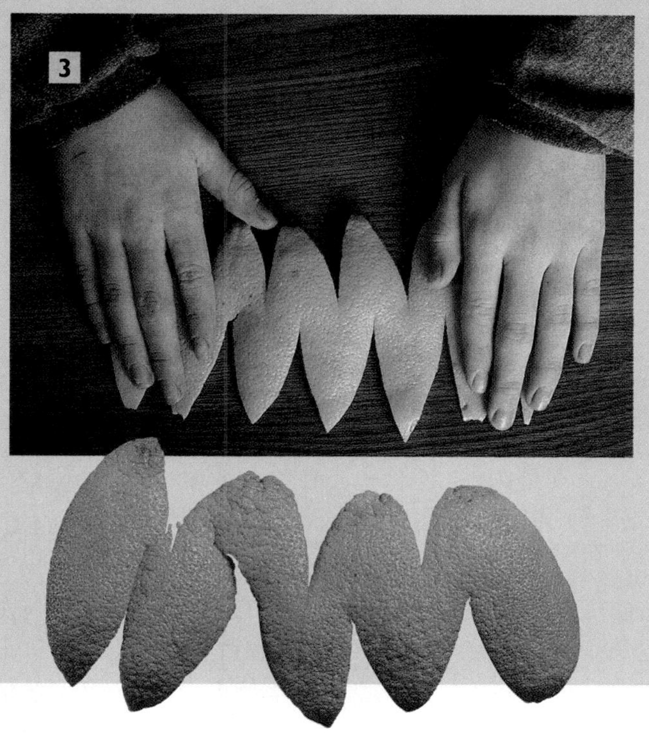

Getting It All on the Map

In 1569, a geographer named Gerardus Mercator (juh RAHR duhs muhr KAYT uhr) created a flat map to help sailors navigate long journeys around the globe. To make his map flat, Mercator expanded the area between the longitudes near the poles. Mercator's map was very useful to sailors. They made careful notes about the distortions they found on their journeys. More than 400 years after he made it, those notes and the Mercator **projection,** or method of putting a map of the Earth onto a flat piece of paper, is used by nearly all deep-sea navigators.

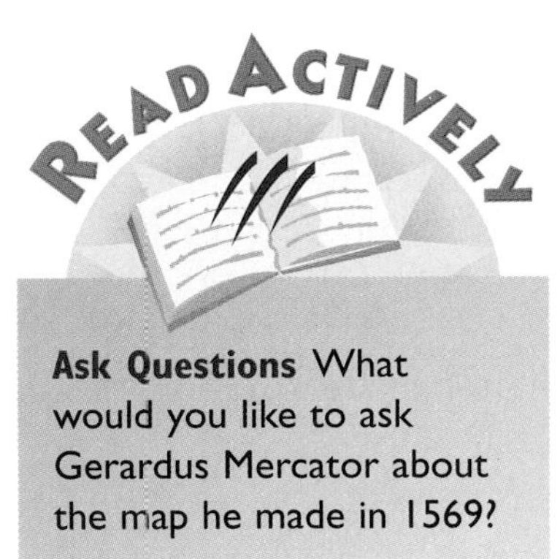

Ask Questions What would you like to ask Gerardus Mercator about the map he made in 1569?

When Mercator made his map, he had to make some decisions. He made sure that the shape of the landmasses and ocean areas was similar to the shapes on a globe. But he had to stretch the spaces between the longitudes. This distorted the sizes of some of the land on his map. Land near the Equator was about right, but land near the poles became much larger than it should be. For example, on Mercator's map Greenland looks bigger than South America. Greenland is actually only one eighth as large as South America.

The World: A Mercator Projection

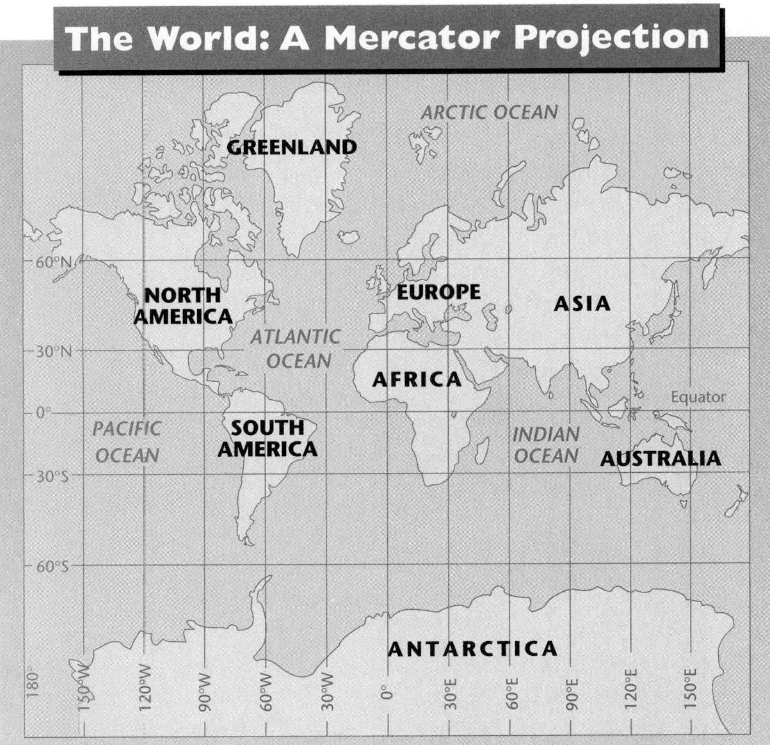

Map Study Mercator maps make areas near the poles look bigger than they are. This is because on a globe, the lines of longitude meet at the poles, but on a flat Mercator map, they are parallel. However, Mercator maps are useful to navigators because the longitude and latitude lines appear straight. Navigators can use these lines and a compass to plot a ship's route. **Place** Here Greenland looks bigger than it really is. It actually is about the size of Mexico. What other areas do you think might look larger than they should? Why?

Geographers call a Mercator projection a conformal map. It shows correct shapes but not true distances or sizes. Other mapmakers used other techniques to try to draw an accurate map. For instance, an equal area map shows the correct size of landmasses but their shapes are altered. The Peters projection on the next page is an equal area map.

Mapmakers have tried other techniques. The interrupted projection (see next page) is like the ripped peel of an orange. By creating gaps in the picture of the world, mapmakers showed the size and shape of land accurately. The gaps make it impossible to figure distances correctly. You could not use this projection to chart a course across an ocean.

Today, many geographers believe Arthur Robinson's projection is the best world map available. This projection shows the size and shape of most of the land quite accurately. Sizes of the oceans and distances are also fairly accurate. However, even a Robinson projection has distortions, especially in areas around the edges of the map.

There are many other types of projections. Each has advantages and drawbacks. It all depends on how you want to use each one. The illustrations on this page and the next page show several projections.

The World: Interrupted, Equal Area, and Peters Projections

Interrupted Projection

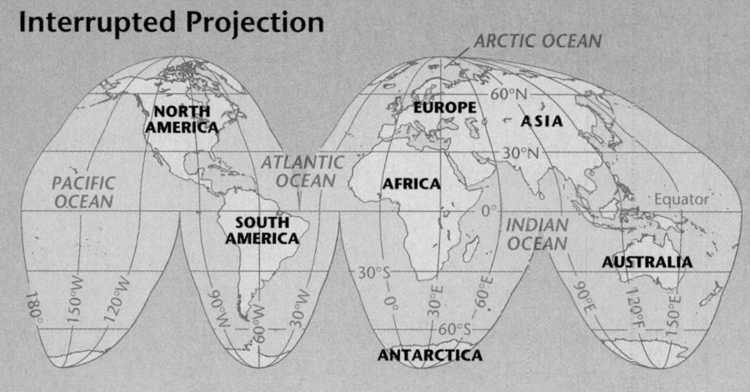

Map Study There are many ways to show a globe on a flat map. The interrupted projection map, on the left, shows the real sizes and shapes of continents. The equal area map, below left, shows size accurately. The Peters projection, below, shows land and ocean areas and correct directions accurately. **Location** Compare each projection with the more accurate Robinson projection below. What do each of these three projections distort?

Equal-Area Projection

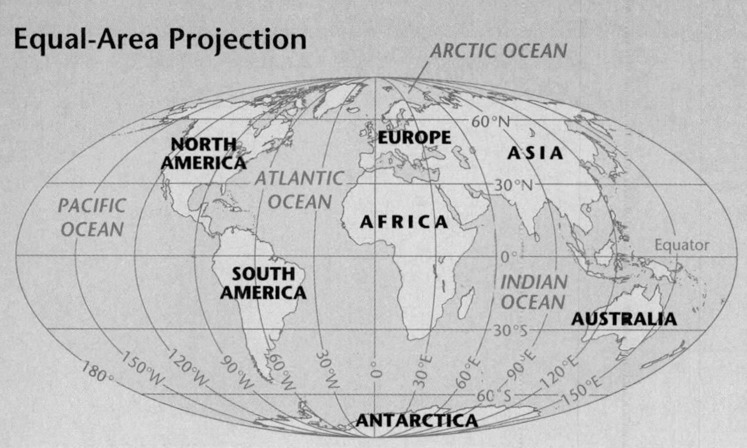

Peters Projection

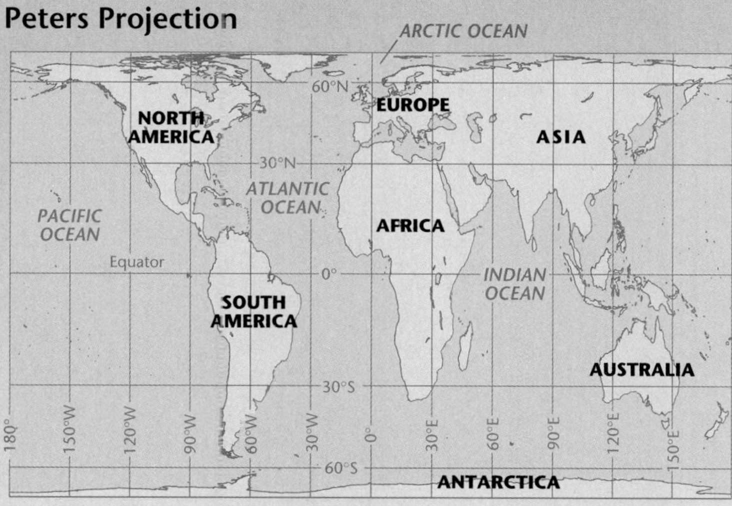

The World: A Robinson Projection

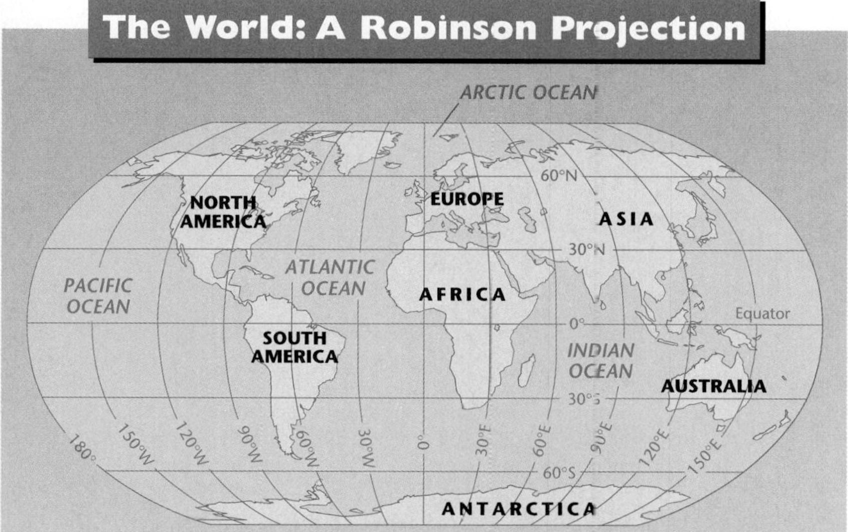

Map Study In 1988, the National Geographic Society adopted the Robinson projection as its official projection for world maps. While the Robinson projection does distort the globe a little, it shows the sizes and shapes of countries most accurately. **Movement** Do you think the Robinson projection would be as useful to a navigator as the Mercator projection? Why or why not?

The Parts of a Map

Look at the two maps below. One is an imaginary pirate map. The other is a map of the Grand Bahama Island, in the Caribbean Sea. Believe it or not, the pirate map has some features that you will find on any map. Of course, regular maps don't have the X that tells where the treasure is, but you will find a mark of some sort that shows your destination.

A Pirate Map and a Road Map

Map Study Almost all maps have some things in common. A compass rose shows direction. A key explains special symbols. A grid often shows longitude and latitude. The road map below has a grid of numbers and letters to help locate places.
Location What airport is located at B-1?

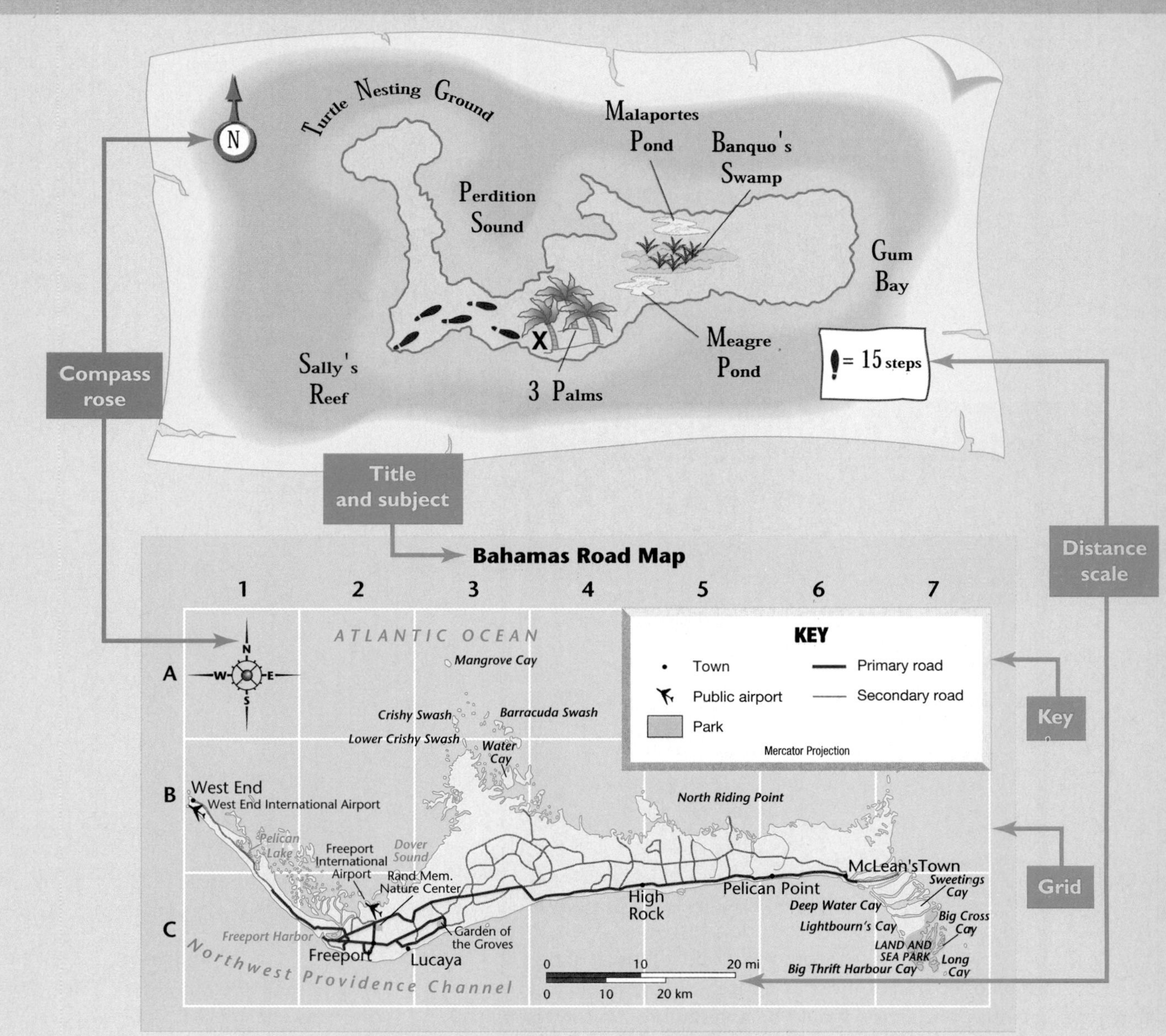

The pirate map has an arrow pointing north. On the regular map, you will find what geographers call a **compass rose,** which is a model of a compass. It tells the **cardinal directions,** which are north, south, east, and west.

On a pirate map, marks will tell you how many paces to walk to find the treasure. On a conventional map, an indicator for scale tells you how far to go to get to your destination. The scale tells you that one inch on the map represents a particular distance on the land. Scales vary, depending on the map. On one map, an inch may equal one mile. On another map, an inch may equal 100 miles.

On the pirate map, special symbols indicate landmarks such as small ponds, a swamp, or a distinct group of trees. Regular maps also have symbols. They are explained in the section of the map called the **key,** or legend. It may include symbols for features such as national and state parks, various types of roads, sizes of towns and cities, or important landmarks.

A regular map includes some things that the pirate map doesn't. For instance, the pirate map doesn't have a map title. On a regular map, a title tells you the subject of the map.

A treasure map does not have a grid, either. Some regular maps use a grid of parallels and meridians. Remember that parallels show latitude, or distance north and south of the Equator. Meridians show longitude, or distance east and west of the Prime Meridian. On some maps, the area is too small for longitude and latitude to be helpful. These maps usually have a grid of letters and numbers to help people find things.

Every part of a map has a very simple purpose. That is to make sure that people who use maps have accurate information they need. The more you know about maps, the easier it will be for you to use them well—even if you're hunting for buried treasure!

Connect What parts of a map do you think are most helpful to you?

1. **Define** (a) globe, (b) scale, (c) distortion, (d) projection, (e) compass rose, (f) cardinal direction, (g) key.
2. **Identify** (a) Gerardus Mercator, (b) Arthur Robinson.
3. What are some advantages and disadvantages of using a globe to show the Earth's surface?
4. Why are there so many different types of map projections?
5. How can knowing the parts of a map help you?

Critical Thinking

6. **Making Comparisons** You are planning a hiking trip with your family to a nearby state park. Your family uses two maps: a road map and a map of the park. What advantages does each map have?

Activity

7. **Writing to Learn** Think of a place that you like to visit. How would you tell a friend to get there? Make some notes about directions and landmarks you could include in a map. Then make a map that shows your friend how to get there.

Expressing Problems Clearly

Geographers know that geography is not just about maps and where places are. Geography is about change. After all, the Earth is always being changed by natural forces. You and the nearly six billion other people on the planet also change it. Geographers use geography to view and understand these changes.

"Geography," as one of the world's leading geographers put it, "turns out to be much more, and much more significant, than many of us realized."

Are you still having a problem understanding what geography is? You can help yourself by expressing that problem clearly.

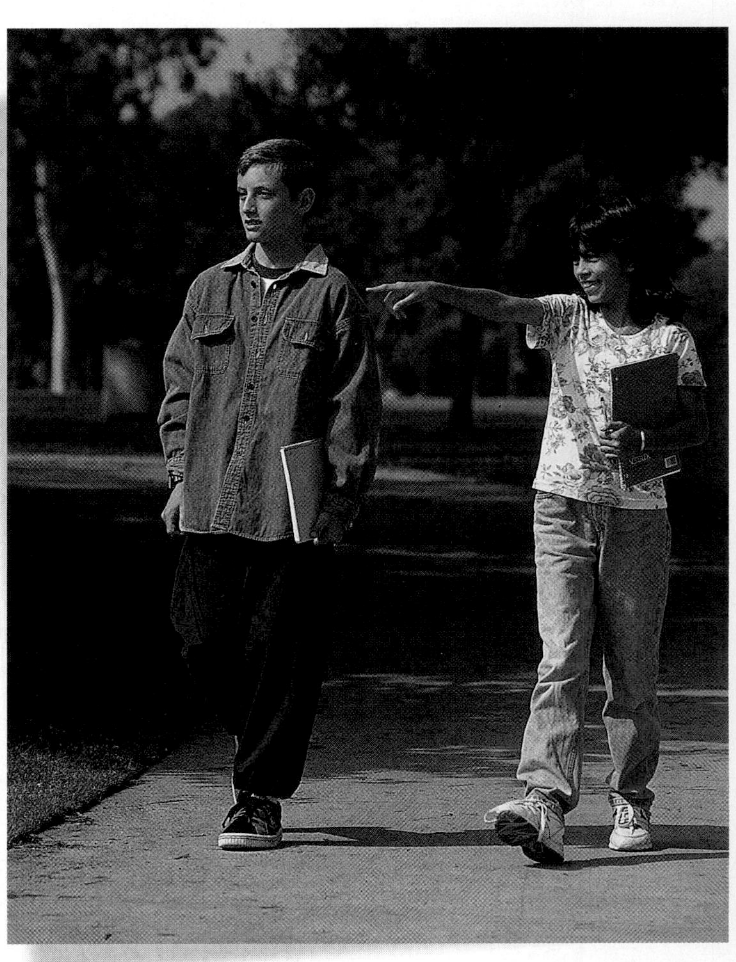

▲What can a geography walk teach you about your surroundings?

Get Ready

One way geographers help organize their study of the Earth is to use the five themes of geography. Look for them in Chapter 1. Understanding the five themes will help you express the meaning of geography.

Try It Out

A. Identify the problem. You may think that geography is only about maps and the names of countries. You need to know what geography really is.

B. Think about exactly what the problem is. You know that the five geography themes should help you figure out what geography is. But maybe you have trouble understanding the five themes.

C. Put the problem into words. Write a sentence that tells the problem. There are many sentences that will work. Perhaps you will think of one something like this.

> What are the five geography themes, and how are they connected to what I know about the world?

Apply the Skill

Practice understanding the five themes of geography by going for a geography walk. Find out how the themes are reflected in the world around you. You don't have to walk near mountains or rivers. You can walk near your home or school.

1. **Take a notebook and a pencil.** You will need to take notes on your walk. Put into the notebook a list of the five geography themes and their definitions.
2. **Take someone with you.** Walk with a family member or a friend. Be sure to walk in a safe place.
3. **Look for geography.** As you walk, look for examples of the five themes. Does a delivery truck drive by? That is an example of movement. Is it carrying bread? Wheat for the bread was grown on a farm. That's human-environment interaction.
4. **Record the geography around you.** Find as many examples of each theme as you can. Record each one in your notebook.

> "...a solid understanding of geography is a vital, basic ingredient for a rounded, full understanding of the world."
>
> —Kenneth Star, author

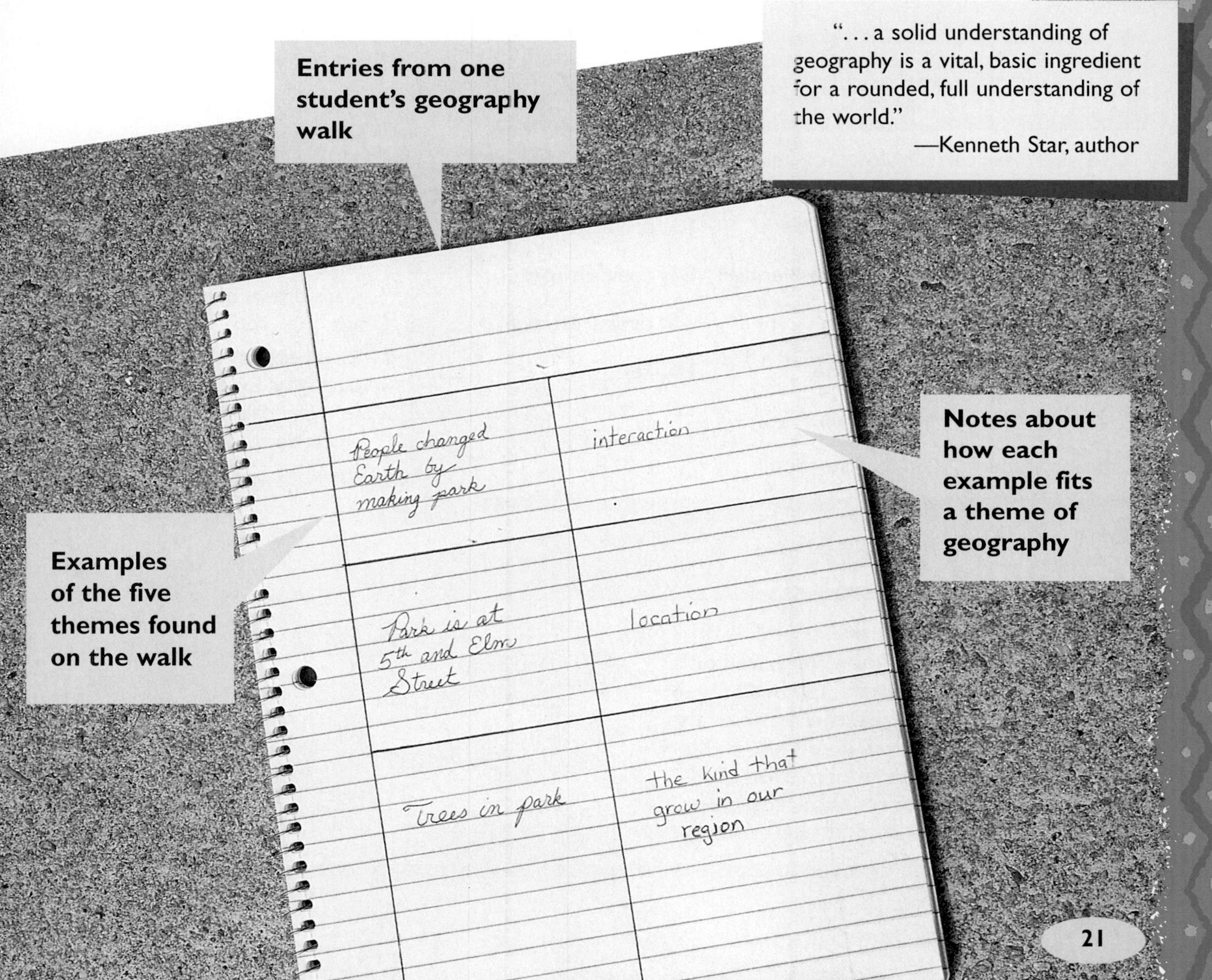

Entries from one student's geography walk
People changed Earth by making park
interaction
Park is at 5th and Elm Street
location
Trees in park
the kind that grow in our region
Examples of the five themes found on the walk
Notes about how each example fits a theme of geography

Review and Activities

Reviewing Main Ideas

1. (a) What two questions do geographers always ask about a place? (b) What do geographers use to help answer the questions?
2. Explain how geographers locate any spot on the Earth.
3. You read in the newspaper that geographers are part of a team of people planning a new highway in your area. List and describe three geography themes that the team might use.
4. If you had to make a map, how would you show the Earth so that the size and shape of its features and the distances between them were accurate?
5. An ocean navigator uses one particular map to determine the best route from New Hampshire to Florida. An official who must solve an argument about which country owns a certain piece of land uses a different kind of map. Why do these two people use different maps?

Reviewing Key Terms

Use each key term below in a sentence that shows the meaning of the term.

1. geography
2. latitude
3. parallel
4. degree
5. Equator
6. longitude
7. meridian
8. Prime Meridian
9. plain
10. globe
11. scale
12. distortion
13. projection
14. compass rose
15. cardinal direction
16. key

Critical Thinking

1. **Recognizing Cause and Effect** Explain why today's maps are more accurate than maps drawn hundreds of years ago.
2. **Expressing Problems Clearly** Explain why there are so many different types of map projections.

Graphic Organizer

Choose a place that interests you. It might be a place you know very well or a place you have never seen. Fill in the web chart on the right. Write the name of the place in the center oval. If you know the place well, list facts or information under each theme. If you don't know the place, list questions that would fit each theme.

Map Activity

The Globe

For each place listed below, write the letter from the map that shows its location.

1. Prime Meridian
2. Equator
3. North Pole
4. South Pole
5. Europe
6. Africa
7. South America
8. North America

Place Location

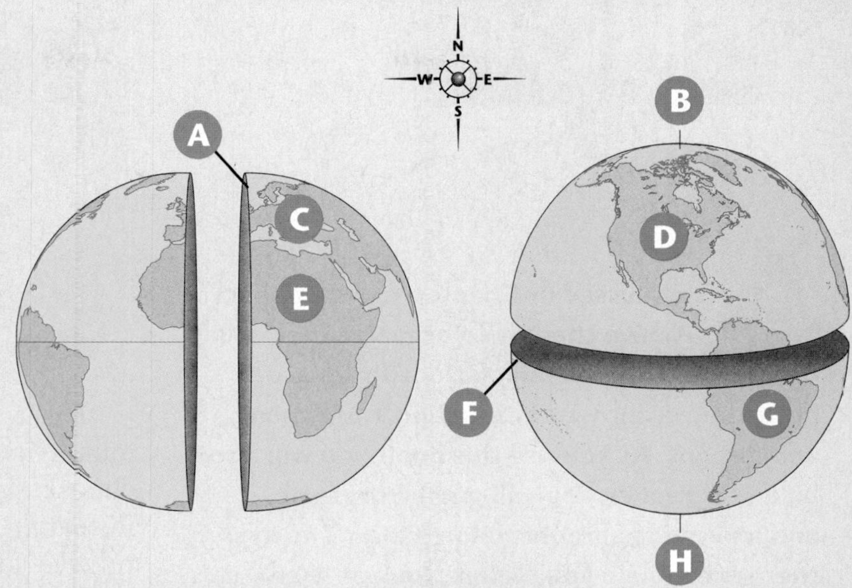

Writing Activity

Writing a Paragraph Write a paragraph describing ways that you have seen people use maps. You may include such things as road maps, maps for seats in a sports arena or areas in a museum, or even hand-drawn maps to a friend's house.

Take It to the NET

Activity View interactive political and physical maps of any place in the world. For help in completing this activity, visit **www.phschool.com.**

Chapter 1 Self-Test To review what you have learned, take the Chapter 1 Self-Test and get instant feedback on your answers. Go to **www.phschool.com** to take the test.

Skills Review

Turn to the Skills Activity.

Review the steps for expressing problems clearly. Then complete the following: (a) Name one strategy you can use to help you express problems clearly. (b) How can expressing problems clearly help you to solve problems?

How Am I Doing?

Answer these questions to help you check your progress.

1. Can I list the five themes of geography and describe how they are used?
2. Do I understand the advantages and disadvantages of different ways of showing the Earth's surface?
3. What information from this chapter can I include in my journal?

A Five-Theme Tour

As discussed in Chapter 1, geographers use five themes to organize their study of the world and its people: location, place, human-environment interaction, movement, and regions. As you use this book, you will also be a geographer. You will gather, organize, and analyze geographic information. The five themes can help you. Before you use them, however, it helps to thoroughly know what they mean. A good way to explore the themes is through real-life examples.

Purpose

In this activity, you will plan a world tour. Your destination is either the world's mountains or the world's rivers. As you plan your tour, you will also explore the five geography themes.

Decide Where You Will Go

First, select the mountain tour or the river tour. Then, use a physical map of the world to choose five places you will visit along the way. Research each place so you can describe its relative location. That is, you will be able to write down descriptions such as "The Nile River in northeast Africa flows through Sudan and Egypt." This is an example of the theme of location, which answers the question "Where is this place?"

◀ ▲ Tourists enjoy the Nile River and the sights of Egypt.

Describe the Places on Your Tour

Use the theme of place to write an exciting description of each place on your tour. The theme of place answers the question "What is this place like?" Include both physical and human characteristics. Physical characteristics are the natural features of the Earth. Things related to people are human characteristics. Your research will help you focus on what makes your places unique.

Next, focus on the theme of human-environment interaction. This theme answers the questions: "How do people use this place? How and why have people changed this place?" For each place on your tour, gather information that answers these two questions. Add the information to your descriptions.

Plan a Travel Route

The theme of movement answers the question "How has this place been affected by the movement of people, goods, and ideas?" To explore this theme, choose just one place. Do research to plan a travel route from your community to that place.

Call or visit a travel agent to find the number of miles for each section of the journey. Add the distances together to find the total number of miles for the trip.

Learn About the Language

The theme of regions answers the question "How is this place similar to and different from other regions?" To help you learn about this theme, focus on the same one special place. Do research to find out what languages people speak there. Then find other places in the world where people speak the same languages. This activity will show you one type of region—a language region. Your place belongs to a group of places that share something similar: the same language.

Do additional research to make a chart of some common words in the languages spoken in your place. For instance, you might find the words for "hello," "good-bye," "thank you," and "please." These are words a visitor will need to know.

Links to Other Subjects

Writing descriptions of places	**Language Arts**
Adding distances in miles	**Math**
Creating a brochure	**Art**

Create a Travel Brochure

Now, use the information you have gathered to create a brochure about the places you will visit on your tour. The brochure will tell everyone about your plans. Include the descriptions you wrote for each place on the tour. Also include your travel route and language chart. Decorate the brochure with drawings or magazine pictures.

ANALYSIS AND CONCLUSION

Write a summary that tells which type of tour you planned—mountains or rivers. Be sure to answer the following questions in your summary.

1. How did the process of planning your tour help you learn about the five themes?
2. Which of the five themes do you think are most important in your tour?

Earth's Physical Geography

SECTION 1
Our Planet, the Earth

SECTION 2
Land, Air, and Water

SECTION 3
Climate and What Influences It

SECTION 4
How Climate Affects Vegetation

PICTURE ACTIVITIES

Before we had satellites in space, people could only imagine how the Earth truly looked. Now, satellites let people see the Earth's land and water beneath a swirling mix of clouds. The following activities will help you get to know your planet.

Be a global weather forecaster

Weather forecasters use satellite pictures like the one above to see weather patterns. The white areas in the picture are clouds. What land areas do you recognize? How do you recognize them? On the day this picture was taken, what areas seem cloudier? Swirling patterns may indicate storms. Do you see any storm patterns?

Become an Earth expert

Watch especially for one of these topics as you read this chapter: Beneath the Earth's Surface, On the Earth's Surface, and Beyond the Earth's Atmosphere. Which one would you like to be an expert on?

Our Planet, the Earth

Reach Into Your Background

What is spring like where you live? What is winter like? How long do these seasons last where you live? If you can answer these questions, consider yourself an amateur geographer. You have noticed the changes in your region at different times of the year.

Questions to Explore

1. How does the Earth move in space?
2. Why do seasons change?

Key Terms

orbit
revolution
axis
rotation
low latitudes
high latitudes
middle latitudes

Key Places

Tropic of Cancer
Tropic of Capricorn
Arctic Circle
Antarctic Circle

"The Sky Father opened his hand. Within every crease there lay innumerable grains of shining maize [corn]. In his thumb and forefinger he took some of the shining grains and placed them in the sky as brilliant stars to be a guide to humans when the bright sun was hidden."

This is part of an ancient myth of the Pueblos, who lived in what today is the southwestern United States. They used the story to explain the appearance of the night sky.

▼ Thousands of years ago, Native Americans laid this wheel out in Wyoming's Bighorn Mountains. They may have used it to track the movements of the stars.

The Earth and the Sun

The Earth, the sun, the planets, and the twinkling stars in the sky are all part of a galaxy, or family of stars. We call our galaxy the Milky Way because the lights from its billions of stars look like a trail of spilled milk across the night sky. Our sun is one of those stars. Although the sun is just a tiny speck in the Milky Way, it is the center of everything for the Earth.

Predict What causes day to change into night?

Understanding Days and Nights The sun may be about 93 million miles (150 million km) away, but it still provides the Earth with heat and light. The Earth travels around the sun in an oval-shaped path called an **orbit.** It takes $365\frac{1}{4}$ days, or one year, for the Earth to complete one **revolution,** or circular journey, around the sun.

As the Earth revolves around the sun, it is also spinning in space. The Earth turns around its **axis**—an imaginary line running through it between the North and South poles. Each complete turn, which takes about 24 hours, is called a **rotation.** As the Earth rotates, it is daytime on the side facing the sun. It is night on the side away from the sun.

Understanding Seasons At certain times of the year, days are longer than nights, and at other times, nights are longer than days. This happens, in part, because the Earth's axis is at an angle. At some points in the Earth's orbit, the tilt causes a region to face toward the sun for more hours than it faces away from the sun. Days are longer. At other times, the region faces away from the sun for more hours than it faces toward the sun. Days are shorter.

The Earth's tilt and orbit also cause changes in temperatures during the seasons. The warmth you feel at any time of year depends on how directly the sunlight falls upon you. Some regions receive a great deal of fairly direct sunlight, while other regions receive no direct sunlight. Special latitude lines divide up these regions of the world. You can see them on the map on the next page.

How Night Changes Into Day

Chart Study This diagram shows how places on the Earth move from night into day. Today, it takes almost 24 hours for the Earth to make one complete rotation. But when the Earth first formed millions of years ago, it spun 10 times faster. A full cycle of day and night on the Earth lasted just over two hours. **Critical Thinking** As time passes, the Earth spins more and more slowly. What will eventually happen to the length of a day? Find North America on the globe. Which coast gets daylight first?

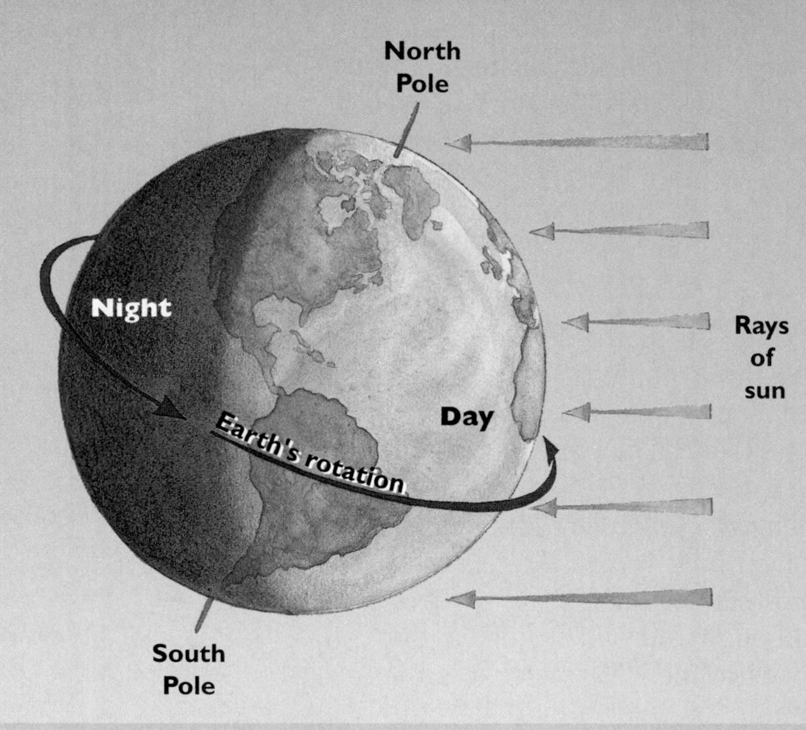

Zones of Latitudes

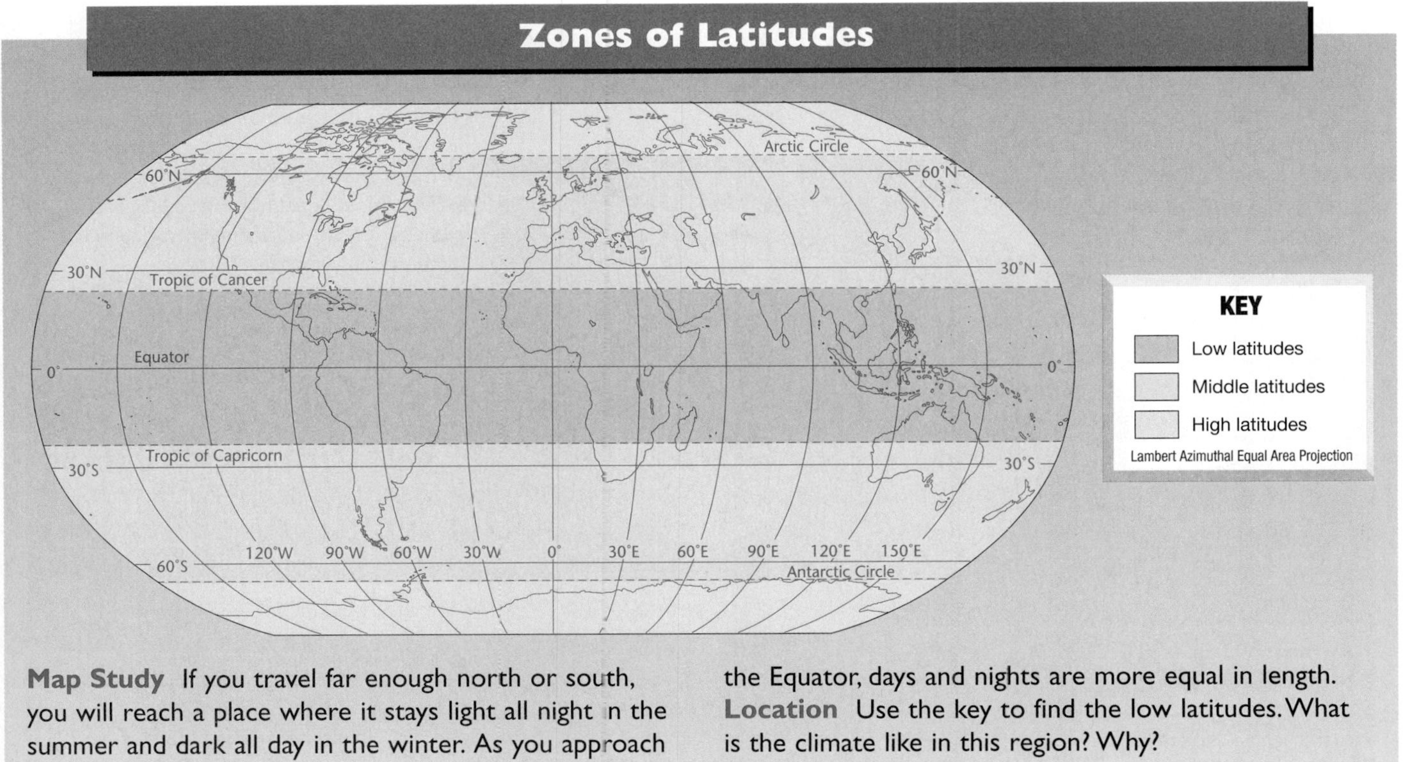

Map Study If you travel far enough north or south, you will reach a place where it stays light all night in the summer and dark all day in the winter. As you approach the Equator, days and nights are more equal in length. **Location** Use the key to find the low latitudes. What is the climate like in this region? Why?

Looking at Latitudes

Look at the diagram on the next page. In some places on the Earth, the sun is directly overhead at particular days during the year. One place is the Equator, an imaginary latitude line that circles the Earth at 0°, exactly halfway between the North Pole (90°N) and the South Pole (90°S). On about March 21 and September 23, the sun is directly over the Equator. On those days, all over the Earth, days are almost exactly as long as nights. People call these days the spring and fall equinoxes.

Two other imaginary latitude lines lie $23\frac{1}{2}°$ north and $23\frac{1}{2}°$ south of the Equator. At $23\frac{1}{2}°$N is the Tropic of Cancer. Here, the sun shines directly above on June 21 or 22. This is the first day of summer, or the summer solstice (SOHL stiss), in the Northern Hemisphere. At $23\frac{1}{2}°$S is the Tropic of Capricorn. Here, the sun shines directly above on December 21 or 22. This is the first day of winter, or the winter solstice, in the Northern Hemisphere. The seasons are reversed in the Southern Hemisphere. When would the summer solstice occur there?

The area between the Tropic of Cancer and the Tropic of Capricorn is called the **low latitudes,** or the tropics. Any location in the low latitudes receives direct sunlight at some time during the year. In this region, it is almost always hot.

Two other latitude lines set off distinct regions. To the north of the Equator, at $66\frac{1}{2}°$N, is the Arctic Circle. To the south of the Equator, at $66\frac{1}{2}°$S, is the Antarctic Circle. The regions between these circles and the poles are the **high latitudes,** or the polar zones. The high latitudes receive no direct sunlight. It is very cool to bitterly cold.

Midnight Sun Earth's axis is at an angle, which makes the Earth seem to lean. When the North Pole leans toward the sun, the sun never sets. At the same time, the South Pole leans away from the sun, so at the South Pole, the sun never rises. This lasts for six months. When the South Pole leans toward the sun, this pole has six months of continuous sunlight. Sunlight at the poles falls at an angle, so the poles receive very little heat.

Seasons of the Northern Hemisphere

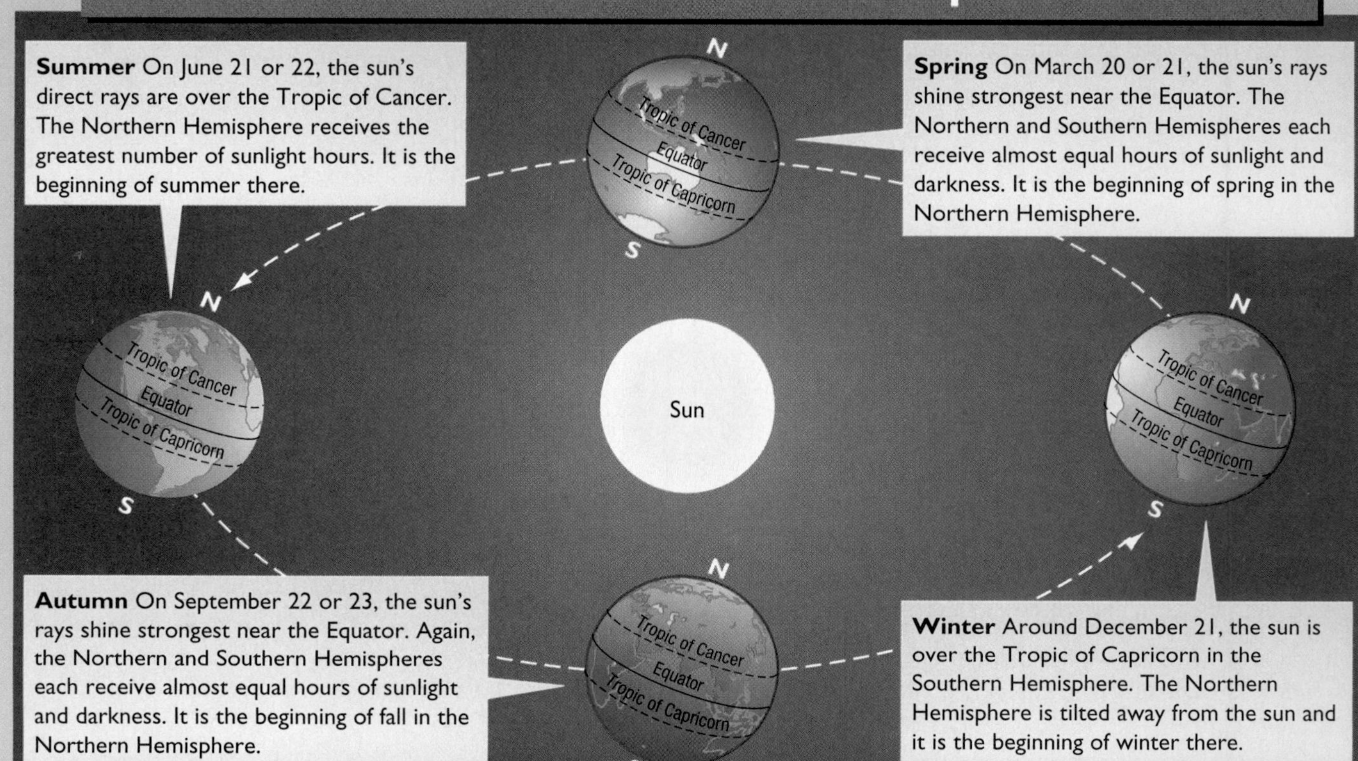

Summer On June 21 or 22, the sun's direct rays are over the Tropic of Cancer. The Northern Hemisphere receives the greatest number of sunlight hours. It is the beginning of summer there.
Spring On March 20 or 21, the sun's rays shine strongest near the Equator. The Northern and Southern Hemispheres each receive almost equal hours of sunlight and darkness. It is the beginning of spring in the Northern Hemisphere.
Autumn On September 22 or 23, the sun's rays shine strongest near the Equator. Again, the Northern and Southern Hemispheres each receive almost equal hours of sunlight and darkness. It is the beginning of fall in the Northern Hemisphere.
Winter Around December 21, the sun is over the Tropic of Capricorn in the Southern Hemisphere. The Northern Hemisphere is tilted away from the sun and it is the beginning of winter there.
Sun
N
S
Tropic of Cancer
Equator
Tropic of Capricorn

Chart Study As the Earth moves around the Sun, summer changes to fall and fall changes to winter. But the warmest and coldest weather does not start as soon as summer and winter begin. Why? Oceans and lakes also affect the weather, and they warm up and cool off slowly. **Critical Thinking** Australia lies in the Southern Hemisphere. What is the season in Australia when it is winter in the United States?

Two areas remain: the **middle latitudes,** or the temperate zones. At some times of the year, these areas receive fairly direct sunlight. At other times, they receive fairly indirect sunlight. So, the middle latitudes have seasons: spring, summer, winter, and fall. Each lasts about three months and has distinct patterns of daylight, temperature, and weather.

SECTION 1 REVIEW

1. **Define** (a) orbit, (b) revolution, (c) axis, (d) rotation, (e) low latitudes, (f) high latitudes, (g) middle latitudes.
2. **Identify** (a) Tropic of Cancer, (b) Tropic of Capricorn, (c) Arctic Circle, (d) Antarctic Circle.
3. The Earth revolves and the Earth rotates. Explain the difference between the two.
4. Why are seasons different in the Northern and Southern hemispheres?
5. What causes the Earth to have seasons?
6. Describe conditions in the high, middle, and low latitudes.

Critical Thinking

7. **Drawing Conclusions** What would happen to plant and animal life if the Earth did not tilt on its axis? Why?

Activity

8. **Writing to Learn** Write a storybook for a young child explaining the relationship between the Earth and the sun.

Land, Air, and Water

Reach Into Your Background

Think of one of your favorite outdoor activities, such as skiing, cycling, or hiking. Tell how the shape of the land helps you enjoy it.

Questions to Explore

1. What forces shape the land?
2. What are the Earth's major landforms?

Key Terms

landform
mountain
hill
plateau
plain
plate tectonics
plate
weathering
erosion
atmosphere

Key Places

Ring of Fire
Pangaea

Listen to the words of Megumi Fujiwara, a Japanese medical student who lived through the Great Hanshin Earthquake in 1995.

> "Early that morning, I had awakened hearing explosions and feeling my body rising. I knew immediately that it was an earthquake and expected the shaking to last only a moment. It didn't, and after landing back on my futon [bed], I lay frozen, listening to windows rattling and breaking [and] seeing objects flying above. Then everything blacked out. I awoke some time later, inhaling dust and unable to see anything. [I] found myself outside at ground level, rather than in my second-story apartment. Open sky had replaced my ceiling."

Fujiwara was lucky. The Great Hanshin Earthquake killed 5,500 people when it struck Kobe (KOH bay), Japan, on January 17, 1995.

Forces Inside the Earth

Japan knows about earthquakes because it is part of what geographers call the "Ring of Fire." About 90 percent of the world's earthquakes and many of the world's active volcanoes occur on the Ring, which circles the Pacific Ocean. Earthquakes and volcanoes are two forces that shape and reshape the Earth. They provide clues about the Earth's structure, and they are one reason why the Earth's surface constantly changes.

What Is the Earth Made Of? To understand events like volcanoes and earthquakes, you must study the Earth's structure. Pictures of the Earth show a great deal of water and some land. The water covers about 75 percent of the Earth's surface in lakes, rivers, seas, and oceans. Only 25 percent of the Earth's surface is land.

In part, continents are unique because of their **landforms,** or shapes and types of land. **Mountains** are landforms that rise usually more than 2,000 feet (610 m) above sea level. They are wide at the bottom and rise steeply to a narrow peak or ridge. **Hills** are lower and less steep than mountains, with rounded tops. A **plateau** is a large, mostly flat area that rises above the surrounding land. At least one side of a plateau has a steep slope. **Plains** are large areas of flat or gently rolling land. Many are along coasts. Others are in the interiors of some continents.

Predict Why do scientists think the Earth once had only one, large landmass?

Pangaea: The Supercontinent For hundreds of years, as geographers studied the Earth's landforms, they asked "where" and "why" questions. When they looked at the globe, they thought they saw a relationship between landforms that were very far apart.

The World: Continents, Oceans, and Seas

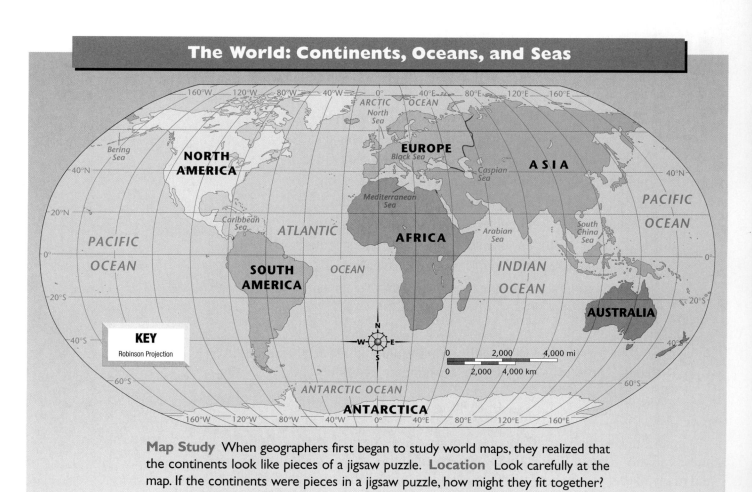

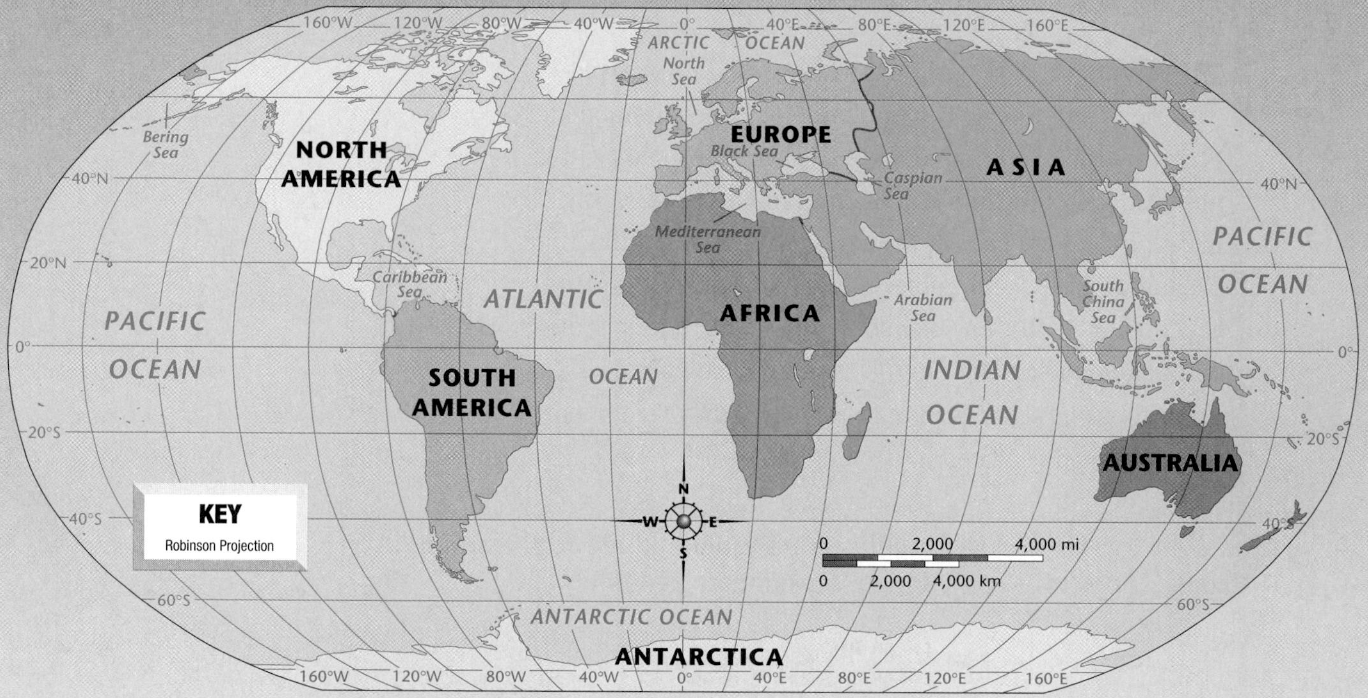

Map Study When geographers first began to study world maps, they realized that the continents look like pieces of a jigsaw puzzle. **Location** Look carefully at the map. If the continents were pieces in a jigsaw puzzle, how might they fit together?

The Movement of the Continents

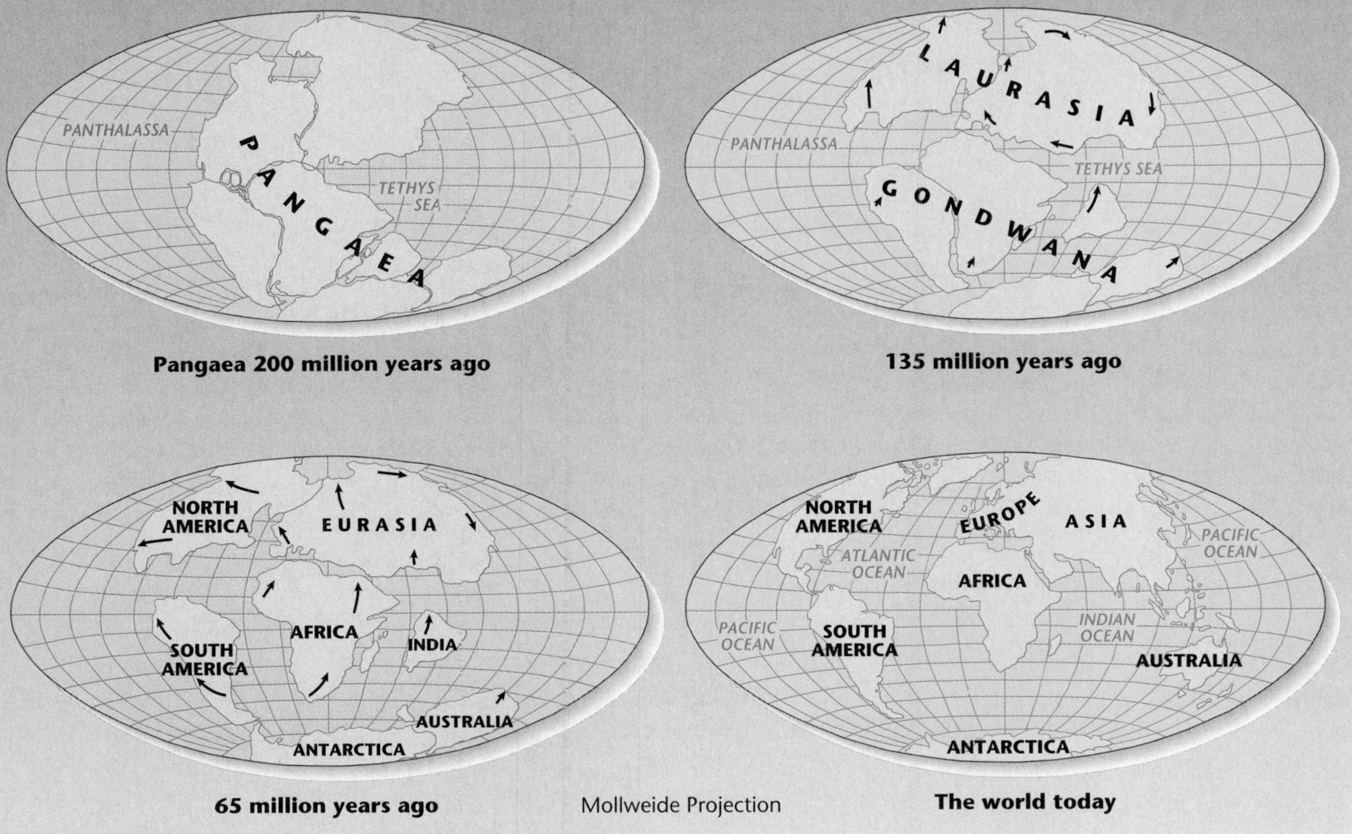

Pangaea 200 million years ago

135 million years ago

65 million years ago

Mollweide Projection

The world today

Map Study The first animals to walk on land lived on Pangaea. Birds and dinosaurs first appeared on Laurasia and Gondwana, and dinosaurs died not long after the continents began to separate. Humans did not appear until two million years ago. **Movement** If you were a scientist trying to prove the theory of plate tectonics, what clues would you look for?

Today, geographers theorize that millions of years ago the Earth had only one huge landmass. They called it Pangaea (pan JEE uh). Scientists reasoned that about 200 million years ago, some force made Pangaea split into several pieces, and it began to move apart. Over millions of years, the pieces formed separate continents.

But why did the continents separate? To explain this question, geographers use a theory called **plate tectonics.** It says the outer skin of the Earth, called the crust, is broken into huge pieces called **plates.** The continents and oceans are the top of the crust. Below the plates is a layer of rock called magma, which is hot enough to be fairly soft. The plates float on the magma, altering the shape of the Earth's surface. Continents are part of plates, and plates shift over time. We cannot see them move because it is very slow and takes a long time. When geographers say a plate moves quickly, they mean it may shift two inches (five cm) a year.

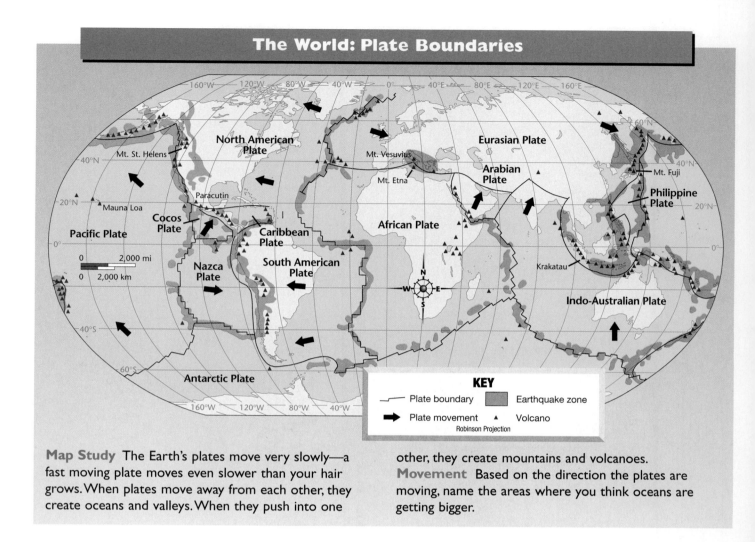

The World: Plate Boundaries

KEY
Plate boundary
Earthquake zone
Plate movement
Volcano
Robinson Projection

Map Study The Earth's plates move very slowly—a fast moving plate moves even slower than your hair grows. When plates move away from each other, they create oceans and valleys. When they push into one other, they create mountains and volcanoes. **Movement** Based on the direction the plates are moving, name the areas where you think oceans are getting bigger.

A New Island For thousands of years, magma from underwater volcanoes built up until it rose above sea level to create the Hawaiian islands. Today, a new island, named Loihi (low EE hee), is forming. Already two miles (3.2 km) high, it has 3,000 feet (914 m) to go before it breaks the ocean's surface. Loihi erupts almost all the time. It causes earthquakes and tidal waves that threaten the other islands.

Volcanoes, Earthquakes, and Shifting Plates Look at the map of plate boundaries on this page. It shows that plates move in different directions. In some places, plates move apart, and magma leaks out through cracks in the crust. In the oceans, over time, the cooling rock builds up to form lines of underwater mountains called ridges. On either side of the line, the plates move away from each other.

In other places, the plates push against one another, forcing one plate under the other. Tremendous pressure and heat builds up. Molten rock races upward, exploding onto the surface and producing a volcano.

Along plate boundaries, there are many weak places in the Earth's crust. When plates push against one another, the crust cracks and splinters from the pressure. The cracks are called faults. When the crust moves along faults, it releases great amounts of energy in the form of earthquakes. These movements can cause dramatic changes.

Forces on the Earth's Surface

Forces like volcanoes slowly build up the Earth; other forces slowly break it down. Often, the forces that break the Earth down are not as dramatic as volcanoes, but the results can last just as long.

Weathering is a process that breaks rocks down into tiny pieces. Three things cause weathering: wind, rain, and ice. Slowly but surely, they wear away the Earth's landforms. Hills and low, rounded mountains show what weathering can do. The Appalachian Mountains in the eastern United States once were as high as the Rocky Mountains of the western United States. Wind and rain weathered them into much lower peaks. Weathering helps create soil, too. Tiny pieces of rock combine with decayed animal and plant material to form soil.

Once this breaking down has taken place, small pieces of rock may be carried to new places by a process called **erosion.** Weathering and erosion slowly create new landforms.

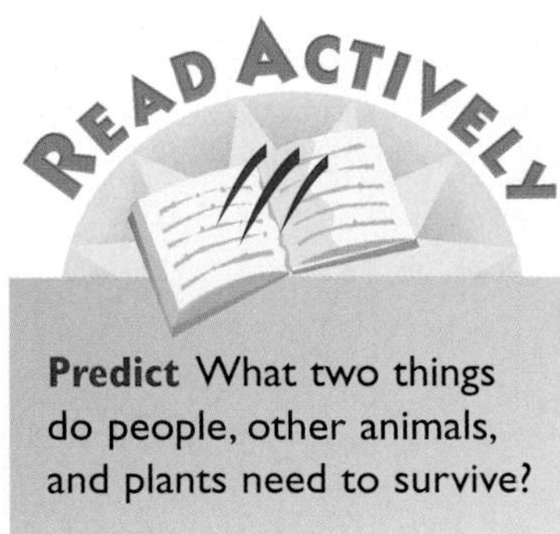

Predict What two things do people, other animals, and plants need to survive?

Air and Water: Two Ingredients for Life

The Earth is surrounded by a thick layer of special gases called the **atmosphere.** It provides life-giving oxygen for people and animals and life-giving carbon dioxide for plants. The atmosphere also acts like a blanket. It holds in the amount of heat from the sun that makes life possible. Winds, as you can see in the map below, help to distribute this heat around the globe.

About 97 percent of the Earth's water is found in its oceans. This water is salty. Fresh water, or water without salt, makes up only a tiny percentage of all the Earth's water. Most fresh water is frozen at the

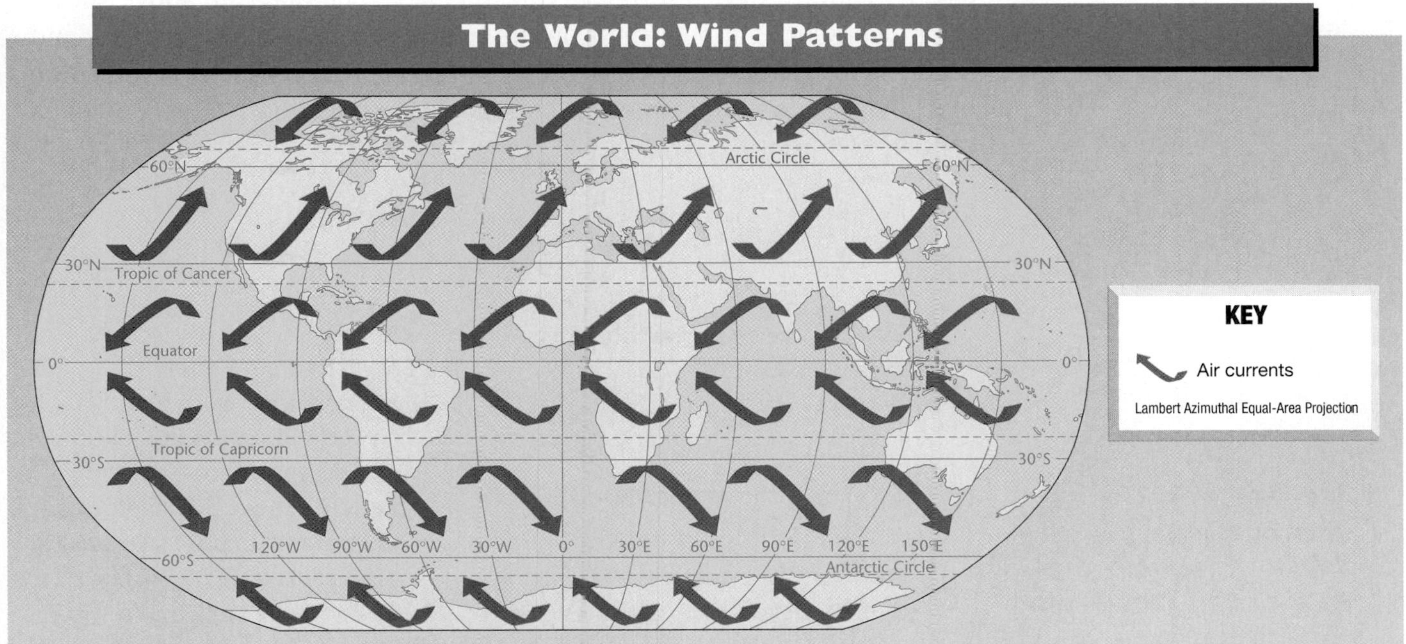

Map Study What makes the wind blow? Part of the answer is that the sun warms some areas of the Earth more than others. Since heat always flows toward cooler areas, warm air moves into areas of cooler air, creating winds. **Movement** Which way does the air flow between the Tropic of Cancer and the Arctic Circle—toward the tropics or toward the Arctic Circle? Why?

The Water Cycle

Chart Study Ocean water is too salty to drink or to irrigate crops. However, the oceans are a source of fresh water. How does this happen? When water evaporates from the ocean's surface, salt is left behind. The water vapor rises and forms clouds. The rain that falls to the Earth is fresh. **Critical Thinking** Once rain has fallen, how does water return to the ocean?

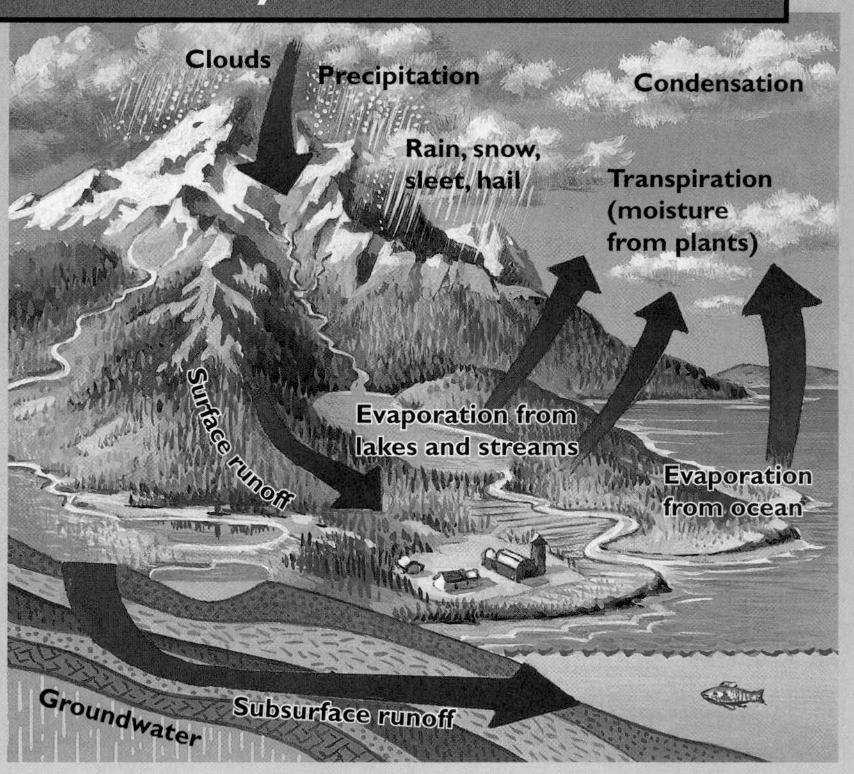

North and South poles. People need fresh water for many things. This fresh water comes from lakes, rivers, and rain. Also, much fresh water, called groundwater, is stored in the soil itself. The diagram above shows the movement of all the water on the Earth's surface, in the ground, and in the air. The Earth does have enough water for people. However, some places have too much water and other places have too little.

1. **Define** (a) landform, (b) mountain, (c) hill, (d) plateau, (e) plain, (f) plate tectonics, (g) plate, (h) weathering, (i) erosion, (j) atmosphere.
2. **Identify** (a) Ring of Fire, (b) Pangaea.
3. Why are there earthquakes and volcanoes?
4. What forces on the Earth's surface break down rocks?
5. Why is the atmosphere important?

Critical Thinking

6. **Distinguishing Fact From Opinion** What facts support the theory of plate tectonics?

Activity

7. **Writing to Learn** Suppose you were able to see the region you live in 10,000 years from now. Describe how the landforms might look. Explain what might have caused those changes.

Climate and What Influences It

Reach Into Your Background

Thunderstorms can knock down power lines and trees. Hurricanes can destroy whole communities. What is the worst weather you have experienced? How did you feel? How did you stay safe?

Questions to Explore

1. What is climate?
2. How do landforms and bodies of water affect climate?

Key Terms

weather
temperature
precipitation
climate

Key Names and Places

Gulf Stream
Peru Current
California Current
St. Louis
San Francisco

In late May 1996, a tornado's furious winds tore down the movie screen of a drive-in theater in St. Catherine's, Ontario, Canada. Ironically, the week's feature movie was *Twister,* a film about tornadoes.

Richard and Daphne Thompson spend their time tracking tornadoes in Oklahoma. Daphne Thompson recalls one particular storm: "The car was hit by 50- to 70-mile-per-hour gusts," she says. "Tumbleweeds were blowing so hard one left a dent in the car."

Weather or Climate?

These two stories show that weather like tornadoes can be dangerous. Or is it "climate" like tornadoes? What is the difference between weather and climate?

Every morning, most people check the temperature outside before they get dressed. But in some parts of India, people have very serious reasons for watching the **weather,** or the day-to-day changes in the air. In this region, it rains only during one period of the year. No one living there wants the rainy days to end too soon. That rain must fill the wells with enough fresh water to last through the coming dry spell.

▼ Tornadoes can easily flatten buildings. Tornado winds are the most powerful and violent winds on the Earth.

The World: Climate Regions

Map Study Many factors, including nearness to the Equator and to bodies of water, affect climate. **Regions** What are the two major climate regions of South America? What is the major climate region of North Africa?

80°N
60°N
40°N
Tropic of Cancer
20°N
0°
Equator
Tropic of Capricorn
60°S
Antarctic Circle
120°W
80°W
40°W
160°W
ATLANTIC OCEAN
PACIFIC OCEAN
N
S
E
W

KEY

Tropical
- Tropical wet
- Tropical wet and dry

Dry
- Semiarid
- Arid

Mild
- Mediterranean
- Humid subtropical
- Marine west coast

Continental
- Humid continental
- Subarctic

Polar
- Tundra
- Ice cap
- Highlands
- Ice pack

Robinson Projection

Weather is measured primarily by temperature and precipitation. **Temperature** is how hot or cold the air feels. **Precipitation** is water that falls to the ground as rain, sleet, hail, or snow.

Climate is not the same as weather. The **climate** of a place is the average weather over many years. Weather is what people see from day to day. A day is rainy or it is dry. Climate is what people know from experience happens from year to year.

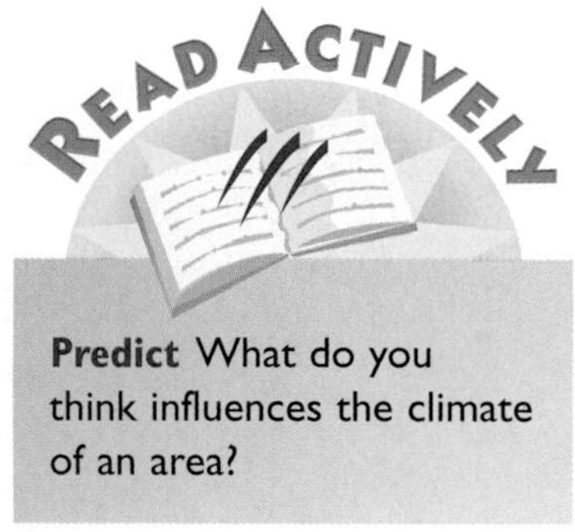

Predict What do you think influences the climate of an area?

Latitude, Landforms, and Climate The Earth has many climate regions. Some climates are hot enough that people rarely need to wear a sweater. In some cold climates, snow stays on the ground most of the year. And there are places on the Earth where between 30 and 40 feet (9 and 12 meters) of rain fall in a single year. Geographers know climates are different in the low, middle, and high latitudes, because latitude affects temperature. Major landforms such as mountains also affect climates in neighboring areas. Wind and water also play a role.

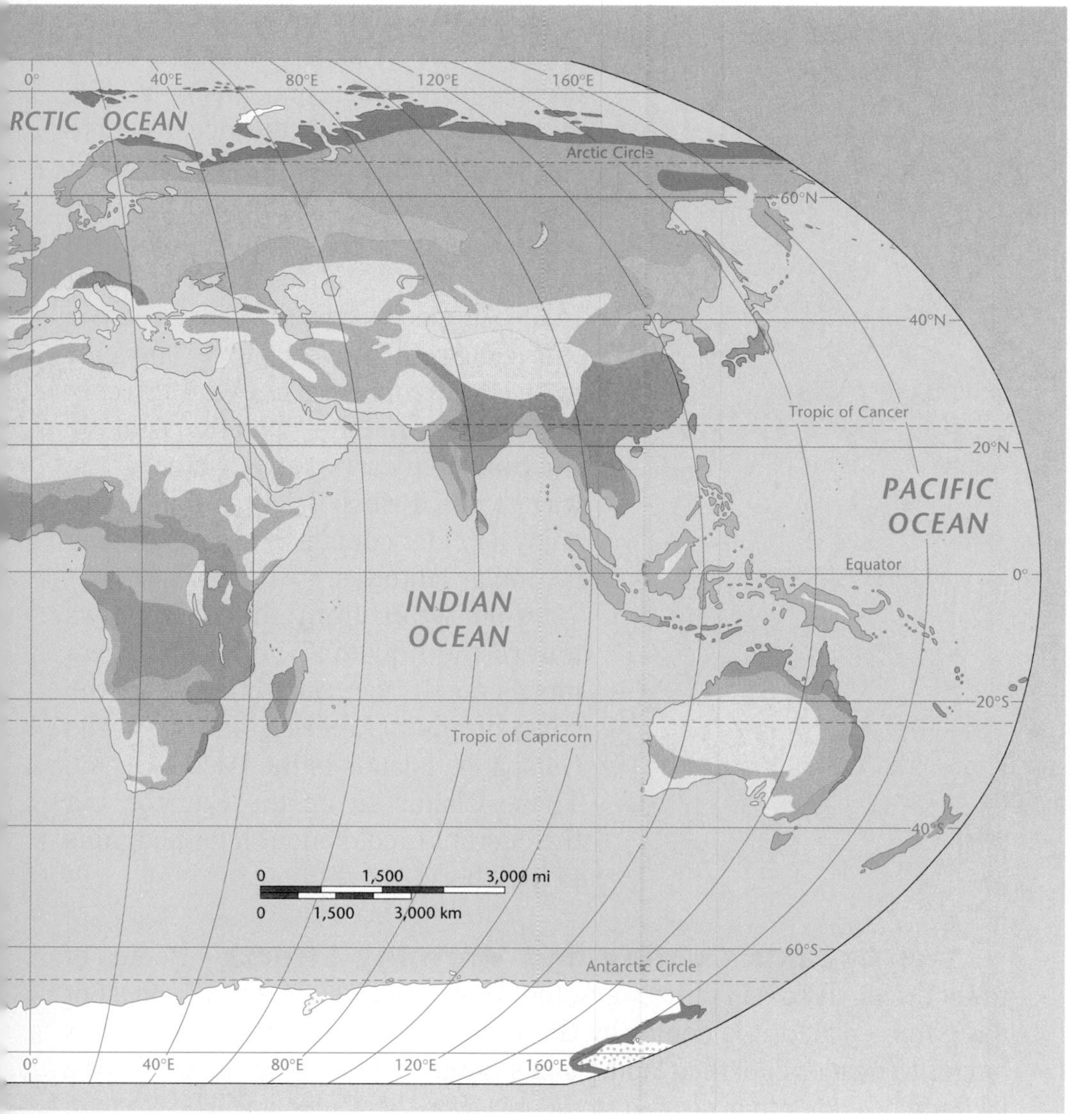

Smog Normally, air is cooler at higher altitudes. During a temperature inversion, however, a layer of warm air sits on top of the cooler air. The warm air traps pollution near the ground. This mixture of dangerous smoke and fog is called smog. The brown air seen in cities such as Los Angeles and Denver is smog caused by car exhaust.

Wind and Water

Without wind and water, the Earth would overheat. If you sit in the sun for a while on a hot day, you will feel warmer and warmer. The same thing could happen to the tropical regions of the Earth if wind and water did not help spread the sun's heat.

The Blowing Winds In part, the Earth's rotation creates our winds. Because of it, air moves in an east-west direction, as the map at the end of the last section shows. Two other factors make air move in a north-south direction: (1) Hot air rises and circulates toward regions where the air is not as hot. (2) Cold air sinks and moves toward regions where the air is warmer. As a result, hot, moist air from the Equator rises in the atmosphere, then moves toward the North Pole or the South Pole. Cold, dry air from the poles moves toward the Equator. This movement helps keep the Earth from overheating.

Relief and Precipitation

Chart Study As moist air blowing from the ocean rises up a mountain, it cools and drops its moisture. **Critical Thinking** Describe the climate on a mountain's leeward side—or side away from the wind.

Ocean Currents: Hot and Cold The Earth's rotation also creates ocean currents, which are like fast-moving rivers in the oceans. Like winds, ocean currents travel great distances. As you can see on the map on the next page, warm water from near the Equator moves north or south. In the Atlantic Ocean, the Gulf Stream, a warm current, travels north and east from the tropics. The Gulf Stream merges with the North Atlantic Current to to carry warm water all the way to the British Isles. People there enjoy a milder climate than people living in similar latitudes.

Cold water from the poles flows toward the Equator. The Peru Current moves north from Antarctica, along the coast of South America, and on to the Galapagos Islands in the Pacific Ocean. These islands sit on the Equator, but the current is cold enough for penguins to live there.

The Ocean's Cooling and Warming Effects Bodies of water affect climate in other ways, too. Have you gone to a beach on a hot day? You learned it is cooler by the water. That is because water takes longer to heat or cool than land. So in summer, a place near the ocean or a lake will be cooler than an area farther away. In the winter, it will be warmer.

For example, consider two places in the United States—San Francisco, California, and St. Louis, Missouri. Both cities have an average annual temperature of about 55°F (13°C). Their climates, however, are quite different. San Francisco borders the Pacific Ocean. The California Current passes by the city, carrying cool water from the waters off Alaska. In winter, the ocean current is warmer than the air, so the current gives off warmth and the air temperature rises. A San Franciscan traveling to St. Louis in December would find it much colder there than at home. In summer, the current is colder than the air, so the current absorbs heat, making the air temperature fall. A San Franciscan probably would find the summer months in St. Louis uncomfortably warm.

Ask Questions What would you like to know about the raging storms that are part of the Earth's climate?

Raging Storms Wind and water can make climates milder, but they also can create storms. Some storms cause great destruction. Hurricane Andrew, for example, struck south Florida in the early morning hours of August 24, 1992, and left 160,000 people homeless. Julius Keaton recalls what happened:

"I heard one window break, so I jumped up and put a mattress against it. But I guess that storm really wanted to get in, 'cause it blew out another window and beat down the front door."

Hurricanes are wind and rain storms that form over the tropics in the Atlantic Ocean. The whirling winds at the center of a hurricane travel over 73 miles (122 km) per hour and can reach speeds of more than 100 miles (160 km) an hour. Hurricanes produce huge waves called storm surges, which flood over shorelines and can destroy homes and towns. Typhoons are similar storms that take place in the Pacific Ocean.

Hurricanes and typhoons affect large areas. One single hurricane can threaten islands in the Caribbean Sea, the east coast of Mexico, and the southern coast of the United States. Other storms are just as dangerous, but they affect smaller areas. Tornadoes, for example, are swirling funnels of wind that can reach 200 miles (320 km) per hour. The winds and the vacuum they create in their centers can wreck almost

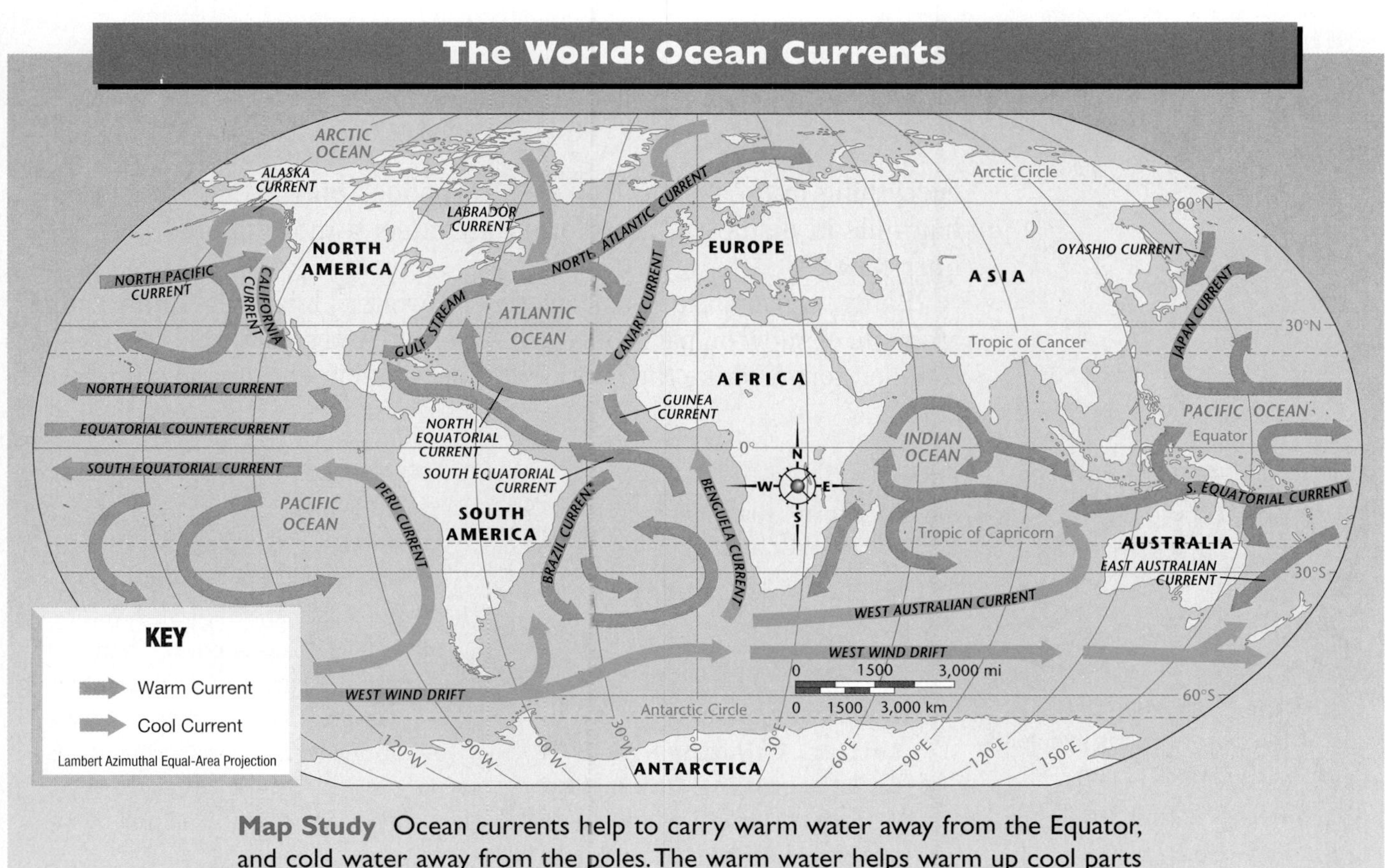

Map Study Ocean currents help to carry warm water away from the Equator, and cold water away from the poles. The warm water helps warm up cool parts of the Earth, while the cold water cools down warm areas. **Regions** Which ocean currents affect the coasts of North America?

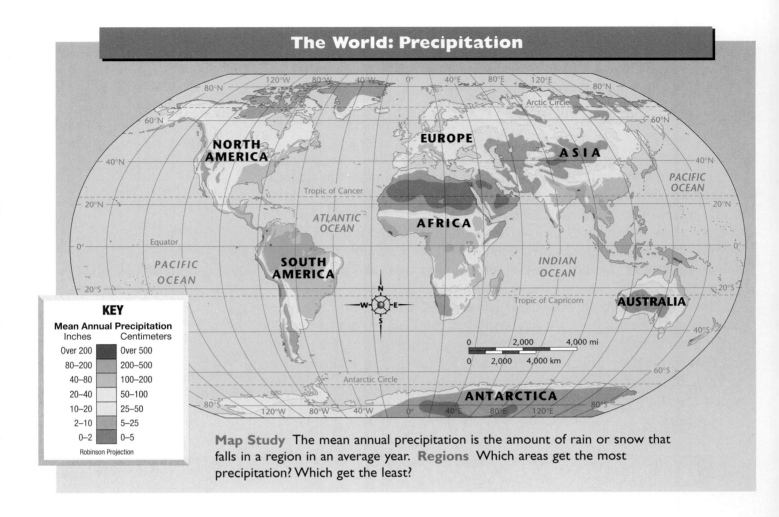

The World: Precipitation

KEY

Mean Annual Precipitation

Inches	Centimeters
Over 200	Over 500
80–200	200–500
40–80	100–200
20–40	50–100
10–20	25–50
2–10	5–25
0–2	0–5

Robinson Projection

Map Study The mean annual precipitation is the amount of rain or snow that falls in a region in an average year. **Regions** Which areas get the most precipitation? Which get the least?

everything in their path. However, tornadoes only average about one-half mile in diameter. Therefore, they affect a more limited area than hurricanes.

Some storms are less severe. In winter, blizzards dump huge amounts of snow on parts of North America. And severe rainstorms and thunderstorms strike the continent most often in spring and summer.

1. Define (a) weather, (b) temperature, (c) precipitation, (d) climate.

2. Identify (a) Gulf Stream, (b) Peru Current, (c) California Current, (d) St. Louis, (e) San Francisco.

3. Explain the difference between weather and climate.

4. How does latitude affect climate?

5. How do mountains affect neighboring climates?

Critical Thinking

6. Recognizing Cause and Effect Explain how currents from the tropics affect climates far away.

Activity

7. Writing to Learn Check a newspaper's local weather forecasts for the last several weeks. Make a chart. Then write a paragraph about your climate. Use what you know about your region's climate to describe the weather as normal or abnormal for this time of year.

How Climate Affects Vegetation

Reach Into Your Background
Make a list of some plants and trees native to your area. How much rain and sunlight do they seem to need? How do they react to unusual weather?

Questions to Explore

1. Where are the Earth's major climate regions?
2. What kinds of vegetation grow in each climate region?

Key Terms
vegetation
canopy
tundra
vertical climate

Key Place
Great Plains
Arctic Circle

Suppose you live in Arizona. You may walk past cactus plants on the way to school. In Minnesota, you may see leafy trees that change color in the fall. In Georgia, you may see Spanish moss draped along bald cypress trees. All these differences are related to climate.

▼ Cacti have waxy skins that hold water in. Prickly spines protect a cactus from being eaten by animals that want its water.

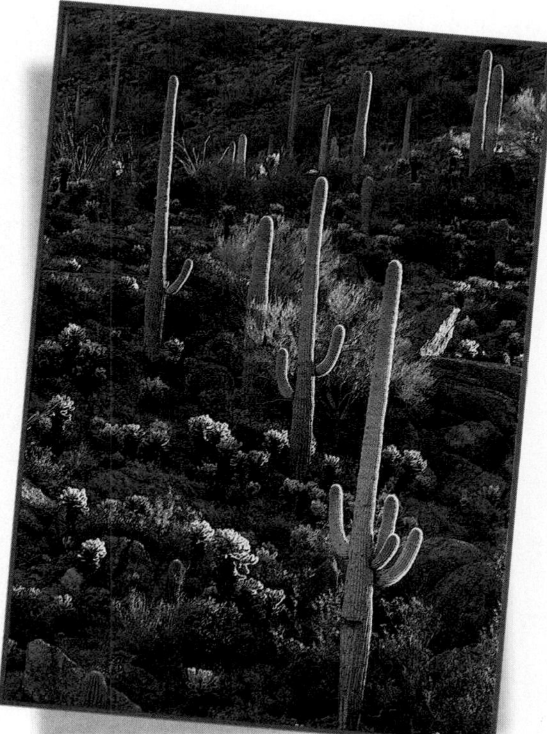

Climate and Vegetation

A climate must provide plants with water, sunlight, and certain nutrients, or elements, plants use as food. Also, plants have features, called *adaptations,* that enable them to live in their particular climate. That means that over a very long time, small, accidental changes in a few individual plants made them better able to survive in a particular place.

How do geographers use such information? They can predict the kinds of plants they will find in a climate. Geographers discuss five broad types of climates: tropical, dry, moderate, continental, and polar. Each has its unique **vegetation,** or plants that grow there naturally.

Tropical Climates In the low latitudes, you will find two types of tropical climates. Both are hot and wet. A tropical wet climate has two seasons—one with a great deal of rain and one with a little less rain. A tropical wet and dry climate also has two seasons: one with much rain and one with very little rain. The vegetation associated with these climates is tropical rain forest.

Because growing conditions are so perfect—there is so much light, heat, and rain—thousands of kinds of plants grow in a rain forest. Some trees rise 130 feet (40 meters) into the air. Their uppermost branches create a **canopy.** Little sunlight can break through this dense covering of leafy branches. Other types of trees, which are adapted to the shade, grow to lower heights. Thousands of kinds of vines and ferns thrive in the rain forest.

Predict What kinds of adaptations would the vegetation of dry climates need to develop?

Dry Climates Arid and semiarid climates are very hot but receive very little rain. Since there is so little moisture, vegetation in dry regions is sparse. Plants grow far apart in sandy, gravelly soil. Their shallow roots are adapted to absorb scarce water before it evaporates in the heat. Some plants have small leaves, which lose little moisture into the air through evaporation. Other plants flower only when it rains so that as many seeds survive as possible.

The World: Natural Vegetation

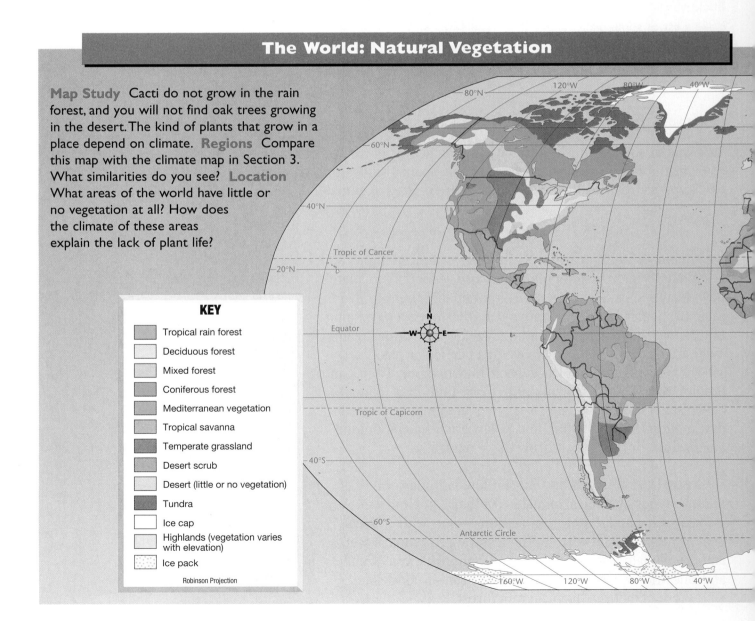

Map Study Cacti do not grow in the rain forest, and you will not find oak trees growing in the desert. The kind of plants that grow in a place depend on climate. **Regions** Compare this map with the climate map in Section 3. What similarities do you see? **Location** What areas of the world have little or no vegetation at all? How does the climate of these areas explain the lack of plant life?

KEY

- Tropical rain forest
- Deciduous forest
- Mixed forest
- Coniferous forest
- Mediterranean vegetation
- Tropical savanna
- Temperate grassland
- Desert scrub
- Desert (little or no vegetation)
- Tundra
- Ice cap
- Highlands (vegetation varies with elevation)
- Ice pack

Robinson Projection

80°N 60°N 40°N 20°N Tropic of Cancer Equator Tropic of Capicorn 40°S 60°S Antarctic Circle 160°W 120°W 80°W 40°W N S E W

Moderate Climates Moderate climates are found in the middle latitudes. There are three types: Mediterranean, marine west coast, and humid subtropical. In all three climate types, rain is moderate. There are seasonal changes, but temperatures hardly ever fall below freezing.

Moderate climates have a wide variety of vegetation. Forests of deciduous trees, which lose their leaves in the fall, grow here. So do tall shrubs, low bushes—or scrub—wildflowers, and a variety of grasses. The Mediterranean climate receives most of its rain in winter and summers are hot and dry. In this climate, plants have leathery leaves, which hold in moisture during the dry summers. Of the three moderate climates, the humid subtropical climate has the most precipitation, heat, and humidity. It supports many types of vegetation. Most marine west coast climates are mountainous and are cooled by ocean currents. Therefore, they support more forests than grasses.

To Be a Leader

In the 1970s, Michael Stewartt was a charter airplane pilot in Alaska. Every day he flew over its vast forests, where he could see the damage to national forests from clear-cut logging. Lawmakers should see this for themselves, he thought. So, Stewartt founded LightHawk, an environmental plane service that took people on educational "tours" in the air. LightHawk continues today. It also creates plans for change.

A Study in Contrasts

Antarctica (right) is an "icy desert"—a world of permanent ice and snow. In contrast, Oregon (below) is a world of constant green, teeming with life. **Critical Thinking** How do you think humans could adapt to living in each of these environments?

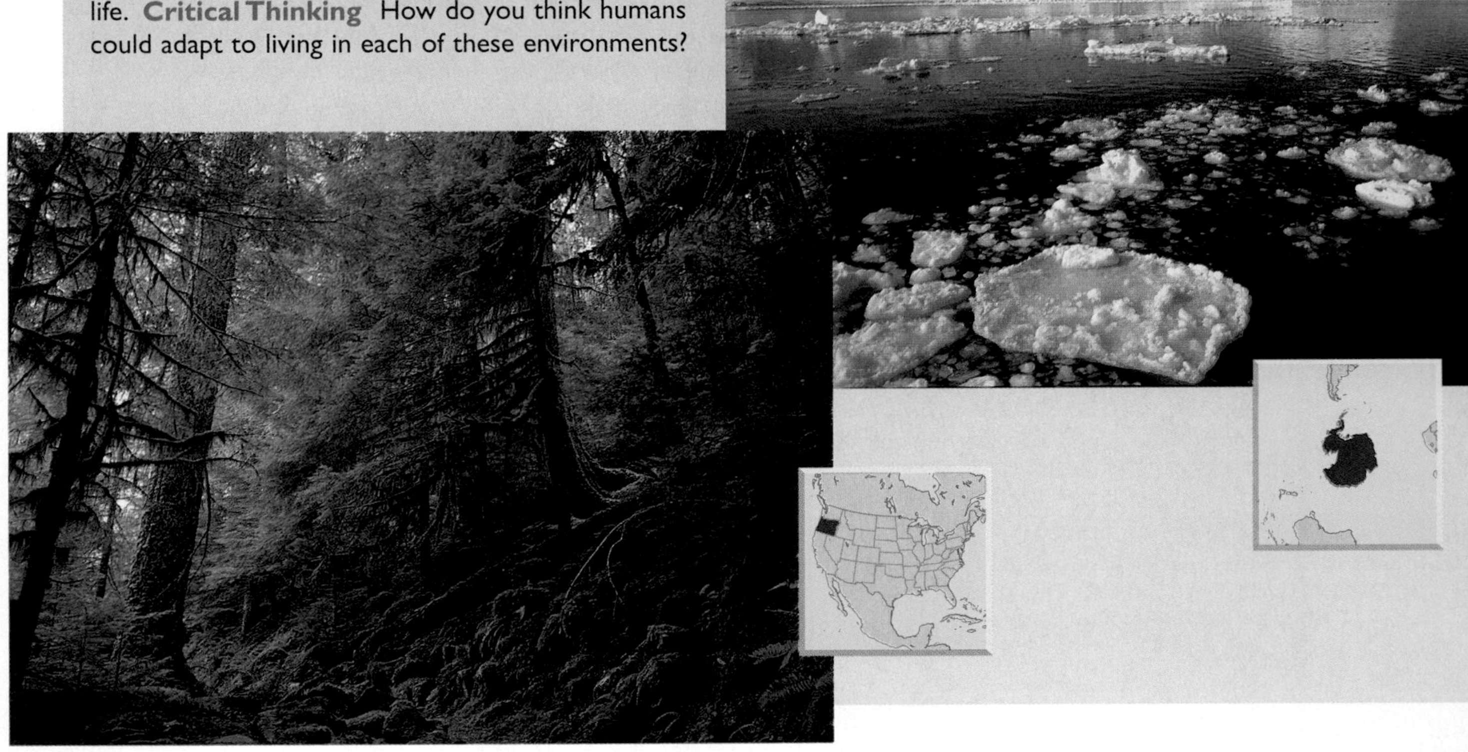

Plant Fossils In ancient rocks in Wyoming, scientists have found fossils of palm trees. Centuries ago, sediments such as sand or ash buried the plants quickly. Over thousands of years, the buildup continued. Slowly, the plants turned to rock. Scientists study fossils to learn about ancient climate and vegetation. Scientists also learn how climate and vegetation have changed over time.

Continental Climates In a humid continental climate, summer temperatures are moderate to hot, but winters can be very cold. This kind of climate supports grasslands and forests. Grasses tend to be tall. The first European settlers on the Great Plains of the United States noted that the grass there was high enough to hide a horse and its rider! Certain areas in this climate region support large deciduous forests. In areas where winters are colder, coniferous forests are found. Coniferous trees have needles, not leaves, and have cones to produce seeds. These adaptations provide protection through the winter.

Regions with subarctic continental climates are much drier, with cool summers and cold winters. Grasses are much shorter. Some subarctic continental areas have huge coniferous forests. Others, however, have few trees.

Polar Climates and Their Vegetation The polar climates of the high latitudes are cold all year around. The **tundra,** which lies along the Arctic Circle, has short, cold summers and long, even colder winters. No trees grow here. Low shrubs bloom during brief summers. Mosses and strange plants called lichens (LY kuhns) grow on the surfaces of rocks. In the northern regions of the tundra, it is even colder and precipitation is very scarce. Only low grasses, mosses, lichens, and a few flowering plants grow.

A Vertical Climate

The climate at the top of Mount Everest, in Nepal in Southeast Asia, is like Antarctica's. But Mount Everest is near the Tropic of Cancer, far from the South Pole. Why is it so cold at the top of the mountain? A mountain is an example of **vertical climate,** where the climate changes according to the mountain's height.

Picture yourself on a hike up a mountain in a moderate climate. Grasslands surround the base of the mountain, and temperatures are warm. You begin to climb and soon enter a region with less precipitation than below. There are short grasses, like those in a continental climate. As you climb higher, you move through deciduous forests. It is cooler and drier here. Slowly the forests change to coniferous trees.

As you continue to climb, you find only scattered, short trees. Finally, there are only low shrubs and short grasses. Soon it is too cold and dry even for them. Mainly you see only the mosses and lichens of a tundra. And at the mountain top, you find an icecap climate, where no vegetation grows.

Vertical Climate Zones

Vertical climate zones determine land use. At an elevation of 6,762 feet (2,061 m), this Swiss village can grow hay and graze cattle. **Critical Thinking** What activities do you think happen at the higher elevations seen in this photograph?

1. **Define** (a) vegetation, (b) canopy, (c) tundra, (d) vertical climate.
2. **Identify** (a) Great Plains, (b) Arctic Circle.
3. Why do polar climates have sparse vegetation?
4. What climate region has the most varied vegetation? Why?
5. How are continental climates different from moderate climates?

Critical Thinking

6. **Drawing Conclusions** Choose a climate region. Explain why certain kinds of plants do *not* grow there.

Activity

7. **Writing to Learn** Research three different cities. Find out what climate and vegetation regions they are in. Write an essay explaining how climate and vegetation affects everyday life in these cities.

Using Special Geography Graphs

"Everybody talks about the weather," Mark Twain is supposed to have said, "but nobody does anything about it." The great humorist was both right and wrong. People have always talked about the weather. Where we live and what we do are all affected by weather and climate.

Because weather is such a big part of life, people have tried to do something about it. For example, hundreds of years ago people in Europe tried to get rid of thunderstorms by ringing church bells. Today, people "seed" clouds with chemicals to try to cause rainfall.

Trying to "do something" about the weather is not very successful. Geographers have managed to do one thing very well, however. That is to gather information about weather and climate. One of the ways geographers do this is by making a climate graph. It usually shows average precipitation and average temperature.

Get Ready

A climate graph is really two graphs in one. Look at the climate graph on this page, for the city of São Paulo, Brazil. The graph has two parts: a line graph and a bar graph. The line graph shows temperature. The scale for temperature is along the graph's left side. The bar graph shows precipitation. The scale for average precipitation in inches is along the right side of the graph. Finally, along the bottom of the graph are the labels for months of the year.

A good way to learn more about climate graphs is to make one of your own. You will need:

- a sheet of graph paper
- a lead pencil
- two different colored pencils

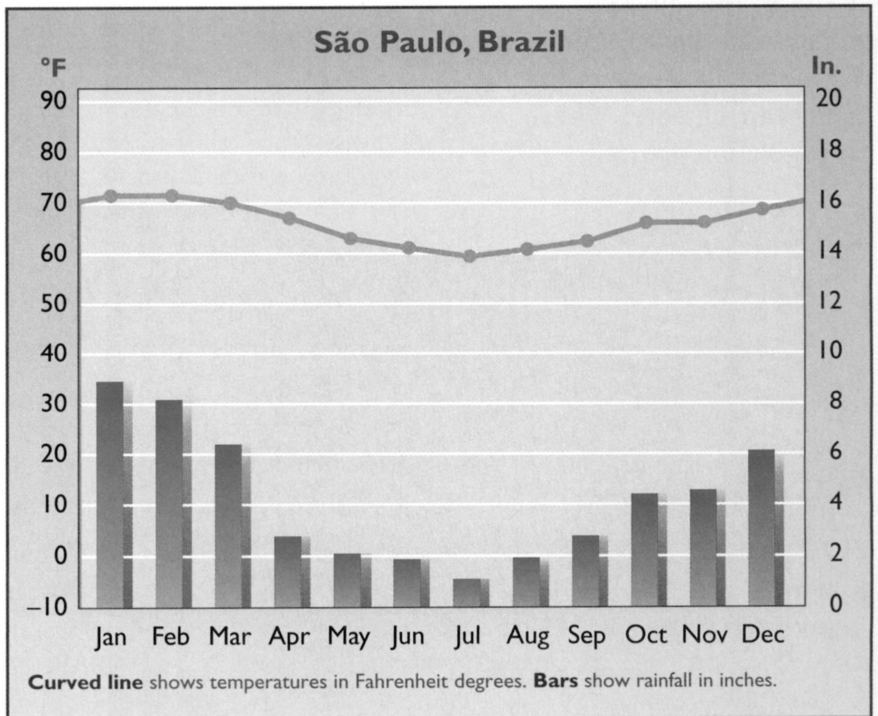

Curved line shows temperatures in Fahrenheit degrees. **Bars** show rainfall in inches.

▶ During which months do you think most thunderstorms occur in South Carolina?

Try It Out

A. Draw a grid. Use the graph paper and the lead pencil to draw a large square. Divide the square into 10 horizontal rows and 12 vertical rows.

B. Label the grid. At the top of the graph, write Charleston, the name of the city you will graph. Using the lead pencil, copy the labels on the climate graph as shown on the previous page. Put labels for temperature on the left side of the graph. Put labels for precipitation on the right side. Finally, put labels for the months of the year along the bottom of the graph.

C. Make a line graph. The data on this page is for Charleston, South Carolina. Use the temperature data to plot a line graph. Use the climate graph on the opposite page as a model. Plot your line graph with one of the colored pencils.

D. Make a bar graph. Now use the data for precipitation to make a bar graph. Use the climate graph on the opposite page as a model. Plot your bar graph with the other colored pencil.

Charleston, South Carolina		
	Temperature (Fahrenheit)	Precipitation (inches)
January	48	3.5
February	51	3.5
March	58	4.5
April	65	3.0
May	73	4.0
June	78	6.5
July	82	7.0
August	81	7.0
September	76	5.0
October	67	3.0
November	58	2.5
December	51	3.0

Apply the Skill

Use the steps below to practice reading your climate graph.

1. **Compare differences in temperature.** (a) Which month has the highest temperature in Charleston? (b) Which month has the lowest?

2. **Compare differences in precipitation.** (a) Which months have the highest precipitation? (b) Which month has the lowest?

3. **Describe the climate.** Temperature and precipitation are two major factors that determine a climate. Using the information presented in the climate graph, how would you describe Charleston's climate?

CHAPTER 2

Review and Activities

Reviewing Main Ideas

1. What causes day and night?
2. Why are the seasons at higher latitudes different from seasons at latitudes near the Equator?
3. How do plate tectonics shape the Earth?
4. What is the difference between weathering and erosion?
5. Why can two places have the same average temperatures but still have different climates?
6. How are climates closer to the poles similar to the tops of vertical climates?
7. (a) List five major climate regions in the world. (b) Then choose one of them and describe plants that live there.

Reviewing Key Terms

Use each key term below in a sentence that shows the meaning of the term.

1. orbit
2. revolution
3. axis
4. rotation
5. plate tectonics
6. weathering
7. erosion
8. atmosphere
9. weather
10. temperature
11. precipitation
12. climate
13. vegetation
14. tundra
15. vertical climate

Critical Thinking

1. **Identifying Central Issues** How does water affect a region's landforms and climate?
2. **Recognizing Cause and Effect** Why is the Earth continually changing form?

Graphic Organizer

Copy the chart on a separate sheet of paper. Select three climates from tropical, dry, moderate, continental, or polar. Write one term in each box of column 1. In column 2, write temperature, precipitation, plus other important information.

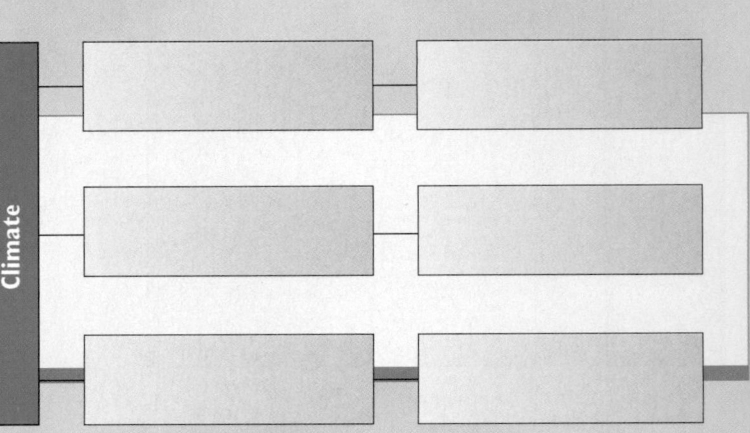

Map Activity

North America

For each place listed below, write the letter on the map that shows its location. Use the Atlas at the back of the book to complete the exercise.

1. Tropic of Cancer
2. Appalachian Mountains
3. Rocky Mountains
4. Arctic Circle
5. Great Plains

Place Location

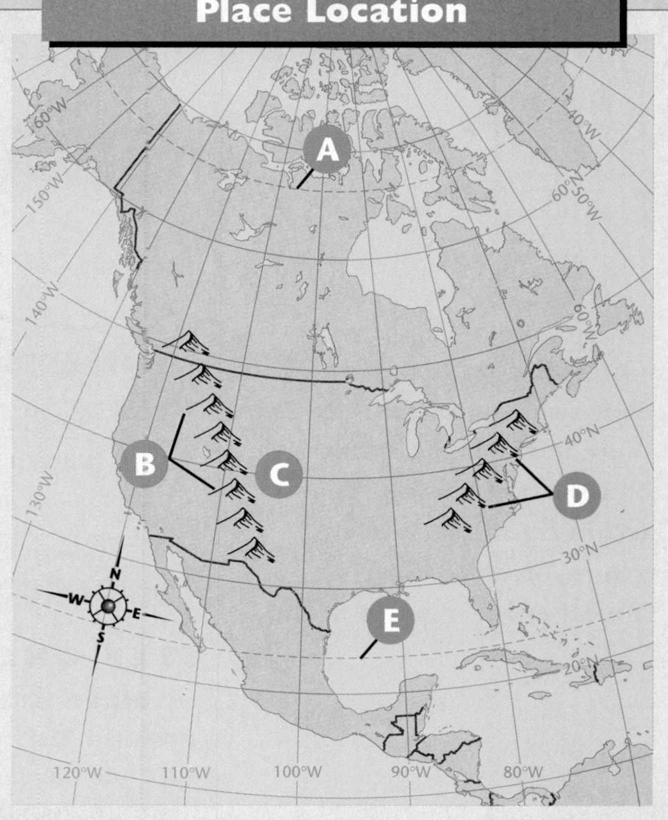

Writing Activity

Writing a News Report

Choose a well-known natural disaster such as Hurricane Mitch or the eruption of Mount St. Helens. Find out where it happened, why it happened, and what were the immediate and long-term effects. Then, write a news report that explains the natural disaster in geographic terms.

Take It to the NET

Activity Study your local weather using maps and charts. Describe changes in the weather throughout the day. For help in completing this activity, visit **www.phschool.com**.

Chapter 2 Self-Test To review what you have learned, take the Chapter 2 Self-Test and get instant feedback on your answers. Go to **www.phschool.com** to take the test.

Skills Review

Turn to the Skills Activity.

Review the steps for understanding special geography graphs. Then complete the following: (a) What two kinds of information are included in a climate graph? (b) How does a line graph help geographers describe a climate?

How Am I Doing?

Answer these questions to help you check your progress.

1. Do I know how the Earth's movements through space create day, night, and seasons?
2. Do I understand the forces that shape the Earth?
3. Can I explain the influences on the Earth's weather and climate?
4. Do I know why the Earth's climates support a variety of vegetation?
5. What information from this chapter can I include in my journal?

The Earth's Seasons

We take seasons for granted. Summer always follows spring, and winter follows fall. Anywhere in the United States, you can usually tell when the seasons begin to change. Two factors cause seasons. One is the way the Earth revolves, or travels around the sun. The other is the angle of the Earth's axis.

Purpose

In this activity, you will make a model that shows how the revolution of the Earth around the sun causes the seasons.

Materials

- masking tape
- marker
- lamp
- globe

Procedure

STEP ONE

Make a model of the Earth's path around the sun. Use masking tape to mark a spot on the floor for the "sun." Following the diagram, use the tape to mark the Earth's orbit around the sun. Next, label the tape where each season begins. Now, tape the globe firmly to its frame. Because the Earth's rotation does not

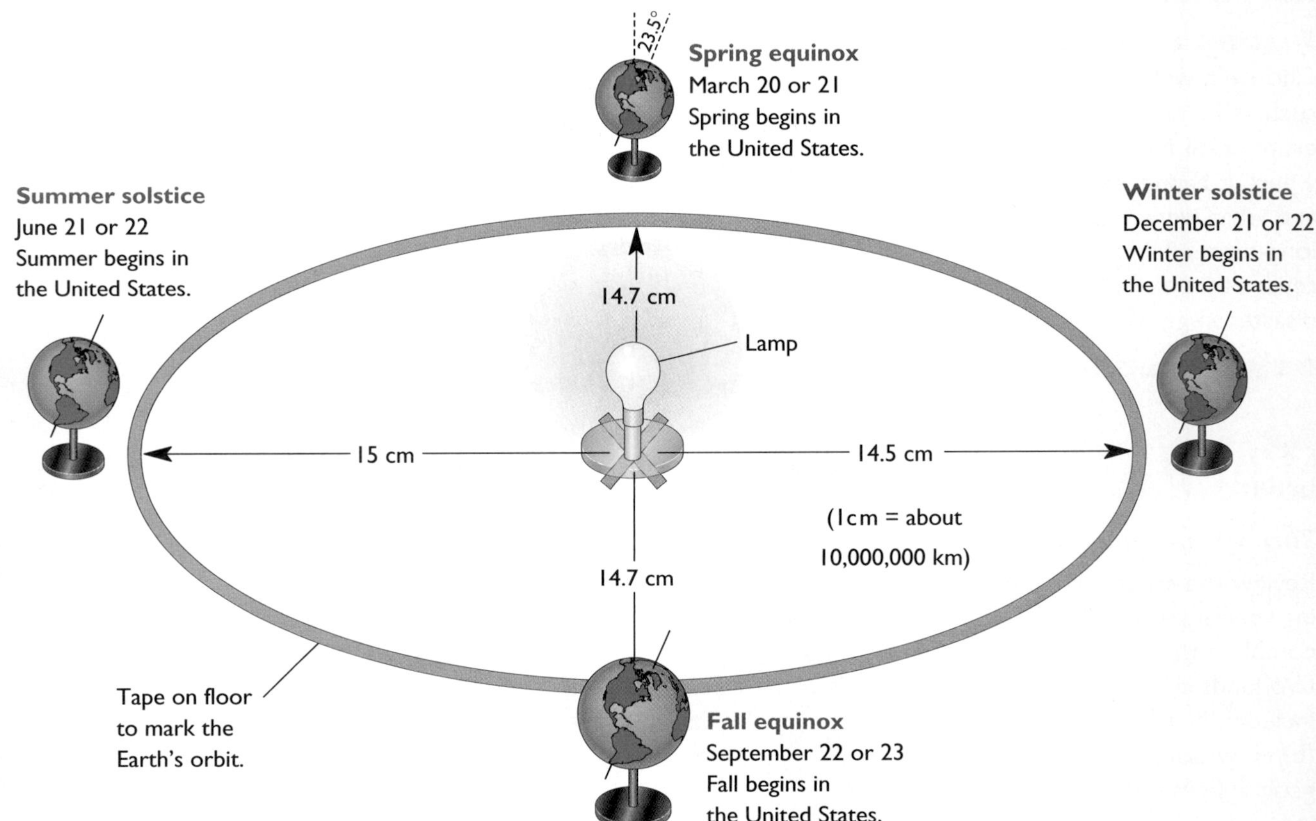

affect the seasons, the globe can remain in place. Put a lamp on the mark for the sun. Remove the shade and turn on the lamp.

STEP TWO

Show winter in the United States. Move the globe to the spot in the orbit where the season is winter in the United States. Be sure that the Earth's axis matches the position in the diagram. Notice that at other times of the year the Earth will be farther from the sun. Something besides distance must cause the season to be winter.

Let the globe sit for five minutes. Study how the sun's light hits the globe. Then, feel it by placing one hand on the Northern Hemisphere and the other on the Southern Hemisphere. Because of the tilt of the Earth's axis, the Northern Hemisphere gets less direct sunlight from the sun than the Southern Hemisphere. That means that the Northern Hemisphere receives less energy from the sun. So temperatures are cooler in the United States than in the Southern Hemisphere.

STEP THREE

Show spring in the United States. Place the globe on the floor at the spot where it is spring in the United States. Line up the Earth's axis correctly. Let the globe sit for five minutes. Place one hand on the Northern Hemisphere and the other on the Southern Hemisphere. Both hemispheres should feel about the same. Notice how the sun's light strikes the Earth. All parts of the Earth get about the same amount of energy.

STEP FOUR

Show summer in the United States. Place the globe at the spot where the season is summer in the United States. Notice that the Earth is farther from the sun than it was in winter. Line up the axis correctly. Let the globe sit for five minutes. Study the effect of the sun on both the Northern and Southern hemispheres. This time, because of the tilt of the axis, the Northern Hemisphere gets more direct sunlight from the sun, and therefore energy, than the Southern Hemisphere. Now, it is summer in the United States.

STEP FIVE

Show fall in the United States. Place the globe on the floor at the spot where it is fall in the United States. Line up the axis correctly. Let the globe sit for five minutes. Study both the Northern and the Southern hemispheres. Again, both hemispheres should feel about the same because all parts of the Earth get about the same amount of energy.

Observation

1. Which affects the seasons more—the angle at which the sun's rays hit the Earth or its distance from the sun? Explain your answer.
2. Which season does the Southern Hemisphere have when it is winter in the Northern Hemisphere?
3. When will you have about the same amount of daylight as night—January 8, July 20, or September 22? Explain your answer.

ANALYSIS AND CONCLUSION

1. If the Earth was not tilted on its axis, how do you think the seasons would be affected? Explain your answer.
2. In a science fiction story, the Earth's orbit is disturbed. The planet travels in a straight line, not around the sun. How would this affect the seasons?

CHAPTER 3

Earth's Human Geography

PICTURE ACTIVITIES

Many people live in New York City, Los Angeles, and other large American cities. To learn more about these people, carry out the following activities.

Study the picture

Look at this crowd of people hurrying along a busy New York City street. Many have come from other countries. List some places you think people in New York City might be from.

Rename the city

With a population of over eight million, New York City has more people than many small countries. The city has enough business and industry to be a country. What would you name the crowded "country" of New York City? Why?

Where Do People Live?

Reach Into Your Background
Would you like to live in a city or in the country? List some interesting things you could do if you lived far from a city. List the things you would enjoy most about city life.

Questions to Explore

1. Where do most of the world's people live?
2. What factors affect population density?

Key Terms
population
population distribution
demographer
population density

Key Places
Nile River valley

Imagine that you go to school in Tokyo, the capital of Japan. Every day you ride the train to school. What is it like? You probably must stand up for your two-hour ride. Every day more and more people jam the train. Often the car is so crowded that special station guards push people inside so the doors can close behind them.

This is not an exaggeration. The country of Japan is smaller than California. But it is home for over 126 million people. Over 34 million of them live in Tokyo and its suburbs. Public transportation, roads, and living space are extremely crowded.

▲ At rush hour in Tokyo, white-gloved guards jam two more passengers onto an already full train.

What Is Population Distribution?

The world's **population,** or total number of people, is spread unevenly over the Earth's surface. Some places have large numbers of people. In other places, the population is very small. **Population distribution** describes the way the population is spread out over the Earth.

Rising Ocean Levels Suppose world temperatures rose enough to melt Earth's glaciers and polar ice caps. A recent government report said the oceans are rising, although this may be only temporary. However, some scientists say ocean levels may rise $1\frac{1}{2}$ feet by 2100. Cities like San Francisco, Sydney, and Rio de Janeiro, which lie along ocean coastlines, would flood.

The reasons population is distributed as it is may seem unclear. Scientists called demographers try to figure it out. **Demographers** study the populations of the world. They examine such things as rates of birth, marriage, and death. And they look at the reasons why people choose to live in certain areas.

Why Is Population Distribution Uneven? To answer this question, demographers start with the idea that people are choosy. Recall an important fact about the Earth's surface. Many of the Earth's landforms are rugged mountains, hot deserts, and dry land with little vegetation. Few people can live in these places.

Many factors make a location a good place for people to live. Most major civilizations of world history began along bodies of water. Rivers and lakes form natural "roads" for trade and travel. Also, rivers and lakes supply fresh water for drinking and farming. People also prefer areas of flat, fertile soil. There they can grow food and build easily. Therefore, plains and valleys are easy to settle. Flat coastal areas make it easy for people to trade by ship with other countries. Look at the maps on this page and the opposite page to see how landforms affect where people live.

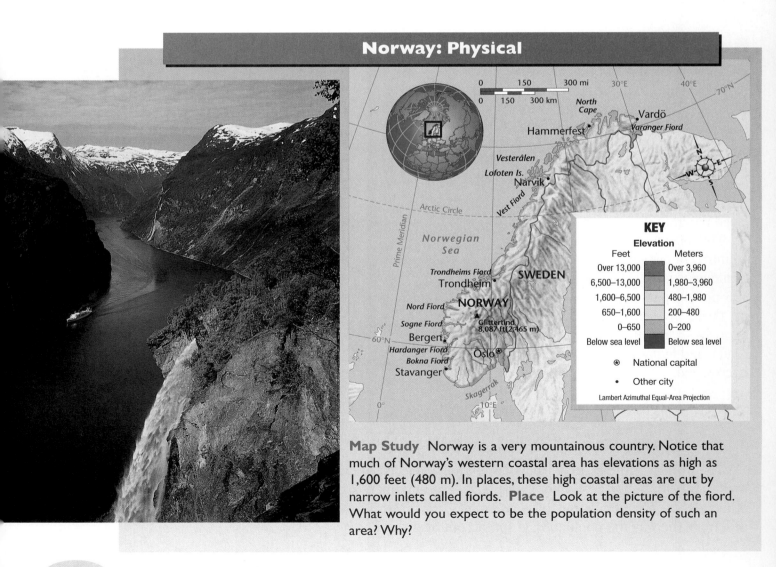

Norway: Physical

Map Study Norway is a very mountainous country. Notice that much of Norway's western coastal area has elevations as high as 1,600 feet (480 m). In places, these high coastal areas are cut by narrow inlets called fiords. **Place** Look at the picture of the fiord. What would you expect to be the population density of such an area? Why?

Other factors affect where people live. People prefer areas where the climate is not too hot or too cold, and where there is adequate rainfall. These places make it easier to raise food crops and animals. People also prefer places with natural resources to build houses and make products. For instance, few trees grew on the American Great Plains. Few people settled there at first. They went on to other regions.

Continents Populous and Not Populous These reasons explain why more than 81 percent of the Earth's people—about 4.9 billion—live in Asia, Europe, and North America. These continents total only about 53 percent of the world's land. However, they have fertile soil, plains, valleys, and other favorable landforms. They also have fresh water, rich natural resources, and good climates.

Other continents have smaller populations partly because it is harder to live there. For example, Australia is about three million square miles, about as large as the continental United States. Only about 19 million people live in Australia, however. About the same number of people live in just the state of New York. Australia's environment is mostly desert or dry grassland. There are few rivers and little rainfall. As a result, most people live along the coasts, where conditions are better.

In Africa, too, landforms and climates limit population. Africa has about 20 percent of the world's land. But it has only about 13 percent of the world's population. Africa has two of the world's largest deserts, one

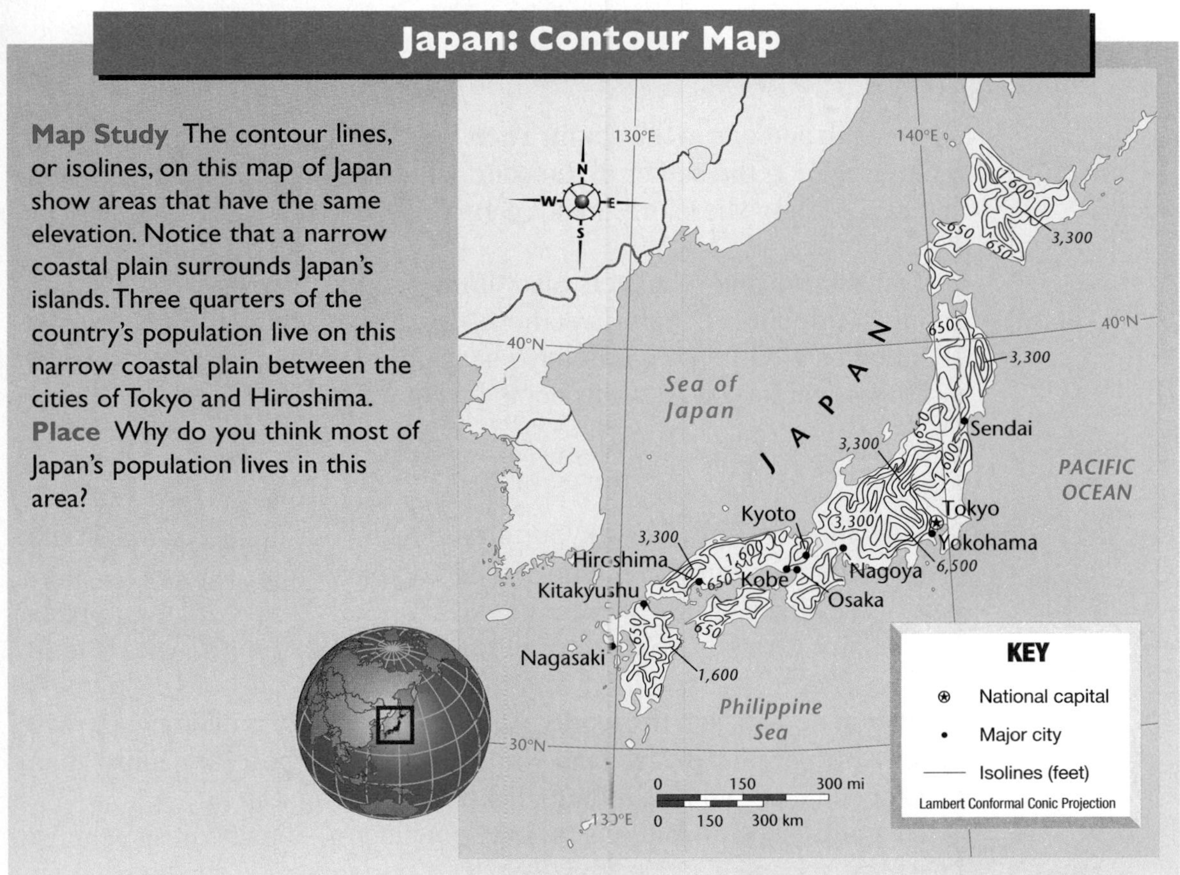

Map Study The contour lines, or isolines, on this map of Japan show areas that have the same elevation. Notice that a narrow coastal plain surrounds Japan's islands. Three quarters of the country's population live on this narrow coastal plain between the cities of Tokyo and Hiroshima. **Place** Why do you think most of Japan's population lives in this area?

City, Suburb, Countryside

In many countries, people can choose to live in very different places. For example, these photographs show apartments in Boston's Back Bay (above), houses in a Texas suburb (above right), and farms dotting the rich land near Lancaster, Pennsylvania (right). **Critical Thinking** What factors might cause people to choose homes in the city, the suburbs, or the country?

in the north and one in the south. Then there are broad bands of land that get little rain. In the center of the continent, along the Equator, there is a vast rain forest. Therefore, many people in Africa live along its narrow coasts.

Landforms and climates also limit South America's population. About 340 million people live there. Most live along the continent's Atlantic coast. Other regions have soaring mountains, vast dry plains, and thick rain forests. Fewer people live in these areas.

What Is Population Density?

How many people live on your street or in your neighborhood? The average number of people who live in a square mile (or square kilometer) is called **population density.** In every city and country, population density varies from one area to another. In a country with a high density, people are crowded together. Japan has one of the highest population densities in the world. Almost all of its 126 million people live on only 16 percent of the land. In Tokyo alone, there are more than 25,000 people per square mile (9,664 people per sq km).

In contrast, Canada has a low population density. It is almost 9 persons per square mile (three persons per sq km). Canada is bigger than the United States. But only about 31 million live there. Many factors affect Canada's population. For instance, its cool climate has a short growing season. This limits farming.

Connect Would you rather live in a place where the population density is high or low? Explain why.

Studying Population Density How do demographers measure population density? They divide the number of people living in a place by the number of square miles (or sq km) of that place. For example, California's population is 33,871,648 people. Its land area is 155,973 square miles (403,970 sq km). Therefore, California's average population density is 217.2 persons per square mile (83.8 persons per sq km).

Remember that population density is an *average*. People are not evenly distributed over the land. New York City has a very dense population. However, New York state has many fewer people per square mile. Even in the city, some areas are more densely populated than others.

On a world population density map, different colors show how world population is distributed. Darker colors show areas with heavy population. Find the world population density map in the Activity Atlas. Find the most densely populated areas of each continent. Now, find these places on the world physical map in the Activity Atlas. Compare the landforms to the population density. Notice that people tend to live on level areas near bodies of water.

Find the Nile River valley in Egypt. This region is very densely populated. In some areas the population density is about 5,000 people per square mile (1,930 per sq km). This is one of the highest population densities in the world. Why do so many people live here? If you think it is because the Nile is a great source of water and the land around it is flat and fertile, you are right. The land beyond the river is desert. Life there is difficult.

Some people do live in areas most of us would find uncomfortable. The Inuit and the Sami people live in frozen Arctic regions. Herders in desert regions of Africa and Asia survive in places that would challenge most people. Over many generations, these people have developed ways of life suited to their environments.

1. **Define** (a) population, (b) population distribution, (c) demographer, (d) population density.
2. **Identify** Nile River valley.
3. How do the physical characteristics of a country tend to affect its population distribution?
4. Why is it important to understand that population density is an average?

Critical Thinking

5. **Making Comparisons** A large percentage of the world's population lives on a small percentage of the world's land. How do the population distributions in Japan and Canada reflect this fact?

Activity

6. **Writing to Learn** You are a demographer studying your community. Make a list of questions to ask and possible sources for answers. Include in your list some population issues that are important to your community.

A Growing Population

Reach Into Your Background

If you called a hospital in your community, you could find out how many babies were born last week. Multiply that number by all the hospitals in the world. Then, add the number of babies who were not born in hospitals. Subtract from this figure the number of people who died both in and out of hospitals. That's one way to find out how much the world's population increased in seven days.

Questions to Explore

1. How fast is the world's population growing?
2. What challenges are created by the world's growing population?

Key Terms

birthrate
death rate
life expectancy
Green Revolution

Imagine that all the years from A.D. 1 to A.D. 2000 took place in just 24 hours. Now you have an imaginary clock to measure how fast the world's population is growing. The list below shows that the Earth's population doubled several times in those 24 hours.

12:00 AM	200 million people in the world
7:48 PM	Population doubles to 400 million
10:12 PM	Population doubles to 800 million
11:00 PM	Population doubles to 1.6 billion
11:36 PM	Population doubles to 3.2 billion
11:59 PM	Population will double to 6.4 billion

How large was the world population at 12:00 AM (A.D. 1)? At 10:12 PM? During those 24 hours, how many times did the world's population double? How long did it take for the world population to double the first time? The last time?

Population Growth Is Worldwide

The example above makes it easy to see that world population has grown rapidly. Even more important, the rate of growth has increased greatly in modern times. For example, in 1960 the world population was 3 billion. By 2000—only 40 years later—it had climbed to more than 6 billion people.

Population Birthrate and Death Rate During different historical periods, populations grew at different rates. Demographers want to understand why. They know that population growth depends on the birthrate and the death rate. The **birthrate** is the number of live births each year per 1,000 people. The **death rate** is the number of deaths each year per 1,000 people. By comparing birthrates and death rates, demographers can figure out population growth.

Better Health Care for the Young

A mother and baby await medical help at the Kenyatta National Hospital in the East African country of Kenya. **Critical Thinking** How has modern medical care helped to increase the world's population growth?

For centuries, the world population grew slowly. In those years, farmers worked without modern machinery. Food supplies often were scarce. Many thousands died of diseases. As a result, although the birthrate was high, so was the death rate. The **life expectancy,** or the average number of years that people live, was short. A hundred years ago in the United States, men and women usually lived less than 50 years.

Reasons for Population Growth Today Today, things have changed. The birthrate has increased dramatically. The death rate has slowed. As a result, populations in most countries have grown very fast. In some countries, the population doubles in less than 20 years. People live longer than ever. In the United States, for example, the average life expectancy for women is about 80 years and for men about 73 years.

Two scientific developments have made this possible. First, new farming methods have greatly increased the world's food supply. Starting in the 1950s, scientists developed new varieties of important food crops and new ways to protect crops against insects. Scientists developed new fertilizers to enrich the soil so farmers can grow more crops. Scientists also discovered ways to raise crops with less water. These changes in agriculture are called the **Green Revolution.**

The second set of scientific advancements came in medicine and health. Today, new medicines and types of surgery treat health problems that used to kill people, such as heart disease and serious injuries. Researchers also have created vaccines to fight diseases such as smallpox, polio, and measles, and antibiotics to fight infections. As a result, many more babies are born and stay healthy, and people live many more years.

Hydroponics How can you grow a plant without soil? People called hydroponics farmers grow plants in water and necessary nutrients. The techniques are used where there is no soil, such as on ships. Today some groceries sell hydroponic vegetables. Some scientists say hydroponics may help feed the world's rapidly growing population.

Life Expectancy in Selected Countries, 2000

Graph Study Life expectancy, or the number of years a newborn baby can expect to live, has soared in many countries since 1900. In some countries, however, life expectancy remains low. Which countries on this chart have the highest life expectancies? Which have the lowest? **Critical Thinking** What has contributed to the rise in life expectancy over the last century?

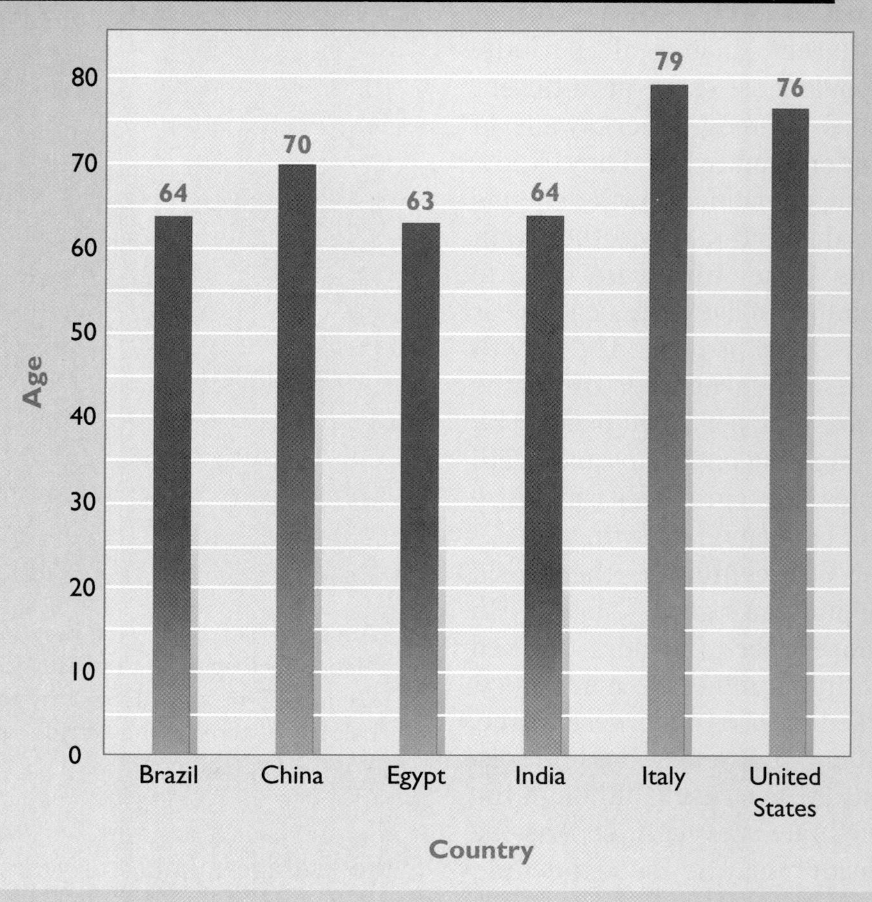

The Challenges of Population Growth

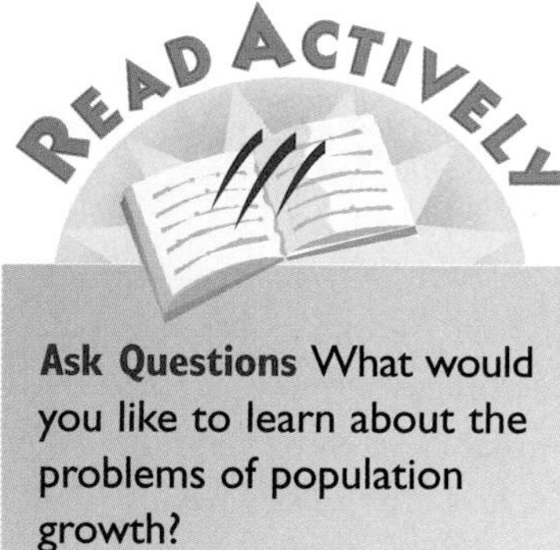

Ask Questions What would you like to learn about the problems of population growth?

Today, food supplies have increased and people live longer. Even so, the people in many countries still face very serious problems. Growing populations use resources much faster than stable populations. Some nations, like those in Southwest Asia, face shortages of fresh water and energy. In Asia and Africa, food supplies cannot keep up with the growing population. Often, these countries do not have enough money to purchase imported food.

Population growth puts pressure on all aspects of life. The population of many countries is increasing so fast that many people cannot find jobs. There are not enough schools to educate the growing number of children. Decent housing is scarce and expensive. Public services like transportation and sanitation are inadequate.

The problems created by rapid population growth are most visible in South Asia. The region is home to about a quarter of the world's population. According to a World Bank study, South Asia is also home to about a quarter of the world's poor. Out of every 14 children born, one will die before reaching the age of one.

World Population Growth, A.D. 1200–2000

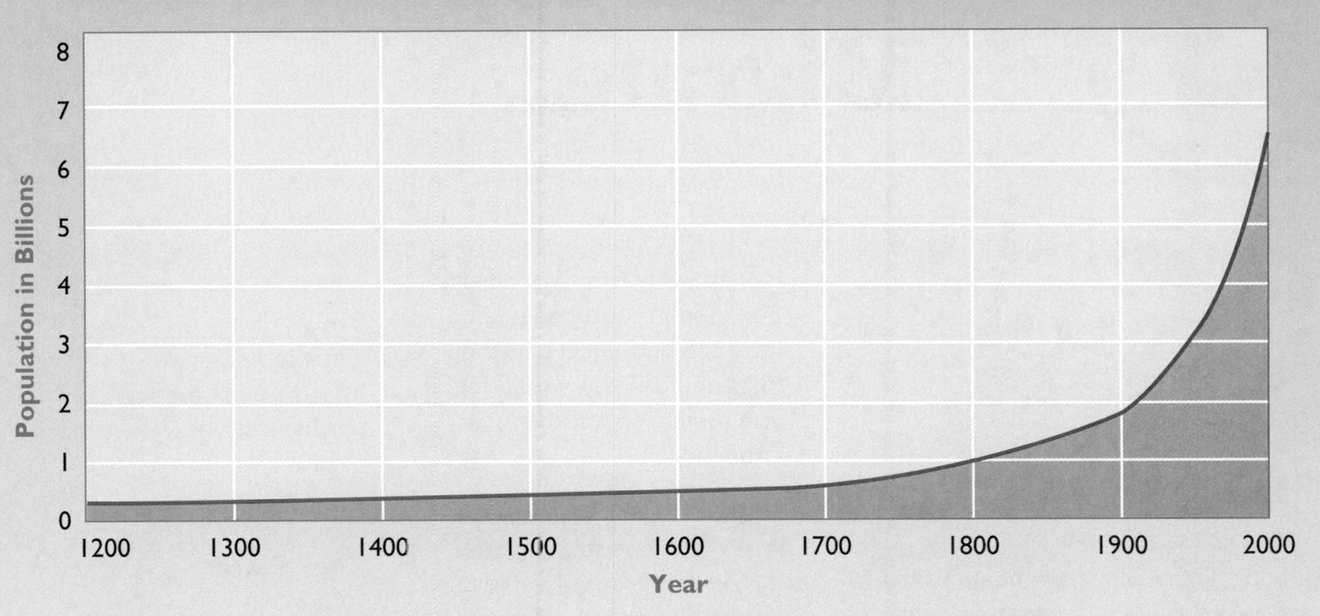

Graph Study For hundreds of years, the world's population rose very slowly. Recently, however, the rate of growth has skyrocketed.

Critical Thinking How does the graph show the change in the growth of the world's population?

Rapid population growth also affects the environment. For instance, forests in areas of India and Pakistan are disappearing. People cut the trees to use the wood for building and for fuel. Cutting forests affects the supply of clean air. Before, tree roots held soil in place. Now heavy rainfall may wash away the soil.

Look at the population changes indicated in the graph on this page. It shows how rapidly change has occurred in the last 300 years. The Earth's resources must now be shared by six times as many people than in earlier times. All the Earth's people must work to meet this challenge.

1. **Define** (a) birthrate, (b) death rate, (c) life expectancy, (d) Green Revolution.
2. Why has the world's population increased so dramatically in the last four or five decades?
3. How have science and technology contributed to the growing population?

Critical Thinking

4. **Drawing Conclusions** The world's population has been growing at a fast rate. What are some of the dangers of a rapidly increasing population?

Activity

5. **Writing to Learn** World hunger is one of the major concerns caused by rapid population growth. Write one or two suggestions to help solve this problem.

Why People Migrate

Reach Into Your Background
There may have been a time in your life when you or your family moved to a new home. Or perhaps a close friend moved away from your neighborhood. You probably felt a little sad and uncertain then. Imagine how you would feel if you moved to another country!

Questions to Explore

1. Why do people migrate?
2. What are some important population issues?

Key Terms
migration
immigrant
"push-pull" theory
urbanization
rural area
urban area

Key Places
Cuba
Vietnam
Jakarta

Roberto Goizueta was the former head of Coca-Cola, one of the largest companies in the world. Yet when he came to the United States from Cuba in 1960, he had nothing. This is how he described his escape from Cuba:

> "When my family and I came to this country [the United States], we had to leave everything behind . . . our photographs hung on the wall, our wedding gifts sat on the shelves."

▼ On July 4, 1996—Independence Day—hundreds of people celebrate receiving their citizenship in El Paso, Texas.

Like millions of others who came to the United States, Roberto Goizueta helped the nation become a land of prosperity.

Migration: The Movement of People

For centuries people have moved from one place to another. This is called **migration. Immigrants** are people who leave one country and move to another. From 1881 to 1920, almost 23.5 million Europeans moved to the United States. Since 1971, nearly 700,000 people migrated here from the country of Vietnam.

Over 995,000 came from Central America, and over 4.2 million came from Mexico. More than 2.4 million immigrants came from the Caribbean islands.

Demographers use the **"push-pull" theory** to explain immigration. It says people migrate because certain things in their lives "push" them to leave. Often, the reasons are economic. Perhaps people cannot buy land or find work. Or changes in a government may force people to leave.

For instance, in 1959 there was a revolution in Cuba. Some Cubans lost land and businesses. Many fled to America to find safety and a better life. In the 1800s, many Scandinavians moved to Minnesota and Wisconsin. They wanted their own land, which was scarce in Scandinavia. Some also left to escape religious persecution.

What about the "pull" part of the theory? The hope for better living conditions "pulls" people to a country. Cubans settled in Florida because it was near their former home. It already had a Spanish-speaking population. Also, Florida's climate and vegetation are similar to Cuba's. Scandinavians were "pulled" by the United States government's offer of free land for immigrants willing to set up farms. They also moved to a familiar place. The long, cold winters in Minnesota and Wisconsin were similar to those in northwestern Europe.

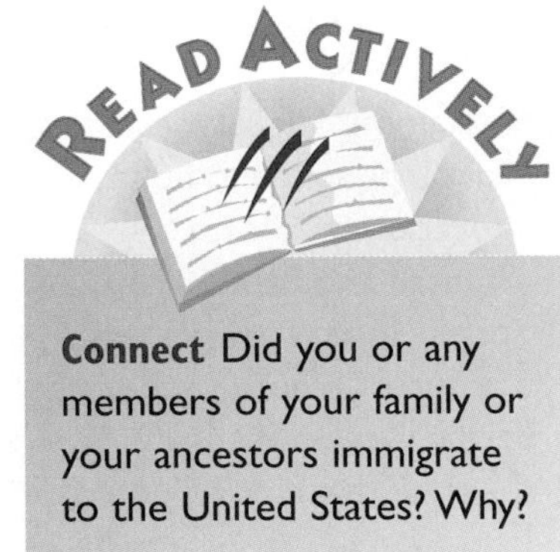

Connect Did you or any members of your family or your ancestors immigrate to the United States? Why?

Cuba and Florida: Climate Regions

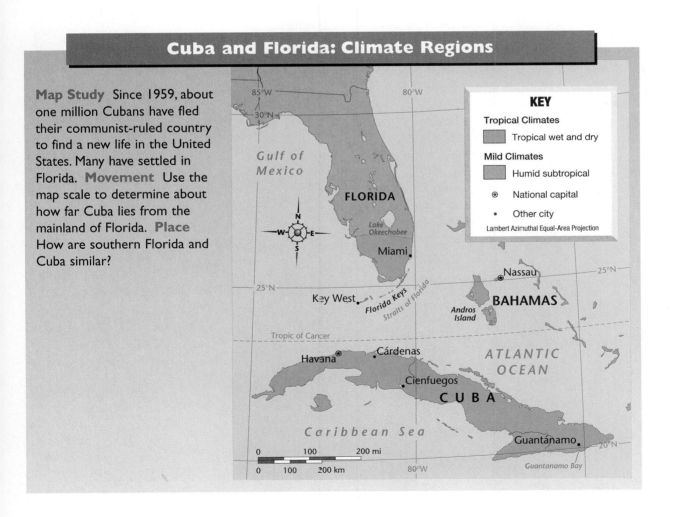

Map Study Since 1959, about one million Cubans have fled their communist-ruled country to find a new life in the United States. Many have settled in Florida. **Movement** Use the map scale to determine about how far Cuba lies from the mainland of Florida. **Place** How are southern Florida and Cuba similar?

KEY

Tropical Climates

Tropical wet and dry

Mild Climates

Humid subtropical

National capital

Other city

Lambert Azimuthal Equal-Area Projection

Settlement of Polynesia Not all people end up in a location by choice. Thousands of years ago people settled in Polynesia, a group of islands in the Pacific Ocean. Scholars theorize that these people left eastern Asia in search of new land. Then violent storms blew them off course. Ocean currents carried these people to the islands they now call home.

Irish Immigrants in the United States Demographers use the push-pull theory to explain the great Irish immigration in the 1840s and 1850s. In those years, 1.5 million people left Ireland for the United States. Why did so many Irish people come to America? Ireland was a farming nation. In the 1840s, disease destroyed its main crop—potatoes. Hunger and starvation pushed people to migrate. Also, England ruled Ireland very harshly. There were very few ways for Irish people to improve their lives. These things also pushed people to move. Job opportunities pulled Irish families to the United States.

Vietnamese Come to the United States The push-pull theory also explains Vietnamese immigration. These people came from southeastern Asia to the United States. After many years of war between North and South Vietnam, peace came in 1975. North Vietnam had won. Soon, it extended its communist form of government to South Vietnam. This was a serious change for many South Vietnamese. Thousands left the country. They were not welcome in nearby Asian countries. But the United States and the South Vietnamese had been allies during the war. The United States accepted the immigrants. That pulled the Vietnamese here.

An Irish-American President

John Fitzgerald Kennedy was elected President of the United States in 1960. His great-grandfather migrated to the United States from Ireland. Like many other immigrants to this country, Irish Americans have made many important contributions. President Kennedy is shown here delivering a speech at the University of California, Berkeley, in 1962.

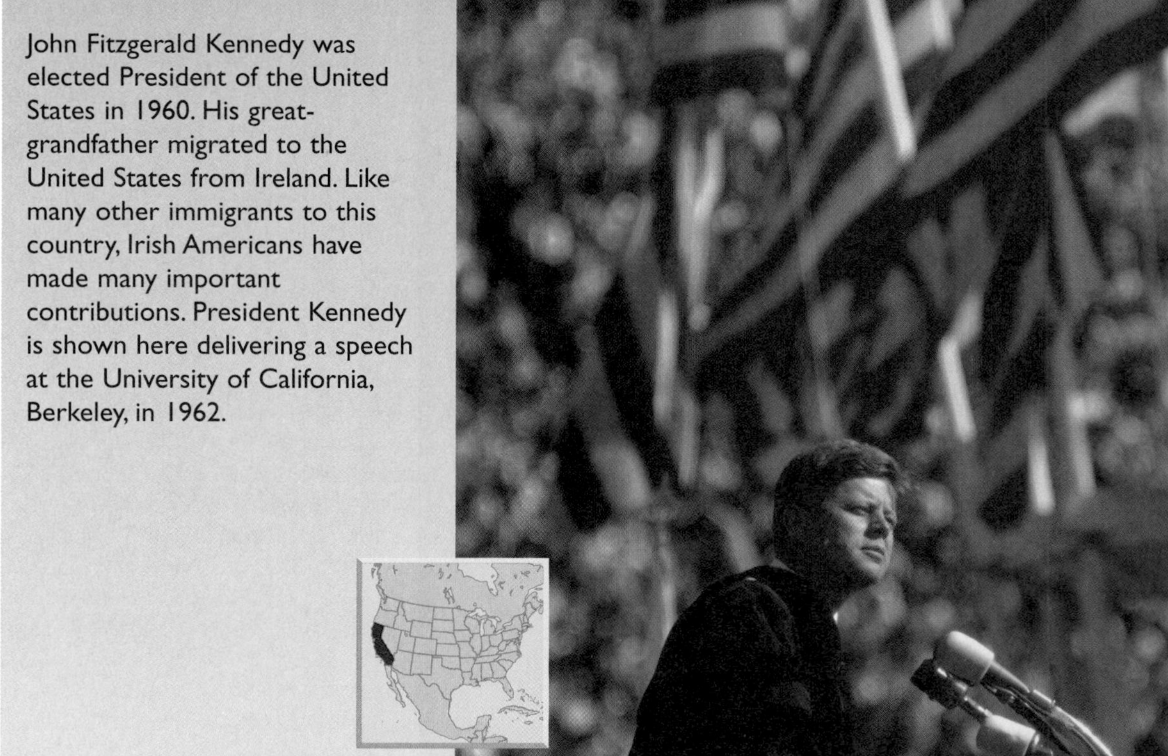

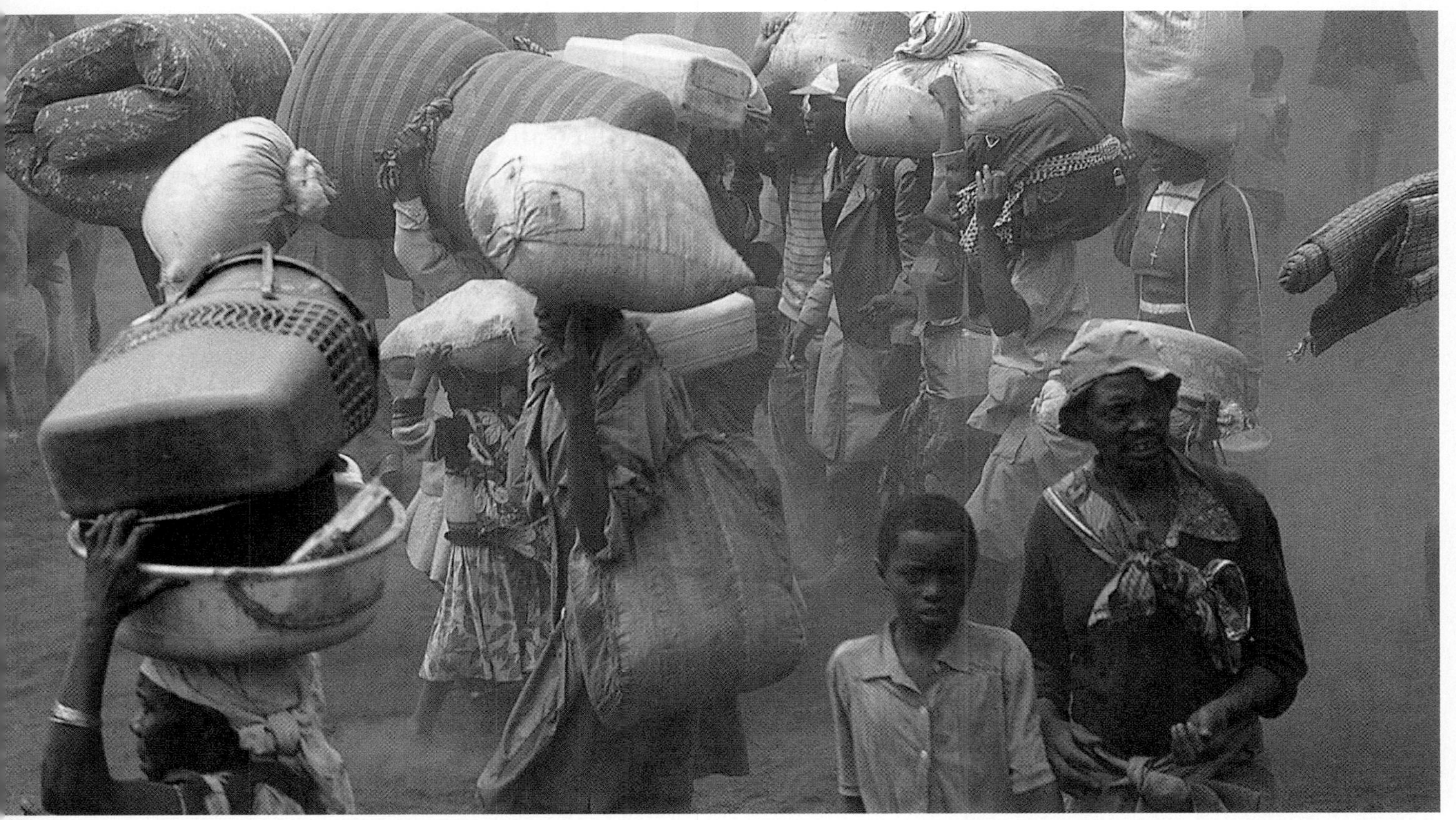

▲ Sometimes war forces people to migrate. In 1995, thousands of refugees fled a brutal civil war in the Central African country of Rwanda.

Other Kinds of Immigration Sometimes, people are forced to migrate. Australia was colonized by the English. Some were convicts serving their sentences in Australia. When their sentences were done, they stayed. War also forces people to migrate. In the mid-1990s, war broke out among three ethnic groups in Yugoslavia, in Eastern Europe. Many refugees fled to escape the warfare. Also, victorious soldiers of one group often forced entire communities of other groups to leave. Millions of immigrants flooded into countries in Eastern and Western Europe.

Other people leave their countries for a few years to help their families. Young men from Morocco and Turkey often go to Europe to find work. They leave their families behind. For a few years they work hard and save their money. Then they return home.

The World Becomes More Urban

Migration also occurs within a country. This happens in the United States. Americans migrate more than citizens of any other country, but most move from one state to another. Recently, the population has shifted from the northeastern states to the southern and southwestern states. People may be searching for better job opportunities or a better climate. This growth in urban areas of southern states has put great stress on services. Southwestern cities, for example, are developing new ways to ensure an adequate supply of fresh water.

Ask Questions What questions would you like to ask someone who plans to migrate to a city from a rural area?

One of the biggest challenges to today's nations is people migrating to cities from farms and small villages. In recent years, the population of major cities has grown tremendously. The movement of people to cities and the growth of cities is called **urbanization.** What pushes people from rural areas? What pulls people to cities?

Growing Cities, Growing Challenges Cities in Indonesia are an example. In the past, most Indonesians were farmers, fishers, and hunters. They lived in **rural areas,** or villages in the countryside. Recently, more and more Indonesians have moved to **urban areas,** or cities and nearby towns. Its urban population is increasing rapidly. For example, in 1978, about 4.5 million people lived in the capital of Jakarta. By 2000, its population was about 11 million. And demographers estimate that by 2015 the population will have risen to about 21 million.

Jakarta is not unique. In South America, too, large numbers of people are moving from rural to urban areas. São Paulo, Brazil, is now the largest city in South America. The city has hundreds of tall office buildings, stores, banks, businesses, and small factories. In 1995, its population was nearly 16 million. By 2015, it is expected to be 21 million.

The problem in cities like São Paulo is that too many people are coming too fast. Cities cannot keep up. They cannot provide housing,

World Urban and Rural Populations, 1800–2000

Graph Study In countries all over the world, city populations have soared, while rural populations have fallen. What percentage of the world's population lived in cities in 1800? What percentage of the world's population lived in cities in 2000? **Critical Thinking** Based on the graph, what do you predict will happen to the world's rural and urban populations by the year 2050?

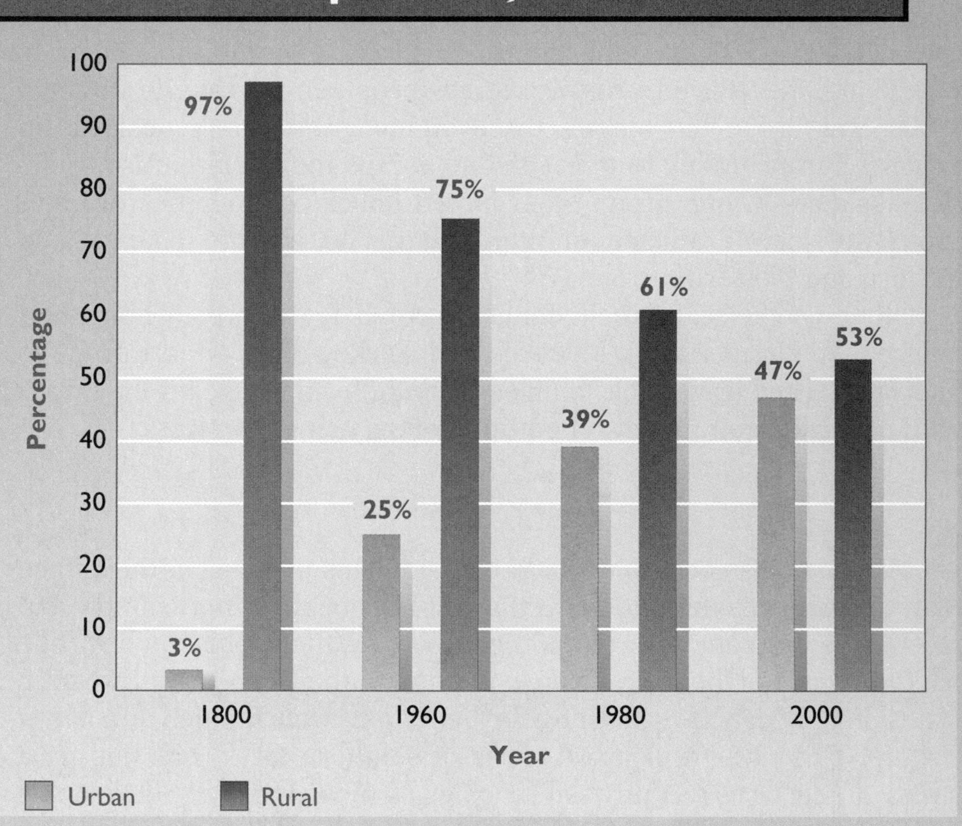

Crowded Conditions in Cairo, Egypt

Across the world, growing cities face special challenges. Sometimes, there is not enough housing for newcomers to the cities. Sometimes, newcomers cannot afford the housing that is available. Until they find better housing, many newcomers build whatever shelters they can. These shelters are in Cairo, Egypt's capital.

jobs, schools, hospitals, and other services that people need. The country as a whole also suffers. With fewer farms, there is less food.

If you visited São Paulo, you would see why some migrants have a hard life. Schoolrooms are crowded. The city's four million cars and buses pollute the air. Traffic noise echoes day and night. Traffic jams and crowds often make it a struggle to get around.

With so many daily problems, why do immigrants flock to São Paulo and other big cities? Most are seeking a better life for their families. They are looking for jobs, decent houses, and good schools. Above all, most want more opportunities for their children.

Visualize Visualize what it would be like to move to a city like São Paulo, Brazil.

1. **Define** (a) migration, (b) immigrant, (c) "push-pull" theory, (d) urbanization, (e) rural area, (f) urban area.
2. **Identify** (a) Cuba, (b) Vietnam, (c) Jakarta.
3. What are some of the reasons why people migrate from place to place?
4. Why have some immigrants left their homelands to live in the United States?

Critical Thinking

5. **Making Comparisons** What is the difference between migration within a country and migration from one country to another?

Activity

6. **Writing to Learn** When too many people migrate from rural to urban areas, it can mean hardships. List suggestions and ideas to help people decide whether to migrate to the city.

Using Distribution Maps

Imagine yourself in a spaceship, floating high above the Earth. Although there is no day or night in space, you can see day and night on the planet beneath you. Half the Earth is lit by the sun, and half of it is in darkness. As you begin to glide over the night side, the Earth comes between you and the sun. Looking out of the spacecraft, you see that in many places there are small smudges of light spaced across the dark land. Some huge areas are brightly lit.

You are seeing the lights of human settlement. They include firelight, street lights, floodlights in parking lots, and the combined effect of millions of lights in homes. Where there are people, there is light. The distribution of the light reflects the distribution of people on the planet. The term geographers use to refer to where people live on the planet is population distribution. Floating over the Earth, you are looking at a living population distribution map of the Earth.

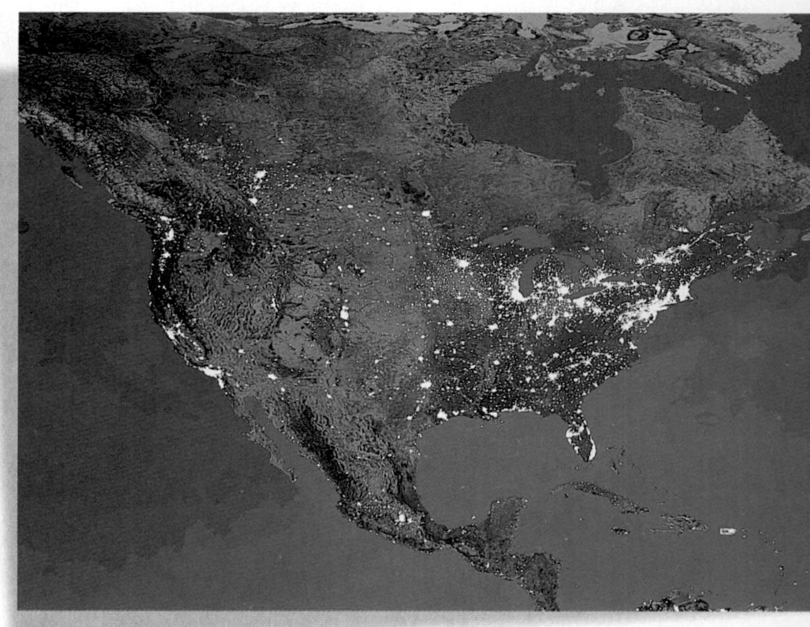

Get Ready

Why do geographers study population distribution? People live all over the world, yet population is concentrated in certain places. Consider this. Nearly six billion people live in the world. Yet all of us, standing close to each other, could easily fit into the state of Connecticut! Why do we live where we do? Figuring out this answer and the reasons behind it are basic to understanding human life on the Earth. The first step is to find out where we do live. A population distribution map shows this best.

To see how population distribution maps are made and used, make and use one of your own. You will need paper, a pen, and a ruler.

Try It Out

A. Draw a map of your school. Use a large sheet of paper. Use the ruler to draw straight lines. Show and label classrooms, hallways, and so on.

B. Make a key for your map. Use stick figures as symbols. Each figure will represent five people. See the example on the next page.

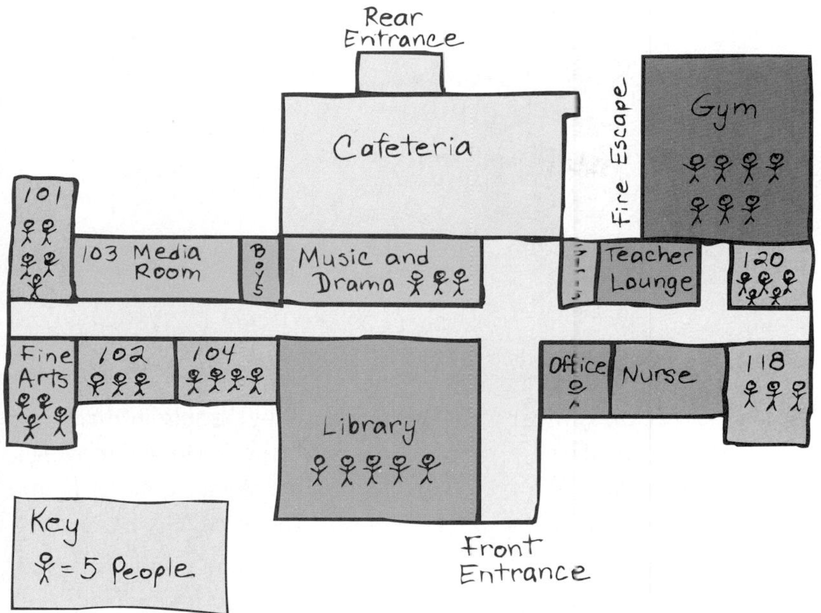

C. **Add stick-figure symbols to your map.** Remember to put the symbols where the people are. Put the right number of symbols to show how many people are in each room. If there are 24 students and 1 teacher in your classroom, for example, you would draw 5 stick-figure symbols on the part of the map that shows your classroom.

D. **Give your map an appropriate title.** You have just made a population distribution map. It answers the same two questions that any such map does: Where are the people? How many people are in each place? Your map also provides clues about another question. Why is the population distributed in the way it is? See if you can answer this question about your school map.

Apply the Skill

Now that you see how population distribution maps are made and what questions they answer, you can learn a great deal from one of Mexico. Use the map here to answer these questions.

1. **Read the map key.** Look at the key to get a sense of what the map is about. How is population represented on the map? How many people does each symbol stand for?

2. **Answer the "where" and "how many" questions that population distribution maps can answer.** Where do most of the people of Mexico live?

3. **Answer the "why" question that population distribution maps can address.** Why do you think the population of Mexico is distributed the way it is? Think about physical factors such as climate and landforms as well as historical factors.

4. **Think about distribution maps generally.** This map shows population distribution. Other maps show the distribution of such things as natural resources, technology, and wealth. Find another type of distribution map and share it with the class.

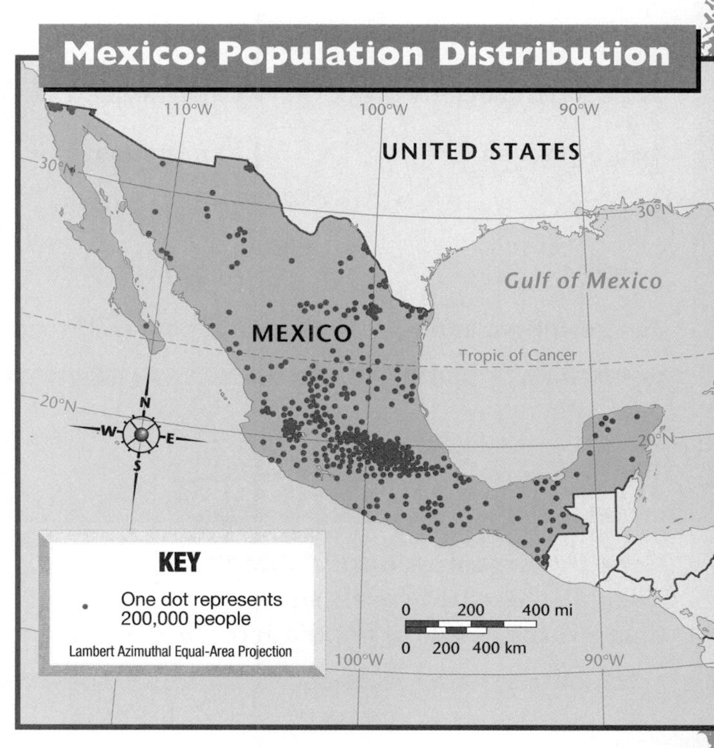

Review and Activities

Reviewing Main Ideas

1. How does geography affect where people settle?
2. (a) List the three continents with the most population and the four continents with the least population. (b) Choose one continent in each group and describe its landforms. Explain how those landforms affect population.
3. What kind of region is most attractive to new settlers? Which is least attractive?
4. Why does the Nile River valley of Egypt have such a high population density?
5. What factors have caused a rapid increase in human population?
6. Explain why people in many parts of the world are moving from rural areas to cities. Name two of these cities.
7. What are some conditions that push people to leave their country and pull them to migrate to another country?

Reviewing Key Terms

Use each key term below in a sentence that shows the meaning of the term.

1. population
2. population distribution
3. population density
4. urbanization
5. rural
6. urban
7. Green Revolution
8. life expectancy
9. birthrate
10. death rate
11. migration
12. immigrants
13. demographer
14. "push-pull" theory

Critical Thinking

1. **Recognizing Cause and Effect** How have Africa's landforms and climate limited its population?
2. **Identifying Central Issues** Explain the meaning of this statement: "Today, many countries of the world are becoming more urban." What does this statement tell about the movement of people in those countries?

Graphic Organizer

Copy the organizer onto a sheet of paper. Then fill the empty ovals with other effects that are the result of population growth.

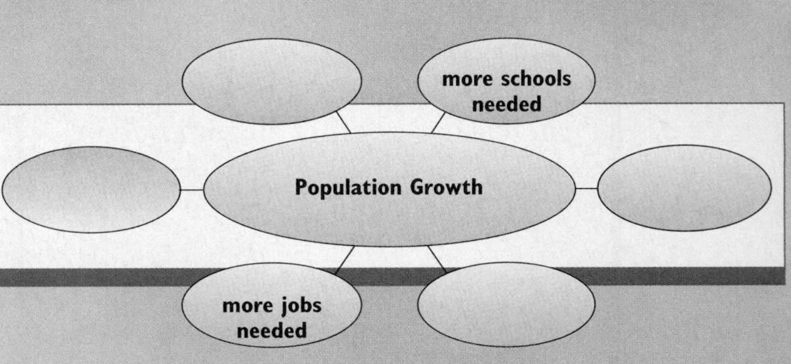

Map Activity

Place Location

Continents

For each place listed below, write the letter from the map that shows its location.

1. Asia

2. Antarctica

3. Africa

4. South America

5. North America

6. Europe

7. Australia

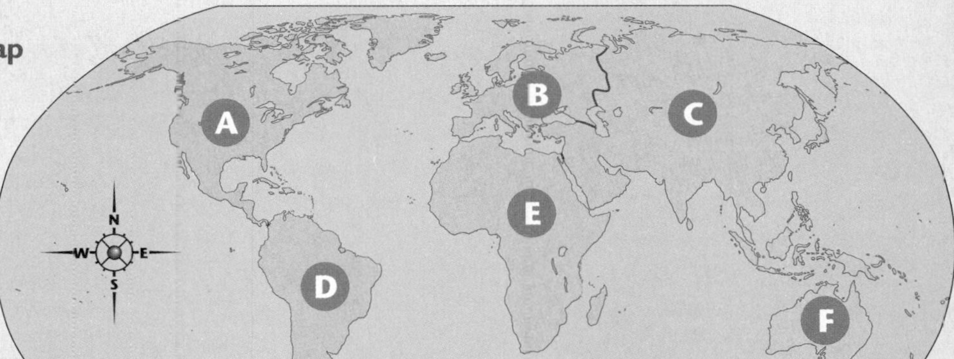

Writing Activity

Writing to Learn

Find out how the population of your state has changed in the last 50 years. Write a paragraph that explains the main reasons why people migrated to or from your state.

Take It to the NET

Activity Find the population in your state in 1990 and 2000. How did the population change? For help in completing this activity, visit **www.phschool.com**.

Chapter 3 Self-Test To review what you have learned, take the Chapter 3 Self-Test and get instant feedback on your answers. Go to **www.phschool.com** to take the test.

Skills Review

Turn to the Skills Activity.

Review the steps for using distribution maps. Then complete the following: (a) What can you learn from a population distribution map? (b) Would you learn more if you compared a population distribution map with a landform map or a climate map? Explain your answer.

How Am I Doing?

Answer these questions to help you check your progress.

1. Do I understand why the world's population is distributed unevenly?

2. Can I identify the continents with the highest population density? The continents where fewer people live?

3. Can I describe how the Earth's landforms and climates affect where people live?

4. Do I understand why many people move from rural to urban areas?

5. What information from this chapter can I include in my journal?

My Side of the Mountain

BY JEAN CRAIGHEAD GEORGE

Reach Into Your Background

Has your electricity ever gone out during a storm or a power failure? Suppose you had no electricity at all, or your home had no heating system. Without modern technology, how would you cope with the natural world around you?

Most people would have a hard time. But Sam Gribley, the fictional hero of the novel *My Side of the Mountain,* decided to live close to nature. He went to the Catskill Mountains in New York state and built a treehouse in a tall hemlock tree. His only companion was his falcon, Frightful. This excerpt tells how Sam managed during his first winter in the mountains.

Questions to Explore

1. What did Sam learn about nature as he lived alone in a forest in winter?
2. What skills did Sam need to survive alone in the wilderness?

hemlock (HEM lahk) *n.* pine trees with drooping branches and short needles
copse (kahps) *n.* a thicket of small trees or shrubs

Connect What would you do to pass the time if you did not have television, radio, or other electronic gadgets?

I lived close to the weather. It is surprising how you watch it when you live in it. Not a cloud passed unnoticed, not a wind blew untested. I knew the moods of the storms, where they came from, their shapes and colors. When the sun shone, I took Frightful to the meadow and we slid down the mountain on my snapping-turtle-shell sled. She really didn't care much for this.

When the winds changed and the air smelled like snow, I would stay in my tree, because I had gotten lost in a blizzard one afternoon and had to hole up in a rock ledge until I could see where I was going. That day the winds were so strong I could not push against them, so I crawled under the ledge; for hours I wondered if I would be able to dig out when the storm blew on. Fortunately I only had to push through about a foot of snow. However, that taught me to stay home when the air said "snow." Not that I was afraid of being caught far from home in a storm, for I could find food and shelter and make a fire anywhere, but I had become as attached to my hemlock house as a brooding bird to her nest. Caught out in the storms and weather, I had an urgent desire to return to my tree, even as The Baron Weasel returned to his den, and the deer, to their copse.

◀ Sunrise over Mongaup Pond in the Catskill Mountains, New York

We all had our little "patch" in the wilderness. We all fought to return there.

I usually came home at night with the nuthatch that roosted in a nearby sapling. I knew I was late if I tapped the tree and he came out. Sometimes when the weather was icy and miserable, I would hear him high in the trees near the edge of the meadow, yanking and yanking and flicking his tail, and then I would see him wing to bed early. I considered him a pretty good barometer, and if he went to his tree early, I went to mine early too. When you don't have a newspaper or radio to give you weather bulletins, watch the birds and animals. They can tell when a storm is coming. I called the nuthatch "Barometer," and when he holed up, I holed up, lit my light, and sat by my fire whittling or learning new tunes on my reed whistle. I was now really into the teeth of winter, and quite fascinated by its activity. There is no such thing as a "still winter night." Not only are many animals running around in the breaking cold, but the trees cry out and limbs snap and fall, and the wind gets caught in a ravine and screams until it dies.

yank (yangk) *v.* the sound made by a nuthatch
barometer (bah RAH muh tur) *n.* an instrument for forecasting changes in the weather; anything that indicates a change
whittle (witl) *v.* to cut or pare thin shavings from wood with a knife
teeth of winter the coldest, harshest time of winter

EXPLORING YOUR READING

Look Back

1. How has Sam's relationship with the weather changed?

Think It Over

2. Sam's relationship with his environment is different from most people's. In places, he talks about wind and trees as if they were alive. Think about your relationship with nature. How is it like Sam's? How is it different?

Go Beyond

3. What things does Sam do without that you take for granted?

Ideas for Writing: Essay

4. How might you decide what to wear to school in the morning without hearing a weather forecast? Write an essay that explains to your classmates how to watch for weather signs.

Cultures of the World

PICTURE ACTIVITIES

Have you ever jumped for joy? The Inuits of Alaska toss *one another for joy. People gather in a circle, grab the sides of an animal skin blanket, and use it to toss one another sky-high. The people here are celebrating a whaling festival. The Inuits also toss one another to celebrate the arrival of spring or a religious holiday or a successful hunt.*

Look for clues

What can you find out about where the people in this picture live? List the clues you find. Explain what they tell you about the place shown.

Write a letter

Write a letter to someone in this photograph. Describe your thoughts about the tossing ceremony. Tell them about an activity you enjoy. Explain how these two activities are similar and different.

What Is Culture?

Reach Into Your Background

You and the people you know have certain ways of doing things. You have a way of celebrating birthdays. You have a way of greeting your friends. You have a way of eating a meal. You have a way of speaking. You have ways of gesturing. Many of the ways you do things are unique to you alone. Others you share with people around you.

Questions to Explore

1. What is culture?
2. How do cultures develop?

Key Terms

culture
cultural trait
technology
cultural landscape
agriculture

"All right, students," your teacher says, "time to clean the room. Kaitlyn—I'd like you to sweep today. Guy and Keisha, please use these feather dusters to clean our shelves and windowsills. Eric and Bobby, you can do the lunch dishes today. Serena and Zack, please empty the wastebaskets and take out the trash."

Would you be surprised if this happened in your classroom? Would you pitch in—or complain? In Japan, students would pitch in to help keep their classrooms clean. Hard work and neatness are important lessons. Although Japanese schools are similar to American ones, there are differences. Japanese students generally spend more time studying than many American students. In Japan, most children go to school five days a week and often on Saturdays for half a day. Many students do many hours of homework every afternoon and evening and over vacations.

Japanese students, like many American students, also enjoy sports, music, drama, and science. They join teams and clubs. They paint and take photographs. They play baseball, soccer, and tennis. They do karate and judo. They play musical instruments.

▼ These students in Japan are listening closely as their classmate speaks. How is your own classroom like this one? How does it differ?

Culture: A Total Way of Life

READ ACTIVELY

Predict What do you think the word *culture* means?

What if you met students from Japan? You would probably ask many questions. "How do you feel about cleaning your classroom?" you might ask. When you heard about how much homework they do, you might also ask "How do you find time to have fun?" Later, you might wonder about other things. What do Japanese students eat for lunch? What kinds of music do they like? What makes them laugh?

Answers to these questions will tell you something about the culture of Japan. **Culture** is the way of life of a group of people who share similar beliefs and customs. The language Japanese students speak and the way they dress are both a part of their culture. So are the subjects Japanese students study and what they do after school.

Elements of Culture Culture includes the work people do, their behaviors, their beliefs, and their ways of doing things. Parents pass these things on to their children, generation after generation. A particular group's individual skills, customs, and ways of doing things are called **cultural traits.** Over time, cultural traits may change, but cultures change very slowly.

Some elements of a culture are easy to see. They include material things, such as houses and other structures, television sets, food, or clothing. Sports, entertainment, and literature are also visible elements of culture. The things you cannot see or touch are also part of culture. They include spiritual beliefs, ideals, government, and ideas about right and wrong. Language is also a very important part of culture.

▼ How people live is part of their culture. Different cultures sometimes interact with their environment in similar ways. In mountainous Japan, farmers build terraces on the hillsides to increase the amount of land available for farming. Terrace farming is also used in other cultures, including those in South America and South Asia.

Culture and Costume

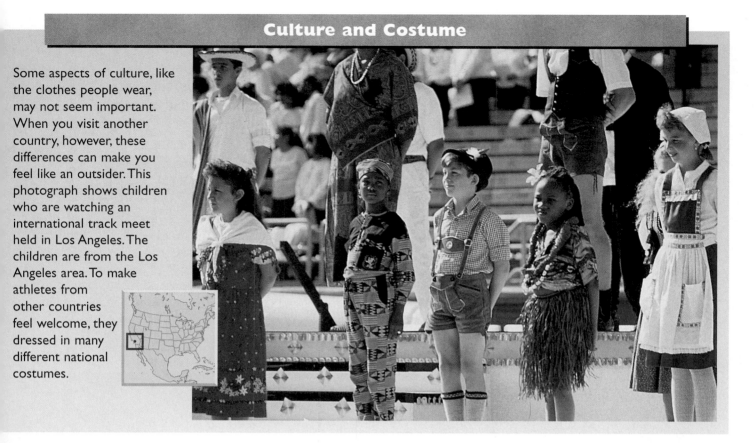

Some aspects of culture, like the clothes people wear, may not seem important. When you visit another country, however, these differences can make you feel like an outsider. This photograph shows children who are watching an international track meet held in Los Angeles. The children are from the Los Angeles area. To make athletes from other countries feel welcome, they dressed in many different national costumes.

People and Their Land Geographers study culture, especially activities that relate to the environment. These things are part of the theme of human-environment interaction. Geographers want to know how landforms, climate, vegetation, and resources affect culture. For example, fish and seaweed are popular foods in Japan, a nation of islands. These islands are mountainous, with little farmland. Therefore, the Japanese get food from the sea.

Geographers are also interested in the effect people have on their environment. Often the effect is tied to a culture's **technology,** or tools and the skills people need to use them. People use technology to take advantage of natural resources and change the environment. Technology can mean tools like computers and the Internet. But technology also means stone tools and the ability to make them. Geographers use levels of technology to see how advanced a culture is.

A group's **cultural landscape** includes any changes to its environment. It also includes the technology used to make the changes. They vary from culture to culture. For example, Bali, in Indonesia, has many mountains. Therefore, people carved terraces in them to create flat farmland. Other regions, such as central India, have much level land. Farmers there would not develop a technology to create terraces.

Think about your culture. What do people eat? What are the houses like? What kind of work do people do? Can you identify some beliefs and values of your culture? In your mind, describe your culture. You may find it is harder to look at your own culture than at someone else's.

Working Together
Sometimes the old ways are best. Two Bolivians, Bonifacia Quispe and Oswaldo Rivera, discovered the ancient Aymara Indians cut terraces into the sides of mountains to create flat farmland. Terraces are easier to irrigate and fertilize than slopes. In 1986, Quispe and Rivera taught the method to today's Aymara farmers. These farmers then grew 28 times more food.

The Development of Culture

Cultures develop over a long time. Geographers say early cultures went through four stages: the invention of tools, the discovery of fire, the growth of **agriculture**, or farming, and the use of writing.

Technology and Weather Forecasting

Technology is a very important part of culture because it changes the way we do things. For thousands of years, people have looked up at the sky to try to forecast the weather. Today, meteorologists—scientists who study the weather—still look up at the sky. However, they use very advanced technology, including various kinds of satellites, to do their job. Our ancestors could do little more than guess about the weather. Modern meteorologists, however, can make highly accurate forecasts about the weather several days into the future. Below is a diagram of a weather tracking satellite system.

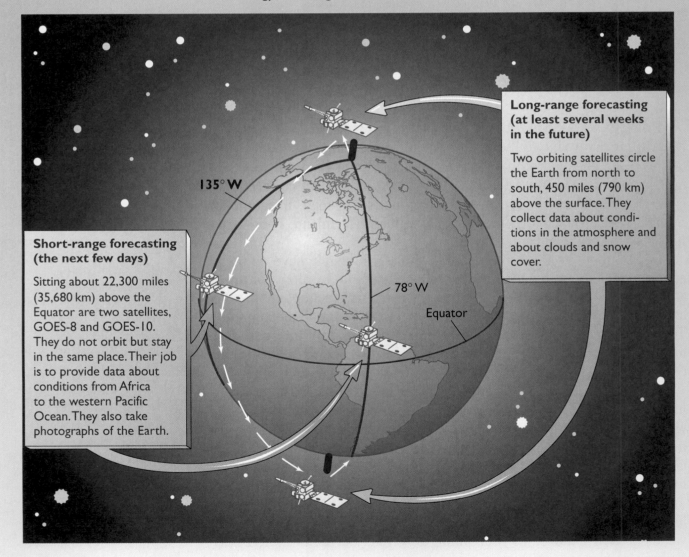

Long-range forecasting (at least several weeks in the future)

Two orbiting satellites circle the Earth from north to south, 450 miles (790 km) above the surface. They collect data about conditions in the atmosphere and about clouds and snow cover.

135° W

78° W

Equator

Short-range forecasting (the next few days)

Sitting about 22,300 miles (35,680 km) above the Equator are two satellites, GOES-8 and GOES-10. They do not orbit but stay in the same place. Their job is to provide data about conditions from Africa to the western Pacific Ocean. They also take photographs of the Earth.

Early Technology For most of human history, people were hunters and gatherers. Traveling from place to place, they collected wild plants, hunted game, and fished. Wood and stone tools and weapons helped them hunt, prepare food, and do other work. Later they learned to make and use fire, so some people began living in colder climates.

The Start of Agriculture Then, people discovered how to grow crops and tame wild animals to use as food or to help them with work. Now people no longer had to spend all their time following herds or moving from campsite to campsite in search of wild plants. Over time, societies relied on farming for most of their food. Historians call this great change the Agricultural Revolution.

By 3,000 years ago, the Agricultural Revolution had changed much of the world. Agriculture provided a steady food supply. Birthrates rose; death rates fell; population increased. Agriculture also led to the creation of cities and complex societies. Some people produced food, and others developed special skills. For example, people became potters, tailors, or metal workers. People began to develop laws and government. To record information, they developed writing. Now, people could store knowledge and pass it on to others. When a culture creates a writing system, it is called a civilization.

Early civilizations also created unique forms of art and music. They organized their beliefs into religions, with priests, temples, and ceremonies. Their roads and canals became features of the landscape. People learned to control and change their environment. Because of technological inventions such as irrigation and terracing, people could grow more and better crops in more areas. People spread over more and more regions. As they moved, they made changes to the Earth's landscape.

The Domestication of Grain Early people gathered the seeds of the wild grains for food. However, about 10,000 years ago, people in Southwest Asia decided to try to plant wild wheat to tide them over. The first crop was poor. But farmers saved seeds from the best plants and tried again the next year. Over time, this led to today's domesticated wheat.

1. **Define** (a) culture, (b) cultural trait, (c) technology, (d) cultural landscape, (e) agriculture.
2. If someone asked you to describe your culture, what would you tell them?
3. Describe four important developments in human culture. Tell why they are important.

Critical Thinking

4. **Recognizing Cause and Effect** Agriculture encouraged people to settle in one area and provided a steady food supply. How did agriculture lead to civilization?

Activity

5. **Writing to Learn** Find a photograph of a familiar scene in your town or city. List at least ten features of your culture shown in the photograph.

Social Groups, Language, and Religion

Reach Into Your Background

Even if you can't speak a word of Chinese, Italian, French, or Spanish, you can probably get Chinese, Italian, French, or Spanish food. Here is a list of four restaurants: Hoy Hing, Bella Vista, Café de Paris, Casa Mexico. Where would you go for enchiladas? For egg rolls? You know where to go because you connect food and language. Both are parts of culture. What else is part of culture?

Questions to Explore

1. Why is social organization important to cultures?
2. What elements make cultures distinct from one another?

Key Terms

social structure
nuclear family
extended family
ethics

▼ The end of Ramadan means a joyous celebration for these Egyptian Muslims.

It is still dark when the muezzin (moo EZ in) calls the people of Cairo to prayer. Roosters crow. As you wake, you remember that today is the first day of Ramadan (ram uh DAHN). During this religious season, Muslims, followers of the religion of Islam, eat and drink nothing from sunrise to sunset. This year, Ramadan will be special. Young children do not fast during Ramadan, but now you are 12. Now you are old enough to join the fast.

You are excited and a little nervous. You want to fast. It is a way to praise Allah, and it shows you are an adult. Still, you wonder if you can go all day without eating or drinking. You join your family for the *suhoor* (soo HOOR), the meal eaten before daybreak. Your parents and grandparents smile at you proudly. In the evening, you will join them for the *Iftar* (if TAHR), or the meal eaten after dark. That meal will taste especially good. And a month from now, when you celebrate the end of Ramadan, you will be prouder than ever. Every year you receive gifts, but this year they will be very special. You will give the prayers of thanksgiving, knowing you have joined with Muslims all over the world to celebrate Ramadan.

How Society Is Organized

Although the children of Cairo join with Muslims all over the world to celebrate Ramadan, they do so within their own households. Every culture has a **social structure.** This is a way of organizing people into

Families Come in All Sizes

In the United States, a mother, father, and their two sons enjoy a day in the park (top left). In Malaysia, children join their parents, aunts, uncles, and grandparents to make music (top right). In the mountains of Tibet, a mother leads her child on a yak (bottom). As these pictures show, a family can be as small as two people or as large as a roomful of people.

Ask Questions What questions would you like to ask about different kinds of families?

smaller groups. Each smaller group has particular tasks. Some groups work together to get food. Others protect the community. Still others raise children. Social structure helps people work together to meet the basic needs of individuals, families, and communities.

The family is the basic, most important social unit of any culture. Families teach the customs and traditions of the culture. Through their families, children learn how to dress, to be polite, to eat, and to play.

Kinds of Families All cultures do not define family in the same way. In some cultures, the basic unit is a **nuclear family,** or a mother, father, and their children. This pattern is common in industrial nations such as the United States, Great Britain, and Germany. Adults often work outside the home. They usually have money to buy what they need. They depend on the work of machines like vacuum cleaners and automobiles.

Other cultures have extended families. An **extended family** includes several generations. Along with parents and their children, there may be grandparents, aunts, uncles, cousins, and other relatives who live with them or close by. In extended families, older people are very respected. They pass on traditions. Extended families are less common than they used to be. As rural people move to cities, nuclear families are becoming more common.

Cultures also differ when deciding who is in charge in families. Many cultures have patriarchal (PAY tree ar kal) families. That means men make most family decisions. But some African and Native American cultures have matriarchal (MAY tree ar kal) families. In these, women have more authority than in patriarchies. Today, family organization is changing. Men and women have started to share family power and responsibility.

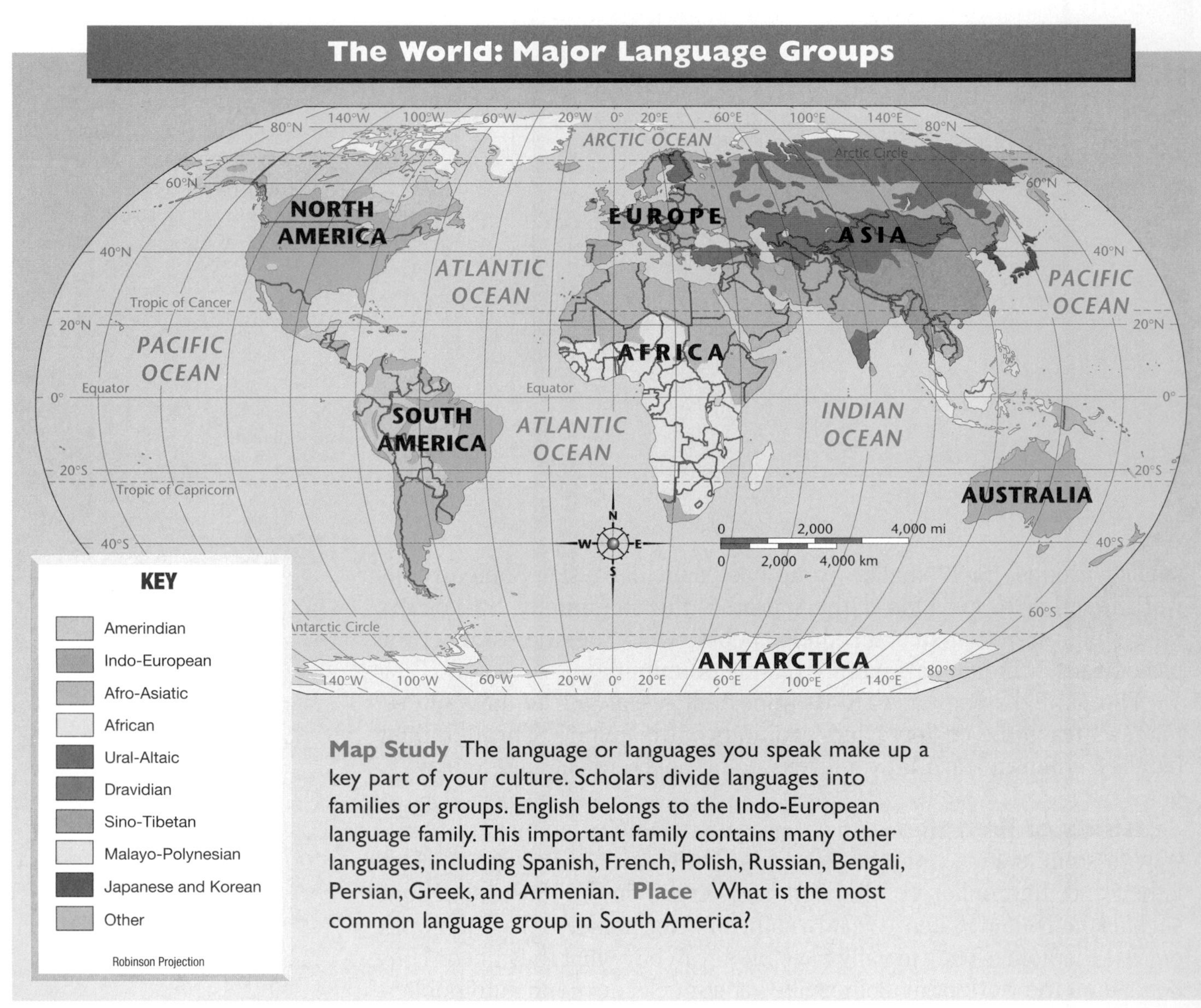

Map Study The language or languages you speak make up a key part of your culture. Scholars divide languages into families or groups. English belongs to the Indo-European language family. This important family contains many other languages, including Spanish, French, Polish, Russian, Bengali, Persian, Greek, and Armenian. **Place** What is the most common language group in South America?

Social Classes Cultures also have another kind of social organization—social classes. These rank people in a culture. A person's status or position may come from such things as wealth, land, ancestors, or education. In some cultures in the past, it was often hard—or impossible—for people to move from one social class to another. Today, people in many societies can improve their status. They can get a good education, make more money, or even marry someone of a higher class.

Language

Culture is a total way of life. Whoever you are, wherever you live, you are part of the culture of your society. You learn your culture from your family or from others. You also learn a great deal through language. Think of how hard it would be if you had no way to say, "Meet me by the gate after school," or "I'll have a tuna sandwich." How could you learn if you could not ask questions?

All cultures have language. In fact, every culture is based on language. It lets people communicate everything they need to share in their culture. Without language, people could not pass on what they know or believe to their children.

A culture's language reflects the things that its people think are important. For example, English has the word *snow* and several adjectives for the white stuff that falls in some places in winter. But the Inuits of North America have over 13 words for snow. Why? Where the Inuits live, snow covers the ground for a good part of the year. Snow is a more important part of their environment than it is to people of other cultures. The Inuits, therefore, have created words to meet their needs. All cultures have their own unique terms.

In some countries, people speak different languages. For example, the official language of Egypt is Arabic. It is spoken by most Egyptians. But some Egyptians speak Italian, Greek, or Armenian. Canada has two official languages, French and English, and Native Americans there speak a number of languages. People who speak these languages are culturally different in some ways from other people in their country. They may celebrate different festivals, wear different clothes, or have different customs for such things as dating or education.

Ancient Alphabets The Phoenicians were ancient traders along the Mediterranean Sea. Their alphabet had 22 letters, and they wrote from right to left. The Greeks saw this writing system and based their own alphabet on it—with one difference. The Greeks, like us, wrote from left to right. We owe our alphabet, in part, to these two ancient cultures.

Ways of Believing

Language is basic to cultures. Other basics are values and religion. At the beginning of this section, you read about Ramadan, a religious celebration of Muslims, followers of the religion of Islam. Ramadan is a very important part of Islam. And Islam is a major part of Egyptian culture. Other religions are important in other cultures.

Religion helps people understand the world. Religion can provide comfort and hope for people facing difficult times. And religion helps answer questions about the meaning and purpose of life. It helps define the values that people believe are important. Religions guide people in **ethics,** or standards of accepted behavior.

Predict Why are religions an important part of cultures?

The World: Major Religions

KEY

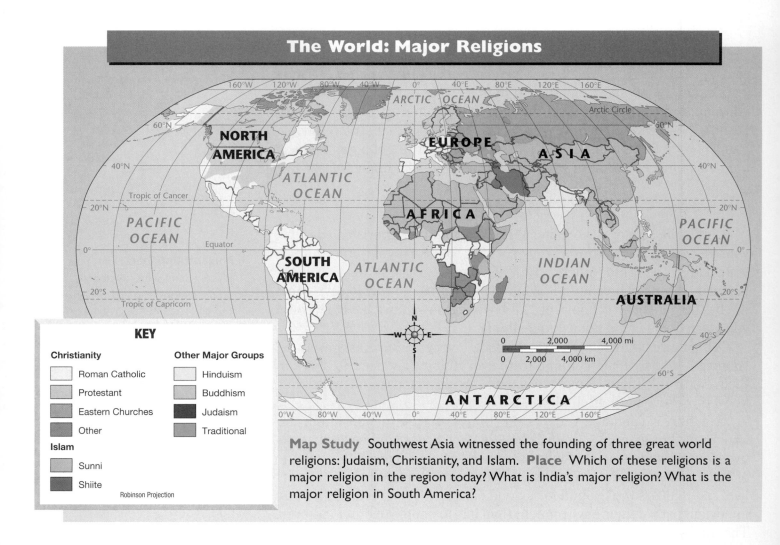

Christianity
- Roman Catholic
- Protestant
- Eastern Churches
- Other

Islam
- Sunni
- Shiite

Other Major Groups
- Hinduism
- Buddhism
- Judaism
- Traditional

Robinson Projection

Map Study Southwest Asia witnessed the founding of three great world religions: Judaism, Christianity, and Islam. **Place** Which of these religions is a major religion in the region today? What is India's major religion? What is the major religion in South America?

Religious beliefs vary. Some religions such as Islam, Judaism, and Christianity believe in one god. Other religions worship more than one god. But all religions have prayers and rituals. Every religion celebrates important places and times. Most religions expect people to treat one another well and behave properly.

1. **Define** (a) social structure, (b) nuclear family, (c) extended family, (d) ethics.
2. What is the basic unit of a culture's social structure?
3. What are three important features of a culture?
4. Explain the difference between a matriarchy and a patriarchy.
5. What is the role of religion in a culture?

Critical Thinking

6. **Recognizing Bias** How do you know that one language is not better than another?

Activity

7. **Writing to Learn** Make notes about your own culture. Draw three circles labeled "social structure," "language," and "religion." In each circle, make notes about your own culture's social structure, language, and religion. Include information about others in your family or neighborhood whose culture influences you.

Economic and Political Systems

Reach Into Your Background

Many schools are polling places where people vote. You may have seen adults going into the gym or another part of your school to use a voting machine or mark a ballot. Signs nearby often urge people to vote for a candidate or a certain way on an issue. Perhaps your student body holds elections, too. They are part of the political process in many places in the United States.

Questions to Explore

1. What is an economic system?
2. How do governments differ in their structure?

Key Terms

economy
producer
goods
services
consumer
capitalism
socialism
communism
government
direct democracy
monarchy
constitution
representative democracy
dictator

Muhammad Yunnus is a professor of economics in the country of Bangladesh. Bangladesh (bahng gluh DESH) is a very poor nation in South Asia. Yunnus wanted to understand how the people in his country really lived. His goal was to help them. He knew Bangladeshis ate only one or two meals a day. Though many had not gone to school, they were intelligent. Yunnus knew they were hard-working and could be trusted.

In the early 1970s, Yunnus met Sufiya Khatun. She made bamboo stools. But she earned only two cents a day because she had so few stools to sell. If she had more money for supplies, she could make more. But Sufiya had no way to borrow money to buy supplies. At first, Yunnus thought he would simply give her the small sum she needed. Then he wondered if others in the village were also like Sufiya. He found 42 people that needed to borrow about $26 each for their businesses.

Yunnus was shocked. So little money meant the difference between success and failure. But banks would not

▼ Most of Muhammad Yunnus's customers are women seeking to open small businesses. This woman used her loan to start a weaving shop.

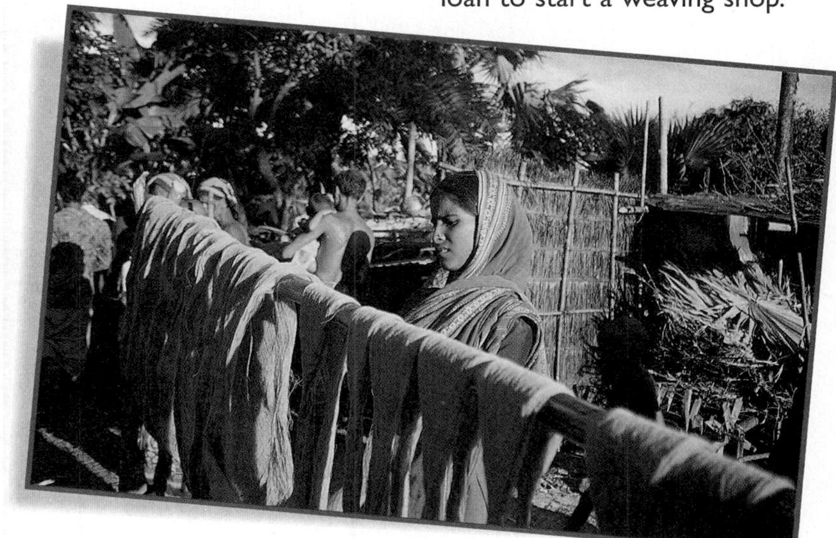

bother with such small loans. In 1976, Yunnus decided to do something about this situation. He started up a bank to loan small amounts of money only to poor people. Every borrower must join a group of five people. Every group member is responsible for the loans of every other member, so members must all trust and help each other. To build trust, they meet once a week to talk over their problems.

Yunnus's bank is called the Grameen Bank, which means "village bank." Today, the Grameen Bank has more than 1,000 offices and has loaned money to 2 million customers. Its interest rates are fairly high, but 98 percent of its loans are paid back. People in other countries are starting banks like Grameen. There are even some in the United States.

Connect Think about each member of your family and what he or she does. Is each a consumer, a producer, or both? Explain why.

Economic Systems

Banks like the Grameen help people become productive members of their nation's economy. An **economy** is a system for producing, distributing, and consuming goods and services. Owners and workers are **producers.** They make products, such as bamboo baskets or automobiles. Those products are called **goods.** Some products are really **services** that producers perform for other people. They may style hair, provide hotel rooms, or heal diseases. **Consumers** are people who buy and use the goods and services.

There are two categories of businesses. Basic businesses are essential for a nation to function. They include things like transportation, communication, and electricity. Non-basic industries are "nice but not necessary." They may make products such as compact disks or sports equipment. Services can also be basic or non-basic businesses. Hospitals are basic businesses. Singing telegram companies are non-basic businesses.

◄▼ Neighbors in the New York town of Ithaca have a very interesting system of exchange. Instead of paying dollars, they trade "Ithaca Hours" for goods like fresh bread, as well as for services like babysitting. Each hour is worth $10—the average hourly wage in Ithaca. "Prices" depend on the amount of labor involved in producing the good or service.

Capitalism Replaces Communism

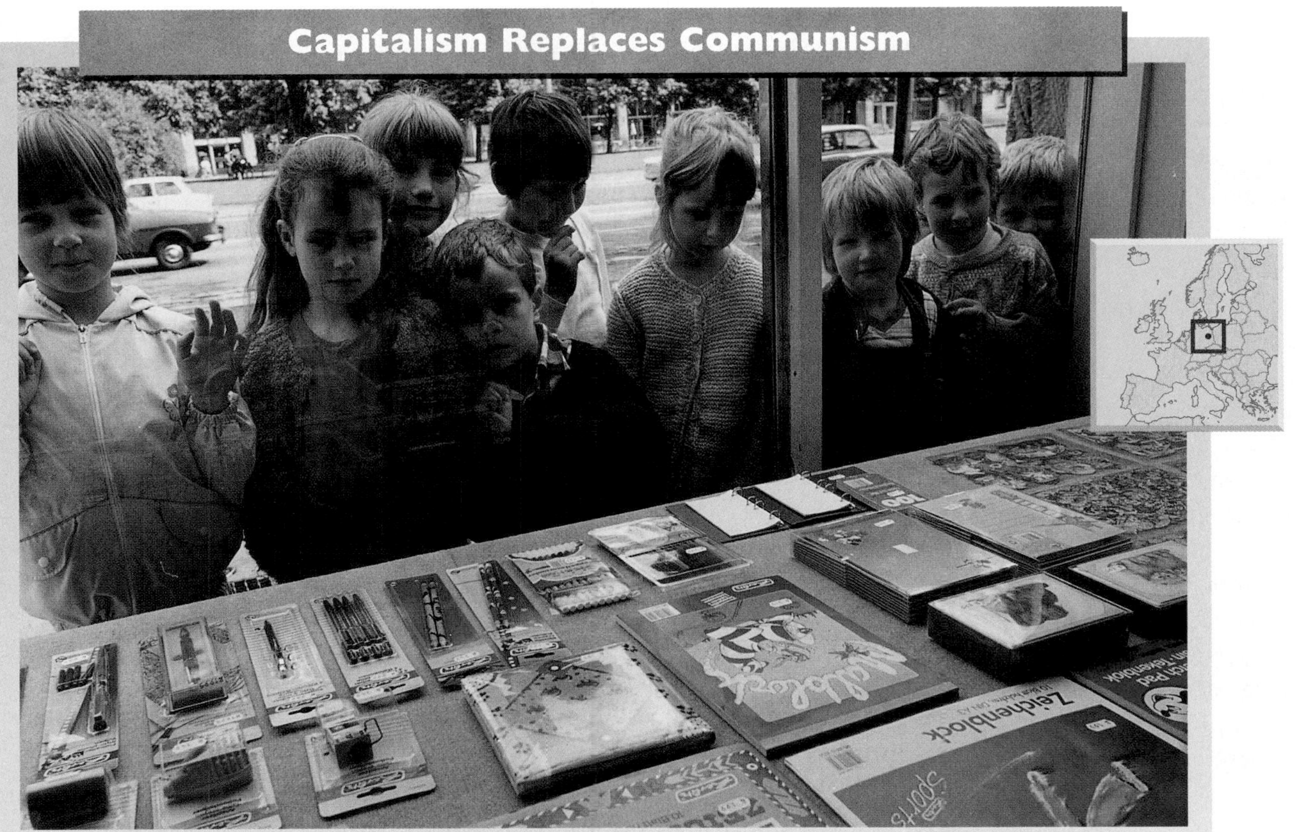

This photograph was taken in Berlin shortly after Communist East Germany united with capitalist West Germany. These East German children had never seen so many different school supplies before. The supplies came from the West, where the free market forces businesses to compete for customers.

Predict What do you think the three basic types of economic systems are?

Cultures choose the way they want to organize their economies. Today, most cultures choose from three basic systems: *capitalism, socialism,* and *communism.*

In **capitalism,** most basic and non-basic businesses are privately owned. Workers produce the goods or services. When a company sells its products, it earns profits, or money. The owners decide how much to pay workers and how to use profits.

The consumer is important in capitalism. Companies make products, but consumers might refuse to buy them. Successful companies supply goods or services that consumers need, want, and can afford. Capitalist countries include the United States, South Africa, and Japan. Capitalism is also called a free-market economy.

In **socialism,** the government owns most basic industries. It runs them for the good of society, not for profit. The government decides how much to pay workers and how much to charge for goods. It uses profits to pay for services such as health and education. Non-basic industries and services follow the capitalist model. They are privately owned, and consumers decide which products to buy. A few countries follow socialism or have socialistic programs. These countries include Spain, Portugal, and Italy.

Quebec In Quebec, a province in Canada, many people are descendants of French settlers. So, they speak both French and English. Some residents want Quebec to become a separate nation. This has led to much political debate. Canada is a democracy, so residents of Quebec could vote on the issue. For now, Quebec has decided to remain part of Canada, but the argument continues.

In **communism,** the central government owns all property, such as farms and factories, for the benefit of its citizens. It controls all aspects of citizens' lives, including prices of goods and services, how much is produced, and how much workers are paid. Today, only a few of the world's nations practice communism. They include Cuba, China, and North Korea.

Hardly any nation has a "pure" economic system. For example, the United States has a capitalistic economy. However, state, local, and federal governments provide educational services, build and repair roads, and regulate product safety. In communist countries, you will find some private businesses such as small farms and special stores.

Political Systems

Small groups of people can work together to solve problems that affect them all. But that is impossible in complex cultures. Still, they also have to resolve conflicts between individuals and social groups. People also need protection from other countries and cultural groups. Communities need laws, leaders, and organizations that make decisions. **Government** is the system that sets up and enforces a society's laws and institutions. Some governments are controlled by a few people. Others are controlled by many.

Ask Questions What would you like to find out about different kinds of government?

Lacquer Painting

Olga Loceva
Age 14
Russia
Under communism, traditional Russian arts and crafts, such as lacquer painting of boxes and vases as shown here, were discouraged. Since the collapse of the Soviet Union, many Russians have begun to practice these arts once again. What traditions do you value? How would you feel if the government banned those traditions?

Direct Democracy The earliest governments were probably simple. People lived in small groups and practiced **direct democracy.** That means everyone participated in running the day-to-day affairs of the group. Chiefs or elders decided what was right or what to do. Decisions were based upon the culture's customs and beliefs. Today, government plays much the same role for complex cultures.

▲ In the United Kingdom's constitutional monarchy, the monarch has little authority. The real power is wielded by Parliament, an elected body similar to our Congress.

Monarchy Until about 100 years ago, one of the most common forms of government was a **monarchy.** In this system, a king or queen rules the government. The ruler inherits the throne by birth. Monarchies still exist today. Sweden, Denmark, the United Kingdom, Spain, and Swaziland are examples. But the rulers of these countries do not have the power their ancestors did. Instead, they are constitutional monarchs. Their countries have **constitutions,** or sets of laws that define and often limit the government's power. In a constitutional monarchy, the king or queen is often only a symbol of the country.

Representative Democracy A constitutional monarchy usually is a **representative democracy.** That means citizens elect representatives to run the country's affairs. Democracy comes from the Greek word *demos,* which means "common people." In a representative democracy, the people indirectly hold power to govern and rule. They elect representatives, who create laws. If the people do not like what a representative does, they can refuse to re-elect that person. They can also work to change laws they do not like. This system ensures that power is shared. The United States, Canada, and Israel are examples of representative democracies.

Dictatorship "If I ruled the world. . . . " Have you ever said or heard those words? It's fun to think about. You could give away free ice cream. You could give 12-year-olds the right to vote. Maybe you could end war and poverty.

◀ Josef Stalin was one of the world's cruelest dictators. He ruled the former Soviet Union from 1929 until 1953. He controlled every aspect of Soviet life and jailed or executed anybody who opposed him.

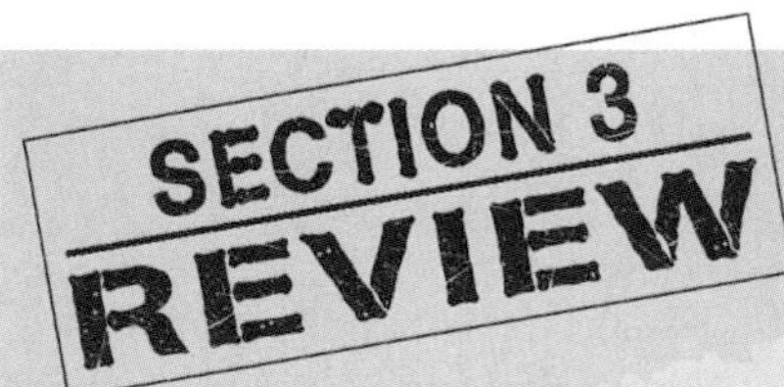

Of course, no one person rules the world. There are some countries, though, where one person rules. A government leader who has almost total power over an entire country is called a **dictator.**

Dictators decide what happens in their countries. They make the laws. They decide if there will be elections. When dictators take over, they often make promises that sound good. They may promise to end crime or to make a country strong. Sometimes they keep their promises. More often, they do not. Either way, people lose the right to make their own decisions.

SECTION 3 REVIEW

1. **Define** (a) economy, (b) producer, (c) goods, (d) services, (e) consumer, (f) capitalism, (g) socialism, (h) communism, (i) government, (j) direct democracy, (k) monarchy, (l) constitution, (m) representative democracy, (n) dictator.
2. Describe the three main types of economic systems.
3. Which form of government gives power to make decisions to the greatest number of people—a monarchy, a democracy, or a dictatorship?

Critical Thinking

4. **Drawing Conclusions** You hear on the news an announcement from the newly elected leader of a foreign country. The announcement states that the country's representatives will not meet. It also says that no elections will be held until further notice. What kind of a government does this country have? How do you know?

Activity

5. **Writing to Learn** You are working on a project to increase voting in your community. A statewide election is approaching. On behalf of your project, write a letter to a newspaper. In it, describe two reasons why people who are eligible to vote should do so.

Cultural Change

Reach Into Your Background

If you like to listen to rap, rock, folk, or jazz music, you like music from many different cultures. The rhythms you like might have come from Ireland, Jamaica, or Peru. You probably like some artists from different countries, too. Name some music you like that you think is a cultural blend.

Questions to Explore

1. What causes cultures to change?
2. Why has the rate of cultural change been increasing?

Key Terms

cultural diffusion
acculturation

Most people think that blue jeans are typical American clothes. But many cultures contributed to them. Blue jeans were created in the United States in the 1800s, by Levi Strauss, a German salesman who went to California. He made the jeans with cloth from France, called *serge de Nîmes.* The name was shortened to denim. Strauss dyed the denim with indigo, a plant from India and China. The indigo colored the denim dark blue.

In the 1980s, the Japanese and the French developed stonewashing. It made brand-new denim jeans look worn. Then, an Italian company created acid-washed jeans. Today, jeans are still popular in America. They are also very popular in Britain, the former Soviet Union, India, and parts of Africa. And the name *jeans*? It's French, for Italian sailors who wore sturdy cotton pants. What is more American than jeans?

▼ Blue jeans are a popular form of casual wear across the world. These blue-jeans clad dancers are from Barcelona, Spain.

Always Something New

Just as jeans have changed over time, so, too, has American culture. Cultures change all the time. Because culture is a total way of life, a change in one part changes other parts. Changes in the natural environment, technology, and new ideas affect culture.

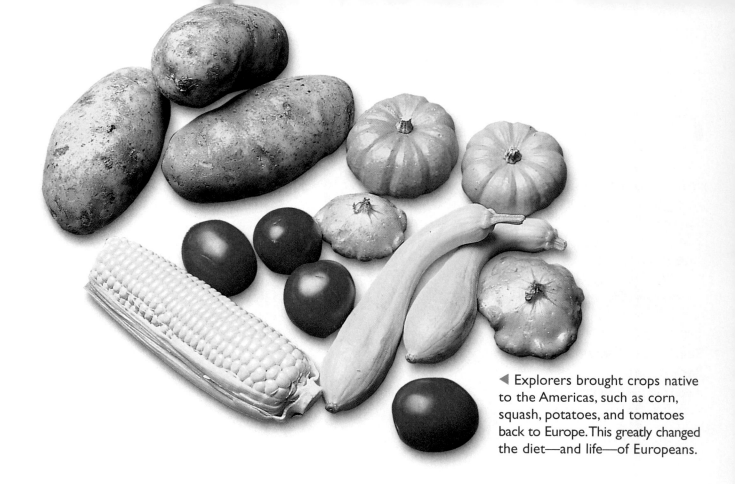

◀ Explorers brought crops native to the Americas, such as corn, squash, potatoes, and tomatoes back to Europe. This greatly changed the diet—and life—of Europeans.

A Change in the Environment If the weather changes long enough, the climate will change. That affects the kinds of food people can grow. It affects the kinds of clothes they wear. Changes in climate affect ways of making a living. But other changes can affect a culture, too.

A New Idea New ideas also change a culture. People used to take nature for granted. They thought anyone could use resources without damaging the overall supply. Since the 1950s, people in the United States and all over the world have become concerned about the environment. They recycle and work to protect endangered species and preserve forests. People also realized that we can use up or pollute many natural resources. The desire to save nature is a cultural change.

Predict What are some changes that technology has made in our culture in modern times?

Technology Equals Change Cultural change has been going on for a long time. New technological discoveries and inventions may have had the most effect on cultures. The discovery of fire helped early people to survive colder climates. When people invented wood and stone tools and weapons, ways of living also changed. Hunters could kill animals such as the mammoth and the giant bear. These animals had been too large to hunt without weapons.

Think of how technology has changed the culture of the United States. Radio and television brought entertainment and news into homes. Such things as TV dinners and instant information are now part of our culture. Computers change how and where people work. Computers even help people live longer. Doctors use computers to treat patients. Radio, television, and computers add new words to our language. *Broadcast, channel surfing,* and *hacker* are three. What other new words can you think of?

Sharing Ideas People are on the move all over the world. People come to the United States from other countries. Americans travel to other countries. In the process, they all bring new things such as clothing and tools with them. They also bring ideas about such things as ways to prepare food, teach children, or worship and govern. Sometimes a culture adopts these new ideas. The movement of customs and ideas is **cultural diffusion.**

The blue jeans story is a good example of cultural diffusion. Jeans were invented in the United States but now are popular around the world. People in other countries made changes to jeans. People in the United States adopted the changes. The process of accepting, borrowing, and exchanging ideas is called **acculturation.**

You can see cultural diffusion and acculturation if you study the history of baseball. It began as an American sport, but today it is played all over the world. That is an example of cultural diffusion. The Japanese love baseball. However, they changed the game to fit their culture. This change is an example of acculturation. Americans value competition. They focus on winning. But in Japan, a game can end in a tie. The

Tuning In to Cyberspace
Many record companies are now on the Internet. They talk about things like a band's latest musical release and upcoming tours. Some let people hear a band's music before buying it. Some bands have even tried live concerts over the Internet. This could be a big cultural change—listening to live performances at home instead of at a concert!

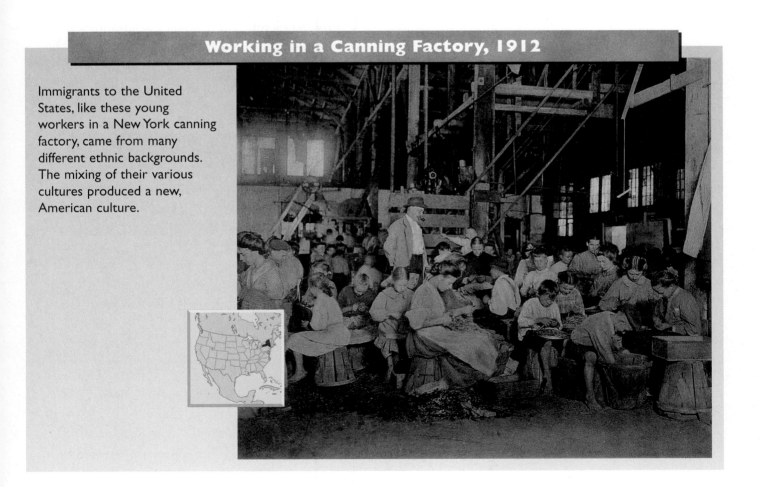

Working in a Canning Factory, 1912

Immigrants to the United States, like these young workers in a New York canning factory, came from many different ethnic backgrounds. The mixing of their various cultures produced a new, American culture.

Ask Questions Imagine you meet someone on the Internet from another culture. What questions would you ask to learn more about his or her culture?

Japanese do not mind a tie game for several reasons. For instance, in Japan, how well you play is more important than winning. Also, people try hard not to embarrass someone.

Technology and the Speed of Change

What's the fastest way to get from your house to Japan? A jet plane? A phone call? A television broadcast? The Internet? A fax? All these answers can be right. It depends on whether you want to transport your body, your voice, a picture, an interactive game, or a sheet of paper.

For thousands of years, cultures changed slowly. People moved by foot or wagon or sailing ship, so ideas and technology also moved slowly. Recently, technology has increased the speed of change. People no longer have to wait for a newcomer to bring changes. Faxes and computers transport information almost instantly. Magazines and television shows bring ideas and information from all over the world to every home. This rapid exchange of ideas speeds up cultural change.

A Global Village A village is a small place where people all know each other. It doesn't take long to get from one place to another. Today, many people call the Earth a "global village." That is because modern transportation and communications tell everyone about faraway people, businesses, and governments almost instantly.

Technology has brought many benefits. Computers let scientists share information about how to clean up oil spills. Telephones let us instantly talk to relatives thousands of miles away. In the Australian Outback, students your age use closed-circuit television and two-way radios to go to school in their own homes.

International Travel

Chart Study More and more people visit foreign countries each year. In 1998, 56 million Americans traveled to other nations. That's nearly the population of California and Texas combined. **Movement** How have today's forms of transportation, such as jet planes, affected international travel? **Critical Thinking** How do you think the increase in international travel has affected the "global village"?

Year	U.S. Travelers to Foreign Countries	Foreign Visitors to the United States
1980	22 million	22 million
1985	35 million	25 million
1990	45 million	40 million
1995	51 million	43 million
1998	56 million	46 million

Keeping Traditions Alive

In recent years, people across the world have made greater efforts to preserve their traditions. In this picture, for example, young people from 20 Native American nations perform a dance at a gathering near Lake Casitas, California. **Critical Thinking** Why do you think it has become more important in recent years for people to preserve their traditions?

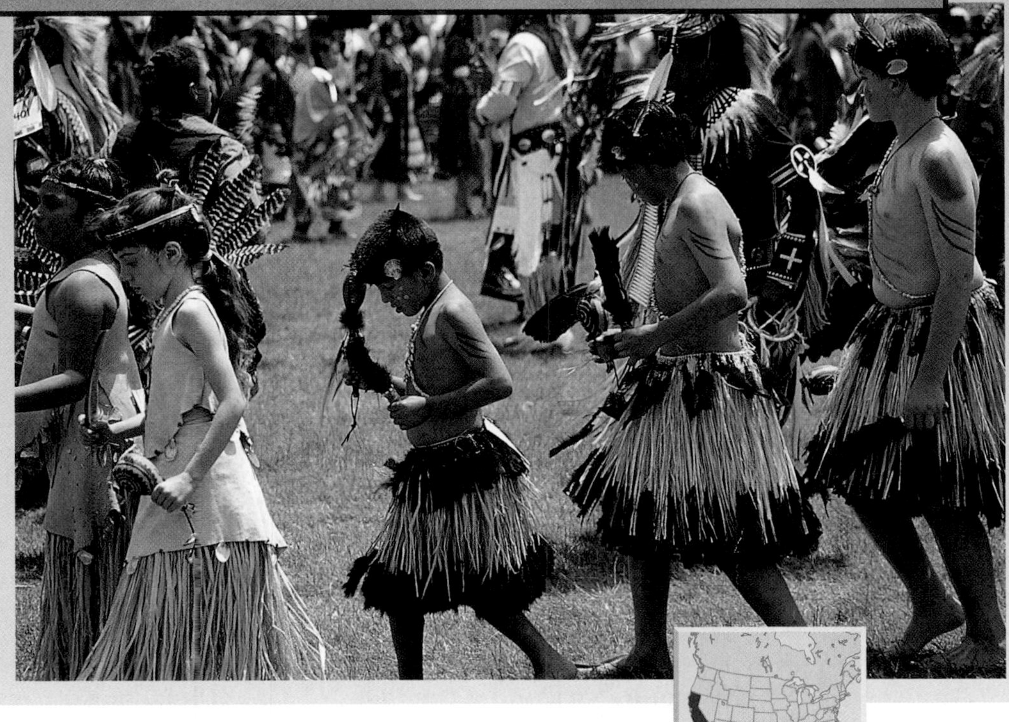

Information Overload? Change can help, but it can also hurt. If things change too fast, people can become confused, and culture is threatened. Valuable traditions can disappear. Once important sources of knowledge are lost, they can never be regained. In many parts of the world, people are working to save their own cultures before it is too late. They do not want to lose what is good in their culture. They understand it is important to remember where they came from if they are to understand where they are going.

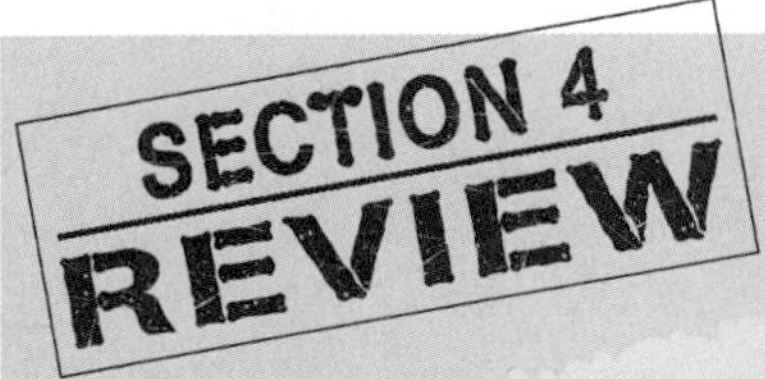

1. **Define** (a) cultural diffusion, (b) acculturation.
2. List three things that can cause a culture to change.
3. Explain the meaning of the term "global village."

Critical Thinking

4. **Distinguishing Fact From Opinion** A friend who has a computer tells you she has an e-mail pal in Singapore. "You learn more by having a pen pal on the Internet than by having one through regular mail," she says. You point out that you get drawings and photos in the mail from your pen pal in Turkey. Which of you has stated a fact? Which has stated an opinion? How do you know?

Activity

5. **Writing to Learn** Interview an older person about what changes she or he has seen in the culture over the years. Write two paragraphs summarizing what they say.

Locating Information

Rhonda was puzzled. "Did you hear that?" she whispered to Denise. "He just told me to shrink the panic! What does he mean?" Rhonda and Denise were staying in the home of a family in Argentina, a country in South America. They had traveled there as exchange students. The family had a mother, a father, a young girl, and a teenage boy. Rhonda had just told the teenage boy that she felt nervous about finding her way around.

That's when he turned to her and said, "Achicar el panico! I'll help you." Rhonda knew "achicar el panico" translated as "shrink the panic" in English. But what did it mean? The boy smiled at her puzzled look. "In Argentina, that's how we say 'chill out!'" he said. Rhonda smiled back.

"I get it," she said. "I guess I also need help learning the slang you use here!"

You know that people in different cultures live lives that are very different from yours. But do you know just how different? Even little things like slang can have completely different meanings. Before you travel to another country, it helps to learn as much about its culture as possible. The trick, believe it or not, is to build a pyramid!

Get Ready

This pyramid is not a real pyramid, of course, but a "pyramid of knowledge." There

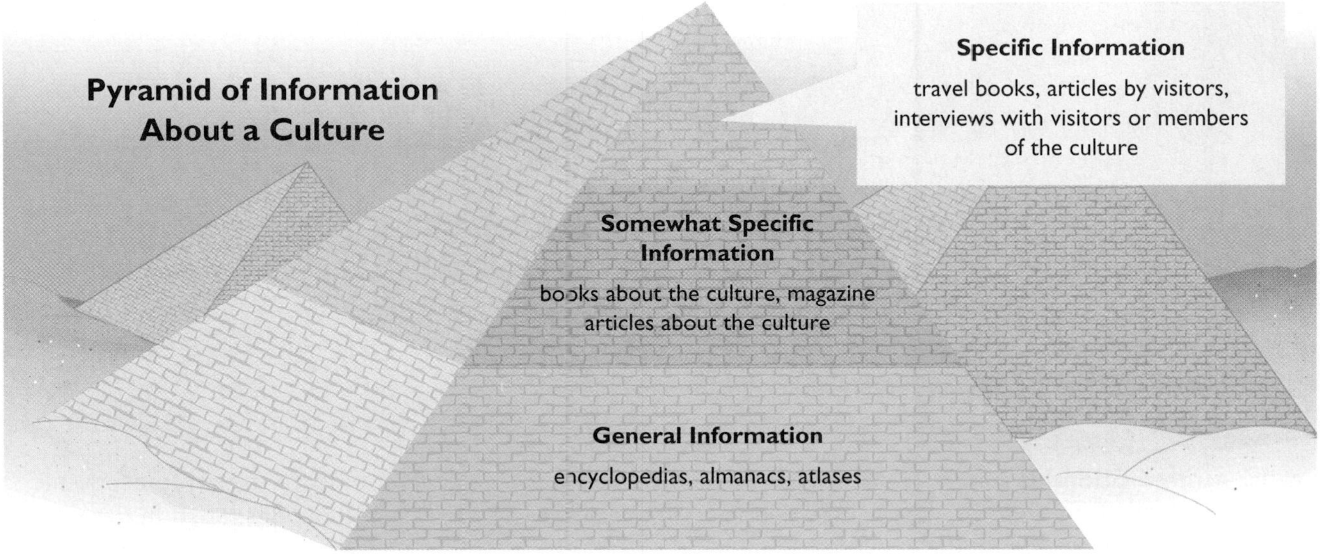

Pyramid of Information About a Culture

Specific Information

travel books, articles by visitors, interviews with visitors or members of the culture

Somewhat Specific Information

books about the culture, magazine articles about the culture

General Information

encyclopedias, almanacs, atlases

are thousands of sources of information about the peoples and cultures of the world. By organizing your search into the form of a pyramid, you can easily learn what you need to know. You will build your pyramid in a library.

Try It Out

Follow the steps below to build a pyramid of knowledge. As you work, refer to the diagram.

A. Choose a culture to learn about. You might choose a culture in a country in Europe, Latin America, Africa, or Asia.

B. Build a base of general information. Pyramids are built from the bottom up. The base of your pyramid of knowledge about a culture is general information. This includes such things as the correct name of a cultural group, its geographic location, the language the people speak, the population, and so on. Find this information by consulting the sources listed in the diagram of the pyramid.

C. Build the middle of the pyramid with more detailed information. The middle of the pyramid is made up of more detailed information about how people live in the culture. What are schools like? What customs are important? What are some common foods? What types of jobs do people have?

D. Build the top with specific information. Complete the pyramid by building the very top. It is made up of specific information about how individuals in the culture interact. Find out, for example, what proper greetings are and what certain gestures mean. Learn how to say basic phrases such as "How do you do?" and "Good-bye" in the language of the culture. Add specific information about anything else that interests you.

You can see you have learned a great deal about the culture in a short time. It takes a lifetime to develop a deep understanding of any culture. But by building a pyramid and continually adding to it, you can add to what you know.

Apply the Skill

Building a "pyramid of knowledge" is as simple as 1-2-3:

1. **Build the base.**
2. **Build the middle.**
3. **Build the top.**

As the pyramid grows, so does your knowledge. Practice applying this skill the next time you have any assignment requiring research. Find general information first, then more detailed information, and then very specific information. Work your way from the bottom to the top.

Review and Activities

Reviewing Main Ideas

1. What is the relationship between the environment people live in and their culture?
2. Describe three developments that have affected human culture.
3. Explain how the technology used in a culture reveals things about the culture's daily life, work, and values.
4. Why was the Agricultural Revolution so important in human history? What changes did it bring about?
5. Explain three important ways in which cultures can differ from one another.
6. Compare the three economic systems described in this chapter: capitalism, socialism, and communism.
7. Explain why people formed governments.
8. Why has culture changed more rapidly in modern times than in the past?

Reviewing Key Terms

Use each key term below in a sentence that shows the meaning of the term.

1. culture
2. technology
3. cultural landscape
4. social structure
5. nuclear family
6. extended family
7. economy
8. producer
9. goods
10. services
11. capitalism
12. socialism
13. government
14. constitution
15. representative democracy
16. dictator
17. cultural diffusion
18. acculturation

Critical Thinking

1. **Identifying Central Issues** Why is no culture exactly like any other culture?
2. **Expressing Problems Clearly** Why do you think people in one culture sometimes do not understand people in another?

Graphic Organizer

Think about how having less fresh water would affect society. Copy this cause-effect organizer. Then consider these topics: social organization, language, economic system, or government. Fill in the boxes, explaining how a water shortage might affect each topic.

Less Fresh Water

Vocabulary Activity

Many terms in this chapter compare and contrast similar ideas or activities. For instance, in capitalism, businesses are run by private individuals, but in communism, businesses are run by government. On a separate sheet of paper, explain how these terms compare and contrast similar ideas or activities.

1. goods and services
2. direct democracy and representative democracy
3. nuclear family and extended family

Writing Activity

Writing a Public Service Message

Your town or city is going to have a culture fair. The fair will introduce people to new cultures. It will also introduce people to different cultures within the United States. Write a public service message for a local radio station. A public service message includes the time, place, and purpose of a cultural event. Your notice should tell people why and how they should get involved with the culture fair.

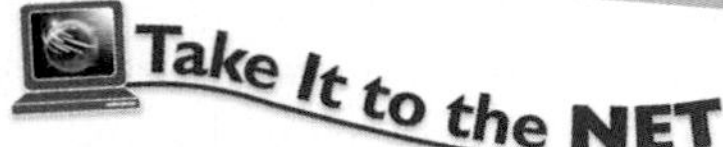

Activity Learn how to say common phrases in different languages. For help in completing this activity, visit **www.phschool.com.**

Chapter 4 Self-Test To review what you have learned, take the Chapter 4 Self-Test and get instant feedback on your answers. Go to **www.phschool.com** to take the test.

Skills Review

Turn to the Skills Activity.

Review the steps for locating information. Then complete the following: (a) How can building a pyramid of knowledge help you to locate information? (b) Explain the difference between general information and specific information.

How Am I Doing?

Answer these questions to help you check your progress.

1. Do I understand how environment affects culture and how culture affects environment?
2. Can I list the major elements of culture and the forms that they take?
3. Can I describe the ways that cultures change?
4. What information from this chapter can I include in my journal?

Rough Country

BY DANA GIOIA

Reach Into Your Background

Think about the area where you live. It has many characteristics that make it unique. Perhaps there is a flood plain, hills, flat land, or an earthquake fault. Perhaps there are special stores or restaurants in your neighborhood. Perhaps the people who live there speak several languages. Or, perhaps, when you first think about it, you cannot see anything about your neighborhood that is different from anywhere else.

Most people are so used to their surroundings that they do not pay any attention to them. But Dana Gioia goes into great detail to explain why "Rough Country" is a very special place. As you read the poem, notice how Gioia emphasizes the unique nature of "Rough Country."

Questions to Explore

1. What characteristics make the country described in the poem "rough"?
2. What is so special about this spot in the country?

Rough Country

Give me a landscape made of obstacles,
of steep hills and jutting glacial rock,
where the low-running streams are quick to flood
the grassy fields and bottomlands.
                                        A place
no engineers can master—where the roads
must twist like tendrils up the mountainside
on narrow cliffs where boulders block the way.

Where tall black trunks of lightning-scalded pine
push through the tangled woods to make a roost
for hawks and swarming crows.
                                        And sharp inclines
where twisting through the thorn-thick underbrush,
scratched and exhausted, one turns suddenly
to find an unexpected waterfall,

glacial (GLAY shul) *adj.* from a glacier; here, rocks left behind by a glacier
bottomlands *n.* low land through which a river flows; flood plain
tendril (TEN drihl) *n.* thread-like part of a climbing plant that supports the plant

not half a mile from the nearest road,
a spot so hard to reach that no one comes—

a hiding place, a shrine for dragonflies
and nesting jays, a sign that there is still
one piece of property that won't be owned.

Visualize What does this place look like in your mind's eye?

◀▼ Where do you call home? Some people live in the Canadian Rockies, and others live in Washington farmlands. What unique features might you find if you lived in those places?

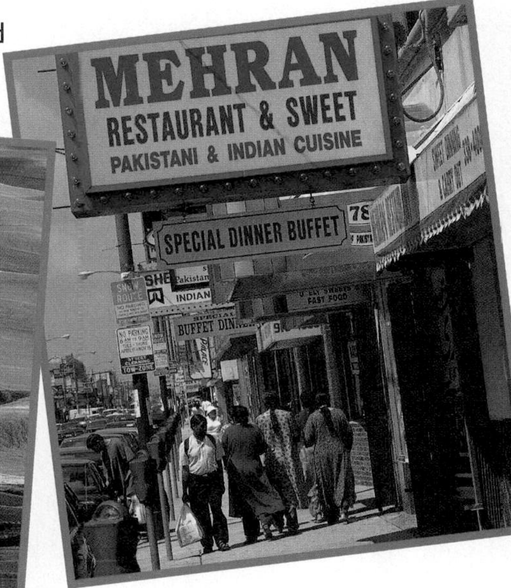

▲ What might you find if you lived in Chicago, Illinois?

Look Back

1. What human activities would be difficult or impossible in this place?

Think It Over

2. In the fourth stanza of "Rough Country," the poet describes a hike that suddenly opens onto a waterfall. What makes the waterfall seem especially beautiful to the poet?

Go Beyond

3. In "Rough Country," the poet describes "one piece of property that won't be owned." Antarctica is another place that no one "owns." No country can claim any part of it. Why might people think a place was so important that no one should own it?

Ideas for Writing: Poem

4. Think about the place where you live. Make a list of its characteristics, and draw a picture of it. Then, write a poem about your place. Finally, compare your poem with "Rough Country."

Earth's Natural Resources

SECTION 1
What Are Natural Resources?

SECTION 2
How People Use the Land

SECTION 3
People's Effect on the Environment

PICTURE ACTIVITIES

Think of the power of a waterfall as it tumbles from high places to low ones. Today, dams like this one on the Brazil-Paraguay border create waterfalls. In the process, they harness river power to create electricity for homes and businesses. This helps economies grow. A dam across a river also has a huge effect on the environment. The dam holds back the water of the river. It floods acres of land and creates a lake. Sometimes such lakes flood forests, farmland, and even towns and villages.

Examine both sides of an issue

Think about how this dam changes the natural landscape and how it helps people. Make a list of the advantages and disadvantages of such a project.

Study the picture

Each country has natural resources. From this picture, what resources do you think Brazil has? As you read this chapter, think about how a country's wealth relates to its land and climates.

What Are Natural Resources?

Reach Into Your Background
How much do you throw away each day? How much do you recycle? What do you own that is made of recycled material? Jot down your answers.

Questions to Explore
1. What are natural resources?
2. What is the difference between renewable and nonrenewable natural resources?

Key Terms
natural resource
raw material
recyclable resource
renewable resource
nonrenewable resource
fossil fuel

What can we do with the garbage we create? People are searching for answers. Some are unique. In 1995, architect Kate Warner built a house in Martha's Vineyard, Massachusetts. She used materials most people call trash. The builders mixed concrete with ash left over from furnaces that burn trash. Then they used the mixture to make the foundation of the house. To make the frame of the house, they used wood left over from old buildings, not fresh lumber. Warner wanted glass tiles in the bathroom. So she had glassmakers create them out of old car windshields. "We ask people to recycle, but then we don't know what to do with the stuff," Warner says. "By making use of waste materials, the manufacturers of these new building materials are creating exciting new markets and completing a loop." In this loop, materials are used over and over again. Garbage becomes a natural resource.

▼ Factories make new steel for bicycles and buildings by combining iron and other natural resources with recycled or "scrap" steel.

Natural Resources

Kate Warner is one of many people who want to use the Earth's natural resources wisely. These people believe this is the only way for humans to survive. A **natural resource** is any useful material found in the environment. Usually when people talk about natural resources, they mean such things as soil, water, minerals, and vegetation. A natural resource, then, is anything from the Earth that helps meet people's needs for food, clothing, and shelter.

The World: Natural Resources

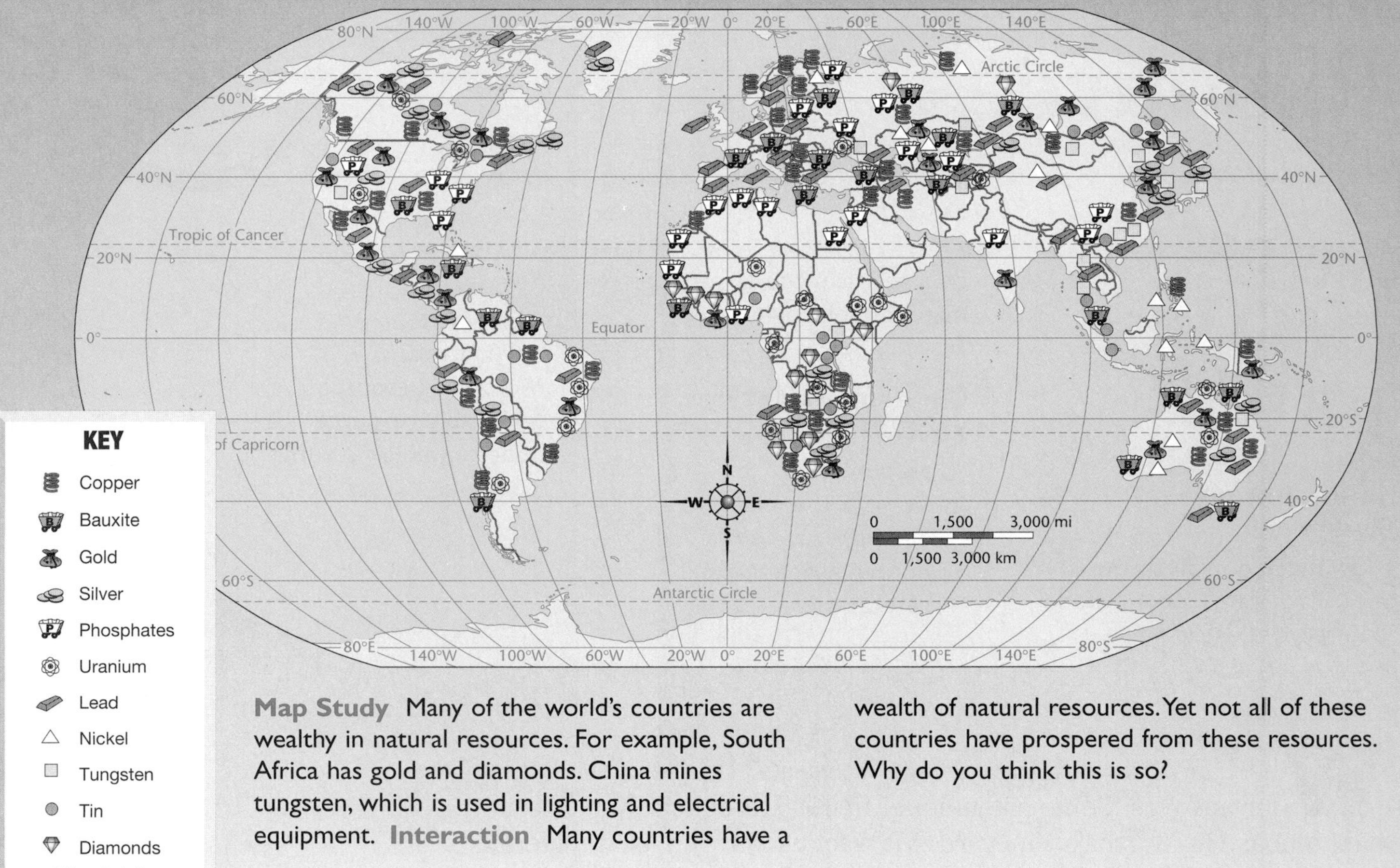

Map Study Many of the world's countries are wealthy in natural resources. For example, South Africa has gold and diamonds. China mines tungsten, which is used in lighting and electrical equipment. **Interaction** Many countries have a wealth of natural resources. Yet not all of these countries have prospered from these resources. Why do you think this is so?

All people need food, clothing, and shelter to survive. People drink water. People eat the food that the soil produces. So do the animals that provide eggs, cheese, and meat. People get such things as fish and salt from the ocean. Homes are made from wood, clay, and steel. Every day you benefit from the natural resources in the environment.

People can use some resources just the way they come from nature. Fresh water is one. But most resources must be changed before people use them. For example, people cannot just go out and cut down a tree to make a house. Even if they want to build a log cabin, they must cut the tree into pieces first. For a modern home, the wood must have the bark shaved away. Then the wood is cut into boards of various sizes. Resources that must be altered, or changed, before they can be used are called **raw materials.** Trees are the raw material for paper and wood.

Three Kinds of Resources The environment is full of natural resources. But not all resources are alike. Geographers divide them into three groups. The first group of resources cycle naturally through the environment. They do so because of the way the Earth works. In the water cycle, water evaporates into the air and falls as rain, snow, hail, or sleet. This happens over and over again. Therefore, the Earth has the same amount of water, although there may be too much of it in some places and not enough in others. For this reason, geographers call water a **recyclable resource.** Some other materials that cycle through natural processes as recyclable resources are nitrogen and carbon.

A second group of resources includes trees and other living things on the Earth. These things are different from recyclable resources. It is possible for people to gather plants or hunt animals until they no longer exist. But it does not have to happen. For example, a timber company may cut down all the trees in an area. But the company may then plant new trees to replace the ones they cut. Every day the people of the world eat many chickens and ears of corn. But farmers and chicken ranchers make sure there are always more corn plants and chickens to replace the ones people eat. If a resource can be replaced, it is called a **renewable resource.** If people are careful, they can have a steady supply of renewable resources.

The third group of resources is called **nonrenewable resources.** When they are used up, they cannot be replaced. Most nonliving things, such as minerals, coal, natural gas, and petroleum—or oil—are nonrenewable resources. So are metals. City recycling programs are often eager to recycle aluminum cans and plastic bottles. That is because these cans and bottles are made of nonrenewable resources.

Visualize Visualize the world if people do not take care to replace renewable resources. What would your town or city look like?

Ancient Energy: Fossil Fuel Often people take some things for granted. Lights turn on when a switch is flicked. The house is warm in winter or cool in summer. The car runs. All of these things require

Rain Forests: A Fragile Resource

Rain forests once covered millions of acres in Asia. Today, the rain forests of Asia are rapidly disappearing. Using heavy equipment to harvest the most valuable woods, loggers often damage huge areas of forest. In this photograph of the Malaysian rain forest, notice the sawmills that process the valuable tropical lumber and the roads that carry the wood out of the area. Once this rain forest is cut down, it will be very difficult to replace.

fossil fuels, which include coal, natural gas, and petroleum. Fossil fuels were created over millions of years from the remains of prehistoric plants and animals. These fuels are no longer being created. As a result, fossil fuels are nonrenewable resources. If people continue using coal, natural gas, and petroleum at today's rate, the Earth will run out of fossil fuels in 100 to 200 years.

A Special Resource: Energy

Imagine that you are in your room, reading your geography book. What items around you require energy? Some are obvious. A clock, a radio, or a lamp all use energy directly, in a form called electricity. Others are not so obvious because they use energy indirectly. Consider a water glass on a dresser or athletic shoes on the floor. These things were manufactured in a factory, and that process uses energy.

What about things made of plastic—a toy, a comb, or a pen? If you have a rug, it may be made of a synthetic material that looks like wool but is really a kind of plastic. These things are manufactured, so they use energy indirectly. But they also use energy directly. The reason is that plastics are made from petroleum, and petroleum is an energy source.

Getting everything to your room required energy, too. Your family bought them at a store, so you used energy to travel back and forth. The store bought them from a manufacturer, which required more energy. It takes a great deal of energy to put a small plastic glass in your room. So it is easy to see why people value energy sources so highly.

Top Petroleum Consumers

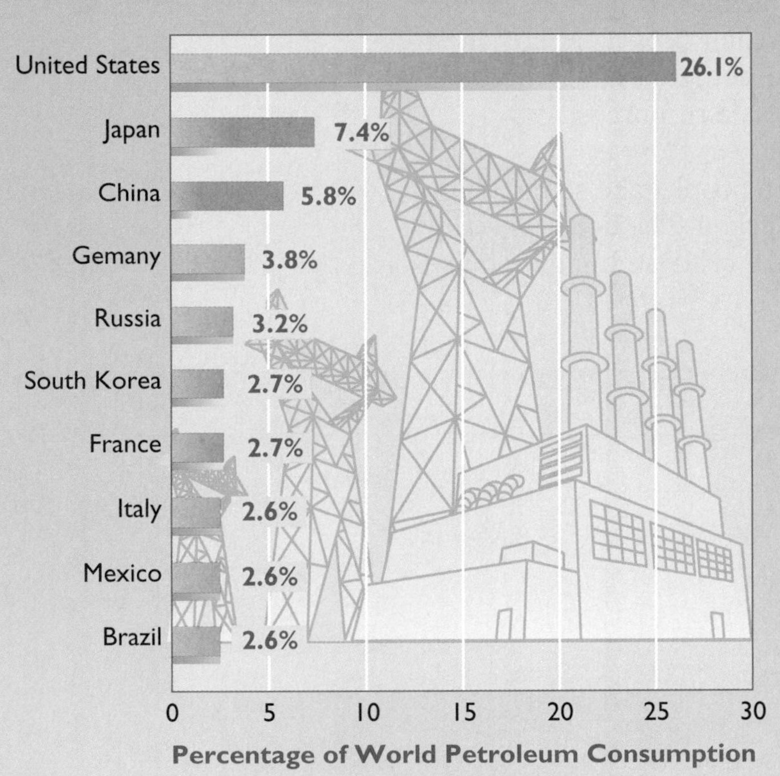

Source: Energy Information Administration

Chart Study Products made from petroleum are used to provide heat for buildings and power for automobiles, airplanes, and factories. People use so much petroleum that experts think that world supplies will be almost exhausted in 100 to 200 years. **Critical Thinking** What countries consume the most petroleum? Think of some ways that these countries could reduce their consumption of petroleum.

Energy "Have's" and "Have Not's" Everyone in the world needs energy. But energy resources are not evenly spread around the world. Certain areas are rich in some energy resources. Others have very few.

Top Petroleum Producers

Chart Study Petroleum is a nonrenewable resource, one that cannot be replaced once it is used. As a result, it is very valuable. Countries that have deposits can sell petroleum for a profit. **Critical Thinking** Compare this chart with the one on the previous page. Notice that the United States uses more than twice as much petroleum as it produces. How does Russia's production compare with its consumption?

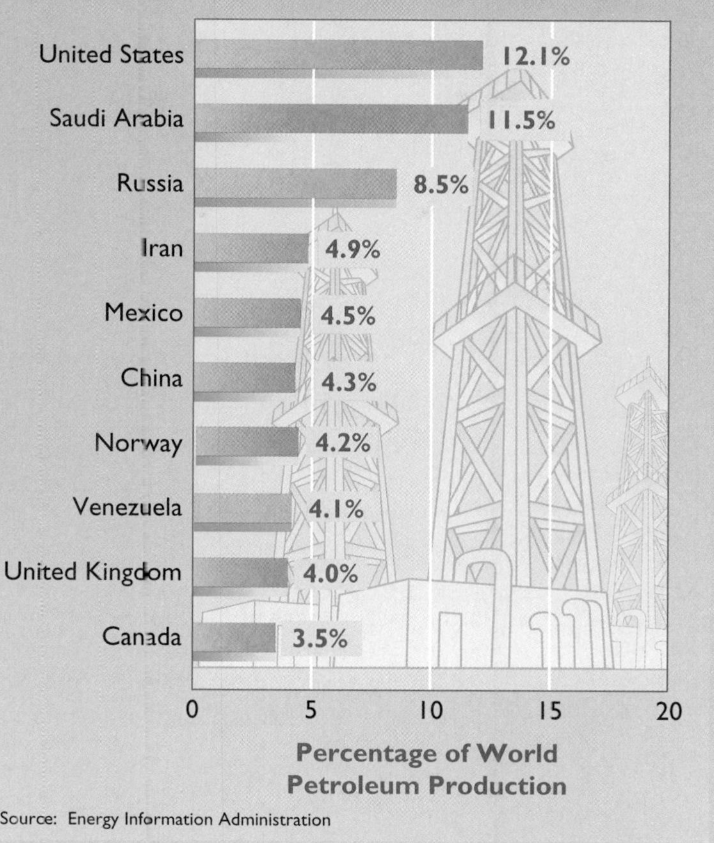

Source: Energy Information Administration

Countries like Saudi Arabia and Mexico have huge amounts of oil. Others, like the United States and China, have coal and natural gas. Countries with many rivers, such as the countries of Northwestern Europe, can use water energy to create electricity. Others, such as Japan, have very few energy sources. These countries must buy their energy from other countries.

Growing Needs and the Search for New Supplies In 1973, members of the Organization of Petroleum Exporting Countries (OPEC) decided to sell less of their oil. In the United States, this caused a shortage of gasoline, which is made from oil. When there is a shortage of something, it is more expensive. The price of gas more than doubled. Drivers sat in long lines at gas stations. Companies that used fuel oil to make electricity sent notices to families and businesses. The notices asked people to use as little electricity as possible. How could OPEC members have such an effect on the United States?

The answer is that just because a country uses large amounts of energy does not mean that country has its own large energy resources. The biggest users of energy are industrial countries like the United States and the nations of Western Europe. Japan, which has few petroleum resources of its own, uses over twice as much energy as all of

Connect What things can you and your family do to use fewer fossils fuels in your everyday life?

Oil From Under the Ocean

In the chilly waters of the North Sea, European companies drill deep wells to tap the area's large oil deposits. Increased production of North Sea oil may reduce the world's demand for oil from Southwest Asia. **Critical Thinking** How might technological improvements such as more modern drilling rigs cut the cost of oil?

Africa. If a country does not have enough energy resources of its own, it must buy them from other countries. In the 1970s, the United States used so much energy that it had to begin buying oil from OPEC members. When producing countries limited the supply of oil, they could charge much more for their product. The United States had to pay whatever the producing country asked. The oil shortages in the 1970s and again in the early 2000s made people see they needed to find more sources of energy.

SECTION 1 REVIEW

1. **Define** (a) natural resource, (b) raw material, (c) recyclable resource, (d) renewable resource, (e) nonrenewable resource, (f) fossil fuel.
2. (a) Name two renewable resources. (b) What are two nonrenewable resources?
3. Name some ways that people use fossil fuels.
4. What is the difference between indirect energy use and direct energy use?

Critical Thinking

5. **Expressing Problems Clearly** Explain why people must be careful about how they use nonrenewable resources.

Activity

6. **Writing to Learn** Early pioneers in North America used forests and grasslands as they pleased. Write a paragraph explaining why it might have been less important then to replace those resources.

How People Use the Land

Reach Into Your Background

How many manufactured, or factory-made, items do you use in a day? What natural resources were used to make them? Make a list of these resources.

Questions to Explore

1. What are the stages of economic development?
2. How do different cultures use land?

Key Terms

manufacturing
developed nation
developing nation
commercial farming
subsistence farming
plantation
foreign aid

"All this water started flowing, but we were told it was restricted for use only by the oil company and we were not allowed to use it," said Li Lixing, a Chinese farmer. "We had to go at night and secretly take some for our crops." Li Lixing lives in a village by the banks of the Huang He. People have farmed here for hundreds of years. In Li's region, the government wants to help the economy by supporting businesses like the oil company. Farmers, therefore, face problems.

Many countries face problems of limited resources, increasing population, and growing demand. Studying how countries use their natural resources shows three basic patterns of economic activity.

Stages of Resource Development

Water from the Huang He is essential for Chinese farmers like Li. But industry needs resources, too. Which group is more important? In some cultures, industry comes first. In others, farmers do. Geographers study how people in different cultures use land and develop their resources. This tells geographers much about a culture. Geographers also compare land use and resource development all over the world.

First-Level Activities Geographers study three stages of economic activity. In the first, people use land and resources directly to make products. They may hunt, cut wood, mine, and fish. They also may herd animals and farm. This is the first stage of activities. People are beginning to develop their land. About half the world's population works in first-level activities. In countries like the United States, however, fewer people do this kind of work every year.

Harvesting Corn

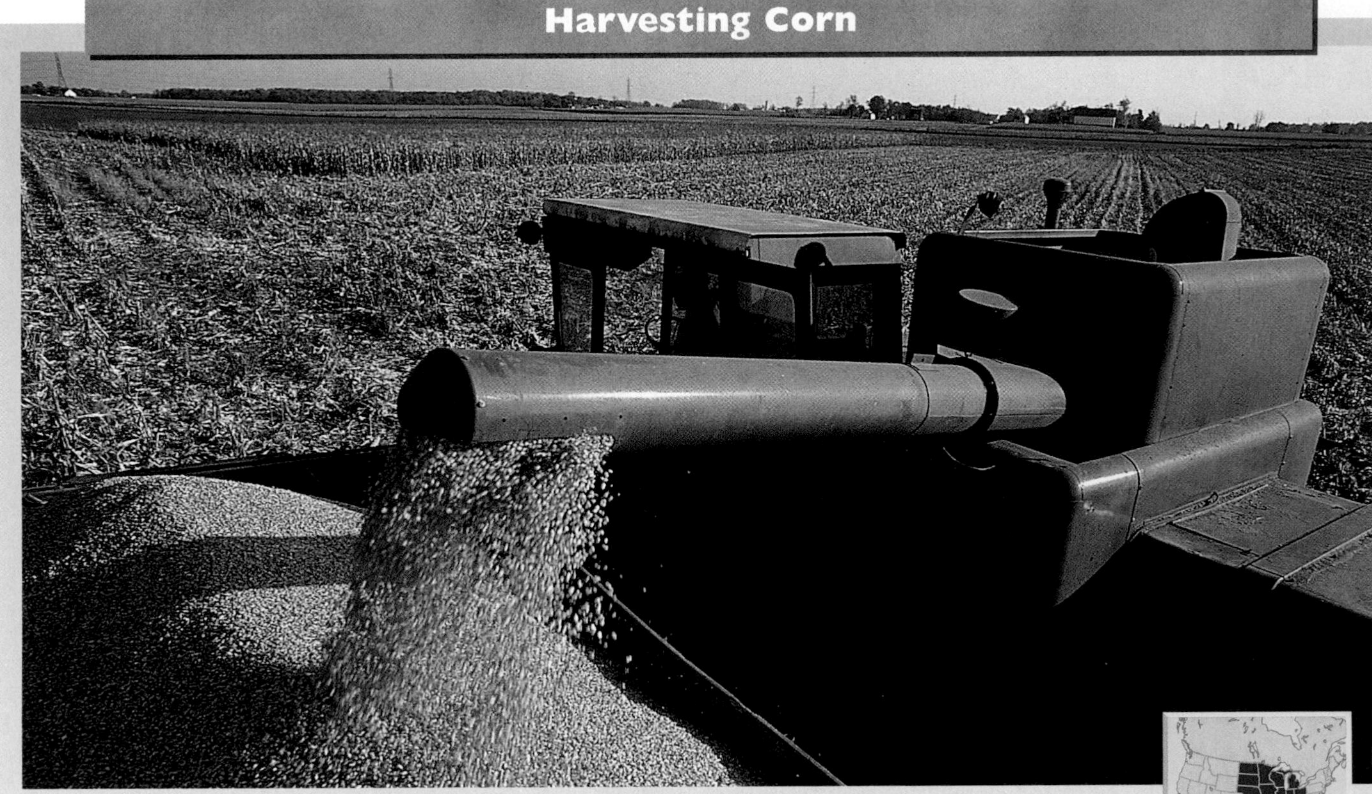

Farmers in the midwest United States are part of the first level of economic activity. Before you eat this corn, it may be frozen, canned, or processed. It may be made into corn meal, cornflakes, corn tortillas, grits, or even corn muffins. Then it must be delivered to a store where you can buy it.

Second-Level Activities Suppose a farmer takes his corn crop to a mill and has the miller grind the corn into corn meal. This is an example of the second step in developing a resource. People turn raw materials into things they use. When a product is processed, it is changed from a raw material into a finished product. That process is called **manufacturing.** The farmer can pay the miller for his service and take the corn meal back home. Or the miller can sell the corn meal to someone else for further processing. Manufacturing may turn the farmer's corn crop into cornflakes for your breakfast.

Connect Think about members of your family and friends who work. Do they do first-, second-, or third-level activities?

Third-Level Activities In the third stage, a person delivers boxes of corn flakes to a local grocery store so you can buy one. In this stage, products are distributed to people who want them. People who distribute products do not make them. They produce a service by making sure products are delivered to people who want and need them.

Industrial nations require service industries. Transportation systems carry products from manufacturer to consumer. Communication for people and businesses comes from telephones, computers, and satellites. Other services—doctors' offices, shopping malls, and fast-food stores—are part of everyday living.

Economic Patterns: Developed and Developing Countries

Today, most manufacturing takes place in factories. Two hundred years ago, that was not so. People produced goods in their homes or small shops. Then came a great change. People invented machines to make goods. They built factories to house the machines. They found new sources of power to run the machines. This change in the way people made goods was called the Industrial Revolution.

The Industrial Revolution created a new pattern of economic activity. It separated countries into two groups—those with many industries and those with few. Countries that have many industries are called **developed nations.** Countries with few industries are called **developing nations.** People live differently in developed and developing nations.

Industrial Societies: Providing Goods and Services

Only about one quarter of the people in the world live in developed nations. These nations include the United States, Canada, Japan, Singapore, Australia, and most European countries. People in these nations use goods made in factories. Their industries consume great amounts of raw materials. They also use power-driven machinery. Businesses spend money on technology, transportation, and communications. Factories produce goods for the country's citizens and extra goods to sell to other countries.

▼ In a Detroit factory, a worker carefully assembles the same part on each automobile that comes down the power-driven assembly line.

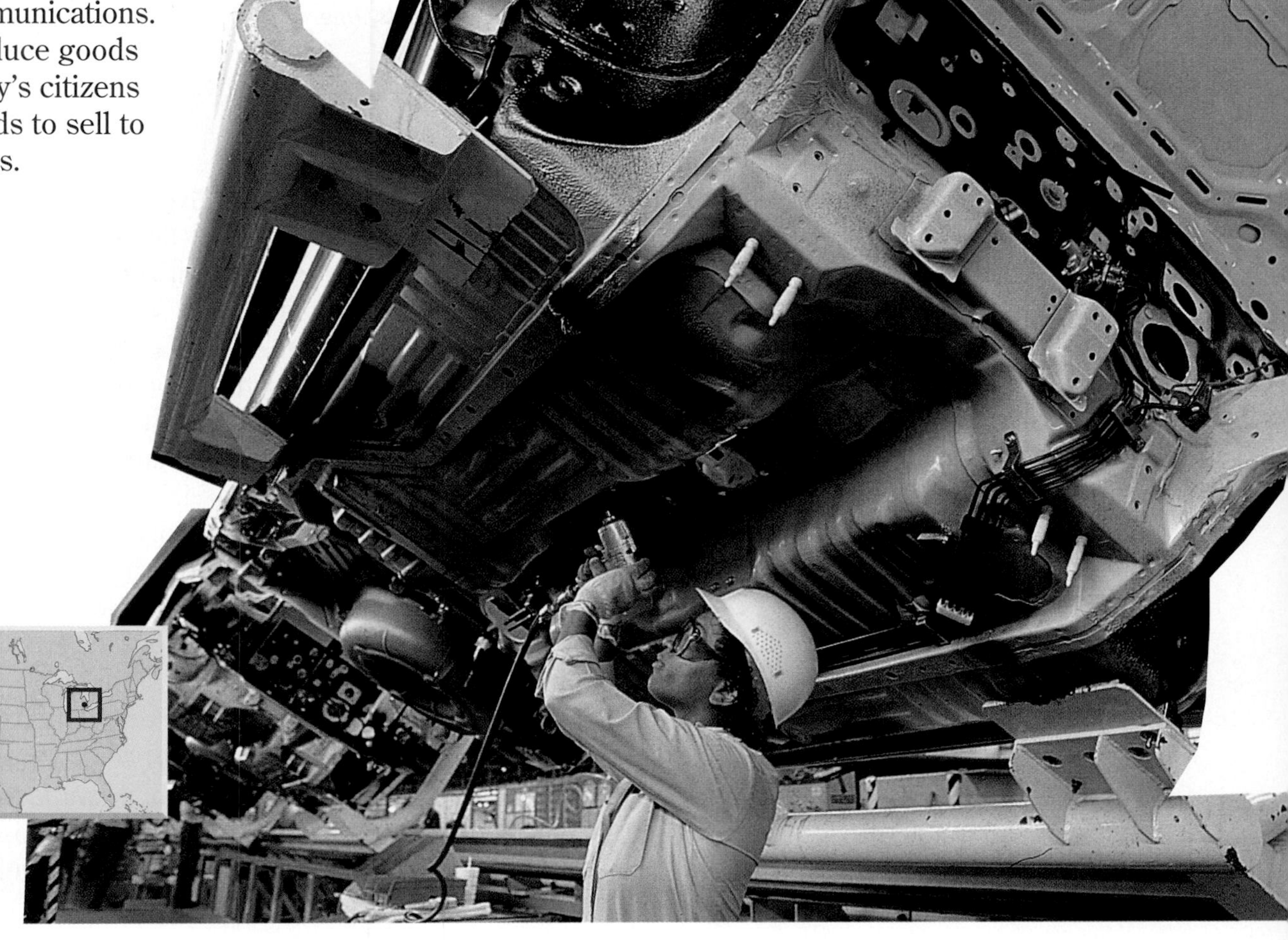

The World: Economic Activity

KEY

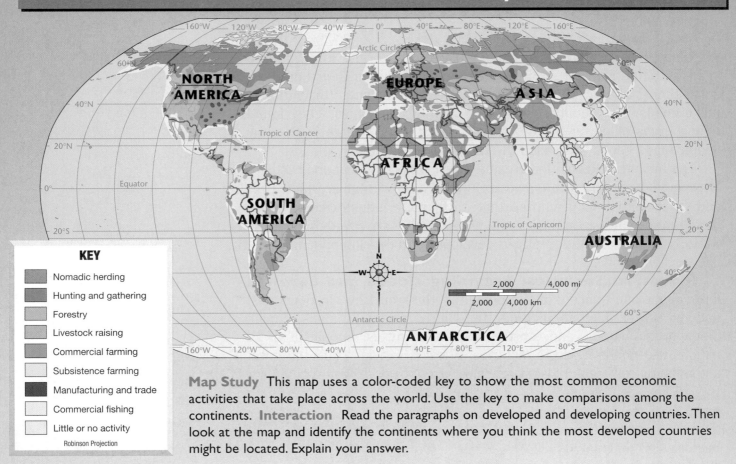

- Nomadic herding
- Hunting and gathering
- Forestry
- Livestock raising
- Commercial farming
- Subsistence farming
- Manufacturing and trade
- Commercial fishing
- Little or no activity

Robinson Projection

Map Study This map uses a color-coded key to show the most common economic activities that take place across the world. Use the key to make comparisons among the continents. **Interaction** Read the paragraphs on developed and developing countries. Then look at the map and identify the continents where you think the most developed countries might be located. Explain your answer.

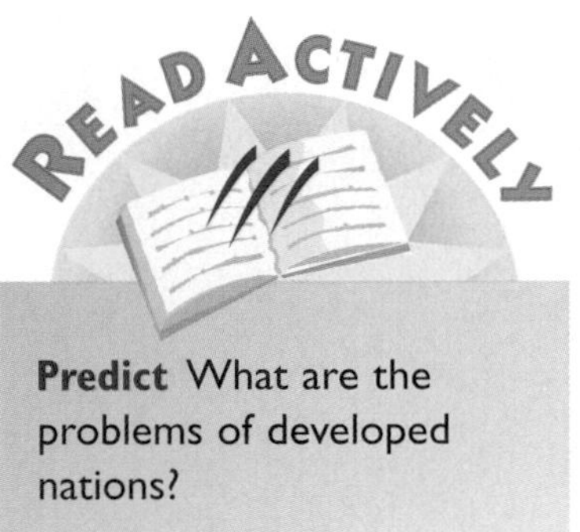

Predict What are the problems of developed nations?

In developed countries, most people live in towns and cities. They work in business and industry. Machines do most of the work. Most people have enough food and water. Most citizens can get a good education and adequate health care.

Developed nations rely on **commercial farming** to produce enough food for their people. Commercial farms are very large. Companies run most of them, not single families. These farms rely on modern technology, so they often need far fewer workers than small traditional farms. Commercial farms are very successful. In the United States, a few million farmers raise enough food to feed more than 280 million people. There is plenty left over to sell to other countries.

People in developed nations depend on each other. Farmers rely on industries for goods and services. City people depend on farmers for food. Anything, like wars and natural disasters, that stops the movement of goods and services can make life hard for everyone.

Developed nations can have some serious problems. Unemployment is a challenge. Not everyone can find a job. Manufacturing can also threaten the environment with air, land, and water pollution. Heavy production uses up natural resources, so shortages develop. Developed nations are working to solve these problems.

Developing Nations It is important to remember that every culture is not like that of the United States. Most of the people of the world live in developing countries. Many of these countries are in Africa, Asia, and Latin America.

Developing countries often do not have great wealth. Many people work at **subsistence farming.** That means farmers raise enough food and animals to feed their own families. The farms require much labor, but they do not yield many crops. Often, the only commercial farms are **plantations.** These farms employ many workers but are owned by only a few people. Plantations usually raise a single crop for export, such as bananas, coffee, sugar cane, or tea.

In some developing countries, certain groups herd animals that provide families with milk, meat, cheese, and skins. In the deserts of Africa and Asia, vegetation and water are scarce. Herders in these regions are nomads. They travel from place to place to find food and water for their animals. In some developing nations, some people live as hunter-gatherers. Such groups are found in the Kalahari Desert in Africa and the Amazon region of South America.

A Nation of Herders The Tuareg of the Sahara in northern Africa herd camels, goats, sheep, and cattle. They travel along the edge of the great desert. Here there are seasonal rains so there is pasture for the herds. Men and women are equals in Tuareg culture. Both can own their own herds of animals and other property.

Challenges in Developing Nations Developing countries often face great challenges. These include disease, food shortages, unsafe water, poor education and health services, and changing governments. Farmers often rely on one or two crops. That puts farmers at risk if the crops fail. Thousands move to cities, but jobs there are often scarce.

Some challenges are connected to rapid population growth. It strains resources. For example, in the late 1990s, the supply of fresh water began to become a problem. As populations grow, they need more water. Larger populations also need more food. This means that farms need more water. Industries also require large amounts of fresh water.

Developing countries are working to improve their people's lives. One way is to use their natural resources or sell them to other countries. Some countries have grown richer by selling natural resources, such as oil and other minerals, to others.

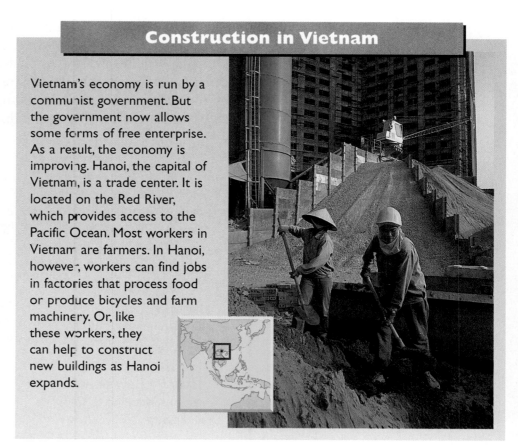

Construction in Vietnam

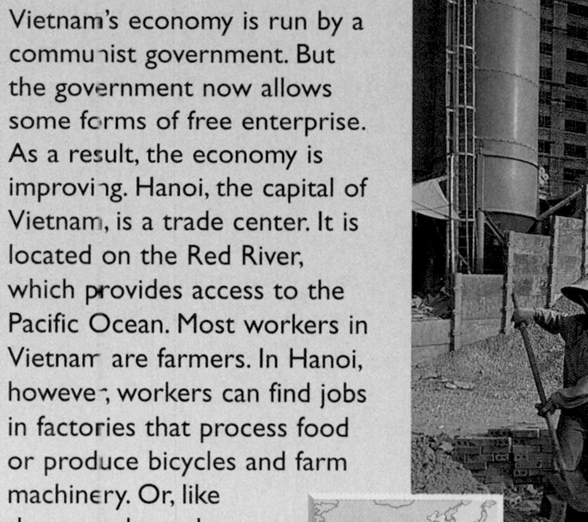

Vietnam's economy is run by a communist government. But the government now allows some forms of free enterprise. As a result, the economy is improving. Hanoi, the capital of Vietnam, is a trade center. It is located on the Red River, which provides access to the Pacific Ocean. Most workers in Vietnam are farmers. In Hanoi, however, workers can find jobs in factories that process food or produce bicycles and farm machinery. Or, like these workers, they can help to construct new buildings as Hanoi expands.

▶ This woman works in the city of Bangalore, India. In recent years, many Indian businesses have improved their services by using computers.

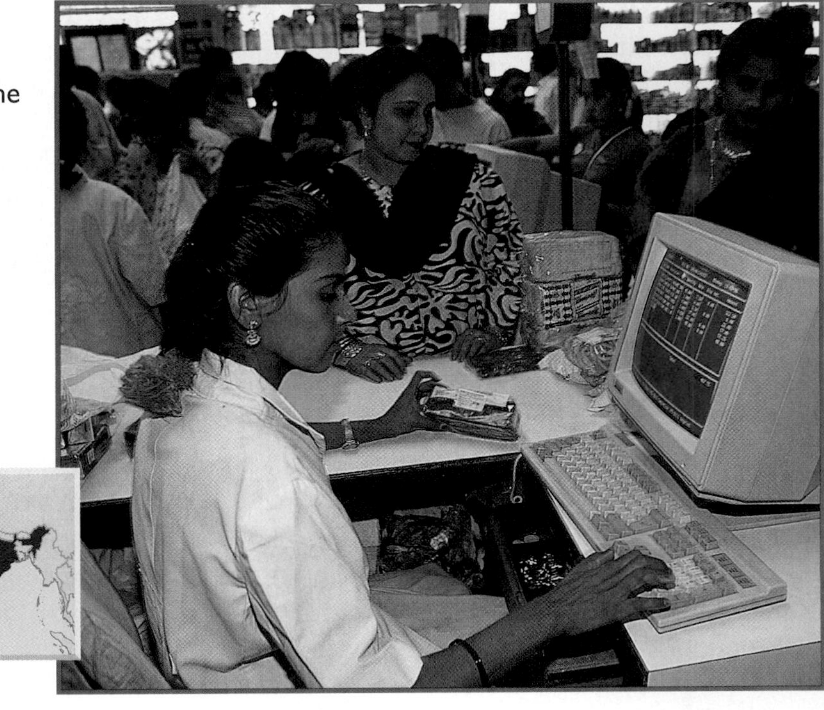

Developing countries sometimes receive help from developed nations. The help could be in the form of **foreign aid,** or gifts and loans from one government to another or from the United Nations. This aid is often used for special projects, such as building roads to move food and other goods from one area to another. Sometimes conflicts arise when the two governments do not agree on the best way to use foreign aid funds.

Sometimes help comes from businesses in developed countries. They may build factories in developing nations. This provides jobs and money for people. Sometimes building communication systems helps spread new ideas for farming and industries.

1. **Define** (a) manufacturing, (b) developed nation, (c) developing nation, (d) commercial farming, (e) subsistence farming, (f) plantation, (g) foreign aid.
2. What are the characteristics of a developed nation? Of a developing nation?
3. How is subsistence farming different from commercial farming?
4. How can countries use their natural resources?
5. What challenges face developed nations? Developing nations?

Critical Thinking

6. **Identifying Central Issues** How are developing nations working to improve their people's lives?

Activity

7. **Writing to Learn** People who work at your school have jobs in a service industry. Interview a teacher, a server in the cafeteria, or a receptionist in the office. Find out what that person's duties are and what that person likes about his or her job. Write a brief profile for your school newspaper.

People's Effect on the Environment

Reach Into Your Background
Many of the environmental problems we face are the result of actions people took in the past. Now people pay more attention to environmental issues. Make a list of things you and your community are doing to improve the environment.

Questions to Explore

1. How do people's actions affect the environment?
2. What are people doing to improve the environment?

Key Terms
ecosystem
deforestation
habitat
acid rain
ozone layer
global warming
recycle

Try to picture the United States as one huge desert. Africa's Sahara is even bigger than that. What's more, the Sahara is spreading. Wangari Maathai of Kenya, in East Africa, works to stop it. She heads Africa's Green Belt Movement. It urges people in a dozen African countries to plant trees. Tree roots hold valuable topsoil in place, stopping the spread of the desert. When their leaves fall to the ground, trees add nutrients to the soil. This will make rich soil good for other plants. Since 1977, this organization has planted more than 10 million trees.

▼ Coral reefs, like this one, take millions of years to construct. They can be completely destroyed in a matter of decades by such things as water pollution.

Danger to Land, Water, and Air

Wangari Maathai is saving forests in Africa. Other people around the world are also working to preserve the environment. If we learn to identify environmental problems, we too can protect our world.

The Sahara is a desert. The Amazon River valley is a rain forest. The Great Plains is an area of grasslands. Each of these regions is an **ecosystem,** a place where living elements depend on one another—and on nonliving elements—for their survival. Living elements are plants and animals. Nonliving elements are water, soil, rocks, and air. Desert birds cannot live in a rain forest. Grassland plants cannot survive in a desert. Living things are tied to their ecosystems.

Death of a Sea The border between Kazakstan and Uzbekistan in western Asia runs through the Aral Sea. Until about 1960, this shallow sea was the fourth largest inland lake or sea in the world. Two rivers fed into the Aral. Then people started diverting the water for irrigation projects. By 1987, the Aral Sea had less than half as much water as before. Its fish were dead. Fishing villages now sat far from the water's edge. Some experts believe it may take 30 years to repair the damage done to the Aral Sea.

If one part of an ecosystem changes, other parts are also affected. For example, ecosystems that have standing water like puddles have mosquitoes. They lay their eggs on the surface of water. A rainy summer produces more standing water. This means that more mosquito eggs will hatch. A dry summer means less water and fewer mosquitoes.

Some changes can destroy an ecosystem. Probably the greatest loss of ecosystems is happening in South America. Rain forests cover more than one third of the continent. They are home for more species, or kinds, of plants and animals than anywhere else in the world. But South Americans need land for farms, so they are cutting down the forests. This process is called **deforestation.** When the forests are gone, many plant and animal species become extinct, or die out.

Protecting Endangered Species How can we prevent species of animals and plants from dying out? One way is through laws. In 1973, Congress passed the Endangered Species Act. It gave the government power to protect not only species that might become extinct but also the places that they live, or their **habitats.** Today, the act protects almost 1,000 kinds of living things in the United States that are threatened, or endangered.

Extinction has many causes. People may build houses or businesses on land that is the habitat of particular animals or plants. The air, soil, or water may be too polluted for a species of plant or animal to survive. Sometimes, a species is hunted until it disappears. Usually, more than one thing threatens a species. The goal of the Endangered Species Act is to stop extinction. But people disagree about the law. Some think humans should be allowed to use natural resources as they need them. Others think people should stop doing things that hurt other species.

Factories and Acid Rain Often, endangered animal species are just one sign of an ecosystem with problems. Visitors to the New York's Adirondack Mountains see an ecosystem in trouble. Its vast forests are centuries old. But today, the needles of the spruce trees are brown, and birch trees have no leaves at all. There are few fish in the rivers. Frogs, certain kinds of birds, and many insects are hard to find. What happened?

According to scientists, **acid rain** is to blame. Acid rain is rain that carries

Saving the Gray Whale

Temporarily trapped in Alaska's ice, this gray whale may survive to make its yearly journey down the Pacific Coast to Mexico. Whaling nearly destroyed the world's population of gray whales. Protection as an endangered species, however, brought their numbers back up.

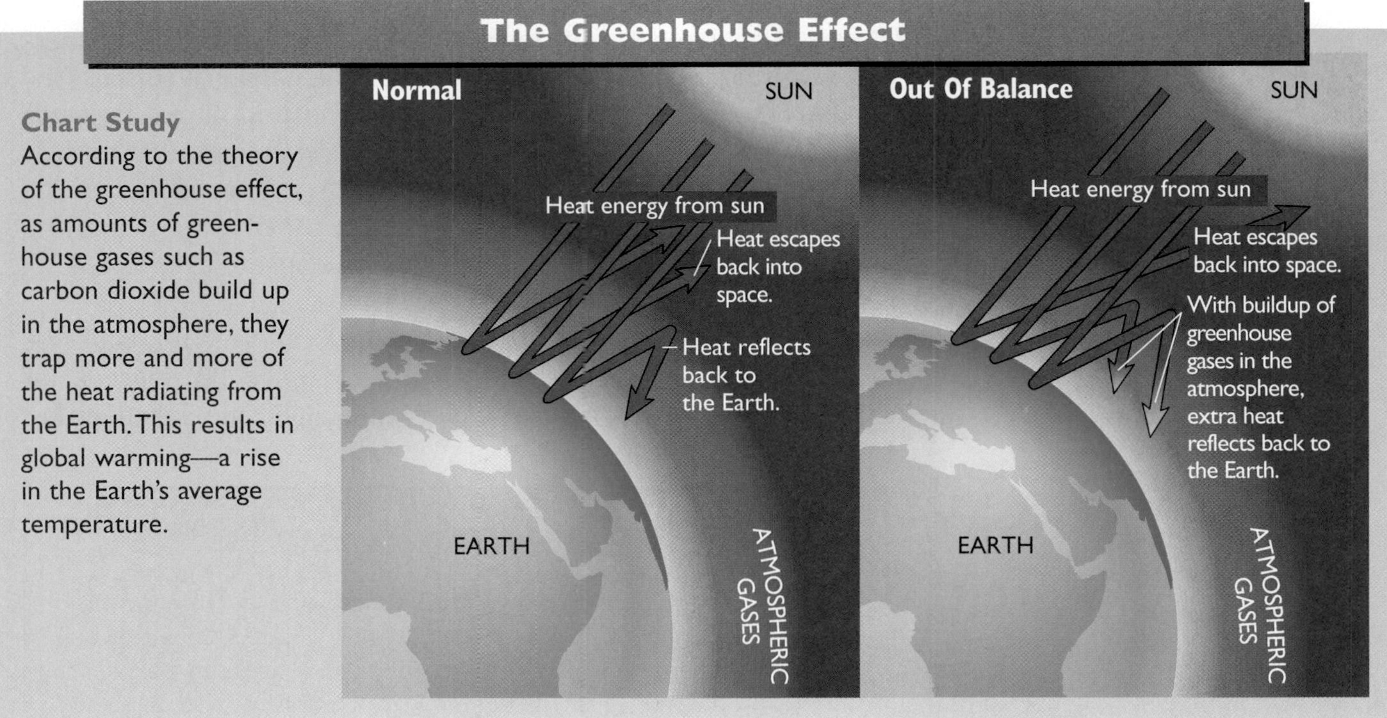

Chart Study
According to the theory of the greenhouse effect, as amounts of greenhouse gases such as carbon dioxide build up in the atmosphere, they trap more and more of the heat radiating from the Earth. This results in global warming—a rise in the Earth's average temperature.

dangerous chemicals. The fossil fuels used by industries and automobiles release chemicals into the air. The chemicals combine with water vapor in the air, making the rain as acid as vinegar.

Canada and the United States now have laws to reduce acid rain. By 2000, the countries had reduced rain acidity by almost 25 percent. Factories are installing new devices called filters and scrubbers to clean up the fumes they release. Car makers have added devices to reduce the dangerous chemicals in car exhaust.

Rivers and Sewage Pollution People have always dumped waste products into rivers, lakes, and oceans. These wastes can harm or destroy living things in the water. They also endanger people. Water creatures take in substances from the water. Little fish eat the creatures, big fish eat the little fish, and animals and people eat the fish. The substances pass from one living thing to another. Some of these substances are poisons.

Fertilizers and pesticides from farms also pollute water. (Pesticides are chemicals that kill insects.) Rainwater washes the substances into lakes and rivers. There, the fertilizers cause water plants to grow too fast, and they use up oxygen needed by fish and other water life.

The Ozone Layer and Ultraviolet Rays In the 1970s, scientists realized that chemicals called chlorofluorocarbons (CFCs) were destroying the atmosphere's **ozone layer.** This is a layer of gas in the upper part of our atmosphere. The ozone layer blocks most of the harmful ultraviolet rays from the sun. These rays cause skin cancer in humans. They also damage other forms of life.

READ ACTIVELY

Connect What are some things you and your friends could do to protect the environment?

Until recently, aerosol spray cans, refrigerators, and air conditioners used CFCs. In 1987, many nations met in Montreal, Canada, to discuss the ozone layer. They reached an agreement called the Montreal Protocol, which said that nations would limit their use of chemicals that destroy ozone, including CFCs. Over the past few years, this action has helped the ozone layer. But scientists continue to monitor the use of ozone-destroying substances, and search for safer chemicals for people to use.

Global Warming The summer of 1995 in New England was unusually hot and dry. Temperatures stayed above 90 degrees for weeks. Heat and drought caused water shortages and killed crops.

EXPLORING TECHNOLOGY

A Sun-Powered House

If you have spent a few hours outside on a hot summer day, then you are well aware of the heating power of the sun. Scientists knew all about it, too. They also knew that if they could find a way to store that power, they would have a cheap, abundant source of energy. The diagram below shows how they solved the problem of storing the heat of the sun.

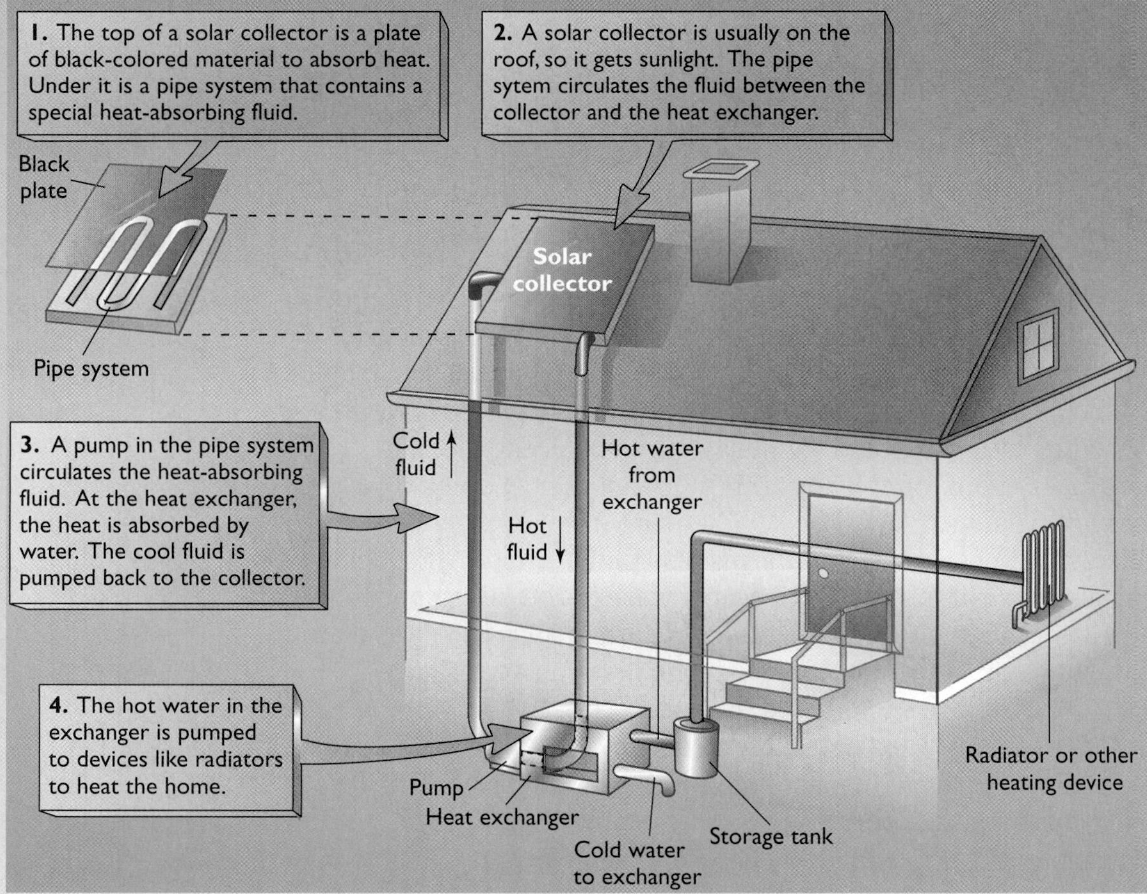
1. The top of a solar collector is a plate of black-colored material to absorb heat. Under it is a pipe system that contains a special heat-absorbing fluid.
2. A solar collector is usually on the roof, so it gets sunlight. The pipe sytem circulates the fluid between the collector and the heat exchanger.
Black plate
Pipe system
Solar collector
3. A pump in the pipe system circulates the heat-absorbing fluid. At the heat exchanger, the heat is absorbed by water. The cool fluid is pumped back to the collector.
Cold fluid
Hot fluid
Hot water from exchanger
4. The hot water in the exchanger is pumped to devices like radiators to heat the home.
Pump
Heat exchanger
Cold water to exchanger
Storage tank
Radiator or other heating device

Some scientists feared this was the start of **global warming,** a slow increase in the Earth's temperature. Global warming may be caused by gases like carbon dioxide that are released into the air. They are called greenhouse gases. Industrial countries produce about 75 percent of these gases. They are released when fossil fuels burn. These fuels produce most of the world's electricity. They also run the world's 550 million cars, buses, and trucks. Developing countries produce these gases when they burn forests to clear land and use wood for heating and cooking.

Normally, heat on the Earth escapes back into space. Some scientists theorize that greenhouse gases trap the heat and reflect it back to Earth. The result is a rise in the Earth's average temperature.

The Challenge of Energy

Because pollution is often tied to using fossil fuels, scientists are exploring other ways to get inexpensive energy. Their research concentrates on nuclear power, water, wind, and the sun. Individuals can protect the environment, too. For example, the United States produces more waste than any other nation in the world. To change that, people now **recycle**, or re-use old materials to make new products. Today, most American cities have recycling programs.

CITIZEN HEROES

Citizen Action Lee Botts of Chicago, Illinois, has spent the last 30 years working to protect the Great Lakes. She fought for a ban on deadly chemicals and on construction of nuclear power plants on the lakes. She also helped establish Indiana Dunes National Park. What is she most proud of? Building organizations that help all citizens get involved. Protecting the environment is, she believes, everybody's job.

◀ It looks as if a fire burned these trees near the peak of Mount Mitchell in North Carolina. In fact, acid rain killed them.

1. **Define** (a) ecosystem, (b) deforestation, (c) habitat, (d) acid rain, (e) ozone layer, (f) global warming, (g) recycle.
2. How do fossil fuels create pollution?
3. Why is global warming a problem?
4. What alternatives to fossil fuels are scientists researching?

Critical Thinking

5. **Expressing Problems Clearly** Explain why some species are endangered. Why do people disagree about reserving land for them?

Activity

6. **Writing to Learn** Write a persuasive paragraph explaining why fresh water should be protected. Include facts to support your reasons.

Writing for a Purpose

Have you ever testified before Congress about pollution? Or stopped a company from pumping poison into a river? Or organized a demonstration to make people more aware of the environment? You may think kids your age do not do such things. But the kids of KAP do.

KAP stands for Kids Against Pollution. These young people work to stop pollution. Nineteen students in Closter, New Jersey, formed KAP in 1987. Today, there are more than 13,000 KAP chapters across the United States and in other countries. KAP's motto is "Save the Earth Not Just For Us But For Future Generations."

One of KAP's main weapons is writing. It can be very powerful. KAP members use the power of persuasive writing, or writing that tries to show other people how their point of view can help solve a problem.

Get Ready

Writing to persuade means taking a stand and trying to convince others to agree with your opinion. There are four basic steps:

1. **Decide what your opinion is.** Your opinion is the position you plan to take. For example, suppose your opinion is "Our city should make a law to require people to recycle newspapers."

2. **Choose your audience.** Your audience is the people to whom you will be writing. You might write to a senator or a mayor. You might write to the general public in a magazine article or letter to the editor of a newspaper.

3. **Find support for your opinion.** Your writing must give reasons for your opinion and the facts to support each reason. For example, the statement "Recycling would prevent burying six tons of paper trash in our town's landfill every month" is a fact that supports an opinion. Find as many facts as you can to support your opinion. They will help make your message stronger.

4 **Write persuasively.** Finally, write a letter or an essay. Present one idea at a time, and defend it with facts. Although persuasive writing emphasizes facts, it often includes an appeal to emotions. Add a sentence or two that does this. KAP's motto, for instance, is an emotional appeal. The combination of facts and emotion can make persuasive writing work.

Try It Out

Suppose you are concerned about the growing amount of litter in a local park. Follow these four steps to write a persuasive letter.

A. What is your opinion? Decide upon a plan to solve the park's problem. Should there be stronger anti-litter laws? Should people be urged to litter less, or should they be required to participate in a community cleanup? Choose one of these opinions or develop your own solution.

B. Who is your audience? If you want a local law passed, write to a member of your local government. To address your fellow citizens, write to the editor of a local newspaper.

C. Why do you hold this opinion? Identify at least two reasons for your opinion. Then support each reason with facts.

D. How will you persuade your audience to agree with your opinion? Before you write your letter, make an outline. Start your letter with a catchy opening. Then present your reasons in logical order. In the conclusion, sum up your arguments and appeal to people's emotions.

Apply the Skill

Now, apply the skill to the real world. Choose a topic, and write a persuasive letter about it to the editor of your local newspaper. Try to persuade your fellow citizens to agree with your opinion.

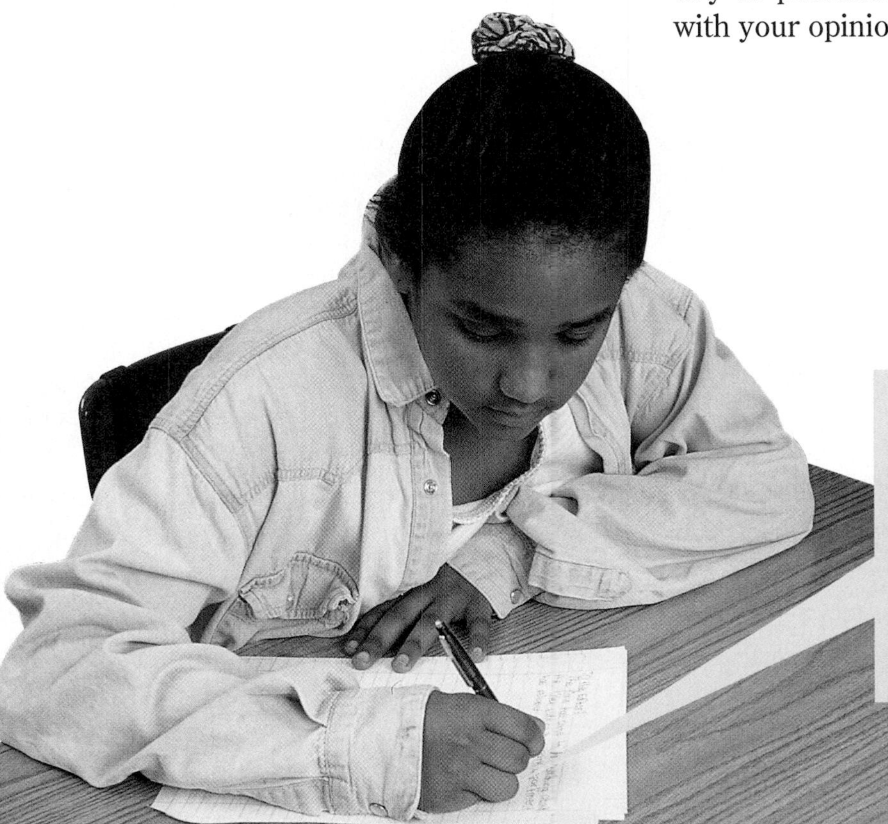

To the Editor:
The time has come to do something about the litter ruining Peace Park. First of all, the Parks Department has released a study that shows littering has increased 10 percent in two years.

Review and Activities

Reviewing Main Ideas

1. (a) Name two natural resources. (b) Describe how they are used.
2. What is the difference between renewable resources and nonrenewable resources?
3. (a) What kind of nation has mainly agricultural activities? (b) What kind of nation has mainly industrial activities?
4. Why is commercial farming part of a developed nation instead of a developing nation?
5. How can foreign aid help a developing nation?
6. Why might one simple change in an ecosystem have many effects in the system?
7. Acid rain hurts forests and lakes. How could acid rain endanger people?
8. What can governments do to protect endangered species?
9. Why is recycling a good use of natural resources?
10. How can people work to prevent global warming?

Reviewing Key Terms

Use each key term below in a sentence that shows the meaning of the term.

1. natural resource
2. raw material
3. recyclable resource
4. renewable resource
5. nonrenewable resource
6. fossil fuel
7. manufacturing
8. developed nation
9. developing nation
10. commercial farming
11. subsistence farming
12. plantation
13. foreign aid
14. ecosystem
15. deforestation
16. habitat
17. acid rain
18. ozone layer
19. global warming
20. recycle

Critical Thinking

1. **Identifying Central Issues** Do you think people should do more to protect the environment? Use facts from the chapter to support your answer.
2. **Recognizing Cause and Effect** Think about the problems that arose during the oil shortage of 1973. It affected the supply of gasoline and heating fuel. Write a paragraph about how a gasoline shortage today would affect the lives of people in your family.

Graphic Organizer

Copy and fill in the table to show how pollution damages the environment and suggest some solutions.

Sources	Damage to Environment	Possible Solutions
Water Pollution		
Land Pollution		
Air Pollution		

Writing Activity

Writing a Letter
Become part of the global community by contacting an organization that works to protect the environment. Two groups are listed here. Describe what you have learned about threats to the environment. Explain how you use natural resources responsibly. Find out if the organization has suggestions for other actions.

Addresses:

Greenpeace
1436 U Street NW
Washington, D.C. 20009

World Wildlife Fund
1250 24th Street, NW
Washington, D.C. 20037

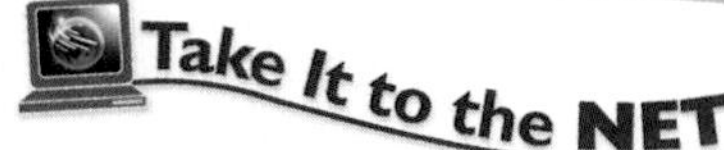

Activity Read the most recent news on geographical issues and programs in your state. For help in completing this activity, visit **www.phschool.com**.

Chapter 5 Self-Test To review what you have learned, take the Chapter 5 Self-Test and get instant feedback on your answers. Go to **www.phschool.com** to take the test.

Skills Review

Turn to the Skills Activity.

Review the steps for writing for a purpose. Then complete the following: (a) Why do you think that it is important to know your audience when you are writing to persuade? (b) Do you think that you need to do research in order to write to persuade? Why or why not?

How Am I Doing?

Answer these questions to help you check your progress.

1. Can I describe natural resources and how different countries use them?
2. Do I understand how the stages of economic development are related to a nation's wealth?
3. Can I identify some threats to the environment?
4. What information from this chapter can I include in my journal?

GEOGRAPHY
TOOLS AND CONCEPTS
PROJECT POSSIBILITIES

The chapters in this book have some answers to these important questions.

- **GEOGRAPHY** What is the Earth's geography like?
- **HISTORY** How has the world's population changed over time?
- **CULTURE** What is a culture?
- **GOVERNMENT** What types of government exist in the world today?
- **ECONOMICS** How do people use the world's resources?

Doing a project shows what you know about geography! The knowledge and skills you have gained will help you do a great job.

Project Menu

Now it's time for you to find your own answers by doing projects on your own or with a group. Here are some ways to make your own discoveries about geography.

The Geography Game
Every place in the world has unique characteristics. Use them to create a geography game with your classmates. Choose a country. Find one fact each about its (1) physical features, (2) climate, (3) population, (4) cultures, and (5) natural resources. These facts will be clues in the game. Practice writing them out until they are short and clear. Clues should not be too easy or too hard. They must provide enough information so that someone can figure out the answer. Now make five playing cards. On one side of each card, write a clue. On the other side, write the name of your country.

Divide into three teams. Each team needs the Atlas in the back of this book. Mix up the cards. Have your teacher or a volunteer pick a card and read the clue to team one. Members have 30 seconds to agree on an answer. If it is correct, the team earns one point. If not, the next team has a chance. Play until the cards are gone. The team with the most points wins.

From Questions to Careers

JOBS IN THE EARTH SCIENCES

People who want to preserve the Earth often have jobs in the sciences. Environmental engineers may figure out how to clean up oil spills or make better use of natural resources. Soil scientists find ways to increase the crops a farmer can grow on a piece of land, or they may work on soil conservation. Ethnobotanists study how certain cultures use plants, especially as medicines. These jobs require a college degree.

Some jobs that help preserve the Earth require less education. People who assist scientists are called technicians. Usually they need only an associate's degree, which takes two years. Technicians may work in agriculture, chemistry, energy, or weather research. All these jobs are vital to helping preserve the environment.

▼A scientist and technician are shown collecting water quality samples from a stream.

World News Today
Collect newspaper and magazine articles about natural resources, economies, and businesses in countries around the world. Display the clippings on a poster. Choose one country, and study the relationship between its economy and its natural resources. Prepare a five-minute speech to tell your class what you found.

Focus on Part of the Whole The world and its population are extremely varied. Choose a particular region or country. If you are working with a group, have each person choose a different country on a continent. Learn everything you can about the land's physical geography, the population, and the lifestyles of the people there. Use encyclopedias, almanacs, or other books.

Set up a display based on your research. Prepare a large map that includes important physical features of the land. Add captions that explain how the land's physical geography affects people's lives.

Desktop Countries
What countries did your ancestors come from? Select one and do some research on it. Interview someone, perhaps a relative from there, or read about it. Find a recipe you can prepare to share with the class. Then make a desktop display about your country. Write the name of the country on a card and put it on your desk. Add a drawing of the country's flag or map, or display a souvenir. On place cards, write several sentences about each object. Take turns visiting everyone's "desktop countries."

EUROPE AND RUSSIA

Europe is a continent filled with countries. Russia is one country that actually lies on two continents—Europe and Asia. Together, Europe and Russia form a gigantic landmass. Together, they also form a rich pattern of different cultures, histories, and languages that stretch back hundreds of years.

GUIDING QUESTIONS

The readings and activities in this book will help you discover answers to these Guiding Questions.

1. **GEOGRAPHY** How has physical geography affected the environment and cultures of Europe and Russia?
2. **HISTORY** How have the people of Europe and Russia been shaped by historical experiences?
3. **CULTURE** What values and traditions do the people of Europe and Russia have in common?
4. **GOVERNMENT** How have changes in government affected Russia and some European nations?
5. **ECONOMICS** How have Russian and European economies developed into what they are today?

PROJECT PREVIEW

You can also discover answers to the Guiding Questions by working on projects. You can find several project possibilities on pages 302–303.

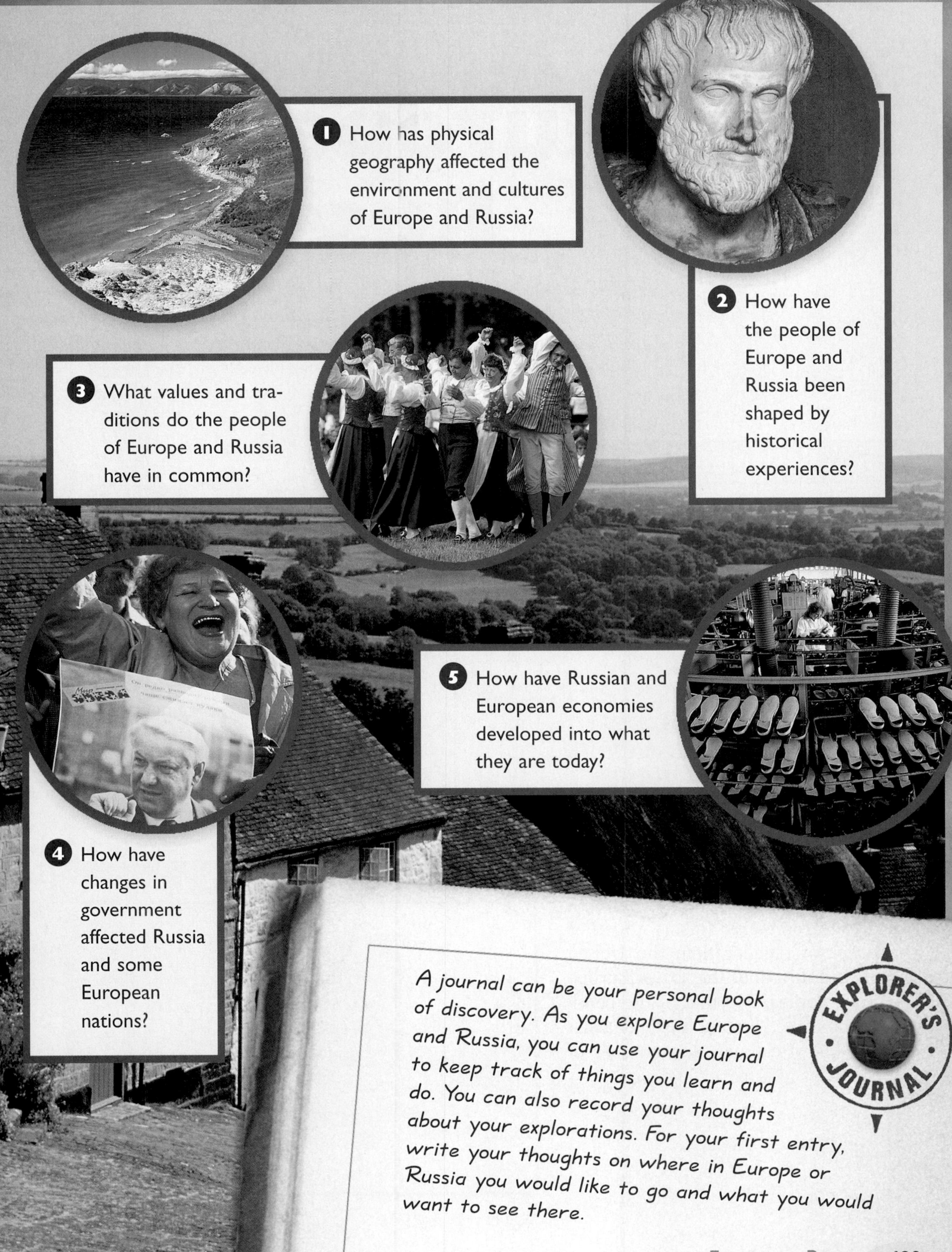

1 How has physical geography affected the environment and cultures of Europe and Russia?

2 How have the people of Europe and Russia been shaped by historical experiences?

3 What values and traditions do the people of Europe and Russia have in common?

4 How have changes in government affected Russia and some European nations?

5 How have Russian and European economies developed into what they are today?

EXPLORER'S JOURNAL

A journal can be your personal book of discovery. As you explore Europe and Russia, you can use your journal to keep track of things you learn and do. You can also record your thoughts about your explorations. For your first entry, write your thoughts on where in Europe or Russia you would like to go and what you would want to see there.

Discovery Activities About

Europe and Russia

Learning about Europe and Russia means being an explorer and a geographer. No explorer would start out without first checking some facts. Begin by exploring the maps of Europe and Russia on the following pages.

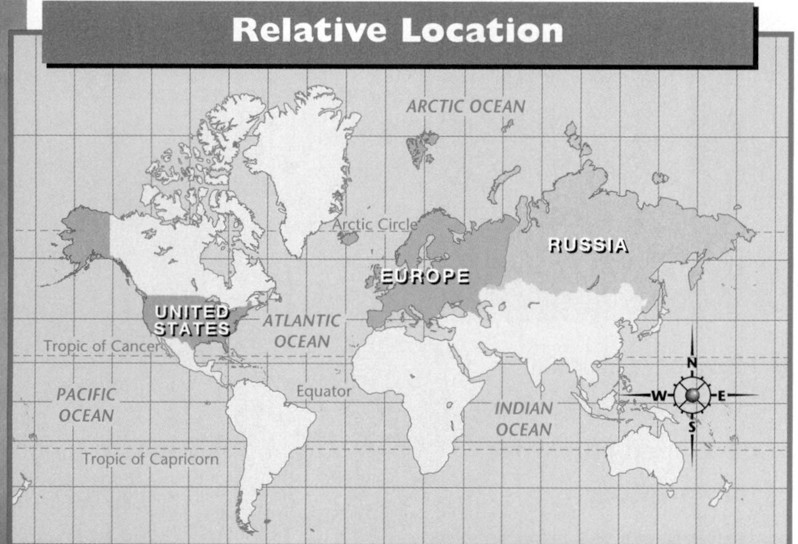

LOCATION

1. Explore Europe and Russia's Location
A geographer must know where a place is located in order to study it. Use the map at left to describe Europe and Russia's location relative to the United States. Which ocean separates Europe and Russia from the United States? Which is closer to the Equator, Europe and Russia or the United States? Which is closer to the Arctic Circle? Many people think the climates of Europe and the United States are similar. Look at the map. Then list three reasons why this might be so.

PLACE

2. Explore Europe and Russia's Size
Are Europe and Russia together larger or smaller than the United States? How does the size of Europe alone compare to that of the continental United States? Based on what you know, estimate the number of countries in Europe.

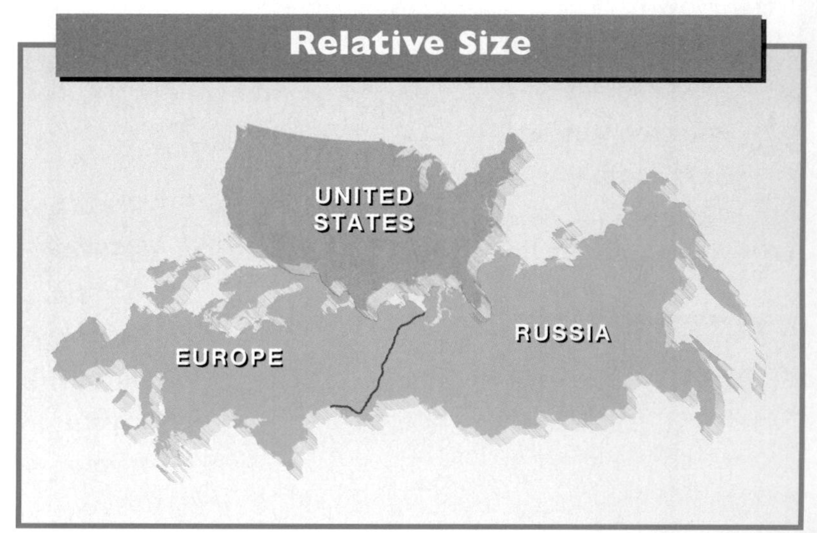

PLACE

3. Explore Europe and Russia Russia is not only the largest country on Eurasia, the large landmass upon which Europe and Asia are located, but it is also the largest country in the world. Some of the smallest countries in the world are also located in Europe. Which European countries are the smallest? Europe is surrounded by several important seas. What are the names of the seas that surround Europe?

REGIONS

4. Predict Climate and Its Effects Find the Arctic Circle on the map. In regions north of the circle, there is a day when the sun never sets and a day when it never rises! Regions this far north are also very cold. Which countries have areas that lie north of the Arctic Circle? How do you think the cold climate affects the way people in these areas live?

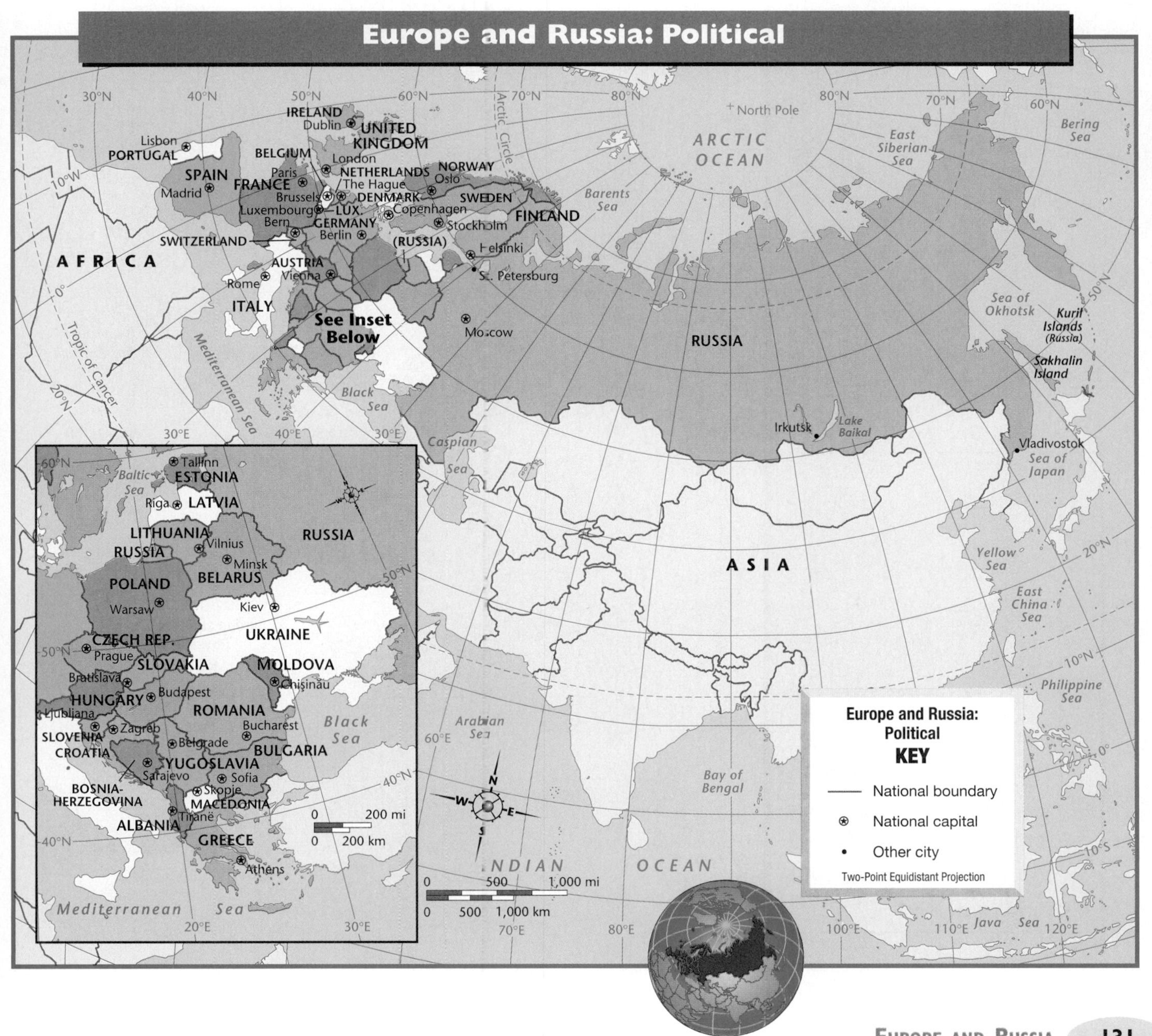

LOCATION

5. Identify the Mountains of Europe and Russia The Alpine mountain chain stretches through much of central and southern Europe. It includes the Pyrenees, the Alps, the Carpathians, the Balkans, and the Caucasus. Find these mountains on the map. Locate the Ural Mountains. They form the border between the western part of Russia that is in Europe and the eastern part that is in Asia.

LOCATION

6. Locate Europe's Peninsulas Europe has several major peninsulas. A peninsula is a piece of land that is almost completely surrounded by water. Which peninsula is farthest north? What bodies of water border this peninsula? Name Europe's other peninsulas. Notice that even the continent of Europe itself is one big peninsula!

Europe and Russia: Physical

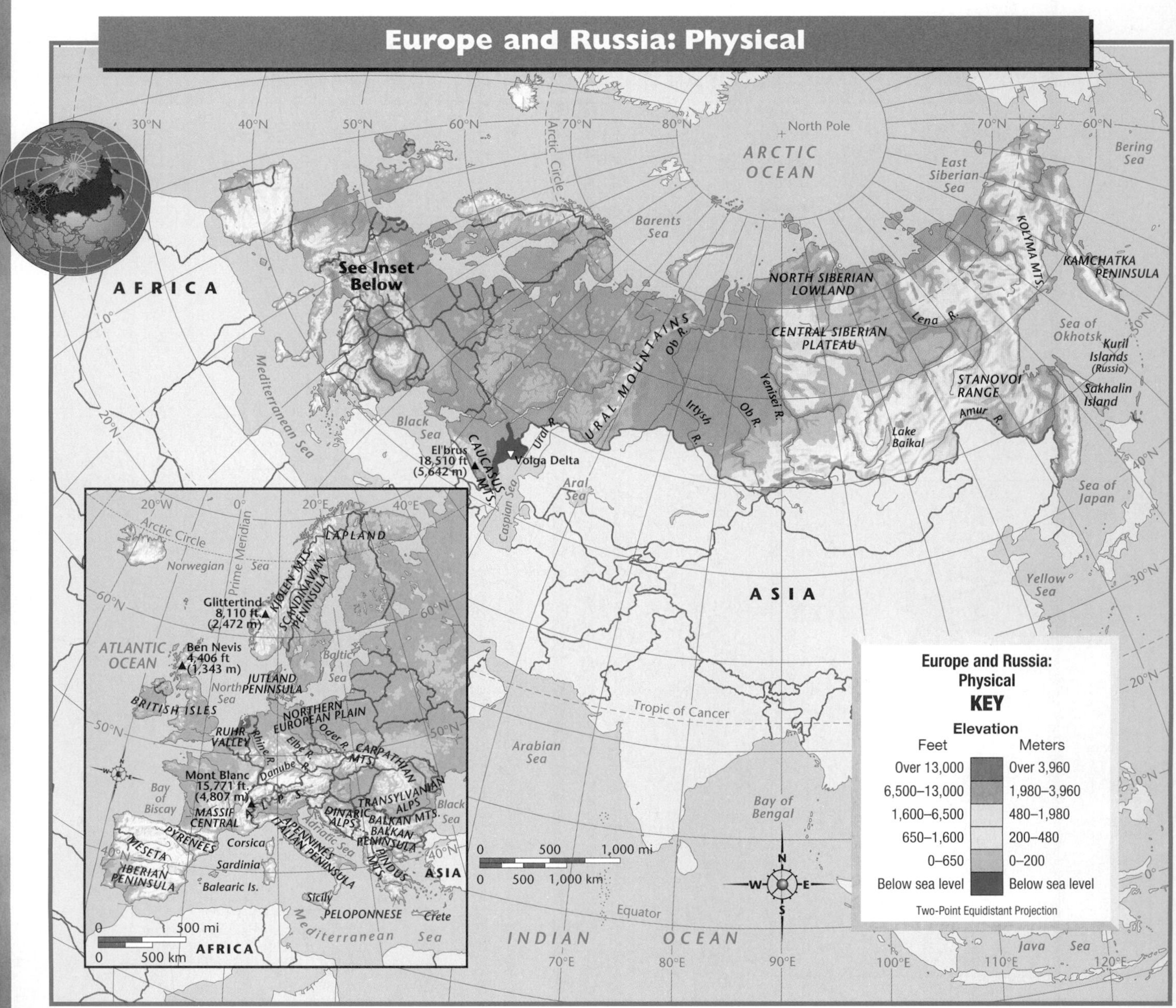

MOVEMENT

7. **Plan Geo Leo's Trip on the Rails** Geo Leo wants to explore Europe and Russia by train. Read the goals he has set for his trip. Then, use the map below to help him plan generally which routes he should take. Estimate the distance of each route.

A. *"After my plane lands in Paris, I want to travel to Warsaw by the shortest route."*

B. *"From Warsaw, I want to go as far north as possible on my way to Moscow."*

C. *"From Moscow, I want to travel to Rome. I want to pass through as many major cities as I can on the way."*

D. *"From Rome, I will need to head straight back to Paris. What's the shortest route I can take?"*

BONUS

Using the physical map on the previous page and the map below, describe the physical features over which Geo Leo will travel during his train trip.

Europe and Russia: Major Railroad Lines

KEY
Railroads
National capital
Other city
Robinson Projection

PLACE

8. **Compare Population Densities** Population density is the average number of people living within a certain area. Compare the parts of Europe that have many people to the parts that have only a few people. Do the same for Russia. How would you describe the population densities of the two regions? What geographic features might explain the low population density of countries like Finland and Norway? What other factors might affect population?

INTERACTION

9. **Analyzing Population Charts** Find the five largest cities in Europe on the map. Which cities are located on the coast? Which cities are located far inland? How do you think life in these cities is different due to their inland or coastal locations? Study the chart on the next page. Which two cities are located in Russia? How would you describe the rest of the country's population density?

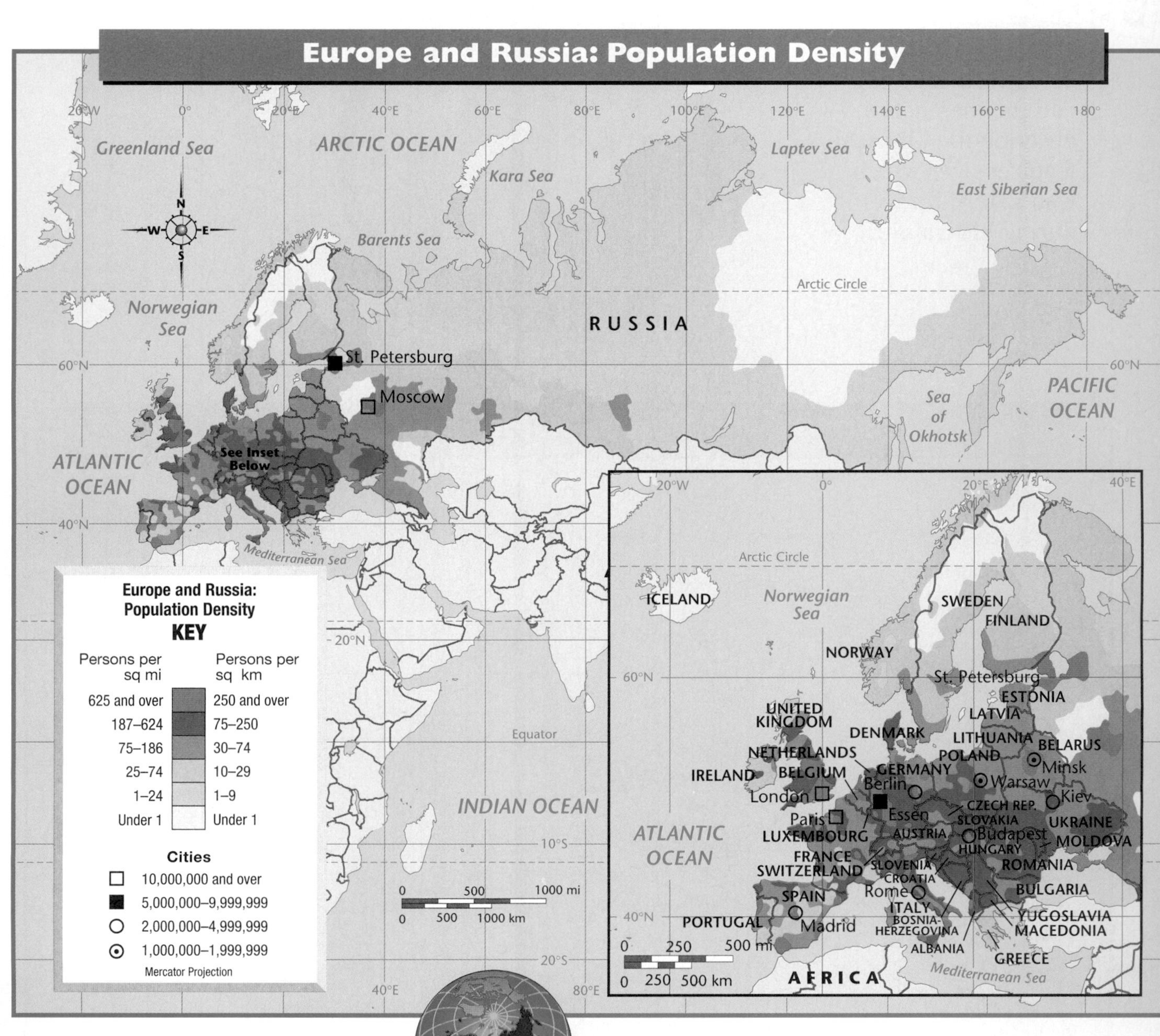

REGIONS

10. Compare Climates in Europe and Russia As you can see on the map below, Europe and Russia have a wide variety of climates. What are its major climates? Compare Russia's climates to those in Europe. Does Europe have a greater or lesser variety of climates? Look at the Five Most Populated Cities chart. In which climate regions are the two most populated cities in Europe and Russia located?

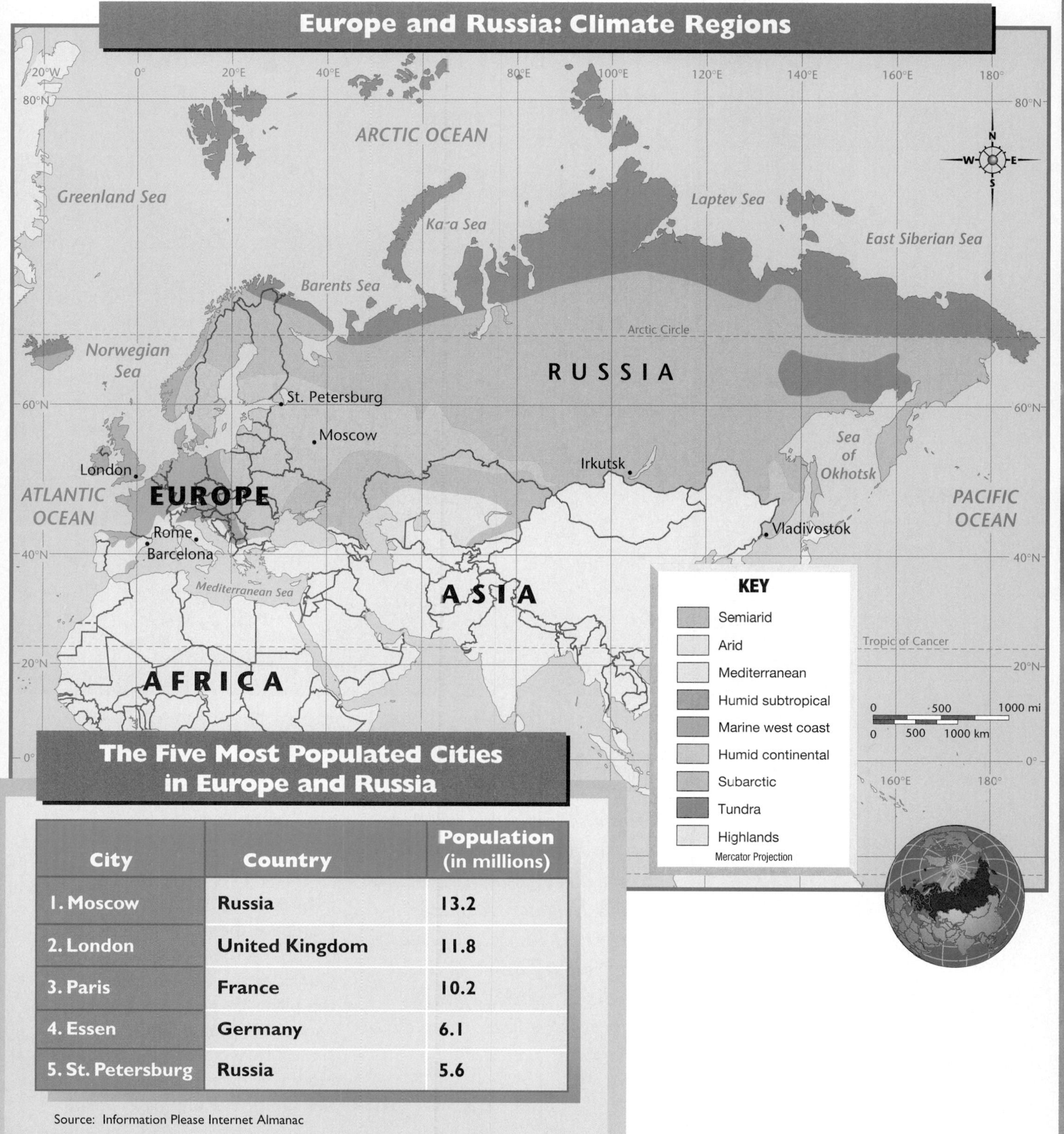

The Five Most Populated Cities in Europe and Russia

City	Country	Population (in millions)
1. Moscow	Russia	13.2
2. London	United Kingdom	11.8
3. Paris	France	10.2
4. Essen	Germany	6.1
5. St. Petersburg	Russia	5.6

Source: Information Please Internet Almanac

CHAPTER 6

EUROPE AND RUSSIA
Physical Geography

PICTURE ACTIVITIES

Water and land have affected where and how people live in Europe and Russia. The picture shows a freighter traveling the Rhine (ryn) River in Germany. To get yourself thinking about the ways in which geography affects people's lives, complete the following activities.

Study the picture

How do you think water is being used? What is the land used for? How can these uses of water and land help certain areas of Europe to grow?

Make a comparison

Compare the area shown in the picture to the area where you live. Consider the features of the land, the plant life, and what you can tell about the climate. How is the area similar to the area where you live? How is it different? Make a list of the similarities and differences.

Land and Water

Reach Into Your Background

How are land and water used where you live? Do you live near fertile plains, forested mountains, or an ocean coast? Do you live in a farming region or an industrial city? Think of the physical features of your area. Then list two ways in which these features have affected your way of life.

Questions to Explore

1. What are the main physical features of Europe and Russia?
2. How have the physical features of Europe and Russia affected where and how people live?

Key Terms

polder
population density
peninsula
plateau
tributary
navigable

Key Places

Europe
Russia
Eurasia
Ural Mountains
Alps
Siberia

If you cross a farm field in the Netherlands (NETH ur luhndz), you might well be walking where sea waves once roared. Water once covered more than two fifths of the country. Centuries ago, the people of the Netherlands began an endless battle to make land where there was water. They built long walls called dikes to hold back the water. They pumped the water into canals that empty into the North Sea. They also created patches of new land called **polders** (POHL durz).

The polders that lie below sea level are always filling with water. Netherlanders must continually pump them out. In early times, they set whirling windmills to do this work. Now they use pumps with powerful motors. Keeping the polders dry has always been important because the richest farmlands and the largest cities in the Netherlands are located on polders.

▼ Polders, like the ones shown on either side of this canal, make up about 3,000 square miles (7,770 sq km) of the Netherlands.

Why have the Netherlanders worked so hard to make new land? Consider the country's **population density,** or average number of people living in an area. The Netherlands has about 1,002 people per square mile (466 people per sq km). By comparison, the world average is about 116 people per square mile (46 people per sq km). The Netherlanders need all the land they can get.

Europe, in general, has a much higher population density than most of the world. By comparison, Russia has a much lower population density—only about 22 people per square mile (9 people per sq km). Few people live in the vast plains and mountains of eastern Russia. The poor soil and cold climate make it a difficult place to live.

Size and Location

Europe and Russia are parts of Eurasia, the world's largest landmass. This landmass is made up of two continents, Europe and Asia. The country of Russia stretches over both continents. About one fourth of Russia is in Europe; the rest is in Asia. Find the Ural (YOOR ul) Mountains on the physical map of Asia in the Atlas at the back of the book. These mountains mark the dividing line between Europe and Asia.

A Small Continent and a Large Country Europe is a small continent. Only Australia is smaller. While Europe lacks size, it has many different countries. Some 47 countries are located on the continent. As you might guess, most of the countries are small. Many are the size of an average state in the United States. Russia, on the other hand, is the largest country in the world. It is almost twice the size of Canada or the United States.

Far to the North

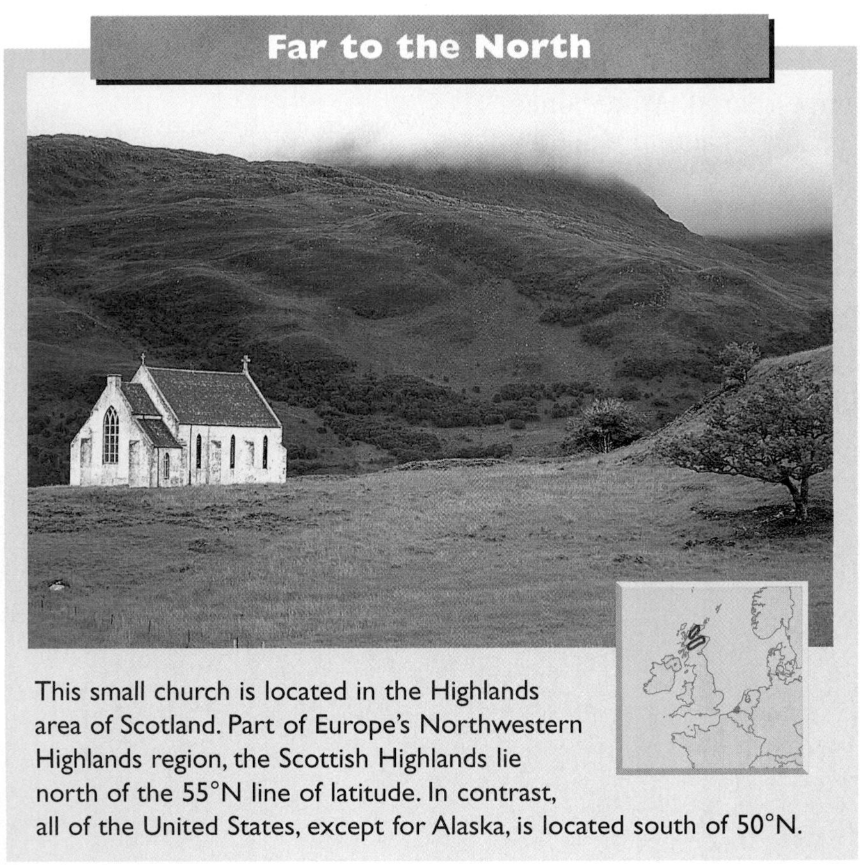

This small church is located in the Highlands area of Scotland. Part of Europe's Northwestern Highlands region, the Scottish Highlands lie north of the 55°N line of latitude. In contrast, all of the United States, except for Alaska, is located south of 50°N.

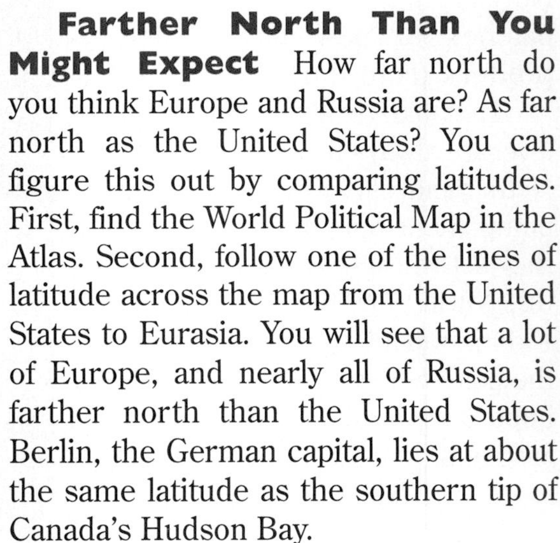

Farther North Than You Might Expect How far north do you think Europe and Russia are? As far north as the United States? You can figure this out by comparing latitudes. First, find the World Political Map in the Atlas. Second, follow one of the lines of latitude across the map from the United States to Eurasia. You will see that a lot of Europe, and nearly all of Russia, is farther north than the United States. Berlin, the German capital, lies at about the same latitude as the southern tip of Canada's Hudson Bay.

Major Landforms of Europe and Russia

Look again at the physical map of Europe in the Atlas and study the shape of Europe. The continent of Europe forms a **peninsula** (puh NIN suh luh), a body of land nearly surrounded by water. The European peninsula juts out into the Atlantic Ocean. Look closely, and you will see that Europe has many smaller peninsulas with bays. These bays include many harbors, or sheltered bodies of water, where ships can dock. Good harbors have enabled Western European countries to become world leaders in the shipping industry.

Now find Russia on the political map of Asia in the Atlas. Notice that Russia lies on the Arctic Ocean. This body of water is frozen for most of the year and cannot be used for shipping. Between Russia and the countries of Europe, however, there are no physical features that form travel barriers. Movement between these two regions has always been easy.

Visualize If you flew in a plane over Europe and Russia, what physical features would you see?

Plains and Uplands of Europe Within the peninsula of Europe are four major land regions: the Northwestern Highlands, the North European Plain, the Central Uplands, and the Alpine Mountain System. Find these regions on the map on the next page.

The Northwestern Highlands stretch across the far north of Europe. These old mountains have been worn by wind and

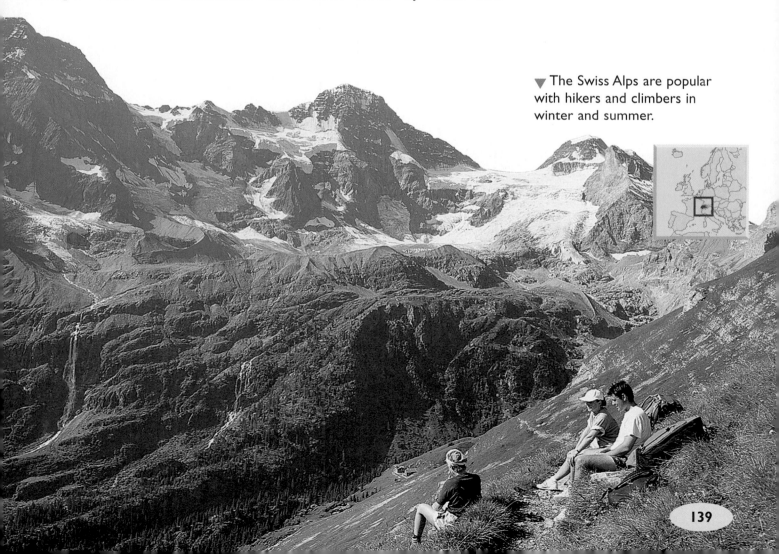

▼ The Swiss Alps are popular with hikers and climbers in winter and summer.

weather. Because they have steep slopes and thin soil, they are not good for farming, and few people live here. Large parts of this region have fewer than 25 people per square mile (10 people per sq km). But the forests here support a successful timber industry.

Notice on the map below that more than half of Europe is covered by the North European Plain. Can you see where this plain begins and ends? It includes most of the European part of Russia and reaches all the way to France. This region has the most productive farmland and the largest cities in Europe.

In the center of southern Europe are the Central Uplands. What do you think uplands are? You probably guessed that this is a region of highlands. In fact, it is made up of mountains and **plateaus** (pla TOHZ), or large raised areas of mostly level land. Most of the land in this region is rocky and not good for farming. But the uplands have other uses. In Spain, people raise goats and sheep here. In Portugal, people mine the uplands for minerals.

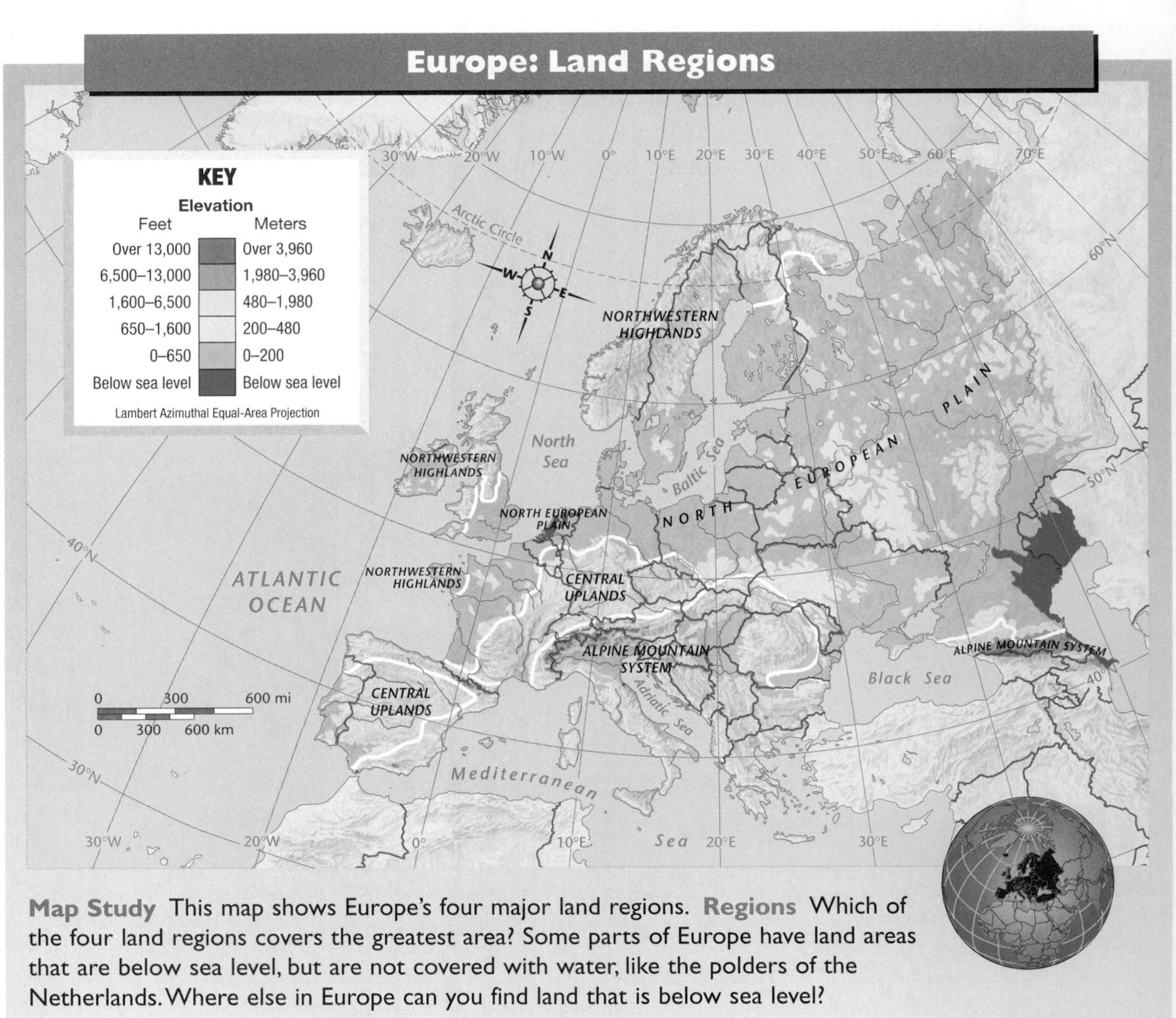

Map Study This map shows Europe's four major land regions. **Regions** Which of the four land regions covers the greatest area? Some parts of Europe have land areas that are below sea level, but are not covered with water, like the polders of the Netherlands. Where else in Europe can you find land that is below sea level?

Strawberry Fields in Siberia

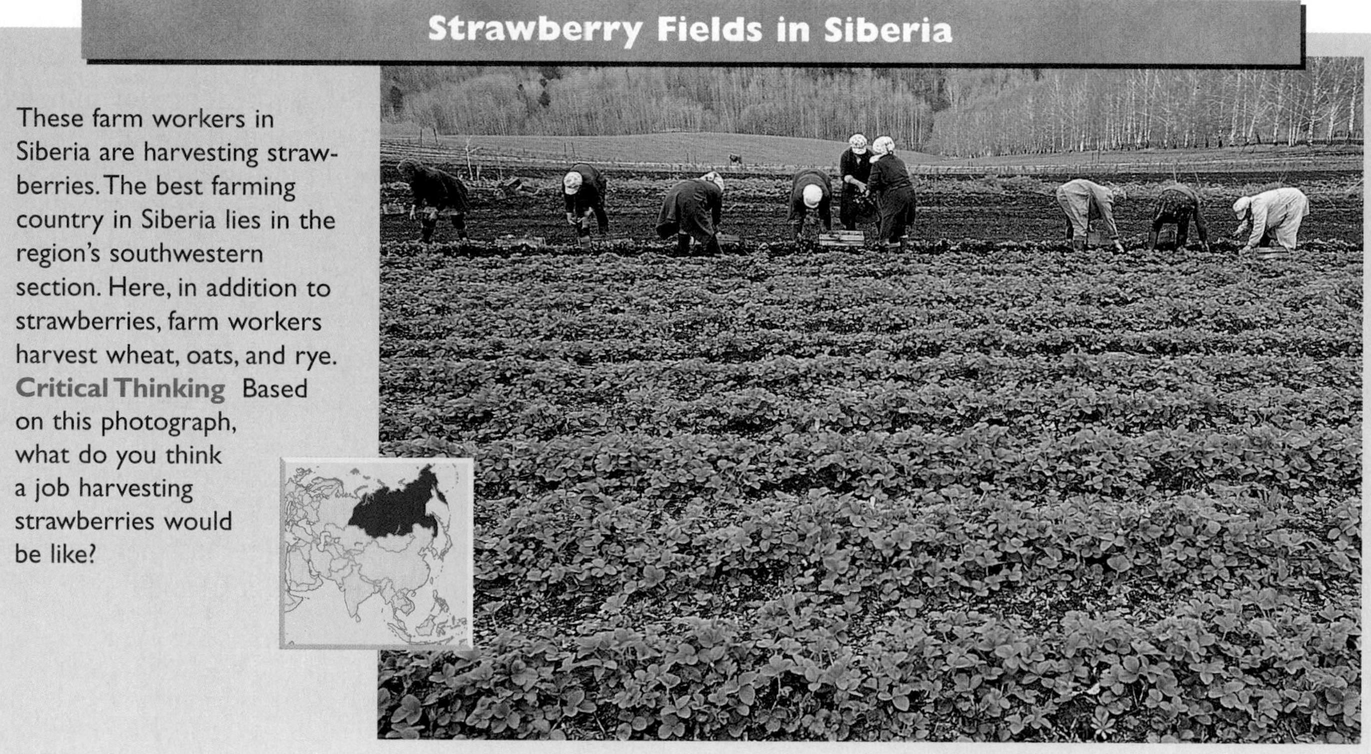

These farm workers in Siberia are harvesting strawberries. The best farming country in Siberia lies in the region's southwestern section. Here, in addition to strawberries, farm workers harvest wheat, oats, and rye. **Critical Thinking** Based on this photograph, what do you think a job harvesting strawberries would be like?

Are you ready to see a spectacular landform? Look for the Alpine Mountain System. These mountains stretch from France to the Balkan Peninsula. The Alps are the highest and most beautiful mountains in this system. They are also a popular vacation place. Some families make a living from small-scale farming in the mountain valleys and meadows of the Alps.

Russian Plains and Uplands Europe and the western part of Russia share the North European Plain. Russia's largest cities, Moscow (MAHS kow) and St. Petersburg, are in this region. Most of Russia's industries are here, too. There are more people living in this region than in any other part of Russia.

Where the plains end, the uplands begin. On the eastern border of the European Plain you will find the Ural Mountains. To the east of the Urals is the Asian part of Russia—a region known as Siberia (sy BIHR ee uh). This region makes up about 75 percent of Russian territory, but it has only about 20 percent of Russia's people. The region's harsh climate has limited settlement there.

If you continue east into Siberia from the Ural Mountains, you will cross the largest plain in the world—the West Siberian Plain. This low, marshy plain covers more than one million square miles (2.58 million sq km), but it rises only 328 feet (100 m) above sea level. Farther east is the Central Siberian Plateau, which slopes upward from the West Siberian Plain. If you travel still farther east, you will need to watch your step. The East Siberian Uplands include more than 20 active volcanoes among the rugged mountains and plateaus.

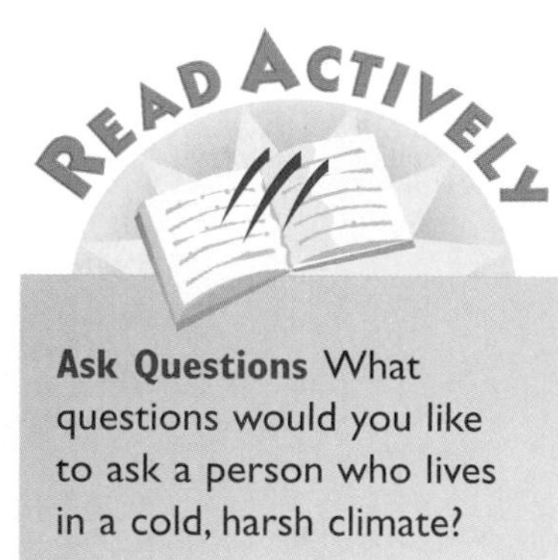

Ask Questions What questions would you like to ask a person who lives in a cold, harsh climate?

Legends of the Rhine The cliffs, castles, and gorges of the Rhine River have inspired many stories. On the Lorelei Cliff, it is believed that a beautiful maiden named Lorelei would sing. The power and beauty of her songs would echo through the cliffs. According to this legend, her songs would attract boatmen, and bring them to their death.

The Rivers of Europe and Russia

The highlands of Europe and Russia are the source for many important rivers. High in the Alps in Switzerland (SWIT sur lund), melting glaciers create two streams that combine to form the Rhine River. Winding through forests and plains, the Rhine makes a journey of 865 miles (1,391 km), from Switzerland to the Netherlands and the North Sea. Along its course through Germany, the river flows past old castles on cliffs and smoky mills and factories.

The Rhine River serves as a major highway. Canals and tributaries (TRIB yoo tehr eez) connect it to the furthest reaches of Western Europe. A **tributary** is a river or stream that flows into a larger river.

The longest river on the continent of Europe is Russia's Volga (VAHL guh) River. It flows 2,291 miles (3,687 km) through western Russia and empties into the Caspian (KAS pih un) Sea. The Volga has many tributaries and canals. They link the Volga to the Arctic Ocean and the Baltic

The Deepest Lake on Earth

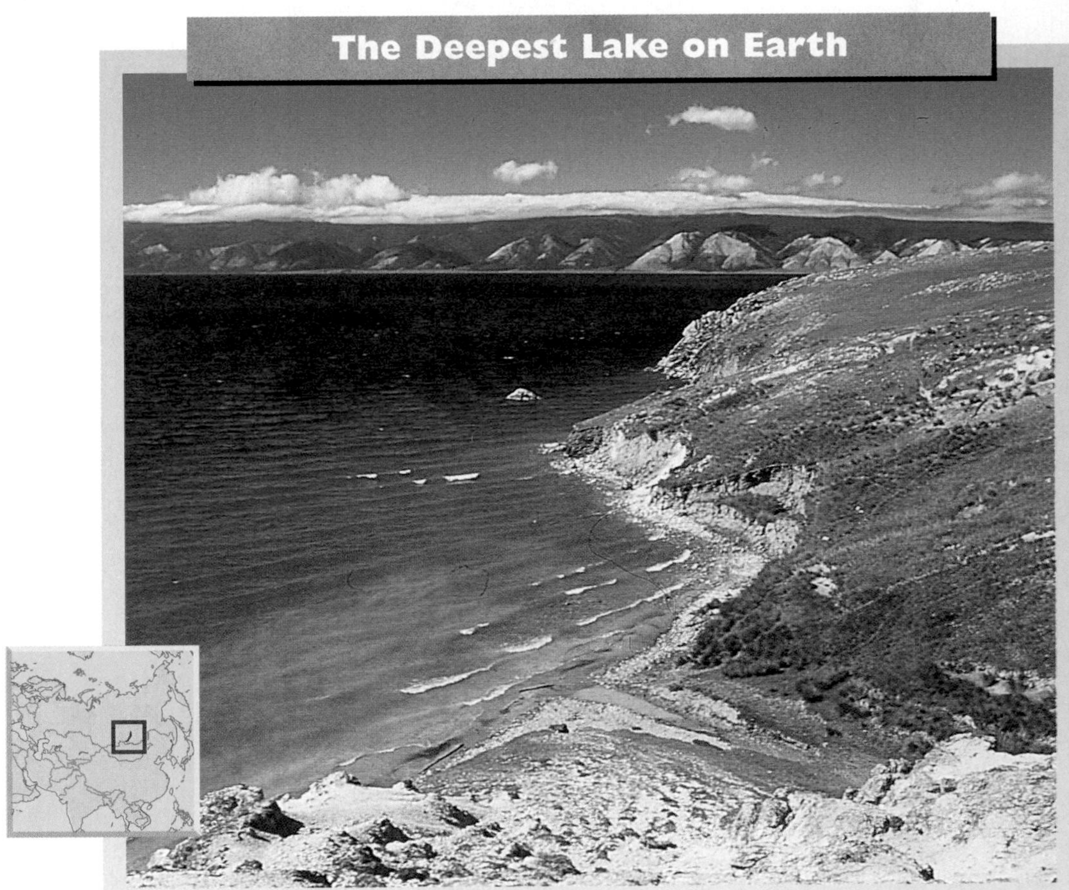

Lake Baikal, Russia, holds about one fifth of Earth's fresh water. More than 300 rivers and streams flow into Lake Baikal from the surrounding mountains. Because Lake Baikal holds so much water, it affects the weather in the area around it. The land near the lake is cooler in the summer and warmer in the winter than land that lies farther away. **Critical Thinking** What other bodies of water can change the weather?

The Danube River

The Danube River flows from the mountains of Germany through eight countries before it empties into the Black Sea in Romania. It is the second longest river in Europe—only Russia's Volga River is longer. Because it is both navigable and long, the Danube is an important trade route. Ships from the Mediterranean can travel as far as this port in Braila, Romania, before their cargo is transferred to smaller vessels. **Critical Thinking** At one time, composers wrote music celebrating the beauty of the Danube River. Today, that beauty has been dimmed by air and water pollution from factories. What parts of this photograph are hard to see because of smog?

Sea. Unfortunately, the Volga freezes for most of its length for three months of each year. During the winter months, it is not **navigable** (NAV ih guh bul), or clear enough for ships to travel.

Other Russian rivers freeze, too. Some of them are frozen for five or more months of the year. And many flow north to the frozen Arctic Ocean, which is also not navigable. These rivers do not serve as dependable trade routes.

1. **Define** (a) polder, (b) population density, (c) peninsula, (d) plateau, (e) tributary, (f) navigable.
2. **Identify** (a) Europe, (b) Russia, (c) Eurasia, (d) Ural Mountains, (e) Alps, (f) Siberia.
3. What are the major physical features of Europe and Russia?
4. Give two examples of ways in which physical features have affected life in Europe and Russia.

Critical Thinking

5. **Drawing Conclusions** Think about the areas of Europe and Russia that are the most densely populated. What physical features attract people to settle in those areas?

Activity

6. **Writing to Learn** Which physical feature described in this section are you most interested in learning more about? Why? In your journal, make a list of the things you would like to learn about this physical feature.

Climate and Vegetation

Reach Into Your Background

Do you live where it is warm year round? Or do you live in an area with warm summers and cold winters? Think of the climate in your area. Identify three ways in which it affects your way of life.

Questions to Explore

1. How do oceans and mountains affect climate in Europe and Russia?
2. What different climates and kinds of vegetation do Europe and Russia have?

Key Terms

rain shadow
prairie
tundra
permafrost
taiga
steppe

Key Places

Barcelona
Irkutsk

It is February in Barcelona (bar suh LOH nuh), Spain. Twelve-year-old Nicholas wakes up to the sun streaming through his bedroom window. It's another warm day, and the temperature is already 65°F (18°C). Nicholas dresses quickly in shorts and a T-shirt and eats a breakfast of thick hot chocolate and *churros,* twisted loops of fried dough. He wants to get out and play soccer with his friends on this sunny Saturday morning.

At the very same moment, it is late afternoon in Irkutsk (ihr KOOTSK), a city in southern Siberia. Vasily (VAS uh lee) returns home from a day of cross-country skiing. He takes off his fur hat, gloves, boots, ski pants, and coat. The day has been sunny but cold, with an average temperature of −15°F (−11°C). Now Vasily warms up with a dinner of *pelmeny* (PEL muh nee), chicken broth with meat-filled dumplings.

▼ In the snowy Siberian winter, skiing is a good way to get from place to place.

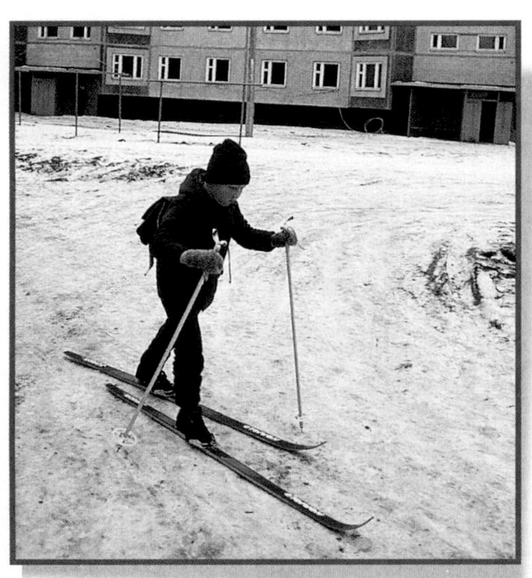

A Wide Range of Climates

Nicholas and Vasily live in vastly different climates. Barcelona, where Nicholas lives, lies on the Mediterranean Sea. Here, the summers are hot and dry, and the winters are mild and rainy. In Irkutsk, Vasily's home in Siberia, summers are short, and the winters are long and very cold. Temperatures in winter can drop to −50°F (−45°C). Snow covers the ground for about six months of the year.

Two Cities, Two Climates

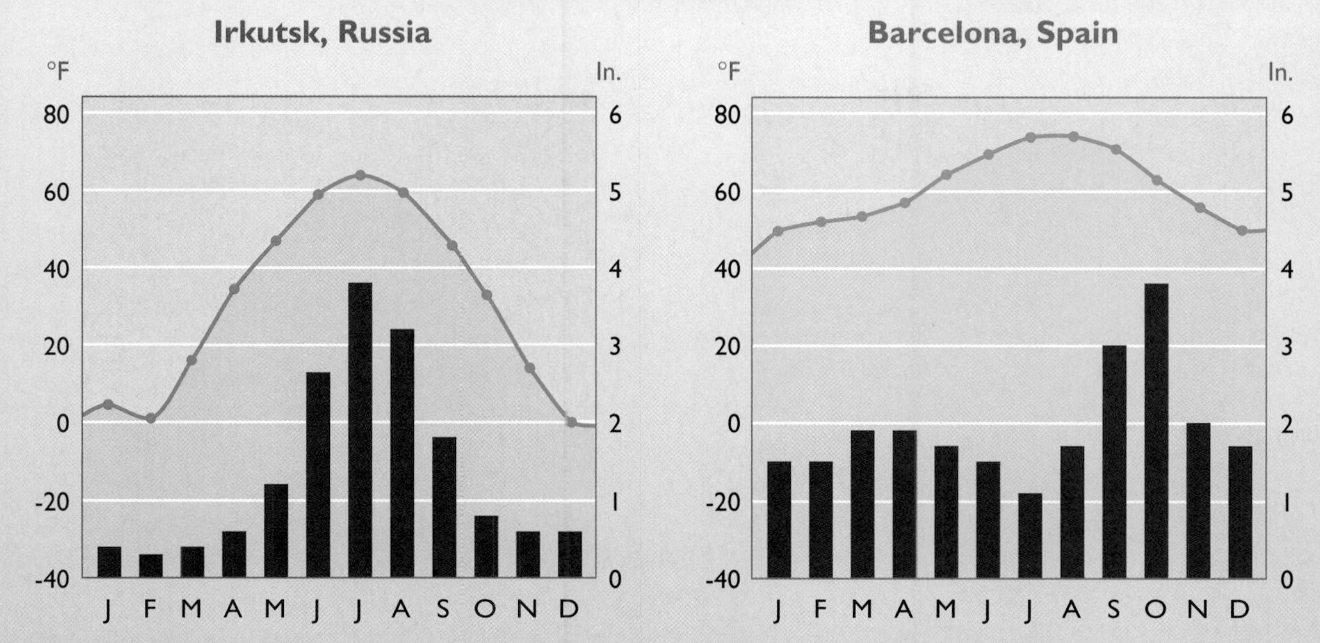

Curved lines show temperatures in Fahrenheit degrees. **Bars** show precipitation in inches.

Graph Study Siberia, where the city of Irkutsk is located, endures the coldest winters of any place in the world except Antarctica. In contrast, Spain, where Barcelona is located, enjoys mild weather throughout the year. **Critical Thinking** Find Irkutsk and Barcelona on the climate regions map in the Activity Atlas. How do you think location influences the climates of these two cities?

Oceans Affect Climate You can partly explain the difference between the climates of Barcelona and Irkutsk by looking at the two cities' distances from an ocean or a sea. Areas that are near an ocean or a sea have fairly mild weather year round. Areas that are far from the ocean often have extreme weather.

Look at the map on the next page and find the Gulf Stream. Notice how it becomes the North Atlantic Current as it crosses the Atlantic Ocean. This ocean current carries warm water from the tropical waters of the Gulf of Mexico to northwestern Europe. Also, winds blowing from the west across the Atlantic Ocean are warmed by this powerful ocean current. The warm waters and winds bring mild weather to much of northwestern Europe.

London is farther north than any city in the continental United States, but it has mild weather. How is this possible? The North Atlantic Current is the reason. But the most dramatic effect of the North Atlantic Current can be seen in northern Norway. Snow and ice cover most of this area in winter. Yet Norway's western coast is free of ice and snow all year. Snow melts almost as soon as it falls. Norway's ice-free ports have helped to make it a great fishing country.

The ocean affects climate in other ways. Winds blowing across the ocean pick up a great deal of moisture. When these winds blow over land,

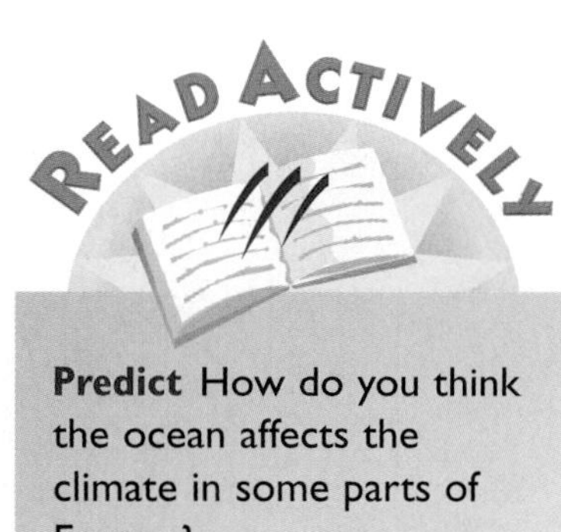

Predict How do you think the ocean affects the climate in some parts of Europe?

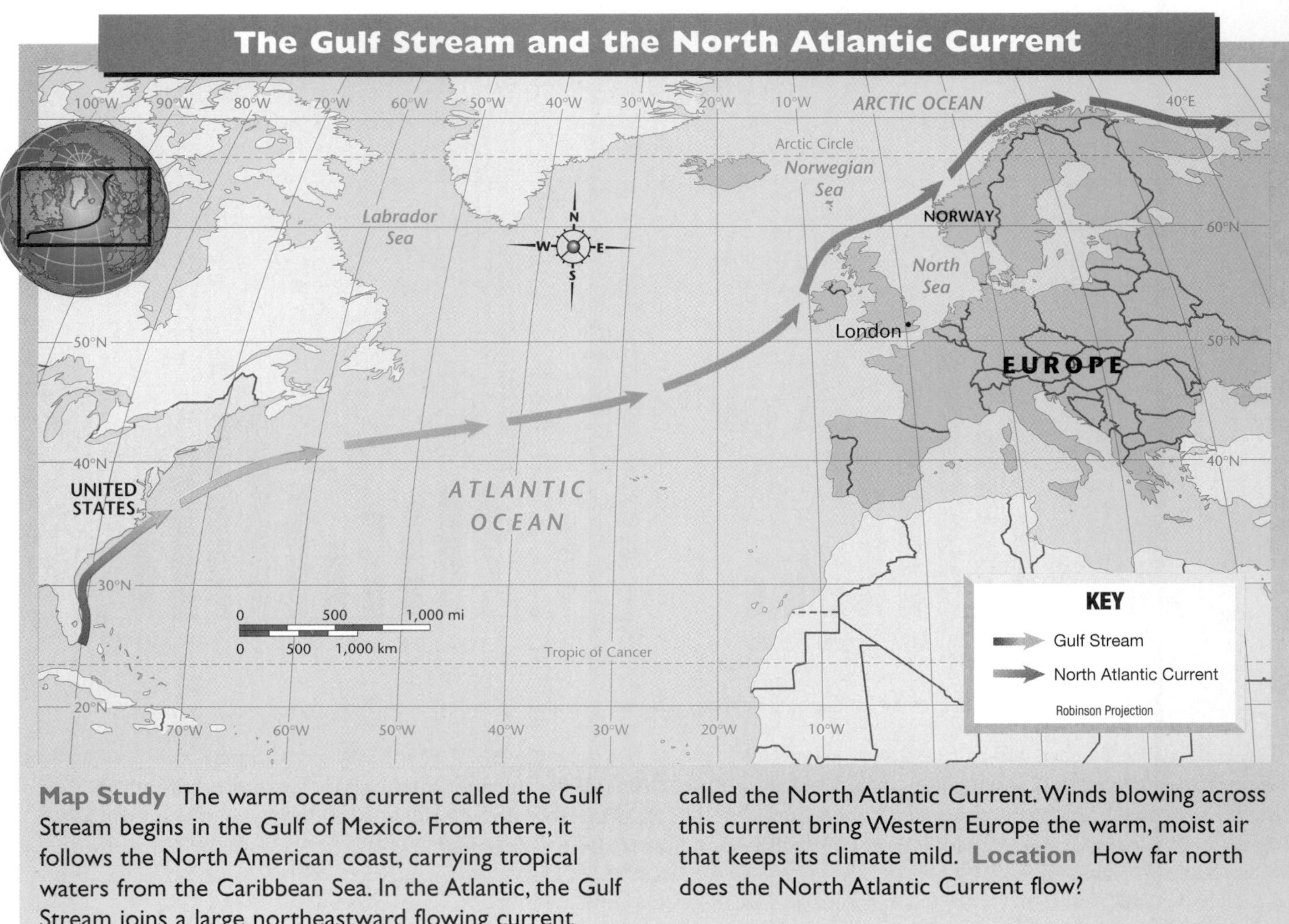

Map Study The warm ocean current called the Gulf Stream begins in the Gulf of Mexico. From there, it follows the North American coast, carrying tropical waters from the Caribbean Sea. In the Atlantic, the Gulf Stream joins a large northeastward flowing current called the North Atlantic Current. Winds blowing across this current bring Western Europe the warm, moist air that keeps its climate mild. **Location** How far north does the North Atlantic Current flow?

they drop the moisture in the form of rain. Winds blowing from the west across the Atlantic bring a fairly wet climate to much of Western Europe.

Mountains Affect Rainfall Mountains also affect the amount of rainfall in an area. In Europe, areas west of mountains receive heavy rainfall. These areas include parts of Great Britain, France, Germany, and Norway. Areas east of mountains have much lighter rainfall.

Why is this so? As winds rise up a mountain, they cool and drop their moisture. The air is dry by the time it reaches the other side of the mountain. Areas on the leeward side of a mountain, or away from the wind, are in a rain shadow. A **rain shadow** is an area on the dry, sheltered side of a mountain that receives little rainfall.

Major Climate Zones of Europe and Russia

Earlier, you read that oceans affect climate. Look at the climate regions map in the Activity Atlas to see a good illustration of this. Notice that much of northwestern Europe has a marine west coast climate. The

North Atlantic Current helps make the climate mild all year. Moisture-carrying winds from the Atlantic Ocean make these areas rainy through all the seasons. In London, the capital of Great Britain, rain is a part of life. Many people who live here are in the habit of carrying an umbrella every day.

Look again at the map. Notice the climate region that surrounds the Mediterranean Sea. It is easy to remember the name of this type of climate—Mediterranean, just like the sea. Remember that Barcelona, where Nicholas lives, is on the Mediterranean. In this kind of climate, summers are hot and dry. Winters are mild and rainy. Look at the climate graph earlier in the section to see the average monthly temperatures and rainfall for Barcelona.

Some inland areas far away from the ocean have a humid continental climate. In these areas, winters are long and cold. But summers can be blazing hot!

Now find Irkutsk, Russia, on the map. Notice that it is located in a huge subarctic climate zone. Here summers are short, and winters are long and cold. You can see how cold it is all year by looking at the climate graph for Irkutsk. The northernmost areas of Europe and Russia have a tundra climate. In these areas it is just plain cold! On the warmest days, temperatures rarely get above 40°F (5°C).

Hot and Cold Iceland's Loki volcano lies beneath Vatnjokul, Europe's largest glacier. In the fall of 1996, Loki erupted. This created a deep crack in the glacier some 6 miles (10 km) long. Melting ice and eruptions of water from a huge "underground lake" beneath the glacier flooded the surrounding area.

My Family in Winter

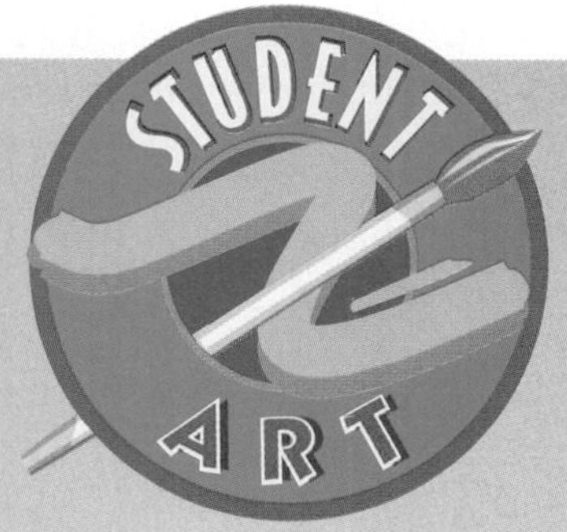

Helin Tikerpuu
13 years old
Estonia

This student has painted her family on a skiing trip. **Critical Thinking** Based on this picture, do you think Helin's family skis just for fun? Or do you think their ski trip has a more practical purpose? Explain your answer.

The Vegetation of Europe and Russia

The natural vegetation, or plant life, of Europe and Russia is as varied as the climate. And vegetation regions are related to climate regions. Compare the climate map with the natural vegetation maps below and on the next page to see how the climate and vegetation bands overlap.

Forests and Grasslands of Europe The natural vegetation of much of Europe is forest. However, most of these forests have been cleared to make way for farms, factories, and cities. In northern Europe, you can still find large coniferous (koh NIF ur us) forests, which have trees with cones that carry and protect the seeds.

The central and southern parts of the North European Plain were once covered by grasslands, called **prairies.** Like the forests, most of the prairies have also been cleared. Today, the land is used for farming.

The Russian Tundra, Forests, and Grasslands Russia has three great vegetation zones: the tundra, the forests, and the grasslands. The tundra and forest zones extend across Siberia. Grasslands cover southwestern Russia.

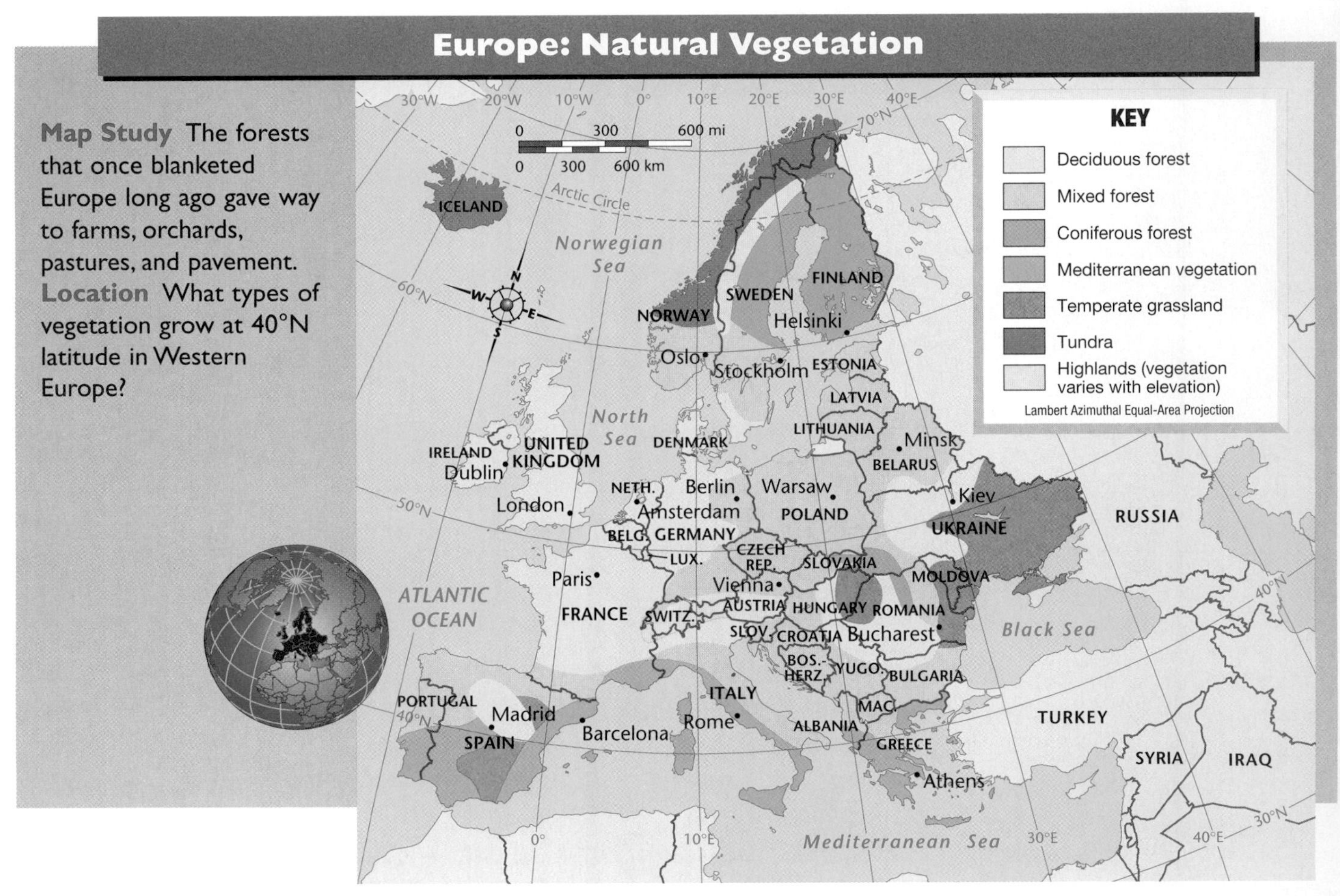

Map Study The forests that once blanketed Europe long ago gave way to farms, orchards, pastures, and pavement. **Location** What types of vegetation grow at 40°N latitude in Western Europe?

Map Study Far from the Equator and from warm ocean currents, Russia's cool climate supports three types of vegetation. **Regions** Which type of vegetation covers the largest area? In the far north, what type of vegetation grows? Which region provides Russia's rich farmland?

The **tundra** is a treeless plain where grasses and mosses grow. Here, winters last up to nine months and the ground is **permafrost,** or permanently frozen soil. When the top surface of the permafrost thaws, fantastic growth spurts take place.

Russia also has more than its share of forests. One, called the **taiga** (TY guh), covers more than 4 million square miles (6.4 million sq km). It is the largest forest in the world.

The Russian grasslands are called **steppes.** The soil of this region is fertile and black and good for farming. The steppes are similar to the Great Plains of the United States.

1. Define (a) rain shadow, (b) prairie, (c) tundra, (d) permafrost, (e) taiga, (f) steppe.

2. Identify (a) Barcelona, (b) Irkutsk.

3. How does the North Atlantic Current affect the climate of northwestern Europe?

4. What are the major climate and vegetation regions of Europe and Russia?

Critical Thinking

5. Recognizing Cause and Effect How do oceans and mountains affect climate?

Activity

6. Writing to Learn Plan a trip to one of the cities mentioned in this section. Decide what time of year you want to go. Based on the climate of the city you have chosen, make a list of the clothes you will pack.

Using Regional Maps

Do you dream of someday traveling around the world? Just by crossing Russia, you can travel halfway around the world.

Russia is the largest country on the planet. It reaches across Europe and Asia. When it is noon at one end of the country, it is close to midnight at the other. How can this be?

Get Ready

There is such a big time difference because Russia stretches across 10 of the world's 24 time zones. Why do we have time zones?

Suppose every clock in the world showed the same time at once. At noon, the sun would be rising in some places and setting in others. It would be very confusing.

The Earth has 24 time zones—one for each hour of the day. Noon everywhere is always about when the sun is at its highest point.

You may someday be talking on the phone with people in Russia. If you understand time zones, you can avoid calling someone at 3:00 A.M. The best way to understand time zones is by learning how to read a time zone map.

Try It Out

The map on the next page shows time zones across the globe. Compare the number of time zones in the United States and in Russia. Use the time zone map to complete the following steps:

A. Find the time zone boundaries. The boundaries are shown by solid lines. Notice that they are mostly straight, but sometimes bend to follow political boundaries. Why do you think this is so?

B. Understand the difference between time zones. The difference in time between one time zone and the next is one hour. (Each time zone represents the distance the Earth rotates in one hour.) As you travel west of the Prime Meridian, the time becomes one hour earlier for every time zone you cross. As you travel east of the Prime Meridian, it becomes one hour later for every time zone you cross. Note the two sets of labels on the map on the next page. At the top are hours labeled A.M. and P.M.

The Prime Meridian is labeled 12 noon. The numbers below the map show the time difference in hours from 12 noon.

C. Follow a three-step process to use the map.

Step 1. The United States covers 6 of the 24 time zones. Find your location on the map. Check what time it is now.

Step 2. Locate the place for which you wish to know the time. Notice its time zone.

Step 3. If the place is in the same time zone as your location, the time is the same as your time. If it is in a different time zone, look at the times in the key below the map to see how many hours away it is. Then add or subtract the hours from your current time. Remember, if the place is east of where you are, add to your time. If it is west of where you are, subtract from your time.

Write down your current time. Now calculate the current time for the five United States cities shown on the time zone map.

Apply the Skill

Russia is the widest country on the Earth. In other words, it stretches across more time zones than any other country does.

1. **Consider the differences in time.** Study the map. In Russia, how many hours' difference is there between the time zone farthest east and the time zone farthest west? When it is 3 P.M. in Moscow, what time is it in Perm? What time is it in Novosibirsk? What time is it in Vladivostok? When it is lunch time in St. Petersburg, what part of the day is it in Anadyr?

2. **Think about the challenges posed by these great differences.** Write a paragraph to answer this question: What challenges might the Russian government and businesses face by having to work with so many different time zones?

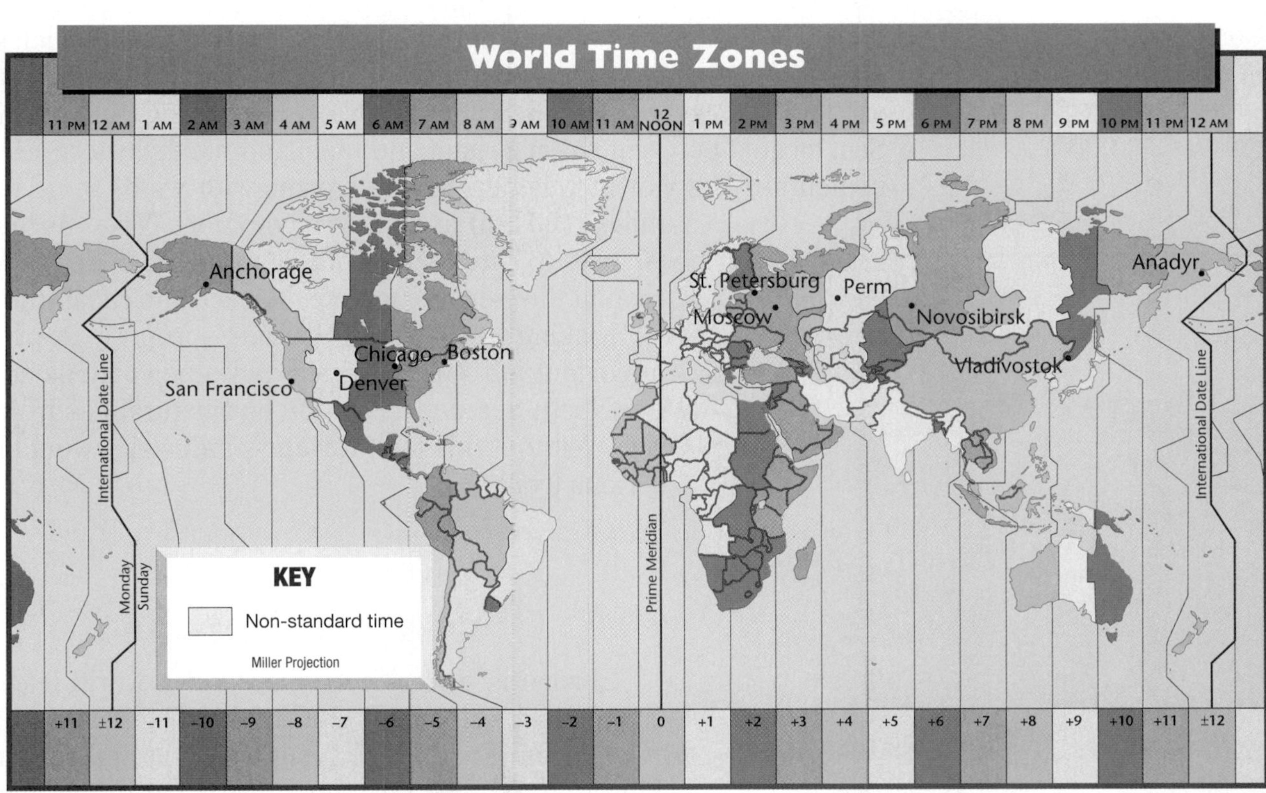

Natural Resources

Reach Into Your Background

The United States has many natural resources. Which resources do you think are most important? Why?

Consider these questions as you read about the natural resources of Europe and Russia.

Questions to Explore

1. What are the major natural resources of Europe and Russia?
2. How do Europe and Russia differ in their use of natural resources?

Key Terms

loess
hydroelectric power
fossil fuel
reserves

Key Places

North Sea
Ruhr
Silesia

How would you like to live and work on an ocean? Oil workers on the North Sea work to pump oil from deep beneath the ocean floor. They anchor a tower called an oil rig over an oil field. In such a rig, oil workers live and work as if they were on a ship. But oil workers cannot sail for the safety of a harbor when a big storm is stirring. And the North Sea, located between Great Britain and mainland northwestern Europe, sometimes has violent weather. Severe storms with winds of up to 100 miles (160 km) an hour are common. Waves as high as 90 feet (27 m) batter oil rig platforms. Crews work around the clock to operate, inspect, and repair the rigs.

▼ On a North Sea oil rig, workers brave icy seas and foul weather to drill for underwater petroleum deposits.

Making sure a rig operates properly is a very important job. Great Britain and other nations around the North Sea depend on oil and natural gas from the rigs. Without this fuel, Europe's industries would be in serious trouble.

Resources of Western Europe

Europe is a wealthy region and a world leader in economic development. Part of this wealth and success comes from Europe's rich supply of natural resources. This region's most important natural resources include fertile soil, water, and fuels.

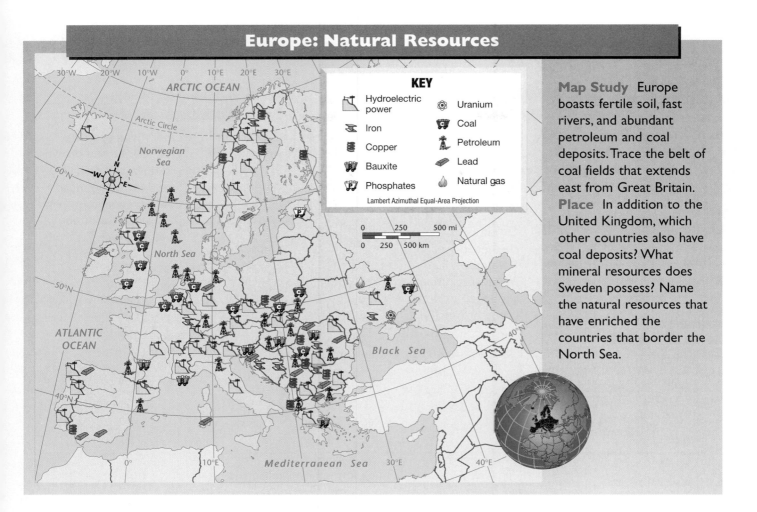

Europe: Natural Resources

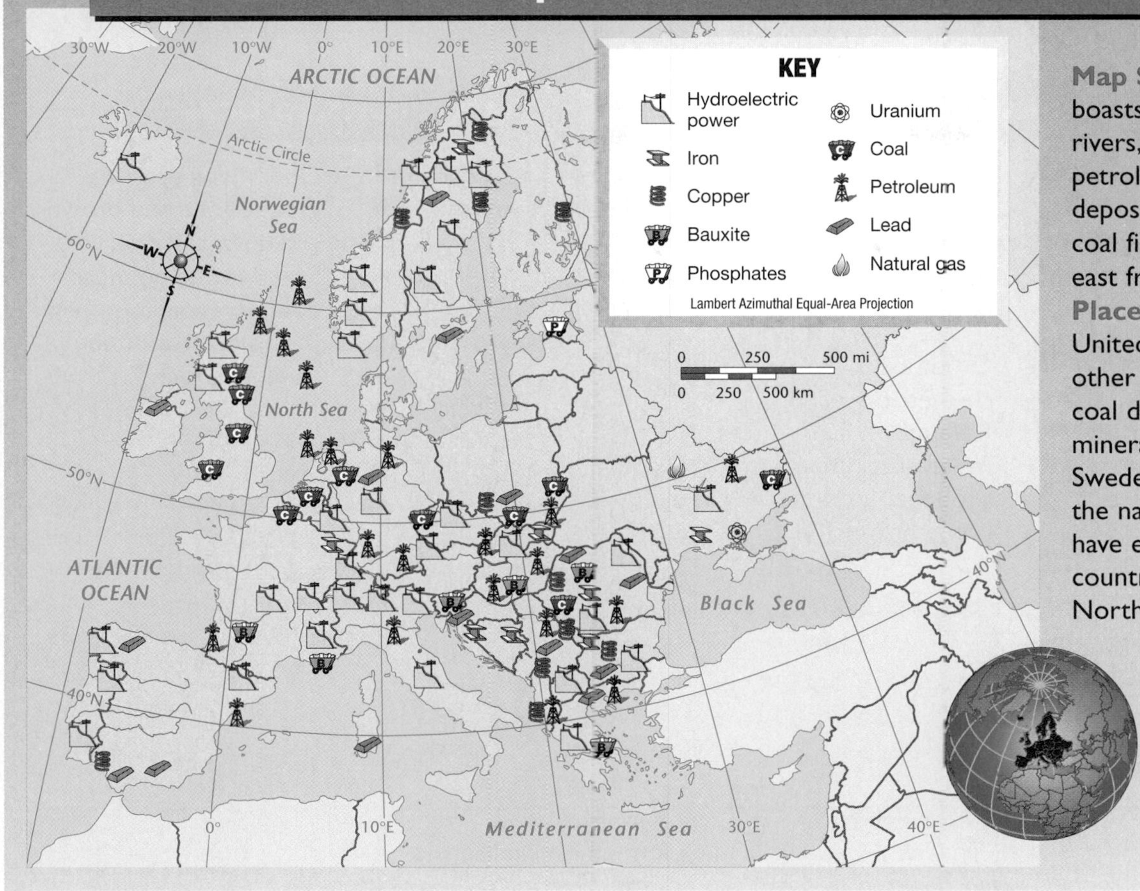

KEY

- Hydroelectric power
- Iron
- Copper
- Bauxite
- Phosphates
- Uranium
- Coal
- Petroleum
- Lead
- Natural gas

Lambert Azimuthal Equal-Area Projection

0 250 500 mi
0 250 500 km

Map Study Europe boasts fertile soil, fast rivers, and abundant petroleum and coal deposits. Trace the belt of coal fields that extends east from Great Britain. **Place** In addition to the United Kingdom, which other countries also have coal deposits? What mineral resources does Sweden possess? Name the natural resources that have enriched the countries that border the North Sea.

Fertile Soil Why do you think soil is one of the most important natural resources? You have probably guessed that it is important because it is needed to grow food. Much of Western Europe is covered with rich, fertile soil, especially the region's broad river valleys.

Wind helps create the fertile soil of the North European Plain. Over thousands of years, winds have deposited a type of rich, dustlike soil known as **loess** (LOH es). This soil, combined with plentiful rain and a long growing season, enables European farmers to produce abundant crops.

Loess in China Winds blowing from Mongolia and the Gobi carry loess to the Huang He valley. The river carries the soil downstream and, during floods, deposits it across the North China Plain. This fertile soil makes the plain one of China's most important farming areas.

An Excellent Supply of Water Western Europe's water is another important resource. People need water to drink. Water nourishes crops. Water can also be used to produce electricity, an important source of energy for industries. To be used as a source of energy, water must flow very quickly. The force of water from a waterfall or a dam can be used to spin machines called turbines (TUR bynz). Spinning turbines generate, or create, electric power. Power generated by water-driven turbines is called **hydroelectric** (hy droh ee LEK trik) **power.**

Many countries in Europe have good locations for the development of hydroelectric power. Some rivers that flow down through the mountains have been dammed to create hydroelectric power. Norway

From Fossils to Fuel

From Plankton to Oil

1. Drifting throughout the oceans and fresh water of the Earth are tiny marine plants and animals called **plankton**. Plankton that died millions of years ago settled on the ocean floor.

2. Over the years, the plankton was covered with mud and sand. The weight of this material gradually changed the plankton into oil. The oil remained trapped inside **porous rock** that also formed.

3. With huge machinery people dig through the rock and remove the trapped oil, called **crude oil**.

4. Crude oil must then be cleaned, or refined. **Refined oil** is used to make many important products, including home heating oil.

From Plants to Coal

1. **Peat** is made of decayed plant material.

2. Over millions of years, material built up over ancient peat deposits. The pressure of this material gradually changed the peat into **brown coal**.

3. Continuing pressure gradually turned brown coal into soft coal. **Soft coal** is the most common coal found on the Earth. It is often used in industry.

Chart Study The fossil fuels coal and oil formed over millions of years. Oil formed when plankton died and was covered with mud. The plankton decayed and the mud turned to rock, filled with pockets of oil. Coal started with swamp-growing plants whose decayed remains formed a substance called peat. **Critical Thinking** What is the difference between crude oil and refined oil?

gets almost all of its electric power from water. Hydroelectric power also keeps factories in Sweden, Switzerland, Austria, Spain, and Portugal humming.

Connect What kinds of natural resources have you used so far today?

Fuels Like flowing water, fossil fuels provide a source of energy for industries. **Fossil fuels** include coal, oil, and natural gas. They are so named because they developed from fossils, or the remains of ancient plants and animals.

You already know that Great Britain has large deposits of oil and natural gas. Norway does as well. Great Britain also has large coal fields, as does Germany. The largest coal deposits in Germany are located in the Ruhr (roor), a region named for the Ruhr River. Because of its fuel resources, the Ruhr has long been one of Western Europe's most important industrial regions.

An abundance of coal, along with another mineral, iron ore, gave Western Europe a head start in the 1800s, when industries grew rapidly. Today, Europe remains a leading world industrial power.

Resources of Eastern Europe

Now, shift your view from Western to Eastern Europe. Turn back to the map showing Europe's natural resources. Notice that Eastern Europe has similar resources to those of Western Europe. Place a finger on the area around 50°N and 15°E. This is where Poland, the Czech (chek) Republic, and Germany come together. This area is called Silesia (sy LEE shuh). Large deposits of coal here have made Silesia a major industrial center.

Ukraine (yoo KRAYN), a large country in Eastern Europe, has coal deposits, too. It also has several other fuel resources—oil and natural gas. However, its most important resource is probably its soil. This black earth, or *chernozem* (CHEHR nuh zem), is very fertile. Not surprisingly, farming is an extremely important activity in Ukraine.

A Slovakian Steel Factory

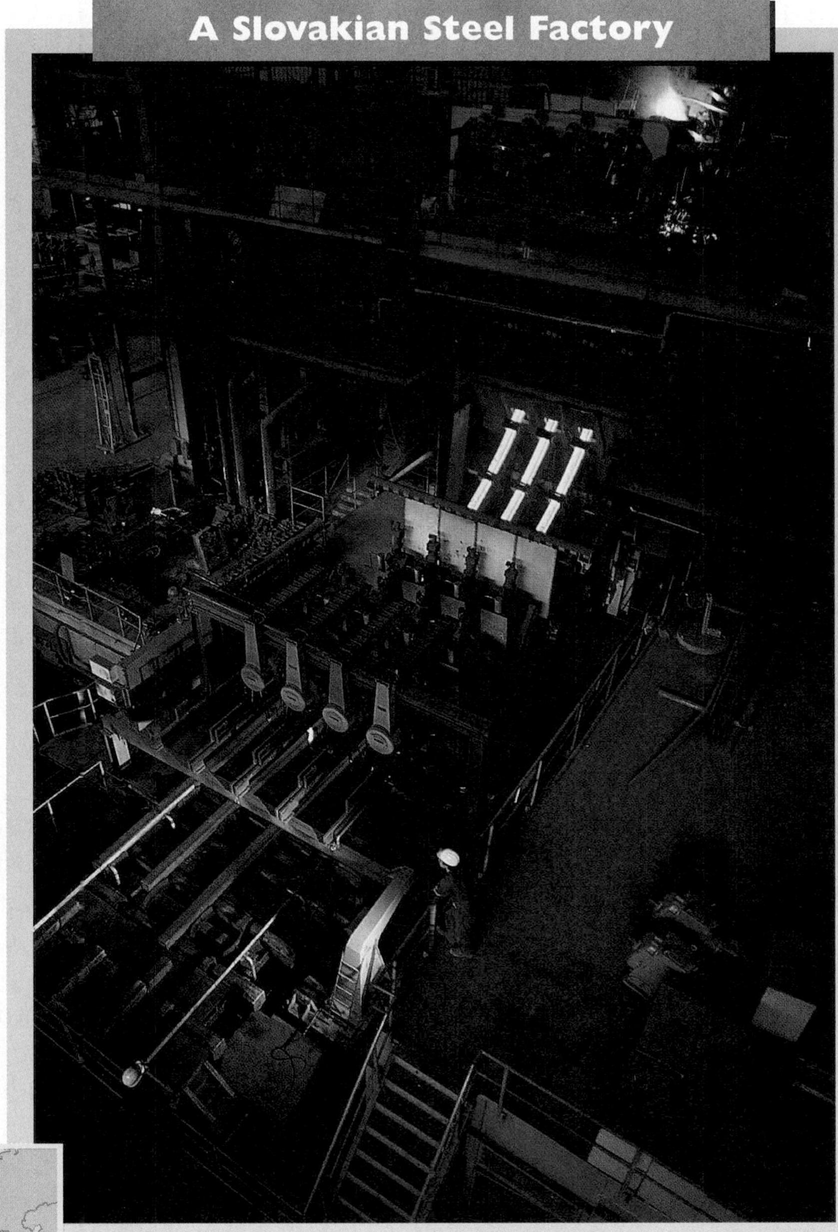

Slovakia has large deposits of iron ore. However, it does not have enough iron to supply all its factories, so it imports some. This photograph shows steel being made out of iron at the steelworks in the Slovakian town of Podbrezova. **Critical Thinking** Steel is very strong and can be molded into many different shapes. What products do you know of that are made out of steel?

Resources of Russia

Russia has developed its natural resources far less than Western Europe. Russia has a huge variety of resources—even more than the United States. Our country has used its resources to become the richest nation on earth. You might wonder why Russia has not done the same. The answer is that Russia's harsh climate, huge size, and few navigable rivers have made it difficult to turn resources into wealth.

Russia: Natural Resources

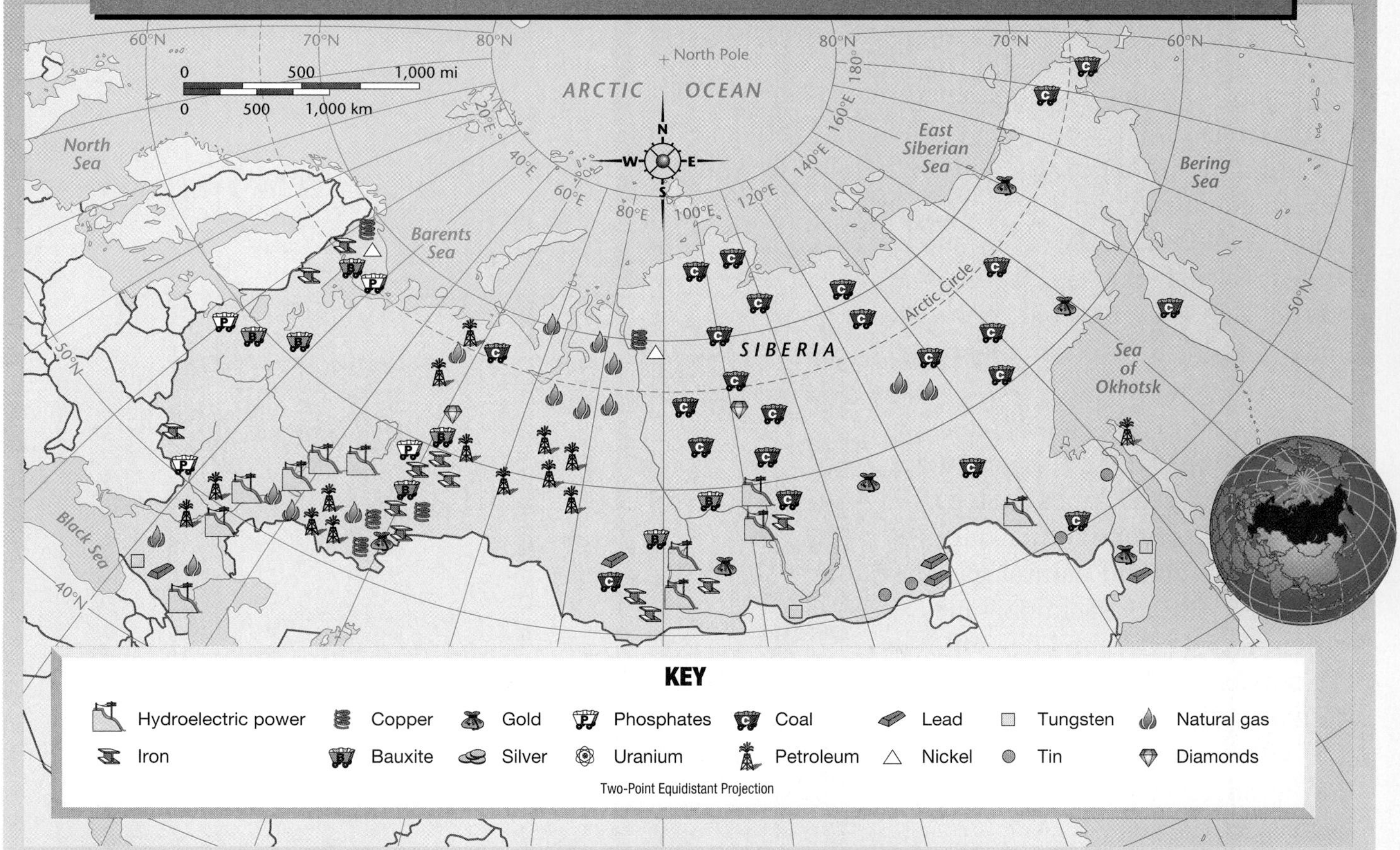

ARCTIC OCEAN
North Pole
North Sea
Barents Sea
East Siberian Sea
Bering Sea
Sea of Okhotsk
Black Sea
SIBERIA
Arctic Circle

KEY

Hydroelectric power · Copper · Gold · Phosphates · Coal · Lead · Tungsten · Natural gas
Iron · Bauxite · Silver · Uranium · Petroleum · Nickel · Tin · Diamonds

Two-Point Equidistant Projection

Map Study Under Russia's permafrost lie coal, oil, natural gas, diamonds, and gold. **Regions** Name five other Russian resources. **Movement** How might the rivers of Siberia be used to transport resources from remote regions when they are frozen in the winter?

Russia's Fossil Fuels and Iron Ore Russia can proudly claim the title of the world's largest oil producer. It also has the largest **reserves,** or available supply, of natural gas in the world. And scientists estimate that the country has about one third of the world's coal reserves.

In addition, Russia has the world's greatest reserves of iron ore, which is used to make steel. Many of these deposits are in the part of Russia that is on the continent of Europe. That is one reason why most of Russia's industry is west of the Ural Mountains.

Predict How is the direction of a river's flow important for transporting resources?

The Special Case of Siberia Look at the map above. Notice that most of Russia's deposits of oil, natural gas, and coal are located in Siberia. Three fourths of the Russian forest lies here, too. This forest holds half of the world's reserves of softwood timber. Siberia is far from the population and industrial centers of the country, however. Retrieving these resources is not easy.

Russia's huge size presents a major challenge. Transporting Siberian resources to areas where they are needed can be a struggle.

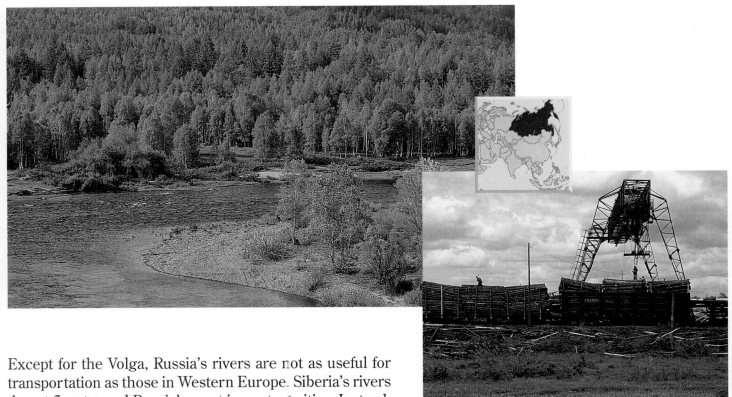

Except for the Volga, Russia's rivers are not as useful for transportation as those in Western Europe. Siberia's rivers do not flow toward Russia's most important cities. Instead, they flow north into the Arctic Ocean. In spite of these problems and the very cold weather, Russia is continually finding ways to move the resources from Siberia. Pipelines carry oil and natural gas, and railroads transport coal to European Russia.

The efforts to get to the resources and use them have created a new challenge—protecting the environment. Some of the world's worst cases of pollution are found in Siberia. Nuclear waste has been dumped into rivers for 40 years. Air pollution from factories is very high. Scientists not only have to find ways to develop Russia's valuable resources, they must also consider how to restore polluted areas.

▲ Siberia's forests (above left) are one of Russia's most important resources. Loggers transport wood from these forests to other parts of Russia by train (above). Unlike coal and oil, forests are a renewable resource if they are managed carefully.

1. Define (a) loess, (b) hydroelectric power, (c) fossil fuel, (d) reserves.

2. Identify (a) North Sea, (b) Ruhr, (c) Silesia.

3. Describe the main natural resources of Western Europe, Eastern Europe, and Russia.

4. Explain how Western Europe and Russia differ in their development of natural resources.

Critical Thinking

5. Drawing Conclusions Russia is richer in natural resources than Western Europe. Yet Russians are generally not as wealthy as Western Europeans. How does geography help explain this?

Activity

6. Writing to Learn What do you think is Europe and Russia's most important natural resource? What makes that resource so important? Write a paragraph explaining your choice.

Review and Activities

Reviewing Main Ideas

1. Describe the land and rivers of Europe and Russia.
2. How have physical features aided Europe's growth and hurt Russia's growth?
3. Describe the climates of Europe and Russia.
4. Describe the vegetation of Europe and Russia.
5. What effect do large bodies of water have on climate in Europe and Russia?
6. Identify the main natural resources of Western Europe, Eastern Europe, and Russia.
7. Compare the development of natural resources in Western Europe and Russia.

Reviewing Key Terms

Use each key term below in a sentence that shows the meaning of the term.

1. polder
2. peninsula
3. plateau
4. tributary
5. rain shadow
6. prairie
7. tundra
8. permafrost
9. steppe
10. hydroelectric power
11. fossil fuel
12. reserves

Critical Thinking

1. **Making Comparisons** Choose one of the land regions of Europe or Russia. Compare it with the area where you live. Consider the landscape, climate, and vegetation.
2. **Recognizing Cause and Effect** Think about what you have learned about the rivers of Europe and Russia. Explain why the direction in which rivers flow is important.

Graphic Organizer

Copy the chart onto a separate sheet of paper. Then, using information from the chapter, fill in the empty boxes.

	Physical Features	Climate	Vegetation	Natural Resources
Europe				
Russia				

Map Activity

Europe and Russia

For each place listed below, write the letter from the map that shows its location. Use the maps in the Atlas at the back of the book to help you.

1. Europe
2. Ural Mountains
3. Alps
4. Siberia
5. Rhine River
6. Volga River
7. North Sea

Writing Activity

Writing a Travel Brochure

Write a travel brochure for Americans who want to visit Siberia. Provide descriptions of the land, climate, and plant life. Suggest clothing for the trip.

Take It to the NET

Activity Use the Internet to learn more about the climates and landforms of Europe and Russia. Make a map showing what you have learned. For help in completing this activity, visit **www.phschool.com**.

Chapter 6 Self-Test To review what you have learned, take the Chapter 6 Self-Test and get instant feedback on your answers. Go to **www.phschool.com** to take the test.

Skills Review

Turn to the Skills Activity.

Review the steps for using a time zone map. Then, use the U.S. time zone map to find the current time for the following places:

a) where you are
b) Boston, Massachusetts
c) Anchorage, Alaska

How Am I Doing?

Answer these questions to help you check your progress.

1. Can I identify and describe the main physical features of Europe and Russia?
2. Can I give some examples of how physical features, climate, and vegetation affect life in Europe and Russia?
3. Can I identify important natural resources of Europe and Russia?
4. What information from this chapter can I include in my journal?

CHAPTER 7

EUROPE AND RUSSIA

Shaped by History

SECTION 1
From Ancient Greece to Feudal Europe

SECTION 2
Renaissance and Revolution

SECTION 3
Industrial Revolution and Nationalism

SECTION 4
Imperial Russia

SECTION 5
The Rise and Fall of the Soviet Union

PICTURE ACTIVITIES

This is the Colosseum in Rome. It is an example of the ancient Romans' great skill in building. To help you understand the importance of this building, complete the following activities.

Write a caption

Identify the main features of this building. Then write a caption describing these features.

Sketch an American landmark

Sketch a building you think is a symbol of the United States. You might choose the United States Capitol or the Empire State Building in New York City. How is this building important to Americans? What do you think of when you see a picture of it?

From Ancient Greece to Feudal Europe

Reach Into Your Background

The accomplishments of ancient Europe still have an impact on our world. What U.S. accomplishments do you know about? Think of some great things Americans have done. Explain why people remember these achievements today.

Questions to Explore

1. What were the main accomplishments of the ancient Greeks and Romans?
2. What was the impact of Christianity and feudalism on life during the Middle Ages?

Key Terms

Middle Ages
democracy
city-state
policy
empire
Pax Romana
feudalism
manor
serf

Key People and Places

Alexander the Great
Augustus
Constantine
Athens
Rome

For many years now, on a special morning in April, thousands of people from around the world have come together in a small Massachusetts town. At noon, they begin a marathon race that requires great strength and willpower. The race ends in the city of Boston, some 26 miles (42 km) away.

But what does the Boston Marathon have to do with European history? To find out, you need to go back 2,500 years to a story about the ancient Greek city of Athens. In 490 B.C., the people of Athens were at war with the Persians. The Athenians finally won at the Battle of Marathon. To announce their victory, an Athenian soldier named Pheidippides (fuh DIP uh deez) ran all the way to Athens, about 25 miles (40 km) away. Pheidippides reached Athens and shouted, "Rejoice, we conquer!" as he entered the city. Then he died.

The story of Pheidippides may or may not be true. But the Greeks loved the story, and people all over the world still run long races called marathons. In repeating this race, people show how history lives on. This

▼ The glory of ancient Greece inspires each running of the Boston Marathon. Shown here is Moses Tanui of Kenya, the winner in the 1996 men's race.

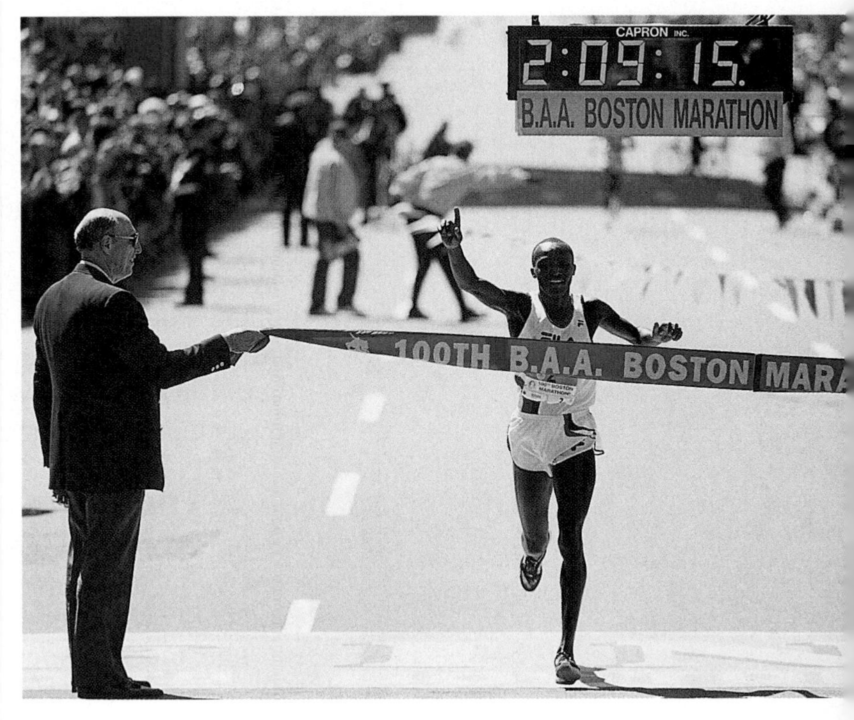

Greece's Accomplishments Live On

Chart Study Greece, whose ideas influence us to this day, borrowed ideas from older civilizations in Mesopotamia and Egypt. But the Greeks sometimes failed to give much credit to these other societies. In fact, the famous Greek thinker Plato bragged, "Whatever the Greeks have acquired from foreigners, they have, in the end, turned into something finer." **Critical Thinking** Which of Greece's achievements do you think has had the most important influence on our lives today? Why?

Area of Achievement	Influence on Modern Society
Drama	Aristotle created the rules for drama known as *The Poetics*. These rules are still used in plays and movie scripts.
Architecture	Many modern building designs reflect the common Greek styles known as Ionic, Doric, and Corinthian.
Science	The ancient Greeks introduced many principles of modern medicine, physics, biology, and mathematics.
Politics	The democratic ideals of government by the people, trial by jury, and equality under the law were formed in Athens around 500 B.C.
History	Herodotus collected information from people who remembered the events of the Persian wars. This method of research set the standard for the way history is recorded today.

chapter discusses three periods in the history of Europe and Russia—ancient times; recent times; and the time between the two, called the **Middle Ages.** We will see how the past affects the present in Europe and Russia.

The Greek Heritage

The Athenians and other ancient Greeks were Europe's first great philosophers, historians, poets, and writers. They did not accept old ways and old thinking. Instead, they observed plants, animals, and the human body. In the process, they invented today's scientific way of gathering knowledge. The Greeks also invented ideas about how people should live. One idea was **democracy** (dih MAHK ruh see), a kind of government that citizens run themselves.

Connect How was democracy in Athens different from today's democracy in the United States?

The Power of Democracy In ancient times, there were over a hundred **city-states** in Greece. Each was both a city and an independent nation. This gave the Greeks plenty of chances to try different kinds of government. Many of their city-states were democracies.

The most famous Greek city-state was Athens. In this city-state, every male citizen voted on laws and government **policies,** or the methods and plans a government uses to do its work. Citizens were either elected or chosen at random for government positions.

Democracy was a fresh idea for the Greeks, but it was not the same as what we call democracy today. Citizens in Greece owned slaves. Non-Greeks, women, and slaves were not citizens. They could not vote. Still, the Greek idea that citizens should have a voice in their own government had a strong impact on people in later times.

▲ The Greek thinker Aristotle, shown here in this marble sculpture, was Alexander the Great's teacher. Later, Alexander spread Aristotle's ideas across an empire.

Greek Ideas Spread Greek ideas might have stayed within their city-states if not for a young man named Alexander, later called Alexander the Great. At age 20, he became king of Macedonia (mas uh DOH nee uh), in northern Greece. But he was not satisfied with this small kingdom. In 334 B.C., Alexander set out to conquer the world. In only 10 years, he conquered an empire almost as big as the United States. An **empire** is a collection of lands ruled by a single government.

In all his new lands, Alexander established Greek cities, the Greek language, and Greek ideas. At the time of his death, in 323 B.C., Greek culture linked the entire Mediterranean world. The people who next ruled the region, the Romans, borrowed much from the Greeks.

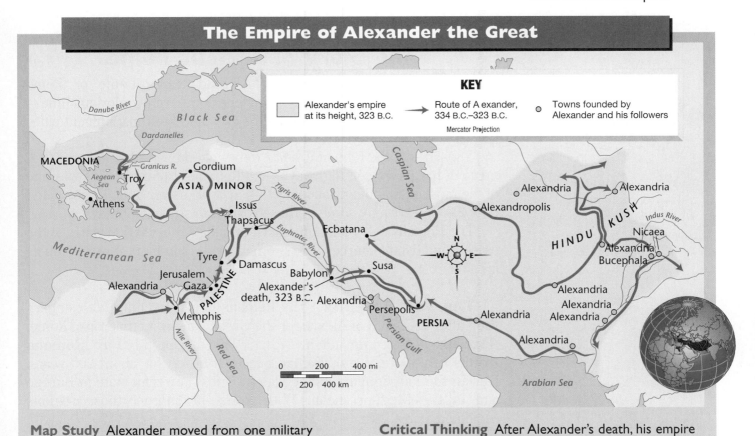

The Empire of Alexander the Great

KEY

Alexander's empire at its height, 323 B.C.

Route of Alexander, 334 B.C.–323 B.C.

Towns founded by Alexander and his followers

Mercator Projection

Map Study Alexander moved from one military victory to the next without losing a single battle. **Movement** How many towns did Alexander and his followers establish?

Critical Thinking After Alexander's death, his empire split into pieces. Why do you think Alexander's empire was difficult to keep united?

Peace Through Strength

Even during the Pax Romana, Roman citizens continued to serve in the military. They kept the peace by stopping revolts in Egypt, Germany, and Britain. This carving showing Roman soldiers is on a column honoring Antoninus Pius, the emperor of Rome from A.D. 138-161. Antoninus Pius ruled Rome during the calmest period of the Pax Romana.

Visualize Visualize the building of roads and aqueducts without modern equipment.

The Glory of Ancient Rome

Have you ever heard the saying "All roads lead to Rome" or "Rome was not built in a day"? These expressions come from a glorious time—when the Roman Empire ruled a huge area and built magnificent cities and structures.

The cities of the Roman Empire were linked by roads—about 50,000 miles of hard-surfaced highways. The Roman system of roads was one of the most outstanding transportation networks ever built. Constructed over 2,000 years ago, some of these roads are still used today.

The Romans also built aqueducts, or canals that carried water to the cities from distant sources. Like Roman roads, some of these aqueducts are still in use.

The Pax Romana The Romans began building their empire soon after the death of Alexander the Great. The first emperor of Rome, Augustus, took command in 27 B.C. This began the **Pax Romana** (pahks roh MAH nah), or Roman peace. It lasted for about 200 years. During the Pax Romana, Rome was the most powerful state in Europe and in the Mediterranean. With Rome in charge, these regions remained stable.

Roman Law One of Rome's greatest gifts to the world was a system of laws. Roman lawmakers were careful and organized. They did not pass their laws on by word of mouth. Instead, they wrote them down. When a judge made a decision, he based it on written law. His decision was also put in writing to guide other judges. After a while, the law became so complex that the Romans organized it. Today, the legal system of almost every European country reflects the organization of ancient Roman law.

Roman laws protected all citizens. At first, citizens included only people who lived in Rome, except slaves. In time, however, the term came to include people all over the empire. The idea thus protected the rights of all citizens, not just the powerful and wealthy. Modern ideas about law and citizenship are based on this idea.

The Decline of Rome Hundreds of years of warfare followed the Pax Romana. People outside the empire grew strong and broke through Roman lines of defense. Sometimes they even entered Rome itself. There they terrorized, looted, and destroyed. The empire needed more and more soldiers. To pay for the wars, the government raised taxes. This hurt the empire's economy. The empire had grown too big for one person to govern, so it was divided into two empires, one in the eastern Mediterranean and one in the west. The eastern empire remained healthy. But the western one continued to weaken.

The Volcano and the City of Pompeii The city of Pompeii stood at the foot of a volcano called Mt. Vesuvius. In A.D. 79, the volcano erupted. Smoke, ash, and cinders rained on the city. In two days, the eruption covered the city with about 20 feet (6.6 m) of ash. It sealed the city like a volcanic "time capsule." Archaeologists have uncovered Pompeii's buildings, almost perfectly intact. They have even found loaves of bread in ovens!

◀This statue shows Augustus, who ruled Rome from 27 B.C. to A.D. 14. He declared that he had "found Rome brick and left it marble." Indeed, during the reign of Augustus, Rome's first emperor, the Romans constructed many buildings and built roads, bridges, and aqueducts.

The weakening of the Roman Empire in Western Europe led to a time of uncertainty. The powerful laws of the great Roman government no longer protected people. People had to look elsewhere for something to protect them.

Europe in the Middle Ages

Picture a building like a hollow mountain of stones. Each stone has been cut and set in place by careful workers. The building's graceful arches sweep to the sky. This building is a cathedral—a great church. Many cathedrals were built in Europe during the Middle Ages.

Today, a building can be raised in a few months. But in the Middle Ages, it took as long as 100 years to build a cathedral. People devoted so much time and energy to building cathedrals because they believed that the work was God's wish. Such strong religious faith was a key part of life in Europe during the Middle Ages.

▼ Paris's Notre Dame Cathedral took about 150 years to complete. It was one of the first buildings constructed with flying buttresses, which are supporting arches on the outside of the building.

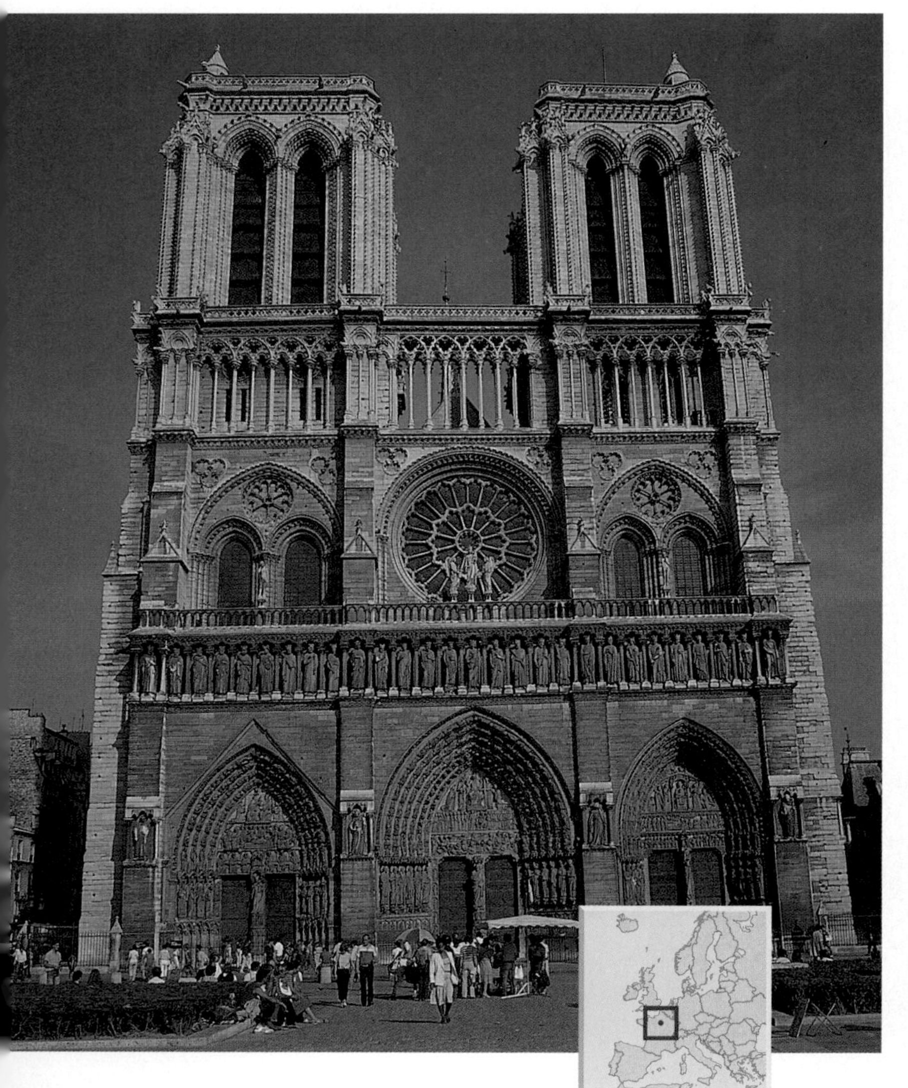

Christian Faith The religion of Christianity arose from the life and teachings of Jesus, who lived in a region called Palestine. After Jesus' death, his followers began spreading his teachings. These followers taught that Jesus was the Son of God.

One person who became a Christian, or follower of Jesus Christ, was a Roman emperor named Constantine. Christianity spread quickly throughout the Roman Empire. Later, the empire collapsed. Government, law and order, and trade broke down. But Christianity remained. The people of Europe, living in a period of difficulty and danger, drew strength from Christianity. In such dark times, faith was like a welcoming light.

Feudalism Christianity was one important part of people's lives during the Middle Ages. Another was **feudalism** (FYOOD ul iz um), which is a way to organize society when there is no central government. In feudalism, leaders called lords ruled the local areas. Lords swore oaths of loyalty to a more powerful leader, such as a king. In return, the king allowed the lord to own a piece of land called a **manor.** The lord owned all the crops and received all income from the land. He collected taxes, maintained order, enforced laws, and protected the **serfs,**

Feudal Society

Chart Study
European society in the Middle Ages was shaped like a pyramid. At the bottom were serfs, who made up 90 percent of the population. Above the serfs were the nobles, made up of knights, lords, and the king. Though there were many fewer nobles than serfs, the nobles had nearly all the wealth and power.
Critical Thinking
How did the feudal system tie different social groups together?

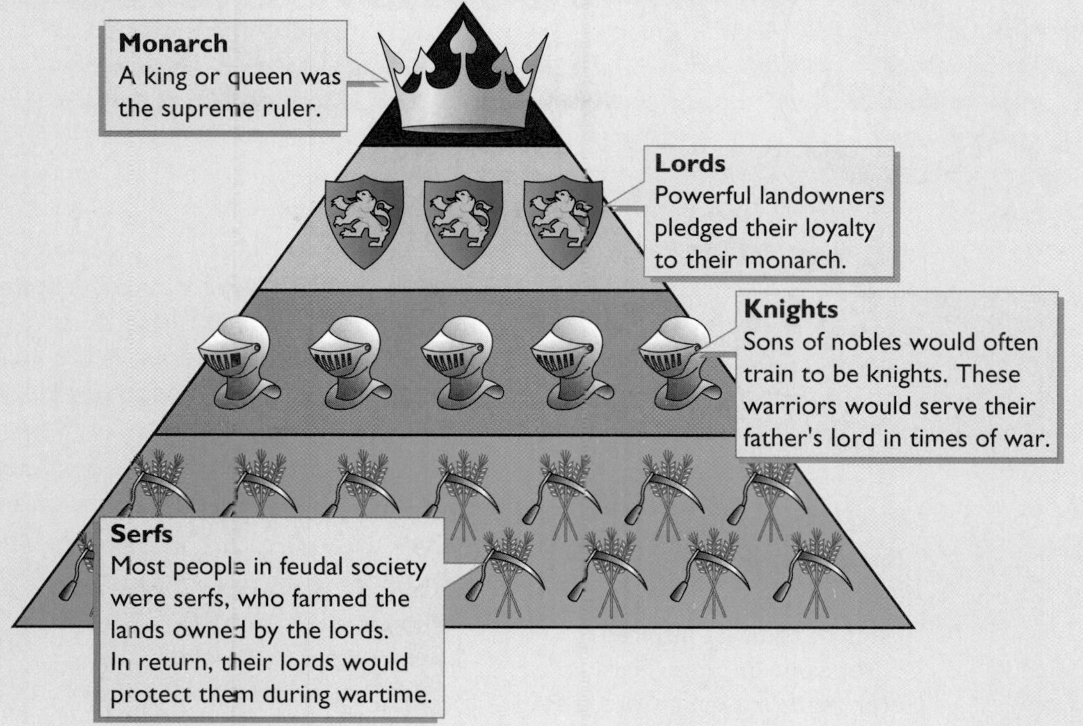

the people who lived on the land and farmed it. Serfs were not slaves, but they could not leave without the lord's permission. They owned no land and depended on the lord for protection in times of war.

Monarch
A king or queen was the supreme ruler.
Lords
Powerful landowners pledged their loyalty to their monarch.
Knights
Sons of nobles would often train to be knights. These warriors would serve their father's lord in times of war.
Serfs
Most people in feudal society were serfs, who farmed the lands owned by the lords. In return, their lords would protect them during wartime.

As centuries passed, life in Europe changed. Trade increased. Many serfs bought their freedom from the lords and moved to towns, which offered excitement and opportunity. Towns grew into cities. By the 1400s, a new way of life had begun to develop in Europe.

1. **Define** (a) Middle Ages, (b) democracy, (c) city-state, (d) policy, (e) empire, (f) Pax Romana, (g) feudalism, (h) manor, (i) serf.
2. **Identify** (a) Alexander the Great, (b) Augustus, (c) Constantine, (d) Athens, (e) Rome.
3. What were the most important ideas given to us by (a) the ancient Greeks and (b) the ancient Romans?
4. What role did Christianity play during the Middle Ages?
5. What did feudalism provide during the Middle Ages?

Critical Thinking

6. **Making Comparisons** Describe some ways in which Europe under the Pax Romana was different from Europe in the Middle Ages.

Activity

7. **Writing to Learn** You are a Roman governor in Britain, far from your home and family in Rome. Write a journal entry describing the things you miss about Rome. Be as specific as you can.

Renaissance and Revolution

Reach Into Your Background

Tales of rich and wondrous lands to the east inspired European explorers. Have you ever read or seen stories that made you want to travel to distant lands? Think of a list of places that you would like to visit. Write a few sentences telling how you learned about them and why you want to visit them.

Questions to Explore

1. Why did Europeans begin to look outward to other continents?
2. How did the Age of Revolution change science and government?

Key Terms

Renaissance
humanism
monarch
middle class
absolute monarch
revolution
colony
Scientific Revolution

Key People

Marco Polo
Michelangelo
Louis XIV

▼ More than 100 years after Marco Polo's departure from Venice in 1271, illustrations like this celebrated his adventures.

The time is about A.D. 1295. The place is a prison in an Italian city called Genoa (JEN uh wuh). An explorer named Marco Polo lies on a cot, telling stories to a fellow prisoner. The tales are amazing because Marco Polo has had quite a life! For a time, he was a messenger of the great Mongol (MAHN gul) emperor Kublai Khan (KOO bly kahn), ruler of China. Polo also traveled across burning deserts and sailed south of the Equator. He visited the Spice Islands, sources of cinnamon, nutmeg, and cloves—spices that Europeans loved. He earned great riches, only to be robbed on his way home to Italy.

These stories were published in a book we know today as *The Travels of Marco Polo.* From the very beginning, the book was a great success. Two hundred years later, Marco Polo's book inspired Christopher Columbus, another explorer. When Columbus sailed west from Europe, he was searching for a new route to the rich lands Marco Polo had described: China, Japan, and India.

The Renaissance in Art

Leonardo da Vinci (above), one of the best-known artists of the Renaissance, is famous for his painting, *Mona Lisa* (left). But he also excelled as a scientist, an engineer, and an inventor.

Glories of the Renaissance

Columbus's search for a new route to wealth was only one example of the energy sweeping Europe. The changes began in Italy in the 1300s and spread over the continent. Traders were busy buying and selling again. The rich were becoming even richer. They had the time to enjoy art and learning—and the money to support artists and scholars. This period is called the **Renaissance** (REN uh sahns), which refers to a "rebirth" of interest in learning and art. The Renaissance reached its peak in the 1500s.

Renaissance scholars and artists rediscovered the ancient world. Once again, people learned about its great poetry, plays, ideas, buildings, and sculpture. What they learned changed them. They began writing fresh, powerful poetry. They built glorious new buildings and filled them with breathtaking paintings. People began to focus on improving this world rather than hoping for a better life after death. In trying to understand the world around them, they looked at the ideas of Greek and Roman thinkers. This new approach to knowledge was called **humanism.**

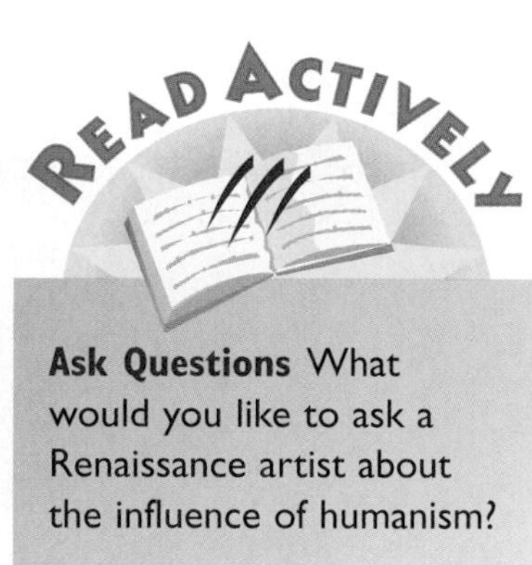

Ask Questions What would you like to ask a Renaissance artist about the influence of humanism?

Humanism affected every part of the Renaissance. For example, in the early Middle Ages, statues had been carved as stiff symbols. But during the Renaissance period, statues carved by artists such as Michelangelo (my kul AN juh loh), an Italian sculptor, were lifelike. In fact, some people say that no better sculptor than Michelangelo has ever lived.

More Trade, Stronger Rulers

In the Renaissance, people also began to travel outside of Europe more often. In the 1400s, Portuguese explorers traveled along the western coast of Africa. There they traded in gold, ivory, and slaves. This trade was very profitable. Finally, the Portuguese reached the Indian Ocean. They set up new trade routes for the most profitable goods of all—spices. Rulers of other European countries envied the Portuguese. Spain, France, England, and the Netherlands all wanted a share of the trading wealth. Then, in 1492, Christopher Columbus found even more possibilities for wealth. Far to the west were two vast continents: the Americas.

The Effects of Trade Europeans raced to the Americas in search of wealth. Precious minerals, such as gold and silver, and trade goods, such as fur and tobacco, poured into Europe. Most of the wealth went to European **monarchs** (MAHN urks), rulers such as kings and queens. Some of it went to traders and merchants. These people formed a group between the poor and the very rich. They became the **middle class.** The taxes paid by the middle class made monarchs even wealthier. Soon, kings no longer needed the support of feudal lords. Feudalism declined, local lords grew weaker, and kings gained power.

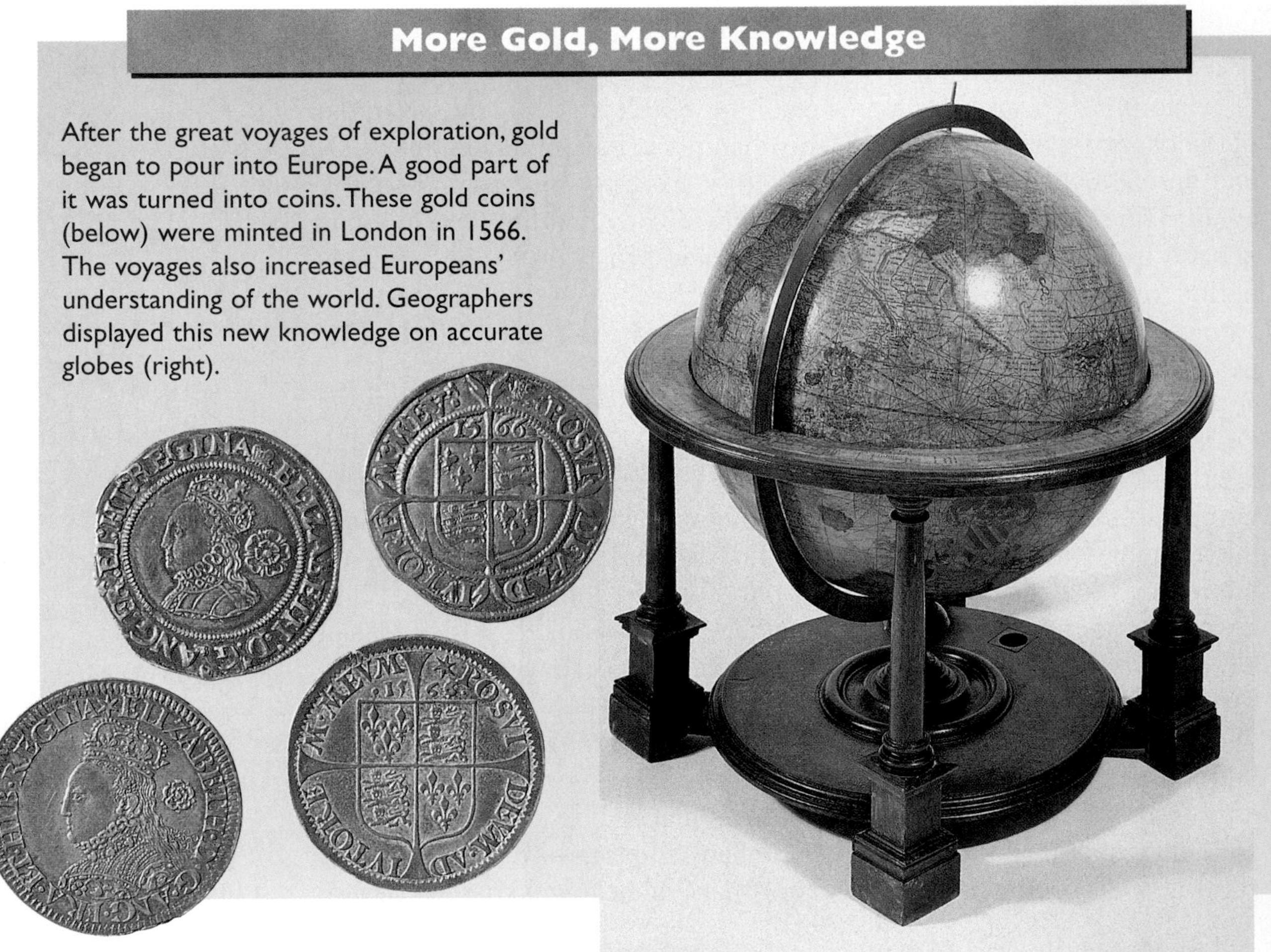

More Gold, More Knowledge

After the great voyages of exploration, gold began to pour into Europe. A good part of it was turned into coins. These gold coins (below) were minted in London in 1566. The voyages also increased Europeans' understanding of the world. Geographers displayed this new knowledge on accurate globes (right).

The Age of Monarchs

From 1643 to 1715, the king of France was Louis XIV. One of Europe's most powerful kings, Louis XIV ruled at a time when France was a leading world power. Like other kings of his time, Louis was an **absolute monarch;** that is, he exercised complete power over his subjects. As he said, "I am the state." His wishes were law, and no one dared to disagree with him. Like other European monarchs, Louis believed that his power to rule came from God. To oppose him was the same as opposing God.

Louis used his power to make people pay heavy taxes. These taxes, in part, paid for his very expensive lifestyle. But Louis also wanted to make France strong. Other rulers wanted the same thing for their countries. Over time, these monarchs made their countries stronger and more unified. As these changes took place, people began thinking again about government. What should it be? What should it do for them?

Hall of Mirrors

Twelve miles from Paris, the palace at Versailles with its glittering Hall of Mirrors advertised the French king's wealth. Paintings on the ceiling illustrate the royal family's accomplishments.

Revolutions in Government and Science

The 1600s and 1700s are often called the Age of Revolution. A **revolution** is a far-reaching change. European thought, beliefs, and ways of life all changed. This period was the beginning of the modern age of science and democracy that we know today.

Revolutions in Government One sign of revolution was that people began questioning their governments. For instance, people wondered if kings should have all the power. In the 1600s, when England's king refused to share power with Parliament (PAHR luh munt), the elected legislature, he was overthrown. England had no monarch for several years. This change in power failed, and the monarchy returned. But this event showed that the people, not the monarch, should decide which type of government is best for them.

This idea of government spread to North America, where Great Britain had 13 colonies. A **colony** is a territory ruled by another nation,

A Share in Two Revolutions In 1776, Thomas Paine wrote *Common Sense,* a pamphlet urging the American colonies to fight for independence. The pamphlet sold more than 500,000 copies and greatly influenced the American Revolution. Later, Paine wrote *The Rights of Man,* in which he defended the French Revolution of 1789.

The French Revolution

On July 14, 1789, an angry French mob seized control of the Bastille, a prison (below). The people were angry at King Louis XVI and the queen, Marie Antoinette (right), because the monarchs were spending money on clothes and building projects at a time when the poor in Paris were starving. Eventually, the king and queen were both executed.

Predict How might humanism have affected science?

usually one far away. In 1776, the colonies rebelled against the British king. The colonists defeated the British and formed the independent nation of the United States. And in 1789, 13 years after the Americans declared their independence, there was a revolution in France. The French Revolution overthrew the French monarchy once and for all.

The Scientific Revolution There was also a revolution in science. For centuries, European scientists had studied nature to explain how the world fit with their religious beliefs. During the Age of Revolution, that approach changed. Scientists began to watch carefully to see what really happened in the world. They would base their theories on facts. They would not try to make the facts fit their religious beliefs. This change is called the **Scientific Revolution.**

The Scientific Revolution required new procedures. These procedures make up what is called the scientific method, in which ideas are tested with experiments and observations. Scientists do not accept an idea as correct unless several tests prove that it is.

Using the scientific method, scientists made dramatic advances. For example, in the Middle Ages, Europeans believed that the Earth was at the center of the universe. Later, Renaissance scientists challenged this belief. Then, during the Scientific Revolution, scientists used a new form

The Scientific Method

Chart Study A revolution in thinking paved the way for the scientific method, which today's scientists still use. Employing this method, scientists began to record what they could actually observe instead of what they merely believed to be true. Followers of the scientific method usually repeat their work many times, in order to make sure that their conclusions are accurate. **Critical Thinking** Why do you think scientists should repeat their work before coming to a conclusion?

STEP ONE
State the problem.

STEP TWO
Gather information about the problem.

STEP THREE
Form a hypothesis, or educated guess.

STEP FOUR
Experiment to test the hypothesis.

STEP FIVE
Record and analyze data.

STEP SIX
State a conclusion.

of mathematics called calculus (KAL kyoo lus). It helped them learn how the moon and planets move. Their work led to better ideas about such things as gravity.

By the end of the Age of Revolution, Europe was a continent of powerful nations. They were bustling with trade and bursting with new scientific ideas. Europe was about to begin a new kind of revolution. This time it would be an economic one—the rise of industry.

1. **Define** (a) Renaissance, (b) humanism, (c) monarch, (d) middle class, (e) absolute monarch, (f) revolution, (g) colony, (h) Scientific Revolution.
2. **Identify** (a) Marco Polo, (b) Michelangelo, (c) Louis XIV.
3. How did Europeans' desire for wealth lead to voyages of exploration?
4. How did the art of the Renaissance differ from the art of the Middle Ages?
5. How did government and science in Europe change during the Age of Revolution?

Critical Thinking

6. **Identifying Central Issues** Explain how trade affected the power of kings during the 1500s and 1600s.

Activity

7. **Writing to Learn** Marco Polo's writings excited readers and made them want to explore the world just like he had. Think about a place that you have visited. What makes it special? What details make you like it—or dislike it? Then write about the place in a way that would make a reader want to go there, too.

Interpreting Diagrams and Illustrations

Sandra bolted through the front door of her grandmother's house.

"Hey, Grandma! Dad just told me that you went to France once, before I was born."

"Yes, I did," said her grandmother. "I went to visit my mother's family. But I was much younger then."

"What was it like? What did you do there?" Sandra wanted to know all about it.

"Well, that little town looked a lot different than it does now—that was 40 years ago."

"Did they have knights and castles then?" Sandra asked eagerly.

Her grandmother laughed. "Oh, no, it wasn't *that* long ago. But you can see for yourself. I think I still have my pictures from that trip. Shall we get them out?"

Sandra nodded.

"There's just one problem," her grandmother warned. "You'll understand the pictures, but all the writing is in French!"

Get Ready

There are many kinds of illustrations—maps, photographs, paintings, drawings, and diagrams, to name a few. Often, diagrams and illustrations are explained by captions and annotations. Annotations are labels that include extra information. They help you understand diagrams and illustrations.

To get the most out of any illustration, you need to study carefully both the illustration itself and all of the annotations. You may find this even more useful when you look at illustrations of life long ago. These illustrations can bring history alive for you. They can help you picture life in other times and other places.

◀ You can learn how to interpret diagrams and illustrations by making one of your own. In addition to the labels shown on this mailbox, the student might have added a caption such as "The post office collects the mail and delivers it to the recipients."

Try It Out

Of course, the world today is much different than the world young people lived in hundreds of years ago. Far in the future, the world will be much different than it is now. Students many years from now will read in their history books about the way *you* live. You can help them out by creating an illustration to help them picture "life long ago"—your life today.

A. Choose your subject. Draw an illustration of something that is common today but might not be common in the future. Perhaps chalkboards will be replaced by computers, or automobiles by personal jets. Be sure to draw something you know well.

B. Illustrate your subject. Using a pencil and unlined paper, draw your subject. Try to be as accurate as possible. Imagine that the students of the future will never have seen the real thing.

C. Add annotations to your illustration. Write brief notes explaining the main features of what you have drawn. Try to have your annotations explain the object's parts. Tell how they are used or how they relate to each other.

Apply the Skill

Now that you have made your own illustration and annotations, you can read one by someone else. Complete the following steps.

1. **Study the illustration.** Look it over in a general way. What is the subject of this illustration? From what time period is it? Does it show something as it really looked, or does it show how something might have looked?

2. **Read the annotations.** The annotations provide key information about the illustration. What are the main parts of a manor? Who lived in the manor house? How were the fields divided? What was the demesne (dih MAYN)? How were the meadows used? Where did the serfs live?

3. **Think about the illustration.** After you have studied the illustration and read the annotations, take another look. This time, imagine yourself as the lord of the manor, or as a serf who worked there. What was life like for you? Write a journal entry from this point of view. Try to capture the sights, sounds, and smells of life on the manor.

A Medieval Manor

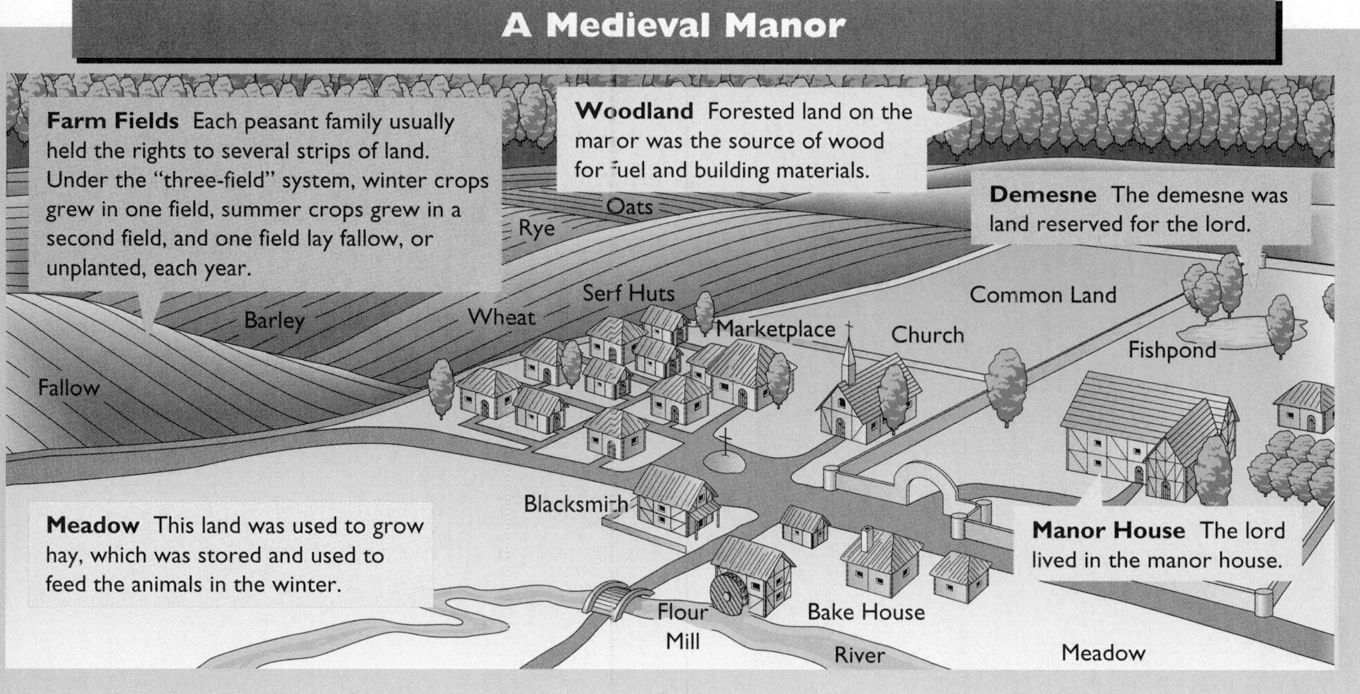

Industrial Revolution and Nationalism

Reach Into Your Background

Have you ever spent a whole day working very hard? Perhaps you helped with spring housecleaning or took part in a car wash. Do you remember how tired you were at the end of the day? During the Industrial Revolution, many people your age worked in factories 12 hours a day, 6 days a week.

Questions to Explore

1. How did the Industrial Revolution change life in Europe?
2. How did nationalism change Europe?

Key Terms

Industrial Revolution
textile
imperialism
nationalism
alliance

It was dawn. Thick, black smoke rose from the tall smokestack of the factory. Dust blew through the air and settled over the crowded rows of houses. The smoke and the roar of machines showed that the factory workday had begun.

Inside, women and children worked at rows of machines that wove cotton thread into cloth. Their work was dirty, noisy, and dangerous. The day before, a worker had caught his hand in a machine and was severely injured. Today, another worker stood in his place. Both were only 13 years old. No matter what, the machines kept going. Workers fed them thread for 12 hours every day—6 days out of every 7. Vacations did not exist.

You could see scenes like this all across Europe in the early 1800s. The great age of factories had begun. Products that once had been made by people in homes or in small shops were now made by machines in huge factories. This change is called the **Industrial Revolution.** The new factories caused great suffering. But as time went by, the rise of industry brought an easier way of life to people all over the world.

▼ This late 1800s picture shows smoke belching from factories beside the Don River in Sheffield, an industrial city in northern England.

From Spinning Wheel to Spinning Mule

During the Industrial Revolution, spinning wheels (below) were replaced by spinning mules (left) that could spin up to 1,300 times as much thread in the same amount of time. Special buildings, called factories, were built to house the spinning mules. **Critical Thinking** How do you think the shift from spinning wheel to spinning mule affected the average worker?

The Industrial Revolution

Did you ever wonder what life would be like without factories? You would have to make everything you need at home or buy it from a small shop nearby. People produced goods this way until about the late 1700s. Then, inventors began to create machines that could make goods quickly and cheaply. Huge factories housed the machines. People left their homes to work in the factories and keep the machines running. This was a revolution in the way goods were made. It was also a revolution in the ways people lived and worked.

Changes in Production The Industrial Revolution began in Great Britain. The first machines were invented to speed up the spinning of thread and the weaving of **textiles,** or cloth products. The new factories made their owners very wealthy. Businesspeople in other countries saw this and decided to try the same thing. Factories sprouted up all over Europe and in the United States. By 1900, factories produced almost all goods made in the United States and most of Western Europe.

Changes in Society The Industrial Revolution changed life across Europe. For hundreds of years, families had farmed the land. Now they moved to industrial centers to work in factories. Cities grew rapidly. People were packed into cramped, dirty housing. Because of unclean and crowded conditions, diseases spread rapidly.

Urbanization When industrialization took hold in Europe, people moved from the country to the cities in huge numbers. In 100 years, the population of London grew from 831,000 to 4.5 million. The population of Paris grew from 547,000 to 2.9 million.

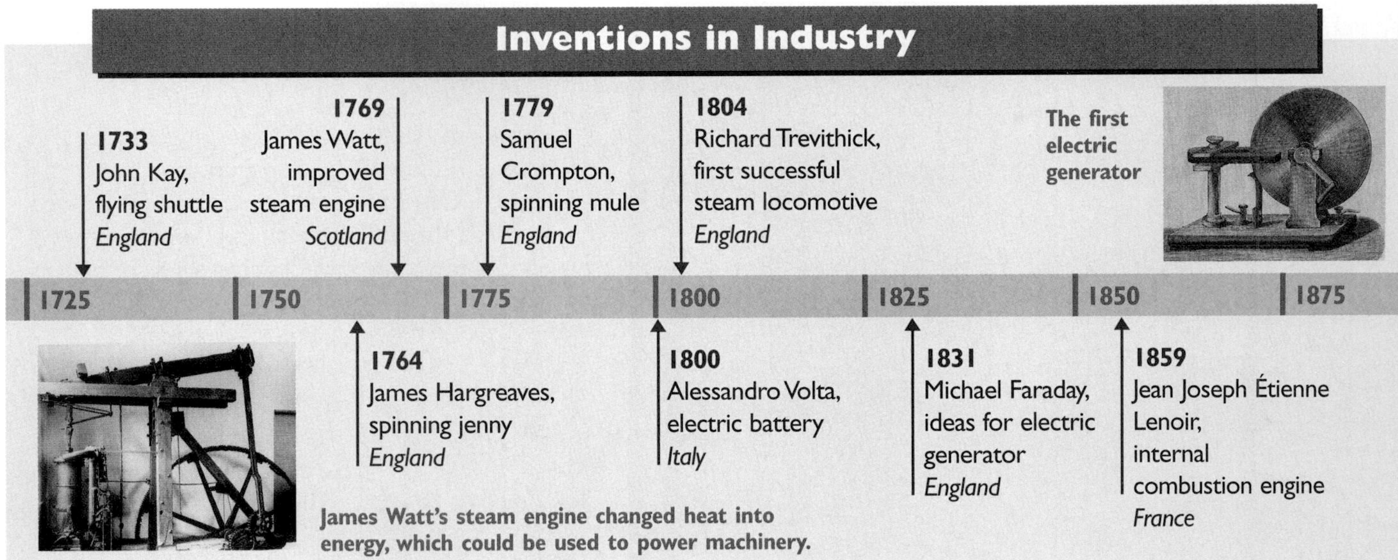

James Watt's steam engine changed heat into energy, which could be used to power machinery.

▲ As you read the time line, find the inventions that could be used to produce power. These inventions paved the way for machines that required more energy than humans or animals could provide.

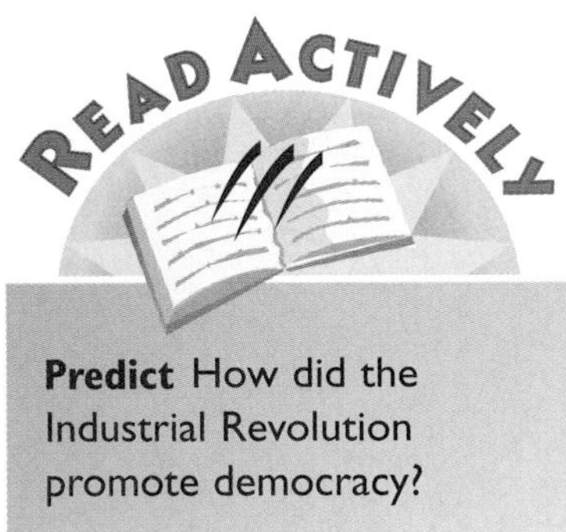

Predict How did the Industrial Revolution promote democracy?

The changes were difficult for many people. For a long time, factory owners took advantage of workers. Wages were low. Factory conditions were not safe. However, workers slowly began to form labor unions and to demand better working conditions. In the early 1900s, governments began passing laws to protect workers. Conditions improved and wages rose.

Changes in Government Government had to respond to workers' complaints. Making and selling goods was a big part of a country's economy. This meant that workers had become very important. As a result, the Industrial Revolution helped give working people a bigger voice in government. Many European nations became more democratic.

At the same time, though, European governments were becoming more aggressive abroad. During the 1800s, many European nations took over other countries and turned them into colonies. This is called **imperialism.** European nations were making more goods than their people could buy. They needed more customers. Colonies could supply those buyers. Colonies also provided raw materials, such things as cotton, wood, and metals, that industry needed.

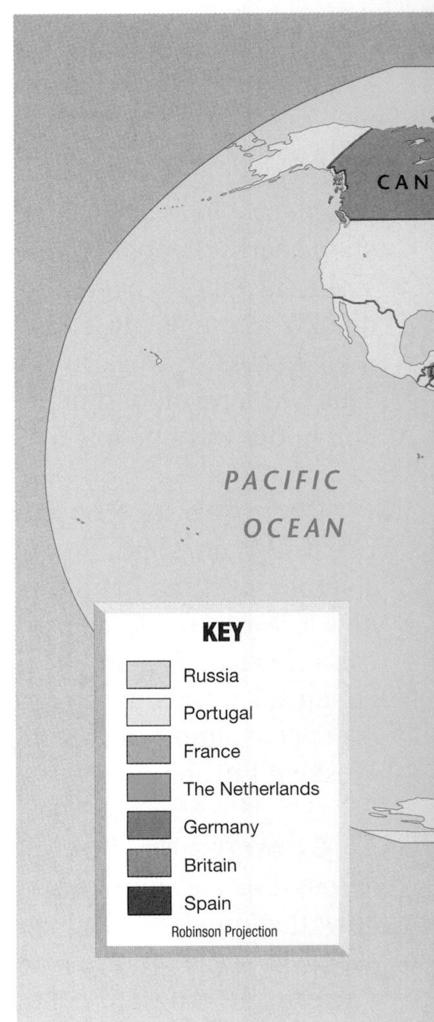

The late 1800s are called the Age of Imperialism. Most of Africa was divided up by the European nations of Belgium, France, Italy, Spain, Portugal, Germany, and Great Britain. These countries also took over much of Southeast Asia and many South Pacific islands. In time, struggles among the colonial powers would bring disaster to Europe.

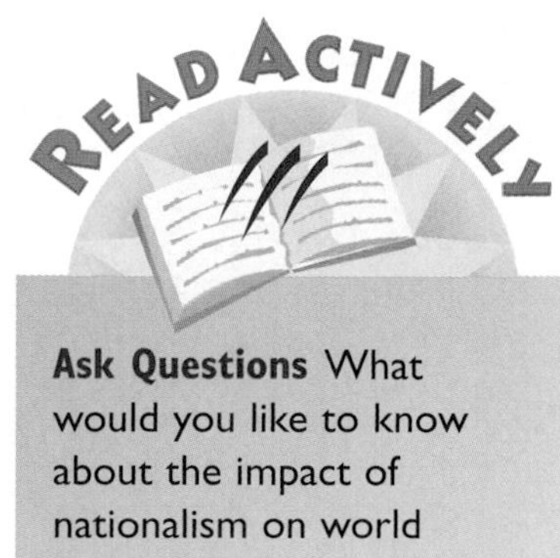

Ask Questions What would you like to know about the impact of nationalism on world history?

A Century of War and Nationalism

At the start of the 1900s, the people of Europe were filled with **nationalism,** or pride in one's country. Nationalism can either be a destructive or creative force, depending on how people express it.

Destructive Nationalism Nationalism can be very destructive. It can make one nation harm another in an effort to get ahead. It can also prevent nations from working with one another. Then anger and hatred can erupt between countries. Between 1900 and 1950, destructive nationalism played a part in causing two world wars and the deaths of millions of people.

European Imperialism, 1900

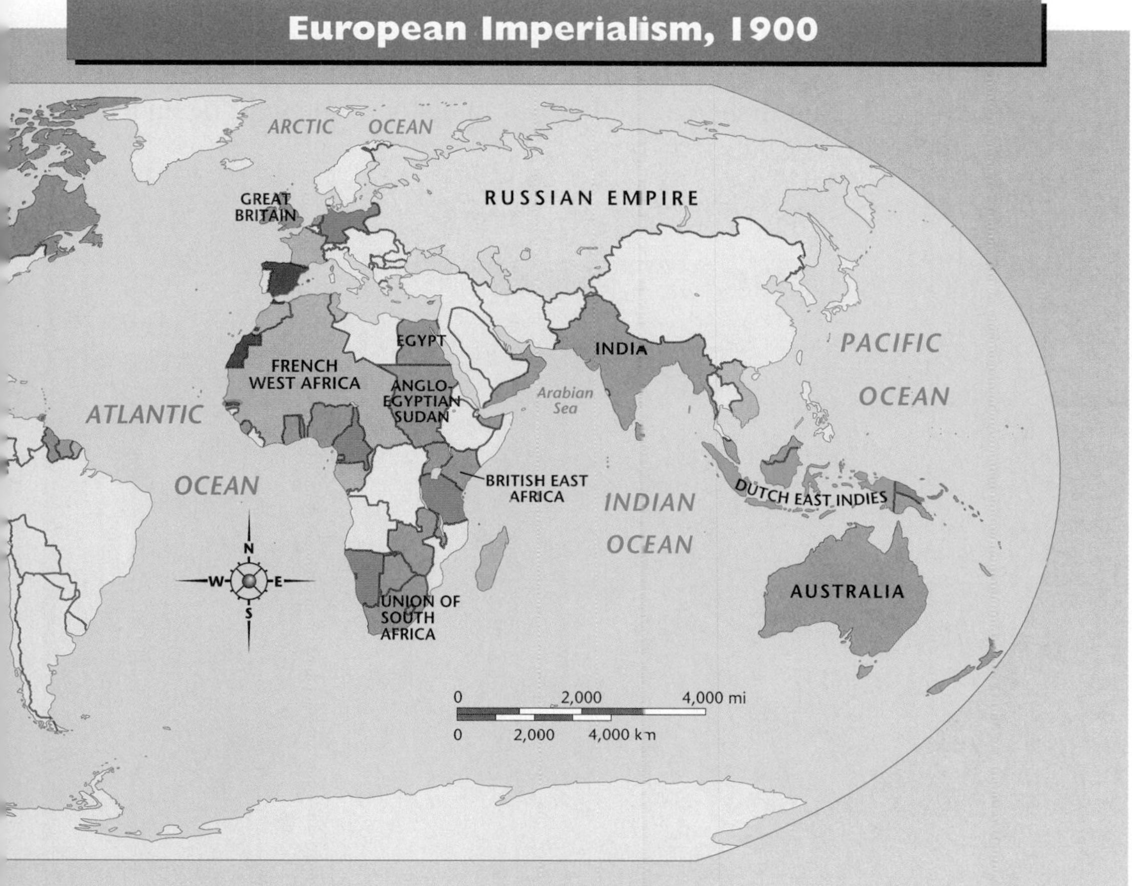

Map Study Europe's history of colonizing other parts of the world did not begin in 1900. European countries began colonizing the Americas in the 1500s. Most of the Americas had become independent by 1900. **Regions** What three European countries had the largest empires in 1900?

Working Together
Jeannine Picabia was 18 in 1941. She worked with a French medical group that traveled to places where prisoners were questioned by German soldiers. She listened carefully to the conversations. One day she decided to go to an American government building in France to tell what she had heard. Secretly, for the rest of World War II, she gathered information for the forces that were trying to defeat Germany.

During the early 1900s, European nations feared one another. Each nation was afraid another would invade or try to take over its territory. To protect themselves, nations made **alliances** (uh LY un sez), or agreements with one another. In such alliances, a nation promises to protect its friends if someone attacks them. Soon, Europe was divided into two alliances. On one side were Germany, Austria-Hungary, and Turkey. On the other side were Great Britain, France, and Russia.

In 1914, fighting between the alliances broke out into what is now called World War I. By the end of the war, in 1918, over 9 million soldiers had been killed. About 13 million civilians, or nonsoldiers, had also died. Europe had lost almost a whole generation of young men.

But nationalism still burned like a flame. In 1939, another war broke out. This war was called World War II. Again there were two alliances. On one side were the Axis Powers—Germany and Italy, which were joined by Japan. These countries wanted to increase their national wealth and power. Therefore, they took control of other countries. They quickly captured most of Europe and parts of China and the South Pacific. Germany also attacked the Soviet Union, a nation made up of Russia and several smaller regions.

In time, the United States joined the Allies—Great Britain and the Soviet Union—in the battle against the Axis Powers. More than 50 nations took part in this war, which was the most destructive ever fought. More people died, more property was damaged, and more money was spent than in any other war in history. The fighting ended in August 1945. The Allies had won.

▼ One of the most frightening weapons of World War I was poison gas. These Russian soldiers are caught in a German gas attack.

A Tunnel Connecting Britain to France

During the Ice Age, France and Great Britain were connected by a low plain. Later, the English Channel separated Britain and France—but not forever. In 1987, France and Great Britain began working together to dig a tunnel under the English Channel. In 1994, these men dug the breakthrough hole linking Britain and France. They exchanged flags and shook hands. Today trains carry passengers and freight through the Channel Tunnel, which many people call the Chunnel. **Critical Thinking** What do you think kept Great Britain and France from building the Chunnel earlier?

Creative Nationalism After the war, all of Europe was in ruins. It was time to rebuild. The European nations were sick of imperialism and war. After hundreds of years, they were no longer world leaders. Now the world looked on the United States and the Soviet Union as leading nations.

Europeans began learning to work together. They became trading partners, not competitors. A new type of nationalism began, a European nationalism. People have not forgotten that they are French, or British, or German. At the end of the 1900s, however, Europeans were working hard to build a common European community. It helped carry them into the new century in peace.

1. **Define** (a) Industrial Revolution, (b) textile, (c) imperialism, (d) nationalism, (e) alliance.
2. What changes occurred in the lives of ordinary people during the Industrial Revolution?
3. What changes in government occurred in industrialized nations during the Industrial Revolution?
4. Give an example of creative nationalism.

Critical Thinking

5. **Identifying Central Issues** The Industrial Revolution caused many changes. Name two changes that helped bring about imperialism.

Activity

6. **Writing to Learn** After World War II, colonies in Africa and Asia demanded their freedom from the European colonial powers. Suppose you were a citizen of a colony. Write a paragraph explaining why you would want to be free from European rulers.

Imperial Russia

Reach Into Your Background

The rulers of Russia could do almost anything they wanted. They could make any laws and carry out any plans they chose. Imagine being able to make any changes you wanted in the United States. What would you change? What would you keep the same?

Questions to Explore

1. How did Russia develop into a huge empire by 1900?
2. How did the serfs' living conditions lead to opposition to the czars?

Key Terms

westernization
czar

Key People

Catherine the Great
Golden Horde
Peter the Great
Nicholas II

At dawn on June 28, 1762, a maid awakened Catherine in her rooms at a small palace outside St. Petersburg, Russia. Catherine's supporter, Aleksei Orlov (ul yik SEEAY ur LAHF), was waiting for her. "Time to rise," he told her. "Everything is prepared." Catherine hurried to a coach waiting to whisk her to St. Petersburg.

▼ This picture shows Catherine the Great wearing the crown of the empress of Russia.

As the coach hurried along, Catherine may have remembered how she had first come to Russia, 17 years before. At age 16, she had been brought here from Germany to marry Peter, who later became emperor. Peter was a weak and foolish ruler. Now Catherine was hoping to remove him from the throne and become empress herself. Would the Russian people support her?

As Catherine's coach rattled down St. Petersburg's main street toward the Winter Palace, crowds streamed out to cheer her on. When she arrived at the palace, she was greeted by government, military, and church leaders. Their support helped make Catherine the new Empress of Russia.

Catherine was witty and charming. She loved the arts, literature, philosophy, and French culture. Under her rule, the court at St. Petersburg glittered with French actors and dancers, German teachers and craftspeople, and artistic treasures from foreign lands. Her court attracted the greatest minds of Europe. She dreamed of creating a great nation, as glorious as France under Louis XIV. Little wonder that she was called Catherine the Great.

Catherine cared about Russia. She built schools and hospitals and gave people more religious freedom. Early in her rule, she became interested in ideas about liberty. She even thought about freeing the serfs, the peasant farmers who worked on the estates of wealthy landowners. Then there was a violent serf revolt, and Catherine changed her mind. She strengthened control over the serfs and crushed their attempts to gain freedom.

Though Catherine did not make Russia a land of freedom, she did make Russia a grand empire. By her death in 1796, she had expanded her nation's borders southward to the edge of the Black Sea. She had also taken over parts of Poland in the west. Her expansion followed a pattern of empire-building that had been taking place in Russia for many centuries.

As Catherine's rule shows, the history of Russia is a story with three themes: (1) expansion; (2) harsh treatment of the common people; and (3) slow **westernization,** a process of becoming more like Western Europe. As you read Russia's story, notice how these three themes show up again and again.

Predict What changes do you think took place because of Mongol rule?

Building a Vast Empire

Russia began as a small country called Muscovy (MUHS kuh vee), or Moscow. In the early 1100s, Kiev (KEE ev) was the most important city in the region. It was home to the grand prince. Other, lesser princes ruled their own lands. They continually fought among themselves. Each hoped to gain enough power to become the grand prince. In 1238, Mongol conquerors, who were called the Golden Horde, swept into the region from Asia. Weakened by the struggles among themselves, the princes were defeated quickly. In 1240, the Mongols conquered Kiev and the whole territory became part of the Mongol empire.

A Mongol Archer

Russians called Mongol warriors like this archer the Golden Horde after the color of their tents. The Mongols plundered and burned Kiev and other Russian towns. They killed so many Russians that a historian claimed "no eye remained to weep for the dead."

Life Under the Golden Horde

The Golden Horde dominated Russia for almost 250 years. The Mongols mostly wanted two things: to collect heavy taxes and to force the Russians to serve in the Mongol army. The conquerors appointed a Russian prince to handle the day-to-day

Map Study Between 1300 and 1584, Russia was a small area around Moscow. Then, during the 1600s and 1700s, the country pushed its borders both to the east and to the west. In the 1900s, Russia became part of the Soviet Union. **Regions** Locate the Ural Mountains, the natural feature that mapmakers consider to be the boundary between Europe and Asia. In 1584, was Russia mostly in Europe or mostly in Asia? In 1955?

affairs of the country. To make sure that the people did not rebel, the Mongols attacked the country from time to time. Because Russia was cut off from the West by the Mongols, Russia did not take part in the Renaissance of art and learning that was changing Western Europe.

The Rise of Moscow During the early 1330s, the Mongols selected Ivan I of Muscovy to be grand prince. Ivan collected taxes for the Mongols. In return, they let him keep some of the money. Ivan the Moneybag, as he was soon called, began to buy land and expand the size of Muscovy.

As Muscovy grew stronger, the Mongol empire began to fall apart. In 1480, Ivan III, Grand Prince of Muscovy, challenged Mongol control by refusing to pay taxes. The Golden Horde was too weak to force its wishes on Ivan and take back control of Russia.

Rise of the Czars As Muscovy became more powerful and spread its control over Russia, its grand prince became known as a **czar** (zar), or emperor. The first czar, Ivan IV, was crowned in 1547. He was also known as Ivan the Terrible. He was cruel and distrusted others. But he increased Russia's size by conquering Mongol lands in the southeast and by conquering western Siberia.

After Ivan IV's death, Russia lived through nearly 30 years of war. Finally, in 1613, Michael Romanov (ROH muh nawf) became czar. He was the first in a long line of Romanovs who ruled Russia until 1917. The Romanovs expanded Russian territory through the 1600s.

In 1689, Peter the Great came to power. A strong leader, Peter started to bring Western European ideas and culture to Russia. In 1697, he sent a group of Russian officials to visit Western Europe. His goals were to find out about western culture and methods and to meet with European officials. Peter went along, dressed as a minor official. On his return to Russia, he started new schools and reorganized his government and the army. He hired foreign professors, scientists, and advisors. He encouraged Russians to adopt western customs.

Visualize Visualize Peter the Great in disguise in meetings with European officials.

◀The Winter Palace at St. Petersburg, completed in 1762, was the world's largest royal palace. It was the winter home of the czars until 1917.

Peter also enlarged Russia. He believed that Russia must have good seaports to become a world power, so he conquered land on the Baltic (BAWL tik) and Black seas. Czars who followed Peter, including Catherine the Great, continued to expand Russia's borders, gaining territories in Poland, Turkey, China, and Sweden. With many lands under its rule, Russia truly became an empire.

Peace Between Russia and Japan Between 1904 and 1905, Japan and Russia fought over control of Manchuria, in northeastern Asia, and Korea, a peninsula in East Asia. Finally, U.S. President Theodore Roosevelt arranged a peace conference in Portsmouth, New Hampshire. For his role in the settlement, Roosevelt was awarded the Nobel Peace Prize in 1906.

The Fall of the Czars

Russia was becoming powerful, but the lives of its serfs had not improved. For hundreds of years, Russia had been divided into two groups—the very rich and the very poor. Tension between the two groups began to rise.

In 1855, a new czar, Alexander II, came to the throne. He, too, wanted Russia to be more like European nations. One way to do that, he believed, was to have the czars and the wealthy give up some of their powers. In 1861, a few years before Abraham Lincoln ended slavery in the United States, Alexander freed the serfs and gave them their own land. Towns were given more control over their own affairs. However, Alexander's son, Czar Alexander III, reversed many of his father's reforms. The country again came under harsh rule.

In 1894, Nicholas II became czar. He would be the last. After Russia was badly beaten in a war with Japan in 1904 and 1905, unrest grew among serfs and workers. On January 22, 1905, thousands of workers in

The Russian Famine of 1892

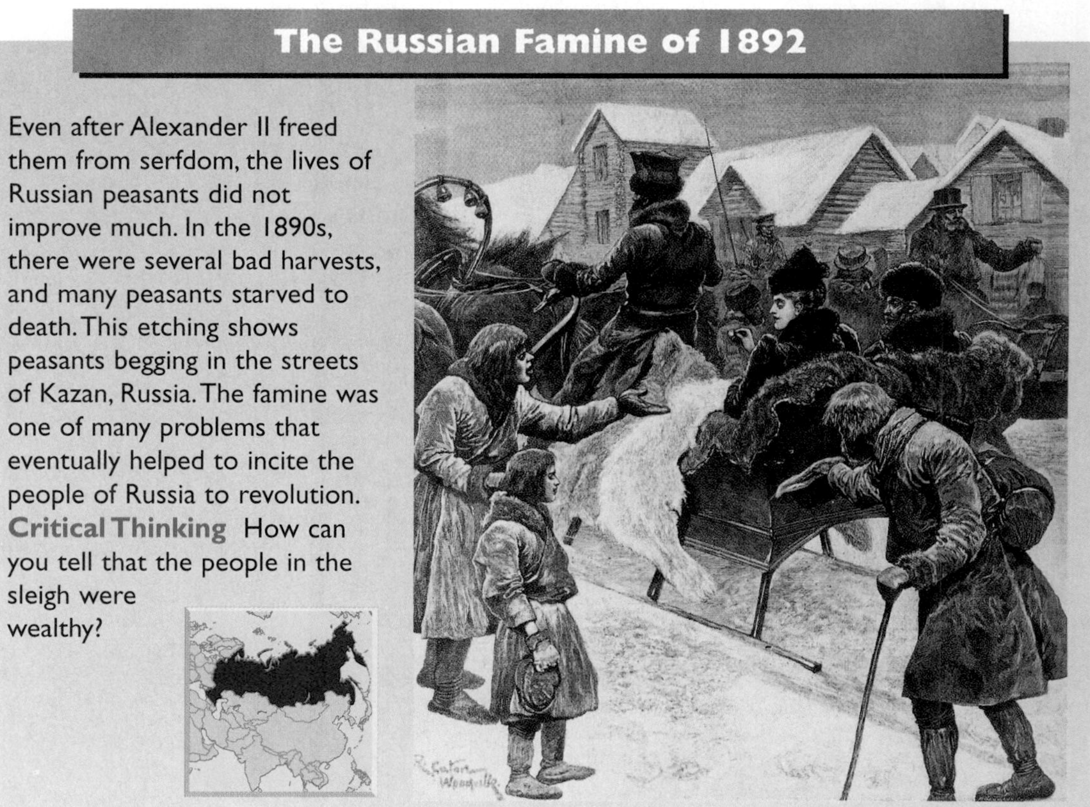

Even after Alexander II freed them from serfdom, the lives of Russian peasants did not improve much. In the 1890s, there were several bad harvests, and many peasants starved to death. This etching shows peasants begging in the streets of Kazan, Russia. The famine was one of many problems that eventually helped to incite the people of Russia to revolution. **Critical Thinking** How can you tell that the people in the sleigh were wealthy?

The Czar and the Czarevitch

Czar Nicholas II (right) and his son Alexis posed for a photograph shortly before the Russian Revolution of 1917. Alexis was the czarevitch, which means that he was the next in line to the throne. If the Russian Revolution had not taken place, he would have become the next czar. **Critical Thinking** Czars, like all monarchs, must learn to be strong leaders. What skills do you think the young czarevitch needed to learn in order to become czar?

St. Petersburg marched on the Winter Palace to ask the czar for reforms. They were met by troops, who fired into the crowd, killing hundreds.

After this mass killing, known as Bloody Sunday, Czar Nicholas was forced to agree to establish the Duma (DOO mah), a kind of congress. Members were elected by the people. The Duma held power, along with the czar, until 1917. Progress toward reform had been made. Some people wanted more, however, as you will read in the next section.

1. **Define** (a) westernization, (b) czar.
2. **Identify** (a) Catherine the Great, (b) Golden Horde, (c) Peter the Great, (d) Nicholas II.
3. What territories did the princes of Muscovy and the czars take to expand Russian territory?
4. How did Russian czars treat the serfs?
5. Which rulers did the most to westernize Russia?

Critical Thinking

6. **Identifying Central Issues** At the beginning of the section, you learned about three themes in Russian history. How do the reigns of Ivan I, Ivan IV, and Peter the Great express those themes?

Activity

7. **Writing to Learn** You are Peter the Great. Write a journal entry about the ways in which you would like to make Russia a better and stronger country.

The Rise and Fall of the Soviet Union

Reach Into Your Background
Imagine going shopping and finding only one style of shoes or one type of shirt. What if the grocery store had row after row of empty shelves? How would your life be different?

Questions to Explore

1. What is communism and why did it fail in the Soviet Union?
2. What happened in the Soviet Union under Lenin and Stalin?

Key Terms
revolutionary
communism
civil war
dictator
Cold War
consumer goods

Key People
Vladimir Lenin
Josef Stalin
Mikhail Gorbachev

▼ A rival said that the fiery Lenin—shown here making a speech in Red Square, Moscow—was so determined that "even when he sleeps, he dreams of nothing but the revolution."

On the afternoon of April 16, 1917, a small group of Russians gathered at a railroad station in a German town. Among them was a man named Vladimir Lenin. Earlier, Lenin had been exiled to Siberia. He had been spreading ideas that the government thought were **revolutionary**—ideas that could cause a revolution, or the overthrow of a government. Then the government gave him permission to leave Russia.

Now the Germans were supplying a train to take Lenin back to Russia. The Germans made two rules. No member of Lenin's group could leave the train or talk to any Germans during their journey. The Germans, too, knew that ideas can be more powerful than any army. Germany was at war with Russia and hoped that Lenin would cause changes in Russia. And he did. Lenin led one of the most important revolutions in history.

Grigory Rasputin—The Czar's Adviser

Grigory Rasputin, an adviser to the czar's family, is often accused of having helped to bring about the Russian Revolution. Rasputin had some success treating the czar's son, Alexis, who suffered from a serious illness. As a result, Rasputin had a great deal of influence with the czar and the czarina, the czar's wife. Some people think Rasputin convinced the czar and czarina to make bad decisions in the years leading up to the revolution. Supporters of the czar feared Rasputin's growing power. A group of them murdered him in 1916.

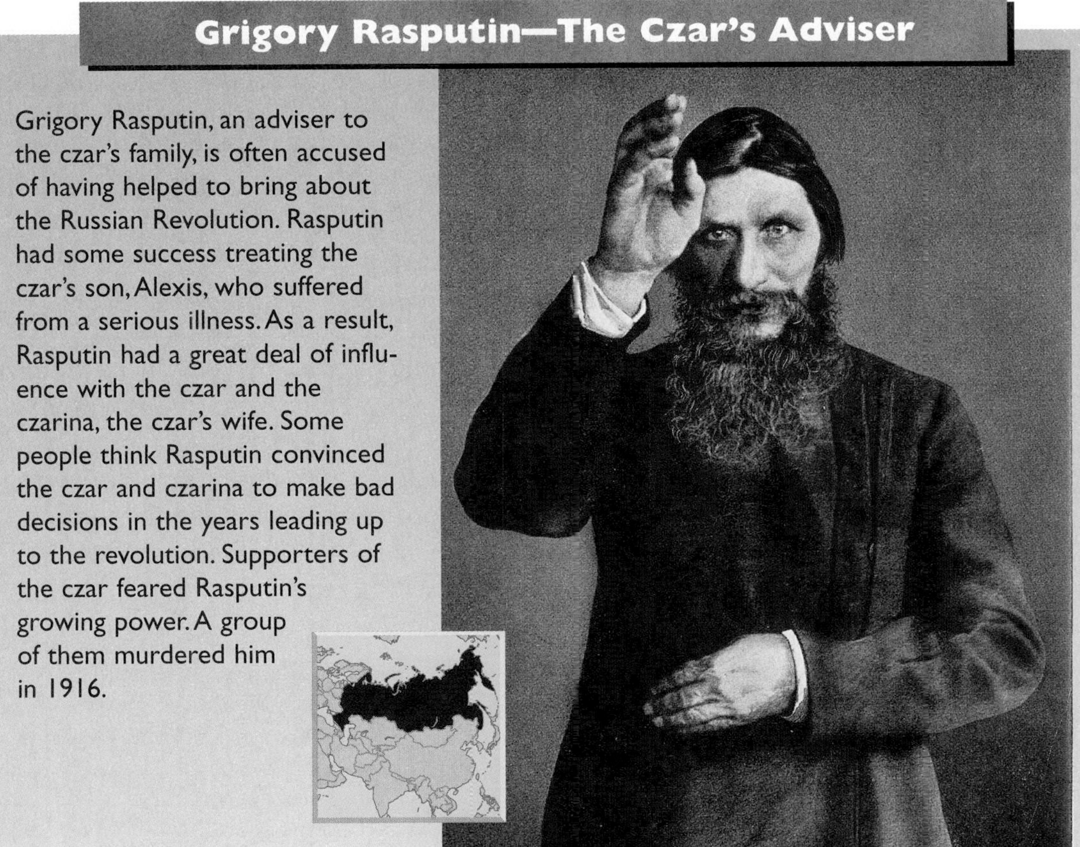

The Russian Revolution

To understand why the Germans helped Lenin, you need to go back to 1914. That year, Russia entered World War I, fighting against Germany. It was a harsh war. Millions of Russian soldiers were killed or wounded. At home, people suffered severe food and fuel shortages. By March 1917, the Russian people began rioting. Troops were sent to put down the uprising. However, they joined the people instead. The czar was forced to give up his throne. A weak government took over.

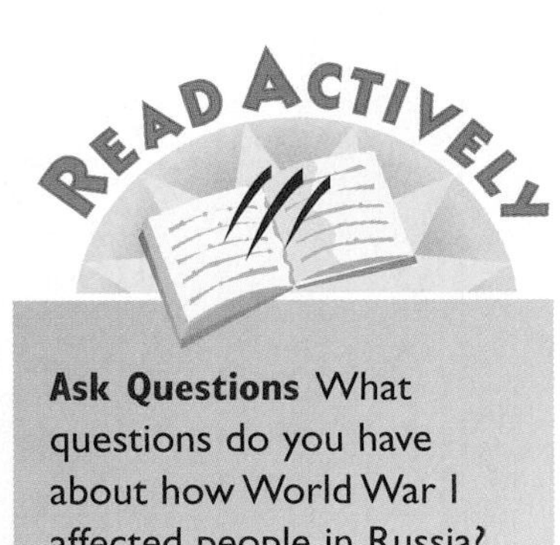

Ask Questions What questions do you have about how World War I affected people in Russia?

In November 1917, Lenin and his supporters pushed the weak government aside. Lenin knew the Russians wanted peace more than anything else. In March 1918, Russia signed an agreement with Germany and withdrew from World War I. This was just what the Germans had hoped for.

As the new leader of Russia, Lenin wanted a communist government. **Communism** (KAHM yoo nizum) is a theory that says the government should own the farms and factories for the benefit of all the citizens. Everyone should share the work equally and receive an equal share of the rewards.

In theory, communism appealed greatly to many of the Russian people. Remember the deep split between Russia's rich and poor? For hundreds of years, Russia's poor had suffered terrible hardships while the rich lived in luxury. In a communist nation, everyone is supposed to be equal. Lenin told the workers and serfs that communism would bring fairness and equality to all Russians.

Building a Communist State

The treaty with the Germans ended the war, but peace did not come. After the Communists came to power, there was a terrible **civil war,** a war between groups inside a country. On one side were the Communists. On the other were many groups opposed to them.

The Russian civil war lasted three years and cost millions of lives. Finally, the Communists won. In 1922, Lenin created the Union of Soviet Socialist Republics (U.S.S.R.), also called the Soviet Union. The Soviet Union was made up of Russia and smaller areas, or republics, under Russian control.

Lenin began taking steps to turn the Soviet Union into a communist country. He jailed and even killed people who opposed him. Such people were enemies of the revolution, he said. Lenin died in 1924. He was followed by Josef Stalin, whose rule would be even more harsh.

▼ This World War II Soviet poster shows a worker holding up a red flag bearing the portraits of Lenin and Stalin. The slogan encourages the Soviet people to produce more for the war effort.

Stalin's Dictatorship Josef Stalin was a **dictator** (DIK tayt ur), a leader who has absolute power. Stalin did not care about the suffering his decisions caused. For example, he wanted to build industry in the Soviet Union. He knew that factory workers would need plenty of food. Therefore, Stalin forced serfs to give their farm products to the government. When the serfs opposed the plan, Stalin sent millions of them to prison camps in Siberia. Most died there. And when people questioned him about other actions, Stalin simply got rid of them. He sent them to the camps, or had them executed. All of the Soviet Union lived in terror of Stalin.

The Fight for Stalingrad

When the Germans invaded the Soviet Union during World War II, they had to contend with the combined forces of bad weather and the Soviet army. First, rain caused German tanks to get stuck in the mud. Then, bitterly cold temperatures gave soldiers frostbite and caused machinery to break down. Finally, they had to fight determined Soviet soldiers who were ready to defend their country regardless of the cost. This picture shows Soviet soldiers in their victorious battle for the city of Stalingrad, which is now known as Volgograd. **Critical Thinking** How do you think the weather helped the Soviet soldiers to win victory over the Germans?

World War II In 1939, Stalin signed an agreement with the Germans. It stated that the two countries would not fight each other. But the Germans invaded anyway. In 1941, three million German soldiers, with tanks and airplanes, drove deep into the Soviet Union.

For a time, a German victory appeared likely. Soviet cities were destroyed, and millions of soldiers died or were captured. But the Soviet people, helped by the harsh Russian winter, fought bravely. In 1943, the Soviets began pushing the Germans back toward their own borders. By 1945, Soviet troops had captured Berlin, the capital of Germany.

The Cold War

After World War II, the United States and the Soviet Union were the world's two strongest countries. They were so much stronger than other countries that people called them "superpowers." Relations between the superpowers were very tense, though the two sides never fought each other. This time of tension without actual war, which lasted roughly from 1945 until 1991, is called the **Cold War.**

Causes of the Cold War Two things caused the tension. First was the problem of Eastern Europe. During World War II, the Soviet army moved westward all the way to Berlin. As the army advanced, it freed Eastern European countries the Germans had conquered. But after the war, Soviet troops did not leave. The Soviets forced these countries

Worried About War Many people during the Cold War feared that the United States and the U.S.S.R. would attack each other and destroy the world. Grace Paley's "Anxiety" is a story about people living with this fear. In the story, an old woman tells a young father to treat his daughter well because her future "is like a film which suddenly cuts to white."

A Voice of Protest By the age of 32, Andrei Sakharov was one of the Soviet Union's best scientists. In 1961, Sakharov began speaking out against the testing of nuclear bombs. As a result, he lost his job and was exiled to Siberia. He quickly became a hero to many Russians and in 1975 was awarded the Nobel Peace Prize.

to become communist. Most contact with the West was cut off. British leader Winston Churchill said that it was as if an "iron curtain" had fallen across Eastern Europe, dividing East and West.

Second, the Soviets tried to expand their power beyond Eastern Europe. They encouraged rebels in other nations to turn to communism. The United States was determined to stop this. The superpowers often backed opposing sides in conflicts in Asia and Africa. The superpowers also built powerful weapons to use against one another. By the 1960s, they had enough nuclear (NOO klee ur) bombs to destroy the entire world.

Collapse of an Empire During the Cold War, the Soviet Union's economy did not grow fast enough. The government invested most of its money in heavy industries, such as steel. It paid little attention to **consumer goods,** such as cars or blue jeans, that the common person might enjoy.

By the early 1980s, almost all of the Soviet people had lost faith in the communist system. They did not want the government to control almost every part of their lives. In the mid-1980s, one Soviet leader responded. Mikhail Gorbachev (mee khah EEL GOR buh chawf), who took power in 1985, made many changes in the Soviet system. He allowed more personal freedom. He also reduced government control of the economy.

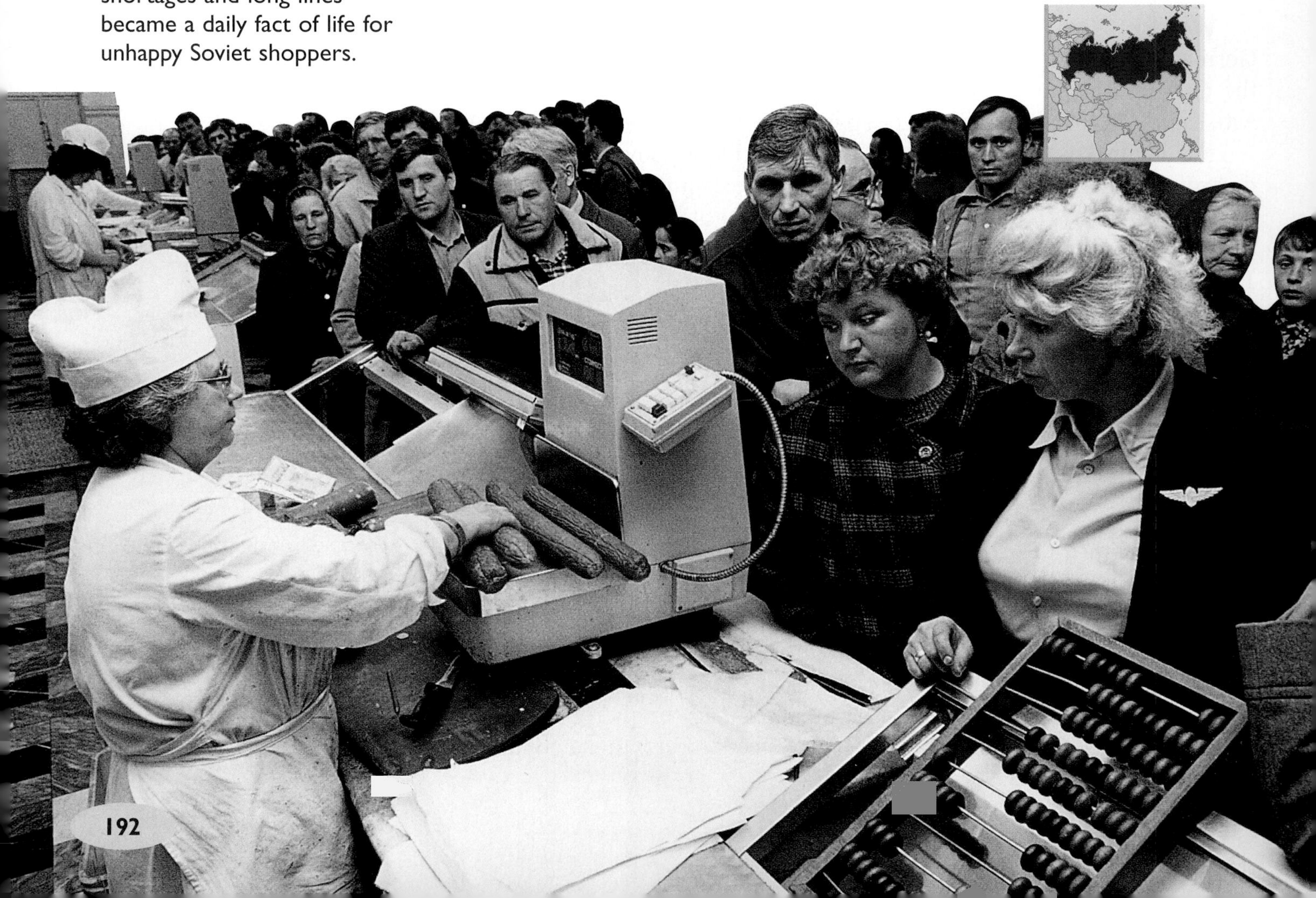

▼ Under communism, food shortages and long lines became a daily fact of life for unhappy Soviet shoppers.

Plenty to Buy

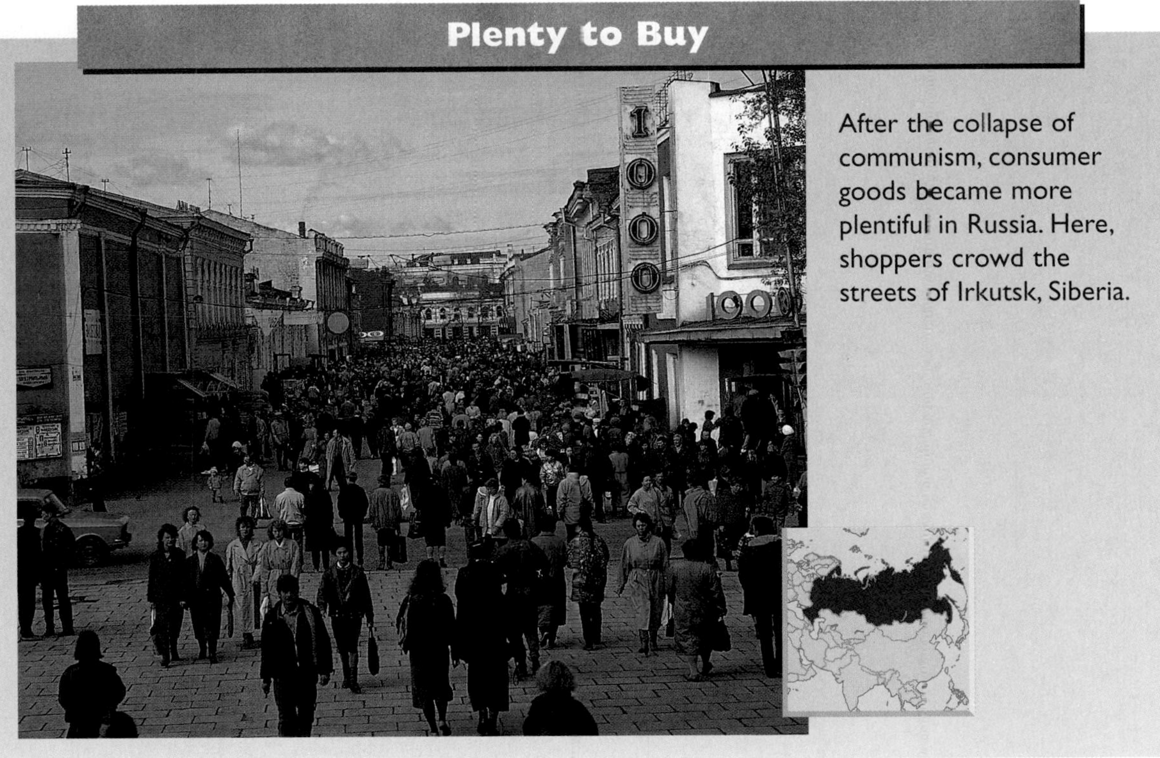

After the collapse of communism, consumer goods became more plentiful in Russia. Here, shoppers crowd the streets of Irkutsk, Siberia.

Often, when people have a taste of freedom, it makes them want more. By the late 1980s, this happened across Eastern Europe and the Soviet Union. Eastern European countries abandoned communism. And the Soviet republics demanded their independence. They wanted to decide their own futures. Finally, at the end of 1991, the Soviet Union broke apart. Russia and most of the former Soviet republics became independent nations.

Today, Russia faces a huge challenge. For hundreds of years, the Russian people have suffered hardships, under the czars and under communism. Now Russians control their own fate. It is up to them to build a new way of life.

1. **Define** (a) revolutionary, (b) communism, (c) civil war, (d) dictator, (e) Cold War, (f) consumer goods.
2. **Identify** (a) Vladimir Lenin, (b) Josef Stalin, (c) Mikhail Gorbachev.
3. How did Lenin become leader of the Soviet Union?
4. Why was Josef Stalin feared?
5. Why were the people of the Soviet Union unhappy with the communist government?

Critical Thinking

6. **Recognizing Cause and Effect** Why did the Germans send Lenin back to Russia?

Activity

7. **Writing to Learn** Some people in Russia want to go back to the old communist way of life. Write a paragraph arguing against returning to communism.

Review and Activities

Reviewing Main Ideas

1. What accomplishments of the ancient Greeks and Romans affect our world today?
2. How did Christianity and feudalism affect the lives of people in the Middle Ages?
3. How did renewed trade affect Europe's interest in the world?
4. List two important changes made during the Age of Revolution.
5. How did the Industrial Revolution change life for people in Europe?
6. How did nationalism help to cause World War I and World War II?
7. Explain how Russia gained territory and became an empire.
8. Why did the Russian people come to oppose the czars?
9. What changes did Lenin and Stalin make in the Soviet Union?
10. Why did the Soviet Union collapse?

Reviewing Key Terms

Use each key term below in a sentence that shows the meaning of the term.

1. democracy
2. empire
3. feudalism
4. Renaissance
5. humanism
6. monarch
7. colony
8. Scientific Revolution
9. Industrial Revolution
10. imperialism
11. nationalism
12. alliance
13. communism
14. civil war
15. dictator
16. Cold War

Critical Thinking

1. **Recognizing Cause and Effect** Describe causes that led to the fall of the Roman Empire.
2. **Making Conclusions** How were the main ideas of the Renaissance different from common ideas of the Middle Ages?
3. **Identifying Central Issues** How was Russia under the czars different from the Soviet Union under communism?

Graphic Organizer

Copy the chart on a sheet of paper. Fill in the empty boxes with important events that happened in Western Europe and in Russia for each century listed.

	Western Europe	Russia
1300s		
1500s		
1700s		
1900s		

Map Activity

Europe and Russia

For each place listed below, write the letter from the map that shows its location. Use the maps in the Activity Atlas to help you.

1. Athens
2. Rome
3. Italy
4. Great Britain
5. St. Petersburg

Place Location

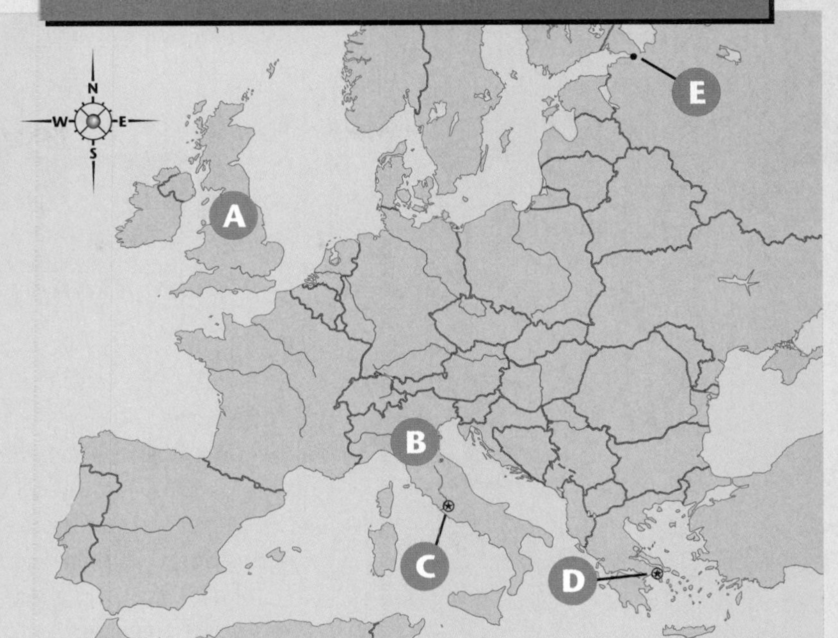

Writing Activity

Writing an Interview

Choose a historical figure from this chapter. Write a "personal interview" with that person. First, think of questions that you would like to ask. Do research to learn how that person might have answered the questions. Then write the "interview" as if you were asking that person the questions and he or she were answering them.

Take It to the NET

Activity View artifacts of Russian czars and learn some fun facts about Russian history. For help in completing this activity, visit **www.phschool.com**.

Chapter 7 Self-Test To review what you have learned, take the Chapter 7 Self-Test and get instant feedback on your answers. Go to **www.phschool.com** to take the test.

Skills Review

Turn to the Skills Activity.

Review the steps for interpreting diagrams and illustrations. Then, find a diagram or illustration somewhere else in this book. Following the steps, write a brief paragraph detailing your interpretation.

How Am I Doing?

Answer these questions to help you check your progress.

1. Can I list the major accomplishments of the Greeks and the Romans?
2. Do I understand how people's views of the world changed during the Renaissance?
3. Do I understand how the Industrial Revolution changed European life?
4. Can I identify Russia's important rulers and their accomplishments?
5. Do I understand what communism is and why it did not work in the Soviet Union?
6. What information from this chapter can I include in my journal?

FROM

Pearl in the Egg

BY DOROTHY VAN WOERKOM

Reach Into Your Background

In Europe in the Middle Ages, an average day for a person your age looked quite different than an average day today. For one thing, a twelve-year-old at that time was seen as much closer to being an adult. People in those days did not live as long as they do today. A 20-year-old person was considered middle-aged!

Pearl in the Egg was the name of a real girl who lived in the 1200s. Historians know little about her except her name. Dorothy Van Woerkom has written a book of historical fiction about Pearl. Her descriptions of Pearl's life are based on what historians know about life in the 1200s. At that time, people in Europe were just beginning to use family names. Usually they gave themselves names that described their work or their families in some way.

In this part of Pearl's story, you will see something of a typical day in her life.

Questions to Explore

1. What does this story tell you about the life of a serf?
2. What can you learn from this story about work on a feudal manor?

Pearl set the bowl of cabbage soup down on the floor near the rushlight. She knelt beside the box of straw that was her father's bed. She wiped his forehead, listening to his heavy breathing.

"Please, Fa," she coaxed. She broke off a piece from a loaf of black bread and dipped it into the soup. She placed it on his lips, letting the soup trickle into his mouth. She ate the chunk of bread, and dipped another.

"I will be in the fields until the nooning," she said, "so you must try to eat a little now. See, I have put a bit of dripping in the soup."

She forced the warm, mild liquid down his throat until the bowl was half empty. She drank the rest herself, chewing hungrily on the lump of fat that the sick man had not been able to swallow.

Again she wiped his face, and then she blew out the light. She crossed the smooth dirt floor, and pulled a sack from a peg on the wall near the door as she left the hut. Outside, the sky was gray with the dawn. Ground fog swirled around her feet. The air smelled of ripening grain and moist earth.

From other huts of mud and timber, serfs hurried out into the

rushlight *n.:* a lamp made with grease and part of a rush, or swamp plant
dripping *n.:* fat and juices drawn from cooking meat
serf *n.:* peasant farmers who worked the land as slaves of wealthy landowners

early morning mist. Some, like Pearl, would spend the day in their own small holdings in the fields. It was the time for harvesting their crops, which would feed their families through the winter. Others, like Pearl's older brother, Gavin, had already left for work in the manor fields to bring in Sir Geoffrey's crops.

Sir Geoffrey was lord of the manor, which included his great stone house and all the land surrounding it. He owned this tiny village. He even owned most of the people in it. A few, like the baker, the miller, and the soapmaker, were freemen and free women. They worked for themselves and paid the lord taxes. For tax, Sir Geoffrey collected a portion of everything they produced. No one in the village had money.

But the serfs were not free. They could never leave the manor, or marry without the lord's permission. They could not fish in the streams or hunt in the forest. They owned only their mud huts and small gardens, called holdings, and an ox or cow, or a few geese or sheep. The serfs also paid taxes. Each year they gave Sir Geoffrey a portion of their crops. He took a share of their eggs; if a flock of sheep or geese increased, he took a share; and if a cow had a calf, he took that also. On certain days of the week each family had to send a man—and an ox if they had one—to help plow the lord's fields, harvest his crops, and do their work. Each woman had to weave one garment a year for the lord and his family.

The sun was up when Pearl reached the long furrows of her field, where the flat green bean pods weighed down their low bushes. She bent to see if the leaves were dry. Wet leaves would wither when she touched them.

The sun had dried them. Pearl began filling her sack, wondering how she could finish the harvest all by herself before the first frost. She had other plots to work as well.

Now that their father was ill, twelve-year-old Gavin was taking his place for three days each week in the manor fields. Sir Geoffrey would get *his* crops safely in! But if the frost came early, or if the only one left at home to work was an eleven-year-old like Pearl, that was of small matter to Sir Geoffrey.

Pearl stood up to rub her back. A serf's life was a hard life. Her father's was, and his father's before him. She sighed. Who could hope to change it?

Old Clotilde came swaying up the narrow path between her field and Pearl's. She waved her empty sack by way of greeting and squatted down among her plants.

"How be your Fa this morning?" she asked Pearl.

"He took some soup. But he wanders in his head. He thinks I am my mother, though she's been dead three summers now."

furrows *n.:* rows in the earth made by a plow

Clotilde (kluh TILD)

▼ This painting from the Middle Ages shows peasants working in a field.

▶This wall painting from the 1300s shows the kind of hunt Pearl saw.

"Ah, and he'll join her soon, Big Rollin will." Clotilde's wrinkled face was nearly the same dirty gray as her cap. "They all do, soon as they take a mite of sickness. For the likes of us to stay alive, we must stay well! Get the priest for him! He won't plow these fields again."

Before Pearl could reply, the shrill blare of a hunting horn sounded across the meadow, followed by the baying of hounds on the trail of a wild boar. Startled to their feet, the serfs watched the terrified boar running in and out among the rows of crops.

bowmen *n.:* men with bows and arrows; archers
defiant *adj.:* bold or resistant

"Run, lest you get trampled!" Clotilde screamed, dashing down the path toward the forest. The others followed her. Someone pulled Pearl along as she stumbled forward, blinded by angry tears, her fingers tightly gripping her sack.

Connect Why does Pearl shed tears of anger?

The hounds came running in pursuit of the boar. Behind the hounds rode the hunting party of twenty horsemen, led by Sir Geoffrey. At the rear was another man Pearl recognized. Jack, one of Sir Geoffrey's bowmen, had come upon her one day as she scrounged for dead branches near the edge of the forest. He had baited her with cruel words, rudely ruffling her hair with the shaft end of an arrow.

"Jack's my name. What's yours?" he had demanded, taking pleasure in her discomfort. For answer she had spat at him, and he had pressed the arrow's metal tip against her wrist until she'd dropped her bundle. Laughing, he had scattered the branches with his foot and grabbed her hair.

"Spit at me again, girl, and that will be the end of you!" Though his mouth had turned up in a grin, his eyes had been bright with anger. His fingers had tightened on the nape of her neck, bending her head back. She stared up at him, frightened, but defiant.

"Perhaps you need a lesson in manners right now," he'd said, raising his other hand. He probably would have struck her, but for the rattle of a wagon and the tuneless whistle signaling someone's approach. He had let her go with a suddenness that had left her off balance, and had stalked away.

Shaken, Pearl had turned to see Sir Geoffrey's woodcutter driving out of the forest with a wagonload of wood for the manor house.

Now Pearl shuddered at the memory; but Jack was taking no notice of her. His eyes were on the boar and on his master. If the boar became maddened during the chase and turned on one of the hunters, Jack was ready with his arrows to put an end to the beast.

Over the meadow they galloped, and onto the fields. They churned up the soft earth, trampled down the precious bean plants, crushed the near-ripe ears of the barley and oats, tore up the tender pea vines. They chased the boar across the fields and back again, laughing at the sport.

When they had gone, Pearl ran back to her field. She crawled in the turned-up earth, searching for unbroken bean pods. The other serfs were doing the same.

"What is the matter with us?" she demanded of Clotilde, "Why do we stay silent, with spoiled crops all around us, just so Sir Geoffrey will have his sport?"

"Shish!" Clotilde warned, looking quickly around to see who might have heard. "Do you want a flogging for such bold words? Hold your tongue, as you see your elders do."

flogging *n.:* beating or whipping

For the rest of the morning they worked in silence. At midday, Pearl picked up her half-filled sack. It should have been full by now. She glared fiercely across the meadow at the manor house, but she held her tongue.

Pearl returned home to find that her father had worsened. When she could not rouse him, she went for the priest.

Look Back

1. Why does Pearl work alone in her family's holdings?

Think It Over

2. Why did the serfs give Sir Geoffrey a portion of their crops every year?

3. What did the serfs use instead of money?

4. What did Clotilde mean when she said, "Do you want a flogging for such bold words?"

Go Beyond

5. The feudal system existed for more than 400 years. Why do you think it did not change for such a long time?

6. Based on what you know about Pearl, how do you think she might act the next time she sees the lord or one of his men?

Ideas for Writing: Story

7. Write an addition to Pearl's story that tells how she got the name Pearl in the Egg.

Cultures of Europe and Russia

PICTURE ACTIVITIES

In many cities and towns in Europe and Russia, people live and work among things that remind them of their cultural backgrounds. This is a picture of Cologne (kuh LOHN), Germany. To learn more about Cologne's culture, complete the following activities.

Study the picture

Find a modern building and a historic one. For what use do you think each building was constructed?

Draw conclusions

From looking at the picture, what conclusions can you draw about the people of Cologne? Do they have a modern way of life? Do they value their cultural background? How do you know?

The Cultures of Western Europe

Reach Into Your Background
Think about your community and your way of life. Now think of another community that you have visited or heard about from relatives or friends. How are the ways of life in each community different? How are they the same? List some differences and similarities.

Questions to Explore

1. What makes the cities of Western Europe great cultural centers?
2. How do people of the many countries of Western Europe interact with one another?

Key Terms
urbanization
immigrant
multicultural
tariff

Key Places
Paris
London
Madrid
Berlin

The train speeds down the track with hardly a whisper. As the passengers sit in their comfortable seats, they can look out the window at the highway next to the railroad. They know that the cars are traveling at 60 miles (96 km) per hour, but the cars seem to be moving backward. That's because the train is traveling *three times faster* than the cars—about 180 miles (289 km) per hour.

Would you like to take a trip like that? You can if you go to France, which has the world's fastest trains. Great Britain, too, has speedy rail travel. Some British trains reach speeds of 140 miles (225 km) per hour. In Western Europe, high-speed trains have made travel between countries easy and fast. Europeans can be in another country in a matter of hours. You will soon see how such easy movement through Western Europe affects the culture of the region.

▼ France's high-speed trains travel about 47 times faster than a person can walk.

Visualize Visualize a European city street with modern and old buildings.

Cultural Centers

When people travel in Europe, they are usually heading for a city. People travel from small towns and villages to cities to find jobs. Some people go to cities to go to school. People also travel to cities to enjoy the cultural attractions. These include museums, concerts, restaurants, nightclubs, and stores.

Most Western European cities are a mix of the old and the new. Public buildings and houses from the Middle Ages are a common sight. They stand next to modern apartments and office buildings. Cars and buses drive along cobblestone streets once used by horse-drawn carriages. Monuments stand for leaders who lived hundreds of years ago.

Each city in Western Europe is different from the other. Paris, the capital of France, attracts scholars, writers, and artists from all over the world. England's capital, London, is known for its grand historic buildings and lovely parks. The Spanish capital city of Madrid (muh DRID) is known as a friendly place where people meet in cafes to relax after work. The German city of Berlin is always full of activity.

▲"The Mousetrap," a play by mystery writer Agatha Christie, has been playing continuously in London since its opening in November 1952.

▼ This glass pyramid houses the entrance to the Louvre, a famous art museum in Paris.

Let's focus on life in Germany for a moment. Most visitors to Germany think that the Germans are efficient. In other words, Germans do their work without waste or extra effort. Visitors get this idea from what they see. In Germany, cities, streets, and buses are clean. Hotels are well run. German cars are well designed and long-lasting. Travel is swift on an excellent system of four-lane highways. Travel is equally fast on high-speed trains.

But life in Germany is not all hard work and fast-paced activity. Many workers enjoy up to six weeks of vacation each year. Outdoor recreation is popular. Mountains and highlands allow skiing, hiking, and camping. The country's many rivers, as well as the North and Baltic seas, are good for swimming and boating. Those who prefer city life enjoy the museums, concerts, and plays.

Oktoberfest in Munich, Germany

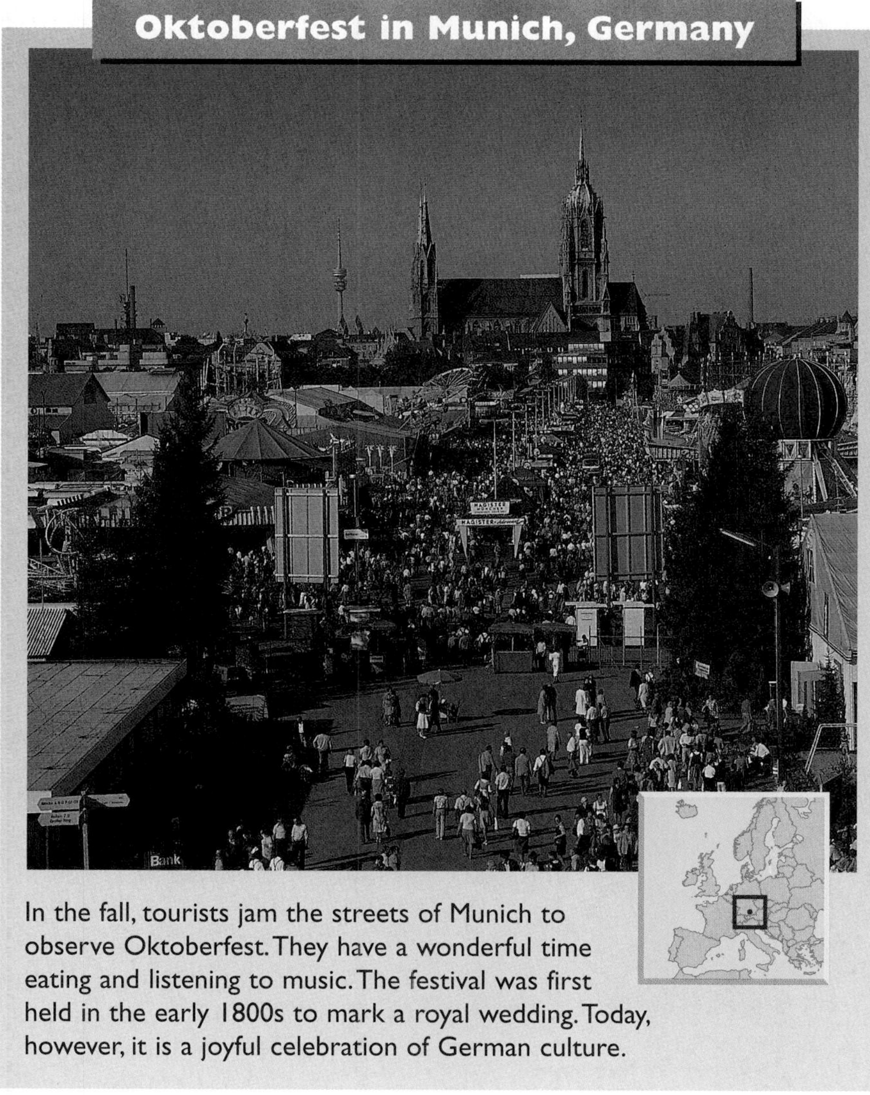

In the fall, tourists jam the streets of Munich to observe Oktoberfest. They have a wonderful time eating and listening to music. The festival was first held in the early 1800s to mark a royal wedding. Today, however, it is a joyful celebration of German culture.

Growing Cities, Growing Wealth

People in most Western European countries enjoy a similar lifestyle. That's because these countries are prosperous, or wealthy. This prosperity is based on industry. Factories in Western Europe make consumer goods that are in great demand around the world. Western European workers also make steel, cars, machines, and many other vital products.

Industry and the Growth of Cities Industry has been developing in Western Europe since the late 1700s. It has not always been so important to the economy, however. In the past, farming played a bigger role.

About 200 years ago, there were few machines to help do farmwork. To meet basic food needs, most of the people worked on farms. Gradually, things changed. New and better farm machines were invented. These machines could do tasks that once required many workers. Farmers also learned ways to improve soil quality and fight insects. With these advances, farms could produce more and better crops with fewer workers.

This revolution in farming came at the same time as the Industrial Revolution. Thus, as the need for farmworkers fell, the need for industrial workers grew. Many people began moving to cities, where

The Labor Force in Selected Western European Countries

Chart Study Today, most people in the Netherlands, Norway, Spain, and Austria make a living as service workers. A service is any task that one person does for another—like selling groceries, typing a letter, or teaching a class. Workers in industry make products, such as clothing, automobiles, and video games. Agricultural workers grow crops and raise livestock. **Critical Thinking** Of the four countries shown here, which two have the most service workers? Which two have the most industrial workers? Would you expect to find service and industrial workers in cities or rural areas? Why?

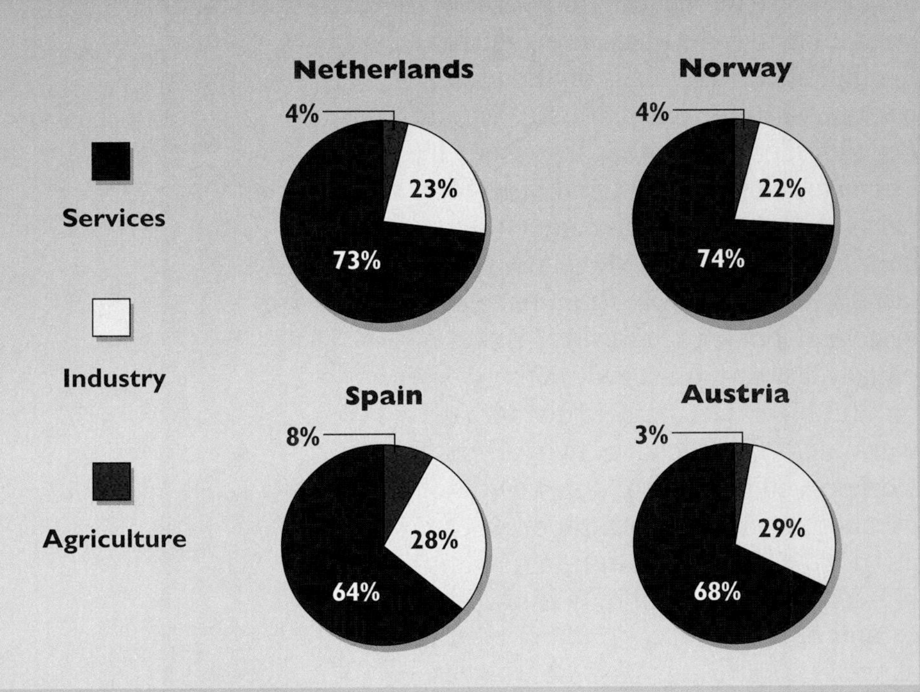

Devoted to Nature
Writers of the English Romantic Age (1798–1832) reacted strongly to the events of their time. They disliked the way the Industrial Revolution changed the ways people lived. In "My Heart Leaps Up When I Behold," William Wordsworth describes the beauty of a rainbow and wishes every day was bound "each to each by natural piety," which means living each day in devotion to nature.

the factories were. This growth of cities, known as **urbanization** (ur bun ih ZAY shun), sped up after World War II. The United States provided billions of dollars to help Western Europe recover from the war. With this help, the region's industries came back stronger than ever. And even more people left rural areas to work in cities.

Today most Western Europeans work in factories or in service industries such as banking and food service. And most Western European workers earn good wages and have a comfortable life.

A Home for Immigrants Life in Western Europe was not always so good. In the 1800s and early 1900s, millions of Western Europeans left Europe. Most went to the United States, Canada, and the countries of South America. They left in search of a better life.

Since World War II, the direction of human movement has changed. No longer are large numbers of people leaving Western Europe. As industry developed in the postwar years, more workers were needed. As a result, people began moving to Western Europe. Today, **immigrants** (IM uh grunts), or people who move to one country from another, make up about 6 percent of the workers in Western Europe. Most are from Eastern Europe, North Africa, South Asia, and the Middle East.

Yang-Mee Tang is an example. She moved to London to start a career in business. Her homeland was Mauritius (maw RISH ee us), an island in the Indian Ocean, off the eastern coast of Africa. Yang-Mee is learning to get around London on the "tube," or subway. She is learning a much different lifestyle from her lifestyle in Mauritius. "There is so much to do here!"

says Yang-Mee. "In my hometown in Mauritius, everything shuts down at around 10:00 P.M. But every night in central London, the streets are still crowded with people at 1:00 A.M."

Immigrants do not simply leave their cultures when they leave their homelands. They bring their languages, religious beliefs, values, and customs. But most immigrants make changes in their ways of life. They may change the way they dress. They may try new foods and discover new ways of cooking. Most of them learn the language of their new country.

In many ways, immigration has changed the cultures of Western Europe. In countries like Britain and France, people from many different backgrounds live and work together. They learn about one another's way of life. In the process, the cultures blend and change. In this way, many Western European countries have become multicultural. A **multicultural** (mul tih KUHL chur ul) country's way of life is influenced by many different cultures.

LINKS ACROSS THE WORLD

Staying in the Neighborhood Have you ever been to Chinatown or Little Italy? New immigrants feel most comfortable with people from their own country—and often form their own little cities within a city. For example, early Italian and Russian immigrants in New York would combine their money to build a church or synagogue. They also formed social clubs where they could meet and talk in their first language.

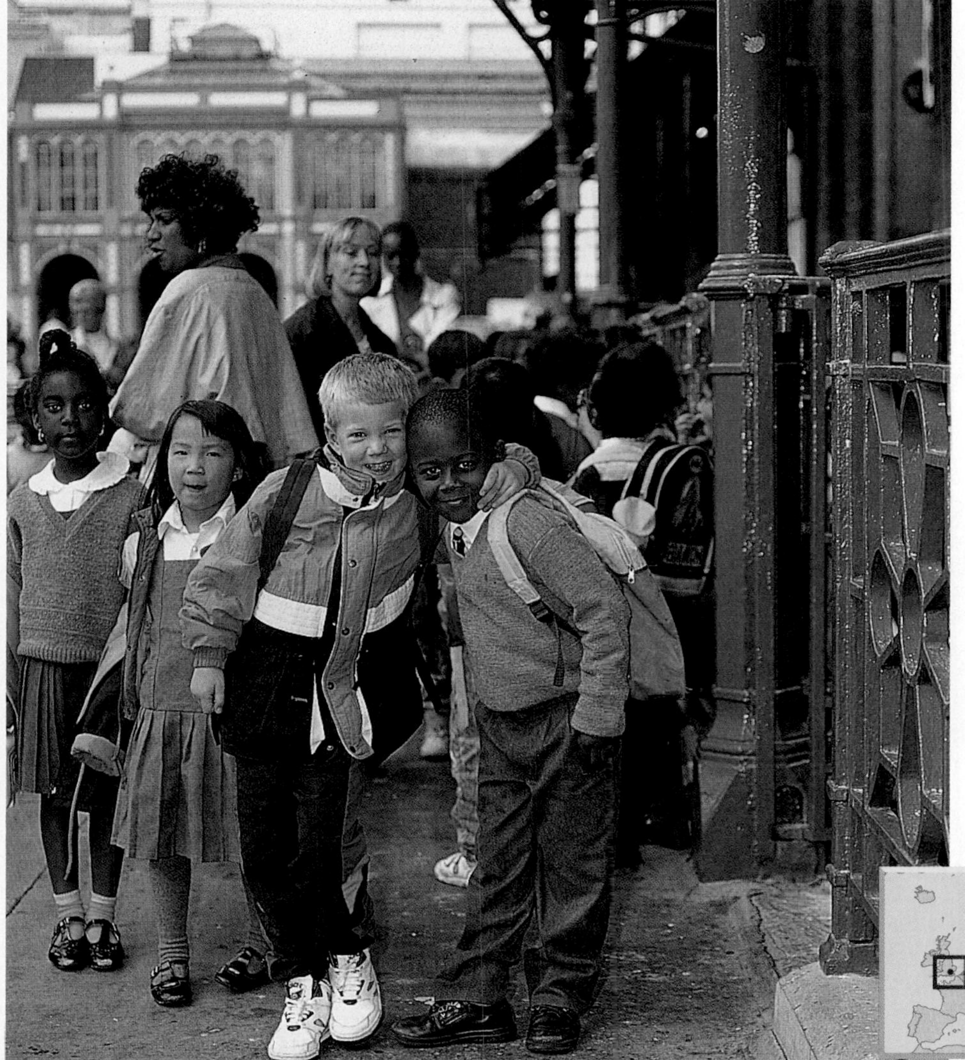

◀These British children are on a school field trip to the West End, London's shopping and entertainment district.

Predict How do you think open borders help Western Europe grow and succeed?

Open Borders

Turn to the political map of Europe in the Activity Atlas in the front of your book. Notice that most European countries are small and close together. Picture a high-speed train traveling across Europe. It's little wonder that travelers can get from one country to another in a matter of hours. Ideas, goods, and raw materials can travel quickly as well. The open exchange of ideas and goods has helped make Western Europe prosperous.

It was not always so easy for people, goods, and ideas to move throughout Western Europe. Changes began around 1950, when France and Germany agreed to work together to help rebuild after World War II. Other nations soon joined them. Now there is an organization called

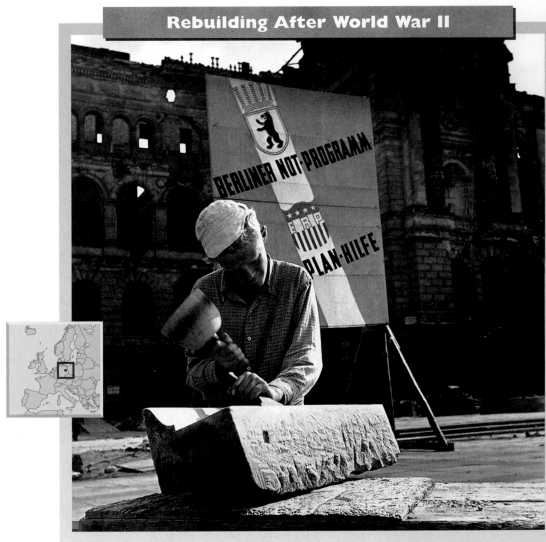

Rebuilding After World War II

After World War II, Germany lay in ruins. The Allied countries worked together to rebuild West Germany and make it a democracy. This man is helping to repair and repaint the Titaina Palace, West Berlin's largest concert hall. The Allies also helped to rebuild homes and factories. **Critical Thinking** Why do you think it was important to the Allies to rebuild Germany as a democracy?

Europe's New Money—the Euro

To make it easier for member nations to trade among themselves, the European Union adopted a single currency called the European Currency Unit, or ECU. Later, the ECU was renamed the Euro. In 1999, consumers began using the Euro, but only through checks, credit cards, or bank transfers. Actual bank notes and coins replaced the national currencies of participating EU members in 2002. **Critical Thinking** How might the Euro make travel and trade among the European countries easier?

the European Union (EU). In 1999, the EU had 15 member nations and plans for adding at least three more. The EU works to expand trade in Europe. One way to do this is to end **tariffs**, or fees that a government charges for goods entering the country. The EU hopes to create a "united states" of Europe, where people, money, goods, and services move freely among member countries.

1. **Define** (a) urbanization, (b) immigrant, (c) multicultural, (d) tariff.
2. **Identify** (a) Paris, (b) London, (c) Madrid, (d) Berlin.
3. How did the growth of industry affect cities in Western Europe?
4. Why is there ease of movement among the countries in Western Europe?

Critical Thinking

5. **Drawing Comparisons** This section describes how the lives of many immigrants to Western Europe change when they settle in their new country. What effect do you think the immigrants have on the way of life in their new home?

Activity

6. **Writing to Learn** Write down two facts about Western Europe that you were surprised to learn. How has this new information changed the way you think about Western Europe?

Summarizing Information

How many words are in this sentence? You should count seven words. How many words do you think are in this paragraph? When you finish reading it, count them.

You can easily count the words in a sentence or a paragraph. But how many ideas do you think are on this page? What about in this entire book?

Think of all the books, magazines, and newspapers you read at school and at home. They all give you a mind-boggling amount of information. No one person could remember them all. You are not expected to. But you can summarize the basic ideas to help yourself remember them.

Get Ready

Summarizing information is a good skill to have. It will help you pick out the main points of what you read. It will also help you study for tests. Most important, it will help you make sense of all the ideas you read or hear about.

You may not know it, but you have already done a lot of summarizing. How can that be? People summarize without even knowing it. For example, suppose someone asked you, "How was math class?" You would not answer with every detail. You would tell the main things that happened, along with a just a few important details. That is just what a summary is: a description of the main points along with a few important details.

Try It Out

To see how easy summarizing is, try this exercise. Write a summary of yesterday. Your goal will be to describe the main points of your day from when you woke up to when you went to sleep. Follow these steps to write your summary.

A. Work from start to finish. When you summarize, you will do best to start at the beginning and work through to the end. When summarizing your day, start with when you woke up.

B. List the main points. Remember that a summary describes the main points, not every little detail. List only the main things that you did yesterday.

C. Add some details to the list. Although you do not want to list too many details, it helps to list a few that will later jog your memory. For example, you might write "ate breakfast" as a main point. You can add the details of what you ate if the meal was special in some way. As you make your list, add details after some of the main points.

D. Turn your list into a summary. Summaries are often in paragraph form. Once you have made your list, you can add transitions to make it into a paragraph. Transitions are words that connect one idea

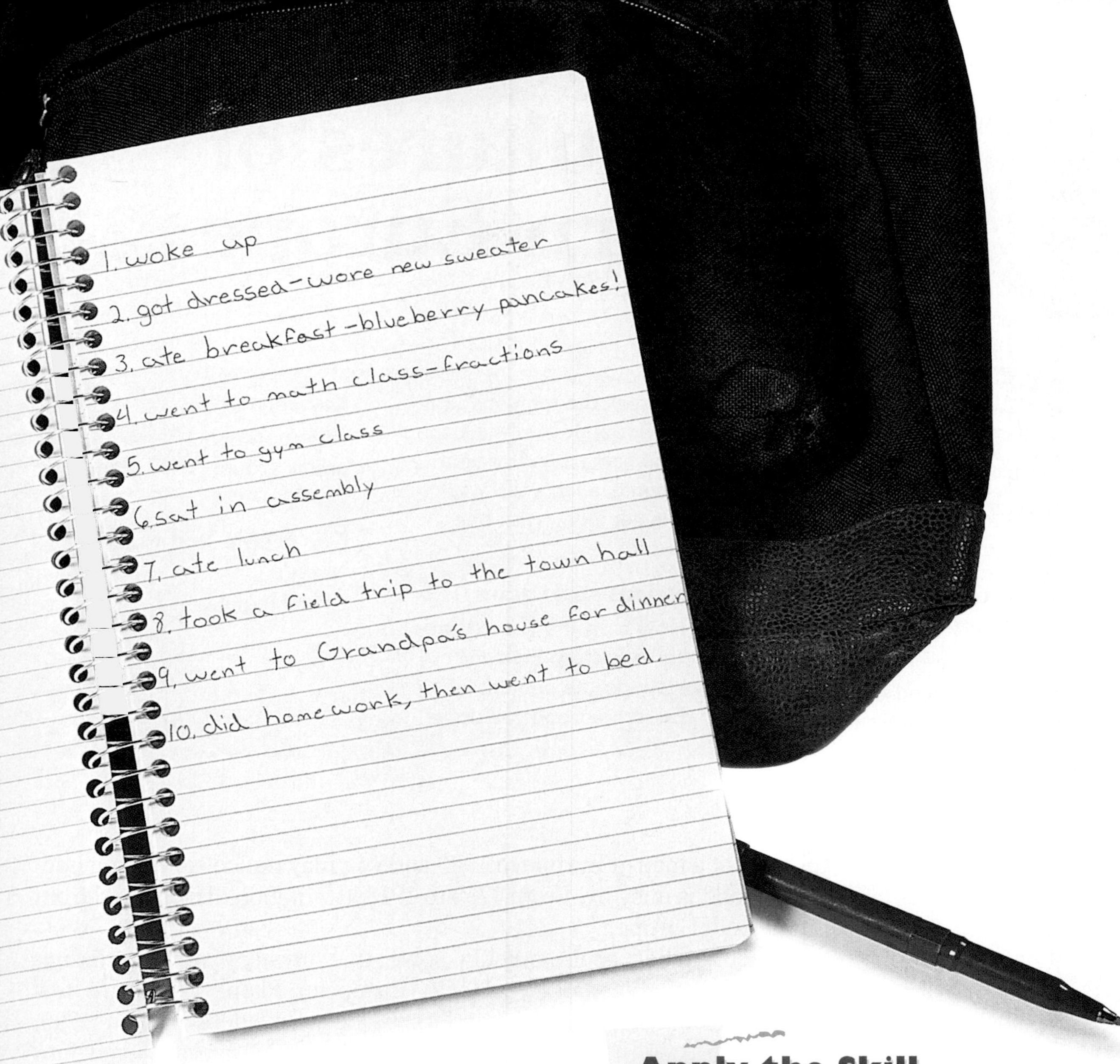

to the next by showing how the ideas are related to each other. For example, if your list reads "1) woke up, 2) got dressed, 3) ate breakfast," you might write, "First, I woke up. Then, after I got dressed, I ate breakfast."

1. woke up
2. got dressed-wore new sweater
3. ate breakfast-blueberry pancakes!
4. went to math class-fractions
5. went to gym class
6. sat in assembly
7. ate lunch
8. took a field trip to the town hall
9. went to Grandpa's house for dinner
10. did homework, then went to bed.

Congratulations! You have just summarized an entire morning in a single paragraph.

Apply the Skill

Summarizing a day is good for diary writing, but not much help in your schoolwork. However, the steps you just took will help you in school when you apply them to what you read or hear.

Practice by writing a summary of this chapter. Follow the four steps you took when summarizing your day. The headings in the chapter will help you pick the main points to list. Topic sentences in paragraphs will also help you find main points and interesting details. Remember to turn your list into a written summary. When you have finished, reread your summary. How can your summary help you remember what was in the chapter and help you prepare for a test?

The Cultures of Eastern Europe

Reach Into Your Background

Are the people of your community a blend of several cultures? Or do most people come from the same cultural group? How do you think the cultural background of your community affects the way people get along with one another?

Questions to Explore

1. How have the Slavs shaped life in Eastern Europe?
2. How do the peoples of Eastern Europe get along?

Key Terms

migration
ethnic group
dialect

Key People and Places

Slovakia
Czech Republic

Look at a map of Europe in 1900 and you may notice something odd. Poland is missing. From 1795 to 1918, this nation disappeared from the maps of Europe.

A geographer could quickly solve this mystery of the missing country. Poland lies on the North European Plain. There are few mountains or other natural barriers to keep invaders out. In 1795, Russia, Prussia, and Austria moved into Poland and divided it among themselves. Poland did not become independent again until the end of World War I.

▼ Poland is not shown on this map of Europe, which was drawn in 1870.

Movement throughout much of Eastern Europe is easy. For thousands of years, groups have entered or crossed this region. This movement from place to place, called **migration** (my GRAY shun), is still happening today.

There are many reasons for migration in Eastern Europe. Long ago, people moved to find places with a good supply of natural resources. Sometimes people moved to escape enemies. In more recent times, people have fled places where their religious or political beliefs put them in danger. And they have often moved to find a better life.

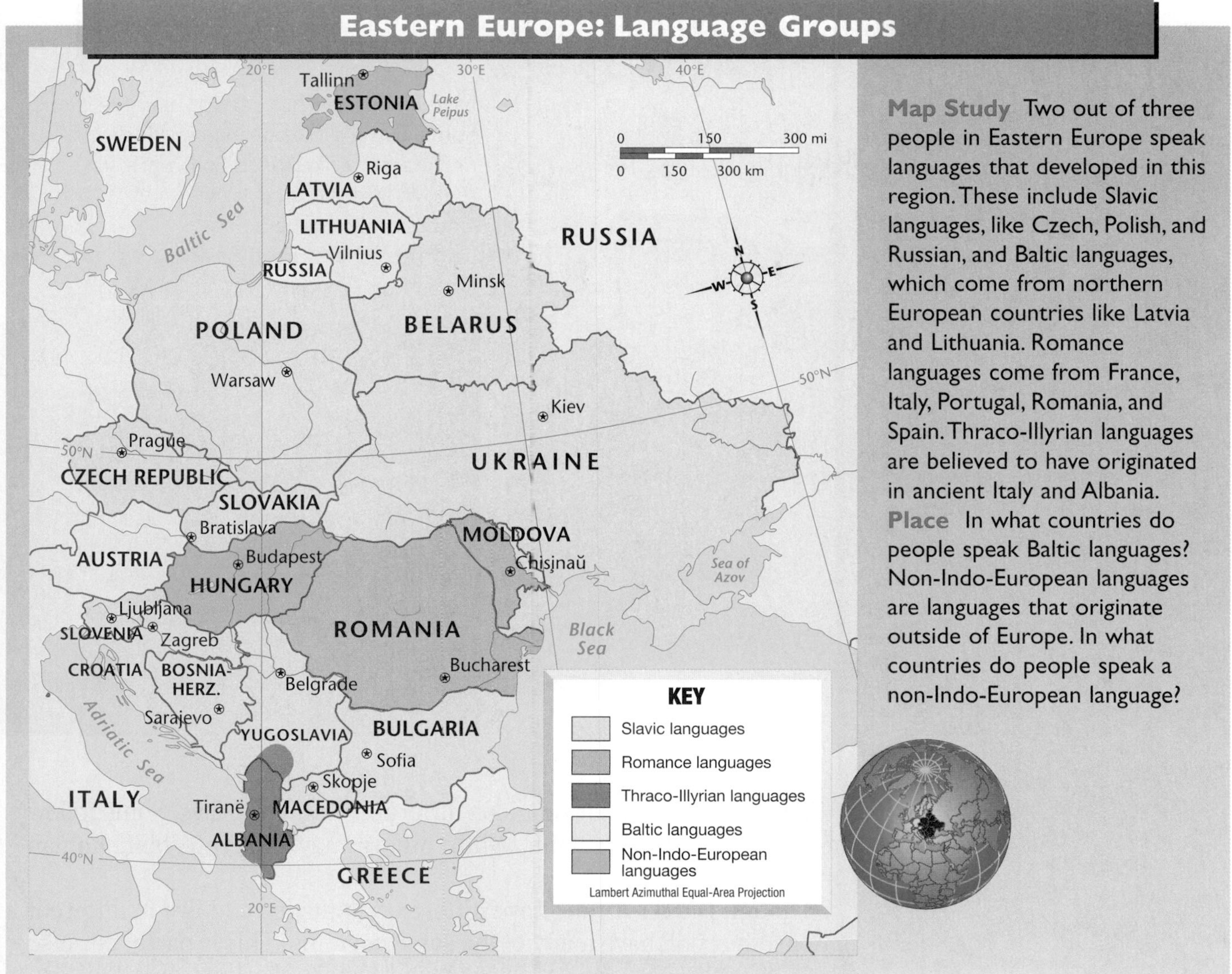

Eastern Europe: Language Groups

Map Study Two out of three people in Eastern Europe speak languages that developed in this region. These include Slavic languages, like Czech, Polish, and Russian, and Baltic languages, which come from northern European countries like Latvia and Lithuania. Romance languages come from France, Italy, Portugal, Romania, and Spain. Thraco-Illyrian languages are believed to have originated in ancient Italy and Albania. **Place** In what countries do people speak Baltic languages? Non-Indo-European languages are languages that originate outside of Europe. In what countries do people speak a non-Indo-European language?

Ethnic Groups in Eastern Europe

Among the groups that long ago migrated to Eastern Europe were the Slavs (slahvz). These people first lived in the mountains of modern Slovakia (sloh VAH kee uh) and Ukraine. By the 700s, they had spread south to Greece, east to the Alps, and north to the coast of the Baltic Sea.

Slavic Cultures Today, the Slavs are one of the major ethnic groups in Eastern Europe. People of the same **ethnic group** share things, such as a culture, a language, and a religion, that set them apart from their neighbors. Two thousand years ago, there was a single Slavic language. But as the Slavs separated, different Slavic languages developed. Today, some 10 Slavic languages are spoken in Eastern Europe. These include Czech, Polish, and Russian.

Also, even two Slavs who speak the same language may not speak the same dialect. A **dialect** (DY uh lekt) is a different version of a language that can be found only in a certain region.

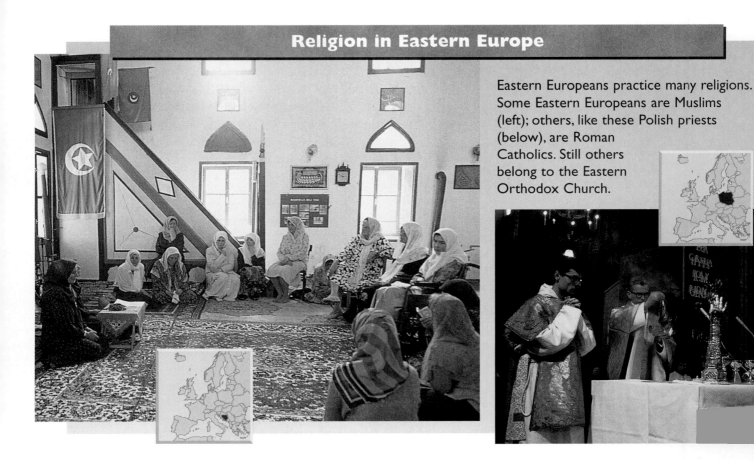

Eastern Europeans practice many religions. Some Eastern Europeans are Muslims (left); others, like these Polish priests (below), are Roman Catholics. Still others belong to the Eastern Orthodox Church.

There are also major religious differences among Slavs. Some follow the Eastern Orthodox faith, while others may be Protestant, Roman Catholic, or Muslim.

Though the Slavs now have different languages and live in different nations, they still have many of the same customs. This is partly because Eastern Europe has fewer factories and factory workers than Western Europe. Large numbers of Eastern Europeans still live in rural areas and work as farmers. Customs change more slowly in rural areas than in cities.

Predict What happens when different groups cannot solve their differences?

Other Ethnic Groups Such countries as Poland, Croatia (kroh AY shuh), Slovenia (sloh VEE nee uh), and the Czech Republic are almost entirely Slavic. But many other ethnic groups live in Eastern Europe. About 90 percent of the people of Hungary belong to an ethnic group called the Magyars (MAG yarz). In the country of Romania, most people belong to yet another ethnic group, the Romanians. Similarly, the Bulgars of Bulgaria and the Albanians of Albania are separate ethnic groups. And people belonging to the German ethnic group live in several of the countries of Eastern Europe.

Ethnic Conflict

In some Eastern European countries, people of different ethnic groups live together in harmony. But in other places, there have been ethnic conflicts.

Czechs and Slovaks: A Peaceful Division For most of the 1900s, Czechoslovakia (check uh sloh VAH kee uh) was a single country. The two main ethnic groups were the Czechs and the Slovaks. The Czechs lived mostly in a western region called Bohemia. Czechs and Slovaks lived in the central region of Moravia. The Slovaks lived mostly in the eastern region of Slovakia. Hungarians, Ukranians, Germans, and Polish people also lived in these areas.

Czechoslovakia was a parliamentary democracy from 1918 to 1935. After World War II, the Soviet Union controlled Czechoslovakia. Almost overnight, the Communist party took over the country. Many people were not happy with the Communist government. For example, writers and scientists could not gain work unless they were members of the Communist party. From the 1960s to the 1980s, students and writers formed groups promoting a return to democracy. Vaclav Havel, a playwright, was a major voice of protest. He spoke out against the government for more than 20 years and was repeatedly put in jail. The government urged him to move out of the country, but he always refused. In 1988, he explained his reasons for staying in Czechoslovakia.

Glassware The people of northern Bohemia, in the Czech Republic, have been making glass since the 1200s. In the 1700s, glass factories made Bohemia one of the wealthiest parts of Europe. The glassware from this region is often decorated with castles, people, and animals. One artist, Caspar Lehmann, engraved glass and copper and bronze tools shaped like wheels.

Prague Castle

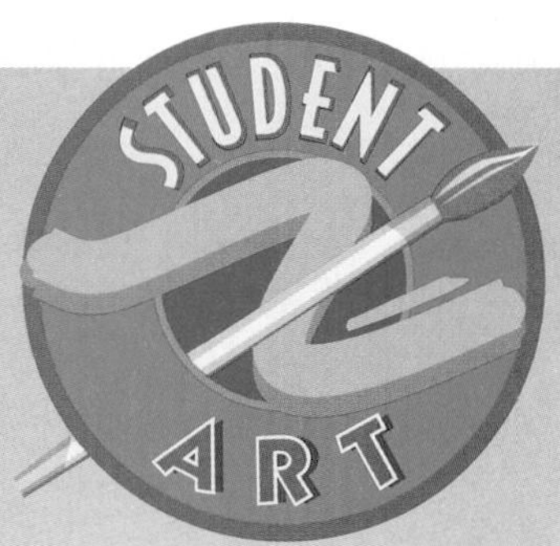

Darina Vassova
10 years old
Czech Republic

Prague Castle was a symbol of unified Czechoslovakia for many years. It was the home of the president of the country, and before that, it was the home of kings. Prague Castle still houses many valuable works of art. It stands high on a hill above the Vlatva River. **Critical Thinking** Why do you think Czechs built Prague Castle on a hill above a river? What are the benefits of such a location?

> “I am Czech. This was not my choice, it was fate. . . . This is my language, this is my home. I live here like everyone else. I don’t feel myself to be patriotic, because I don’t feel that to be Czech is to be something more than French, English, or European, or anybody else. . . . I try to do something for my country because I live here.”

Mass protests forced the communist government to consider changes. In 1989, the Communist party gave up its power and worked in cooperation with the democratic groups. This generally nonviolent change in power from a communist government to a democratic system is called the Velvet Revolution. Havel later was elected president of Czechoslovakia.

The Czechs and the Slovaks had strong ideas about the future of their groups. Both sides disagreed about how to carry out the goals of the newly democratic country. In 1993, they agreed to separate, and the countries of the Czech Republic and Slovakia were born. Perhaps because most Czechs and Slovaks already lived in separate parts of the country, the split was peaceful.

Eastern Europe: Political

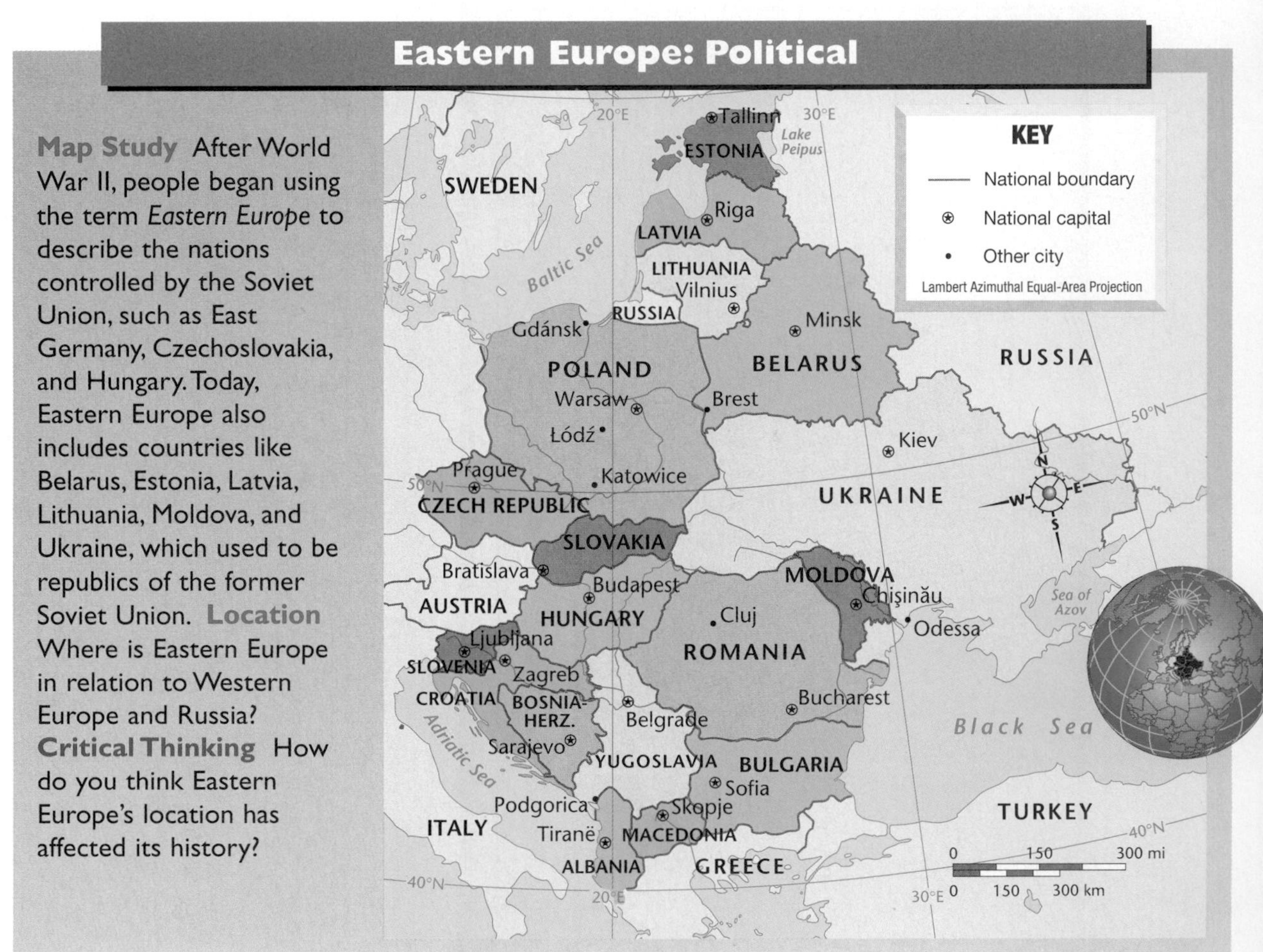

Map Study After World War II, people began using the term *Eastern Europe* to describe the nations controlled by the Soviet Union, such as East Germany, Czechoslovakia, and Hungary. Today, Eastern Europe also includes countries like Belarus, Estonia, Latvia, Lithuania, Moldova, and Ukraine, which used to be republics of the former Soviet Union. **Location** Where is Eastern Europe in relation to Western Europe and Russia? **Critical Thinking** How do you think Eastern Europe's location has affected its history?

◀ In the war-torn country of Bosnia-Herzegovina, United Nations troops struggle to keep a fragile peace among the warring parties.

When Ethnic Groups Clash But not all ethnic conflicts in Eastern Europe have ended peacefully. In Yugoslavia (yoo goh SLAH vee uh), most Yugoslavs were part of the same ethnic group—the Slavs. However, various groups within the country had distinct religions and cultures. These differences led to the breakup of Yugoslavia in the early 1990s. The new countries of Bosnia-Herzegovina (BAHZ nee uh hert suh goh VEE nuh), Croatia, Slovenia, Serbia and Montenegro, and Macedonia were formed. The breakup of Yugoslavia led to many problems in the new countries of the region. War broke out, and thousands of people, mainly Bosnians, were killed. In 1995, NATO forces helped bring peace to the region. NATO (North Atlantic Treaty Organization) is an alliance between the United States, Canada, and other western nations. NATO was formed in 1949 with the goal of protecting the interests of the member nations and promoting international cooperation.

By 1999, conflict had again broken out, this time between the Serbs and ethnic Albanians who live in Kosovo, a province of Serbia. As a result, NATO forces were again sent to the region. Though a cease-fire was reached, tensions remain, and the future of the region is uncertain.

1. **Define** (a) migration, (b) ethnic group, (c) dialect.
2. **Identify** (a) Slovakia, (b) Czech Republic.
3. Why are the Slavs important in Eastern Europe?
4. Give an example of Eastern Europeans (a) getting along with one another and (b) being in conflict with one another.

Critical Thinking

5. **Recognizing Cause and Effect** This section explains that Slavs in rural areas follow customs that have lasted for centuries. Why do you think customs change more slowly in rural areas than in urban areas?

Activity

6. **Writing to Learn** Write a paragraph about how you think ethnic conflicts affect the ways in which people think of other ethnic groups. How can people's attitudes make it harder to solve these conflicts?

The Cultures of Russia

Reach Into Your Background

Do you and your family celebrate certain holidays each year? Why are these holidays important? Do other people in your community observe these holidays, or do they observe different ones?

Questions to Explore

1. How have ethnic groups in and around Russia affected Russian history?
2. How are the people of Russia reconnecting with their traditions?

Key Terms

heritage
repress
propaganda

Key People and Places

Leo Tolstoy
Peter Tchaikovsky
St. Petersburg

▼ Under communism, worship in Soviet churches was forbidden. Now, the doors of churches all over the former Soviet Union are open again for worshippers.

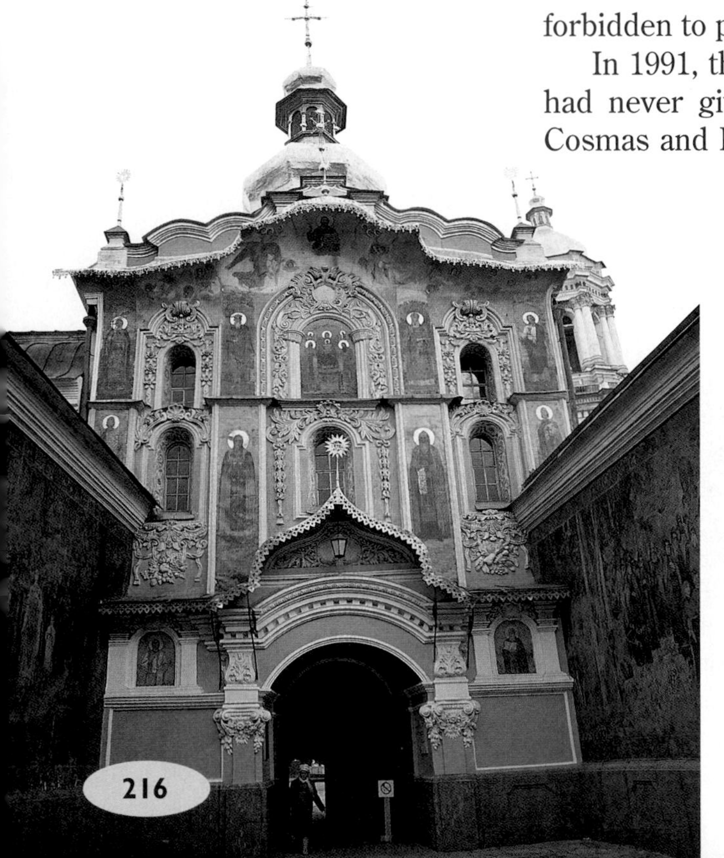

For many years, Russians passing the Church of Saints Cosmas and Damian in Moscow never heard a choir. They never saw a bride and groom leave the church. They never heard religious services. The only sound they heard was the hum of machines printing government documents. The communist government of the Soviet Union owned the church and used it as a printing shop. In the Soviet Union, people were forbidden to practice religion.

In 1991, the Soviet Union collapsed. Two years later, Russians who had never given up their faith took back their church. Now Saints Cosmas and Damian is filled with people singing songs of worship. In recent years, hundreds of other churches in Moscow have reopened their doors. The same return to religion can be seen in places of worship across all of Russia.

Russia's Ethnic Mix

The Russian Orthodox religion, a branch of Christianity, has been a powerful bond among Russians for hundreds of years. It is part of the Russian **heritage** (HEHR ut ij), or the customs and practices that are passed from one generation to the next. Another part of the Russian heritage is ethnic. More than 80 percent of the Russian people belong to the ethnic group of Russian Slavs. These people generally speak the Russian language and live in western parts of the country.

Other Ethnic Groups Besides the Slavs, more than 75 different ethnic groups live in Russia. Most of the minority groups live far from the heavily populated western areas. The Finns and Turks live in regions of the Ural and Caucasus (KAW kuh sus) mountains. Armenians and Mongolians live along Russia's southern edges. The Yakuts (yah KOOTS) live in small areas of Siberia. These groups speak languages other than Russian. They also follow different religions. Muslims make up Russia's second-largest religious group, after Russian Orthodox believers. Many followers of Buddhism (BOOD izum) live near Russia's border with China.

United or Divided? When the Soviet Union came apart, some non-Russian ethnic groups broke away from Russia and formed their own countries. Since that time, other ethnic groups have tried to break ties with Russia.

The new Russian government has tried to keep the country unified by giving ethnic groups the right to rule themselves. At times, however, groups have called for complete independence from Russia. In response, the Russian government has sent the army to **repress,** or put down, the independence movements.

The East-West Split In 1054, it was official. The Christian Church was split into the Eastern Orthodox Church (which included the Russian Orthodox Church) and the Roman Catholic Church. The leaders of each church excommunicated each other; each man said that the other man could not belong to his church. It was not until 1965 that the two sides officially removed the excommunications.

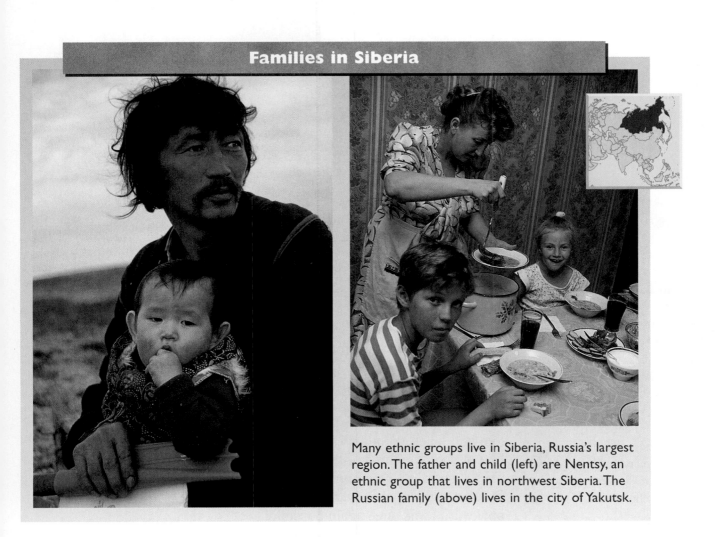

Families in Siberia

Many ethnic groups live in Siberia, Russia's largest region. The father and child (left) are Nentsy, an ethnic group that lives in northwest Siberia. The Russian family (above) lives in the city of Yakutsk.

A Monument to Heroic Workers

Socialist realism was the only acceptable style of art in the Soviet Union. Socialist realist paintings and sculptures showed idealized—or perfect—views of heroic workers and farmers, often struggling against great odds. The only purpose of socialist realist art was to further the aims of the Soviet government. **Critical Thinking** This sculpture in Moscow is a monument to Soviet workers. The two workers are holding aloft a hammer and sickle, the symbols of the Soviet Union. What aspects of socialist realist art does this sculpture illustrate?

Russian Ballet Sergei Diaghilev created the Ballets Russes—a Russian ballet company—in 1909. He had a flair for using unusual dance and music in his shows. In one ballet, the music was so strange that the audience complained—and the dancers were unable to hear the music from the nearby orchestra pit.

Russian Culture and Education

Russia has produced many great artists, thinkers, and writers. Russia's artistic heritage includes outstanding architecture, fine religious paintings, great plays, and intricate art objects like the Fabergé (fah ber ZHAY) egg on the opposite page. Novelist Leo Tolstoy (TOHL stoy) wrote powerful stories of life in Russia in the 1800s. Peter Tchaikovsky (chy KAWF skee) composed moving classical music. Russian painters, such as Vasily Kandinsky (kan DIN skee), were leaders in the modern art movement in the early 1900s. In a way, creating works of art is a tradition among Russians.

Under communism, the creation of great new works of art nearly came to a halt. The Soviet government believed that the purpose of art was to glorify communism. The government banned any art it did not like and jailed countless artists. The only art that the government did like was **propaganda**—the spread of ideas designed to support some cause, such as communism. With the collapse of communism, the Russian people eagerly returned to their artistic traditions. Creating new works was once again possible.

Elegant St. Petersburg An important center of Russian culture is the city of St. Petersburg. Visitors to the city can clearly see the Russian mixture of European and Slavic cultures. This city has many Western influences. Peter the Great founded it in 1703. His goal was to create a Russian city as beautiful as any Western European city.

Elegant is the best word for St. Petersburg. The Neva (NEE vuh) River winds gracefully through the city. Along the river's banks are palaces, and public buildings hundreds of years old. St. Petersburg's

A Fabergé Egg

EXPLORING TECHNOLOGY

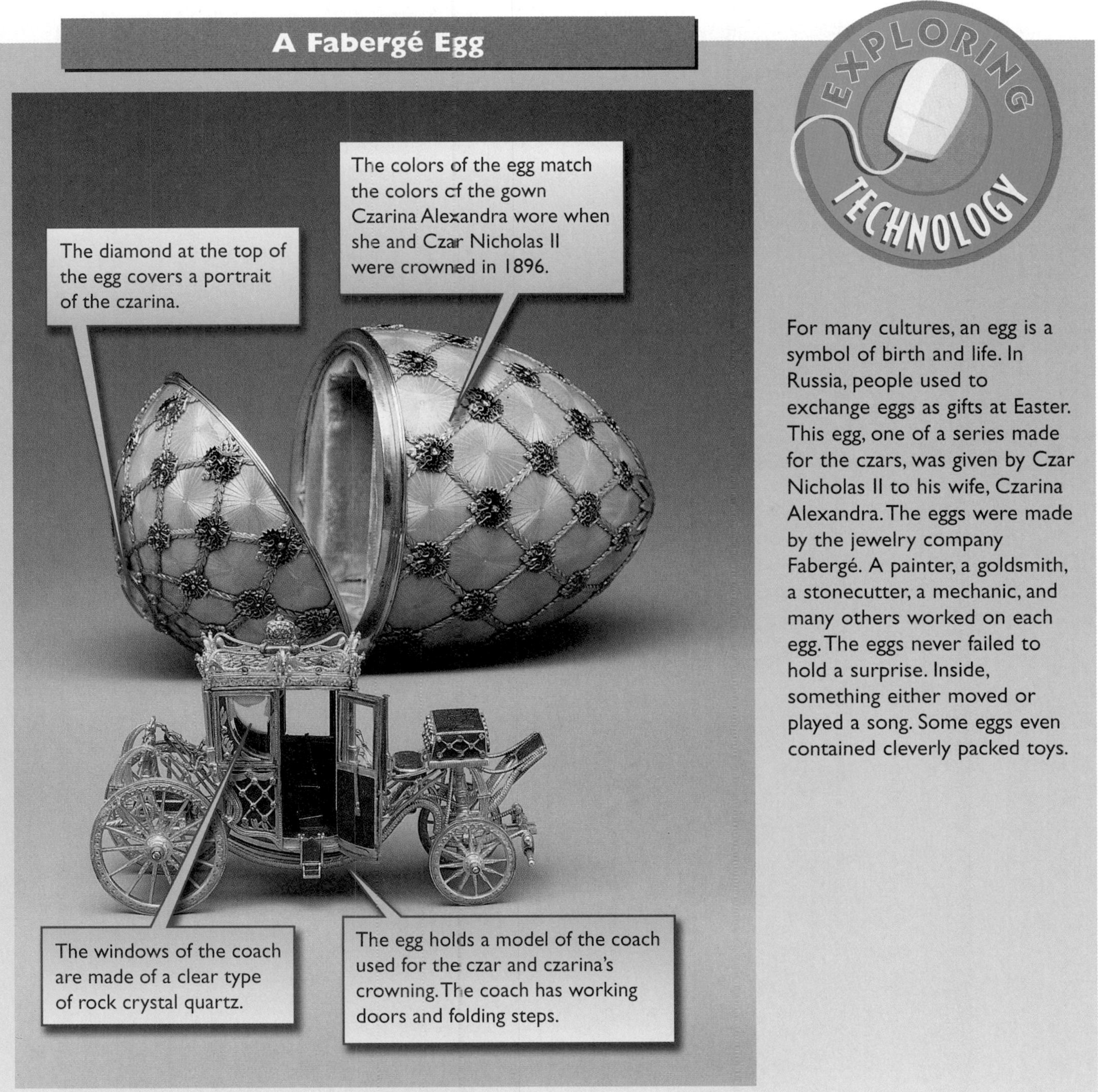

The colors of the egg match the colors of the gown Czarina Alexandra wore when she and Czar Nicholas II were crowned in 1896.
The diamond at the top of the egg covers a portrait of the czarina.
The windows of the coach are made of a clear type of rock crystal quartz.
The egg holds a model of the coach used for the czar and czarina's crowning. The coach has working doors and folding steps.

For many cultures, an egg is a symbol of birth and life. In Russia, people used to exchange eggs as gifts at Easter. This egg, one of a series made for the czars, was given by Czar Nicholas II to his wife, Czarina Alexandra. The eggs were made by the jewelry company Fabergé. A painter, a goldsmith, a stonecutter, a mechanic, and many others worked on each egg. The eggs never failed to hold a surprise. Inside, something either moved or played a song. Some eggs even contained cleverly packed toys.

grandest sight, the Winter Palace, is on the Neva. This more than 1,000-room palace, shown in the pictures below, was the winter home of Russia's czars. Part of the palace is the Hermitage (HUR mih tij) Museum. This museum houses one of the world's finest art collections.

Education in Russia One of the few strengths of the old Soviet Union was its offer of free public education. Under this system, the number of Russians who could read and write rose from about 40 percent to nearly 100 percent.

Russian Treasures

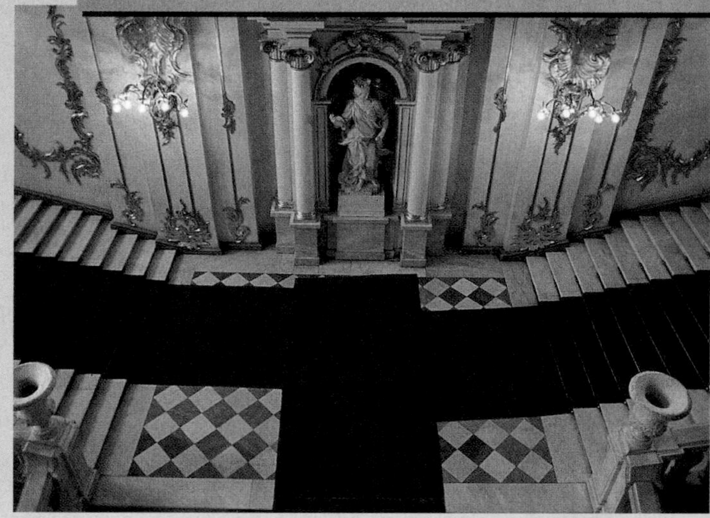

Visitors to St. Petersburg's Hermitage Museum can view priceless art objects in the Emblem Hall (below) and climb the Grand Staircase where czars once walked (left). **Critical Thinking** Why do you think it is important to Russians to preserve the homes of czars even though Russia is no longer ruled by a czar?

The new Russia has continued free public schooling for children between ages 6 and 17. Schools are updating their old courses of study, which told only the communist point of view. New courses, such as business management, are preparing students for the new, noncommunist Russia. Some private schools run by the Orthodox Church offer similar courses, as well as religious instruction.

These changes show that Russia is trying to recover the riches of its past even as it prepares for a new future. Religion and art, two important parts of Russia's cultural heritage, can now be freely expressed. And Russia's young people, unlike their parents, can grow up deciding their future for themselves.

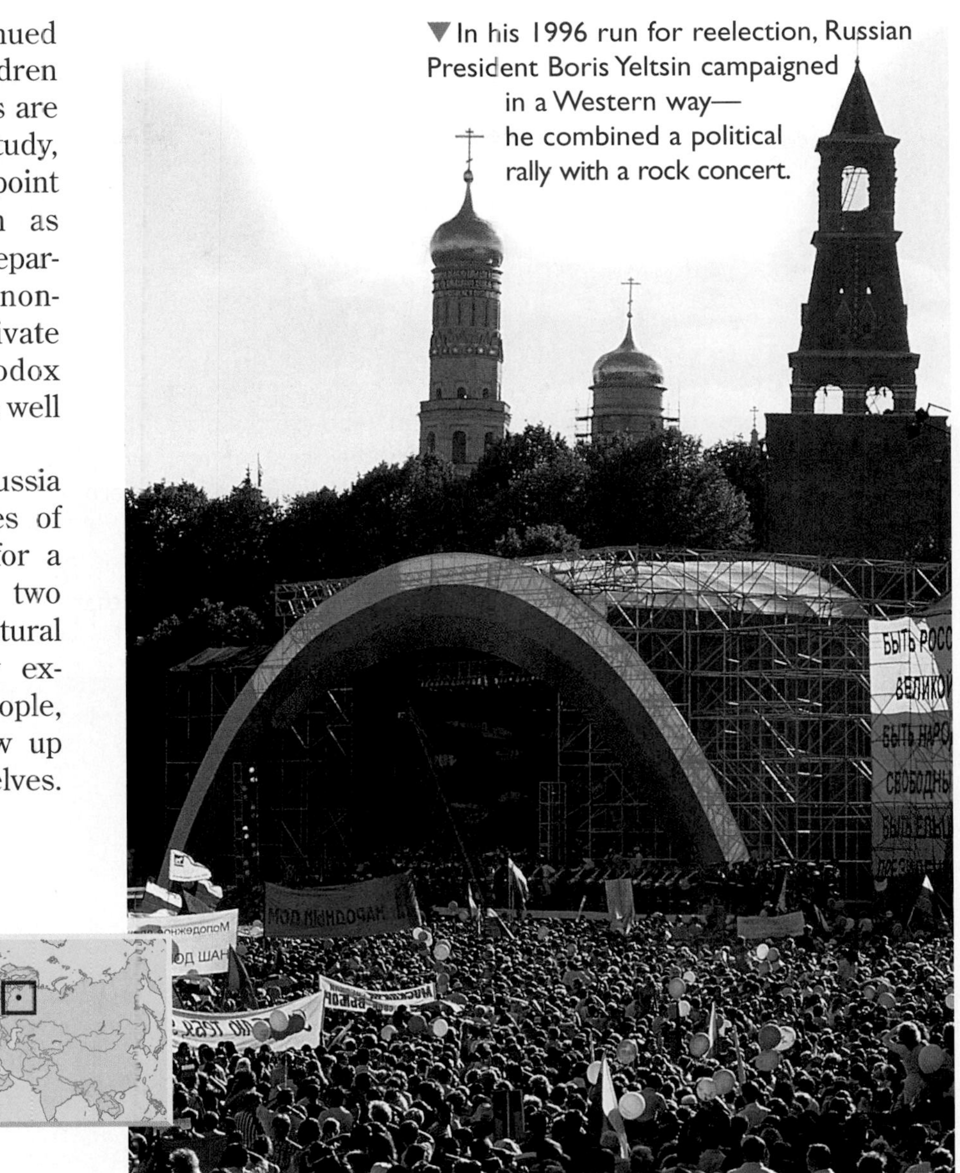

▼ In his 1996 run for reelection, Russian President Boris Yeltsin campaigned in a Western way—he combined a political rally with a rock concert.

SECTION 3 REVIEW

1. **Define** (a) heritage, (b) repress, (c) propaganda.
2. **Identify** (a) Leo Tolstoy, (b) Peter Tchaikovsky, (c) St. Petersburg.
3. (a) What is Russia's major ethnic group? (b) How has the government treated Russia's smaller ethnic groups?
4. What are some examples of ways in which Russians are reconnecting with their past?

Critical Thinking

5. **Recognizing Cause and Effect** How have the political changes in Russia led to changes in education?
6. **Expressing Problems Clearly** How has Russia's ethnic mix created challenges for the new Russian government?

Activity

7. **Writing to Learn** What predictions might you make about Russia's culture in the next 10 years? Give reasons for your predictions.

Review and Activities

Reviewing Main Ideas

1. What features make many cities in Western Europe great centers for culture?
2. How do open borders and free trade affect the way Western Europeans live?
3. (a) Who are the Slavs? (b) Why are the Slavs an important part of the population of Eastern Europe?
4. How was the breakup of Czechoslovakia different than the breakup of Yugoslavia?
5. How have non-Russian ethnic groups reacted to recent events in Russia?
6. What traditions are Russians reviving following the collapse of the Soviet Union?

Reviewing Key Terms

Match the definitions in Column I with the key terms in Column II.

Column I

1. to put down
2. the movement of people from place to place
3. people who share a language, culture, and religion
4. a variation of a language
5. customs passed on from one generation to the next
6. influenced by many different cultures
7. spread of ideas designed to support a cause
8. a fee that the government charges for goods entering the country

Column II

a. **multicultural**
b. **migration**
c. **heritage**
d. **ethnic group**
e. **dialect**
f. **propaganda**
g. **repress**
h. **tariff**

Critical Thinking

1. **Drawing Conclusions** Why do Western Europeans generally have a higher standard of living than Eastern Europeans?
2. **Identifying Central Issues** How has life changed for the Russian people since the collapse of the Soviet Union?

Graphic Organizer

Copy the chart onto a separate sheet of paper. Then fill in the empty boxes to complete the chart.

	How the Lives of Its People Are Changing	What Is Special About Its Cultures	Relations Among Different Ethnic Groups or Countries
Western Europe			
Eastern Europe			
Russia			

Map Activity

Europe and Russia

For each place listed below, write the letter from the map that shows its location. Use the maps in the Activity Atlas to help you.

1. France
2. Ukraine
3. Russia
4. Germany
5. Slovakia
6. St. Petersburg

Place Location

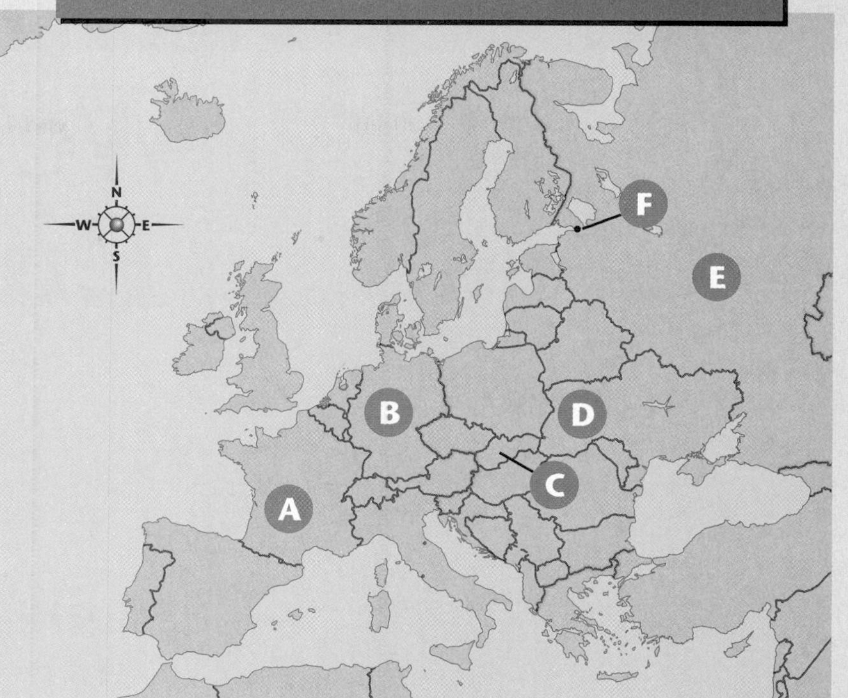

Writing Activity

Writing a Travel Guide

If you had friends who were visiting Europe and Russia for the first time, what information would you want to share with them? Starting with the title "A Guide to Europe and Russia," write a brief travel guide your friends can use to plan an educational and enjoyable trip. Mention interesting places and activities, and provide background information on the cultures of the people they will meet.

Take It to the NET

Activity Explore the Web sites of Russian cities and use the information to create a brochure on Russian culture. For help in completing this activity, visit **www.phschool.com.**

Chapter 8 Self-Test To review what you have learned, take the Chapter 8 Self-Test and get instant feedback on your answers. Go to **www.phschool.com** to take the test.

Skills Review

Turn to the Skills Activity.

Review the steps for summarizing information. Then, write a one-paragraph summary of your last weekend.

How Am I Doing?

Answer these questions to help you check your progress.

1. Do I understand how and why the people of Western Europe are coming together?
2. Can I identify different ethnic groups in Eastern Europe?
3. Can I describe the heritage of the Russian people?
4. What information from this chapter can I include in my journal?

CHAPTER 9

Exploring Western Europe

MAP ACTIVITIES

This map shows Western Europe, the region you will be reading about in this chapter. To help you get to know Western Europe, complete the following activities.

Understanding geography

Western Europe is sometimes called a "peninsula of peninsulas." Use information from the map to explain why.

Study the map

Follow the outlines of the countries. Look for familiar shapes. For example, Italy looks like a boot. Spain and Portugal look like a square attached to the rest of Europe. Describe the shapes of other countries.

Great Britain

A Democratic Tradition

Reach Into Your Background

What does the word *tradition* mean to you? Identify two or three American traditions. Compare them to the British traditions you read about in this section.

Questions to Explore

1. How did democracy develop in Britain?
2. How does Britain's status as an island nation affect the way of life of its people?

Key Terms

Parliament
representative
constitutional monarchy

Key People and Places

Queen Elizabeth II
King John
Buckingham Palace

The line of tourists seems to go on forever. Every few feet along the line, a different language is spoken. You can hear English, French, Arabic, and Japanese. Despite the difference in languages, all the tourists are talking about the same thing: the British crown jewels.

The jewels are kept under guard in a large building called the Tower of London. The beautiful collection includes crowns worn by Great Britain's kings and queens. After a long wait, the tourists reach a motorized walkway, which slowly carries them past the bulletproof case. Their eyes widen with wonder at the sight of huge diamonds, bright rubies, and cool sapphires (SAF eyerz).

British history comes alive in and around the Tower. On Tower Green, nobles went to their deaths on the executioner's block. In the Bloody Tower, the young King Edward V and his brother were said to have been murdered. The Wakefield Tower holds rings and royal symbols of

▼ St. Edward's crown, one of several crowns kept at the Tower of London, is a copy of a crown worn by Edward the Confessor. He ruled England from 1042 to 1066.

kings and queens. All these places are watched over by guards called Beefeaters. They wear colorful red costumes like those worn by the guards in the 1500s.

United Kingdom: Resources and the Economy

Labor Force

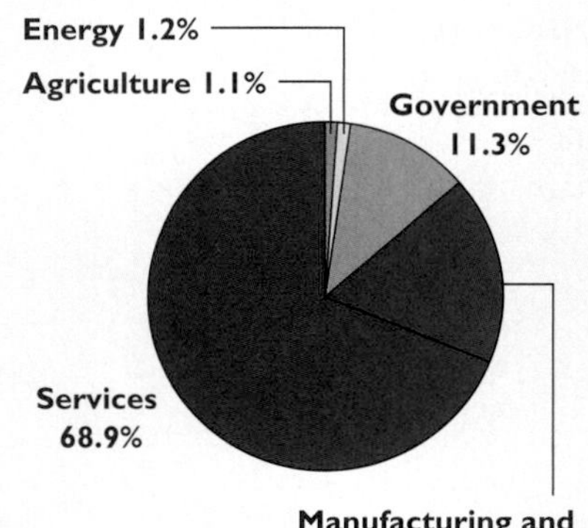

Source: CIA World Factbook 2000

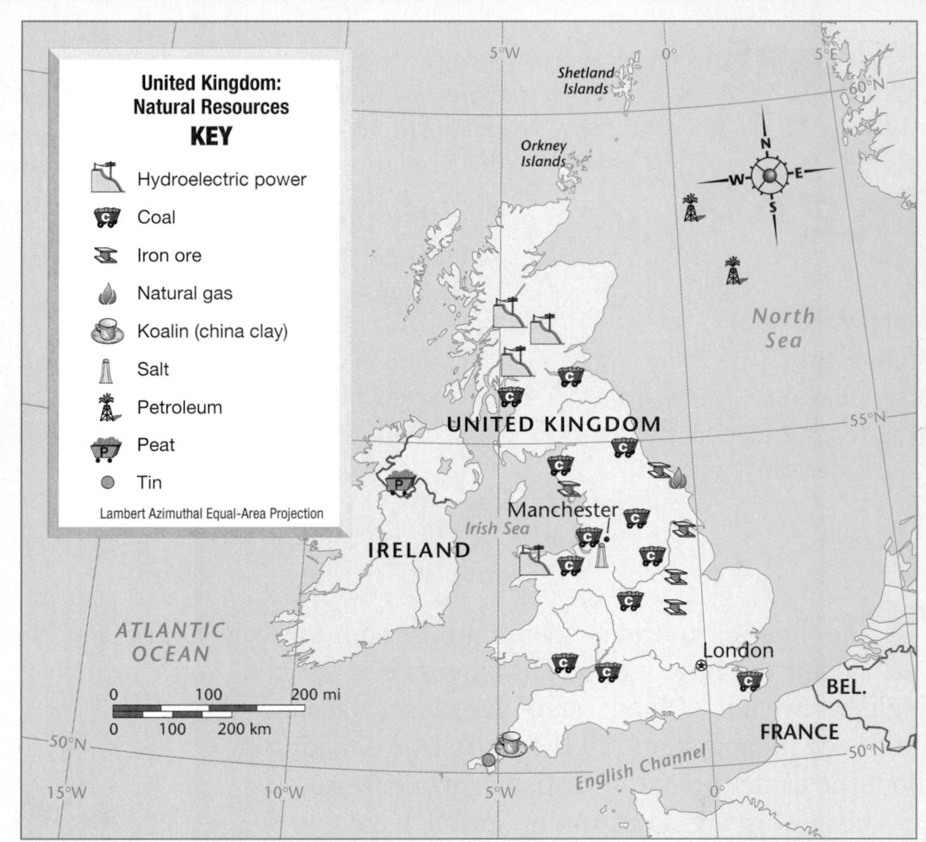

Major Export Destinations

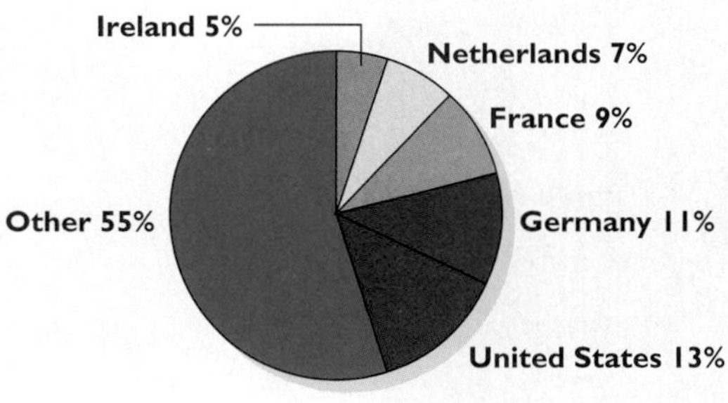

Major Sources of Imports

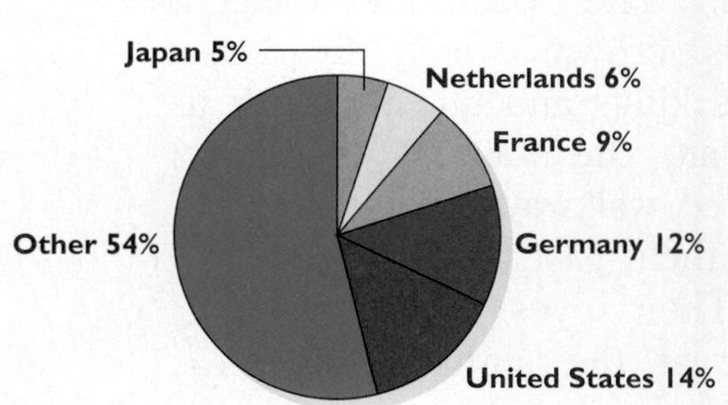

Source: Dorling Kindersley World Desk Reference

Take It to the NET

Data Update For the most recent data on the United Kingdom, visit **www.phschool.com.**

Economics The map and charts show the natural resources, workforce, and trading partners of the United Kingdom. **Map and Chart Study** (a) Describe the location of energy sources—coal, oil, and natural gas—found in the United Kingdom. (b) Which type of economic activity employs the most people in the United Kingdom? (c) From which country does the United Kingdom receive the most imports?

A Democratic Heritage

Visitors standing inside the Tower of London may forget that Great Britain is a modern nation. In the Tower, Britain's long tradition of kings and queens seems as strong as ever. Great Britain is still a monarchy, headed by Queen Elizabeth II. She is a symbol of Britain's past and its customs. But Great Britain also has a strong democratic government. This country served as one of the first models of a modern democracy.

The roots of British democracy go back many hundreds of years. During the Middle Ages, British kings could not take major actions without the approval of a group of rich nobles. Over time, the power of this group grew. In 1215, the group forced one English monarch, King John, to sign a document called the Magna Carta, or "Great Charter." The Magna Carta strengthened the power of the nobles and limited the power of the king.

In time, the group of nobles became known as the **Parliament.** This word comes from the French word *parler* (PAHR lay), which means "to talk." The Parliament later gained more power. It helped to decide the kinds of taxes paid by citizens. It elected people from each area to serve as **representatives.** A representative represents, or stands for, a group of people. In time, the people themselves elected these representatives. Such changes helped to make Britain a true democracy.

Ask Questions What questions would you like answered about Great Britain's system of government?

British Parliament, Present and Past

The modern Parliament consists of the House of Commons, whose members actually govern the nation, and the House of Lords (above). This 300-year-old illustration of Parliament in session (right) shows how the governing body looked in 1295 when King Edward I reigned.

A Ceremonial Monarchy

Britain's Queen Elizabeth II (above left) was crowned in 1953. The red-coated officers (above right) who guard her stand at stiff attention. The Queen may approve or reject laws passed by Parliament, but no British monarch has rejected a law since the 1700s. The Queen and members of her family also sponsor charity events, participate in important national ceremonies and parades, and represent Britain on trips to other countries.

Democracy and Monarchy

Today, the monarchy serves as an important symbol of Britain's past. It also helps to unify, or bring together, the British people. The British honor the monarchy in many ways. When the queen is in London, a royal flag is flown over her home at Buckingham (BUK ing um) Palace. Whether she is there or not, a short ceremony called the changing of the guard takes place every day. Trumpets blare and guardsmen march back and forth at the palace gate.

However, Britain's monarchs today do not have the power to make laws or collect taxes. Great Britain is now a **constitutional monarchy.** A constitution is a set of laws that describes how a government works. In a constitutional monarchy, the power of kings and queens is limited. The laws state what they can and cannot do. This is very different from the absolute monarchy in France during the time of Louis XIV. British laws are made by Parliament, not by the king or queen.

Britain Looks Outward

Parliament today governs all of the United Kingdom, which includes Great Britain (England, Scotland, and Wales) and Northern Ireland. The southern part of the island of Ireland became an independent country in the 1920s. Though *United Kingdom* is the country's official name, people often use *Britain* or *Great Britain* instead. This is because most of the people live on the island of Great Britain.

Building an Empire As an island nation, Great Britain is more difficult to invade than other European countries. During World War II, it was one of the few European countries that was not captured by the Germans. But as an island, Britain has limited natural resources. It must trade with other nations for resources. For this reason, trade has always been important to Britain.

In the 1500s, Britain began building a large empire. Its empire grew to include colonies on six continents. The colonies provided Britain's factories with raw materials. They also provided places to sell the goods made in Britain's factories. The colonies, then, helped Britain become a world economic power.

The Brightest Jewel Rare spices, silks, and other riches attracted the British East India Company to India in the 1600s. In time, the company gained great power in India. But the company misused its power, so the British government took over. By the mid-1800s, Britain controlled three fifths of India. Many people called India the "brightest jewel" in the British "crown" of colonies.

British Empire, 1900

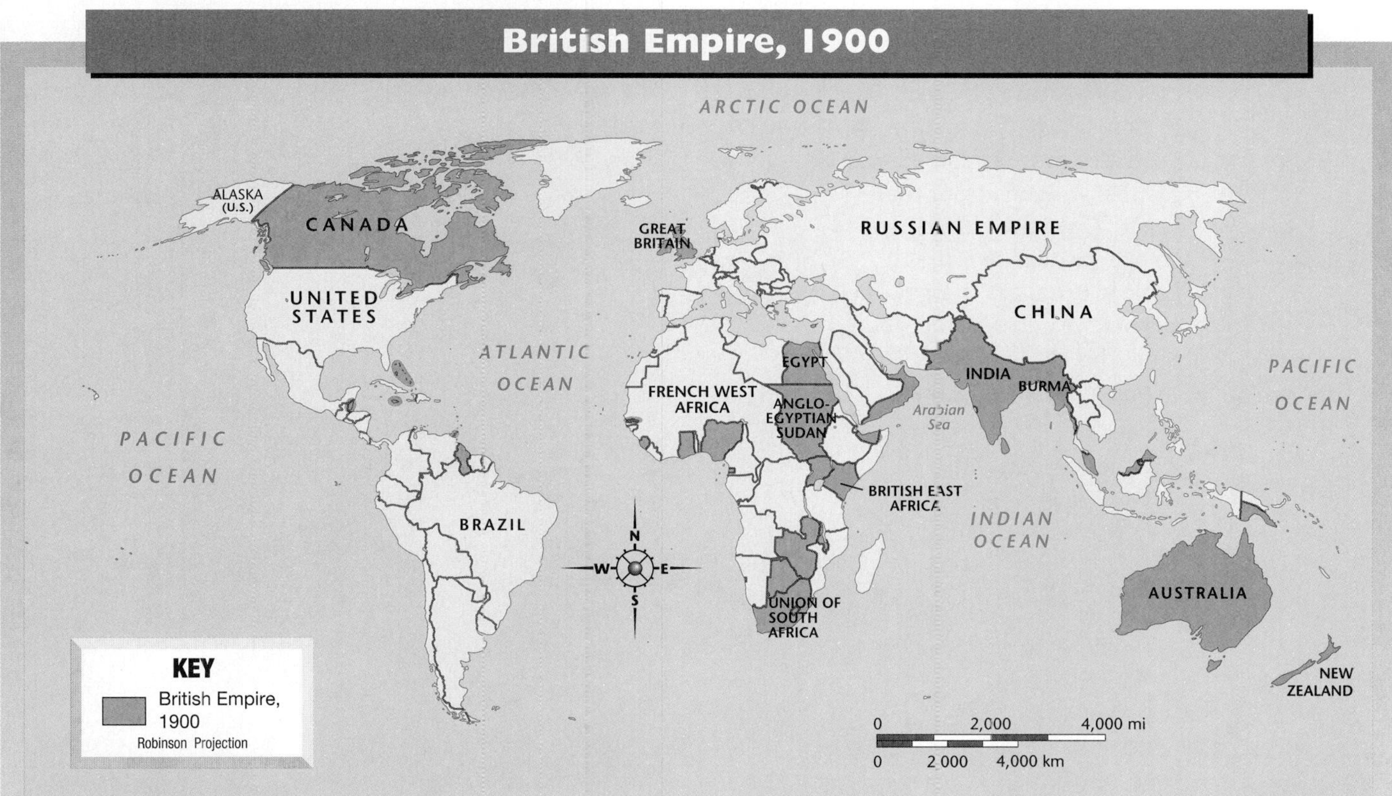

Map Study By 1900, the British Empire had reached its high point. At that time, it included approximately one fourth of the world's land and people. As the 1900s dawned, one writer noted that the area under British control had grown by "over two acres of new territory every time the clock has ticked since 1800." **Location** List, along with their continents, at least three British colonies.

At one point, Britain had so many colonies around the world that people said, "The sun never sets on the British Empire." Fighting the two World Wars weakened Britain, however. After the World Wars, Great Britain's empire fell apart. Most of its colonies gained their independence. Britain maintained close economic ties with its former colonies. However, it now had to compete with other countries to buy and sell in these markets.

A Community Member Britain's industrial base remains strong. It has good supplies of fossil fuels—especially oil from deposits beneath the North Sea. It continues to export many manufactured goods, such as clothing and electronic products. However, Britain is not as strong a world power as it was before the World Wars.

A Natural Gas Refinery

Great Britain uses natural gas in factories that produce automobiles, ships, steel, textiles, and many other products. Several deposits of natural gas lie under the North Sea, east of Great Britain. Great Britain produces most of the natural gas that it needs from these fields. **Critical Thinking** Unlike gasoline, which is a liquid, natural gas is a gas, like air and steam. What do you think the challenges of shipping a gas might be?

Flags of the European Union

In 2001, the European Union had 15 members. Some of their flags are shown here. Many more European countries are working their way through the EU application process. **Critical Thinking** How might membership in the EU benefit the British economy?

Britain can no longer rely on its colonies to boost its economy. To be successful in the modern world, Britain has had to change its approach to trade. In 1973, Britain joined what is now called the European Union (EU), a group of nations that promotes trade among its members.

Britain today is a leading member of the EU. Its expertise in areas such as shipping and finance have strengthened the EU in global trade. In turn, easier access to European markets has helped replace the trade Britain lost when its empire collapsed. With new links to the resources and markets of other European countries, the British look forward to a bright economic future.

1. **Define** (a) Parliament, (b) representative, (c) constitutional monarchy.
2. **Identify** (a) Queen Elizabeth II, (b) King John, (c) Buckingham Palace.
3. How did Britain become a constitutional monarchy?
4. How has the location of Great Britain affected how the country has developed?

Critical Thinking

5. **Drawing Conclusions** Why do you think Britain holds on to its monarchy even though the monarch now has very little power?

Activity

6. **Writing to Learn** Write one or two paragraphs describing the places you would go and the things you would do if you visited London.

France

Preserving a Culture

Reach Into Your Background
Do you have a special way of doing something? Is it dancing, playing a sport, dressing, or something else? As you read this section, you will see that the French, too, have special ways of doing things.

Questions to Explore

1. In what parts of their culture do the French people take special pride?
2. How is the culture of other nations affecting French culture?

Key Terms
emigrate

Key Places
Aix-en-Provence
Paris

▼ Carrying baguettes—long, crusty loaves of bread—two young girls stroll through France's countryside.

Catherine and Victoire are sisters. Both are in their 20s—just one year apart in age. The two look so much alike that some people think they are twins. They grew up in the south of France, in a city called Aix-en-Provence (eks ahn praw VAHNS). It is a quiet, pretty town, a trading center for olives, almonds, and wine.

Catherine and Victoire may look alike, but they are very different. Catherine still lives in Aix. She is married and has two children. Her husband works as a pastry chef, making cakes and other desserts. He learned how to make them from a master chef. He follows French recipes that were created 150 years ago.

Victoire is single and lives in Paris, the capital of France. She works for a publisher. Her job is to get American books translated into French. She has worked on science fiction books, westerns, and even vampire novels! Of course, she speaks English very well. In her apartment, she listens to American rock bands or watches American television programs. Her favorite restaurant serves only American food.

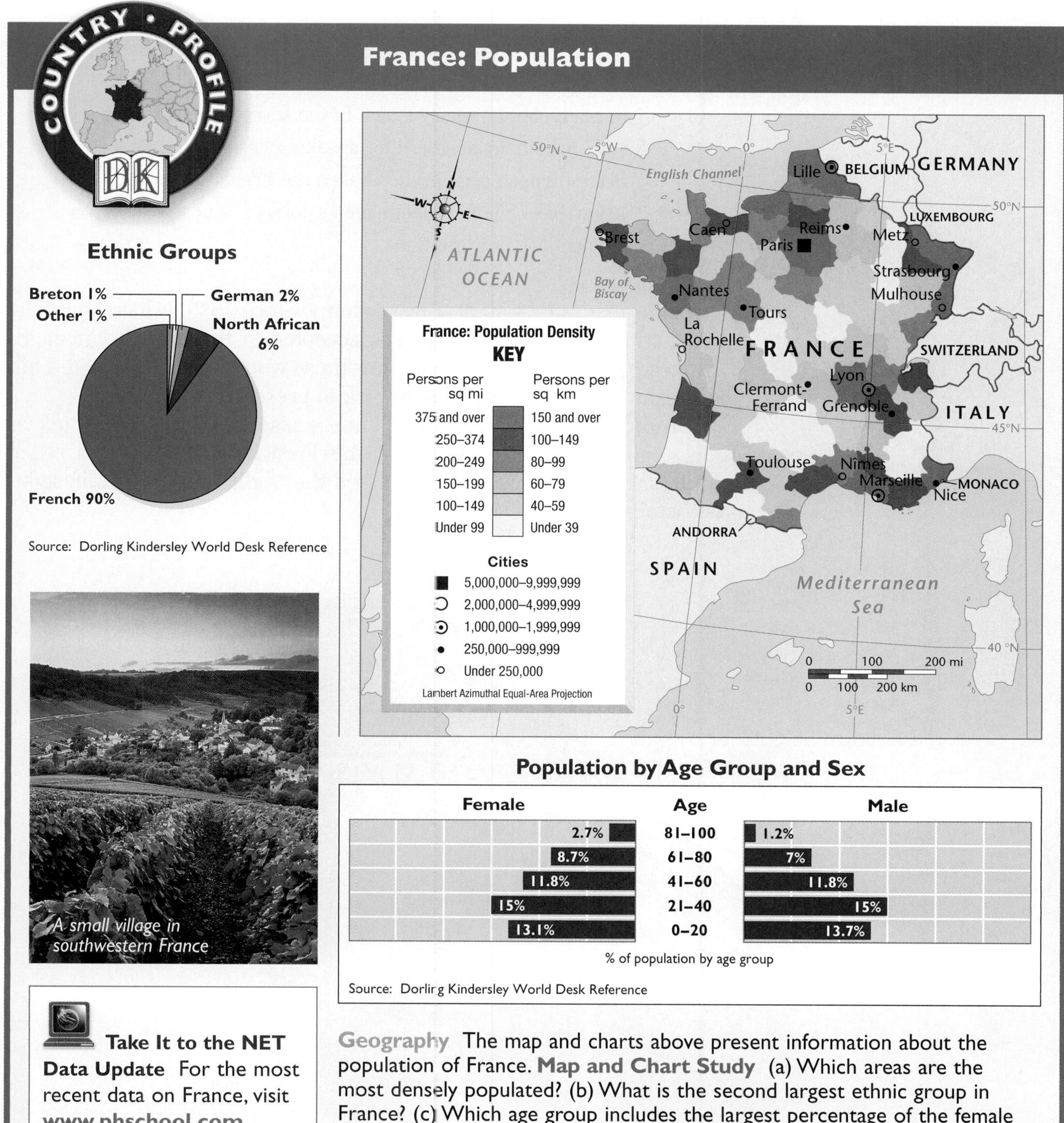

A small village in southwestern France

Take It to the NET

Data Update For the most recent data on France, visit **www.phschool.com**.

Geography The map and charts above present information about the population of France. **Map and Chart Study** (a) Which areas are the most densely populated? (b) What is the second largest ethnic group in France? (c) Which age group includes the largest percentage of the female population?

Pride in French Culture

Catherine and Victoire show us two sides of the French character. Each side values French culture differently. Catherine sums up her attitude this way:

> "We French are as modern as anyone else. But there is something very special about our culture. Take our language. It's very exact. In the seventeenth century [we] invented a standard for speaking correct French. Since then, an organization called the French Academy has tried to keep our language as correct as possible. We French love our traditions."

Connect Think of two or three foreign words that are part of the American language.

Catherine is right about the Academy. Since 1635, it has published dictionaries that give all the words accepted in the French language. The Academy makes rules about how these words should be used. This is an example of how the French work to preserve their culture.

On the other hand, French culture is also changing. Films, television, tourists, and trade have put the French in contact with other cultures. These cultures have changed the traditional French lifestyle. As Victoire explains:

▶ This billboard on Galeries Lafayette, a huge department store in Paris, announces to English speakers that it is the "Capital of Fashion."

"There are plenty of articles in the French papers about the need to keep the French language pure. How are we going to do that, is what I want to know! At my publishing company most of us use a few foreign words to describe some of our activities. In the new France there are plenty of modern things that we didn't have any words for. We had to borrow them from the Americans!"

Building Chartres Cathedral

"The bigger the better" may have been the motto of architects and builders in the Middle Ages. Without the help of modern machinery or electric power, they built towering cathedrals like this one at Chartres, France. At the time, many people could not read or write, so cathedrals were built with scenes from the Bible carved in stone or shown in stained-glass windows. It took over 100 years to build most cathedrals, but the people of Chartres built this one in only 30 years. What part of the cathedral do you think was the hardest to build? Why?

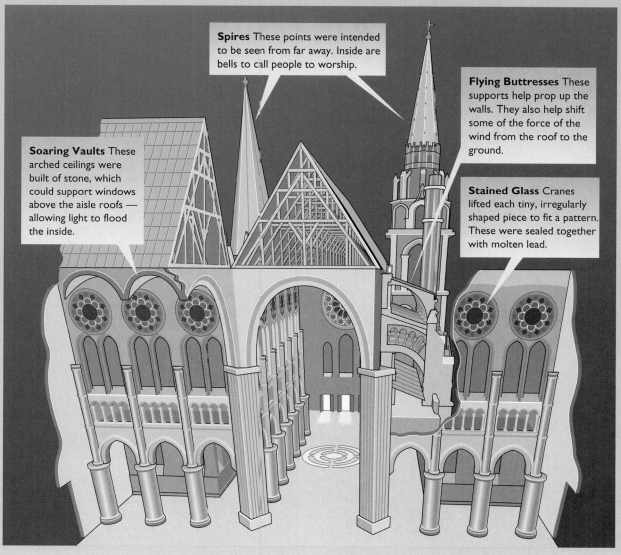

Spires These points were intended to be seen from far away. Inside are bells to call people to worship.

Flying Buttresses These supports help prop up the walls. They also help shift some of the force of the wind from the roof to the ground.

Soaring Vaults These arched ceilings were built of stone, which could support windows above the aisle roofs — allowing light to flood the inside.

Stained Glass Cranes lifted each tiny, irregularly shaped piece to fit a pattern. These were sealed together with molten lead.

Going Home to Paint Paul Cézanne was one of the greatest painters of his time. He lived in both Paris and Aix-en-Provence—where he was born—for most of his life. In 1883, he went to the countryside near his home town. He painted mountains, seashores—even his gardener. When he was outdoors, Cézanne tried to learn from nature. He believed that nature showed him what he needed to paint.

Victoire is referring to words like *sandwich, weekend, toast,* and *parking.* These words are a sign of France's close ties with other nations. These close ties mean that other cultures affect life in France. They also mean that French culture affects life in other nations.

Highlights of French Culture In 1805, a French pastry chef named Marie-Antoine Carême (muh REE ahn TWAHN kuh REM) began making desserts for rich and powerful people in France. His cakes and puddings delighted all. Some cakes looked like buildings or monuments. Some puddings looked like birds or flowers.

In 1833, Carême wrote a book on the art of French cooking. His book was similar to the dictionary of the French Academy. It set strict standards of excellence. Ever since Carême's book was published, French cooking has been one of the most respected kinds of cooking in the world.

The French have also set standards in the fashion industry. In 1947, a French fashion designer named Christian Dior (dee OR) caught the attention of the industry. His clothing designs were fresh and new. During World War II, women had worn shoulder pads and short, straight skirts. In contrast, Dior's "New Look" featured narrow shoulders and long, full dresses. His fashions became popular all over the world. Dior made Paris the center of the fashion industry.

Fashion's "New Look"

Women in your grandmother's generation might have worn evening dresses such as these, designed in the 1950s by French fashion designer Christian Dior (center). **Critical Thinking** High-fashion clothing by European designers remains popular today. Why do you think this is so?

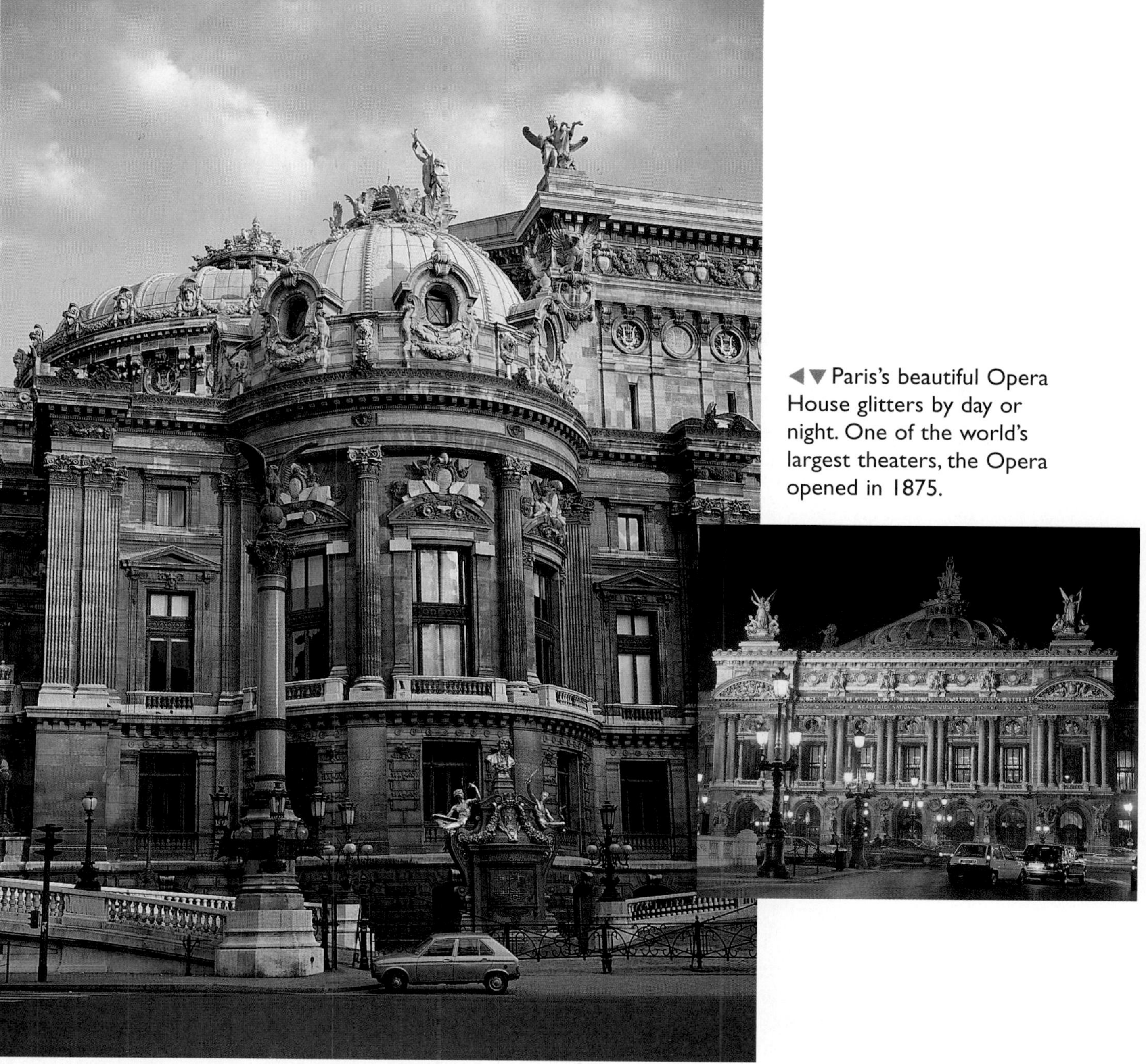

◀▼ Paris's beautiful Opera House glitters by day or night. One of the world's largest theaters, the Opera opened in 1875.

French cooking and fashions are only two examples of the influence of French culture on the rest of the world. France has also produced world-famous poets, philosophers, painters, and politicians. And some of the best wine in the world comes from France. The roots of this success go back centuries. They are based on the French system of education, methods of farming, and outlook on life.

Holding on to Tradition In Aix, many French traditions continue. Catherine feels that the city of her birth is an important part of who she is. Her father, grandmother, and great-grandmother live in Aix. Her family has lived there since the 1400s! Catherine says that good French pastry chefs, like her husband, are born with the talent "in their blood." Once she even checked the city's records to see if her husband's ancestors were pastry chefs.

Changes in French Life

Like many French citizens, Catherine believes French culture is unique and valuable. Yet she, too, agrees that life in France is changing. And the French people and government are beginning to deal with the changes.

READ ACTIVELY

Predict When immigrants move to a new place, how do they change the culture?

The New Immigrants Immigrants have been moving to Western Europe since World War II. Many people in French colonies started **emigrating,** or moving away, from their homelands to France. They came from Algeria (al JIR ee uh), Senegal (sen ih GAWL), Vietnam (vee ut NAHM), and other former French colonies.

When France joined the European Union, immigrants from other countries in Europe moved to France in search of work. The native French people had questions about the immigrants. Would the newcomers take jobs away from people already in France? Would the newcomers understand French culture? Would the cultures of the newcomers change French traditions?

The debate about the new immigrants continues. But their influence can be seen, especially in the big cities. In Paris, Arab, African, and Asian cultures are very strong. In other large cities in France, it is common to hear people speaking languages other than French. Every year, there are more and more restaurants and grocery stores that sell foreign food.

In an immigrant neighborhood in Paris, people buy and sell foods that are both new and familiar (below). Immigrants from West and North Africa, some of France's newest residents, can browse at book shops that feature Arabic and French-language books about Islam and Africa (right).

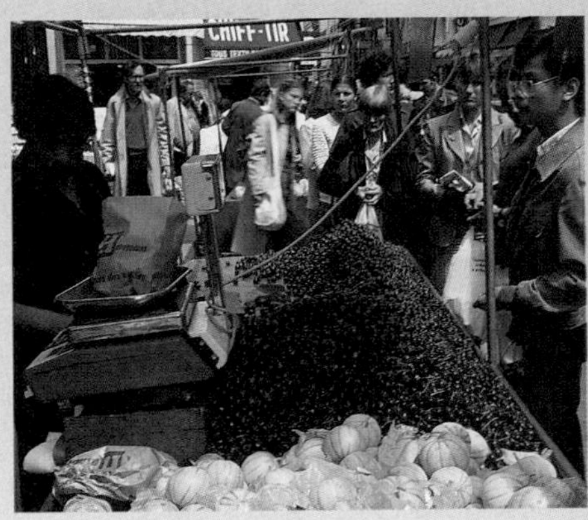

Some French people, like Catherine, continue to follow traditional French ways. And some French politicians support her point of view. The French government passed a law that makes it illegal to use certain foreign words in advertisements, business, and education. This law aims to protect the French language from foreign influences. Another law was passed to deal with citizenship. This law states that children born in France of parents born in other countries are not all French citizens.

Like her sister, Victoire is proud of French culture. But Victoire disagrees with the new language law. She believes France should accept foreign influences. Victoire also disagrees with the citizenship law. A few years ago, she and some friends protested against it in public.

▲ The theme park based on France's favorite cartoon character, Astérix, has added a new attraction every year since it opened.

American Influence In 1992, a strong foreign influence showed up just outside of Paris: the EuroDisney (YOO roh diz nee) theme park. This was the first Disney park to be built in Europe. Many French people cannot believe how big it is. The park is one fifth of the size of Paris.

At EuroDisney, visitors from all over Europe get to sample American culture. EuroDisney has a section called Main Street, U.S.A., with an American-style city hall. It also has a hotel that looks like a Wild West town, a camp with log cabins, and a California-style restaurant.

When the theme park opened, French reactions were mixed. Some French people loved it and brought their families to enjoy the rides, exhibits, and food. Other people were not so happy. They disliked the bright colors, cartoon characters, and fake scenery in the park.

After a slow start, EuroDisney has become a success. However, most visitors come from Great Britain, Germany, and other European countries—not France. Many French people prefer to go to another, smaller theme park called Parc Astérix (uhs STA riks). It is based on a French comic strip character.

1. **Define** emigrate.
2. **Identify** (a) Aix-en-Provence, (b) Paris.
3. How has Catherine shown pride in French culture?
4. How has Victoire shown that she is open to new ideas from outside of France?

Critical Thinking

5. **Recognizing Bias** Describe the views of those who agree and those who disagree with France's language law.

Activity

6. **Writing to Learn** Think about making a visit to Catherine or Victoire. What would you like to talk about? What would you like to see in Aix or Paris?

Using the Writing Process

James ran the entire three blocks home from the library. He threw open the front door and dropped his books and coat in the hall. Then he ran upstairs. His uncle Steven found him an hour later at his desk, scribbling madly.

"What are you doing, James?"

James barely looked up from his paper. "I'm writing about the Berlin Wall. I can't believe it stood in place for all those years and then the people just knocked it down!"

Uncle Steven picked up the paper. He read a few sentences and frowned.

"James, I can see in your writing that you're very excited about it, but it's kind of a jumble. What are you trying to say?"

James shrugged. "I just want to write down everything I know."

"It's tempting, I know, but you can't just throw everything into one pot like a soup. You have to plan your work. Remember, writing is a process."

Get Ready

Using the writing process means following a certain kind of method when writing. It means that people do not just sit down and write a paper all at once. Writing is not a single act. Instead, writing is a process, or a series of steps.

Most things you do in life are processes. For example, when you brush your teeth, you might follow these steps: 1) pick up your toothbrush and toothpaste, 2) put toothpaste on the brush, 3) brush your teeth, and 4) rinse. When you think about it, you can see how you go through processes every day of your life.

Writing is the same way. It involves a series of steps called the writing process. By simply following the steps, you can complete any writing assignment.

Try It Out

The writing process is shown in the diagram at right. Refer to the diagram as you read the description of each step. Use it to complete the activity that follows.

A. Prewriting This first step is what you do before you start to write. (*Pre-* means "before.") Prewriting involves two steps: deciding what you will write about, and finding the information you will need.

B. Drafting Drafting means organizing your information in a logical and interesting way. Make an outline and write a rough draft of your work. If you discover that you need more information, return to the prewriting step.

C. Revising Revising is, in many ways, the most important step. Professional writers often revise their work three, four, or even more times until they are happy with it. When you revise, you change your writing to make it clearer and more enjoyable to read. If necessary, you can reorganize your ideas by returning to the drafting stage.

D. Proofreading Reread your writing and correct any errors in grammar, usage, spelling, and punctuation. Fix even the smallest problems to make your writing as good as it can be. This step is especially important because a lot of little mistakes can hurt a piece of writing as much as a few big mistakes can.

The Writing Process

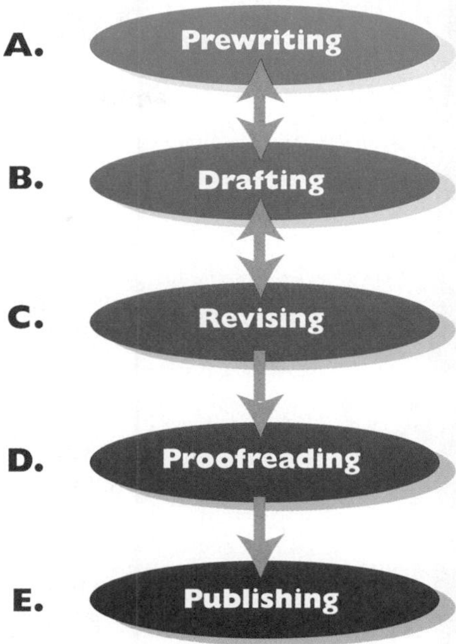

E. Publishing Publishing is the final step. Publishing means sharing your writing with an audience. You might do this by turning it in to the teacher, posting it on the bulletin board, or reading it aloud to your classmates.

To help you apply the skill next time you have a writing assignment, do the following now. On a clean sheet of paper, copy the flowchart that shows the writing process. Write a brief description of each step underneath the step in the flowchart.

Apply the Skill

Use the writing process every time you have a writing assignment, from one-paragraph reports to long themes. You should even use it to answer essay questions on tests.

Now that you understand the writing process, put it to work. Your assignment is to use the writing process to write a paragraph that describes life in present-day rural France.

Sweden

A Welfare State

Reach Into Your Background
Do you know someone who has received some kind of help from the government? Do you think people need more government help, or should they do more for themselves? In Sweden, the government provides many services—such as hospital care and a college education—at little or no cost.

Questions to Explore

1. How does the Swedish government care for the needs of its people?
2. What economic challenges face the Swedish government, and how is it meeting these challenges?

Key Terms
benefit
welfare state
national debt

Olof Hylten-Cavallius (OHL uhf HIL tuhn kuh VAHL yuhs) is a Swedish banker. He thinks his third heart attack was the luckiest thing that ever happened to him. That is because it was not until the third heart attack that doctors agreed to give Olof an operation. Now his heart is close to normal.

The doctors who performed Olof's operation were experts in their field. The hospital had all the latest equipment, and the care afterwards was excellent. The operation would have cost Olof about $20,000 in the United States. But in Sweden, it cost him next to nothing. How did Olof manage to get such an expensive operation at such a low cost?

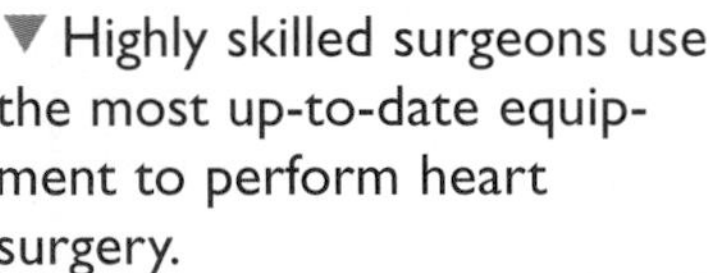

▼ Highly skilled surgeons use the most up-to-date equipment to perform heart surgery.

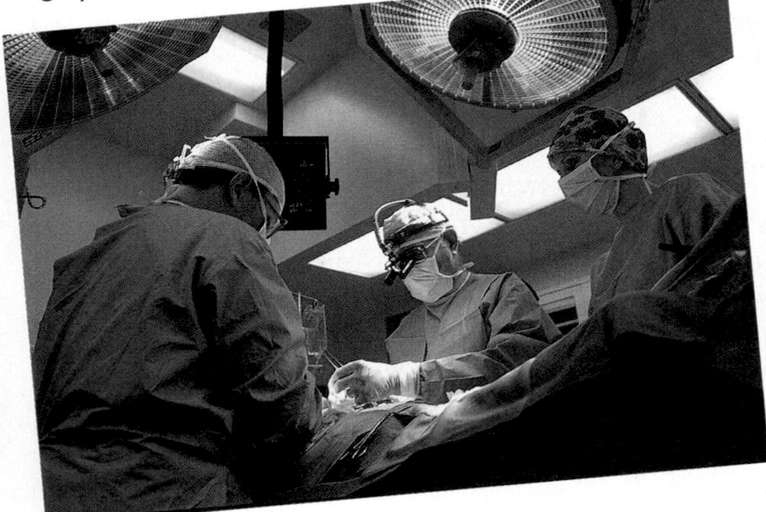

Life in a Welfare State

Olof's operation is just one example of the free—or nearly free—services in Sweden. Elisabet Ray, a school teacher, provides another example. She is happy that her daughter is going to college. This education costs nothing. Does this sound amazing to you? As you may know, college in the United States can cost more than $20,000 a year.

COUNTRY • PROFILE

Sweden: People and the Environment

The Five Most Populated Cities

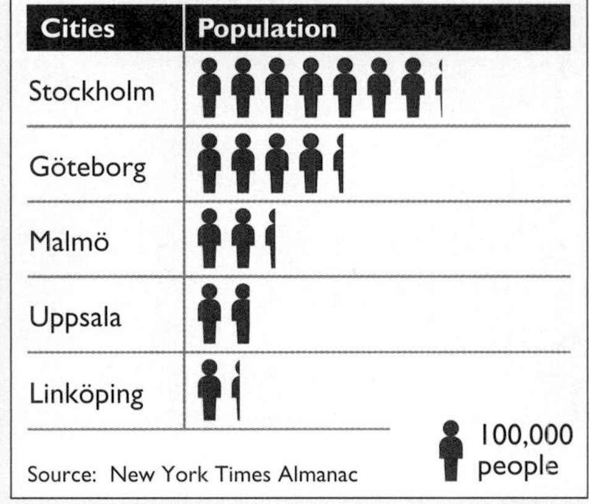

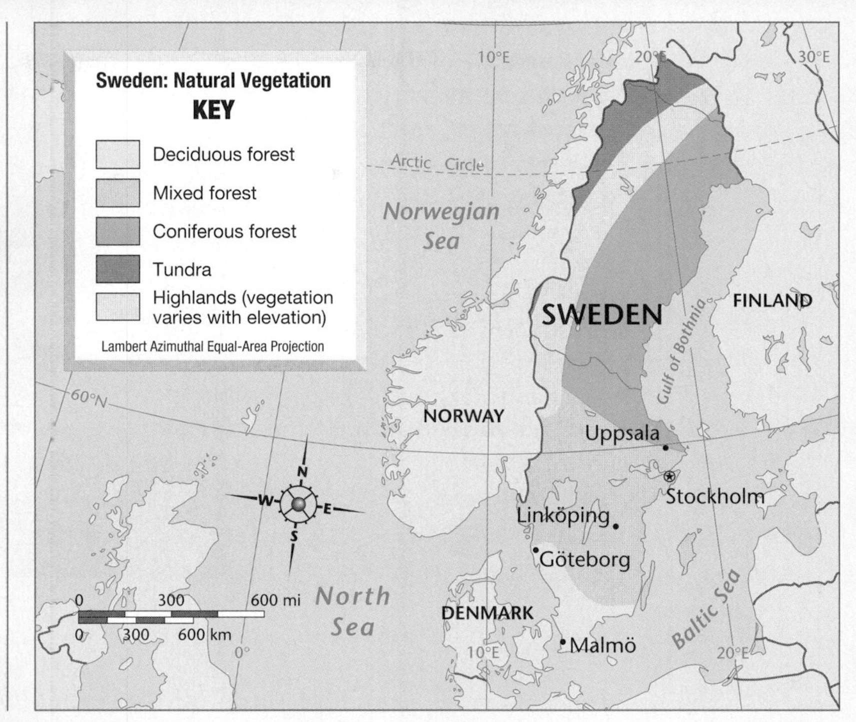

A busy street in Stockholm

Weather Chart

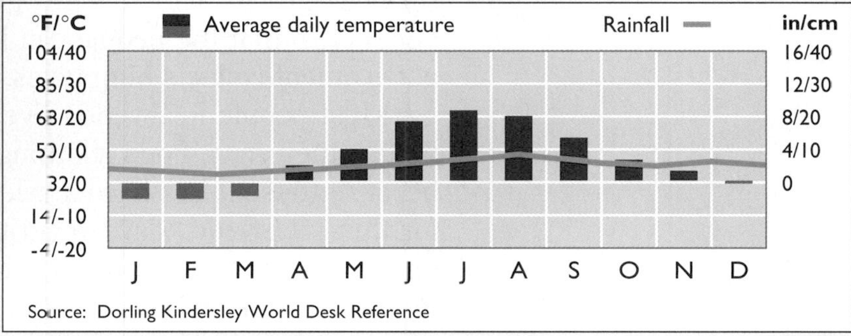

Take It to the NET Data Update For the most recent data on Sweden, visit **www.phschool.com**.

Geography The map and charts above present information about land use and climate in Sweden. **Map and Chart Study** (a) In which months does Sweden experience the lowest average temperature? (b) In which vegetation regions are the five most populated cities located?

Elisabet's family received other forms of help, too. When Elisabet's son Patrick was born, she took nine months off work so that she could take care of him. Her husband also took the time off from his job. During their time away from work, they received monthly checks for 90 percent of their salaries.

When Elisabet went back to work, she needed to take her son to a childcare center. Elisabet's family received help for this care, too. Until her son reaches the age of 16, Elisabet will receive more than $100 a week to pay for child care. Most countries do not have such benefits. A **benefit** is a free service or a payment.

Predict How do you think the Swedish government pays for services for its citizens?

Shopping in Sweden

Consumer goods are expensive in Sweden. For the most part, this is because of the taxes the Swedish government collects. First, consumer goods are more expensive to make because companies pay heavy taxes on the raw materials they need. Second, a sales tax is charged when the goods are sold in stores. **Critical Thinking** How might your life be different if you had to pay more for goods like shoes than you currently pay?

Where do all of these benefits come from? In Sweden, they come from the government. Sweden is a **welfare state.** This means that many services are paid for by the government. The government provides benefits so that the people can live well. To pay for these services, the government collects high taxes.

Most people in Sweden live this way. They pay high taxes on the money they earn. Food, clothing, and other consumer goods are costly because these items have a sales tax of about 20 percent. In exchange for this, all Swedes have security. Whether they are rich or poor, they know their children will get a good education. Medical costs are low. Rents are affordable.

Sweden's Difficult Past

Life in Sweden was not always so secure. By the late 1800s, industry had grown in the United States and most of Europe. But Sweden was far behind. There were few factories or railroad lines, or even good roads. Farming methods had not changed much since the Middle Ages. Many people were very poor. By the end of the century, 1.5 million Swedes had left the country in search of a better life. Most of them settled in the United States.

Building a Welfare State

After World War II, a political party called the Social Democrats became powerful in Sweden. The Social Democrats promised a better life for Swedes. From 1946 to 1976, the party changed Sweden into a welfare state.

As part of the government benefits program, all workers receive five weeks of paid vacation. Most workers generally take their vacation at the same time during the summer. For five weeks in the summer, the nights in this far-northern country are very short. It is daylight for most of the day. Many factories and businesses shut down during this period.

Swedish people take more days off for being sick—and get paid for them—than the workers of any other Western country. Some of this money comes from the government. And when Swedish workers retire, they receive a monthly payment from the government that nearly equals the pay they received when they were working.

In Sweden, welfare benefits are for everyone. Many Swedes do not mind paying high taxes because they enjoy the benefits. Mona Sahlin (MOH nuh SAH lin), a Swedish politician, summed up the Swedish way of thinking:

> "If you are a Social Democrat, you think it is terrific to pay taxes. For me, taxes are the finest expression of what politics are all about."

A welfare system means something very different in the United States than it does in Sweden. Our welfare system only helps people in great need—people who cannot afford medical care or food. And the rules about who can receive welfare benefits in the United States are becoming stricter. Sweden, too, is changing its rules about welfare benefits.

The Forecast: Sunny All Day and Night Near the Earth's polar regions, the sun can be seen 24 hours a day in six-month periods. At the North Pole, the sun is out from about March 20 to September 23. At the South Pole, the sun remains above the horizon from September 23 to March 20. In the northern part of Sweden, the sun stays out day and night for a few days around June 21. The Swedes celebrate this as Midsummer's Eve, with maypoles, dancing, and music.

▼ In midsummer, when the sun shines 24 hours a day, many people in Sweden stay up and celebrate with traditional dances.

Businesses in Sweden

Peter Wallenberg is a Swedish banker. His family owns more than 40 percent of Sweden's corporations. Most businesses in Sweden, like most businesses in the United States, are owned by individuals. **Critical Thinking** How do businesses help people in the community?

Problems and Solutions

Everyone in Sweden receives benefits, but some people are wealthier than others. The Wallenberg family, for instance, owns more than 40 percent of the corporations in Sweden. Families like the Wallenbergs live in great luxury. But in Sweden, some people are struggling with the costs of living. Lately, a number of Swedes have been just getting by.

Connect What would you do if you had to wait a long time for medical help when you really needed it?

Sweden's Troubles For the last 20 years, Sweden's economic growth has stalled. Because of the high taxes on groceries, clothing, and other goods, people buy fewer items than they would like to. Thus there is less spending to boost the economy. Also, Sweden's long vacations mean that workers spend less time on the job. This makes Swedish companies less productive.

There are also problems with the health care system. Medical care is not always available when it is needed. People often wait a long time to receive help.

The government is facing budgetary problems. To supply more benefits, the government has had to borrow money. Some Swedes think the amount their government owes, or the **national debt,** has gotten out of control. The government has increased taxes and cut some spending to try to control national debt.

Finding Solutions Government and private businesses must both try to solve these problems. The government needs to reduce benefits and spend less money. And businesses need to earn more. The more money businesses earn, the more money, in the form of taxes, will go to the government.

One way for businesses to grow is to take advantage of Sweden's natural resources. Sweden has high-grade iron ore and makes enough steel for itself and for export. Each year, half of Sweden's electricity is made by hydroelectric turbines that use Sweden's fast rivers and many waterfalls. Sweden's vast forests support the timber industry, which supplies Sweden's needs and those of other countries.

Swedish companies have had trouble competing with firms in other countries. Most Swedish products are of high quality. But the Swedes have not been able to make them as quickly and cheaply as other countries. Some companies have found a solution to this problem. A Swedish automaker, for example, has made a partnership with an American company. Using the methods of American auto factories, the Swedes can now make a car in less than 40 hours. It used to take them four days.

The Graying of Sweden
Sweden has 1.5 million retired people out of a population of about 8.9 million. This means that about one out of six people is retired. This is the highest proportion in the world. The Swedish government is having trouble taking care of so many retired people. Some studies say that unless the government reforms its welfare benefits, there will not be any money left by 2015. Raising taxes to cover benefits for every-one has been proposed—but it is not a popular idea.

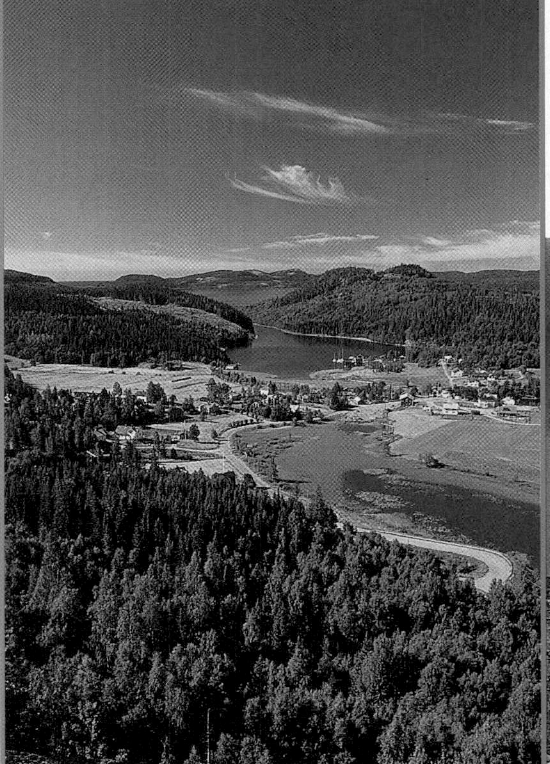

◄▼ Natural resources, such as large forests (left), helped Sweden to build thriving industrial cities such as Stockholm (below). Wood products make up a large amount of Sweden's exports.

Sweden's Dala Horses

In this picture, a craftworker puts the finishing touches to a dala horse. These small figures are carved out of wood, painted red or blue, and decorated with floral designs. For Swedes, the dala horse is a symbol of hope and good luck. And for Swedes who no longer live in Sweden, it represents their homeland. In fact, the dala horse has become an important export item. Some 20 percent of dala horses made in Sweden are exported to the United States alone.

Improving the economy means changing the ways things are done in Sweden. Mats Thourslund (mahts THORZ luhnd), a professor at a Swedish university, said:

> "Sweden will not be that different from other countries in the future. We have been used to having our kids in day-care centers and old people cared for by the system, leaving the rest of us free to do whatever we want. But the party is over."

When Thorslund says, "the party is over," he means the country will be providing fewer services in order to spend less money. Making this happen is Sweden's biggest challenge today.

SECTION 3 REVIEW

1. **Define** (a) benefit, (b) welfare state, (c) national debt.
2. Describe some of the benefits that Swedish citizens receive.
3. What natural resources can help the Swedish economy?

Critical Thinking

4. **Recognizing Cause and Effect** What has caused Sweden to want to change its welfare system?

Activity

5. **Writing to Learn** Think about the welfare systems in the United States and Sweden. Write a paragraph about what you think the United States and Sweden might learn from each other.

Italy

Two Ways of Life

Reach Into Your Background

Do you think the region in which you live should help other regions develop new industries? Why or why not?

Questions to Explore

1. How have the differences in the environments of northern and southern Italy affected the lives of Italians?
2. How are Italians attempting to speed the development of southern Italy?

Key Term

manufacturing

Key Places

the Vatican
Rome
Milan
Locorotondo

Can you solve this riddle? A magazine photographer spent about a year exploring a certain country, yet the country is so tiny that he was able to walk around it in 40 minutes. Its population is only about 1,000. But one billion people look to its leader for guidance. What is the country?

The tiny nation is called the Vatican (VAT ih kun). It is the world headquarters of the Roman Catholic Church. Its leader is the pope. Every day, Roman Catholics all over the world look to him for leadership.

▼ This aerial view of Vatican City shows the grand dome of St. Peter's Church, which dominates the skyline.

Country Within a Country

The Vatican is a country within a country. Located within Rome, the capital of Italy, the Vatican is an independent city-state. A city-state is both a city and an independent nation. The Vatican has its own money and stamps. It is a member of the United Nations. It also has its own radio station, newspaper, fire department, and supermarket.

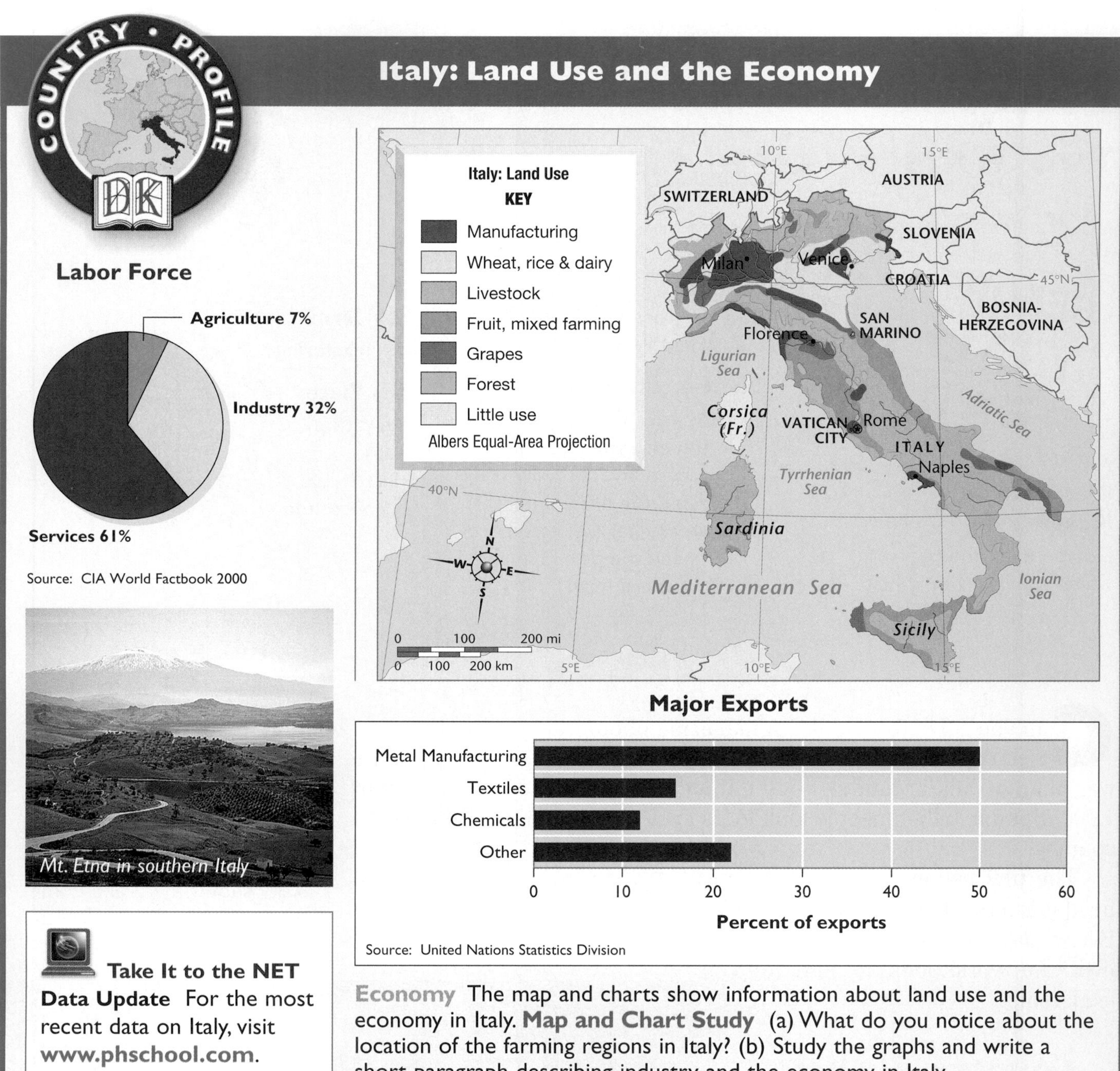

READ ACTIVELY

Visualize What would it be like to visit the Sistine Chapel? What would it feel like to be surrounded by art?

Every day, Catholics and non-Catholics stream into this little country. They come here to see St. Peter's Church. The Vatican's palace and art museum is also a popular attraction.

The Sistine (SIS teen) Chapel, located inside the Vatican, contains many world-famous paintings, sculptures, and other works of art. Tourists crowd into this chapel, but there is nearly perfect silence inside. No one is allowed to speak above a whisper. Everyone leans back to see the scenes painted on the ceiling. Some scenes were painted by the famous artist Michelangelo. It is the most famous and perhaps the most beautiful ceiling in the world.

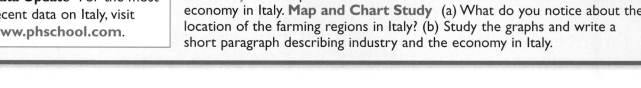

Church and Family

Roman Catholicism unites about one billion people around the world. And it especially unites Italians. Not every Italian is Catholic, but Italy's history is closely tied to the history of Catholicism. Until recently, Catholicism was the official religion of the country.

The Roman Catholic Church provides a common focus for Italians throughout the country. For most Italians, the pope is symbolic of a father. The Church is a giant family to which they belong. Many Italians expect the Church to help them with their daily decisions—just as good parents help their children.

This way of living has existed for hundreds of years. Today, in the small towns of the countryside, life is organized around the larger family of the Church and the smaller family in the home. In the cities, these ties may not be as strong.

Divisions Between North and South

A common belief in Catholicism has helped Italians unify their nation. Until the 1800s, Italy was made up of many separate city-states, territories, and small kingdoms. In 1870, the Italian people unified these areas into one nation. Still, the Italy of today seems divided into two different countries—the north and the south. The ways of life in the two areas set them apart.

The Risorgimento: "Rising Again" The Risorgimento was a movement in the 1800s to inspire the Italian people to unite as one nation. Poets and philosophers tried to create a sense of nationalism. Today, Italian schoolchildren learn about and celebrate the movement. Cities have streets and squares that bear the names of many of the Risorgimento's heroes.

The Pope

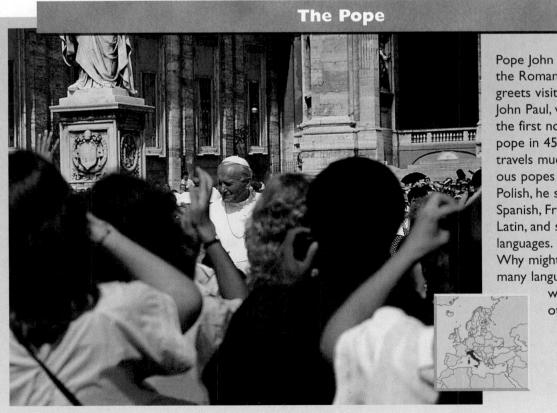

Pope John Paul II, the leader of the Roman Catholic Church, greets visitors to Vatican City. John Paul, who is Polish, was the first non-Italian to become pope in 450 years. John Paul travels much more than previous popes did. In addition to Polish, he speaks English, Spanish, French, German, Italian, Latin, and several Slavic languages. **Critical Thinking** Why might the ability to speak many languages help a pope who often travels to other countries?

A Cross Between Art and Fashion Futurism was an artistic movement that centered in Italy in the early 1900s. Futurists celebrated the future and criticized traditions. They glorified technology by painting images of a speeding car or the motion of a powerful train. An artist named Fortunato Depero, a Futurist painter, also designed men's vests. These vests had "Futurist" designs on them—such as mechanical figures.

Life in the North Milan (mih LAN) is typical of northern Italy. Abundant minerals, fast rivers, and a developed economy have brought wealth to the area. Many international businesses are located here.

Milan is one part of a triangle of cities—with the cities of Turin and Genoa—that are home to most of Italy's **manufacturing** industries. Manufacturing is the process of turning raw materials into finished products.

Milan has a flashier side, too. Every season, people interested in fashions crowd into Milan to see collections from clothing designers. Italian fashion has become so important that Milan is second only to Paris as a fashion capital. Milan's factories also produce cars, planes, leather goods, and plastics.

Like many European cities, Milan is a mix of the old and the new. In a 300-year-old palace, you can see what may be the oldest public library in Europe. Millions of dollars have been spent to keep it in good condition. Less than a mile away, you can drive past modern steel-and-glass office buildings. These buildings cost millions of dollars to construct.

▼▶ Italy has both new and old attractions, such as this high-tech shoe factory in Milan (below) and a centuries-old burial place in Rome (right).

▲ This band is playing music for the tarantella, one of southern Italy's most popular folk dances. Tarantella music is lively, so the dancers must skip, run, and hop as they dance. Italian legend states that dancing the tarantella can cure someone who has been bitten by a tarantula spider.

A Town in Southern Italy Southern Italy is very different from Milan. Southern Italy is mostly agricultural. Fertile areas near the coast get enough rainfall to grow abundant crops. Olives, tomatoes, fruits, and other crops are grown here. Inland, people barely make a living because of the thin soil and dry climate. These people follow a traditional way of life.

Locorotondo (loh koh roh TAWN doh) is a small town located in the southernmost part of Italy. It is on the "heel" of the Italian "boot." Farming is the way most people here make a living. Wheat, olives, and fruits are grown here. Fishing is also an important industry.

The people here talk about northern Italy as if it were another country. They know little of the high fashions of Milan or the noisy city of Rome. Southern Italian traditions and the family still rule everyday life.

Many religious events are celebrated in the streets of town. The procession of the Feast of Corpus Christi takes place every year, several weeks after Easter. It celebrates the presence of Jesus Christ. In this festival event, women hang their wedding clothes over their balconies and place flowers on them. Additional such displays are set up on the streets around town. People walk together around the town, from church to church and display to display.

The traditional way of life may change as the economy of southern Italy changes. After World War II, Puglia (POOL yah)—the region that Locorotondo lies within—became one of the main areas for land reform. Large farms were divided into smaller farms and sold. Today the Italian government is using tax money to modernize parts of the southern region. New schools and hospitals are being built. The government is also rebuilding factories in the south's large cities, such as Naples (NAY pulz) and Syracuse (SIHR uh kyoos).

A Call for Independence

During a speech in Venice in 1996, Umberto Bossi, the leader of the Northern League, demanded independence for Padania, the League's name for northern Italy.

Politics and the Two Italys

Northern and southern Italy are so different that some Italians think the two regions should be separate countries. In 1996, a political party known as the Northern League won 10 percent of the vote in a national election. The Northern League wants to turn northern Italy into a separate country. If this happens, people in northern Italy will no longer have to support the poorer southern part of Italy with their taxes.

It is not likely that the Northern League will get its way. No matter how much Italians disagree, they will never lose their strong Italian identity. Religion and family will probably keep the people of Italy unified for many years to come.

1. **Define** manufacturing.
2. **Identify** (a) the Vatican, (b) Rome, (c) Milan, (d) Locorotondo.
3. List three differences between life in Milan and life in a southern Italian village.
4. How has the government tried to help the development of southern Italy?

Critical Thinking

5. **Drawing Conclusions** Do you think northern Italy should try to help develop southern Italy? Why or why not?

Activity

6. **Writing to Learn** Work with a partner. One of you will write a letter to a relative about life in northern Italy. The other will write a response from the point of view of a southern Italian.

Germany

A Nation Reunited

Reach Into Your Background

What is it like to see a friend whom you have not seen in a long time? Do you sometimes find that you do not know the person as well as you once did? As you read this section, you will see how two parts of Germany separated and then came together again.

Questions to Explore

1. Why was Germany divided and how did it become reunited?
2. How are Germans dealing with the issues of a reunited nation?

Key Terms

Holocaust
reunification

Key People and Places

Adolf Hitler
Berlin

One day in 1961, Conrad Schumann, a 19-year-old policeman, stood guard at a barbed-wire fence. His job was to shoot anyone who tried to get across the fence. East Berlin (bur LIN), where Schumann was standing, was part of East Germany. East Germany had a communist government. The fence was built to prevent East Berliners from escaping to West Berlin. From West Berlin, people could reach democratic West Germany.

To Schumann, the fence was a terrible thing. He could see the buildings of West Berlin on the other side. They seemed very beautiful. On television, he had seen a program from West Berlin. It showed people dancing to American music, shopping for colorful clothing, and speaking their views freely. In East Germany, the government did not approve of American music and free speech. The stores had few interesting things to buy.

Schumann thought about all these things. Then he made a decision and jumped over the barbed wire. A moment later, he was on the other side—in the freedom of the West.

Just a few days after Schumann jumped to freedom, the barbed-wire fence was replaced by a concrete wall. The Berlin Wall separated families and friends. On one side of it, communism ruled. On the other side, the people did.

▼ At first, the Berlin Wall was only barbed wire. As you can see, Conrad Schumann jumped over it easily. Later, he said, "I had no desire to shoot my fellow citizens, and I knew that they were about to put up a much stronger wall."

COUNTRY • PROFILE

Germany: Population

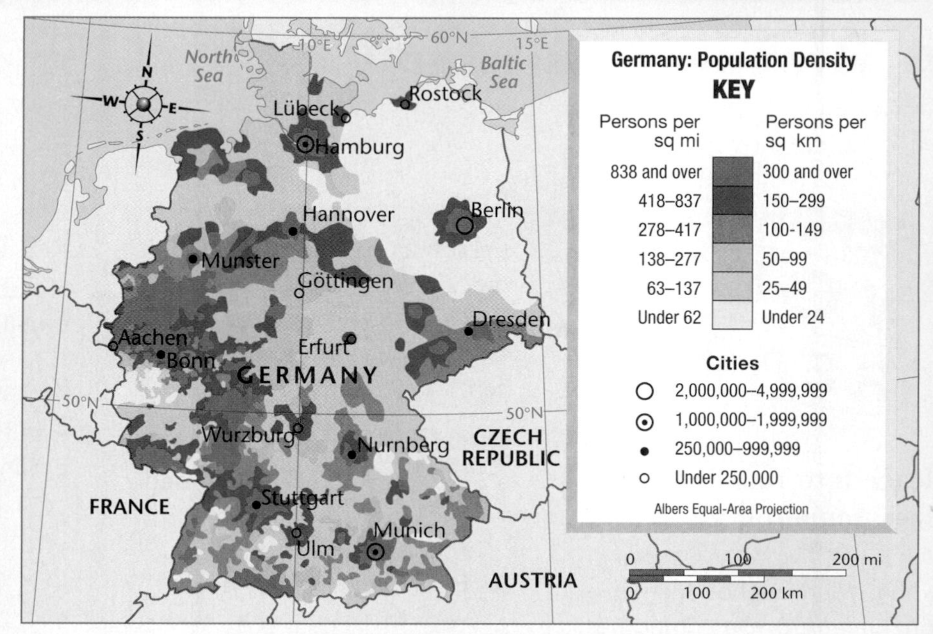

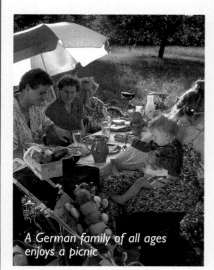

A German family of all ages enjoys a picnic

Geography The map and charts on the right describe the people of Germany and where they live. **Map and Chart Study** (a) Which regions of Germany are least populated? (b) In Germany's oldest age group, are more people male or female?

Population by Age Group and Sex

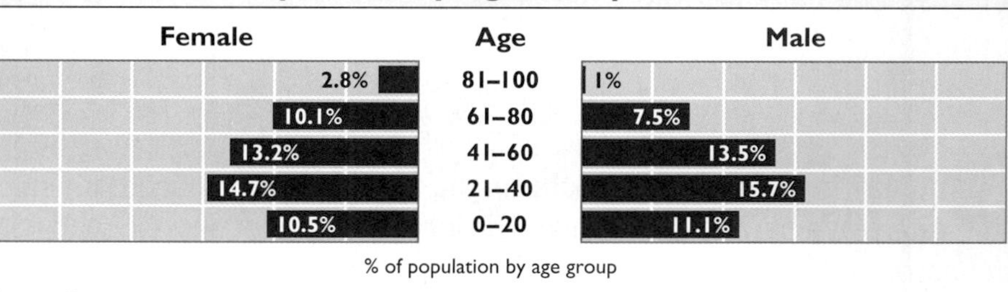

Urban and Rural Population

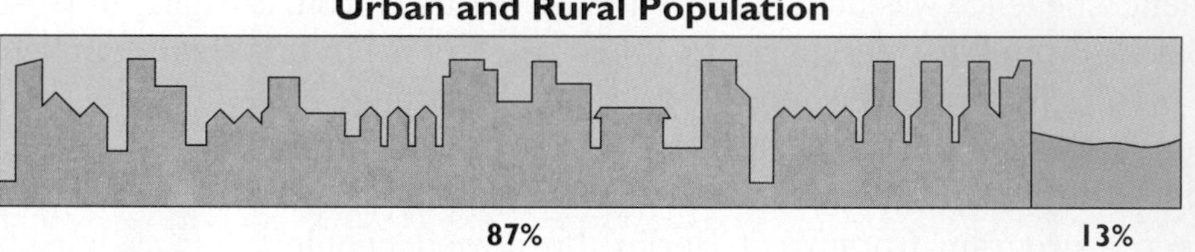

Source: Dorling Kindersley World Desk Reference

Take It to the NET
Data Update for the most recent data on Germany, visit **www.phschool.com**.

Germany's Tragic Past

To understand the importance of the Berlin Wall, you need to understand part of Germany's past. After losing World War I in 1918, the German government had to pay billions of dollars as punishment for attacking other countries. To make things even worse, the German economy collapsed. Prices soared. Germans everywhere felt desperate.

Hitler and World War II Adolf Hitler (AY dahlf HIT lur), a young German soldier, had wept bitterly in 1918 when he learned that Germany had lost the war. He promised himself that his country would never suffer such a defeat again. Hitler became deeply involved in politics. In speech after speech, he promised to make Germany great again. By 1933, this once unknown soldier was dictator of Germany.

Hitler blamed Germany's economic problems on German Jews. He spread hateful theories about Jews, Gypsies, and other ethnic groups in Germany. He claimed they were inferior to, or not as good as, other Germans. He claimed that Germans were a superior ethnic group—and should lead Europe.

Many people did not believe Hitler's threats. But Hitler was deadly serious. He ordered attacks on neighboring countries and forced them under German rule. His actions led to the start of World War II in 1939. Great Britain, the Soviet Union, and the United States joined other nations to stop Hitler and the Germans. By the end of the war, Europe was in ruins. People around the world learned that the Germans had forced countless Jews, Gypsies, Slavs, and others into brutal prison camps. Millions of people were murdered in these camps. Most of them were Jews. This horrible mass murder of six million Jews is called the **Holocaust** (HAHL uh kawst).

The Cold War At the end of the war, the Americans, the British, the French, and the Soviets divided Germany. The American, British, and French sections were joined into a democratic country called West Germany. The Soviet Union created a communist system in East Germany.

Albert Einstein Born in 1879 to Jewish-German parents, Albert Einstein was a quiet child who grew into one of the greatest scientists of all time. His famous equation, $E=mc^2$, describes the relationship between mass and energy and led the world into the atomic age. Einstein settled in the United States in 1933 and gave up his German citizenship. He became a citizen of the United States in 1940.

Divided Berlin

Map Study When the United States, Great Britain, France, and the Soviet Union divided Germany into two parts, they also divided Germany's capital, Berlin. The city of Berlin was located well inside East Germany. At one point, the Soviet Union tried to take over West Berlin by blocking all the roads, railways, or waterways leading to the city, so that the two million people living in West Berlin could not get food or supplies. The United States, Great Britain, and France organized a huge airlift to supply West Berlin until the Soviet Union ended its blockade. **Movement** What challenges do you think would face people living in a city that is isolated within enemy territory?

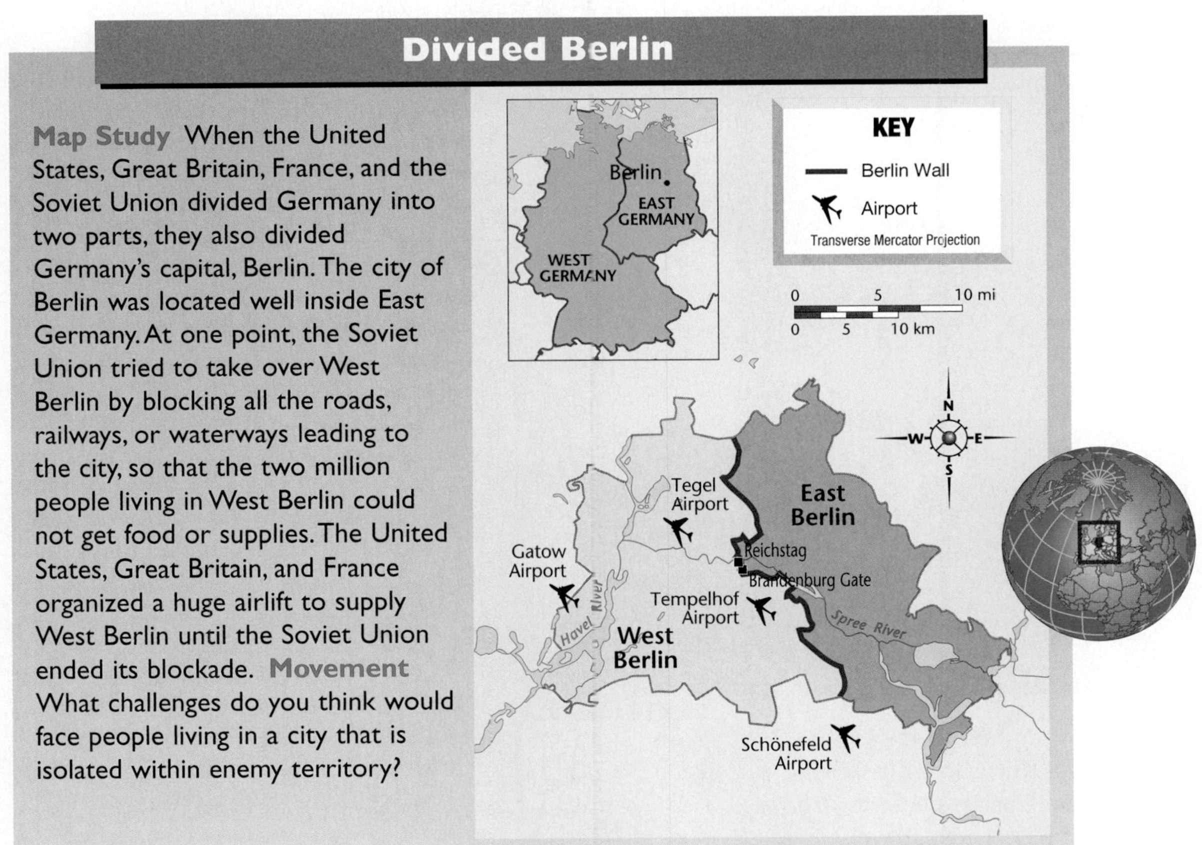

Berlin was in the Soviet part of Germany. But the western half of it, called West Berlin, became part of democratic West Germany. This turned the Western half into an island of democracy in the middle of communism. The Berlin Wall separated the two halves of the city. But it divided more than Berlin. It was a symbol of a divided world. Little wonder that some people called it the "Wall of Shame."

During the Cold War, the United States and Western Europe became partners. These countries had democratic governments and were against communism. Eastern European countries had communist governments and were partners with the Soviet Union. Soviet troops stayed in Eastern Europe to make sure that these countries remained communist.

Think about the effects of the Cold War on European countries. Recall that these countries are small and close together. Family, friends, and relatives were separated by Cold War borders. Even some who had managed to escape to the West suffered. For example, Conrad Schumann, who jumped over to the western side, could no longer see his sister, brother, and mother. They remained in East Berlin. The idea that he could not even visit his mother filled him with sadness.

East Germans led far different lives than West Germans. The communist government required people to obey without asking questions. It even encouraged people to spy on family members and

Easing International Tensions

Soviet and Western leaders often met to try to ease tensions. Soviet leader Nikita Khrushchev is shown meeting with French President Charles de Gaulle (above right) and U.S. President John F. Kennedy (above).

Free at Last!

During the summer of 1989, many East Germans took vacations in other Eastern European countries. They had no intention of returning, however. Rather, they planned to flee to West Germany. Here, a group of East Germans celebrate as they prepare to go through the Czech-West German border. **Critical Thinking** In the summer of 1989, the Soviet Union and Eastern European countries such as Czechoslovakia were still under communist rule. Why do you think that no efforts were made to prevent East Germans from fleeing to the West?

neighbors. Children were taught to respect only those things that helped communism. Things from the West—including movies, music, books, and magazines—were seen as harmful to communism.

The Communists Weaken In time, communist rule started to change. One reason was that the East German economy was falling further behind the West German economy. The average West German had a much better life than the average East German. To keep East Germans happy, the government softened its rules. Some East Germans could then visit West Germany. Conrad Schumann's mother, who was then in her late seventies, was allowed to see him. But he still was not allowed to go to East Berlin to see her. If he crossed the border, he would be arrested and put in prison.

In the late 1980s, changes in the Soviet Union helped to cause the collapse of East Germany. Soviet leader Mikhail Gorbachev made it clear that he would not use force to protect communism in Eastern Europe. Fear of the Soviets had helped keep the East German government in power. Now this fear was gone. Gorbachev told the East German leaders to make more reforms, but they refused. Without any support from the people, East Germany's government collapsed.

The Berlin Wall collapsed as well. On November 9, 1989, crowds of Germans began scrambling over the wall. Some people raced to see friends and relatives. Others just wanted to enjoy a different life. People

Visualize Visualize the collapse of the Berlin Wall. Describe some of the sights and sounds of this momentous event.

The Wall Comes Down

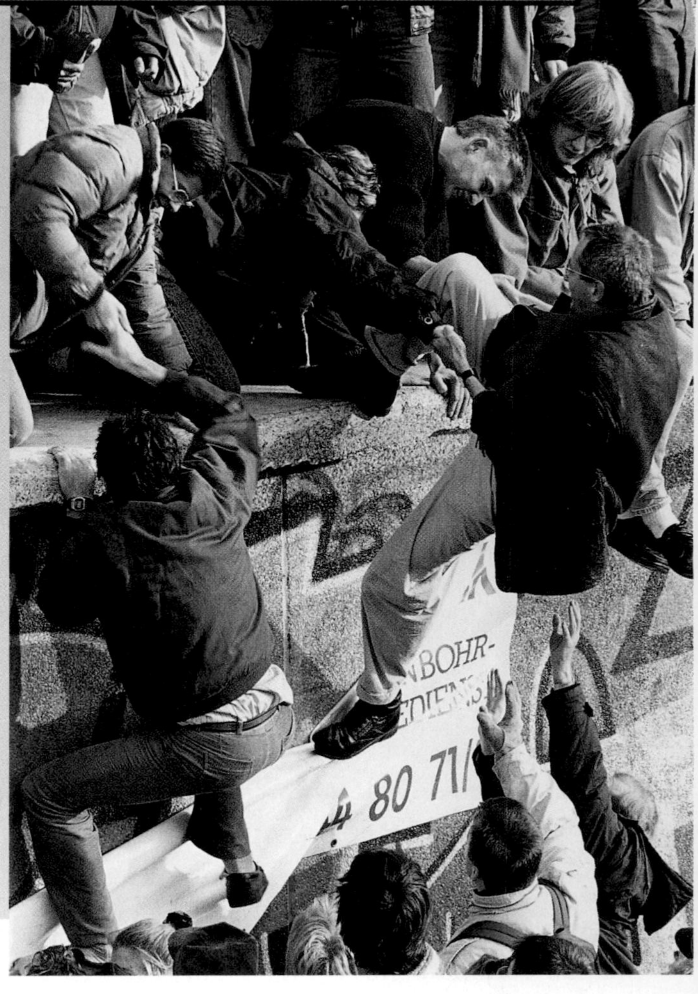

Crowds began to destroy the Berlin Wall on November 9, 1989. They held a huge party on and around the wall, while people from both sides helped each other up and over. Three million people from East Germany visited West Germany the first weekend after the wall came down, and 2,500 decided to stay there permanently. **Critical Thinking** Judging from the behavior of the crowds, how do you think Germans felt about the Berlin Wall?

helped each other over the top of the wall to the other side. Crowds tore at the wall and took it apart block by block. Less than a year later, the governments of East and West Germany united. Germany had become a single country again.

Germany Reunited

Ask Questions What questions might you ask East Germans about their views on reunification?

Most Germans were thrilled about the fall of the Berlin Wall. The cultures of East and West Germany had remained similar in many ways. People in both Germanys spoke the same language and ate the same foods. They knew the same German composers, writers, and painters. Still, the process of becoming unified again, called **reunification** (ree yoo nuh fih KAY shun), would not be easy.

Germans spent millions of dollars to rebuild the economy of what was East Germany. For the first time since World War II, East Germans are enjoying modern televisions, cars, and washing machines. They have new shopping malls and better roads.

Easterners may have more televisions and cars, but they have fewer jobs. In communist East Germany, people were guaranteed a job and

▲ Since the fall of communism, many new stores and coffee shops have opened in Alexanderplatz, East Berlin's main shopping area.

food to eat. There are no such guarantees under the Western democratic system. This is one of the prices of freedom, and most former East Germans are willing to pay it.

When Germany was reunited in 1990, so was Berlin. The next year, the German legislature restored this city to its traditional role as the nation's capital. By 1999, most government offices had moved back to Berlin from the West German capital of Bonn.

The cost of moving the capital has been enormous. It has led to budget cuts and the elimination of many public service jobs. Still, Germans believe that the move will benefit the "new Germany." Berlin's central location, they say, will aid reunification by linking Germans in the east with Germans in the west.

1. **Define** (a) Holocaust, (b) reunification.
2. **Identify** (a) Adolf Hitler, (b) Berlin.
3. Describe (a) the events that led to the division of Germany and (b) the events that led to its reunification.
4. How has the reunification of Germany affected life in the former East Germany?

Critical Thinking

5. **Making Comparisons** Compare personal freedom in East and West Germany during the Cold War.

Activity

6. **Writing to Learn** Write a journal entry from the point of view of an East Berliner. Describe the night the Berlin Wall was torn down. How did you feel? Whom and what did you want to see?

Review and Activities

Reviewing Main Ideas

1. How does the monarchy unify Great Britain?
2. If Great Britain were on the European continent, would life for the British be different? Explain your answer.
3. Why have the French made laws forbidding the use of foreign words?
4. What aspects of foreign culture are becoming a part of France?
5. How do Sweden's mineral reserves benefit its economy?
6. Why have most Swedes not worried about medical care or money for retirement in the past?
7. Why might a person from Milan have a hard time adapting to life in southern Italy?
8. How has northern Italy tried to develop southern Italy?
9. (a) How was Germany divided? (b) Why was it reunified?
10. What kept Germans unified in their thinking even when their country was divided?

Reviewing Key Terms

Decide whether each statement is true or false. If it is true, write *true*. If it is false, change the underlined term to make the statement true.

1. Parliament is the group of people that governs Britain.
2. A representative is someone who represents, or stands for, a group of people.
3. In a welfare state, the power of kings and queens is controlled by laws about what they can and cannot do.
4. To immigrate is to move away from a country.
5. Swedes enjoy the national debt they receive from the government.
6. Milan is a manufacturing center.
7. Many European Jews were killed during the Holocaust.
8. Germans celebrated the reunification of their nation.

Critical Thinking

1. **Making Comparisons** (a) How is Sweden like the former East Germany? (b) How is it different?
2. **Drawing Conclusions** How do you think Germany will change in the future? How might Germans react to these changes?

Graphic Organizer

Copy the chart onto a separate sheet of paper. Then fill in facts you have learned about each country.

Country	Government	Economy	Culture
United Kingdom			
France			
Sweden			
Italy			
Germany			

Map Activity

Western Europe

For each place listed below, write the letter from the map that shows its location.

1. Aix-en-Provence
2. London
3. Sweden
4. Italy
5. Berlin

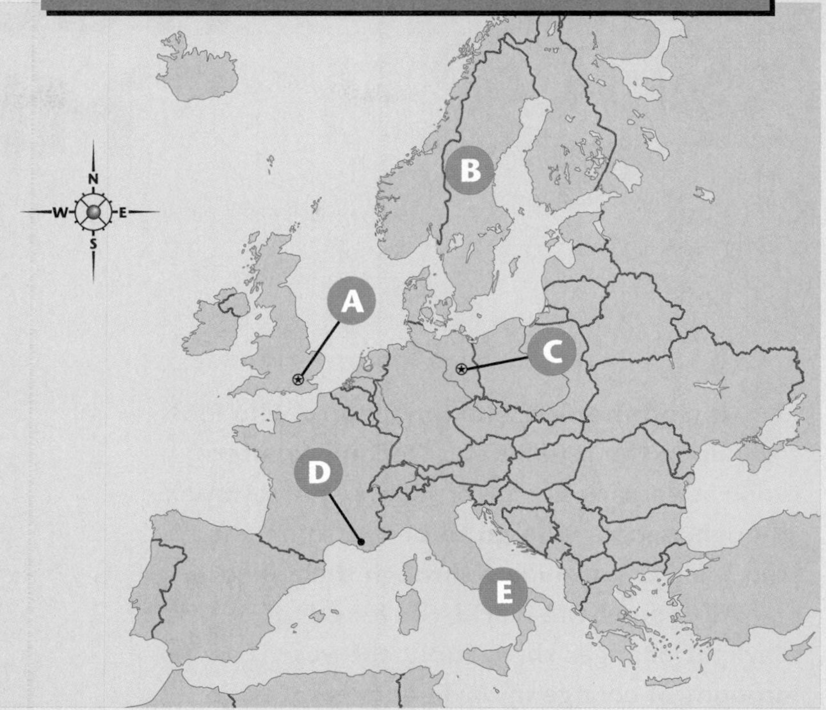

Writing Activity

Writing a Travel Journal
Imagine that you have traveled to each country in this chapter. Write a journal entry describing some of the traditions you encountered.

Take It to the NET

Activity Use a clickable map to take a virtual tour around the museums and monuments of Paris. For help in completing this activity, visit **www.phschool.com.**

Chapter 9 Self-Test To review what you have learned, take the Chapter 9 Self-Test and get instant feedback on your answers. Go to **www.phschool.com** to take the test.

Skills Review

Turn to the Skills Activity.

Review the steps for using the writing process. Then, follow the steps to write a one-page paper about one aspect of life in Western Europe.

How Am I Doing?

Answer these questions to help you check your progress.

1. Do I understand why tradition is important in Great Britain?
2. Do I understand why France has tried to preserve its traditional culture?
3. Do I understand what kind of welfare state Sweden is?
4. Do I understand how and why people are working to unify two separate regions in both Italy and Germany?
5. What information from this chapter can I include in my journal?

Tracking the Midnight Sun

In Hammerfest, Norway, people who look up in the middle of a December afternoon see a dark sky full of stars. In the summer, though, people who go to bed at midnight can see the sun shining through their windows.

All around the world, the length of daylight changes throughout the year. The amount of change in daylight is greatest in areas near the North or South Pole. Because Hammerfest is in the Arctic, near the North Pole, there is a huge difference in the number of light hours during summer days and winter days.

Purpose

The length of daylight changes as the Earth makes its yearly orbit around the sun. Because of the tilt of the Earth's axis, the Northern Hemisphere faces the sun during summer. It faces away from the sun during winter. In this activity, you will make a model that shows why arctic Scandinavia and Russia have midnight suns in summer and dark days in winter.

Materials

- unshaded lamp
- tangerine or orange
- masking tape
- marker
- pencil
- metric tape measure

Procedure

STEP ONE

Make a model of the Earth. Holding your tangerine or orange around its middle, push your pencil through the fruit's core. The fruit represents the Earth. The pencil represents the Earth's axis, or the imaginary line around which the Earth turns. The point where the pencil emerges represents the North Pole. With your marker, draw a line all the way around the fruit, halfway between the two ends of the pencil. This circle represents the Equator. Next, measure the distance in centimeters between the "Equator" and the "North Pole." Then use your marker to draw a circle around the fruit approximately seven ninths of the distance from the "Equator" to the "North Pole." This circle represents the 70° latitude. Areas north of the 70° latitude are considered arctic areas. Make a dot just above this line to represent Hammerfest, Norway.

STEP TWO

Make a model of the Earth's path around the sun. Place the unshaded lamp on the floor. With the masking tape, mark a circle on the floor with the lamp at its center. This line shows the Earth's orbit. Next, mark the tape at four points equally spaced around the orbit. Label the points "arctic spring," "arctic summer," "arctic autumn," and "arctic winter." Turn on the lamp.

STEP THREE

Show what happens when it is summer in the Arctic. Hold the fruit at the level of the lamp's lightbulb and place it above the spot on the floor labeled "arctic summer." Refer to the diagram to tilt the "Earth's" axis correctly. The Earth turns on its axis about once every 24 hours, or once each day. Where the Earth faces the sun, it is daytime. Where the Earth faces away from the sun, it is night. Slowly turn the "Earth" on its axis. Notice where the lamp's light hits the fruit. Notice what parts of the fruit are in shadow. Study the amount of light and shadow in the Arctic.

STEP FOUR

Show what happens when it is winter in the Arctic. Hold the fruit at the level of the lightbulb and place it above the spot on the floor marked "arctic winter." Line up the axis as before. Slowly turn the fruit on its axis. Study the amount of light and shadow that hits the Arctic.

Observations

1. In the Arctic, is the length of daylight more affected by the Earth's rotation or the tilt of the Earth's axis? Explain your answer.
2. During summer, how much of the day is light in Hammerfest? How much is light during winter? Why?

ANALYSIS AND CONCLUSION

1. If the Earth were not tilted on its axis, how do you think life in the Arctic would be different? Explain your answer.
2. Suppose that the Earth orbited around the sun but never rotated on its axis. How much daylight would Hammerfest receive during the summer? Autumn? Winter? Spring? Explain your answer.

CHAPTER 10

Exploring Eastern Europe and Russia

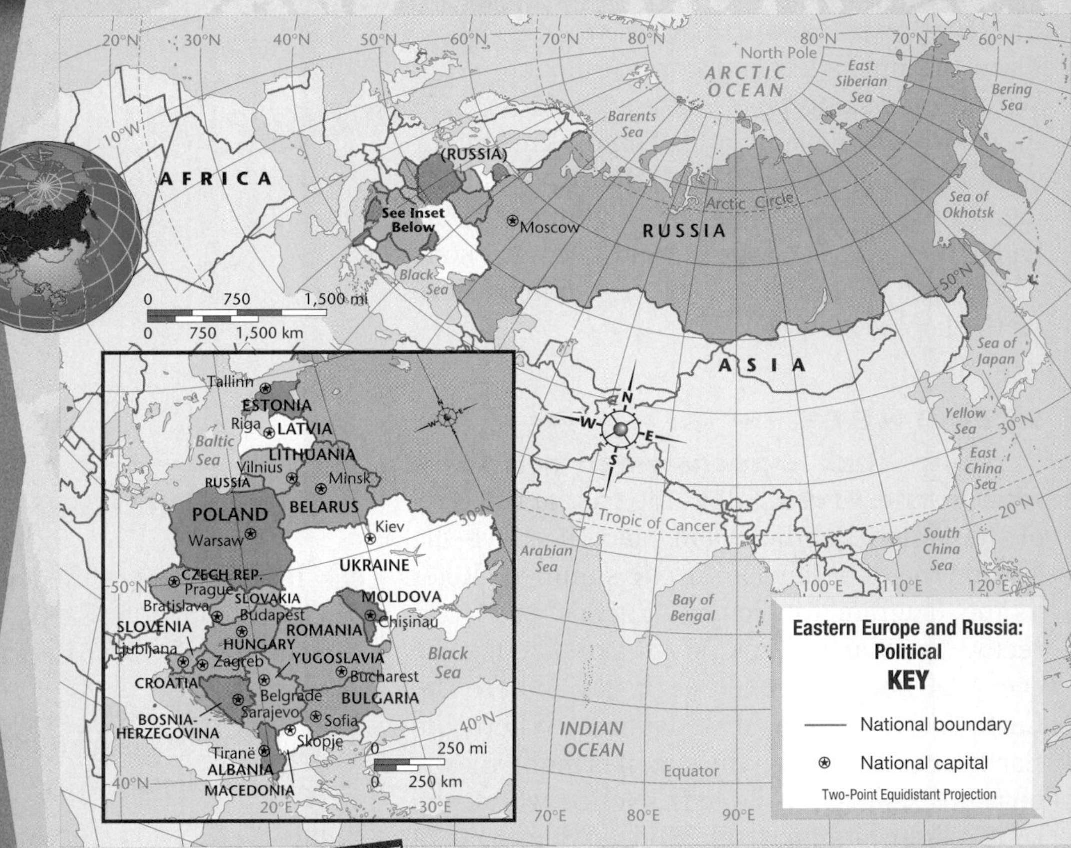

The countries of Eastern Europe and Russia have undergone many changes. Some have come about peacefully and others have come about with much struggle. To help you get to know Eastern Europe and Russia, complete the following activities.

Study the map

Which countries border the Baltic Sea? Which countries do not share a border with any bodies of water?

Make historical connections

Many countries in Eastern Europe once had communist governments. How do you think the location of these countries helped communism dominate the area?

Poland

Tradition and Change

Reach Into Your Background

Think of your own hometown 20 years from now. Do you think it will be very different? What things about it would you like to see changed? What would you like to stay the same?

Questions to Explore

1. What traditions remain strong in the Polish countryside?
2. How is life changing in Polish towns and cities?

Key Terms

free enterprise
shrine

Key People

Pope John Paul II

In 1989, Poland's communist government came to an end, and many things changed. Meet two brothers-in-law who are like the two faces of Poland. One man has changed with the times. The other sticks to old ways.

The first is Janusz Rajtar (YAHN uhsh RY tuhr). He owns a grocery store in a small city. The new non-communist government lets him keep most of his profits. He has saved money and gotten a loan. Now he is thinking of expanding his business. You can tell how well he is doing when you see his family. He and his wife dress in the latest fashions. His three young sons have new clothes, too.

Janusz Rajtar's brother-in-law, whose name is Janusz Podolak, has not been quite so lucky. He still wears the loose-fitting overalls that people wore during communist days. When the communist government fell, he grew poorer. He is a peasant farmer in a region where most farmers still use horses to plow the land. During the time of communist rule, the government kept his farm going by paying some of his costs. Now all of that is over.

▼ Now that Poland is no longer communist, its businesses are thriving.

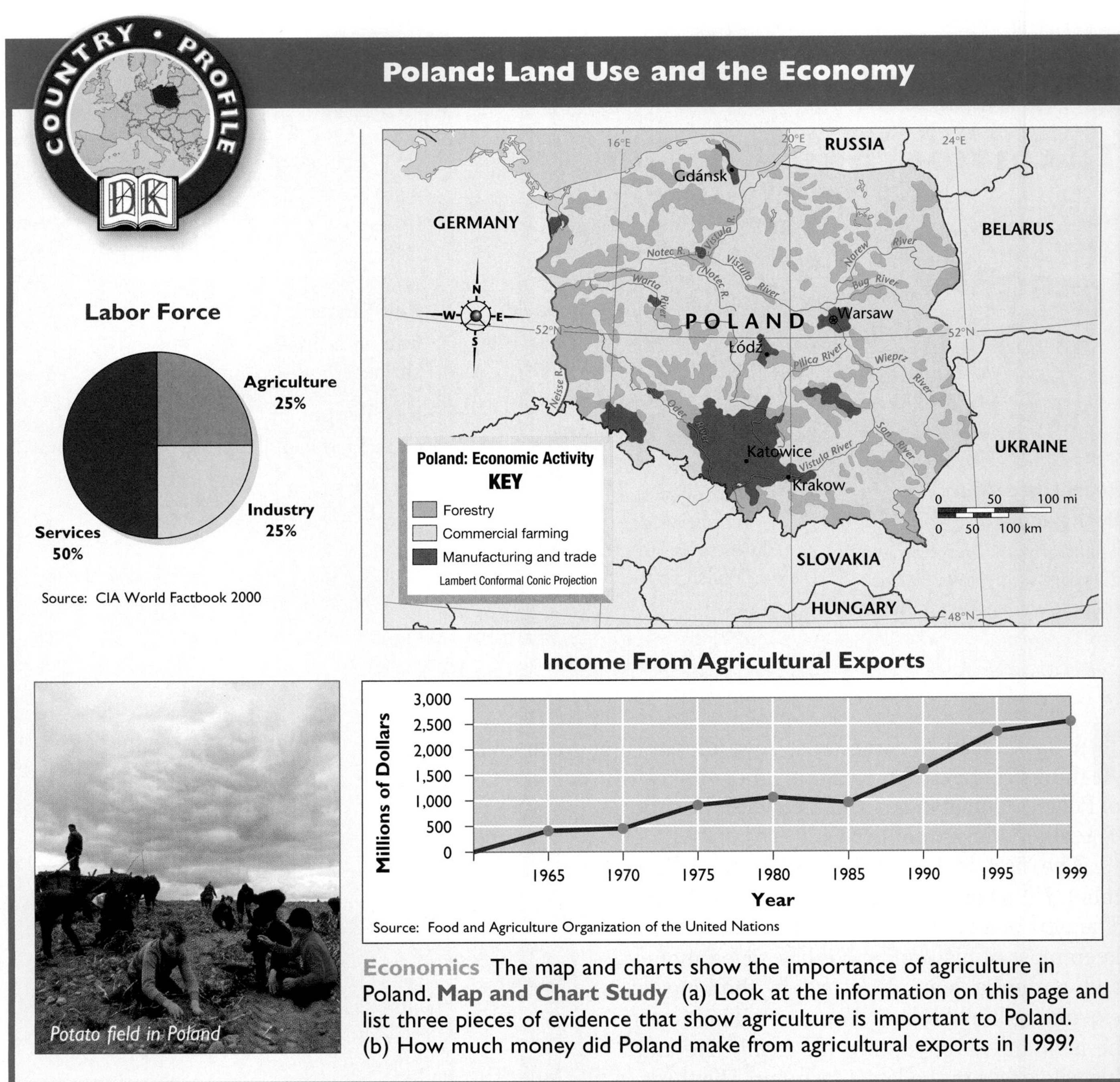

Economics The map and charts show the importance of agriculture in Poland. **Map and Chart Study** (a) Look at the information on this page and list three pieces of evidence that show agriculture is important to Poland. (b) How much money did Poland make from agricultural exports in 1999?

Take It to the NET

Data Update For the most recent data on Poland, visit **www.phschool.com**.

Tradition in Poland

Since Poland's communist government fell, the country has moved away from a communist economy in which the government owned and ran all the businesses. Instead, Poland has adopted the **free enterprise** system, or capitalism. In it, people can run their own businesses. But not all of life in Poland has changed. As you travel in the countryside, you see signs of a way of life that existed long before communist rule.

The Polish Countryside For a look at tradition in Poland, you might visit the northeast corner of the country. Here, the Polish border has shifted many times. Again and again, other countries have seized this area. Sometimes, it belonged to Russia. At other times, it was controlled by Lithuania (lith oo AY nee uh) or Germany. There were even times when other countries took over all of Poland. But no matter what happened, the traditions of Polish life stayed the same. This is true even today.

After World War II, Poland became a communist nation. At public festivals, Poles had to pledge loyalty to communism. When crops did not grow, Poles relied on money from the communist government. When Poles were sick, they went to doctors who were paid by the government. When they were too old to farm, they knew they would receive a government pension.

Now all that has changed. It is up to the farmer to save money for old age. If the crops fail, the farmer must try to borrow money to start again. Learning this new way of life has been hard for some Poles.

Ask Questions What questions might you ask about life in Poland under communism?

Polish Catholicism The years of communist rule did not change the love most Poles have for the Roman Catholic Church. For hundreds of years, Catholicism has been at the center of Polish tradition. The communist government tried to discourage Catholicism, but it did not succeed. Today, most Poles still are Catholic.

Polish Catholicism is unique. Poles have their own way of observing Catholic holidays and their own way of prayer. An example of Polish religious life can be seen in northeastern Poland, in the forest of

Poland's Solidarity Movement

Polish workers put pressure on the Communist government throughout the 1980s by rallying under the banner of Solidarity, an independent labor union (left). Their rallies often were broken up by the police (below). Today, Solidarity is a leading political party with many representatives in the Polish parliament.

Brightly Colored Eggs

Christians across the world give decorated eggs as gifts at Easter. The brightly colored eggs pictured here are similar to those Polish people might exchange. Don't try to peel off the shells, however. These eggs are made of wood. **Critical Thinking** What other celebrations or religious holidays involve the exchange of special gifts?

Biaolowiza (bee AHL uhv yezh uh). Not far from the forest is the holy mountain of Grabarka. A church sits at the top of the mountain. In mid-August, visitors climb this mountain to visit the church. Each visitor plants a cross in the earth. Among the trees on the mountainside are hundreds of crosses. Some are as tall as trees, others as tiny as flowers. You can see such **shrines,** or holy places, all over Poland.

Polish Catholics felt tremendous pride in 1978, when a Pole was selected as pope of the Catholic Church. Pope John Paul II quickly became the most widely traveled Catholic leader in history. He also made the world more aware of Poland, which was struggling under communism. On his visit to Poland in 1979, about one million Poles went wild with joy in greeting him. Mothers held babies over their heads for the pope's blessing. The crowd sang hymns and threw flowers toward the stage on which he sat. For most of these people, the pope stood for traditional Poland. He was a symbol of a part of Poland that they hoped would never die.

The Wisent For centuries the European bison, or wisent, roamed forests from Western Europe to Siberia. These animals are related to the North American buffalo. The wisent eat grasses, ferns, leaves, and tree bark. By 1600, loss of habitat wiped out almost all of the wisent. Now, thanks to special programs, about 1,500 wisent live in Poland. They make their home in the forest of Biaolowiza.

The Polish Language Like Roman Catholicism, the language of the Poles has also stood the test of time. Some foreign rulers banned the use of Polish in schools and in the government. The communists did not ban Polish but did force Polish schoolchildren to learn Russian, the main language of the Soviet Union.

Today, the Polish language is alive and well. It ties the people of the nation together. And it gives them the strong feeling that being Polish is something different and special. As a Slavic language, it also links the nation to other Slavic nations in Eastern Europe.

Changes in Towns and Cities

If you are looking for the newer Poland, you will find it in the larger towns and cities. Ever since the fall of communism, Poland has undergone rapid change. The biggest of these changes have come in Poland's economy.

Predict What do you think new businesspeople in Poland must do to succeed?

Making Business Grow With the end of communist rule, Poles were free to find new ways to make money. Small businesses soon blossomed all over Poland's capital, Warsaw. At first, traders set up booths on the streets. They sold everything they could find, from American blue jeans to old Soviet army uniforms.

Slowly but surely, some traders earned enough money to take over stores that the government had once owned. Poland's economy began growing faster than any other in Eastern Europe. Today, the standard of living of its people is growing stronger every day.

Standard of Living in Eastern European Countries

Country	Number of Televisions per 1,000 People	Number of Telephones per 1,000 People
Albania	89	40
Czech Republic	446	371
Hungary	438	405
Lithuania	364	321
Poland	414	228
Romania	201	167
Yugoslavia	27	214
United States	847	653

Source: The World Almanac 2001

Chart Study One way to study a country's economic health is to take a look at its basic services, such as communications. Televisions and telephones are two important tools of communication in today's world. This chart lists several Eastern European countries and shows how many people have TVs and telephones in each. It also shows the same for the United States. **Critical Thinking** Study the information in the chart. Which country probably has the weakest economy? Why?

People like store owner Janusz Rajtar are doing well in the new Poland. To find the best products for his store, Rajtar rises at 4:00 A.M. to buy fruits and vegetables at the local farmers' market. By 7:00 A.M., he is behind his desk at a second job, working in an office. Then, at 3:00 P.M., he is back at the grocery store.

Looking Toward the Future Janusz Rajtar is benefiting from his hard work. But people like Janusz's brother-in-law are working harder and are not benefiting. Farmers, with no government support, find it hard to compete in the European market. Many young people in rural areas feel that they have little chance to make a decent living. Some have moved to the city in the hope of finding jobs.

Migration to the cities, however, can cause overcrowding. Today, 65 percent of all Poles live in towns or cities, a huge increase from just 50 years ago. In response, the government is building apartment buildings and expanding suburban areas.

The new life is good in some ways and hard in others. Many Poles have things they never had before. In 1989, only half of the homes in Poland had color televisions. Now, almost every home has one. On the streets of Warsaw, some people make telephone calls on cellular phones and wear the new clothing fashions. For these people, the new way of life is good.

▼ Forests once covered Poland's flat landscape, but for centuries most of the country has been cleared for farming. This picture shows Poland's fertile farmland and the traditional wooden houses near the city of Krakow, in the foothills of the Carpathian Mountains. Many of Poland's farmers still sow their fields by hand.

Old Market Square, Warsaw, Poland

Years ago, merchants sold their wares in Warsaw's Old Market Square. People did their shopping on special market days. Today, Old Market Square is not only a shopping area, but also a place to meet friends and watch free entertainment. Street performers regularly attract large and enthusiastic audiences.

But in Warsaw, you can also see people with nothing to do. This, too, is a change. There are more people without jobs than there were under communism. The Poles will have to find ways to deal with such challenges. The Polish people are ready to do whatever is needed because for the first time in many years, their future is in their own hands.

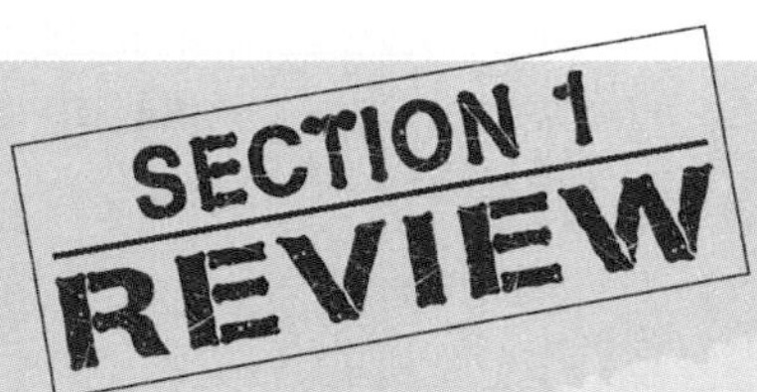

1. **Define** (a) free enterprise, (b) shrine.
2. **Identify** Pope John Paul II.
3. What features of country life show the traditional side of Poland?
4. What are some of the changes taking place in Poland?

Critical Thinking

5. **Making Predictions** What do you predict will happen to the Polish economy in the future? Give reasons for your predictions.

Activity

6. **Writing to Learn** Use library resources to find a book or encyclopedia article about Polish history. Read about the fall of communism in Poland. Then, write a brief summary of what you have read.

Yugoslavia

A Region Tries to Rebuild

Reach Into Your Background

Think about how you identify yourself as a person. How would you feel if someone who didn't know you disliked you just because of who your parents were? In Yugoslavia, people have been in this situation for many years.

Questions to Explore

1. What are some of the differences among the people who live in Yugoslavia?
2. What happened to Yugoslavia after communist leader Tito died?
3. What changes have taken place in Yugoslavia since the signing of the peace treaty in the 1990s?

Key Terms

United Nations
economic sanctions

Key People and Places

Sarajevo
Belgrade
Marshal Tito

In January 1984, the people of Sarajevo (sah rah YAY voh), a beautiful old city in Yugoslavia, were filled with a spirit of anticipation. They had proudly won the right to host the Winter Olympics of 1984. To prepare for these games, they had built new hotels and restaurants. They had erected ski lifts and carved ski racing trails into the mountains. New bobsled runs and an elegant skating complex were waiting for the athletes. A shiny new Olympic Village had been built to welcome athletes and visitors to the Games.

▼ The Olympic Center was destroyed during the civil war that took place in Yugoslavia in the 1990s.

Ten years later, most of these facilities lay in ruins. So did much of Sarajevo. Bombings destroyed many of its fine old buildings. How could this have happened? The answer is war—civil war that broke up Yugoslavia and shattered the grand city.

Land of Many Cultures

Yugoslavia is located in a region of southeastern Europe called the Balkans. Most of its people are Slavs. However, the Slavs are made up of many ethnic groups. Before the breakup of Yugoslavia, the largest Slavic groups in the country were the Serbs and Croats (kroh ATS). Slovenes,

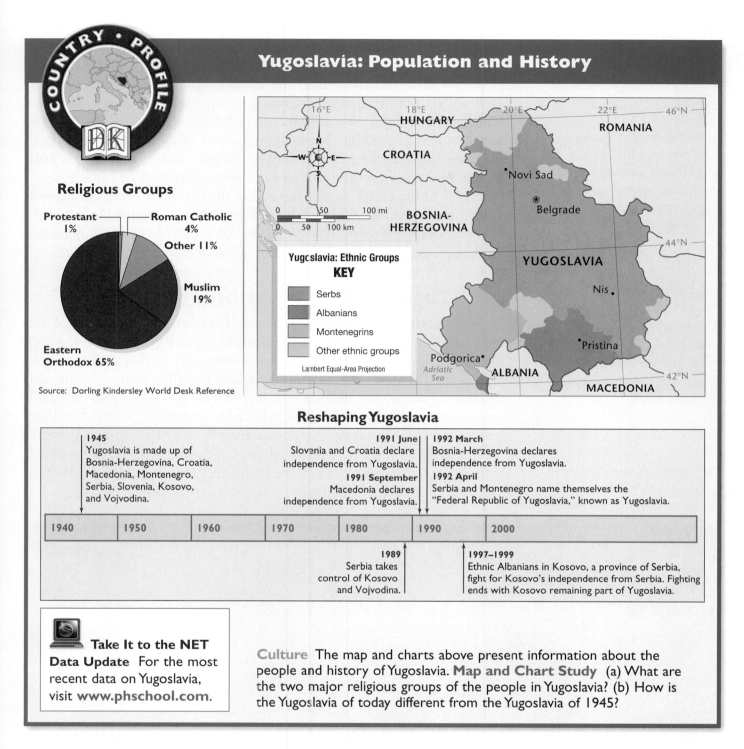

COUNTRY • PROFILE

DK

Yugoslavia: Population and History

Religious Groups

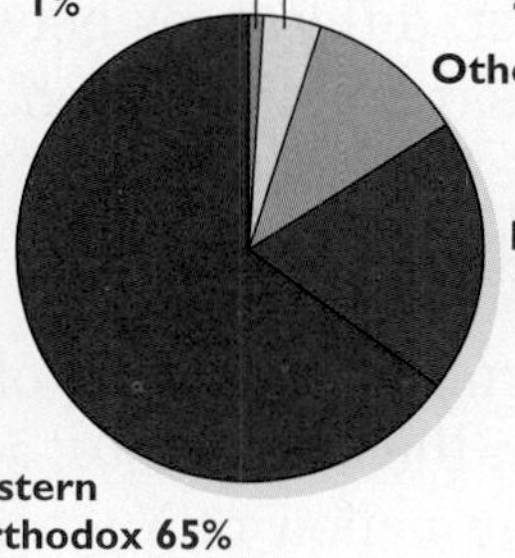

- Protestant 1%
- Roman Catholic 4%
- Other 11%
- Muslim 19%
- Eastern Orthodox 65%

Source: Dorling Kindersley World Desk Reference

Yugoslavia: Ethnic Groups

KEY

- Serbs
- Albanians
- Montenegrins
- Other ethnic groups

Lambert Equal-Area Projection

16°E 18°E 20°E 22°E 46°N 44°N 42°N

HUNGARY, ROMANIA, CROATIA, BOSNIA-HERZEGOVINA, YUGOSLAVIA, ALBANIA, MACEDONIA, Adriatic Sea

Novi Sad, Belgrade, Nis, Pristina, Podgorica

0 50 100 mi
0 50 100 km

Reshaping Yugoslavia

1945 Yugoslavia is made up of Bosnia-Herzegovina, Croatia, Macedonia, Montenegro, Serbia, Slovenia, Kosovo, and Vojvodina.

1989 Serbia takes control of Kosovo and Vojvodina.

1991 June Slovenia and Croatia declare independence from Yugoslavia.

1991 September Macedonia declares independence from Yugoslavia.

1992 March Bosnia-Herzegovina declares independence from Yugoslavia.

1992 April Serbia and Montenegro name themselves the "Federal Republic of Yugoslavia," known as Yugoslavia.

1997–1999 Ethnic Albanians in Kosovo, a province of Serbia, fight for Kosovo's independence from Serbia. Fighting ends with Kosovo remaining part of Yugoslavia.

1940	1950	1960	1970	1980	1990	2000

Take It to the NET
Data Update For the most recent data on Yugoslavia, visit **www.phschool.com.**

Culture The map and charts above present information about the people and history of Yugoslavia. **Map and Chart Study** (a) What are the two major religious groups of the people in Yugoslavia? (b) How is the Yugoslavia of today different from the Yugoslavia of 1945?

Montenegrins (mahn tuh NEH grinz), and Macedonians (mas uh DOH nee unz) were smaller Slav groups.

While many of these groups share a Slavic heritage, there are also differences among them. One is language. Three different languages are used by the groups—Serbo-Croatian, Slovenian, and Macedonian. Both Serbs and Croats speak Serbo-Croatian, but they use different alphabets to write the language.

Religion is another major difference among the groups. Most Serbs, Montenegrins, and Macedonians belong to the Christian Orthodox Church. Croats and Slovenes are mainly Roman Catholic. Other Serbs are Muslim.

Connect What kinds of ideas can cause barriers between people?

Writer in War During World War II, Germany invaded Yugoslavia. To protest against this, people in Sarajevo started a newspaper called *Oslobodjenje* in 1943. It is still published today, despite the civil war. *Oslobodjenje's* office has been bombed. The newspaper has suffered from shortages of electricity, paper, and ink. It has few reporters left. And still it continues, keeping hope alive.

Historic Regional Tensions How did these differences arise? They began centuries ago when the Roman Empire broke up into eastern and western regions. The Cyrillic alphabet and the Christian Orthodox Church became dominant in the eastern empire, and the Latin alphabet and Roman Catholic Church were dominant in the western empire. Serbs, Montenegrins, and Macedonians developed cultures influenced by the east. The Croats and Slovenes who had settled to the northwest developed cultures influenced by the west.

Then, in the 1300s, a group known as the Ottoman Turks conquered much of the Balkan region. They brought their religion, Islam, with them. Some Serbs converted to Islam. After that, differences between Christians and Muslims added to the ethnic tensions in the region.

Yugoslavia—A Nation Torn Apart

For hundreds of years, the Ottoman Turks ruled the peoples of the Balkans. When the Ottoman empire broke up in the early 1900s, some Balkan peoples formed independent states. The nation of Yugoslavia was formed in 1918. This new nation joined together various ethnic and religious groups. But making one united nation out of these separate groups was not easy. The Serbs, who were Yugoslavia's largest ethnic group, set up a central government in the city of Belgrade. This government failed to win the support of other ethnic groups, and resentment of it grew. Yugoslavia faced a new challenge in 1941. During World War II, Germany and Italy invaded and occupied Yugoslavia.

▼ Yugoslav soldiers approach a German fort in what is now Slovenia during World War II.

Communism—Its Rise and Fall In 1945 the war ended. The leader of the Yugoslav fight against Germany, Joseph Broz Tito, became head of the government. Marshal Tito, as he was usually called, built the government on communist political and economic principles. Yugoslavia was a federal state, divided into smaller units called republics. Each ethnic group lived in a republic where it was in the majority. For example, Croatia was home to most of the Croats. All republics, however, contained peoples of other ethnic groups.

Yugoslavia became a firm ally of the Soviet Union. Later Tito wanted to develop his own policies and relations with other countries, especially those of the West. This put him in conflict with the Soviet dictator, Joseph Stalin. In 1948, Stalin expelled Yugoslavia from the Soviet Union's communist group of nations in Eastern Europe. Tito then became less hostile to the United States and nations of Western Europe. He continued to rule Yugoslavia according to communist principles, but he also had good relations with anti-communist nations.

Breakup Leads to War Tito's strong government reduced ethnic tensions. During Tito's time, people began to identify themselves as citizens of Yugoslavia. But after his death in 1980, politicians struggled for power. Their struggle encouraged ethnic nationalism and

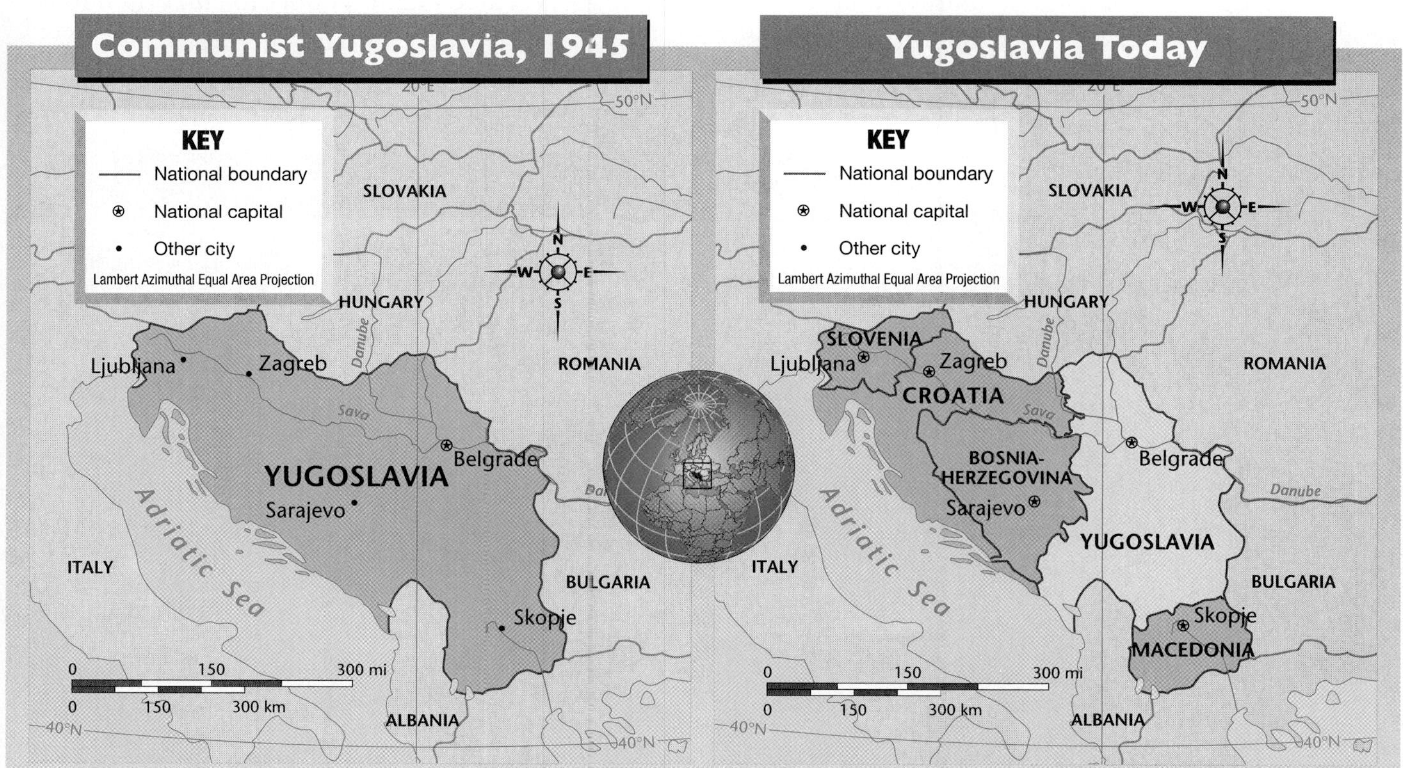

Map Study In the 1990s, several regions declared themselves independent of Yugoslavia. Yugoslavia is now half the size it was during Tito's rule. **Location** What countries now occupy areas that were once part of Yugoslavia? In what country is Sarajevo now located?

Connect How would you feel if you and some of your friends or members of your family were on opposite sides in a war?

independence movements. The first republics to break away from Yugoslavia were Slovenia and Croatia. They declared themselves independent nations in 1991. Macedonia and Bosnia-Herzegovina followed later that year. By 1992 only two republics—Serbia and Montenegro—remained part of Yugoslavia.

The breakup of Yugoslavia led to terrible violence and bloodshed. Croats and Serbs battled over disputed borders. Croats forced Serbs living in Croatia to return to Serbia. Serbia made Croats living in Serbia return to Croatia. Bosnia-Herzegovina was torn apart by civil war.

Bosnia-Herzegovina

In Bosnia-Herzegovina, tensions among different ethnic groups led to a long and bitter war. Sometimes Christian Serbs and Croats fought on the same side to win land controlled by Bosnian Muslims. At other times Serbs, backed by Yugoslavian president Slobodan Milosevic, fought Croats for land. People on all sides were mistreated by their enemies. Many people were killed. Others had their homes blown up and were forced to move away from where they had lived peacefully for years, just because they were Serbs or Croats.

During the war, Sarajevo, the capital of Bosnia-Herzegovina, was almost completely destroyed. Homes and schools were bombed. People were shot as they tried to go about their daily business. Serb armies cut Sarajevo off from the rest of the world, causing people to run out of food and other supplies.

The Long War in Bosnia

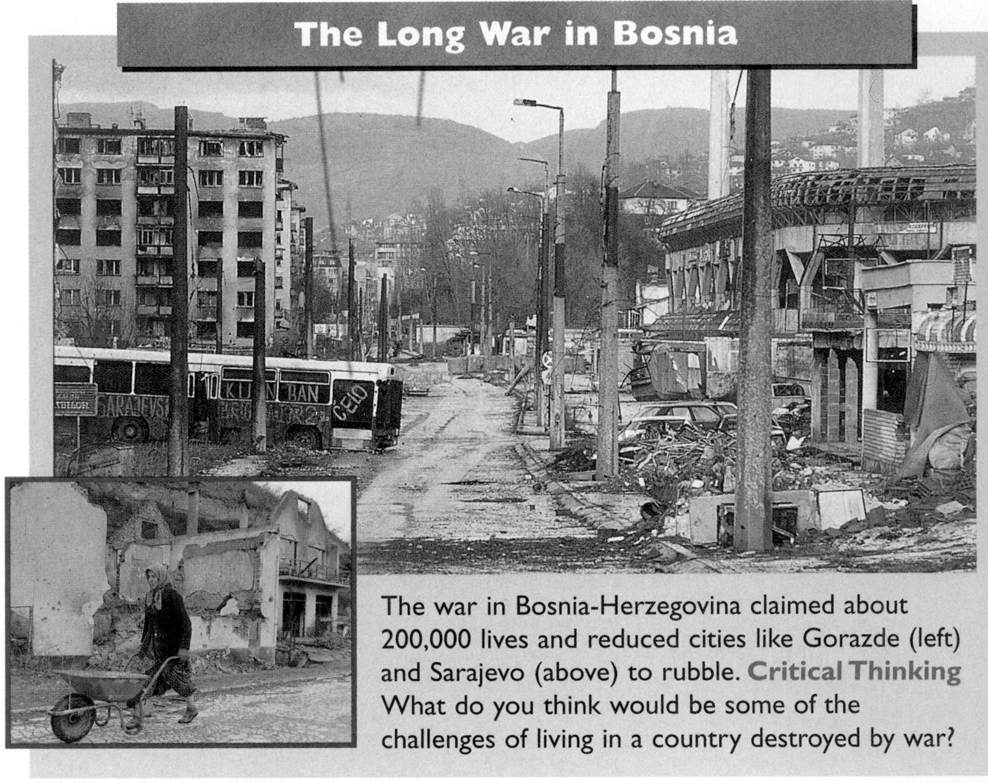

The war in Bosnia-Herzegovina claimed about 200,000 lives and reduced cities like Gorazde (left) and Sarajevo (above) to rubble. **Critical Thinking** What do you think would be some of the challenges of living in a country destroyed by war?

In 1992 the United Nations sent troops to the city to bring in supplies. The **United Nations** is an international group that was founded in 1945, after World War II. Its member countries work together to bring about peace and cooperation. A few years later, the Serbs, Croats, and Bosnian Muslims signed a peace treaty. After years of war, the people of a much smaller Yugoslavia hoped that the peace would last.

The Region's Future

Though a peace treaty was signed, trouble in the region did not end. Tensions between different ethnic groups still existed. Russian and NATO forces, sent in by Western countries, helped keep peace but often introduced new conflicts.

▼Slobodan Milosevic was arrested in Yugoslavia in 2001 and turned over to a United Nations tribunal to face charges of crimes against humanity.

Many Serbs were unhappy with President Slobodan Milosevic, known for his cruel treatment of people who were not Serbs. The United States and Europe held Milosevic responsible for the violence. They placed **economic sanctions** on Yugoslavia to show their disapproval. Economic sanctions are actions to limit trade with nations that have violated international laws.

In 2000, Yugoslavia held new presidential elections. Vojislav Kostunica was elected, replacing Milosevic. To show their approval of the new president, the United States and European nations promised to lift the sanctions against Yugoslavia.

What lies ahead for Yugoslavia? The destruction that occurred in the 1990s presents its population of over 10 million with deep economic problems. The country hopes to move toward a more stable and peaceful time, but it will have to overcome its recent history of ethnic conflict.

1. **Define** (a) United Nations, (b) economic sanctions.
2. **Identify** (a) Sarajevo, (b) Belgrade, (c) Marshal Tito.
3. Describe the similarities and differences among Yugoslavia's ethnic groups.
4. What challenges face Yugoslavia and the former nations of Yugoslavia in the future?

Critical Thinking

5. **Recognizing Cause and Effect** Why might the presence of NATO peacekeeping forces in Yugoslavia lead to new conflicts?

Activity

6. **Writing to Learn** Suppose that you work for the United Nations. Write a letter to the leader of one of Yugoslavia's ethnic groups explaining why the group should strive for peace.

SKILLS
ACTIVITY

Recognizing Cause and Effect

Have you ever played with dominoes? It's fun to stand them up in a line and then topple them over. By pushing just the first domino, you set up a chain reaction that eventually knocks all of the dominoes down. In 1988, students in the Netherlands set up 1.5 million dominoes! By pushing just one, they were able to topple nearly all the rest.

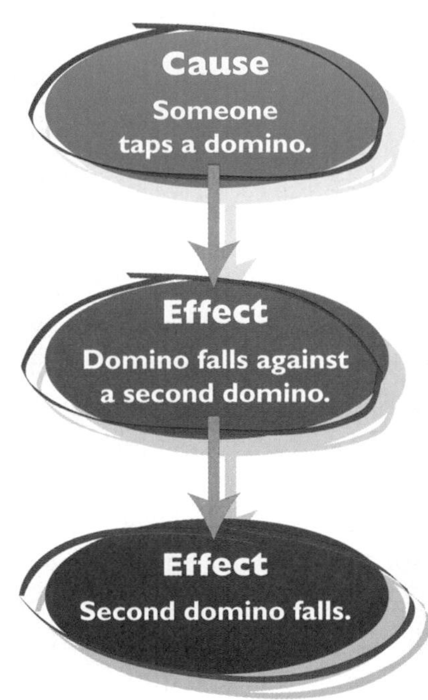
Cause
Someone taps a domino.
Effect
Domino falls against a second domino.
Effect
Second domino falls.

Get Ready

Toppling dominoes is fun, but it also teaches a lesson in cause and effect. A *cause* is something that makes something else happen. The *effect* is what happens. Someone taps the first domino. It falls over. The falling domino hits a second domino and it falls, too. The tapping of the first domino is the cause, and the effect is the fall of the second domino.

Cause and effect can explain the relationship between events. History is full of causes and effects. For example, a big cause of the French Revolution was the fact that a small number of people owned most of the country's wealth. An effect of the revolution was that France's king, who was very wealthy, was thrown out of power.

A single event can have more than one cause or more than one effect. In France, for example, the revolution had many effects besides the fall of the monarchy. Also keep in mind that not all events are linked by cause and effect. For example, if a girl claps her hands, and it then begins to rain, her claps did not cause it to rain. Learning to correctly recognize causes and effects will help you understand history.

Try It Out

Causes and effects can be shown in cause-effect diagrams, like the one pictured to the left. You can see how events can have more than one cause or more than one effect.

To understand how cause-effect relationships work, make a cause-effect diagram about the most recent presidential election. You can learn about this event by looking it up in an almanac or other source. To make your cause-effect diagram, complete the following steps:

A. Identify the event. Your diagram will explain the most recent presidential election. Write the event in the middle of a clean sheet of paper and circle it.

B. Identify the causes. What caused the election to take place? You should be able to identify at least two causes. Write them to the left of the event, and draw a circle around each one. Then, draw an arrow from each cause to the event to show that they made the event happen.

C. Identify the effects. Identify at least two effects of a presidential election. For example, was the President reelected? Write the effects to the right of the event, and circle each one. Then, draw an arrow from the event to each effect to show that they resulted from the event.

Now look your diagram over to see how it works. Notice that it reads from left to right, just as books do. By following the arrows, you can trace the causes and effects of events.

▼A line of falling dominoes is an example of the relationship between cause and effect.

Apply the Skill

Read the paragraph below. Look for cause-and-effect relationships between the events. Words and phrases such as "because," "so," and "as a result" will give you clues that a cause-and-effect relationship exists.

Poland After Communism

In 1989, communism in Poland ended, and Poland adopted the free enterprise system. In this kind of system, people can open and run their own businesses free from government control. The fall of communism meant that the government no longer controlled the creation of jobs. As a result, many government jobs disappeared. The loss of jobs forced people to look for jobs elsewhere. Because of free enterprise, small companies now have the freedom to grow naturally. Growing companies have created new and better jobs for some people, but other people remain jobless.

When you have finished reading the paragraph, go back and read the underlined events. Find at least one cause and one effect of each underlined event, and write them down. As you are looking, remember that the effect of one event can also be the cause of another.

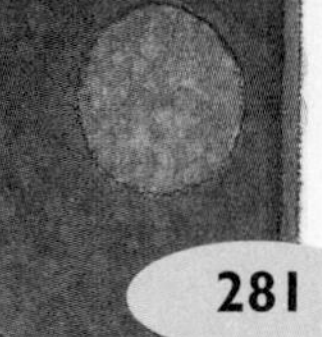

Ukraine

People Working Together

Reach Into Your Background

Have you gained more independence as you have grown older? What kinds of problems has your new independence brought you? How have you solved them? The newly independent people of Ukraine have solved many of their problems by working together.

Questions to Explore

1. How have the natural resources of Ukraine shaped the history of that nation?
2. How did the accident at Chernobyl affect the environment of Ukraine?

Key Terms

chernozem
collective

Key Places

Kiev
Chernobyl
Kharkov

How many people, linked hand-to-hand, would it take to cover 300 miles (483 km)? The people of Ukraine can tell you, because they did it in 1990. It took about 500,000 Ukrainians to make a human chain this long. It stretched from Kiev, Ukraine's capital, to the city of Lvov (lvawf). The chain was a symbol of their protest against Soviet control of Ukraine. It also proved that Ukrainians know how to work together to solve their problems. Today, people in Ukraine are enjoying independence and still working together.

▼In 1990, the people of Ukraine rallied to protest Soviet control of their country.

Ukraine's Path to Freedom

For hundreds of years, Ukraine had struggled to be independent. You can see why if you look at Ukraine's location. This huge land lies between the nations of Europe and Russia. In fact, the name *Ukraine* means "borderland." Look at the political map of Eastern Europe and Russia at the beginning of this chapter. Notice that to the west of Ukraine are Poland, Slovakia, and Hungary. To the east of Ukraine is Russia. The map makes it easy to see that Ukraine is open to invasion by its neighbors.

Ukraine: Agriculture and the Economy

Major Export Destinations

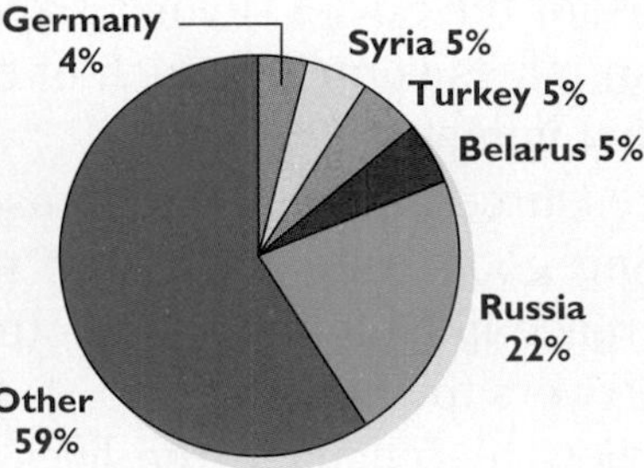

Source: Dorling Kindersley World Desk Reference

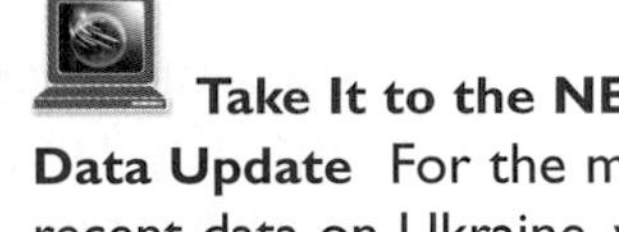

Take It to the NET

Data Update For the most recent data on Ukraine, visit **www.phschool.com**.

Ukrainian port on the Black Sea

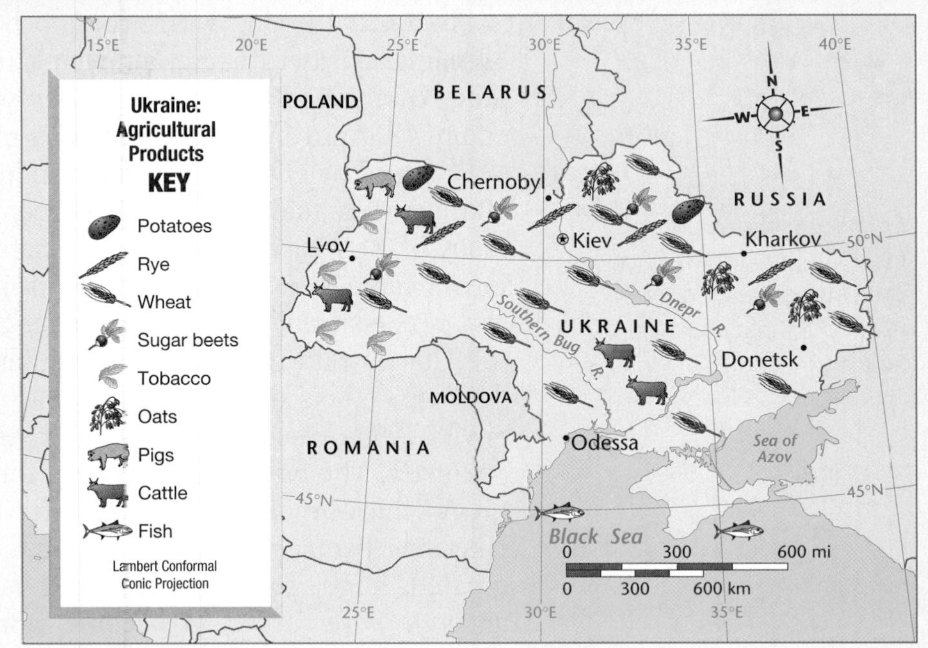

Top 10 Wheat Producers in Europe, 2000

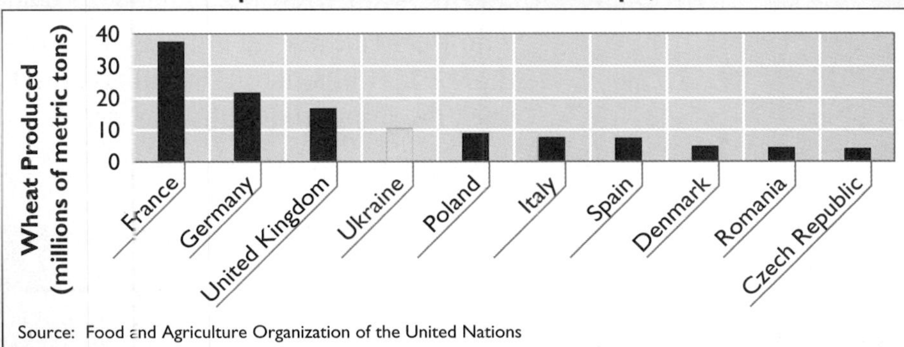

Source: Food and Agriculture Organization of the United Nations

Economics The map and charts highlight the importance of agriculture to Ukraine's economy. **Map and Chart Study** (a) How does Ukraine rank among European wheat producers? (b) Near what cities is wheat grown in Ukraine? (c) What country receives the most exports from Ukraine?

Location has been only part of the problem. The other has been Ukraine's vast natural resources, which attract invaders. As a result, at one time or another, Poland, Czechoslovakia, and Romania have taken slices of Ukraine. During World War II, the German army invaded Ukraine to gain its natural resources. But the most difficult neighbor of all has been Russia. It ruled Ukraine for much of the time between the late 1700s and the fall of the Soviet Union in 1991.

Predict What kinds of natural resources would encourage one country to try to take over another?

Supplying the Soviets A hundred years ago, Ukraine, which then was part of the Russian empire, was one of Europe's leading grain producing regions. Ukraine produced so much grain that people called it the "breadbasket of Europe." Why is Ukraine so productive? Over half of the country is covered by a rich, black soil called **chernozem** (CHER nuh zem).

Connect How would you feel if all the resources of the United States were used to benefit another country?

In 1922, Ukraine was forced to become part of the Soviet Union. Ukrainian farmers began supplying the rest of the Soviet Union with food. By the end of the 1980s, they were producing 25 percent of the country's grain and 30 percent of its meat.

Under Soviet rule, Ukrainian industries grew. In time, factories in Ukraine were making about 25 percent of the country's goods. Further, many of the weapons, ships, and machines for the Soviet Union's armed forces came from Ukraine. And Ukrainian mines supplied much of the iron ore, coal, and other minerals for Soviet industries.

The Soviets used other Ukrainian resources as well. Ships used Ukraine's ports on the Black Sea to bring goods into and out of the Soviet Union. Several of Ukraine's rivers reach like highways into other countries. The Soviets made use of these rivers to ship goods.

All the economic changes under Soviet rule changed the lives of Ukraine's people. The Soviet rulers took farms away from farmers and created huge government-owned farms called **collectives.** Most farmers were forced to become workers on these collective farms. (Some farmers were sent instead to cities to work in the new factories.) All the crops from the collectives went to the government. The people who worked the land got very little of the food they grew. As a result, in the 1930s millions of Ukrainians died of hunger. Over the years, however, life improved on the farms.

Golden Fields of Wheat

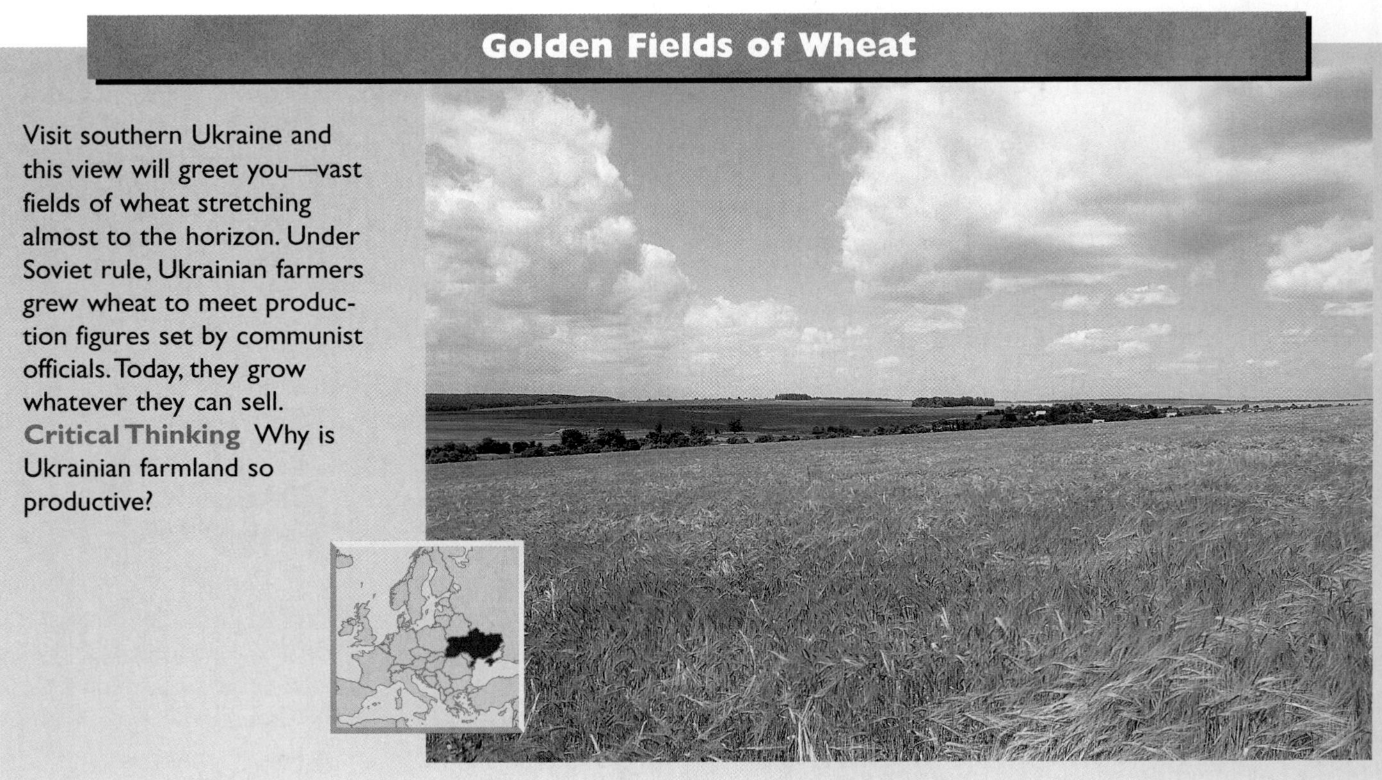

Visit southern Ukraine and this view will greet you—vast fields of wheat stretching almost to the horizon. Under Soviet rule, Ukrainian farmers grew wheat to meet production figures set by communist officials. Today, they grow whatever they can sell. **Critical Thinking** Why is Ukrainian farmland so productive?

Odessa, Ukraine

The city of Odessa is one of Ukraine's greatest assets. Located on the Black Sea, it is a center of shipping and manufacturing.

Building an Independent Economy Ukrainians won their independence from the Soviets in 1991. Since then, they have worked together to build up their economy and change to a new way of life. Like people in other former Soviet republics, Ukrainians are having to learn how to start new businesses, make goods, and keep prices under control. However, they have had some important successes. For example, very few Ukrainians are without work. Recently, less than 4 percent of the people who could work were unemployed. In contrast, 5 to 15 percent of workers are unemployed in the rest of Europe.

Issues After Independence

Now that Ukrainians are independent, they must decide many important issues for themselves. For example, should their national language be Russian or Ukrainian?

Choosing a Language Under Soviet rule, the official language was Russian. Books and newspapers were published only in Russian. Lessons in school were taught only in Russian, using Russian textbooks. As a result, many Ukrainians speak only Russian, especially in the cities and in the eastern part of the nation. Russian is also the language of ethnic Russians, who make up about one fifth of the people. Ukrainian is widely spoken only in rural areas and in the western part of the nation.

After the Nuclear Accident at Chernobyl

In the days after the Chernobyl nuclear power accident, there was always at least one helicopter in the air near the reactor. From the helicopters, people used hand-held radiation counters (right) to check the levels of radiation in the air. Despite the unsafe conditions, the Soviet Union began operating the Chernobyl reactor again six months later. People returned to Chernobyl to work, but not to live. Years after the accident, the Chernobyl area (below) remained deserted. **Critical Thinking** What challenges do you think might face people who returned to work at Chernobyl after the accident?

Still, many people want the country to return to its own language. Speaking Ukrainian could tie the country together. It could also free Ukraine from its Soviet past. Elementary schools have begun using Ukrainian in the early grades. In later grades and high school, Russian is still used. In the coming years, however, that will change. Most Ukrainians are pleased about the change. One teacher said, "Language is the anchor of our independence."

READ ACTIVELY

Ask Questions What do you want to know about the explosion at the nuclear power plant in Chernobyl?

Accident at Chernobyl One of the biggest issues facing independent Ukraine grew out of a terrible event during the Soviet period. When it was under Soviet rule, Ukraine sent resources to the Soviet Union. In return, it received Soviet natural gas and oil. But Ukraine's industries needed even more energy. So the Ukrainians built five nuclear power plants. These supply about one third of the country's electricity.

Nuclear power is created with a special radioactive metal called uranium. When atoms, or very tiny pieces, of uranium are split, heat is released. The heat turns water into steam. The steam turns large machines called generators, which produce electricity.

This process must be kept under tight control. If too much heat is produced too quickly, it could destroy the entire building. Then poisonous gas would escape into the air.

In 1986, there was an explosion at the Chernobyl (CHER noh bul) nuclear plant, 65 miles (105 km) from the city of Kiev. Poisonous gases filled the air. Some people died at once. Others had serious health problems that killed them slowly or left them suffering. More than 100,000 people had to be moved out of the area because it was no longer safe to live there.

Even after 10 years, much of Ukraine's soil and water was still poisoned. Some towns and farmland remain abandoned to this day. With the help of other nations, the Ukrainians are cleaning up the poison around Chernobyl. It may take up to a hundred years to repair the damage. But the Ukrainians are determined to bring back the land they love.

Antinuclear Protests

Ukraine has a strong antinuclear movement. Some Ukrainians who are opposed to nuclear power wear masks and hoist banners in protest.

Life in Ukraine

Independence has already changed life in Ukraine. For example, the Kreshchatik (kree SHAH tik), the main street in Kiev, often is jammed with people. Along this street are many parks, stores, and restaurants. People sell ice cream and hot dogs covered with a thin red sauce that Ukrainians love. Newsstands are filled with magazines and newspapers, many of which have been published only since independence. At a local market, farmers sell cheese or produce from their own farms. This, too, only became possible after independence.

LINKS ACROSS THE WORLD

The Spread of Poison Winds blew Chernobyl's poisonous gases across Europe. In England, Germany, and Spain the gases poisoned milk, meat, and leafy vegetables. In Belarus, one fifth of the farmland was poisoned. And in Norway, Sweden, and Finland, the reindeer herds of the Sami ate poisoned grasses. Almost the whole herd—about 180,000 animals—had to be killed.

◀ To symbolize the deadly nature of the Chernobyl accident, a protester plants crosses near a nuclear power station.

Folk Museum in Ukraine

Near Kiev, Ukraine, the Museum of Folk Architecture features a traditional farmhouse. A loom, used to weave cloth, sits in the middle of the room shown here. It reminds visitors of a time when people made cloth, furniture, and tools for themselves. People on farms also grew the vegetables and grains that they ate, collected eggs from the chickens they raised, and raised cows and goats for milk and meat. **Critical Thinking** Life in Ukraine and elsewhere has changed in many ways since the days when this traditional farmhouse was used. Name some aspects of life that have not changed.

Other Ukrainian cities are also alive with the new spirit of freedom. Not far from Kiev is the city of Kharkov. Located near huge reserves of iron ore and coal, it is the busiest industrial center in the nation. But Kharkov is not all work. While you are there, you can listen to fine music or watch a play.

As you travel through Ukraine, you can see that it is in the early stages of a new time in its history. The people have always wanted freedom, and now they have it in their grasp. They know that independence is not easy. But with the land's great resources and the people's ability to work together, the Ukrainians have a good chance to make independence work.

1. **Define** (a) chernozem, (b) collective.
2. **Identify** (a) Kiev, (b) Chernobyl, (c) Kharkov.
3. How has Ukraine's location affected its history?
4. Why do many Ukrainians want to make Ukrainian the official national language?

Critical Thinking

5. **Distinguishing Cause and Effect** In recent years, some Russian leaders have declared that they want Ukraine to become a part of Russia. Why would they want this to happen?

Activity

6. **Writing to Learn** Write a letter to one of the people who was forced to leave his or her home because of the Chernobyl explosion. You can offer comfort or advice and/or ask questions about the accident.

Russia

A Large and Diverse Country

Reach Into Your Background
What other states in the United States have you visited? What other towns or cities have you seen? Were they very different from where you live? In Russia, as you will see, there are great differences from one region of the nation to another.

Questions to Explore

1. How do ways of life differ in a land as large as Russia?

2. What problems do Russians have today in unifying their country?

Key Terms
investor

Key Places
Kemerovo
Moscow

Inessa Krichevskaya (in ES uh kree CHEV sky uh) has surprising feelings about change in Russia. "You know," she says, "it's a very difficult period in our country right now, but we will just have to live through it, because this is the right direction. . . . We can never go back to what was before."

Why are Inessa's feelings so surprising? For more than 30 years, she was a loyal Communist. She lived and worked in the city of Moscow as an engineer. Like all other Russians, she always expected that the government would send her monthly checks when she grew too old to work. That was part of the communist system. But then Russia switched to the free enterprise system. Now Inessa is in her 60s and is retired. The amount she receives from the government is much less than she expected. Inessa gets about 1,300 rubles a month—only about $8.

The fall of communism caused other hardships for Inessa. During a march for democracy, her son was killed by soldiers. Still, Inessa believes that the changes are moving her country in the right direction, toward freedom. "My son, and the others who turned out that night, just wanted some sort of free life," she explains.

What kind of life have the people of Russia found as their country has turned toward a new system? To answer that question, let's look at two parts of Russia: Siberia and Moscow.

▼ After the collapse of communism, Russia's people joyfully used their right to speak freely about politics.

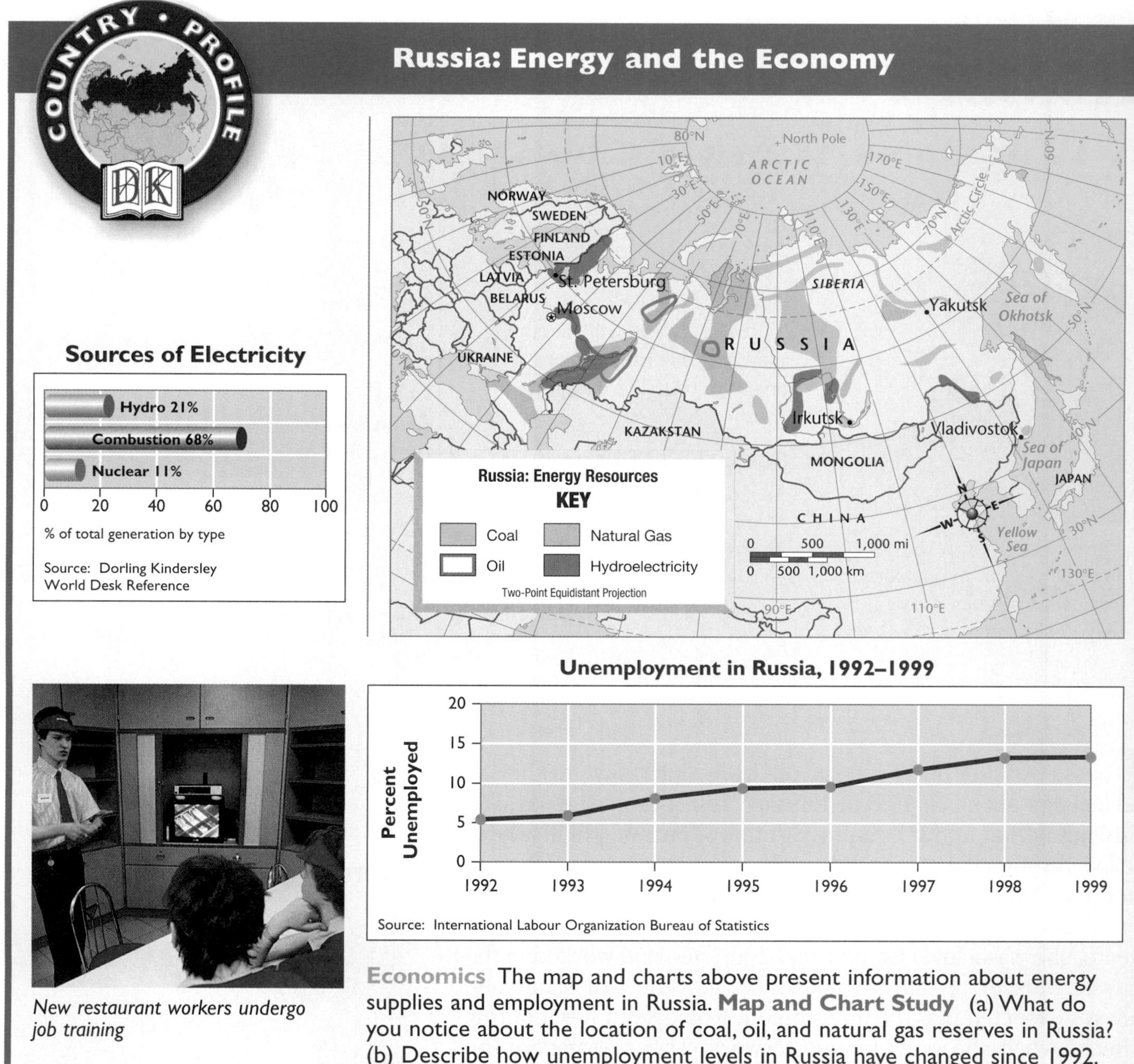

New restaurant workers undergo job training

Economics The map and charts above present information about energy supplies and employment in Russia. **Map and Chart Study** (a) What do you notice about the location of coal, oil, and natural gas reserves in Russia? (b) Describe how unemployment levels in Russia have changed since 1992. (c) What type of energy is generated the most in Russia?

Take It to the NET

Data Update For the most recent data on Russia, visit **www.phschool.com**.

Life in Siberia

During the Soviet years, the government tried to change Siberia, the huge region of eastern Russia. It built factories to take advantage of the region's rich reserves of coal, gold, iron, oil, and natural gas. The government built the Trans-Siberian Railroad to transport materials to and from Siberia. But today, many of the factories are outdated. In the Siberian city of Kemerovo (KEM uh roh voh), factories still release black smoke into the air. Other buildings in the town are crumbling. Rusty cars move slowly down the muddy streets.

Siberian Industry: A Mixed Blessing

Black smoke belches into the cool air in the Siberian town of Ulan Ude (oo LAHN oo DAY) along the Trans-Siberian Railroad. The railroad, completed in 1905, helped to link Siberia's rich natural resources to more densely populated areas of Europe. When towns along the tracks of this railroad became industrial centers, the number of available jobs increased. But so did pollution.

In the Villages As Kemerovo shows, the changes of free enterprise have come slowly to cities in this region. Change is even slower in rural areas. Life in many villages is almost like life on the American frontier more than 100 years ago. Many homes have no running water, so water has to be hauled from wells once a week. Sometimes the wells freeze in the winter. Then people have to drink and cook with melted snow.

Despite problems like these, Siberians know how to survive and enjoy life in their frigid climate. They follow a strict timetable so they can take advantage of changes in the seasons. Before winter comes they start collecting nuts and honey. Tractors work overtime to harvest crops before the frost. In winter, some families hang huge pieces of meat from their porches. Temperatures in winter are so cold that the meat freezes solid and does not spoil.

During winter, women wearing many layers of clothing leave their log cabins to fetch firewood. Inside the log cabins, it is warm and cozy. That is because many cabins have large stoves used both for cooking and for heating. When the nights become really cold, the family may spread a straw mat on top of the stove and sleep there to stay warm.

During the winter, the meals are hearty. To catch fresh fish, men cut holes through the ice that covers the rivers. At home, the women may also cook homemade goose soup or dumplings stuffed with meat. Or perhaps the family will make a meal of some of the meat they have frozen.

READ ACTIVELY

Visualize Visualize life in a Siberian village.

Believe it or not, some Siberians start their day by bathing in a pitcher of ice-cold water! They believe that it strengthens their body against the cold. Sometimes, they pour water to make a huge puddle in front of their houses. The water freezes quickly, and the children then play ice hockey.

While the children are playing, the adults might decide to have a Siberian-style sauna (SAW nuh), or steam bath. They crowd into a shack filled with hot steam scented with pine. There they sit until they can stand the heat no longer. Then they rush out of the sauna dripping with sweat and roll in the snow to cool down.

READ ACTIVELY

Ask Questions What do you want to know about how the fall of the Soviet Union affected life in Siberia?

Changing Ways Traditional ways still continue in Siberia. But the fall of communism and the arrival of free enterprise are starting to affect life in the region. Under the communist system, everyone was guaranteed a job. Now Siberians who work in factories and coal mines must worry about losing their jobs. On the other hand, for the first time in more than 70 years, Siberians are able to buy their own homes. Before, they had to live in houses that belonged to the state. People can also now buy stock in the companies in which they work.

Life in Moscow

Moscow, where Inessa lives, has gone through many changes since the fall of communism. At first, business took off. Investors from everywhere, including the United States, came to Moscow to make money. An **investor** is someone who spends money on improving a business in the hope of getting more money when the business succeeds. Some investors become very wealthy. When the first American fast-food chain in Russia opened in Moscow, people lined up in the streets to try it out. The restaurant served 30,000 people on the first day. Within a few years, however, things had changed.

▼During the long Siberian winter, a horse-drawn sleigh hauls supplies (right) and a red-cheeked Siberian child plays on his toboggan (below).

Building Anew in Moscow

Since the fall of communism, people in Moscow, Russia's capital, have started over. They have constructed new buildings and started many new businesses. Russians still face many challenges, but they have made great progress over the past few years. The number of cars in Russia has tripled, and the streets of the capital, once empty, are always busy. **Critical Thinking** How does starting a new business create jobs?

Challenges for Ordinary Russians Moscow is the capital of Russia. It has a population of more than 9 million people. In big cities like Moscow, new wealth has brought big changes. Just outside the city, a new skyscraper reaches the sky. At its top is a fine restaurant, enclosed in stone and glass. The building is the world headquarters of Gazprom (GAHS prahm), Russia's only natural gas company. Started by a former Communist official, and mostly owned by the state, it makes a huge amount of money.

The head of Gazprom is one of Russia's richest people. Many other former government leaders have become wealthy in the new Russia. Another group of newly rich Russians leads criminal gangs. Criminal gangs often force people who own businesses to pay them money. The ordinary Russians who own or work in these businesses suffer. Laws meant to protect people are often not enforced.

Connect What things make a business in your neighborhood a success?

Ordinary Russians have been working hard since the collapse of communism in Russia. For the first time, they have been able to fulfill their dreams of starting their own new business or opening a small factory. They have been studying Western ways of doing business and gaining knowledge from the Internet, which has become popular in Russia. Unlike during Soviet times, ordinary Russians can own appliances and can sometimes afford to travel.

Yet ordinary Russians are at a disadvantage in the new Russia, especially when the economy does not thrive. In 1998, the value of the ruble fell, causing prices of goods to skyrocket and bringing heavy

Boris Yeltsin
In August 1991, some members of the Communist party tried to take over the Soviet government. They arrested the Soviet leader, Mikhail Gorbachev, and sent troops to take over government buildings. Boris Yeltsin, president of Russia, refused to leave one government building. He urged citizens to stand between the building and the soldiers. And he told the soldiers to join the people. The army did. The communist revolt fell apart. Yeltsin's courage made him a hero across the country.

inflation. In addition, Russia faced a severe food shortage, forcing Russians to change their diets and to seek food aid from the United States.

The economy continued to struggle at the start of the 21st century but still, most Russians try to face the future with optimism. Vlad Olkhovski (vlad ohl HAWV skee) is starting a new travel agency. There used to be only one travel agency for all of Russia. But Vlad hopes that he can attract customers to his new agency. Vlad explains his approach this way:

> "We have learned that the only way you can prosper is to be the best in your market, be professional and be reliable. In America, of course, these are old lessons. But it's an entirely new [way of thinking] for people here."

Tradition and Change The collapse of communism has changed Moscow. But old Russian ways survive alongside the new. After all, Russia is a huge country with many different ways of life. On Moscow's streets you will see poor people who have come from the countryside to buy things, just as they have always done. You will see people from Mongolia wearing the traditional padded silk jackets of their region. And you will see young Russians wearing blue jeans, with haircuts in the latest American style.

On very cold winter days, some people in Moscow go to the parks to celebrate an old tradition: picnicking in the snow. At these picnics they make shish ke-bab by piercing pieces of meat with a sharp stick. Then they roast the meat over an open fire.

Moscow's art, theater, and dance also show great variety. On one evening, people might attend the Bolshoi (BOHL shoy) Ballet. Dancers

▶GUM, Moscow's biggest department store, stands at the city's center. Its shelves are now stocked with goods rarely seen by ordinary Russians in communist times. On weekends, when the economy is doing well, up to 25,000 people a day shop here.

Russian Art

The collapse of communism has freed artists to experiment with bold modern styles in painting (left) and sculpture (above).

from this famous Russian school of ballet have performed around the world. On another evening, people might go to see a group of folk dancers from northern Russia. Wearing jeweled caps and robes with laced sleeves, the dancers twirl and stamp their feet to traditional folk songs.

The differences between Siberia and Moscow show us the challenges that Russia must meet in the future. Can a country with many different ethnic groups and an area of more than 6 million square miles (9 million sq km) hold itself together? Will the old ways and new ways become one common way for everyone? The answers to these questions are not yet clear. But Russians are united in the hope for a better future for all.

1. **Define** investor.
2. **Identify** (a) Kemerovo, (b) Moscow.
3. What do Siberians do to survive in their very cold climate?
4. How does Moscow show the variety of Russian life?

Critical Thinking

5. **Recognizing Cause and Effect** What problems might a country have if it includes many ethnic groups that speak many different languages?

Activity

6. **Writing to Learn** Choose and conduct research on one of Russia's 100 ethnic groups. Find answers to these questions: Where do the people live? What language do they speak? What is their religion? What is their relationship to the rest of the country? Then write a brief report on the group.

Review and Activities

Reviewing Main Ideas

1. What parts of Polish life have not changed?
2. What forces are changing some basic parts of Polish town life and country life?
3. What conflicts led to the breakup of Yugoslavia?
4. (a) Name some things that Serbs, Croats, Slovenes, Montenegrins, and Macedonians have in common. (b) Name some differences.
5. (a) What are the natural resources of Ukraine? (b) How have they affected its history?
6. How did the explosion at Chernobyl damage Ukraine's rich soil?
7. What are some differences between the lifestyle in Siberia and that in Moscow?
8. How have recent events affected the people of Russia in different ways?

Reviewing Key Terms

Use each key term below in a sentence that shows the meaning of the term.

1. free enterprise
2. shrine
3. United Nations
4. economic sanctions
5. chernozem
6. collective
7. investor

Critical Thinking

1. **Making Comparisons** Compare life in a Polish village to life in Siberia. How are they alike? How are they different?
2. **Expressing Problems Clearly** What do you think would help bring lasting peace to the former Yugoslavian nations?

Graphic Organizer

Copy the chart onto a separate sheet of paper. Then fill in the empty boxes to complete the chart.

	Country	Recent Challenges	Possible Solutions
Warsaw			
Sarajevo			
Chernobyl			
Moscow			

Map Activity

Eastern Europe

For each place listed below, write the letter from the map that shows its location.

1. Ukraine
2. Kiev
3. Sarajevo
4. Bosnia-Herzegovina
5. Yugoslavia

Place Location

Writing Activity

Writing an Advertisement

Write an advertisement for Janusz Rajtar's shop in Warsaw. In the advertisement, explain why people should buy from Rajtar instead of from older stores that used to be run by the government.

Take It to the NET

Activity Learn more about Poland's history, culture, economy, geography, and demographics. For help in completing this activity, visit **www.phschool.com.**

Chapter 10 Self-Test To review what you have learned, take the Chapter 10 Self-Test and get instant feedback on your answers. Go to **www.phschool.com** to take the test.

Skills Review

Turn to the Skills Activity.

Review the steps for recognizing cause and effect. Then, list three unrelated events of your own life history. For each event, name at least one cause and one effect.

How Am I Doing?

Answer these questions to help you check your progress.

1. Do I understand the clash between tradition and change in both Poland and Russia?
2. Do I understand some of the causes of the breakup of Yugoslavia?
3. Do I understand how Ukraine's natural resources have helped and hurt that country?
4. Do I know some of the changes talking place in Russia?
5. What information from this chapter can I include in my journal?

Plan a New Railroad Line

Siberia, the vast Asian region of Russia, has many natural resources, but it has few transportation routes. The region's major rail line, the Trans-Siberian Railroad, was completed in 1905. The route is thousands of miles long, but it covers only a part of Siberia. An addition to the rail line would make it easier for people to move throughout the region.

Purpose

In this activity, you will plan a new branch of the Trans-Siberian Railroad. As you work on the activity, you will learn about Siberia's resources.

Draw a Resource Map

A new rail line in Siberia would transport some of the region's many natural resources to other parts of Russia. Look in an encyclopedia for Siberia and for Russia. Make a list of Siberian mineral resources. Next to each item on the list, note its uses. Draw a small symbol, or picture, to represent each resource. Then draw a map of Siberia. Put the symbols on the map to show where these resources can be found.

Make a Circle Graph

Money to build a new rail line will come from cities and towns located along the line, from the Siberian regional government, and from the Russian national government. Using the figures below, draw a circle graph to show the percentages of the total money each source would contribute.

- Cities and towns 15%
- Regional government 32%
- National government 53%

Decide on a Route

Look at some maps of Siberia, including your mineral resources map. Then decide where you think a new rail line should run.

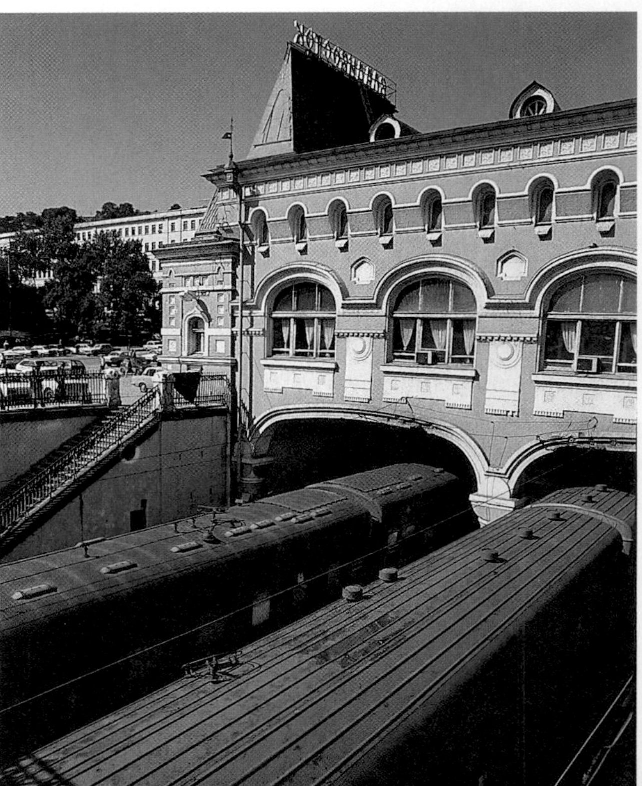

▶ A Trans-Siberian Railroad station

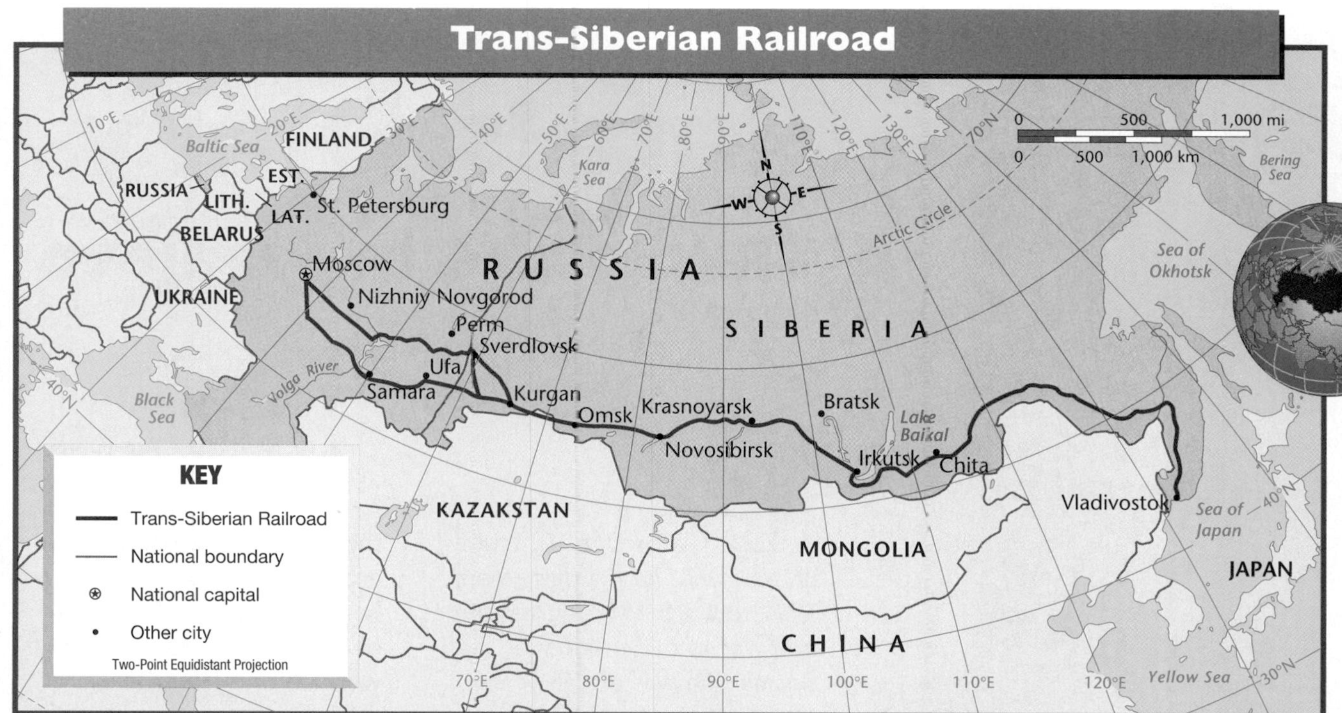

Write down a list of cities and towns the route might pass through. On your list, write the distances between the cities and towns. Figure out the total distance of the route. Finally, circle the places where the line will start and end.

Write a Proposal

Write a proposal to persuade the national government to build a new rail line in Siberia. Start with a brief history of the Trans-Siberian Railroad. Then tell where the new rail line will run, what purpose it will serve, and how the project will be paid for.

Write a Railroad Song

Once a new rail line is built, people need to hear about it. Write a song that will advertise the new railroad. In your song lyrics, describe the features of the new train. Tell about the resources and wildlife of Siberia. Try to use the rhythm and sounds of a train in your own rhythm and melody.

Links to Other Subjects

Making a mineral resource chart .... **Earth Science**

Making a circle graph .... **Math**

Determining routes and distances .... **Math**

Writing a proposal .... **Language Arts**

Writing a song .... **Language Arts & Music**

ANALYSIS AND CONCLUSION

Write a summary explaining what you've learned from planning and proposing the railroad extension. Be sure to answer the following questions in your summary:

1. What have you learned about the geography of Siberia and its mineral resources?
2. What did you learn about writing an effective proposal and song?

FROM

Zlata's Diary
A Child's Life in Sarajevo

BY ZLATA FILIPOVIĆ

Reach Into Your Background

To whom do you tell your secret thoughts? Many people write in a diary or journal what they would tell no other person. Diaries can give people hope and courage, especially during hard times.

Zlata Filipović (ZLAH tah FIL uh POH vich) kept a diary from 1991 through 1993, during the civil war in the country of Bosnia. She was eleven years old when she began her diary, which she called Mimmy. At that time, life in the city of Sarajevo (sar uh YEH voh) was normal for Zlata and her parents. In the spring of 1992, however, their lives changed when war broke out around them. Schools closed. Zlata's family, like many others, spent their days in the basement to avoid gunfire. Food and water became scarce. In December of 1993, Zlata and her parents were able to leave Bosnia safely.

Questions to Explore

1. What do these diary entries tell you about war?
2. How do you think the experience of living through a war affected Zlata?

Thursday, May 7, 1992

Dear Mimmy,

I was almost positive the war would stop, but today . . . Today a shell fell on the park in front of my house, the park where I used to play and sit with my girlfriends. A lot of people were hurt. From what I hear Jaca, Jaca's mother, Selma, Nina, our neighbor Dado and who knows how many other people who happened to be there were wounded. Dado, Jaca and her mother have come home from the hospital, Selma lost a kidney but I don't know how she is, because she's still in the hospital. AND NINA IS DEAD. A piece of shrapnel lodged in her brain and she died. She was such a sweet, nice little girl. We went to kindergarten together, and we used to play together in the park. Is it possible I'll never see Nina again? Nina, an innocent eleven-year-old little girl—the victim of a stupid war. I feel sad. I cry and wonder why? She didn't do anything. A disgusting war has destroyed a young child's life. Nina, I'll always remember you as a wonderful little girl.

Love, Mimmy,
Zlata

shrapnel *n.:* fragments of a bomb, mine, or shell

◀ Zlata with her diary in a library building ruined by the war.

Thursday, December 3, 1992

Dear Mimmy,

Today is my birthday. My first wartime birthday. Twelve years old. Congratulations. Happy birthday to me!

The day started off with kisses and congratulations. First Mommy and Daddy, then everyone else. Mommy and Daddy gave me three Chinese vanity cases—with flowers on them!

As usual there was no electricity. Auntie Melica came with her family (Kenan, Naida, Nihad) and gave me a book. And Braco Lajtner came, of course. The whole neighborhood got together in the evening. I got chocolate, vitamins, a heart shaped soap (small, orange), a key chain with a picture of Maja and Bojana, a pendant made of a stone from Cyprus, a ring (silver) and earrings (bingo!).

The table was nicely laid, with little rolls, fish and rice salad, cream cheese (with Feta), canned corned beef, a pie, and, of course—a birthday cake. Not how it used to be, but there's a war on. Luckily there was no shooting, so we could celebrate.

It was nice, but something was missing. It's called peace!

Your Zlata

Connect How can people celebrate one thing while being sad about another? Explain why you think people do this.

Melica (MEE lit zuh)
Kenan (KEN ahn)
Naida (NY duh)
Nihad (NEE hahd)
Braco Lajtner (BRAHT zoh LYT nur)
Maja (MY uh)
Bojana (BOY ah nuh)

EXPLORING YOUR READING

Look Back

1. What bad experiences does Zlata record in her entries? What good experiences does she write about?

Think It Over

2. How would you describe Zlata's outlook on her world?
3. Why do you think Zlata treats her diary as a friend?

Go Beyond

4. How do you think the war has changed Zlata?

Ideas for Writing: Diary

5. Keep a diary for a week, writing one entry each day. Write about what makes you happy as well as things that bother or upset you. At the end of the week, write an entry telling what you think about keeping a diary.

EUROPE AND RUSSIA
PROJECT POSSIBILITIES

The following questions will help you direct your reading about Europe and Russia:

- **GEOGRAPHY** How has physical geography affected the environment and cultures of Europe and Russia?
- **HISTORY** How have the people of Europe and Russia been shaped by historical experiences?
- **CULTURE** What values and traditions do the people of Europe and Russia have in common?
- **GOVERNMENT** How have changes in government affected Russia and some European nations?
- **ECONOMICS** How have Russian and European economies developed into what they are today?

These projects will give you the chance to show what you know about Europe and Russia!

Project Menu

The chapters in this book have some answers to these questions. Now it's time for you to find your own answers by doing projects on your own or with a group. You can make your own discoveries about Europe and Russia.

Changing Climates It's not always easy to get used to life in a new climate. Someone who moved from Norway to Greece, for example, might be surprised about the way the climate affects how the Greek people live. Choose a European country near the Arctic or one near the Mediterranean. Find out about ways of life that have to do with the climate. Look for details about housing, clothing, food, and recreation.

Based on what you find, write a guide for someone moving to that region from the other end of the continent. Include special tips for things like very hot or cold days, comfortable sleeping, or special snacks.

From Questions to Careers

INTERNATIONAL TRADE

The United States trades many goods and services with Europe and Russia. This trade is important to people in both places. Many international businesspeople work to make this trade happen. Some Americans work in Europe, and some stay here.

There are many careers in international trade. People with careers in international marketing and sales sell products and services to customers in other countries. Shipping companies transport products by boat or by plane. Sailors, pilots, shippers, and handlers make shipping possible.

When people work in other countries, they often need translators. English is the most common language for international business, so some Americans can work in Europe without knowing other languages. However, all who work with other countries must know something about those countries. International managers train workers in the cultures of their trade partners.

▼ Many people have careers in international shipping, as this man does.

Olympic Cities Plan an Olympic season in a European city. As you read this book, keep track of cities that you find interesting. Research them at the library or on the Internet.

After you have gathered your information, choose a city that you think would do a good job of hosting either the summer or winter Olympics. Write a proposal to Olympic officials, explaining what the city has to offer to the Olympics. Include maps or pictures of your city with your proposal.

Tourism in Eastern Europe Many former communist countries would like to have more tourists, who bring money to their economies. Choose a country in Eastern Europe. Read about parts of the culture and landscape that might interest visitors—for example, ski slopes in Slovakia.

Create a travel advertisement for that country. Write your own text and use pictures that you draw or cut out from magazines.

Folklore Corner Create a library of folk and fairy tales from countries throughout Europe. As you read about a country in this book, find a traditional tale from that country. Think about how the stories reflect the country's culture.

With your classmates, build a Folklore Corner in your classroom. Create a display of books of folk tales. Include objects, drawings, and photographs that represent the culture in these tales. Label each tale with its country of origin.

AFRICA

The name Africa may have come from the Latin word *aprica*, meaning "sunny." In much of Africa, the sun does shine brightly. Each morning, the African sunrise awakens one eighth of the world's population in more than fifty countries. In the chapters that follow, you'll spend the day with some of them.

GUIDING QUESTIONS

The readings and activities in this book will help you discover answers to these Guiding Questions.

1. **GEOGRAPHY** What are the main physical features of Africa?
2. **HISTORY** How have historical events affected the cultures and nations of Africa?
3. **CULTURE** How have Africa's cultures changed?
4. **GOVERNMENT** What factors led to the development of different governments across Africa?
5. **ECONOMICS** What factors influence the ways in which Africans make a living?

PROJECT PREVIEW

You can also discover answers to the Guiding Questions by working on projects. You can find several project possibilities on pages 480–481.

1. What are the main physical features of Africa?

2. How have historical events affected the cultures and nations of Africa?

3. How have Africa's cultures changed?

4. What factors led to the development of different governments across Africa?

5. What factors influence the ways in which Africans make a living?

Explorer's Journal

A journal can be your personal book of discovery. As you explore Africa, you can use your journal to keep track of the things you learn and do. You can also record thoughts about your journey. For your first entry, write your thoughts on where in Africa you would like to go and what you would want to see there.

DISCOVERY ACTIVITIES ABOUT

Africa

Learning about Africa means being an explorer and a geographer. No explorer would start out without first checking some facts. Begin by exploring the maps of Africa on the following pages.

Relative Location

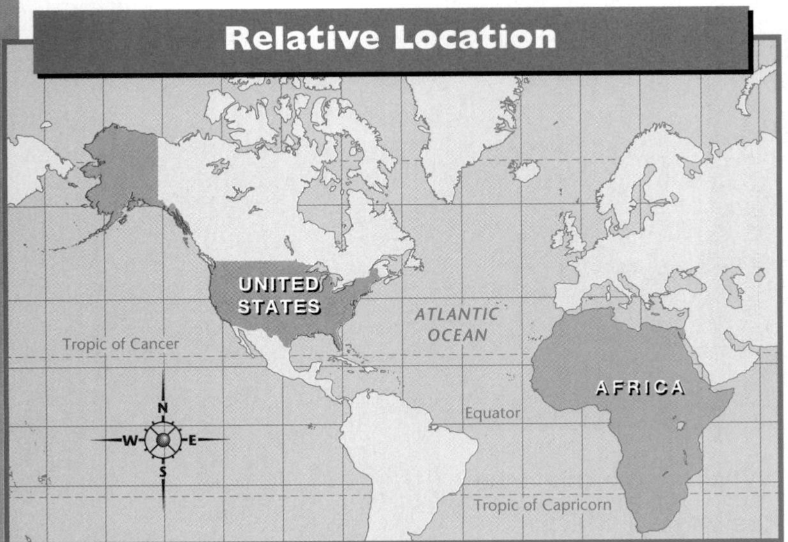

LOCATION

1. **Explore Africa's Location** One of the first questions a geographer asks about a place is "Where is it?" Use the map to describe Africa's location relative to the United States. What ocean lies between Africa and the United States? Note that the Equator extends through Africa. What role might the Equator play in the climates of nearby countries? How do you think climates of the United States might differ from the climates of Africa?

REGIONS

2. **Explore Africa's Size** How big is Africa compared to the United States? On a separate sheet of paper, trace the map of the United States and cut it out. How many times can you fit it inside the map of Africa?

Relative Size

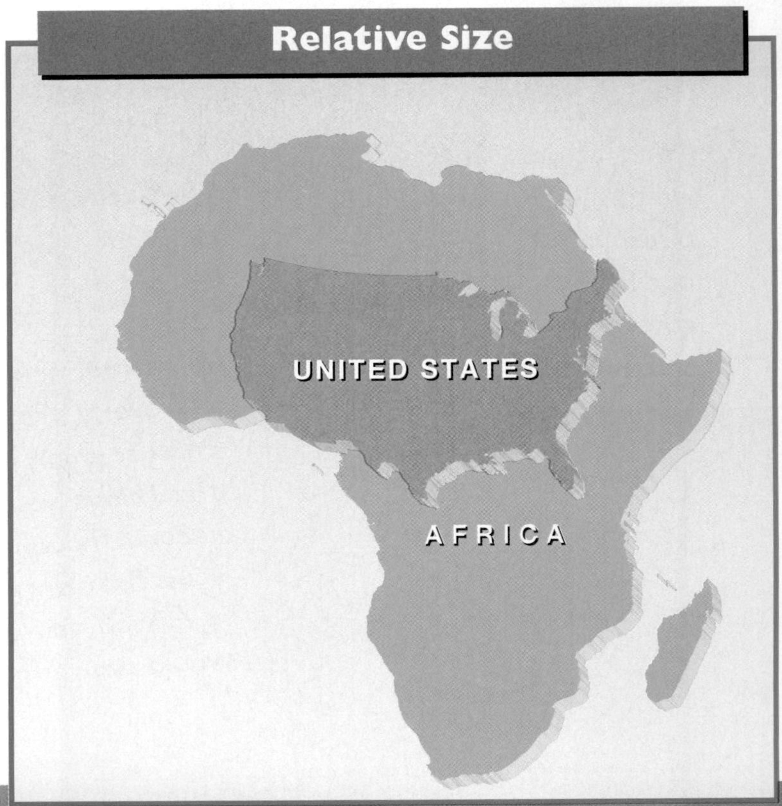

PLACE

3. **Find Africa's Lakes** There are several large lakes in Africa. Name four of them. What countries do they border? In what part of the continent do you find the most lakes?

MOVEMENT

4. **Predict How Location Affects Economic Wealth** Fifteen African nations are landlocked. That is, they do not border any ocean. Find them on the map. Landlocked nations are often poor. How do you think a landlocked location might affect a nation's economy?

Africa: Political

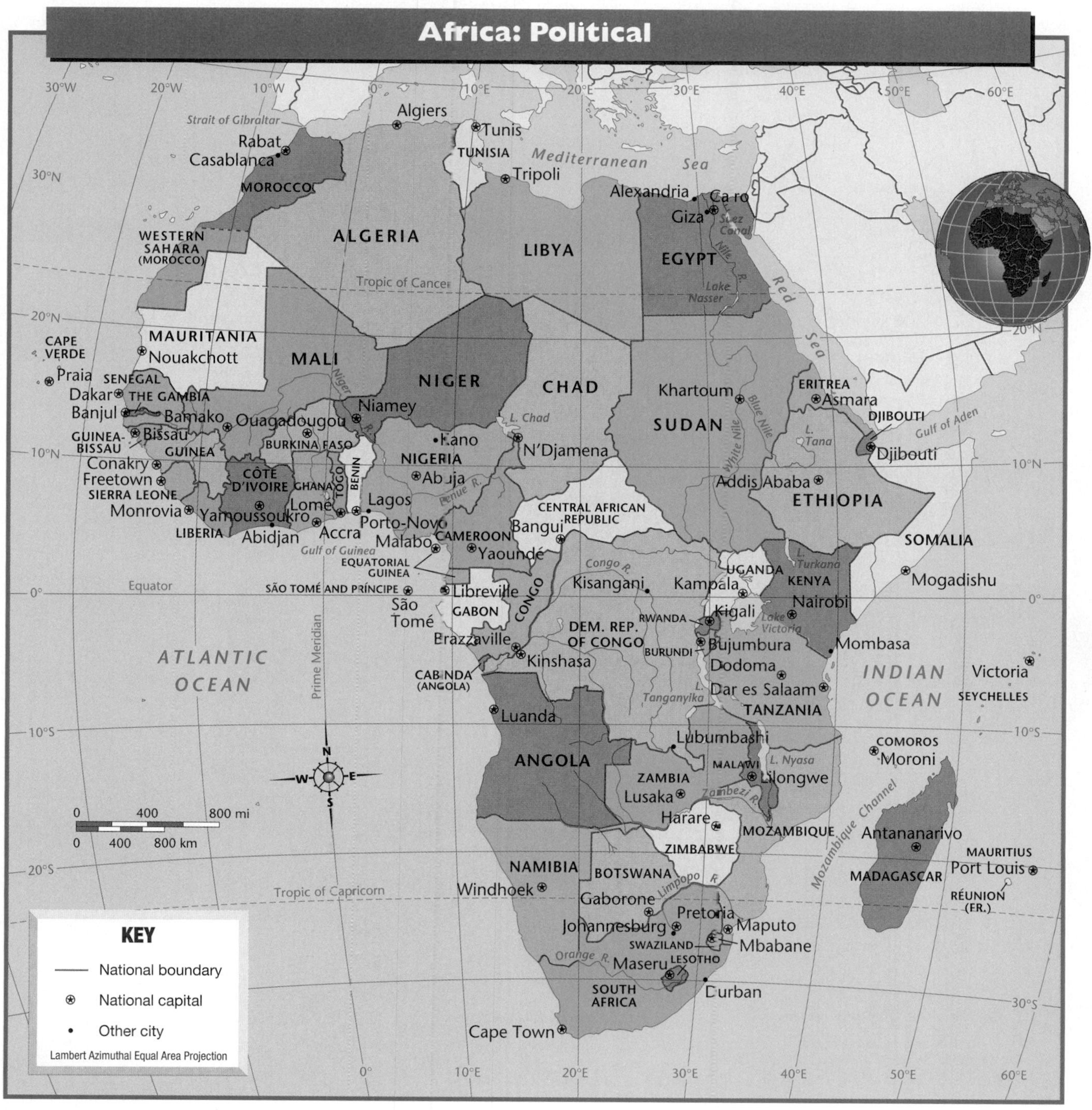

PLACE

5. Investigate Africa's Physical Features Parts of Africa's coasts have very narrow strips of flat plains. Cliffs rise steeply from these plains. The interior is high and somewhat flat, forming a huge plateau. Find Southern Africa on the map below. It extends south of 10ºS. The cliffs arise where the dark green areas meet the light green areas. Trace these cliffs with your finger. Note that in some places they extend nearly along the coast. Is Africa's plateau higher in the western part of the continent or the southeastern part?

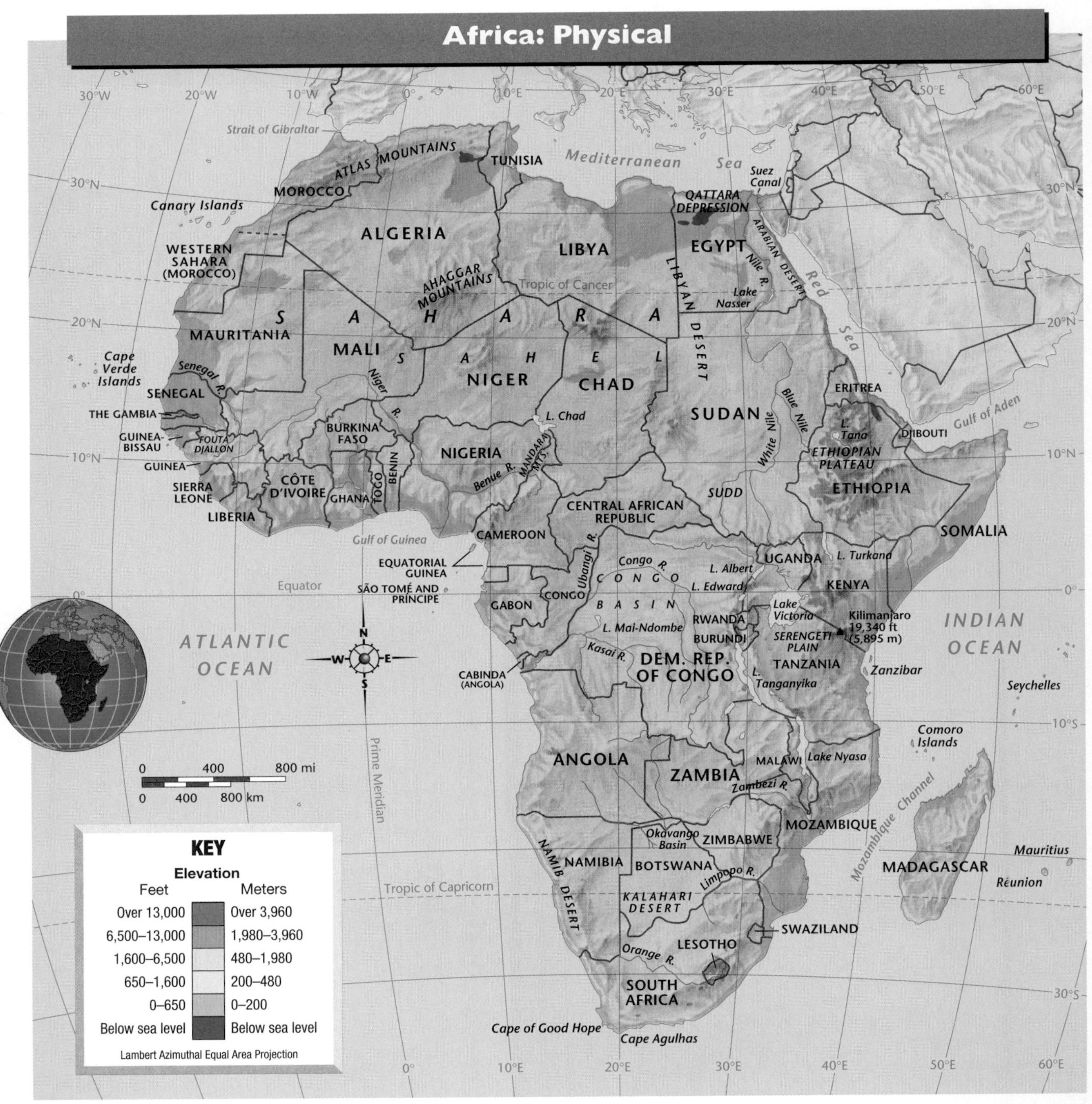

REGIONS

6. Find Geo Cleo Geo Cleo has gone off on one of her flying trips. This time she's gone to Africa, but she hasn't told anyone exactly where in Africa she's traveling. Read the messages Geo Cleo radioed from her plane. Then use the map below and the maps on the two previous pages to locate the city described in each message.

A. *I'm in a region of tall grasses and few trees, or a savanna. I've landed in a city in Ethiopia near 10°N and 40°E.*

B. *Not too many places in Africa have Mediterranean vegetation. And I'm not even anywhere near the Mediterranean Sea! I am flying over a city on a very narrow coastal plain. The cliffs here are really steep.*

C. *Today, I flew above tropical rain forests growing right along the Equator. Going north, I saw these magnificent forests change into open grasslands, or savanna. I've just landed in a city in the savanna region north of where the Benue River meets the Niger River.*

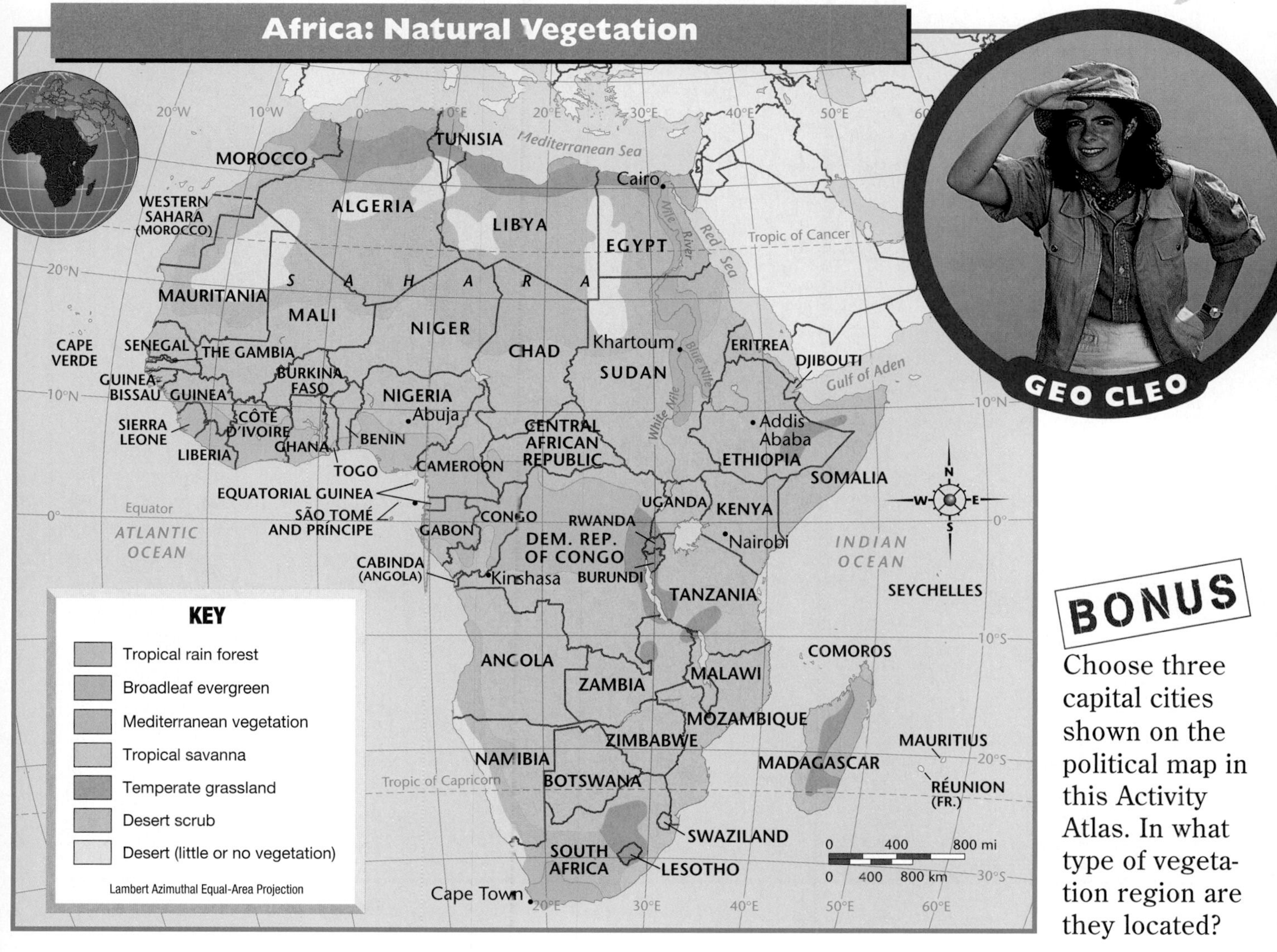

BONUS

Choose three capital cities shown on the political map in this Activity Atlas. In what type of vegetation region are they located?

INTERACTION

7. Estimate the Impact of Deforestation Deforestation means a loss of trees and forest. Deforestation contributes to droughts, increased temperatures, and the loss of animal life. In already dry areas, such as lands bordering the Sahel, fewer trees and vegetation creates new desert areas. Human activity is the main cause of deforestation. Farmers and lifestock herders cut or burn down trees to make farming and grazing lands. The map on this page shows deforestation in Africa today. Which regions are most affected by deforestation? How would the loss of all vegetation, including farm crops, affect people in these regions?

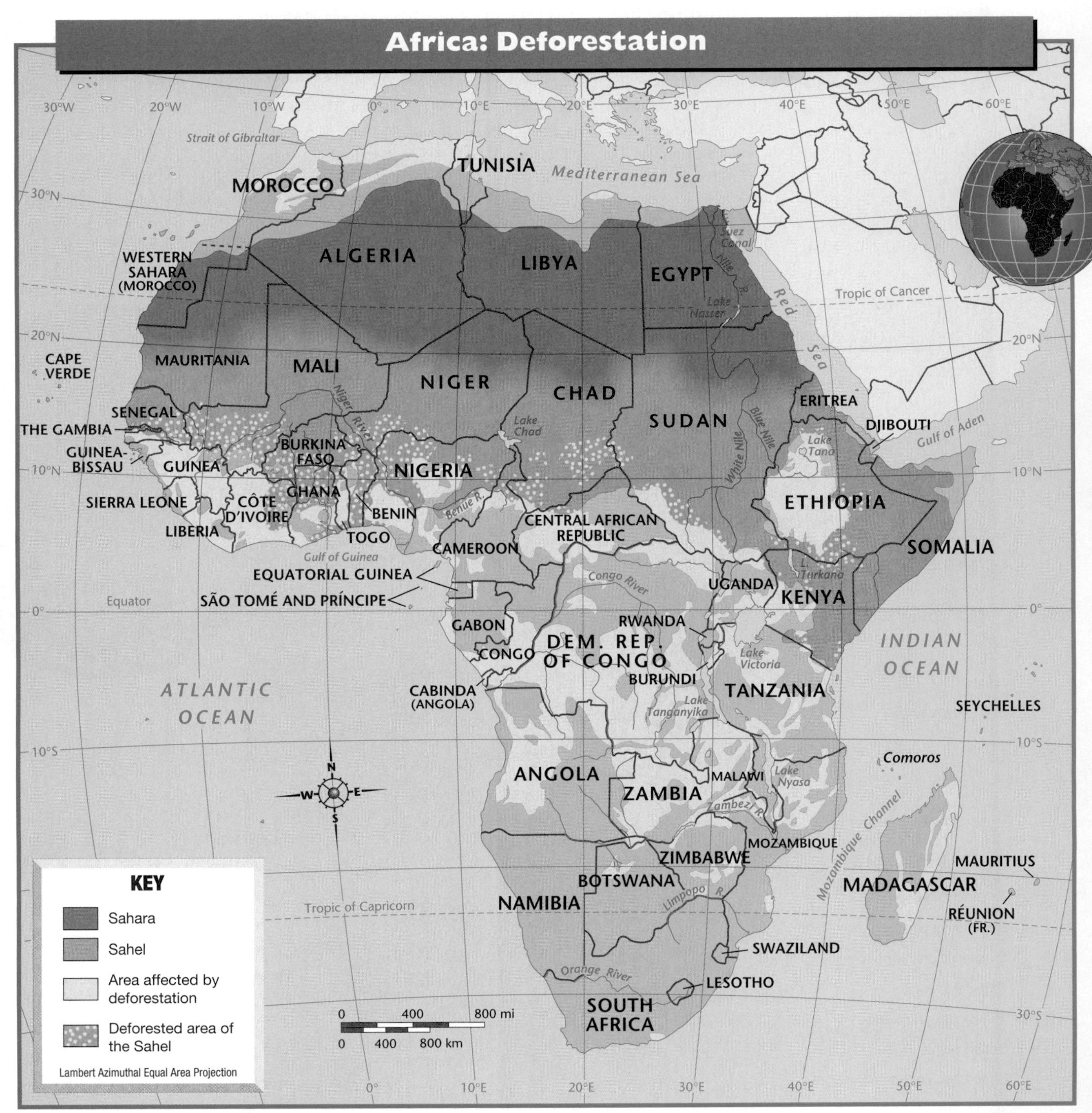

REGIONS

8. Analyze Temperatures Across the Continent The map below shows the average temperatures on the continent of Africa. Use this map and the map on the previous page to answer the following questions. What are the average temperatures in the Sahara? In the Sahel? How do the temperatures in southern countries such as Lesotho differ from countries such as Gabon that are located along the Equator? Why do you think the temperatures in extreme northern and southern parts of Africa are similar?

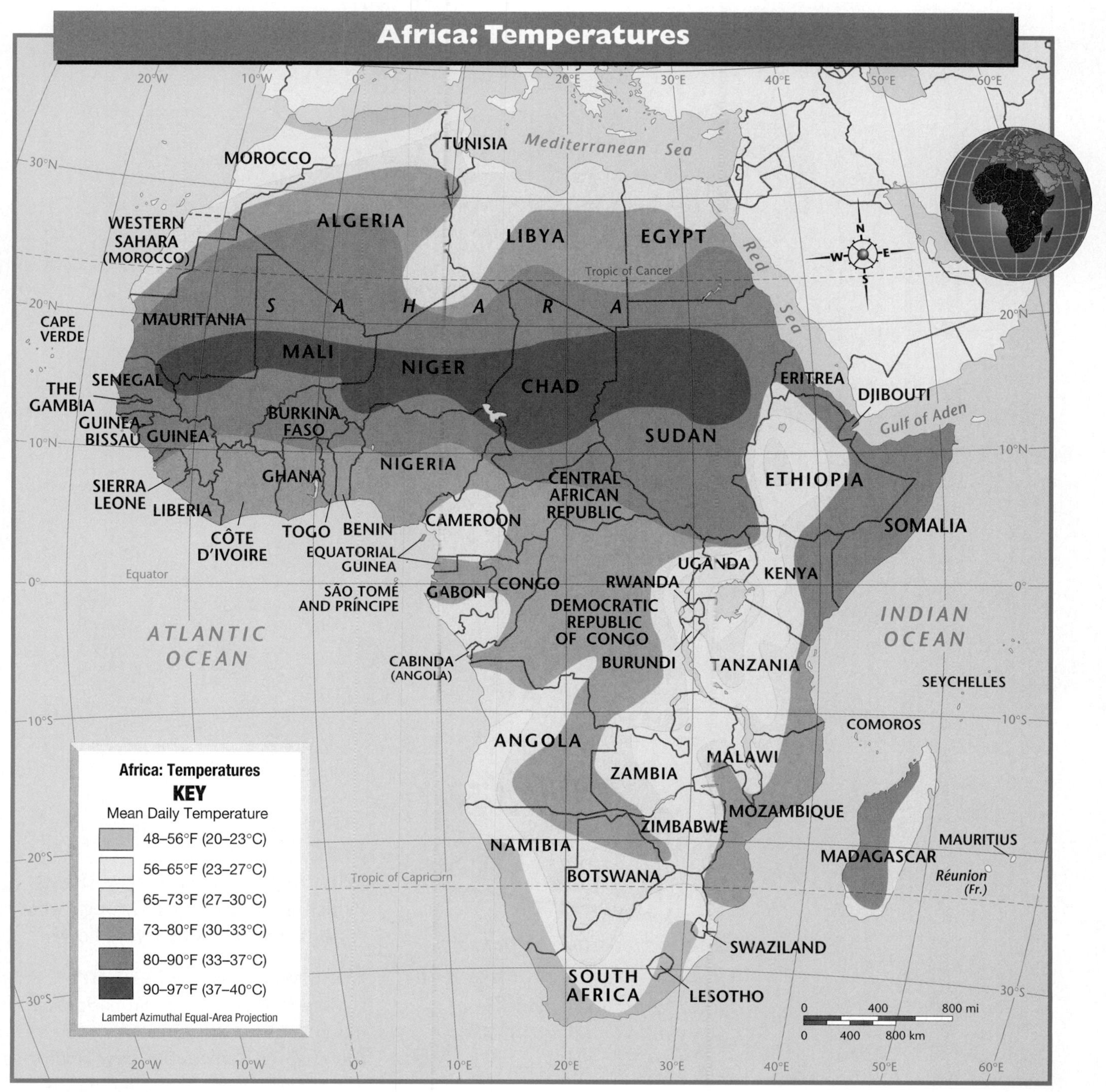

CHAPTER 11

AFRICA
Physical Geography

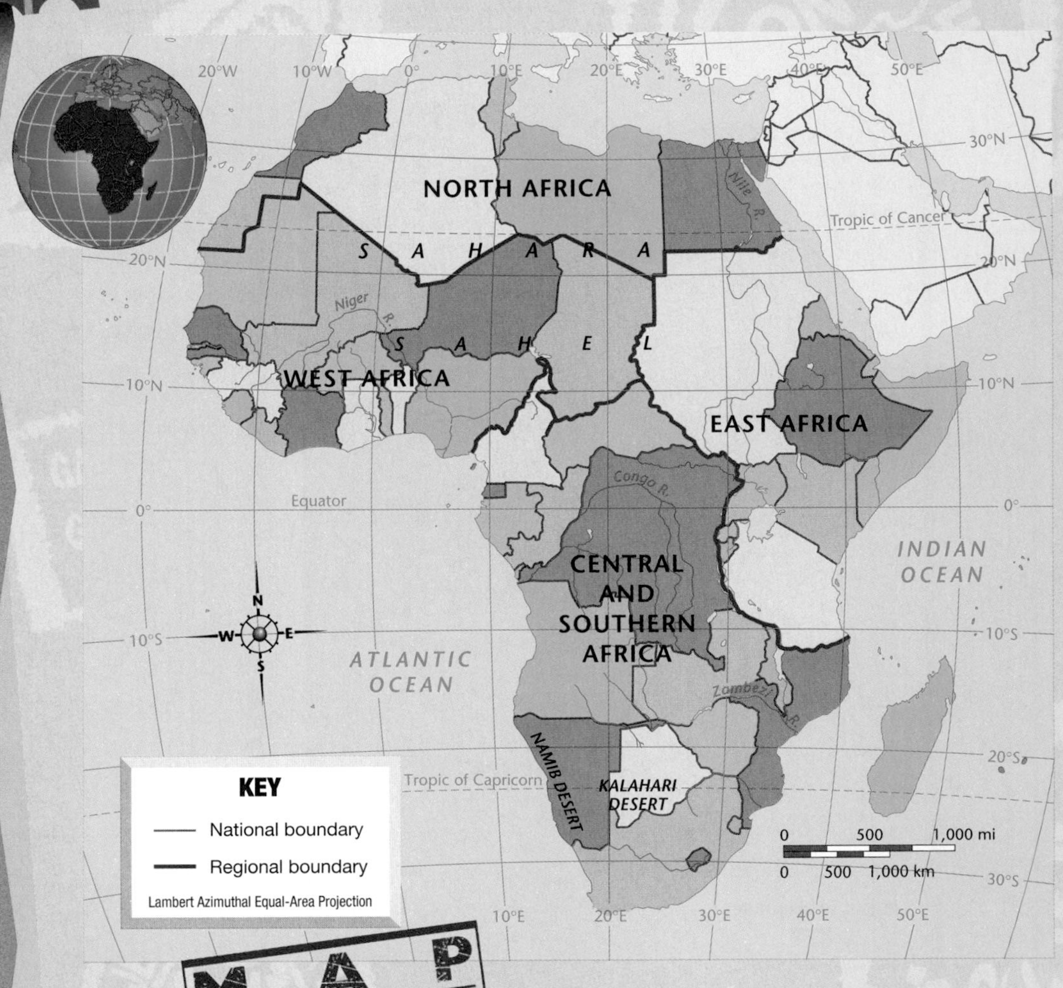

MAP ACTIVITIES

This map shows four regions of Africa. Each region contains many different landforms and climates. Start exploring the geography of Africa by doing the following activities.

Study the map

What region of Africa is the largest? Which is the smallest? Through what regions do the major rivers flow?

Consider the geography

Notice that some African nations are much larger than others. As you read this chapter, think about how landforms and climate might have affected the political boundaries of Africa.

Land and Water

Reach Into Your Background
Think about the state in which you live. What different landforms are in your state? Are there any mountains or valleys? How do these landforms affect your daily life?

Questions to Explore

1. Where is Africa located?
2. What are Africa's most important landforms?

Key Terms
plateau
elevation
escarpment
rift
cataract
silt
fertile
tributary

Key Places
Sahara
Great Rift Valley
Nile River
Congo River
Niger River
Zambezi River

Scientists believe that over 200 million years ago, dinosaurs easily walked from the continent of Africa to the continent of South America. That's because Africa and South America were connected. Find Africa on the world map in the atlas at the back of this book. As you can see, it would be pretty hard to walk from Africa to South America today. How did Africa and South America become separated? About 190 million years ago, forces within the Earth caused South America and Africa to move apart, forming the southern part of the Atlantic Ocean.

▼ Scientists found the bones of one type of dinosaur on more than one continent. This clue made them suspect the continents were once connected.

The Four Regions of Africa

Africa can be divided into four regions: (1) North, (2) West, (3) East, and (4) Central and Southern. Each of these regions contains many different climates and landforms.

North Africa is marked by rocky mountains and seemingly endless stretches of the world's largest desert, the Sahara. Find the Sahara, which is almost the size of the United States, on the physical map in the Activity Atlas. What countries include part of the Sahara?

West Africa, the continent's most populated region, consists mostly of grasslands. The soil in the grasslands is good for farming. Find West Africa on the map at the beginning of the chapter. What geographic features border this region to the north and south?

East Africa contains many mountains, and **plateaus,** large raised areas of mostly level land. The east also has areas of grasslands and hills. Find East Africa on the map at the beginning of this chapter. What East African countries have sea coasts?

Much of Central and Southern Africa is flat or rolling grassland. The region also contains thick rain forests, mountains, and swamps. The Namib (NAHM eeb) Desert of the country of Namibia and the Kalahari (kal uh HAHR ee) Desert of Botswana are in this region.

▼ In the Atlas Mountains of Morocco (below), some people adapt to steep slopes by building houses along the sides of the mountains. Some people living in the lush rain forests of the Democratic Republic of Congo (inset, upper left) take advantage of the tropical vegetation by gathering honey from bees' nests in the trees.

Africa's Major Landforms

Africa can be described as an upside-down pie. If you were to slice Africa in half from east to west, you would see that much of the continent is a plateau that drops off sharply near the sea.

The Plateau Continent Africa is often called the "plateau continent." That is because the elevation of much of the land area is high. **Elevation** is the height of land above sea level.

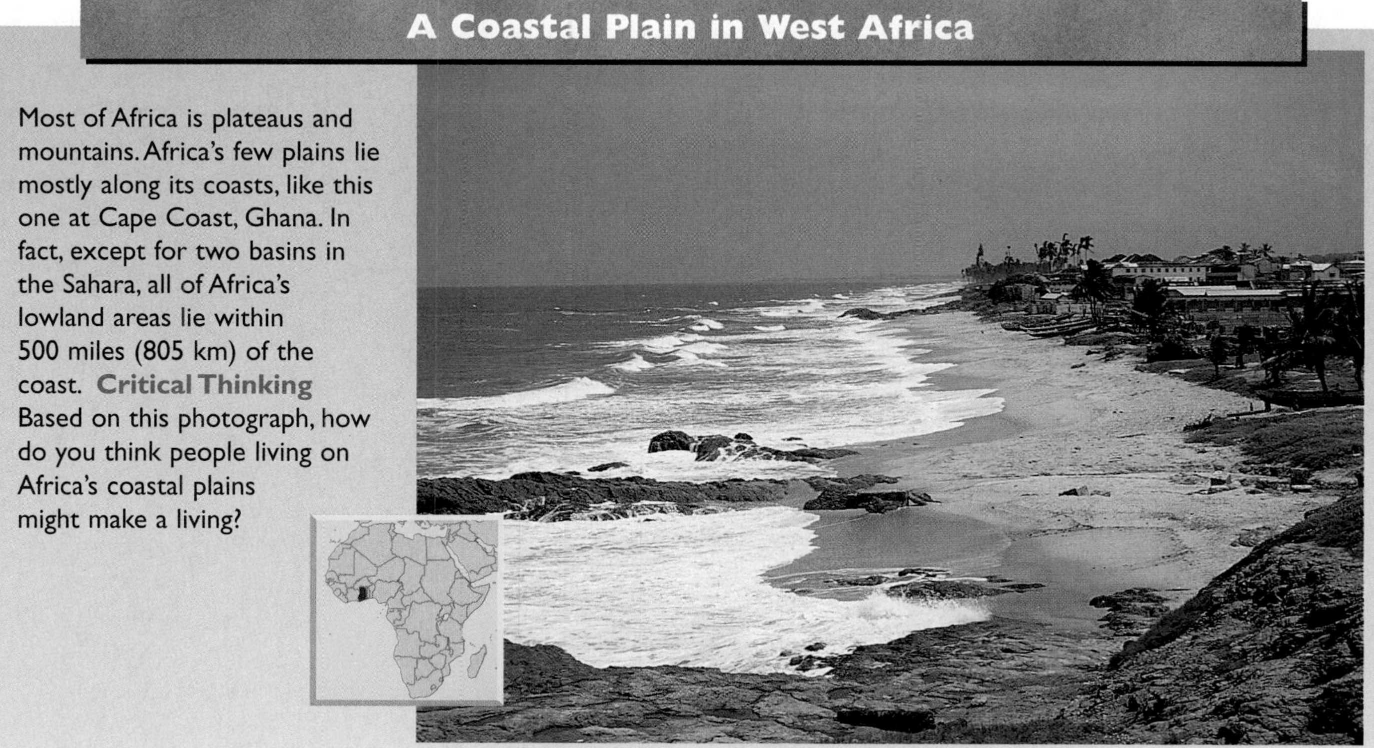

A Coastal Plain in West Africa

Most of Africa is plateaus and mountains. Africa's few plains lie mostly along its coasts, like this one at Cape Coast, Ghana. In fact, except for two basins in the Sahara, all of Africa's lowland areas lie within 500 miles (805 km) of the coast. **Critical Thinking** Based on this photograph, how do you think people living on Africa's coastal plains might make a living?

Each of Africa's four regions has mountains. The highest are in East Africa. Mount Kilimanjaro is Africa's tallest mountain. It rises to a height of 19,341 feet (5,895 m).

Coastal Plains Edge the Continent Along much of Africa's coast is a strip of coastal plain. This strip of land is dry and sandy at some points. It is marshy and moist at other places. Look at the political map in the Activity Atlas. Find the city of Accra, in the West African country of Ghana (GAHN uh). Here, the coastal strip is only 16 miles (25 km) wide. It ends at a long **escarpment,** or steep cliff, that is about as high as a 100-story skyscraper.

Connect What part of the United States contains a deep trench?

The Great Rift Valley Mount Kilimanjaro is located on the edge of the Great Rift Valley in East Africa. The Great Rift Valley was formed millions of years ago, when the continents pulled apart. A **rift** is a deep trench. The rift that cuts through East Africa is 4,000 miles (6,400 km) long. Most of Africa's major lakes are located in or near the Great Rift Valley.

Africa's Rivers

Four large rivers carry water from the mountains of Africa's plateaus to the sea. They are the Nile, the Congo, the Zambezi, and the Niger (NI jur). The rivers are useful for traveling. But they are broken in places by **cataracts,** or rock-filled rapids. Cataracts make it impossible for ships to sail from Africa's interior to the sea.

The Great Rift Valley

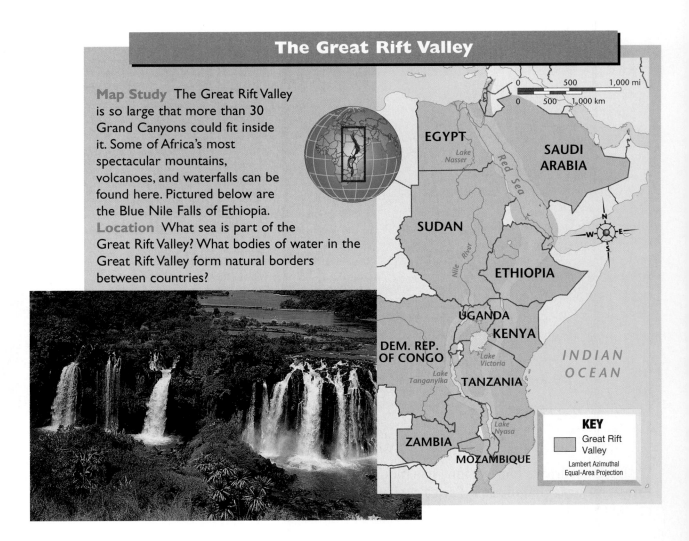

Map Study The Great Rift Valley is so large that more than 30 Grand Canyons could fit inside it. Some of Africa's most spectacular mountains, volcanoes, and waterfalls can be found here. Pictured below are the Blue Nile Falls of Ethiopia. **Location** What sea is part of the Great Rift Valley? What bodies of water in the Great Rift Valley form natural borders between countries?

EGYPT
Lake Nasser
Red Sea
SAUDI ARABIA
SUDAN
Nile River
ETHIOPIA
UGANDA
KENYA
DEM. REP. OF CONGO
Lake Victoria
Lake Tanganyika
TANZANIA
INDIAN OCEAN
Lake Nyasa
ZAMBIA
MOZAMBIQUE
0 500 1,000 mi
0 500 1,000 km
N S E W

KEY
Great Rift Valley
Lambert Azimuthal Equal-Area Projection

The Nile River The Nile is the longest river in the world. Its length, more than 4,000 miles (6,400 km), is almost twice the width of the United States. The sources of the Nile are the White Nile in the country of Sudan and the Blue Nile in the highlands of Ethiopia. From these two sources, the river flows north and spills into the Mediterranean Sea.

People have farmed the land surrounding the Nile for thousands of years. At one time, the Nile flooded its banks regularly. Farmers planted their crops to match the flood cycle of the river. The floods provided water for the crops and left behind a layer of **silt,** which is the tiny bits of rock and dirt that build up on the bottoms of rivers and lakes. Silt helps make soil **fertile,** or containing substances that plants need in order to grow well.

The Mississippi River Like the Nile in Africa, the Mississippi River in North America occasionally overflows its banks. It also leaves behind silt, which fertilizes the farmland along the river's banks.

About 30 years ago, Egypt's government built the Aswan High Dam to control the flooding of the Nile. As the water backed up behind the dam, it created Lake Nasser. Lake waters are channeled to water crops that grow in the desert. Water rushing through the dam makes electricity.

The Congo River The Congo River flows through the rain forest of the country of Congo (KAHNG oh) in Central Africa. Look at the map at the beginning of the chapter. What ocean does the Congo River flow into? At 2,900 miles (4,677 km), the Congo is Africa's second-longest river. It is fed by hundreds of **tributaries,** or small rivers and streams that flow into a larger river. People in this region grow grains and cassava to make into porridge. Cassava is a starchy plant a little like a potato. They also catch fish in the Congo with basket traps.

The Niger River Africa's third-longest river, the Niger, begins its journey in Guinea (GIN ee). The river flows north and then bends south for 2,600 miles (4,180 km). The Niger provides water for farms in the river valley. People make a living catching fish in the river.

The Zambezi River The fourth-longest of Africa's rivers, the Zambezi, is in southern Africa. It runs through or forms the borders of six countries: Angola, Zambia, Namibia, Botswana, Zimbabwe (zim BAHB way), and Mozambique (moh zam BEEK). The Zambezi is 2,200 miles (3,540 km) long. Boats can travel about 460 miles (740 km) of the river.

A River Without a Delta
The Congo River's current is so strong that the river does not form a delta as it flows into the ocean. Instead, the river has cut a deep, wide canyon beneath the sea for a distance of about 125 miles (200 km).

The Congo River

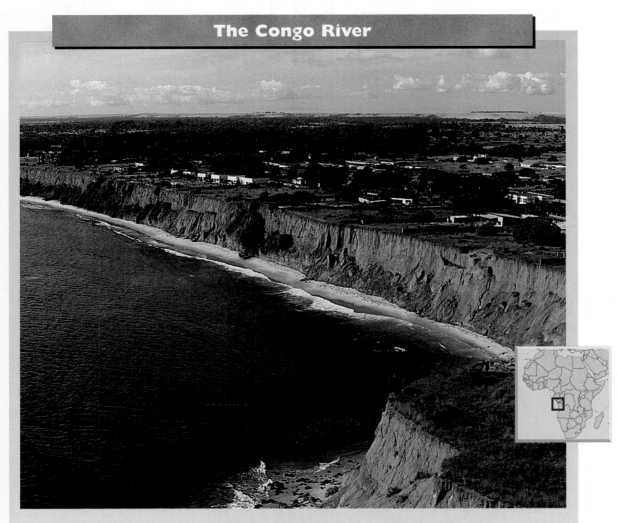

The Congo River flows very fast—every second, the equivalent of more than 100 swimming pools full of water flows past its mouth.

Victoria Falls

The African name for Victoria Falls means "The Smoke That Thunders." Victoria Falls lies on the Zambezi River, which crosses 2,200 miles (3,540 km) and six countries. It is broken by many waterfalls. **Critical Thinking** Based on this photo, why do you think the Zambezi River is not used as a major trade route?

People have used the Zambezi's strong current to make electricity. About halfway to its outlet in the Indian Ocean, the Zambezi plunges into a canyon, creating Victoria Falls. People can sometimes see the mist and spray of the falls from up to 40 miles (65 km) away.

1. **Define** (a) plateau, (b) elevation, (c) escarpment, (d) rift, (e) cataract, (f) silt, (g) fertile, (h) tributary.
2. **Identify** (a) Sahara, (b) Great Rift Valley, (c) Nile River, (d) Congo River, (e) Niger River, (f) Zambezi River.
3. Why is Africa called the "plateau continent"?
4. (a) How do people use the rivers of Africa? (b) What makes them difficult to use?

Critical Thinking

5. **Drawing Conclusions** Most of the people in North Africa live north of the Sahara near the Mediterranean Sea. If the Sahara were a grassland with rivers and forests, would this change where people in North African countries live? Why?

Activity

6. **Writing to Learn** List several landforms in Africa you would like to visit. Explain why you would like to go there and what you would do on your trip.

Climate and Vegetation

Reach Into Your Background
Think about the climate where you live. What kind of weather do you have in the summer? What kind of weather do you have in the winter? What are the months when you have summer? What are the months when you have winter?

Questions to Explore

1. What types of climates and vegetation are found in Africa?
2. How do climate and vegetation affect how Africans make a living?

Key Terms
irrigate
oasis
savanna
nomad

Key Places
Sahel
Namib Desert
Kalahari Desert

A trip to Africa sounds like a great adventure. But packing for the trip might prove harder than you think. What would you pack for a two-week journey to Africa? As you read about Africa's climates and vegetation, see if you would add any items to your list.

▼ If you visit Botswana during the rainy season, be prepared to get wet. Floods like this one, on the Okavango River Delta, are common.

What Influences Climate?

Look at the climate map on the following page. Find the Tropic of Cancer and the Tropic of Capricorn. As you can see, much of Africa lies between these two lines of latitude. This means that most of Africa is in a tropical climate region. Notice that the Equator runs through this midsection of the continent. These regions are usually hot.

Many parts of Africa are indeed hot. But much of Africa is not. That is because location near the Equator is not the only influence on climate. The climate of a place may depend on how close it is to large bodies of water. Major landforms also affect climate. So does the elevation of a place.

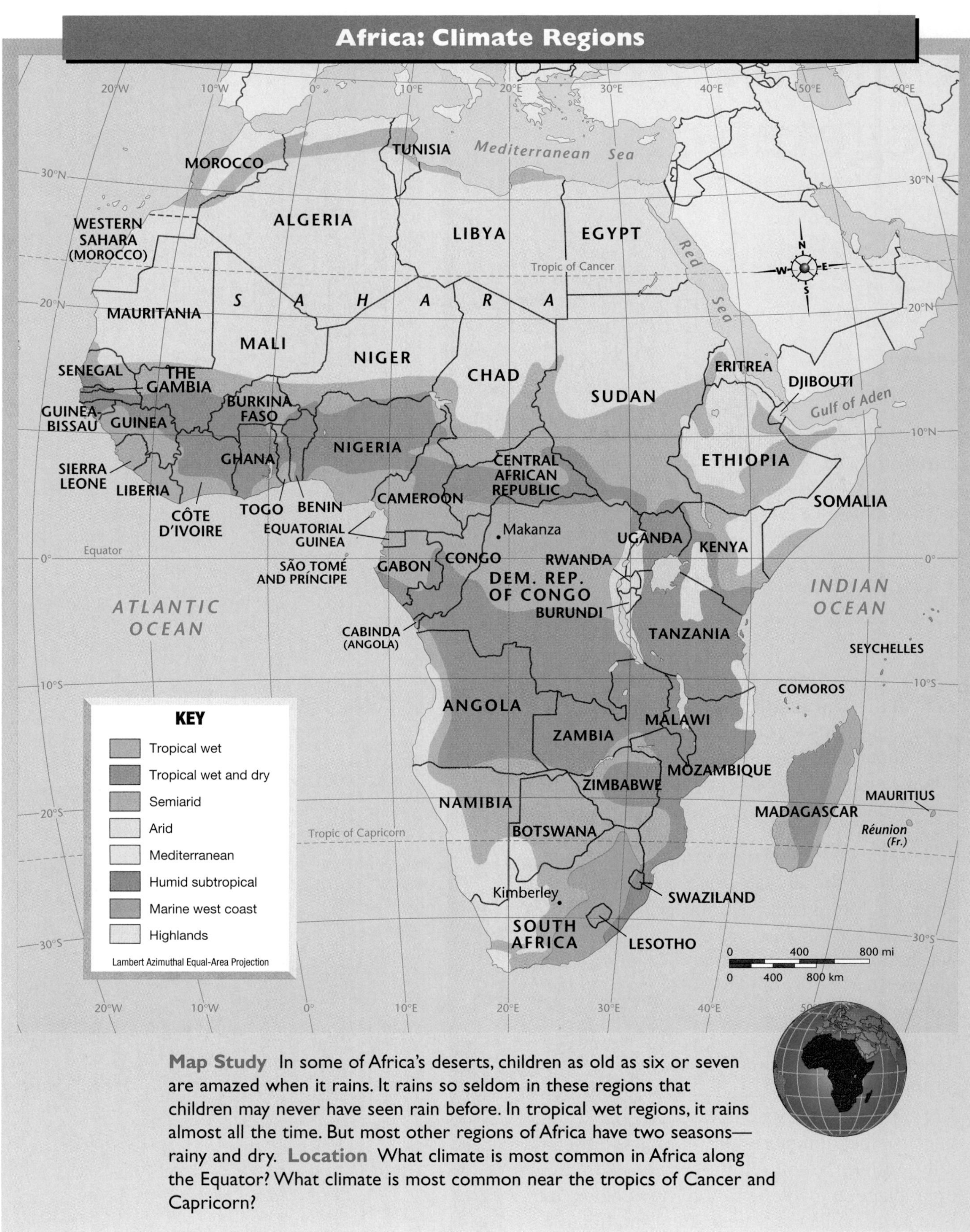

Map Study In some of Africa's deserts, children as old as six or seven are amazed when it rains. It rains so seldom in these regions that children may never have seen rain before. In tropical wet regions, it rains almost all the time. But most other regions of Africa have two seasons—rainy and dry. **Location** What climate is most common in Africa along the Equator? What climate is most common near the tropics of Cancer and Capricorn?

Distance From the Equator Africa's location near the Equator means that most of the continent is warm. A place's location in relation to the Equator influences the seasons. North of the Equator, winter and summer occur at the same time as they do in the United States. South of the Equator, the seasons are reversed. For example, July in South Africa is the middle of winter.

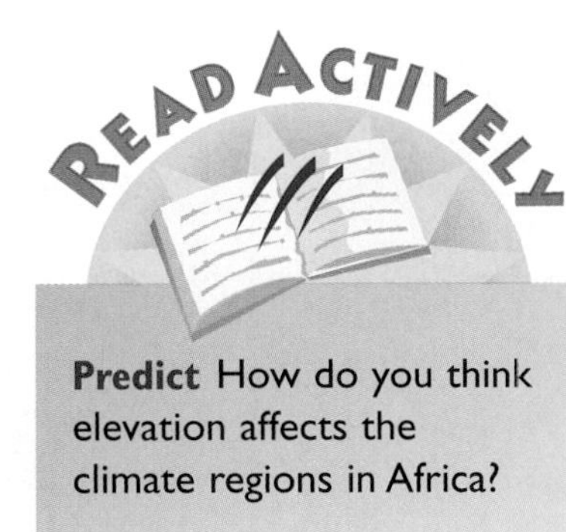

Predict How do you think elevation affects the climate regions in Africa?

Higher, Cooler: The Role of Elevation Elevation, or height above sea level, also affects climate. The higher the elevation, the cooler a place tends to be. Mount Kilimanjaro, Africa's highest peak, is located very close to the Equator. Yet ice and snow blanket the peak of Kilimanjaro year round.

The countries of Ethiopia and Somalia provide another example. They are about the same distance from the Equator, yet they have different climates. Ethiopia is on a very high plateau. Much of Ethiopia has mild temperatures and much rain. Farmers there grow a wide range of crops—including coffee, dates, and cereals. Because Ethiopia usually gets plenty of rain, many farmers there do not **irrigate,** or artificially water, their crops.

Somalia is at a much lower elevation than Ethiopia. Its climate is hot and dry. Farming is possible only in or near an oasis, where crops can be irrigated. An **oasis** is a place where springs and fresh underground water make it possible to support life in a region that gets little rain.

Unpredictable Rainfall Rainfall varies greatly from one region of Africa to another. Along parts of the west coast, winds carry moisture from the warm ocean over the land. Rainfall averages more than 100 inches (250 cm) per year. Compare that to your own height in inches. Forty inches (100 cm) of rain might fall during June alone. But in parts of the Sahara in the north and Namib Desert in the south, it may not rain at all for several years in a row.

Farmers who live in dry regions can never be sure whether there will be enough rain for their crops. Some farmers

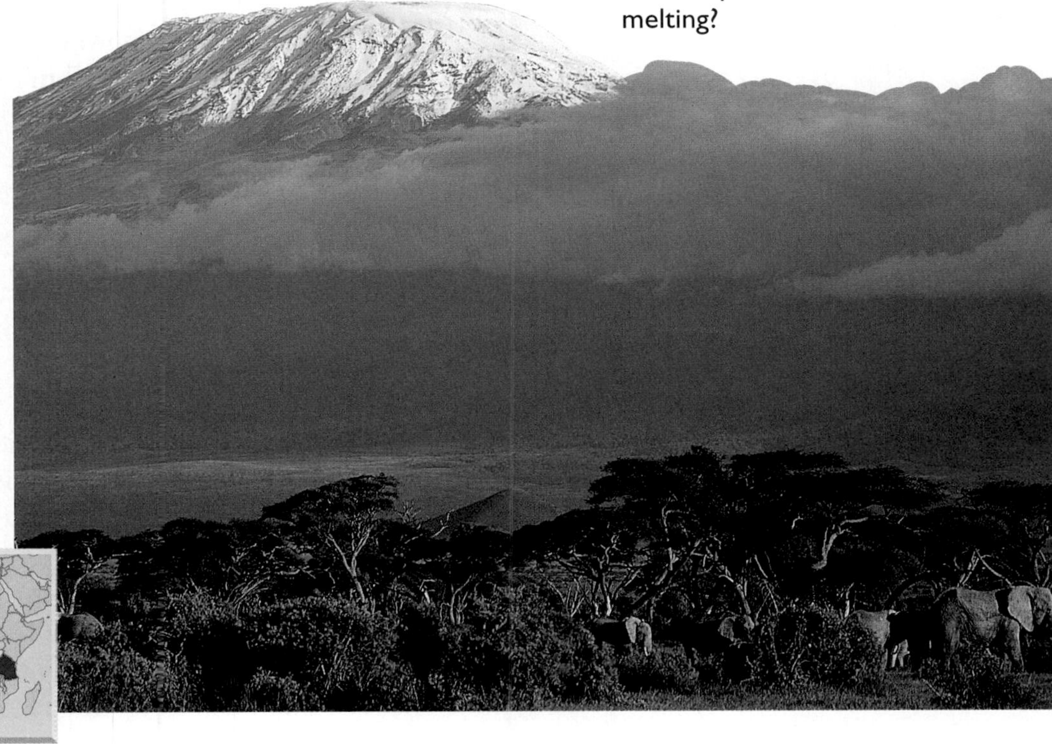

▼ What clue in this picture shows that it is Mount Kilimanjaro's high elevation that keeps its snow from melting?

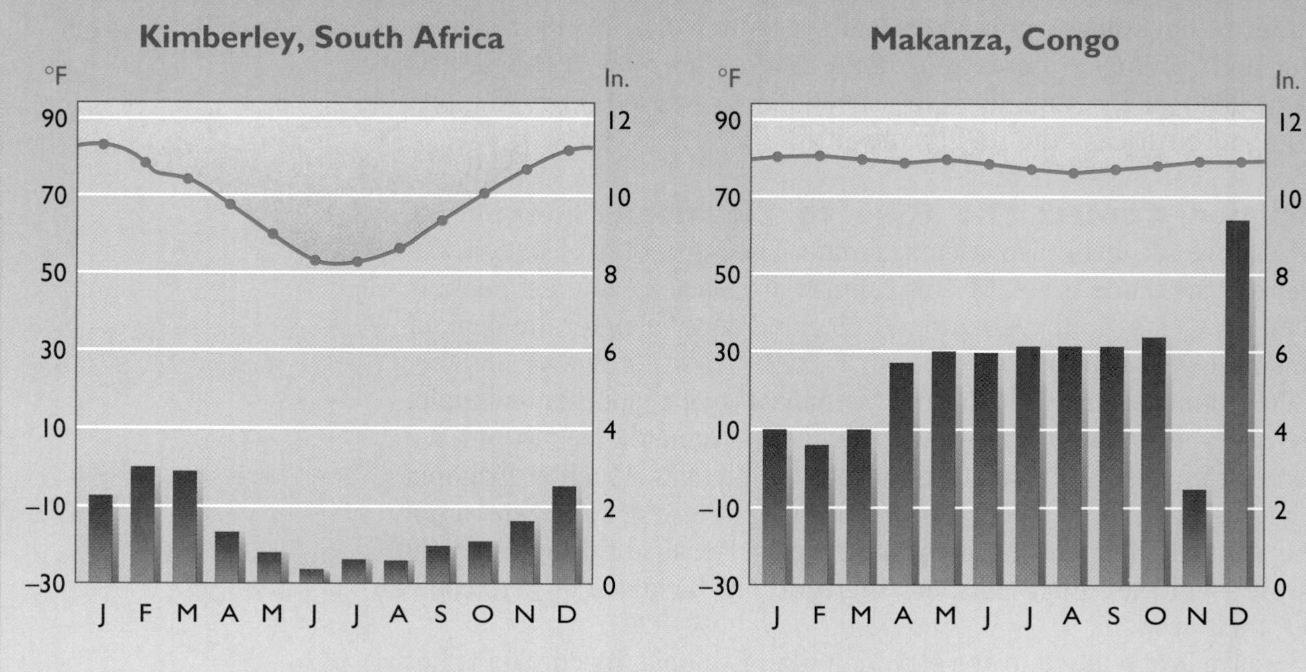

Chart Study The vegetation of Kimberley, South Africa, is mostly desert scrub. Makanza, Congo, lies in a tropical rain forest. **Critical Thinking** What differences do the climate charts show that would explain why Kimberley is in a warm, dry region while Makanza is in a tropical rain forest?

choose to plant a variety of crops, each needing different amounts of rainfall. These farmers hope they will have at least one successful crop. The charts on this page show rainfall in two cities that have very different climates. Which city do you think would have the best climate for farming?

READ ACTIVELY

Visualize Visualize the rain forest in the country of Cameroon. What might it look like and sound like?

Vegetation

Look at the vegetation map in the Activity Atlas. Near the Equator are rain forests. Farther from the Equator lies a region of tall grasses, called the **savanna.**

Tropical Rain Forests Tropical rain forests are regions where it rains nearly all the time. The moisture supports a rich environment of trees, plants, and animals. Find the tropical rain forest region on the vegetation map. The tropical rain forest region used to be much larger. It covered much of Central Africa. Through the years, people cut trees from the forest to use the wood or to clear land for farming. Rain forest lands, however, do not make good farmland. Once the trees are cut down, heavy rains wash away the nutrients that make soil fertile.

Tropical Savannas Much of Africa north and south of the rain forest is tropical savanna. Tall grasses, thorny bushes, and scattered trees grow in the savanna region. Some grasses grow as high as a person's head.

The climate of the tropical savanna is tropical wet and dry. This means that the savanna has two seasons: dry and wet. During the dry season, farming is impossible. Trees lose their leaves and rivers run dry. People use the season to trade, build houses, and visit friends. In the wet season, the land turns green, and farmers plant their crops.

▲ The acacia tree produces a substance that is used in candy, glue, and ink. It grows in tropical savanna regions.

Deserts in Africa Beyond the savanna lie the deserts. The immense Sahara extends across most of North Africa. This desert covers almost as much land as the entire United States.

The southern edge of the Sahara meets the savanna in a region called the Sahel (SAH hil), which is the Arab word for shore or border. The Sahel is very hot and dry. It receives only 4 to 8 inches (10 to 20 cm) of rain per year. Small shrubs, grass, and some trees grow there.

The Namib and Kalahari deserts extend over much of Namibia and Botswana in Southern Africa. These deserts, like the Sahara, feature landscapes of bare rock, towering rock formations, sand dunes, and a few areas of small bushes and grass.

A journalist traveling in the Namib Desert described the region:

> "There was sand everywhere, an impossible amount of sand covering thousands of square miles and heaping into dunes as high as 1,200 feet. The ultimate sandpile. It was uniformly fine and found its way into everything. I blinked sand from my eyes, blew it from my nose, spit it from my mouth and throat."

The Oldest Sunscreen In the United States, people often wear sunscreen to protect their skin from sunburn. But it is hard to get sunscreen in the Sahara. Instead, desert nomads cover themselves from head to toe in long, loose robes.

Nomads make their living in the Sahara. **Nomads** are people who move around to various places to make a living. Some nomads are traders, and others hunt game and gather food. Most nomads are herders, however. They travel to places where they know they can get water and food for their herds of goats, camels, or sheep.

Some nomadic herders live mainly in the mountainous areas. In spring, they leave their winter grazing grounds in the foothills and head

▶These Berber nomads are traveling across the country of Morocco, through the Sahara.

up into the mountains. Other nomads live mainly in the flat desert areas. During the dry season, they set up tents near oases. When the rainy season comes, they move their goats and camels to better pastures.

Building Good Health

Connect Do you know of any diseases that are spread by insects in the United States? If so, how do people keep the disease from spreading?

The climate people live in can affect their health. Throughout Africa there are regions that present health risks to livestock and humans. In rain forest regions, the moist environment is home to many disease-carrying insects. Even in the drier grasslands, disease and illness take their toll.

Nearly one fifth of Africa is home to the tsetse (TSET see) fly, a pest that makes raising cattle almost impossible. The bite of the fly kills cattle and brings a disease called sleeping sickness to humans. African researchers, together with cattle herders, have worked to find ways to control the spread of the tsetse fly. Cattle herders in Kenya are setting traps for flies. Herders in the country of Uganda use netting sewn into a tent that contains poison to catch flies.

1. **Define** (a) irrigate, (b) oasis, (c) savanna, (d) nomad.
2. **Identify** (a) Sahel, (b) Namib Desert, (c) Kalahari Desert.
3. What three factors affect the climate of Africa?
4. What most affects farming in Africa, rainfall or temperature? Explain.

Critical Thinking

5. **Recognizing Cause and Effect** If Mount Kilimanjaro were located in Canada instead of Kenya, would the climate at its peak be much different? Why or why not?

Activity

6. **Writing to Learn** Now that you know more about the climate and vegetation in Africa, make your new packing list for a two-week trip to Africa. Explain why you are bringing each item. (Hint: you may want to decide exactly which regions of Africa you will be visiting before you make the list.)

Natural Resources

Reach Into Your Background
Have you ever heard the saying, "Don't put all your eggs in one basket?" What do you think this saying means?

Questions to Explore

1. What are Africa's major natural resources?
2. How are Africans developing these resources?

Key Terms
subsistence farming
cash crop
economy
diversify

"**Tete Quarshie:** I have a humble request to make of you, my noble friend. I hope you will not turn deaf ears to my cries. Here, in this load, I bear the seeds of a wonderful tree which, if cultivated in this land, will bless its sons everlastingly with wealth, and people far and near with health. These are the seeds of the cacao tree which I have brought with me from across the sea. . . . Would you, therefore, be kind enough to grant me a mere acre of land in this neighborhood to try my luck, and yours, and that of this country as a whole?"

These words come from a short play, *Cocoa Comes to Mampong.* The play tells the story of cocoa in the West African country of Ghana. Cacao trees, from which cocoa and chocolate are made, used to grow only in Central and South America. As people in the Americas, Europe, and Africa began to trade with one another, they found that cacao trees could be grown in West Africa. In the play, the people granted the land to Tete Quarshie, who raised the first successful crop of cacao in Ghana.

▼ To make milk chocolate from cacao beans, shown below, chocolate makers grind the beans, and then mix them with lots of milk and sugar.

Farming Equipment
Corn and wheat farmers in the United States often use heavy machines to work the land. Most African farmers could not use such machines. They would destroy the thin layer of topsoil on most African farms.

Agricultural Resources

Some Africans are farmers living in areas with fertile soil and much rain. But most Africans have land that is hard or impossible to farm because of poor soil or too little rain.

Farming to Live The map on the next page shows how much of Africa's land is used for **subsistence farming.** Subsistence farmers raise crops to support their families. They sell or trade a few crops for other items they need. In northern African countries such as Morocco, farmers raise barley and wheat. They also irrigate fields to grow fruits and vegetables. Farms at Saharan oases in Egypt produce dates and small crops of barley and wheat.

In countries that contain dry tropical savanna, such as Burkina Faso (bur KEE nuh FAH soh) and Niger, subsistence farmers grow grains. In regions with more rainfall, farmers also grow vegetables, fruits, and

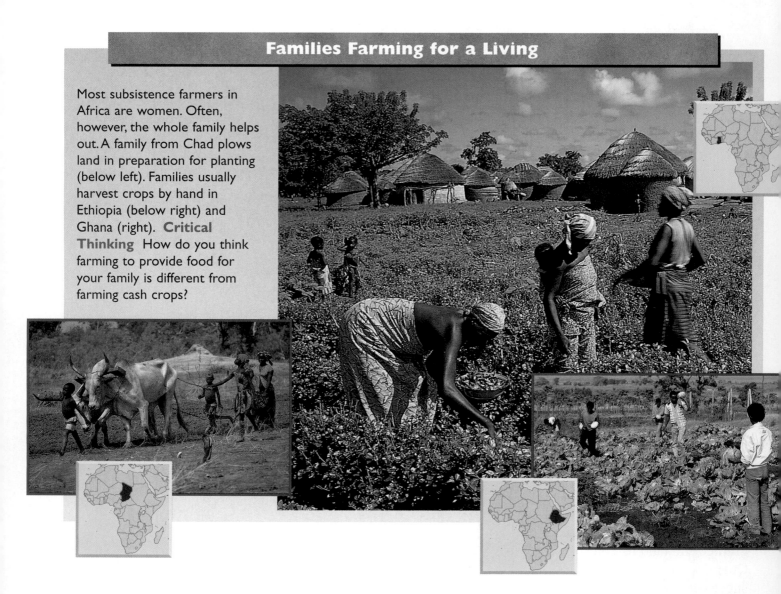

Families Farming for a Living

Most subsistence farmers in Africa are women. Often, however, the whole family helps out. A family from Chad plows land in preparation for planting (below left). Families usually harvest crops by hand in Ethiopia (below right) and Ghana (right). **Critical Thinking** How do you think farming to provide food for your family is different from farming cash crops?

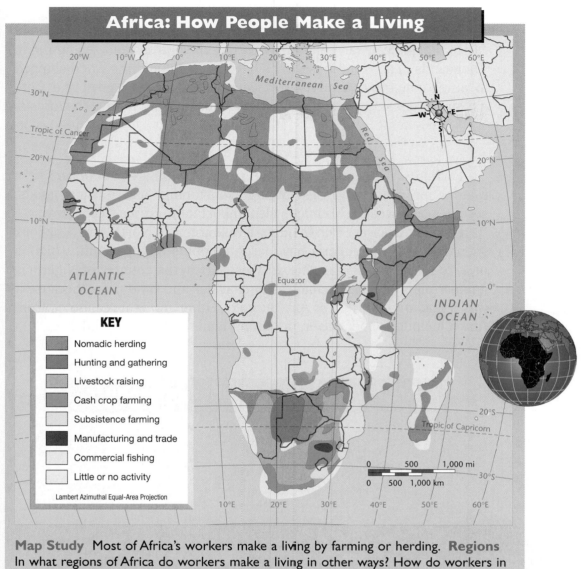

Africa: How People Make a Living

KEY
- Nomadic herding
- Hunting and gathering
- Livestock raising
- Cash crop farming
- Subsistence farming
- Manufacturing and trade
- Commercial fishing
- Little or no activity

Lambert Azimuthal Equal-Area Projection

Map Study Most of Africa's workers make a living by farming or herding. **Regions** In what regions of Africa do workers make a living in other ways? How do workers in these areas make a living? **Critical Thinking** Why do you think that some parts of Africa have little or no economic activity?

roots such as yams and cassava. Tapioca, which is used in the United States to make pudding, is made from cassava. In West Africa, corn and rice are important crops. People in many of Africa's cultures fish or raise goats or poultry.

Crops for Sale In all regions of Africa, farmers raise crops to sell. These are called **cash crops.** Farmers in Côte d'Ivoire (koht deev WAR), Ghana, and Cameroon grow cash crops of coffee and cacao. Farmers in Kenya, Tanzania, Malawi, Zimbabwe, and Mozambique grow tea as a cash crop.

In recent years, more and more farmers have planted cash crops. As more land is used for cash crops, less land is planted with crops to feed families. In some regions, this practice has led to food shortages when cash crops have failed.

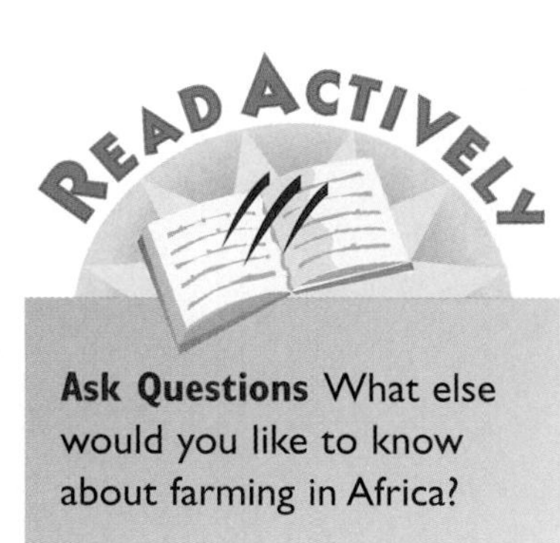

Ask Questions What else would you like to know about farming in Africa?

Harvesting Trees Hardwood trees grow in all four regions of Africa. People can earn money by cutting down trees and selling them. Thousands of acres of these trees have been cut and the wood shipped to other countries. A number of countries, such as Kenya and Côte d'Ivoire, are planting trees by the thousands in order to save the forests.

Mineral Resources

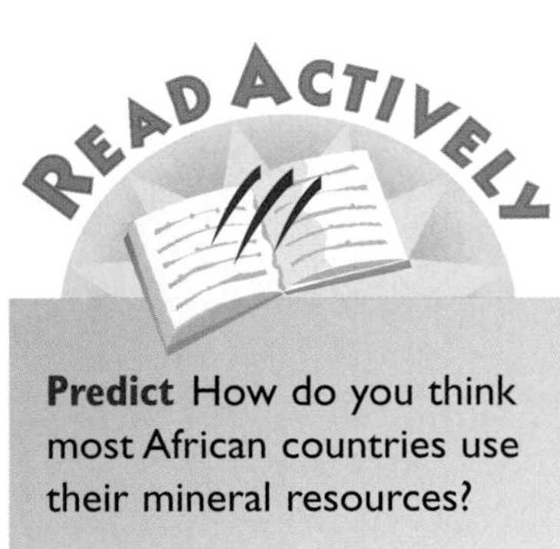

Predict How do you think most African countries use their mineral resources?

Farming is the major part of Africa's economy. An **economy** is a system for producing, distributing, consuming, and owning goods, services, and wealth. Mining is also important to Africa's economy.

Parts of Africa are rich in mineral resources. In North Africa, nations such as Libya and Algeria have large amounts of petroleum, which is used to make oil and gasoline. In West Africa, the country of Nigeria is a major oil producer. Ghana was once called the Gold Coast because it was a leading exporter of African gold. Other mineral resources from Africa include copper, silver, uranium, titanium, and diamonds.

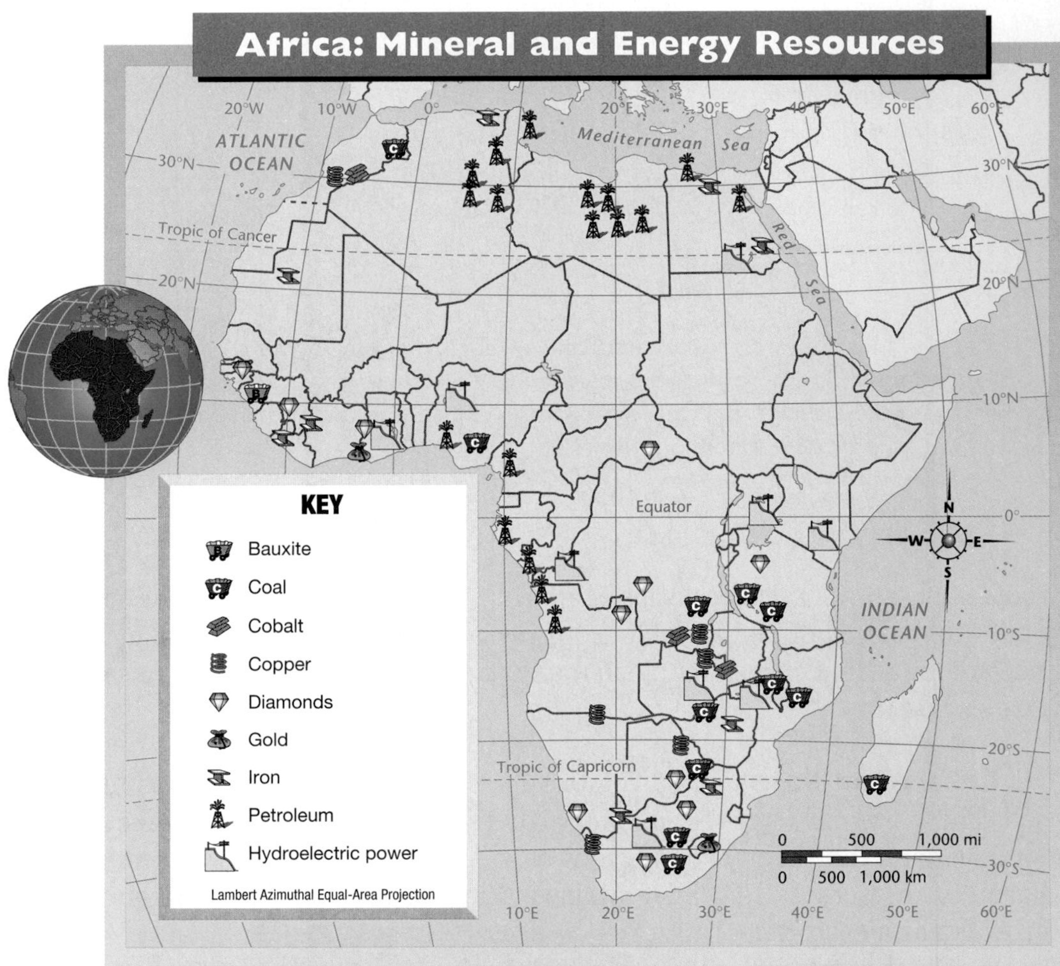

Map Study Most of Africa's people work in agriculture, yet most of Africa's exports are produced by miners. **Regions** Southern Africa is famous for its diamond industry. What other regions of Africa produce diamonds? **Interaction** Which resource shown on this map can be used without being used up?

Balancing Crops, Minerals, and Industry

Most of Africa's workers are farmers. When an economy of a nation is dependent on one kind of industry, such as farming, it is called a specialized economy. In Africa, specializing in just farming makes the economy sensitive to rainfall and to the price of crops. For that reason, African countries are now trying to diversify their economies. To **diversify** means to add variety. These countries are working to produce a variety of crops, raw materials, and manufactured goods. A country with a diverse economy will not be hurt as much if a major cash crop fails or if world prices for one of its major mineral exports suddenly drops.

Mining requires many workers and costly equipment. Throughout much of Africa, foreign companies mine African resources and take the profits. This system does little to help African economies. In addition, Africa has few factories to make products from its own raw materials. Therefore, many African countries want to diversify their economies to include manufacturing.

▼ All over Africa, people are moving to cities to apply for jobs in factories like this one. These men work on the assembly line at the Livingstone Car Plant in the country of Zambia.

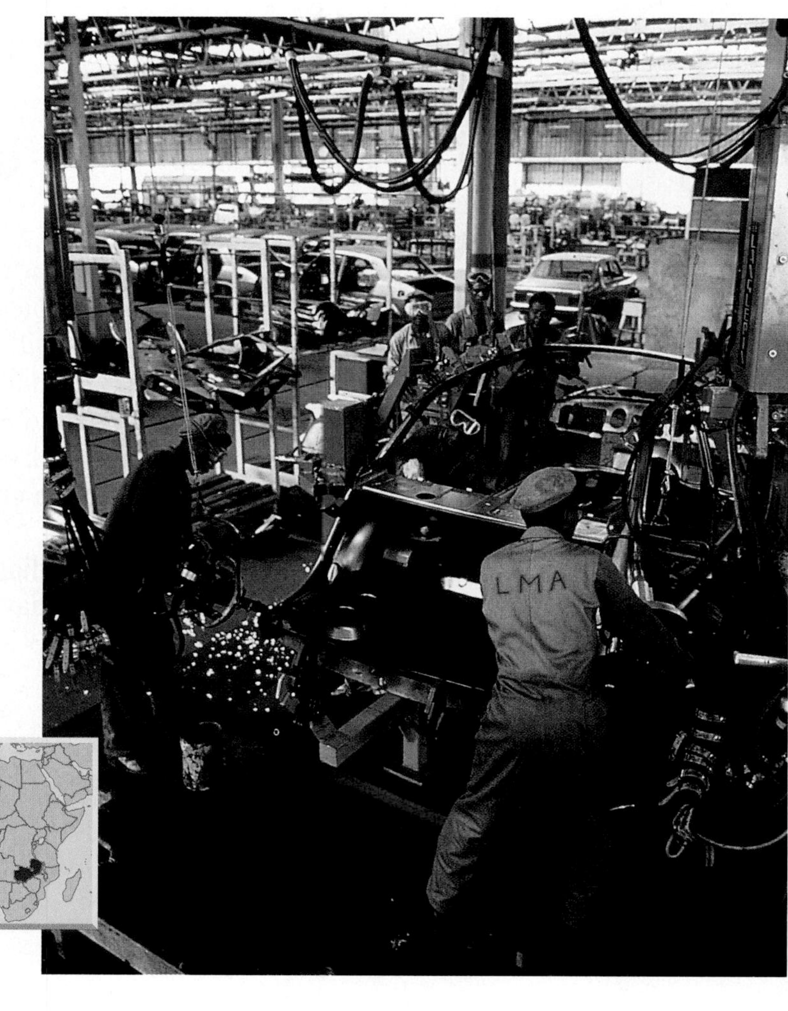

SECTION 3 REVIEW

1. **Define** (a) subsistence farming, (b) cash crop, (c) economy, (d) diversify.
2. Why are African governments working to diversify their economies?
3. Compare subsistence farming with farming to raise cash crops. How are they similar? How are they different?

Critical Thinking

4. **Identifying Central Issues** What are some important natural resources in Africa?

Activity

5. **Writing to Learn** List some of Africa's natural resources that you and your family use. Then, write a paragraph that explains which you would miss most if you did not have it—and why.

Interpreting Diagrams

Africa is a giant. More than three times bigger than the United States, it covers close to 11,700,000 square miles (more than 30,000,000 sq km). That is about one fifth of all of the land in the world. If you drove across Africa at its widest point going 65 miles (105 km) per hour, without stopping for gas or sleep, it would take you about 72 hours. Traveling north-to-south, the trip would take about 77 hours.

A quick look at a world map will impress upon you Africa's great length and width. But the map will not show you its enormous elevations, or height.

One of the most effective ways to see Africa's elevations is to study a cross-sectional diagram of this gigantic land.

Get Ready

You already know that a diagram is a figure drawn to explain something. A *cross section* is basically a slice of something viewed from the side. For example, if you were to cut an apple in half, and look at the exposed cut, you would be looking at a cross section of the apple. If you drew a picture of what you saw, you would have a cross-sectional diagram of that apple.

You can get a good idea of a cross-sectional diagram by making one of your own—and having some fun as you do it. You'll need:

- modeling clay
- a butter knife
- pen and paper

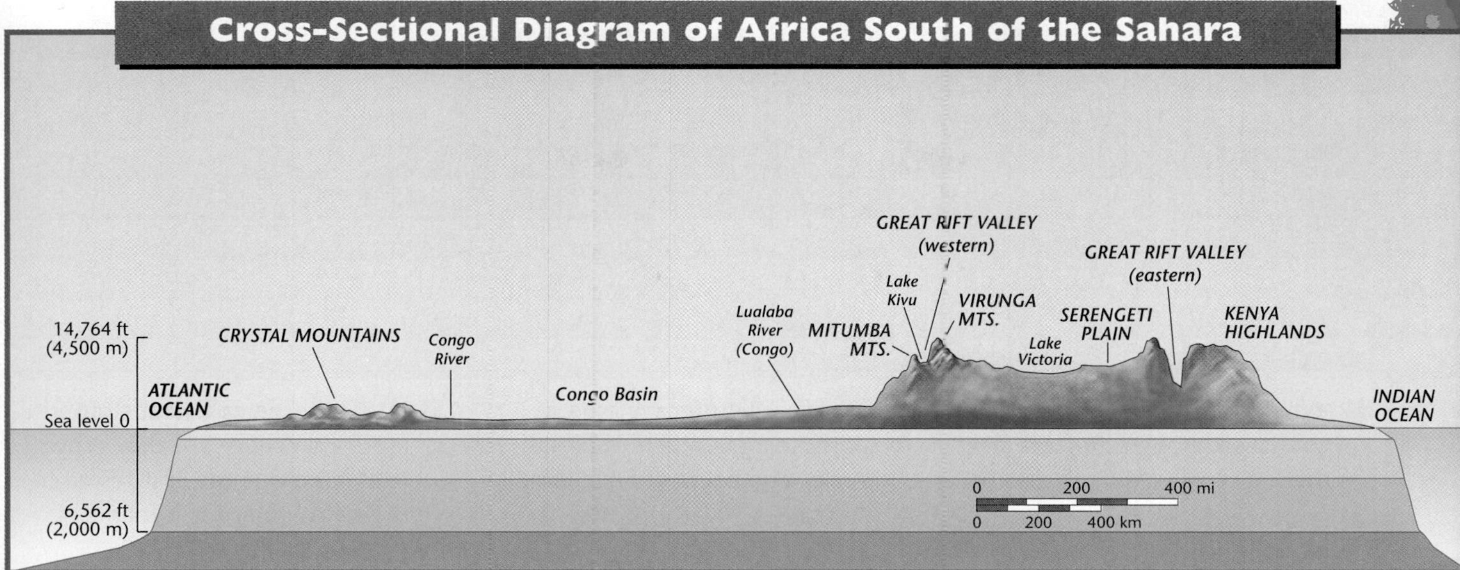

Try It Out

A. Create a continent. Take a fist-sized ball of modeling clay and shape it into an imaginary continent. First, flatten it out. Then mold the continent into any shape you want. Mold mountain ranges, valleys, plateaus, and any other landforms you wish.

B. Cut the cross section. When you've finished, put your "clay continent" flat on a table. Use the butter knife to cut it in half at its widest point.

C. Look at your result. Pick up one-half of your continent and look at the cut edge. You are looking at a cross section of your imaginary continent.

D. Sketch what you see. By sketching a side view of your model, you have made a cross-sectional diagram of your imaginary continent. How does the diagram reflect the vertical shape of the continent? Write the answer on the back of your cross-sectional diagram.

Apply the Skill

The illustration above is a cross-sectional diagram of Africa south of the Sahara. Use it to complete the following steps.

1. **Understand the diagram.** Just as you cut your clay continent at a certain place, the cross-sectional diagram of Africa shows the continent "cut" at a certain place. Does this cross section show Africa from east to west or from north to south? How is elevation indicated on the diagram? What geographic features are labeled on the diagram?

2. **Learn from the diagram.** What is the lowest point on the diagram? What is the highest point? How large a range in elevation is this? How far below the surrounding landscape does the Great Rift Valley drop?

Review and Activities

Reviewing Main Ideas

1. Why are some parts of Africa cold even though they are near the Equator?
2. List four major physical features of Africa. Choose one and describe what it is like.
3. Explain why there is little or no farming in much of North Africa and parts of Southern Africa.
4. How is subsistence farming in Africa different from farming to raise cash crops?
5. (a) List three cash crops raised in Africa. Where are they grown? (b) Name one mineral resource of Africa. Where is it found?
6. Explain why many African nations are trying to diversify their economies.

Reviewing Key Terms

Use each key term below in a sentence that shows the meaning of the term.

1. plateau
2. elevation
3. escarpment
4. rift
5. cataract
6. silt
7. fertile
8. tributary
9. irrigate
10. oasis
11. savanna
12. nomad
13. subsistence farming
14. cash crop
15. economy
16. diversify

Critical Thinking

1. **Identifying Central Issues** Explain the meaning of this statement. Give an example to support it. "People in Africa tend to live in grassland regions."
2. **Recognizing Cause and Effect** How did the yearly flooding of the Nile affect farmers in the Nile Valley? How did the building of the Aswan Dam affect the farmers?

Graphic Organizer

Copy the chart onto a sheet of paper. Then fill in the empty boxes to complete the chart.

	Amount of Rainfall	Temperature	Crops Grown
Desert	Little or none	Hot	Dates, barley, wheat in or near oases
Tropical Savanna			
Uplands and Mountain Regions			

Map Activity

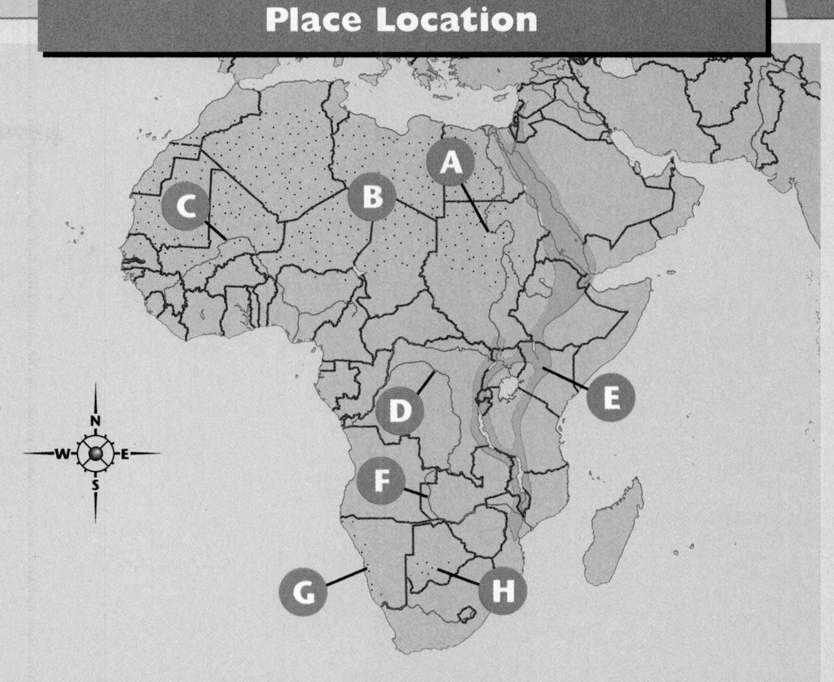

Africa

For each place listed, write the letter from the map that shows its location.

1. Nile River
2. Congo River
3. Sahara
4. Namib Desert
5. Zambezi River
6. Kalahari Desert
7. Niger River
8. Great Rift Valley

Writing Activity

Writing a Short Report Describe some problems Africans face that are caused by Africa's landforms or climate. Give some examples of how Africans are solving these problems.

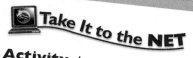

Activity Learn more about Africa's land and take a fun online quiz to test your knowledge. For help in completing this activity, visit **www.phschool.com**.

Chapter 11 Self-Test To review what you have learned, take the Chapter 11 Self-Test and get instant feedback on your answers. Go to **www.phschool.com** to take the test.

Skills Review

Turn to the Skills Activity.

Review the steps for interpreting a diagram. Then complete the following: (a) In your own words, describe what a cross-sectional diagram is. (b) What information can you find on a cross-sectional diagram?

How Am I Doing?

Answer these questions to check your progress.

1. Can I describe the location of Africa?
2. Do I understand how climate influences farming activity in Africa?
3. Can I identify some mineral resources of Africa?
4. Can I name some large landforms in Africa?
5. What information from this chapter can I include in my journal?

CHAPTER 12

AFRICA

Shaped by Its History

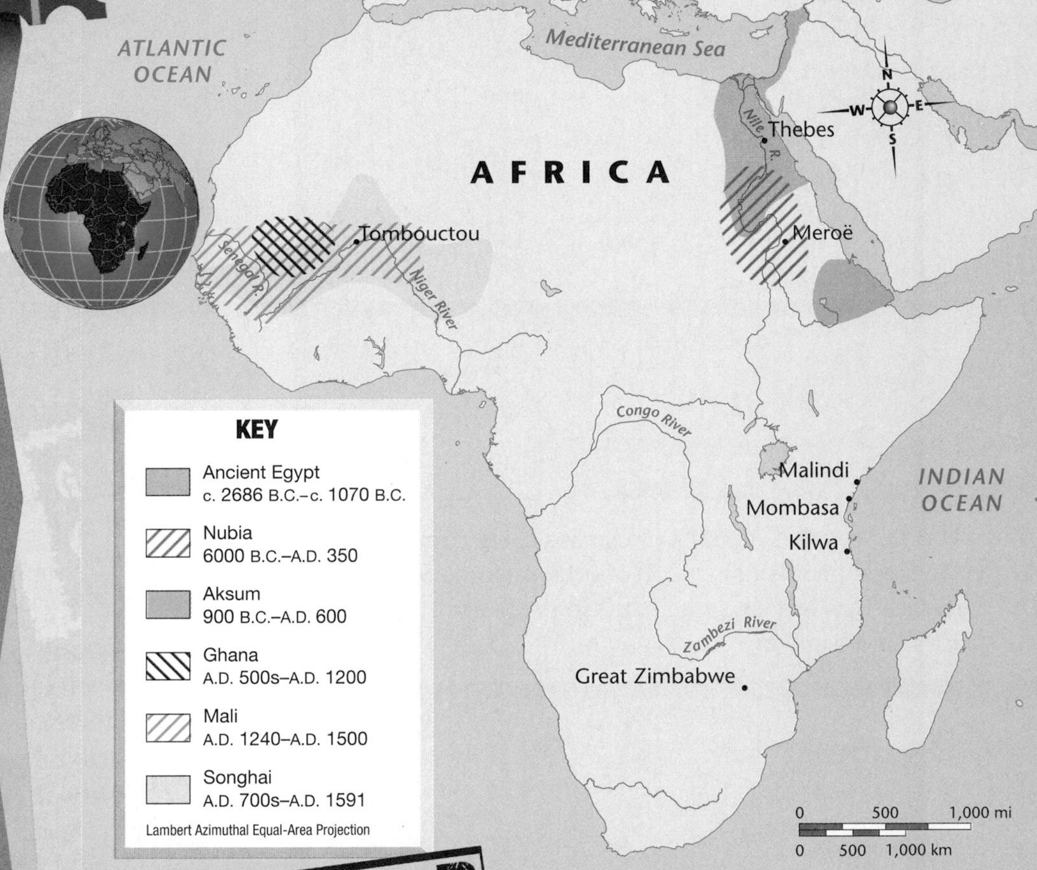

MAP ACTIVITIES

This map shows some of Africa's great empires, kingdoms, and cities. Note that they did not all exist at the same time. Start exploring the history of Africa by doing the following activities.

Study the map

Compare this map with the political map of Africa in the Activity Atlas. Which countries took their names from early empires and kingdoms?

Consider locations

Notice that most of these empires and cities are close to rivers or oceans. How do you think the locations of empires and cities affected their development?

Africa's First People

Reach Into Your Background

What are some of the things you remember from your past? Do you remember your very first day of school? What is the earliest birthday you can remember? All those things are part of your personal history.

Questions to Explore

1. What techniques did early Africans use to get food?
2. How did important ideas and discoveries spread throughout Africa?
3. What civilizations arose along the Nile River?

Key Terms

hunter-gatherer
domesticate
surplus
civilization
migrate
ethnic group

Key People and Places

Louis Leakey
Egypt
Nubia

Today the dry sands of the Sahara cover most of North Africa. But until about 4,000 years ago, this large area held enough water to support many people and animals. Scientists think that Africa's first farmers lived there. Paintings on cliffs and cave walls tell their story.

But the history of people in Africa is even older. Several million years earlier, the continent's first people lived in East Africa. We know this because of the stones and bones they left behind. These East Africans were the very first people to live on the Earth.

▼ This painting was found in Algeria. The horns on this woman's helmet show that the Sahara may once have supported animal life.

Hunter-Gatherers

The earliest humans probably survived by gathering wild fruits, nuts, and roots. These **hunter-gatherers** also hunted animals for meat and clothing. They made tools out of wood, animal bones, and then stone. The first use of stone tools marks the beginning of a period scientists call the Stone Age.

These stone tools worked very well. The scientist Louis Leakey found some of the first evidence of early people in East Africa. He also taught himself to make and use their tools. Using a two-inch, 25,000-year-old stone knife, Leakey could skin and cut up a gazelle in just 20 minutes.

Early Farming

When hunter-gatherers settled down in one area and began farming, they faced longer, harder work days. Farmers spent many hours tilling the soil, planting seeds by hand, tending fields, harvesting crops, and caring for domesticated animals. They used only tools such as these, which they could make by hand. Farmers used axes (left) to clear the land. After butchering a cow, sheep, or goat, farmers used scrapers (top) to clean the hide, and cleavers (bottom) to cut the meat. **Critical Thinking** Since farming is harder work than hunting and gathering, why would a hunter-gatherer want to become a farmer?

The Thirst Zone Africa's first farmers probably lived in Algeria, in North Africa. Thousands of years ago, more rain fell in this region. But today, much of North Africa is known as the "Thirst Zone." People need to drink about 2.5 quarts (2.4 l) of water per day. People also use water for washing and farming. All in all, each person needs at least 21 quarts (20 l) of water per day. In the Thirst Zone, only about five quarts (5 l) of water per person is available.

Farming and Herding

Between 10,000 and 6,000 years ago, hunter-gatherers began to farm and to herd animals. The first farmers probably planted wild grains such as wheat, barley, sorghum, and millet. At first, gatherers just protected the areas where these grains grew best. Then, they began to save some seed to plant for the next year's crop.

Later, people began to **domesticate** plants, or adapt them for their own use. They threw away seeds from weaker plants and saved seeds from stronger ones. People domesticated animals by breeding certain animals together.

Domesticating plants and animals meant people could plant their own crops. They did not have to travel to places where grains were already growing. As a result, they could settle in one place. Most people settled where the land was fertile, or productive. Some communities produced a food **surplus**, or more than they needed. Surpluses allowed some people in the community to do work other than farming.

Civilizations on the Nile

Over hundreds of thousands of years, some Stone Age groups became civilizations. A **civilization** is a society with cities, a government, and social classes. Social classes form when people do a variety of jobs. As a result, some people are rich, some are poor, and others are middle class. Civilizations also have architecture, writing, and art. One civilization arose on the Nile River about 5,000 years ago.

◀ This Egyptian wall painting shows Nubian princes arriving in Egypt. At first, Egypt ruled Nubia, but later, Nubia conquered much of Egypt.

Egypt Each summer, the Nile River flooded its banks. It left a layer of fertile silt that was ideal for farming. People began farming along the banks of the Nile by around 4000 B.C. They settled in scattered villages. Over the centuries, these villages grew into the civilization of ancient Egypt.

Ancient Egypt was ruled by kings and queens called pharaohs (FAY rohz). The people believed the pharaohs to be gods as well as kings. When pharaohs died, they were buried in pyramids. People painted murals and picture-writings called hieroglyphics (hy ur oh GLIF iks) on the walls in the pyramids.

Egyptian civilization included more than just the pyramids. The Egyptians were advanced in paper-making, architecture, medicine, and mathematics.

Visualize What does a pyramid look like?

Nubia Starting in about 6000 B.C., several civilizations arose south of Egypt. This area was called Nubia. The final and greatest Nubian kingdom arose in the city of Meroë (MER oh ee) during the 500s B.C. It thrived until about the middle of the A.D. 300s. Meroë was probably the first place in Africa where iron was made.

The Bantu Migrations

By about 500 B.C., West Africans had learned to heat and shape iron. They used it to form parts of tools such as arrowheads, ax heads, and hoe blades. The strong iron tools made farming easier and created food surpluses. As a result, West Africa's population increased.

Around 2,000 years ago, a group of people who spoke Bantu (BAN too) languages began to **migrate,** or move, out of West Africa, perhaps looking for new land to farm. Over hundreds of years, these

Routes of the Bantu Migrations

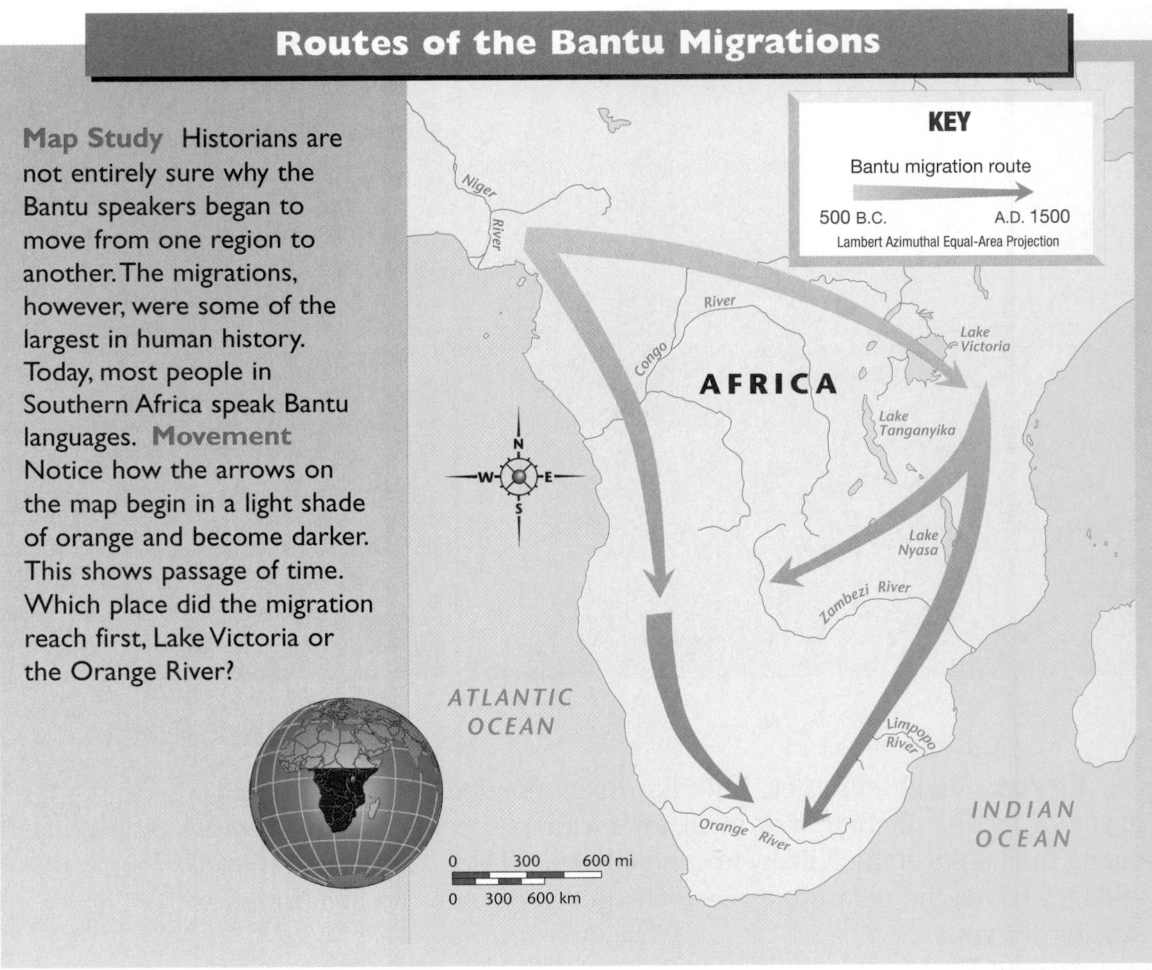

Map Study Historians are not entirely sure why the Bantu speakers began to move from one region to another. The migrations, however, were some of the largest in human history. Today, most people in Southern Africa speak Bantu languages. **Movement** Notice how the arrows on the map begin in a light shade of orange and become darker. This shows passage of time. Which place did the migration reach first, Lake Victoria or the Orange River?

Bantu-speakers settled in Central and Southern Africa. They introduced farming, herding, and iron tools to these regions. Today, people in this part of Africa belong to hundreds of **ethnic groups,** or groups that share languages, religions, family ties, and customs. But almost all of these ethnic groups speak Bantu languages.

1. **Define** (a) hunter-gatherer, (b) domesticate, (c) surplus, (d) civilization, (e) migrate, (f) ethnic group.
2. **Identify** (a) Louis Leakey, (b) Egypt, (c) Nubia.
3. How did iron tools, farming, and herding spread to Southern Africa?
4. Name some achievements of ancient Egyptian and Nubian civilizations.

Critical Thinking

5. **Drawing Conclusions** How did early Africans adapt to their environment?

Activity

6. **Writing to Learn** Make a poster that illustrates, step-by-step, an important idea from this section. For example, you might show how scientists learn about early people or how ideas spread from one part of Africa to another.

Kingdoms and Empires

Reach Into Your Background

What things do you own or have at home that were made in other countries? What things were made in the United States? Make a short list and share it with a classmate.

Questions to Explore

1. How did trade enrich Africa's kingdoms and city-states?
2. How did the religion of Islam spread to different parts of Africa?

Key Terms

Quran
pilgrimage
Swahili
city-state

Key People and Places

Mansa Musa
Aksum
Ghana
Mali
Songhai
Tombouctou
Kilwa
Zimbabwe

In the year A.D. 1, a Greek writer made a list of things you could buy in Adulis, East Africa. Adulis was the most important city in Aksum, a bustling trade center along the Red Sea. There, you could buy:

> "Cloth made in Egypt . . . many articles of flint glass . . . and brass, which is used for ornament and in cut pieces instead of coin; sheets of soft copper, used for cooking utensils and cut up for bracelets and anklets for the women; iron, which is made into spears used against the elephants and other wild beasts, and in their wars."

▼ These beads are from Zimbabwe, but thanks to the traders of Aksum, they could have journeyed all the way to Europe or India.

Aksum

Aksum was located in East Africa. If it still existed today, it would be in the countries of Ethiopia and Eritrea. Around 1000 B.C., African and Arab traders began settling along the west coast of the Red Sea. They were the ancestors of the people of Aksum. Over time, Aksum came to control trade in

Ask Questions What questions do you have about trade in ancient Africa?

the Red Sea. Aksum came to power after the Nubian kingdom of Meroë fell. By then, Aksum controlled a trade network that stretched from the Mediterranean Sea to India.

Ideas, as well as goods, traveled along trade routes. The Christian religion traveled to Aksum along these routes. In the mid-300s, many people in Aksum became Christian. Aksum became a center of the early Ethiopian Christian Church. But Aksum began to decline in the 600s. Then Arabs took control of much of the region's trade.

West African Kingdoms and Trade Routes

▶ **Map Study** Three kingdoms—Ghana, Mali, and Songhai—ruled West Africa for hundreds of years. Their rule was based on control of trade with North Africa. **Place** What West African kingdom controlled the largest area?

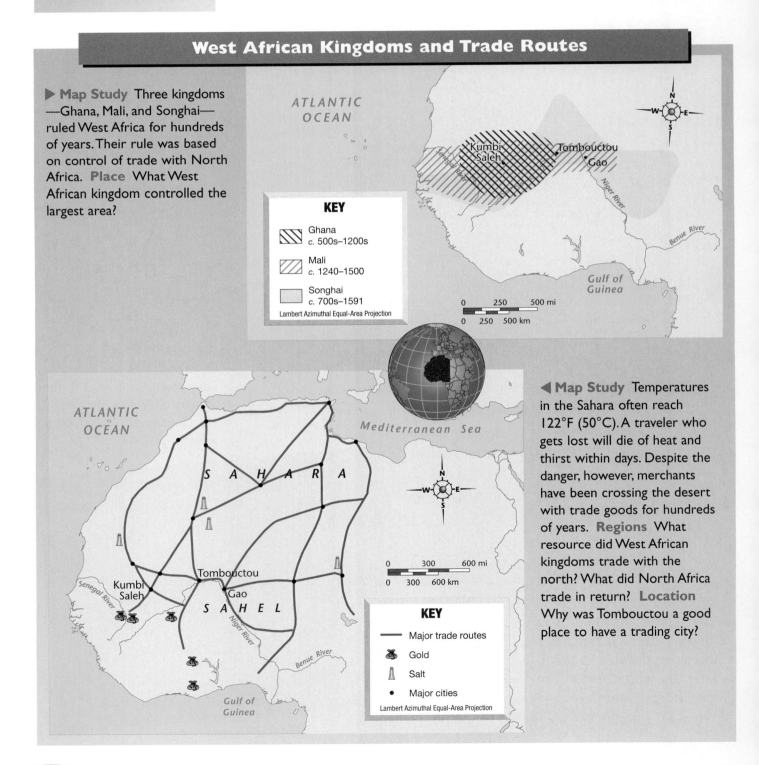

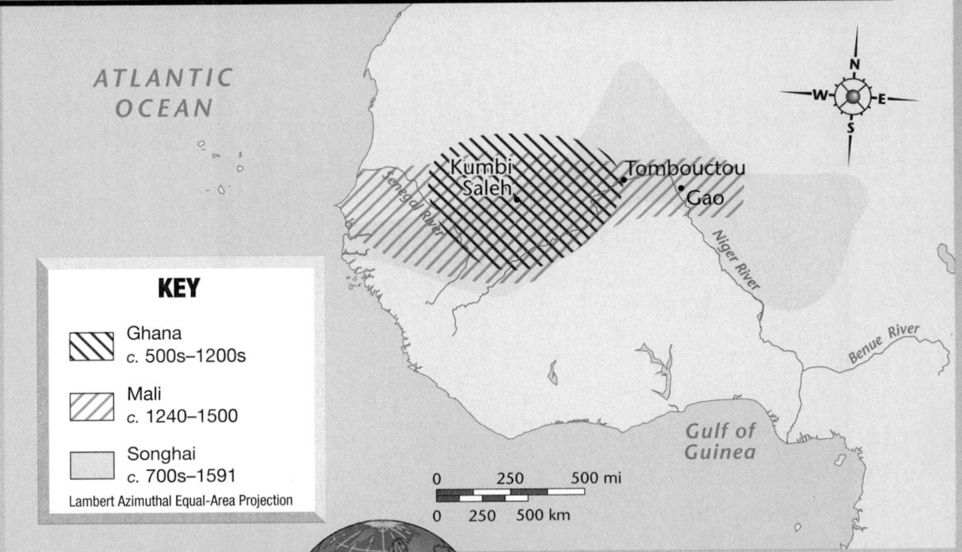

ATLANTIC OCEAN
Kumbi Saleh
Tombouctou
Gao
Senegal River
Niger River
Benue River
Gulf of Guinea

KEY
Ghana c. 500s–1200s
Mali c. 1240–1500
Songhai c. 700s–1591
Lambert Azimuthal Equal-Area Projection

0 250 500 mi
0 250 500 km

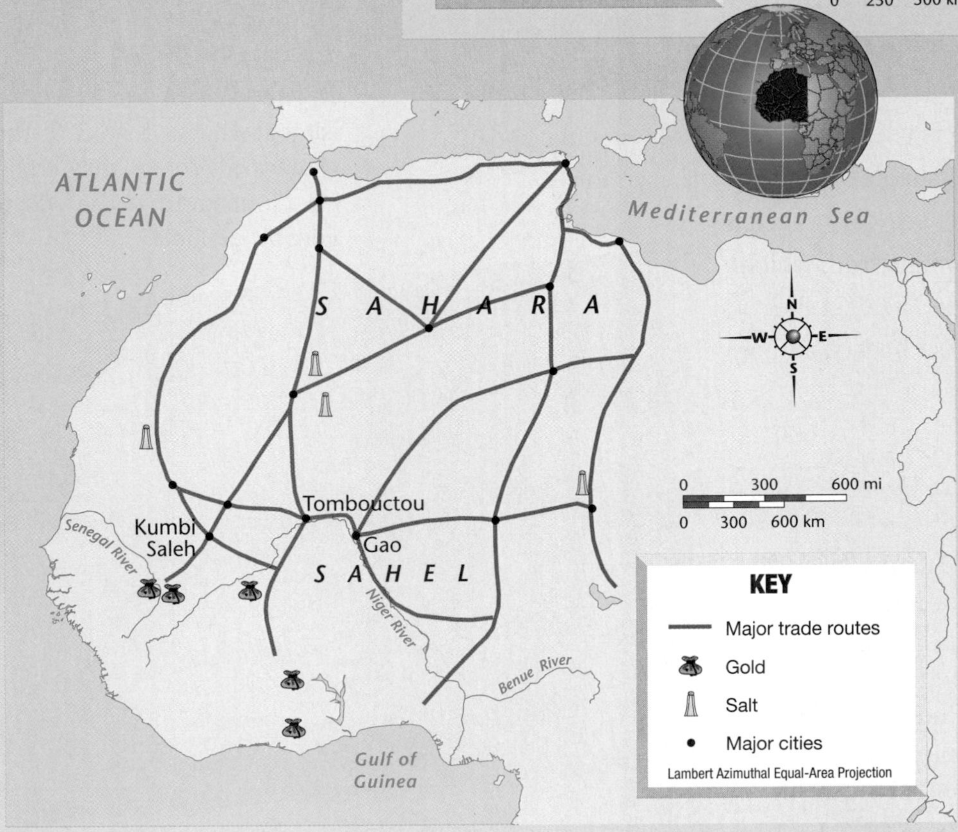

ATLANTIC OCEAN
Mediterranean Sea
SAHARA
SAHEL
Kumbi Saleh
Tombouctou
Gao
Senegal River
Niger River
Benue River
Gulf of Guinea

0 300 600 mi
0 300 600 km

KEY
Major trade routes
Gold
Salt
Major cities
Lambert Azimuthal Equal-Area Projection

◀ **Map Study** Temperatures in the Sahara often reach 122°F (50°C). A traveler who gets lost will die of heat and thirst within days. Despite the danger, however, merchants have been crossing the desert with trade goods for hundreds of years. **Regions** What resource did West African kingdoms trade with the north? What did North Africa trade in return? **Location** Why was Tombouctou a good place to have a trading city?

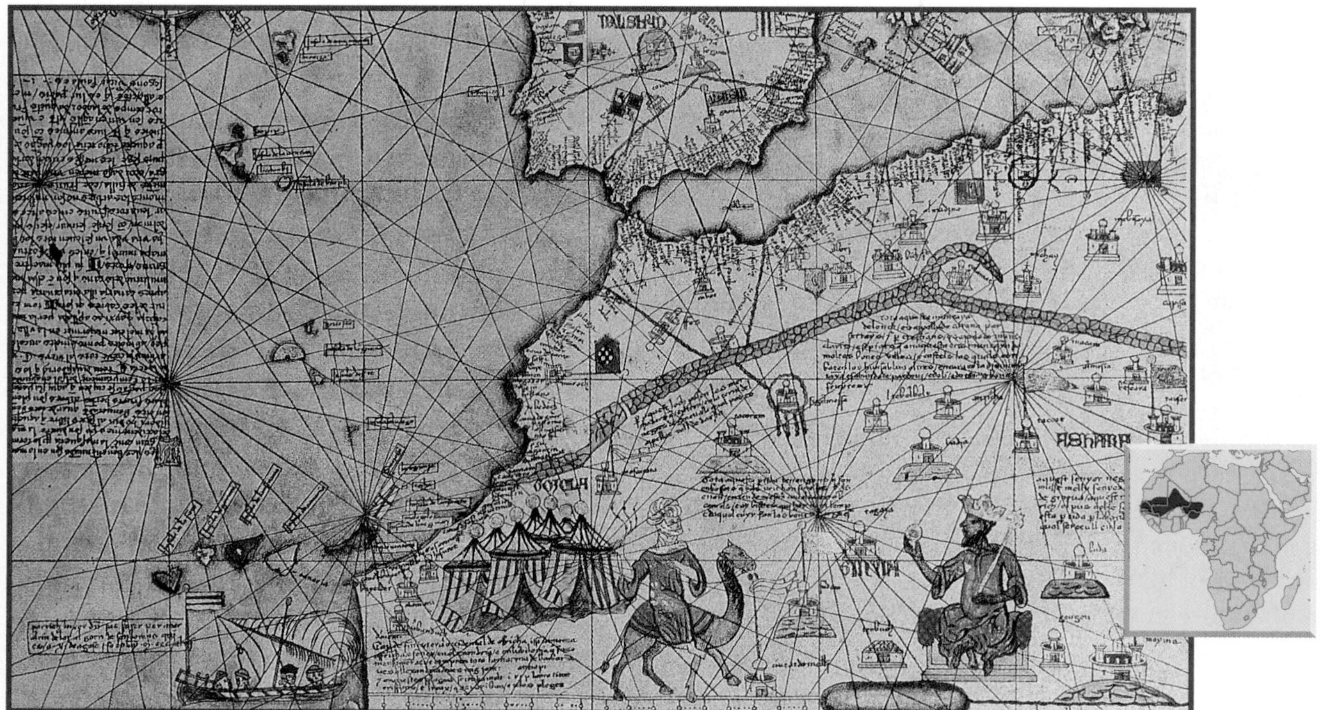

▲ Impressed with Mansa Musa's gold, Europeans included a picture of him on their maps of Africa. He appears in the lower right-hand corner of this map.

West African Kingdoms

As Aksum declined, great kingdoms arose on the other side of the continent, in West Africa. The power of these kingdoms was based on the trade of salt and gold. People need salt to survive, especially in hot areas like West Africa. The people of West Africa had no local sources of salt. However, they had plenty of gold. For the people of North Africa, the opposite was true. They had salt, but no gold.

A brisk trade between North Africa and West Africa quickly grew. Control of this trade brought power and riches to three West African kingdoms—Ghana (GAH nuh), Mali (MAH lee), and Songhai (SAWNG hy).

Ghana Look at the map on the previous page. Note that the kingdom of Ghana was located between the Senegal and Niger rivers. From this location Ghana controlled trade across West Africa. Ghana's kings grew rich from the taxes they charged on the salt, gold, and other goods that flowed through their land. The flow of gold was so great that Arab writers called Ghana "land of gold." But in time, Ghana lost control of the trade routes. It gave way to a new power, the kingdom of Mali.

Visualize Visualize the court of the king of Ghana. How would you know you were in the presence of wealth and power?

Mali and the Spread of Islam The kingdom of Mali arose in the mid-1200s in the Upper Niger Valley. The word Mali means "where the king lives." Mali's powerful kings controlled both the gold mines of the south and the salt supplies of the north. In Mali, the king was called Mansa, which means "emperor."

Mali's most famous king, Mansa Musa, gained the throne about 1312. His 25-year reign brought peace and order to the kingdom. An Arab visitor to Mali found "safety throughout the land. The traveler here has no more reason to fear thieves than the man who stays at home."

The Spread of Islam From Arabia, Islam began to spread west through Southwest Asia and North Africa in the 600s. But Islam also spread east—to central Asia, India, Pakistan, Bangladesh, and Indonesia. The Muslim community in the country of Indonesia is one of the largest in the world.

Mansa Musa based his laws on the **Quran** (koo RAHN), the holy book of the religion of Islam. Over the centuries, Muslim traders had spread their religion into many parts of Africa. Muslims are followers of Islam. Mansa Musa and many of his subjects were Muslims.

In 1324, Mansa Musa made a **pilgrimage**—a religious journey—to the Arabian city of Mecca. Muslims consider Mecca a holy place. Muhammad, the prophet who first preached Islam, was born there. Mansa Musa brought 60,000 people with him on his pilgrimage. Eighty camels each carried 300 pounds (136 kg) of gold. Along the way, Mansa Musa gave people gifts of gold.

Mansa Musa's pilgrimage brought about new trading ties with other Muslim states. It also displayed Mali's wealth. Hearing the reports, Europe's rulers grew interested in African gold.

Songhai After Mansa Musa's death around 1332, Mali declined. Mali was finally destroyed by an empire called Songhai. In time, Songhai became West Africa's most powerful kingdom. Songhai's rulers controlled important trade routes and wealthy trading cities.

The wealthiest trading city, Tombouctou (tohn book TOO), also was a great Muslim learning center. People said of Tombouctou:

> "Salt comes from the north, gold from the south, and silver from the city of white men. But the word of God and the treasures of wisdom are only to be found in Tombouctou."

Invaders from North Africa defeated Songhai in 1591. But Songhai people still live near the Niger River, and Islam remains important in the region.

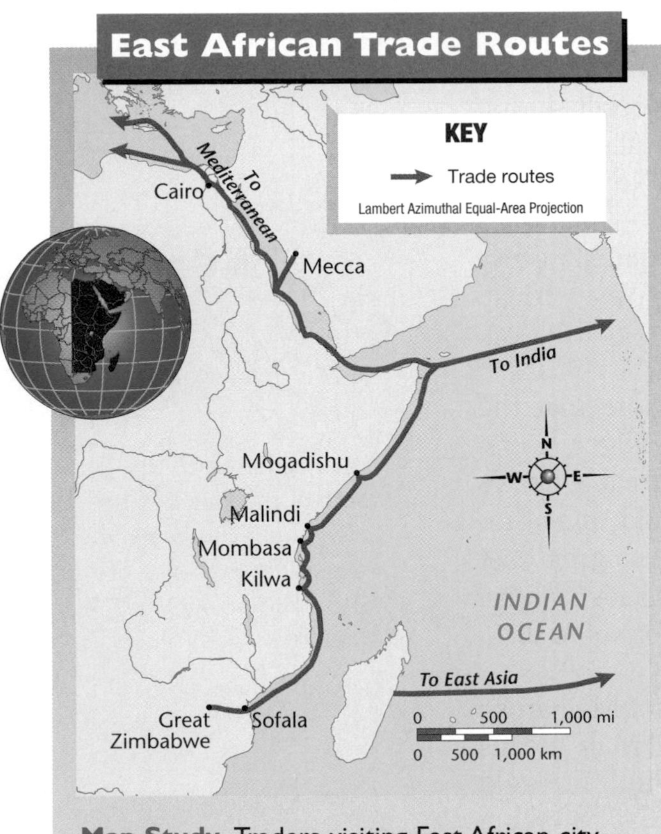

Map Study Traders visiting East African city-states could buy gold from Africa, cotton from India, and porcelain from China. **Location** How were the East African city-states ideally located to become centers of trade?

East African City-States

As in West Africa, trade helped East African cities to develop. Around the time that Aksum declined, trading cities arose along East Africa's coast. Traders from these cities used seasonal winds to sail northeast to India and China. They carried animal skins, ivory, and gold and other metals. When the winds changed direction, the traders sailed with them. They brought many goods, including cotton, silk, and porcelain.

Trade affected the culture of coastal East Africa. Some of the traders who visited the area were Muslims. Many of them settled and introduced Islam to East Africa. In time, a new language developed in the area. Called **Swahili** (swah HEE lee), it

Trade in East Africa

As early as A.D. 1100, traders in East Africa bought and sold goods from many parts of the world. Traders bought animal skins, gold, ivory, or elephant tusks (above left) from Africa, and sold them in India and China.

From India, traders brought back cloth, grain, oil, and sugar. From China, they brought back dishes and vases made of porcelain, a hard substance made by baking clay (above right).

was a Bantu language with some Arab words mixed in. Today, many East Africans still speak Swahili.

Some East African cities grew into powerful city-states. A **city-state** is a city that has its own government and often controls much of the surrounding land. Among the greatest of these city-states were Malindi (muh LIN dee), Mombasa (mahm BAH suh), and Kilwa (KIL wah). Look at the map on the previous page. How do you think the locations of these city-states helped them to become important trade centers?

Kilwa Ibn Batuta (IHB uhn ba TOO tah), a Muslim traveler from North Africa, visited Kilwa in 1331. He had seen great cities in China, India, and West Africa. But Batuta wrote that Kilwa was "one of the most beautiful and best-constructed towns in the world." In Kilwa, people lived in three- and four-story houses made of stone and sea coral.

Kilwa and other East African city-states grew rich from trade and taxes. Traders had to pay huge taxes on goods they brought into the city. "Any merchant who wished to enter the city paid for every five hundred pieces of cloth, no matter what the quality, one gold [piece] as entrance duty," reported one visitor. "After this, the king took two thirds of all the merchandise, leaving the trader one third."

In the early 1500s, Kilwa and the other city-states were conquered by the European country of Portugal. The Portuguese wanted to build their own trading empire.

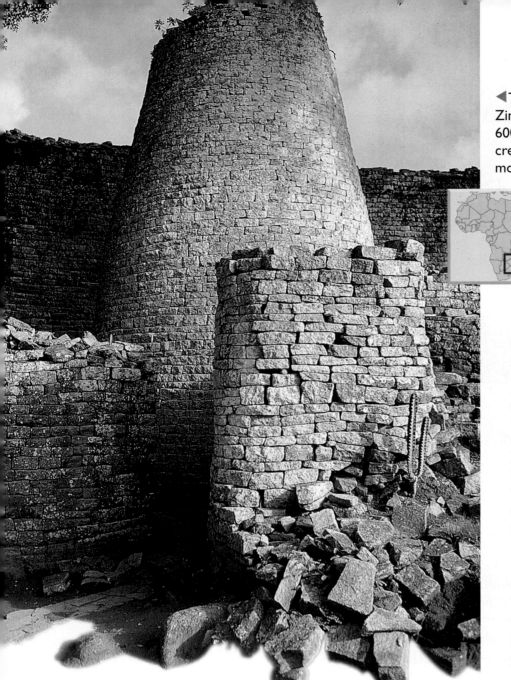

◀The walls of Great Zimbabwe are more than 600 years old. Builders created them without using mortar or cement.

Zimbabwe South and inland from the East African city-states lay another great trading civilization. Great Zimbabwe (zim BAH bway) was located near the bend of the Limpopo (lim POH poh) River in Southern Africa. Great Zimbabwe reached its peak about the year 1300. Today only ruins of it remain. But once, more than 200 gigantic stone buildings covered the area. (Great Zimbabwe means "stone dwelling.")

Upon seeing the ruins in the late 1800s, European explorers did not think that Africans had the skill to build them. They were wrong. The builders were the Shona, a group of Bantu speakers who had lived in the region since the 900s.

1. Define (a) Quran, (b) pilgrimage, (c) Swahili, (d) city-state.

2. Identify (a) Mansa Musa, (b) Aksum, (c) Ghana, (d) Mali, (e) Songhai, (f) Tombouctou, (g) Kilwa, (h) Zimbabwe.

3. On what was the wealth and power of the city-states based?

4. How did Islam become a major religion in West and East Africa?

Critical Thinking

5. Drawing Conclusions How did Ghana, Mali, and Songhai become wealthy from gold and salt even though they did not mine either one?

Activity

6. Writing to Learn You are a traveler visiting one of the West African kingdoms or city-states. Write a short letter home about some of the things you see.

The Conquest of Africa

Reach Into Your Background

What actions would you take to get something you really wanted? What would you do to hold on to something that was already yours?

Questions to Explore

1. Why did European contact with Africa increase?
2. What were the effects of European rule in Africa?

Key Terms

colonize

Key People and Places

Gorée
Cape of Good Hope
Olaudah Equiano

On the island of Gorée (gaw RAY), off the coast of the West African country of Senegal, stands a museum called the House of Slaves. It honors millions of Africans who were enslaved and shipped across the Atlantic Ocean. Many Africans passed through this building. Their last view of Africa was an opening called "The Door of No Return." Beyond it lay the ocean and the slave ships bound for the Americas.

Europeans on the Coast

The Atlantic slave trade began in the 1500s and continued through the late 1800s. But contact between Europeans and Africans began long before that. In North Africa, Europeans traded for gold from the empires of Ghana and Mali, and for salt from the Sahara. Why do you think Europeans' first contacts with Africans took place in North Africa?

After 1500, Europe's relationship with Africa changed. It had begun as trade between equals. But it turned into the enslavement and forced migration of millions of Africans. The African slave trade ended in the 1800s. Then Europeans wanted Africa's natural resources. By 1900, European countries had divided Africa among themselves.

▼The Door of No Return in Senegal led to a pier, where slave ships were waiting to sail to the Americas.

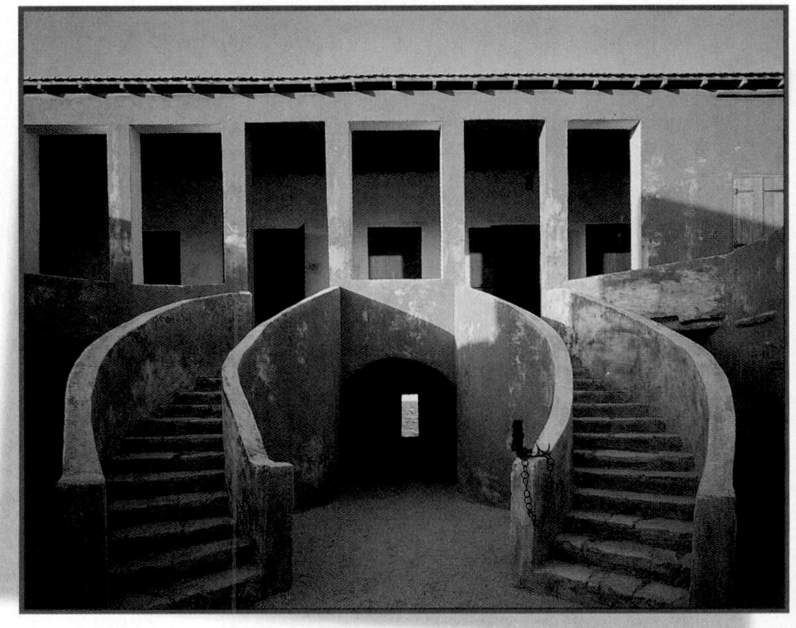

Europeans and the Americas Christopher Columbus sailed extensively along the coast of western Africa. He traveled several times to the Portuguese trading post in the Gold Coast. On these journeys, he sometimes found pieces of wood floating from the west. These signs helped to convince Columbus that there was land to the west. Such convictions increased his desire to take the journey westward.

In the 1400s, Portuguese explorers began exploring the coast of West Africa. They wanted to trade directly for West African gold and ivory, instead of dealing with North African merchants. They also wanted to trade with Asia.

Many inventions helped the Portuguese explore Africa's coast. The Portuguese used a lateen sail, a triangle-shaped sail designed in North Africa. The lateen sail allowed ships to sail against the wind as well as with it. And better instruments, such as the astrolabe (AS troh layb), helped sailors navigate at sea. With these improvements, Portuguese sailors became the first Europeans to travel south along Africa's coasts.

At first, both Africans and Europeans traded together as equals. Africans traded gold, cotton, ivory, skins, metal objects, and pepper. In return, Europeans traded copper, brass, and clothing. Europeans brought corn, cassava, and yams from the Americas. These plants became food crops in Africa. Some Africans also became Christians.

But soon this balance was upset. In 1498, three Portuguese ships rounded the tip of Southern Africa and sailed north along Africa's east coast. The wealth of the East African city-states amazed the Portuguese. More Portuguese ships followed—not to trade but to seize the riches of the city-states. Portugal controlled trade on East Africa's coast until well into the 1600s.

The Dutch, French, and English soon followed the Portuguese. They set up trading posts along Africa's coasts, where sailors could get supplies. The Dutch built a trading post on the Cape of Good Hope at Africa's southern tip. Soon, settlers arrived. They moved inland, building homes and farms.

▼ In 1482, the Portuguese built this fort, Elmina Castle, in Ghana to protect and supply its trade with West Africa.

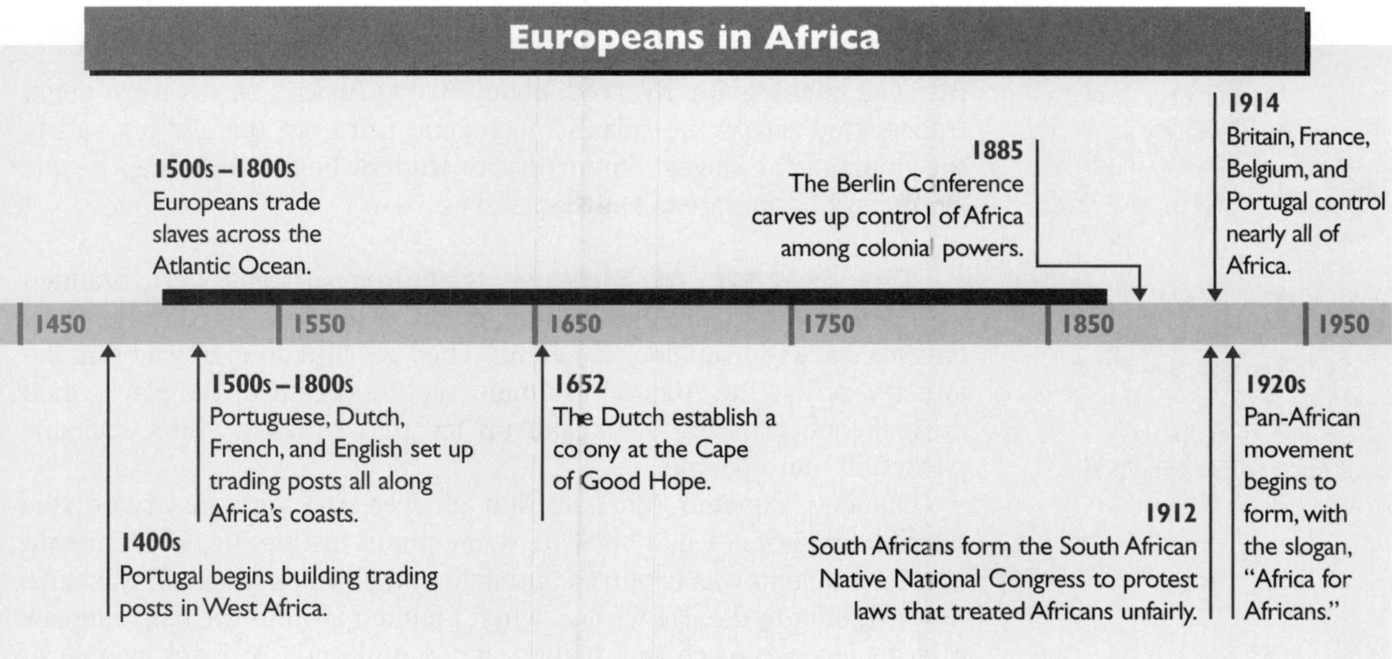
Europeans in Africa
1500s–1800s
Europeans trade slaves across the Atlantic Ocean.
1885
The Berlin Conference carves up control of Africa among colonial powers.
1914
Britain, France, Belgium, and Portugal control nearly all of Africa.
1450
1550
1650
1750
1850
1950
1500s–1800s
Portuguese, Dutch, French, and English set up trading posts all along Africa's coasts.
1652
The Dutch establish a colony at the Cape of Good Hope.
1400s
Portugal begins building trading posts in West Africa.
1912
South Africans form the South African Native National Congress to protest laws that treated Africans unfairly.
1920s
Pan-African movement begins to form, with the slogan, "Africa for Africans."

▲ Africans resisted European colonization, but, as this time line shows, Europe slowly took control of more and more of Africa. Why do you think it was possible for Europeans to colonize Africa?

As Europeans spread out, sometimes by force, their relations with Africans worsened. But the growing trade in enslaved Africans poisoned future contacts between Africans and Europeans the most.

The Atlantic Slave Trade

Before the 1500s, slavery was common in Africa. But slaves usually won their freedom after a few years. Some became important citizens among the people who had enslaved them. Slaves could even be bought out of slavery by their own people.

Then the European powers began to build colonies in North and South America. They practiced a new type of slavery there. The Europeans treated slaves like property, not like people. Freedom in the future was out of the question. The African slave trade did not end until the 1800s. By then, millions of Africans had been taken from their homelands, never to return.

The Demand for Slaves Spanish, Portuguese, and Dutch settlers in the Americas needed workers for their plantations and mines. At first they enslaved Native Americans. But many Native Americans became sick and died from diseases or brutal working conditions. Others ran away. To replace them, the Europeans started to import enslaved Africans.

The Europeans thought that Africans would make good slaves. Africa's climate was similar to that of the Americas. Africans were skilled farmers, miners, and metal workers. They also did not know the territory. It would be almost impossible for them to escape.

By the 1600s, Portuguese traders were trading goods for African slaves. Some African groups refused to join the trade. But other groups sold slaves captured during battles. In return, the Europeans gave the Africans cheap guns. By 1780, about 80,000 African slaves were being transported across the Atlantic each year. But even this did not satisfy the demand for slaves. Some African leaders began to kidnap people from neighboring areas to sell as slaves.

Visualize Visualize the inside of a slave ship. What do you think it would have been like to cross the Atlantic in these conditions?

The Horror of Slavery Captured Africans were branded with hot irons. In the slave ships, captives lay side by side on filthy shelves stacked from floor to ceiling. They got little food or water on the journey across the Atlantic. As many as 20 percent of the slaves died during each crossing. To make up for these losses, ships' captains packed in more people.

Olaudah Equiano (oh LOW duh ek wee AHN oh), described this horrible experience in a book he wrote about his life. In 1756, at about age 11, Equiano was captured and sold at a slave auction. He was sure he was going to die. He wrote, "when I looked around the ship and saw a large furnace of copper boiling and a multitude of black people of every description chained together . . . I no longer doubted of my fate."

Equiano proved luckier than most African slaves. In time, he was able to buy his freedom. For most slaves, freedom was little more than a distant dream.

The Cramped Journey Across the Atlantic

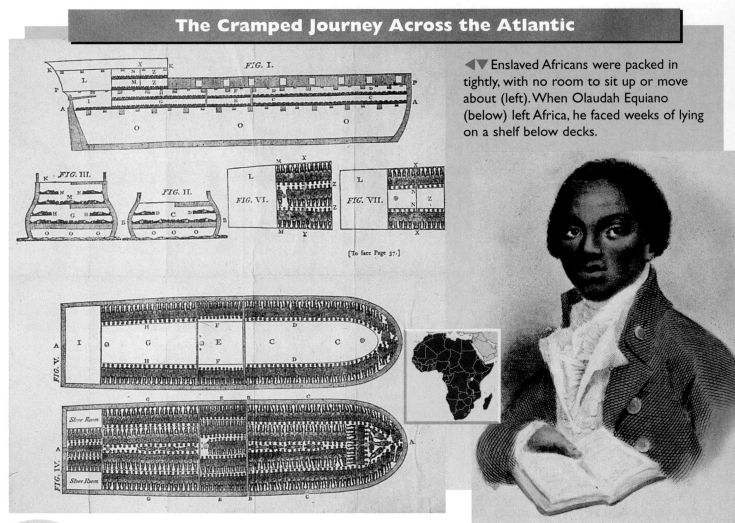

◀▼ Enslaved Africans were packed in tightly, with no room to sit up or move about (left). When Olaudah Equiano (below) left Africa, he faced weeks of lying on a shelf below decks.

The Effects of Slavery on Africa Some Africans grew wealthy from the slave trade. The slave trade, however, was a disaster for West Africa. The region lost more than a large number of its population to slavery. It lost many of its youngest, healthiest, and most capable people. Robbed of their families and their skilled workers, many African societies were torn apart.

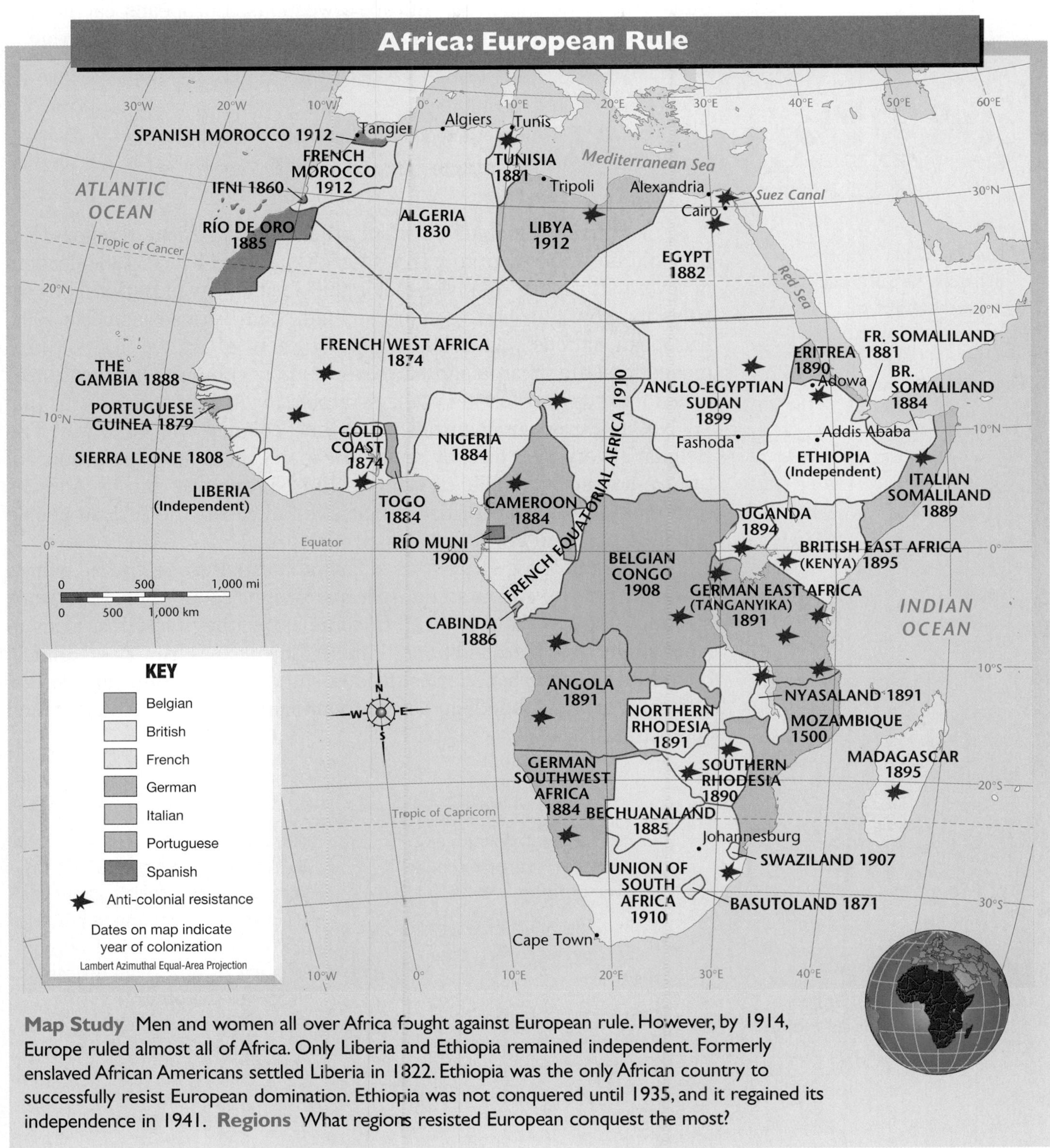

Map Study Men and women all over Africa fought against European rule. However, by 1914, Europe ruled almost all of Africa. Only Liberia and Ethiopia remained independent. Formerly enslaved African Americans settled Liberia in 1822. Ethiopia was the only African country to successfully resist European domination. Ethiopia was not conquered until 1935, and it regained its independence in 1941. **Regions** What regions resisted European conquest the most?

Europeans Carve Up Africa

After the slave trade ended, Europeans then began to raid Africa's interior for resources. They wanted the resources to fuel the new factories that were springing up all across Europe. Europeans also saw Africa as a place to build empires.

Africans fiercely resisted European conquest. But their cheap guns proved no match for Europe's weapons. Europeans carried the Maxim gun, the first automatic machine gun. A British author wrote at the time:

> "Whatever happens we have got
> The Maxim-gun; and they have not."

Ask Questions What questions do you have about the effect of European colonization on the people of Africa?

Europeans competed with each other to gain African territory. But they did not want to go to war with each other over it. In 1884, leaders of several European countries met in the German city of Berlin. They set rules for how European countries could claim African land. By 1900, European nations had colonized many parts of Africa. To **colonize** means to settle an area and take over its government. One newspaper called this rush for territory "the scramble for Africa."

Not all European countries ruled their colonies the same way. The Belgian government directly ran the Belgian Congo (now the country of the Democratic Republic of Congo). But Nigeria was run by Africans who took orders from British officials. In all cases, the African people had little power in government.

The scramble for Africa caused lasting harm. Europeans had gained power in part by encouraging Africans to fight each other. Europeans also took the best land to farm. In some areas, they forced Africans to labor under terrible conditions. Finally, Europeans drew new political boundaries. These boundaries divided some ethnic groups and forced differing groups together. These boundaries were to cause much conflict in Africa.

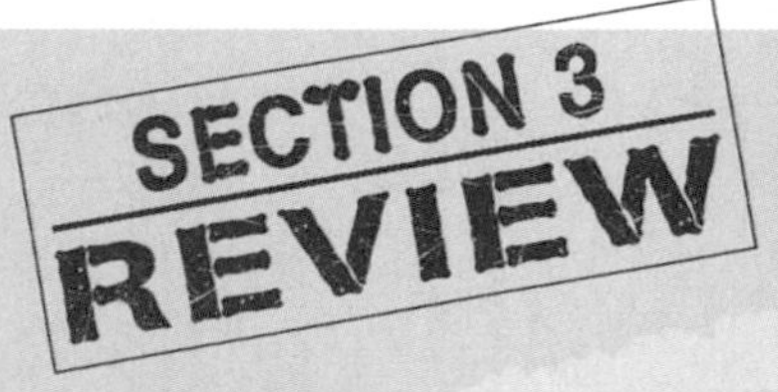

1. **Define** colonize.
2. **Identify** (a) Gorée, (b) Cape of Good Hope, (c) Olaudah Equiano.
3. How did relations between Africa and Europe change over time?
4. In what different ways did the Europeans govern their African colonies?

Critical Thinking

5. **Identifying Central Issues** How did the European conquest affect Africa?

Activity

6. **Writing to Learn** Write two brief editorials about the European conference in Berlin. Write one editorial from the point of view of an African. Write the other from the point of view of a European who attended the conference.

Independence and Its Challenges

Reach Into Your Background

People have different ideas about what independence means. For some, it means having the freedom to make their own decisions. What does independence mean to you?

Questions to Explore

1. What techniques did African nations use to win independence from European powers?
2. What challenges did new African leaders face after independence?

Key Terms

nationalism
Pan-Africanism
boycott
democracy

Key People

Robert Mugabe
Léopold Sédar Senghor
Kwame Nkrumah

On April 18, 1980, the people of Rhodesia took to the streets. They had recently elected Robert Gabriel Mugabe (mu GAHB ee) as Prime Minister. It was the first free election in Rhodesia's history. People waited excitedly through the night. At midnight, the British flag came down for the last time. People cheered loudly. At that moment, the British colony of Rhodesia became the independent country of Zimbabwe.

The fight for independence had been hard and sometimes violent. Now, Prime Minister Mugabe asked all the people to work together. They would have to build a new nation. "The wrongs of the past must now stand forgiven and forgotten," said Mugabe. Zimbabwe was one of the last African countries to win independence. But the movement for freedom in Zimbabwe had begun many years before.

▼ Zimbabwe's flag went up for the first time when the country became independent of Great Britain.

The Growth of Nationalism

Many Africans dreamed of independence after Europe's scramble for Africa in the late 1800s. In 1897, Mankayi Sontanga (mun KY ee suhn TAHN guh) put this dream to music. His song, called "Bless, O Lord, Our Land of Africa," expressed the growing nationalism of Africans. **Nationalism** is a feeling of pride in one's homeland.

Education and Nationalism Many African leaders worked to encourage pride in being African. The colonial powers had drawn political borders that brought together many ethnic groups. Some of these groups were old rivals. African leaders saw that to end colonial rule, they would have to build a spirit of togetherness.

Nationalism grew during the early 1900s. In 1912, Africans in South Africa formed a political party. Today this party is the African National Congress (ANC). Party members protested laws that limited the rights of black South Africans. Five years later, African lawyers in British West Africa formed the West African National Congress. This group also worked to gain rights for Africans, including the right to vote.

LINKS ACROSS THE WORLD

The Right to Vote African Americans have also struggled to win the right to vote. By law, African American men received the right to vote in 1870. African American women received the right to vote at the same time as other American women, in 1920. But violence often prevented African Americans from exercising their right to vote. Change came about slowly as the result of a nonviolent social movement. Today, African Americans can exercise their right to vote in peace.

Pan-Africanism In the 1920s, Africans formed a movement called **Pan-Africanism.** This movement stressed unity and cooperation among all Africans. Pan-African leaders tried to unify all Africans, whether they lived in Africa or not. Their slogan was "Africa for Africans." The movement won many supporters.

One of the greatest leaders of Pan-Africanism was Léopold Sédar Senghor (san GAWR) of Senegal. Senghor was a poet as well as a political leader. He encouraged Africans to look carefully at their traditions. They should be proud of their culture, he said. Senegal became independent in 1960, and Senghor became its first president.

Pan-Africanism in the U.S.

W.E.B. Du Bois was one of the first leaders of the movement to gain equal rights for African Americans in the United States. Du Bois also was an early leader of the Pan-African movement. He worked with African leaders, such as Jomo Kenyatta and Kwame Nkrumah, to make plans for African countries to become independent.

Fighting for Democracy in World War II

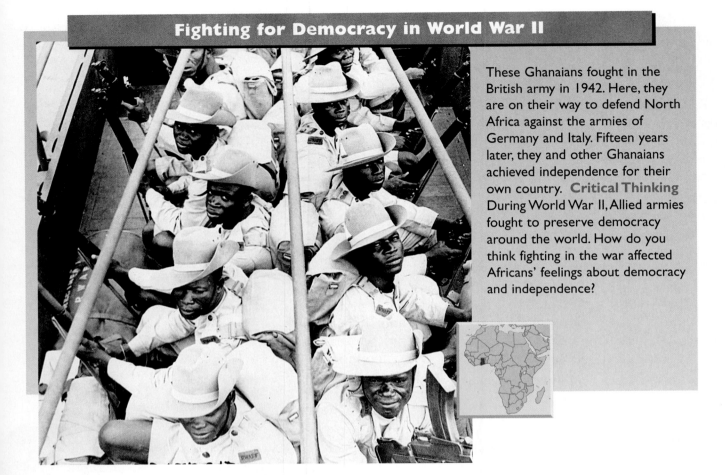

These Ghanaians fought in the British army in 1942. Here, they are on their way to defend North Africa against the armies of Germany and Italy. Fifteen years later, they and other Ghanaians achieved independence for their own country. **Critical Thinking** During World War II, Allied armies fought to preserve democracy around the world. How do you think fighting in the war affected Africans' feelings about democracy and independence?

World War II

A major boost to African independence came unexpectedly in the 1930s and 1940s, out of the global conflict called World War II. A group called the Allies included Great Britain, France, and the United States. They fought the armies of Germany, Italy, and Japan, who were invading much of the world. German and Italian forces invaded North Africa.

Africa played a huge role in support of the Allies. The colonies supplied metals for guns and other equipment. Allied planes used their airfields to move supplies into Asia. African soldiers fought and died to help free Europe from conquest. About 80,000 soldiers from Tanganyika alone served in the British Army.

Africans came home victorious. Now, they wanted their own freedom. One soldier said, "We have been told what we fought for. That is 'freedom.' We want freedom, nothing but freedom."

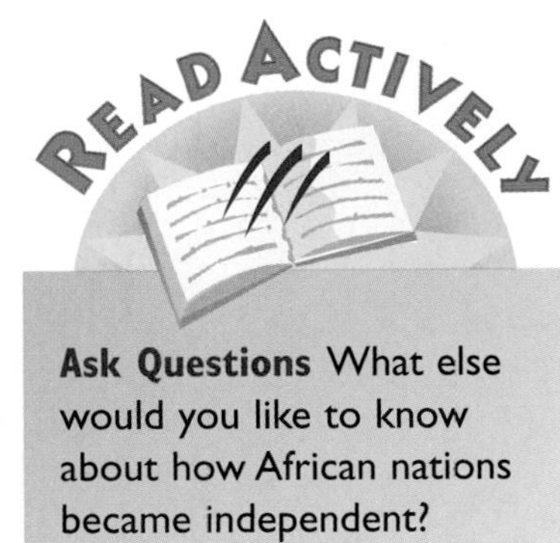

Ask Questions What else would you like to know about how African nations became independent?

Different Paths to Independence

The war not only inspired Africans to win their freedom. It also weakened colonial powers like Great Britain. Many people in Britain felt that they could no longer afford a colonial empire. The United States and the Soviet Union—Britain's allies during the war—began to speak out against colonialism.

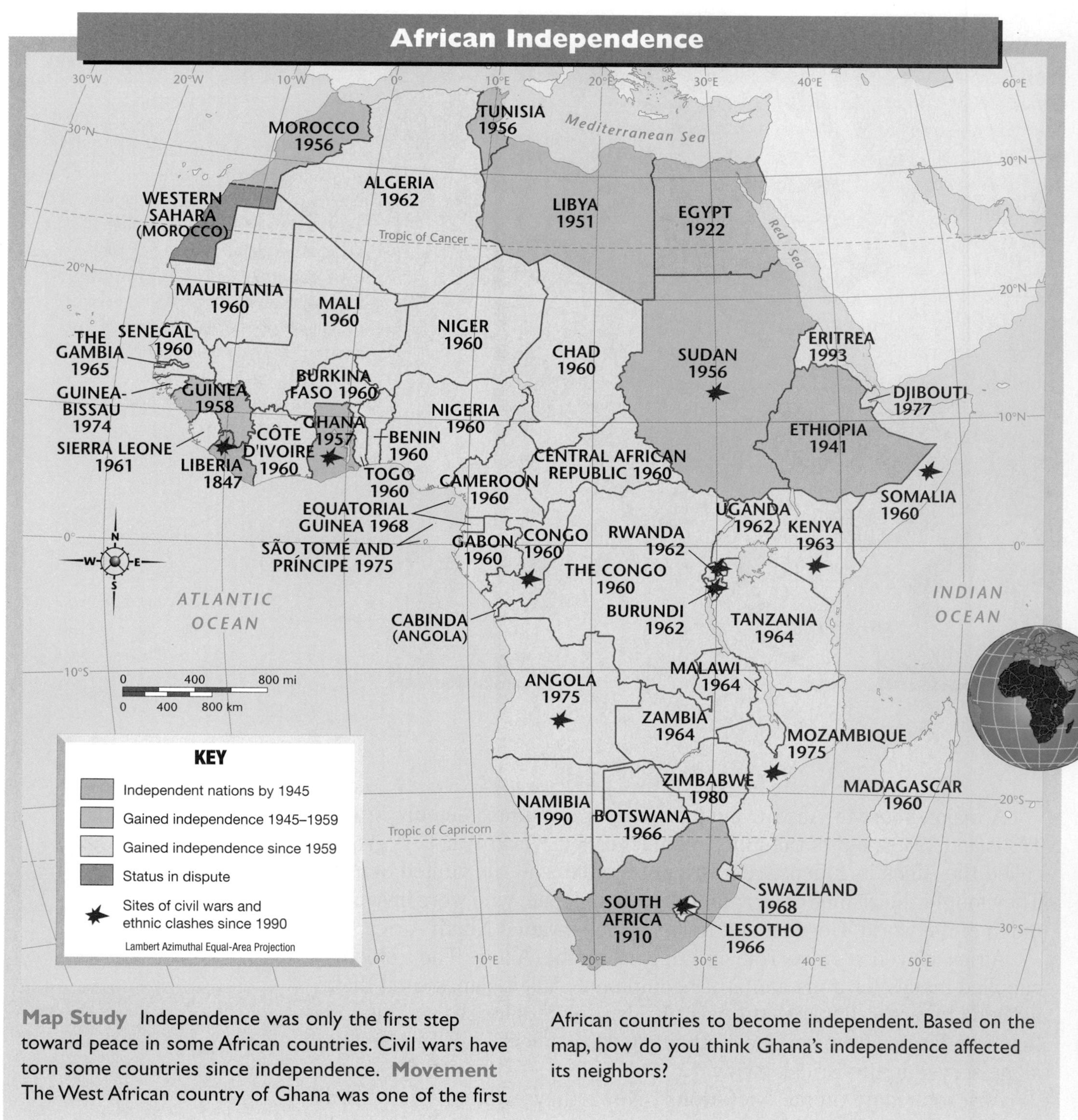

African Independence

Map Study Independence was only the first step toward peace in some African countries. Civil wars have torn some countries since independence. **Movement** The West African country of Ghana was one of the first African countries to become independent. Based on the map, how do you think Ghana's independence affected its neighbors?

British leader Harold Macmillan realized that Britain would not be able to keep its African colonies. "The winds of change are blowing across Africa," he said. Soon, European countries began to give up their African colonies.

Some colonial powers let go willingly, while others fought to keep power. Ghana won its independence from Britain peacefully. But Algeria, a former French colony, had to fight for its freedom.

From Gold Coast to Ghana In the British West African colony of the Gold Coast, Kwame Nkrumah organized protests against British rule in the early 1950s. These protests took the peaceful form of strikes and boycotts. In a **boycott,** people refuse to buy or use certain products or services. The British threw Nkrumah in jail for his actions. But the protests continued without him. In 1957, he achieved his goal: independence for the Gold Coast. The country took the new name of Ghana, after the great trading kingdom that lasted until the 1200s. It was a name that recalled Africa's earlier greatness. Released from prison, Nkrumah became Ghana's first president in 1960.

War in Algeria The French people who had settled in Algeria thought of it as more than a colony. To them, it was part of France. Algerians disagreed. They were willing to fight for the right to govern themselves. A bloody war began in Algeria in 1954. The eight-year struggle cost the lives of 100,000 Algerians and 10,000 French. But by 1962, the Algerians had won.

The Challenges of Independence Africa's new leaders had spent many years working for independence. But they had little experience actually governing a country. The colonial powers had rarely allowed Africans to share in government. And even after agreeing to independence, the colonial powers did little to prepare the new leaders. As a result, some new governments in Africa were not very stable.

In some African countries, military leaders took control of the government by force. Military governments are not always fair. The people often have few rights. Further, citizens may be jailed if they protest. But this form of government has held together some African countries that otherwise would have been torn apart by war.

Other African countries have a long history of democracy. In a **democracy,** citizens help to make governmental decisions. Some countries have made traditional ways a part of governing. For example, in Botswana, lively political debates take place in "freedom squares." These outdoor meetings are like the traditional *kgotla* (KUHT luh), in which people talk with their leaders.

▼ Children wave goodbye to the British governor shortly after Ghana became independent.

Gambians Celebrate Independence

The Gambia won its independence from Great Britain through peaceful elections in 1965. Schoolchildren celebrate Gambian independence every year. **Critical Thinking** How is this celebration similar to Fourth of July celebrations in the United States?

Connect The United States is a democratic country. How does democracy in the United States affect you?

Most African countries are less than 50 years old. In contrast, the stable, democratic country of the United States is over 200 years old. Many Africans feel that building stable countries will take time. One leader commented, "Let Africa be given the time to develop its own system of democracy."

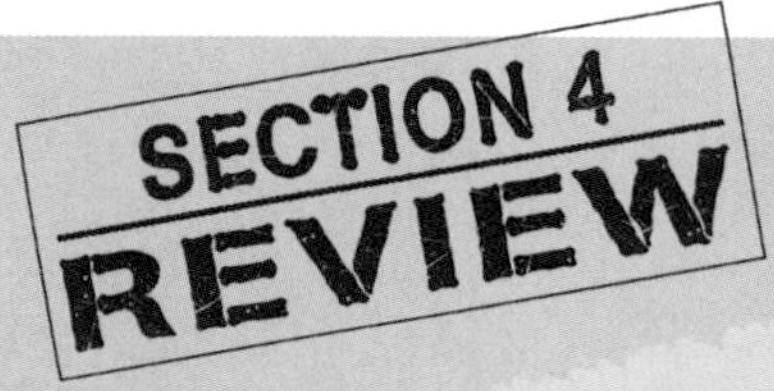

1. **Define** (a) nationalism, (b) Pan-Africanism, (c) boycott (d) democracy.
2. **Identify** (a) Robert Mugabe, (b) Léopold Sédar Senghor, (c) Kwame Nkrumah.
3. Compare Ghana's road to independence to that of Algeria.
4. In what ways did colonial rule cause problems for African countries after independence?

Critical Thinking

5. **Recognizing Cause and Effect** How did World War II boost the independence movement in Africa?

Activity

6. **Writing to Learn** Research one African country that won its independence after 1950. Write a headline and a short article for a newspaper that might have appeared on the day your country became independent. Compile all the articles from your class to create a bulletin board display about African independence.

Issues for Africa Today

Reach Into Your Background

As you have grown, you have become more independent. What challenges are you facing as you grow older? How have you met your challenges?

Questions to Explore

1. What challenges do African countries face today?
2. What actions may help Africans meet some of their challenges?

Key Terms

commercial farming
hybrid
literacy
life expectancy

Key Places

Niger
Senegal

In the past, nothing grew during the dry season in the Sahel. Farmers had to travel to cities to find work. Now, the West African country of Niger has a new irrigation program. This makes it possible for farmers to grow a second crop during the dry season. Farmer Adamou Sani (AH duh moo SAH nee) says that raising two crops a year means that he can stay on village land.

> "Dry-season crops are such a normal practice now that everyone grows them. Before, each year after the harvest, I went to the city to look for work. But today, with the dry-season crops, I have work in the village. Truly it is a good thing."

▼ Farmers in Niger use irrigation canals to bring water from the Niger River to their crops.

Niger's irrigation program is one way Africans are improving their lives. Africans are also finding ways to meet economic, social, and environmental challenges.

Economic Issues

The colonial powers saw Africa as a source of raw materials and a market for their own manufactured goods. They did little to build factories in Africa. African countries still have little industry. Most economies are based on farming and mining.

A South African Gold Mine

South Africa's gold miners work day and night in a mammoth mine more than two miles underground. South Africa produces more than half the world's gold. The gold from this mine will make jewelry, coins—and even teeth—for people around the world. What do you think it would be like to work in a gold mine?

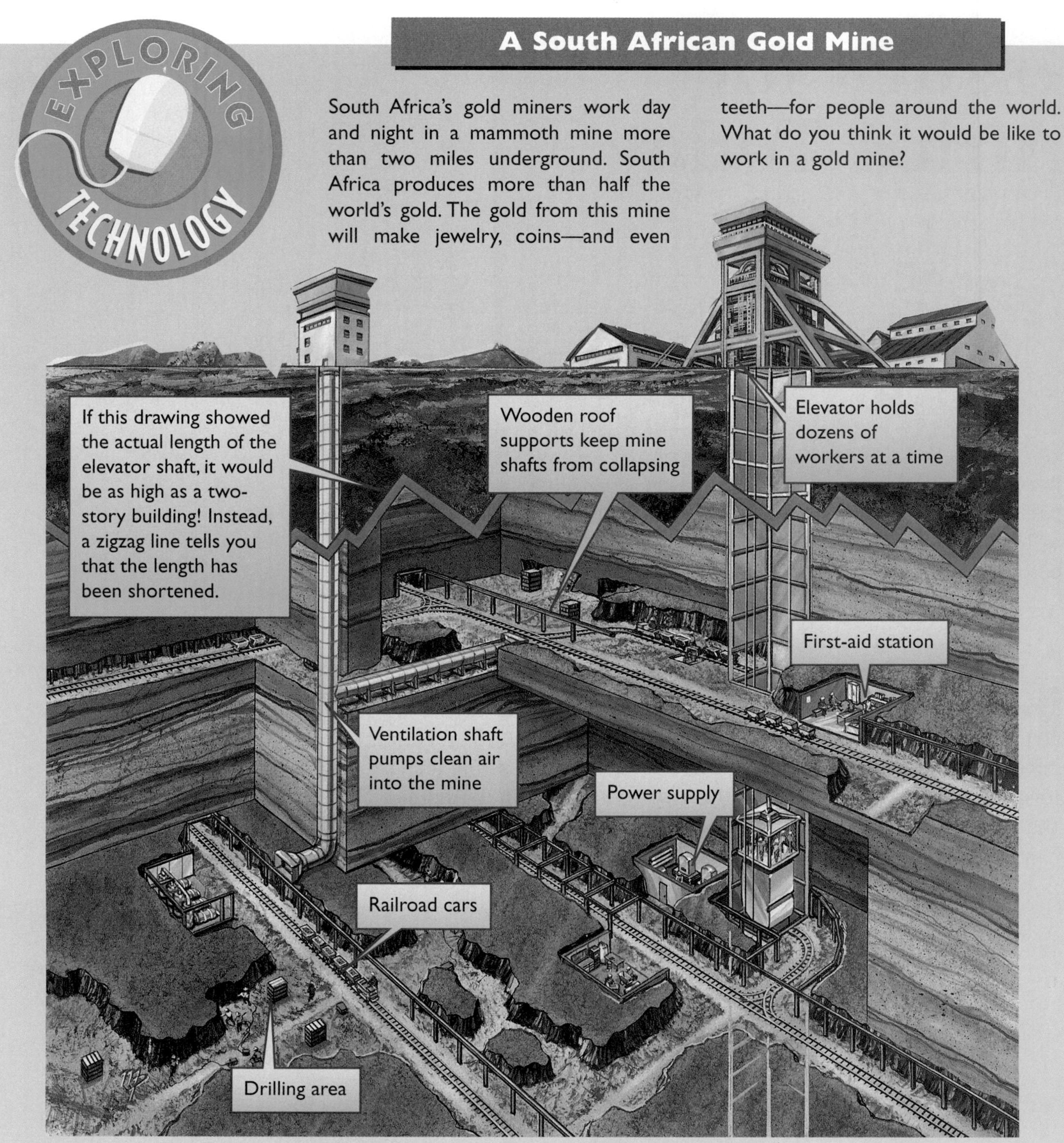

EXPLORING TECHNOLOGY
If this drawing showed the actual length of the elevator shaft, it would be as high as a two-story building! Instead, a zigzag line tells you that the length has been shortened.
Wooden roof supports keep mine shafts from collapsing
Elevator holds dozens of workers at a time
First-aid station
Ventilation shaft pumps clean air into the mine
Power supply
Railroad cars
Drilling area

Farming and Mining Farming is the most important activity in Africa. About 75 percent of workers are farmers. And more than half of what Africa sells overseas are farm goods. Africans practice two kinds of farming—subsistence and commercial. With subsistence farming, farmers work small plots of land. They raise just as much food as their families need. **Commercial farming** is the large-scale production of cash crops such as coffee, cocoa, and bananas for sale.

Many African nations have rich mineral resources. They export minerals to other countries. Nigeria has oil and coal. Congo and Zambia have copper, while South Africa has gold. Look at the diagram on the previous page. How does South Africa produce its gold?

Economic Challenges About 75 percent of African countries have economies that are specialized—they depend on exporting one or two products. The Gambia depends on peanuts, while Zambia relies on the export of copper. As a result, African economies are sensitive to the rise and fall of world prices. A fall in prices hurts economies that depend on the sale of one crop or mineral.

African countries are now trying to depend less on one export. They are trying to diversify their economies. For example, Senegal became independent in 1960. At the time, it earned more than 80 percent of its money by exporting peanuts. Today, Senegal has other industries such as fishing, fish processing, and mining. Peanuts account for only 9 percent of the money Senegal makes from exports.

World Copper Prices

Year	Cents Per Pound (kg)
1990	123.16 (271.52)
1991	109.33 (241.03)
1992	107.42 (237.01)
1993	91.56 (208.86)
1994	111.05 (244.82)
1995	138.33 (304.97)
1996	109.04 (240.39)
1997	106.92 (235.72)
1998	78.64 (173.37)

Source: United States Geological Survey

Chart Study Congo and Zambia both rely on copper mining for most of their income. Copper is used to make coins, wire, tubes, and jewelry. **Critical Thinking** Based on these prices, what challenges do you think might face a country that gets most of its income from selling copper?

African nations face another economic problem—how to feed a growing population. Many governments are trying to help farmers grow more. One method they use is to develop hybrid plants. A **hybrid** is made by combining different types of the same plant. In the early 1980s, farmers in Zimbabwe who grew hybrid corn doubled their harvests. Today, most of Zimbabwe's corn comes from hybrids.

Predict What problems do you think can arise when a nation depends on one crop or resource?

Social Issues

African nations also must provide social services to a growing population. In the areas of health care and education, many African nations are working to keep their traditions alive while adapting to the modern world.

Education African children must often add to their family's income by working on family farms or selling goods in the market. When girls and boys go to school, families sacrifice. But many Africans gladly make this sacrifice in order to improve their lives.

▶ How is this school in Zimbabwe similar to your school? How is it different?

In South Africa, parents often help to build new schools. Even so, the schools are often overcrowded. As a result, students take turns attending. The headmaster at one such school said that students "who couldn't cram into the desks knelt on the floor or stood on their toes so as not to miss a word the teacher was saying."

The number of people who can read and write varies from country to country. But in all countries, more people have learned to read since independence. When the Portuguese left Mozambique in 1975, only 10 percent of the people in Mozambique were literate. **Literacy** is the ability to read and write. Today about 40 percent of the people are literate. In Tanzania, progress has been even more dramatic. At the time of independence only 15 percent of Tanzania's people were literate. Today, about 68 percent of Tanzanians can read and write.

Virtual Eritrea Eritrea is a country in East Africa along the Red Sea. It won independence from Ethiopia in 1993. Now, Eritreans are using Internet technology to help them meet the challenges of self-rule. They have formed Dehai, an on-line community. Dehai is an Internet newsgroup. About 500 Eritreans living in other countries use Dehai to discuss issues related to Eritrea's new constitution.

Health Like literacy, **life expectancy**—how long an average person will live—differs from country to country. In Morocco, life expectancy is between 67 and 71 years. In Southern Africa, however, the average life expectancy is under 50 years. In the Southern African country of Botswana, it is only 40 years.

The main reason for low life expectancy in Africa is disease. Insects spread diseases such as malaria. Unclean drinking water and living conditions help spread other diseases. Viruses, or tiny germs, spread diseases like measles and AIDS. AIDS is caused by a virus, called HIV. This virus attacks healthy cells in people's bodies. People with AIDS get very sick, and often die.

Though AIDS exists around the world, it is the worst in Southern Africa. Many people who are poor cannot afford drugs that might help them. Many people have not had access to education, so they could not learn how to prevent the disease. In Southern Africa, millions of people have died from AIDS. Millions more are sick because of it. African governments are working with the World Health Organization and other groups. Together, they work to prevent and treat AIDS, and overcome other health problems.

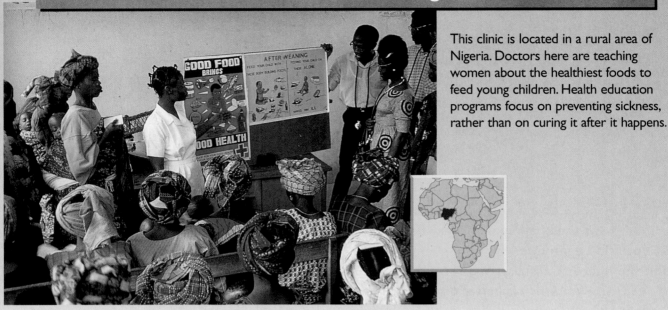

This clinic is located in a rural area of Nigeria. Doctors here are teaching women about the healthiest foods to feed young children. Health education programs focus on preventing sickness, rather than on curing it after it happens.

The Environment

Like the United States, Africa faces a number of environmental challenges. About two thirds of Africa is desert or dry land. And more and more of Africa is turning into desert. Forests are being cut down, which causes soil to wash away. This reduces the amount of land on which food can be grown. This, in turn, threatens many Africans with starvation.

But science can help feed Africans and save Africa's environment. Irrigation projects, hybrids, and vegetation that holds water in the ground have all increased crop harvests. To fight soil erosion, farmers in Nigeria now plant food crops such as yams in long rows. Between the rows they plant trees that hold the soil in place.

African nations still face many challenges. They are meeting them by using their resources, increasing education, and keeping traditions alive in a changing world.

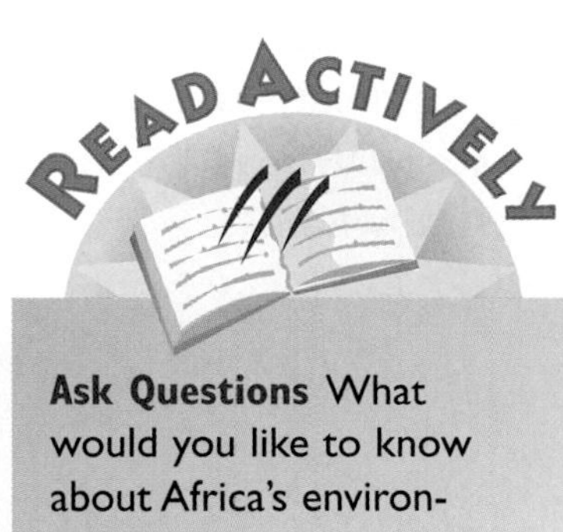

Ask Questions What would you like to know about Africa's environment?

1. **Define** (a) commercial farming, (b) hybrid, (c) literacy, (d) life expectancy.
2. **Identify** (a) Niger, (b) Senegal.
3. Why are African nations trying to diversify their economies?
4. List two challenges African countries face and describe the steps African countries are taking to meet these challenges.

Critical Thinking

5. **Drawing Conclusions** In what ways have Africans shown the high value they place on education?

Activity

6. **Writing to Learn** You are the economic adviser to the president of an African country. Write a brief report on some steps the president might take to improve the economy.

Recognizing Bias

When Latisha got to class, she looked at the chalkboard. Every day, Mr. Copeland began class by writing something on the board to discuss:

Life in West Africa is better than life in North Africa.

"Well, class? What do you think about that?" Mr. Copeland asked.

Latisha wondered how someone decided what made life better in one place than another. She raised her hand.

"That statement does not tell the whole story! Whose life are you talking about? And when?"

Mr. Copeland smiled. "Latisha, you've hit the nail on the head. The statement on the board does not tell the whole story—it may even be completely untrue. It shows you an example of *bias*."

Get Ready

To be biased is to lean to a particular point of view. Sometimes, people who write about something only know one side of the story.

Other people leave out information on purpose to give their own viewpoint. Biased writing takes a side, even if at first it seems not to.

You need to be able to recognize bias in writing. It is the only way you can know whether you're getting a fair picture of a situation. When you read, you can look for certain clues that will point out a writer's bias.

Try It Out

To determine whether a writer is biased, do the following:

A. Look for opinions. Opinions are beliefs that cannot be proved. They are the opposite of facts, which can be proved. Biased writing often contains opinions disguised as facts. For example, the statement "Life in West Africa is better than life in North Africa" may sound like a fact, but it is an opinion.

B. Look for loaded words and phrases. Loaded words and phrases carry a hidden meaning. They give a positive or negative impression. Read this sentence: "The coastline of Nigeria is so beautiful it takes your breath away." The words "so beautiful it takes your breath away" are loaded. They give a very positive impression. However, this hidden meaning cannot be proved. It is not fact.

C. Look for what isn't there. Biased writers often leave out information that does not support their bias. For example, the writer might say "the Mali empire failed," but leave out the fact that before it declined, it succeeded for centuries.

◀ Everything you read was written by someone. You need to use your skills to sort out whether or not to believe what the writer says.

D. Think about the tone. Tone is the overall feeling of a piece of writing. It shows the writer's attitude toward the subject: "From burning desert to steamy tropics, the climates of Africa are unbearable." This sentence gives you the clear impression that the writer has negative feelings about the climates of Africa. Unbiased writing provides the facts and lets the reader form his or her own conclusions.

Apply the Skill

The selection in the box is a biased, one-paragraph description of the early African empire of Ghana. To spot the bias, follow steps A through D. Consider these questions: Are there any opinions disguised as facts in the selection? What words give a positive or negative impression of the West African kingdoms? What important facts about West African kingdoms does the writer fail to include? How would you describe the tone of the writing? Positive? Negative? After you have finished, describe the West African kingdoms in one paragraph without bias.

West African Kingdoms

Between the 3500s and the 1500s, West Africa was a terrible place to live. People couldn't even survive without salt. They were forced to trade their most precious gold just to get enough salt to stay alive. In the kingdom of Ghana, the kings forced people to pay money just to carry salt, gold, and other goods through the land. The Ghanaian kingdom became so weak that it fell to the crushing power of the kingdom of Mali.

Review and Activities

Reviewing Main Ideas

1. List some of the ways in which early Africans made a living.
2. What were Africa's earliest civilizations like?
3. List several effects of the Bantu migrations.
4. How did Africa's kingdoms and city-states become wealthy?
5. (a) How did the relationship of Europeans and Africans begin? (b) How did it change?
6. Explain two effects of the Atlantic slave trade on Africa.
7. What factors helped lead to independence for many African countries?
8. Describe two types of government used in African countries after independence.
9. How are Africans working to improve their economies?
10. How are Africans working to improve social conditions?

Reviewing Key Terms

Use each key term below in a sentence that shows the meaning of the term.

1. hunter-gatherer
2. surplus
3. civilization
4. migrate
5. ethnic group
6. Quran
7. city-state
8. colonize
9. nationalism
10. Pan-Africanism
11. democracy
12. commercial farming
13. literacy
14. life expectancy

Critical Thinking

1. **Recognizing Cause and Effect** Many of Africa's cities and countries are located along trade routes. How has trade affected Africa's history?
2. **Expressing Problems Clearly** The Atlantic slave trade lasted from the 1500s to the 1800s. Then the "scramble for Africa" began. How did the slave trade and the scramble for Africa affect traditional African cultures?

Graphic Organizer

Copy the web onto a sheet of paper. Then fill in the empty spaces to complete a web of African history.

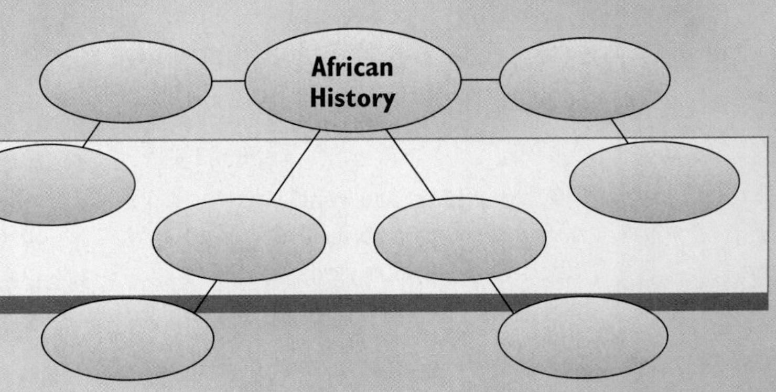

Map Activity

Africa

For each place listed below, write the letter from the map that shows its location.

1. Senegal
2. Great Zimbabwe
3. Tombouctou
4. Cape of Good Hope
5. Kilwa
6. Kingdom of Mali
7. Nubia
8. Aksum

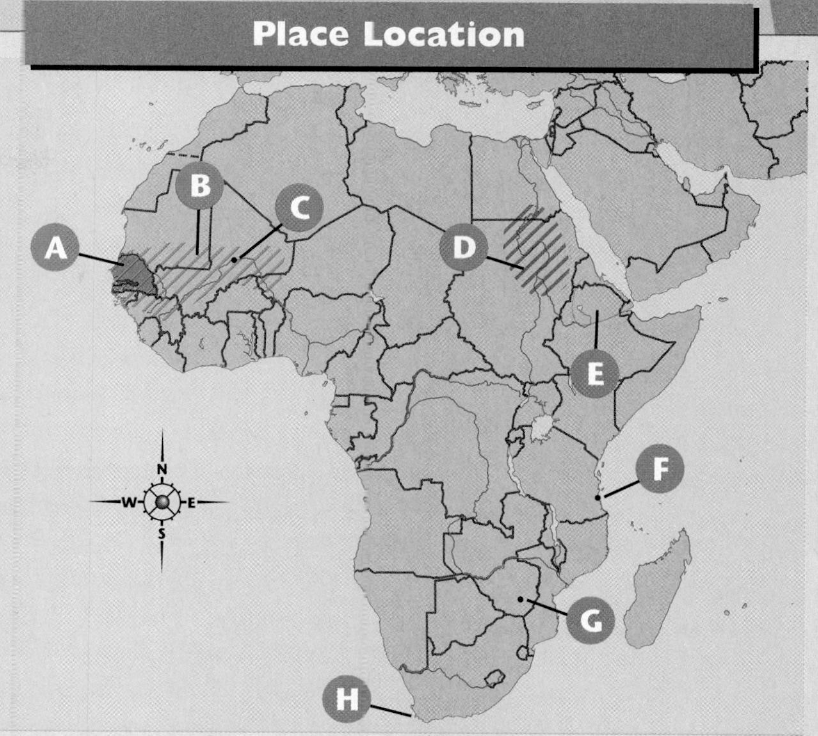

Writing Activity

Writing a Speech

In the 1800s, many people in the United States spoke out against slavery. They were called abolitionists, because they wanted to abolish, or put an end to, slavery.

Pretend that you are an abolitionist living in the 1800s. Use what you have learned about the slave trade to write a speech that will help persuade people that slavery is wrong.

Take It to the NET

Activity Read more about the Swahili language and learn how to speak Swahili. For help in completing this activity, visit **www.phschool.com.**

Chapter 12 Self-Test To review what you have learned, take the Chapter 12 Self-Test and get instant feedback on your answers. Go to **www.phschool.com** to take the test.

Skills Review

Turn to the Skills Activity.

Review the steps for recognizing bias. (a) In your own words, explain the difference between biased and unbiased writing. (b) How can you determine whether a writer is biased?

How Am I Doing?

Answer these questions to check your progress.

1. Can I explain how early humans lived in Africa?
2. Can I identify the ancient civilizations of Africa and name their accomplishments?
3. Do I understand how European rule affected Africa?
4. Can I identify the challenges that African nations have faced since independence?
5. What information from this chapter can I include in my journal?

CHAPTER

13

Cultures of Africa

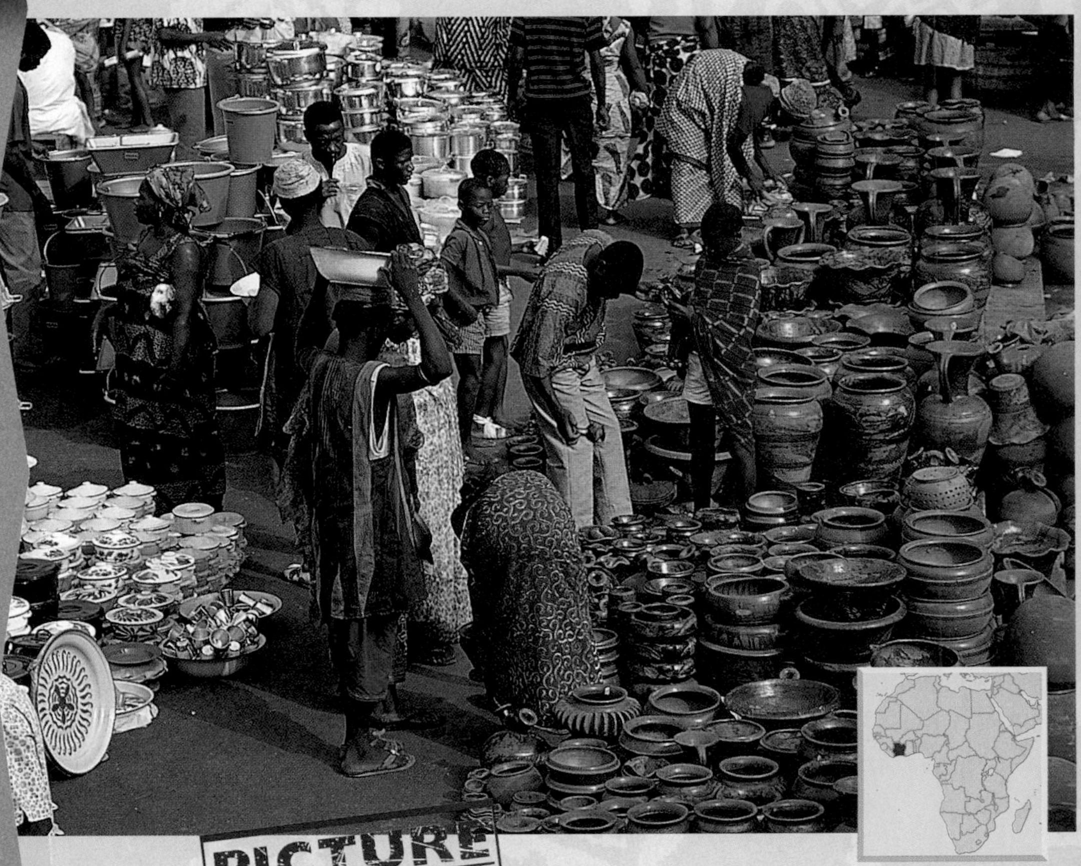

PICTURE ACTIVITIES

An African market brings together a wide variety of people and goods. Here you can buy baskets, spices, or a lamb. You can get a haircut, listen to a storyteller, or watch acrobatic dancers perform. To help you begin to understand Africa's cultures, do the following activities.

Look for clues

From this picture, what can you tell about how these Africans live? How do they dress? What kinds of products do they make and sell?

Make a list of questions

Pick a person in the picture whose life you would like to know more about. Make a list of questions that you would ask this person if you could. As you read, see if some of your questions are answered.

The Cultures of North Africa

Reach Into Your Background

Suppose you have been given the assignment of describing your way of life to students in North Africa. How would you answer the following questions: What is a day in your life like? What is your school like? What is your home like? Think about your answers as you read this section.

Questions to Explore

1. What is culture?
2. How does Islam influence life in North Africa?
3. How has their Mediterranean location affected the cultures of North Africa?

Key Terms

culture
cultural diffusion

Key Places

Sahara
Mediterranean Sea

Thirteen-year-old Meena lives in the city of Marrakech (muh RAH kehsh) in Morocco, a country in North Africa. Every morning she works in a factory, weaving carpets. She learned to weave carpets from her mother, who learned the skill from her mother. Carpets play an important role in Moroccan life. They are an export. And in some Moroccan homes, they serve as more than just floor coverings. They are used as chairs, beds, and prayer mats. In the afternoon, Meena leaves the factory to attend school. Her day ends at sunset, when she hears the crier who calls out from the nearby mosque, a Muslim house of worship. Muslims are followers of the religion of Islam. When she hears the call, Meena recites this prayer in Arabic: "There is no God but God, and Muhammad is His prophet."

▼ Moroccan weavers decorate their carpets with intricate designs. Which of these carpets would you buy? What would you use it for?

What Is Culture?

Meena's way of life is different in some ways from yours. That is partly because her culture is different.

Building With Adobe
Adobe comes from an ancient Egyptian word. It refers to a brick made of earth and straw. Arabs brought adobe-making techniques to Spain. Later, the Spanish brought the use of adobe to what is now the southwestern United States. People in the Southwest still build adobe homes.

Culture is the way of life of a group of people who share similar beliefs and customs.

Culture has many elements. Culture includes food, clothing, homes, jobs, language, and so on. It also includes things that are not so easy to see, such as how people view their world and what their religion is. These ideas shape the way people behave. Meena, for example, takes time from her activities to pray several times a day.

Cultures in different places have common elements. In many rural villages in Morocco, for example, houses are made of thick adobe, a type of brick made from sun-dried clay. Thick adobe walls help keep out the heat. Across the globe, in Mexico, and in the southwestern United States, many people in rural areas also live in adobe houses.

The Influence of Islam

Religion is an important part of North African culture. Islam is the religion of most North Africans. More than 95 percent of North Africans practice Islam and are called Muslims.

Like Jews and Christians, Muslims believe in one God. Allah is the Arabic word for God. Muslims believe that Muhammad was God's final messenger. They also believe that the Old Testament prophets and Jesus were God's messengers. The main duties of a Muslim are outlined in the Five Pillars of Islam, shown in the chart on the next page.

▼ Adobe bricks fall apart if they are often exposed to cold or wet weather. They can only be used in hot, dry climates. The picture below shows adobe houses in Morocco.

The Five Pillars of Islam

Duty	Description
Declaration of Faith	Declaring belief in one God and in Muhammad as God's final messenger
Prayer	Reciting prayers five times a day: at dawn, at midday, in the afternoon, at sunset, and in the evening
Almsgiving	Giving a portion of one's wealth to the needy
Fasting	Not eating or drinking from sunrise to sunset during the ninth month in the Muslim year, Ramadan
Pilgrimage	Making the *hajj*, or pilgrimage to Mecca, at least once in a lifetime if able

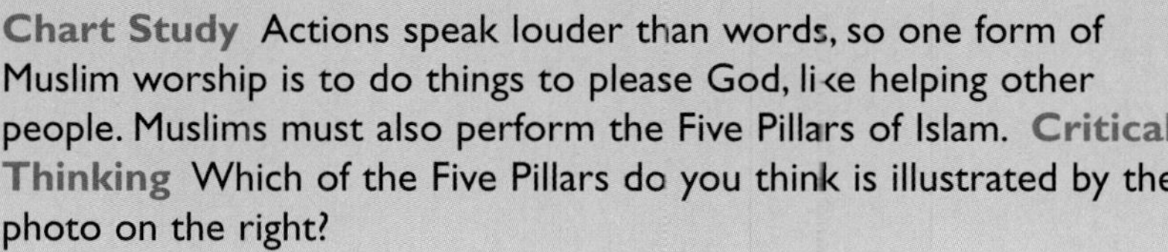

Chart Study Actions speak louder than words, so one form of Muslim worship is to do things to please God, like helping other people. Muslims must also perform the Five Pillars of Islam. **Critical Thinking** Which of the Five Pillars do you think is illustrated by the photo on the right?

Five Pillars of Islam

The sacred book of Islam is the Quran. Besides teaching about God, the Quran provides a guide to life. Like the Bible, the Quran forbids lying, stealing, and murder. It also prohibits gambling, eating pork, and drinking alcohol.

The Islamic system of law is based on the Quran. Islamic law governs all aspects of life, including family life, business practices, banking, and government.

Islam Unifies the People of North Africa Islam and the Arabic language unify the different peoples of North Africa. These peoples are spread out over a large area that includes the following countries: Egypt, Libya, Tunisia, Algeria, and Morocco. People here have many different backgrounds and ways of life.

An ethnic group is a group of people who share language, religion, or cultural traditions. Most North Africans are Arabs. But the region has other ethnic groups, too. The largest of these is the Berbers who live mainly in Algeria and Morocco. Most Berbers speak Arabic as well as Berber. Some live in cities, but most live in small villages in rugged mountain areas. They make their living by herding and farming. The Tuareg (TWAH rehg) are a group of Berbers who live in the Sahara, the

North Africa's Rural and Urban Areas

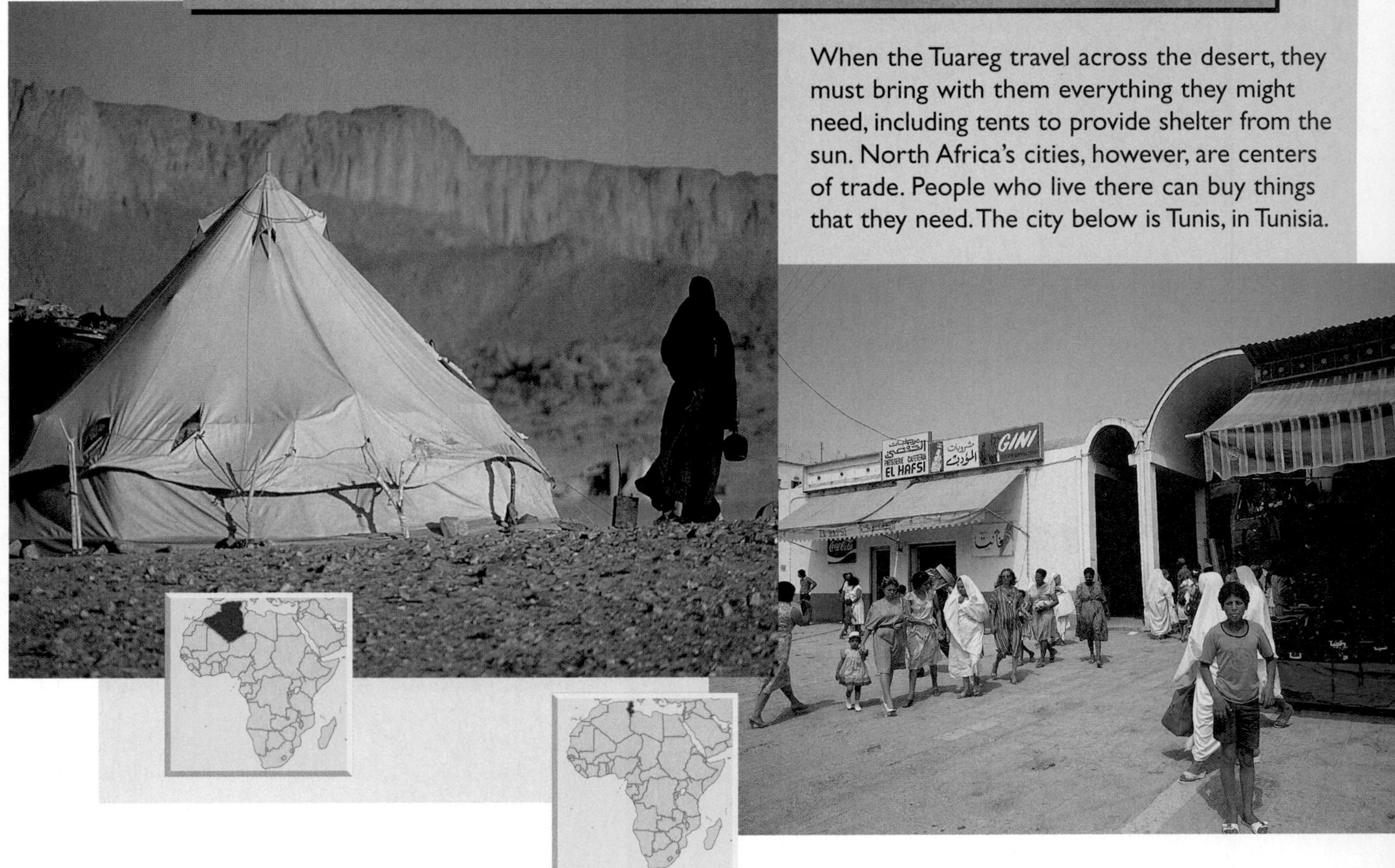

When the Tuareg travel across the desert, they must bring with them everything they might need, including tents to provide shelter from the sun. North Africa's cities, however, are centers of trade. People who live there can buy things that they need. The city below is Tunis, in Tunisia.

great desert that stretches across North Africa. The Tuareg herd camels, goats, and other livestock.

In parts of rural North Africa, some people live much as their parents and grandparents did. But traditional and modern ways of life mix in towns and large cities like Cairo (KY roh), Egypt, and Tunis, Tunisia. Like Meena, who weaves carpets, some city people work at traditional crafts. Others are architects, engineers, scientists, and bankers. Some sell baskets in outdoor markets. Others sell television sets in modern stores.

Arab and Berber, urban and rural, architect and herder—the peoples of North Africa live vastly different lives, yet almost all consider themselves fellow Muslims. Islam forms a common bond of culture among North Africans.

READ ACTIVELY

Visualize What sights might you see if you were walking through an outdoor market in a North African city? How would these sights be different from what you might see inside a modern supermarket?

Cultural Change in North Africa

North Africa's mix of traditional and modern ways of life shows that culture does not stay the same forever. It changes all the time.

How Culture Spreads Cultural changes often occur when people travel. As they travel, people bring their customs and ideas with them. They also pick up new ideas and customs. In this way, customs and ideas spread from one place to another. The movement of customs and ideas is called **cultural diffusion.** The word *diffuse* means "to spread out."

Connect What cities in the United States are centers of trade?

A Mediterranean Outlook One factor that has aided the diffusion of culture in North Africa is location. Find North Africa on the map below. North Africans have long viewed their region as a gateway to three continents: Africa, Europe, and Asia. Can you see why? This Mediterranean outlook dates back to early history.

Because of its location, North Africa has been a hub of trade. Throughout history, the people of North Africa have traded with people in Europe, Asia, and other parts of Africa. Thus, they have influenced, and been influenced by, cultures in all these places.

The mixing of cultures in North Africa did not occur only through trade. It also occurred through conquest. North Africa is home to one of the world's oldest civilizations—ancient Egypt. The ancient Egyptians developed trade links with ancient civilizations in both Europe and Southwest Asia. They both conquered and were conquered by other empires. These conquests helped bring about cultural diffusion.

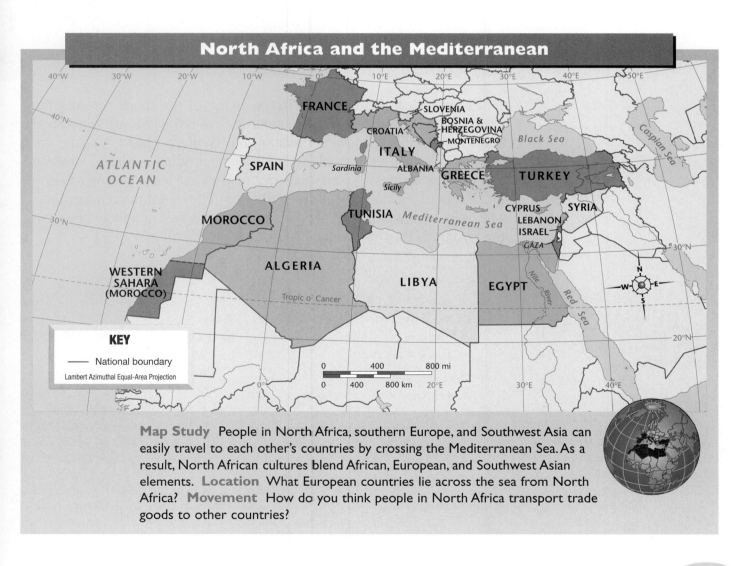

North Africa and the Mediterranean

KEY

—— National boundary

Lambert Azimuthal Equal-Area Projection

Map Study People in North Africa, southern Europe, and Southwest Asia can easily travel to each other's countries by crossing the Mediterranean Sea. As a result, North African cultures blend African, European, and Southwest Asian elements. **Location** What European countries lie across the sea from North Africa? **Movement** How do you think people in North Africa transport trade goods to other countries?

▶ Muslims often build a large, empty space into the middle of their mosques. Why? In countries with more than one culture and religion, Muslims use mosques as community centers. The empty space can be used for many different kinds of activities, including education.

Preserving Muslim Culture One of the more recent influences on North Africa is Western culture. Some Muslims are concerned that their countries are becoming too Western. More people are wearing Western clothes, buying Western products, seeing Western films, and adapting Western ideas. Some Muslims fear that this will lead to the loss of Muslim values and traditions. They want to preserve their way of life. All over Africa, people face the challenge of how to preserve the traditions they value as their countries modernize.

SECTION 1 REVIEW

1. **Define** (a) culture, (b) cultural diffusion.
2. **Identify** (a) Sahara, (b) Mediterranean Sea.
3. How does Islam affect everyday life in North Africa?
4. How has North Africa's location contributed to cultural diffusion?

Critical Thinking

5. **Making Comparisons** Which aspects of North African culture are similar to and which are different from your culture? Make a list of the similarities and differences.

Activity

6. **Writing to Learn** What traditions in your culture do you think are worth preserving? Write an essay describing the customs you value most.

The Cultures of West Africa

Reach Into Your Background
How much do you know about different ethnic groups in the United States? Make a list of three or four groups. Jot down notes about each group's culture. Does the group speak a language other than English? What special customs or beliefs does the group have?

Questions to Explore

1. Why does West Africa have such a variety of cultures?
2. What effects do family ties have on West African culture?
3. How has urbanization affected the cultures of West Africa?

Key Terms
cultural diversity
kinship
nuclear family
extended family
lineage
clan
griot

In Mauritania, North Africa meets West Africa. Here, the Sahara merges into the savanna, or grasslands. Hamadi (hah MAH dee) is a teacher in a small village school in southern Mauritania. Although the country's official language is Arabic, Hamadi teaches French in the school. But at home, he speaks Poular, the language of the Halpoular, one of Mauritania's main ethnic groups.

▼ Children in Mauritania do not always have paper and pencils, but that doesn't stop them from learning. Instead, they use slates and chalk.

Cultural Diversity of West Africa

Being able to speak more than one language is useful in Africa, and especially in West Africa. Seventeen countries make up this region. West Africa also has hundreds of ethnic groups. Because of its many ethnic groups, West Africa is famous for its **cultural diversity**—it has a wide variety of cultures. Unlike the ethnic groups of North Africa, West Africans are not united by a single religion or a common language.

Predict How do you think the cultural diversity of West Africa affects the lives of its people?

West Africans Speak Many Languages Think about your community. Imagine that the people who live nearby speak a different language. How would you communicate with them? Suppose you wanted to shop in a store, eat in a restaurant, or attend a sports event in the next town. It might seem like visiting another country.

This situation is real for many West Africans. The hundreds of ethnic groups in West Africa speak different languages. Sometimes groups in neighboring villages speak different languages.

To communicate, most West Africans speak more than one language. Many speak four or five languages. They use these different languages when they travel or conduct business. This practice helps unify countries with many ethnic groups.

West Africans Have Many Ways of Making a Living West Africa's ethnic groups differ in more than just the language they speak. Like North Africans, West Africans have many ways of making of a living. Most West Africans live in rural areas. A typical village consists of a group of homes surrounded by farmland. The village people grow food for themselves and cash crops to sell.

In the Sahara and the dry Sahel just south of the Sahara, many people herd cattle, goats, sheep, or camels. Along the coast, most West Africans make a living by fishing. Some West Africans live in large cities where they may work in hospitals, hotels, or office buildings.

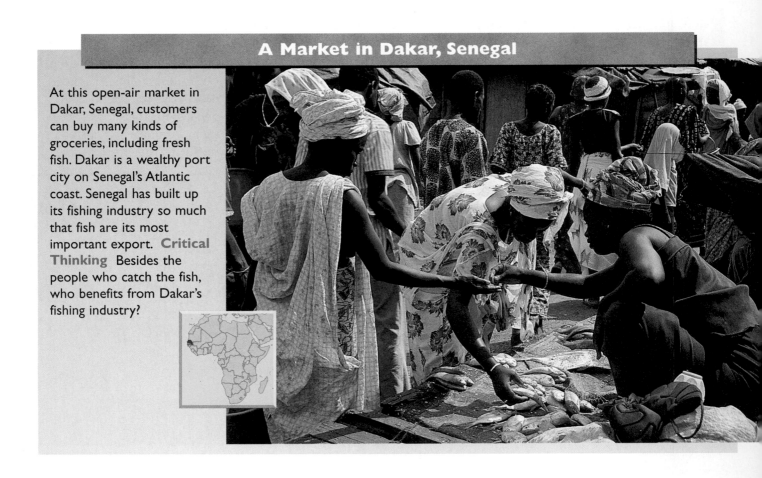

A Market in Dakar, Senegal

At this open-air market in Dakar, Senegal, customers can buy many kinds of groceries, including fresh fish. Dakar is a wealthy port city on Senegal's Atlantic coast. Senegal has built up its fishing industry so much that fish are its most important export. **Critical Thinking** Besides the people who catch the fish, who benefits from Dakar's fishing industry?

Life in West Africa

Ways of making a living in West Africa vary from country to country. Most people in Mali (below left) make a living growing crops such as grains, corn, potatoes, yams, and cassava. But in some countries, such as Côte d'Ivoire, almost half the people live and work in cities. The University of Côte d'Ivoire (below right), in the largest city of Abidjan, employs hundreds of people.

Belonging to Groups

Like North Africans, West Africans see themselves as members of a number of groups. Just as you belong to a family, an ethnic group, and a country, so do West Africans.

Connect How do people outside your immediate family help to raise you?

The Strong Ties of Kinship One of the strongest bonds West Africans have is **kinship,** which refers to a family relationship. The first level of kinship is the **nuclear family,** which consists of parents and their children. The next level is the **extended family,** which includes other relatives besides parents and children. It may include grandparents, aunts, uncles, and cousins. Many West Africans live in extended families.

Extended families work together and take care of each other. Family members care for the elderly and those who are sick or less well-off. They make decisions together. And they watch over all the children in the village. This custom is reflected in the well-known African proverb, "It takes a village to raise a child." Neighbors always pitch in and help one another. Thus, kinship adds to a strong sense of community.

Larger Groups: Lineages and Clans In many rural areas, kinship reaches beyond extended families. A group of families may trace their descent back to a common ancestor. Such a group forms a **lineage.** Several lineages form a **clan.** The people in a clan all have roots back to an even earlier ancestor.

Tracing Lineage Different traditions also govern the way groups trace their lineage. Some groups are matrilineal. They trace their lineage through women ancestors. Property is passed on to children through the female side of a family. In a matrilineal society, if people marry outside the clan, the husband comes to live with the wife's clan. The result is that the village has a core of women who live there. The men they marry are newcomers, who move into the homes of the local women. Most groups, however, are patrilineal. They trace their descent through the male side of a family.

Changes in Family Life

Although traditional family ties remain strong in West Africa, family life is changing. More people are moving from rural villages to urban areas, or cities. This trend, called urbanization, is occurring throughout Africa and the world.

▼ In places like Tombouctou, Mali, where the climate is hot, some families in rural areas do many household chores outside.

The Streets of Lagos

Bus drivers must find their way carefully through the crowded streets of Lagos, Nigeria. Like people all over Africa, many of these people have come to Lagos to find work. **Critical Thinking** Why do you think it would be easier to find a job in a city than in a rural area?

Many young men come to West Africa's cities to find jobs. The women often stay in the rural homes. They raise the children and farm the land. The men come home from time to time to visit their families and to share what they have earned.

Keeping Traditions Alive

In West Africa today, people are adapting to change in various ways. But most West Africans still keep strong family ties. People still pass their history, values, and traditions on to the young.

One important way in which West African traditions are being preserved is through storytelling. Traditional West African stories are spoken rather than written. The stories teach children cultural values. A storyteller called a **griot** (GREE oh) passes this oral tradition from one generation to another. The oral tradition of West Africa tells the histories of ethnic groups and kinships. Stories of tricksters, animal fables, proverbs, riddles, and songs are also part of West Africa's oral tradition. This Yoruba proverb reflects the value placed on passing on traditions: "The young can't teach traditions to the old."

West African Folk Tales West Africa has a rich tradition of folk tales. One type of tale is the escape story, in which a clever person thinks of a way out of an impossible situation. One tale from Benin is about a cruel king who orders his people to build him a new palace. He tells them that they must start at the top and build down. The people despair. Then a wise old man invites the king to begin by setting the first stone in place. The people are saved.

A Griot Tells a Tale

When a griot tells a story, it can take all night or even several days. The audience does not mind, because the stories are usually scary, funny, or exciting. This griot, from Côte d'Ivoire, is telling these children a legend from their history. The children pay careful attention, because the griot acts out parts of the story as he goes along.

West African traditions have greatly influenced other cultures, especially American culture. About half of the enslaved Africans who were brought to the United States came from West Africa. They brought with them the only things they could: their ideas, stories, dances, music, and customs. The stories of Brer Rabbit as well as blues and jazz music have their roots in West Africa. Today, West African culture—the stories, music, dances, art, cooking, clothing—is more popular than ever. Griot guitarists and other musicians from West Africa have international followings. In recent years, three Nobel Prize winners for literature have been African. One of them, Wole Soyinka (WOH lay shaw YING kah), is from the West African country of Nigeria.

SECTION 2 REVIEW

1. **Define** (a) cultural diversity, (b) kinship, (c) nuclear family, (d) extended family, (e) lineage, (f) clan, (g) griot.
2. In what ways is West Africa culturally diverse?
3. Describe the importance of family ties to West Africans.
4. How has urbanization changed the lives of West Africans?

Critical Thinking

5. **Drawing Conclusions** How has the extended family helped to develop a sense of community among West Africans?

Activity

6. **Writing to Learn** Imagine that you live in a small village in an extended family in West Africa. Make a list of the advantages and disadvantages of your way of life.

The Cultures of East Africa

Reach Into Your Background
Think about the language you speak. How many words can you identify that come from another language? What about the words *banjo, canyon,* or *succotash? Banjo* comes from an African language, possibly Kimbundu. *Canyon* comes from Spanish. *Succotash* comes from Narragansett, a Native American language. See if you can find other examples.

Questions to Explore

1. How has location affected the development of East African cultures?
2. What role does the Swahili language play in East African cultures?
3. How and why are ideas about land ownership changing in East Africa?

Key Terms
plantation

Key People and Places
East Africa
Julius Nyerere

Alemeseged Taddesse Mekonnen (ah LEM uh seh ged tah DAY say meh KOH nen) is an Ethiopian who works in a bakery in St. Louis, Missouri. Before coming to the United States, he lived with his extended family in Gonder, a city in northern Ethiopia. His father owned a large store there. Mekonnen speaks three languages: Amharic, Arabic, and English. At home, in Ethiopia, Amharic was his first language. Because he is Muslim, he learned Arabic to study the Quran. And he learned English in school, as other Ethiopians do.

Mekonnen misses life with his close-knit family in Ethiopia. "At home we ate every meal together. If anyone was missing, we waited until they came home," he says. Mekonnen hopes to return home someday. He lives in the United States, but his heart is in Ethiopia.

▼ Shown below is the city of Gonder, in northern Ethiopia. Ethiopia is one of the countries in East Africa.

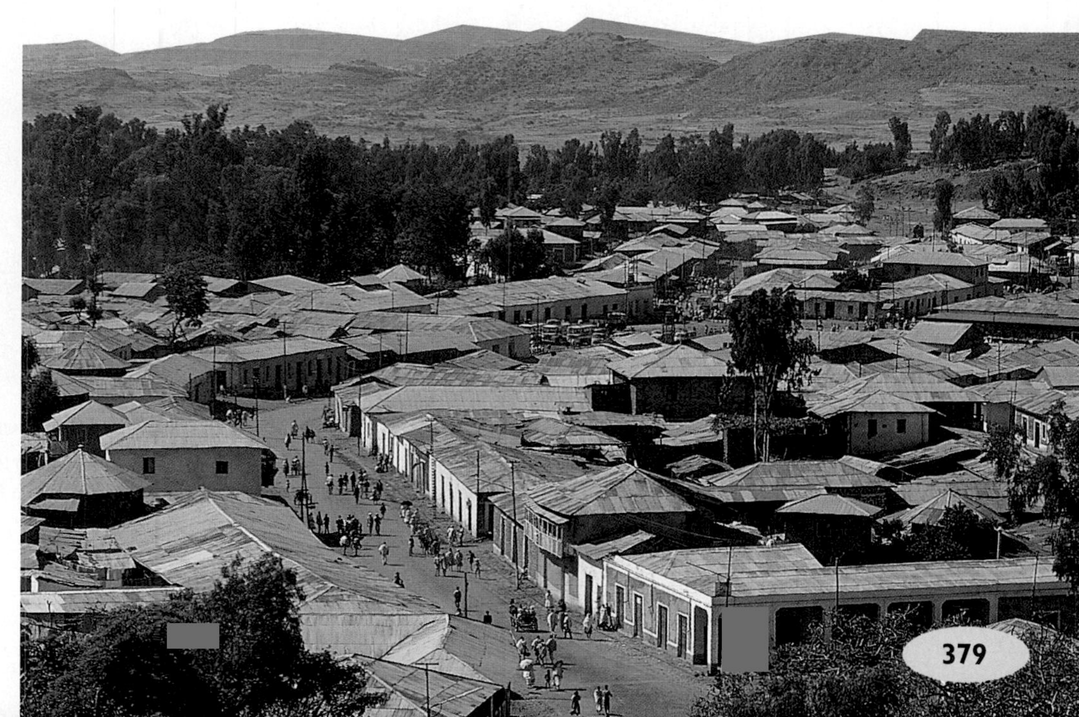

Living Along the Indian Ocean

Knowing three languages is not unusual for an East African, just as it is not for a West African. In Ethiopia alone, more than 70 different languages are spoken. Like West Africa, East Africa has many ethnic groups who speak different languages. The region has great cultural diversity.

East Africa's diversity is the result of its location. Many ethnic groups have migrated to East Africa from other regions of the continent. For example, about 2,000 years ago, Bantu-speaking peoples migrated to East Africa from West Africa. In addition, East Africa has a long coastline along the Indian Ocean. The ocean connects the people of East Africa to people living across the ocean to the east. These people include Arabs, Indians, and other Asians. The connection extends even to countries as far away as China and Malaysia.

This link dates back to early times. Arab traders began to settle in the coastal villages of East Africa nearly 2,000 years ago. They brought Arab culture into East Africa, where it mixed with various African cultures. This mixture produced the Swahili culture.

Lunch Time for a Kenyan Family

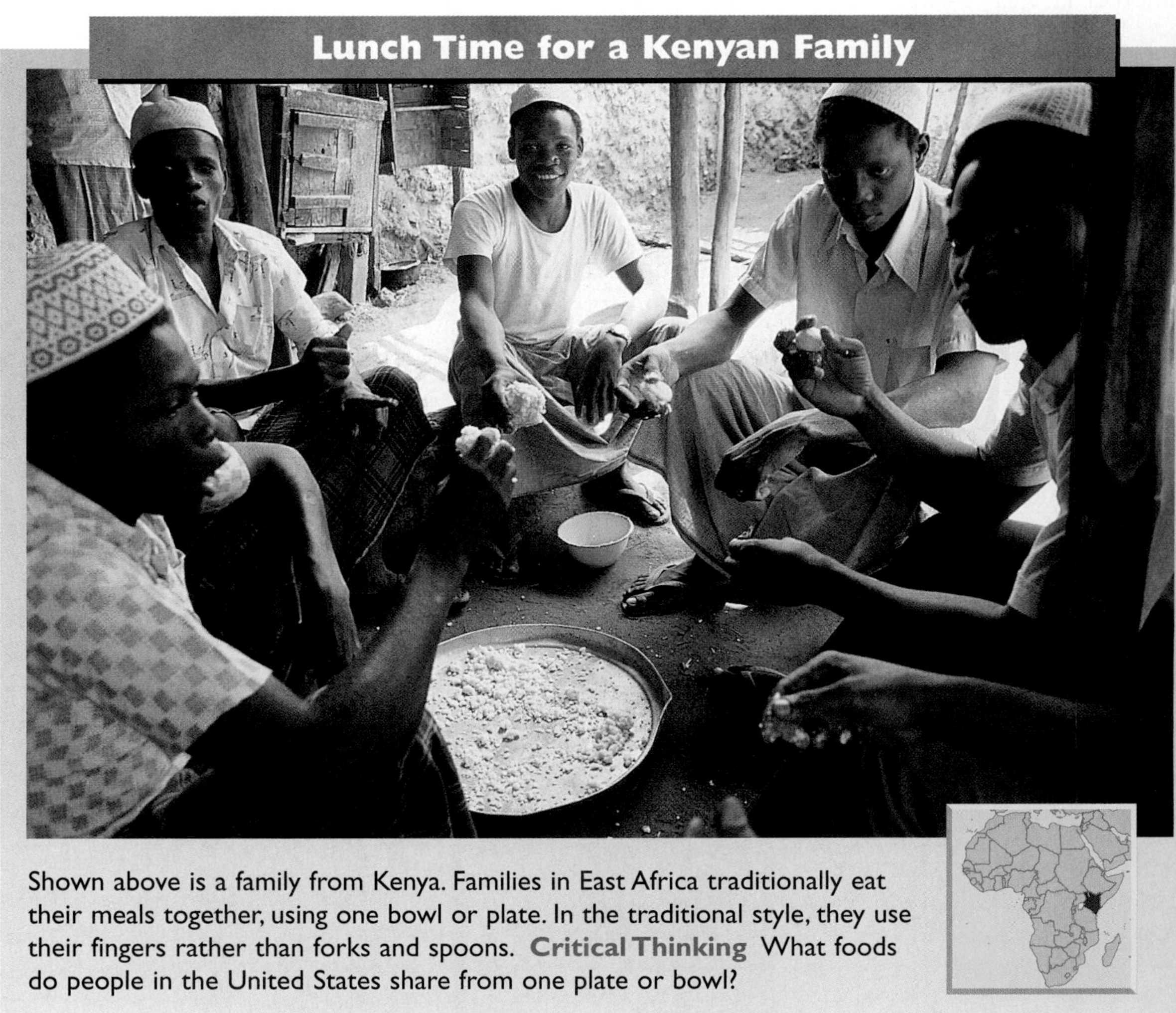

Shown above is a family from Kenya. Families in East Africa traditionally eat their meals together, using one bowl or plate. In the traditional style, they use their fingers rather than forks and spoons. **Critical Thinking** What foods do people in the United States share from one plate or bowl?

Kampala, Capital City of Uganda

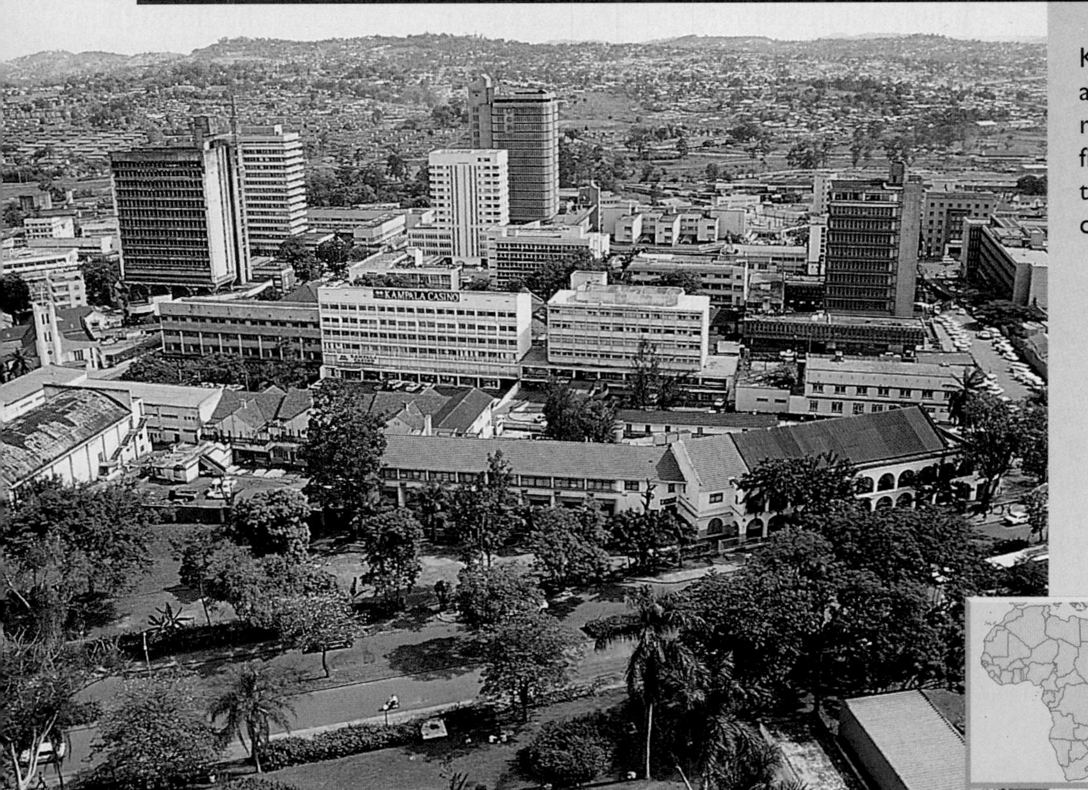

Kampala is Uganda's largest city and leading trade center. It is a religious center as well. You can find Muslim mosques, Hindu temples, and Christian churches here.

Swahili Culture

The Swahili are Africans who have mixed African and Arab ancestry. They live along the east coast of Africa from Somalia to Mozambique. Their language is also called Swahili. It is a Bantu language, but it contains many Arabic words. The Swahili are just one of hundreds of ethnic groups in East Africa. But their language is widely used for business and communication among many ethnic groups throughout the region.

Swahili is the first language of about 49 million people worldwide. It also serves as the second language of millions of East Africans. Swahili is the official language of Kenya and Tanzania. In Tanzania, children are educated in Swahili through the primary grades. Later, they learn English as well. By promoting the use of Swahili, these nations are trying to preserve their African heritage.

A Mixture of Religions

Like languages, religious beliefs in East Africa reflect the cultural diversity of the region. Both Islam and Christianity have large followings in the region. Islam was introduced into East Africa by Arab traders. The Romans introduced Christianity into some of their North African territories. Later, it spread into Ethiopia. In the 1800s,

Kwanzaa Swahili culture and language have also come to the United States. Many African Americans celebrate Kwanzaa (KWAN zah), a holiday based on a traditional African harvest festival. The word *Kwanzaa* is related to the Swahili word for "first." Kwanzaa is based on a set of values that also have Swahili names. These include *umoja* (oo MOH juh), or unity; *kuumba* (koo OOM buh), or creativity; and *imani* (ee MAHN ee), or faith.

Europeans pushed into Africa and spread Christianity farther. In addition, traditional religions remain alive in East Africa and throughout the continent.

Agatha Mbogo Agatha Mbogo wanted to help her rural community of Embu, Kenya. But in her community, it is unusual for women to be political leaders. With little money and no experience, Mbogo ran for a district council seat—and won. That gave her the courage to run for mayor in 1994. Despite facing a veteran mayor, she was elected by the all-male district council.

Changing Ideas About Land

In East Africa, as in the rest of Africa, most people live in rural areas, where they farm and tend livestock. The ways in which they view and work the land are part of the culture of East Africans.

Before Land Was Owned Before Europeans took over parts of Africa in the 1800s, individual Africans did not own land. People did not buy or sell land. The very idea of owning land did not exist. Families had the right to farm plots of land near the village, but the actual plots might vary in size and location over time.

Traditionally, extended families farmed the land to produce food for the whole group. Men cleared the land and broke up the soil. Women then planted the seed, tended the fields, and harvested the crops. Meanwhile, the men herded livestock or traded goods. This division of roles still exists in many parts of Africa today.

The Rise and Fall of Plantations The idea of privately owned land was introduced into many parts of Africa by European settlers. In parts of East Africa, the British set up plantations. A **plantation** is a large farm where cash crops are grown. When many African countries became independent, they broke up the old colonial plantations. They sold the land to individual Africans.

Some land in East Africa is still available to buy. But much of it is poor farmland in areas where few people live. In fertile areas like the Ethiopian Highlands and the Rift Valley, land for farming is scarce. Many people live in these areas where the farmland is fertile. In densely populated countries, such as Rwanda and Burundi, conflicts have developed over land.

Where Is Home?

Connect How do you feel when you return home after being away for a long time?

Traditionally, Africans feel a strong bond to the land where they grew up. Like the rest of Africa, East Africa is becoming increasingly urban. Yet even people who spend most of their time in a city do not call it home. If asked where home is, an East African will name the village of his or her family or clan. Most people consider their life in the city temporary. They expect to return to their villages at some time.

Tanzania's former president Julius Nyerere (nyuh RAIR ay) is one example. Nyerere continued to be involved in world affairs, but far from Dar es Salaam, the capital city of Tanzania. After he stepped down as

◀ The coastal city of Mombasa, Kenya, began as a trading center in the 1200s. One of its chief exports was ivory. Today, metal arches shaped like elephant tusks memorialize Kenya's ivory trade. While cities like Mombasa can be beautiful and exciting, to most East Africans a city can never really be home.

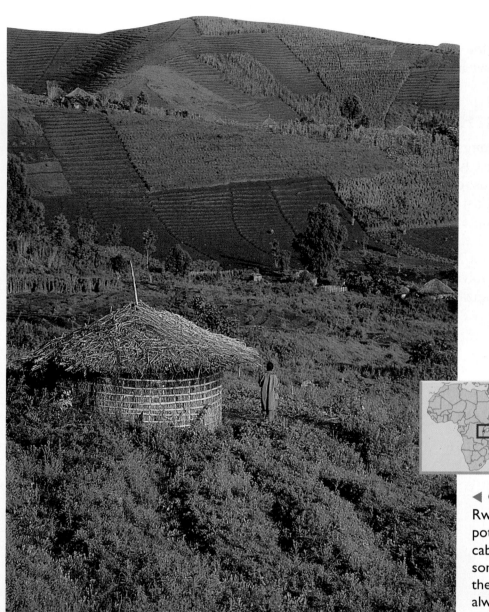

president in 1985, Nyerere moved back to his home village. There, until his death in 1999, he grew corn and millet on his farm. He spent his mornings working in the fields. In an interview in 1996, Nyerere said: "In a sense I am a very rural person. I grew up here, and [working in] Dar es Salaam was a duty. I did my duty and after retiring in 1985, I came back here and said, 'Ah, it's good to be back.'"

Other East Africans feel the same. They do their duty by earning money in the city. But, their homes—and their hearts—are in their rural villages.

◀ On his family farm in Rwanda, this farmer grows potatoes, corn, beans, and cabbage. East Africans sometimes move away from their farms, but they almost always hope to return to them one day.

1. **Define** plantation.
2. **Identify** (a) East Africa, (b) Julius Nyerere.
3. Describe some ways in which East Africa's location along the Indian Ocean has affected its cultures.
4. Why is Swahili spoken by so many people in East Africa?
5. Explain the changes in ideas about land ownership in East Africa.

Critical Thinking

6. **Making Comparisons** How did traditional East African ideas about land differ from the ideas of Europeans who took over parts of Africa?

Activity

7. **Writing to Learn** Write a description of the place that you consider home. Tell what it means to you and explain why.

The Cultures of Central and Southern Africa

Reach Into Your Background

Think of a goal you had to work hard to achieve at home or at school. Why was it important to you to achieve your goal? Think about the plan you made and the strategies you used to achieve your goal. What obstacles did you have to overcome? How did you feel when you finally succeeded?

Questions to Explore

1. How has the country of South Africa influenced the entire region of Southern Africa?
2. How did migrant labor give rise to a new group identity among the peoples of Southern Africa?
3. How does Central Africa reflect the cultural diversity of all of Africa?

Key Terms

migrant worker

Key Places

Republic of South Africa
Democratic Republic of Congo

The African National Congress (ANC), a political party in the Republic of South Africa, played a key role in gaining political and civil rights for all South Africans. Until 1991, Europeans in South Africa had denied equal rights to blacks, who make up a majority of the population. Three countries—Tanzania, Zambia, and Zimbabwe—adopted the ANC anthem for their national anthems. Here are the words to the ANC anthem:

> "Bless, O Lord, our land of Africa
> Lift its name and make its people free.
> Take the gifts we offer unto Thee
> Hear us, faithful sons.
> Hear us, faithful sons."

▼ These teenagers sang the ANC anthem for the opening of Parliament in Cape Town, South Africa.

The Pull of South Africa

Ask Questions What questions do you have about South Africa's influence on the rest of Southern Africa?

South Africa is just one country in Southern Africa, but it has had, by far, the greatest impact on the region. Its political and economic influence has touched the lives of millions of people.

Political Influence of South Africa Until the 1990s, a European minority ruled South Africa. In 1923, they separated South Africans into categories based on skin color. People of African descent were classified as black, people of European descent as white, and people of mixed ancestry as colored. Asians, who were mostly from India, formed the fourth category. Blacks, coloreds, and Asians could not vote and did not have other basic rights. For nearly 70 years, these groups struggled to gain their rights.

The struggle for basic rights created a sense of nationalism among black South Africans. White settlers, not blacks, had established the nation of South Africa. But as blacks struggled to gain political rights, they began to think of themselves as members of the nation. They wanted to take part as equal citizens in running the nation. The struggle for majority rule in South Africa lasted so long that it inspired similar movements in Namibia and what is now Zimbabwe.

Economic Influence of South Africa South Africa is the richest and most industrialized country on the continent of Africa. It produces two fifths of the manufactured goods, half of the minerals, and one fifth of the agricultural products of the entire continent. Its economic power and needs have affected all of Southern Africa because its demand for labor has been so great. To provide a labor force for the mines, South African companies used workers from throughout Southern Africa.

To get jobs in South Africa, hundreds of thousands of workers migrated from nearby countries. Workers were allowed to stay in South Africa for only a short time. New workers were always needed. A large force of **migrant workers,** people who move from place to place to find work, was soon created.

A South African Gold Miner

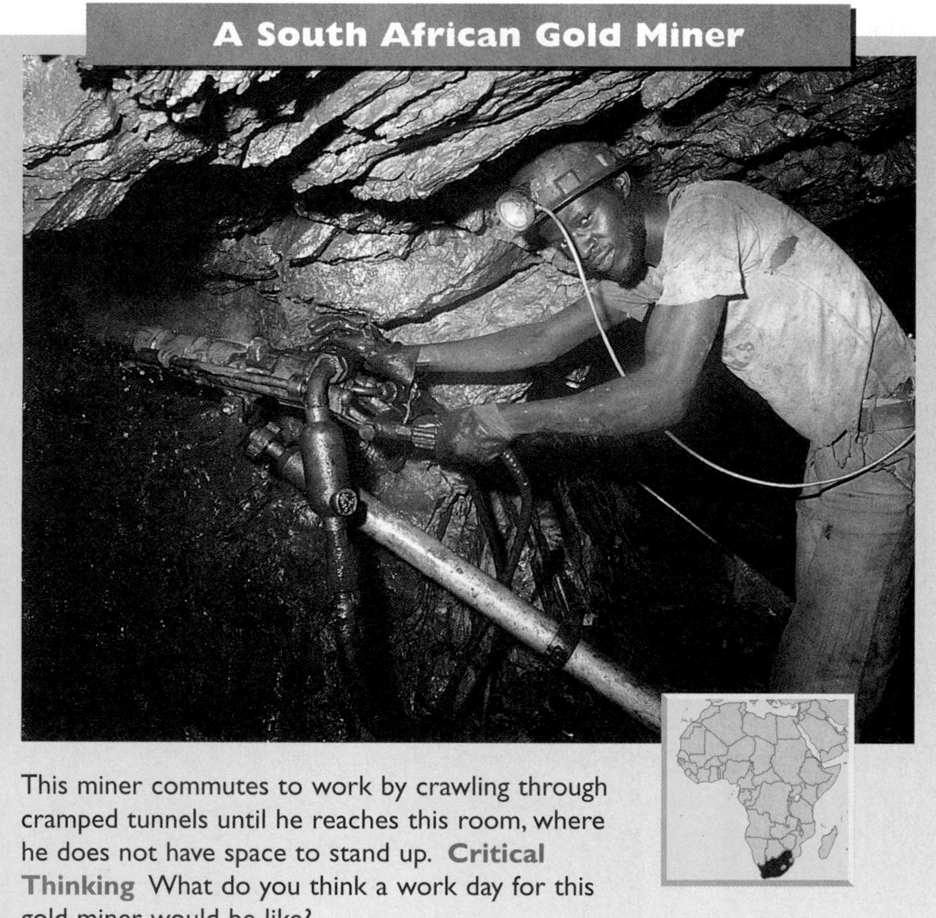

This miner commutes to work by crawling through cramped tunnels until he reaches this room, where he does not have space to stand up. **Critical Thinking** What do you think a work day for this gold miner would be like?

The Fight for Equal Rights

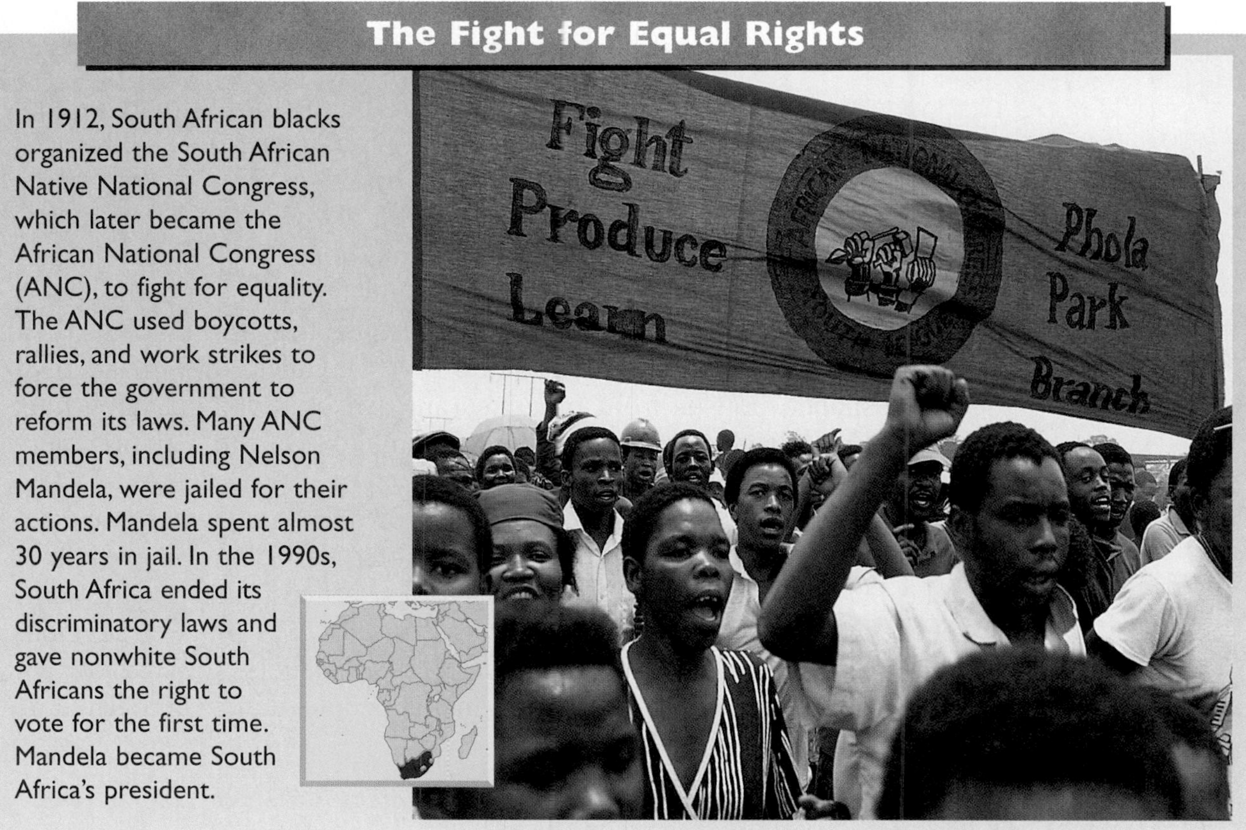

In 1912, South African blacks organized the South African Native National Congress, which later became the African National Congress (ANC), to fight for equality. The ANC used boycotts, rallies, and work strikes to force the government to reform its laws. Many ANC members, including Nelson Mandela, were jailed for their actions. Mandela spent almost 30 years in jail. In the 1990s, South Africa ended its discriminatory laws and gave nonwhite South Africans the right to vote for the first time. Mandela became South Africa's president.

Migrant Workers Form a New Group Identity

Mine workers in South Africa were from many countries. They lived together in compounds, or fenced-in groups of homes. They were far from their families, clans, and ethnic groups. They worked long hours in dangerous conditions for low wages.

Predict How do you think South Africa's mines affected its culture?

A Person Is a Person Because of People The migrant mine workers came to rely on one another. They began to think of themselves as a group—as workers. This kind of group identity was new for Southern Africans. It was not based on family or ethnic group. Group identity is very important in Africa. This is reflected in the African proverb "A person is a person because of people." It means that a person is who he or she is because of his or her relationships with other people. The migrant workers formed a new identity based on how they related to each other as workers.

Mine Workers Form a Union In the 1980s, the mine workers in South Africa formed a union—the National Union of Mineworkers. This union was illegal at the time. But it played a leading role in the drive for equal rights. The union workers sometimes went on strike in support of their causes. Thus, the new identity of the mine workers led them to take group action.

Tradition and Change in Central Africa

Like people in Southern Africa and the rest of Africa, Central Africans have gone through many cultural changes in the 1900s. But many people in the region also follow old traditions. Like the rest of the continent, Central Africa displays great cultural diversity. The country of the Democratic Republic of Congo alone has about 200 ethnic groups.

One ethnic group in Congo is the Mbuti (em BOO tee), who live in the rain forests. The Mbuti are unique because they live much as their ancestors did. In forest camps of 10 to 25 families, they make their dome-shaped houses from branches and leaves. For food, they hunt wild animals and gather wild plants. The culture of the Mbuti is more than 3,000 years old.

In contrast, millions of people live in crowded shantytowns or cinder-block apartments in Kinshasa, the largest city in Congo. They walk or take buses or trucks to work in factories, offices, and hotels. Some people are Roman Catholics or Protestants. Others practice religions that blend Christian and traditional African beliefs. Still others are Muslims. On Saturday evenings, many people dance and listen to Congolese jazz in city dance halls.

Barkcloth Art The Mbuti of Congo use only renewable resources. For example, they make some of their cloth out of tree bark. Men pound the bark with mallets until it is almost as soft as velvet. Then women draw shapes and patterns on the cloth. Many art galleries in the United States and Europe collect Mbuti barkcloth drawings.

At Work in Cameroon

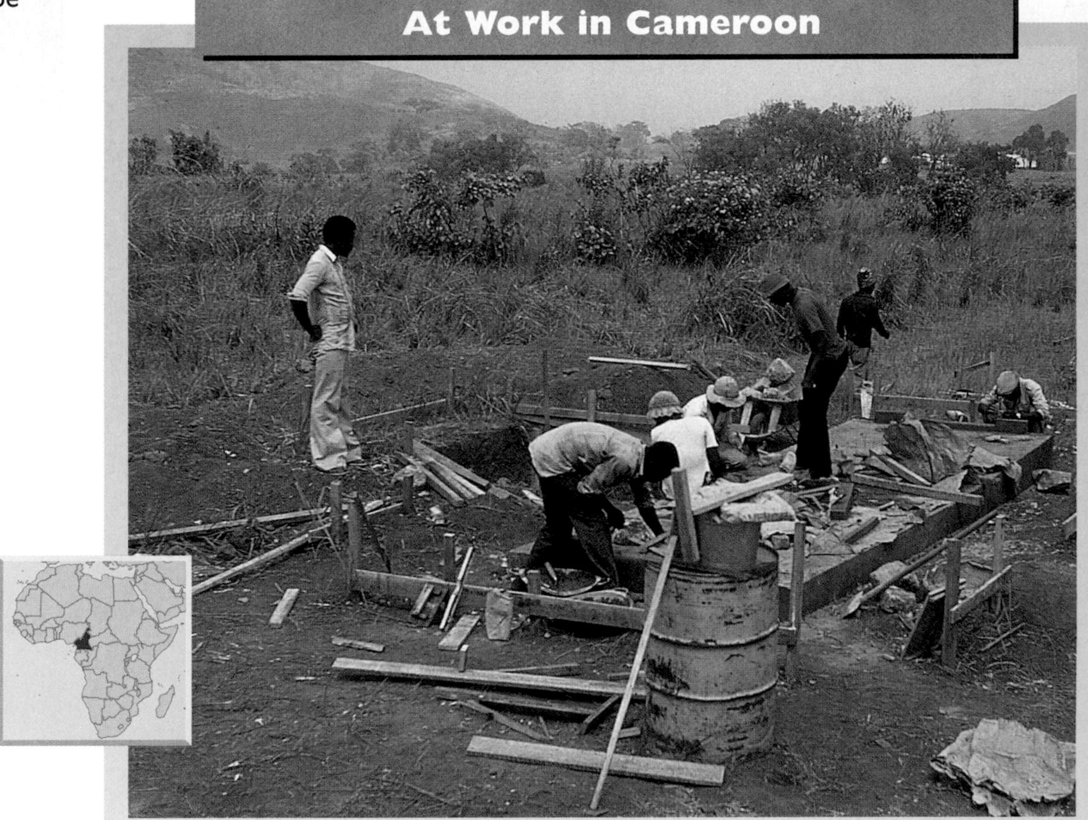

Cameroon is a country in northwest Central Africa. Most people in Cameroon live in rural areas and make a living by farming or by herding cattle. These men are building farm structures used in taking care of cattle.

A Modern City in an Old Location

Kinshasa is Congo's capital. People have lived here since the late 1400s, making a living by fishing or trading on the Congo River. Today, people still fish on the Congo River, and it remains an important source of transportation. However, Kinshasa is also a center of government and industry.

What one writer said about North Africa applies to Southern Africa as well. To define the real North African, he said, "you have to define which one you mean: the rich or the poor, the Berber women of the mountains or the college girls on motorbikes...." Old, new, and mixtures of the two live on in all regions of Africa.

1. **Define** migrant worker.
2. **Identify** (a) Republic of South Africa, (b) Democratic Republic of Congo.
3. Describe the political and economic effects South Africa has had on the entire region of Southern Africa.
4. What was unusual about migrant workers in South Africa forming a group identity as workers?
5. In what ways are the cultures of Central Africa like those in other parts of Africa?

Critical Thinking

6. **Recognizing Cause and Effect** What positive and/or negative effects might South Africa's labor needs have had on the economies of nearby countries?

Activity

7. **Writing to Learn** Consider the life of a mine worker in a South African gold mine in the 1970s. Write the first verse of a song protesting miners' living and working conditions and wages.

Assessing Your Understanding

Imagine you have a pen pal, a student your age from Africa. In one of her letters, she asks you this question: "What is your school like?" How would you answer?

You might describe it as a large school, or a small one. You could say whether it is in a rural area or in the heart of a big city. You could describe your school building, the classes you take, your teachers, your friends, and so on. This would be easy for you, because school is such a big part of your life. The classes you take, the people you see, and the books you read all seem normal to you.

But have you ever wondered what school is like for a person your age in Africa? You could ask your pen pal. Depending on where your pen pal lives, though, the answer would be different. A school in a big city in Egypt is very different from a school in rural Uganda. But every school in Africa has at least one thing in common with your school—students are there to learn. Like other students, if you want to study new things, you must learn to assess your understanding.

Get Ready

What does "assessing your understanding" mean? It means checking to see how well you understand something you are reading or studying. If you assess your understanding as you go along, you will know what areas you need to read or think more about to make sure you understand. You can concentrate on studying those things. This can help you to get better grades. For example, by assessing your understanding before a test, you can predict what grade you will get on the test. And you will know exactly what you need to study if you want to get a higher grade. It can help you get more out of your reading. If you realize something does not make sense to you, you can use some strategies such as rereading or making a graphic organizer to help you understand the information.

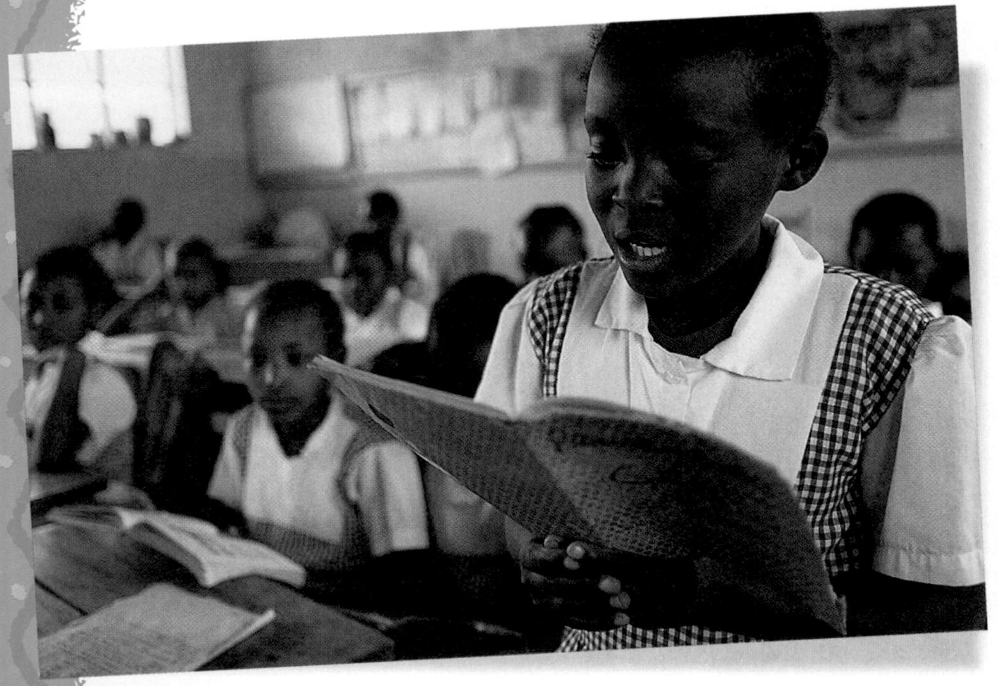

Try It Out

A good way of assessing your understanding is to play a simple game called "Do I Understand?" To play, choose one assignment you completed recently. Then ask yourself the questions on the checklist.

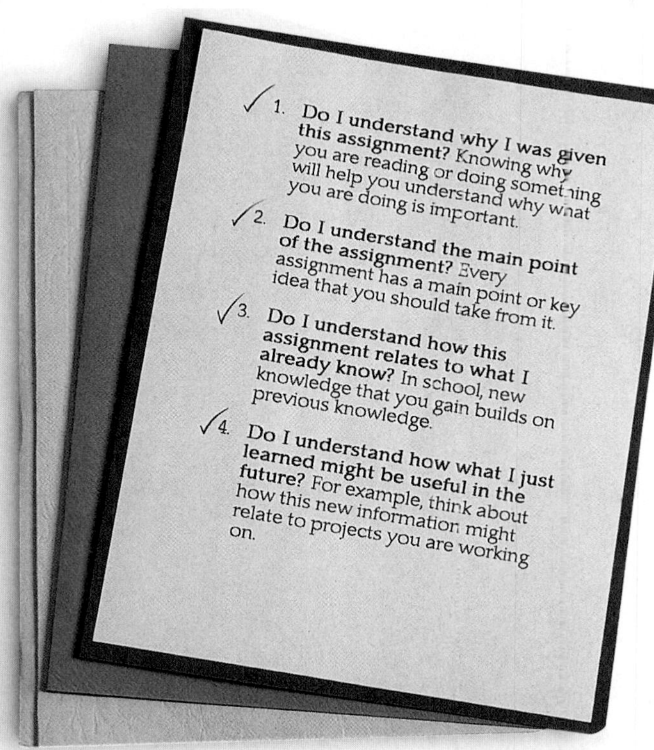

1. **Do I understand why I was given this assignment?** Knowing why you are reading or doing something will help you understand why what you are doing is important.
2. **Do I understand the main point of the assignment?** Every assignment has a main point or key idea that you should take from it.
3. **Do I understand how this assignment relates to what I already know?** In school, new knowledge that you gain builds on previous knowledge.
4. **Do I understand how what I just learned might be useful in the future?** For example, think about how this new information might relate to projects you are working on.

Apply the Skill

Practice assessing your understanding with the short reading assignment in the box, "An African School" by David Lamb.

1. Now, reread Question 1 in the list above. Why is it worthwhile to learn about a school in Kenya? What key ideas about the school does the writer try to communicate?
2. Reread Question 2. What do you think is the main point of "An African School"?
3. Reread Question 3. How does the writer's description fit with what you have already learned about Africa? Consider such things as languages, climate, and the condition of the school. Does anything in the reading assignment surprise you, or is it what you expected?
4. Look at Question 4. What are two ways that the knowledge you have just gained could help you in the future?

An African School

The Njumbi primary school [is] not far from the town of Karai in Kenya. . . . The headmaster, Michael Mathini, an energetic . . . man of thirty who rides a bicycle to work, greeted us at the door. He led us into his office and pointed with great pride to a wall graph showing that his students scored above the national average in the annual. . .examination.

The school has 620 students . . . and seventeen teachers who earned from $80 to $135 a month. . . . In the first-grade classroom across from Mathini's office, thirty or forty boys and girls were learning to count. . . They applauded . . . each time one of them gave the teacher the right answer. . . an ancient wooden radio sat on another teacher's desk and the dozen or so teenagers there strained through the heavy static to hear the creative writing lesson being broadcast in English from Nairobi.

Review and Activities

Reviewing Main Ideas

1. Describe how Islam has influenced the culture of North Africa.
2. What factor has greatly aided cultural diffusion in North Africa?
3. How is West Africa culturally diverse?
4. What role do family ties play in West African culture?
5. Explain how location has affected East African cultures.
6. How does the language of Swahili help unite the people of East Africa?
7. Why is the idea of privately owned land fairly new to East Africans?
8. How has South Africa affected the cultures of the entire region of Southern Africa?
9. What major effect did migrant labor have on the people of Southern Africa?
10. How is Central Africa like other parts of Africa?

Reviewing Key Terms

Use each key term below in a sentence that shows the meaning of the term.

1. culture
2. cultural diffusion
3. cultural diversity
4. kinship
5. nuclear family
6. extended family
7. lineage
8. clan
9. griot
10. plantation
11. migrant worker

Critical Thinking

1. **Identifying Central Issues** Explain why the proverb "A person is a person because of people" is particularly suited to African culture.
2. **Drawing Conclusions** What benefits and problems have come with modernization in Africa?

Graphic Organizer

Copy the chart onto a sheet of paper. Then complete the chart by describing one or more key features of the cultures of each region.

The Cultures of Africa				
Region	North Africa	West Africa	East Africa	Central and Southern Africa
Culture				

Map Activity

Africa

For each place listed below, write the letter from the map that shows its location.

1. Mediterranean Sea
2. North Africa
3. West Africa
4. East Africa
5. Central and Southern Africa

Place Location

Writing Activity

Writing a Dialogue

An exchange student from an African country has come to stay at your home for six weeks. You and your family are sharing your first dinner with the visitor. Write a dialogue in which you ask your visitor about African culture. Use what you have learned in this chapter to write your visitor's answers.

Take It to the NET

Activity Read an African fable and research the setting of the story. Use what you learn to write your own African fable. For help in completing this activity, visit **www.phschool.com.**

Chapter 13 Self-Test To review what you have learned, take the Chapter 13 Self-Test and get instant feedback on your answers. Go to **www.phschool.com** to take the test.

Skills Review

Turn to the Skills Activity.

Review the steps for assessing your understanding. Then look at the Writing Activity on this page. Ask yourself questions to assess whether you understand the reason for this writing assignment.

How Am I Doing?

Answer these questions to check your progress.

1. Can I describe the cultural diversity of Africa?
2. Do I understand the role of kinship in African cultures?
3. Can I explain how urbanization has changed the way of life of many Africans?
4. What information from this chapter can I include in my journal?

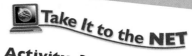

The Language of Music

In the United States, you can hear music at parties, in concerts, on the radio, or even in supermarkets. It has many purposes. Music also has many roles in the cultures of African countries. Music may be used to send messages or to tell a story. It may organize work or celebrate a special occasion. In the United States, it is not uncommon to perform music by itself. People in African countries, however, rarely play music by itself. Most often, they combine music with dance, theater, words, games, or visual art.

Traditional African instruments include xylophones, lutes, harps, horns, flutes, clarinets, bells, and drums. Musicians can study for years to master their art, just as they do in the United States. In many African cultures, drums play an important role in traditional and modern music.

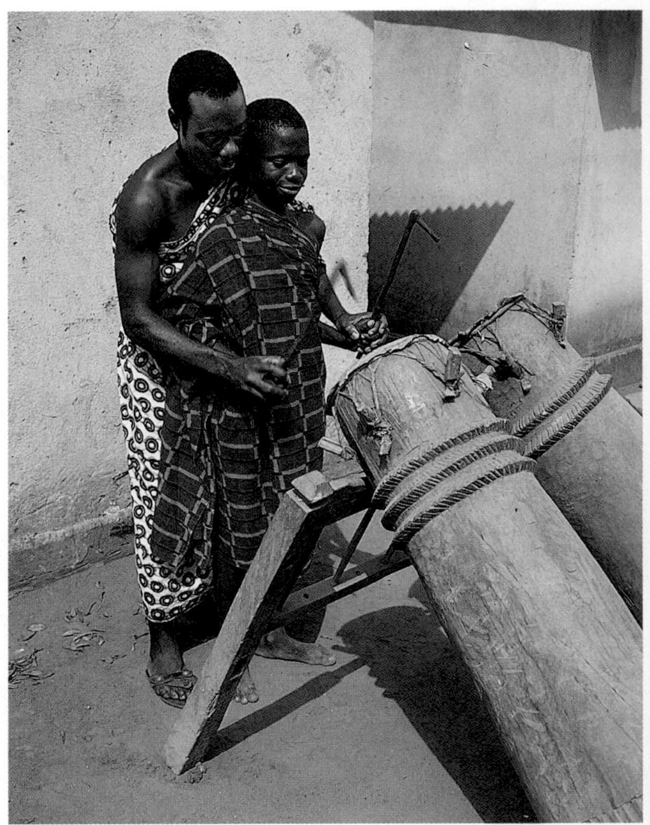

Purpose

In this activity, you will research traditional African drums and make your own drum. As you work on this activity, you will learn how Africans make and use drums.

Research African Drums

Traditionally, drums have been the most important instrument in African music. There are many types of drums, including the slit drum, the obodo, and the kettle drum. Use the information on this page to get you started. Then use encyclopedias, the Internet, and other resources to find out more about traditional African drums and how they differ. When you do research, look under subject headings such as African Arts, African Music, and Musical Instruments. You should also search under the names of specific drums.

Write down the names of several African drums. Then choose one drum to model your own after. Learn as much as you can about this kind of drum, including what materials it is made from, how it is played, how it is used, and where it is used.

Build Your Own Drum

Once you have chosen a traditional African drum as a model, you can build your own drum. You may want to use items such as buckets, cans, or cartons for the body of your drum. For the head of the drum, you might use cloth, plastic, or paper. Also consider the following questions:

- How will you attach the head of the drum to the body?
- Is one side of the drum open or are both sides covered?
- How will you strike your drum?

If possible, use materials that are similar to the materials the traditional drums are made from. Experiment with different methods to see which sounds best.

Play Your Drum

Figure out how you can use your drum in a way similar to the one you are modeling. For example, if the drum you are modeling was used to communicate messages across a long distance, think of a rhythmic code you can use to play a message to your classmates across the playground. If the drum was used as part of a drum group, you may want to write a short piece of music and play it with your classmates. If the drum accompanied a chant or song telling the history of a community, write a song telling a story about something that has happened to you or someone you know.

Links to Other Subjects

Researching African instruments	**Music**
Researching traditional materials	**Life Science**
Building a drum	**Physical Science**
Communicating over distance	**Language Arts**
Using a drum as part of a drum group	**Math (rhythms), Music**
Writing a chant to accompany a drum	**Language Arts, Music**
Writing a paragraph comparing drums	**Language Arts**

Compare Drums

After you have built your drum and practiced with it, write a paragraph comparing your drum to its African model. You may want to present your work to the class and perform a piece of music.

Write a summary that describes how you built and used your drum. Be sure to answer the following questions in the summary.

1. How is your drum similar to and different from the African drum you used as a model?
2. What factors affect the way your drum sounds?
3. How did you adapt the original uses of the model drum?

Exploring North Africa

SECTION 1
Egypt
HEARING THE CALL OF ISLAM

SECTION 2
Algeria
THE CASBAH AND THE COUNTRYSIDE

MAP ACTIVITIES

Six countries make up the region of North Africa. Find them on the map above. To help you get to know this region, do the following activities.

Size up the region

Which country in the region looks the largest? Which country looks the smallest? What body of water lies on the region's northern boundary?

Consider the location

Find the major cities of North Africa shown on this map. How close are they to the Mediterranean Sea? How do you think that nearness to the sea might have affected North Africa's cultures?

Egypt

Hearing the Call of Islam

Reach Into Your Background

You probably have a favorite holiday that you look forward to all year. Think about what you do during the holiday. What special foods do you eat? What different songs do you sing? Why do you and your family celebrate on that holiday?

Questions to Explore

1. How does religion affect Egypt's culture?
2. How has the role of Islam in Egypt changed in recent times?

Key Terms

bazaar
fellaheen

Key Places

Cairo

At noon, the restaurants in Cairo stand empty. Egyptian teenagers try not to think about pita bread or sweet dates. Only certain people, such as the very young or those who are sick, eat regular meals. Is there a food shortage in Egypt? No, it's the Muslim holiday of Ramadan (ram uh DAHN). Muslims are followers of the religion of Islam. For a month, Muslims fast from dawn to dusk. A fast is a period when people go without food. During Ramadan, Muslims eat only when the sun is down.

But Muslims do more than fast during Ramadan. They also think of those who are less fortunate than themselves. And they try not to get angry when things go wrong.

▼ More people live in Cairo than in any other city in Africa. Most of the people who live here are Muslim Arabs.

Islam in Egypt

Egypt is located in North Africa, where many of the world's Muslims live. Egypt is across the Red Sea from Saudi Arabia, where the messenger of Islam, Muhammad, was born. Islam spread from Saudi Arabia across North Africa. Today, the countries in this area have populations that are mostly Muslim. Islam is the major religion in Egypt. In fact, Islam is the country's official religion.

COUNTRY • PROFILE

Egypt: Population

A crowded street in Cairo

Culture The map and charts present information about the people of Egypt and where they live. **Map and Chart Study** (a) How does Egypt's geography affect where people live? (b) Use the information in the map and charts to write a brief paragraph about the people of Egypt.

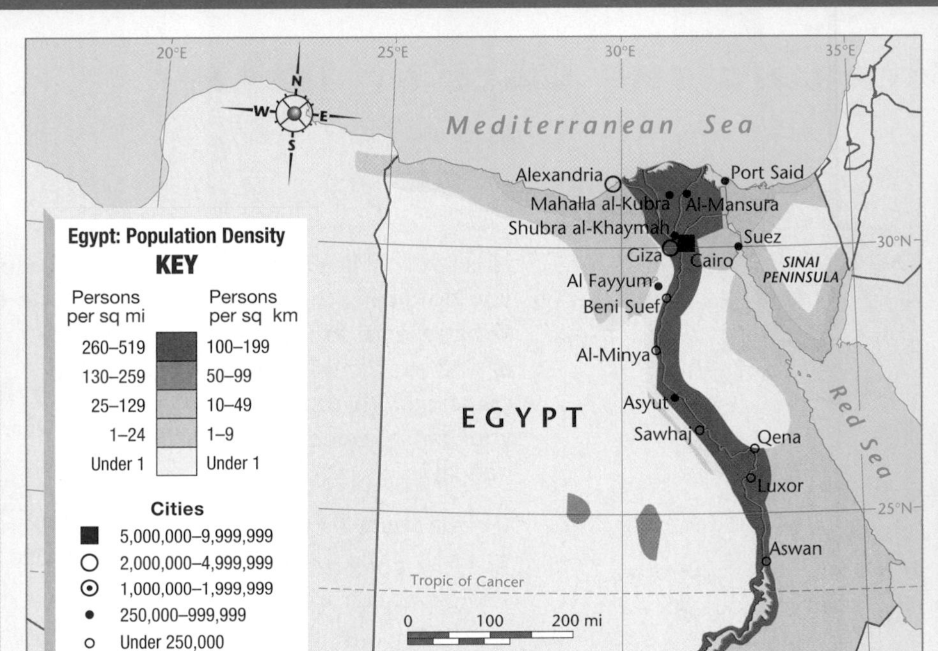

Population by Age Group and Sex

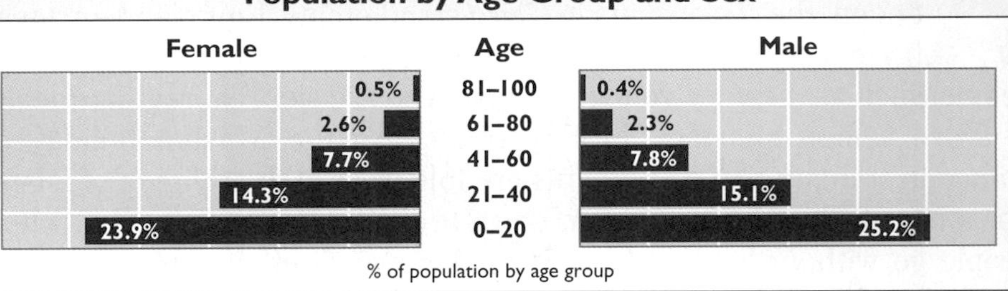

Urban and Rural Population

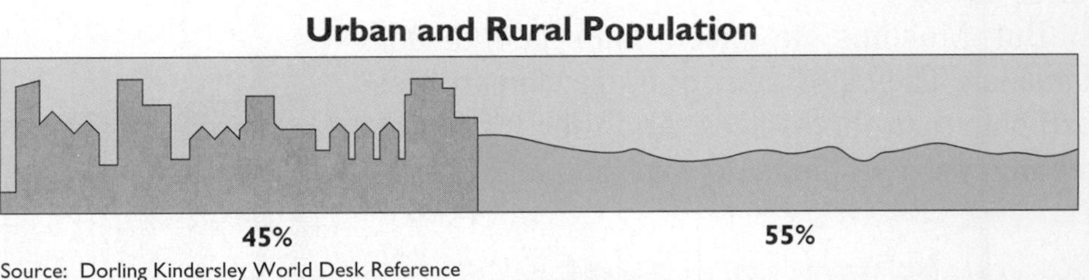

Source: Dorling Kindersley World Desk Reference

Take It to the NET
Data Update For the most recent data on Egypt, visit **www.phschool.com**.

Teachings and Practices The Quran is the sacred book of the Muslims. It contains the basic teachings of Islam. Muslims believe that the Quran contains the words of God, which were revealed to Muhammad during the month of Ramadan. Muslims also believe that the Jewish Torah and the Christian Bible are the word of God.

Recordings of the Quran have become very popular in Egypt. As Ahmed Abdel Rahman (AH med AHB del RAHK mahn), a record store manager in Cairo, says, "You can get bored by a song after a few days. But no one gets bored listening to the Quran." During the day, many Egyptians listen to the recordings on audiotapes or on the government radio station.

Islam's Contribution to Science

Muslim scholars do not limit themselves to studying the Quran. From the 600s on, Muslims have studied art, literature, philosophy, math, astronomy, and medicine. Muslim mathematicians invented algebra, and Muslim astronomers accurately mapped the locations of the stars. A Muslim astronomer drew this illustration of a comet in the 1500s. **Critical Thinking** What practical purpose do you think Muslim scholars may have had for studying astronomy?

"I have two ears," says Saad Eddin Saleh (SAH ahd EH deen SAH leh), a carpenter in Cairo, "one for work, and one for listening to the Quran."

The Quran requires that Muslims pray five times a day. Many Egyptians pray in a mosque, a building used for Muslim worship. During prayer, Muslims face in the direction of Mecca, Saudi Arabia, where Islam's holiest shrine is located. A mosque may also offer religious training for schoolchildren. The young students who attend these schools learn to read and memorize the Quran.

Ask Questions What else would you like to know about the religion of Islam?

An Islamic Renewal The Quran is one of the main sources of Sharia (sha REE ah), or Islamic law. The Sharia is also based on the words and deeds of Muhammad, and on comments written by Muslim scholars and lawmakers. Muslims in North Africa and Southwest Asia try to renew their faith by living each day according to Sharia.

Praying and fasting are two of the ways that Egyptian Muslims have brought their religion into their daily lives. But the Quran includes many teachings that govern day-to-day life. It stresses the importance of honesty, honor, and giving to others. It also requires Muslims to love and respect their families.

Most Muslims in Egypt agree that the laws of Egypt should be based on Islamic law. In 1978, Egypt's government studied its laws and discovered that most already were in agreement with Sharia. But in recent years, some Egyptians have said that all of Egypt's laws should match Islamic law. And this has led to disagreements among Egyptian Muslims.

King Tut's Clothes
Scientists are studying the clothes of Pharaoh Tutankhamen, the boy who became ruler of Egypt at the age of nine, in about 1333 B.C. They have learned that Egyptian clothing had no hooks or buttons. King Tut had to tuck, wrap, and tie his clothes on. Because of their clothing, ancient Egyptians had to take small steps and walk carefully.

▼Some Egyptian women veil their faces, while others do not. Why do you think a woman would choose to veil her face? Why might she not?

Dressing Modestly One part of the debate about Sharia has centered on how women should dress in public. Muhammad taught that men and women are equal in the eyes of God. And Islamic law requires that both men and women dress modestly in public. Men and women must wear loose-fitting clothing that covers most of the body. Sharia requires that women cover all parts of their body except their hands, face, and feet.

However, some Muslims believe that women should also veil their faces, except for the eyes. They believe that covering the face is an important way for women to show their Muslim faith. Many other Muslims, including some government leaders, disagree. In 1994, these leaders banned female public school students from veiling their faces. This upset many Egyptians who were not strongly religious. They feel that the kind of veil a woman wears should be a matter of individual choice.

Life in Egypt

People in Egypt's cities and villages alike practice Islam. However, except for the time they spend in prayer, people in the cities and the villages live very different lives.

City Life Nearly half of all Egyptians live in cities. Cairo, the nation's capital and largest city, is home to about six million Egyptians. More people live in Cairo than in Los Angeles and Chicago combined. It is the largest city in Africa. Some

A Traffic Jam in Cairo

Some people think that Cairo is the loudest city in the world because of its honking horns and roar of car engines. More than 14 million people live in the city and surrounding urban areas, but even more drive or take buses and trains in from the suburbs during the day. At night the streets are empty, but it can be difficult to find even one open parking space.

parts of Cairo are more than 1,000 years old. Other parts of Cairo look just like a Western city. Most people live in apartment buildings with electric fans or air-conditioning. However, they often shop in traditional open-air markets called **bazaars.**

Many people move to the cities from rural areas. They hope to find jobs and better education. As a result, Cairo is very crowded. There are traffic jams and housing shortages. Some people live in tents that they have set up on rowboats on the Nile. Others live in homes they have built in the huge graveyards on the outskirts of Cairo. So many people live in the graveyards that they are considered suburbs of the city, and the government has provided the graveyards with electricity.

Connect How does urban life differ from rural life in the United States?

Rural Life Most of the people in Egypt's rural areas live in villages along the Nile River or the Suez Canal. In Egyptian villages, most of the people make their living by farming. Egypt's rural farmers are called ***fellaheen*** (fel uh HEEN). Most of the fellaheen do not own land. Land is scarce because the river banks are so narrow. Some fellaheen farm small, rented plots of land. Others work in the fields of rich landowners.

Many of the fellaheen live in homes built of mud bricks or stones. Most of these homes are small. They have one to three rooms and a courtyard that the family often shares with its animals. The roofs of village houses are flat. The fellaheen use their roofs as places to store food and firewood, spread dates out to dry, and dry wet clothes.

▲ With power from a water buffalo, a fellaheen woman runs a traditional machine that separates the seeds of grain from the plants.

Egypt's people differ from each other in many ways. Some live in cities, while others live in rural areas. Some people make a living by programming computers, while others farm using ancient techniques. Despite their differences, however, most Egyptians are unified by one thing—their faith in Islam. Egyptian Muslims hope that renewing their faith every day will help them to maintain traditional values and customs in a modern age.

1. **Define** (a) bazaar, (b) fellaheen.
2. **Identify** Cairo.
3. Give two examples of how Islam affects everyday life in Egypt.
4. Compare the lives of city and village dwellers in Egypt.

Critical Thinking

5. **Identifying Central Issues** How have Egyptian Muslims tried to renew their faith?

Activity

6. **Writing to Learn** In a journal entry, describe how the clothes people wear and the music they listen to may reflect their beliefs. Use examples from your own experience as well as from this section.

Algeria

The Casbah and the Countryside

Reach Into Your Background
How do you adapt to the climate in your area? How do you change your schedule or your choice of clothing based on the weather?

Questions to Explore

1. What are some differences and similarities between the Berbers and the Arabs of Algeria?
2. How is life in Algerian cities different from life in the villages?

Key Terms
terrace
souq
casbah

Key People and Places
Sahara
Berber
Arab

Like people in many parts of the world, Algerians adapt to their climate by resting during the hottest hours of the day. Journalist William Langewiesche described part of his visit to Adrar, an oasis city in the Algerian Sahara, as follows:

> "We . . . waited out the hot midday hours, drinking brown water from a plastic jug. The water was brown because Miloud had mixed in cade oil. The cade is an evergreen bush that grows in the Atlas Mountains. Saharan nomads use its oil to seal the inside of goatskin water bags. Miloud did not have a goatskin, but he came from a long line of desert travelers. He bought the oil in small bottles and added it to his water for flavor and good health. The mixture smelled of pine sap and tasted of clay. . . . But I would have drunk anything. I had been for a walk."

▼ The Tuareg, a nomadic Berber group, normally relax under tents during the hottest hours of the day. This Tuareg man is brewing green tea.

Algeria: Climate and Physical Features

Percent of Land Covered by the Sahara

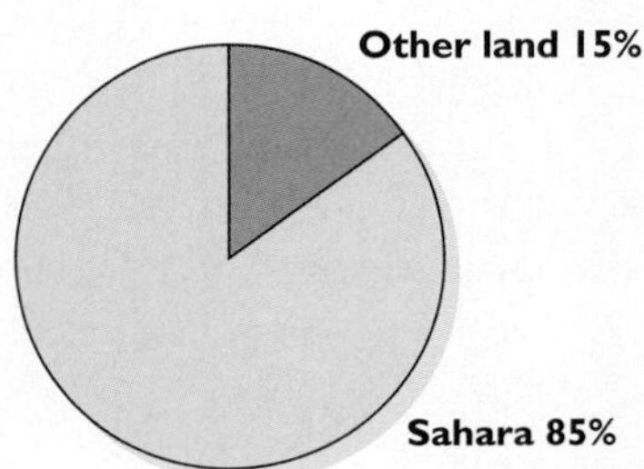

Source: Infoplease Internet Encyclopedia

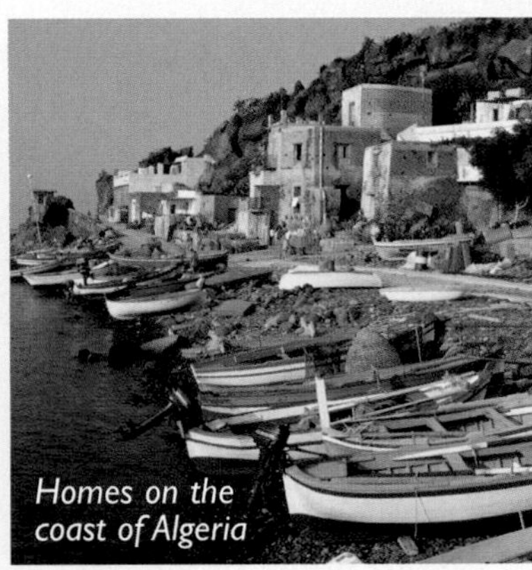

Homes on the coast of Algeria

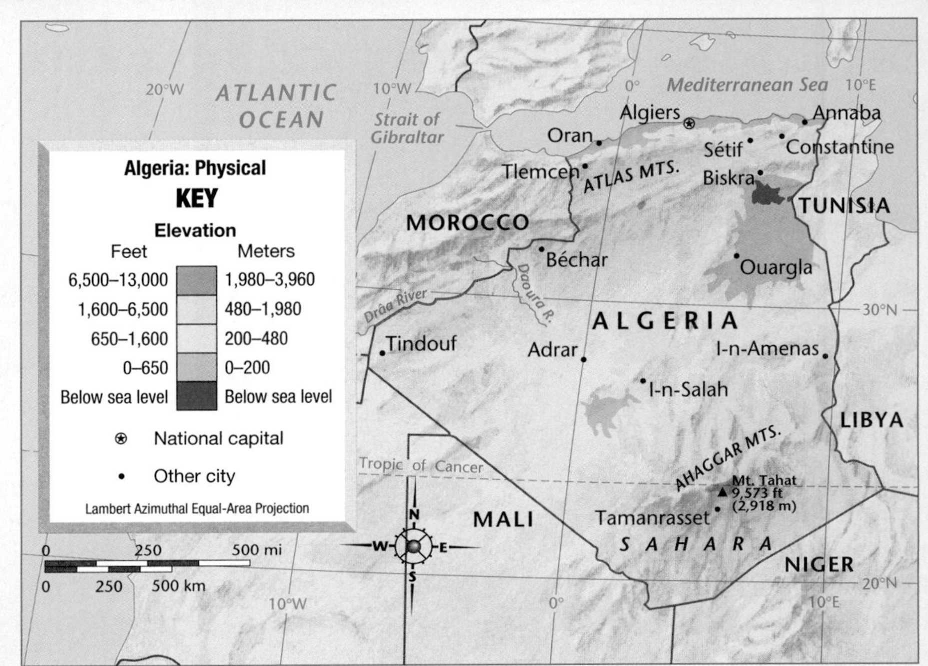

Weather Chart

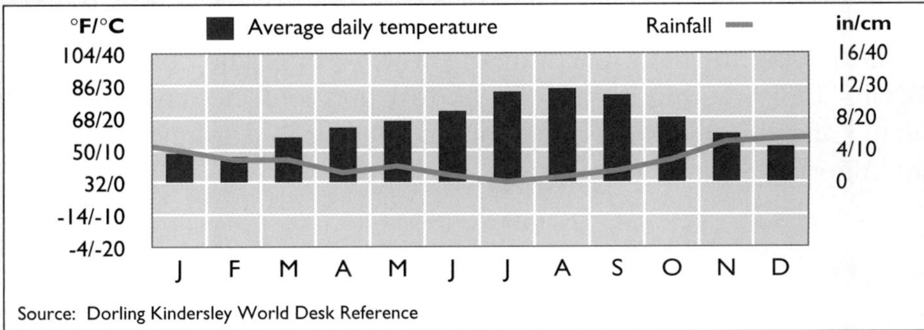

Source: Dorling Kindersley World Desk Reference

Take It to the NET
Data Update For the most recent data on Algeria, visit **www.phschool.com.**

Geography The map above shows Algeria's elevation and physical features. The charts provide information on Algeria's climate and environment. **Map and Chart Study** (a) Why do you think most people in Algeria live in coastal areas? (b) In which three months does Algeria receive the most rainfall?

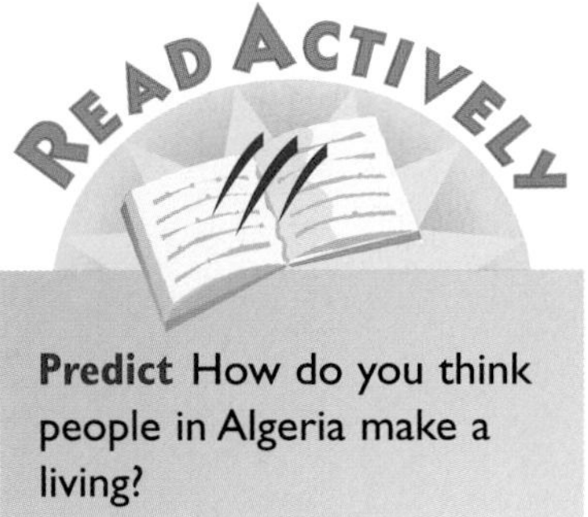

Predict How do you think people in Algeria make a living?

Algeria's People

The temperature outside while Langewiesche was walking was 124°F (51°C). To survive in that heat, people must drink enough water to produce 2 to 4 gallons (8 to 16 l) of sweat a day. Look at the map in the Country Profile. The Sahara covers all of Algeria south of the Atlas Mountains. Water is in short supply in this area. For this reason, fewer than three percent of Algeria's people live here. But because of their resourcefulness, Berber and Arab nomads have survived in the Sahara for hundreds of years.

The Berbers The Berbers and the Arabs are Algeria's two main ethnic groups. The Berbers have lived in North Africa since at least 3000 B.C. No one knows exactly where they came from, but many historians think they migrated from Southwest Asia. They settled in the Atlas Mountains and on plains near Algeria's coast. More than 90 percent of Algerians still live near the coast, where the weather is milder than in the Sahara.

Some Berbers live in Algeria's cities. Most, however, live in villages in rural areas. Many Berbers continue to follow traditional ways of life. Berber households form an extended family, which includes more relatives than just a mother, a father, and their children. Each Berber house has an open courtyard in the back. The windows in the house face the courtyard, not the street. Each married couple in a family has its own home, opening onto the family courtyard. In this way, grandparents, parents, sons, daughters, and cousins can all live close together.

Family is so important to the Berbers that their village governments are based on it. The head of each family is a member of the village assembly, which makes laws for the village.

Most families in Berber villages make a living by farming and herding. They get up as soon as it is light. In the middle of the day, when the sun is hottest, people rest for several hours. Then they work until dark. Farmers use wooden plows drawn by camels. They grow wheat and barley and raise livestock. In the mountains, the Berbers build **terraces,** or platforms cut into the mountainside, for their crops. The terraces increase the amount of farmland and stop the soil from washing away when it rains.

The Professional Poet Many Berber villages have a professional poet. The poet is always a woman who improvises songs in one of the Berber languages. A chorus of women accompany the poet with their voices and with small drums.

A Desert Lifestyle

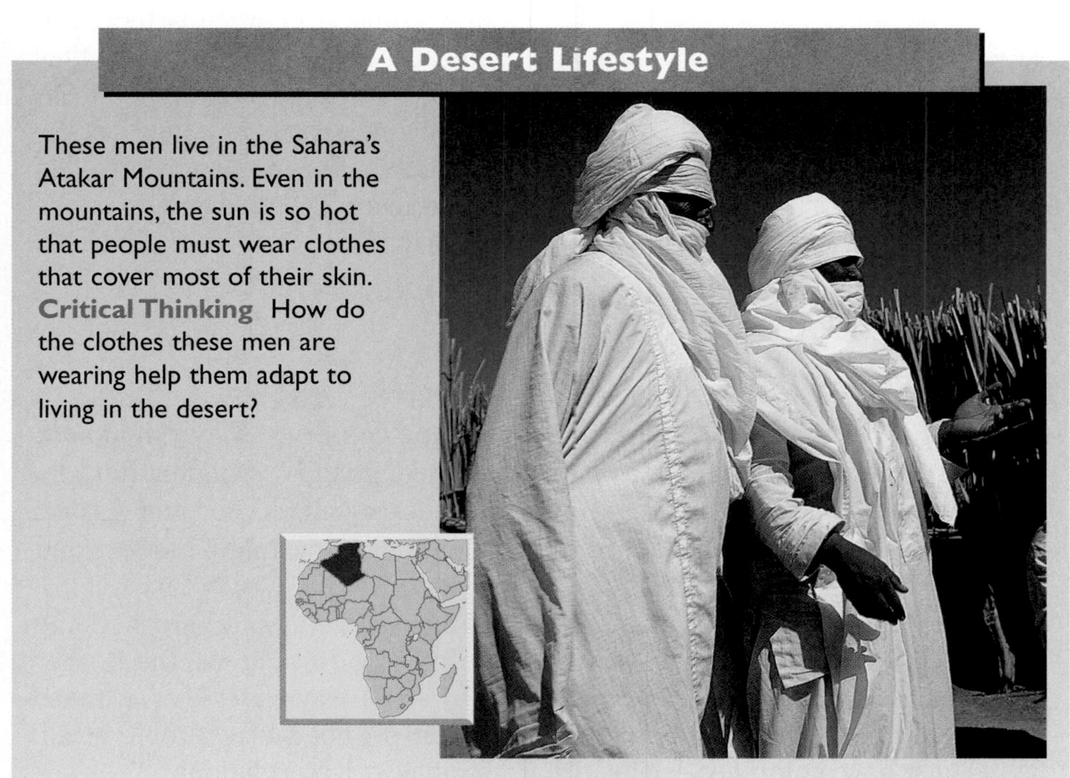

These men live in the Sahara's Atakar Mountains. Even in the mountains, the sun is so hot that people must wear clothes that cover most of their skin. **Critical Thinking** How do the clothes these men are wearing help them adapt to living in the desert?

Arabs in Algeria The Berber way of life changed in the A.D. 600s, when Arabs spread across North Africa. The Arabs conquered North Africa gradually, over hundreds of years. Peace in the region came about when most Berbers accepted the religion of Islam.

Arab traditions are like Berber traditions in many ways. For example, both Muslim Arabs and non-Muslim Berbers traditionally live with extended families. However, Arabs and Berbers do differ.

Muslim Arabs created a central government in Algeria that is based on Islam. The Berber tradition is for each village to govern itself. But Berbers adapted to Arab rule by keeping their own governments along with the new one.

Another difference between the Berbers and the Arabs was that most Arabs were nomads. They usually camped near a well or stream in the summer and herded animals across the desert during the rest of the year. As a result of Arab influence, many Berbers of the hills and plains changed from a farming to a nomadic lifestyle. Sometimes there were conflicts between farmers and nomads. More often, however, they achieved peaceful settlement. Usually, the farmers would let the nomads' herds graze on their land in exchange for livestock and goods. The farmers also sold grains to the nomads. Most Berbers today are farmers, but some Berber nomads still migrate across the Sahara.

An Algerian Market

Traditionally, Algerians bought goods in open-air markets. Shopkeepers in Algeria today still put some of their goods outside their stores, so that Algerians can continue to enjoy shopping in the open air. This shop is in the town of El Dued.

Berbers and Arabs Today

Berbers and Arabs have mixed over the centuries. Today, it is hard to recognize a Berber or an Arab based on language or religion. Berbers and Arabs alike are Muslim. Most Berbers speak Berber and Arabic. Because France ruled Algeria for part of its history, many Berbers and Arabs also speak French.

Most Berbers and many Arabs in Algeria live in rural areas. Some are farmers, while others are nomads. In some rural areas, the Berber way of life has hardly been touched by Arab ways. Berbers in these areas speak Berber languages, and some do not speak Arabic at all. Many have combined Islam with traditional African religions.

Visualize Visualize yourself walking through a village in rural Algeria. What would you see? What might you see along a city street?

Old and New

◀▲ Algiers, the capital of Algeria, has a modern section of high-rise buildings, shown at the left. The old section of the city (above) is called the Casbah. What clue shows that the Casbah was not built in the 1900s?

Life in the Cities Berbers and Arabs who live in Algeria's cities have the most in common with each other. More than half of Algeria's people live in cities, and most speak Arabic. Mosques and open-air marketplaces called ***souqs*** (sooks) fill the cities. Older parts of the cities are called ***casbahs*** (KAHZ bahz). The houses and stores here are close to each other on narrow, winding streets. Newer parts of the cities look like cities in Europe and the United States. They have tall buildings and wide streets.

The Berbers and the Arabs of Algeria have had many conflicts in the past. However, there have also been long periods during which they learned from each other peacefully. Algeria's future will continue to mix Berber and Arab, old and new.

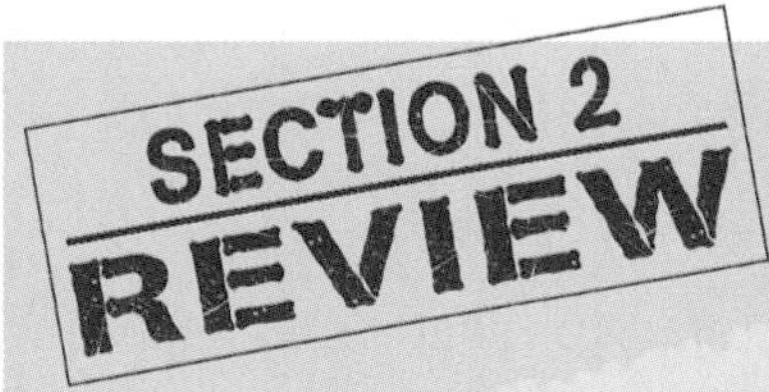

SECTION 2 REVIEW

1. **Define** (a) terrace, (b) souq, (c) casbah.
2. **Identify** (a) Sahara, (b) Berber, (c) Arab.
3. How did the Berber way of life change when Arabs came to North Africa?
4. How are Arabs and Berbers similar today?

Critical Thinking

5. **Drawing Conclusions** What differences might have caused conflicts between Berbers and Arabs? How did Berbers and Arabs sometimes overcome their differences?

Activity

6. **Writing to Learn** Suppose that you were a member of a Berber village assembly at the time that the Arabs first came to North Africa. Write a speech in which you discuss the possible impact of this change on your community.

Using Regional Maps

Have you ever seen anyone try to drive around town with a map of the whole world?

It would never work. A world map is useful for looking at the world as a whole. You can easily see the shapes and locations of the continents and oceans. They do not show you street names, however. Because they cover such a large area, world maps lack the detail to show much about a specific part of the world.

That is why we have regional maps. You already know that a region is an area of the Earth that shares some common characteristics. A regional map is a map of a region. Regional maps are probably the most common type of map. Road maps and bus maps are regional maps. So are the weather maps you see on the news. Throughout your life, you will see regional maps in newspapers and magazines, in textbooks and on television. It pays to know how to use them.

Get Ready

Regional maps focus on one part of the world, showing it in greater detail. Because of this detail, you can learn a lot about the region that is shown on the map. Since regions can be defined by many different characteristics—landforms, economies, political boundaries, and so on—there are many different types of regional maps. But if you learn how to read one type of regional map, you can use your skills to help you read others.

Try It Out

Follow these steps to read the map in column two on the next page.

A. Identify the region. What region is shown on the map? What defines the region?

B. Use the map key to learn about the region. What basic information is shown on the map? What do the solid lines represent? What do the single dots represent?

C. Use the regional map as a tool. What landforms can be found on either side of the Nile River valley? Where are most cities in the Nile River valley located?

D. Extend your learning. Why might the Nile River be important to people in Egypt? How is the Nile related to the location of Egyptian cities?

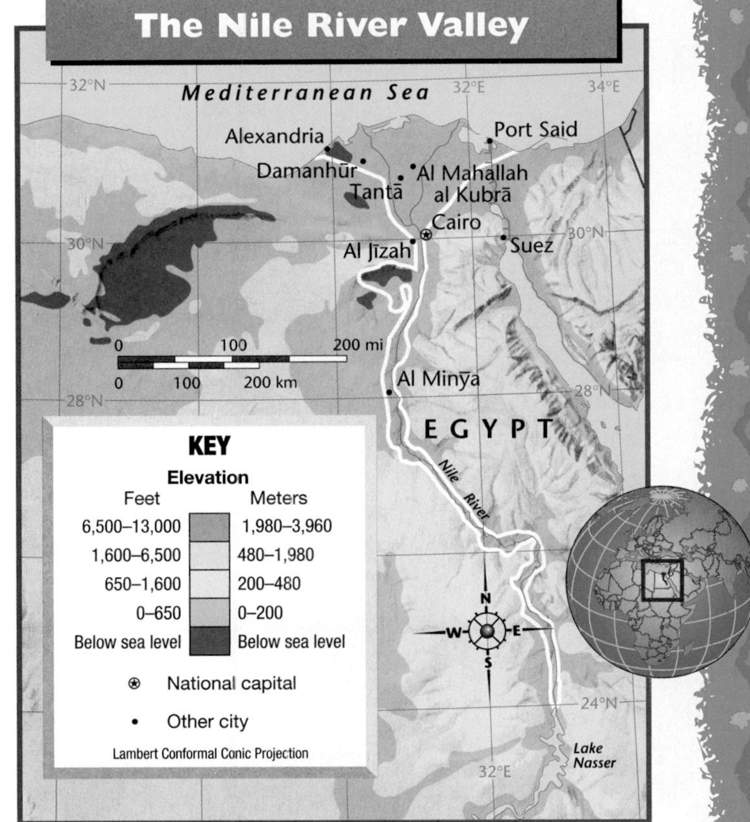

Apply the Skill

The map below is a regional map of North Africa. Work independently to apply the four basic regional map reading skills to this map.

1. **Identify the region.** What region is shown on the map? What defines the region?

2. **Use the map key to learn about the region.** What basic information is shown on the map? What physical features are identified on this map?

3. **Use the regional map as a tool.** How many countries are in North Africa? Which countries are they? Do you see any bodies of water in North Africa?

4. **Extend your learning.** Why would this map be useful in learning about the ways of life of this region? How might it help you understand the history of the region? What do you think might have been very important to people of this region?

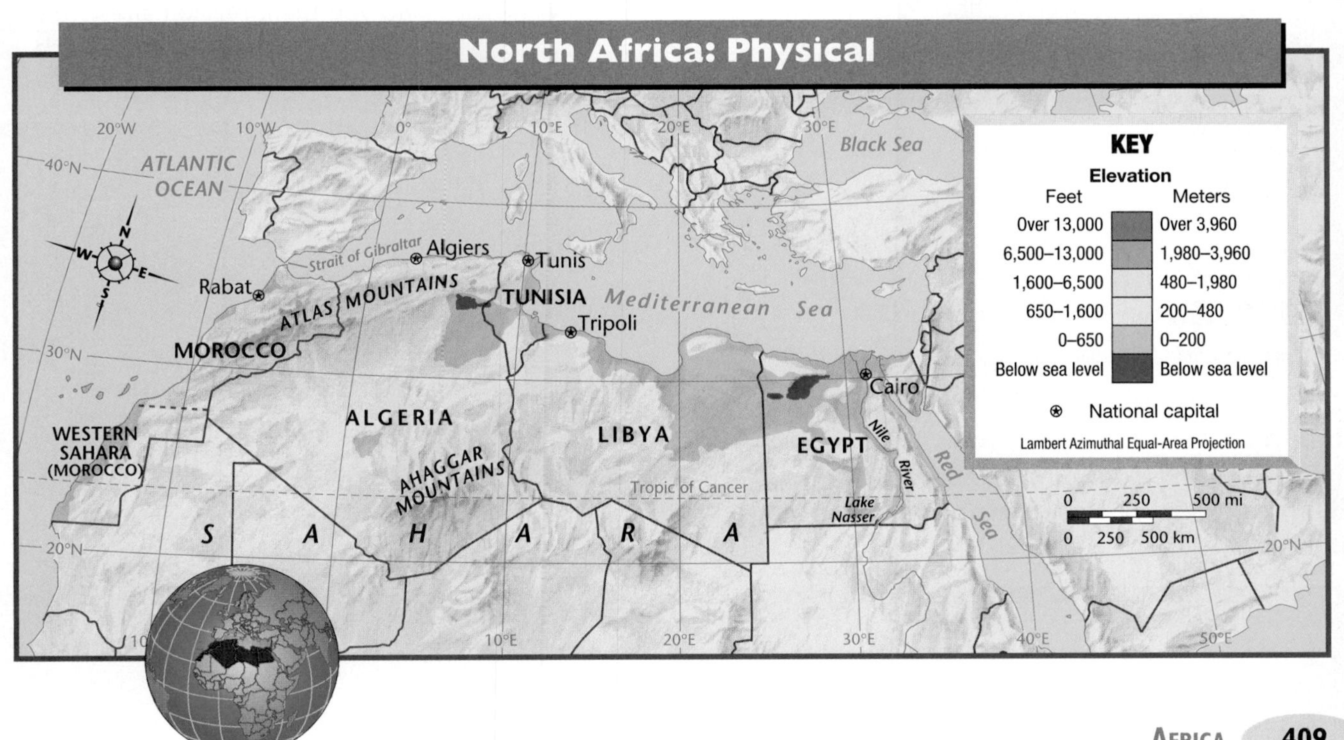

Review and Activities

Reviewing Main Ideas

1. Why do most Muslims study and memorize parts of the Quran?
2. How do Egyptians show their faith in Islam in their daily lives?
3. How does life in Egypt's cities differ from life in Egypt's rural areas?
4. Explain what Berbers and Arabs in Algeria have in common and what sets them apart.
5. How does Algeria's geography affect the people who live there?
6. How do Algeria's cities blend the old and the new?

Reviewing Key Terms

Decide whether each statement is true or false. If it is true, write "true." If it is false, change the underlined term to make the statement true.

1. A traditional Egyptian open-air market is called a <u>casbah</u>.
2. Egypt's rural farmers are called <u>fellaheen</u>.
3. <u>Souqs</u> are platforms cut into the side of a mountain.
4. In Algeria, an open-air market may be called a <u>nomad</u>.
5. The old section of Algiers is called the <u>Sharia</u>.

Critical Thinking

1. **Recognizing Cause and Effect** Why do you think that the Berbers who lived in isolated areas maintained their language and traditions after Arabs came to Algeria?
2. **Drawing Conclusions** How do you think religion affects the way people in Egypt and Algeria feel about their communities?

Graphic Organizer

Copy the web onto a sheet of paper and then complete it. Narrow your focus each time you move to a new level on the web. Fill in the web with as many people and ideas as you can.

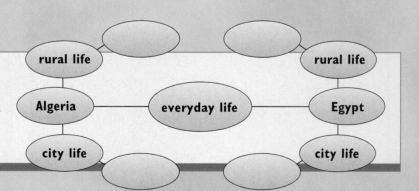

rural life
Algeria
city life
everyday life
rural life
Egypt
city life

Map Activity

North Africa

For each place listed below, write the letter from the map that shows its location.

1. Cairo
2. Algeria
3. Mediterranean Sea
4. Egypt
5. Sahara

Place Location

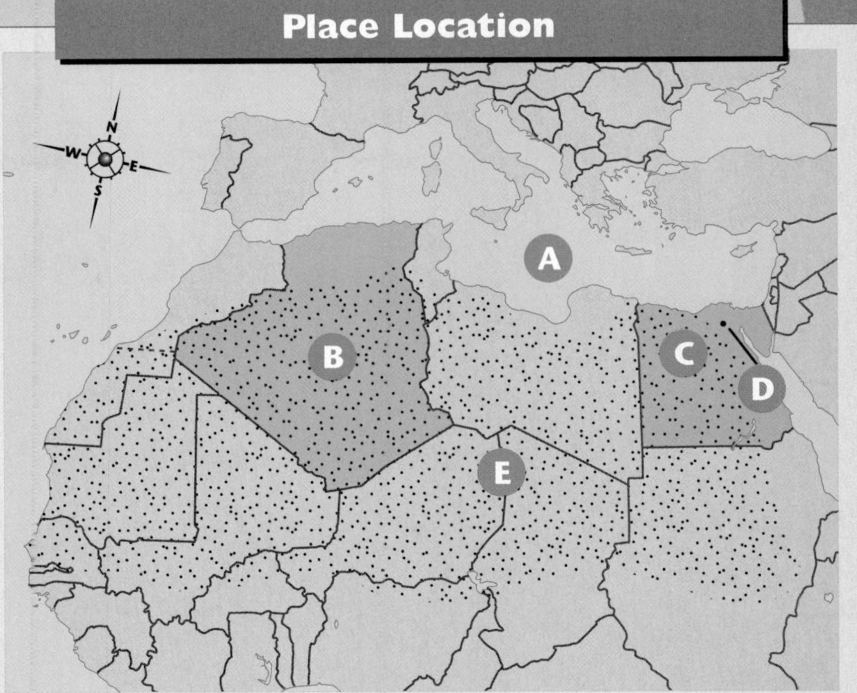

Writing Activity

Writing a Poem

The Berber languages are rarely written down. Most Berber history is preserved by professional poets. Pretend that you are a professional poet living in the 600s, when Arabs first came to North Africa. Write a poem explaining some of the differences and similarities between Arabs and Berbers.

Take It to the NET

Activity Learn more about Algeria and write a report on what you find most interesting. For help in completing this activity, visit **www.phschool.com.**

Chapter 14 Self-Test To review what you have learned, take the Chapter 14 Self-Test and get instant feedback on your answers. Go to **www.phschool.com** to take the test.

Skills Review

Turn to the Skills Activity.

Review the steps for using regional maps. Then answer the following questions: (a) How can you use the map key to help you learn about a region? (b) How can you use a regional map as a tool?

How Am I Doing?

Answer these questions to check your progress.

1. Do I understand how Islam has influenced life in both Egypt and Algeria?
2. Can I identify some historic events that have shaped the modern cultures of North Africa?
3. Do I understand how cultures in North Africa compare to other African cultures I have studied?
4. What information from this chapter can I include in my journal?

CHAPTER 15

Exploring West Africa

SECTION 1
Nigeria
ONE COUNTRY, MANY IDENTITIES

SECTION 2
Ghana
FIRST IN INDEPENDENCE

SECTION 3
Mali
THE DESERT IS COMING

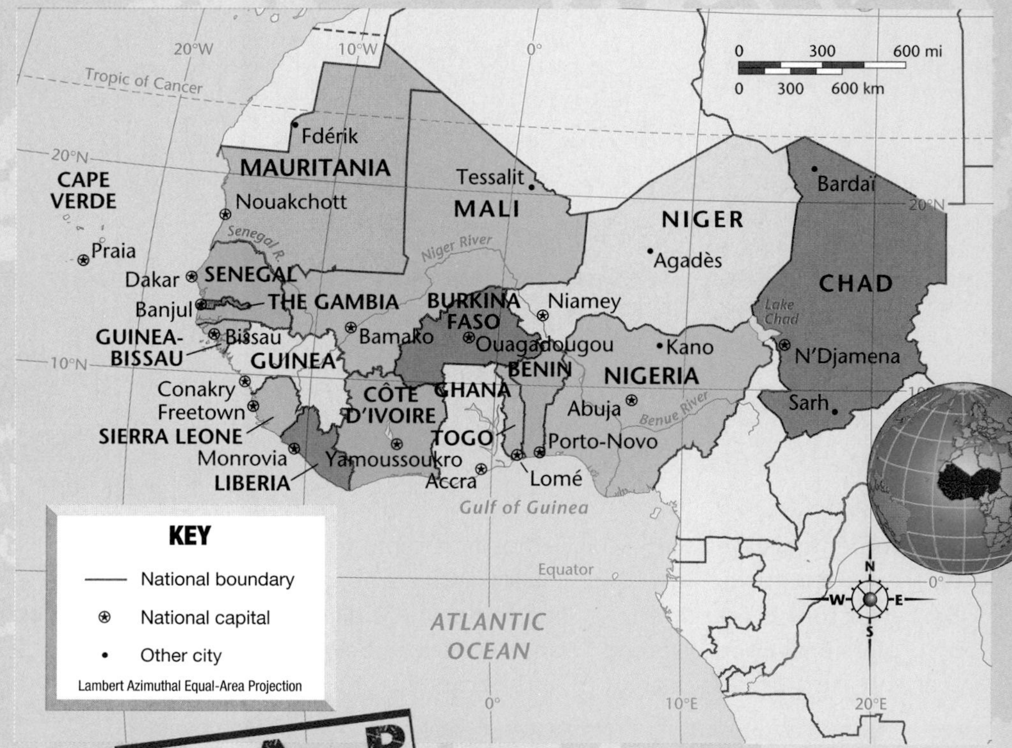

MAP ACTIVITIES

Seventeen countries make up the region of West Africa. To help you get to know this region, do the following activities.

Consider the location

What ocean do many of West Africa's countries border? What capitals of West African countries are close to rivers and lakes? What cities are far from rivers and lakes?

Think about the cities

Where are many of West Africa's cities? What factors might explain the locations of West African cities?

Consider the climate

Nearness to the Equator is one factor that can influence a country's climate. Where does most of West Africa lie in relation to the Equator and the Tropic of Cancer? Based on West Africa's location, what do you think its climate might be like?

Nigeria

One Country, Many Identities

Reach Into Your Background
Think about the ways in which you use language in daily life.

How would you communicate with people who do not speak your language?

Questions to Explore

1. What are Nigeria's main ethnic groups?
2. How are Nigeria's main ethnic groups similar to and different from each other?

Key Terms
multiethnic
census

Key Places
Lagos
Abuja
Kano

The language of England is English. The language of Spain is Spanish. The language of Greece is Greek. But the language of Nigeria is not Nigerian. In fact, there is no such language as Nigerian. Nigerians speak about 400 languages!

The languages of Nigeria match its ethnic groups. Nigeria's three most widely spoken languages are Hausa, Yoruba, and Igbo. There are places called Hausaland, Yorubaland, and Igboland. Most people in Hausaland are Hausa and speak Hausa. Most people in Yorubaland are Yoruba and speak Yoruba. And most people in Igboland are Igbo and speak Igbo. But these places are not countries. In fact, Hausaland and Yorubaland both lie partly in Nigeria and partly in other countries.

Nigeria's History

Why are there so many ethnic groups and languages within one country? Before Europeans arrived, what is now Nigeria was ruled by many ethnic groups, including the Hausa, the Yoruba, and the Igbo. But when Europeans drew Nigeria's borders, they did not think about ethnic groups. Look at the map in the Country Profile. You can see that Nigeria's borders do not match the borders of any one ethnic group.

Nigeria contains so many ethnic groups in part because it is so big. Nigeria is about as big as the states of California, Arizona, and New Mexico combined. More people live in Nigeria than in any other country in Africa. Its population is nearly twice that of Ethiopia, the second most populous country in Africa. And Nigeria is **multiethnic,** which means that many ethnic groups live within its borders.

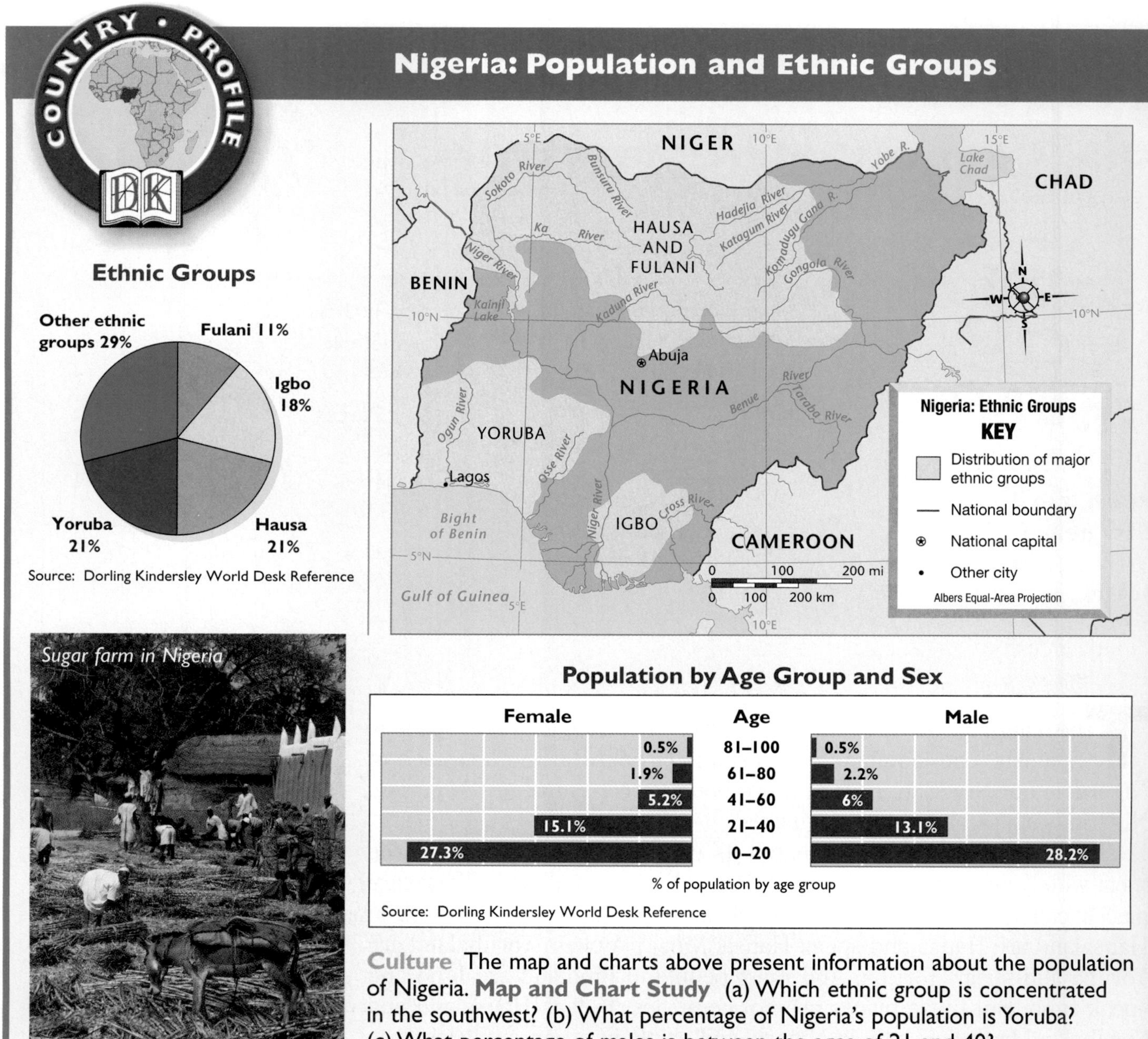

Culture The map and charts above present information about the population of Nigeria. **Map and Chart Study** (a) Which ethnic group is concentrated in the southwest? (b) What percentage of Nigeria's population is Yoruba? (c) What percentage of males is between the ages of 21 and 40?

Take It to the NET

Data Update For the most recent data on Nigeria, visit **www.phschool.com**.

The Colonial Legacy The Hausa, the Fulani (FOO lah nee), the Yoruba, and the Igbo were each governing their own regions when Europeans arrived. In the late 1400s, Portugal began to buy slaves in West Africa. Later, Great Britain, the Netherlands, and other countries entered the slave trade.

By 1914, Great Britain had taken over the government of Nigeria. The borders of the British colony of Nigeria included part of Hausaland, part of Yorubaland, and Igboland.

Nigeria became independent in 1960. Ethnic groups that had always lived separately then worked together to create one nation. To help unify the country, in 1991 the government moved the nation's capital from Lagos, in the south, to Abuja (ah BOO jah). The new capital is located in the central portion of the country, where several ethnic groups live.

Unifying the large number of ethnic groups in Nigeria was not easy. Only a few years after the country became independent, fighting broke out among some groups. A military group took control of the government in 1967. This began a long period in which various military groups ruled. Many of Nigeria's people struggled to create a democratic government free of military rule. Finally, on May 29, 1999, military leaders gave up their power to a new democracy controlled by the people.

Pidgin How do people talk to each other when they speak different languages? One way is to create a language that includes a little of each language. This kind of language is called pidgin. Nigerian pidgin mixes English words with the grammar of Nigerian languages. Enslaved Africans and their captors may have been the first people in Africa to use pidgin.

Three Different Ways of Life

Making Abuja the capital helped bring Nigeria together, because it meant that the capital would be close to more than one ethnic group. The Hausa, the Fulani, the Igbo, and the Yoruba each live in different regions. Most Hausa and Fulani live in the north. The Igbo live mainly in the southeast, and the Yoruba in the southwest. Many smaller ethnic groups live in central Nigeria and throughout the country.

The Hausa and Fulani: Traders of the North Both the Hausa and the Fulani built city-states in northern Nigeria. The Fulani conquered Hausaland in the early 1800s. Many Hausa and Fulani have intermarried since that time. The Hausa and the Fulani make up about 32 percent of Nigeria's people. Together, they are called the Hausa-Fulani. Most Hausa and Fulani are Muslims.

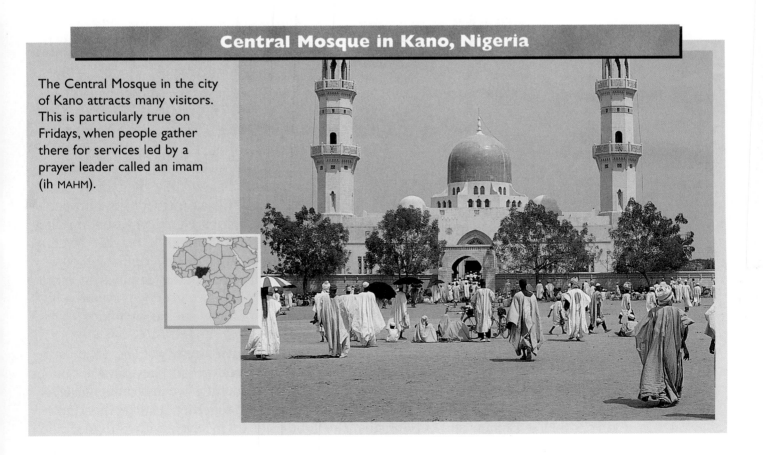

Central Mosque in Kano, Nigeria

The Central Mosque in the city of Kano attracts many visitors. This is particularly true on Fridays, when people gather there for services led by a prayer leader called an imam (ih MAHM).

Calabash Carver in Kurmi Market

A carver decorates a calabash, or empty gourd, at his stall in Kano's Kurmi Market. A plain calabash makes a light and inexpensive bowl. A highly decorated calabash may, in time, become very valuable. At the Kurmi Market, you can buy crafts from not only Nigeria, but also many other African countries.

For hundreds of years, the Hausa-Fulani have made an important part of their living by trading. Hausa-Fulani traders dealt in goods from as far away as Spain, Italy, and Egypt. The Hausa-Fulani built cities at the crossroads of trade routes. Each of these cities had its own ruler, was enclosed by walls, and had a central market. Kano, the oldest city in West Africa, is a Hausa city. Kano has been a center of trade for over 1,000 years. The Kurmi Market in Kano is one of the largest trading centers in Africa. People from around the world visit its thousands of stalls. These stalls sell everything from fabrics and dyes to electric appliances.

Ask Questions What would you like to know about the differences among the Hausa-Fulani, the Yoruba, and the Igbo?

The Yoruba: Farmers Near the Coast The Yoruba are Nigeria's second largest ethnic group. About 20 percent of Nigeria's people are Yoruba. By about A.D. 1100, the Yoruba had built several city-states. Many Yoruba still live in the city-state they built more than 500 years ago, Lagos. In the 1800s, Lagos was a center for the European slave trade. Many Yoruba were sold into slavery and sent to the Americas. But today, Lagos is a more peaceful center of trade. Its streets are lined with hundreds of small shops that sell many kinds of goods.

Most Yoruba are farmers. They live with their families in large compounds. Each compound has several houses grouped around a big yard. A Yoruba community is made up of many such compounds.

The Igbo: A Tradition of Democracy The Igbo have traditionally lived as rural farmers in the southeast. They have not built any large cities like Kano or Lagos. Instead, they live in farming villages. The people in each village work closely together. Unlike the Hausa-Fulani and the Yoruba, the Igbo rule themselves with a democratic council of elders. Instead of one or two leaders making decisions for an entire village, members of the council work together to solve problems.

The southeast was the first area of Nigeria to be affected by the arrival of Europeans. During colonial times, the Igbo were often educated by Christian missionaries. Many people in the south converted, or changed their religion, to Christianity. During British rule, some Igbo attended European or American universities and became teachers, doctors, and lawyers. Today, many Igbo have left rural villages and work in Nigeria's towns and cities.

Tensions sometimes arise between the Igbo and the other two major groups. In 1967, the Igbo tried to leave Nigeria to start their own country. For two and a half years the country was torn by war. In the end, Nigeria stayed united, and people tried to put the war behind them.

Counting Heads It is hard to know exactly how many people belong to each ethnic group. Nigeria has tried to count its people. A count of all the people in a country is called a **census.** In Nigeria,

▼▲ Cities like Lagos (below) are not new to Nigeria. The skyscraper below is very modern, but the Yoruba built Lagos in the 1400s. The Yoruba traditionally trade in cities and farm (above) in rural areas.

▶ Kano's airport was closed for three days during Nigeria's 1991 census. No one could fly in or out of the country.

whenever a census is taken, it causes debate. This is because the largest ethnic group will have the most power in Nigeria's government.

In 1991, Nigeria conducted an unusual census. On November 26, the country was cut off from the outside world. No one could enter or leave the country for three days. And no one in Nigeria was allowed to move from one place to another between 7 A.M. and 7 P.M. Hundreds of thousands of census takers went from house to house, making a count of the people. The census showed that over 88 million people live in Nigeria, and that the Hausa-Fulani are the country's largest ethnic group. This gives them more political power than other groups.

Over the years, many Nigerians have challenged the census results. In 1963 and 1973, for example, some ethnic groups charged that other ethnic groups had reported too large a number of people. Nigerians hope that by taking accurate censuses, they will be able to hold the many ethnic groups together.

1. **Define** (a) multiethnic, (b) census.
2. **Identify** (a) Lagos, (b) Abuja, (c) Kano.
3. What are the three largest ethnic groups in Nigeria, and where does each group live?
4. Why might taking a census create tension in Nigeria?

Critical Thinking

5. **Cause and Effect** How did the arrival of Europeans in Nigeria affect the ethnic groups that live in the region?

Activity

6. **Writing to Learn** Currently, Nigeria does not have one national language. Based on what you have learned about this country, do you think a national language might be useful? Why or why not? Write a paragraph explaining your opinion.

Ghana

First in Independence

Reach Into Your Background

Think about a turning point in your own life, such as moving to a new community or beginning a new school. What was different after that turning point? What remained the same?

Questions to Explore

1. What changes did Kwame Nkrumah bring to Ghana?
2. How has life in Ghana changed since independence?

Key Terms

sovereignty
coup

Key People

Kwame Nkrumah
Jerry Rawlings

In 1935, Kwame Nkrumah, a 26-year-old student, sailed from Ghana to the United States. At that time, Ghana was called the Gold Coast. It had been ruled by Great Britain for over 60 years. Nkrumah's visit to the United States was a turning point in his life. He was well aware that the people of his country did not have true freedom or equality. When Nkrumah saw the Statue of Liberty for the first time, it made him determined to bring freedom not only to his country, but to the whole continent. As he looked at the statue, he thought, "I shall never rest until I have carried your message to Africa."

▼ Kwame Nkrumah, the first leader of independent Ghana, showed his respect for African traditions by wearing traditional clothing.

Moving Toward Independence

In 1947, Nkrumah returned to the Gold Coast. The Gold Coast was named for its gold, which is one of the country's most important natural resources. The Country Profile on the next page shows the country's other important resources. But while the Gold Coast had many resources, most of its people were poor. Nkrumah believed that the people should benefit from the wealth of their own country. He began traveling all over the country. He convinced the people to demand independence from Great Britain.

COUNTRY • PROFILE

DK

Ghana: Natural Resources and the Economy

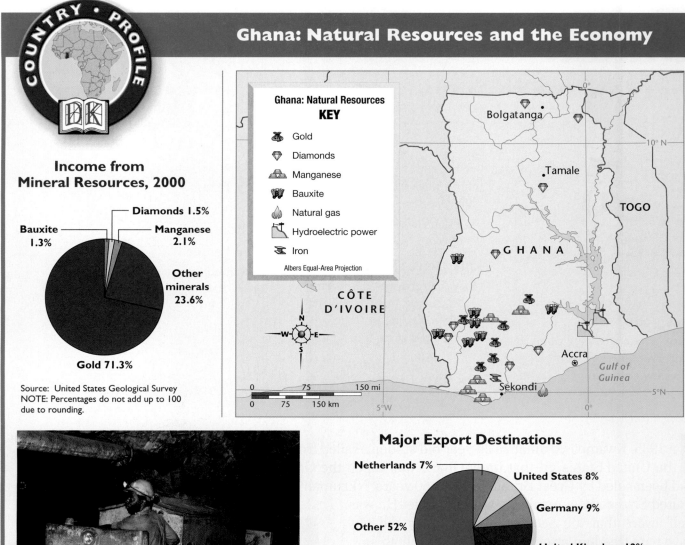

Income from Mineral Resources, 2000

Diamonds 1.5%
Bauxite 1.3%
Manganese 2.1%
Other minerals 23.6%
Gold 71.3%

Source: United States Geological Survey
NOTE: Percentages do not add up to 100 due to rounding.

Ghana: Natural Resources
KEY
- Gold
- Diamonds
- Manganese
- Bauxite
- Natural gas
- Hydroelectric power
- Iron

Albers Equal-Area Projection

Bolgatanga
Tamale
TOGO
GHANA
CÔTE D'IVOIRE
Accra
Sekondi
Gulf of Guinea
10° N
5° N
5° W
0°
N
S
E
W
0 75 150 mi
0 75 150 km

A miner drives a train through a gold mine in Ghana

Source: Dorling Kindersley World Desk Reference

Economics The map and charts above provide information about Ghana's natural resources. **Map and Chart Study** (a) Where in Ghana are gold and diamonds mined? (b) What percent of Ghana's exports are received by the United States?

Take It to the NET
Data Update For the most recent data on Ghana, visit **www.phschool.com.**

Traditional Government in Ghana During the 1900s, Africans who were ruled by European countries pushed to become independent. But the European countries did not want to give up their colonies. Some Europeans claimed that the colonies were not ready to rule themselves. Kwame Nkrumah answered this with a question.

> "Wasn't the African who is now unprepared to govern himself governing himself before the advent [arrival] of Europeans?"

The Akan are the largest ethnic group in Ghana. When the Akan give power to a new leader, they also give a warning:

> "Tell him that
> We do not wish greediness
> We do not wish that he should curse us
> We do not wish that his ears should be hard of hearing
> We do not wish that he should call people fools
> We do not wish that he should act on his own initiative
> We do not wish that it should ever be said 'I have no time.
> I have no time.'
> We do not wish personal abuse
> We do not wish personal violence."

If the leader does not rule fairly, the people can give power to a new ruler. In this way, the Akan are democratic. The people have control over who rules them.

While the Europeans were trading in gold and slaves on the coast, some Akan groups formed the Asante kingdom. This kingdom became very rich from trade. It controlled parts of the northern savanna and the coastal south. The Asante used all their power to try to stop the Europeans from taking over West Africa.

The Influence of Colonialism In 1874, Great Britain made the Gold Coast a colony. But it let the leaders of various ethnic groups continue to rule their people. Even today, there are at least 75 ethnic groups in Ghana, and their leaders are powerful people.

To Be a Leader The Asante did not submit to colonial rule without a fight. In 1900, Asante Queen Yaa Asantewa led a war against the British. Although the British were armed with modern rifles and machine guns, it took them more than three months to defeat the queen and her troops. Because of Yaa Asantewa's rebellion, the British began to treat the Asante more respectfully. In her memory, Asante children still sing a song about "Yaa Asantewa, the warrior woman who carries a gun and a sword of state into battle."

All That Glitters Is Gold

The leader of the Asante is called Asantehente. His power is symbolized by the Golden Stool, which sits in a place of honor on a chair beside him. If a leader does something wrong, the people may take the stool away. The Golden Stool is made of wood and decorated with real gold. **Critical Thinking** What does this picture tell you about the economic status of the Asante?

▼ Since colonization, many Ghanaian women purchase machine-made cotton fabrics, instead of traditional kente cloth, for everyday dresses and head scarves.

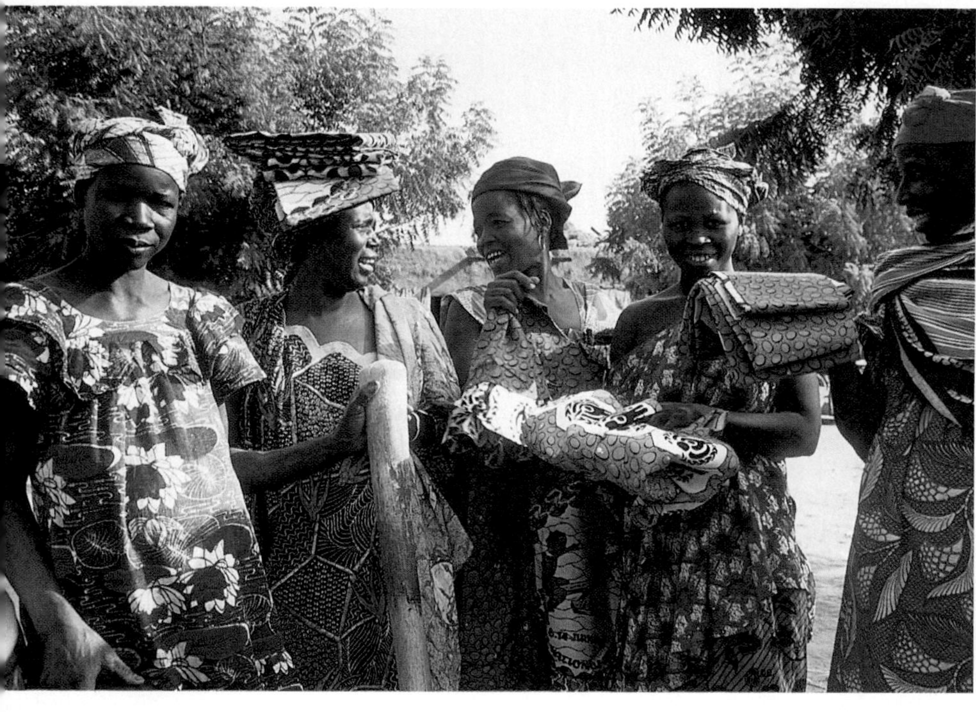

The British were most interested in controlling the economy of the Gold Coast. They encouraged farmers to grow cocoa. Then, the British sent the cocoa to factories in Britain, where it was made into chocolate. The British also exported timber and gold. As these raw materials left the country, goods from other countries were shipped in. This led to a problem that was typical of much of colonial Africa. People grew fewer food crops because growing cash crops like cocoa brought in more money. Food, therefore, had to be imported. People also spent more time on farming and less on traditional crafts. The British sold food and factory-made goods to the people of the Gold Coast. Soon, they began to depend on these imports.

The British also built schools in the Gold Coast. Foreign missionaries ran the schools. Christianity began to replace traditional religions. By the time Ghana became independent in 1957, many new ideas and lifestyles had come to traditional communities. Many people blended the new ways and the old African ways. Kwame Nkrumah, for example, was a Christian. But he also believed in parts of the traditional African religion. Nkrumah's respect for old and new ways helped him govern when Ghana became independent.

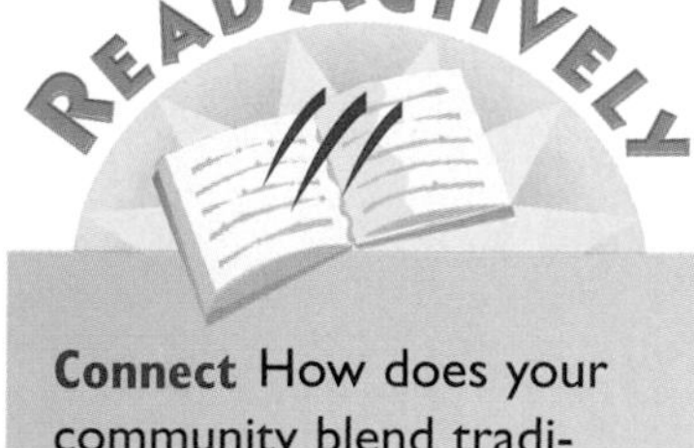

Connect How does your community blend traditional ways of life with modern ways?

Independence

In 1957, some 22 years after making his pledge to the Statue of Liberty, Nkrumah gave a moving speech to his people. Great Britain, he said, had finally agreed to grant them **sovereignty** (SAHV run tee), or political independence. Cheering, the people carried Nkrumah through the streets. Crowds sang victory songs to celebrate a dream come true.

Nkrumah became the leader of the new country. Later, he became the president. The government changed the country's name from the Gold Coast to Ghana, after an African kingdom that had ruled the region hundreds of years ago. Ghana was the first African colony south of the Sahara to become independent.

Since independence, Ghana has worked to balance new technology with traditional culture. Modern health care, electricity, transportation, and education are things that most Ghanaians want. Sometimes, however, these changes happened too quickly.

Nkrumah's Government Is Overthrown Nine years after being carried through the streets as a hero, Nkrumah was thrown out of office by a military **coup** (koo), or takeover. Army officers led the coup. Most Ghanaian citizens did not protest. In fact, many celebrated. People pulled down statues of Nkrumah.

How did this hero become an enemy? Nkrumah had big plans for Ghana. He borrowed huge amounts of money to make those plans happen fast. He spent millions of dollars to build a conference center. He spent millions more to build a super-highway. In addition, he made a deal with an American company to build a dam on the Volta River. The dam was to provide electricity and irrigation for people in rural areas. But when world prices for cocoa, Ghana's chief export, fell, Ghana could not pay back its loans. Many people blamed Nkrumah for the country's economic problems.

Nkrumah's downfall did not end Ghana's problems. The country alternated between military and democratically elected governments. Few were successful. In the meantime, people began to think better of Nkrumah. Many felt that he had done his best to help the country. When he died in 1972, he was hailed as a national hero. Leaders around the world mourned his death.

Ghana's Economy and Culture Today In the 1980s, Ghana's president, Jerry Rawlings, tried to reform Ghana's politics and economy. Rawlings stressed the traditional African values of hard work and sacrifice. Ghanaians supported Rawlings, and as a result, Ghana's economy began to grow.

Ghana is still dependent on the sale of cocoa. Even so, the economy has grown so much that Ghana has been able to build better roads and irrigation systems. The government under new president John Kufuor, elected in 2000, plans to improve education and health care. People have formed groups so they can voice concerns about issues that affect their lives.

Ghana's culture, as well as its economy, has benefited from Rawlings's renewal of

Nkrumah Toppled

Pulled down by angry citizens, the headless statue of Kwame Nkrumah lies on the grounds of the central police station in Accra. Nkrumah was out of the country when he was overthrown, in February 1966. He never returned to Ghana, but lived in exile in the nearby country of Guinea.

Talking Drums The talking drums of West Africa are used to send messages. The "language" of the talking drums is characterized by high and low tones. A drummer can relay a message to another drummer up to 20 miles away! In West Africa, news reports on the radio are often preceded by the drum beats that mean news is coming.

traditional values. Ghana now has special centers that have been set up to keep the country's traditional culture alive. People who visit Ghana may bring new ideas, but they also learn from Ghana's rich traditional culture. Art from Ghana is valued around the world. Ghana's culture can also be seen in daily life. Most people in Ghana live in small villages. Traditional dancing can be found even in the most modern dance clubs. In all forms, traditional Ghanaian culture exists alongside new ideas.

▼ Ghanaian crafts are popular all over the world. Below right are stamped *adinkra* cloth and woven *kente* cloth. Below left are handcrafted beeswax candles.

1. Define (a) sovereignty, (b) coup.

2. Identify (a) Kwame Nkrumah, (b) Jerry Rawlings.

3. How did colonization affect Ghana's economy?

4. Why did Kwame Nkrumah believe that Ghana should be independent?

Critical Thinking

5. Recognizing Cause and Effect Kwame Nkrumah went from being a Ghanaian hero to an unpopular figure. What caused this change in people's attitudes?

Activity

6. Writing to Learn Write about one or two changes you would like to see in your country or community. What obstacles might be in the way of this change? How could those obstacles be overcome?

Mali

The Desert Is Coming

Reach Into Your Background

Think about how the environment you live in affects your daily life. How does the clothing you wear reflect the climate? Are there sports or other activities that take place in only certain seasons?

Questions to Explore

1. How does the environment in Mali affect the country's economy?
2. How are the challenges faced by Mali typical of the challenges faced by other countries in the Sahel?

Key Terms

desertification
drought
erode

Key Places

Tombouctou
Sahara
Sahel

Outside the Hotel Bouctou in Tombouctou, Mali, sand piles up against buildings. It coats the fur of camels. It gives a yellowish tint to everything in sight. Inside, manager Boubacar Toure (boo buh CAR too RAY) sits in a lobby that is covered with a fine layer of red sand. Only 4 of his hotel's 29 rooms are taken. He is waiting for the river to rise, hoping that it will bring customers.

But each year, the river rises a little later. "Ten years ago the first boat arrived on July 1," says Tombouctou politician Moulaye Haidara (moo LAH ee HY dah rah). "Five years ago it was July 15. Now, we're lucky it's here by early August. In another five years, who knows?"

▼ Tombouctou's narrow streets used to attract crowds of tourists and traders. Now the city is slowly being covered with sand.

Mali's Environment

Tombouctou wasn't always so empty. From the 1300s to the end of the 1500s, Tombouctou was an important trade center. Caravans from North Africa crossed the Sahara to trade goods at Tombouctou. The Sahara covers much of West Africa, and it is getting bigger. The Sahara covers about one third of Mali. Few people live in the Sahara, however. Some Malians live in the savanna, the one area of the country that gets enough rain for farming. Other Malians live in the Sahel, the partly dry lands south of the Sahara. Tombouctou is in the Sahel.

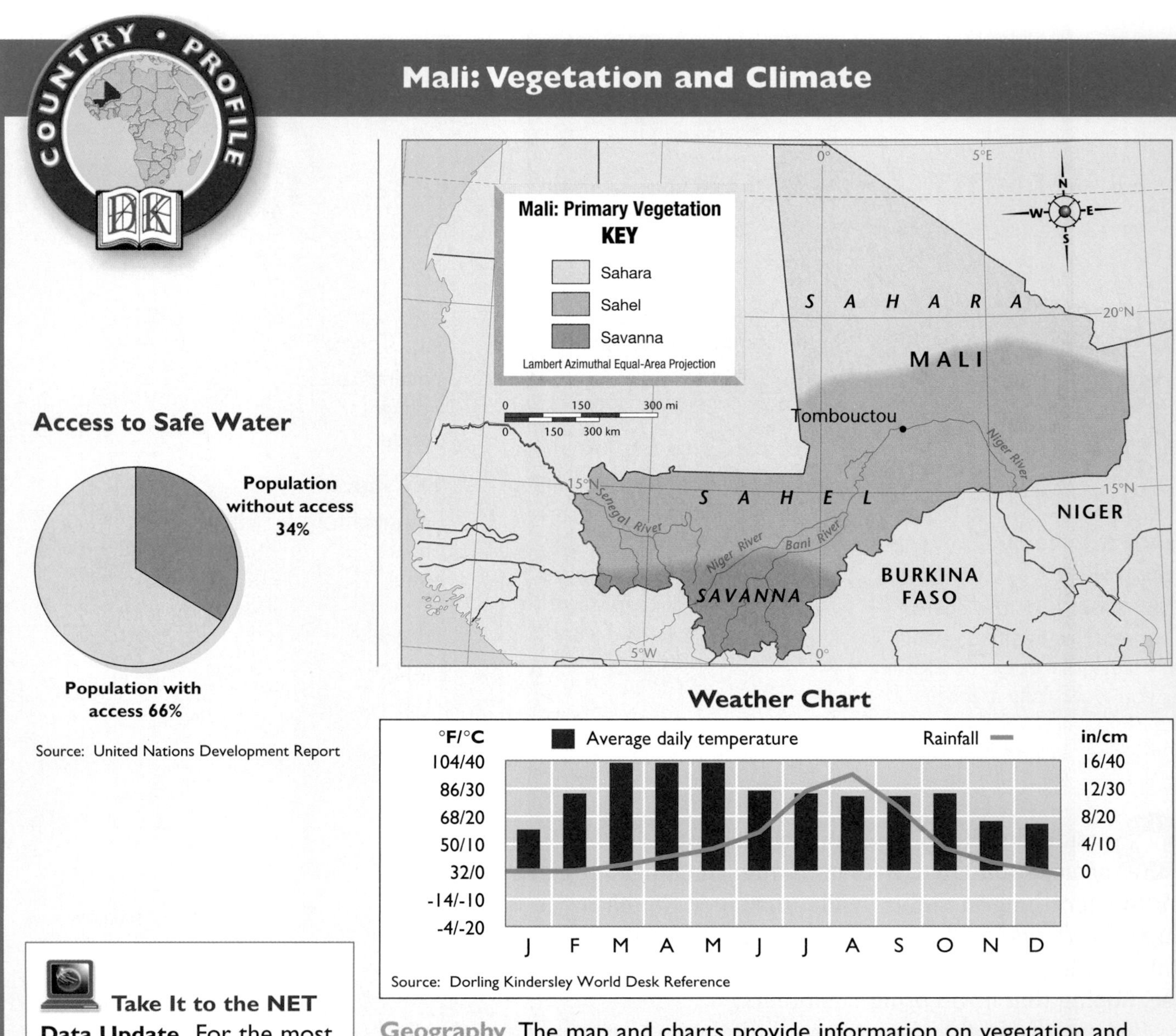

Take It to the NET

Data Update For the most recent data on Mali, visit **www.phschool.com.**

Geography The map and charts provide information on vegetation and climate in Mali. **Map and Chart Study** (a) Describe how Mali's vegetation changes from north to south. (b) Why do you think such a large percentage of Mali's population is without access to safe water?

READ ACTIVELY

Ask Questions What would you like to know about life in the Sahel?

Life in the Sahel The Sahel is a zone between the desert and the savanna. Eleven African countries lie partly in the Sahel. The Sahel stretches through the middle of Mali. Look at the map in the Activity Atlas. What other countries are in the Sahel? The large, dry Sahel affects the economy of every country it touches. But people who live in the region have long used the resources of the Sahel to earn their living.

People have lived in the Sahel for thousands of years. For a long time, they did very well and even grew rich. The region's grasslands provide food for animal herds. And the Sahel's location between the Sahara and the savanna is important. People traveling south must pass through the Sahel before reaching the savanna. For this reason, Tombouctou became a wealthy center of learning and business.

Once European ships began trading along Africa's coast, trade through the Sahara decreased. Tombouctou and other trade cities declined. But life in Tombouctou still follows certain traditional patterns. As in past times, caravans still carry huge blocks of salt into Tombouctou. And women still bake bread in outdoor ovens in the traditional way.

The Desert Comes Closer Mali has little industry. Most people make their living by trading, farming, and herding. However, all of these kinds of work are being threatened by **desertification,** the change of fertile land into land that is too dry or damaged to support life. In Mali and other countries of the Sahel, the desert is spreading south. Even the wetter lands in southwest Mali are in danger.

The region facing the greatest threat is the Sahel. The people of the Sahel whose way of life is most affected by desertification may be the Tuareg (TWAR ehg). The Tuareg have lived in the desert and the Sahel for hundreds of years. Wrapped from head to toe in blue cloth, with only their eyes showing, the Tuareg gallop across the land on fast camels. They live a nomadic life, moving their herds of goats, sheep, and camels

Dogon Granary Doors
The Dogon live in a wetter part of Mali. They work as farmers. They use granaries to store grain. These granaries are made of twigs and mud but have very stylized wood doors. The Dogon believe the tree from which the wood came contains a spirit that protects the stored grain. Although the rain and sun often wear down the granaries, the Dogon transfer the symbolic door from one granary to another.

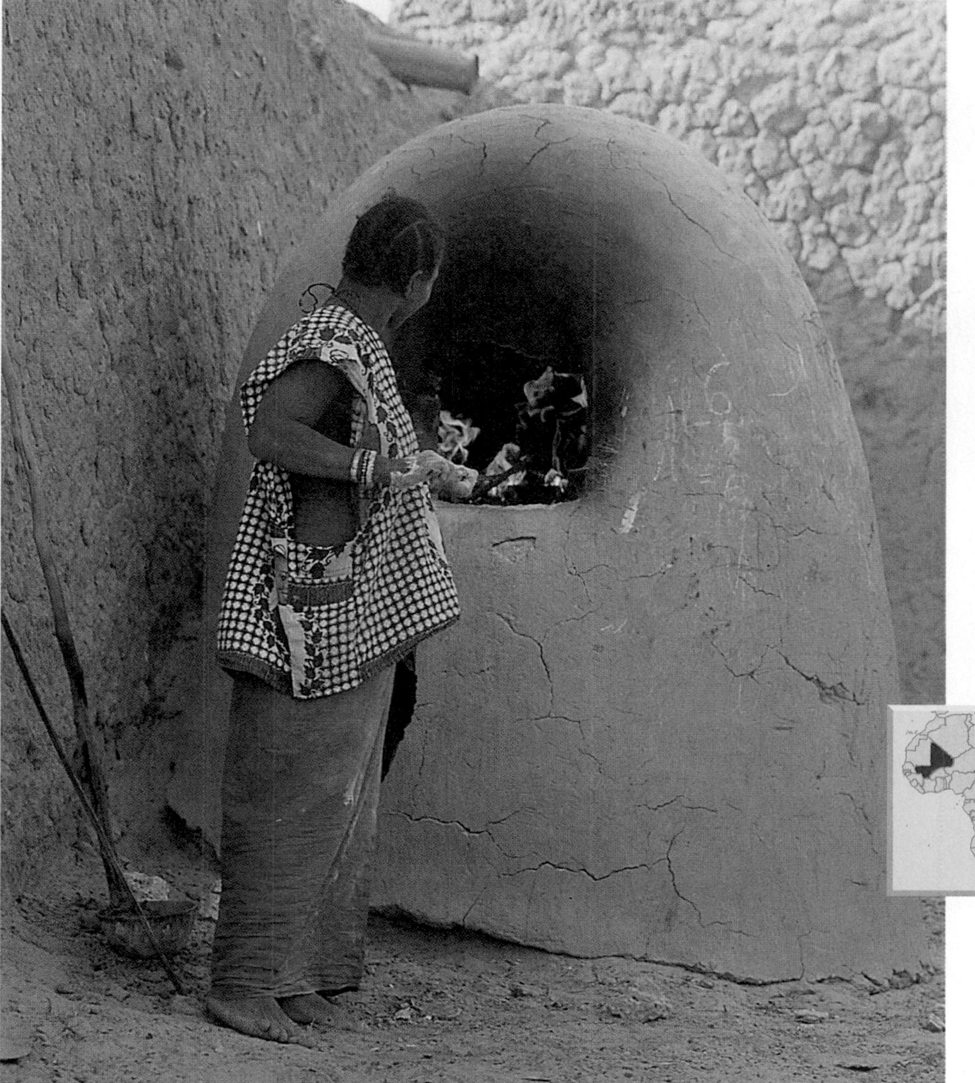

◀ Baking bread outside makes sense when average daily temperatures exceed 90°F (32°C). An oven inside would only heat your house up more.

south in the dry season and north in the wet season. Most Tuareg have never lived permanently in one place. The desertification of countries like Mali and Niger is threatening their way of life.

A Change in Lifestyle Major droughts in the 1970s and 1980s made life very difficult for the Tuareg. A **drought** is a time when there is little or no rain. Facing water and food shortages, some Tuareg settled on farms or in cities. Others built camps outside Tombouctou.

Ibrahim Ag Abdullah and his wife Fatimata are Tuareg. They live in a camp near Tombouctou. In the morning, Ibrahim Abdullah rides his camel into the city. Instead of tending his herds, Ibrahim Abdullah now sells camel rides to tourists. Fatimata Abdullah draws water from a well built by the government and grows vegetables. But the Abdullahs want to return to their nomadic life. "Each time I earn a little money, I buy a goat or a sheep. I save up so I can have enough animals to return to the desert," says Ibrahim Abdullah. But this way of life will only be possible if the Sahel's grasslands are maintained.

▼ This picture shows a Tuareg man dressed in traditional style. The Tuaregs' name for themselves means "free people." Clustered in small groups throughout the southwest Sahara, these nomads resist being controlled by any government. The Tuareg practice their own form of Islam, which keeps many elements of their original religion.

Preserving the Environment

Many people around the world are worried about the Sahel. The United Nations has created a committee to fight desertification. First people must understand why the fertile land changes into unusable desert.

Some environmentalists think that overgrazing can cause desertification. They say that grazing large herds of animals **erodes** the soil, or wears it away. That allows the desert to take over. When there are no roots to hold soil in place, the fierce winds of the Sahel blow it around. Yellow dust clouds fill the air. This loose soil is one reason that Tombouctou is slowly being covered in sand.

Other environmentalists say that grazing does not increase desertification. They think that grazing may actually help grasses grow once the area gets enough rain. These scientists think that long periods of

Desertification and the Economy

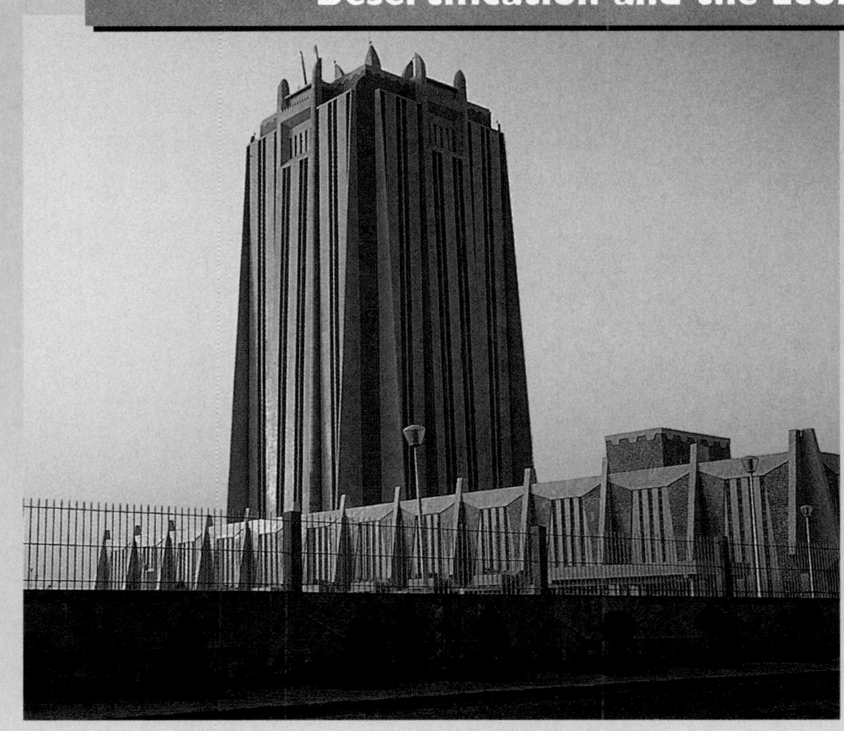

This is the West Africa Regional Bank in Bamako, Mali's capital and largest city. Desertification has hurt Mali's economy by making it harder for farmers to grow cash crops. Now Mali's government is trying to encourage people to start their own businesses, as well as encouraging existing businesses to come to Mali.

drought turn land into desert. Over the last 25 years, the Sahel has had much less rain than it did in the 70 years before. If these scientists are right, a few years of good rainfall could stop desertification. The Tuareg would not have to change their way of life.

Currently, Mali's government is studying the problem. Mali is working with the United Nations to educate people in rural areas about better ways to use land. The government is also irrigating and planting in some areas to create a greenbelt. In 2000, it set forth an action plan for tackling desertification.

1. **Define** (a) desertification, (b) drought, (c) erode.
2. **Identify** (a) Tombouctou, (b) Sahara, (c) Sahel.
3. How does Mali's geography affect how people make a living?
4. How does desertification affect the people who live in the Sahel?

Critical Thinking

5. **Drawing Conclusions** Many Tuareg living around Tombouctou are now depending on the tourist trade for income. Based on what you have learned about Tombouctou, what will be some of the challenges of this new occupation?

Activity

6. **Writing to Learn** Overgrazing may contribute to the desertification of the Sahel. What common North American activities may present a threat to the environment? Do you think those activities should be discouraged? Why or why not?

Using Distribution Maps

Do you think in pictures? Most people do. They try to visualize what they read about. For example, if you read a story about a trip along the Niger River, you may imagine a wide river with dense forest along its banks. You may try to picture, in your own mind, what the writer saw. Thinking in pictures is a natural way to make sense of the world.

Geographers think in pictures, too. For them, of course, the pictures are often maps. There is an old saying: "A picture is worth a thousand words." This is especially true when the picture is a distribution map.

Get Ready

A distribution map is a map that shows how something is distributed. In other words, it shows where something is located. A "population distribution map" shows where people live. It is one of the most common distribution maps. A "resource distribution map" shows where resources are found. You can make a distribution map that shows how nearly anything is distributed. The location of ethnic groups, languages, vegetation, schools—and almost anything else you can think of—can all be indicated on distribution maps.

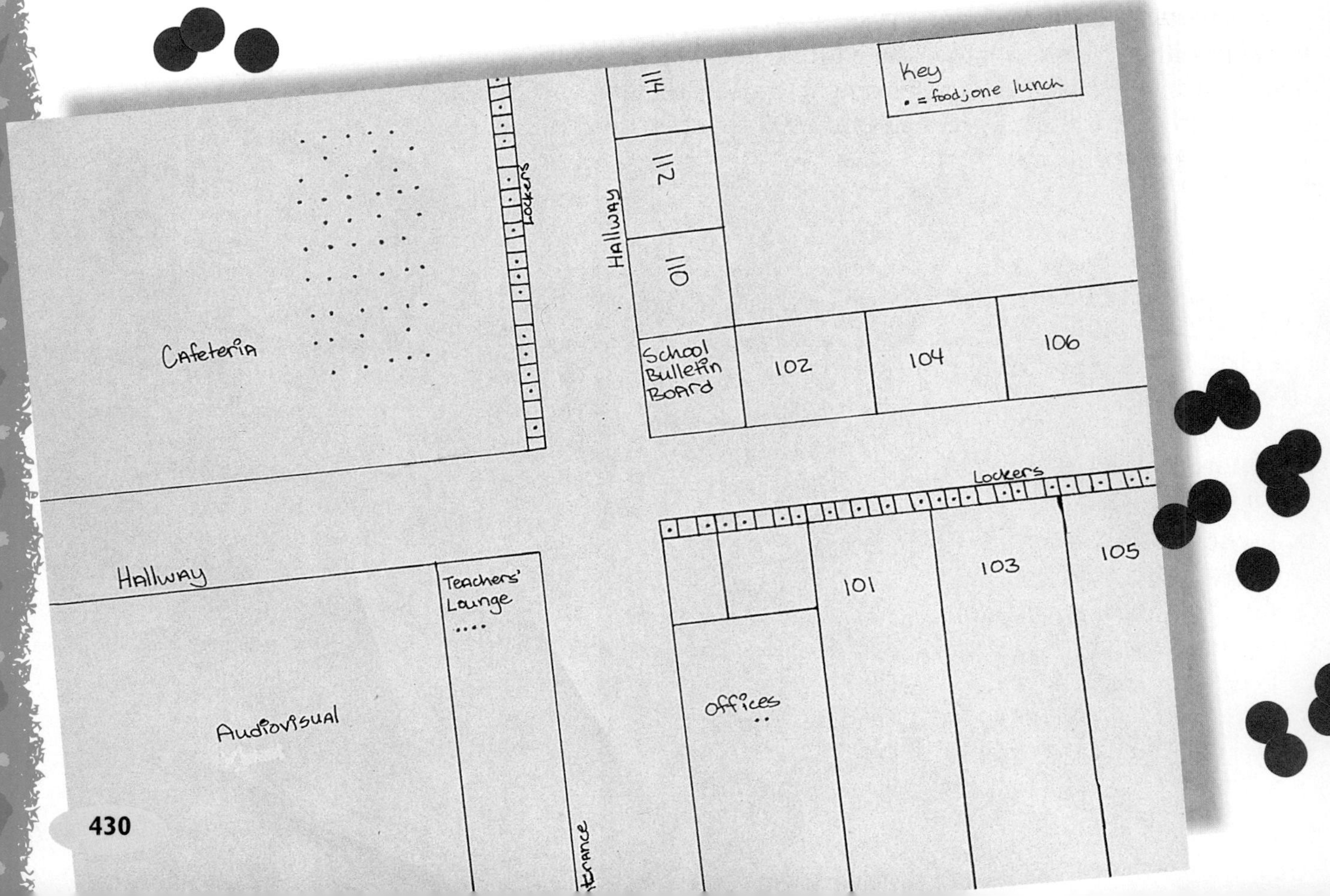

Try It Out

Imagine a map of your school. What would a "food distribution map" of your school look like? Chances are, it would indicate that food is located in the cafeteria, in student lunchboxes, and perhaps in the teacher's lounge.

How would this work exactly? To find out, make that map. Sketch a map, or floor plan, of your school. Make a map key that uses a symbol to indicate "food." One symbol on the map will indicate one food item, two symbols will represent two food items, and so on. Now mark the map with the symbols. When you're done, you'll probably have a map with many symbols in the cafeteria and some others scattered throughout the school.

Every distribution map tells you three basic things:

A. What is distributed Your map shows the distribution of food.

B. Where it is distributed By looking at the symbols, you can see where the food is located.

C. How many are distributed Because each symbol represents a certain number of food items, the map tells you approximately how many food items are located in each room in the school.

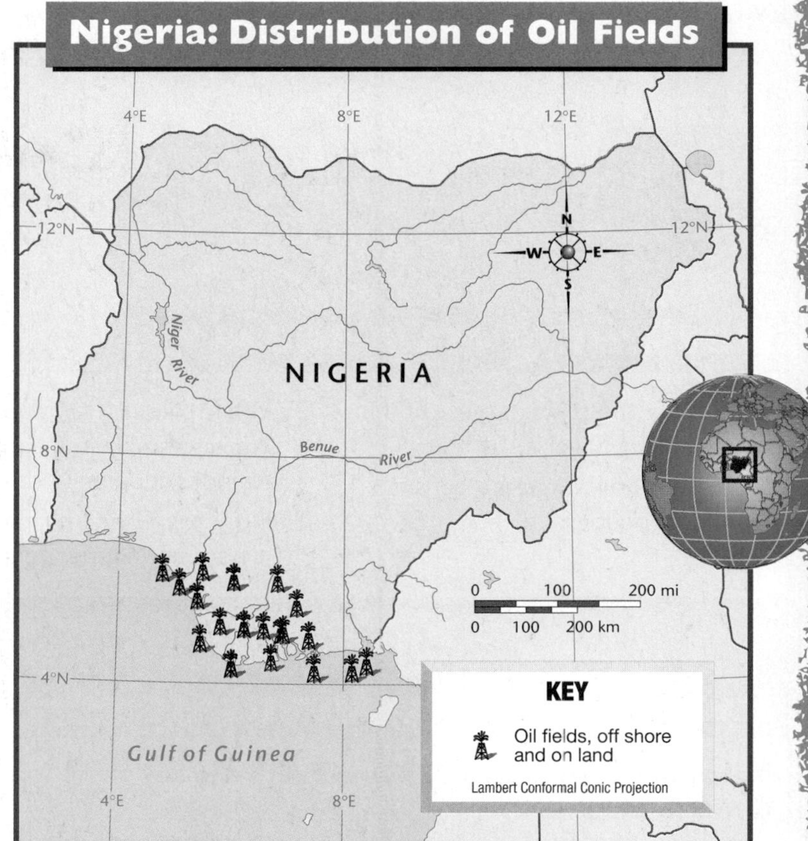

Apply the Skill

Now that you see how distribution maps are made and what three things they tell you, you can use what you have learned to read a real distribution map. Use the distribution map on the right to answer the following questions.

1. **Determine what is distributed.** What resource does this map show the distribution of?

2. **Determine where it is distributed.** How is the distribution indicated on the map? In what part or parts of Nigeria is this resource located?

3. **Determine how many are distributed.** How many symbols are shown on the map?

4. **Organize what you have learned.** Using the map as a guide, write a paragraph that explains the information on the map. After you have completed your paragraph, write another paragraph explaining whether or not you think the map is a more useful way of communicating this information than writing.

5. **Make a connection to the real world.** Explain why this map would be useful to each of the following people: the president of an oil company, an officer in the Nigerian armed forces, a member of the Nigerian government, a member of the government of neighboring Cameroon.

Review and Activities

Reviewing Main Ideas

1. Identify the three largest ethnic groups of Nigeria.
2. Explain how Nigeria's census affects politics.
3. What role did Kwame Nkrumah play in Ghana's move to independence?
4. How has Ghana changed since it became independent?
5. How has desertification affected the life of the Tuareg?
6. Describe two possible causes of desertification.

Reviewing Key Terms

Match the definitions in Column I with the key terms in Column II.

Column I

1. to wear away
2. composed of many ethnic groups
3. a group distinguished by race, language, religion, or cultural traditions
4. the change of fertile land into land that is too dry or damaged to support life
5. a long period of little or no rainfall
6. a systematic counting of the population
7. a sudden overthrow of a ruler or government
8. a country's freedom and power to decide on policies and actions

Column II

a. **drought**
b. **erode**
c. **census**
d. **ethnic group**
e. **multiethnic**
f. **coup**
g. **desertification**
h. **sovereignty**

Critical Thinking

1. **Making Comparisons** Compare Ghana's geography to that of Mali. How do you think each country's geography has affected its history?
2. **Recognizing Cause and Effect** How did the colonial histories of Nigeria and Ghana affect those countries after independence?

Graphic Organizer

Copy the chart onto a sheet of paper. Fill it in to show how Nigeria's Hausa-Fulani, Yoruba, and Igbo groups are similar and different.

	Hausa-Fulani	Yoruba	Igbo
Region of Nigeria			
Ways of Making a Living			

Map Activity

West Africa

For each place listed below, write the letter from the map that shows its location.

1. Nigeria
2. Ghana
3. Sahara
4. Tombouctou
5. Lagos
6. Abuja
7. Sahel
8. Mali

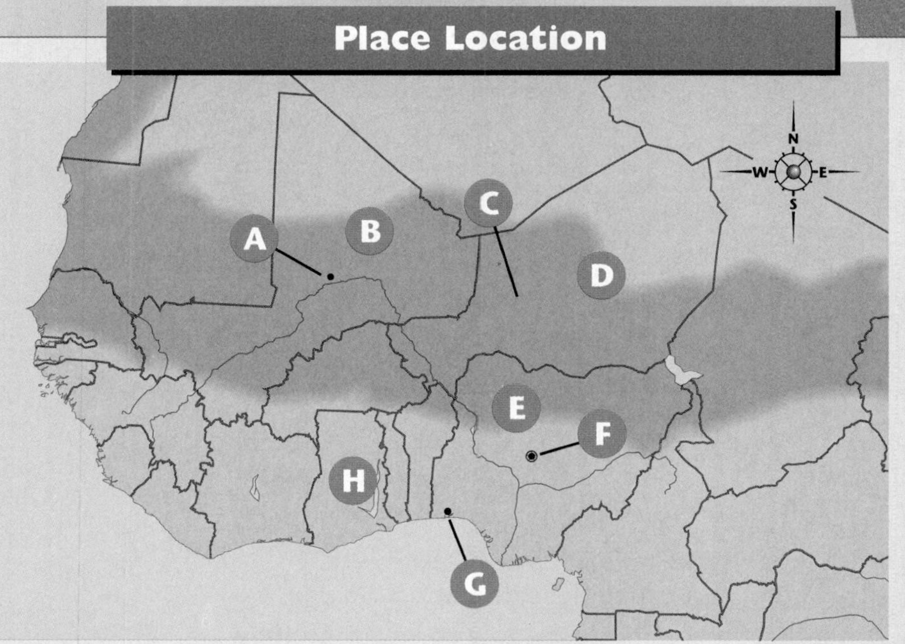

Writing Activity

Writing a News Report

Choose one of the recent events described in this chapter and write a news report about it. Remember to describe these five things for your readers: who, what, where, when, and why.

Take It to the NET

Activity Read about a girl's trip to Ghana, her parents' homeland. According to the author, how is life in Ghana different from life in the United States? For help in completing this activity, visit **www.phschool.com**.

Chapter 15 Self-Test To review what you have learned, take the Chapter 15 Self-Test and get instant feedback on your answers. Go to **www.phschool.com** to take the test.

Skills Review

Turn to the Skills Activity.

Review the three basic types of information a distribution map provides. Then answer the following questions: (a) What would a vegetation distribution map of Mali tell you? (b) What would a natural resources distribution map tell you about Ghana?

How Am I Doing?

Answer these questions to check your progress.

1. Can I describe the main geographic features of West Africa?
2. Do I understand how cultures in West Africa compare to other African cultures I've studied?
3. Can I identify some historic events that have shaped the modern cultures of West Africa?
4. What information from this chapter can I include in my journal?

Desertification

Desertification occurs when land that was once fertile becomes a desert. The land becomes dry and salty, underground water dries up, erosion occurs, and plant life dies. Changes in climate, such as a long drought, can cause desertification. So can people. For example, people sometimes allow animals to graze so much that most plants are killed.

Purpose

The Sahara is expanding into the edge of the savanna, or the Sahel. The desertification of the Sahel affects not only the environment, but also the people living there. In this activity, you will explore one cause of desertification.

Materials

- three-sided box
- blow-dryer
- piece of sod as wide as the box
- sand
- goggles

Procedure

STEP ONE

Set up your experiment. Place the box so that the open end is in front of you. Put on your goggles. Lay the sod in the box, with some space between the sod and the back of the box.

Pour the sand in a pile across the open end of the box, directly in front of the sod. Hold the blow-dryer at the open end of the box so that it will blow across the sand toward the sod.

STEP TWO

Create a windstorm over good land. Use the blow-dryer to create "wind." Lift handfuls of sand and let it sift through your fingers in front of the blow-dryer, so that the sand is blown across the grass. This represents the sandy winds that blow across the desert and over grassy lands. Do this for about one minute, holding the blow-dryer no higher than the top of the sod. Note how much sand gets caught in the grass.

STEP THREE

Begin the desertification process. Thin the vegetation by removing about half of the grass in the sod. This is similar to what happens when vegetation is grazed or dies from climate change. Use the blow-dryer and handfuls of sand to create another windstorm, again for one minute. How much sand is in the sod this time? How does the grass look?

STEP FOUR

Continue the desertification process. This time remove almost all of the grass in the sod. This represents more overgrazing and the death of vegetation. Make a final one-minute windstorm. How much sand is in the sod now? How does the sand affect the soil?

Observations

1. What happened to the sand as it blew across the grass?
2. What happened to the remaining grass and topsoil as the sand blew across the "overgrazed" sod?
3. Imagine you are a cattle herder who needs to feed your cattle. You know that if you let your animals graze, you might contribute to desertification. But if your animals do not eat, they will die. What would you do? The agricultural officials in your region want to know your decision. Write them a letter explaining your decision.

ANALYSIS AND CONCLUSION

1. Why do you think that it is important to people living in the Sahel to slow desertification?
2. Pretend you are a journalist on a photo shoot. You see a farmer allowing animals to feed in an area where there is little vegetation. You know the farmer has no other place to let the animals graze. You take a photograph. Write an article to accompany your photograph.

The Distant Talking Drum

POEMS FROM NIGERIA
BY ISAAC OLALEYE

Reach Into Your Background

Have you lived in your hometown all your life, or have you moved from place to place? How do you think it would feel to live somewhere far from where you grew up?

Writers who have moved far away from their homes often write about the place where they grew up. Many writers feel that writing helps them deal with their feelings of homesickness. Some writers respond to other changes in their lives, or to the loss of a friend or family member, in the same way.

Isaac Olaleye, the author of these poems, grew up in Nigeria and lived there for many years. He moved to England and lived there for several years. Now he lives in the United States.

Questions to Explore

1. What can you learn from these poems about the ways that many Nigerians make a living?
2. What can these poems teach you about some features of Nigerian culture?

My Village

Èrín is the name
Of my African village.
Laughter is what Èrín means
In the Yoruba language.

In streams,
Women and children
Still collect water in gourds
and clay pots,
Which they balance on their
heads.

Electric light has not shone in
my village.
With ruby-red palm oil
Poured into a clay vessel
We see at night.

My village of Èrín is peaceful,
Like a hidden world.
It's ringed by radiant green
And surrounded by five
streams.

Like a stream,
The love
For my village
Flows.

Visualize How can people make light using palm oil?

gourd *n.:* a fruit with a hard skin, such as a melon or a pumpkin
radiant *adj.:* bright

Village Weavers

Men and women
Weave cloth
From yarns
Dyed in herbs
In colors of green, blue,
    black, and red.

Thick and heavy cloth
They weave.
Cloth thick for the sun,
Tough for the field,
And fancy for feasts.

In alleys,
Or under the shadow of
    trees,
From morning to evening
Their hands and feet
Are busy weaving.

They work happily,
Singing and laughing,
So their mouths
Also keep busy.

Connect Do you like to keep your mouth busy talking when your hands are busy working? Why or why not?

◀ This Nigerian man is weaving in a workshop.

EXPLORING YOUR READING

Look Back

1. How do the people of the village use the cloth that the weavers weave?

Think It Over

2. Do you think the people in the poems live in rural or urban Nigeria? Why?
3. Why do you think that the author describes Èrín as peaceful?
4. How do you think the people in the village spend most of their time? Why?

Go Beyond

5. No electricity means no televisions, no light bulbs, and no air conditioning. How would your life be different without electricity? How would your life be the same? For example, you would not watch television, but you would still play with your friends. Think of other examples.

Ideas for Writing: Hometown Poem

6. If you were going to write a book of poems about your hometown, what topics would you write about? Make a list. Then choose one topic from your list and write a poem. Use Olaleye's poems as a model.

CHAPTER 16

Exploring East Africa

SECTION 1
Ethiopia
CHURCHES AND MOSQUES

SECTION 2
Tanzania
WHEN PEOPLE COOPERATE

SECTION 3
Kenya
SKYSCRAPERS IN THE SAVANNA

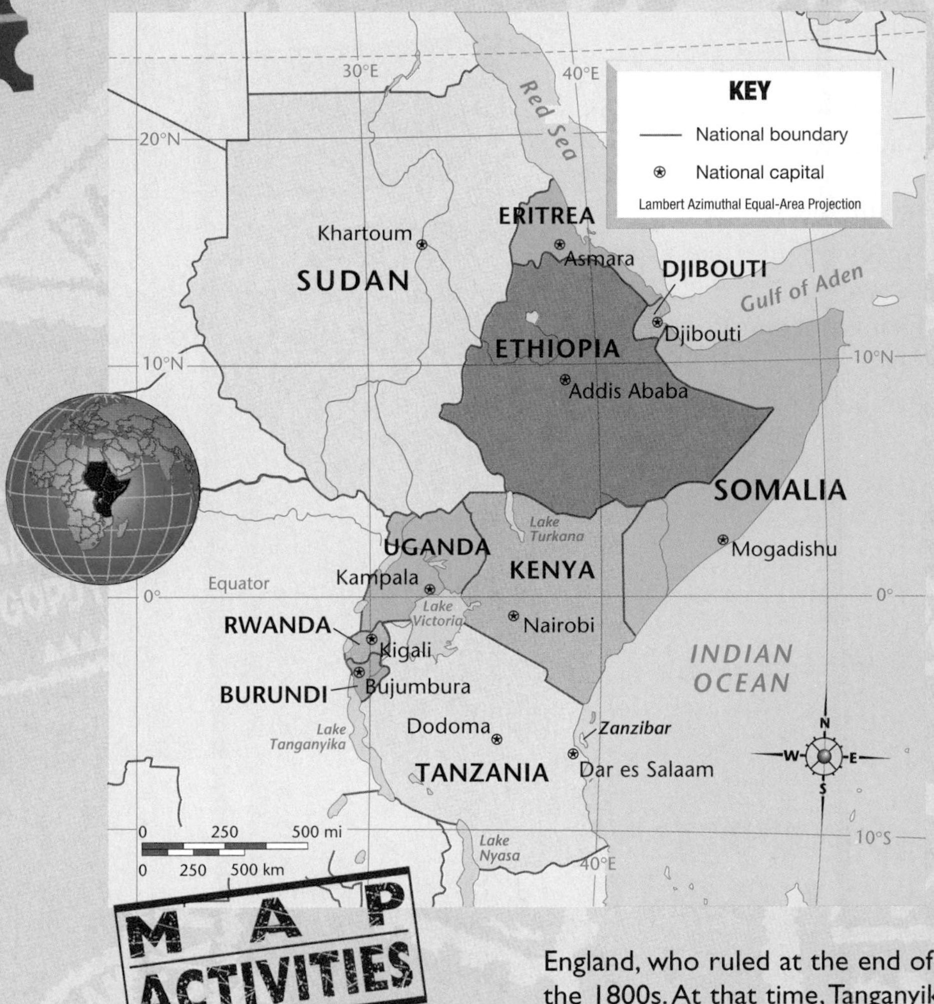

MAP ACTIVITIES

The borders of many East African countries were set by the Europeans who started colonies there. Borders often follow rivers and mountains. To get to know this region, do the following activities.

Rename a lake

Find Lake Victoria on the map. It was named after Queen Victoria of England, who ruled at the end of the 1800s. At that time, Tanganyika and Kenya were ruled by Great Britain. (Tanganyika later became part of the country of Tanzania.) Use features on the map to help you rename the lake.

Consider location

The countries of East Africa are located between the Red Sea, the Gulf of Aden, and the Indian Ocean. How do you think East Africa's location might have affected its history and cultures?

Ethiopia

Churches and Mosques

Reach Into Your Background

Think about the subjects you study in school. Why is it important for you to be able to read and write? Why is it important for you to learn history and math? What might your life be like if you could not go to school? What kind of jobs could you do if you did not go to school?

Questions to Explore

1. What religions can be found in Ethiopia?
2. Why did Christianity in Ethiopia develop in a unique way?

Key Terms

monastery

Key Places

Lalibela
Addis Ababa

As a young boy, Iyasus Moa (ee YAH soos MOH uh) went to school and learned to read and write. But he dreamed of studying music and painting. He also wanted to learn another language, so Iyasus traveled to Tigray (TEE gray), in northern Ethiopia. He walked a distance that today would take three days to drive. Did he plan to enter a university in Tigray? No. The year was A.D. 1220, and there were no universities in Ethiopia. Iyasus entered a Christian **monastery.** This is a place where priests live, work, and study. A priest who lives in a monastery is called a monk.

Iyasus studied hard for many years. He became a monk. He also became a famous teacher and artist. His students built monasteries and schools all over the country.

▼ The Debre Bizen monastery sits about 8,000 feet (2,438 m) up in the mountains of Eritrea, which was part of Ethiopia until 1993.

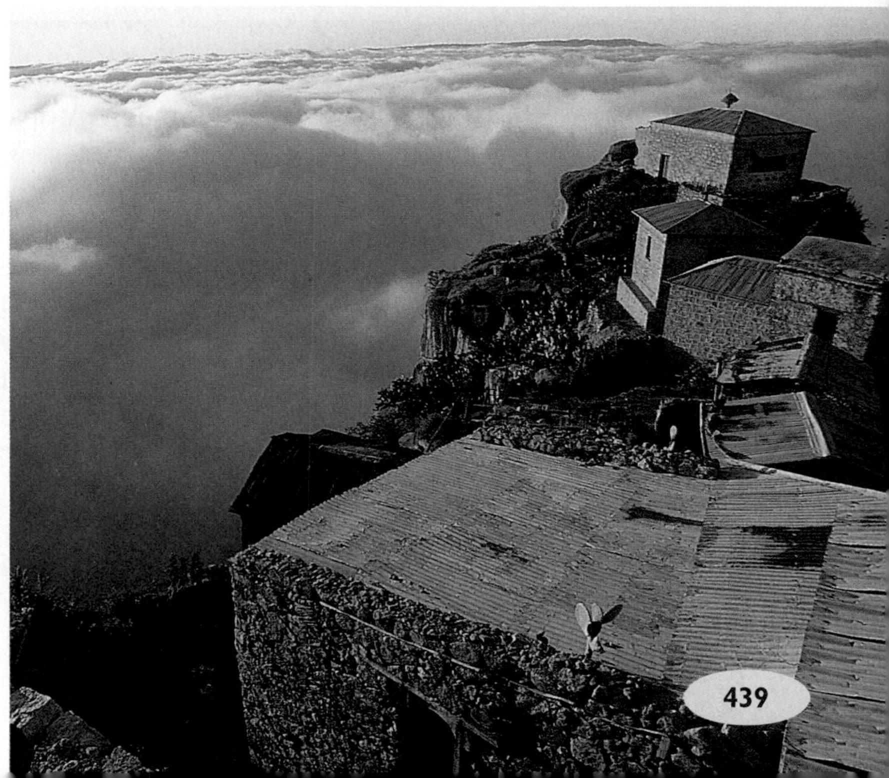

Religions of Ethiopia

Iyasus Moa lived in Ethiopia, a country in East Africa. He studied Geez (gee EZ), one of the world's oldest languages. Geez is an ancient form of the language spoken by the Amhara, one of Ethiopia's larger ethnic groups. The Amhara were writing their language by A.D. 400. Ethiopia and

Ethiopia: Population and Ethnic Groups

Ethnic Groups

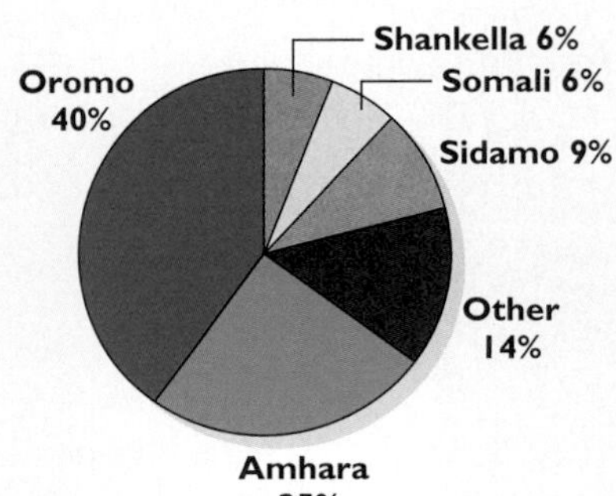

Source: Dorling Kindersley World Desk Reference

Ethiopia: Population Density

KEY

Persons per sq mi	Persons per sq km
160–685	62–265
78–159	20–61
15–77	6–19
Under 15	Under 6

Cities

- 2,000,000–4,999,999
- 1,000,000–1,999,999
- 250,000–999,999
- Under 250,000

Lambert Conformal Conic Projection

0 200 400 mi
0 200 400 km

SUDAN, ERITREA, Red Sea, YEMEN, DJIBOUTI, Gulf of Aden, SOMALIA, KENYA, UGANDA, INDIAN OCEAN, Adwa, Mekele, Gonder, Bahir Dar, Dese, Dire Dawa, Harer, Addis Ababa, Bedele, Nazret, Jima, 15°N, 10°N, 5°N, 25°E, 30°E, 35°E, 40°E, 45°E

Population by Age Group and Sex

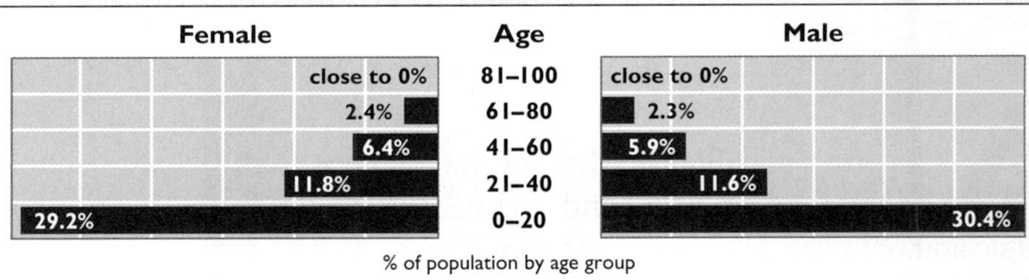

Source: Dorling Kindersley World Desk Reference

Take It to the NET

Data Update For the most recent data on Ethiopia, visit **www.phschool.com.**

Culture The map and charts provide information about the people of Ethiopia. **Map and Chart Study** (a) Which regions of Ethiopia are the least populated? (b) What is the largest ethnic group in Ethiopia? (c) Which age group makes up the largest percentage of the male population?

Church History The Egyptian Coptic Church was one of the first to leave the rest of the Christian Church. Later, the Christian Church divided even more. Today, there are many denominations, or types, of Christian churches.

Egypt are the only African countries that have a written history dating back to ancient times. Much of Ethiopia's history was preserved by monks like Iyasus, who copied books by hand.

The religion Iyasus studied was also very old. It had spread to Ethiopia along trade routes. Ethiopia was a center of trade. Look at the physical map of Africa in the Activity Atlas. Find the Nile River and the Red Sea. The main source of the Nile River is in Ethiopia's highlands. Ethiopia used to include the countries that today are Eritrea, Djibouti, and Somalia. These countries border the Red Sea. As people traded goods along the Nile River and the Red Sea, they also learned about each other's religions.

Ethiopian Christianity Alexandria, a city in Egypt, was one of the first centers of Christianity. Over time, Christians in Alexandria came to differ with Christians in Rome and Constantinople. In A.D. 451,

Egyptian Christians separated from the rest of the Christian Church. They formed the Coptic Christian Church. Coptic Christianity slowly spread from Egypt to Ethiopia.

Ethiopian Christians were isolated from Christians in other parts of the world. Ethiopia's mountains made it hard for people in the interior to travel to other areas. Some people traveled along the Nile River and the Red Sea. With the spread of Islam, however, these travel routes were cut off to Ethiopian Christians.

Islam In the 600s, Arabs began to spread across North Africa. They brought their religion, Islam, with them. Muslim Arabs did not take over Ethiopia, but they moved into the areas around it. Over time, Arab traders built cities along trade routes. Eventually, Muslim Arabs came to control trade in the entire region. And, in time, some Ethiopians adopted the Muslim faith.

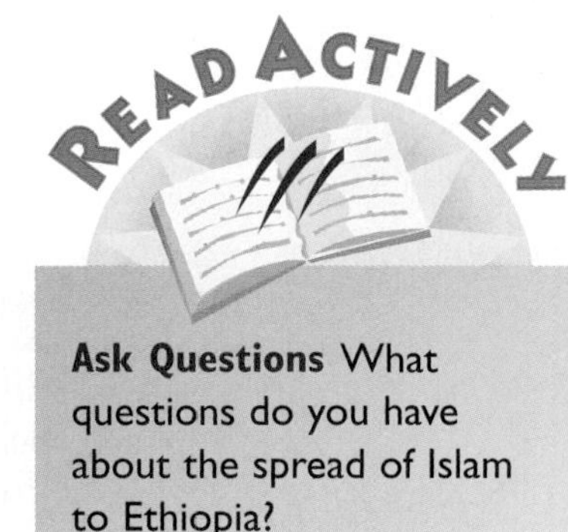

Ask Questions What questions do you have about the spread of Islam to Ethiopia?

Christians and Muslims As Muslim Arabs took control of Ethiopia's coastal regions, Ethiopian Christians began moving inland. Finally, Christian Ethiopia was surrounded by Muslim-controlled areas. As a result, Christians in Ethiopia had little contact with Christians elsewhere. The Ethiopian Christian Church developed into a unique form of Christianity. The Ethiopian Church still uses its own traditions and literary language, Geez.

Throughout Ethiopia's history, Christians and Muslims have sometimes fought over religious issues. They were at war with each other in the 1500s. But, for the most part, Christians and Muslims have lived together peacefully in Ethiopia. Today, about 35 percent of Ethiopians are Christians, and some 45 percent are Muslims. The rest practice traditional African religions.

▼ Ethiopian Christians and Muslims both have histories that are rich in literature and education. The page at left is from the Quran and the page at right is from a hand-painted Christian document.

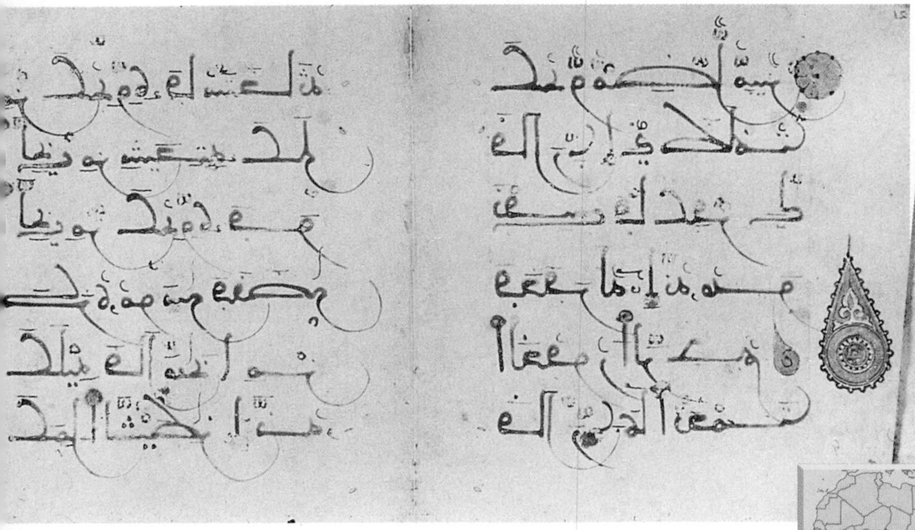

The Churches of Lalibela

Most churches are built from the bottom up. In the 1100s, however, Ethiopians carved 11 churches from the top down. Workers carved the roof first. They worked their way from the top of the church to the bottom. They always left enough rock in place so that they could stand on it and still reach the area, inside or outside, that they were carving. How might carving a church starting at the top be easier than starting at the bottom? How might it be harder?

Because the churches at Lalibela were underground, Ethiopian Christians were able to hide them from invaders by piling earth on the roofs.

Workers carved the roof, windows, and floors of each church on a slight incline, to allow the heavy summer rains to run off.

Each church is connected to other churches by underground passages carved out of rock.

Workers used hand tools to carve each church out of solid underground rock. Some churches took 150 years to complete.

Contrasting Ways of Life

Most Ethiopians, regardless of their religious background, live in rural areas. What is life like for rural Ethiopians? A look at the town of Lalibela (lah lih BEL uh) provides some clues.

Lalibela Lalibela was the capital of Christian Ethiopia for about 300 years. Rural Ethiopia also has many towns with Muslim shrines and tombs.

Services such as electricity and running water are rare in rural Ethiopia. No one in Lalibela has electricity and there are more donkeys than cars. The people who live around Lalibela make a living by farming. In some areas, people make a living by herding cattle or fishing. Some families specialize in jobs such as woodworking and beekeeping.

A Growing City

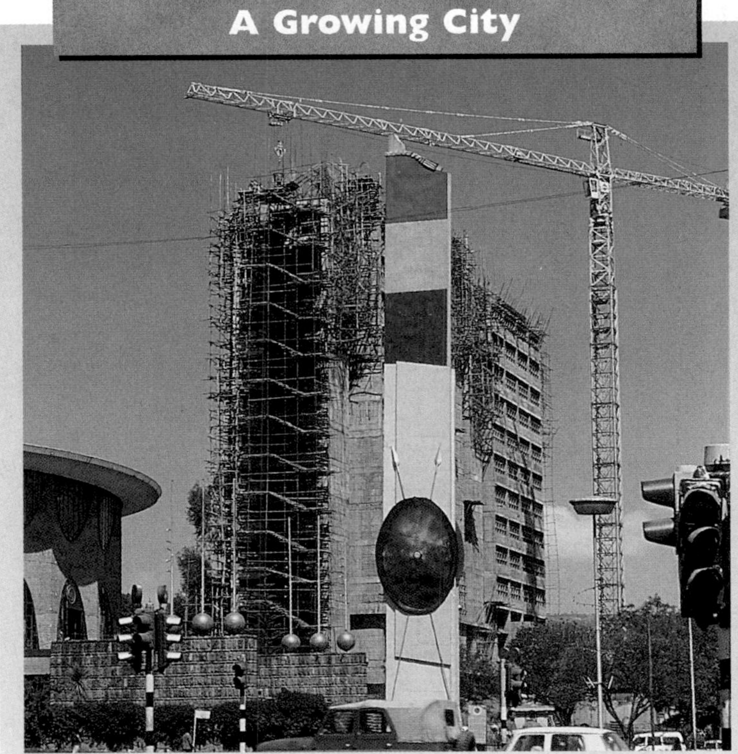

The population of Addis Ababa is growing. New buildings are always being constructed. This one lies near the center of the city.

Addis Ababa Some 200 miles (322 km) south of Lalibela lies Ethiopia's capital city, Addis Ababa (ad uh SAB uh buh). It has all the conveniences of city life—running water, electricity, and modern hospitals. The city also has a more traditional, rural side. In some areas, houses are made not of concrete and stone, but of wood and dried mud. And some families still wash their clothes in the river, leaving them to dry on the riverbanks.

Addis Ababa's mix of modern and traditional ways of living illustrates the outlook of many Ethiopians. While expressing great pride in their past, they look toward the future with confidence.

Connect How is your community a mix of old and new?

1. **Define** monastery.
2. **Identify** (a) Lalibela, (b) Addis Ababa.
3. How did Ethiopia's geography affect its role in the ancient world?
4. Why did Christian beliefs in Ethiopia differ from those of Christians in the rest of the world?

Critical Thinking

5. **Making Comparisons** How is life in Ethiopia's rural areas different from life in Addis Ababa? How is life similar in both areas?

Activity

6. **Writing to Learn** Write a paragraph encouraging travelers to visit the historic churches of Ethiopia. In your paragraph, explain how the Ethiopian Christian Church has been affected by the country's history.

Tanzania

When People Cooperate

Reach Into Your Background

Think about how you feel when things are about to change. Are you excited or nervous? Are you a little unsure about what the future might hold?

Questions to Explore

1. How is Tanzania's government changing?
2. What challenges have these changes produced?

Key Terms

lingua franca
foreign debt
multiparty system

Key People and Places

Dar es Salaam
Julius Nyerere
Zanzibar

In October 1995, the capital of Tanzania, Dar es Salaam, looked ready for a celebration. Flags hung from almost every building. Crowds of people chanted and sang in the streets. Why all this joy? Was it a special holiday? Had a Tanzanian sports team won a championship? Neither. An election was about to start. It would be the first election in over 30 years to include more than one political party. Finally, voters would have a real choice among candidates with differing views.

▼ In October 1995, happy citizens rallied in Tanzania's capital, Dar es Salaam, as the country prepared to hold its first multiparty general elections.

Tanzanians felt joyful, but they did not know what the future might hold. Their feelings were rooted in Tanzania's history.

Tanzania's History

Look at the map of Tanzania in the Country Profile. You can see that Tanzania lies on the Indian Ocean. Its location has made this area a center for trade. The people on the coast of East Africa traded with the ancient Greeks, Romans, Arabs, and Persians.

In the last 2,000 years, this part of East Africa has been ruled mostly by Arabs, who settled here, and by the Germans and the British, who did not. The British named the area Tanganyika. Tanganyika became independent in 1961. In 1964, it joined with the island of Zanzibar to form the nation of Tanzania.

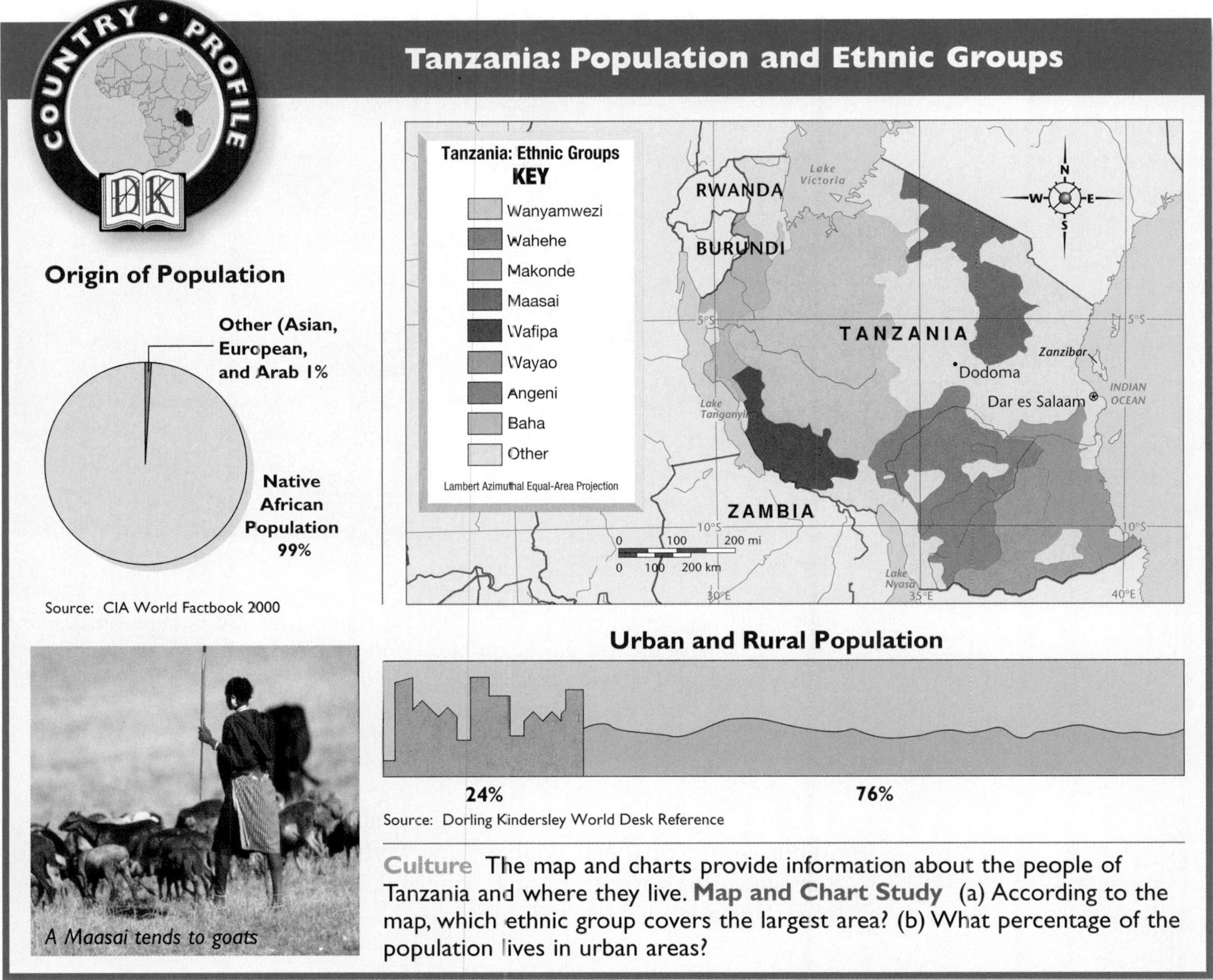

Culture The map and charts provide information about the people of Tanzania and where they live. **Map and Chart Study** (a) According to the map, which ethnic group covers the largest area? (b) What percentage of the population lives in urban areas?

Nyerere's Changes

When Tanzania became independent, most of its people were poor. Few were literate. Literacy is the ability to read and write. Tanzania's new president was Julius Nyerere. According to Nyerere, the new republic had serious problems:

> "We had 12 medical doctors in a population of 9 million. About 45 percent of children of school-going age were going to school, and 85 percent of the population was illiterate."

Nyerere also worried about keeping the peace among Tanzania's 120 ethnic groups. In many African nations, ethnic groups fought each other after independence. Nyerere wanted to make sure that would not happen in Tanzania.

Take It to the NET
Data Update For the most recent data on Tanzania, visit **www.phschool.com.**

Julius Nyerere—Tanzania's First Leader

After Julius Nyerere became Tanzania's first president, he also became famous for living simply. He drove a tiny compact car and would accept only a small salary. After he stepped down as president, he lived in a simple home on his family farm.

To bring about this goal, Nyerere adopted unusual social policies. While some of these policies met with approval both at home and abroad, others were sharply criticized. Even today, debate continues over Nyerere's legacy in Tanzania.

Swahili To help all the ethnic groups feel like part of one country, Nyerere made Swahili the national language. Swahili is an old Bantu language that contains many Arabic words. It is probably Africa's most widely spoken language, with as many as 50 million speakers. In the many countries of East Africa, Swahili is a ***lingua franca.*** This means that East Africans can use it to talk to each other if they speak different languages at home.

Nyerere's decision to adopt Swahili as Tanzania's national language had an important result. It made it less likely that the government would be controlled by just one ethnic group.

The One-Party System Nyerere also feared that political parties in Tanzania would be based on ethnic groups. Then, to win an election, a candidate from one party might promote hatred toward an ethnic group whose members belonged to another party. This had happened in other newly independent African nations.

To avoid ethnic conflict, Nyerere pushed to have only one political party. Voters still got to choose among several candidates. But all the candidates were members of the same party. Critics complained that having just one party encouraged corruption in government.

Working Together When Tanzania became independent, it did not have enough educated citizens to run the government. Many people had to moonlight, or work more than one job. For example, Amri Abedi was the mayor of Dar es Salaam, the leader of a regional government, and the Minister of Justice—all at the same time.

Economic Changes Next, Nyerere turned to the economy. He told Tanzanians that independence meant *uhuru na kazi* (oo HOO roo nah KAH zee)—"freedom and work." This was his way of saying that only hard work could end poverty. Nyerere said that Tanzania should be self-reliant and not depend on other nations.

One part of self-reliance was *ujamaa* (oo JAH mah), which is Swahili for "togetherness" or "being a family." Tanzania's economy is based on farming. Nyerere called for all farmers to live in ujamaa villages, where they could work together and share resources. He knew that it would be easier for the government to provide clean water, education, and other services if people lived in organized villages. At first, some farmers volunteered to move to the ujamaa. Then Nyerere's government began to use force, and sometimes violence, to get others to move.

Predict Do you think Nyerere's policies helped Tanzania? Why or why not?

A Mixed Legacy Tanzania had experienced great change by the time Nyerere stepped down as president. The country had a national language, and had avoided ethnic conflict. Education and literacy had improved greatly. Nyerere was proud of his success. He commented:

> "When I stepped down, 91 percent of the adult population was literate, 100 percent of the children of schoolgoing age were going to school, not just for four years, but for seven years. We did not have enough

An Ujamaa Village

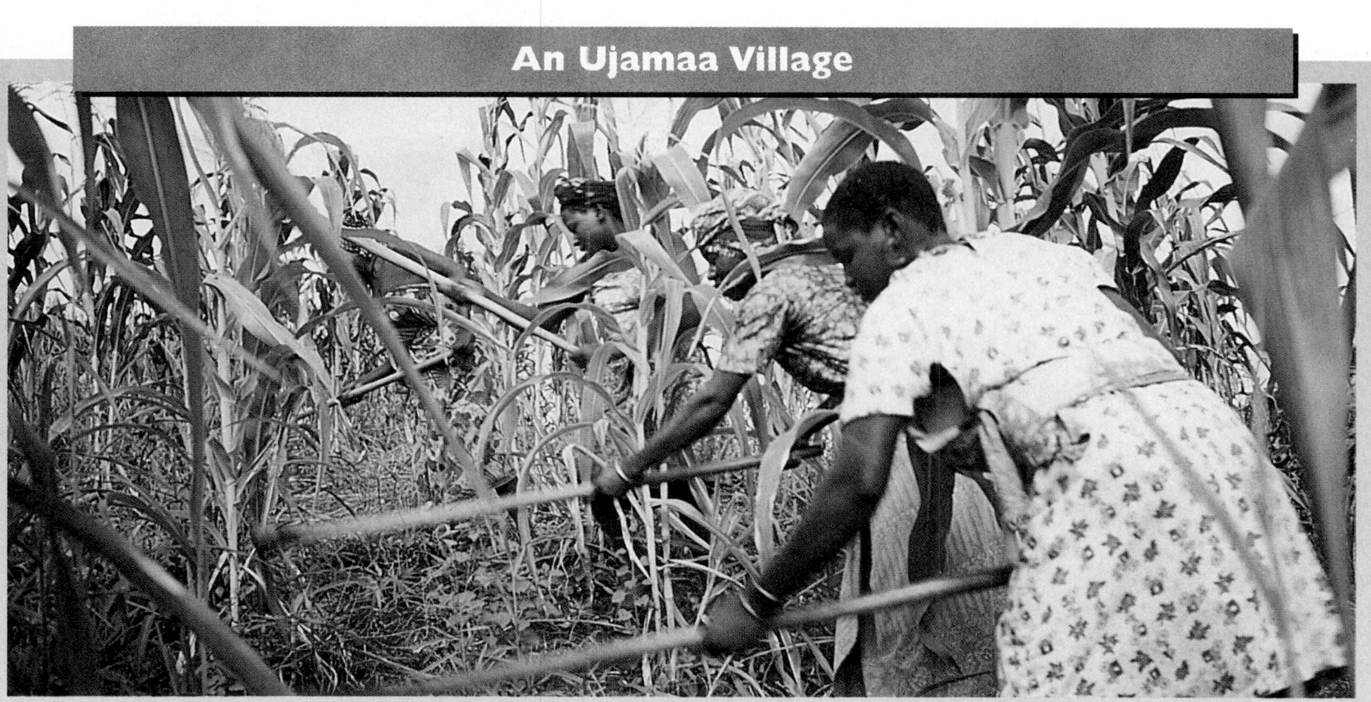

The ujamaa villages were supposed to boost farm production. Communities could then sell their surplus produce. Some people, like the women hoeing corn above, were glad to take part in ujamaa. Many other Tanzanians, however, resisted leaving the small family farms where their ancestors were buried. In the long run, Tanzania ended the ujamaa program.

> engineers, but we had thousands of engineers trained by ourselves. We did not have enough doctors, but we had many more than twelve, we had thousands trained by ourselves. That is what we were able to do ourselves in a short period of independence."

However, Tanzania was still one of the poorest countries in the world. The economy had suffered, and the ujamaa program had failed. Many farm families had refused to move to the new villages. Crop production had fallen throughout the nation.

Nyerere retired in 1985 and a new president was elected. Nyerere continued to work with leaders of other nations to study the challenges that face Africa. In 1996, he led an effort to stop a civil war in a nearby country, Burundi. Then Nyerere retired to the village where he had been born. He had never owned a fancy car or had a lot of money. But he had won respect for all the efforts he had made as the founding father of Tanzania. He died in 1999.

Connect How are elections in the United States like elections in Tanzania today?

Tanzania Today

After Nyerere left office, Tanzania's new leaders changed some of his unsuccessful programs. To begin with, they ended ujamaa. They also decided that farms should put more effort into producing cash crops to sell. They also asked foreign countries for more help. Tanzania

A Cash Crop That Smells Sweet

Tanzania's island of Zanzibar is the biggest producer of cloves in the world. People use cloves as a spice. A clove tree must grow for five years before it will begin to flower (right). When it does, farmers pick the buds by hand before the flowers open. They dry the cloves in the sun until they turn dark brown (below).

is still very poor. It has a huge **foreign debt,** or money owed to foreign countries. But the economy is improving.

Tanzania's new leaders also changed the election system. In 1992, the government started to allow new political parties to form. When a country has two or more political parties, it has a **multiparty system.** The first elections under the multiparty system were held in October 1995. Members of more than 10 parties ran for office. In the end, Nyerere's party won the most votes. But the election raised some issues that divided people. For example, one party suggested that the island of Zanzibar should no longer be part of Tanzania. This is exactly what Nyerere worried about.

As Tanzania's leaders face new challenges, they may keep in mind Nyerere's words: "There is a time for planting and a time for harvesting. I am afraid for us it is still a time for planting."

▲ New farming methods and seeds are helping some Tanzanian farmers to grow more than they could in the past. Changes like these are helping to improve Tanzania's economy.

1. **Define** (a) lingua franca, (b) foreign debt, (c) multiparty system.
2. **Identify** (a) Dar es Salaam, (b) Julius Nyerere, (c) Zanzibar.
3. What changes did Julius Nyerere bring to Tanzania?
4. What challenges faced Tanzania in the 1990s?

Critical Thinking

5. **Identifying Central Issues** Why did Julius Nyerere want a one-party system? Do you think he was right? Why or why not?

Activity

6. **Writing to Learn** How does Nyerere's slogan, "uhuru na kazi," or freedom and work, apply to the kind of independence that comes from growing up? Write a paragraph explaining how you have experienced uhuru na kazi as you have grown older.

Using Isolines to Show Elevation

"What on Earth is this?"

Alicia stared at the map. She could not imagine the purpose of the strange lines she was looking at.

"Those are isolines," her teacher, Ms. Washington, answered. "And they are not really on Earth. They are imaginary lines that people draw on maps. Think about the borders of countries. You can't see borders in the real world—there are no big, painted lines on the ground. Isolines are like that. They exist only on maps, to show information."

"Okay," Alicia said. "What do they show?"

"These isolines show elevation. By understanding isolines, you can make a flat map stand up! Let me show you how to figure them out."

Get Ready

Ms. Washington is right. Isolines do make flat maps stand up, in a way. How? Start with the word *isolines* itself. It comes from the Greek word *iso,* which means "equal," and the English word *lines.* Isolines outline equal parts of a map. When isolines are used to show elevation, they outline different parts of the map at the same elevation. Isolines that show elevation are also called contour lines because their pattern shows the contour, or shape, of the land. If you understand how to read isolines, you can see a two-dimensional map in three dimensions!

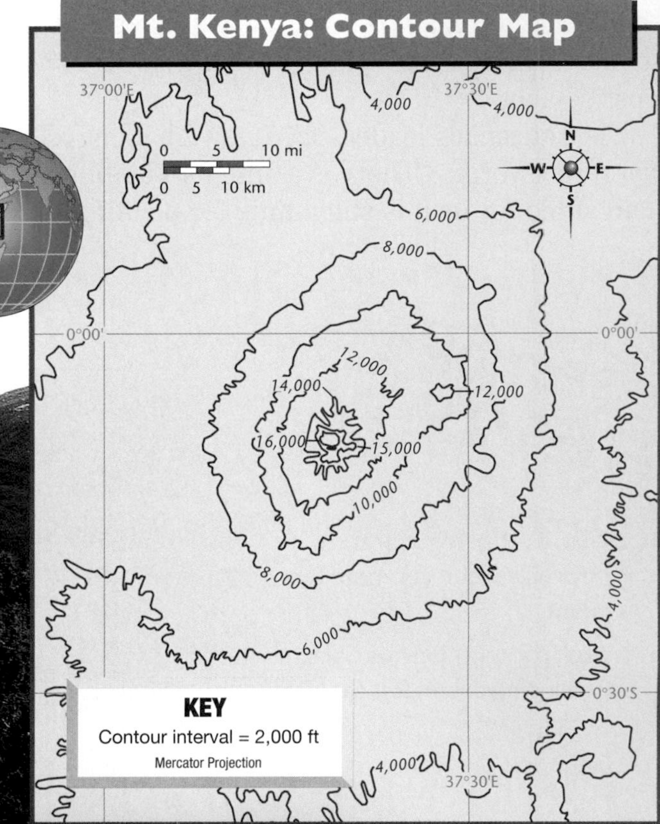

Look at the opposite page. The picture on the left shows how a landform looks from the side. To the right, the landform is represented by isolines. Do you see how they match? Where the land is steeper, the isolines are closer together. Where the land is flatter, the isolines are farther apart.

Try It Out

You can learn to read isolines by playing a game. All you need are notecards, pens, and a partner.

A. Deal the cards. Deal six notecards to your partner and six to yourself.

B. Draw landforms. You and your partner should each draw a profile, or sideways view, of an imaginary landform on each of your cards.

C. Draw isolines. Now, on your remaining three cards, you and your partner should each draw isolines that represent different imaginary landforms, one per card. The isolines can be any shape you want.

D. Trade Cards. Work with your partner's cards. Draw a profile of the landform based on your partner's isolines, and isolines based on your partner's landforms. When you have finished, check each other's work.

Apply the Skill

The map on this page shows isolines of Ethiopia. Use the map to complete the steps that follow, and try to visualize the contour of the land of Ethiopia.

1. **Remember that isolines connect places of equal elevation.** The isolines on this map are labeled to show elevation. What is the lowest elevation in Ethiopia? What is the highest? What is the difference between each pair of isolines?

2. **Use the isolines to get an idea of landscape.** How would you describe the Ethiopian landscape—hilly, mountainous, flat? Where are the highest parts of the country? Which part of the country is the most rugged?

3. **Use isolines to find the elevation near bodies of water.** Look at the isolines around Lake Tana and Ethiopia's other bodies of water. Which is on higher land, Lake Tana or the rivers in the southeastern part of Ethiopia?

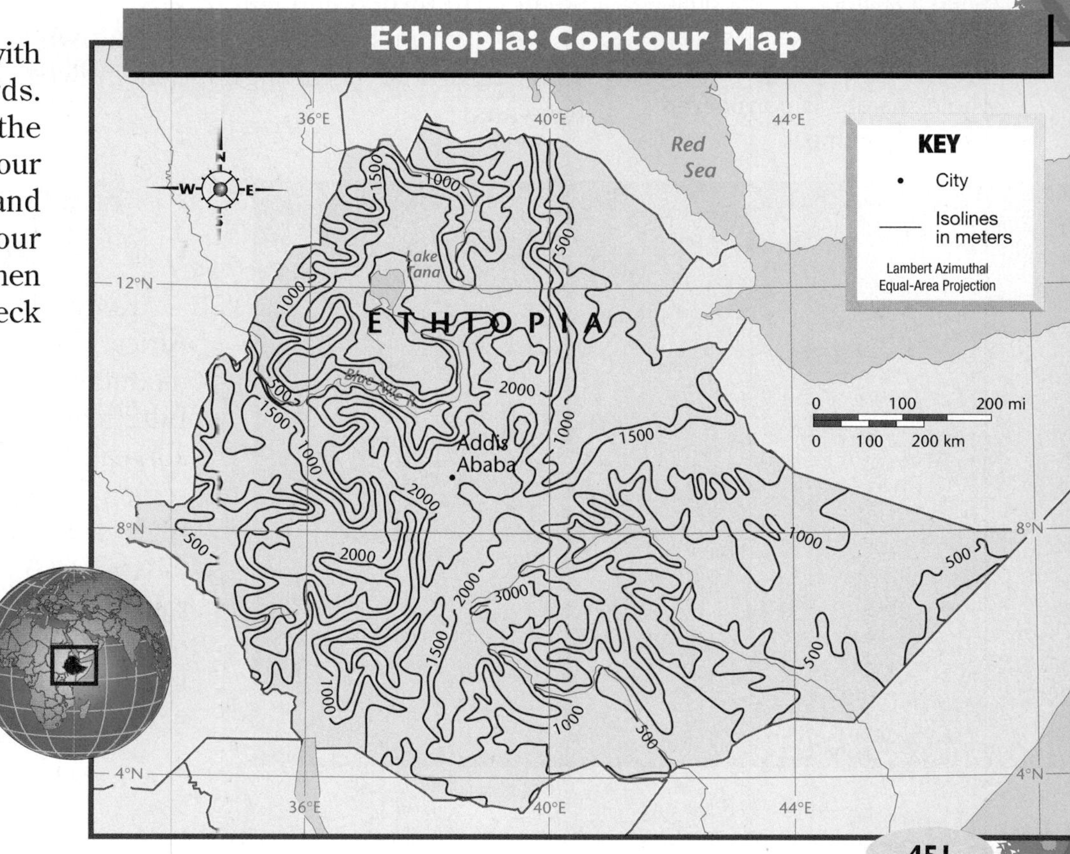

Kenya

Skyscrapers in the Savanna

Reach Into Your Background

How do you stay in touch with friends and family members after one of you moves? How do you cope with feeling homesick when you are away from home?

Questions to Explore

1. How do Kenyans who move to Nairobi from rural areas maintain ties to their homes and families?
2. Why do many more Kenyan men than women move from the country to the city?

Key Terms

harambee

Key People and Places

Jomo Kenyatta
Mount Kenya
Nairobi

"Where is your shamba?" This is a question that two Kenyans usually ask each other when they first meet. A shamba is a small farm owned and run by a Kenyan family. Even Kenyans who live in the city think of the piece of land where they were born as home. They return to it throughout their lives. Land is very important to Kenyans.

▼ This series of buildings is called a shamba. It was built by members of Kenya's Kikuyu ethnic group. The whole shamba is considered the family home.

Kenya's Geography and People

Kenya is a country in central East Africa. Mount Kenya, Kenya's highest mountain, lies just south of the Equator. But its twin peaks are covered with snow all year. Southwest of Mount Kenya is a region of highlands. This region has a high elevation. Its average temperature is 67°F (19°C). The area also gets plenty of rain, so the land is good for farming. Most of Kenya's people are farmers, and they live in shambas dotting the countryside in the highlands.

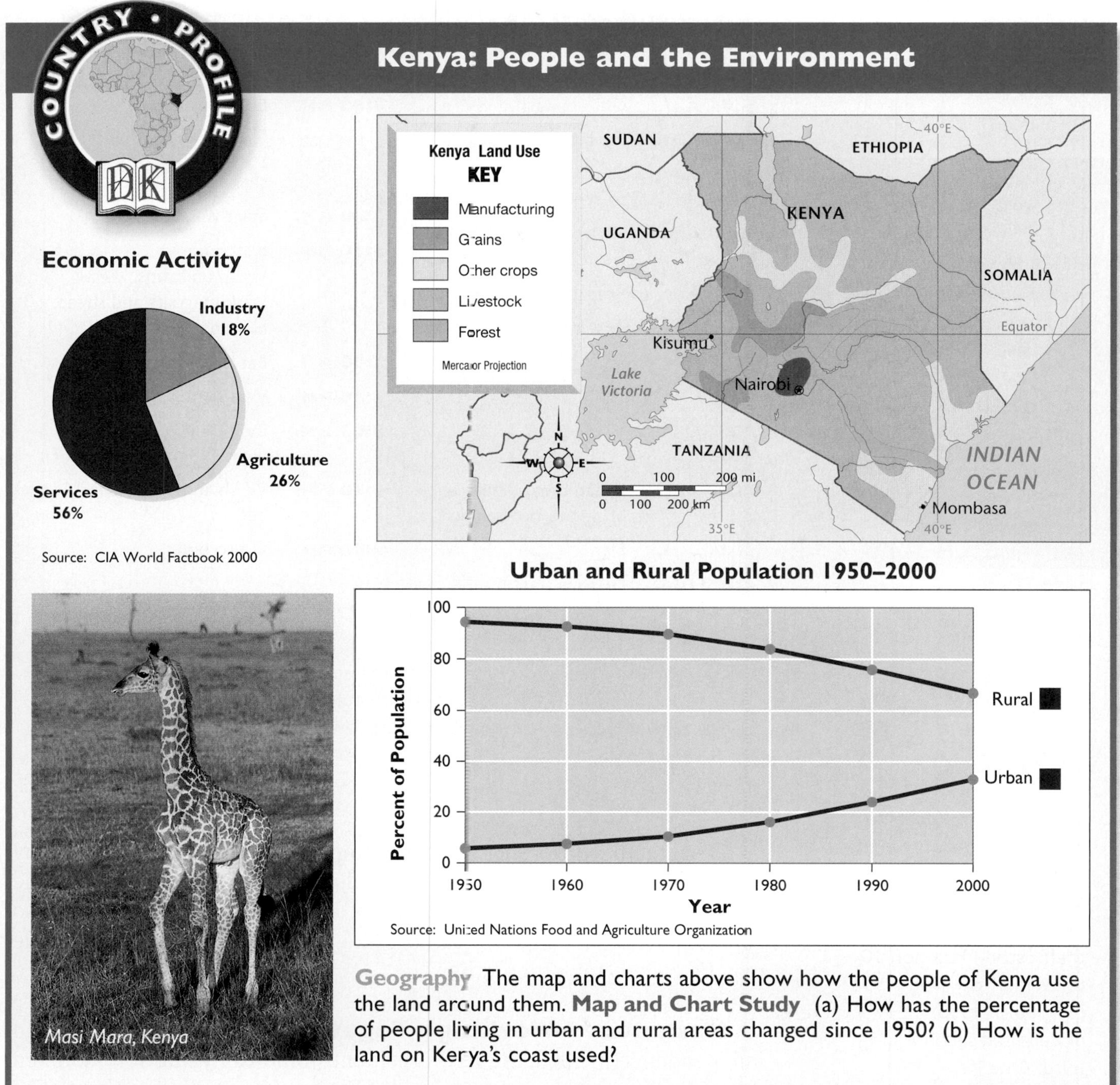

Masi Mara, Kenya

Geography The map and charts above show how the people of Kenya use the land around them. **Map and Chart Study** (a) How has the percentage of people living in urban and rural areas changed since 1950? (b) How is the land on Kenya's coast used?

The land near the coast is warmer than the highlands, but the area also has good farmland. Farther inland, plains stretch across Kenya. Here there is little rainfall. Because of this lack of rain, the plains support only bushes, small trees, and grasses. North of the plains lie deserts, where the temperature can sometimes climb as high as 135°F (57°C).

The Diversity of Kenya's People Nearly all of Kenya's people are indigenous Africans. A few of Kenya's people are of European or Asian descent. Kenyans belong to more than 40 different ethnic groups. Each group has its own culture and language. Most Kenyans are Christian or Muslim.

A Typical Day for Young Kenyans

Time	Activity	Time	Activity
5:45 A.M.	Get up, wash, and dress.	4:00 P.M.	Lessons end. Help clean the school or work on the school shamba.
6:15 A.M.	Eat breakfast.	5:00 P.M.	Start walking home.
6:30 A.M.	Start walking to school.	5:30 P.M.	Reach home. Wash uniforms. Lock up goats and sheep. Help prepare supper.
7:00 A.M.	Arrive at school. Help clean the school.	7:00 P.M.	Eat supper.
7:30 A.M.	Prepare for lessons.	7:30 P.M.	Wash up.
7:45 A.M.	Assembly. Sing national anthem.	8:00 P.M.	Do homework every night.
8:00 A.M.	Lessons start.	8:30 P.M.	Wash and prepare for bed.
10:20 A.M.	Break	9:00 P.M.	Go to bed.
11:00 A.M.	Lessons		
12:45 P.M.	Lunch break. Children bring their own lunch.		
1:00 P.M.	Play.		
2:00 P.M.	Lessons start.		

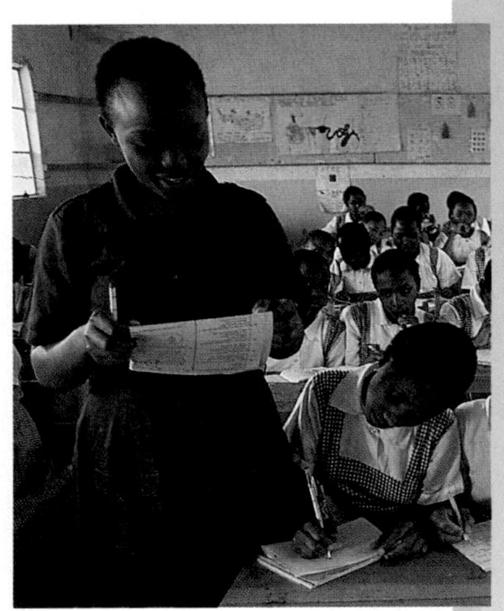

Chart Study Like you, Kenyan children spend most of each day in school. **Critical Thinking** Compare your schedule with this one. How would your day be different if you lived in Kenya? How would it be similar?

Running from Kenya to Boston Kenyan runners work together to train for athletic events—and it pays off. Kenyan runners won the Boston Marathon 10 times in a row, from 1991 to 2000. In 1995, they placed first, second, and third. One Kenyan, Cosmas Ndeti, won the race three times in a row, from 1993 to 1995. And Kenyan athletes have won numerous Olympic medals. No one is sure why Kenyan runners are so good at their sport, but some people think that training in Kenya's high elevations gives runners more endurance.

Despite the differences among Kenya's people, they have many things in common. As much as they value the land, Kenyans also value their families. Many families have six or more children. People also consider their cousins to be almost like brothers and sisters. An uncle may be called "my other father."

Harambee—Working Together After Kenya gained independence in 1963, the new president, Jomo Kenyatta (JOH moh ken YAH tuh), began a campaign he called ***harambee*** (hah RAHM bay). The word is Swahili for "let's pull together." One example of harambee is Kenyatta's approach to education. The government pays for some of a child's education, but not all of it. As a result, in many villages, the people have worked together to build and support schools.

Rural Kenya

The people who live in the rural areas of Kenya are farmers. Most of Kenya's farmers, like farmers all over Africa, are women. They grow fruits and vegetables to eat. They also herd livestock. Men also farm, but they usually raise cash crops, such as coffee and tea. Some women also grow cash crops.

Farming in the Highlands The Kikuyu (ki KOO yoo) are Kenya's largest ethnic group. Many Kikuyu live in shambas on the highlands near Mount Kenya. They build round homes with mud walls and thatched roofs. The Kikuyu grow food and cash crops such as coffee and sisal, which is used to make rope.

Children in a farming village have more responsibilities than most children in the United States. They may begin their day by carrying water from a stream to the village. They milk the cattle or goats and clean their homes before going to school. For fun, Kenyan boys play soccer, and the girls play dodgeball. Kenyan children also make toy cars, dolls, and other toys. Occasionally, someone will bring a truck with a generator, a film projector, and a screen to the village, and the people will enjoy a movie. To see what a typical day is like for a Kenyan child, look at the schedule on the previous page.

READ ACTIVELY

Visualize Kenyan children spend about half an hour walking to school in the morning. Visualize the scenes they might see on their way to school.

Moving to the City

The way of life of many Kenyans is changing. As the population increases, many men and some women are moving to the city to find work. Most women and children, however, stay in the rural areas. Women are the primary caretakers for children, and it is expensive for women with children to move from the country to the city. Many find it easier to support their families by farming.

A Nairobi Street Scene

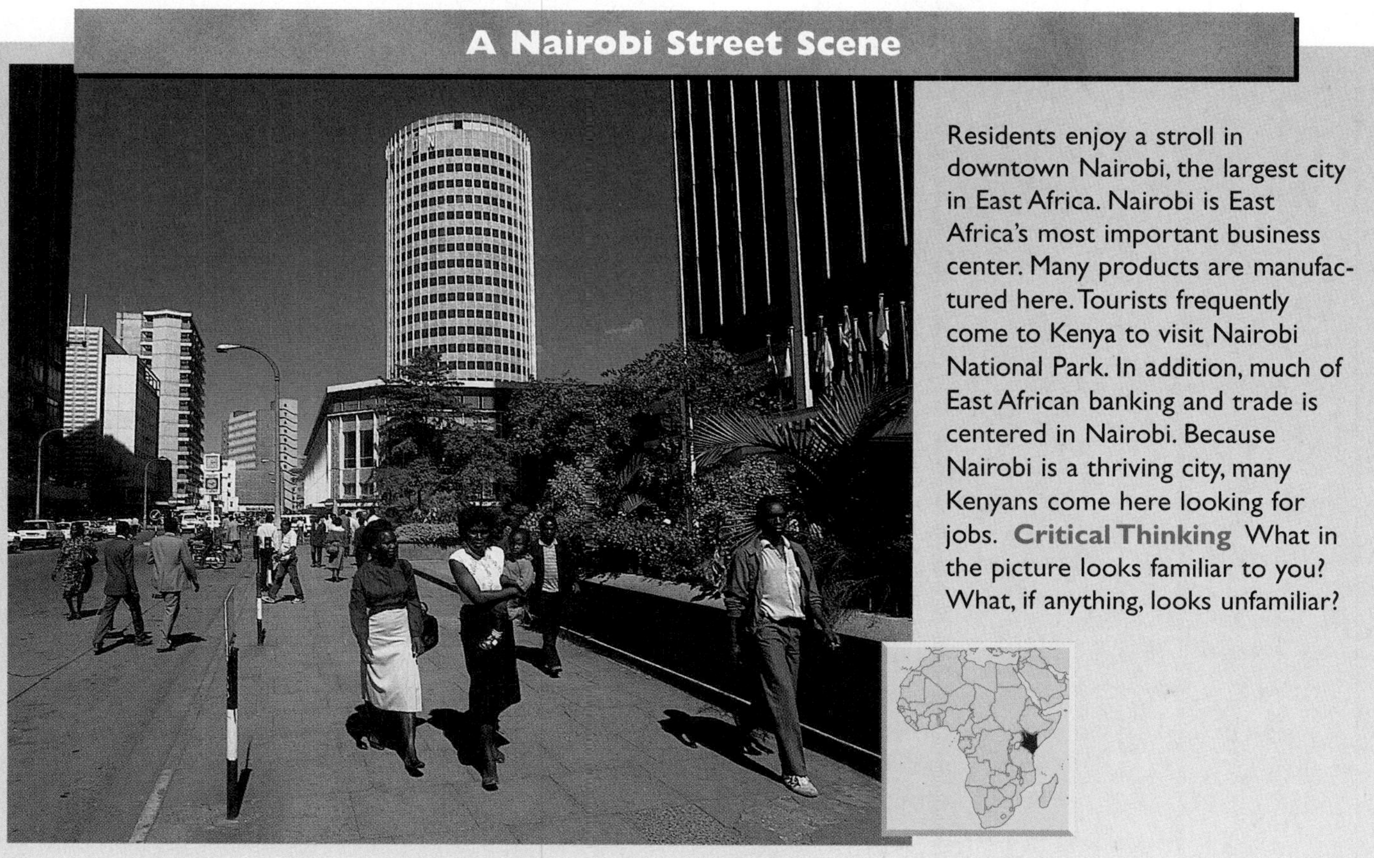

Residents enjoy a stroll in downtown Nairobi, the largest city in East Africa. Nairobi is East Africa's most important business center. Many products are manufactured here. Tourists frequently come to Kenya to visit Nairobi National Park. In addition, much of East African banking and trade is centered in Nairobi. Because Nairobi is a thriving city, many Kenyans come here looking for jobs. **Critical Thinking** What in the picture looks familiar to you? What, if anything, looks unfamiliar?

Ask Questions What more would you like to know about what it's like to live in Nairobi?

Nairobi: Kenya's Capital City Every day, people arrive in Nairobi (ny ROH bee) by train, bus, or *matatu* (muh TAH too)—a minibus. They are new residents of the city. Nairobi's population grew from one million in 1985 to three million in 1995, making it bigger than the city of Chicago in the United States. Many of Nairobi's newcomers walk to their jobs in the city from the outskirts of town. They may walk as far as 10 miles to work, because they cannot afford the few cents that it costs to take the bus.

When men move to Nairobi without their families, they often feel homesick for their loved ones in rural villages. Meanwhile, the women who are left behind in the villages must do twice as much work. Many people in Kenya have responded to this situation in the spirit of harambee—working together.

Women's Self-Help Groups One of the best examples of harambee in rural Kenya are women's self-help groups. Women in rural areas all over Kenya have formed these groups to solve problems in their communities. The women grow cash crops in addition to the crops they grow for their families to eat. Then they sell the cash crops and save the money as a group. The women meet to decide what to do with the money they have saved.

Matatu Ride

Ian Kamau
Age 16
Kenya

Look carefully at the painting. Notice that, like the British, Kenyans have their steering wheels on the right side of vehicles. That's because Kenya used to be a colony of Great Britain. **Critical Thinking** This matatu is bound for Nairobi. Do you think the artist considers a visit to Nairobi a happy event? Why or why not?

In Mitero, a village in the mountains north of Nairobi, Kikuyu women's groups have built a nursery school and installed water pipes for the community. They also loan money to women who want to start small businesses. Sometimes they give money to women who need to buy such things as a cow or a water tank. They also save money individually and use it to educate their children.

However, it is not easy to grow cash crops, grow vegetables for the family, chop firewood, haul water, and take care of children all in one day. One woman commented, "My children were educated through the sweat of my brow."

Men in the City Men who move to the city also work hard. Many are saving money to buy land in the countryside. Men in Nairobi who are from the same ethnic group often welcome each other, share rooms, and help each other.

Moses Mpoke (MOH zuz uhm POHK ay) is a Maasai. The Maasai of Kenya traditionally make a living farming and herding. Mpoke finished high school and now works in Nairobi. He has land in his home village. But the land is too dry for farming, and he could not move his livestock to find good grazing. He left the village to find work.

Now Mpoke is a filing clerk in the city. Mpoke lives outside the city, where he shares a room with two other Maasai. Their friendship makes his life in the city bearable. Like Mpoke, most newcomers to the city are made welcome by relatives or other members of their ethnic group.

Every weekend, Mpoke returns to his village to see his family and friends. Once, as Mpoke sat in his village home, a visitor asked him which was the real Moses Mpoke, the one in the city or the one in the village. He answered:

> "This is the real Moses Mpoke, but the other is also me. In the week, I can live in the city and be comfortable. At weekends, I can live here and be comfortable. The city has not stopped me from being a Maasai."

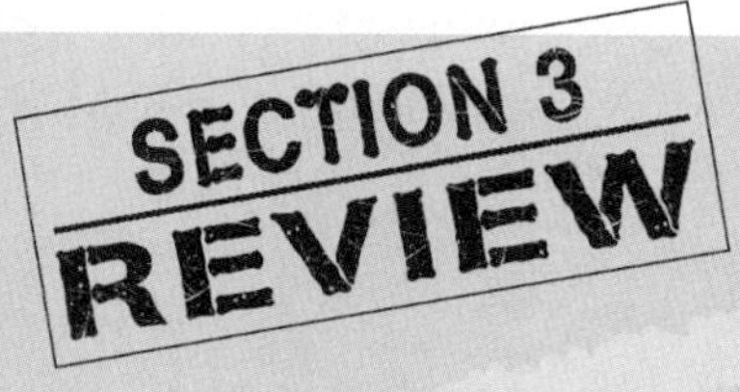

1. **Define** harambee.
2. **Identify** (a) Jomo Kenyatta, (b) Mount Kenya, (c) Nairobi.
3. Describe the daily life of a child in a rural Kenyan village.
4. Why do so many Kenyan men move to Nairobi?

Critical Thinking

5. **Expressing Problems Clearly** How are women in rural villages affected when men move to the city?

Activity

6. **Writing to Learn** Describe an example of harambee in your community.

Review and Activities

Reviewing Main Ideas

1. What are the main religions in Ethiopia? How did they get there?
2. Compare life in Ethiopia's cities with life in its rural communities.
3. Did Nyerere's one-party system achieve its goals? Why or why not?
4. Explain the purpose of an ujamaa village.
5. How do men's and women's lives change when men move to Nairobi?
6. How are Kenyans in rural areas working together to improve their lives?

Reviewing Key Terms

Decide whether each statement is true or false. If it is true, write "true." If it is false, change the underlined term to make the statement true.

1. The Swahili word that means "let's pull together" is <u>shamba</u>.
2. Tanzania owes a huge <u>foreign debt</u> to other countries.
3. A building where priests live and work is a <u>multiparty system</u>.
4. People who speak different languages often communicate by speaking a <u>lingua franca</u>.
5. A country with two or more political parties has a <u>harambee</u>.

Critical Thinking

1. **Making Comparisons** What do you think would be the advantages of a one-party political system? What would be the advantages of a multiparty political system?
2. **Recognizing Cause and Effect** How did the spread of Islam cause Ethiopian Christians to become more isolated?

Graphic Organizer

Copy the web onto a sheet of paper. Then complete the web by filling in the empty circles with the ways that President Nyerere planned to help Tanzania to be self-reliant.

Self-reliance in Tanzania

Map Activity

East Africa
For each place listed below, write the letter from the map that shows its location.

1. Ethiopia
2. Nairobi
3. Tanzania
4. Dar es Salaam
5. Zanzibar
6. Kenya
7. Addis Ababa
8. Lalibela

Place Location

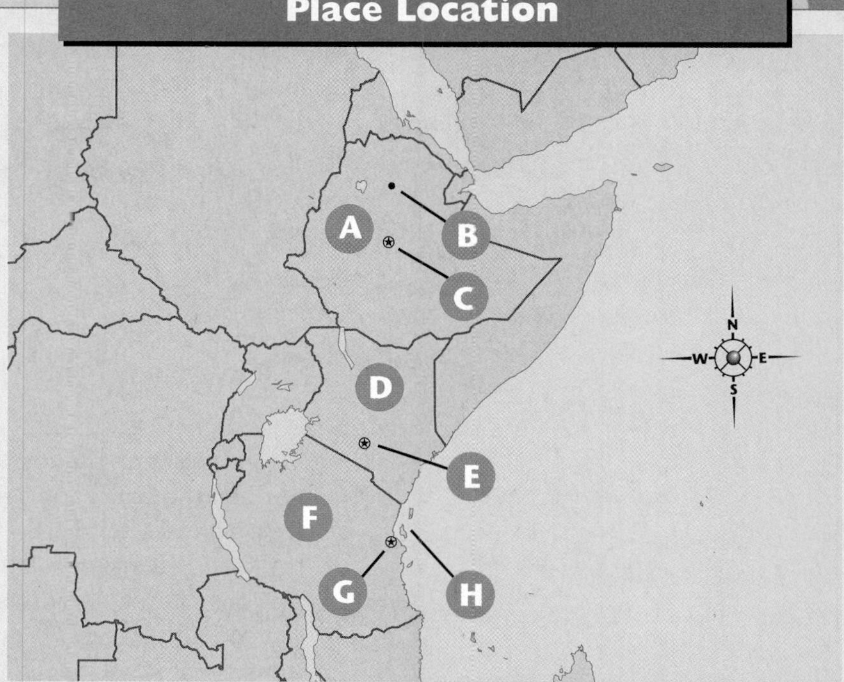

Writing Activity

Writing a Newspaper Opinion Article
Think about your community. Is it growing or getting smaller? Hypothesize about why your community has developed in the way that it has. Is it developing in a way that benefits its citizens? What are some good things about the change in growth in your community? What are some bad things? Write a newspaper opinion article explaining your view.

Take It to the NET

Activity Explore Tanzania's culture, history, attractions, and more. Create a travel brochure including interesting facts about Tanzania and the country's most exciting attractions. For help in completing this activity, visit **www.phschool.com.**

Chapter 16 Self-Test To review what you have learned, take the Chapter 16 Self-Test and get instant feedback on your answers. Go to **www.phschool.com** to take the test.

Skills Review

Turn to the Skills Activity.

Review the steps for using isolines. Then complete the following: (a) Explain what information you can discover by using the isolines on a map. (b) How are isolines used on water maps?

How Am I Doing?

Answer these questions to check your progress.

1. Can I identify the main religions of Ethiopia?
2. Can I explain some of the ways Tanzania's government has changed in recent years?
3. Do I understand why men in Kenya are moving to the cities? Can I explain how their move affects people throughout the country?
4. What information from this chapter can I include in my journal?

A Promise to the Sun

BY TOLOLWA M. MOLLEL

Reach Into Your Background
What does a promise mean to you? Have you ever made a promise that you later discovered you could not keep?

Promises are famous around the world for being easy to make but hard to keep. Making a promise is a serious matter, because a person who accepts a promise trusts that it will be kept. In most cultures, breaking a promise is the same as betraying a person's trust. This Maasai story from East Africa is about just such a broken promise.

Questions to Explore

1. What can you learn from this story about how people in East Africa make a living?
2. What does this story tell you about the values of the Maasai people?

Long ago, when the world was new, a severe drought hit the land of the birds. The savannah turned brown, and streams dried up. Maize plants died, and banana trees shriveled in the sun, their broad leaves wilting away. Even the nearby forest grew withered and pale.

maize *n.:* a type of corn
shrivel *v.:* to wrinkle as moisture is lost
wilt *v.:* to droop
withered *adj.:* shriveled and shrunken from drying out

The birds held a meeting and decided to send someone in search of rain. They drew lots to choose who would go on the journey. And they told the Bat, their distant cousin who was visiting, that she must draw, too. "You might not be a bird," they said, "but for now you're one of us." Everyone took a lot, and as luck would have it, the task fell to the Bat.

Over the trees and the mountains flew the Bat, to the Moon. There she cried, "Earth has no rain, Earth has no food, Earth asks for rain!"

The Moon smiled. "I can't bring rain. My task is to wash and oil the night's face. But you can try the Stars."

On flew the Bat, until she found the Stars at play. "Away with you!" they snapped, angry at being interrupted. "If you want rain, go to the Clouds!"

The Clouds were asleep but awoke at the sound of the Bat

arriving. "We can bring rain," they yawned, "but the Winds must first blow us together, to hang over the Earth in one big lump."

At the approach of the Bat, the Winds howled to a stop.

"We'll blow the Clouds together," they said, "but not before the Sun has brought up steam to the sky."

As the Bat flew toward the Sun, a sudden scream shook the sky:

"Stop where you are, foolish Bat, before I burn off your little wings!"

The Bat shrank back in terror, and the Sun smothered its fire in rolls of clouds. Quickly the Bat said, "Earth has no rain, Earth has no food, Earth asks for rain!"

"I'll help you," replied the Sun, "in return for a favor. After the rain falls, choose for me the greenest patch on the forest top, and build me a nest there. Then no longer will I have to journey to the horizon at the end of each day but will rest for the night in the cool and quiet of the forest."

The Bat quickly replied, "I'm only a Bat and don't know how to build nests, but the birds will happily make you one. Nothing will be easier—there are so many of them. They will do it right after the harvest, I promise—all in a day!"

And down the sky's sunlit paths the Bat flew, excited to bring the good news to the birds.

The birds readily promised to build the nest.

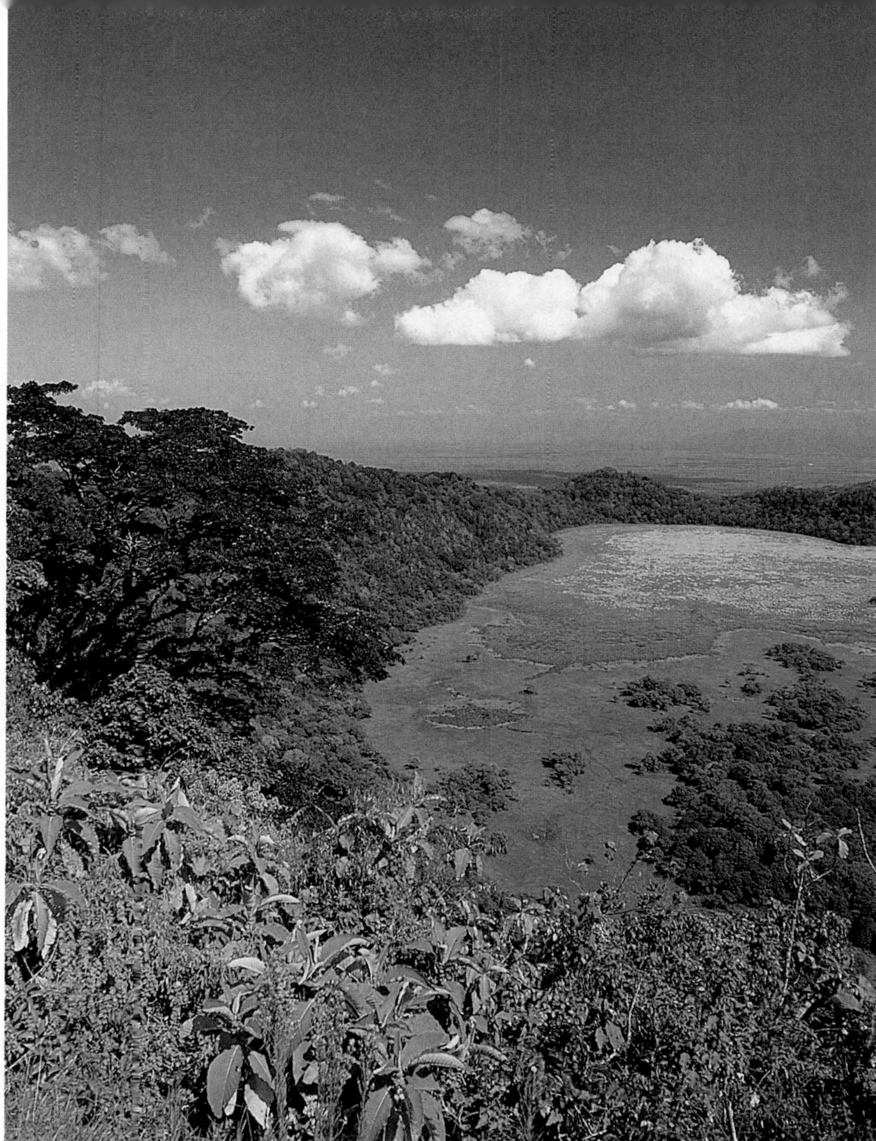

"The very day after the harvest," said the Sparrow.

"All in a day," said the Owl.

"A beautiful nest it'll be," said the Canary.

"With all the colors of the rainbow," said the Peacock.

So the Sun burnt down upon the earth, steam rose, Winds blew, and Clouds gathered. Then rain fell. The savannah bloomed, and streams flowed. Green and thick and tall, the forest grew until it touched the sky. Crops flourished and ripened—maize, bananas, cassava, millet, and peanuts—and the birds harvested. The morning after the harvest, the Bat reminded the birds about

▲ "After the rain falls, choose for me the greenest patch on the forest top, and build me a nest there," the sun said.

horizon *n.*: the place where the Earth and the sky appear to meet

Predict Do you think the birds will ever build the nest for the sun?

throb *v.:* to beat
shriek *v.:* to cry out with a sharp, shrill sound

the nest. Suddenly the birds were in no mood for work. All they cared about was the harvest celebrations, which were to start that night and last several days.

"I have to adorn myself," said the Peacock.

"I have to practice my flute," said the Canary.

"I have to heat up my drums," said the Owl.

"I have to help prepare the feast," said the Sparrow.

"Wait until after the celebrations," they said. "We'll do it then." But their hearts were not in it, and the Bat knew they would never build the nest.

What was she to do? A promise is a promise, she believed, yet she didn't know anything about making a nest. Even if she did, how could she, all on her own, hope to make one big enough for the sun?

The Sun set, and the Moon rose. The celebrations began. The drums throbbed, the flutes wailed, and the dancers pounded the earth with their feet.

Alone with her thoughts and tired, the Bat fell fast asleep.

She awoke in a panic. The Moon had vanished, the Stars faded. Soon the Sun would rise!

Slowly, the Sun peered out over the horizon in search of the nest.

Certain the Sun was looking for her, the Bat scrambled behind a banana leaf. The Sun moved up in the sky. One of its rays glared over the leaf. With a cry of fear, the Bat fled to the forest.

But even there, she was not long at peace. There was a gust of wind, and the forest opened for a moment overhead. The Bat looked up anxiously. Peeking down at her was the Sun.

She let out a shriek and flew away.

As she flew, a cave came into view below. She dived down and quickly darted in.

There, silent and out of reach, she hid from the glare of the Sun.

She hid from the shame of a broken promise, a shame the birds did not feel.

Outside, the celebrations went on. The Owl's drums roared furiously.

▼ The Sun inched down toward the horizon.

The Canary's flute pierced the air. And the Sparrow cheered the Peacock's wild dancing.

The Sun inched down toward the horizon. It lingered over the forest and cast one more glance at the treetops, hoping for a miracle. Then, disappointed, it began to set. The birds carried on unconcerned, the sounds of their festivities reaching into the cave.

But the Bat did not stir from her hiding place that night. Nor the next day. For many days and nights she huddled in the cave. Then gradually she got up enough courage to venture out—but never in daylight! Only after sunset with Earth in the embrace of night.

Days and months and years went by, but the birds didn't build the nest. The Sun never gave up wishing, though. Every day as it set, it would linger to cast one last, hopeful glance at the forest top. Then, slowly, very slowly, it would sink away below the horizon.

Year after year the Sun continued to drag up steam, so the Winds would blow, the Clouds gather, and rain fall. It continues to do so today, hoping that the birds will one day keep their promise and build a nest among the treetops.

As for the Bat, . . . she made a home in the cave, and there she lives to this day. Whenever it rains, though, she listens eagerly. From the dark silence of her perch, the sound of the downpour, ripening the crops and renewing the forest, is to her a magical song she wishes she could be out dancing to.

And as she listens, the trees outside sway and bow toward the cave. It is their thank-you salute to the hero who helped turn the forests green and thick and tall as the sky.

Connect How do you feel if you break a promise?

venture *v.:* to move in the face of danger

embrace *v.:* to hug

EXPLORING YOUR READING

Look Back

1. What favor did the Sun ask of the Bat? Why didn't the Bat keep her promise?

Think It Over

2. What natural events are explained by this story?
3. Based on this story, how dependable do you think the Maasai people consider nature to be?
4. Why do you think that the birds did not feel as ashamed as the Bat?

Go Beyond

5. What lesson does this story teach about how all the different parts of the world relate to each other? What lesson does it teach about how the animals relate to each other?

Ideas for Writing: Short Story

6. Using this story as a model, write a story in which the Bat makes her peace with the Sun.

CHAPTER 17

Exploring Central and Southern Africa

SECTION 1
Democratic Republic of Congo
RICH BUT POOR

SECTION 2
South Africa
THE END OF APARTHEID

MAP ACTIVITIES

This map shows the nations that make up Central and Southern Africa. To help you get to know this region, do the following activities.

Consider the geography

How many countries can you count on this map? Which country is the biggest? The smallest? Which countries are near water? Which countries are landlocked, or surrounded by other countries?

Find the island countries

Look at the west coast of Central Africa. How many countries are completely surrounded by the Atlantic Ocean? Look at the east coast of Central and Southern Africa. How many countries are completely surrounded by the Indian Ocean?

Democratic Republic of Congo

Rich But Poor

Reach Into Your Background
What resources do you think a country needs to provide a good life for its people? Make a list of these resources. Share your list with the rest of the class.

Questions to Explore

1. Why is mining important to Congo's economy?
2. What economic challenges has Congo faced since independence?

Key Terms
authoritarian
nationalize

Key People and Places
Katanga
King Leopold II
Mobutu Sese Seko

Copper mining in what today is the Democratic Republic of Congo began in ancient times. The demand for copper brought Europeans to the area in the early 1900s. In 1930, a mining company found copper in a place called Kolwezi (kohl WAY zee). The company built a mine and hired miners and a host of other workers. Soon a small city of workers' houses arose. Meanwhile, miners started to tunnel down into the Earth for the copper. They found it, too—right under their houses.

The Kolwezi area proved so rich in copper that, at first, miners found that they barely had to scratch the surface to find the mineral. After a time, however, the miners had to dig deeper. Soon, they had dug a huge pit. Miners are still digging for copper there today. The Kolwezi mine in southern Congo is one of the largest open-pit mines in Africa.

▼ In Congo, miners take copper out of the ground in layers, leaving an open pit behind.

Congo's Physical Geography

Since the 1930s, Congo has become one of the world's main sources of copper. Congo also has supplies of many other resources, including gold, diamonds, copper, forests, water, and wildlife. Look at the map in the Country Profile and identify these resources. Congo's minerals and other resources have played an important role in the nation's history.

Democratic Republic of Congo: Natural Resources

Sources of Electricity

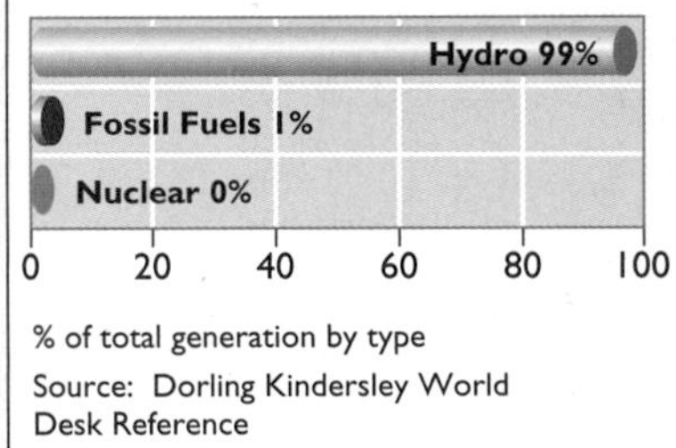

Congo River

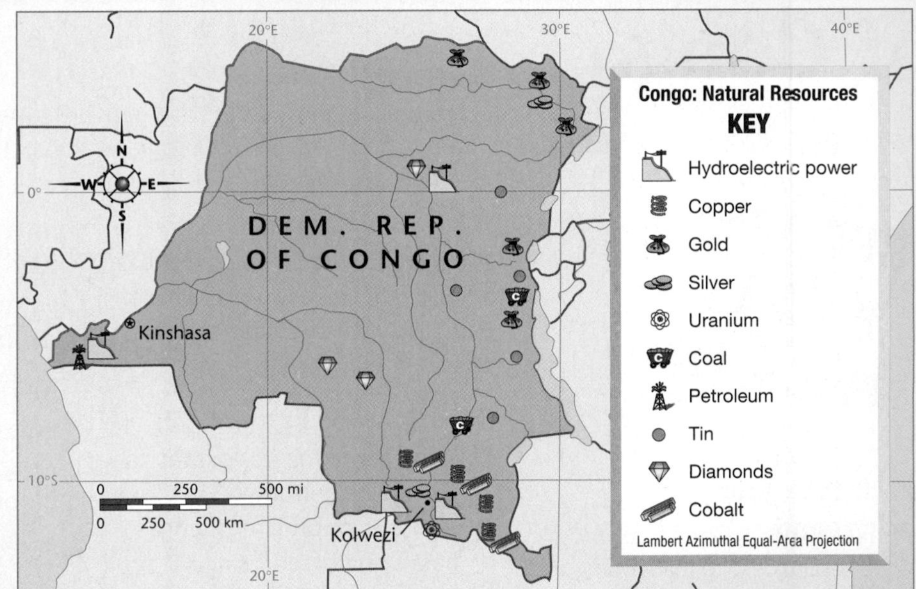

Income from Mining, 1999

Sources	Millions of Dollars
Diamonds	
Petroleum	
Cobalt	
Copper	

(Key: one coin = $50 million)

Source: United States Geological Survey

Economics The map and charts above show information about the natural resources of the Democratic Republic of Congo and how they help the country's people and economy. **Map and Chart Study** (a) Which resources are found in the southern region of the Democratic Republic of Congo? (b) In total, how much money did the Democratic Republic of Congo get from petroleum in 1999?

Take It to the NET

Data Update For the most recent data on the Democratic Republic of Congo, visit **www.phschool.com**.

Connect How do people make a living on the grasslands of the United States?

Forests and Grasslands The Democratic Republic of Congo is located in west Central Africa. Equal in size to the United States east of the Mississippi River, it is Africa's third largest country. Congo has four major physical regions: The Congo Basin, the Northern Uplands, the Eastern Highlands, and the Southern Uplands.

The Congo Basin is covered by a dense rain forest. People who live in this region mostly farm for a living. Most Congolese live in the country's other regions. The Northern Uplands, along the country's northern border, are covered with savanna, or grasslands. The Eastern Highlands have grasslands and occasional thick forests. The Southern Uplands are high, flat plains of grasslands and wooded areas. In these regions, most people make a living by subsistence farming.

A Mineral-Rich Nation While about two thirds of Congo's people work as farmers, mining produces most of the country's wealth. Congo has huge copper deposits in the southern province of Katanga (kuh TAHN guh). The country also has reserves of gold and other minerals. Congo produces more diamonds than any other country except Australia. And Congo has enough water power to run many hydroelectric plants. Congo has developed only a small part of its water power, mainly because the potential is so huge.

Predict How do you think that Congo's mineral resources have affected its history?

Natural Resources in Congo's History

Resources dominate the history of the Democratic Republic of Congo. By the 1400s, the kingdoms of Kongo, Luba, and Lunda ruled much of Central Africa. The power of these kingdoms was based on their knowledge of ironworking. The first Europeans who arrived in the area—the Portuguese in the 1480s—were not interested in iron. They came in search of gold.

Some 400 years later, during the scramble for Africa, King Leopold II of Belgium took control of the area, calling it the Congo Free State. Leopold ruled brutally, forcing Africans to harvest wild rubber without paying them. He grew wealthy while Africans suffered, starved, and died, probably by the millions. Later, Belgian government officials ruled less harshly. But they still were interested only in Congo's resources, especially its copper and diamonds.

During the 1950s, calls for independence echoed throughout Africa, including Congo. After a time of unrest, Congo won its independence in 1960.

Agriculture in Eastern Congo

Although Congo is rich in natural resources, not all Congolese make a living as miners. Many Congolese work as farmers. They grow bananas, cassavas, corn, peanuts, and rice for their families. Others make a living growing cash crops such as cocoa, coffee, cotton, and tea. **Critical Thinking** The fields shown in this photograph are in a hilly area of Congo. How do you think the shape of the land here creates challenges for farmers?

Since Independence

Latin American Economies Like Congo, many Latin American countries used to depend on one resource. These countries have been working to diversify their economies. They are trying to earn more money by growing more types of cash crops. They are also working to build their own industries and mine their own resources without help from foreign countries.

Congo's first years as an independent country were difficult. Various groups fought each other for power. This worried the foreign companies that controlled Congo's mines. The unrest, they feared, might hurt their businesses. In 1965, these foreign companies helped a military leader, Mobutu Sese Seko (muh BOO too SAY say SAY koh), take power. With a strong ruler in control, they thought their businesses would thrive.

Mobutu tried to restore order in the country by setting up an **authoritarian** government. In this form of government, a single leader or small group of leaders has all the power. An authoritarian government is not democratic. Mobutu tried to cut some ties with the colonial past. First he renamed the country Zaire. Then he **nationalized,** or put under government control, industries that had been owned by foreign companies. Mobutu also borrowed money from foreign countries to start projects. Many were promoted by foreigners and were useless.

Mobutu's economic moves failed. Government officials who ran the nationalized companies often made poor managers. Others simply stole their companies' profits. Mobutu and his supporters added to the problem by keeping much of Zaire's wealth for themselves.

Then, in the mid-1970s, the world price of copper fell sharply. Suddenly, Zaire was earning less and less from the sale of its major export. It could not pay back the money it had borrowed, and the country's economy quickly collapsed.

Mobutu responded by cutting government spending. This hit the poor people of Zaire especially hard. Unemployment rose rapidly. When political groups formed to challenge Mobutu's policies, Mobutu cracked down. He threw many of his opponents into prison or had them killed.

Throughout the 1980s, Mobutu continued his harsh rule, and Zaire's economy continued to decline. Calls for reform came from inside and outside Zaire. In the early 1990s, Mobutu's grip on the country weakened. He made desperate promises—promises he wouldn't keep—to stay in power.

At Work in Kinshasa

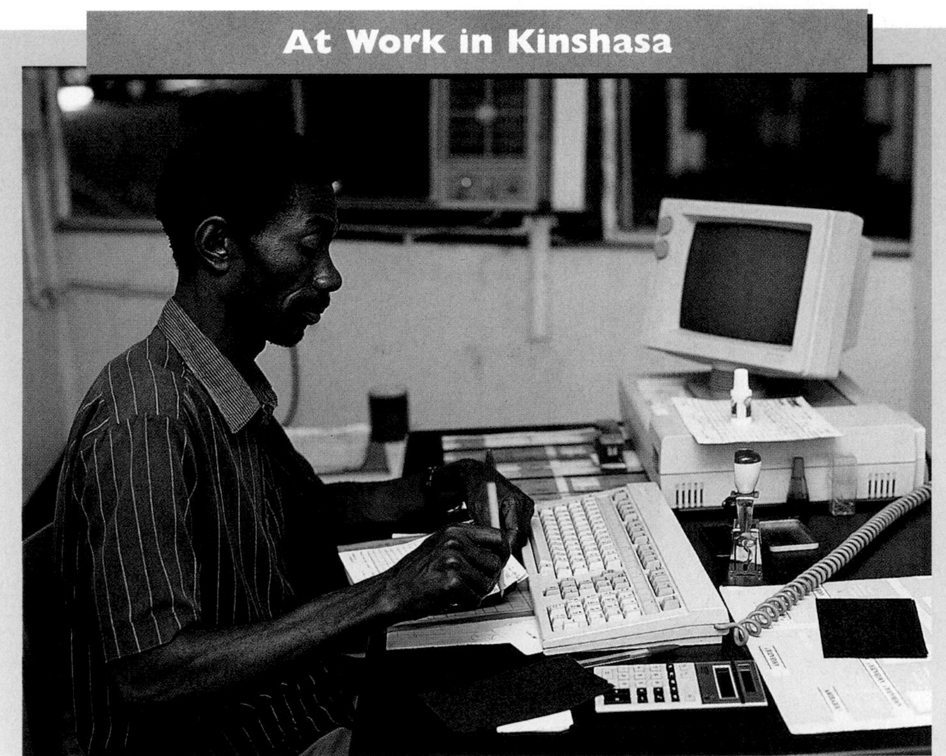

At a truck assembly plant in Congo's capital city, Kinshasa, an employee works on a computer in an air-conditioned office. **Critical Thinking** What kind of work might he be doing? How does this office resemble one in the United States?

In 1996, a minor uprising began in a region of eastern Zaire some 800 miles from the capital, Kinshasa. A small ethnic group there clashed with Zairian troops. The neighboring countries of Uganda, Rwanda, Burundi, and Angola supported the small group. With their help the uprising turned into a rebellion against the Mobutu government. Zaire's army tried to put down the rebellion. Its soldiers, however, were poorly paid and poorly trained. Many of them surrendered or ran away to avoid fighting.

The rebel army gained popular support as it grew in strength. Within months, the rebels had taken control of much of eastern Zaire. Then they turned their sights on Kinshasa. By May 1997, the rebel army was closing in on the capital city. Alarmed, Mobutu fled the country for Morocco. He died there four months later.

The rebels took charge of the capital. Soon they controlled the whole country, which they renamed the Democratic Republic of Congo. They vowed to establish a new constitution and hold national elections. As months went by without the promised reforms, criticism erupted. Rival political groups demanded progress. By early 1998, popular support for the new government was fading.

In August 1998, another armed rebellion began. Uganda and Rwanda supported the new rebels. They seized land in eastern Congo and threatened to overthrow the government. Several other neighbors of Congo, including Angola, Namibia, and Zimbabwe, backed the government. The civil war continued month after month. Neither side was able to achieve victory.

In April 1999, the United Nations took steps to arrange a cease-fire in Congo. It called on both sides to end the fighting and urged Congo's neighbors to withdraw from the country. Still the war drags on. Meanwhile, the people of Congo continue to suffer. Most of them support neither the rebels nor the government. They simply want peace and a chance to rebuild Congo's shattered economy.

Predict Once peace returns to Congo, how will the Congolese people restore their country's economy?

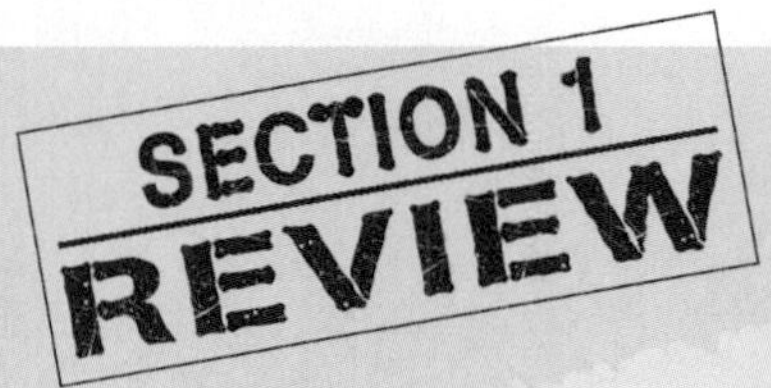

1. **Define** (a) authoritarian, (b) nationalize.
2. **Identify** (a) Katanga, (b) King Leopold II, (c) Mobutu Sese Seko.
3. (a) What are some of Congo's natural resources? (b) What role have they played in Congo's development as a nation?
4. (a) What economic changes did Mobutu Sese Seko make when he took power? (b) How successful were these changes?

Critical Thinking

5. **Drawing Conclusions** Why do you think Congolese people's wages and living conditions have declined since independence?

Activity

6. **Writing to Learn** Write a title and short description for a book about the history of Congo. Design a cover by deciding what images best represent Congo's history.

Organizing Your Time

"Your reports are due Monday," the teacher said on Friday afternoon. To Claudia the teacher's words sounded more like this: "You will not have any fun this weekend. You will not have time to see your friends or play basketball. And if you're lucky, you will finish your report late Sunday night and come to school tired Monday morning."

"There goes the weekend," she muttered to Timothy, who sat at the next desk.

"Oh, I don't know," he responded. "I just need to fix up my final copy, and I'll be done."

"How come you're so far along?"

"Well, I started two weeks ago, when she assigned the reports." He paused. "You haven't started yet?"

"No," Claudia said. "But I guess I'd better get on it."

Has this ever happened to you? Or are you more like Timothy, who got an early start—and then a better grade and free time over the weekend for his efforts? The key is to organize your time.

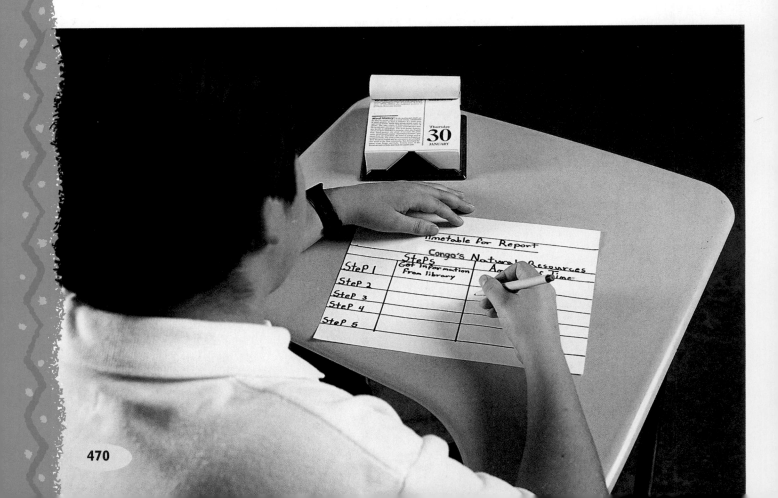

Get Ready

Teachers know how long it takes for students to complete assignments. So they make sure to give you a reasonable amount of time. But they expect you to start assignments soon after they make them. This is the first rule of organizing your time—get started early.

But an early start does not guarantee success. You must also organize your time carefully.

Timetable for Report on Apartheid

	Steps	Amount of Time
Step 1		
Step 2		
Step 3		
Step 4		
Step 5		

Try It Out

First, set a goal. Then identify the steps you need to take to reach it. Put these steps in the form of a chart to make a plan.

A. Set your goal. Include it in the title of your chart. Suppose that your goal is to turn in a one-page report by Friday. The title of your chart might be "Timetable for Report on Congo's Natural Resources."

B. Identify the first step you will need to take to reach your goal. What do you need to find out about Congo's natural resources? How can you find the information?

C. Continue toward your goal. Write every single step in your chart. What will you need to do after you find books and magazine articles about your topic? List the steps you need to carry out to end up with your written report.

D. Estimate the time for each step. Look back over the steps you need to take. Think about the time you need to complete each one. Write the amount of time next to each step in the chart.

Apply the Skill

To see how your chart can help you organize your time, complete these steps.

1. **Identify the steps.** Suppose you must write a two-page paper on the history of apartheid in South Africa. Make a chart of the steps you will take to reach this goal.

2. **Use your chart to organize your time.** You have two weeks to complete this assignment. Estimate how long each step will take. A step might take a few minutes, a few hours, or several days. Next to each step, write how long you think it will take. Remember, *the total amount of time for this assignment cannot be more than two weeks.*

3. **Transfer this information to a calendar.** Copy each step in the chart onto the proper days on the calendar. If you follow the calendar, you will reach your goal.

South Africa

THE END OF APARTHEID

Reach Into Your Background
Have you ever experienced being left out when you should have been included? Maybe you didn't get to do something you had planned, or you weren't chosen for a team. How did you deal with the experience of being unfairly left out?

Questions to Explore

1. How did the people of South Africa change their government and society?
2. How has life changed for the people of South Africa in the years since the end of apartheid?

Key Terms
apartheid
discriminate
homeland

Key People and Places
F. W. de Klerk
Nelson Mandela
Cape Town

▼ Many black South African children go to schools with real classrooms now, but on nice days they enjoy studying outside.

Nomfundo Mhlana, a young black woman, grew up on a white-owned farm. Both of her parents worked every day of the year, her father in the fields, her mother in the house. As a child, she wasn't allowed inside the white family's house, because she might get it dirty or steal something. The first time she went into the house, she was afraid the whites would chase her out.

Today, Mhlana says, "I do have hope that some whites are changing their minds. The whites on the farm now will come into our house and drink some tea with my mother. They also have a daughter who is nineteen, like me, and we are friends."

Life has changed for other South Africans, too. Just outside Johannesburg (joh HAN is burg) is a rural settlement called Orange Farm. Black South Africans escaping poor rural areas and crowded cities founded Orange Farm in 1989. At first, they lived in tents. Children attended school in what used to be chicken coops and horses' stables. Today, more than 900 Orange Farm children attend school in real buildings.

The changes experienced by Mhlana and other South Africans have been a long time coming. For many years, the Republic of South Africa was a divided country.

South Africa: Population and Ethnic Groups

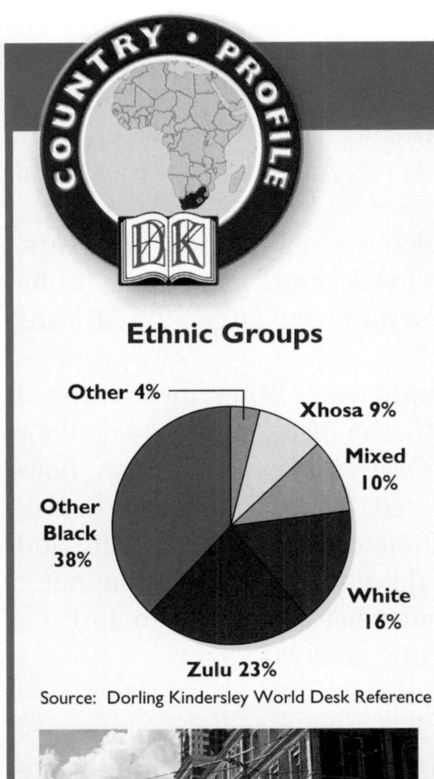

Source: Dorling Kindersley World Desk Reference

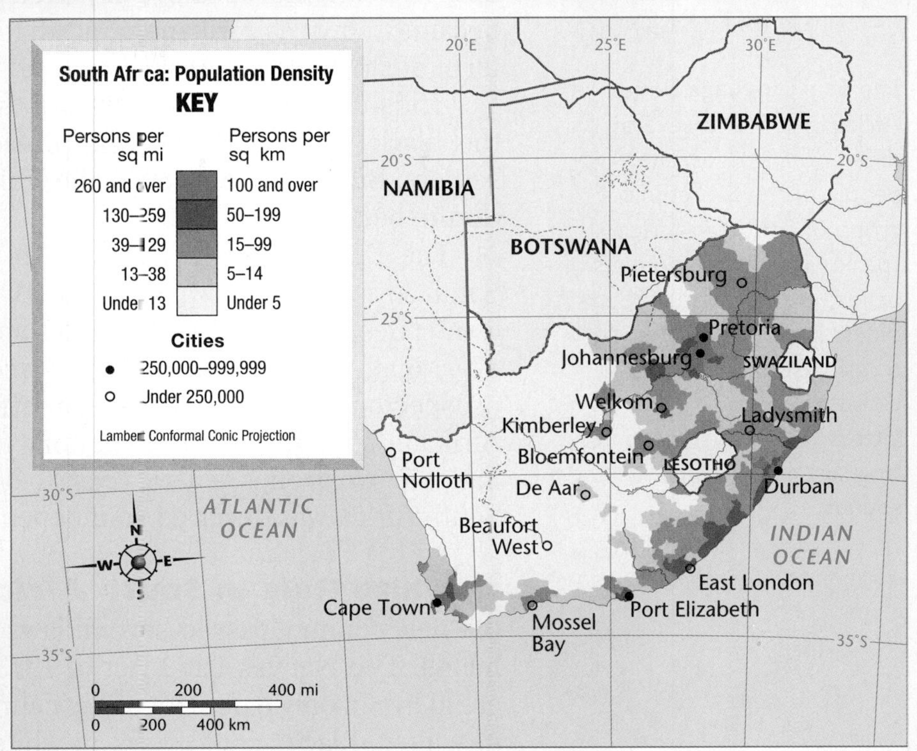

Johannesburg, South Africa

Urban and Rural Population

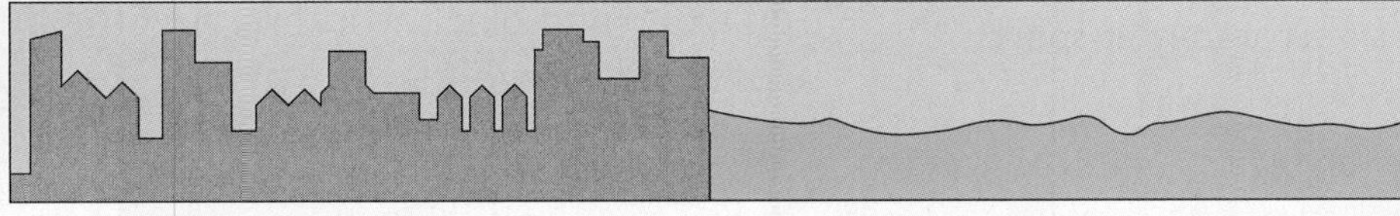

Source: Dorling Kindersley World Desk Reference

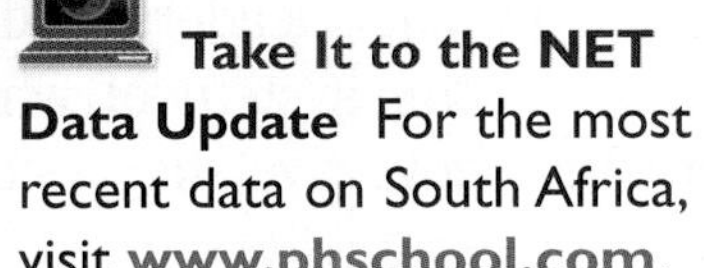
Take It to the NET

Data Update For the most recent data on South Africa, visit **www.phschool.com**.

Geography The map and charts above provide information about the people of South Africa and where they live. **Map and Chart Study** (a) Describe the location of the most densely populated area in South Africa. (b) Do more South Africans live in rural or urban areas?

One Country, Two Worlds

South Africa lies at the southern tip of Africa. Look at the map in the Country Profile. Like the United States, South Africa has seacoasts on two oceans—the Atlantic Ocean and the Indian Ocean. The country of South Africa is larger than the states of Texas and California combined. It is one of the wealthiest African countries. Yet, until recently, white people controlled almost all its riches. Society was divided by law along racial and ethnic lines. How did such a system come to be?

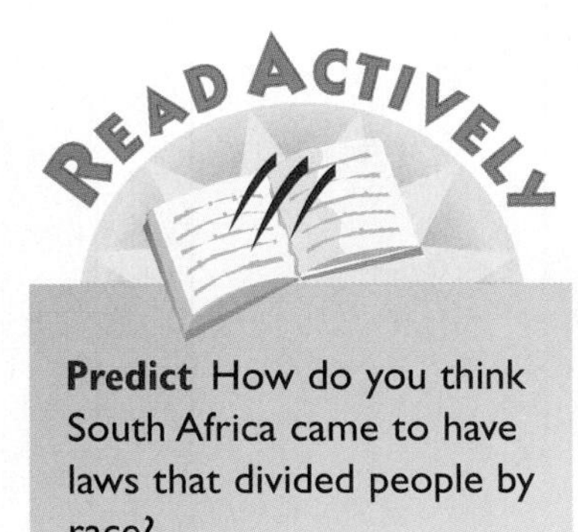

Predict How do you think South Africa came to have laws that divided people by race?

Cultures Clash The ancestors of most of today's black South Africans arrived about 2,000 years ago during the Bantu migrations. White Europeans first arrived in South Africa about 400 years ago. In

The San Language South Africa is home to several different languages. The people of the San ethnic group of Southern Africa speak what many scientists believe is the world's oldest language. In addition to using sounds such as those used to say the letters T, S, or B, the San language also uses click sounds.

1652, Dutch settlers set up a colony at Cape Town on the southern tip of the continent. In time, these people began to think of themselves as not being European. They called themselves Boers. Later, they became known as Afrikaners (af rih KAHN erz). And they spoke a special form of Dutch called Afrikaans.

British and French settlers also settled in South Africa. For years, the black South Africans who already lived there battled the white settlers. But by the late 1800s, the white settlers had forced the Africans off the best land.

The British and Afrikaners also fought each other for control of South Africa. To get away from the British, the Afrikaners founded their own states, Transvaal (tranz VAHL) and Orange Free State. Soon, however, diamonds and gold were discovered in the Transvaal. British prospectors pushed Afrikaners off their farms. The British and Afrikaners fought over the territory for three years. Britain won, but it took the two groups several years to decide what would happen. In 1910, South Africa was declared an independent country.

White Rule in South Africa The white-led government of the new country passed several laws to keep land and wealth in white hands. The Natives Land Act of 1913, for example, stated that blacks could live in only 8 percent of the country. The rest of the land belonged to whites. Blacks could work in white areas—for very low wages. But they could not own land there. Other laws passed in the 1920s separated white and black workers. And the best jobs and the highest pay were reserved for whites.

▼ Under apartheid, blacks and whites were even forced to sit separately at sports events.

In 1948, the Afrikaners' political party, the National Party, won the election and took over the country. Afrikaner leaders added new laws to the system of white power. And they gave the system a new name—**apartheid** (uh PAHR tayt), which is an Afrikaans word meaning "separateness." Apartheid laws placed every South African into a category based on race. The laws also made it legal to discriminate on the basis of race. To **discriminate** means to treat people differently, and often unfairly, based on race, religion, or sex.

Apartheid separated South Africans into four groups—blacks, whites, coloreds, and Asians. Blacks included all Africans. Whites included people of European heritage.

Coloreds were people of mixed race. The term Asians usually meant people from India. Coloreds and Asians had a few rights. Blacks had practically no rights at all.

Apartheid forced thousands of South African blacks to move to 10 poor rural areas called **homelands.** These homelands had the driest and least fertile land. There, black South Africans lived in poverty.

Apartheid affected not only where blacks could live but every aspect of their lives. It denied them citizenship rights, including the right to vote. The system kept blacks and coloreds in low-paying jobs. It put them in poor schools. It barred blacks and coloreds from white restaurants, schools, and hospitals. Apartheid also strengthened the pass laws that required all blacks to stay in homelands unless they could prove they were useful to whites and could "pass" into white areas. In short, apartheid kept whites in control of the country.

First Multiracial Elections, 1994

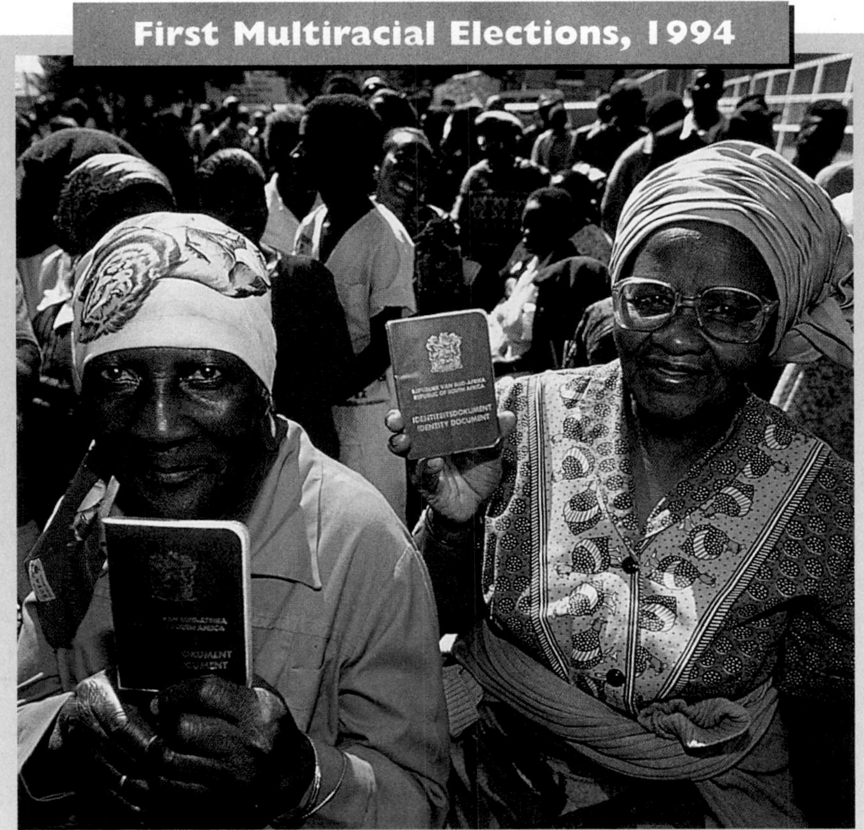

Women in Johannesburg joyously displayed the identification papers that allowed them to vote in the historic election on April 26, 1994. Blacks had to wait in line for as long as eight hours to cast ballots for the first time in their lives. As a 93-year-old woman finally reached the polling booth, she said, "I am happy this day has come. I never thought it could happen here."

The Deadly Struggle Against Apartheid Many South Africans fought apartheid. During the 1950s and 1960s, blacks and some whites took to the streets in peaceful protest against it. The well-armed South African police met them with deadly force. Hundreds of men, women, and children were wounded or killed. Thousands more were thrown in jail. In the 1970s, black students and black workers protested against inequality. The government tried to end these protests with more force. But the demonstrations kept growing, even though thousands of blacks were killed. Many people were willing to risk everything for freedom.

Countries around the world joined the movement against apartheid. Many nations stopped trading with South Africa, or lending it money. Its athletes were banned from the Olympic Games and other international sports events.

In 1990, these struggles began to have an effect. Faced with a weakening economy and continuing protests, South Africa's president, F. W. de Klerk, pushed through laws that tore down apartheid.

To Be a Leader The end of apartheid inspired Ivy Nonqayi to make a change. She made $80 a month tending the big house of a white town councilor, Peb Saunders. Nonqayi wanted jobs and housing for blacks, so in 1995 she took a brave step. She ran for her boss's seat—and easily ousted her. Despite her win, Nonqayi stayed on as Saunders' maid.

In April 1994, for the first time, South Africans of all colors peacefully elected a president. They chose Nelson Mandela, a black man who had spent 28 years in prison for fighting apartheid.

New Challenges

Connect What do you think South Africans could learn from people who remember integration in the United States?

Under Nelson Mandela's government, legal discrimination on the basis of race finally ended. Blacks and some whites welcomed the changes. But many whites who had grown up with the privileges of apartheid were not as happy.

Despite new opportunities for millions of blacks, South Africa has remained a divided society. Blacks and whites usually live in different neighborhoods. Whites still control most of the country's biggest businesses and newspapers. Compared to blacks, whites have better-paying jobs and own more property.

Even though they still hold a lot of power, many whites do not like the recent changes in South Africa. Some oppose government plans to help blacks get jobs. One white woman, for example, wondered whether her white skin would be a drawback when she looked for a job. Other whites fear their children's education will suffer in schools attended by all races. Mandela's government had to find ways to reassure whites

Children of the Orlando Children's Home
Ages 8-15
Soweto, South Africa

In 1989, the children of the Orlando Children's Home in Soweto painted this mural on the wall that surrounds their home. Apartheid had not yet ended. **Critical Thinking** This mural shows many ways of flying away from South Africa. However, it also shows people with parachutes jumping out of the airplanes. What feelings about South Africa do you think the children meant to express when they painted this mural?

Flying Away

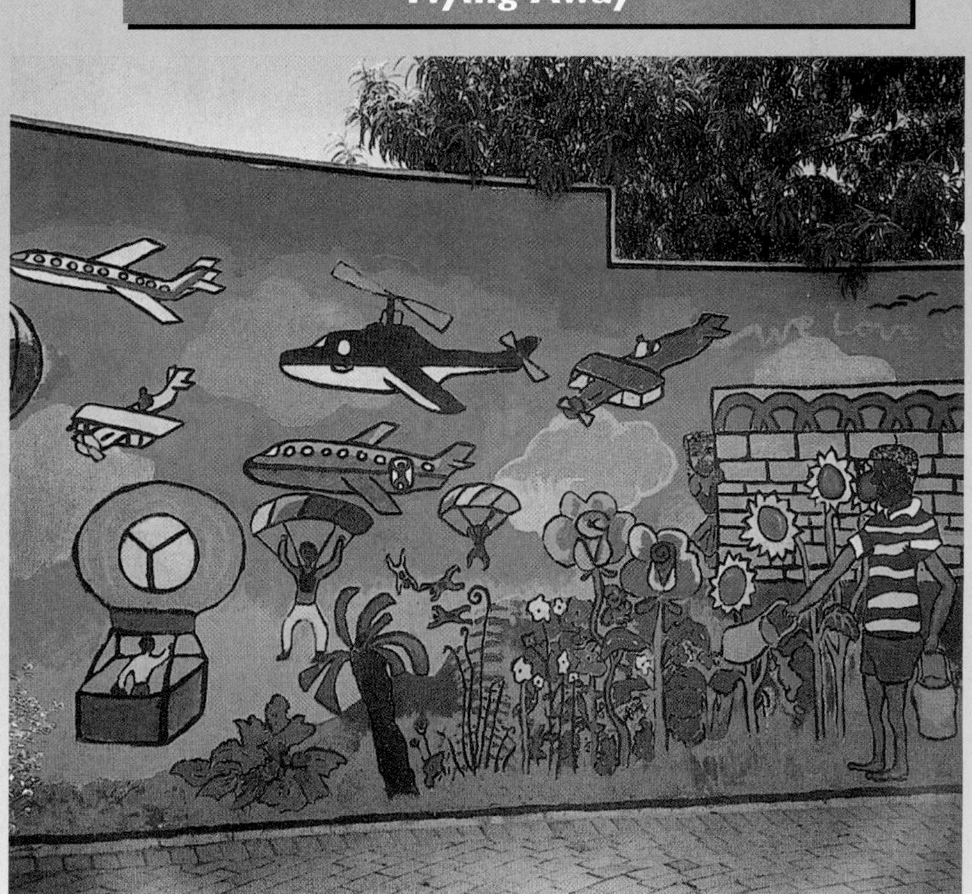

while making certain that blacks had an equal chance for a good life. To meet its challenges, South Africa's government will need the help of all its citizens, regardless of race.

Building a New Nation

Nearly every day, television, radio, and newspapers report on the changes that have taken place in South Africa. Nomfundo Mhlana has been grateful for the changes. But she sees room for more change. She said, "Now that Mandela is president, I think our society is more equal, but I also think whites still have apartheid in their hearts." All South Africans are struggling to build the new South Africa.

David Bailes, a white South African, left the country in the early 1970s because he hated apartheid. Since then, he has been living in the United States. Today, Bailes is thinking about returning to South Africa to live. After a recent visit to Cape Town, he said:

> "There's still a lot of inequality there.... On the surface, things don't appear much different. But you know they are—you can feel it.... South Africa is becoming a brand new country."

Nelson Mandela's government took steps to heal South Africa. It set up a Truth and Reconciliation Commission to examine the crimes of the apartheid era. In 1998, the commission issued its final report. The report condemned acts of murder and torture by both white and black South Africans. The commission also granted amnesty, or forgiveness, to some people who committed crimes. It withheld amnesty from others, which meant they could face trial.

In June 1999, South Africa held its second election open to all races. Mandela's political party stayed in power, and his deputy president replaced him as president. Mandela ended his political career, but his impact on the country continued. Thanks to his leadership, South Africans are working together to build a peaceful and prosperous nation.

▲ In 1993, South Africa's president, F. W. de Klerk, and Nelson Mandela—soon to be elected the first black president of South Africa—share a triumphant moment.

1. **Define** (a) apartheid, (b) discriminate, (c) homeland.
2. **Identify** (a) F. W. de Klerk, (b) Nelson Mandela, (c) Cape Town.
3. How did apartheid affect South Africans?
4. What changes have taken place in South Africa since the collapse of apartheid?

Critical Thinking

5. **Expressing Problems Clearly** What challenges must the South African government meet in order to build a new nation based on equality for all?

Activity

6. **Writing to Learn** Write a letter to a friend, explaining your view of the changes in South Africa.

Review and Activities

Reviewing Main Ideas

1. (a) Describe Congo's four main geographic regions. (b) Which region brings in the most income?
2. How has mining affected the history of Congo?
3. What actions did Mobutu Sese Seko take after coming to power?
4. (a) How did the system of apartheid affect South Africans in their daily lifes? (b) How did South Africans struggle against apartheid?
5. (a) How is life in today's South Africa different than it was under apartheid? (b) How are people still divided by race?
6. What are some challenges faced by the new government of South Africa?

Reviewing Key Terms

Match the definitions in Column I with the key terms in Column II.

Column I

1. form of government in which a single leader or small group of leaders has all the power
2. a system of laws that legalized racial discrimination
3. rural areas in which black South Africans were forced to live
4. to treat people in a different way based on their race, religion, or sex
5. to put under government control

Column II

a. nationalize

b. authoritarian

c. discrimination

d. apartheid

e. homelands

Critical Thinking

1. **Making Comparisons** How did life in Congo stay the same after the rebels took power from Mobutu?
2. **Drawing Conclusions** South Africa's new government is trying to persuade its skilled white workers to remain in the country. Based on what you know about apartheid, why do you think much of South Africa's population lacks these skills?

Graphic Organizer

Copy the flowchart onto a sheet of paper. Then, fill in the empty boxes to show the impact of resources on Congo's history, from the first contacts with Europeans to the present.

Portuguese arrive looking for gold	→		→		→	

Map Activity

Central and Southern Africa

For each place listed below, write the letter from the map that shows its location.

1. Cape Town
2. Johannesburg
3. Kinshasa
4. Democratic Republic of Congo
5. South Africa

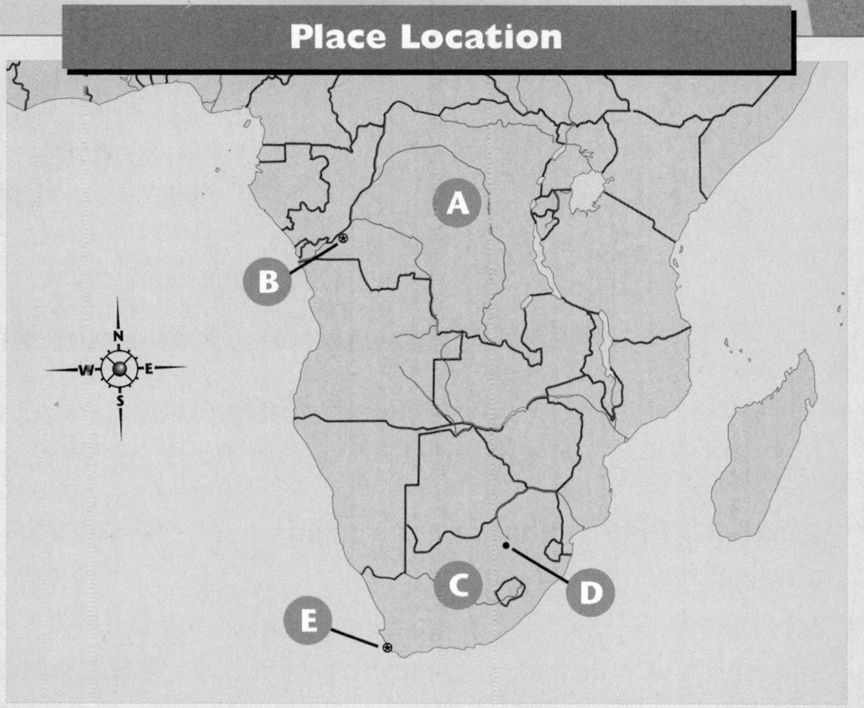

Writing Activity

Writing Interview Questions

Choose either South Africa or Congo. Write a list of five interview questions you would ask someone who has been elected president of the country. Consider the challenges the new president faces. Then exchange questions with a partner. Pretend that you are the president. Write answers to your partner's questions.

Take It to the NET

Activity Explore Southern Africa's ancient civilizations and modern-day culture. For help in completing this activity, visit **www.phschool.com**.

Chapter 17 Self-Test To review what you have learned, take the Chapter 17 Self-Test and get instant feedback on your answers. Go to **www.phschool.com** to take the test.

Skills Review

Turn to the Skills Activity.

Review the steps for organizing your time. Then, in your own words, explain how a flowchart can help you to organize your time.

How Am I Doing?

Answer these questions to check your progress.

1. Can I explain the part that resources have played in Congo's history?
2. Do I understand the problems that have kept modern Congo a poor nation?
3. Can I describe how life has changed for black and white South Africans following the collapse of apartheid?
4. What information from this chapter can I include in my journal?

As you study the vast continent of Africa, you will be reading and thinking about these important questions.

- **GEOGRAPHY** What are the main physical features of Africa?
- **HISTORY** How have historical events affected the cultures and nations of Africa?
- **CULTURE** How have Africa's cultures changed?
- **GOVERNMENT** What factors led to the development of different governments across Africa?
- **ECONOMICS** What factors influence the ways in which Africans make a living?

Show what you know by doing a project!

Project Menu

The chapters in this book have some answers to these questions. Now it's time for you to find your own answers by doing projects on your own or with a group. Here are some ways to make your own discoveries about Africa.

Africa on Stage Write a play about growing up in a country in Africa. Set the scene for your play in one of the African countries you have studied. Choose three or four characters. Next think about plot. What situation, serious or humorous, will the main character face? How will he or she react to the situation? How will the other characters affect the plot?

Write a script for your play that shows the lines each character will speak. Then present your play. Ask classmates to read aloud the parts of your characters. You may wish to videotape your live performance and show it to other classes or your family.

From Questions to Careers

AGRICULTURE

Farmers have always wanted to be able to produce more food. More and more, they face the newer problem of using up too much of the Earth's resources—good soil, land, or grazing material. In some places, people need to farm differently than before because of a changing climate. In Africa and all over the world, people are working on new and different ways of farming that will solve these problems.

Agricultural scientists and farmers work together to develop and try out different farming methods. It may take much time and patience to figure out whether a method works over one or several growing seasons. Engineers invent new machinery, fertilizer, and other products for farmers. Machinists and technicians help manufacture these products. Ecologists study the effects of farming on the surrounding environment.

Agricultural scientists, engineers, and ecologists all go to college. Farmers, technicians, and machinists may go to college or they may have training in specific skills for their jobs. Many farmers learn much of what they know through direct experience.

▲ This modern Nigerian farmer is using equipment suitable for his crops and his land.

Africa in Art The tradition of mask-making has special meaning in some African cultures. Look through books and magazines for information about different mask-making traditions in Africa. Research the kinds of masks people make, the ways of making them, and the meanings that they have. Prepare a mini-museum display with pictures or examples and detailed explanations of the masks and traditions you research.

You may want to try making a mask of your own. Use papier-mâché and your imagination.

Africa 2000 Hold an "All Africa" conference about life in Africa in the twenty-first century. Decide on several major topics for the conference, such as economic growth, agriculture, literature, and arts. Form committees to plan the conference. For example, a speakers' committee can find speakers to discuss the topics. Speakers can be students who have done research on these topics. A scheduling committee can plan the agenda for the conference. A publicity committee can make posters to let other students know about the conference. A food committee can make and serve African foods. A press committee can write news reports. Invite other classes to attend the conference.

ASIA AND THE PACIFIC

Asia and the Pacific islands form a region of extremes, with some of the driest deserts, longest rivers, and highest mountains in the world. In the Pacific east of the Asian continent are chains of islands, peninsulas, and the only continent that is also a country—Australia.

GUIDING QUESTIONS

The readings and activities in this book will help you discover answers to these Guiding Questions.

1. **GEOGRAPHY** What are the main physical features of Asia and the Pacific?
2. **HISTORY** How have ancient civilizations of Asia and the Pacific influenced the world today?
3. **CULTURE** What are the main characteristics of the cultures of Asia and the Pacific?
4. **GOVERNMENT** What types of government exist in Asia and the Pacific today?
5. **ECONOMICS** How do the people of this region make a living?

PROJECT PREVIEW

You can also discover answers to the Guiding Questions by working on creative projects. You can find several project possibilities on pages 670–671.

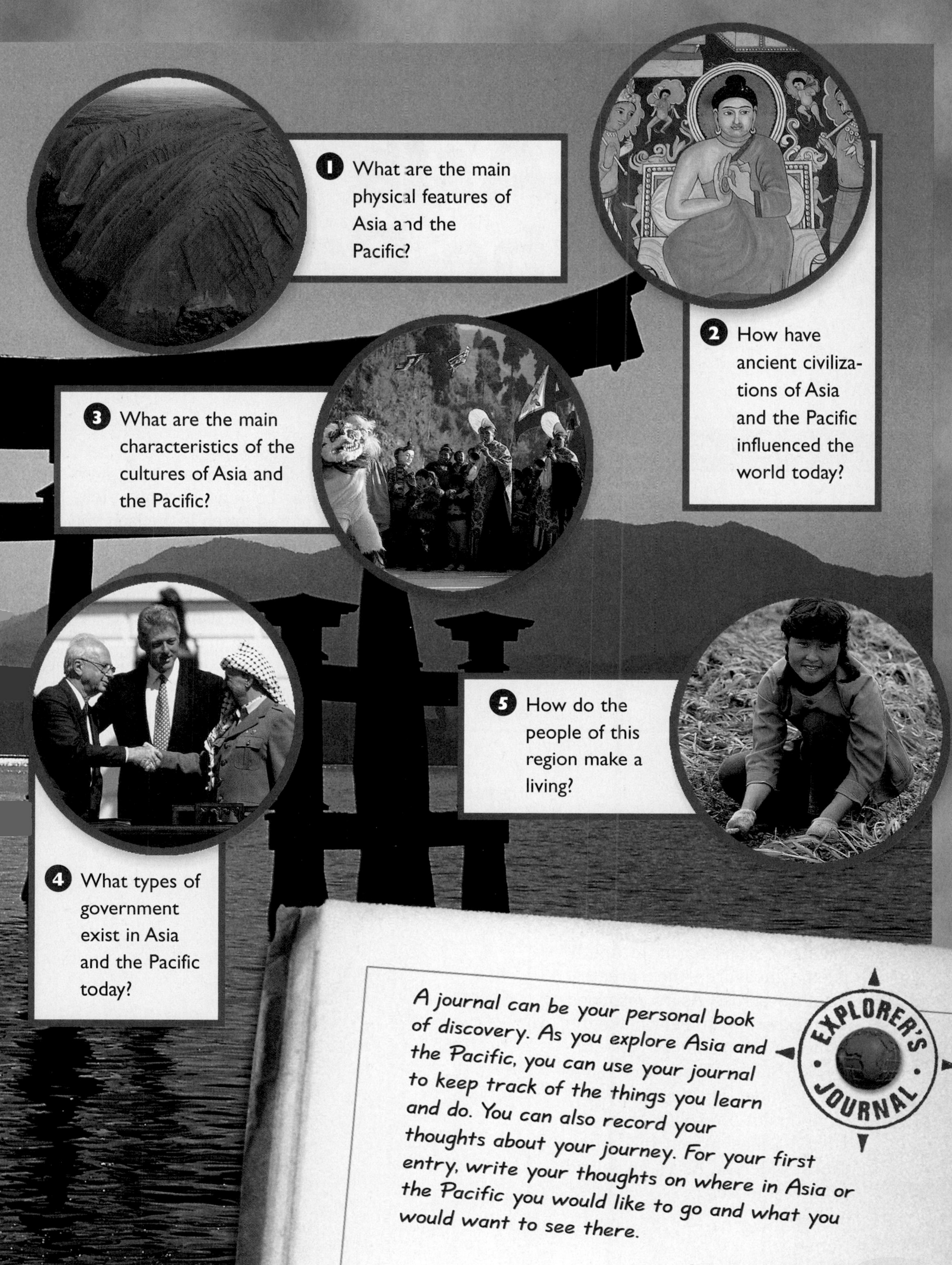

1 What are the main physical features of Asia and the Pacific?

2 How have ancient civilizations of Asia and the Pacific influenced the world today?

3 What are the main characteristics of the cultures of Asia and the Pacific?

4 What types of government exist in Asia and the Pacific today?

5 How do the people of this region make a living?

A journal can be your personal book of discovery. As you explore Asia and the Pacific, you can use your journal to keep track of the things you learn and do. You can also record your thoughts about your journey. For your first entry, write your thoughts on where in Asia or the Pacific you would like to go and what you would want to see there.

Discovery Activities About Asia and the Pacific

Learning about Asia and the Pacific means being an explorer and a geographer. No explorer would start out without first checking some facts. Begin by exploring the maps of Asia and the Pacific on the following pages.

Relative Location

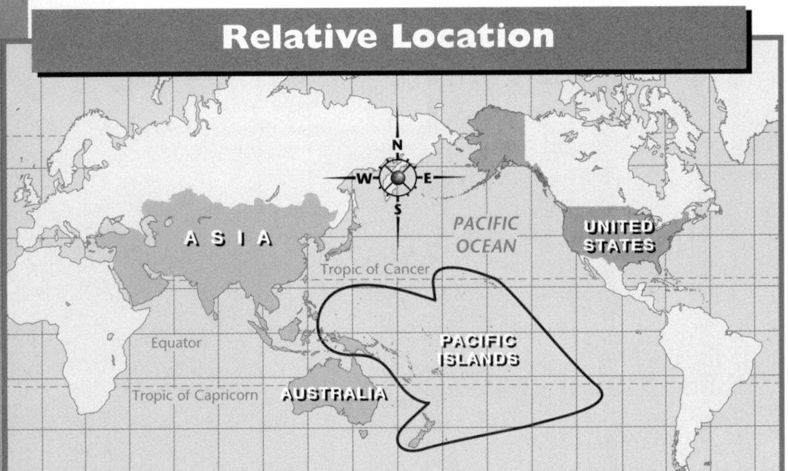

LOCATION

1. **Explore the Locations of Asia and the Pacific Islands** Look at the map at left. The land that is colored green is the land you will be reading about in this book. This area includes Asia, Australia, and the Pacific islands. What ocean lies between Asia and the Pacific islands and the United States? If you lived on the west coast of the United States, in which direction would you travel to reach Asia?

PLACE

2. **Explore Asia's Size** How large is Asia's mainland compared to the continental United States? Use a ruler to measure the greatest distance across Asia's mainland from north to south. Next, measure the greatest distance across Asia's mainland from east to west. Now make the same measurements for the United States. About how many times longer is Asia's mainland from north to south than the United States? About how many times wider is Asia's mainland from east to west?

Relative Size

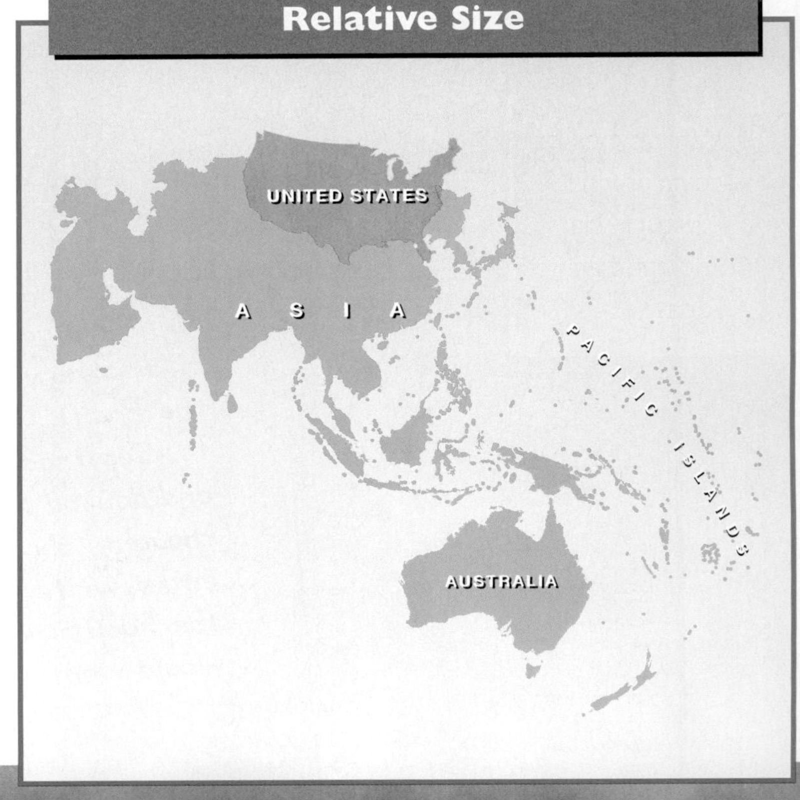

PLACE

3. Explore Countries in Asia Asia is the largest continent on the Earth. The map below shows countries in Asia. Which Asian country on the map do you think is the biggest? Asia also includes many countries that are located on islands. Find three island countries on the map below. What are their names? Asia extends far to the west and east. One country in the western part of Asia is Saudi Arabia. Name three countries that are near Saudi Arabia.

The continent of Asia also includes part of the country of Russia. Russia is such a big country that it is a part of two continents—Europe and Asia. Notice the location of Russia on the map below. Most of Russia lies in Asia. Most Russians, however, live in the European part of Russia. For this reason, geographers often include Russia in discussions of Europe, rather than in discussions of Asia.

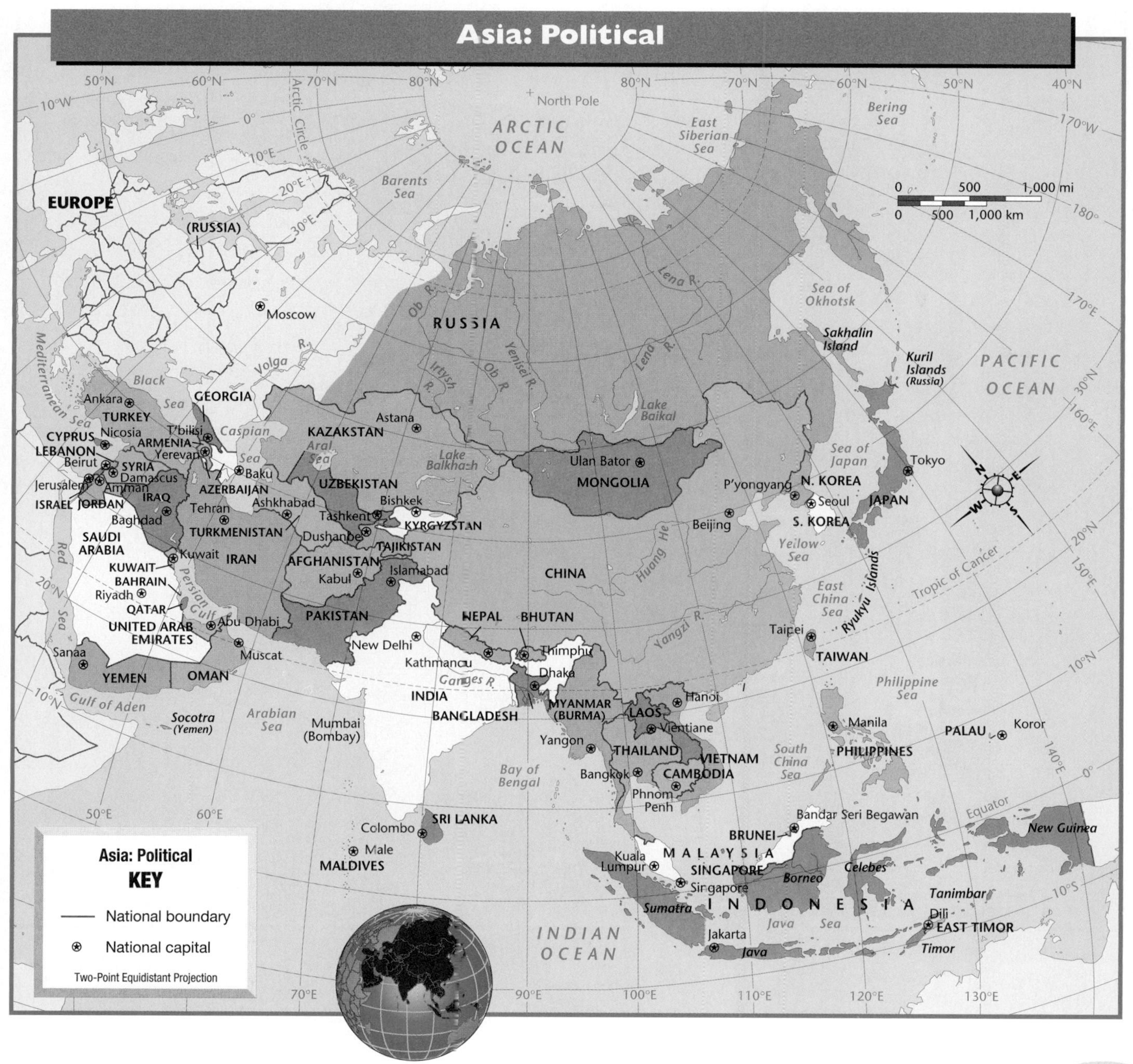

PLACE

4. Identify Asia's Highest and Lowest Points

Asia is a continent of towering mountains, high plateaus, and low-lying plains. Use the elevation key to identify the highest and lowest areas on the map. What elevation do coastal areas usually have? The lowest and highest areas in Asia are also marked on the map. Where is each area located?

LOCATION

5. Find Water Bodies and Peninsulas in Asia

Asia is a region surrounded by bodies of water. Use the map below to locate and name the bodies of water from the eastern side of Asia to the western side. Asia also has several major peninsulas. A peninsula is an area of land almost completely surrounded by water. Asia's major peninsulas are labeled on the map below. What are their names?

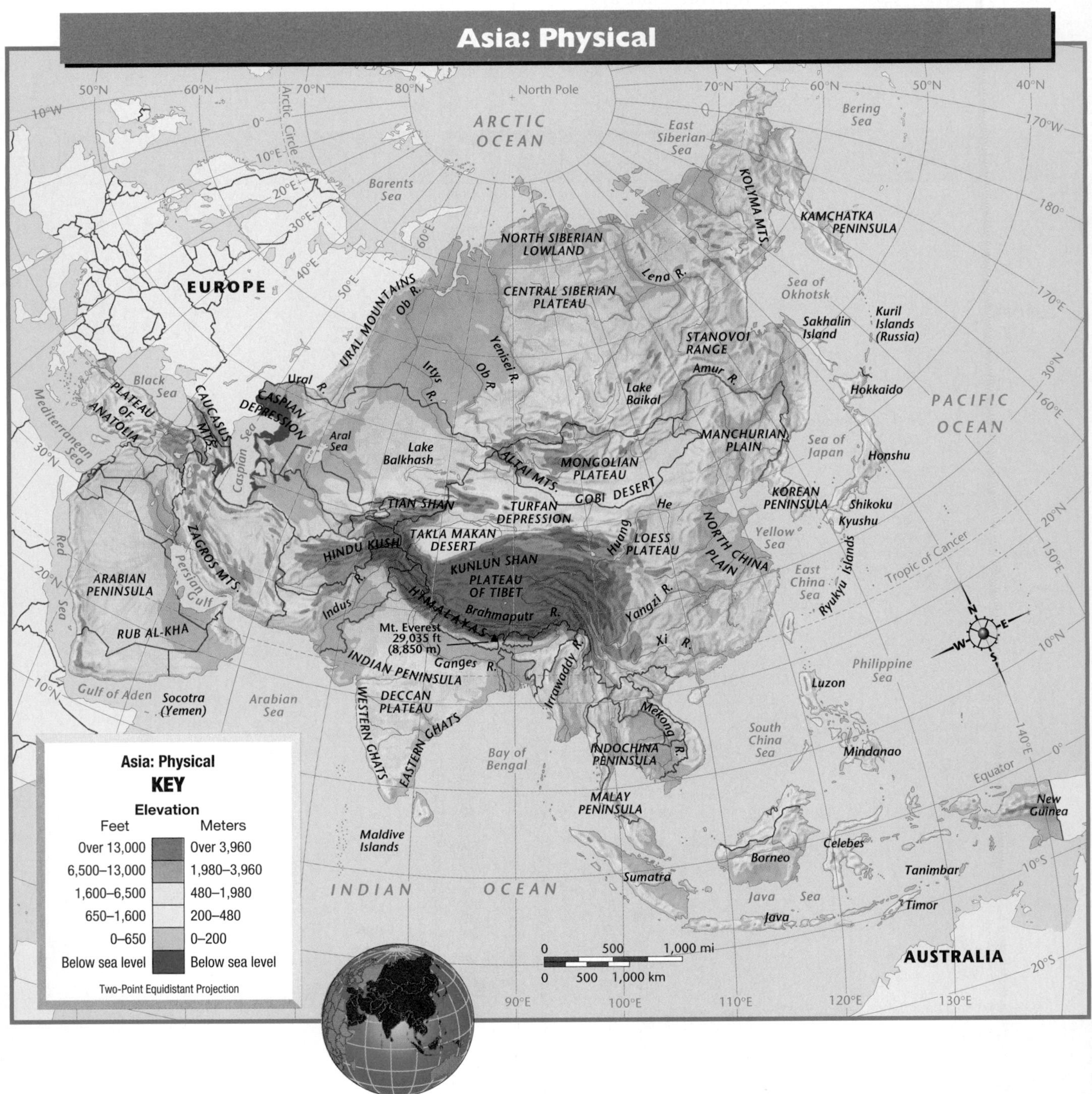

INTERACTION

6. Follow the Asian Monsoons With Geo Cleo

Monsoons are great winds that blow across Southeast Asia and India every winter and summer. Winter monsoons blow dry air across the land and push clouds away from land toward the oceans. Summer monsoons blow clouds and moist air across the land, creating great rains. The map below shows the land use and monsoons in Asia. Use the map to trace Geo Cleo's trip across Asia.

A. *My first stop is in a country that is on a peninsula. To its south is the Indian Ocean. The Bay of Bengal borders its east coast. What's the name of this country? What is the land used for in most of this country?*

B. *I just arrived in a large country with a long eastern coast. Nomadic herding takes place in the western half of the country. Wet monsoons blow from the south, affecting its southeastern coast. In what country am I?*

C. *Find the area on the map called Southeast Asia. Much of this area has a tropical wet climate. What kind of monsoon affects this area most? What two types of farming take place in this area?*

Asia: Land Use and Monsoons

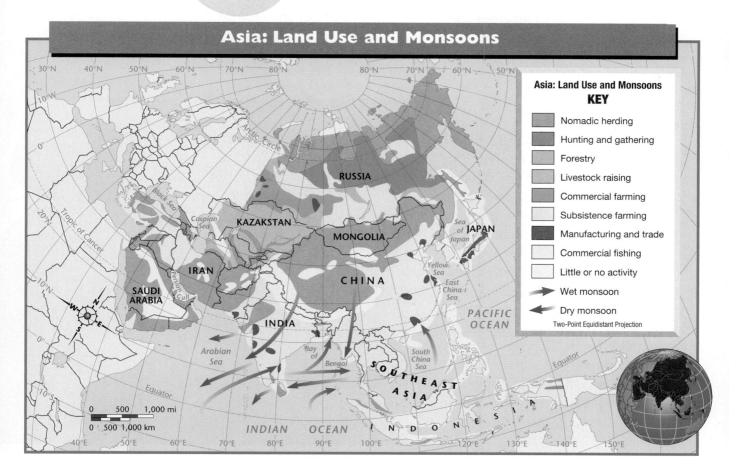

Asia: Land Use and Monsoons

KEY

- Nomadic herding
- Hunting and gathering
- Forestry
- Livestock raising
- Commercial farming
- Subsistence farming
- Manufacturing and trade
- Commercial fishing
- Little or no activity
- Wet monsoon
- Dry monsoon

Two-Point Equidistant Projection

RUSSIA
KAZAKSTAN
MONGOLIA
CHINA
JAPAN
IRAN
SAUDI ARABIA
INDIA
SOUTHEAST ASIA
INDONESIA
Arctic Circle
Black Sea
Caspian Sea
Sea of Japan
Yellow Sea
East China Sea
Persian Gulf
Tropic of Cancer
Arabian Sea
Bay of Bengal
South China Sea
PACIFIC OCEAN
INDIAN OCEAN
Equator
0 500 1,000 mi
0 500 1,000 km

Australia and the Pacific Islands

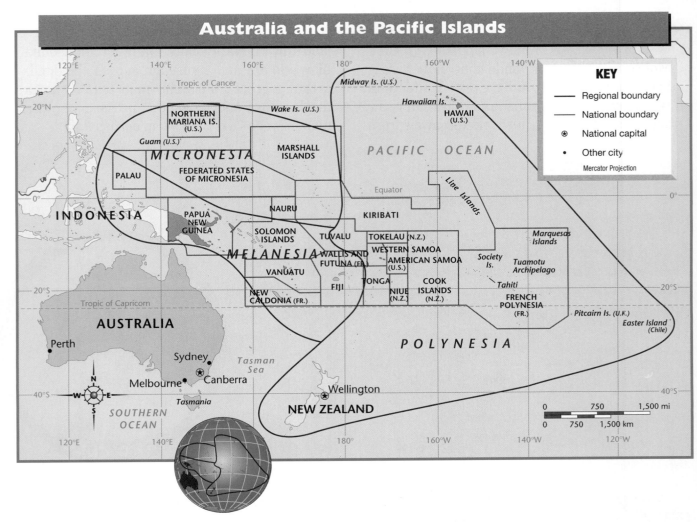

KEY
Regional boundary
National boundary
National capital
Other city
Mercator Projection

120°E 140°E 160°E 180° 160°W 140°W 120°W
20°N 0° 20°S 40°S
Tropic of Cancer
Equator
Tropic of Capricorn

Midway Is. (U.S.)
Hawaiian Is.
HAWAII (U.S.)
Wake Is. (U.S.)
NORTHERN MARIANA IS. (U.S.)
Guam (U.S.)
MICRONESIA
MARSHALL ISLANDS
PACIFIC OCEAN
PALAU
FEDERATED STATES OF MICRONESIA
Line Islands
INDONESIA
NAURU
KIRIBATI
PAPUA NEW GUINEA
SOLOMON ISLANDS
TUVALU
TOKELAU (N.Z.)
Marquesas Islands
MELANESIA
WALLIS AND FUTUNA (FR.)
WESTERN SAMOA
AMERICAN SAMOA (U.S.)
Society Is.
Tuamotu Archipelago
VANUATU
FIJI
TONGA
NIUE (N.Z.)
COOK ISLANDS (N.Z.)
Tahiti
NEW CALDONIA (FR.)
FRENCH POLYNESIA (FR.)
Pitcairn Is. (U.K.)
Easter Island (Chile)
AUSTRALIA
Perth
POLYNESIA
Sydney
Tasman Sea
Canberra
Melbourne
Wellington
Tasmania
SOUTHERN OCEAN
NEW ZEALAND
0 750 1,500 mi
0 750 1,500 km

▼ Much of Australia has a dry climate that produces dramatic landscape.

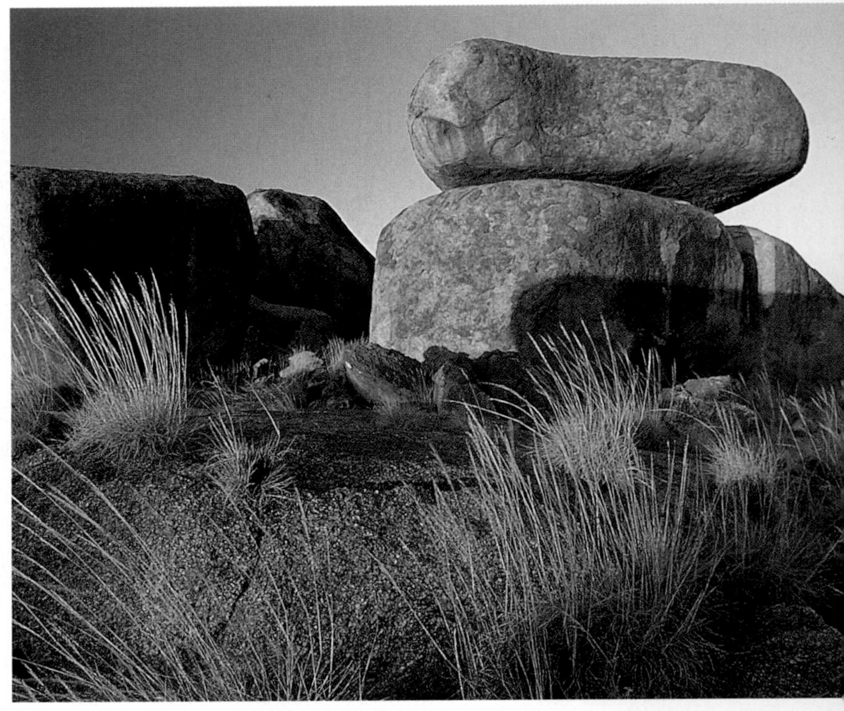

PLACE

7. Explore Australia and the Pacific Islands Australia is both a continent and a country. Find it on the map above. What is Australia's national capital? Most of the Pacific islands are tiny. Two of the larger islands make up the country of New Zealand. Where is New Zealand relative to Australia? The Pacific islands are divided into three groups. They are Micronesia, Melanesia, and Polynesia. They are regions, not countries. Each region is shown on the map above. In which region is Hawaii? Hawaii is also one of the fifty United States.

REGIONS

8. **Trace the Ring of Fire** Many active volcanoes surround the Pacific Ocean. Use the map to name countries with several volcanoes. Now trace these strings of volcanoes with your finger. Why do you think this region is called the Ring of Fire?

REGIONS

9. **Examine Pacific Fault Lines** Fault lines are breaks in the Earth's crust. Beneath the Earth's crust lies hot, liquid rock. Find the fault lines on the map and trace them with your finger. Where do you find volcanoes in relation to fault lines? During earthquakes, the Earth's crust briefly opens, and sometimes liquid rock, or lava, escapes. What might this have to do with volcanoes?

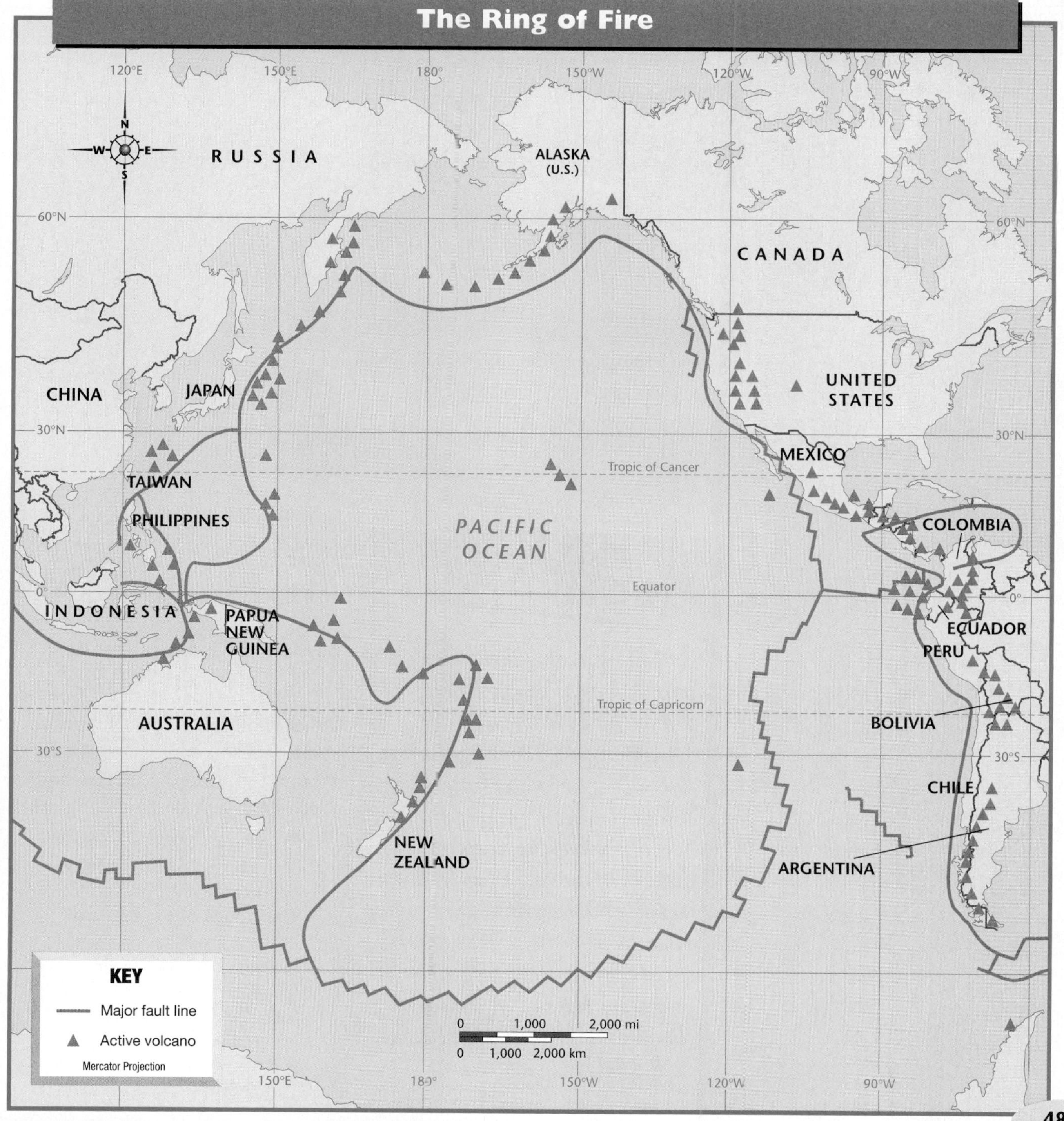

CHAPTER 18

EAST ASIA

Physical Geography

SECTION 1
Land and Water

SECTION 2
Climate and Vegetation

SECTION 3
Natural Resources

PICTURE ACTIVITIES

Sometime during their lives, most Japanese people climb Mount Fuji (FOO jee), a 12,388-foot (3,776-m) volcano that has not erupted since 1707. It takes between five and nine hours to travel the steep trails and reach the top. Clearly, people feel they have a connection to this mountain. To help you understand how physical geography affects the lives of the people of Japan and the rest of East Asia, do the following activities.

Make predictions

Use evidence from the picture to make some predictions about the physical geography of East Asia.

Study the picture

What thoughts do you suppose the Japanese people have about Mount Fuji? Use the picture and these lines written by an emperor in the A.D. 600s to provide clues.

"Lo! There towers the lofty
peak of Fuji.
The clouds of heaven dare
not cross it,
Nor the birds of the air
soar above it.
It baffles the tongue, it
cannot be named,
It is a god mysterious."

Land and Water

Reach Into Your Background

Landforms are important no matter where you live. Make a list of all the physical features in your region that you can think of. Include mountains, hills, valleys, rivers, lakes, streams, oceans, islands, and forests. Be sure to include even those you have never seen. Which of these physical features attract visitors? Why?

Questions to Explore

1. What are the main physical features of East Asia?
2. How does physical geography affect where people live in East Asia?

Key Terms

plateau
desert
fertile
loess
archipelago
peninsula
population density

Key Places

Mount Everest
Himalaya Mountains
Yangzi
Huang He

It was 6:00 P.M. on September 24, 1975, when British climbers Doug Scott and Dougal Haston reached the summit of Mount Everest, on the border of China and Nepal. Their feelings of triumph and joy were mixed with concern. It would soon be night, and they would never make it back to their camp before dark. They would have to spend the night in a quickly built snow cave near the summit. But what they saw made them forget their concerns.

Looking toward the Plateau (pla toh) of Tibet, a huge highland region in southern China, they saw a vast range of small hills. Actually, these hills were mountains—some of which rose to 24,000 feet (7,315 m). They seemed so small next to Everest! Beyond those "hills," Everest cast a huge purple shadow some 200 miles (322 km) across Tibet. "The view was so staggering," Scott said, that it held them "in awe."

East Asia's Landforms

East Asia is a huge region of breathtaking landforms like Mount Everest. A single nation, China, takes up most of its land. In fact, China is the world's third-largest country in land area after Russia and Canada. Mountains, highlands, and **plateaus,** or raised areas of level land, make up much of

▼ Rising 29,035 feet (8,850 m)—about five and a half miles—Mount Everest towers over a group of climbers marching across a snowfield.

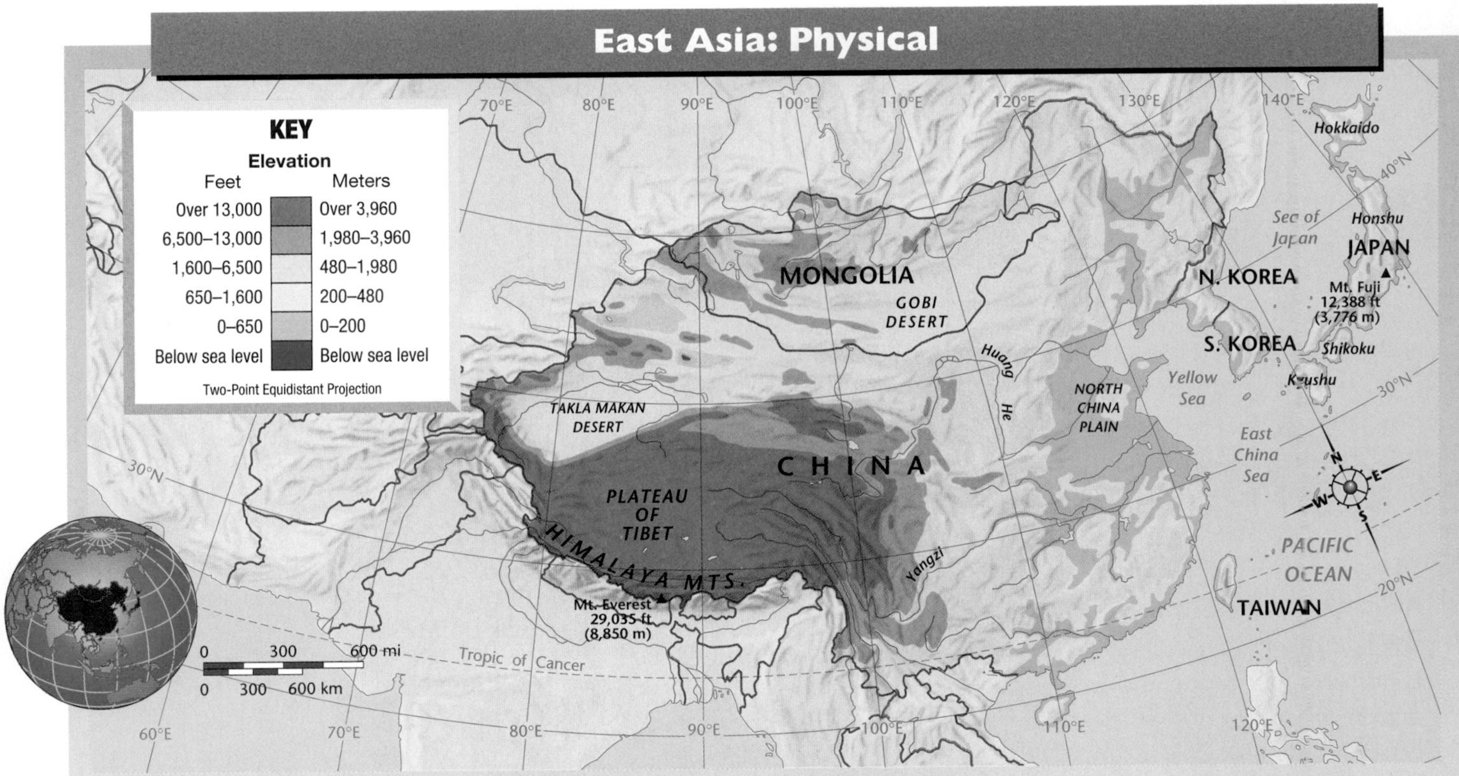

Map Study This map shows the variety of East Asia's landforms. The Himalaya Mountains, whose name means "Snowy Range," border the Plateau of Tibet. Much of this plateau is flat, but its elevation is high. Many rivers of East Asia and other regions of Asia begin in this area. **Place** How can you tell just by looking at the map that China's greatest rivers, the Huang He and the Yangzi, flow toward the east?

Visualize Look at the physical map of East Asia. Visualize the landforms that you would see if you visited the region.

its landscape. The other countries of this region—Mongolia, North Korea, South Korea, Taiwan, and Japan—are mountainous like China. But they lack its wide plains and plateaus. In Japan and the Koreas, narrow plains are found mainly along coasts and rivers.

Powerful natural forces created the rugged landscape of East Asia. About 50 million years ago, a huge piece of a continent collided with Asia. It formed the land we now call India, located southwest of China. The collision caused the Earth's surface to fold and buckle, forming the Himalaya Mountains and other mountain ranges in China, as well as the Plateau of Tibet.

To the east, natural forces also shaped the islands of Japan. Earthquakes forced some parts of the country to rise and others to sink. Erupting volcanoes piled up masses of lava and ash, forming new mountains. Today, in many parts of East Asia, earthquakes and volcanoes are still changing the landscape.

A Land of Extremes China is a land of extremes. It is home to the oldest civilization on the Earth. With more than one billion people, it also has the most people of any nation in the world.

Mountains and deserts take up over two thirds of China. A **desert** is a dry region of extreme temperatures and little vegetation. As you can see from the map on the previous page, western and southwestern China are home to some of the highest mountains anywhere. The Himalaya Mountains contain Mount Everest and other mountains nearly as tall. Part of the Himalayan range is located in the area of China called Tibet. A high plateau surrounded by mountains covers much of Tibet. China's most important rivers, the Yangzi (YAHNG zuh) and the Huang He (hwahng hay), begin in this region and flow east.

The Yangzi flows 3,915 miles (6,300 km) to the East China Sea. It is the only river in East Asia that is deep enough for cargo ships to sail on. More than 400 million people live along the banks of the Huang He. It runs through one of the most fertile regions of China, the wide North China Plain. **Fertile** lands contain substances that plants need in order to grow well. The North China Plain is covered with deposits of **loess** (LOH es), a brownish yellow fertile soil.

Japan: An Island Country Japan is an **archipelago** (ar kuh PEL uh goh), or group of islands, in the western Pacific Ocean. It has four major islands and over 3,000 smaller ones. Every major Japanese city is located on the coast. As the map below shows, most of Japan's people live in coastal areas. Nearly 80 percent of the country is mountainous.

China's Deserts The Takla Makan Desert in western China is one of the world's driest deserts. Raindrops that fall here may evaporate before they touch the ground. Another Chinese desert, the Gobi, is almost twice the size of Texas. Temperatures in the Gobi can range from -40°F (-40°C) in January to 113°F (45°C) in July. In the Badain Jaran Desert, the sands make a singing sound even when there is no wind.

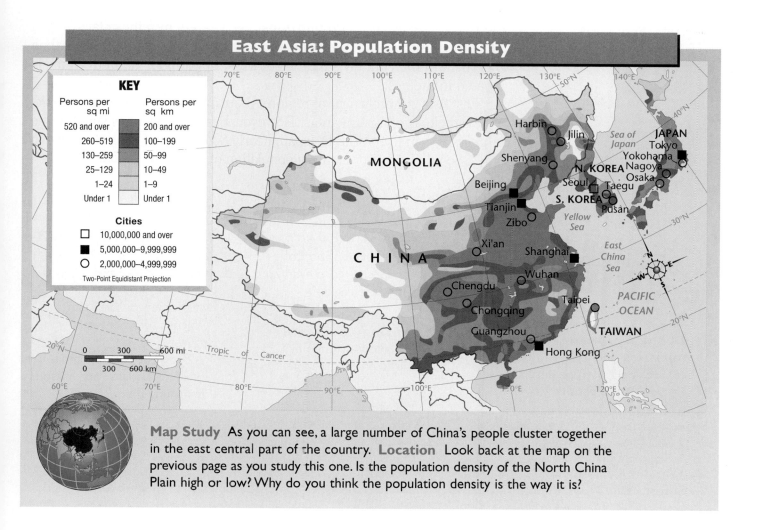

East Asia: Population Density

Map Study As you can see, a large number of China's people cluster together in the east central part of the country. **Location** Look back at the map on the previous page as you study this one. Is the population density of the North China Plain high or low? Why do you think the population density is the way it is?

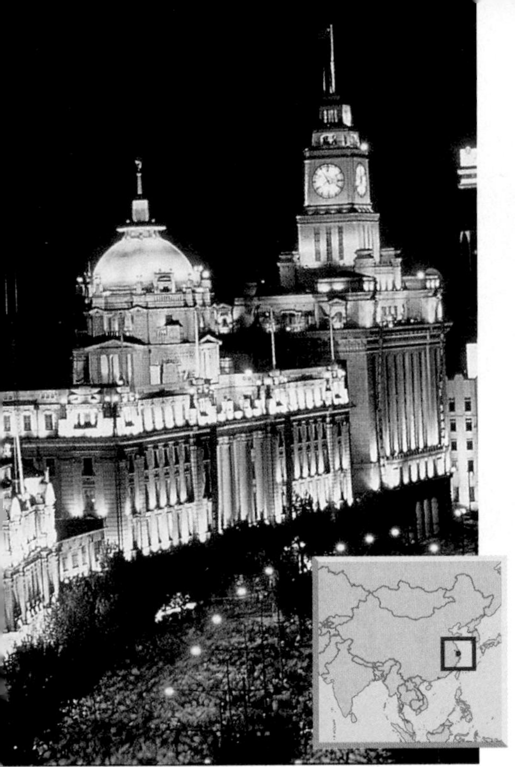

▲ Shanghai, located near the mouth of the Yangzi, is China's leading port. With a population of over 12 million people, it is the largest city in China.

The Koreas: "Land of Golden Embroidery" Rocky peaks, narrow canyons, and rushing streams make Korea a land of great beauty. Sunlight reflecting off the water, some people say, turns the landscape into a "land of golden embroidery."

Korea occupies a **peninsula,** which is a piece of land nearly surrounded by water. The Korean peninsula stretches out into the Yellow Sea and the Sea of Japan. It is one of the world's most mountainous regions. More than 70 percent of the land consists of steep and rocky slopes. Compared with the mountains of China and Japan, however, these ranges are not very high. Since the end of World War II, in 1945, Korea has been divided into two separate countries, North Korea and South Korea.

Geography and Population

As you can see on the map on the previous page, the population of East Asia is not spread evenly across the land. Few people live in the deserts, highlands, and mountains. Yet, almost 1.5 billion people make their homes in this region. This means that people crowd into the lowland and coastal areas, where it is easier to live and grow food. These parts of East Asia have a very high **population density,** or average number of people living in a square mile (or square km).

In East Asia, level ground must be shared by cities, farms, and industries. Almost half the population of Japan is crowded on less than 3 percent of the country's total land. Most of the population of China is located in the east.

East Asia is largely a rural region. About 70 percent of China's people, for example, live in rural areas. However, East Asia also has some of the largest cities in the world. In Japan, nearly 80 percent of the people live in cities. Seoul, South Korea, has a population of about 10 million.

1. **Define** (a) plateau, (b) desert, (c) fertile, (d) loess, (e) archipelago, (f) peninsula, (g) population density.
2. **Identify** (a) Mount Everest, (b) Himalaya Mountains, (c) Yangzi, (d) Huang He.
3. What are the major landforms in East Asia?
4. Why isn't the population of East Asia spread more evenly throughout the region?

Critical Thinking

5. **Recognizing Cause and Effect** How do the physical features of the area affect the lives of people in East Asia?

Activity

6. **Writing to Learn** You are a travel agent with a client who wants to visit East Asia. Which landforms would you suggest that your client visit? Record your recommendations and explain your reasons for making them.

Climate and Vegetation

Reach Into Your Background
How would you describe the climate where you live? How does it affect what you do, wear, and eat? Make a list of five ways in which the climate affects what you do and how you do it.

Questions to Explore

1. What are the major climates and vegetation regions of East Asia?
2. How do climate and vegetation affect people's lives in East Asia?

Key Terms
monsoon
typhoon
deciduous

Key Place
North China Plain

You and your family are visiting Japan in the middle of February. All of you are trying to decide where to go for a long weekend. Your brother wants to go north to the island of Hokkaido (hoh KY doh), where the skiing is perfect. Your parents, though, have had enough of winter. They would like to go to the island of Kyushu (kyoo shoo). The water there may be warm enough for swimming. What would you prefer, sun or snow?

▼ Because it is surrounded by water, Japan has a mild climate. In this picture, people enjoy a walk through a park in Kyoto on a pleasant fall day.

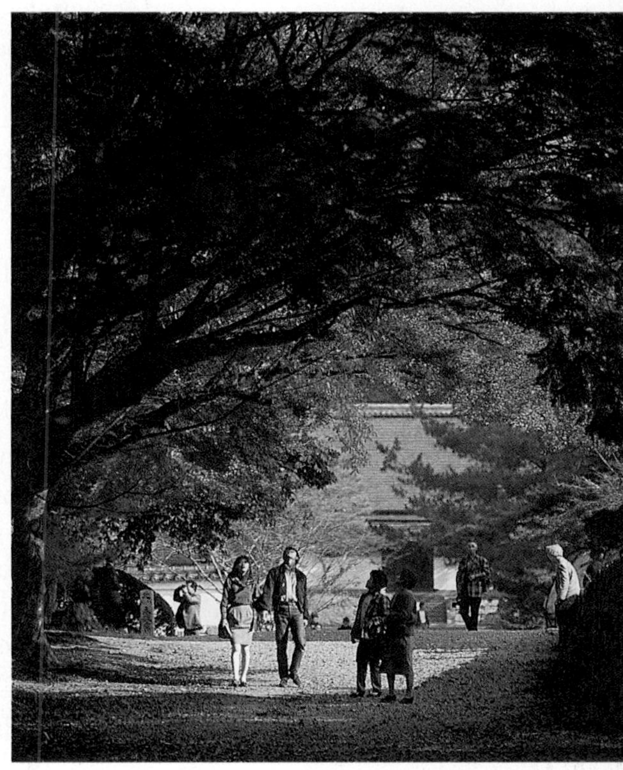

East Asia's Climates

Even though Japan is much smaller in area than the United States, it has similar extremes of weather. People who live in the United States would have the same choices for a February weekend. They could enjoy winter sports in New England, the Midwest, or the Rocky Mountains. Or they might lie on the beach in Florida or California. In fact, much of East Asia, like the United States, has a variety of climates.

East Asia's Climate Regions Look at the climate map on the next page. What climates do you find in the eastern part of this region? A large part of eastern China has a humid subtropical climate—hot summers and cool winters with plenty of rain. To the north is an area of warm summers and cold winters. Because South Korea and Japan are almost

East Asia: Climate Regions

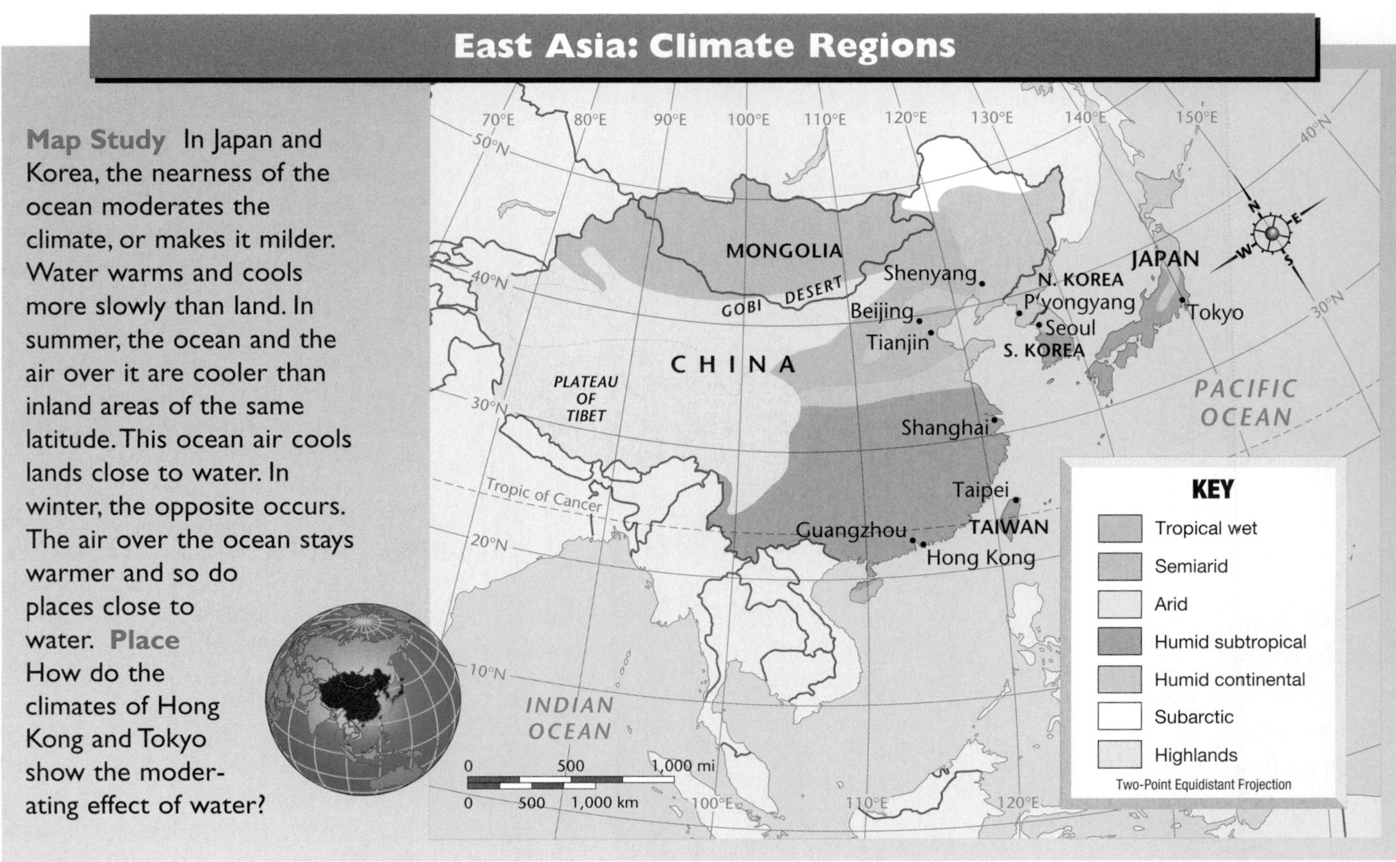

Map Study In Japan and Korea, the nearness of the ocean moderates the climate, or makes it milder. Water warms and cools more slowly than land. In summer, the ocean and the air over it are cooler than inland areas of the same latitude. This ocean air cools lands close to water. In winter, the opposite occurs. The air over the ocean stays warmer and so do places close to water. **Place** How do the climates of Hong Kong and Tokyo show the moderating effect of water?

completely surrounded by water, summers are a bit cooler and winters are a bit warmer than in other places at the same latitude.

In contrast, the northern interior of China is very dry. Here, temperatures can range from very hot to very cold. To the south, the Plateau of Tibet has a cool, dry, highland climate. Look at the map to learn more about the climates of East Asia.

LINKS ACROSS TIME

Divine Winds Typhoons twice saved Japan from invaders. In 1274, Kublai Khan, a great leader of China's Mongol people, sent a fleet of warships to Japan. The Mongols got only as far as the island of Kyushu. A typhoon frightened them back to China. When Kublai Khan tried again in 1281, a typhoon destroyed his huge fleet. The Japanese called this typhoon *kamikaze*, or "divine wind."

Storms in Asia Monsoons strongly affect the climates of East Asia. **Monsoons** are winds that blow across the region at certain times of the year. In summer, Pacific Ocean winds blow west toward the Asian continent. They bring rainfall that starts in June as a drizzle. The Japanese call this the "plum rain" because it begins just as the plums begin to ripen on the trees. The winds cause hot, humid weather and heavier rain in July.

In winter, the winds blow toward the east. The ones that begin in the interior of northern Asia are icy cold and very dry. In parts of China, they produce dust storms that can sometimes last for days. Where they cross warm ocean waters, such as those of the South China Sea, these monsoons pick up moisture. Later, they drop it as rain or snow.

East Asia has hurricanes like those that sometimes strike the southern coastline of the United States during August and September. These violent storms, which develop over the Pacific Ocean, are called **typhoons.** Whirling typhoon winds blow at a speed of 75 miles an hour or more. The winds and heavy rains they bring can cause major damage.

The Influences of Climate

In East Asia, climate influences everything from the natural vegetation, which is shown on the map below, to agriculture. Climate affects what people grow, how often they can plant, and how easily they can harvest their fields.

Vegetation Much of the plant life in East Asia is strong enough to stand seasonal differences in temperature and rainfall. Bamboo, for example, grows unbelievably fast during the wet season in southern China and Japan. Yet it can also survive dry spells by storing food in its huge root system. Shrubs and many small flowering plants in the deserts of China spring up rapidly after summer rains. Then they disappear when dry weather returns. **Deciduous** (dih SIJ oo wus), or leaf-shedding, trees also change with the weather. Maples, birches, and other trees turn the hillsides of Korea and Japan gold, orange, and red once summer gives way to fall.

The Life of the People Climate greatly affects life in East Asia. The region around the Huang He, or Yellow River, in China is a good example. The river gets its name from the brownish yellow loess that is blown by the desert winds. The river picks up the loess and deposits it to the east on the North China Plain. The loess covers a huge 125,000 square mile (32,375,000 hectare) area around the river. This plain is one of the best farming areas in China.

▲ Parts of Japan experience snowy winters, as shown in this scene by a Japanese artist.

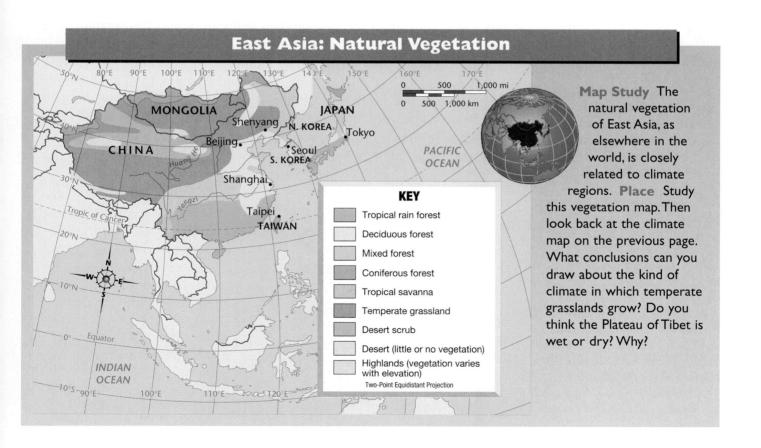

East Asia: Natural Vegetation

KEY

- Tropical rain forest
- Deciduous forest
- Mixed forest
- Coniferous forest
- Tropical savanna
- Temperate grassland
- Desert scrub
- Desert (little or no vegetation)
- Highlands (vegetation varies with elevation)

Two-Point Equidistant Projection

Map Study The natural vegetation of East Asia, as elsewhere in the world, is closely related to climate regions. **Place** Study this vegetation map. Then look back at the climate map on the previous page. What conclusions can you draw about the kind of climate in which temperate grasslands grow? Do you think the Plateau of Tibet is wet or dry? Why?

A River in Flood

Like the Huang He, the Yangzi, China's other great river, sometimes floods. In July 1996 and again in 1998, intense rains caused the Yangzi to overflow, flooding cities and farmland along its banks. The 1998 flood was the worst in 44 years, killing 4,100 people and causing about $30 billion in damages. Here, three workers visit their store in the downtown area of the city of Wuhan. Their only way to get there is by rowboat.

Critical Thinking How might a river like the Yangzi be a blessing and a curse for the people living along its banks?

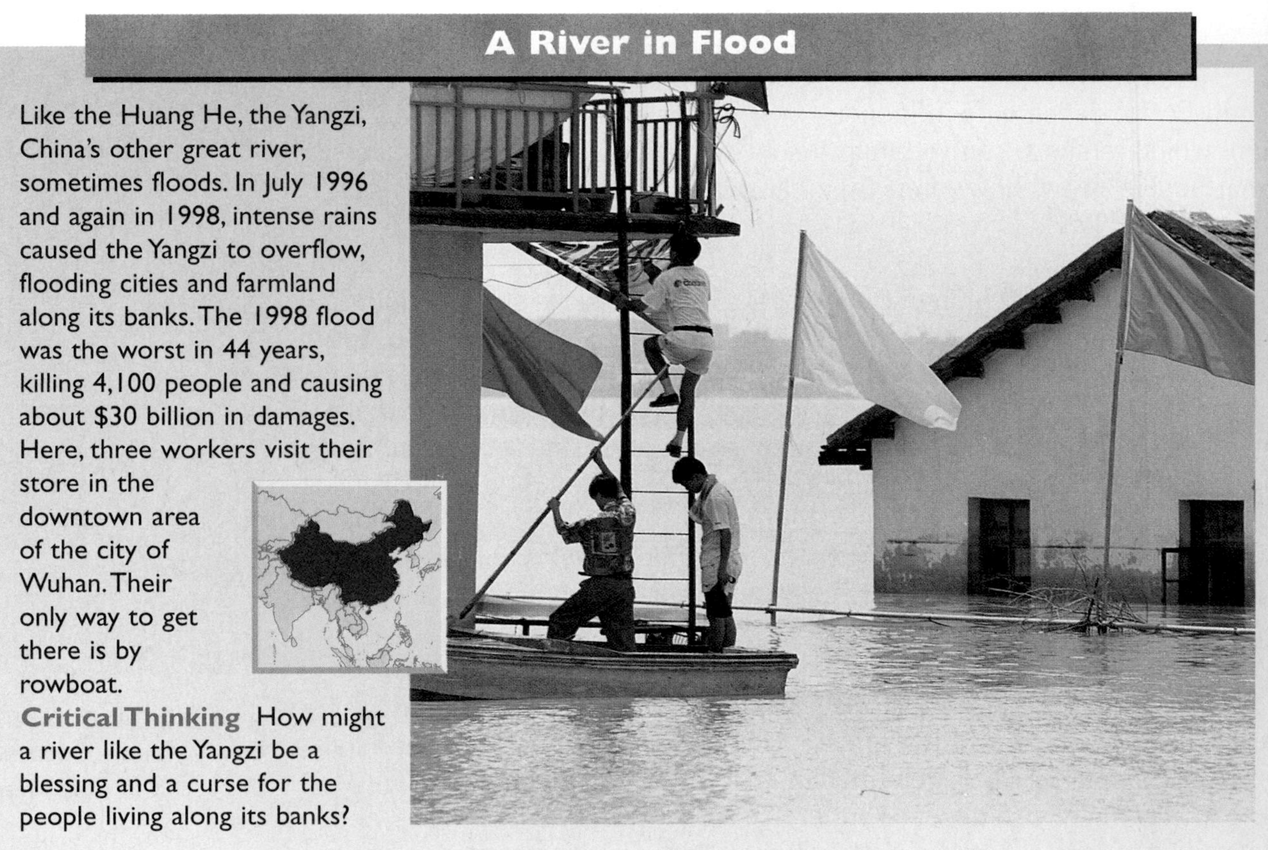

Connect What foods are affected by climate or seasons in your region?

Unfortunately, the Huang He also floods. Today, a system of dams helps control the waters. But the river can still overflow its banks during the monsoons. In the past, damaging floods gave the Huang He its nickname, "China's Sorrow." The river is both a blessing and a curse for Chinese farmers who live along its banks.

The diet of East Asians is also affected by climate and geography. Because rice needs warm weather, it is the main crop—and food—of people in southern China. In the cooler north, wheat and other grains grow better than rice. This means that people in the north eat more flour products, such as noodles.

1. **Define** (a) monsoon, (b) typhoon, (c) deciduous.
2. **Identify** North China Plain.
3. How would you describe the climates of East Asia?
4. How does climate determine what vegetation grows in different parts of East Asia?

Critical Thinking

5. **Identifying Central Issues** Where do you think a farmer moving to East Asia would choose to live? Why? Consider the effects of landforms and climate.

Activity

6. **Writing to Learn** Write a letter to a friend who is planning a long trip to East Asia. Explain to your friend what climate conditions can occur during different times of the year in different areas. Mention the dangers of typhoons and floods. Include suggestions for clothing.

Natural Resources

Reach Into Your Background

Think about all of the different products you use in a day, from the alarm clock that wakes you in the morning to the plate that holds your evening snack. What natural resources were needed to make these items? Does a country have to have natural resources in order to manufacture things?

Questions to Explore

1. What are East Asia's major natural resources?
2. How can East Asia produce enough food to feed its large population?

Key Terms

import
developing country
developed country
export
hydroelectricity
aquaculture
terrace
double-cropping

On some days, oil workers in China's Takla Makan Desert regions battle stinging sand and blowing pebbles. On other days, extreme temperatures may freeze or burn their skin. Trucks sink in the sand as they collect the oil. But no matter how terrible the conditions are, the oil drilling never stops. Scientists estimate that 74 billion barrels of oil may lie beneath the Takla Makan. This amount is three times the oil reserves of the United States. If this estimate is correct, China will have enough oil to fuel its economy. If not, China will have to **import** oil, or buy it from other countries. This will reduce its industrial development.

Using East Asia's Resources

Oil is an important natural resource. But it is just one of many found in East Asia. Although East Asia's lands and waters are filled with natural resources, some are too difficult or too expensive to obtain. The resource map on the next page will help you understand this region's natural resources.

▼ Hot, glowing metal rolls from a machine in this iron and steel plant in Wuhan, China. Iron ore and coal, the resources used to make iron and steel, are found not far from the city.

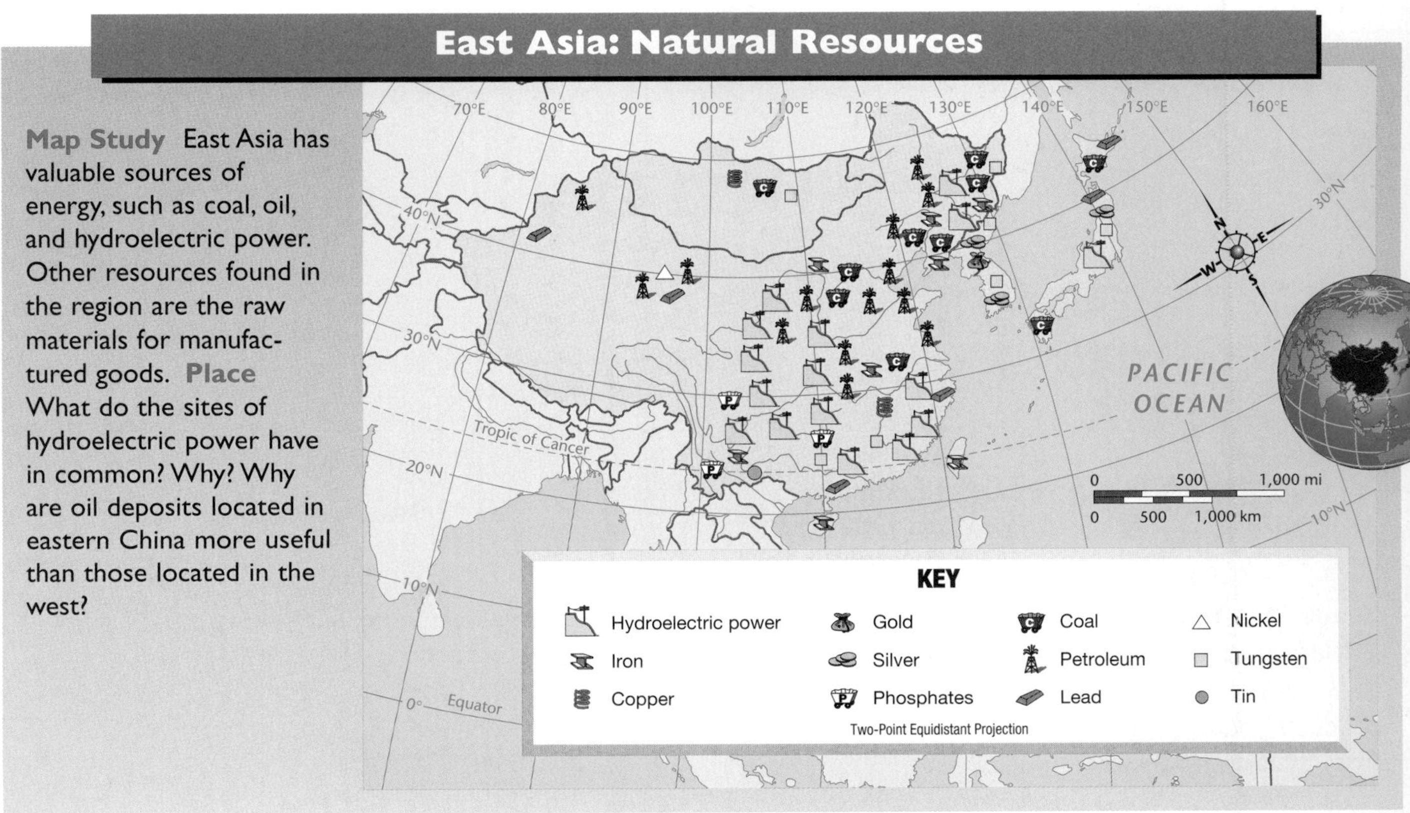

Map Study East Asia has valuable sources of energy, such as coal, oil, and hydroelectric power. Other resources found in the region are the raw materials for manufactured goods. **Place** What do the sites of hydroelectric power have in common? Why? Why are oil deposits located in eastern China more useful than those located in the west?

Minerals The two Koreas have limited mineral resources. Coal and iron, which are used in manufacturing, are plentiful in North Korea. But there is little coal or iron in South Korea, where much more manufacturing takes place. The only minerals that are in large supply in the South are tungsten and graphite. Tungsten is used in electronics. Graphite is a soft mineral used in pencils.

If South Korea could share North Korea's coal and iron, both countries would benefit. But the two do not share resources, since they do not get along. North Korea is a **developing country**—one that has low industrial production and little modern technology. South Korea is a **developed country**—one with many industries and a well-developed economy. Because of its limited resources, South Korea must import the iron, crude oil, and chemicals it needs for its industries from other countries. Nevertheless, it has become one of East Asia's richest economies. It **exports** many manufactured goods, or sells them to other nations.

READ ACTIVELY

Predict What is the difference between a developing country and a developed country?

Japan is a modern industrial society. Yet Japan—like South Korea—has few mineral resources. It imports vast quantities of minerals. Japan is the world's largest importer of coal, natural gas, and oil. It also imports about 95 percent of the iron ore, tin, and copper that its major industries need.

Unlike its East Asian neighbors, China has a large supply of natural resources. For more than 2,000 years, the Chinese have mined copper, tin, and iron. And along with its huge oil reserves, China has one of the world's largest supplies of coal. However, China does not have everything it needs and must import some raw materials.

Forests Parts of East Asia have large forests. However, the nations of this region, like those in other parts of the world, have not treated their forests carefully. In the past, people gave little thought to replacing the trees that they cut down. Farmers needing to heat their homes cut wood without concern. Programs that plant new trees in all four countries may someday allow East Asia to meet its own needs for wood. At present, some countries must still import wood.

Waters The rugged mountains and heavy rainfall of East Asia are perfect for developing water power. Using the power of East Asia's swiftly flowing rivers is important to the region's industrial development. However, building dams to collect water is costly. It is even more costly to build power plants that produce **hydroelectricity.** These plants use the power of running water to generate electricity.

The Pacific Ocean is an important resource for food in East Asia. In areas where cold and warm currents meet, tiny plants thrive. They attract a variety of fish. Some people in East Asia catch fish using poles and nets. Some even train birds called cormorants to help them fish. But fishing is also a big business. Huge boats owned by corporations catch large numbers of fish and shellfish.

East Asians also practice **aquaculture,** or sea farming. In shallow bays throughout the area, people raise fish in huge cages. Artificial reefs provide beds for shrimp and oysters. The lakes and rivers of China are also important sources of food. In fact, almost twice as many freshwater fish are caught in China as in any other country in the world.

Saving Forests Forests once covered two thirds of South Korea. By the early 1970s, many were gone. Then the nation began its forestry program. Workers now plant new trees. They develop new kinds that can fight off diseases and pests. The program limits the number of trees that can be cut. Now, many more trees are growing in South Korea. The trees keep soil from being washed away by rain and floods.

◀ ▼ The Japanese raise oysters not only for food, but also for pearls. Here, a worker plants a tiny "seed" of shell inside an oyster (left). The oyster will cover it with layers of shiny material from its body to form the pearl. Only 1 out of 20 oysters will make a pearl (below).

Visualize Picture some unusual places in your neighborhood where people could grow food plants.

Fertile Lands: A Valuable Resource

In order to feed its large population, East Asia needs to farm every bit of available land. With so many mountains and plateaus, only a small percentage of the land can be cultivated. Only 10 percent of China, 11 percent of Japan, and 14 percent of North Korea can be farmed. South Korea's 19 percent is about equal to the percentage of land farmed in the United States.

Land that in other countries would not be used is used with great care in East Asia. In China, Japan, and parts of Korea, farmers cut ledges called **terraces** into steep hillsides to gain a few precious yards of soil for crops. In China, farmers often plant one type of crop between the rows of another in order to grow more food. Farmers even use the sides of roads and railways lines for planting.

Where climate and soil allow it, farmers practice **double-cropping,** growing two crops on the same land in a single year. In some parts of the south, farmers are even able to grow three crops in a year. In southern Japan, rice seeds are sowed in small fields. When the seedlings are about a foot high, they are replanted in a larger field after wheat has been harvested.

In order to get the most out of their land, the farmers of East Asia have made their local conditions work for them. For example, in northern Japan, farmers raise a special rice that ripens fast. Farmers can harvest it in early fall before the severe winter begins.

▼▶ Terraces increase the amount of land available for farming. Fields of rice cover these terraces in China (below). Women (right) harvest tea grown on sloping hillsides in Japan.

Like this young woman tending rice, about one third of all workers in North Korea earn their living by farming. Better seeds and more irrigation have improved farming in this country. However, a lack of good farmland and several years of poor harvests have led to food shortages.

In Japan, as in other crowded parts of Asia, cattle and other types of livestock are rare. Crops take up far less space than animals, and farmers can get more food from each acre of land by planting.

East Asian farmers will continue finding better ways to farm. They are trying to find new crops with larger yields. They also are looking for better fertilizers and better ways of managing farms. Only then will they be able to keep feeding East Asia's growing population.

1. **Define** (a) import, (b) developing country, (c) developed country, (d) export, (e) hydroelectricity, (f) aquaculture, (g) terrace, (h) double-cropping.
2. What are some of East Asia's most important mineral resources?
3. In what ways are the waters of East Asia an important resource for the people?
4. How have the farmers of East Asia made the best use of their land?

Critical Thinking

5. **Drawing Conclusions** (a) How might natural resources help a nation to become a developed country? (b) How could a nation become developed without many natural resources?

Activity

6. **Writing to Learn** Choose one way that East Asians increase their food supply, such as double-cropping or aquaculture. Research your topic. Then write a five-minute speech to explain the process to your classmates.

Reading Actively

Steve dropped his books on the table. "I just can't seem to get this," he told his sister Lena.

Lena picked up one of her brother's books and looked at it. "What's wrong, Steve? This book is about volcanoes. I thought you were interested in volcanoes."

"I am, but there are no *real* volcanoes in that book. It's just a bunch of words on the page. It all seems to fly right out of my brain!" said Steve.

"I know what you mean," said Lena. "But if you read actively, it sticks a lot better."

Get Ready

Reading actively means using certain strategies to get the most from your reading. Four important reading strategies are described in the Try It Out section on the next page. By reading actively you will enjoy your reading more. You will also learn more. Reading actively can also help you remember what you read. This is important, because much of the information you will learn in your lifetime will probably come from reading.

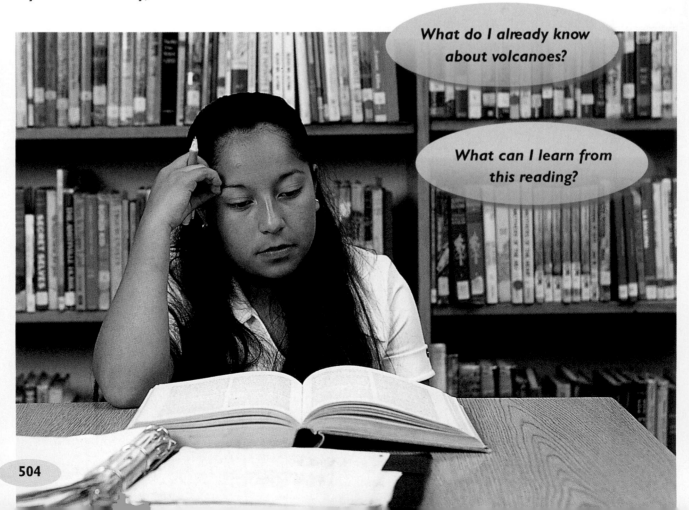

What do I already know about volcanoes?

What can I learn from this reading?

Try It Out

Here are some strategies you can use to read actively.

A. Ask questions. Constantly ask yourself questions as you read. "Why is this information important?" "What made this happen?"

B. Predict. As you read, try to predict what you will read about next. This can help you focus on the topic. After you have read that part, think about whether your predictions matched what you read.

C. Connect. Try to make connections between what you are reading and other things you know or have read and seen. Put yourself in the picture. How would it feel to be part of what you are reading?

D. Visualize. Create pictures in your mind as you read. Think about what you would see if you were actually in the place you are reading about. Add your other senses. What would things sound and smell like?

Apply the Skill

The selection in the next column describes one of the world's most dramatic geographic features. Use the four reading strategies. To do this, get a blank sheet of paper and turn it sideways. Write the four strategies as headings across the top. List ideas under each heading as you read.

Try to apply the four strategies of reading actively every time you read. As you apply them, they will become a natural part of your reading. Then you will be a better reader.

The Ring of Fire

When a volcano starts to erupt, smoke and ash pour from the top. Then comes a huge explosion of hot liquid rock, which pours down the side of the mountain. This amazing event does not happen very often, but it happens in some parts of the world more than others.

The Ring of Fire is a narrow band of volcanoes that almost encircles the Pacific Ocean. It stretches through Japan, the Philippines, the Pacific islands, and New Zealand. It includes the western edge of South America, the middle of Central America, and a mountain range in the western United States.

Most of the world's volcanoes are in the Ring of Fire. So are the ones that are most likely to erupt. Scientists say there are about 540 active volcanoes on the Earth. Most of them are part of the Ring of Fire.

▶ A volcano erupts in the Kilauea crater of Hawaii Volcanoes National Park.

Review and Activities

Reviewing Main Ideas

1. Name three physical features of East Asia.
2. Where do the majority of East Asians live? Why?
3. Name and describe the type of climate found in most of East Asia.
4. How does East Asia's climate affect its natural vegetation?
5. How do both climate and vegetation affect the lives of people in East Asia?
6. What are five natural resources found in East Asia?
7. How do the natural resources of China compare to those of Japan in terms of number and variety?
8. What is the difference between importing and exporting?

Reviewing Key Terms

Use each key term below in a sentence that shows the meaning of the term.

1. plateau
2. desert
3. loess
4. archipelago
5. peninsula
6. population density
7. monsoon
8. typhoon
9. deciduous
10. developing country
11. developed country
12. hydroelectricity
13. aquaculture
14. terrace
15. double-cropping

Critical Thinking

1. **Cause and Effect** How might Japan's lack of natural resources affect its economy?
2. **Drawing Conclusions** About two thirds of China's land is covered by mountains and deserts. What conclusion about China's farmland can you draw from this?
3. **Drawing Conclusions** The Yangzi is the only river in East Asia that is deep enough for cargo ships to sail on. How might this affect the population density of the lands surrounding the river? Of East Asia?

Graphic Organizer

Copy the diagram onto a sheet of paper. Then fill it in so that it compares and contrasts the natural resources of China and Japan.

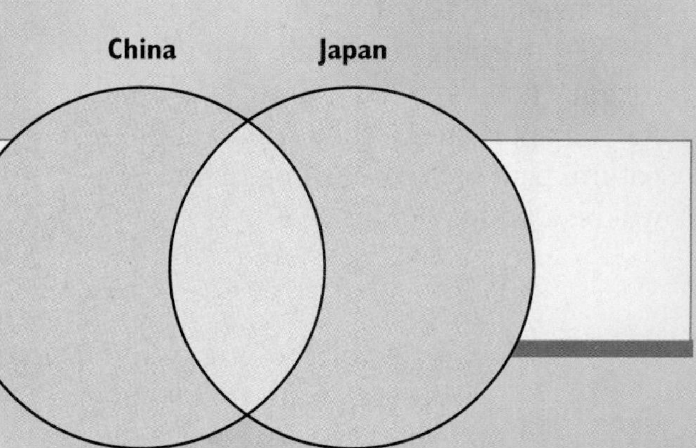

Map Activity

East Asia
For each place listed below, write the letter from the map that shows its location.

1. Mount Fuji
2. Mount Everest
3. North China Plain
4. Himalaya Mountains
5. Yangzi
6. Huang He

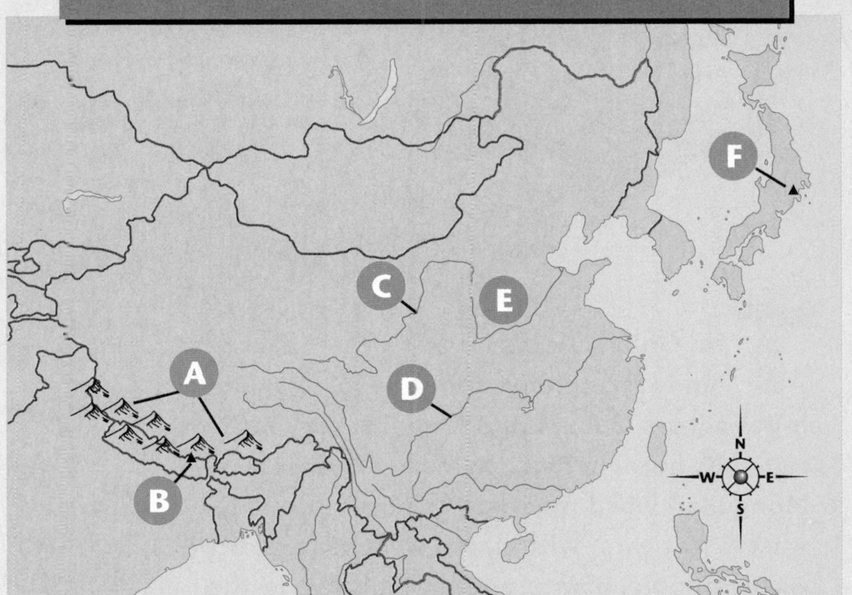

Take It to the NET

Activity Research the volcanoes found in Japan. Write a science news article on the volcano you find most interesting. For help in completing this activity, visit **www.phschool.com**.

Chapter 18 Self-Test To review what you have learned, take the Chapter 18 Self-Test and get instant feedback on your answers. Go to **www.phschool.com** to take the test.

Writing Activity

Writing a Pamphlet
China's Huang He has created rich soil for the surrounding lands. This makes these lands the best agricultural areas in China. However, China's monsoon season causes the river to overflow frequently. Do some research to find out how people protect fields from flood damage. Write a pamphlet that contains suggestions for the farmers who live along the banks of the Huang He to protect their crops.

Skills Review

Turn to the Skills Activity.
Review the four strategies for reading actively. Make notes as you ask questions, predict, connect, and visualize while reading this section. Explain how these strategies helped you read better.

How Am I Doing?

Answer these questions to help you check your progress.

1. Can I identify the main geographic features of East Asia?
2. Do I understand how climate has affected the vegetation and population of East Asia?
3. Can I identify the most important natural resources in East Asia?
4. What information from this chapter can I include in my journal?

Crossing the Great Gobi

The Gobi is Asia's largest desert. Barren lands stretch for about 500,000 square miles across China and Mongolia. Very little rain falls here. In fact, the name *Gobi* is a Mongolian word meaning "place without water." Yet even with harsh weather and little water, people, plants, and animals live in the desert. How do they survive?

Purpose

In this activity, you will plan a trip through the Gobi to study desert survival. As you learn more about life in the desert, you will plan for your own survival as well. Look in your library for books on deserts, their vegetation and animal life, books on East Asia, and books on the Gobi in particular.

Investigate Desert Life

People who live in desert climates have invented special ways of preserving water and staying cool during the day and warm at night. Research the people who live in the Gobi. What kinds of houses do they build? How do they dress? What advice might they give someone not used to desert life? Write a list of ways that people live in the desert. Draw pictures to illustrate your list.

Chart Your Trip

How many days' worth of supplies should you pack for your trek? Come up with an estimate and justify your answer. First, find and trace a map of the Gobi. Draw a dotted line on

the map to chart the path of your trip. Now, use the map scale to determine how many miles you are planning to travel. To decide how many miles to travel each day, answer these questions. Write your answers on a sheet of paper.

- How many hours a day will you need for rest and for your research? How many hours are left for travel?
- How many miles an hour do you think your truck can cross the desert sand?
- What might slow you down? How much time will you plan for emergencies?

Links to Other Subjects

Studying desert peoples .... **Science, Art**
Calculating travel rates and distances .... **Math**
Researching desert health hazards ..... **Health**
Writing a travel journal ...... **Language Arts**
Drawing a desert plant or an animal .... **Art, Science**

Protect Your Health

Desert travel can be hazardous to your health. Some dangers include heatstroke, sunburn, and dehydration. What are the symptoms of each? How can you avoid or treat each condition? Research these questions. Then write a fact sheet on health tips for desert travel.

Keep a Travel Journal

Research the Gobi's animals, plants, people, land, and weather. Then use the information you found to write a journal about your desert travel. Describe what you think it feels like to spend nights and days in the desert. What discoveries, setbacks, or dangers might you encounter? Give details using all your senses—sight, sound, smell, taste, touch.

Draw a Desert Plant or an Animal

Desert species have traits that help them survive. Research one animal or plant species that lives in the Gobi. What helps it survive in the dry desert? Draw a picture of this plant or animal. Include captions to point out special features adapted to desert life.

Write a summary describing what you learned about the Gobi while planning your trip. Be sure to answer the following questions in your summary.

1. What steps would you take to be sure of your own survival in the desert? Why are these steps important?
2. How are people, animals, and plants that live in the Gobi able to survive the desert climate?
3. What are some reasons people might want to visit the desert in spite of its dangers?

CHAPTER 19

EAST ASIA

Cultures and History

PICTURE ACTIVITIES

Perhaps because East Asian cultures are among the oldest in the world, the people of East Asia cherish their past. To help you understand how the past and present mix in East Asia, look at this picture of a boat with the city of Hong Kong in the background. Do the following activities.

Study the picture

Identify what is old and what is new in the picture. Would you rather explore the old or the new? Why?

Make up a title

Write a short title for the picture that expresses the contrasts between the old and new things you see.

Historic Traditions

Reach Into Your Background

Each day, you come into contact with many cultures that may be different from your own. Make a list of the foods, words, clothing, entertainers, sports, and types of music from other countries that you enjoy.

Questions to Explore

1. What are some of ancient East Asia's major achievements?
2. How did Chinese culture influence the rest of East Asia?

Key Terms

civilization
irrigate
emperor
dynasty
migration
clan
cultural diffusion
communist

Key People and Places

Confucius
Commodore Matthew Perry
Great Wall of China
Middle Kingdom

Over two thousand years ago, one of the most important thinkers of ancient times gave this advice to his pupils:

> "Let the ruler be a ruler and the subject a subject.
>
> . . .
>
> A youth, when at home, should act with respect to his parents, and, abroad, be respectful to his elders. He should be earnest and truthful. He should overflow in love to all, and cultivate the friendship of the good.
>
> . . .
>
> When you have faults, do not fear to abandon them."

These words are from the teachings of Confucius (kun FYOO shus), who lived in China about 500 B.C. He taught that everyone has duties and responsibilities. If a person acts correctly, the result will be peace and harmony. Confucius' ideas helped China's government run smoothly for years and Chinese culture to last for centuries.

▼ Chinese people all over the world still admire Confucius. This statue of Confucius stands in the Chinatown section of New York City.

East Asia's Achievements

Ask Questions Think of three questions you might ask about the achievements of China.

Regions of Asia and Africa produced civilizations earlier than China's. A **civilization** has cities, a central government, workers who do specialized jobs, and social classes. Of the world's early civilizations, only China's has survived. This makes it the oldest continuous civilization in the world. Korea and Japan are not as old. But they, too, have long, important histories.

The Glory That Was China For much of its history, China had little to do with the rest of the world. The Great Wall of China was begun in the 600s B.C. as many small walls between warring states. Over time it became a symbol of China's desire to keep the world at a distance. In fact, Chinese leaders had such pride that they named their country the Middle Kingdom. To them, it was the center of the universe.

The Chinese had reason to believe that their civilization was the greatest in the world. They invented paper, gunpowder, silk weaving, the magnetic compass, the printing press, clockwork, the spinning wheel, and the water wheel. Chinese engineers were experts at digging canals, building dams and bridges, and setting up irrigation systems. To **irrigate** means to supply dry land with water by using ditches or canals. Chinese scientists made major discoveries in mathematics and medicine.

Starting in ancient times, China was governed by an **emperor**—a ruler of widespread lands and groups of people. A series of rulers from the same family was a **dynasty.** Chinese history is described by dynasties. The time line below highlights some important events and cultural contributions of several dynasties.

▼ The Chinese made many important achievements during the Han dynasty. When did the Han rule China?

Major Dynasties of China

1500 B.C. | 1000 B.C. | 500 B.C. | A.D. 1 | A.D. 500 | A.D. 1000 | A.D. 1500

Shang
1700 B.C.–1100 B.C.
- Writing
- Wheeled chariots

Zhou
1100 B.C.–256 B.C.
- Confucius lived.
- First canals built

Qin
221 B.C.–206 B.C.
- China took its name from this dynasty.
- Great Wall built
- Standard weights and measures

Han
206 B.C.–A.D. 220
- Chinese trace their ancestry to this dynasty.
- Paper, compass, seismograph invented
- Buddhism comes to China from India.

Tang
A.D. 618–A.D. 907
- Art and poetry flourish.
- Chinese goods flow to Southwest Asia and Europe.
- First book printed

Song
A.D. 960–A.D. 1279
- Block printing
- Paper money

Ming
A.D. 1368–A.D. 1644
- Artists and philosophers make China the most civilized country in the world.

Qing
A.D. 1644–A.D. 1911
- Last dynasty ends with Emperor Pu Yi.

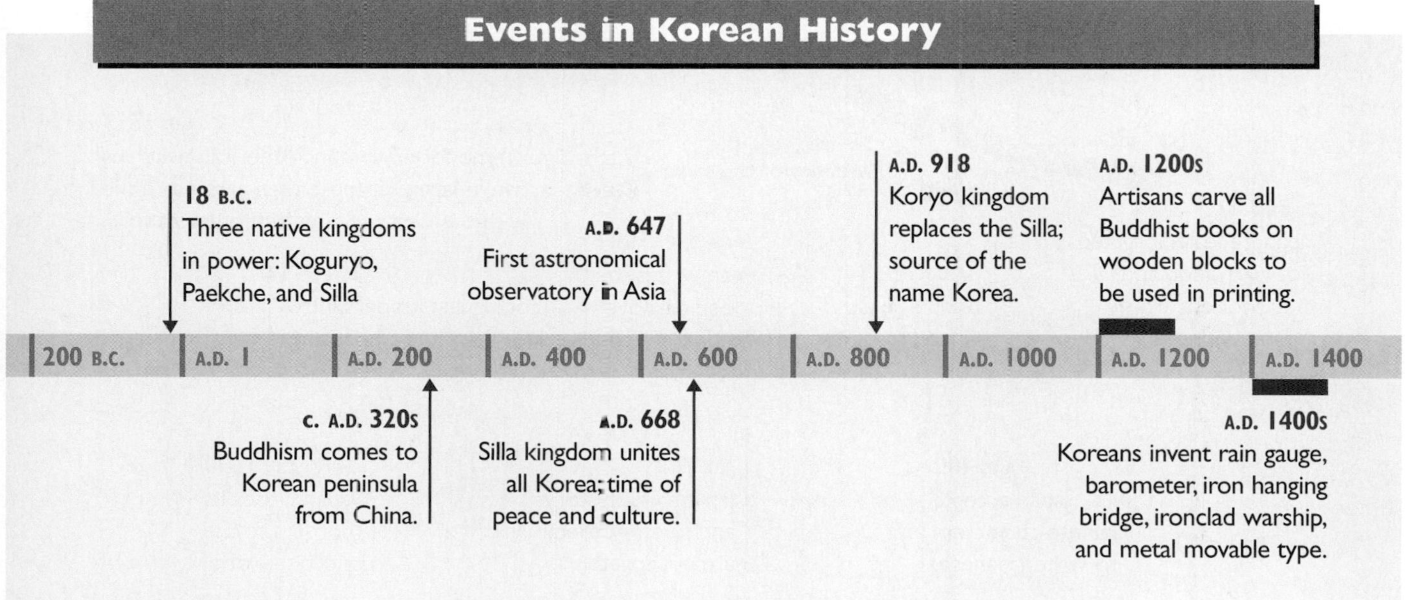
Events in Korean History
18 B.C.
Three native kingdoms in power: Koguryo, Paekche, and Silla
A.D. 647
First astronomical observatory in Asia
A.D. 918
Koryo kingdom replaces the Silla; source of the name Korea.
A.D. 1200s
Artisans carve all Buddhist books on wooden blocks to be used in printing.
200 B.C.
A.D. 1
A.D. 200
A.D. 400
A.D. 600
A.D. 800
A.D. 1000
A.D. 1200
A.D. 1400
c. A.D. 320s
Buddhism comes to Korean peninsula from China.
A.D. 668
Silla kingdom unites all Korea; time of peace and culture.
A.D. 1400s
Koreans invent rain gauge, barometer, iron hanging bridge, ironclad warship, and metal movable type.

▲ Although Chinese culture influenced that of Korea, the Koreans made contributions of their own. What were some of them?

Korea and China Although Korea's original settlers came from north-central Asia, the country's history is closely tied to China. Around 1200 B.C., during a time of troubles in China, some Chinese moved to the Korean Peninsula. Later, other Chinese settled in the southern part of the peninsula. These migrations led to a transfer of Chinese knowledge and customs to the Koreans. A **migration** is a movement of people from one country or region to another to make a new home.

People have lived on the Korean Peninsula for thousands of years. But not until the Silla people gained control was the peninsula unified. The time line above highlights some of the major events and contributions during the country's early history.

Years of Japanese Isolation For much of Japan's history, **clans,** or groups of families who claimed a common ancestor, fought each other for land and power. Around A.D. 500, one clan, the Yamato (yah mah toh), became powerful. Claiming descent from the sun goddess, Yamato leaders took the title of emperor. Many emperors sat on Japan's throne. For a long time they had little power. Instead, shoguns (shoh gunz), or "emperor's generals," made the laws. Warrior nobles, the samurai (sam uh ry), enforced these laws. Together, the shoguns and samurai ruled Japan for more than 700 years.

At first, the Japanese favored trade with their East Asian neighbors. This did not last long, however. Japanese leaders came to believe that isolation, or separation, was the best way to keep the country united. Thus, Japan was isolated from the outside world for many hundreds of years. Although Japanese culture grew, the rest of the world knew little about it until Japan became interested in Western inventions. Japan finally was forced to trade with the West in the 1800s. The time line on the next page shows some key events in Japanese history.

▲ This comic mask is worn in *no* plays, a traditional form of Japanese drama.

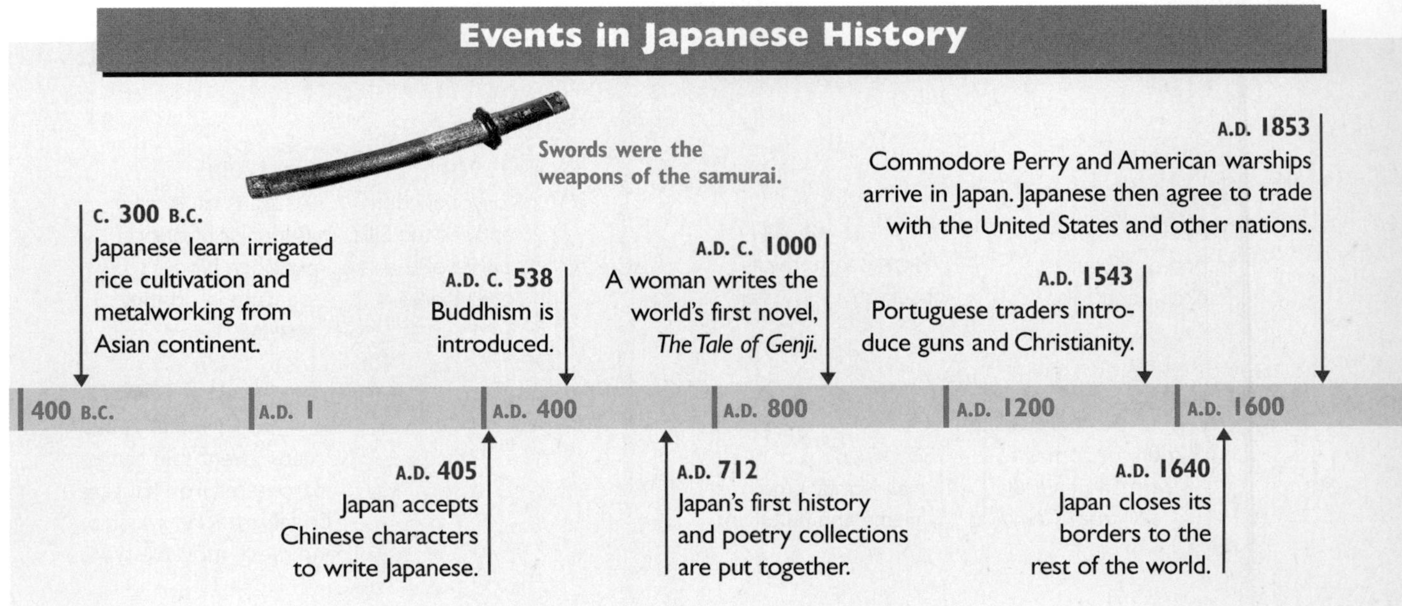
Events in Japanese History
Swords were the weapons of the samurai.
c. 300 B.C.
Japanese learn irrigated rice cultivation and metalworking from Asian continent.
A.D. c. 538
Buddhism is introduced.
A.D. c. 1000
A woman writes the world's first novel, The Tale of Genji.
A.D. 1543
Portuguese traders introduce guns and Christianity.
A.D. 1853
Commodore Perry and American warships arrive in Japan. Japanese then agree to trade with the United States and other nations.
400 B.C.
A.D. 1
A.D. 400
A.D. 800
A.D. 1200
A.D. 1600
A.D. 405
Japan accepts Chinese characters to write Japanese.
A.D. 712
Japan's first history and poetry collections are put together.
A.D. 1640
Japan closes its borders to the rest of the world.

▲ Japan has interacted with outside nations except for one period in its history. When was this? How long did it last?

The Spread of Culture

In ancient times, China was far ahead of the rest of the world in inventions and discoveries. Thus, it is not surprising that many Chinese discoveries spread to Korea and Japan. This **cultural diffusion,** or spreading of ideas, happened early. The teachings of Confucius were among the first ideas to be passed along. The religion of Buddhism (BOOD izm), which China had adopted from India, later spread to Korea and Japan.

Cultural diffusion also occurred between other lands. It was not always friendly. For example, Korean pottery so impressed the Japanese that they captured villages of potters and took them to Japan after an invasion in 1598. East Asian culture, as a whole, owes much to the early exchanges among China, Japan, and Korea. In each case, however, the countries changed what they borrowed until the tradition became their own.

LINKS
ACROSS THE WORLD

West Meets East The West has been greatly influenced by the cultures of East Asia. Noodles and other Chinese food long ago became part of Western cooking. Eastern art influenced the design of Western architecture, gardens, furniture, and fabrics. Traders imported porcelain, pottery made from a fine white clay, from China, Japan, and Korea. Europeans and Americans called it "china" and tried to copy it.

Westerners in East Asia

Although East Asia was not interested in the rest of the world, the world was interested in East Asia. Marco Polo, an Italian merchant, is believed to have visited China in the 1200s. When he returned to Italy, he told people about China. He described a royal palace with walls covered in gold and silver. He told tales about people burning black rocks (coal) to heat their homes. His stories excited the imaginations and the greed of European monarchs and merchants.

The Opening of East Asia In spite of the efforts of China and Japan to remain isolated, Western nations could not be kept away. In the 1800s, Europeans and Americans began to produce great amounts of manufactured goods. East Asia seemed to be a good place to sell these products. Western trading ships began to sail to Asian ports.

Paper as We Know It

Cai Lun, an official of the Han dynasty, is said to have invented paper as we know it about 2,000 years ago. He made it from the bark of the mulberry tree or silk rags. In 1957, scientists discovered a small piece of paper in a Chinese tomb. It might have been made as early as 140 B.C.

Chinese papermakers first chopped up plants or other materials such as hemp rope or old fishing nets. They soaked these materials in water.
Workers pounded the mixture of water-soaked materials until it turned into a watery mush called pulp.
Workers dipped a mesh screen into the pulp. Water drained from the screen, leaving a layer of damp pulp on top. When the pulp dried, it was peeled off the screen to make a sheet of paper. Papermakers used starch or gelatin to strengthen the paper.

In 1853, U.S. Commodore Matthew Perry sailed with four warships to Japan to force it to grant trading rights to the United States. In a few years, the Japanese learned more about Western ways and inventions. They adapted what was useful to them, while preserving their own culture. Japan soon became the strongest nation in Asia.

The opening up of China to Europe was different. Foreign countries wanted to control parts of China and its wealth. As foreign powers entered China, it became clear that the country was not strong enough

Connect What do you think it would be like to live in a country isolated from others?

to protect itself. The British, French, Dutch, Russians, and Japanese gained control over parts of China. Other countries then feared losing the opportunity to share in China's riches. In 1899, the United States announced the policy that China should be open for trade with all nations equally. For a while, nations halted their efforts to divide up China.

New Forces in the Twentieth Century Many Chinese blamed the emperor for the growing foreign influence. In 1911, revolution broke out in China. The rule of emperors ended, and a republic was set up.

Meanwhile, Japan was becoming more powerful. As Japan's industry grew, its leaders sought to control other Asian countries. They wanted to make sure that Japan would have resources to fuel its industries. Japanese attacks on other Asian and Pacific lands led to World War II in East Asia. After years of fighting, the United States and its allies defeated Japan. The United States then helped Japan recover and create an elected government.

After World War II, civil war broke out in China between two groups. The Nationalists wanted to strengthen China so it could manage its own affairs without other nations. The Communists wanted to break the power of the landlords and other wealthy people and drive out all foreign influences. The Communists won the civil war in 1949 and made China a **communist** nation. This means that the government owns large industries, businesses, and most of the country's land.

After World War II, Korea found itself divided into two parts. Communists ruled North Korea. South Korea turned to Western nations for support. In 1950, the two Koreas exploded into a bloody civil war. North Korea invaded South Korea. The United States sent 480,000 troops to help South Korea. The war dragged on for three years, killing about 37,000 U.S. soldiers. More than 2 million Korean soldiers and civilians lost their lives. Neither side won. The battle line at the end of the war, in 1953, remains the border between the two Koreas today.

1. **Define** (a) civilization, (b) irrigate, (c) emperor, (d) dynasty, (e) migration, (f) clan, (g) cultural diffusion, (h) communist.
2. **Identify** (a) Confucius, (b) Commodore Matthew Perry, (c) Great Wall of China, (d) Middle Kingdom.
3. In what ways was ancient China an advanced civilization?
4. Explain how East Asian countries interacted with the West.

Critical Thinking

5. **Expressing Problems Clearly** Why would isolating a country from its neighbors help keep it united?

Activity

6. **Writing to Learn** Research an invention or a discovery of either the Chinese or the Koreans. Write and illustrate an advertisement for it that tells what it is and how it works. Explain the difference it might make in people's lives or why it is important.

People and Cultures

Reach Into Your Background

Do you or a friend own something that has been handed down for generations? Perhaps it is something that was owned by a grandparent or great-grandparent. Perhaps someone bought it on a long-ago trip. List some of the ways in which people keep connections with earlier times.

Questions to Explore

1. How does East Asia's past affect modern-day culture?
2. Who are East Asia's many peoples?

Key Terms

commune
dialect
nomad
homogeneous
ethnic group

The Chinese game *weiqi* (wy chee) has ancient cultural roots. One player has 181 black stones standing for night. The other has 180 white stones standing for day. The goal is to surround and capture the opponent's stones. But to the Chinese, weiqi is more than a game. For centuries, Buddhists have used it to discipline the mind and show behavior. Masters can look at a game record to see exactly when players became too greedy and doomed themselves to defeat. Today, you can see people playing this ancient game in any park in China.

Tradition and Change

In East Asia, tradition mixes with change in a thousand ways. Businesspeople in Western suits greet each other in the traditional way—with a bow. Ancient palaces stand among skyscrapers. Everywhere in Japan, China, and the Koreas, reminders of the past mingle with activities of the present.

Communism and Change in China When the Communists came into power in 1949, they began to make major changes in the Chinese way of life. To begin with, the government ended the old system of land ownership. It created **communes,** communities in which land is held in common and where members live and work together.

▼ This woman from Tibet, in the western part of China, reflects the traditions of her ethnic group in her headdress, jewelry, and the way she carries her baby.

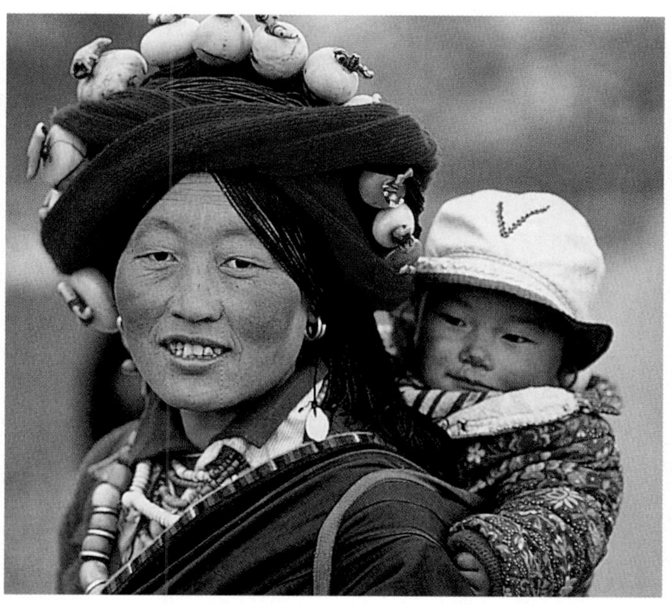

The Ideal Family

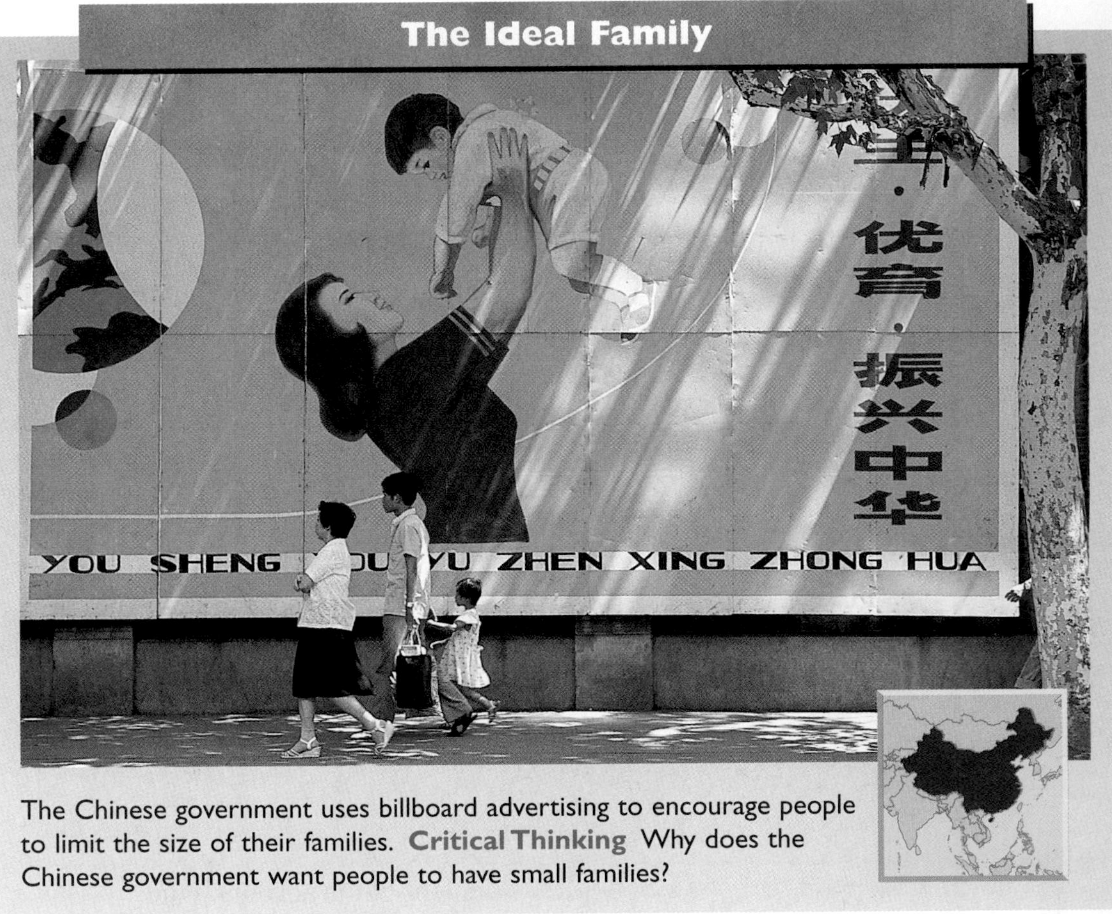

The Chinese government uses billboard advertising to encourage people to limit the size of their families. **Critical Thinking** Why does the Chinese government want people to have small families?

Many Chinese farmers were bitter at losing their land. They were accustomed to living in family groups that worked together in small fields. The farmers resisted the communes. Food production fell, and China suffered terrible food shortages. Only when the government allowed some private ownership did food production grow.

The Communists also tried to slow China's population growth by attacking the idea of large families. Here, they had more success. Chinese couples are supposed to wait until their late twenties to marry. They are not supposed to have more than one child per family. Chinese families with only one child receive special privileges.

Under communism, the position of women has improved. Traditionally, Chinese women worked at home. Now most work in full-time jobs outside the home. One of the first laws the Communists passed allowed a woman to own property, choose her husband, and get a divorce. However, men still hold most of the power, and many marriages are still arranged.

The mixture of old and new affects the lives of all Chinese. The old traditions are strongest in rural areas. Yet even in the cities, a visitor sees examples of the old China. The streets are filled with three-wheeled cabs pedaled like tricycles. Tiny shops sell traditional cures made from herbs. These shops exist side by side with modern hospitals. Even as they are modernizing, the Chinese continue to respect their past.

Changing Korea In Korea, daily life is still affected by long-standing traditions. The family is still important, though the average family is smaller today. A family still looks after the welfare of all its members. In rural areas, grandparents, parents, aunts, and uncles may live in one household. In the cities, a family is usually just parents and children.

As in China, modern ways are much more visible in urban areas. Most Koreans wear modern clothes. They save their traditional dress of trousers or a long skirt with a long jacket for holidays. Also, as is true all over the world, the role of women has changed. Earlier, women had few opportunities. Today, women can work and vote.

Japan's Blend of Old and New Japan is the most up-to-date of the East Asian countries. Japanese work at computers in skyscrapers and ride home on speedy trains. Once they reach home, however, they may follow traditional customs. For example, they may change into kimonos, or robes. They may sit on mats at a low table to have dinner. Japanese students dress like students in the United States, though some wear the headbands of samurai warriors to show that they are getting ready for a challenge.

The Japanese use more modern technology than the rest of East Asia. Still, they try hard to preserve the past. The help given to Japanese artists is a good example. Some years ago, the Japanese saw that traditional arts and crafts were dying out. The government began offering lifetime salaries to some artists. The main task of these artists is to teach young people who will keep the ancient arts alive. Respected by all, these artists are referred to as National Living Treasures.

▼ In Beijing opera, an old form of Chinese drama, actors in rich costumes stage traditional myths and legends.

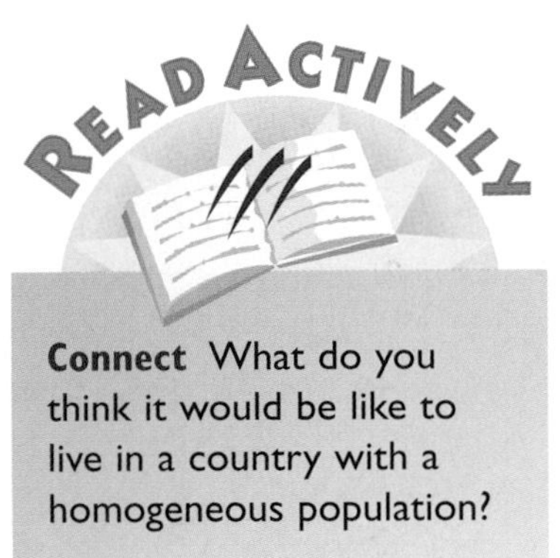

Connect What do you think it would be like to live in a country with a homogeneous population?

East Asia's People

East Asian cultures embrace both the old and the new. Within each of the area's countries, however, the people tend to share a single culture.

China: The Han and Others About 19 of every 20 Chinese people trace their ancestry to the Han, the people of China's second dynasty. As you can see on the map below, the Han live mostly in eastern and central China. Although they have a common language, they speak different **dialects,** or forms of a single language, from region to region. The other Chinese come from 55 different minority groups. These groups live mainly in the western parts of China.

Korea and Japan: Few Minorities Historians believe that the ancient Koreans were descended from many different groups of nomads from Mongolia. **Nomads** are people who have no settled home.

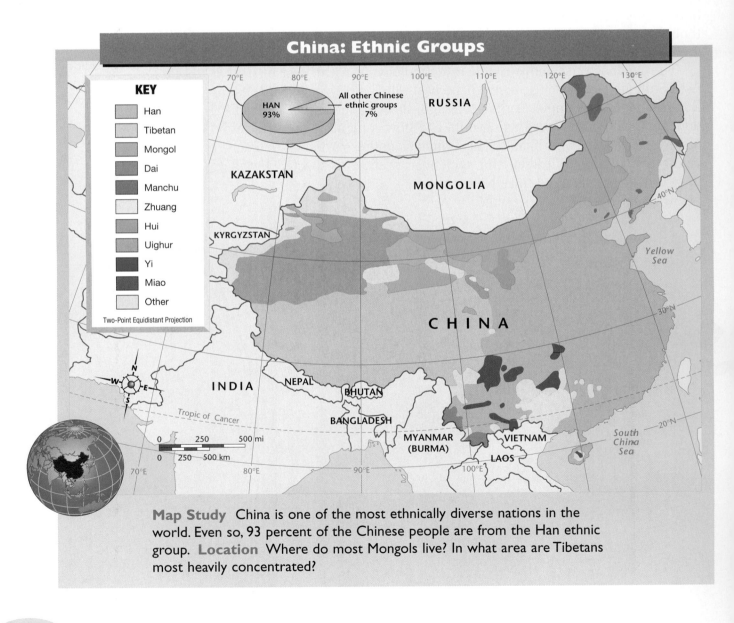

China: Ethnic Groups

KEY: Han, Tibetan, Mongol, Dai, Manchu, Zhuang, Hui, Uighur, Yi, Miao, Other

Two-Point Equidistant Projection

HAN 93%; All other Chinese ethnic groups 7%

RUSSIA, KAZAKSTAN, MONGOLIA, KYRGYZSTAN, CHINA, INDIA, NEPAL, BHUTAN, BANGLADESH, MYANMAR (BURMA), VIETNAM, LAOS, Yellow Sea, South China Sea, Tropic of Cancer

0–250–500 mi; 0–250–500 km

Map Study China is one of the most ethnically diverse nations in the world. Even so, 93 percent of the Chinese people are from the Han ethnic group. **Location** Where do most Mongols live? In what area are Tibetans most heavily concentrated?

The Country in the City

Chen Di
age 12
China

This painting shows a country scene in the city. **Critical Thinking** How do you think the student artist feels about the countryside? Why?

They move from place to place in search of water and grazing for their herds. Over centuries, these groups lost their separate traditions. They formed one **homogeneous** (hoh muh JEE nee us) group. That is, the group's members were very similar. Today, even with the division of Korea into two countries, the population is quite homogeneous. There are few minority groups.

Because it cut itself off from the world for a long time, Japan has one of the most homogeneous populations on the Earth. Nearly all of the people belong to the same **ethnic group,** a group that shares language, religion, and cultural traditions. Minority groups are few. One notable minority group is the Ainu (EYE noo), who may have been Japan's first inhabitants. Small numbers of Koreans and Chinese also live in Japan. However, Japan has strict rules on immigration. It is hard for anyone who is not Japanese by birth to become a citizen.

1. **Define** (a) commune, (b) dialect, (c) nomad, (d) homogeneous, (e) ethnic group.
2. How does East Asia reflect past and present traditions?
3. Why are the populations of Korea and Japan homogeneous?

Critical Thinking

4. **Recognizing Cause and Effect** Why do you think the Communists wanted to slow China's population growth?

Activity

5. **Writing to Learn** You want to make your permanent home in Japan. Write a letter to the Japanese government, asking officials to allow you to do so. Make your letter persuasive by pointing out all of the ways in which the country interests you.

China

Transforming Itself

Reach Into Your Background
Think about the ways in which your community has changed during your lifetime. What new highways and buildings have been built? Are there new places for entertainment? Is there more traffic today? List all of the changes you know about in your community.

Questions to Explore

1. How has communism changed the lives of many Chinese?
2. What steps has China recently taken to improve its economy?

Key Terms
radical
free enterprise

Key People and Places
Mao Zedong
Red Guard
Taiwan

▼ China's streets are no longer packed with bicycles. In modern Shanghai, throngs of walkers share the streets with buses and other motor vehicles.

Visiting China in the early 1980s, an American doctor named Jay Arena made the following comments:

> "Bicycles . . . bicycles . . . bicycles . . . 200 million of them (one out of every five Chinese owns one). Plain clothes . . . no jewelry . . . only stainless steel wristwatches. Courtesy . . . reasonable happiness . . . discipline; a relaxed people. Cities without pet cats, dogs, birds (keeping them is against the law). . . . Respect and affection for old people. . . ."

If you visited China today, you might share some of Dr. Arena's experiences. But you would also notice some changes.

During the early 1980s, for example, the streets of large cities were fairly quiet. Most people traveled by bicycle or bus. At this time, the total number of vehicles in all of China was 100,000. In 2000, over 11 million cars, buses, and trucks crowded the streets of major cities. When Dr. Arena visited China, few houses had running water or flush toilets. Today, China's major cities have high-rise apartment and office buildings. New roads connect rural areas to the cities. Change is speeding up as China works to become an industrial nation.

Tradition and Change

When the Communists took power in 1949 and formed the People's Republic of China, they had few friends among the major nations of the world. The United States had backed the Nationalists. The Soviet Union had been on the Communists' side, but later withdrew its support. The two nations disagreed about how a communist society should be run.

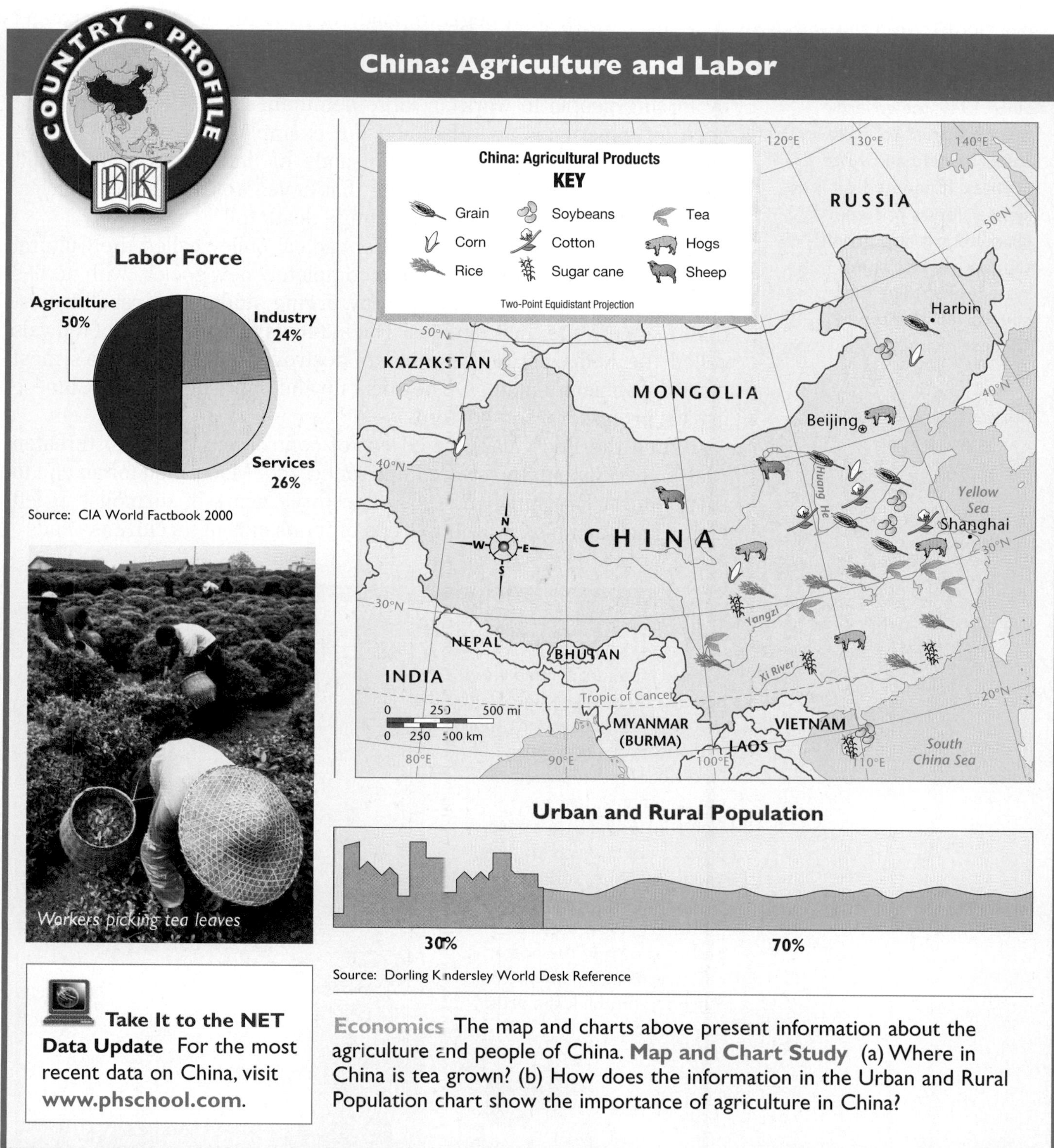

Workers picking tea leaves

Take It to the NET
Data Update For the most recent data on China, visit **www.phschool.com.**

Economics The map and charts above present information about the agriculture and people of China. **Map and Chart Study** (a) Where in China is tea grown? (b) How does the information in the Urban and Rural Population chart show the importance of agriculture in China?

Writing Chinese To write their language, the Chinese use characters, or symbols. Each one is a word or part of a word. To read and write, people must learn thousands of characters. Since 1949, the government has tried to make it easier to read and write Chinese. It adopted simpler forms of some characters. It also promoted the use of *pinyin*, a system of spelling the sounds represented by Chinese characters.

Huge problems faced the Communists when they took control. China had not had peace for almost a century. Most Chinese were extremely poor. Their methods of farming and manufacturing used few machines.

Under the leadership of Mao Zedong (mow zuh dung), China made huge changes. The government seized land from large landowners. In the cities, the government seized all factories and businesses. But Mao was not satisfied. Economic growth was too slow.

In the 1950s, Mao began a policy of **radical,** or extreme, change. This policy, called the "Great Leap Forward," turned out to be a giant step backward. The Communists rushed to increase production by forcing people to work on large communes. But they ignored the need for experience and planning. For example, they ordered a huge increase in steel production. Thousands of untrained workers built backyard furnaces for steel-making that never worked. Mao's policies, and natural disasters, resulted in a huge death toll.

In 1966, Mao introduced another radical policy called the Cultural Revolution. His aim was to create a completely new society with no ties to the past. He began the process by urging students to rebel against their teachers and their families. The students formed bands of radicals called the Red Guard. These bands destroyed some of China's most beautiful ancient buildings. They beat up and imprisoned many Chinese artists, professors, and doctors.

When the Red Guard raged out of control and began to threaten Mao's government, they were imprisoned, too. Mao called for an end to the Cultural Revolution in 1969. The three years of turmoil had left China in a shambles, with hundreds of thousands of its citizens dead.

China's Communist Takeover

"Under Mao's leadership, the people of the valleys and mountains." These words top a poster showing an image of Mao Zedong that celebrates the communist takeover of China in 1949. The purpose of posters like this was to make people feel a part of the revolution. **Critical Thinking** How are the people shown in the poster different from one another? Why do you think the artist made them different?

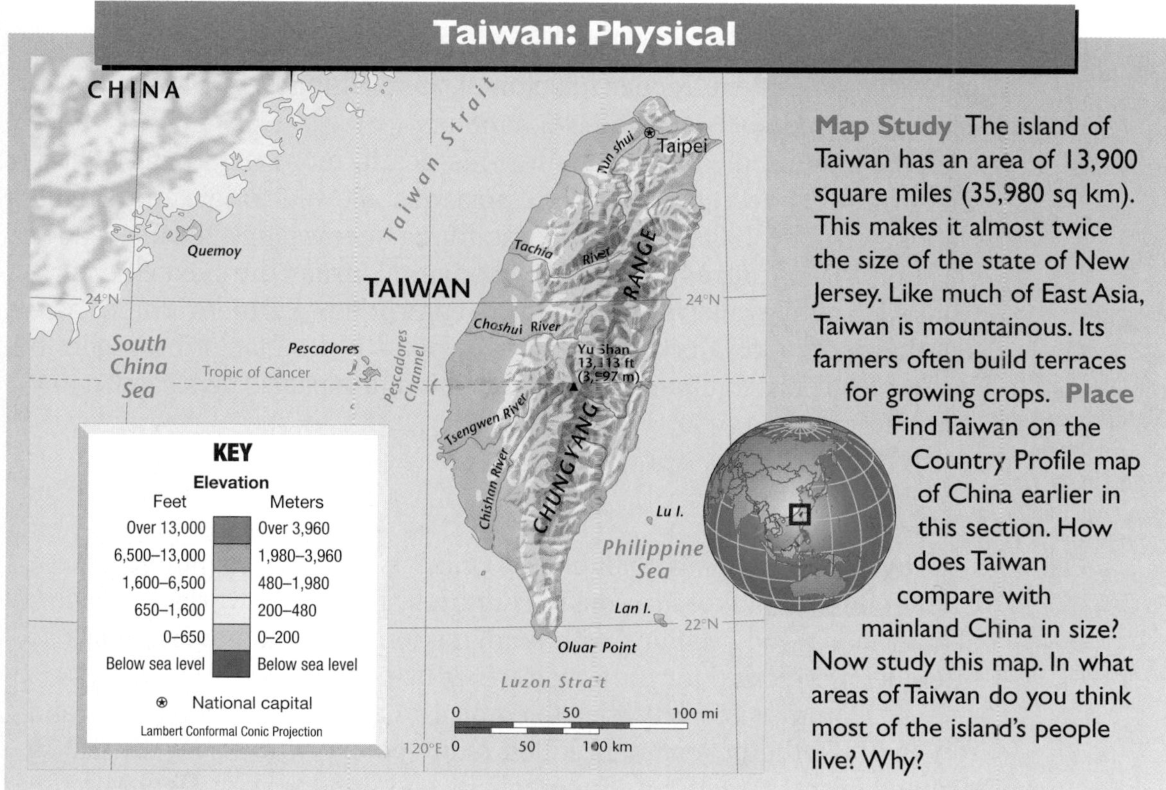

Map Study The island of Taiwan has an area of 13,900 square miles (35,980 sq km). This makes it almost twice the size of the state of New Jersey. Like much of East Asia, Taiwan is mountainous. Its farmers often build terraces for growing crops. **Place** Find Taiwan on the Country Profile map of China earlier in this section. How does Taiwan compare with mainland China in size? Now study this map. In what areas of Taiwan do you think most of the island's people live? Why?

The Growth of Taiwan

After their defeat by the Communists in 1949, the Nationalists fled to Taiwan, an island 100 miles (161 km) off mainland China's southeast coast. They formed a new government called the Republic of China.

The Nationalists followed **free enterprise.** Under this economic system, people choose their own jobs, start private businesses, and can make a profit. Even in the 1950s, Taiwan's free enterprise economy was one of Asia's strongest. The Chinese on Taiwan started programs that increased farm output and brought in more money. This money helped Taiwan build new ports and railroads.

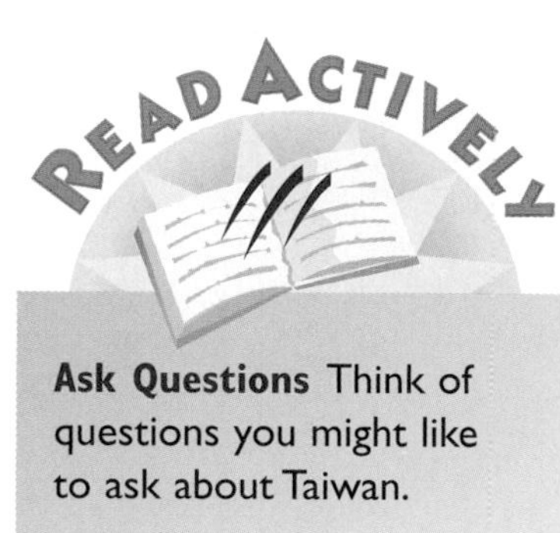

Ask Questions Think of questions you might like to ask about Taiwan.

Taiwan also had the support of foreign countries. Both Taiwan and China claimed to be the "real" China. China said that Taiwan was its province. Taiwan said China was its province. At first, the United States and other western countries supported Taiwan. Taiwan sold computers and other electronic products to the rest of the world. Taiwan's economy grew dramatically. The quality of life greatly improved for its people.

China Faces Its Challenges

Meanwhile, many western countries refused to trade with China. At the same time some of Mao's policies, as you read, hurt the country. During the late 1970s, the Communists realized that they needed new policies in order to secure China's place in the world.

First, China began repairing relations with the West. In 1972, American President Richard Nixon visited China. This historic trip opened up trade between the two nations.

Mao Zedong died in 1976. After his death, more moderate leaders gained power in China. In 1978, China was allowed to join the United Nations. Around 1980, Deng Xiaoping (dung sheow ping) became leader of China. Deng introduced many changes. During the next 20 years, China gradually allowed some free enterprise. Farmers could now sell their crops for a profit. Privately owned Chinese factories began to make electronic equipment, clothes, computer parts, toys, and many other products.

China Today

Today, the People's Republic of China is a major economic power. The products it makes are sold to countries all over the world. China has also formed good relations with many nations. Yet the government has often been criticized for the way it treats its people.

The Communist Party tries to control what Chinese people read and say. In 1989, the government killed many people who had gathered to demand greater freedoms. Such policies did not end with Deng's death in 1997. China's new leader, Jiang Zemin (zhang zuh min), followed Deng's lead in maintaining strict control over the Chinese people. However, the Internet and media make it hard to keep information from the Chinese people.

Many nations question how they should treat a country with such a poor human rights record. Still, most of them continue to remain trade partners with China. China's population makes it a huge market for goods, and China manufactures many items for other countries. In 2001, Beijing was chosen as the site of the 2008 Summer Olympics. People from all over the world will be there to see how China is facing its recent challenges.

1. **Define** (a) radical, (b) free enterprise.
2. **Identify** (a) Mao Zedong, (b) Red Guard, (c) Taiwan.
3. How did early communist policies affect the people of China?
4. In what ways has China's economy changed in recent years?

Critical Thinking

5. **Making Comparisons** Explain the similarities and differences between China today and China under Mao Zedong.

Activity

6. **Writing to Learn** Write a letter giving economic advice to a developing nation. Use what you have learned about China to suggest ways for the country to build a strong economy.

Japan

TRADITION AND CHANGE

Reach Into Your Background

What should a person think about when looking for a job? What makes a good job? Jot down some answers to these questions. Then compare your ideas with what you learn about working in Japan.

Questions to Explore

1. How did Japan become one of the most successful developed nations in the world?
2. How does modern culture exist side by side with traditional culture in Japan?

Key Terms

robot
subsidize
recession
discrimination

Employees of one Japanese electronics company gather each morning to sing the company song:

> "Sending our goods to the people of the world
> Endlessly and continuously,
> Like water gushing from a fountain.
> Grow, industry, grow, grow, grow!"

A Japanese car company hands out a weekly newsletter that includes pep talks to help its employees work more efficiently. In one year, workers cut the time it took to put together some car parts from 90 seconds to 45. At first, a packing task took workers an hour. Three years later, it took only 12 minutes.

A company that makes **robots,** computer-driven machines that do tasks once done by humans, holds an Idea Olympics each year. Employees compete in thinking up ideas to improve the company. Nearly half of the employees work on these ideas on their own time.

▼ Workers in neat uniforms exercise in unison at a seafood plant. The Japanese believe that such group activities make workers more productive.

COUNTRY • PROFILE

DK

Japan: Land Use and the Economy

Labor Force

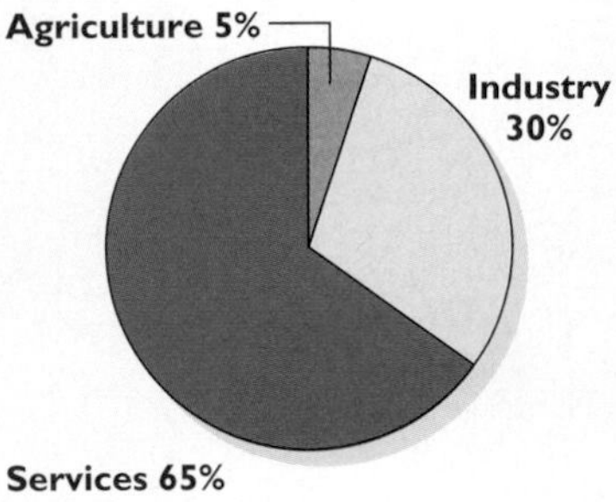

Agriculture 5%

Industry 30%

Services 65%

Source: CIA World Factbook 2000

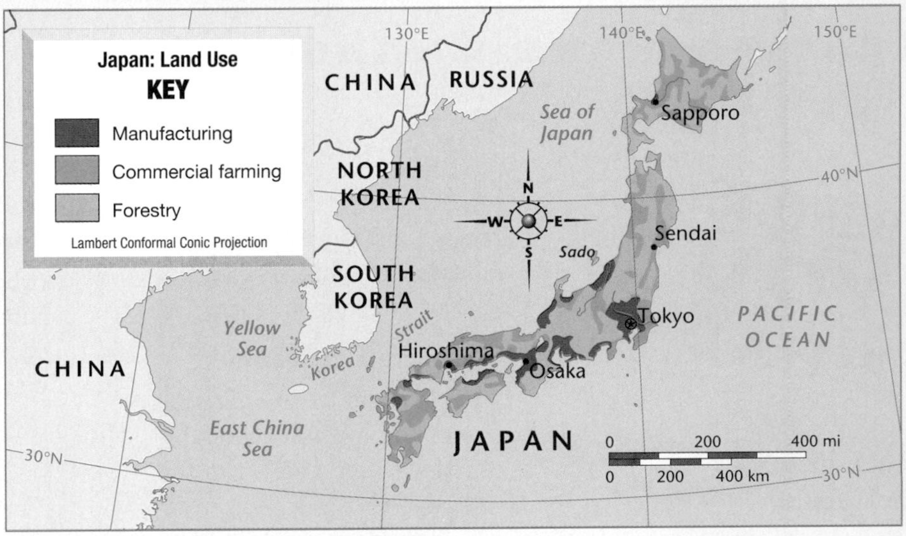

Japan: Land Use

KEY

- Manufacturing
- Commercial farming
- Forestry

Lambert Conformal Conic Projection

130°E 140°E 150°E 40°N 30°N

CHINA RUSSIA Sea of Japan Sapporo NORTH KOREA Sendai Sado SOUTH KOREA Tokyo PACIFIC OCEAN Yellow Sea Korea Strait Hiroshima Osaka CHINA East China Sea JAPAN

0 200 400 mi
0 200 400 km

Automobile factory in Japan

Income from Top Exports, 2000

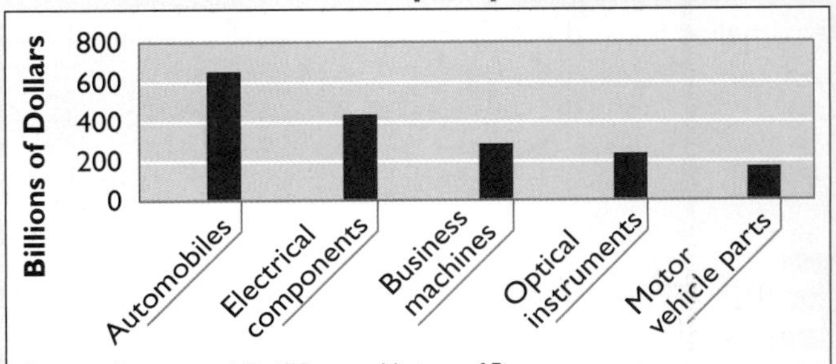

Billions of Dollars: 800, 600, 400, 200, 0

Automobiles; Electrical components; Business machines; Optical instruments; Motor vehicle parts

Source: Customs and Tariff Bureau, Ministry of Finance

Economics The map and charts above present information about the land use and economy of Japan. **Map and Chart Study** (a) How is the land used on Japan's coast? How is the land used in Japan's interior? (b) What is Japan's top export?

Take It to the NET

Data Update For the most recent data on Japan, visit **www.phschool.com**.

Economic Ups and Downs

Some of Japan's ideas have come from outside the nation. Japan has long been known for adopting ideas from other nations and improving them. Once Japan finally opened its ports to other countries in the 1800s, it welcomed new ideas and inventions from the West. For years, the Japanese worked to build major industries. By the 1920s, Japan had become an important manufacturing country. Its economy depended on importing natural resources and exporting manufactured goods.

World War II and Beyond After World War II, Japan was in ruins. Only a few factories were still running. They made shoes from scraps of wood, and kitchen pots and pans from soldiers' steel helmets. The idea that the Japanese might soon be able to compete with the industrial giants of the West seemed impossible.

Tiny Computer Chips

In recent years, Japan has become a leader in computer technology. Here, a manager of a Japanese computer company displays dynamic random access memory, or DRAM, chips. These tiny chips, which measure about 0.5 inches (1 cm) by 0.75 inches (2 cm), are the "brains" of a computer. **Critical Thinking** How did the Japanese government help computer technology and other industries to grow?

Financial aid from the United States helped to rebuild industry. But the main reason Japan became a prosperous industrial nation was its ability to change and grow. The Japanese government helped industries by **subsidizing,** or economically supporting, them. This allowed companies to build large factories and buy modern machines. With more goods to sell, manufacturers could earn more money. Workers also earned more money, so they were able to spend more. This raised the demand for Japanese goods within Japan itself.

Visualize Picture what an industrial robot might be like. What are some tasks it could do?

Since the 1960s, Japan has produced some of the world's most modern industrial robots. By the 1970s, the Japanese were making more watches and cameras than the Swiss and the Germans. By the 1980s, Japan made and sold a large share of the world's cars, electronic goods, skiing gear, and bicycles. Japan also produced huge amounts of steel, ships, televisions, and CDs.

Japan continued to improve on existing products. For example, the pocket calculator was invented in Britain. But the Japanese created better models. In addition, they had some new ideas of their own. You are probably familiar with personal stereos and small, hand-held electronic games. These were invented by the Japanese.

Success Brings Challenges By the 1980s, Japan had one of the world's largest and strongest economies. Japan was so wealthy that it loaned huge amounts of money to other countries. It also led the world in giving aid to developing nations.

Japan's economy depended on exports of its products to the rest of the world. Americans and Europeans eagerly bought Japanese products—particularly cars, television sets, and electronics. Yet Japanese people themselves did not buy many imported goods. Many of

Tiny Trees *Bonsai,* the art of growing trees in pots, is an old tradition in Japan. The goal is to create a small, natural-looking tree 2 inches (5 cm) to 36 inches (91 cm) high. The trees are not naturally small. Growers keep trees tiny by trimming branches and roots. They also bend and wire the branches for a natural look.

them worked too hard to want to spend money in their free time. Also, they preferred to save as much money as they could, which the government had encouraged in the past.

Other countries grew angry because though they bought many Japanese products, the Japanese did not buy theirs. This led to poor trade relations between Japan and other countries. On top of that, in the early 1990s the Japanese economy suffered a severe **recession.** A recession is when an economy and the businesses that support it slow down.

To overcome the recession, companies began laying off their employees. Unemployment in Japan rose. This had some long-term effects on workers. While companies used to hire workers for life, now they hired them only on a temporary basis. In the past, people were given special benefits just for being with a company for a long time. After the recession, many companies only gave benefits to those who they felt performed their jobs the best.

Japan still has one of the strongest economies in the world. As it has done in the past, it is likely to develop new ideas about how to stay strong in the face of its challenges.

The Modern and the Traditional

As elsewhere in East Asia, traditions are important in Japan. Times are changing, but change comes slowly. The role of women is one example. As in the past, being married is the most acceptable position for a Japanese woman. Large companies often have marriage bureaus to introduce their single employees.

School Outing

Like American schoolchildren, these Japanese students enjoy clowning for the camera. Unlike most U.S. students, though, they are dressed in school uniforms. **Critical Thinking** What purpose do you think school uniforms serve?

Japan's hard-working wives and mothers support the economy. Japanese women are in charge of their households. They make housing and schooling decisions, handle the family finances, and take care of major purchases.

Japanese women often work before marriage. In the past, many worked in rice fields, fisheries, and factories, or as nurses or teachers. Today, though, some married women are venturing outside the home in a new direction—as part-time workers.

In the 1980s, the largest group of working women in Japan was the army of "office ladies." They served tea, did light cleaning, held doors, and answered the phone. Today, office ladies are rare. Instead, young graduates who want to work for a few years until they marry and middle-aged women with grown children are crowding the workplace. Often, these women work long hours beside male workers—who get higher salaries and good benefits.

At present, few women become managers in Japanese businesses. Even when they do, they may meet with job **discrimination,** or unequal treatment. For this reason, many young women are not willing to join Japanese firms. Instead, they look for jobs with foreign businesses in Japan. They are also finding jobs in newer fields where there is less discrimination.

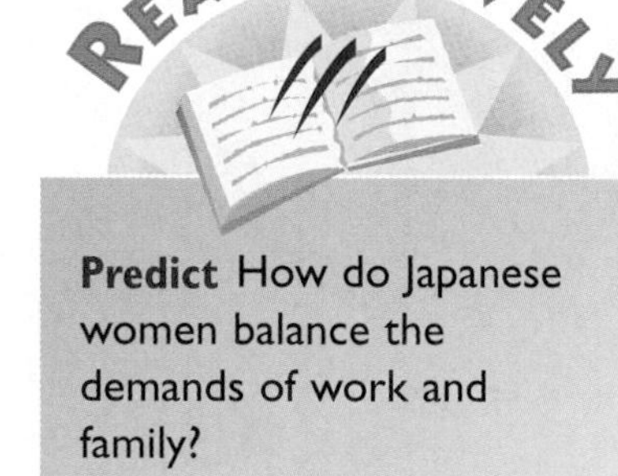

Predict How do Japanese women balance the demands of work and family?

▼ Employees of an American computer firm discuss a technical problem at the company's Japan headquarters.

1. **Define** (a) robot, (b) subsidize, (c) recession, (d) discrimination.
2. What are some reasons for Japan's economic success and for its recent economic downturn?
3. How do the roles played by women illustrate how tradition and change affect Japan today?

Critical Thinking

4. **Drawing Conclusions** How do you think the post-recession changes to hiring practices and benefits affected Japanese workers?

Activity

5. **Writing to Learn** Question several friends or family members about their attitudes toward their jobs. Are they loyal to their employers? Do they feel part of a team? Do they take pride in their work? What incentives do their employers offer? Write a short essay comparing American views with Japanese views.

The Koreas

A Divided Land

Reach Into Your Background
What do you think it would be like to live in a country divided into two parts? Suppose that part of your family lived in the other half and you could not visit or communicate with them. How would you feel?

Questions to Explore

1. How has South Korea become an economic success?
2. Why has North Korea been slower to develop?

Key Terms
diversify
famine

Key Places
Seoul
demilitarized zone

The Korean Peninsula is a tense and divided region. A visitor to South Korea's capital, Seoul (sohl), described that nation's defenses against its northern neighbor this way:

> "If you head south from Seoul in a car, the . . . divider in the highway disappears soon after you leave the city, and for a long stretch, the road is broad and very flat. It becomes, in fact, an emergency airfield by which Seoul could be supplied—or evacuated [emptied]—in the event of war. North of the capital, the highway is marked every few miles by what appear to be overpasses for other highways that were never built. In fact, these massive concrete "bridges" are . . . designed to impede [block] assaulting tanks. In the DMZ, the 155-mile-long buffer zone between North and South Korea, the South Korean Army some time ago discovered three underground tunnels that were built during the past decade by the North Koreans."

▼ South Korean troops patrol a section of the barbed-wire-topped fence that extends along the demilitarized zone. North and South Korea each fear they will be attacked by the other.

DMZ stands for "demilitarized zone." It is a border area between North and South Korea in which no weapons are allowed. The DMZ holds back more than weapons and

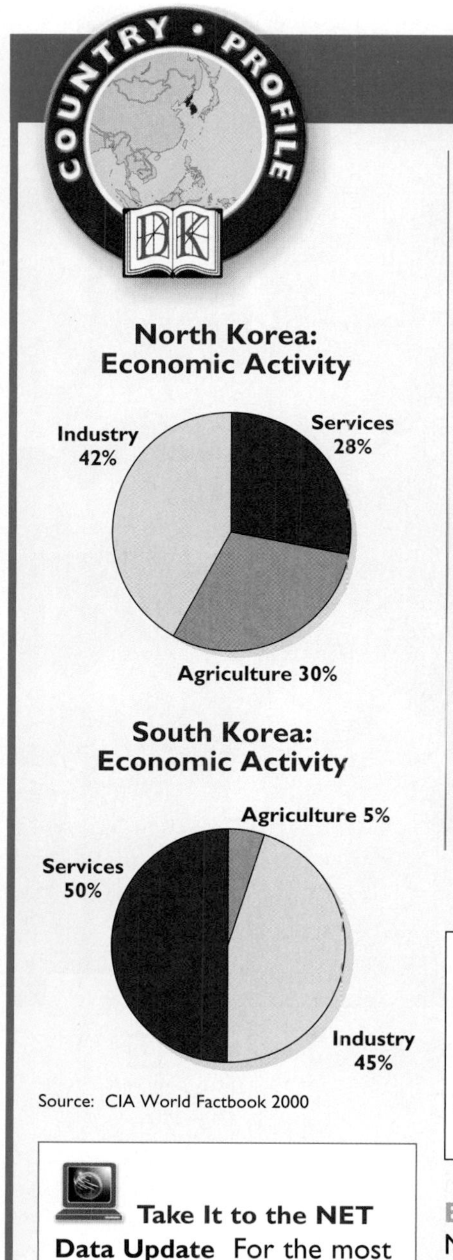

The Koreas: Resources and the Economy

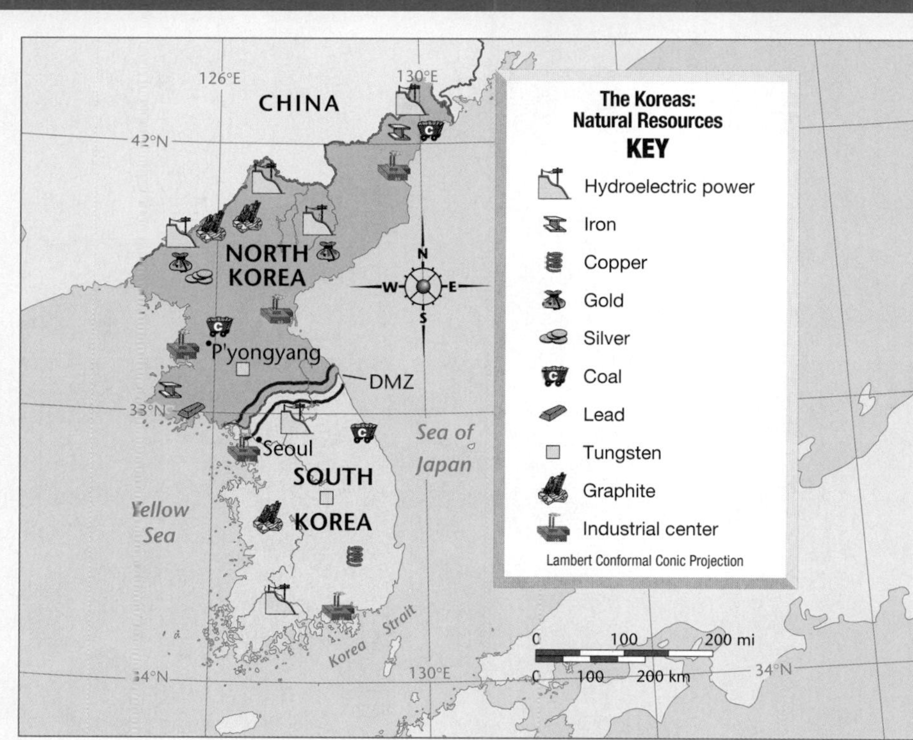

Sources of Electricity

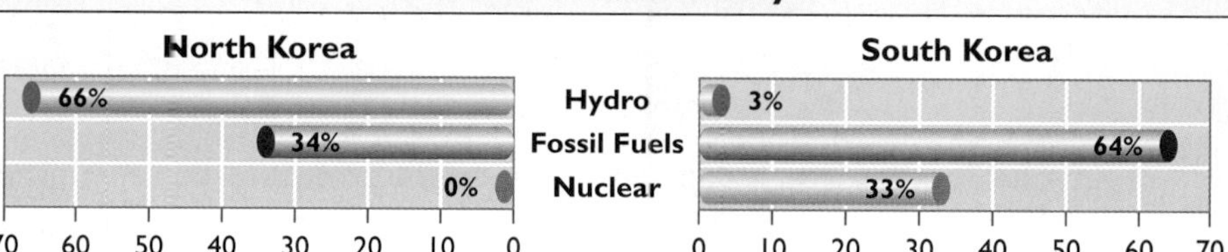

North Korea		South Korea
66%	Hydro	3%
34%	Fossil Fuels	64%
0%	Nuclear	33%

Source: Dorling Kindersley World Desk Reference

Take It to the NET
Data Update For the most recent data on the Koreas, visit **www.phschool.com.**

Economics The map above shows the location of natural resources in North Korea and South Korea. The charts show how these natural resources affect the economy. **Map and Chart Study** (a) Which country has more developed sources of hydroelectric power? (b) Which country has more natural resources?

troops, however. It keeps all people, supplies, and communication from passing between the countries. It also divides two countries that are on very different economic paths.

Economic Growth in South Korea

In the mid-1900s, South Korea had agricultural resources but few industries. A half-century later, South Korea has become a leading economic power. It is one of the world's fastest growing industrial centers.

South Korea is a democracy with an economy based on free enterprise. After World War II, South Korea's factories focused on making

Predict How does South Korea's economy differ from North Korea's economy?

Student Demonstration in Seoul

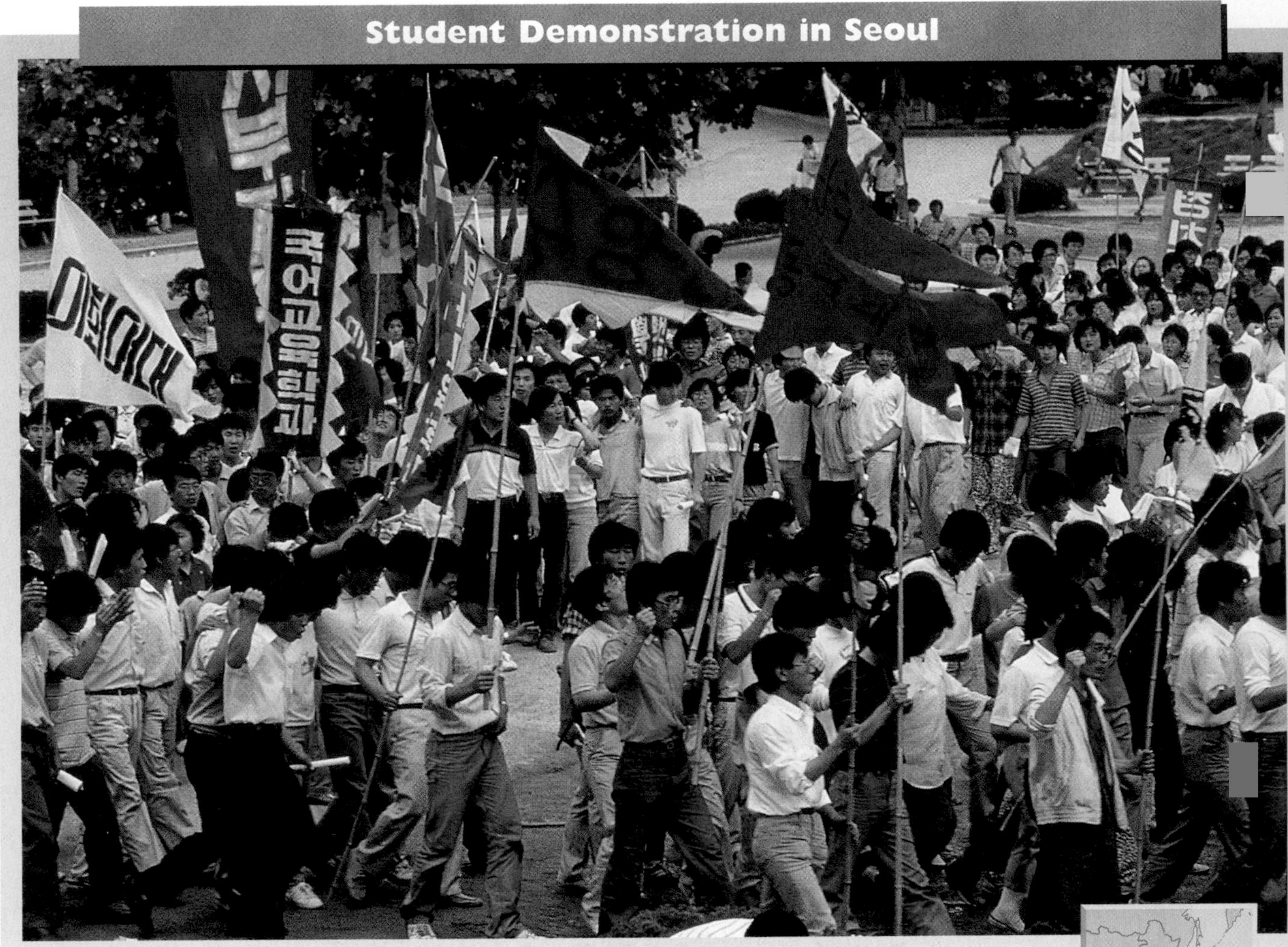

In South Korea, groups often take to the streets to demand higher wages, better working conditions, new government programs, or friendlier relations with North Korea. Here, a group of college students march in such a parade, or demonstration, in Seoul. Sometimes, marchers clash with police. **Critical Thinking** What kinds of slogans do you think might be written on the colorful banners carried by the students?

cloth and processed foods. Later, it developed heavy industry. Today, South Korea is among the world's top shipbuilders. It has a growing electronics industry that exports radios, televisions, and computers. It has large refineries, or factories that process oil. This oil is then used to make plastics, rubber, and other products.

South Korea's change from a farming to an industrial economy has created a building boom. Factories, office and apartment buildings, and roads have sprung up to meet the needs of modern society.

The government of South Korea has focused on industry. But it has also helped farmers. Programs help farmers increase crop production. Other programs improve housing, roads, and water supplies and bring electricity to rural areas.

Despite its successes, South Korea faces a number of challenges. Like Japan, it lacks many natural resources. It must import large amounts of raw materials to keep industry running. Major imports are oil, iron, steel, and chemicals. The cost of living has grown, and wages often cannot keep up.

Peace for the Birds
Korea's DMZ is 2 1/2 miles (4 km) wide. Its north and south edges bristle with barbed wire and explosives. A million soldiers guard it. Yet this hostile area is a peaceful sanctuary for wildlife. The troops on both sides have an unspoken agreement not to disturb the creatures that live or migrate here.

North Korea: Rich in Resources

North Korea is a communist country that has kept itself closed to much of the rest of the world. This has kept out new technology and fresh ideas. Yet North Korea is rich in mineral resources. Until the end of World War II, it was the industrial center of the Korean Peninsula.

Today, however, North Korea cannot compete with South Korea. It still manufactures goods in government-owned factories. These factories produce poor-quality goods. Little has been done to **diversify,** or add variety to, the economy.

Farming methods, too, are outdated in the north. Many farmers burn hillsides to prepare for planting crops. After a few years of this, the good soil can be washed away by rain. Then, the fields can no longer be farmed. In 1995, North Koreans faced **famine,** or a huge food shortage, and starvation. North Korean officials estimated about 220,000 people died from famine between 1995 and 1998. For the first time, North Korea asked noncommunist countries for aid.

In recent years, North Korea and South Korea have taken steps toward improving relations. South Korea provided North Korea with aid to help its northern neighbor overcome its food shortages and economic problems. In June 2000, the leaders of the two countries met in P'yongyang, the capital of North Korea, and agreed to strive for peace and cooperation among the nations. It was the first time leaders of the two nations had met since 1945. Communication between North and South Korea slowed in 2001, but both sides say they will continue peacemaking efforts.

1. **Define** (a) diversify, (b) famine.
2. **Identify** (a) Seoul, (b) demilitarized zone.
3. Discuss the reasons for South Korea's economic success and recent downturn.
4. Why has North Korea's economy lagged behind South Korea's?

Critical Thinking

5. **Making Comparisons** How do the governments of North and South Korea affect their economies?

Activity Journal

6. **Writing to Learn** The division between North and South Korea has cut you off from family members. It has also influenced the way you live. Write a journal entry describing what it is like to live in either North or South Korea.

Reading Route Maps

Tony looked at the clock eagerly. In the last ten minutes of class, Mr. Nelson always held a discussion time, Tony's favorite part of the day.

Mr. Nelson spoke. "Ladies and gentlemen, today we're going to talk about something that has played a great role in the development of civilization. What do you think it is?"

There was silence for a moment as the students thought. "War," said one boy. "Computers," said another. "Books," said the girl behind Tony. After a few minutes, they ran out of ideas.

But then Mr. Nelson said, "What do you think about this one?" He picked up the chalk and wrote one word on the board: *Roads.*

Get Ready

Roads link people together as nothing else does. Roads let people travel to different lands. Roads are the lifeline of trade and the economy. Also, the people who travel on roads carry their ideas and customs with them. How would your life be different in a world without roads?

Roads are shown on route maps. A route is any way that people travel. There are sea routes and air routes. Most routes, however, are roads. To understand history, it helps to understand routes. To understand routes, you need to be able to read a route map.

Try It Out

Reading a route map is simply a matter of reading a map and the routes that are marked on it. Reading a map means reading the title, the key, the scale, the compass rose, and the labels on the map. This helps you understand what the map shows. You then find the routes on the map by following the lines that show them.

Try it out by reading a road map of your own community. Working with a small group, answer these questions:

A. What does the map key show?

B. How are types or sizes of roads shown?

C. What are the main roads that run north and south? East and west?

D. About how long is the longest road in town?

E. Locate your school on the map. What is the most direct route from your school to a major intersection in your community?

Apply the Skill

Now you have practiced with a modern route map of an area close to home. You have all the skills you need to read an ancient route map of an area far away.

The map below shows the Silk Road, which was a collection of trade routes dating from about 300 B.C. This road linked China to the West. Along it, traders carried not only many goods but also many ideas. The road, pictured in the Chinese painting on the opposite page, had a very important effect on the development of cultures and the exchange of ideas. Use the route map of the Silk Road to complete the steps that follow.

1. **Familiarize yourself with the map.** The first step in reading any map is to figure out what it is about. What is the title of the map? In what region of the world was the Silk Road?

2. **Understand what routes are shown.** How is the Silk Road indicated? What was its western end point? What was its eastern end point? Through what major landforms did it pass?

3. **Look at the physical features along the routes.** Along the way, the Silk Road divides and then meets again. What physical feature lies between the divided sections of the road? Why do you think the road divides the way it does? What physical obstacles might have faced the travelers on the Silk Road?

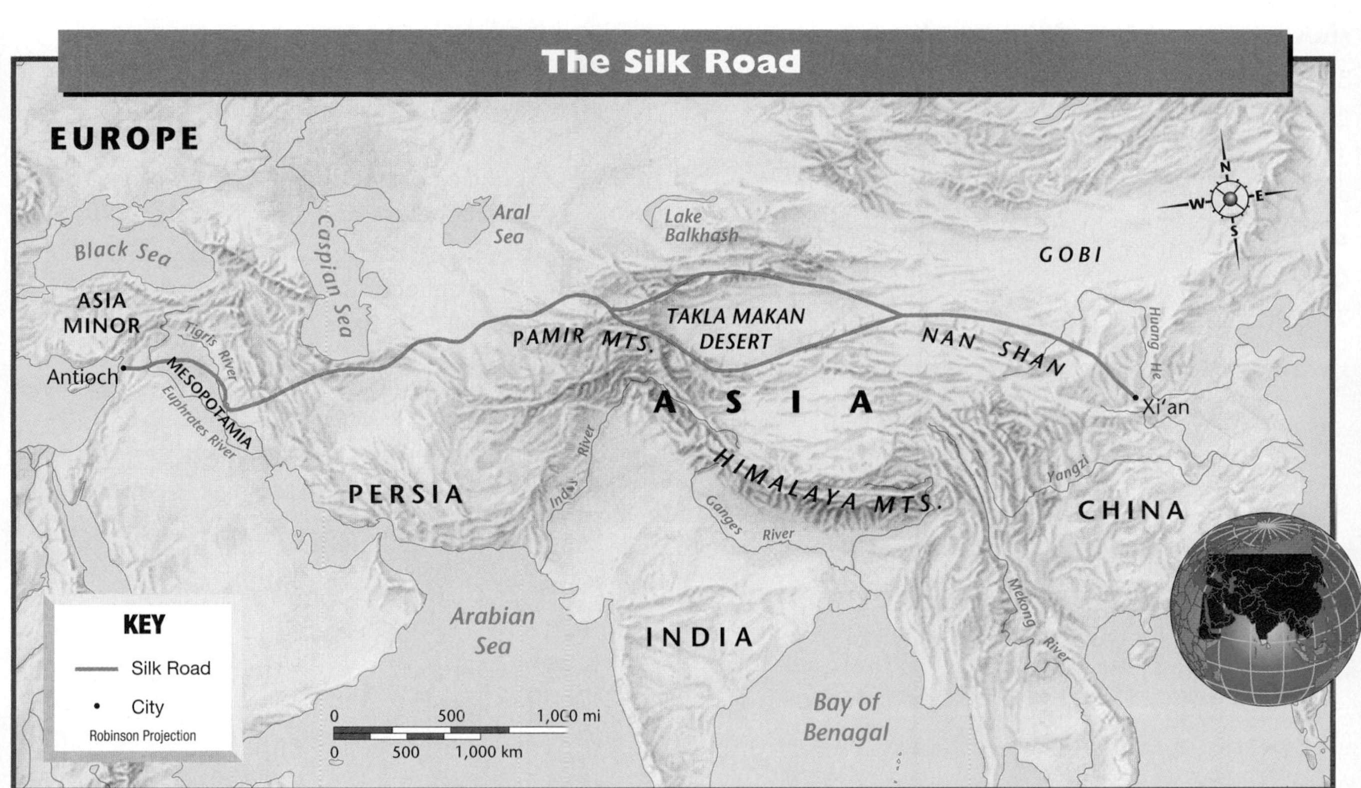

Review and Activities

Reviewing Main Ideas

1. Describe three major achievements of ancient East Asia.
2. In what ways did the West influence East Asia?
3. In what ways do tradition and change exist together in East Asian society?
4. How does China's population differ from the populations of Japan and Korea in terms of ethnic diversity?
5. What economic policies did the Chinese Communists introduce in the 1950s?
6. How did Mao Zedong's policies cause problems for China?
7. What abilities allowed the Japanese to build one of the world's most successful economies?
8. How do modern and traditional cultures exist together in Japan?
9. What economic problems has Japan faced in recent years?
10. Why is North Korea taking much longer than South Korea to improve and modernize its economy?

Reviewing Key Terms

Use each key term below in a sentence that shows the meaning of the term.

1. civilization
2. emperor
3. dynasty
4. migration
5. clan
6. cultural diffusion
7. commune
8. ethnic group
9. dialect
10. radical
11. subsidize
12. recession
13. discrimination
14. diversify

Critical Thinking

1. **Drawing Conclusions** Both ancient China and Japan attempted to isolate themselves from foreign influences. How did this affect both countries?
2. **Making Comparisons** Compare the policies of the communist government of China before and after the late 1970s.
3. **Recognizing Cause and Effect** What effect did Japan's recession of the early 1990s have on the country?

Graphic Organizer

Copy the chart onto a separate sheet of paper. Complete the chart by filling in the blanks.

	People	Type of Government	Type of Economy	Values and Traditions
China				
Japan				
North Korea				
South Korea				

Map Activity

East Asia

For each place listed below, write the letter from the map that shows its location. Use the Atlas in the back of your book to help you.

1. Japan
2. China
3. Taiwan
4. South Korea
5. Hong Kong
6. North Korea

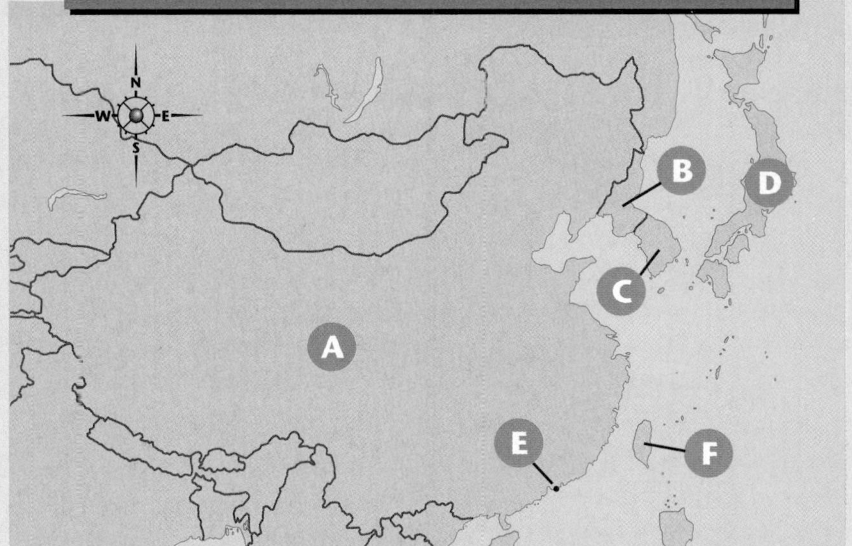

Writing Activity

Writing Sentences

Based on what you have read in this chapter, write five sentences describing how tradition and change exist together in East Asia. Then write five sentences describing how tradition and change exist together in the United States.

Take It to the NET

Activity Learn about the history, culture, and geography of the Korean Peninsula. What is the most interesting fact you learned about Korea? For help in completing this activity, visit **www.phschool.com**.

Chapter 19 Self-Test To review what you have learned, take the Chapter 19 Self-Test and get instant feedback on your answers. Go to **www.phschool.com** to take the test.

Skills Review

Turn to the Skills Activity.

Review the steps for reading route maps. What is the purpose of a route map? Describe the different ways routes or roads can be shown on a route map.

How Am I Doing?

Answer these questions to check your progress.

1. Can I list some of the major cultural developments in East Asia?
2. Can I identify East Asia's many peoples?
3. Do I understand the impact that East Asia's various economies have had on its people?
4. Do I understand how tradition and change exist together in East Asia?
5. What information from this chapter can I include in my journal?

Poems

FROM SOUTH KOREA AND JAPAN

Reach Into Your Background

Think about looking up at the sky when no one else is around. You might see only a tiny cloud in the sunlight. You might hear only a bumblebee buzzing. If you were all alone, you might notice things that are normally very still and quiet.

Nature does not always shout to get your attention. Some poets look and listen in nature for small, still things. When you read these poems, you might think twice about a very simple thing. You might see something lovely or something new that once seemed very ordinary.

Look for still, silent images when you read the following poems by Kwang-kyu Kim from South Korea and by the Japanese poets Hashin and Jōsō.

Questions to Explore

1. What parts of nature are most important in these poems?
2. How do the poems change when you read them aloud?

Loneliness

No sky at all;
no earth at all—and still
the snow flakes fall. . . .

Hashin
Translated by
Harold G. Henderson

Winter

Mountains and plains,
all are captured by snow—
nothing remains.

Jōsō
Translated by
Harold G. Henderson

▲ "View of Mount Haruna Under the Snow," Japanese print, early 1800s.

◀ Mount Fuji, Japanese print, early 1800s.

The Birth of a Stone

In those deep mountain ravines
I wonder if there are stones
that no one has ever visited?
I went up the mountain
in quest of a stone no one had
ever seen
from the remotest of times

Under ancient pines
on steep pathless slopes
there was a stone
I wonder
how long
this stone all thick with moss
has been
here?

Two thousand years? Two
million? Two billion?

No
Not at all
If really till now no one
has ever seen this stone
it is only
here
from now on

This stone
was only born
the moment I first saw it

Kwang-kyu Kim
Translated by
Harold G. Henderson

Ask Questions Where might this poem take place?

Look Back

1. What do the three poems have in common?
2. What questions does the narrator of "The Birth of a Stone" ask about the stone?

Think It Over

3. Explain what the poet of "Winter" means by writing that the mountains and plains are captured by snow.
4. Why do you think the narrator in "Birth of a Stone" wanted to find a stone no one had ever seen?

Go Beyond

5. Think of a place where very few people have ever been. How would you feel if you saw something no one had ever seen?
6. Describe what you think it feels like to be alone in nature.

Ideas for Writing: Poem

7. Spend some time alone outside. You could be in a park, a forest, or any space under the sky. Try to find a place that is quiet, or visit it during a quiet part of the day. Look and listen for things you normally do not notice. Write a poem about what you find.

CHAPTER 20

South and Southeast Asia
Physical Geography

PICTURE ACTIVITIES

This village is built on the Ganges (GAN jeez) River in the country of Bangladesh (bahn gluh DESH). The Ganges River begins in the mountains of India, runs through Bangladesh, and finally empties into the Bay of Bengal. To help you get to know this part of South Asia, do the following.

Write a letter
What would it be like to live in this village? Write a letter to a friend describing your life in this village.

Picture the seasons
Draw pictures of what you think the village would look like during the different seasons of the year. What do you suppose the climate is like in this village? Do you think it snows here? Why or why not?

Land and Water

Reach Into Your Background

Mountains are the most important landform in South Asia. They affect where rain falls—rain that is needed for crops. Think about landforms in your state. Which do you think have the greatest effect on people's lives?

Questions to Explore

1. What are the major landforms of South and Southeast Asia?
2. How do the landforms affect the way people of South and Southeast Asia live?

Key Terms

subcontinent

Key Places

Himalaya Mountains
Ganges River
Indus River
Ring of Fire

Two hundred million years ago, the land now called the Indian **subcontinent** was attached to the east coast of Africa. A subcontinent is a large landmass that is a major part of a continent. Scientists believe that in those times, all of the Earth's continents were joined.

About 200 million years ago, the land shifted and cracked and the continents began to break apart. The Indian subcontinent split off from Africa and crept slowly toward Asia. The landmass moved so slowly that it took about four years to travel the length of an average pencil.

About 40 million years ago, the Indian subcontinent collided with Asia. Just as the front ends of cars crumple in a traffic accident, northern India and southern Asia crumpled where they met. This area is the huge Himalayan Mountain range. The Himalaya Mountains contain the tallest peaks in the world.

▼ A stream fed by melting snow zigzags down through the rugged Himalaya Mountains and across a field of wildflowers in the Lahaul Valley of northern India.

The Indian Subcontinent

The largest nation in South Asia is India. It extends from the Himalaya Mountains down to the narrow tip of the peninsula in the south. Pakistan and Afghanistan (af GAN uh stan) lie to

South Asia: Physical

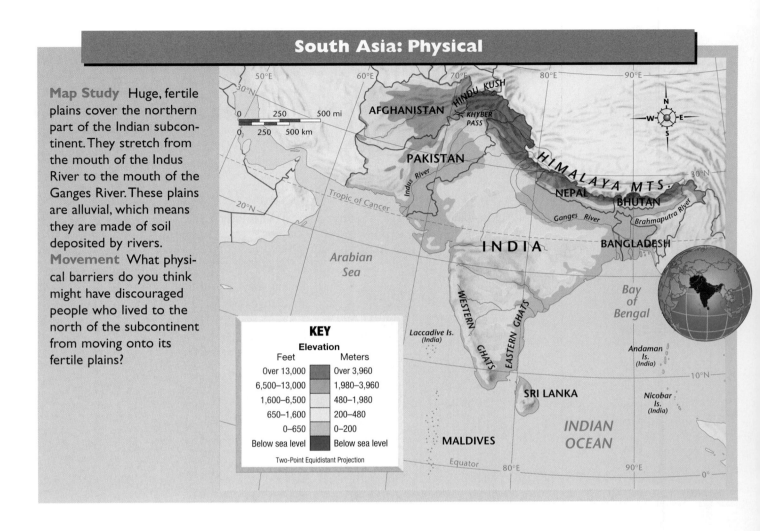

Map Study Huge, fertile plains cover the northern part of the Indian subcontinent. They stretch from the mouth of the Indus River to the mouth of the Ganges River. These plains are alluvial, which means they are made of soil deposited by rivers. **Movement** What physical barriers do you think might have discouraged people who lived to the north of the subcontinent from moving onto its fertile plains?

KEY

Elevation

Feet	Meters
Over 13,000	Over 3,960
6,500–13,000	1,980–3,960
1,600–6,500	480–1,980
650–1,600	200–480
0–650	0–200
Below sea level	Below sea level

Two-Point Equidistant Projection

Predict What effects have the Himalaya Mountains had on the Indian subcontinent?

the west of India. Along India's northern border, the kingdoms of Nepal and Bhutan lie along the slopes of the Himalaya Mountains. To the east sits Bangladesh. The island nations of Sri Lanka (sree LAHN kuh) and the Maldives (MAL dyvz) lie off the southern tip of India.

A Natural Wall The Indian subcontinent has many different landforms and contrasting regions. Perhaps the most dramatic is the Himalayan Mountain range. Find the Himalaya Mountains on the map above. Notice how they form a barrier between South Asia and the rest of the continent.

This huge mountain range stretches some 1,550 miles (2,500 km) from east to west. Mount Everest, the world's tallest mountain, is located in the Himalayas. Everest rises to 29,035 feet (8,850 m). That's about five and a half miles high! Another 30 mountains in the Himalayas soar above 24,000 feet (7,300 m).

As you know, the Himalaya Mountains were formed when two sections of the Earth's crust collided. This collision formed great folds in the Earth's surface. Over time, the movement of these sections has pushed the folds higher and higher. This mountain-building process is still going on today. Scientists estimate that Mount Everest is "growing" about 2 inches (5 cm) each year!

Rivers of Life The mighty Himalaya Mountains provide the subcontinent with one of its most valuable features: life-giving rivers. The two most important rivers in South Asia—the Ganges and the Indus—begin high in the mountains.

The Ganges River flows in a wide sweeping arc across northern India. After turning southward toward the sea, the Ganges is joined by the Brahmaputra (brah muh POO truh) River. They continue their journey through Bangladesh and empty into the Bay of Bengal.

The Indus River gives India its name. It flows westward from the Himalaya Mountains into the country of Pakistan. The lower part of the Indus flows through the hottest and driest part of the Indian subcontinent.

Rivers carry from the mountains the water and minerals necessary for good farming. The plains around the rivers, therefore, are quite fertile. As a result, the plains are heavily populated.

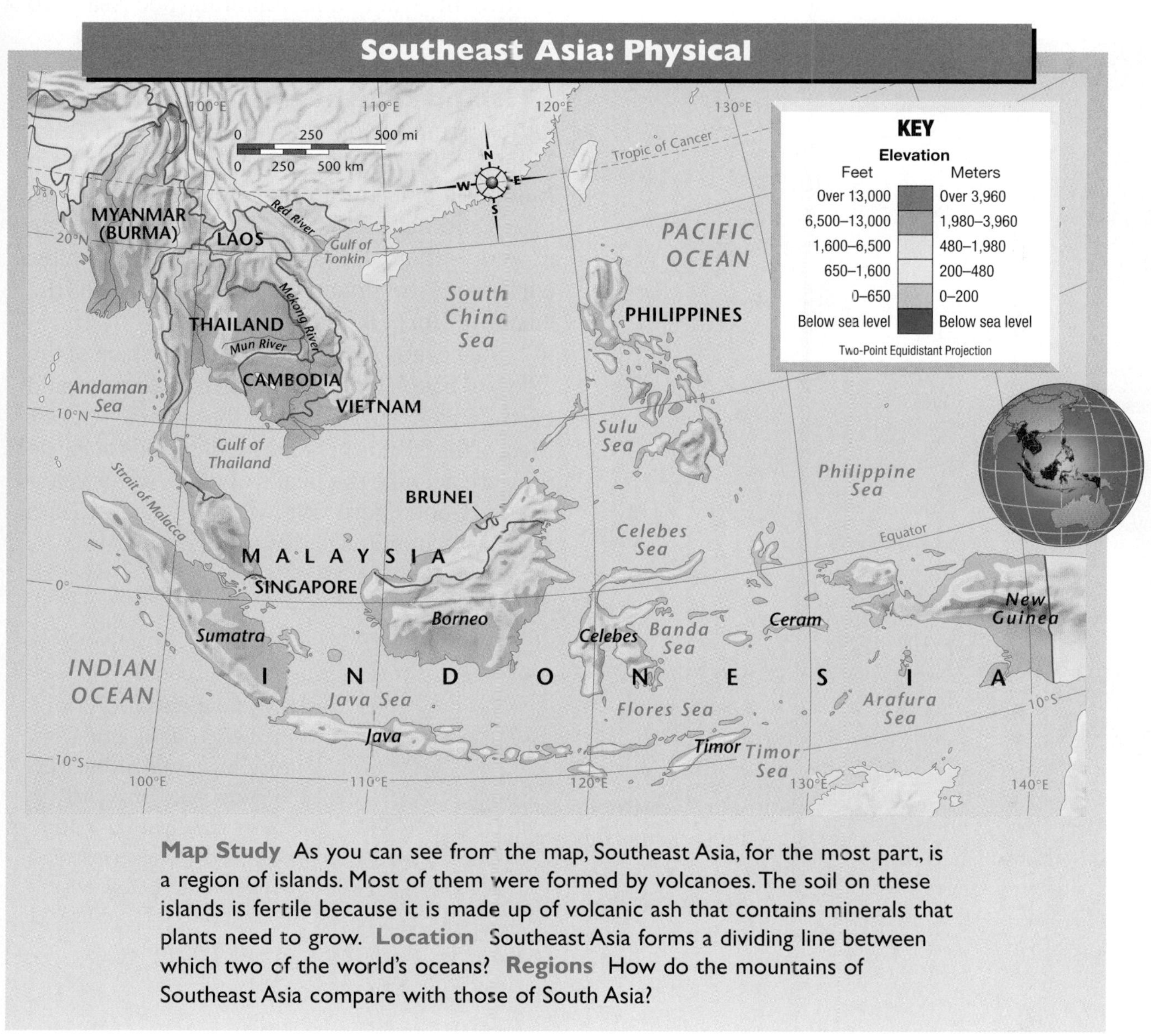

Map Study As you can see from the map, Southeast Asia, for the most part, is a region of islands. Most of them were formed by volcanoes. The soil on these islands is fertile because it is made up of volcanic ash that contains minerals that plants need to grow. **Location** Southeast Asia forms a dividing line between which two of the world's oceans? **Regions** How do the mountains of Southeast Asia compare with those of South Asia?

Southeast Asia

Predict What do you think the Ring of Fire is?

East of the Indian subcontinent and south of China lies the region called Southeast Asia. It is divided into mainland and island areas. The mainland is a giant peninsula that juts south from the main area of Asia. The islands extend east and west between the Indian and the Pacific oceans. Locate the mainland and the islands on the map on the previous page.

Mainland Southeast Asia The nations of mainland Southeast Asia are Vietnam, Cambodia, Laos (LAH ohs), Myanmar (MY ahn mar), Singapore, and Thailand (TY land). Singapore is the smallest of the mainland nations, located at the tip of the Malay Peninsula. The region is about one fifth the size of the United States. Much of this area is covered by forested mountains. The mountains run north and south. Most people live in the narrow river valleys between mountain ranges. Just as on the Indian subcontinent, rivers flow from the north and provide river valleys with the water and minerals necessary to grow crops.

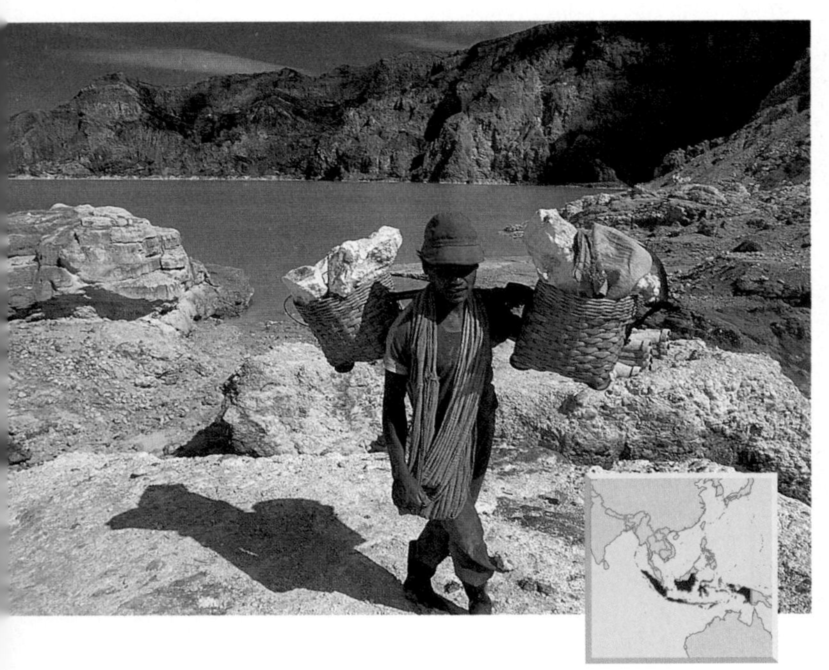

▼ The yellow mineral called sulfur fills the baskets of this Indonesian miner. Sulfur is often produced by volcanic eruptions. It is used in making chemicals.

Island Southeast Asia Four major nations make up island Southeast Asia: Malaysia (muh LAY zhuh), Brunei (broo NY), Indonesia, and the Philippines. The largest of the island nations is Indonesia. It is made up of more than 13,500 islands. Malaysia lies partly on the mainland and partly on the island of Borneo.

The islands of Southeast Asia are part of the "Ring of Fire." This is a region of volcanoes and earthquakes surrounding the Pacific Ocean. Most of the islands here are mountainous because they are actually the peaks of underwater volcanoes. People here live with the fear that a volcanic eruption will destroy their homes.

1. **Define** subcontinent.
2. **Identify** (a) Himalaya Mountains, (b) Ganges River, (c) Indus River, (d) Ring of Fire.
3. What are the main rivers of South Asia?
4. Why are the river valleys of South and Southeast Asia more heavily populated than the mountainous regions?

Critical Thinking

5. **Making Comparisons** List and describe one similarity and one difference between South Asia and Southeast Asia.

Activity

6. **Writing to Learn** Write a two-paragraph description of a television show that focuses on the geography of South and Southeast Asia. Choose one feature, such as rivers, mountains, or islands to write about. Describe the pictures your show might include.

Climate and Vegetation

Reach Into Your Background
How do you feel after it rains for several days in a row? How about after several days of intense heat? South and Southeast Asia have climates that include both of these extremes. Read on to find out how people in the region feel about rain and heat.

Questions to Explore

1. What factors affect climate in South and Southeast Asia?
2. How is vegetation linked to climate in the region?

Key Terms
rain forest

Key Places
Ghat Mountains
Bangladesh
Vietnam

It is a scorching June day in Mumbai (Bombay), India. A hot breeze moves through the city streets like wind blowing from a huge oven. A water vendor pulls a water barrel on a wooden cart. "Water, only one rupee!" he shouts. Selling water, he makes about 40 rupees a day. That is less than $1 in the United States. An average field-worker in India makes only 15 rupees a day—about 30 cents.

Throughout India, schools remain closed. The grass on golf courses outside expensive hotels burns up. Movie theaters have only one show a day to save electricity. Much of India's electricity is produced by the force of fast-moving rivers. When water levels in the rivers fall, there is not enough force to generate power.

The rains brought by the summer monsoons are late again. The monsoons are seasonal winds. They are crucial to the lives of the people of South and Southeast Asia. All of India worries and waits for the first sign of the summer monsoons. If the rains are too late, crops will die and people will go hungry.

▼ Rain and mud are a source of fun for these Indian children. Each summer, they celebrate the return of the life-giving rains.

Predict How do you think monsoons affect the climate of South Asia?

Finally, after several more days, rain starts to fall. Some parts of India receive only a few drops. Other areas are blasted with strong storms and winds. The streets of Mumbai flood during the onslaught. Old buildings collapse.

But in rural parts of India, it is a time of joy and relief. The people here need the summer rains to grow crops. Once the rivers are flowing and the water tanks are full, the constant rain will lose its charm. But for now, people run into the streets and hold out their arms in joy.

The Climates of South Asia

The monsoons are the single most important factor in the climate of South Asia. There are two monsoon seasons. The summer monsoons blow across South Asia from the southwest. During the winter, the winds change direction and blow down from the northeast. Look at the land use and monsoons map in the Activity Atlas and note the directions of the monsoon winds.

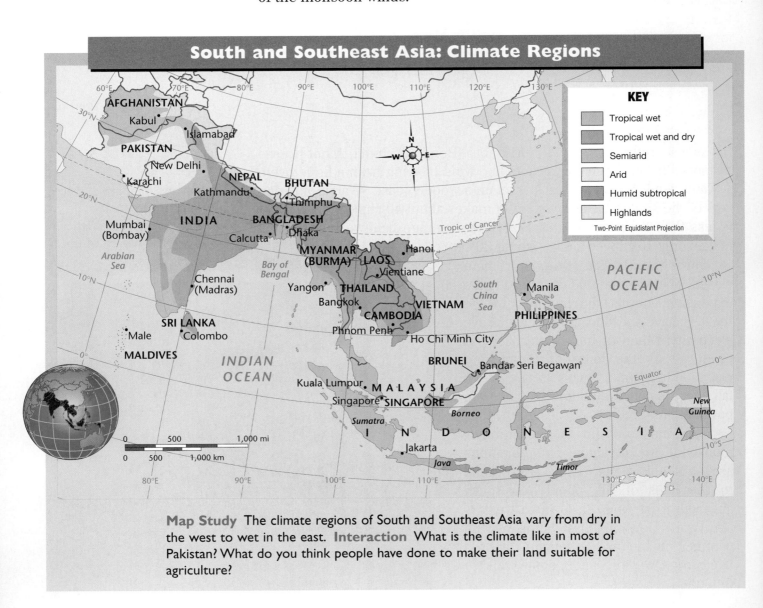

South and Southeast Asia: Climate Regions

Map Study The climate regions of South and Southeast Asia vary from dry in the west to wet in the east. **Interaction** What is the climate like in most of Pakistan? What do you think people have done to make their land suitable for agriculture?

The Summer Monsoons From June to early October, steady winds blow air over the surface of the Arabian Sea and the Indian Ocean. This air picks up a great deal of moisture. Then, it passes over the hot land along the western tip of India and Sri Lanka. The change in temperature makes the air lose its moisture in the form of rain. As the air climbs up over the Ghat (gaht) Mountains, it loses even more moisture. By the time the air gets to the other side of the mountains, it has lost most of its moisture.

As the first heavy rains start falling near the coastline, the coastal lands cool down somewhat. So when the next moisture-filled air mass is blown in from the sea, it travels a little further inland before losing its supply of moisture as rain. In this way, the monsoon rains work their way inland until they finally reach the Himalaya Mountains. Just as the air traveling over southern India loses its moisture as it goes over the mountains, so, too, does the air that reaches the Himalaya Mountains. In fact, the southern mountain slopes of the country of Bhutan are drenched. They get as much as 300 inches (762 cm) of rain every summer.

Mumbai—A Monsoon City

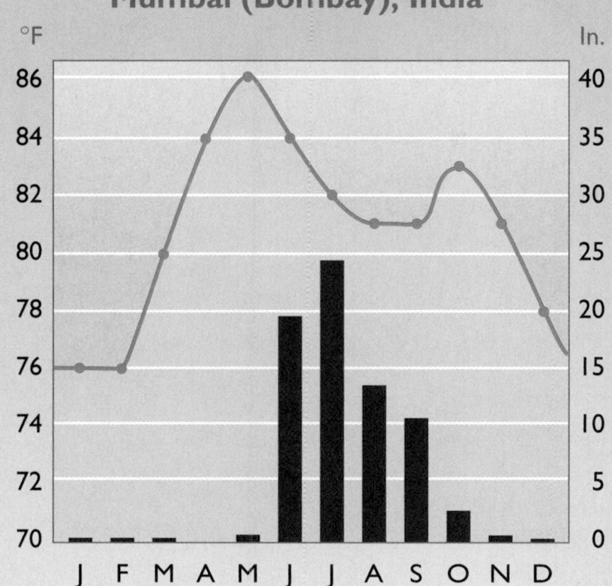

Chart Study This climate graph shows the average monthly temperature and precipitation for Mumbai (Bombay), a city on India's west coast. As you can see on the graph, heavy rainfall occurs in June. This marks the beginning of the summer monsoons. **Critical Thinking** What effect do the summer monsoon winds have on the temperature in Mumbai?

The Winter Monsoons During the winter months in Asia, the monsoons change direction, and winds blow down from the frigid northeast. These winds move dry, cold air toward South Asia. But most of the bitter cold never gets there. The mighty Himalaya Mountains block the cold air. The nations of South Asia are spared. They enjoy dry weather, with temperatures averaging 70°F (21°C).

People and Monsoons The monsoon rains in Asia provide water for half the world's population. But the monsoons affect life in South Asia in other ways as well. In India, students start school in June, after the first rains have fallen. Their long vacation comes during the spring, when hot, stifling temperatures make it hard to concentrate on schoolwork.

In the country of Nepal, fierce monsoon rains can bring mudslides that destroy entire villages. The mud comes from hills that have been

India's Salt Lake During the hot months, the 90-square-mile (230-sq-km) Sambhar Lake in northwestern India is dry. Oddly, during this time the lake bed looks as though it is covered in snow. The white blanket is not snow but a sheet of salt. This salt supply was harvested as far back as the 1500s. It is an important resource for the region even today.

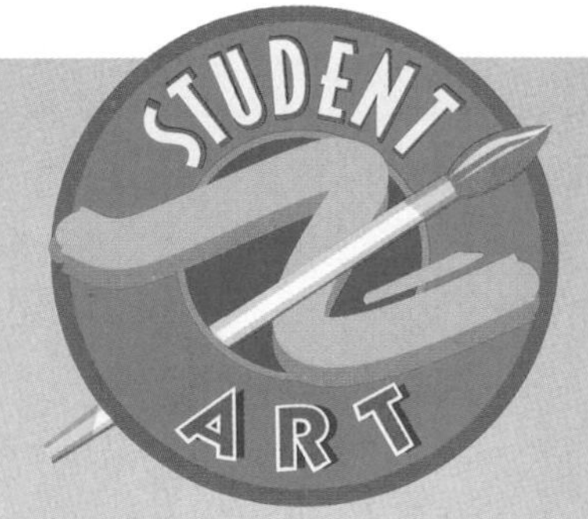

Amita
age 11
India

This park in an Indian city provides a green and pleasant place for many activities. **Critical Thinking** How does this park scene compare with what you might see in a park in the area where you live?

Visualize Visualize rain pouring onto a bare dirt hillside. What do you think happens to such a hill if it rains a long time?

stripped of their trees. Trees keep soil from washing away during heavy rains. Many were cut down to create land for a growing population. Whole hillsides may wash away during rainstorms. In Bangladesh, swollen rivers overflow and flood two thirds of the land. In some years, crops and homes are destroyed and many people lose their lives. To protect against the floods, whole villages in Bangladesh are built on stilts.

The Climates and Vegetation of Southeast Asia

Look at the climate map of South and Southeast Asia at the beginning of this section. Notice that the climate regions in mainland Southeast Asia between Myanmar and Vietnam are similar to those in South Asia. On the west coast of Myanmar, there is a tropical wet climate, just as on the west coast of India. As you move east, the climate changes to tropical wet and dry, and then becomes humid subtropical.

However, when you get to the east coast of Vietnam, the pattern changes. The climate becomes tropical wet. It supports tropical **rain forests**—thick forests that receive at least 60 inches (152 cm) of rain a year. How is this possible? Don't the rains of the summer monsoons come from the southwest? Doesn't most of the summer rain fall on Myanmar?

Vietnam owes its lush coastal rain forest to the winter monsoons. As you already know, winds blow from the northeast during the winter in Asia. As the winter winds blow south from China toward Vietnam, they cross the South China Sea. The air picks up moisture, which it dumps as rain when it hits the coast of Vietnam. The Philippines and much of Indonesia also experience rainy seasons during the winter.

A Green World

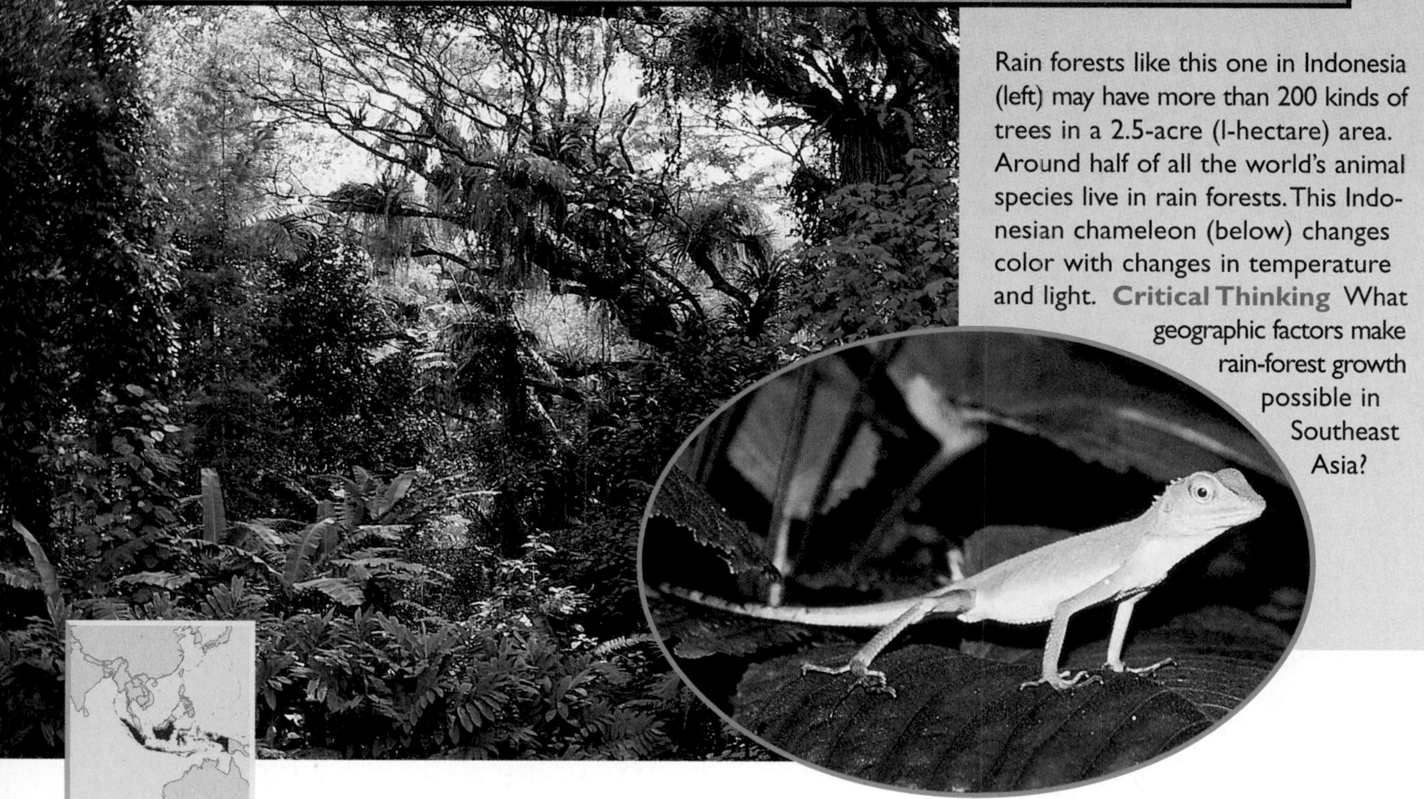

Rain forests like this one in Indonesia (left) may have more than 200 kinds of trees in a 2.5-acre (1-hectare) area. Around half of all the world's animal species live in rain forests. This Indonesian chameleon (below) changes color with changes in temperature and light. **Critical Thinking** What geographic factors make rain-forest growth possible in Southeast Asia?

As you can see on the climate map, much of Southeast Asia has a tropical wet climate. It is covered with rain forests. Southeast Asia contains the second-largest rain forest region in the world. The largest is in South America.

The rain forests of Southeast Asia are lush and thick. However, there are disadvantages to living in the tropical climate of Southeast Asia—typhoons. When typhoons hit land, the high winds and heavy rain often lead to widespread property damage and loss of life.

Connect What parts of the United States are subject to storms like typhoons?

1. **Define** rain forest.
2. **Identify** (a) Ghat Mountains, (b) Bangladesh, (c) Vietnam.
3. Identify the climate zones you would pass through if you traveled eastward across mainland Southeast Asia.
4. Why does the rainy season occur during the summer in India and during the winter in Vietnam?

Critical Thinking

5. **Recognizing Cause and Effect** How might the climate of South Asia be different if the Himalaya Mountains were not there?

Activity

6. **Writing to Learn** Write three weather reports—one for the west coast of India in July, one for central India in December, and a third for the southeast coast of Vietnam in December.

Natural Resources

Reach Into Your Background

Look around you. Can you identify the natural resources that were used to create any of the things you see? For example, what is your pencil made of? How many natural resources can you identify?

Questions to Explore

1. What natural resources do South and Southeast Asia have?
2. How are the resources located throughout the region?

Key Terms

surplus
cash crop

Key Places

Thailand
Java

▼ A sturdy scaffold made of bamboo easily supports the construction of this temple tower in Indonesia. The bamboo poles that run diagonally give added strength to the scaffold.

What grows up to 4 feet (1.2 m) a day, is stronger (for its weight) than both concrete and steel, and has flowers that bloom only once every 20 years? Hints: half of the world's people depend on this material for shelter and food. It is a natural material that can be used to make irrigation pipes, ropes, and bridges. A platform made from this material can support the weight of an elephant.

The answer is bamboo, a type of grass. Some kinds of bamboo look like regular grass. They grow only waist high in small bushes. Other kinds are much bigger. The giant bamboo, which grows deep in the forests of Asia, is about 25 inches (63 cm) around. It towers 120 feet (37 m) into the sky—as high as a 13-story building.

Asians have long recognized the value of this natural resource. "Bamboo is my brother," goes an old Vietnamese saying. And a Chinese poet who lived nearly a thousand years ago wrote, "It is quite possible not to eat meat, but not to be without bamboo."

Land and Water: Precious Resources

Most of the people of South and Southeast Asia make their living from the land. They live in small villages, where they build their own homes, often from bamboo, and grow their own food. Some use the same building and farming methods that their ancestors relied upon thousands of years ago.

Ask Questions Think of three questions to ask about how people live in South and Southeast Asia.

Fertile River Valleys in South Asia Three out of four South Asians still live in the countryside. Most of these people are crowded into fertile river valleys. Here they grow whatever crops the soil and climate of their particular region will allow.

The Life of a Himalayan Farmer Far up in the Himalaya Mountains, near the sources of the mighty rivers of South Asia, live the people of Nepal and Bhutan. The resources they need come from the beautiful land around them.

If you had been born in a small village in Nepal or Bhutan, you would look up at the high mountain peaks with respect. You might spend your day helping your parents tend to the crops of rice, corn, wheat, or barley growing on the terraced slopes. You might pass each day tending a herd of yaks. These are shaggy, oxlike animals that graze on the grassy slopes of the Himalaya Mountains. Your clothing would be made from yak hide and hair. Your diet would include yak milk and meat.

Herding in the Himalayas

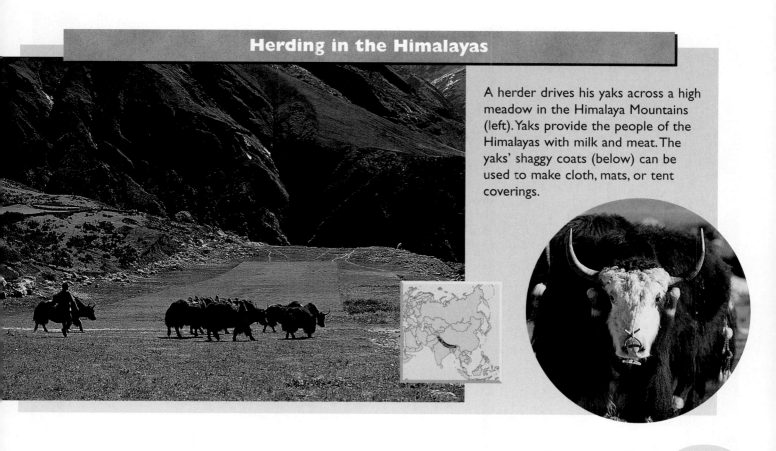

A herder drives his yaks across a high meadow in the Himalaya Mountains (left). Yaks provide the people of the Himalayas with milk and meat. The yaks' shaggy coats (below) can be used to make cloth, mats, or tent coverings.

Fertile River Valleys in Southeast Asia The river valleys between the mountain ranges of mainland Southeast Asia are home to millions of people. Like the people of South Asia, they live in small villages and usually grow their own food. In fact, rural Southeast Asia produces enough rice to feed people in the countryside and in the cities. Thailand produces so much extra rice that it has become a world leader in rice export. In the past, Cambodia, Myanmar, and Vietnam have also produced a rice **surplus,** or more than is needed.

Visualize Visualize a house on stilts during a summer downpour. Can you see a reason for putting a house on stilts?

The Life of a Thai Farmer Life in small farming villages in Southeast Asia differs greatly from the life of a farmer in Nepal or Bhutan. If you had been born in a small village in Thailand, you would probably live in a bamboo house built on stilts near a river. During the monsoon rains, the river might flood, and you would paddle home after school in a small boat. During the dry season, your family's prized possession, a water buffalo, would live between the stilts under your house. There it would be safe from wild animals.

Most of your time would be taken up with growing rice. Soon after planting seeds in boxes, you would transplant the sprouts to the fields just before the rains. Throughout the growing season, you would keep the fields flooded. You would carefully weed between the rice plants. And, at harvest time, you would cut down the rice plants, using a knife or a sickle. All this is hard but needed work. In Thailand, as in many Southeast Asian countries, rice is the most important part of all meals.

▼ Tea is an important cash crop in Sri Lanka. These workers can pick about 40 pounds (18 kg) of tea a day. Harvesting tea is a job traditionally done by women.

Cash Crops Some countries of South and Southeast Asia produce cash crops such as tea, cotton, and rubber. A **cash crop** is one that is raised to be sold for money on the world market.

Cash crops often bring in a great deal of money, but they may also cause problems. They can make the economies of a region dependent on world prices for the crops. When prices are high, the people who produce the crops are able to buy food. But when world prices fall, the cash crops do not bring in enough money. Because you cannot eat tea or rubber, the people who produce these crops sometimes go hungry.

▲The mineral wealth of South and Southeast Asia includes valuable gems. Myanmar, Thailand, Sri Lanka, and India are the source of fine rubies and sapphires.

Other Resources of South and Southeast Asia

South and Southeast Asia are rich in mineral and rain forest resources. Tapping these resources, however, has led to serious problems for the countries of this region.

Mineral Resources of South and Southeast Asia The earth beneath India holds a vast supply of mineral wealth. Iron ore and coal are plentiful. Other important minerals include copper, limestone, and bauxite—an ore used to make aluminum. India has only a small amount of oil. Because of this, India relies heavily on hydroelectric and nuclear power for energy.

The nations of Southeast Asia are also rich in minerals. Indonesia, Myanmar, and the small kingdom of Brunei contain large deposits of oil. Malaysia is the world's leading exporter of tin. And iron can be found in the Philippines, Vietnam, and Malaysia.

Simply having mineral resources does not mean that a country is rich and its people live well. It is risky to depend heavily on money from the export of minerals, just as it is risky to rely on cash crops. When world prices for these minerals fall, so do the profits.

It is better for nations to use their resources to help create their own industries. In recent years, the nations of Southeast Asia have begun to build up their industries. However, they continue to export large amounts of raw materials. The challenge for South and Southeast Asia in the future will be to use their mineral resources to modernize their own nations.

Brunei's Big House
Brunei, on the northwestern coast of the island of Borneo, is only about the size of the state of Delaware. Yet this tiny nation boasts the world's biggest palace, the home of the Sultan of Brunei. This building covers 50 acres (20 hectares)—about the area of 36 football fields—and has 1,788 rooms. The Sultan and the people of Brunei have grown rich from the oil and natural gas resources of the area.

Rain Forests: A Fragile Resource Large areas of South and Southeast Asia have a tropical climate that supports rain forests. These forests contain a great variety of plant and animal life. They are a valuable source of bamboo and timber; dyes, oils, and chemicals used in industry; and medicines to treat diseases. They also produce food products—coffee, bananas, nuts, and spices.

However, the rain forests are in danger. Huge sections of them have been cut down to make more farmland and living space for a growing population. On the island of Java in Indonesia, more than 90 percent of the rain forest has been cleared for farms and tree plantations. Similar destruction is found in every nation of this region with rain forests.

The Asian rain forests contain valuable trees. Teakwood was once used to build ships and is now in demand for furniture. Teak trees take hundreds of years to mature. When the rain forest is thinned by logging, the trees are gone forever. The forest may not have a chance to grow

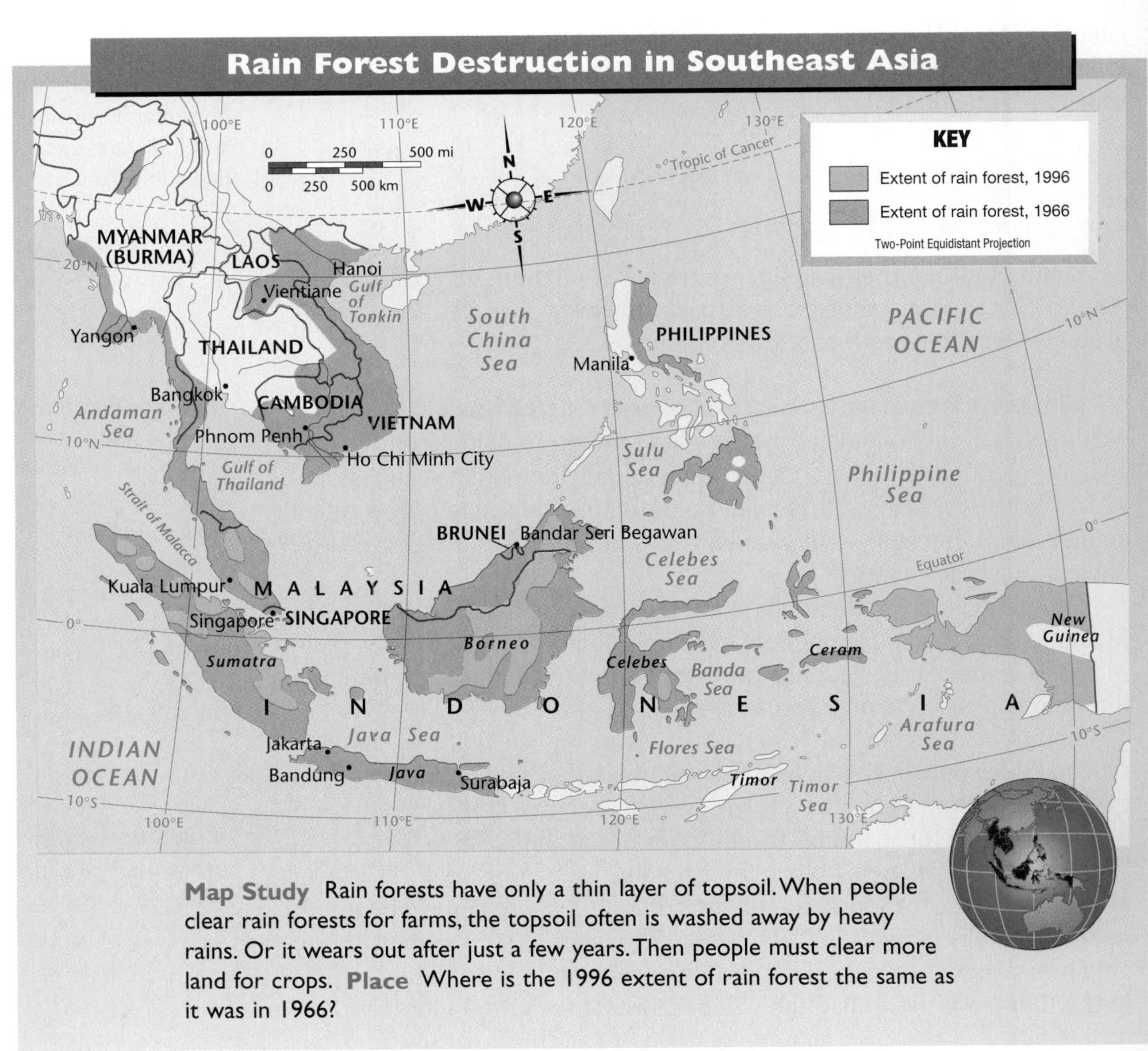

Map Study Rain forests have only a thin layer of topsoil. When people clear rain forests for farms, the topsoil often is washed away by heavy rains. Or it wears out after just a few years. Then people must clear more land for crops. **Place** Where is the 1996 extent of rain forest the same as it was in 1966?

An Endangered Species

The orangutan makes its home in the rain forests of Indonesia. Orangutans like this mother and baby spend most of their lives high in the trees. This quiet, shy animal is an endangered species. **Critical Thinking** What do you think will happen to orangutans if Indonesian rain forests are cut down? Why?

back. The logging of rain forest trees was once carried out slowly. Workers used handsaws to cut the trees and elephants to drag the timber from the forest. But recently, logging has become faster. Chain saws, bulldozers, and trucks now cut and clear the trees.

A Step Toward Conservation Another challenge for the nations of South and Southeast Asia is to balance the need for economic growth with the need for rain forests. Thailand has made some progress toward conserving its remaining rain forests. In 1988, hundreds of people were killed by huge mudslides. The mudslides occurred because trees that had held the soil on the hillsides had been cut down. In 1989, logging in Thailand was banned.

1. **Define** (a) surplus, (b) cash crop.
2. **Identify** (a) Thailand, (b) Java.
3. Name three natural resources of South and Southeast Asia.
4. How do natural resources affect how people live? Give two examples of natural resources and describe their effects on people.

Critical Thinking

5. **Expressing Problems Clearly** The island nation of Sri Lanka is one of the world's leading producers of tea. What might happen to the people of Sri Lanka if tea prices fell very low?

Activity

6. **Writing to Learn** Write a diary entry from the point of view of a farmer living in South or Southeast Asia. What daily tasks might you describe? What would you notice about the weather? Use information from this chapter, conclusions you drew from this information, and your imagination.

Using Isolines to Show Precipitation

If you ever visit Mawsynram, remember to take an umbrella.

Mawsynram, a city in India, is the rainiest place on the Earth. On average, Mawsynram receives about 463 inches (11,873 mm) of rain per year. That is more than ten times as much rain as most cities in the United States receive! It rains an average of $1\frac{1}{4}$ inches in Mawsynram every day.

Mawsynram is in Asia. You will also find the world's largest dry region in the world in Asia—the Arabian Peninsula. While Mawsynram is getting drenched, parts of the Arabian Peninsula do not see rain for years at a time.

It is hard to imagine how the wettest and the driest places in the world can be on the same continent. Asia is the world's largest continent. Rainfall varies greatly all the way across it.

Get Ready

On maps, the amount of precipitation is often shown by isolines. The word *isoline* comes from the Greek word *isos,* which means "equal," and the Latin word *linea.* Isolines are lines on a map that connect parts of an area that are equal in some way. On a map that shows precipitation, they outline areas that have about the same amount of precipitation.

Try It Out

To see how isolines are used to show precipitation, make a simple isoline map of "rainfall" in your own classroom.

A. Make it rain. Take plastic or paper cups of the same size and place one on each desk in your classroom. Fill four cups in one corner of the classroom with three inches of water each. Surrounding those four cups, fill eight cups of water with two inches of water each. Next to these cups, fill three cups each with one inch of water. Leave the remaining cups empty. The arrangement of your cups will vary slightly, depending on your classroom.

B. Draw a map. On the board, draw a rough map of your classroom. Draw a box to show each desk.

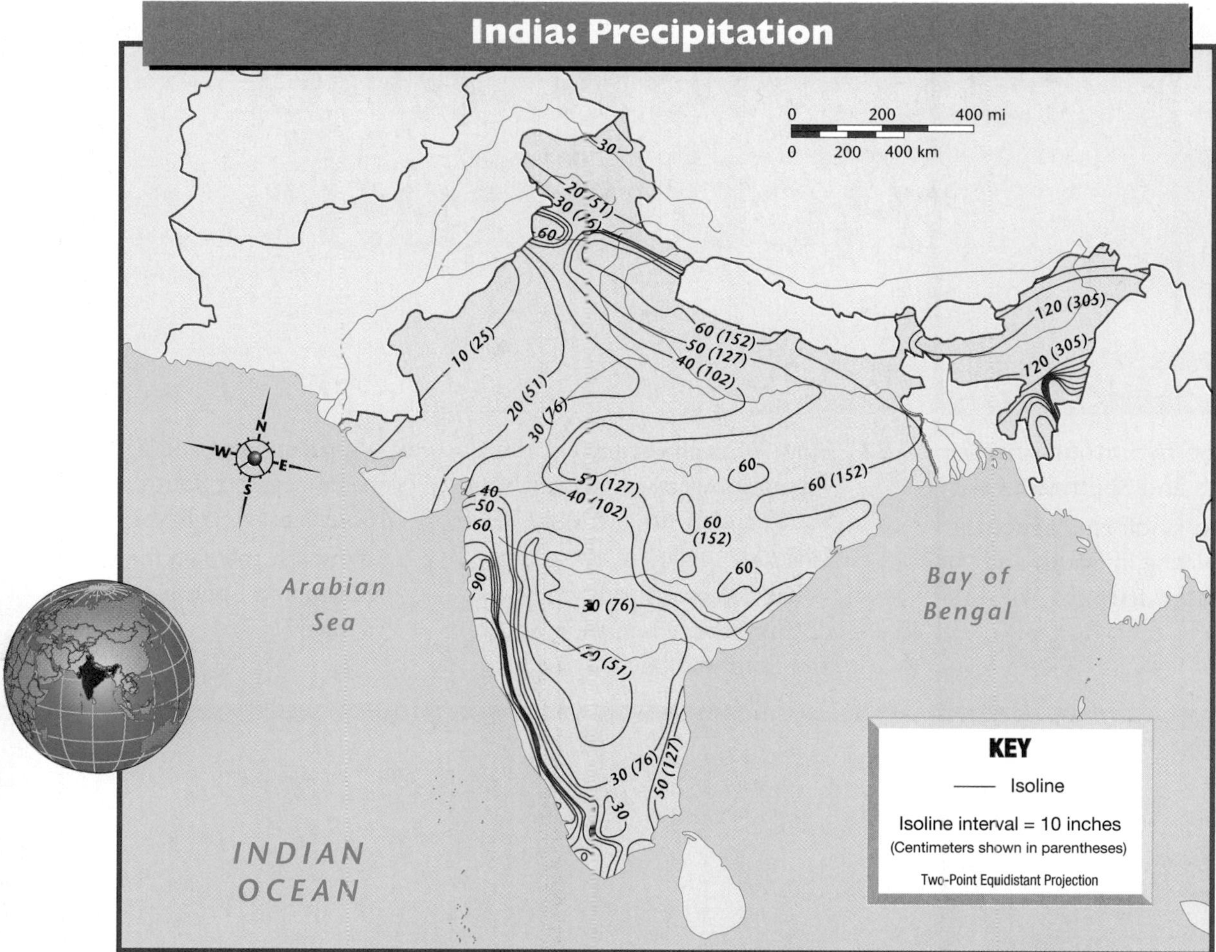

C. Record the precipitation on the map. Count the inches of "rainfall" in each cup. Write each measurement in the box that shows that desk on the map.

D. Draw isolines. Draw one isoline around the entire area of all desks. This line shows the base level of no rainfall. Then draw a single line around the entire area that has *at least* one inch of rainfall. This will also enclose areas with two and three inches of rainfall.

Just inside the one-inch isoline, draw an isoline that surrounds the desks with at least two inches of rainfall. Be sure not to include the desks with only one inch of rainfall. Inside the two-inch isoline, draw an isoline that surrounds only the desks with three inches of rainfall.

E. Read your map. Look at the isolines on your map and think about how they help you to visualize the differences in precipitation throughout your classroom.

Apply the Skill

The same process is used on a larger scale to draw precipitation maps of large regions, countries, or whole continents. The map above is a precipitation map that uses isolines to show average amounts of rainfall in India. Use it to complete the following steps.

1. **Study the isolines.** What is the interval, or difference in amount of precipitation, between isolines? How much rain does the rainiest part of India receive each year? How much rain does the driest part receive?

2. **Use the isolines to find useful information.** Where is the rainiest part of India? Where is the driest part?

Review and Activities

Reviewing Main Ideas

1. Describe two major landforms in South and Southeast Asia.
2. How do landforms affect the people living in South and Southeast Asia?
3. How does climate affect the vegetation growing throughout South and Southeast Asia? Give two examples.
4. What are monsoons, and how do they affect rainfall in South and Southeast Asia?
5. What mineral and agricultural resources do South and Southeast Asia have?
6. Why are the rain forests of South and Southeast Asia in danger?

Reviewing Key Terms

Use each key term below in a sentence that shows the meaning of the term.

1. subcontinent
2. rain forest
3. surplus
4. cash crop

Critical Thinking

1. **Recognizing Cause and Effect** Why would cash crops affect rain forests?
2. **Making Comparisons** What are two similarities between South and Southeast Asia? What are two differences?

Graphic Organizer

Copy the chart onto a sheet of paper. Then fill in the empty boxes to complete the chart.

	Major Landforms	Climate and Vegetation Regions	Natural Resources
South Asia			
Southeast Asia			

Map Activity

South and Southeast Asia

For each place listed below, write the letter from the map that shows its location.

1. Vietnam
2. Nepal
3. India
4. Bangladesh
5. Borneo
6. Thailand
7. Himalaya Mountains

Place Location

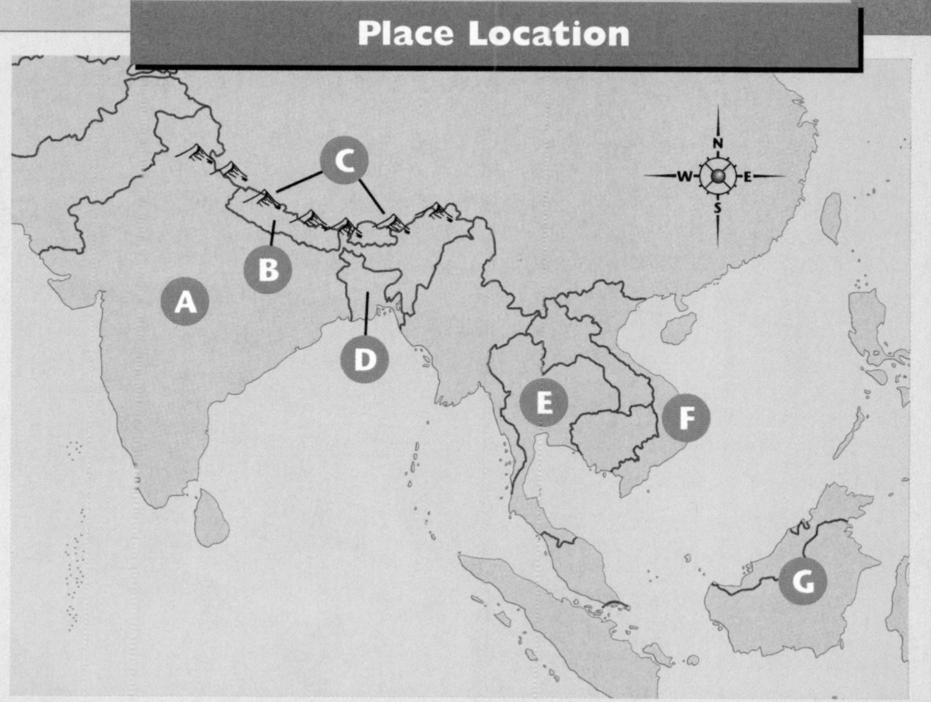

Writing Activity

Writing a Plan

Suppose you were planning a trip to South and Southeast Asia. Write a day-by-day plan for your trip. Explain what places you would visit and when you would go. Include information about the climate, landforms, and natural resources of the regions in your plan. Begin with this entry: "July 1: Fly from New York to Mumbai (Bombay), India. Arrive in Mumbai at 3:00 P.M."

Take It to the NET

Activity Read an article about the impact of a proposed dam in Thailand. What are the advantages and disadvantages of building the dam? For help in completing this activity, visit **www.phschool.com.**

Chapter 20 Self-Test To review what you have learned, take the Chapter 20 Self-Test and get instant feedback on your answers. Go to **www.phschool.com** to take the test.

Skills Review

Turn to the Skills Activity.

Review the use of isolines to show precipitation. Then answer the following questions: (a) What is an isoline? (b) Could isolines connect areas of equal snowfall? Why or why not?

How Am I Doing?

Answer these questions to help you check your progress.

1. Can I describe the major landforms of South and Southeast Asia?
2. Do I know how the monsoons affect the climate and vegetation of South and Southeast Asia?
3. Do I know the natural resources that can be found in the nations of South and Southeast Asia?
4. What information from this chapter can I include in my journal?

South and Southeast Asia

Cultures and History

SECTION 1
The Cultures of South Asia

SECTION 2
The Cultures of Southeast Asia

SECTION 3
India
IN THE MIDST OF CHANGE

SECTION 4
Pakistan
ECONOMIC PROGRESS

SECTION 5
Vietnam
A REUNITED NATION

PICTURE ACTIVITIES

The picture above shows a religious festival in India. Begin your study of India and other countries in South and Southeast Asia by completing the following activities.

Study the picture

What does the picture tell you about the role of religion in everyday life in South and Southeast Asia?

Choose a person

Pick one of the people in the picture. Write a short description of the person. What is the person wearing? What do you think he or she is doing?

The Cultures of South Asia

Reach Into Your Background

Holidays and celebrations are one part of culture. What holidays or celebrations do you or people you know take part in? Think about the things you do to celebrate. Do you eat turkey on Thanksgiving? Do you belong to a group that marches in a parade on the Fourth of July? What else do you do?

Questions to Explore

1. How did invasions affect the cultures of South Asia?
2. What ancient traditions influence the cultures of South Asia today?

Key Terms

caste
colony
boycott
partition

Key People

Siddhartha Gautama
Asoka
Mohandas K. Gandhi

In 1922, scientists digging near the Indus River came upon the ruins of an ancient city they called Mohenjo-Daro (moh HEN joh DAH roh). The city was amazingly well planned, with wide, straight streets and large buildings. It had a sewer system and a large walled fortress. Mohenjo-Daro was part of a civilization that developed about 4,500 years ago.

The people who lived there were part of one of the world's oldest civilizations. Over the centuries, many other people moved into the region. Some came peacefully. Others marched in with swords in their hands. All of these invaders contributed to South Asian culture.

South Asian culture, in turn, influenced cultures of other regions. Hinduism (HIN doo izm) and Buddhism, two religions that developed in South Asia, are practiced by hundreds of millions of people.

▼ The people of Mohenjo-Daro built their city on mounds of earth to protect it from the floods of the Indus River.

New Religions

Between 2000 B.C. and 1500 B.C., invaders known as Aryans (AIR ee unz) swept down on the people of the Indus Valley. Look at the map on the next page and note the route the Aryans took. The Indus Valley farmers were no match for the Aryan soldiers in horse-drawn chariots. The Aryans took control of

The Early History of India

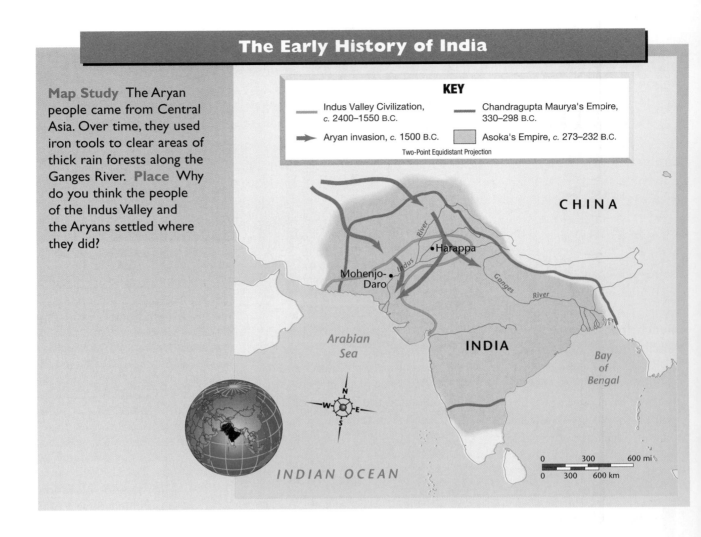

Map Study The Aryan people came from Central Asia. Over time, they used iron tools to clear areas of thick rain forests along the Ganges River. **Place** Why do you think the people of the Indus Valley and the Aryans settled where they did?

KEY

- Indus Valley Civilization, *c.* 2400–1550 B.C.
- Chandragupta Maurya's Empire, 330–298 B.C.
- Aryan invasion, *c.* 1500 B.C.
- Asoka's Empire, *c.* 273–232 B.C.

Two-Point Equidistant Projection

CHINA

Harappa

Mohenjo-Daro

Indus River

Ganges River

INDIA

Arabian Sea

Bay of Bengal

INDIAN OCEAN

0 300 600 mi

0 300 600 km

the area. In time, the Aryans moved eastward to the Ganges River, laying claim to much of northern India.

The Aryans ruled northern India for more than 1,000 years. They introduced new ways of living. For instance, they divided people into three classes—priests, warriors, and ordinary working people. This division grew out of Aryan religious writings called the Vedas (VAY duz). In time, the Aryans drew the conquered people into their class system. By 500 B.C., there was a strict division of classes. Europeans later called it the caste system. Each **caste,** or class, had special duties and work.

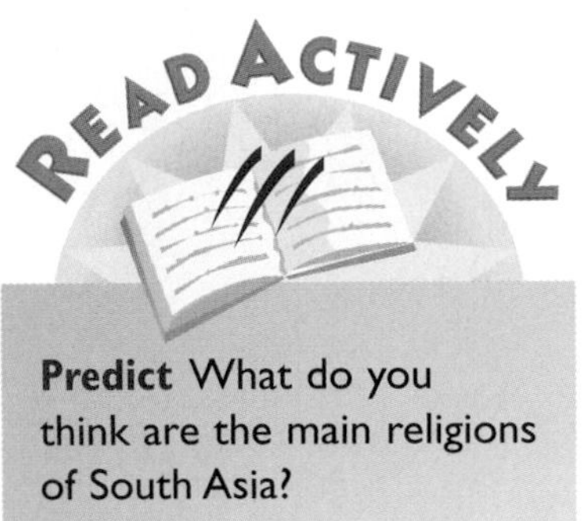

Predict What do you think are the main religions of South Asia?

The caste system became a central part of a new system of belief that also emerged from Aryan religious ideas and practices. This system of beliefs, Hinduism, is one of the world's oldest living religions.

Hinduism Hinduism is unlike other major world religions. It has no one single founder. However, it has many great religious thinkers. Also, Hindus worship many gods and goddesses, but they believe in a single spirit. To Hindus, the various gods and goddesses represent different parts of this spirit. As an old Hindu saying states: "God is one, but wise people know it by many names." Today, Hinduism is the national religion of India and has 700 million followers here.

Buddhism Buddhism, like Hinduism, developed in India. According to Buddhist tradition, its founder was a prince named Siddhartha Gautama (sihd DAHR tuh goh TUH muh). He was born in about 560 B.C., in present-day Nepal. Gautama was a Hindu of high caste. He lived a privileged life, safe from hunger and disease.

When he was 29 years old, Gautama left home to learn about his kingdom. For the first time, he saw people who were hungry, sick, and poor. He became so unhappy that he gave up his wealth. He pledged his life to finding the causes of people's suffering.

Eventually, Gautama found what he believed was the solution. He taught that people can be free of suffering if they give up selfish desires for power, wealth, and pleasure. He then became known as the Buddha, or "Enlightened One." People of all backgrounds, princes and ordinary people alike, flocked to hear his sermons.

For some time after the Buddha's death, Buddhism had a huge following in India. Over time, however, it almost completely died out there.

Ask Questions Think of three questions you might ask about the teachings of the Buddha.

Great Empires

Buddhism had its greatest following in India in the 200s B.C., during the time of a great empire. For hundreds of years, India was divided into many small kingdoms. No one ruler emerged to unite them.

Languages of South Asia

Country	Major Languages	Major Religions
Afghanistan	Pashtu, Dari	Islam
Bangladesh	Bengali (official), English	Islam, Hinduism
Bhutan	Dzongkha (official), Gurung, Assamese	Buddhism, Hinduism
India	Hindi (official), English (official), and 14 other languages	Hinduism, Islam, Christianity, Sikhism
Nepal	Nepali (official) and many others	Hinduism, Buddhism, Islam
Pakistan	Urdu (official), English, Punjabi, Sindhi	Islam
Sri Lanka	Sinhala (official), Tamil (official), and English (official)	Buddhism, Hinduism, Christianity, Islam

Chart Study The chart shows the major religions and languages of South Asia. In India, for example, the people speak over 1,000 different languages and dialects. Note that an official language is one chosen by a nation and used for government business. **Critical Thinking** Why do you think English is a major language in several South Asian countries?

Decimal Numbers By A.D. 600, Indian astronomers were using the decimal system—a numbering system based on tens. Their system also had place values and a zero. This made it easy to add, subtract, multiply, and divide. Europeans were using Roman numerals at this time. They later switched to this decimal, or Hindu-Arabic, system. It is used worldwide today.

The Maurya Empire Around 330 B.C., however, a fierce leader named Chandragupta Maurya (CHUN druh gup tuh MAH ur yuh) conquered many kingdoms. By the time of his death in 298 B.C., he ruled an empire that covered much of the subcontinent.

Chandragupta's grandson, Asoka (uh SOH kuh), continued the conquests. This soon changed, however. After one bloody battle, Asoka gave up war and violence and freed his prisoners. Later he changed his beliefs to Buddhism and vowed to rule peacefully.

Asoka kept his word. He showed concern for his people's welfare. He made laws requiring people to treat each other with respect. He spread the peaceful message of Buddhism throughout his empire.

The Maurya empire collapsed not long after Asoka's death. More than 1,500 years would pass before another empire as great ruled India.

The Mughal Empire In the A.D. 700s, people from the north began moving into northern India. They introduced Islam to the area. Islam is the set of beliefs revealed to the prophet Muhammad. He began teaching these beliefs around A.D. 610 in Southwest Asia. Islam spread westward into North Africa and eastward into Central and South Asia.

Among these Muslims, or followers of Islam, who settled in India were the Mughals (MOO gulz). They arrived in the 1500s and established an empire. Akbar (AK bar), who ruled the Mughal empire from 1556 to 1605, allowed all people to worship freely, regardless of their religion. He also supported the arts and literature.

Akbar's grandson, Shah Jahan (shah juh HAHN), built many grand buildings. Perhaps the greatest is the Taj Mahal (tahzh muh HAHL). He had it built as a magnificent tomb for Mumtaz (mum TAHZ) Mahal, his

Buddhism in India

The religion founded by the Buddha (right) had its greatest following during the rule of Asoka. The stone lions (left) topped one of the pillars that Asoka set up all over India. Asoka had Buddhist writings carved on these pillars. After Asoka's death, Buddhism nearly died out in India, but missionaries carried the religion to Japan, Korea, China, and Vietnam.

▲ It took 20,000 workers 22 years to finish the Taj Mahal, the stunning monument Shah Jahan built to his wife.

wife. The cost of this and other of Jahan's building projects was enormous. It drained the empire of money and, eventually, helped to cause the empire's collapse in the 1700s.

The Jewel in the Crown During the 1700s, 1800s, and 1900s, European nations established many colonies in Asia, Africa, and the Americas. A **colony** is a territory ruled by another nation, usually one very far away. Through trade and war, the nations of Europe made colonies of most of South Asia. Britain took over most of the region, including India. Because of the riches it produced, the British called India the "jewel in the crown" of their empire.

While Britain treasured its empire, many Indians treasured their freedom. A strong independence movement grew up. Its greatest leader was Mohandas K. Gandhi (GAHN dee). He called for people to resist British rule. However, Gandhi stressed that they should do this through nonviolent means. For example, he urged a boycott of British goods. A **boycott** means a refusal to buy or use goods and services. Gandhi was jailed many times for opposing British rule. This only made him a greater hero to his people. Gandhi's efforts played a major part in forcing Britain to grant India its freedom in 1947.

Ask Questions What questions do you have about how India won its freedom from Britain?

Strength Without Violence

Mohandas K. Gandhi urged Indians to resist the British by following Hindu traditions. He preached the Hindu idea of *ahimsa,* or nonviolence and respect for all life. Because of his nonviolent approach, Indians called him *Mahatma,* or "Great Soul." **Critical Thinking** Why do you think that Gandhi's nonviolent methods proved so successful?

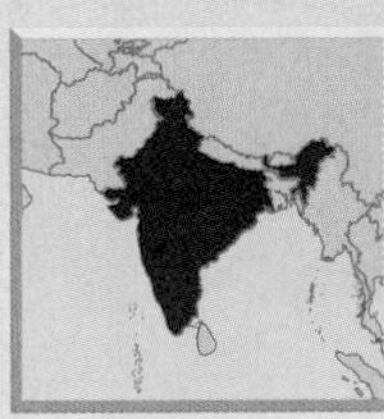

Independence was soon followed by the horror of religious warfare. During the struggle for freedom, Hindus and Muslims had worked together. However, Muslims were a minority. Many feared that their rights would not be protected in a land with a Hindu majority. In 1947, Hindus and Muslims agreed on the **partition,** or division, of the subcontinent into two nations. India would be mainly Hindu. Muslims would be the majority in Pakistan.

This did not stop the fighting. About 1 million people were killed. Gandhi himself was murdered. Conflict between the two nations continued. In 1971, for example, Indian troops helped East Pakistan break away from Pakistan to form the nation of Bangladesh (bahn gluh DESH). Even today, India and Pakistan continue to view each other with distrust.

1. **Define** (a) caste, (b) colony, (c) boycott, (d) partition.
2. **Identify** (a) Siddhartha Gautama, (b) Asoka, (c) Mohandas K. Gandhi.
3. How did the Aryan invasion shape South Asian culture?
4. What religions have influenced the cultures of South Asia?

Critical Thinking

5. **Drawing Conclusions** Why do you think jailing Gandhi made him more of a hero to the people of India?

Activity

6. **Writing to Learn** Write a letter in which the Buddha explains to his family why he gave up his wealth.

The Cultures of Southeast Asia

Reach Into Your Background

Southeast Asia has a great deal of cultural diversity, or variety. Think about the idea of diversity. The United States is culturally diverse, too. Why do you think this is so?

Questions to Explore

1. Why is Southeast Asia a culturally diverse region?
2. What effects did colonial powers have on Southeast Asia?

Key Terms

nationalist

dictator

Key Places

Angkor Wat

Philippines

Deep in the rain forests of Cambodia lies Angkor Wat—the largest temple in the world. Angkor Wat is a Hindu temple. It was built in the A.D. 1100s by the Khmer (kuh MEHR). The Khmer empire included Cambodia and much of Laos, Thailand, and Vietnam. In the 1100s, the empire enjoyed great wealth. Wearing gold and pearls, the king rode on an elephant whose tusks were wrapped in gold. The ruins of Angkor Wat stand as proof of a great civilization.

A Region of Diversity

The Khmer empire was one of many kingdoms in Southeast Asia. Unlike the Khmer empire, however, the other kingdoms were small. Geography had much to do with this. Southeast Asia's mountains kept people protected and apart. People had little contact with those who lived outside their own valley. Each group developed its own special way of life. These factors created a region with a variety of cultures.

Through the centuries, traders, explorers, and travelers passed through Southeast Asia. They brought new ideas and new religions to the region. The people of Southeast Asia blended these new ideas with their own traditions to create unique ways of life.

▼ Angkor Wat is almost one square mile (2.6 sq km) in area. Its inner walls are covered with carvings of figures from Hindu myths.

Dance Class in Cambodia

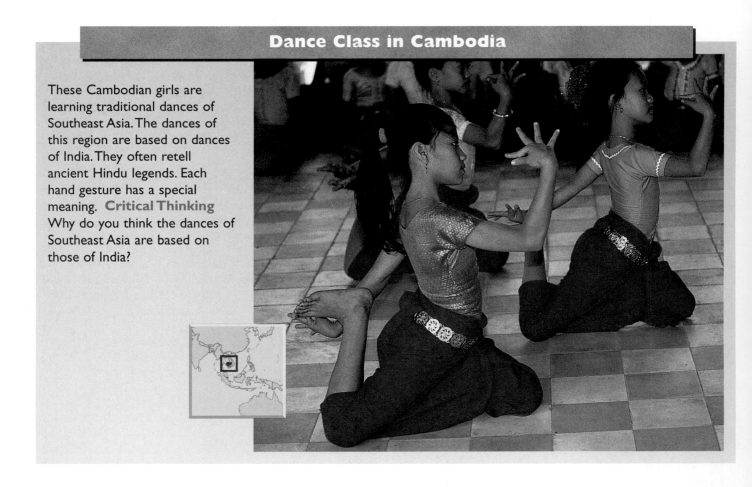

These Cambodian girls are learning traditional dances of Southeast Asia. The dances of this region are based on dances of India. They often retell ancient Hindu legends. Each hand gesture has a special meaning. **Critical Thinking** Why do you think the dances of Southeast Asia are based on those of India?

▼ The Shwe Dagon Pagoda crowns Yangôn, Myanmar's capital city. This famous Buddhist temple is covered with gold.

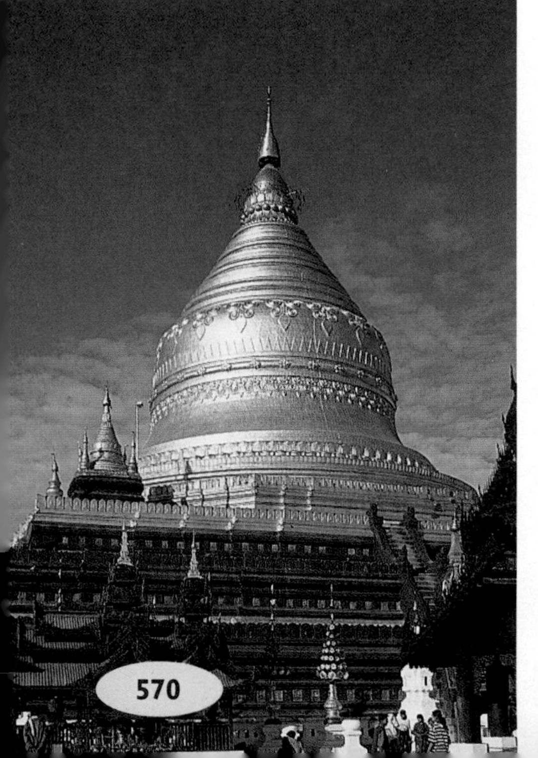

The Influence of China In spite of the mountains, the kingdoms of Southeast Asia always worried about invasion from their powerful neighbor to the north—China. From time to time, Chinese armies swept into Southeast Asia. In 111 B.C., the Chinese took over Vietnam. They ruled the country for more than 1,000 years. During that time, the Vietnamese began using Chinese ways of farming. They also began using the ideas of Confucius to run their government.

The Religions of Southeast Asia The Indians were another influence on Southeast Asia. Nearly 2,000 years ago, Indian traders sailed across the Indian Ocean to the lands of Southeast Asia. Indians introduced the religion of Hinduism to the region. Today, there are Hindus in Bali, in Indonesia, and in parts of Malaysia. Around A.D. 100, Indians brought Buddhism to Southeast Asia. Buddhists eventually outnumbered Hindus in the region. There are many Buddhists in Myanmar, Thailand, Laos, Vietnam, and Cambodia today.

During the 800s and 900s, Arab traders introduced Islam to Southeast Asia. Today, Islam is the religion of millions in Malaysia, Indonesia, the southern Philippines, and other countries. In fact, Indonesia has the largest Muslim population in the world.

European missionaries brought Christianity to the area in the 1500s. Today, most Filipinos are Christian. There are small groups of Christians in other Southeast Asian countries, too.

Colonial Rule in Southeast Asia

Europeans brought more than Christianity to Southeast Asia. Traders from Europe arrived in the region in the 1500s. They hoped to gain control of the rich trade in silks, iron, silver, pearls, and spices. At first, Portugal, the Netherlands, and other European nations built trading posts here. From these small posts Europeans expanded their power. By the 1800s, European nations had gained control of most of Southeast Asia.

Effects of Colonial Rule Outside nations took over Southeast Asian land in order to gain control of the economy. The ruling powers forced their colonies to grow cash crops. On the island of Java, the Dutch forced farmers to grow and sell coffee. This caused rice production to fall. There was not enough food for people to eat.

Colonial rulers built a network of roads, bridges, ports, and railroads in Southeast Asia. Good transportation was essential for the economic

Visualize Visualize a road, bridge, canal, or railroad in your community. How does it make moving people and goods across your region easier?

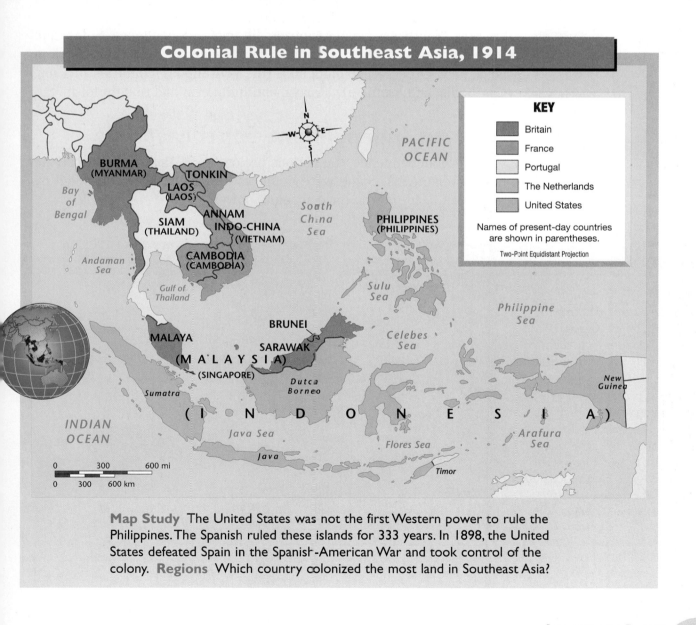

Colonial Rule in Southeast Asia, 1914

KEY
- Britain
- France
- Portugal
- The Netherlands
- United States

Names of present-day countries are shown in parentheses.

Two-Point Equidistant Projection

Map Study The United States was not the first Western power to rule the Philippines. The Spanish ruled these islands for 333 years. In 1898, the United States defeated Spain in the Spanish-American War and took control of the colony. **Regions** Which country colonized the most land in Southeast Asia?

Working Together East Timor takes up half of a small island several hundred miles from the capital of Indonesia, Jakarta. A former Portuguese colony, East Timor was invaded by Indonesia in 1975 and ruled harshly. Some people, however, fought back. Carlos Filipe Ximenes Belo, a Roman Catholic bishop, and José Ramos-Horta, a politician, worked peacefully on behalf of the Timorese people. They were awarded the 1996 Nobel Peace Prize for their efforts. In 1999, East Timor voted to become an independent nation.

success of the colonies. It made it easier to move people and goods across the region. The colonial powers also built schools and universities, which helped to produce skilled workers for colonial industries. In addition, education gave some Southeast Asians the skills to become teachers, doctors, government workers, and more. These educated Southeast Asians would eventually lead the struggle for freedom.

Fighting for Freedom By the early 1900s, nationalists were organizing independence movements throughout Southeast Asia. A **nationalist** is someone who is devoted to the interests of his or her country. By the time World War II broke out in 1939, the Japanese had begun to move into Southeast Asia. During the war, the Japanese drove out the colonial powers. Many Southeast Asians hoped that a Japanese victory would end colonialism in the region. However, Japanese rule proved to be as harsh as that of the former colonial powers.

After the Japanese were defeated in World War II, Western nations hoped to regain power in Southeast Asia. But Southeast Asians had other hopes. They wanted independence.

Most Southeast Asian countries did gain independence. Some, like the Philippines and Burma (now called Myanmar), won their freedom peacefully. Others, like Indochina (the present-day countries of Laos, Cambodia, and Vietnam), Malaya, and Indonesia had to fight for it.

An Independent Southeast Asia

After independence, the nations of Southeast Asia worked to create new governments. Some were democratic. Others were controlled by **dictators,** leaders who have absolute power.

Anti-Chinese Demonstrations

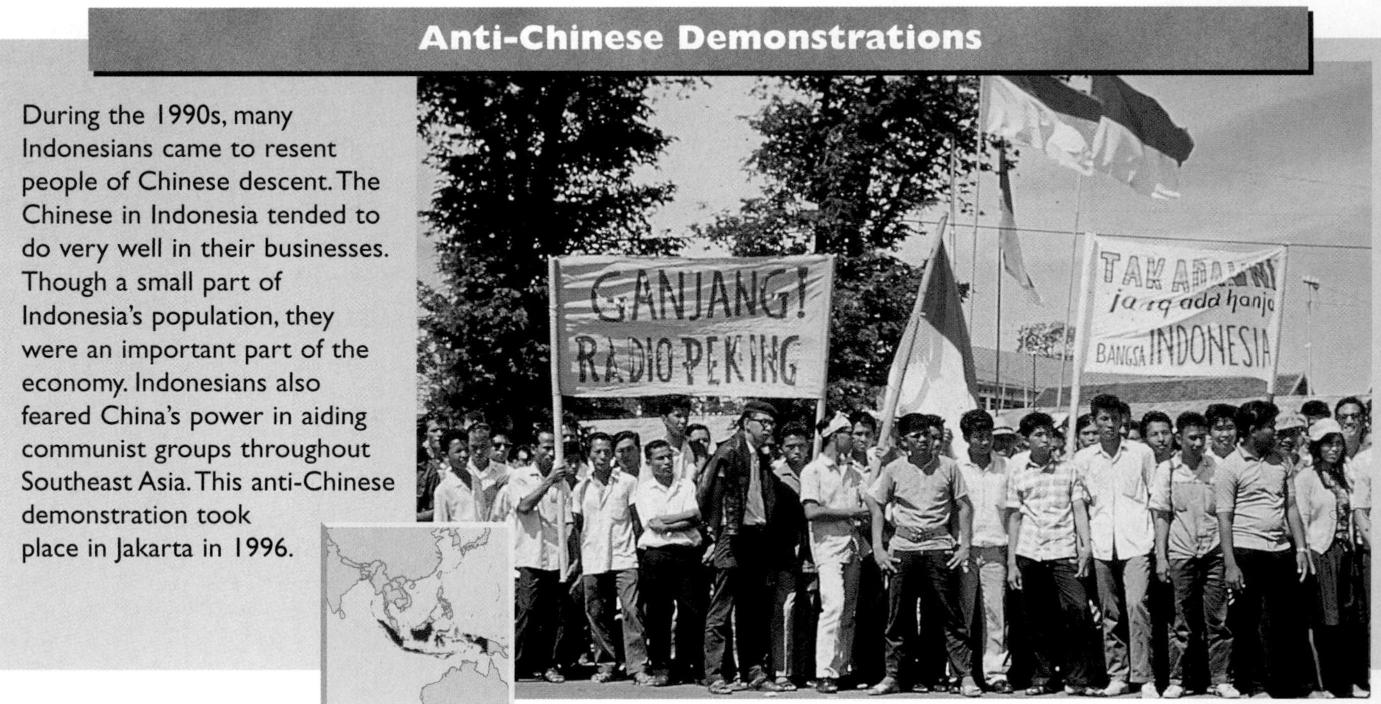

During the 1990s, many Indonesians came to resent people of Chinese descent. The Chinese in Indonesia tended to do very well in their businesses. Though a small part of Indonesia's population, they were an important part of the economy. Indonesians also feared China's power in aiding communist groups throughout Southeast Asia. This anti-Chinese demonstration took place in Jakarta in 1996.

◀ Corazon Aquino (KOR uh zahn uh KEE noh) is shown here campaigning during the 1986 elections in the Philippines. She had restored democracy to the nation after dictator Ferdinand Marcos (MAHR kohs) had been forced to flee. Aquino served as president of the Philippines for six years.

Indonesia won its independence in 1945. In 1965, the army took control of the country. Two years later, General Suharto (soo HAR toe) became president. Suharto used violence to stay in power. During his rule, Indonesia's economy grew rapidly. In 1998, however, an economic collapse brought inflation and food shortages. Indonesians blamed Suharto, and forced him to resign. The next year, Indonesia held its first free elections. Having taken this step toward democracy, Indonesians could concentrate on fixing the economy.

Problems still remained for some people in Indonesia. The East Timorese had lived on the island of Timor for hundreds of years. In the 1600s Portugal took control of the island. In 1975, Indonesia invaded and later annexed East Timor. The Indonesian government ruled the territory harshly. Many people were killed as the Indonesian government tried to suppress a growing movement for independence. Finally, Indonesia's president allowed the East Timorese to choose between remaining part of Indonesia or forming their own independent nation. In September of 1999, the East Timorese voted overwhelmingly for independence.

Though the East Timorese finally had gained independence, their struggle was far from over. Right after the vote, pro-Indonesia militias in East Timor began to terrorize those who had voted for independence. In an attempt to stop the violence, the United Nations sent a peacekeeping force to the island. In addition, the president of Indonesia agreed to set up a commission to investigate human rights violations. Still, the future of East Timor remains uncertain, and the East Timorese have many obstacles to overcome before they can build a new nation.

Connect How did the United States gain its independence? What type of government was created in the United States when it became independent?

1. **Define** (a) nationalist, (b) dictator.
2. **Identify** (a) Angkor Wat, (b) the Philippines.
3. How did China and India affect the cultures of Southeast Asia?
4. (a) Why were many Southeast Asians hopeful when the Japanese invaded the region during World War II? (b) Why were they disappointed?

Critical Thinking

5. **Expressing Problems Clearly** What challenges face the independent nations of Southeast Asia?

Activity

6. **Writing to Learn** Write a speech urging Southeast Asians to support independence from European rule.

India

In the Midst of Change

Reach Into Your Background

What if you had little choice when it came to choosing a job? Suppose that you were expected to work in the same occupation as the rest of your family—an occupation that your family has worked at for hundreds of years. Write a few sentences telling how you would feel about this situation.

Questions to Explore

1. How has independence affected life in India?
2. How are the roles of men and women in India changing?

Key Terms

quota
purdah
parliament

Key People

Indira Gandhi

The whole village had turned up for the Hindu religious service—everyone from members of the highest caste to those of no caste, the Untouchables. After the service, the people sat down to a meal. No one seemed to mind who was sitting next to them. At the end of the meal, lower caste members and Untouchables began to clean up the dining room. Some higher caste members told them to stop, then did the work themselves. Stunned, an Untouchable said, "This is the first time in my life to see such a sight."

▼ An Indian barber shaves a customer. Many barbers in India work in the open air.

A Changing Society

Why did the Untouchable express surprise? Because of the ancient traditions, such as the caste system, in which Indian culture is rooted.

The Caste System Traditional Hindu society divides its followers into four castes. The castes put people in order from the bottom of society to the top. Below the lowest caste are the Untouchables. They are a "casteless" or outcast Hindu group.

Over thousands of years, the caste system grew complex. The main castes divided into hundreds of groups, or subcastes. The people in each subcaste had

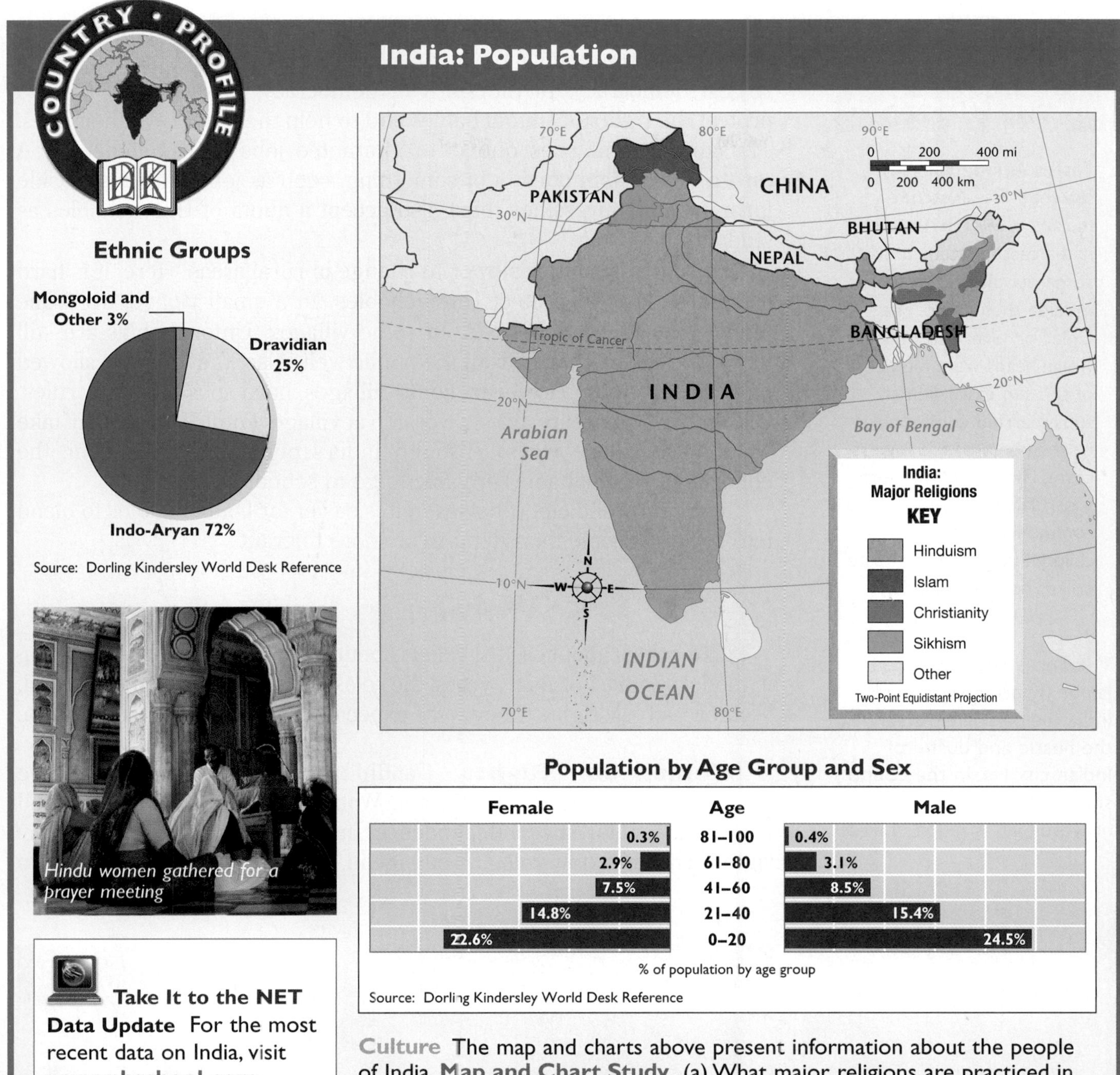

Culture The map and charts above present information about the people of India. **Map and Chart Study** (a) What major religions are practiced in northern India? (b) What percentage of males and females are under 40?

the same job. Shopkeepers, barbers, and weavers, for example, each had their own subcaste. The caste system gave Hindus a sense of order. But for the Untouchables, life was hard. Untouchables could do only the dirtiest work. They were not allowed to mix with people of higher castes.

The System Weakens Today, however, the caste system is weakening. During India's struggle for independence, Mohandas Gandhi began to fight for the rights of Untouchables. He took Untouchables as his pupils. He called them *Harijans,* or children of God.

Castes Among the Natchez The Natchez Indians of North America had a caste system. In it, some people had to marry outside their caste. The Chief, or Great Sun, and village heads were members of the sun caste. Female suns married commoners, or members of the lowest caste. Their children were suns. Male suns also married commoners, but their children belonged to a caste called "honored people."

▼ ▶ This street scene in Jaipur (JY poor), northern India (below), illustrates well the hustle and bustle of Indian city life. In the country-side outside Jaipur (right), however, life is much quieter.

After independence, India became a democracy. With more than three times the population of the United States, India is the world's largest democracy. In the spirit of democracy, India passed laws to protect the rights of Untouchables and to help them improve their lives. The government uses quotas to guarantee jobs to Untouchables. A **quota** is a certain portion of something, such as jobs, that is set aside for a group. Universities must also accept a quota of Untouchables as students.

The caste system is slower to change in rural areas. Here, it is hard to enforce laws to protect Untouchables. In a small village, everyone knows everyone else's caste. In some villages, Untouchables are still forbidden to draw water from the public well. Also, they may be allowed only certain jobs. However, some villages have loosened the rules. Untouchables now are able to worship at village temples. They may take water from village wells. Through India's public school system, the children of Untouchables are able to go to school.

In the crowded cities, however, it is easier for Untouchables to blend into society. People there tend to be more tolerant.

Women in India

Like beliefs about castes, beliefs about men and women are changing in modern India. For many years, the roles of men and women were rigid. Women had few rights. They were expected to marry and have children.

Women Gain Rights Gandhi urged women to play an active part in India's fight against Britain. Women took part in boycotts and prepared leaflets. Since independence, Indian women have gained many rights. They can now vote and engage in business. They are now free to

take part in public life, as well. In 1966, a woman, Indira Gandhi, became prime minister. She was the daughter of Jawaharlal Nehru (juh WA hur lal NAY roo), India's first prime minister.

Indira Gandhi

Indira Gandhi served as prime minister of India for all but three years during the period from 1966 to 1980. Conflict between the Indian government and Sikhs, a religious minority, led to Gandhi's death in 1984. She was assassinated after she ordered an attack on a temple held by armed Sikhs.

Changing Roles for Indian Women In addition to gaining legal rights, women have changed their roles in other ways. Many Muslim women no longer follow the custom of **purdah,** or covering their heads and faces with veils. Many Indian women today have careers and work outside the home. More and more women are entering the fields of science and health care. For example, India has a high percentage of women doctors.

Also, more Indian women than American women hold high government positions. For example, Roda Mistry, who lives in the city of Hyderabad, in central India, is president of the Indian Council on Social Welfare. Before reaching this position, Mistry was a member of the Indian **parliament,** or lawmaking body. She also served as Minister of Tourism and Minister of Women's and Children's Welfare in the Indian government. In her work for the Council on Social Welfare, Mistry has set up shelters for orphans. She also has started programs designed to help poor women find work. Mistry is a well-respected political leader. Her grandchildren call her *Mamaiji,* which means "Grandmother, Sir."

Connect Think about the men and women in your family. How are their lives similar and different?

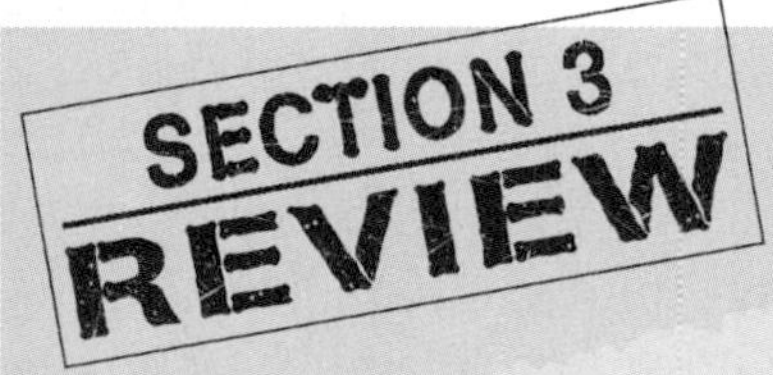

1. **Define** (a) quota, (b) purdah, (c) parliament.
2. **Identify** Indira Gandhi.
3. How is the caste system different in cities and rural villages?
4. What rights have women gained since independence?

Critical Thinking

5. **Drawing Conclusions** Why do you think the Indian government has taken the lead in helping Untouchables?

Activity

6. **Writing to Learn** Write a letter to Roda Mistry. Include some questions you would like to ask her about the roles of women in India.

Pakistan

Economic Progress

Reach Into Your Background

Jot down several goals that you have achieved. Put a star beside those that required the help of other people. Who helped you achieve your goals? How did they help?

Questions to Explore

1. What has Pakistan done to help its farmers?
2. What industrial growth has taken place in Pakistan?

Key Terms

drought
textile
automotive industry

Key Place

Kashmir

▼ Only about 6 percent of Kashmir's land is good for growing crops. Here, farmers have built terraces so they can grow crops on sloping land.

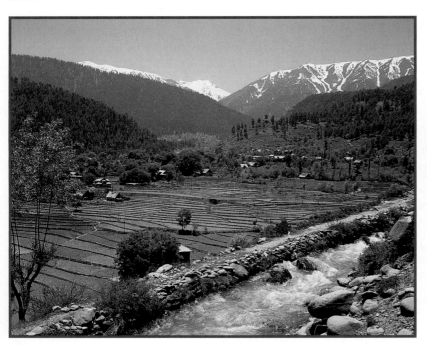

Water. Everyone needs it to survive. Many of us take it for granted. We turn on the tap, and water pours out. But many countries in the world lack water resources. **Drought,** or a long period without rain, is a major problem in Pakistan. It is one cause of the conflict over the region of Kashmir (KAZH mihr).

Kashmir is a land of high mountains and beautiful lakes. The Indus River flows from the high mountains of Kashmir. Therefore, whoever controls Kashmir, controls the water flow of the Indus River. This water is necessary to farmers. They need it to irrigate their crops. Without the Indus River, Pakistan would be a dry, hot desert.

Kashmir is bordered by Pakistan, India, China, and Afghanistan. Both Pakistan and India claim Kashmir. Both wish to control the waters of the Indus. The conflict over Kashmir has led to battles between India and Pakistan. This is how important water is to the region.

An Agricultural Nation

Pakistan fears losing control of the waters of the Indus River. Most Pakistanis are farmers. They rely on the waters to irrigate their fields. Through hard work and clever farming methods, they grow large amounts of wheat, cotton, and sugar cane. Pakistani farmers grow so

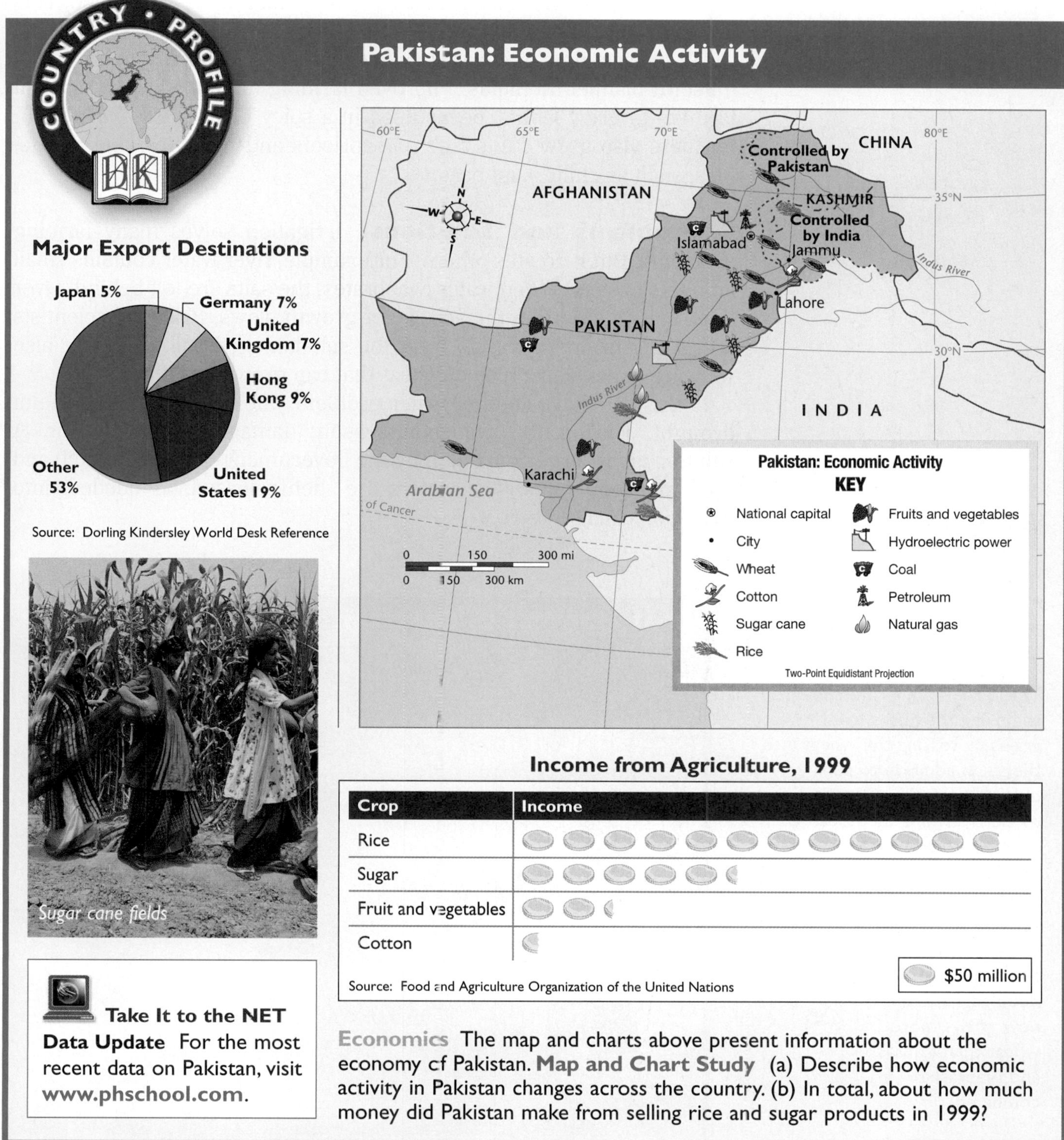

Take It to the NET

Data Update For the most recent data on Pakistan, visit **www.phschool.com.**

Economics The map and charts above present information about the economy of Pakistan. **Map and Chart Study** (a) Describe how economic activity in Pakistan changes across the country. (b) In total, about how much money did Pakistan make from selling rice and sugar products in 1999?

Predict What do you think farmers in Pakistan do to make sure that their crops get enough water?

much rice, they export it to other countries. The great advances the country has made in agriculture could easily be lost without the much-needed water.

Irrigation Produces Larger Crops Pakistanis on the Indus Plain have built thousands of canals and ditches to move water to their fields. In this way, farmers maintain a steady flow of water, even during droughts. As more land is irrigated, more acres are farmed. This increases the amount of crops.

At harvest time, the bright yellow flowers of Pakistan's five kinds of mustard blanket the fields. Improved farming methods allow Pakistani farmers to grow lentils, beans used in a spicy dish called *dhal* (dahl). Farmers also grow fruits, such as apricots and mangoes, and vegetables, such as chilies and peas.

Problems and Solutions Irrigation solves many farming problems. But it creates others. For example, river water contains small amounts of salts. When water evaporates, the salts are left behind. Over time, salts build up in the soil. Plant growth slows. Pakistani scientists are trying to find a way to treat the salt-damaged soil. They are also working to develop a type of wheat that can grow in salty soil.

Pakistanis have another water problem, one that is the opposite of drought. During the monsoon season, damaging floods occur. A solution is the large dams built by the government. The dams catch and hold monsoon rains. The waters are then released, as needed, into irrigation canals.

Wheat Harvest in Pakistan

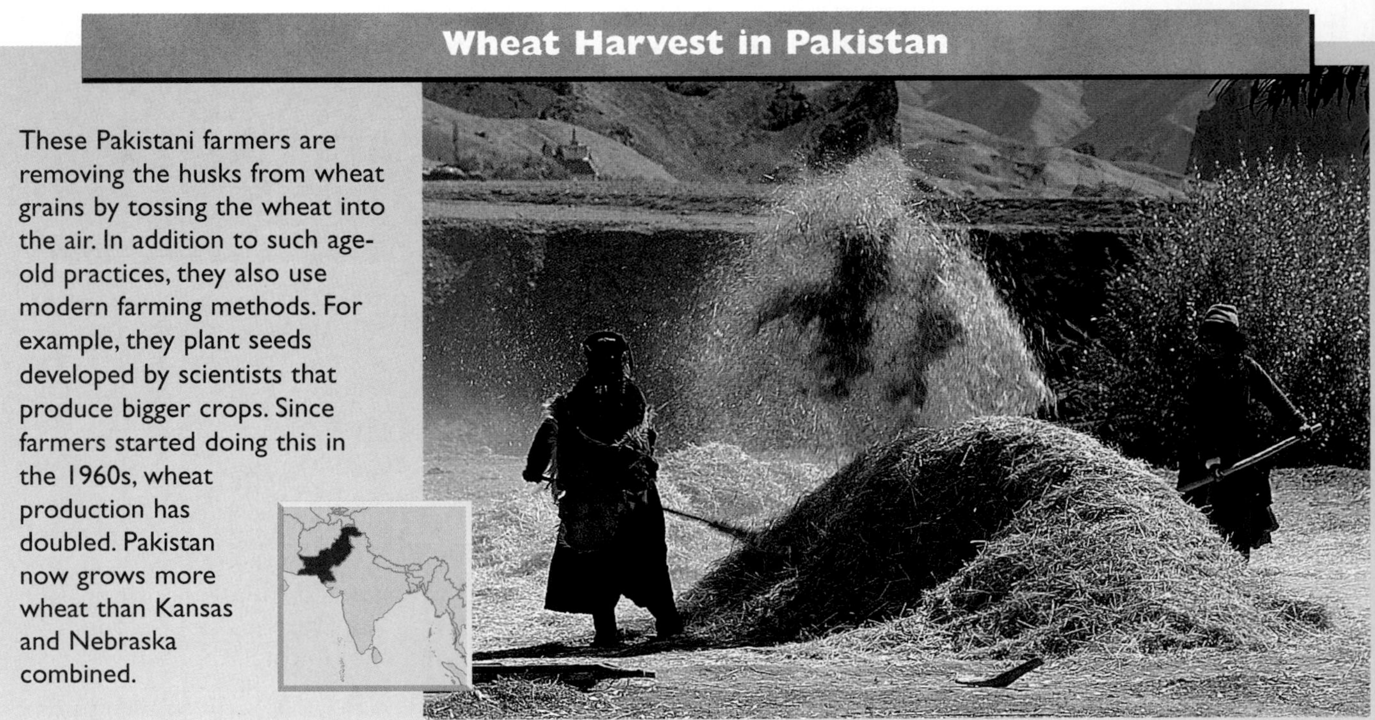

These Pakistani farmers are removing the husks from wheat grains by tossing the wheat into the air. In addition to such age-old practices, they also use modern farming methods. For example, they plant seeds developed by scientists that produce bigger crops. Since farmers started doing this in the 1960s, wheat production has doubled. Pakistan now grows more wheat than Kansas and Nebraska combined.

A New Industry

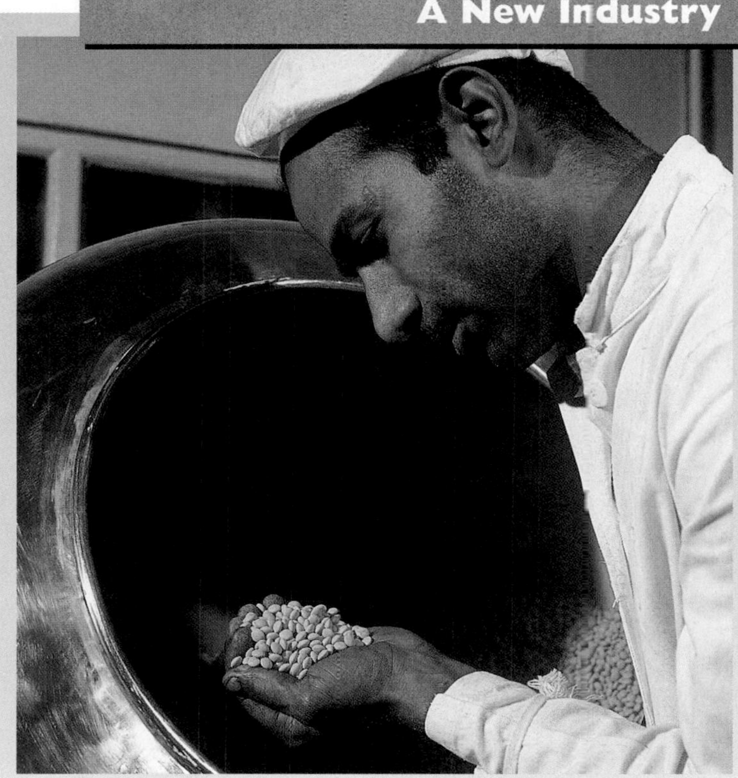

A Pakistani worker checks a handful of pills to make sure they have the correct coating. The making of pharmaceuticals (fahr muh SOOT ih kulz), or medicines and pills, is an important new industry in Pakistan.

Industrial Growth

In addition to helping farmers, dams such as the Tarbela—on the Indus River in northern Pakistan—speed industrial growth. Dams can release rushing water to create hydroelectric energy. In Pakistan, hydroelectric power plants produce electricity to run **textile,** or cloth, mills and other factories. Most industry is located near the sources of hydroelectric power, on the Indus Plain.

Industries Based on Agriculture At independence, Pakistan had few factories. Pakistan has worked hard to build its economy through agriculture and industry. Today, Pakistan is one of the most prosperous countries in Asia. Even so, only a few Pakistanis can afford such things as refrigerators, telephones, and cars. The typical Pakistani family earns about 29,400 Pakistani rupees each year. That is equal to about $490.

Pakistan began its industrial growth by building on what its people knew best: farming. More than half of Pakistan's industrial output comes from turning crops such as cotton into manufactured goods such as socks.

Industries: From Steel to Crafts Although most industry in Pakistan relates to farming, the nation has other industries. The chemical industry produces paint, soap, dye, and insect-killing sprays. The **automotive industry** is one that puts together vehicles such as

A Geologist's Dream The mountains in Pakistan's Salt Range are of little interest to most people except geologists. These scientists learn about the Earth by studying its rocks. This area of Pakistan offers a detailed picture of the Earth's history. It has a series of rocks that range from 570 million years to less than a million years in age.

Traditional Crafts

Many people in Pakistan work in small workshops producing traditional crafts. This worker from Karachi makes wooden trays and boxes that are inlaid with metal designs. Other traditional craft items produced in Pakistan include lace, carpets, pottery, and leather goods. **Critical Thinking** How might the development of traditional crafts help Pakistan's economy?

cars, vans, pickup trucks, tractors, and motorcycles. Several steel mills allow Pakistan to make almost all the steel it needs. This saves money. Producing steel is less costly than buying it from other countries.

Millions of Pakistanis work in small workshops, instead of in large factories. Workshops produce field hockey sticks, furniture, knives, saddles, and carpets. Pakistan is famous for its beautiful carpets. Some sell for as much as $25,000 in Pakistan—and $50,000 in New York or London.

Pakistanis are working hard to improve their future. By building industries and modernizing agriculture, they hope to raise their quality of life.

Connect What products do you use that may have been made in Pakistan?

1. **Define** (a) drought, (b) textile, (c) automotive industry.
2. **Identify** Kashmir.
3. Why is the Indus River crucial to Pakistani farmers?
4. What industries have emerged since Pakistan became a nation?

Critical Thinking

5. **Expressing Problems Clearly** Why is Kashmir important to both India and Pakistan?

Activity

6. **Writing to Learn** Write a dialogue between an Indian and a Pakistani in which each expresses his or her opinion about the fate of Kashmir.

Vietnam

A Reunited Nation

Reach Into Your Background
Write down two or three things you know about the Vietnam War. As you read this section, revise your list, adding new information.

Questions to Explore

1. What conflicts have divided Vietnam?
2. How are the Vietnamese rebuilding their economy?

Key Terms
refugee

Key People and Places
Ho Chi Minh
Ngo Dinh Diem
Ho Chi Minh City

It is summer in northern Vietnam. Villagers cut, harvest, and plow rice fields just as their parents and grandparents did. Unlike their parents and grandparents, however, these villagers are making money. Rice farmers in the village of Phu Do return from the fields to a second job: noodle-making. Farmers in Son Dong carve religious statues from wood in their free time. Potters in Bat Trang, goldsmiths in Dong Sam, embroiderers in Thuong Tin—all are earning money from age-old crafts. Their success helps to rebuild the economy of Vietnam.

▼ These Vietnamese women are making dishes and bowls in a traditional way. It takes great skill to form smooth, round pots from clay without using a potter's wheel.

Decades of Conflict and War

The people of Vietnam are ending a long period of struggle. The struggle began when they fought for independence from France after World War II. Then the country was divided, and civil war followed. North Vietnam fought South Vietnam and its ally, the United States.

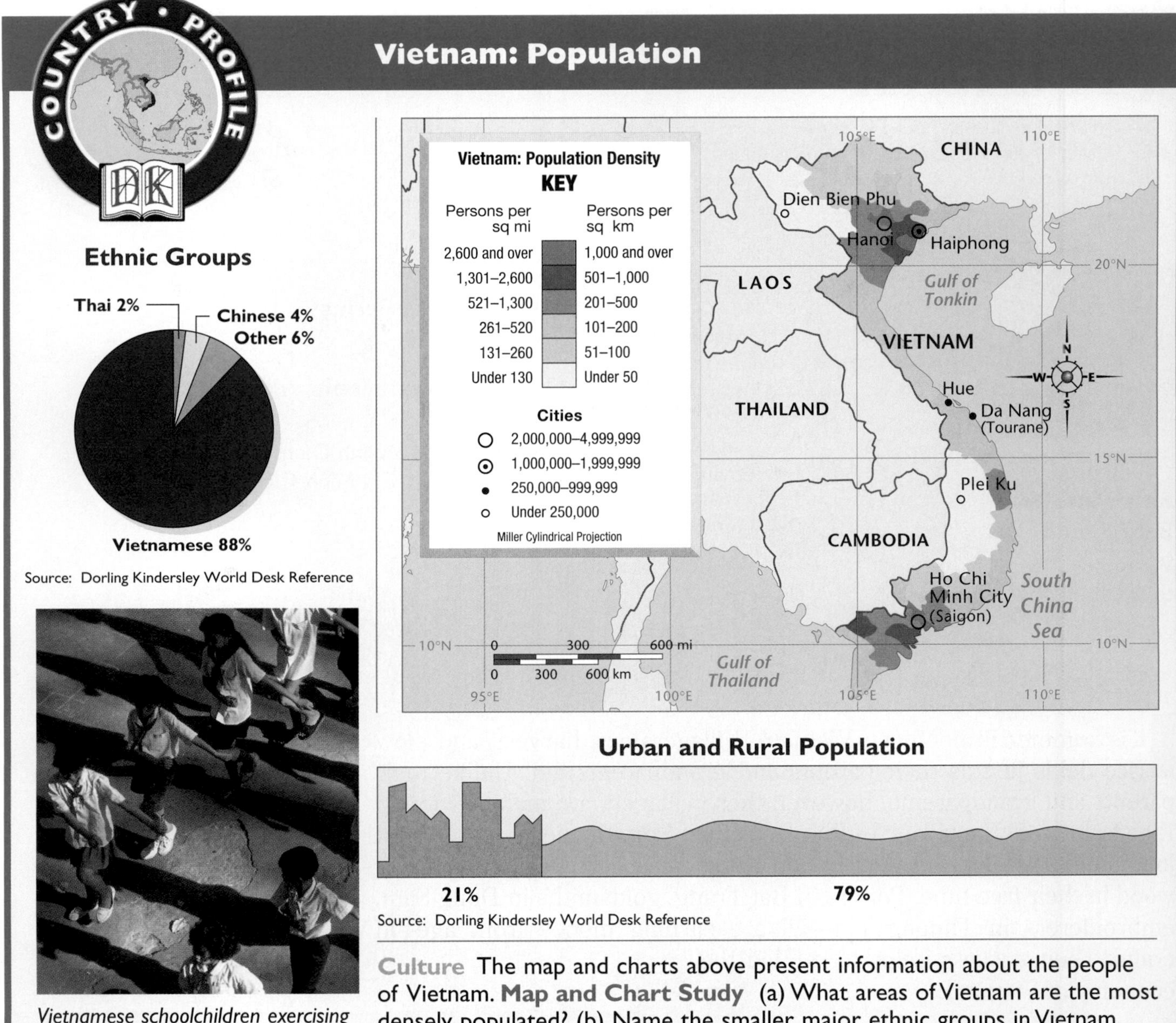

Vietnamese schoolchildren exercising

Culture The map and charts above present information about the people of Vietnam. **Map and Chart Study** (a) What areas of Vietnam are the most densely populated? (b) Name the smaller major ethnic groups in Vietnam.

Take It to the NET
Data Update For the most recent data on Vietnam, visit **www.phschool.com.**

In the mid-1800s, France took over Vietnam as a colony. Vietnam resented French rule. They wanted to have their own government on their own soil. In 1946, they listened to the call to arms of independence leader Ho Chi Minh (hoh chee MIN):

> "Let him who has a rifle use his rifle, let him who has a sword use his sword. And let those who have no sword take up pickaxes and sticks."

Under Ho Chi Minh, the Vietnamese Communists defeated the French. The United States and other democracies did not want Vietnam to become a communist country. After the French defeat, a treaty divided

◀ The United States began sending troops to Vietnam in the mid-1960s. By 1968, more than 500,000 troops were there. About 58,000 Americans died in the Vietnam War.

Vietnam into northern and southern parts. The northern half was controlled by Communists. The treaty said that, eventually, an election would be held to reunite the country under one government.

These elections were never held. Ngo Dinh Diem (noh DIN deh EM), the leader of South Vietnam, refused to uphold his part of the treaty. Instead, he held a vote on whether he should keep ruling South Vietnam. Diem won the election. However, Diem made many enemies within South Vietnam. He ruled until 1963, when he was killed by political opponents.

During these years, Ho Chi Minh and the Communists were trying to take over the south by force. In 1959, they launched a war to achieve this goal. Ho Chi Minh's forces were called the Viet Cong. As they threatened South Vietnam, the United States took an active role in the war. At first, the United States sent thousands of military advisors to help the South Vietnamese. Later, hundreds of thousands of American troops arrived. Through the 1960s, the United States sent more and more troops to Vietnam. By 1968, there were more than 500,000 U.S. troops fighting in Vietnam.

By the 1970s, Vietnam had been at war for more than 30 years. The United States government realized it was fighting a war it would never win. In addition, thousands of people in the United States were calling for an end to the war. By 1973, the United States finally ended its part in the war.

LINKS TO ART

Water Puppets In Vietnam, a type of puppet theater uses a pond for a stage. Water puppet shows started centuries ago. In them, a puppeteer guides wooden figures so that they appear to wade through the water. The puppets are attached to rods and strings hidden underwater. Audiences sit at the water's edge. Stage settings of trees and clouds are also placed on the pond.

After the War

After the United States pulled out, North Vietnam conquered the south. In 1976, the country was reunited under a communist government. Vietnam had been devastated by the war. Millions of Vietnamese had been killed or wounded. Homes, farms, factories, and forests had been destroyed. Bombs had torn cities apart. Fields were covered with land mines, or hidden explosives. The Vietnamese people were worn out. Still ahead was the huge effort of rebuilding.

The Vietnamese Rebuild In the years after the war, the communist government in Vietnam strictly controlled the lives of its citizens. As time passed, however, it was clear that the economy was not growing. Like the Chinese, the Vietnamese had to adapt their approach to economic growth. Although it is still a communist country, Vietnam now allows some free enterprise. This has helped many Vietnamese improve their lives.

Most Vietnamese live in rural areas. In spite of some progress, these areas remain poor. Whole families live on a few hundred dollars a year. Most houses have no indoor toilets or running water. Children suffer from a lack of healthy food. Vietnam is still among the poorest nations in Asia.

▼ Modern cranes and construction projects reflect the growing economy of Vietnam. Here, construction workers lay the foundations for a new office building in Ho Chi Minh City.

Rebirth in Ho Chi Minh City Vietnam's greatest successes have been in rebuilding its cities. Hanoi in the north is the capital. The city of Saigon (sy GAHN) was renamed Ho Chi Minh City. It is the most prosperous city in Vietnam and is the center of trade. Americans who visit Ho Chi Minh City find some of the same things they would find at home. They eat American-style ice cream, drink soda, and watch cable news networks on television. Well-off Vietnamese also feel comfortable here. They buy designer clothing and watches, stereo systems, video recorders, and jewelry. Many of these people run restaurants or hotels, buy and sell land or buildings, or own factories.

Northern Vietnam has been much slower to modernize than the south. Still, the desire for economic success has taken hold in that part of the country. One elderly Vietnamese who fought in the war now says, "I'm astonished by what I see of America on television—automobiles, refrigerators, private homes. Such abundance! The United States ought to be our model."

◀ Like people in many parts of the world, these young Vietnamese women enjoy traveling by motorbike. These vehicles are cheaper than cars and speedier than bicycles.

Le Van Cam, an artisan in a village in the north, explained his economic success story in the new Vietnam:

> "A few years ago, I managed a [factory] that produced rice bowls. My family lived in one room, and all I had was a bicycle. Since the reforms, I've been running my own company. Now I have a big house, a television set, a videocassette recorder, even a washing machine. If I had a garage, I'd buy a car."

Thousands of former **refugees,** people who flee their country because of war, have returned to Ho Chi Minh City. Many developed valuable skills in other lands. Some ex-refugees attended business and law schools in the United States. Today, they use their knowledge of Vietnam and the West to help wealthy foreigners do business in Vietnam.

Visualize Visualize a family living in one room. Then visualize the same family living in a big house. How is life in a big house different from life in one room?

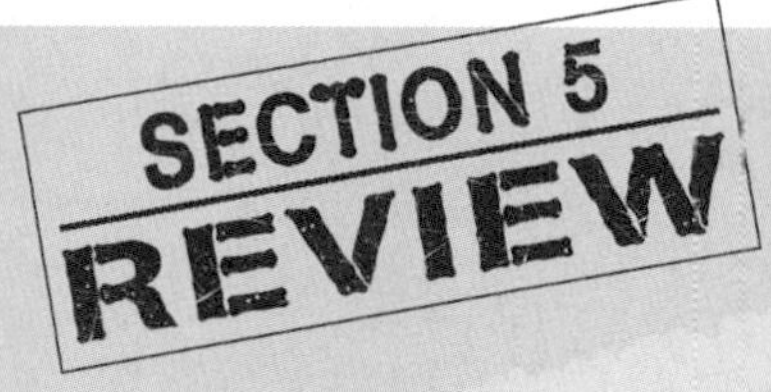

1. **Define** refugee.
2. **Identify** (a) Ho Chi Minh, (b) Ngo Dinh Diem, (c) Ho Chi Minh City.
3. What conflicts have divided Vietnam?
4. What successes has Vietnam had in rebuilding its economy?

Critical Thinking

5. **Understanding Points of View** Why do you think Saigon was renamed Ho Chi Minh City after the war?

Activity

6. **Writing to Learn** Imagine that you are a Vietnamese living in Saigon in 1954. Explain your attitude towards Ngo Dinh Diem and Ho Chi Minh.

Identifying the Central Issue

Have you ever said to someone, "That's not the point!" or "You just don't get it"?

You probably have. Suppose you want to talk to a friend about the big play in a football game. You say, "Wasn't that a great catch Jimmy Brown made?" Then your friend replies by saying, "The closest defender to him was 20 yards away."

You might say, "That's not the point!"

It is frustrating when someone you are talking to does not "get it," or understand your main point. It is just as difficult when you do not "get," or really understand, something you read, because you know that understanding what you read is necessary for you to do well in school and beyond.

Get Ready

Another way to say "getting the point" is "identifying central issues." All the many ideas that relate to a topic are its issues. For example,

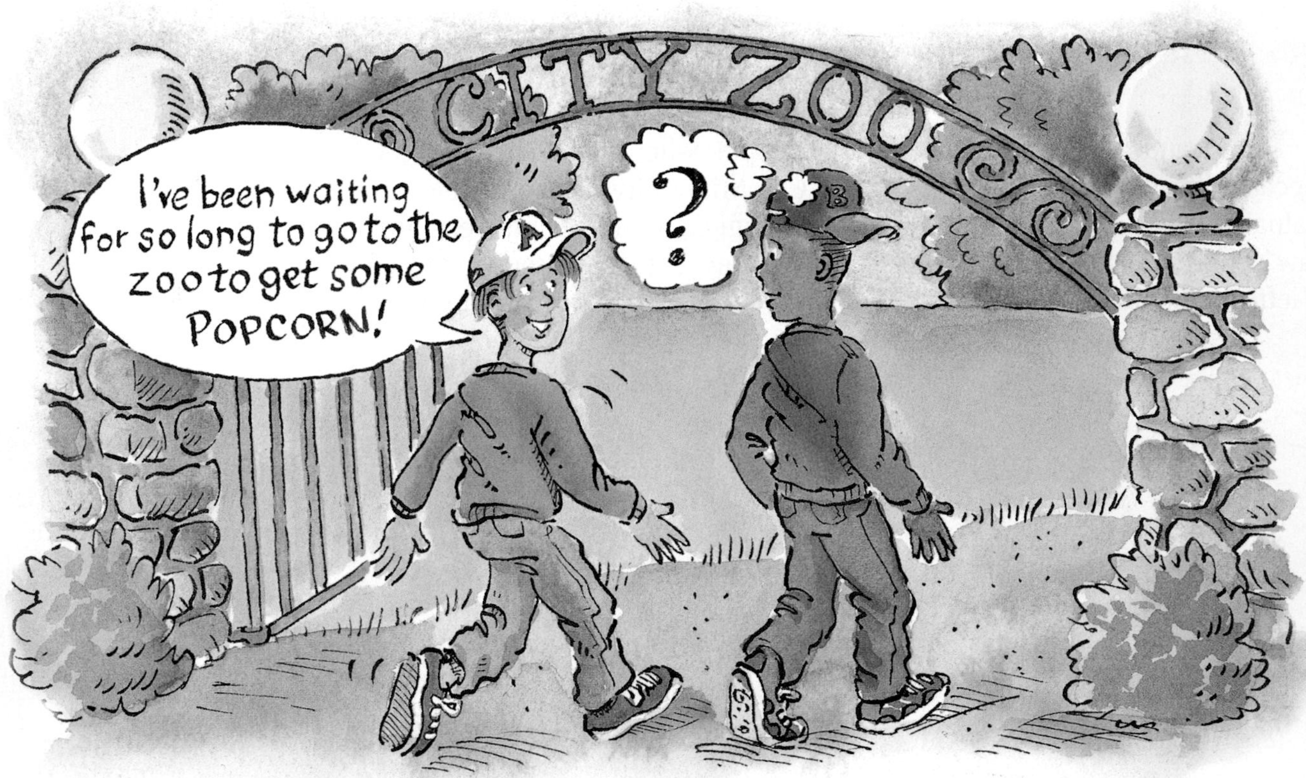

the issues related to a trip to the zoo include the animals, the weather, the crowd, the snacks, and the parking lot. The list is almost endless. But the central issue of a trip to the zoo—the most important idea—is the animals. Can you see why this is so? The central issue is the single most important idea about a topic. All of the other issues are less important than the basic idea behind the zoo—people go to see animals.

Identifying central issues is the way you understand the most important ideas about any topic.

Try It Out

Any paragraph has a central issue, often expressed in the first sentence or two. This is usually followed by details that support the central issue by giving examples or further explanation. When you read a paragraph, be sure to make note of the details and see how they support the central issue.

Read the following paragraph. Then look at the four statements that follow the paragraph. Which statement best describes the central issue of the paragraph—statement A, B, C, or D?

> Like the United States, India has a very diverse population. However, diversity in India has developed somewhat differently from here. For example, the majority of today's American ethnic and cultural groups have come to this country in the last 200 years. Many of India's cultures, on the other hand, have entered the country through many centuries of invasion and migration. Other cultural groups have evolved through many years of isolation from other groups.

A. Some Indian cultures have been isolated for many years.

B. Cultural diversity in India developed differently than it did in the United States.

C. American ethnic groups have immigrated recently.

D. Both the United States and India have many different ethnic groups.

Apply the Skill

In Section 1 of this chapter, read the paragraphs under the heading "New Religions." After you have read the paragraphs, read the statements listed below. Which statement identifies the central issue—statement A, B, C, or D?

A. Aryans invaded the Indus Valley in 1500 B.C.

B. In a caste system, each class has special duties and work.

C. One result of the Aryan invasion of northern India was the formation of Hinduism.

D. The Aryans introduced their class system to India.

Review and Activities

Reviewing Main Ideas

1. What lasting effect did the Aryan invasion have on South Asia?
2. Give proof of Siddhartha Gautama's continuing influence in South and Southeast Asia.
3. What effect did colonial rule have on the development of Southeast Asian economies?
4. How has the caste system weakened since India's independence?
5. Why is helping farmers a major concern of the Pakistani government?
6. Why did the Vietnam War break out?
7. How is Vietnam building its economy today?

Reviewing Key Terms

Use each key term below in a sentence that shows the meaning of the term.

1. caste
2. colony
3. boycott
4. partition
5. nationalist
6. dictator
7. quota
8. parliament
9. purdah
10. drought
11. textile
12. automotive industry
13. refugee

Critical Thinking

1. **Recognizing Bias** Ho Chi Minh spoke of "liberating" South Vietnam when he tried to reunite it with North Vietnam. Why do you think he used the word *liberate*?
2. **Making Comparisons** Compare recent changes in the roles of women in India and the United States.

Graphic Organizer

Copy the web onto a sheet of paper. Then fill in the empty ovals to complete it.

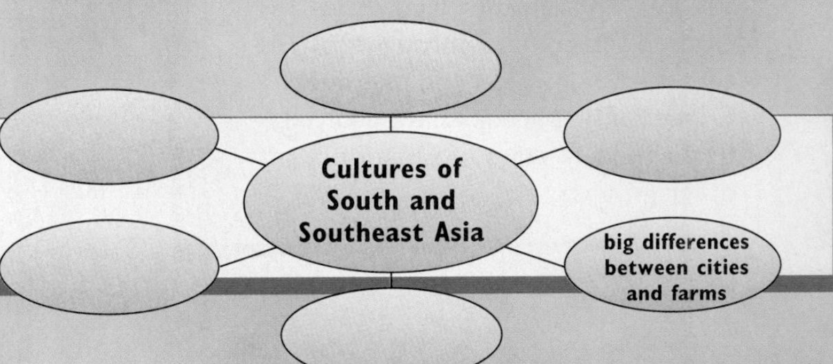

Map Activity

South and Southeast Asia
For each place listed below, write the letter from the map that shows its location.

1. India
2. Pakistan
3. Vietnam
4. Bangladesh
5. Pacific Ocean

Place Location

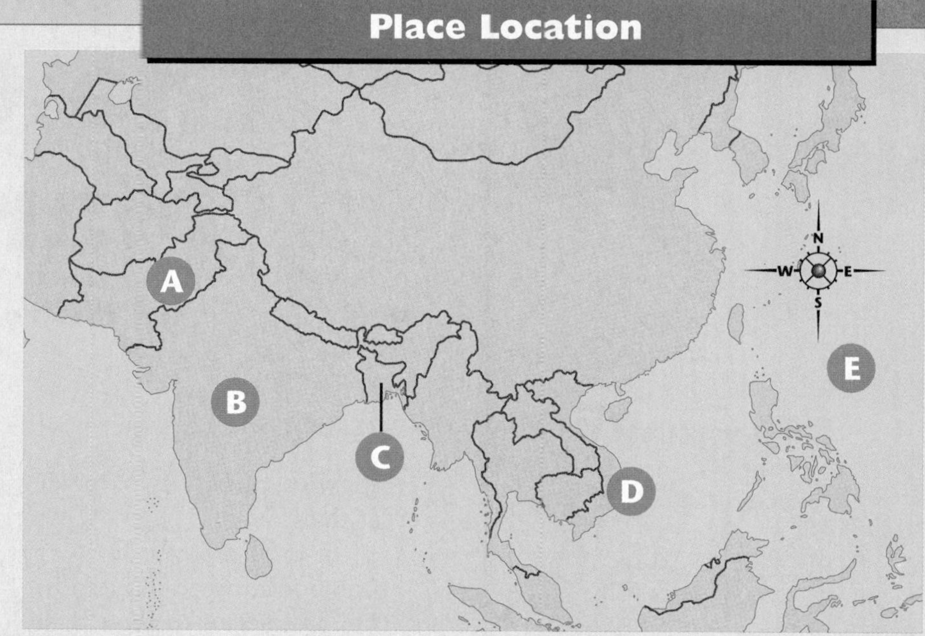

Writing Activity

Write a Newspaper Editorial
Choose one conflict that you read about in this chapter. Write a newspaper editorial that gives your point of view on the conflict.

Take It to the NET

Activity Take a photographic tour of India and see how the people who live there interact with the environment. For help in completing this activity, visit **www.phschool.com**.

Chapter 21 Self-Test To review what you have learned, take the Chapter 21 Self-Test and get instant feedback on your answers. Go to **www.phschool.com** to take the test.

Skills Review

Turn to the Skills Activity.

Review the steps for identifying central issues. Then look back at Section 1 and answer the following questions: (a) What is the central issue? (b) How did you identify the central issue?

How Am I Doing?

Answer these questions to help you check your progress.

1. Do I understand how geography helped shape the cultures of South and Southeast Asia?
2. Can I explain the cultural diversity of these two regions?
3. Can I identify some historic events that shaped the cultures and beliefs of South and Southeast Asians?
4. What information from this chapter can I include in my journal?

FROM

The Clay Marble

BY MINFONG HO

Reach Into Your Background

Think of someone you admire. What special gift or quality does that person have? Some people have the ability to show us a new way of looking at things.

In 1980, civil war in Cambodia forced thousands of Cambodians to leave their homes and move to refugee camps near the border of Thailand and Cambodia. Among these refugees lived many children. There was very little food, and living conditions were poor. *The Clay Marble* tells the story of twelve-year-old Dara, who lives in one such camp. Dara's friend Jantu, another girl in the camp, makes toys out of little scraps and trinkets she finds at the camp.

Questions to Explore

1. What is Jantu's special gift?
2. What does Dara learn from Jantu?

It amazed me, the way she shaped things out of nothing. A knobby branch, in her deft hands, would be whittled into a whirling top. She would weave strips of a banana leaf into plump goldfish or angular frogs. A torn plastic bag and a scrap from some newspaper would be cut and fashioned into a graceful kite with a long tail. A couple of old tin cans and a stick would be transformed into a toy truck.

Whenever Jantu started making something, she would withdraw into her own private world and ignore everything around her. Leaving me to mind her baby brother, she would hunch over her project, her fierce scowl keeping at bay anybody who might come too close or become too noisy. But if I was quiet and kept my distance, she didn't seem to mind my watching her.

And so I would stand a little to one side, holding the baby on my hip, as Jantu's quick fingers shaped, twisted, smoothed, rolled whatever material she happened to be working with into new toys.

"How do you do it?" I asked her one day, after she had casually woven me a delicate bracelet of wild vines.

"Well, you take five vines of about the same length—elephant creeper vines like this work

◀ Cambodian children playing games in a refugee camp near Thailand.

well—and you start braiding them, see. Like this . . . "

"No, I don't mean just this bracelet," I said. "I mean the goldfish, too, and the kites and toy trucks and . . ."

"But they're all different," Jantu said. "You make them different ways."

"But how do you know what to make? Is there some . . . some kind of magic in your hands, maybe?"

Jantu looked puzzled. "I don't know," she said, turning her hands over and examining them with vague interest. They looked like ordinary hands, the finger-nails grimy, the palms slightly callused. "I don't see anything there," she said. "Nothing that looks like magic." She shrugged and dismissed the subject.

Yet the more I watched her, the more convinced I became that Jantu's hands were gifted with some special powers, some magic. How else could anyone explain how she made that wonderful mobile, of two delicate dolls husking rice?

Even from the start, I knew it was going to be something special. For three days Jantu had kept me busy scrounging up a collection of old cloth and string. Then, as I sat cross-legged watching her, she fashioned two straw dolls in sarongs and straw hats and, with dabs of sticky rice, glued their feet onto a smooth branch. Carefully she tied strings connecting the dolls' wrists and waists, so that when one doll bent down, the other one straightened up. Each doll held a long thin club, with which, in turn, one would pound at a tiny mortar as the other doll lifted up its club in readiness. Jantu held up the mobile and showed me how a mere breath of wind would set the two dolls in motion.

Pound and lift, up and down, the two dolls took turns crushing the rice with exactly the same jerky rhythm that real village women pounded it to get the brown husks off. There were even some real grains in the miniature mortar set between the two dolls. It was the cleverest thing I had ever seen.

sarong *n.* (suh RAWNG) a loose garment made of a long strip of cloth wrapped around the body

mortar *n.* a dish in which seed or grain is pounded or ground

Visualize Picture the two dolls in motion. What does the toy look like?

▶ These Cambodian children are in a refugee camp in Thailand.

Children crowded around Jantu, pressing in from all sides to watch her work it. "Let me hold it," I begged, standing next to Jantu. "I helped you find the stuff for the dolls."

Jantu nodded. Breathlessly I held it carefully and blew on it. It worked! One of the dolls bent down and pounded the mortar with its club. The other doll straightened up and waited its turn. I was still engrossed with it when someone shouted a warning: "Watch out, Chnay's coming!"

Even in my short stay at the camp, I'd heard of Chnay. He liked to break things, and he was a bully. An orphan, Chnay made his way to the Border alone. Too young to be recruited into the resistance army, Chnay roamed the fields by himself, scrounging for food and sleeping wherever he liked.

Chnay sauntered up and shoved his way through to us. "What've you got there?" he demanded.

"Nothing," I said, trying to hide the toy behind me.

Laughing, Chnay snatched it away from me. One of the dolls was ripped loose and dropped to the ground.

As I bent over to retrieve it, Chnay pushed me aside. "Leave it," he said. "That's for kids. Look what I have." He thrust his arm out. It was crawling with big red ants, the fierce kind that really sting when they bite. "I'm letting them bite me. See?" he bragged. Already small fierce welts were swelling up on his arm, as some ants kept biting him.

"That's dumb!" I exclaimed. Dodging behind him, I tried to snatch the mobile back from him.

Chnay flung the toy to the ground, scattering straw and red ants into the air.

I grabbed on to his hand, but he was taller than I, and much stronger. He shoved me aside

recruit *v.* to persuade someone to join
resistance army *n.* an army of people resisting, or opposing, the group holding political power in a country
saunter *v.* to walk in an idle or casual manner
retrieve *v.* to get something back again

and stomped on the dolls until they were nothing but a pile of crushed sticks and rags. Then, kicking aside a boy who stood in his way, Chnay strode off, angrily brushing red ants off his arm.

I squatted down beside the bits of dolls and tried to fit them together, but it was no use. The delicate mobile was beyond repair. I could feel my eyes smarting with angry tears. "I should've held on to it more tightly," I said bitterly. "I shouldn't have let him grab it away from me."

Jantu knelt next to me and took the fragments of the dolls out of my hands. "Never mind," she said quietly, putting them aside. "We can always start something new."

"But it took you so long to make it," I said.

Idly Jantu scooped up a lump of mud from a puddle by her feet and began to knead it in her hands. "Sure, but the fun is in the making," she said.

She looked down at the lump of mud in her hands with sudden interest. "Have you ever noticed how nice the soil around here is?" she asked. "Almost like clay." She smoothed the ball with quick fingers, then rolled it between her palms.

When she opened her palm and held it out to me, there was a small brown ball of mud cupped in it. "For you," she announced.

I looked at it. Compared to the delicate rice-pounding mobile, this was not very interesting at all. "I don't want it," I said. "It's just a mud ball."

"No, it's not. It's a marble," Jantu said. Her eyes sparkling, she blew on it. "There! Now it's a magic marble."

I took it and held it. Round and cool, it had a nice solid feel to it. I glanced at Jantu. She was smiling. Slowly I smiled back at her.

Maybe, I thought, maybe she did put some magic in the marble. After all, why else would I feel better, just holding it?

Connect When have you changed the way you feel about something? What made you change?

EXPLORING YOUR READING

Look Back

1. What does Dara think about Jantu's ability to make toys?

2. What did Chnay do to Jantu's dolls?

Think It Over

3. How does Jantu feel about her own abilities?

4. Why do you think Chnay behaves the way he does?

5. What does Dara learn from Jantu?

Go Beyond

6. How might you learn from Jantu to see something differently in your own life?

7. Describe a person you know and admire. What can you learn from that person?

Ideas for Writing: Short Story

8. Write a story about a person who learns something from the example of another person. Write about at least two characters, and be sure that your story has a beginning, a middle, and an end. In your story, show the moment when the person first understands what there is to learn.

CHAPTER 22

Southwest and Central Asia Physical Geography

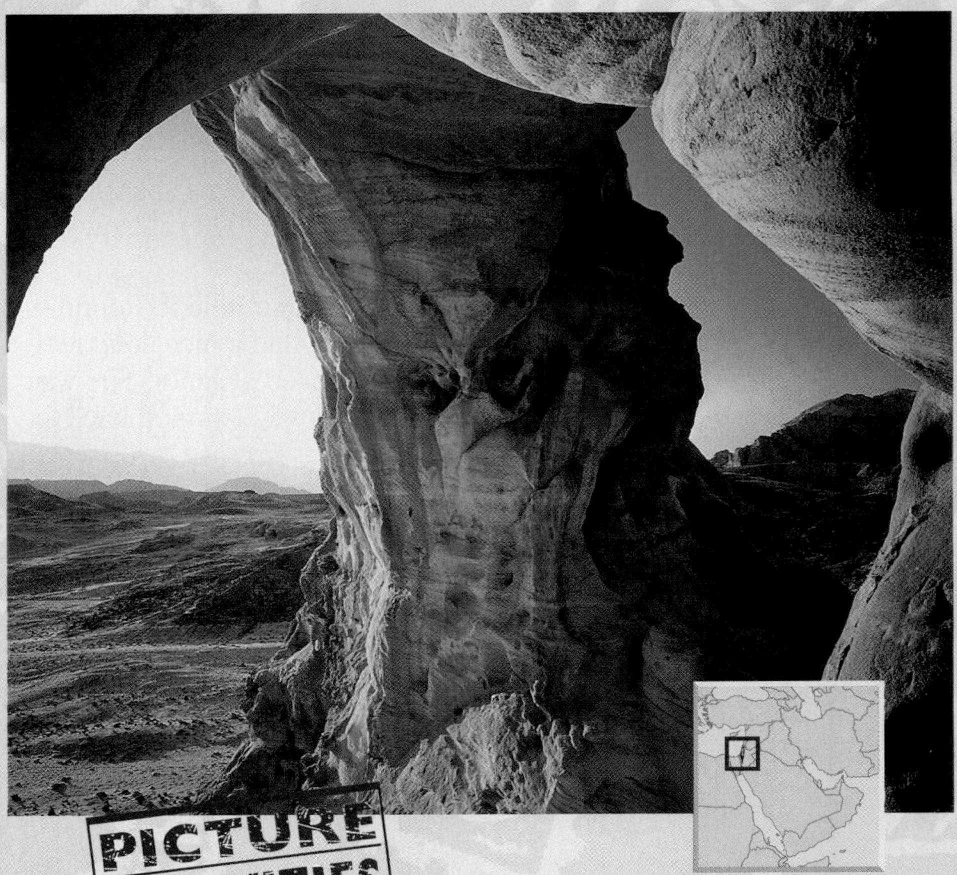

PICTURE ACTIVITIES

The photo above shows natural sandstone arches in Israel, a country in Southwest Asia. Study the picture. Then start your study of this region by doing the following activities.

Write a caption

Write a short caption for the photo that describes the arches.

Decide what to wear

Think about what the weather would be like in the place shown above. Would it be hot or cold? Would it be wet or dry? Would the temperature vary or stay the same? Make a list of the clothing you would pack for a week-long visit to the location.

Land and Water

Reach Into Your Background
Every place in the world has physical features that are unique. What physical features stand out in the area in which you live? Is there a lake, a stream, a hill, or a plateau that everyone in your community knows about? Write down a phrase or two that would help describe this feature to a stranger.

Questions to Explore

1. What are the major landforms of Southwest and Central Asia?
2. Why are Southwest and Central Asia considered a crossroads?

Key Term
oasis

Key Places
Rub al-Khali
Tigris River
Euphrates River
Hindu Kush
Pamirs
Mediterranean Sea

The Rub al-Khali (roob ahl KHAH lee), or "Empty Quarter," of the Arabian peninsula is the largest all-sand desert in the world. Almost nothing lives in this flat, hot territory. Ten years may pass between rainfalls. One sand dune may weigh millions of tons. And the sand dunes do not stay in one place—they gradually move because they are blown by the wind.

▼ The sands of the Rub al-Khali seem to go on forever. Its shifting dunes make it almost impossible to explore or map.

The Dry World

A visitor to the nations of Southwest and Central Asia will see more than just sand, however. The region also includes snowcapped mountains, green valleys, and seacoasts. Look at the physical map of Southwest and Central Asia on the next page. What nations contain mountains? What nations have seacoasts?

Vast Expanses of Desert Despite the region's diversity, its nickname, "the Dry World," is accurate. Southwest and Central Asia contain some of the Earth's largest deserts. The Rub al-Khali is almost as big as the state of

Southwest and Central Asia: Physical

KEY

Elevation

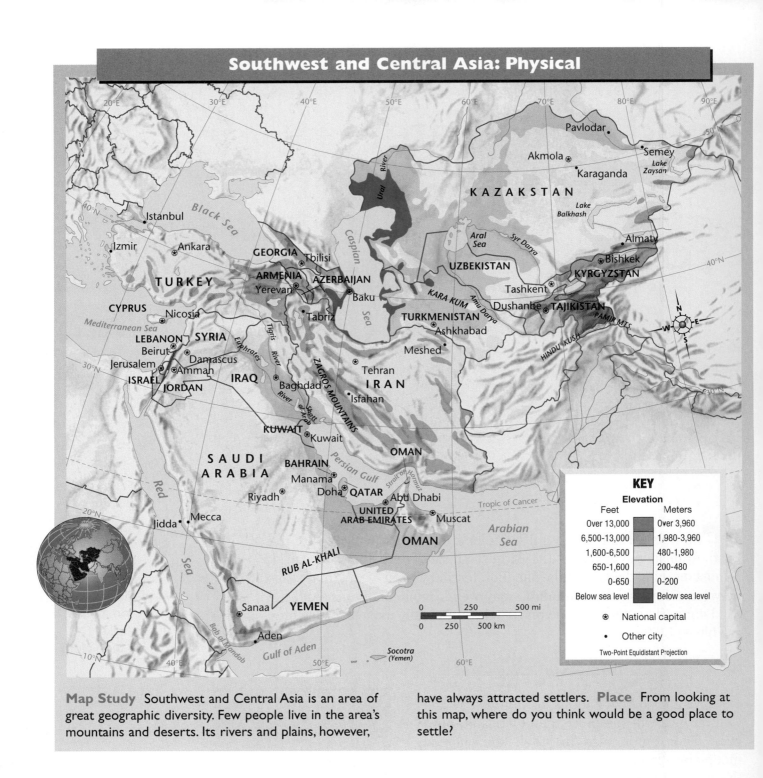

Feet	Meters
Over 13,000	Over 3,960
6,500-13,000	1,980-3,960
1,600-6,500	480-1,980
650-1,600	200-480
0-650	0-200
Below sea level	Below sea level

⊛ National capital

• Other city

Two-Point Equidistant Projection

Map Study Southwest and Central Asia is an area of great geographic diversity. Few people live in the area's mountains and deserts. Its rivers and plains, however, have always attracted settlers. **Place** From looking at this map, where do you think would be a good place to settle?

Visualize Visualize the contrast between an oasis and a gravelly desert.

Texas. In Central Asia, the Kara Kum covers 70 percent of Turkmenistan (turk mun ih STAHN). Most parts of the Dry World get little rain. Water is very valuable in dry regions.

Some of the region's deserts are covered with sand. In others, the land is strewn with pebbles, gravel, and boulders. Travelers passing through any of these dry regions are relieved when they find an **oasis** (oh AY sis), a place where fresh water is available from an underground spring or well. Sometimes, the oasis has enough water to support a community of people. Palm trees provide shade from the sun. Farmers can grow fruits and vegetables. Shepherds can raise livestock such as camels, sheep, and goats.

The Importance of Rivers Few plants grow in most Southwest and Central Asian deserts. However, some of the most fertile soil in the world lies along the Tigris, Euphrates (yoo FRAYT eez), and Ural rivers. When these rivers flood, they deposit rich soil along their banks. More people live in river valleys than anywhere else in the region.

Rivers are not only important as sources of water. They also provide means of transportation. The Tigris and Euphrates rivers, for example, both begin in Turkey and make their way south. They combine to form the Shatt-al-Arab Channel, in Iraq. This channel empties into the Persian Gulf, and gives Iraq its only outlet to the sea.

Mountains as Borders Many rivers begin in Southwest and Central Asia's rugged mountains. These mountains serve as borders between countries and regions. To the east, mountains separate Central and East Asia. The Hindu Kush separate Tajikistan (tah jeek ih STAHN) from Afghanistan. The Pamirs (pah MIHRZ) divide Tajikistan and China.

Sea to Shining Sea Like the mountains of Central Asia, the seas of Southwest Asia separate regions and countries. The Red Sea separates Southwest Asia and Africa. The Mediterranean Sea forms Southwest Asia's western border. The Black Sea borders Turkey to the north. And the Caspian Sea forms part of the boundary between Southwest and Central Asia.

An African Desert Africa's Sahara is the world's largest desert. It is as big as the United States. The Grand Erg Occidental and the Grand Erg Chech are huge sand dunes in the Sahara. They can appear on maps because they stay in one place. Most sand dunes are moved by the wind. Some have been known to move as far as 60 feet (18 m) in a single day in violent winds.

◀▲ The Sea of Galilee (left) is the starting point of Israel's National Water Carrier. This system of pipelines and channels carries water west to the country's coastal cities and south to the Negev Desert. In dry Southwest Asia, plastic shelters are used to keep the moisture in, not to keep the rain out (above).

Where Two Continents Meet

The Turkish city of Istanbul is located on two continents—Europe and Asia. This picture shows a view from the European part of the city looking out across the Sea of Marmara. The building in the center of the picture is the Blue Mosque. It is unusual because it has six minarets. Most mosques have only four of these tall towers. **Critical Thinking** What in the picture suggests that the Sea of Marmara is a busy trade route?

A Crossroads of Continents

Southwest Asia is often called the Middle East. But the Middle East is not in the middle or the east of any continent. Geographers prefer to call it Southwest Asia. The word *middle* is correct in one way, however. In Istanbul, Turkey, you can go from Asia to Europe and never leave the city. This is because the city is built on both sides of a narrow strip of water that forms part of the border between the two continents. To go from Asia to Africa, catch a bus in the Israeli city of Taba and ride to the African nation of Egypt. Southwest and Central Asia are at the crossroads where North Africa, Asia, and Europe meet.

1. **Define** oasis.
2. **Identify** (a) Rub al-Khali, (b) Tigris River, (c) Euphrates River, (d) Hindu Kush, (e) Pamirs, (f) Mediterranean Sea.
3. What are some of the deserts, rivers, mountain ranges, and seas that can be found in Southwest and Central Asia?
4. What continents meet within Southwest and Central Asia?

Critical Thinking

5. **Recognizing Bias** Some of the people who live in Southwest and Central Asia object to the term *Middle East.* Why do you think they object to this term?

Activity

6. **Writing to Learn** Write a description of one of the landforms discussed in this section.

Climate and Vegetation

Reach Into Your Background
The climate that you live in affects the food crops that are grown in your area. Think of some foods that are grown where you live. What are some foods that must be brought in from places with different climates?

Questions to Explore

1. What are the main climates and types of vegetation in Southwest and Central Asia?
2. How do the climate and vegetation affect the people of Southwest and Central Asia?

Key Terms
wadi
arable land

In the winter, the citizens of eastern Kazakstan (kah zahk STAHN) wrap themselves in fur to brave the freezing temperatures. Snow covers the ground as far as the eye can see. Livestock must dig through the ice to feed on the tough grass that lies under it. But the straight, lonely roads of the countryside never need to be plowed. Engineers built the roads slightly higher than the surrounding flatland. The fierce winds keep the roads free of snow.

Nearly 2,000 miles (3,220 km) away, in Iraq, temperatures can climb above 100°F (38°C) in the summer. It is so hot that the air seems to shimmer. Windstorms kick up so much dust that people wrap themselves in robes for protection. And it is so dry that herders and their animals must travel long distances to find water.

▼ This young Bedouin boy may go months without seeing rain. Where he lives—Qatar in Southwest Asia—receives only about 4 inches (10 cm) of rain a year.

Dry Regions

Southwest and Central Asia are regions of huge climate extremes. They have scorching summers followed by bitterly cold winters. In some places, temperatures change drastically every day. When the sun goes down, the temperature often falls 20°F (11°C). Winter or summer, however, one thing remains the same: Southwest and Central Asia are among the largest dry regions on the Earth. Droughts are common here.

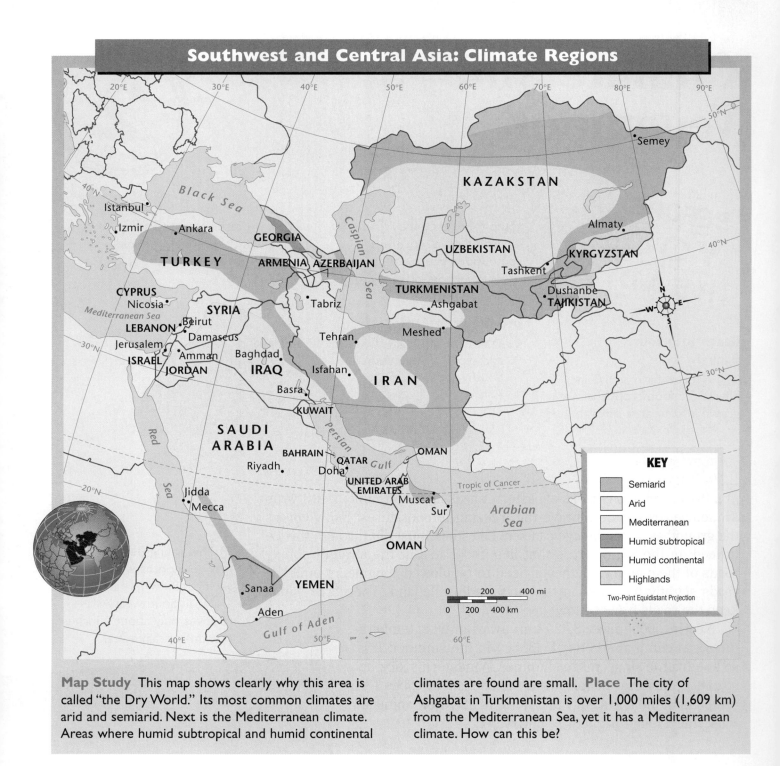

Southwest and Central Asia: Climate Regions

KEY

- Semiarid
- Arid
- Mediterranean
- Humid subtropical
- Humid continental
- Highlands

Two-Point Equidistant Projection

Map Study This map shows clearly why this area is called "the Dry World." Its most common climates are arid and semiarid. Next is the Mediterranean climate. Areas where humid subtropical and humid continental climates are found are small. **Place** The city of Ashgabat in Turkmenistan is over 1,000 miles (1,609 km) from the Mediterranean Sea, yet it has a Mediterranean climate. How can this be?

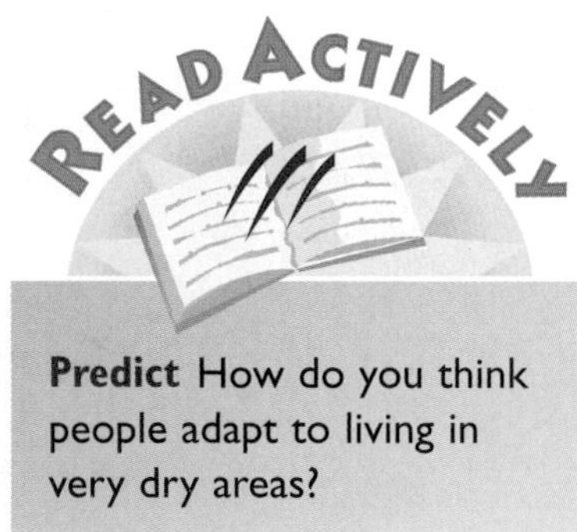

Predict How do you think people adapt to living in very dry areas?

Adapting to Harsh Conditions Even in dry conditions, some plants survive. Plants that grow well in Southwest and Central Asia have adapted to the harsh climate. Some plants survive by growing quickly. They are fully grown before the hottest and driest time of the year. Others have thick, oily skins to protect them from the heat.

Water Where There Was None To grow crops in these regions, however, people must often irrigate their land. Saudi Arabia, for example, has no permanent rivers. It has **wadis** (WAH deez), waterways

▲ Muhammad bin Abdallah Al Shaykh inspects one of the date palms on his farm. These trees produce a sweet, nourishing fruit. In addition, the trunk provides timber, and leaves provide fuel and the makings of baskets and rope.

that fill up in the rainy season but are dry the rest of the year. Rainfall is scarce. People here irrigate their crops by pumping water from deep underground wells.

In other parts of Southwest and Central Asia, wells are not as necessary. People use water from rivers and streams to irrigate the dry areas of the country. Pipes and canals carrying water from rivers snake across the land. This way, the snows melting off the mountains in Tajikistan, for example, can water dry plains that have soil suitable for farming.

A Family Farm in Saudi Arabia Muhammad bin Abdallah Al Shaykh (moo HAM ud bin ub DUL lah al SHAYK) and his family now raise crops on what was once a huge, sandy plain in Saudi Arabia. Only thornscrub, a kind of short, stubby shrub, grew here. Before Muhammad and his family could grow any crops on their land, they had to dig a well more than 600 feet (183 m) into the ground to find water.

Muhammad's family also dug irrigation canals throughout their 20 acres (8 hectares) of farmland. They planted trees to help protect the farm from the fierce desert winds. Then they planted date palms. Dates are an important crop in Southwest Asia. The palms survive well in desert conditions. The picture above shows Muhammad checking on his date palms.

Dates are not the only crop grown by Muhammad's family. They also grow cucumbers, tomatoes, corn, and large crops of alfalfa. The extremely long roots of alfalfa plants can find moisture deeper in the ground. Growing plants with long roots is one way that farmers adapt to a climate of hot summers and cold winters.

Water and Population

Although much of Southwest and Central Asia is extremely dry, some areas are more suitable for living. People tend to settle near coasts, oases, and rivers. The Mediterranean Coast and the river valleys of the Tigris and Euphrates are heavily populated.

Water and Farming

In the dry lands around the city of Avalos in central Turkey, water is scarce. Farmers have to work very hard to raise a few vegetables (right). In the Dalaman River valley in southwest Turkey, water is plentiful. Farmers can grow cash crops such as cotton (below).

Connect What parts of the United States have plenty of arable land?

Most workers in Southwest and Central Asia work on farms. In Turkey and Syria, agriculture is the most important economic activity. But the amount of **arable land,** or land that can produce crops, is limited. In some places, the soil is not fertile. Sometimes there is not enough water to go around. In other places, mountains make it hard to farm. Under such conditions, people have a hard time making a living.

People are using technology to solve some of these problems. In Turkey, people built the Ataturk Dam so they could increase the amount of arable land. A dam blocks the flow of a river so that its water forms a large lake. Water stored in such a lake can be released as it is needed to irrigate land. Scientists and farmers are also developing ways to grow more crops in less space. As industry develops, fewer people will have to make a living farming. But in the meantime, the people of Southwest and Central Asia will continue to grow crops in a dry world.

SECTION 2 REVIEW

1. **Define** (a) wadi, (b) arable land.
2. Describe the climate of Southwest and Central Asia.
3. How has the climate of Southwest and Central Asia affected where people live and what they grow?

Critical Thinking

4. **Expressing Problems Clearly** Few places in Southwest and Central Asia receive enough rainfall for growing crops. What challenges does this create for the people who live in the region?

Activity

5. **Writing to Learn** Write a paragraph describing how the climate that you live in affects you.

Natural Resources

Reach Into Your Background

The lifestyle of Americans today depends on oil products, such as gasoline. For example, every item found in a grocery store was brought there by vehicles powered by gasoline. Think back on the last few days. How would your life have been affected if no gasoline had been available?

Questions to Explore

1. How has petroleum affected Southwest and Central Asia?
2. Why is water considered a most precious resource?

Key Terms

petroleum
nonrenewable resource
standard of living

Key Places

Kuwait
Almaty
Aral Sea

In February 1991, day seemed like night in the oil fields of Kuwait (koo WAYT). Smoke filled the air, and flames shot hundreds of feet into the sky. Iraq was at war with Kuwait near Southwest Asia's Persian Gulf. As Iraqi troops retreated from Kuwait, they set fire to more than 700 oil wells.

The world watched the war in the Persian Gulf with horror. People worried about how the raging oil fires might harm the environment. They also worried that Kuwait's oil reserves might be destroyed forever, or that the price of oil would rise sharply. People around the world relied on Persian Gulf oil. A rise in oil prices could mean hard times for people in most countries.

▲ At the time of the Persian Gulf War, burning oil wells in Kuwait spread air pollution to Iraq, Iran, and other areas of Southwest Asia.

Petroleum: Black Gold

The oil mined in Kuwait is **petroleum** (puh TROH lee um), which formed from the remains of ancient plants and animals. It is found under the Earth's surface. Petroleum deposits take millions of years to form. Petroleum is a **nonrenewable resource**—one that cannot be replaced once it is used. Petroleum is the source of gasoline and other fuels. People all over the world depend on petroleum to fuel cars and trucks, provide energy for industry, and heat homes.

Exploring Technology

To obtain petroleum, workers must drill through layers of rock to reach deposits of oil under the Earth's surface. They begin by building a tall framework called a derrick. The derrick is usually 80 to 200 feet (24 to 61 m) high. It has a system of pulleys and cables that raise and lower the drilling equipment. Some oil deposits are as much as 3.75 miles (6 km) under the Earth's surface. When oil is reached, the drilling equipment is removed. Then, special pipes that let the oil flow up to the surface are put in place.

Drilling for Oil

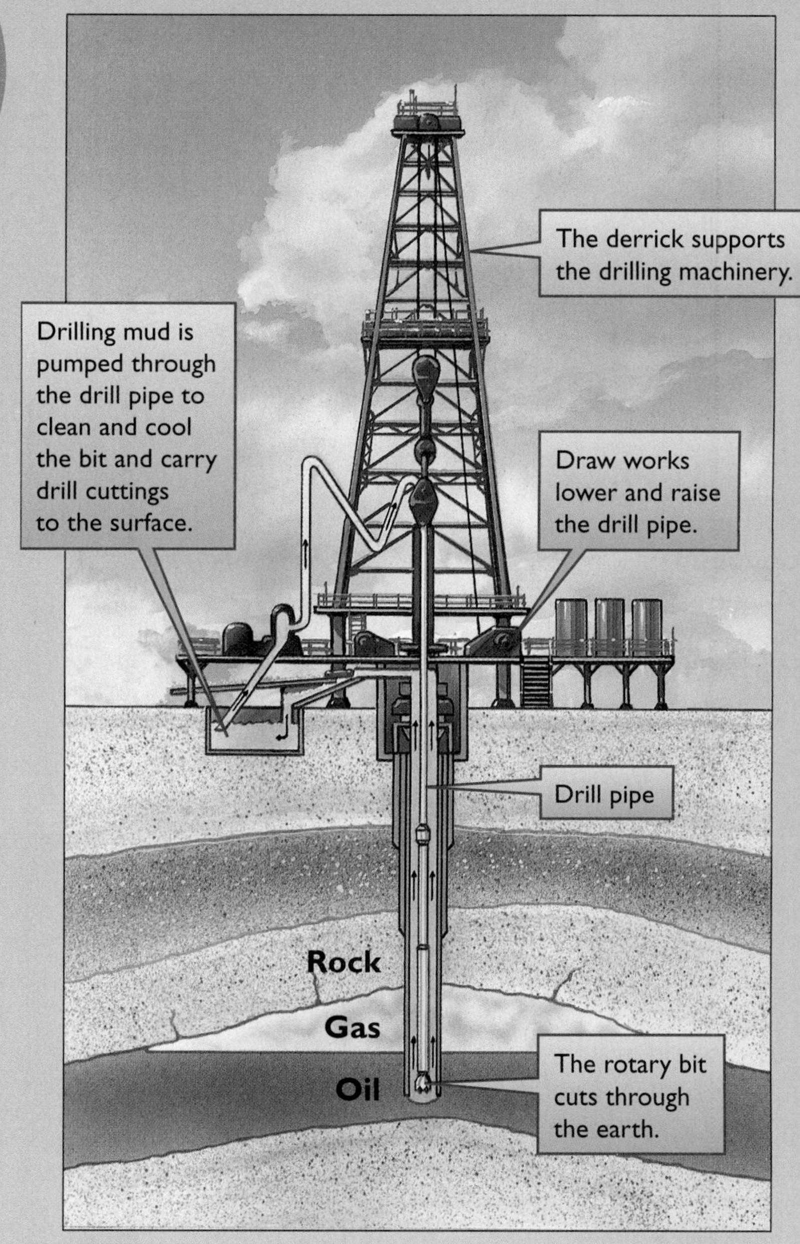
The derrick supports the drilling machinery.
Drilling mud is pumped through the drill pipe to clean and cool the bit and carry drill cuttings to the surface.
Draw works lower and raise the drill pipe.
Drill pipe
Rock
Gas
Oil
The rotary bit cuts through the earth.

Read Actively

Predict What effect do you think reserves of petroleum have on the countries of Southwest and Central Asia?

Petroleum can be found in only a few places around the globe. As a result, petroleum-rich countries play a key role in the world's economy. Southwest Asia is the largest oil-producing region in the world. Central Asia also has a large supply of it. Both regions are greatly affected by their oil wealth.

Southwest Asia: Resources Divided Unequally Petroleum is Southwest Asia's number one export. Oil wealth allows many Southwest Asian countries to increase the **standard of living,** or quality of life, of their people. These countries have enough money to build excellent schools and hospitals and import goods from other countries. They can also import workers. Most of the people living in oil-rich Kuwait are citizens of other countries. Workers from Sudan, Jordan, and Lebanon poured into tiny Kuwait to work. This flow of people is common in the region.

Southwest Asia has more than half of the world's oil reserves. But some countries in the region have little or no oil. These countries tend to have a lower standard of living than their oil-rich neighbors. Why? They do not have the income that petroleum brings. However, these countries benefit from oil wealth in one way. When their citizens work in oil-rich nations, they bring money home.

Central Asia: Attracting Attention Central Asia, too, is rich in natural resources. Kazakstan's oil reserves have changed the face of Almaty (al MAH tee), its largest city. Almaty used to be a quiet city.

Working Together After the Iraqi Army set fire to Kuwait's oil wells, a group of brave oil-firefighters from Texas, led by a man named Red Adair, saved the day. They smothered the fires with nitrogen. The work was dangerous; firefighters breathed smoke; the heat melted desert sands into glass. It took eight months to put out the fires.

Southwest and Central Asia: Natural Resources

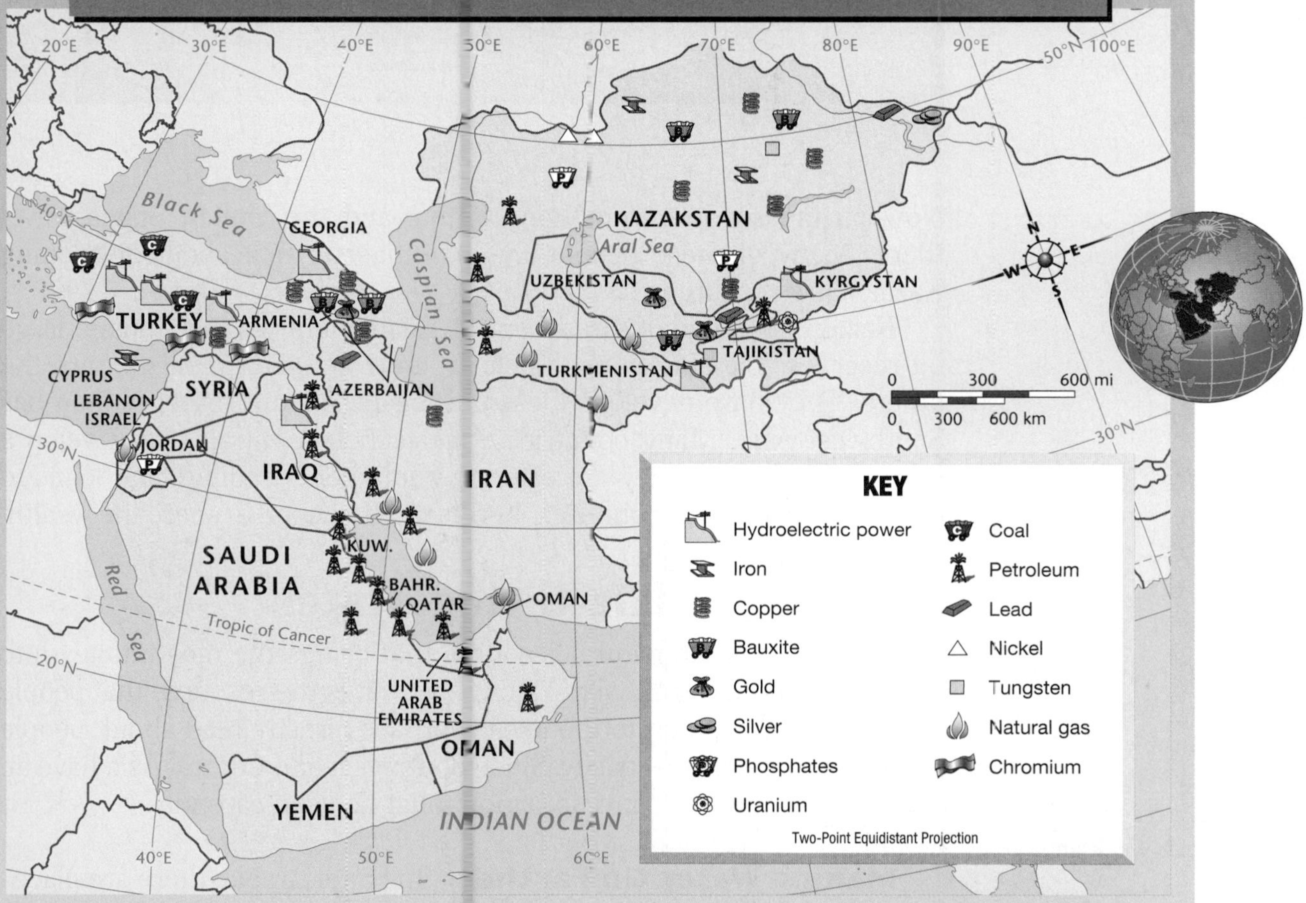

KEY

- Hydroelectric power
- Iron
- Copper
- Bauxite
- Gold
- Silver
- Phosphates
- Uranium
- Coal
- Petroleum
- Lead
- Nickel
- Tungsten
- Natural gas
- Chromium

Two-Point Equidistant Projection

Map Study Saudi Arabia has about one fourth of the world's oil reserves. Its oil fields are located in the eastern part of the country and under the Persian Gulf. **Movement** Why is the location of Saudi Arabia's oil fields an advantage? Look at the physical map at the beginning of Section 1. What would be the disadvantages of having oil fields in the Rub al-Khali?

▶ Today, Almaty is a bustling industrial city. However, it is easy to find peaceful scenes like this one. It shows a Russian Orthodox church at the end of a quiet lane.

Now businesspeople from Italy, China, and the United States travel there. Many of these people are in Almaty to talk about developing Kazakstan's resources.

Kazakstan is one of three Central Asian countries that contain large oil reserves. Uzbekistan (ooz bek ih STAN) and Turkmenistan are the others. They have developed less of their petroleum reserves than has Southwest Asia. Many countries want to help Central Asia develop a larger oil industry. They are offering equipment, training, and loans to Central Asia's oil-rich countries. In return, they hope to share the wealth.

Visualize Visualize water rushing through a creek. Then visualize the creek bed dry, with no water in it. How could a creek be full of water one week and dry the next?

Life-Giving Water

Petroleum is the natural resource that brings the most money into Southwest and Central Asia. Water, however, is the resource that people need most. In addition to the uses you have already read about, people use water to create electricity. Since Southwest and Central Asia have an arid climate, the water in this region must be used carefully.

Making Water Go Farther In Saudi Arabia, there are places where a torrent of muddy water may cut through the dry earth. Along the banks of this rushing wadi, vegetation may sprout. It is a welcome bit of green in the brown landscape. Two weeks later, however, a visitor to the same place may find that the water has disappeared and the creek bed is dry. Throughout much of Southwest and Central Asia, rivers, lakes, and wadis are dry for part of the year. The water they sometimes hold must be used while it is there. Then other sources must be found. As the population in Southwest and Central Asia grows, the demand for water grows, too.

There are few permanent water sources in the region. Southwest and Central Asian countries must conserve the water that they have. In Saudi Arabia, people dig deep wells to tap into water below the surface. People in Kazakstan have built several dams along the Syr Darya (sihr DAR yah) River. They use the water supply created by the dams to irrigate crops.

Stretching Sources to Their Limits The nations of this region have continued to build irrigation systems. But irrigation cannot solve the problem of water scarcity. Too much irrigation can use up the water that is available.

The Aral (A rul) Sea in Central Asia was once the world's fourth-largest lake. Now many boats here rest on dry earth. Two of the rivers that feed the sea were channeled to raise cotton crops in Uzbekistan and Kazakstan. With so much less water flowing into it, the Aral Sea is drying up.

In an area with little rainfall, water that is channeled from a river cannot be replaced. When a river runs through more than one nation, each nation is affected by the others' irrigation systems. For example, in 1989, Turkey built a giant dam on the Euphrates River. Turkey cut the flow of the Euphrates into Syria and Iraq while it filled the lake behind the dam. The dam created new farmland and a supply of electricity for Turkey. But the other countries through which the Euphrates flowed suffered.

The countries of Southwest and Central Asia are trying to work together to preserve their water. They are also trying to make the best use of their oil reserves. Managing these precious resources is important not only to these nations, but to the rest of the world.

Dead Sea Alive With Minerals The Dead Sea, a lake between Israel and Jordan, is too salty to support fish or plant life. But it does help support Israel's economy. The sea is full of minerals. The Israelis take out potash—a mineral used for explosives and fertilizer—as well as table salt and other minerals for export.

1. **Define** (a) petroleum, (b) nonrenewable resource, (c) standard of living.
2. **Identify** (a) Kuwait, (b) Almaty, (c) Aral Sea.
3. What benefits has oil brought to Southwest and Central Asia?
4. List three important uses of water.

Critical Thinking

5. **Making Comparisons** Do you think a person in Chicago looks at water in a different way than a person in Southwest and Central Asia does? What about someone living near the deserts of the southwestern United States?

Activity

6. **Writing to Learn** The economy of Southwest and Central Asia depends on oil and water. Write a paragraph explaining ways in which water and oil can be conserved.

Interpreting Graphs

Look at the picture to the right. It is a standard-size oil barrel. The barrel is about the size of a large trash can. It holds 42 gallons.

Imagine ten of these barrels, filled with oil, standing together in a corner of your classroom. Now imagine 20. Is your classroom filled up yet? If you stacked them, how many could fit into the room? You could probably squeeze in a few hundred.

If just a few hundred barrels of oil would fill your classroom, imagine how much space 22 billion barrels would fill! You probably can't even picture so many barrels. Yet it is important for people to visualize huge numbers like these, because they often represent facts we need to understand.

What kind of visual tool might help you to think about and compare such large numbers? You might try using a graph.

Get Ready

Graphs are helpful because they show a large amount of information in a simple, easy-to-read way. A common type of graph is the bar graph. To help you understand bar graphs, try making a simple one yourself.

Try It Out

Which season is the busiest for birthdays in your class—spring, summer, fall, or winter? You can graph this simple data using the following steps.

A. Gather information. Write down the names of the four seasons: spring, summer, fall, and winter. Poll the class on their birth dates. Count the number of birthdays that occur in the spring and write that number down on your paper next to the word *spring*. Do the same for the other three seasons.

B. Draw the frame of your bar graph. Using the empty graph below as a model, draw and label the horizontal and vertical axes. The horizontal axis is called the *x*-axis. Along this axis you will show the categories of your data—spring, summer, fall, and winter. The vertical axis is called the *y*-axis. The *y*-axis shows value. In your graph, this means the number of birthdays. Make both your *x*-axis and *y*-axis 6 inches long. Space your categories evenly along the *x*-axis. Space your values evenly along the *y*-axis, beginning with zero.

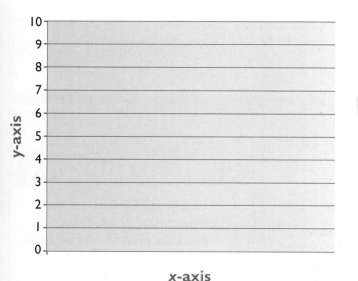

C. Title your bar graph. Write a title above the graph. The title should tell what the graph is about.

D. Draw the bars. Now use the information you gathered in Step A to finish your graph. Begin at the category Spring. Draw a bar beginning from the *x*-axis. The bar should rise only as high as the number on the *y*-axis that matches the number of students having spring birthdays. Do the same for the other three seasons.

E. Study your bar graph. Just by glancing at the bar graph, you can tell when most of the students in your class have birthdays. During which season does your class have the fewest birthdays?

Apply the Skill

Now here's your chance to work with a bar graph that shows very large numbers. Follow these steps to read the bar graph.

1. **Study the labels and the axes.** The title indicates the subject matter of the graph. The labels tell you what each axis represents. What is the subject matter of this bar graph? What information does the horizontal axis show? What information does the vertical axis show? In what order are the countries listed?

2. **Analyze the data in the bar graph.** Which country produces the most oil? Which country produces the least? How much oil does Iraq produce in one year? What about the United Arab Emirates? Which country produces about half as much oil as Saudi Arabia?

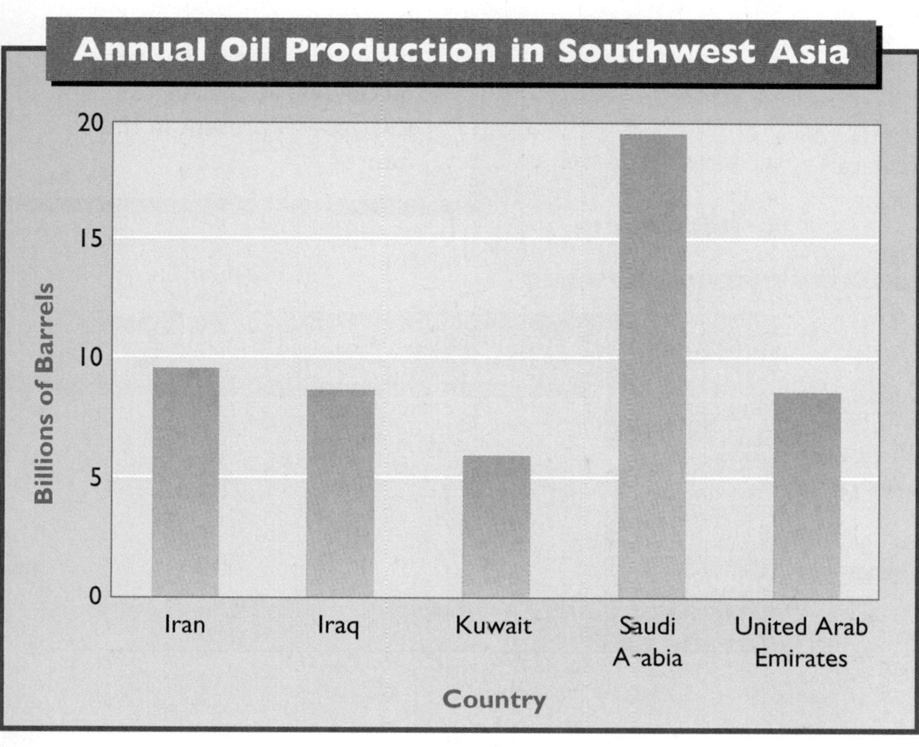

Review and Activities

Reviewing Main Ideas

1. (a) Name one major desert found in Southwest or Central Asia. (b) Name one sea. (c) Name one river. (d) Name one mountain range.
2. Describe why the region of Southwest and Central Asia is known as a crossroads.
3. How does climate affect what grows in Southwest and Central Asia?
4. How does the availability of water in Southwest and Central Asia affect where people settle in the region?
5. What benefits have Southwest and Central Asia gained from their oil reserves?
6. Why is it important for Southwest and Central Asia to conserve water?

Reviewing Key Terms

Match the definitions in Column I with the key terms in Column II.

Column I

1. land that produces crops
2. a measure of the quality of life
3. a type of oil formed from the remains of ancient plants and animals and found underneath the Earth's surface
4. a waterway that fills up in the rainy season but is otherwise dry
5. a natural resource that cannot be replaced once it is used
6. a place in a dry region where fresh water is available from an underground spring or well

Column II

a. **nonrenewable resource**

b. **oasis**

c. **wadi**

d. **standard of living**

e. **arable land**

f. **petroleum**

Critical Thinking

1. **Recognizing Cause and Effect** Most of Southwest and Central Asia has an arid or semi-arid climate. What are three effects of this lack of water?
2. **Expressing Problems Clearly** The populations of Southwest and Central Asian countries are growing very quickly. What challenges might this growth present in the future?

Graphic Organizer

Copy the chart onto a separate sheet of paper, then fill in the empty boxes to complete the chart.

Country	Natural Resources	Major Bodies of Water	Major Areas of Population
Iraq			
Kazakstan			
Saudi Arabia			
Turkey			
Uzbekistan			

Map Activity

Southwest and Central Asia

For each place listed below, write the letter from the map that shows its location.

1. Rub al-Khali
2. Euphrates River
3. Pamirs
4. Mediterranean Sea
5. Kuwait
6. Saudi Arabia
7. Turkey

Place Location

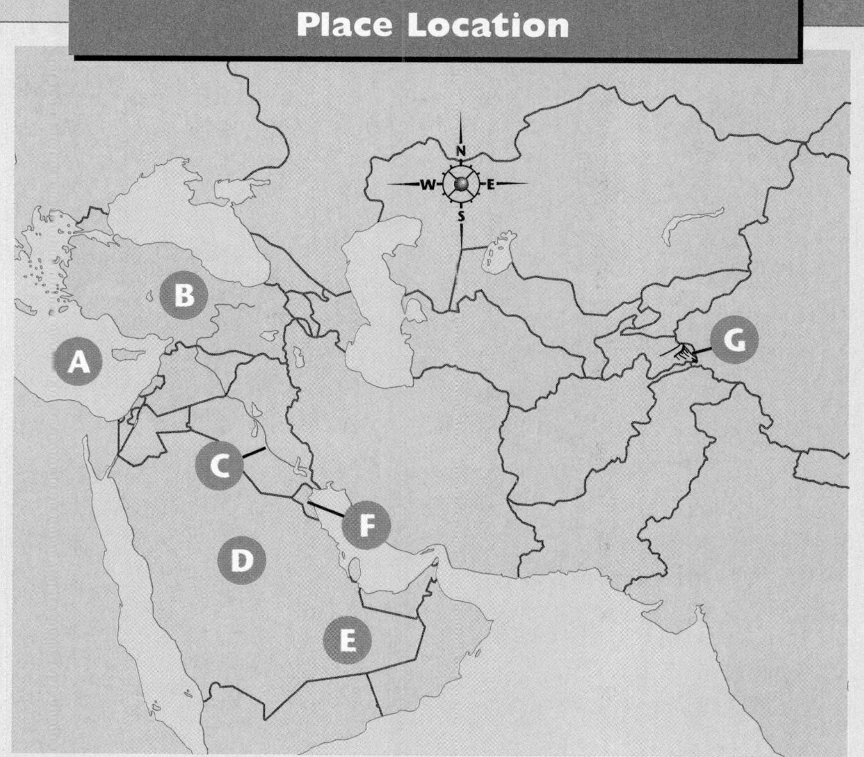

Writing Activity

Writing a Pamphlet

In order to have enough water to meet the needs of the population, irrigation systems must be used throughout Southwest and Central Asia. Sometimes these irrigation systems can cause environmental problems or deprive other countries of water. Select a country in Southwest Asia. Write a pamphlet that describes the advantages a dam might bring to this country. Also, mention possible problems the dam might bring and offer solutions to those problems.

Take It to the NET

Activity Learn more about the geography of Saudi Arabia. Use what you have learned to give a typical daily weather report on a region of your choice. For help in completing this activity, visit **www.phschool.com**.

Chapter 22 Self-Test To review what you have learned, take the Chapter 22 Self-Test and get instant feedback on your answers. Go to **www.phschool.com** to take the test.

Skills Review

Turn to the Skills Activity.

Review the six steps for making and interpreting a bar graph. Then complete the following: (a) What makes bar graphs an easy way to get information? (b) List the steps for reading a graph. Should you always do them in the order given? Why or why not?

How Am I Doing?

Answer these questions to help you check your progress.

1. Can I identify the main geographic features of Southwest and Central Asia?
2. Do I understand how climate has affected the vegetation and population in this region?
3. Can I identify two of the most important natural resources in Southwest and Central Asia?
4. What information from this chapter can I include in my journal?

SOUTHWEST AND CENTRAL ASIA

Cultures and History

SECTION 1
The Cultures of Southwest Asia

SECTION 2
The Cultures of Central Asia

SECTION 3
Israel
BUILDING ITS ECONOMY

SECTION 4
Saudi Arabia
OIL AND ISLAM

SECTION 5
Kazakstan
BEYOND INDEPENDENCE

PICTURE ACTIVITIES

This photo shows the ruins of a ziggurat, a pyramid-like structure in Southwest Asia. People living in what is now the country of Iraq built ziggurats between 2200 B.C. and 500 B.C. The ziggurats were different from the pyramids of ancient Egypt. First, the ziggurats did not have any rooms inside. They were made out of solid mud brick. Second, the sides of each ziggurat were terraced, or shaped like stairs. People planted trees and gardens on the terraces.

Study the picture

How do you think people climbed to the top of the ziggurat? Why do you think people built the ziggurat? How might they have used it?

Consider the architecture

Suppose that you were going to build a model of the ziggurat. How would you start? What materials would you use? What are some of the main steps that would be part of your building process?

The Cultures of Southwest Asia

Reach Into Your Background

Every society has rules. What are some of the rules that you must follow at school, at home, and in your community? What would happen if no one followed these rules?

Questions to Explore

1. What were some of the achievements of the ancient cultures of Southwest Asia?
2. Why has Southwest Asia had a long history of conflict?

Key Terms

deity
muezzin

Key Places

Mesopotamia
Iraq
Palestine

Hammurabi's Code was written about 3,800 years ago in Southwest Asia. People have described its laws as demanding "an eye for an eye." But there was more to the code than that:

> "If the robber is not caught, the man who has been robbed shall formally declare whatever he has lost . . . and the city and the mayor . . . shall replace whatever he has lost for him.
>
> . . .
>
> If a person is too lazy to make the dike of his field strong and there is a break in the dike and water destroys his own farmland, that person will make good the grain [tax] that is destroyed."

The law punished people harshly for wrongdoings. But it also offered justice to people who had been hurt through no fault of their own.

Mesopotamia

Hammurabi ruled the city of Babylon from about 1800 B.C. to 1750 B.C. He united the region along the Tigris and Euphrates rivers. This region is called Mesopotamia, which means "between the rivers."

Ancient Southwest Asia

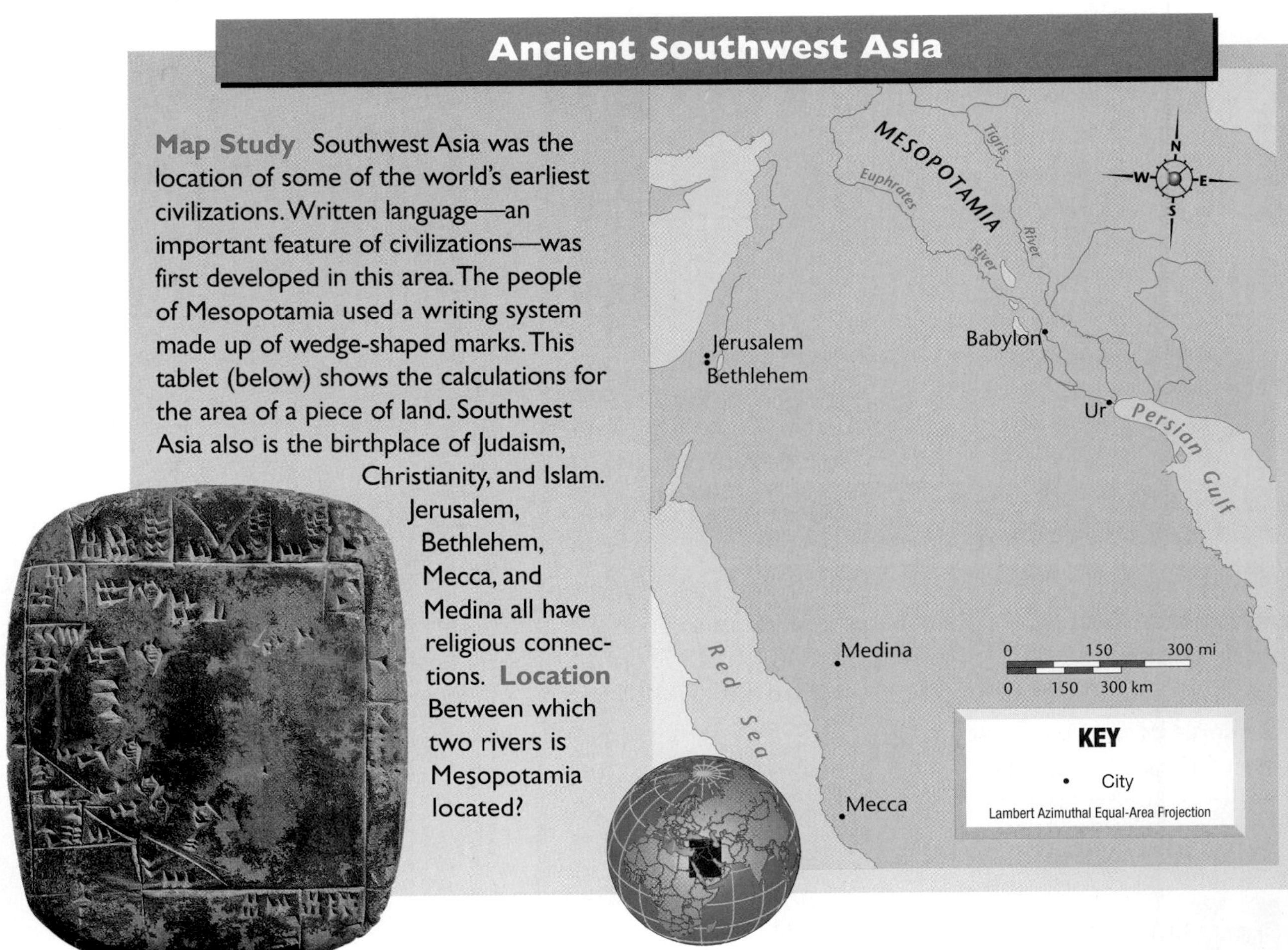

Map Study Southwest Asia was the location of some of the world's earliest civilizations. Written language—an important feature of civilizations—was first developed in this area. The people of Mesopotamia used a writing system made up of wedge-shaped marks. This tablet (below) shows the calculations for the area of a piece of land. Southwest Asia also is the birthplace of Judaism, Christianity, and Islam. Jerusalem, Bethlehem, Mecca, and Medina all have religious connections. **Location** Between which two rivers is Mesopotamia located?

The people of Mesopotamia developed a system of writing. They also produced ideas about law that still affect people today. For example, they believed that all citizens must obey the same set of laws.

People had lived in Mesopotamia for thousands of years, long before Hammurabi united it. By 3500 B.C., the people made the area a center of farming and trade. The Tigris and Euphrates rivers flooded every year, leaving fertile soil along their banks. People dug irrigation ditches to bring water to fields that lay far from the river. Irrigation helped them to produce a crop surplus, or more than they needed.

Many people settled in Mesopotamia. They invented the sailboat and used it to travel on the rivers, trading goods. They developed writing because they needed it to record business deals. People here also exchanged ideas with people from other regions—ideas about agriculture, law, and religion.

Birthplace of Three Religions

Three of the world's religions—Judaism, Christianity, and Islam—have their roots in Southwest Asia. Judaism began when Abraham began practicing it in Mesopotamia around 2000 B.C. Almost 2,000 years later, Jesus, the founder of Christianity, began preaching in what is now Israel. In about A.D. 600, Islam's prophet, Muhammad, began teaching in what is now Saudi Arabia.

People who practice Judaism, Christianity, and Islam all worship the same **deity,** or God. They all study the Bible as part of their heritage. Of the three religions, Islam has by far the most followers in the region today. They are called Muslims.

The sights and sounds of Islam are everywhere in Southwest Asia. One sound is the call of the **muezzin** (moo EZ in), a person whose job is to summon Muslims to pray. Five times a day, wherever they are, Muslims stop what they are doing and pray. In large cities, the call to prayer is broadcast over loudspeakers.

Arabic-speaking Arabs are the largest ethnic group in the region, and Islam is their main religion. But not all Southwest Asians are Arabs. Many Southwest Asians do not speak Arabic and many people, including Arabic-speaking Arabs, practice religions other than Islam.

Judaism is centered in Israel, although Jews live in every part of the world. At the heart of Judaism is the Torah, five books that make up the Jews' most sacred text. The Torah contains the Ten Commandments, laws that Jews believe God gave them through the prophet Moses. The laws established both religious duties toward God and rules for moral and ethical behavior.

Christianity is firmly rooted in Judaism. Jesus, the founder of the Christian religion, was a Jew. Christians adopted the Torah as the first five books of the Old Testament in the Bible. Like Islam and Judaism, Christianity began in Southwest Asia and spread throughout the world.

Visualize Visualize what it would be like to live where everything stopped for prayer five times a day. What might such a town look like? What would it sound like?

Jerusalem, Crossroads of Three Religions

Jerusalem, capital of the country of Israel, is an ancient city. People have been living there since 1800 B.C. Jerusalem is holy to Jews, Christians, and Muslims because events important to their religions took place there. To the left is the silver dome of a Christian church. The golden-domed building is called the Dome of the Rock. It stands over the rock from which Muslims believe the prophet Muhammad rose into heaven to speak with God. **Critical Thinking** Do you think it is easy for three religions to share a holy city? Why or why not?

Conflicts and Challenges

Aswir Shawat is a Kurd from the town of Halabja, Iraq. Kurds are an ethnic group whose people live throughout Southwest Asia. Kurds practice Islam, but have their own language and culture. However, they do not have a country of their own. Their desire for a country has led to conflicts between Kurds and the governments of Iran, Iraq, and Turkey. Shawat describes what happened to him when the Iraqi army attacked his hometown in 1991:

> "Over 5,000 Kurdish people were killed at Halabja, and thousands were injured. My brother and I were saved from death because a few hours before the bombing, we had gone out of town to a village for some reason. . . . We had to go with thousands of people towards the border to Iran. I walked with my grandmother and brother. Nobody took anything with them. We left all our things in Halabja. When we got to Iran, they took us to a camp and gave us a tent. At the camp, we found our mother and grandfather."

READ ACTIVELY

Predict What do you think might happen if two groups of people claimed the same land?

Many people in Southwest Asia have had experiences like Shawat's. The region is a crossroads for Asia, Africa, and Europe. As a result, many groups live here. Religious and ethnic differences have led to disputes.

After World War I, a conflict broke out between Arabs and Jews in Southwest Asia. Judaism has its roots in Southwest Asia. Over the centuries, a few Jews continued to live in their homeland. But many had migrated to other parts of the world. In the late 1800s, Jews from around the world began to dream of returning to Palestine, an area along the eastern shore of the Mediterranean Sea. This alarmed the Arabs who lived there.

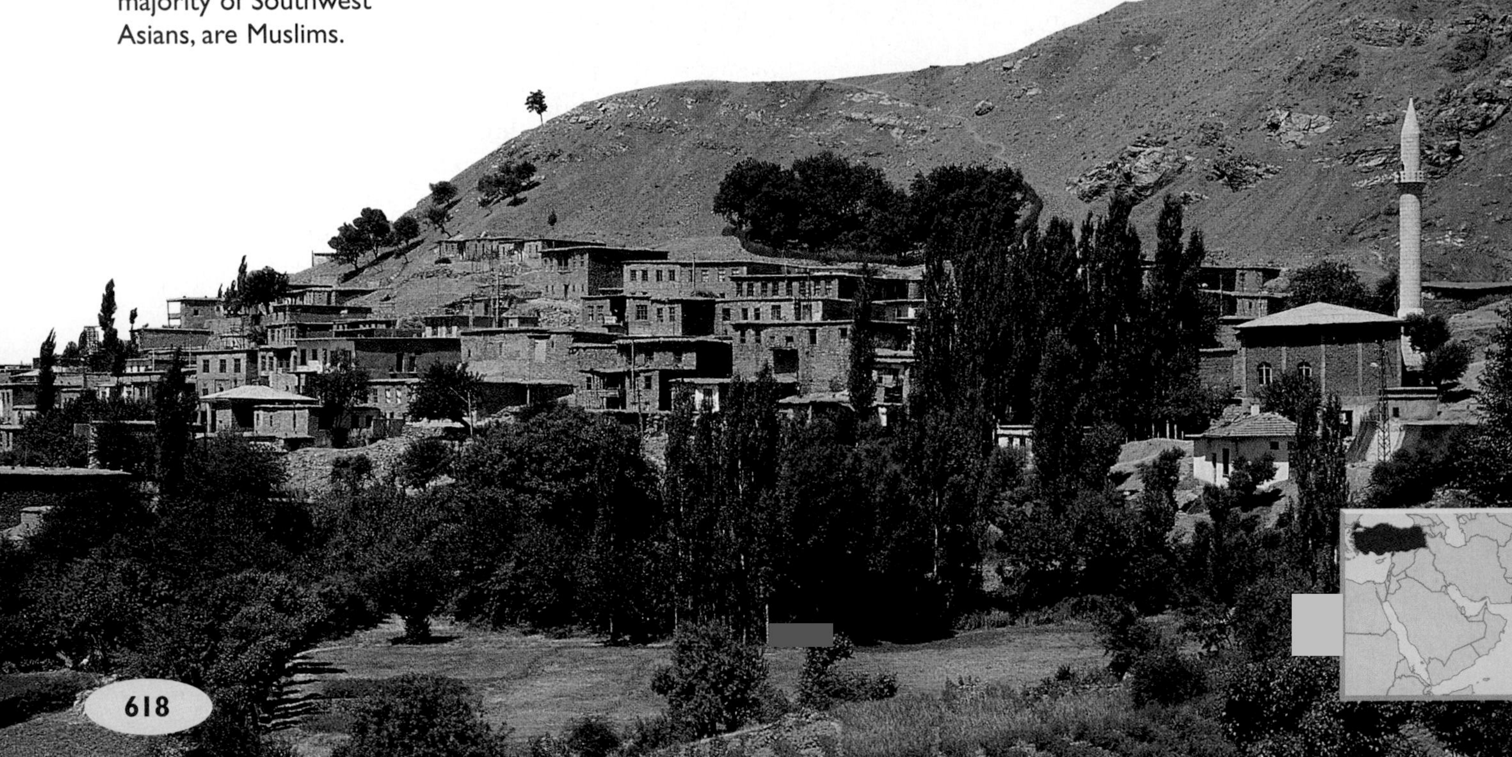

▼ This Kurdish settlement is located in eastern Turkey. Kurds also live in the neighboring countries of Armenia, Iran, Iraq, and Syria. However, they long for their own homeland. Notice the minaret—the tall tower to the right in the picture. Most Kurds, like the majority of Southwest Asians, are Muslims.

Palestine was their homeland, too. When some Jews began moving to Palestine at the end of World War I, tensions rose.

Jews continued to migrate to Palestine during the 1930s. During World War II, millions of Jews in Europe were killed solely because they were Jewish. After the war, many of those who had survived decided to go to Palestine. The United Nations voted to divide Palestine into separate Arab and Jewish states. But neither side was happy with the borders that were chosen. The result was war.

In 1948, Jews formed their own state, Israel. Their state was recognized by the United Nations. Since then, the Arabs of Palestine have lived as refugees in other Arab nations or in Israel, under Israeli rule. Israel has fought a number of bloody wars with the Arab nations that border it.

Arabs and Israelis have been working toward peace. Yasser Arafat is chairman of the Palestinian Liberation Organization (PLO), which seeks to create a Palestinian nation on Israeli land. Israel and the PLO agreed that Palestinians could govern themselves in some Israeli-occupied lands. Then in 1998, Arafat and Israeli Prime Minister Benjamin Netanyahu signed the Wye agreement. This agreement called for Israel to give Palestinians more land, and to release some Palestinian prisoners from Israeli jails.

Though the Wye agreement was easy to sign, carrying it out proved to be difficult. For years neither side could agree on the exact terms. Tensions between the two groups increased. In 2000, fighting broke out among Israelis and Palestinians once again. By early 2001, hundreds of people had been killed. Arafat and Israel's new prime minister, Ariel Sharon, had much work ahead of them to try to work out a peace agreement.

A Handshake for Peace

Former Israeli Prime Minister Yitzhak Rabin (left) shook hands with Yasser Arafat (right). In 1995 U.S. President Bill Clinton invited the two leaders to the White House, where they signed a peace agreement between Israel and the PLO. This event paved the way for the Wye agreement. Although the terms of the agreement could not be settled upon, it is hoped that Arafat and Israel's new prime minister can work them out. **Critical Thinking** Why do you think that many people considered the 1995 meeting a historic occasion?

SECTION 1 REVIEW

1. **Define** (a) deity, (b) muezzin.
2. **Identify** (a) Mesopotamia, (b) Iraq, (c) Palestine.
3. Describe three achievements of the civilizations of ancient Mesopotamia.
4. What three religions have their roots in Southwest Asia?
5. What caused tensions between Arabs and Israelis?

Critical Thinking

6. **Identifying Central Issues** What conflicts over land have existed in Southwest Asia?

Activity

7. **Writing to Learn** Write a paragraph explaining why writing helps people engaged in trading goods.

The Cultures of Central Asia

Reach Into Your Background

Think about how your culture, your education, and the part of the country in which you live affect you. How does your history affect the person you are today? How does your history make you a unique individual?

Questions to Explore

1. What factors have influenced the cultures of Central Asia?
2. What challenges must the people of Central Asia meet on the road to independence?

Key Terms

steppe
collective

Key Places

Kazakstan
Silk Road
Samarkand

Have you ever wished you could change your name? In 1995, the people of Kazakstan did just that. Their republic used to be known as Kazakhstan. The "h" in Kazakhstan was added by Russians to make the name easier to pronounce in Russian.

Russians had a history of misnaming the Kazaks. When Russians first met the Kazaks, they wanted to avoid confusing them with the Cossacks, a southern Russian ethnic group. So Russians called the Kazaks the *Kyrgyz* (kihr GEEZ). Finally, they began calling the Kazaks *Kazakhs* and their country *Kazakhstan*. When the "h" was dropped in 1995, the Kazaks finally had a name for their country that reflected who they really were.

▼ Signs written in the Russian Cyrillic alphabet, like the one on the window below, still can be seen throughout Kazakstan.

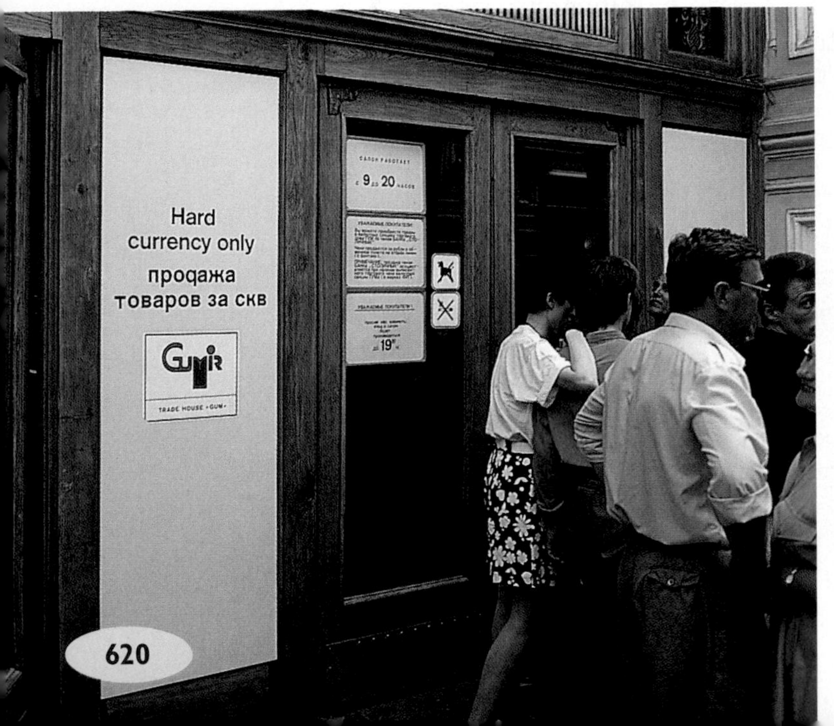

Hard
currency only
продажа
товаров за скв
GUM
TRADE HOUSE • GUM •

Meeting Place of Empires

Kazakstan is the largest country in Central Asia. But the Kazaks are not Central Asia's only ethnic group. Because of the region's central location, dozens of ethnic groups have settled here. Russians still live here, too. Each group that settled in Central Asia brought new ideas and ways of doing things.

◀▼ The rugged Caucasus Mountains are located in western Central Asia (left). In the mountainous areas of Tajikistan, traveling can be difficult even in the mountain valleys (below).

Early History Central Asia is a rugged land. It contains broiling deserts and rocky mountains. Many of Central Asia's ethnic groups first made a living as nomadic herders. They herded livestock across the deserts and the **steppes,** or treeless plains. The nomads took their livestock to places where they knew they could find food and water. On the way, they met other groups and exchanged ideas and customs.

Predict Why do you think the trade route across Central Asia was called the "Silk Road"?

Over 2,000 years ago, a trade route called the Silk Road linked China and Europe. The Silk Road brought the people of Central Asia into contact with the people of East Asia, Southwest Asia, and Europe. For hundreds of years, caravans brought Chinese silk to the West. They carried items such as glass, wool, gold, and silver to the East. Along with goods, the traders exchanged ideas and inventions. Cities like Samarkand, in the country of Uzbekistan, sprang up along the route. These cities became wealthy centers of trade and learning.

The Silk Road generated wealth, but it also attracted invaders. Waves of foreign conquerors fought to control Central Asia. Sometimes the conquerors came from the West. Sometimes they came from the East. Although some ruled for hundreds of years, none lasted. Eventually, a new invader would conquer the area.

Each conqueror left a mark on the region. For example, an ancient Asian people called Persians left large buildings built from stone. In the 300s B.C., the Greeks, led by their warrior king, Alexander the Great, ruled for only a short while. But when they left, their ideas about military organization and strategy remained.

The Different Faces of Central Asia

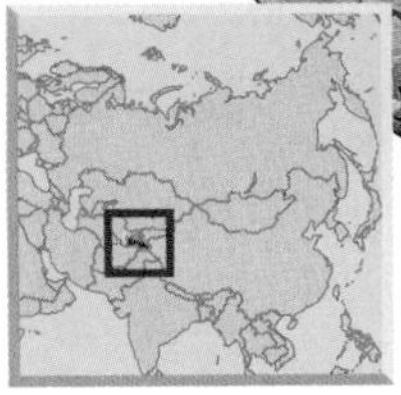

The people of Central Asia represent many different cultures. On the left, a girl takes a short break from picking cotton on a farm in Tajikistan. On the right, a young family waits for a bus on a city street corner in Kazakstan.

Lands for Empires In the 1200s, much of Central Asia was part of the largest land empire the world has ever known. Genghis Khan (GEN giz kahn), a leader of Mongolia, to the north of China, united his nomadic people into a strong fighting force. He conquered much of China and then swept west over Central Asia. At his death in 1227, his empire stretched from the Sea of Japan to the Caspian Sea.

About A.D. 700, the Muslim empire spread across large stretches of Central Asia. The Muslims had the greatest impact on the culture of the region. Many of the people of Central Asia adopted Islam. Today, most people in this region are Muslims.

Under Soviet Rule Europeans soon learned that there were faster ways to trade with China than to use the Silk Road. Ships began carrying goods between China and the seaports of Europe and the Americas. When this happened, trade declined in Central Asia.

This, however, did not stop foreign powers from wanting to control the region. In the 1800s, both Russia and Britain tried to expand their empires into Central Asia. Russia got there first. It captured the city of Tashkent, Uzbekistan, in 1865.

Russia built railroads, factories, and large farms in Central Asia. Some Russians moved into the region, bringing new ways of life. But most people continued to live as they always had. They practiced Islam and lived as nomadic herders.

The outside world, however, was closing in on Central Asia. In 1922, Russian Communists formed the Soviet Union. The Soviets extended communist power over wide areas of Central Asia. The Communists forced people to stop living as nomads. They had to work on **collectives.**

These were farms that were created when the government took over groups of small farms and combined them into large units. Collectives are owned by a country's national government. Soviet collectives did not always produce enough food for people to eat. At least one million Central Asians starved to death during the 1930s.

The Soviets also outlawed the practice of religion. They banned the practice of Islam and tried to stamp out Muslim culture. Many mosques—places of Islamic worship—were torn down. People were expected to celebrate communism, not Islam.

While the Soviets built new industries, schools, and hospitals in Central Asia, they allowed people few freedoms. Critics were jailed, even executed.

Predict What challenges do you think newly independent countries face?

The Challenges of Independence

The Soviet Union ruled Central Asia for almost 70 years. In 1991, the Soviet Union broke up. Then Central Asia in turn broke into five independent countries. Since then, the people of these countries have had to learn to govern themselves.

Each country of Central Asia faces unique challenges. The region's industries are old. Some of these industries pollute the environment. Many people do not have jobs. Health care is poor and hard to get.

▼ After the collapse of the Soviet Union, Muslims in Uzbekistan were again free to worship at their blue-domed mosque in the ancient Silk Road city of Samarkand.

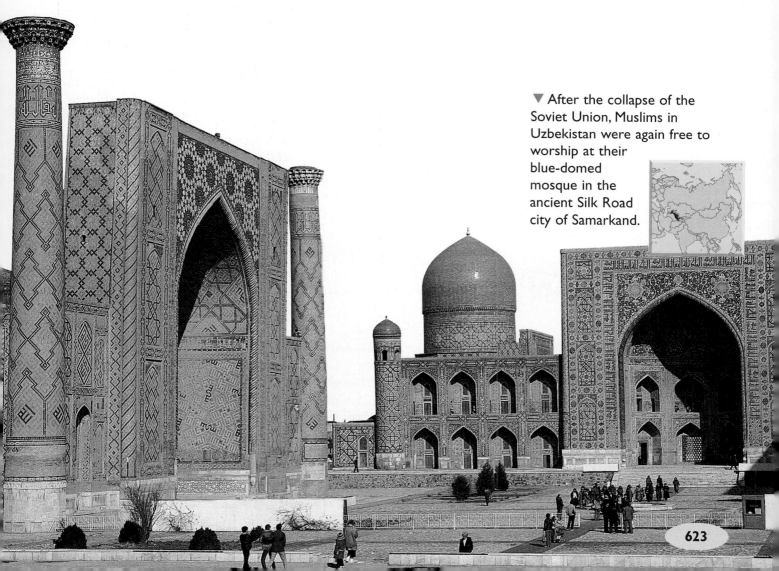

Economies of Central Asian Countries

Chart Study Since gaining political independence from the Soviet Union, the countries of Central Asia are working to become economically independent of their former ruler. **Critical Thinking** What is one product produced by all five nations? How do you think each country might be trying to strengthen its economy?

Country	Economic Activity
Kazakstan	Mining, steel production, and farm machine manufacturing are important industries. Grain and cotton are major crops. Kazakstan is also starting to develop its large oil and natural gas supplies.
Kyrgyzstan	Livestock raising and farming are central to the economy. Cotton, tobacco, fruits, and grains are the major crops. Industries include tanning and textile production.
Tajikistan	Tajikistan's economy is mainly agricultural. Cotton is its most important crop. Its major industries are textile and knitware manufacture and some mining.
Turkmenistan	Turkmenistan has large supplies of natural gas. It is working to export more of this valuable resource. Cotton and sheep production are also important.
Uzbekistan	Although it is a poor country, Uzbekistan is one of the world's largest exporters of cotton. It is also a major producer of gold and natural gas.

However, all the countries of Central Asia now proudly celebrate their culture and Islam. Mosques that had fallen into ruin are being rebuilt. The people of Central Asia are teaching their children about their religion. Neighboring Muslim countries are helping. For example, Saudi Arabia donated one million copies of the Quran, the Muslim holy book, to the nations of Central Asia. The people of Central Asia are working hard to make new lives for themselves since independence.

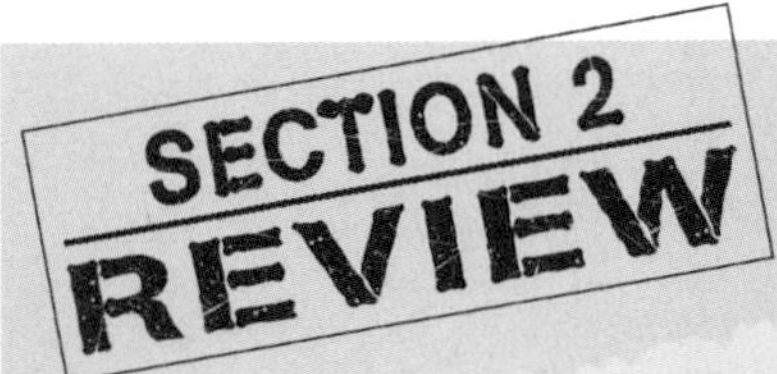

1. **Define** (a) steppe, (b) collective.
2. **Identify** (a) Kazakstan, (b) Silk Road, (c) Samarkand.
3. How has Central Asia's location influenced its history?
4. How did Soviet rule cause problems for the countries of Central Asia?

Critical Thinking

5. **Making Comparisons** The countries of Central Asia face many challenges. Using the chart on this page, compare the tasks confronting the countries of Central Asia.

Activity

6. **Writing to Learn** Write a journal entry telling about a time when you wanted to change your name. Explain why. Or tell why you think your name reflects who you really are.

Israel

Building Its Economy

Reach Into Your Background
Think of a time when you were faced with a nearly impossible challenge. How did you react? What strategies did you use to meet the challenge?

Questions to Explore

1. What are Israel's main economic activities?
2. How do geography and politics affect Israel's economy?

Key Terms
desalination
moshavim
kibbutz

Key Places
Negev Desert
Galilee
Jordan River

Picture a land of rock and sand that is the lowest point on the Earth—1,200 feet (366 m) below sea level. Three to four inches of rain (seven to ten cm) fall each year. Daytime temperatures can exceed 120°F (49°C). This is the Negev Desert, which makes up the southern two thirds of the country of Israel. In this uninviting landscape, Kalman Eisenmann makes a living growing tomatoes, peppers, and melons.

Making the Desert Bloom

Israel is one of the countries of Southwest Asia. Israel's geography is similar to that of the whole region. Two thirds of Southwest Asia is covered by desert. Throughout history, people in desert regions have made a living by herding animals across the desert, not by farming. In Israel, that has changed.

The people of Israel have used technology, new ideas, and hard work to make it possible to farm in the desert. Today, fruits and vegetables grown here are sold around the world. Agriculture has become an important part of Israel's economy.

Technology to the Rescue Kalman Eisenmann grows fruits and vegetables on Negev land that was once barren and dry. He uses an irrigation system that is controlled by a computer.

▼ With the sands of Israel's Negev Desert rising behind them, workers harvest strawberries. This crop is grown under protective plastic sheeting, which keeps water from evaporating into the hot desert air.

COUNTRY • PROFILE

Israel: Agriculture and Climate

Labor Force

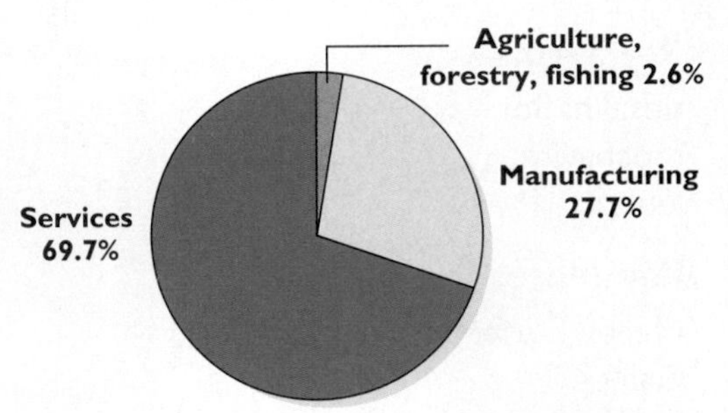

Source: CIA World Factbook 2000

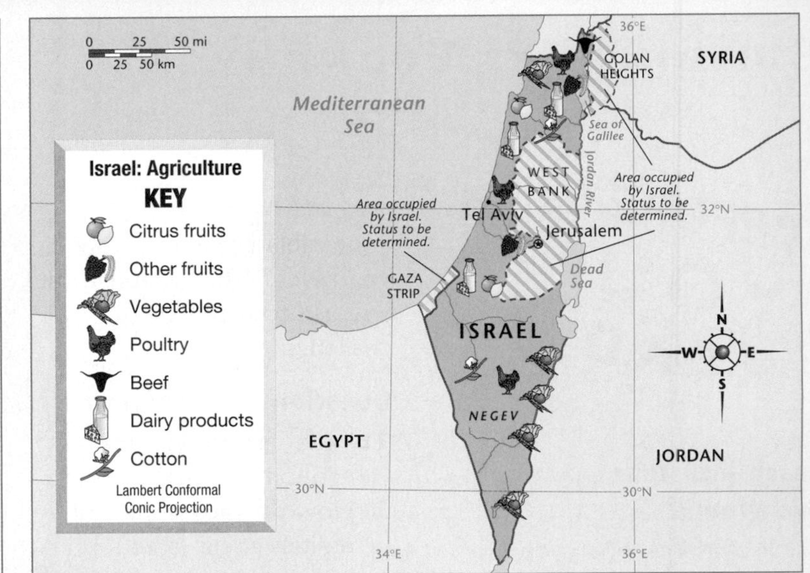

Vineyard in Jerusalem

Weather Chart

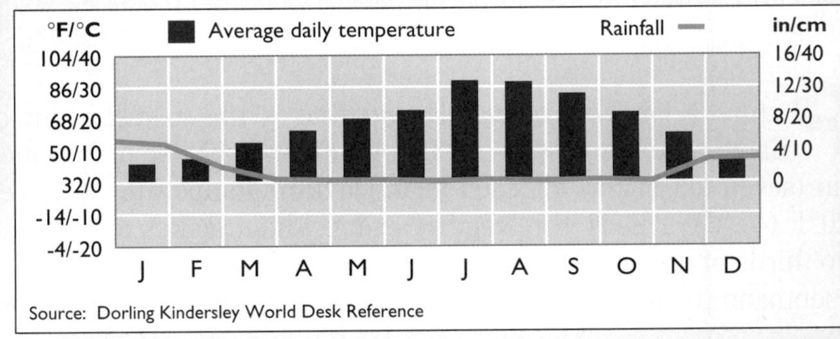

Source: Dorling Kindersley World Desk Reference

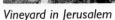

Take It to the NET

Data Update For the most recent data on Israel, visit **www.phschool.com.**

Geography The map and charts above present information about agriculture and climate in Israel. **Map and Chart Study** (a) In what part of the country is beef produced? (b) What is the average amount of rainfall Israel receives in December?

It moves underground water through plastic tubes straight to the roots of the plants. This way of irrigating crops was invented in Israel. When it was developed, few people lived in this desert. But now half a million people live here.

Irrigation, however, could not be used in the Negev without other advances. The water pumped through the system is brackish, too salty to support growth. The Israelis tried **desalination,** or taking the salt out of the water. But that proved too expensive. So the Israelis developed new plants that soak up the water, but not the salt.

Developing new plants is not easy. Many crops were ruined. "I've buried, salted, sunburned, drowned, and otherwise punished thousands of crop varieties," Kalman Eisenmann says.

Even after developing the right kinds of plants, there is more work to be done before desert turns into farmland. Trees must be planted to

Visualize Visualize a desert filled with fruit orchards and vegetable plants. What would be your first reaction?

prevent erosion. Tractors and other equipment must level the surface of the land. But all of this effort pays off. One farmer cuts open a ripe cantaloupe grown on her farm. "Sweet as ice cream," she tells a visitor, handing him a slice.

Working Together Israel became a country in 1948. Since then, it has almost doubled the amount of farmland within its borders. One reason for this success has been cooperation among farmworkers. In Israel, most people who do not live in cities live in **moshavim** (moh shah VEEM), small farming villages. The workers here cooperate. They combine their money to buy equipment. They tell each other about new methods of farming. They also pool their crops to get a better price.

The **kibbutz** (kih BOOTS) is another kind of cooperative settlement found in Israel. People who live on a kibbutz cooperate in all parts of life. They eat together, work together, and share profits equally. The people on a kibbutz do not earn any money while they work there. But the kibbutz provides their housing, meals, education, and health care.

On a kibbutz, people do more than farm. They may also work in factories. Some of these factories make products such as electronic equipment and clothing. Manufacturing is an important part of Israel's economy. The country exports its products to many nations.

Western Wall In A.D. 70, Romans destroyed the Second Temple of Jerusalem, considered most holy by the Jews. Today, a section of the temple still stands. It is part of a larger wall that surrounds a Muslim mosque. The old temple wall, called the Western Wall, is about 160 feet (49 m) long and 60 feet (18 m) high. Long ago, people renamed it the Wailing Wall when they saw Jews praying and mourning near it.

On an Israeli kibbutz, all able-bodied adults work. While some adults tend crops such as oranges (left), others are busy cooking, doing the laundry, or teaching school. Children on a kibbutz may live with their parents, or they may stay in a Children's House, where they eat, sleep, and attend school. This kibbutz kindergarten class (above) is learning how to bake bread. **Critical Thinking** How is life for children on a kibbutz similar to your life? How is it different?

Predict How might a nation's use of the Jordan River affect the lives of people living along the river?

Israel and Its Neighbors

Israel has succeeded in making its dry lands come to life. However, like all countries in Southwest Asia, it must continue to manage its water carefully. To do this, Israel must cooperate with its neighbors.

Sharing the Jordan River Galilee, in northern Israel, is a land of rolling green hills and valleys covered with wildflowers. Farmers pick bananas for market. Picnickers sit near the Sea of Galilee and toss scraps of bread to seagulls. Tourists who come to this fertile region may forget that Israel is a dry land. They may also find it hard to believe that Galilee has been the site of conflict between Israel and its Arab neighbors. The Jordan River, which runs through Galilee, is important both to Israel and to its Arab neighbors.

The Jordan River runs along Israel's borders with Syria and Jordan. It flows into the Dead Sea. In many places, this river is small and muddy. However, in Southwest Asia, the Jordan River is a vital resource. Israel, Syria, and Jordan each irrigate their crops with water from the Jordan. For example, Israel uses water from this river to irrigate part of the Negev Desert.

Each country's use of Jordan River water affects its neighbors. The long conflict between Israel and the Arab states makes it hard for these neighbors to trust each other. Therefore, they watch each other's use of the Jordan River closely. When Israel began building a national irrigation system in the 1950s, Syria tried to stop the project. In the 1960s, Israel tried to stop Syria from channeling some of the river's waters. Today, the country of Jordan worries that it does not have enough water to meet its needs. It plans to build a dam near the Sea of Galilee. No building has begun, because if Jordan starts without Israel's approval, war could result.

▼ All young Israelis—men and women—are required to serve in the armed forces. Here, a woman soldier shows how to put together a gun.

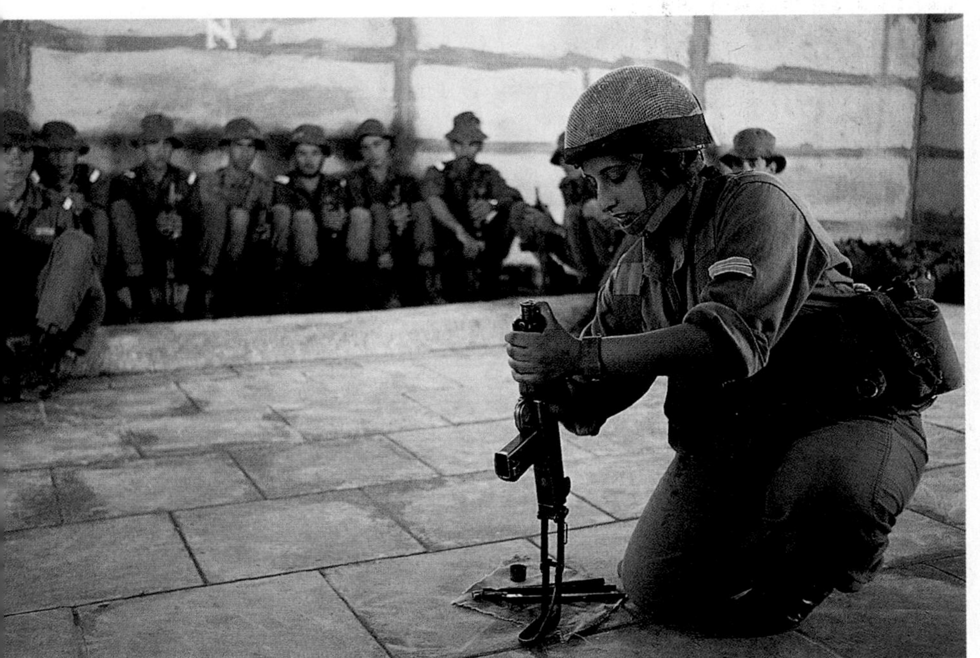

The Price of War After becoming a nation, the Israelis dreamed of enriching their new country. They hoped to provide a home for Jews from around the world. In many ways, this dream came true. The economy developed rapidly. Immigrants came to Israel hoping to find a new life. But Israel's changes cost a great deal of money. Israel received help from the United States and other nations. However, the Israelis have not always had enough money to meet the needs of their growing country.

One expense is the military. Israel maintains a large army. It

West Bank Neighbors

Israel has occupied the West Bank area since the late 1960s. Recently, however, Israel has turned over control of parts of the West Bank to the Palestinians. Not all Israelis are happy with this plan. They want the Israeli army to remain in the area. In this picture, Israeli soldiers in the West Bank town of Hebron watch as two mothers, one Israeli (on the left), one Palestinian, walk with their children.

uses its army in conflicts with Arab nations. These conflicts have taken a toll on all of the countries involved.

Fortunately, Israel and its neighbors are now taking steps that may lead to a lasting peace. In addition, Israel, Syria, and Jordan are starting to cooperate on the issue of water. They have discussed projects that will benefit them all, such as building dams.

Some Arabs and Jews have not waited for Israel and its neighbors to come to an agreement. Mustafa Zuabi is Arab. His friend Palti Sella is Jewish. They live in Galilee, and they have been close friends for years. According to Zuabi, "Thirty-five years ago, I told Palti that peace would come to this land. Because if one Arab and one Jew can be friends, there's hope for all of us."

1. **Define** (a) desalination, (b) moshavim, (c) kibbutz.
2. **Identify** (a) Negev Desert, (b) Galilee, (c) Jordan River.
3. What geographic problems has Israel overcome to build a healthy nation?
4. How have Israelis used technology to overcome obstacles?

Critical Thinking

5. **Expressing Problems Clearly** Why have Israel's relations with its neighbors slowed its economic development?
6. **Drawing Conclusions** Would you enjoy working on a kibbutz? Why or why not?

Activity

7. **Writing to Learn** Israel's economy has benefited from farmers working together. Think about a challenge that has faced your community. Then write a paragraph describing how people can work together to solve it.

Saudi Arabia

Oil and Islam

Reach Into Your Background

In the modern world, gasoline and oil have many uses. What petroleum products do you depend on every day?

Questions to Explore

1. How has oil wealth changed Saudi Arabia?
2. How does Islam affect women in Saudi Arabia?

Key Terms

hajj
diversify

Key Places

Mecca
Riyadh

▼ Each year, over two million Muslims make the hajj to Mecca. Here, huge crowds worship at the Kabah, the holiest site in all of Islam. The Kabah is the cube-shaped structure to the left in the picture.

For more than a thousand years, Muslims from all over the world have been making pilgrimages to Mecca, Saudi Arabia. By going to Mecca, they honor the memory of Abraham, who is said to have built the first house of worship here. The pilgrimage is called the **hajj** (hahj). Muslims must make the hajj once in their lifetime if they can. The hajj used to be long, hard, and dangerous. Muslims traveled across mountains and deserts by foot, horse, or camel to reach Mecca. But in recent years, Saudi Arabia has spent billions of dollars to make the journey safer and more comfortable. Today, many pilgrims travel to Mecca by airplane. Modern hotels line the streets of Mecca.

Oil Wealth

In 1900, Mecca was a small and very poor town. Saudi Arabia was one of the poorest countries in the world. Many of its people made a living by herding livestock through the desert. Like most of the countries of Southwest Asia, Saudi Arabia is mostly desert.

But in the 1930s, everything changed. People discovered oil in Southwest Asia. Oil reserves changed the fortunes of Saudi Arabia and several other countries in the region. It made them rich.

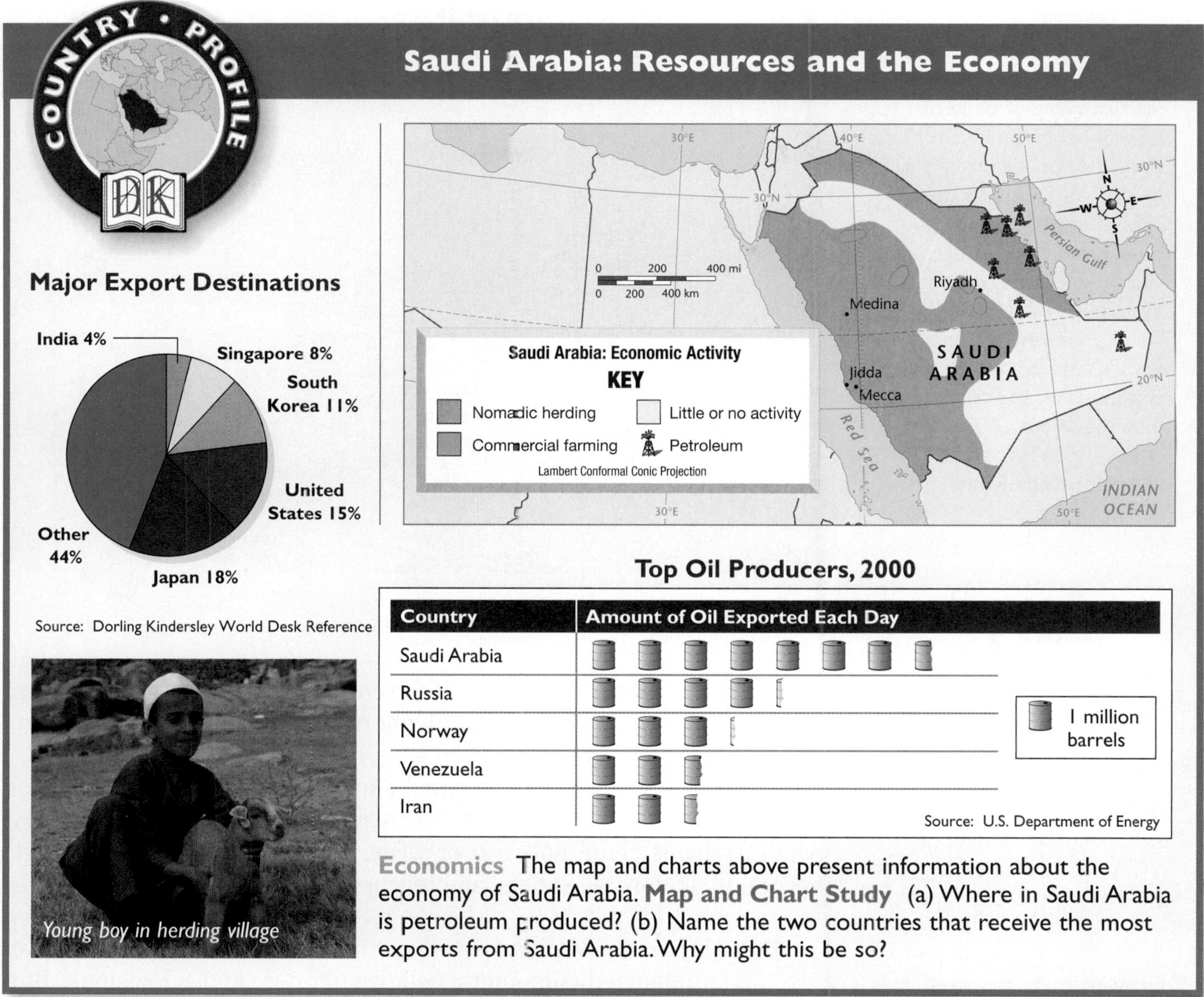

Economics The map and charts above present information about the economy of Saudi Arabia. **Map and Chart Study** (a) Where in Saudi Arabia is petroleum produced? (b) Name the two countries that receive the most exports from Saudi Arabia. Why might this be so?

New Developments When night falls in Riyadh (ree AHD), Saudi Arabia's capital, the skyline begins to glow. The lights of the many apartment and office buildings flicker on. Large buildings line the city streets. When oil prices are high, buildings go up at a rapid pace. Money pours in, allowing communities like Riyadh to modernize. But when oil prices are down, the economy of the entire country is shaken. Many large building projects grind to a stop.

Saudi Arabia has the most important oil economy in the world. Under its deserts lie more than 250 billion barrels of oil. Saudi Arabia has about one fourth of the world's oil. No other country on the Earth exports more petroleum.

Many Saudi leaders think that Saudi Arabia depends too much on oil. The Saudis are trying to **diversify**, or increase the variety of, their economy. They want to create many different ways for the country to earn money. But today, oil exports are still Saudi Arabia's main source of income.

Meanwhile, projects paid for with oil money have changed the lives of all Saudi Arabians. Before the oil boom, there were few roads in Saudi

Take It to the NET
Data Update For the most recent data on Saudi Arabia, visit **www.phschool.com**.

A Modern Capital City

The discovery of oil in the Arabian peninsula in the 1930s brought dramatic changes to Riyadh, Saudi Arabia's capital. Once a small country town, today Riyadh is a modern city with broad highways and skyscrapers of steel and glass. Riyadh ranks as one of the world's fastest-growing cities. Its population has tripled in size since the 1960s. **Critical Thinking** Why do you think oil wealth made Riyadh grow?

READ ACTIVELY

Predict How do modern technology and traditional values exist together in Saudi Arabia?

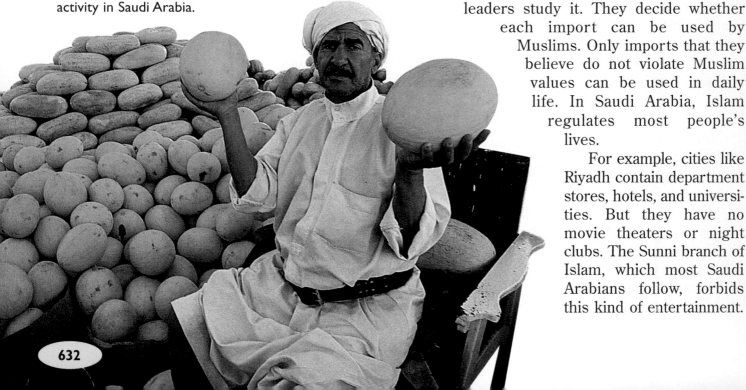

Arabia. Now roads link all parts of the country. In the past, people often lived without electricity and telephones. Now these luxuries are common in Saudi Arabia.

The nation's wealth has also made it possible to build a good school system. Saudi Arabia has built thousands of schools. In 1900, many Saudi Arabians could not read or write. But today, Saudi students are becoming doctors, scientists, and teachers.

▼ Growing fruits and vegetables is becoming an important economic activity in Saudi Arabia.

Traditional Values Using their oil wealth, Saudis have imported computers, cellular phones, and televisions. But before a new gadget is used, the nation's religious leaders study it. They decide whether each import can be used by Muslims. Only imports that they believe do not violate Muslim values can be used in daily life. In Saudi Arabia, Islam regulates most people's lives.

For example, cities like Riyadh contain department stores, hotels, and universities. But they have no movie theaters or night clubs. The Sunni branch of Islam, which most Saudi Arabians follow, forbids this kind of entertainment.

Alcohol and pork are illegal in Saudi Arabia. All shops must close during the five times a day when Muslims pray. Saudi Arabians use Western inventions to improve their lives. But they make sure these inventions do not interfere with their traditions.

The Role of Women in Saudi Arabia

Many laws in Saudi Arabia deal with the role of women. Women are protected in certain ways. They are also forbidden to do some things. The role of women is changing, but traditional values remain strong.

Old Ways and New Professions In Riyadh, women who go out in public cover themselves with a full-length black cloak. Even their faces are usually covered. This is one of the rules of the country. Another rule is that women may not drive cars. At home, women stay in the female part of the house if guests are visiting.

Circles of Wheat In Saudi Arabia, some parts of the desert have what is called "sweet" sand. This sand is not too salty, so plants can grow in it. In a place with sweet sand, wells are dug and fields are planted. Often, the fields are circular, with the well at the center. A long pipe swings around the well, irrigating the field. Wheat, alfalfa, and even pumpkins are grown in such areas.

◀▲ This children's doctor in Riyadh (above) wears western-style clothes in her office. In the street, she wears a traditional full-length black cloak similar to the ones worn by these women in the Saudi city of Jidda (left).

Samira Al Tuwaijri (suh MIH ruh at tuh WAY zhree), a young woman who lives in Riyadh, follows these rules. Tuwaijri is also a doctor in the King Fahd Hospital. She is studying to become a surgeon. "Traditionally, women have always . . . stayed at home to cook and look after the family. Working for a living was just not done," says Tuwaijri.

But when Saudi Arabia built new schools, women became better educated. "Women are no longer content to just stay at home. . . . We are able to compete in a man's world," Tuwaijri says.

Despite the changes, women and men usually still remain separate. Boys and girls go to different schools. They do not socialize with one another. Women choose careers where they will not have to work closely with men. Tuwaijri's patients are all women. "I could have entered general medicine, but I have been brought up strictly and it was difficult to adjust to examining male patients," she says.

The Influence of the Quran Most of the rules governing women's behavior in Saudi Arabia come from the Quran, the holy book of Islam. It requires fair treatment of women. Muslim women could own property long before Western women had that right. However, not all Muslims agree on how to apply the Quran to modern life.

"I suppose it is difficult for those who live in the West to understand why I am not allowed to be photographed," Tuwaijri says. "In Islam, the family is very important and a family decision is accepted by all members without question. . . . Even if I disagreed with it, I would still abide by it."

Like many Saudi women, Tuwaijri is content with her role in a Muslim society. She does not want to live as Western women live. "There are many things in our culture which limit our freedom, but I would not want change overnight," she says. "It is important that we move into the future slowly and with care."

1. **Define** (a) hajj, (b) diversify.
2. **Identify** (a) Mecca, (b) Riyadh.
3. Name three changes that occurred in Saudi Arabia as the country grew wealthy from oil.
4. What happens in Saudi Arabia when oil prices go up? When they go down? Why do many Saudi leaders think their country depends too much on oil?
5. How do Saudi Arabians keep a traditional Muslim way of life even with the changes brought by their oil wealth?

Critical Thinking

6. **Understanding Points of View** What is Samira Al Tuwaijri's point of view about the place of women in her culture?

Activity

7. **Writing to Learn** Saudi Arabians have used their wealth to make changes, but have also maintained traditional ways. Write a paragraph about how your life would change if you became rich. What things about your life would you want to remain the same?

Kazakstan

Beyond Independence

Reach Into Your Background
"The United States is a free country." Think about the meaning of this statement. What does freedom mean to you? What does it mean for a country to be free?

Questions to Explore

1. What unites and divides the people of Kazakstan?
2. What challenges does Kazakstan face now that it is independent?

Key Terms
radiation poisoning

Key Places
Semey
Aral Sea

Who is a Kazak? "If a man cannot name his ancestors for seven generations, he is not Kazak," says one man. He can trace his family history back to the nomads who roamed the steppes. Long ago, nomads recited their family histories to each other when they met on the plains. Kazaks still follow this tradition today.

Today, fewer than half of the people in Kazakstan could pass the count-the-generations test. Until recently, the Soviet Union controlled the country. Members of many ethnic groups moved to the area. Many still live here. Now these citizens are working to fit into the new Kazakstan. Some ask whether they can be citizens of Kazakstan if they can never be true Kazaks.

◀ A group of students gather in a school playground in the western Kazakstan city of Beyneu. Kazak children are required to attend school from ages 7 to 18.

COUNTRY • PROFILE

DK

Kazakstan: Natural Resources

Uranium being shipped out of Kazakstan

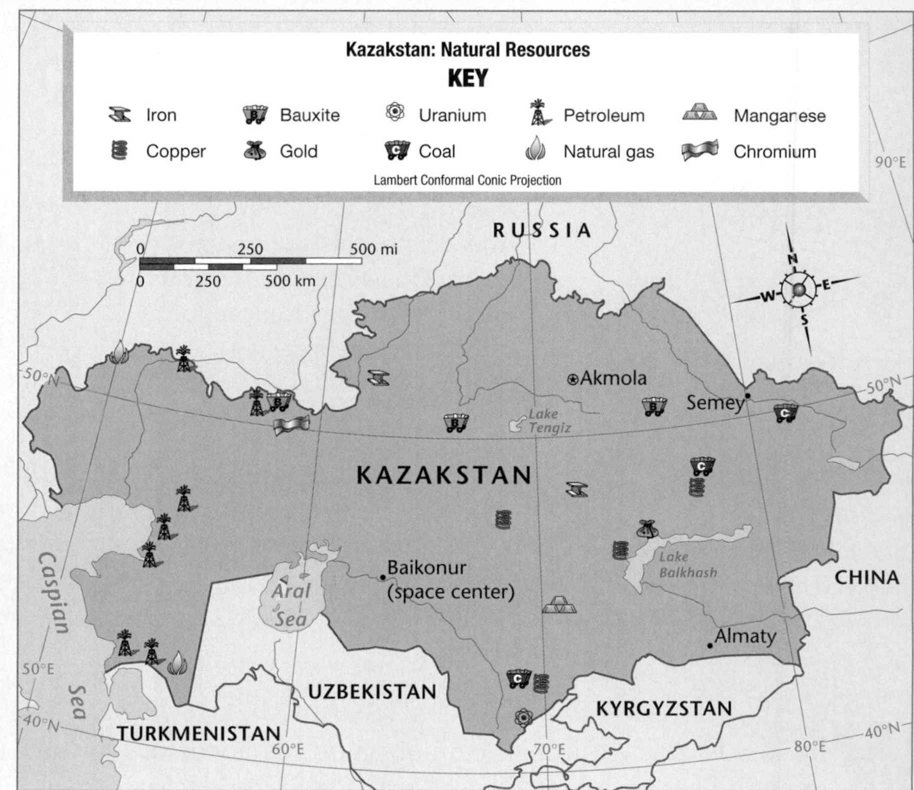

Sources of Electricity

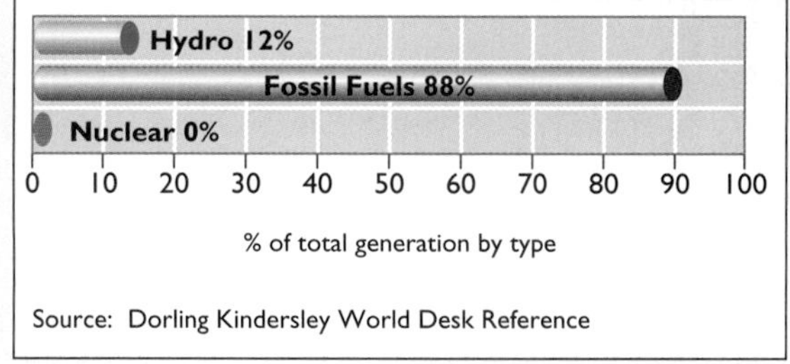

Source: Dorling Kindersley World Desk Reference

Mineral Production

Mineral	Production (metric tons)	Rank in World
Chromium	1,600,000	2nd
Copper	374,000	9th
Lead	34,000	10th

Source: United States Geological Survey

Geography The map and charts above present information about Kazakstan's natural resources and how they are used. **Map and Chart Study** (a) In what part of the country is Kazakstan's main supply of uranium located? (b) What are Kazakstan's main sources of electricity?

Take It to the NET
Data Update For the most recent data on Kazakstan, visit **www.phschool.com**.

Forces Uniting; Forces Dividing

Kazakstan borders Russia in Central Asia. Look at the map above. What country borders Kazakstan to the east? What countries lie along Kazakstan's southern border? The culture of Kazakstan reflects its location between Asia and Europe, to the northwest.

Kazaks in Kazakstan High up on a lonely plateau, Marat Imashev steps out of his tent, which is made of felt carpets. He looks out over his 650 sheep. He, the sheep, a horse, and two camels have been on the move for a month. They are heading toward a place where his flock can nibble on sweet mountain grass. "I know the way without a map," he says. "Kazaks have been grazing sheep on this plateau for centuries."

When Kazakstan became independent, members of the Kazak ethnic group rejoiced. They began to celebrate their heritage. Kazaks designed a symbol for their new country that shows the wooden wheel that holds together a shepherd's tent. They replaced Russian with Kazak as the official state language. They also built mosques around the country so that Kazaks could again practice Islam. These moves frightened many Russians who live in Kazakstan.

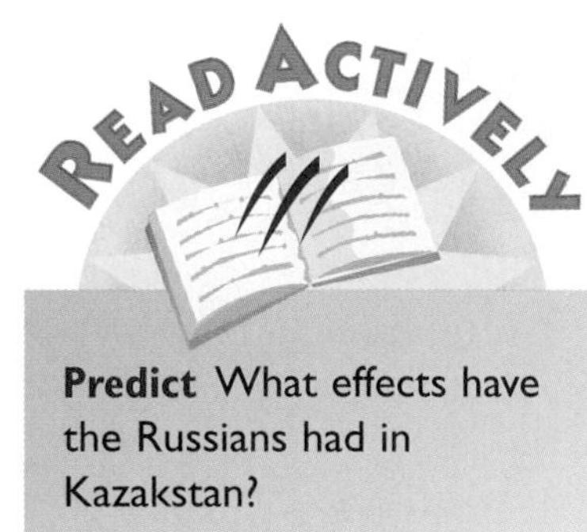

Predict What effects have the Russians had in Kazakstan?

Russians and Kazaks In 1991, almost as many Russians as Kazaks lived in Kazakstan. Most had migrated there since the 1930s to farm. Then Kazakstan became independent. Russians living there worried about what would happen to them.

Today, Russians work at many important jobs in Kazakstan. They speak Russian and have their own schools, theaters, and clubs. Because Russians have some of the best jobs in a land of high unemployment, many Kazaks resent them.

Russian Viktor Mikhailov came to Kazakstan in the 1950s. His job was to turn 60 million acres (24 million hectares) of grazing land into wheat fields. When he arrived in Kazakstan he was surprised to find that the Kazaks bitterly opposed plowing their grazing land under for crops. "We thought we were bringing the future to this country," he says. "And the people say now, 'Why did you come here? You spoiled our pastures. We had a lot of sheep. Now we have no place to herd them.'"

A-OK, Baikonur! Kazakstan will long be remembered for its role in the conquest of outer space. Baikonur (by kuh NOOR), a space center in south-central Kazakstan, was the site of several historic Soviet space flights. In 1957, the first human-made satellite was launched from Baikonur. The earliest manned spacecraft to orbit the Earth blasted off from there in 1961. The first woman in space also began her journey in Baikonur.

Forging Unity Tensions run high between Russians and Kazaks. The new leadership must forge a united country out of these hostile groups. Kazaks are not the majority of the population, but they control the government. This worries the Russians, who do not speak Kazak and are not Muslim.

One Russian leader thinks that both Russian and Kazak should be the official languages. Otherwise, he says, "Russian speakers will not be involved in the government, and all documents will be in Kazak." A Kazak leader does not want Russians in the government. "We do not want them to interfere with the revival of Kazakstan."

Meanwhile, some leaders worry about Russians leaving the country. If they go, they will take their technical skills with them. This nation needs the help of all its citizens.

Kazakstan's Challenges

During Soviet rule, the Soviets used Kazakstan and its resources for their own ends. This is one of the reasons for the tension between Russians and Kazaks today. Many other challenges facing Kazakstan can also be traced to the Soviet period. One of these problems is the damage to the environment.

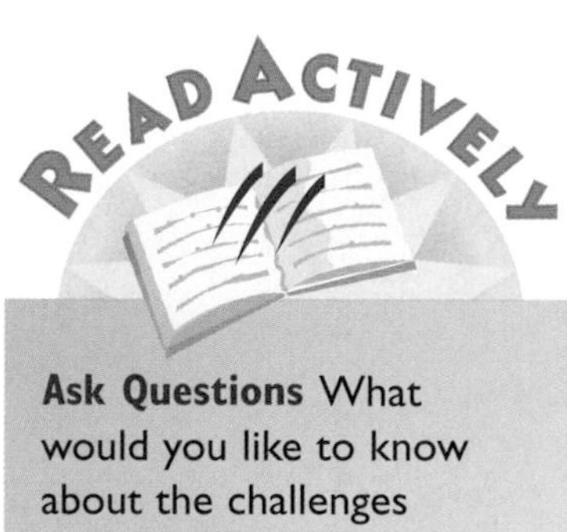

Ask Questions What would you like to know about the challenges Kazakstan faces today?

Nuclear Fallout Semey is a city in northeastern Kazakstan. Before independence, it was known as Semipalatinsk. During the 1950s and 1960s, the skies around it sometimes lit up with a fierce, blinding flash. Giant mushroom-shaped clouds would appear on the horizon. The earth would shake so hard that the walls of houses 50 miles (80 km) from the flashes and clouds would shudder and crack. The Soviet Union was testing nuclear bombs.

The Soviets had a nuclear testing site nearby. In the 1960s, above-ground nuclear explosions were banned. At this point, the Soviets began exploding their nuclear bombs underground. They exploded 600 bombs in about 40 years. Eventually, protests from local people forced the Soviets to stop the explosions.

However, the region is still polluted with nuclear fallout, radioactive particles that fall from nuclear bombs. The pollution from all these explosions will take years to clean up. This pollution has caused problems for the people around Semey. Many babies in the region are born with serious illnesses. Some will never be able to see, hear, or speak. Many people have **radiation poisoning,** a sickness caused by exposure to radiation produced by nuclear explosions. Others have cancer.

Kazakstan also has to clean up after another Soviet experiment. The Soviets tried to grow cotton on land that was not suited to it. Irrigation systems built to water the cotton diverted a great deal of water from the

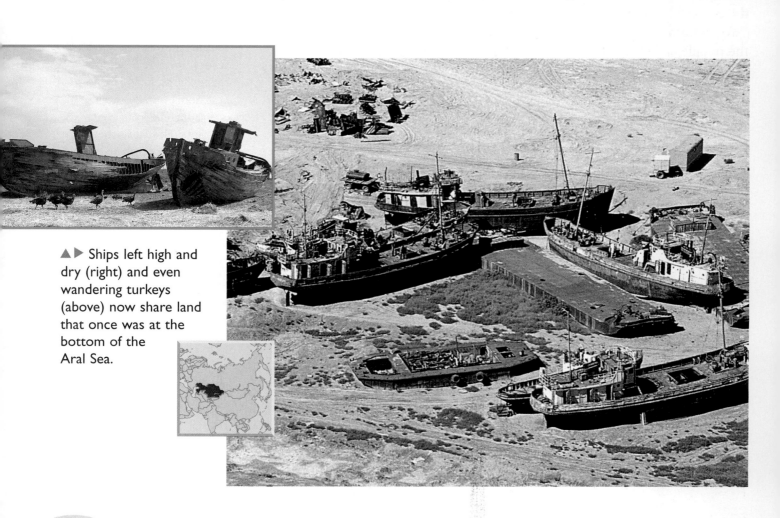

▲▶ Ships left high and dry (right) and even wandering turkeys (above) now share land that once was at the bottom of the Aral Sea.

Market Day in Almaty

The Kazak city of Almaty is located on the old Silk Road trade route. For centuries, the city's markets rang with the shouts of merchants buying and selling goods. Today, the city still has busy markets. However, people visit them to buy local goods, not products from foreign lands. At this market, farmers from the area around Almaty sell their produce.

Aral Sea. As a result, the sea has shrunk in size and its water has become very salty. Some experts believe it may take 30 years to repair the damage done to the Aral Sea.

Discovering Strengths Kazakstan is the largest country in Central Asia. Like all of the new countries of Central Asia, it faces many challenges. But it has some advantages that other nations do not. Kazakstan has many industries. It has the factories and skilled work force it needs to produce manufactured goods. Other countries in the region will need to develop these industries.

Kazakstan is also rich in natural resources. It has coal, lead, zinc, and copper, among other minerals. Most important, it has oil. Kazakstan has already signed an agreement with an American company to start developing the Tengiz oil field. Tengiz is one of the largest oil fields in the world. Resources like this could make the country rich. Oil wealth may help Kazakstan pay the costs of cleaning its environment.

1. **Define** radiation poisoning.
2. **Identify** (a) Semey, (b) Aral Sea.
3. Describe some of the differences between Kazaks and Russians in Kazakstan.
4. What strengths does Kazakstan have in solving its major problems?

Critical Thinking

5. **Recognizing Cause and Effect** How did the years of Soviet rule affect Kazakstan?
6. **Making Comparisons** What are some advantages that Kazakstan has over other nations in the region?

Activity

7. **Explorer's Journal** Write a journal entry explaining how you would feel about Russians living in Kazakstan if you were a Kazak. Then write another journal entry explaining how you would feel about living in Kazakstan if you were a Russian.

Locating Information

Daniel asked Alison, "Do you know what the next concert at the Zip will be?" Alison looked up from her computer screen.

"No, but I can tell you in a few minutes," she said.

"How are you going to do that?" Daniel asked.

"I'll check the Internet," she said.

"Hey, can you show me how?" said Daniel. "I've always wanted to use the Internet, but I don't really understand it."

Get Ready

The Internet is a worldwide network of computers. It is made up of thousands of computers around the globe that communicate over a very complicated network of telephone cables, fiber optic lines, and satellite links. The computers are owned by individuals, schools, businesses, and governments.

People use the Internet to exchange information about nearly every topic. They use it to send words and pictures back and forth to people all over the globe. For example, doctors in the United States use the Internet to share medical information with doctors in China. Music fans share their thoughts about their favorite groups with fans in other countries by sending messages over the Internet.

The World Wide Web is an important part of the Internet. The Web makes information on the Internet easy to find and use. It is made of "Web pages," or individual documents stored in computers on the Internet.

Web pages show information about almost anything at all. For example, many Web pages are set up by stores. By calling up a store's Web page, you can look at the products, read descriptions, and even order items. People have created Web pages about rock groups, families, and whole countries.

As you can imagine, the information on the Internet could fill dozens of libraries. You can use this information for your schoolwork and just for fun. But how can you sort through the pools of information on the Internet to find just what you are looking for?

To start looking, you use special computer programs that will search the Internet for you. These programs are often called search engines.

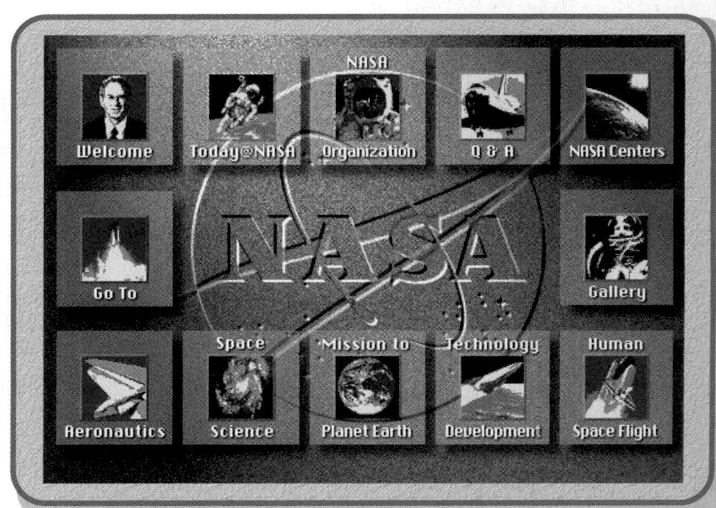

▶ This is a NASA Web page. An Internet user can find more information about any topic named by "clicking" on one of the boxes.

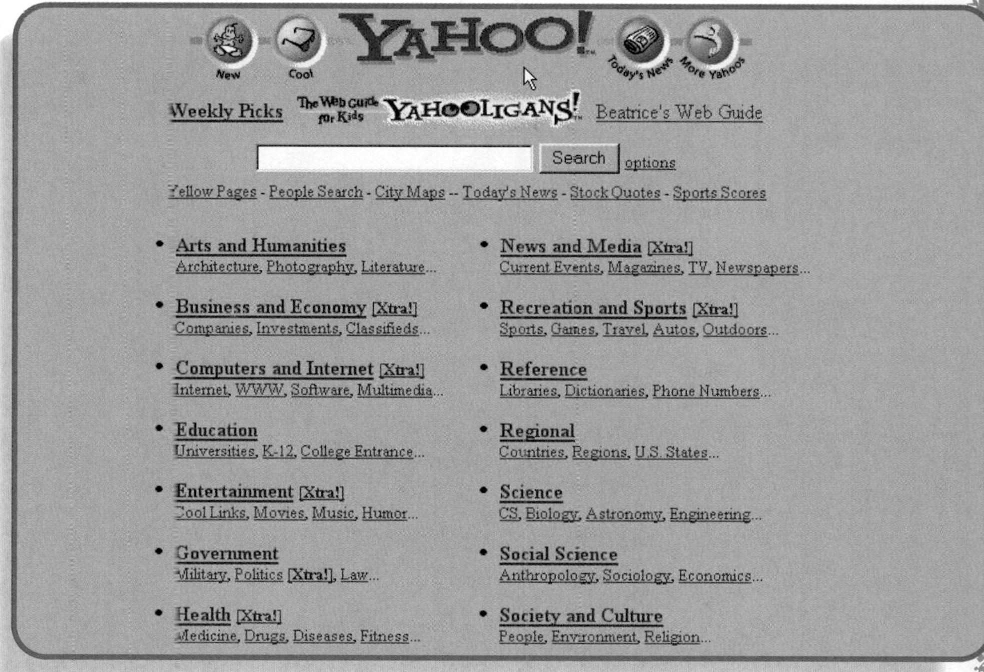

▶ After you type in your topic, this search engine will find references to that topic for you.

Search engines work like the index of a book. In a book index, you locate the topic you want to read about and then turn to the listed pages. On the Internet, you enter your topic and the search engine looks through the Internet for you, listing all of the Internet sites with information about your topic.

Try It Out

The trick to using a search engine is the same as the trick to using a book index—you have to identify the key words for your topic. A key word is a word or phrase that serves as the key to your topic idea. For example, if your topic is "the greatest ballerinas of all time," your keywords might be "ballerina" or "ballet." These words are more specific than "dance," and will probably give better results. Specific key words usually work better than more general ones. Many search engines have useful tips on searching with key words.

A. Identify your key words. What key words would you use to search the Internet and the World Wide Web for information about these topics?
- Your favorite musical group
- Your favorite sports team
- Your home state
- A hobby or interest of yours

B. Begin your search. If you have Internet access, use the search engines to look for your information. Many schools have Internet connections, as do many public libraries. The search engine will respond to your key words with the names of articles or Web pages.

C. Make a selection. Choose the articles or Web pages that look most interesting to you. The network will show you your selection.

D. Read or print out your selection. You can read the information on the screen, or you can print it out to have on paper.

Apply the Skill

Now prepare for an Internet search for information about Central and Southwest Asia. Follow the same steps as in Try It Out, but research the following topics, in addition to any other ideas you have:

- Typical food in Kazakstan
- History of Israel
- Architecture in Saudi Arabia

Review and Activities

Reviewing Main Ideas

1. What were the accomplishments of the early Mesopotamians?
2. List two conflicts that trouble Southwest Asia.
3. How did Central Asia's location affect its history and cultures?
4. Identify two challenges that the countries of Central Asia face today.
5. How is Israel's agriculture affected by its geography?
6. Explain how Israel's relationship with its neighbors affects its economy.
7. List two ways in which Saudi Arabia has spent some of its oil money.
8. How have the lives of Saudi Arabian women remained the same since the oil boom? How are they different?
9. Explain why there is tension between the Kazaks and the Russians living in Kazakstan.
10. What strengths will help Kazakstan face the challenges of independence?

Reviewing Key Terms

Use each key term below in a sentence that shows the meaning of the term.

1. deity
2. muezzin
3. steppe
4. collective
5. desalination
6. moshavim
7. kibbutz
8. hajj
9. diversify
10. radiation poisoning

Critical Thinking

1. **Identifying Central Issues** Each country in Southwest and Central Asia is unique. However, all these countries have certain similarities. What characteristics do most of the countries in this region share?
2. **Making Comparisons** Israel and Kazakstan are both very young countries. In what ways are these countries alike? In what ways are they different?

Graphic Organizer

Copy the diagram onto a sheet of paper, then fill in the empty boxes to complete the chart.

	Israel	Saudi Arabia	Kazakstan
Traditional Way of Making a Living			
Modern Changes to How People Make a Living			

Map Activity

Southwest and Central Asia

For each place below, write the letter from the map that shows its location. Use the maps in the Activity Atlas at the front of the book to help you.

1. Israel
2. Saudi Arabia
3. Kazakstan
4. Silk Road
5. Negev Desert

Place Location

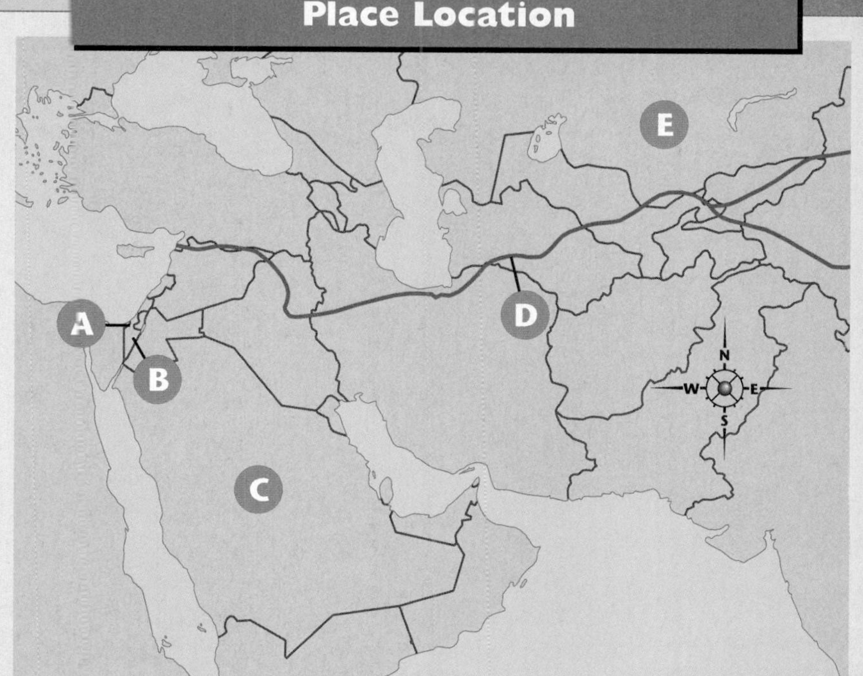

Writing Activity

Writing a Progress Report

All of the countries in Southwest and Central Asia face challenges as they enter the future. Choose one of the countries covered in this chapter and write a progress report about it. Remember to address the problems the nation faces and the solutions being put forward to address those problems.

Take It to the NET

Activity Browse the exhibits at the Israel Museum. Which exhibit did you find most interesting? For help in completing this activity, visit **www.phschool.com.**

Chapter 23 Self-Test To review what you have learned, take the Chapter 23 Self-Test and get instant feedback on your answers. Go to **www.phschool.com** to take the test.

Skills Review

Turn to the Skills Activity.

Review the way to find information on the Internet. Then complete the following: (a) How is a search engine like an index? (b) Give examples of how you would narrow a topic down to one or more key words.

How Am I Doing?

Answer these questions to help you check your progress.

1. Can I describe the main geographic features of Southwest and Central Asia?
2. Do I understand how cultures in Southwest and Central Asia compare to other Asian cultures I have studied?
3. Can I identify some historic events that have shaped the modern cultures of Southwest and Central Asia?
4. What information from this chapter can I include in my journal?

CHAPTER

24

The Pacific Region

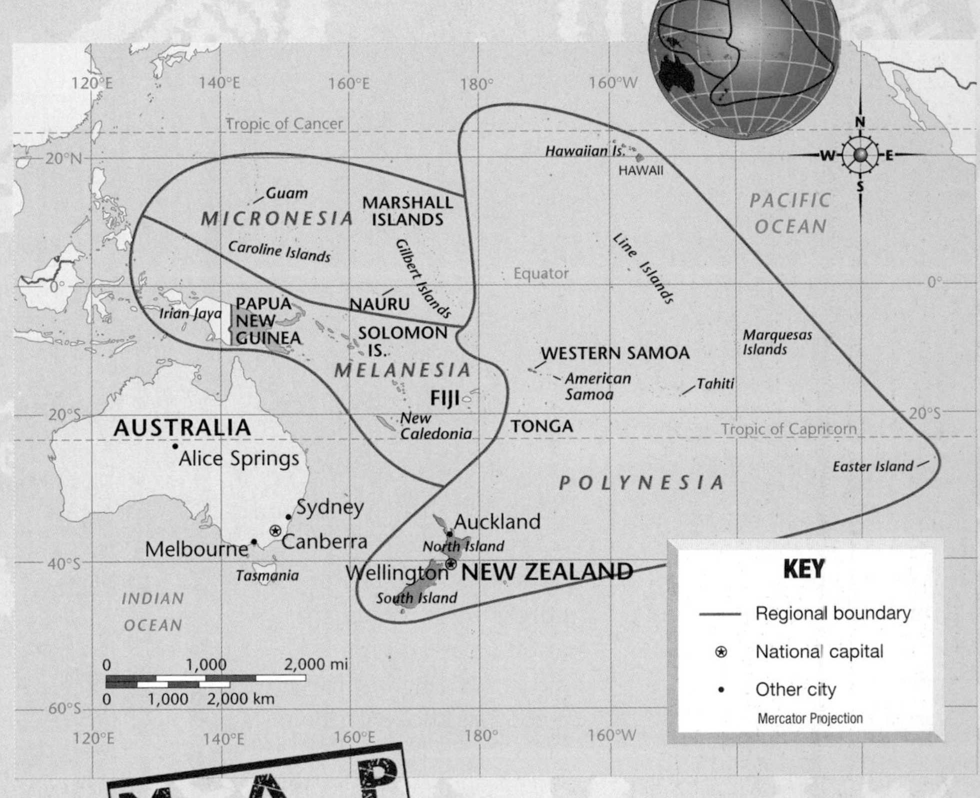

MAP ACTIVITIES

The Pacific region includes the continent of Australia and many islands. The largest islands are those that make up New Guinea and New Zealand, but there are thousands of others. To learn more about the lands and the people of this region, do the following activities.

Study the map

Look at the map scale. What important fact does the map scale tell you about the Pacific region? Name the three large groups of Pacific islands.

Make connections

The Pacific region is one of the largest in the world. But only about 29 million people live here. That is less than 1 percent of the world's population. Why do you think so few people live in this region?

Physical Geography of Australia and New Zealand

Reach Into Your Background

Do you live in a crowded city or in a small town? How close to your neighbors do you live? What are some of the advantages and disadvantages of living in a city? In a small town? Think about these questions as you read about Australia and New Zealand.

Questions to Explore

1. What are the major physical features of Australia and New Zealand?
2. How has physical geography affected the climate, vegetation, and animal life of the region?

Key Terms

marsupial
tectonic plate
geyser
fiord

Key Places

Great Dividing Range
Outback
North Island
South Island
Canterbury Plain

What bird is strange looking, has a long bill, does not fly, and only comes out at night to hunt? If you said a kiwi, you are right. The people of New Zealand are so proud of this unusual bird that they have made it their national symbol. The people even call themselves "Kiwis." The bird is one of many unique animals found in New Zealand and its neighbor to the west, Australia.

▼ The Kiwi has no tail. It is the only bird with nostrils at the tip of its beak. These help it sniff out insects and berries.

Unique Environments

Australia and New Zealand lie between the Pacific Ocean and the Indian Ocean. Both are in the Southern Hemisphere, south of the Equator. This means that their seasons are the opposite of those in the United States. They are far from other landmasses, which has made them unique.

New Zealand and Australia are so far from other large landmasses that many of their animals and plants are found nowhere else on the Earth. Only in New Zealand can you find kiwis and yellow-eyed penguins. Eighty-four percent of the vegetation in New Zealand's forests grows nowhere else. Australia has many unique creatures, such as the kangaroo and the koala. These animals are biologically unique, too.

Australia and New Zealand: Physical

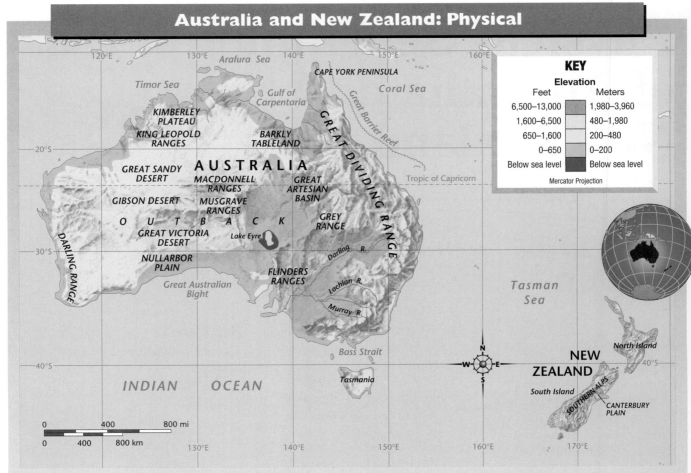

Map Study Apart from the Great Dividing Range, most of Australia is quite flat. The huge area to the west of the Great Dividing Range is made up of plains or low plateaus. In contrast, New Zealand is mountainous or hilly. **Location** Where are most of Australia's deserts located? **Place** Which of New Zealand's two islands is more mountainous?

Ask Questions What would you like to learn about the animals of Australia and New Zealand?

They are **marsupials** (mar SOO pea ulz), or animals that carry their young in a body pouch. Marsupials are found elsewhere in the world. The opossum of North America, for instance, is a marsupial. But in Australia, almost all mammals are marsupials. This is not true anywhere else on the Earth.

The uniqueness of New Zealand and Australia is the result of forces beneath the Earth's surface. The outer "skin" of the Earth, or the crust, is broken into huge pieces called **tectonic plates.** Australia, New Zealand, and the Pacific islands are all part of the Indo-Australian plate. Once, it was part of a landmass that included Asia. Then, several hundred million years ago, the plate broke away. Slowly—only an inch or two each year—it moved southeast in the Pacific Ocean.

As the plate moved, the distance between the islands and Asia increased. Over the centuries, small changes occurred naturally in the islands' animals and plants. For instance, many birds have lost the ability to fly, even though they still have small wings. Because of the islands' isolation, these living things did not spread to other regions.

Australia: A Continent and a Country

Australia is the Earth's largest island and smallest continent. It is about as large as the continental United States. That means the part of the United States located between Canada and Mexico. Australia has a much smaller population than the United States. Most Australians live on a narrow plain along Australia's eastern and southeastern coasts. Australia's physical geography explains why.

Find the region along Australia's east coast on the map on the opposite page. This plain has Australia's most fertile farmland and receives ample rain. Winds flowing westward across the Pacific Ocean pick up moisture. As the winds rise to cross the Great Dividing Range—mountains just to the west of the coastal plain—the moisture falls as rain. These winds not only bring rain. They also help make the climate mild and pleasant. Also, Australia's most important rivers, the Murray and Darling, flow through the region. Most Australians live here, in cities.

The rest of Australia is very different. Just west of the Great Dividing Range is a rain shadow. This is a region that gets little precipitation because of a mountain range. This area is made up of semiarid plateaus and desert lands. Since rain seldom falls here, and there are few rivers, people depend on wells for fresh water. Farther west, the huge central plain called the Outback is desert and dry grassland.

▼ The Great Barrier Reef (below) is located off Australia's northeast coast. Measuring about 1,250 miles (2,010 km) in length, it is the largest coral reef in the world. Ayers Rock (below left), is 1.5 miles (2.4 km) long and 1,100 feet (335 m) high. This huge, red rock is a major landmark in Australia's Outback.

Shaped by Volcanoes

Now look at the map and find New Zealand, which lies about 1,200 miles (1,900 km) southeast of Australia. Made up of two islands, New Zealand is much smaller than Australia. The climate is not as hot, because New Zealand is farther from the Equator. Here, the landforms have been shaped by volcanoes. They, in turn, were caused by the movement of tectonic plates. Where plates meet, there often are earthquakes and volcanoes. New Zealand is located where the Pacific plate meets the Indo-Australian plate. Like other island groups, New Zealand's North Island and South Island were formed by volcanoes when these plates collided.

New Zealand is one of the largest countries in the Pacific region—about the size of the state of Colorado. Both its islands have highlands, forests, lakes, and rugged, snowcapped mountains. Although New Zealand is more than 1,000 miles (1,600 km) long, no place is more than 80 miles (129 km) from the sea. The country has a mild climate and plenty of rainfall.

In the middle of North Island lies a volcanic plateau. Three of the volcanoes are active. The volcano called Mount Egmont, however, is inactive. North of the volcanoes, **geysers** (GY zurz), or hot springs, shoot scalding water over 100 feet (30.5 m) into the air. New Zealanders use this energy to produce electricity.

South Island has a high mountain range called the Southern Alps. Mount Cook, the highest peak in the range, rises to 12,349 feet (3,764 m). Glaciers cover the mountainsides. Below, crystal-clear lakes

LINKS ACROSS THE WORLD

Steam Heat Geysers are found in three places in the world: the northwestern United States, Iceland, and New Zealand. In these places, movements of tectonic plates have created deep cracks in the Earth's crust. Water seeps down into the cracks until it reaches very hot rocks. The heat raises the temperature of the water until it is so hot that it bursts upward in a shower of water and steam.

Building New Zealand's Volcanoes

Chart Study New Zealand's volcanoes were formed when the Pacific and Indo-Australian plates crashed together. The Pacific plate slid downwards into the Earth, forcing the edge of the Indo-Australian plate upwards. Friction and heat from inside the Earth melted the rock at the edges of the two plates. This molten rock, or magma, rose to the surface, causing volcanic eruptions. **Critical Thinking** Which is the Pacific plate, the one on the left of the diagram or the one on the right?

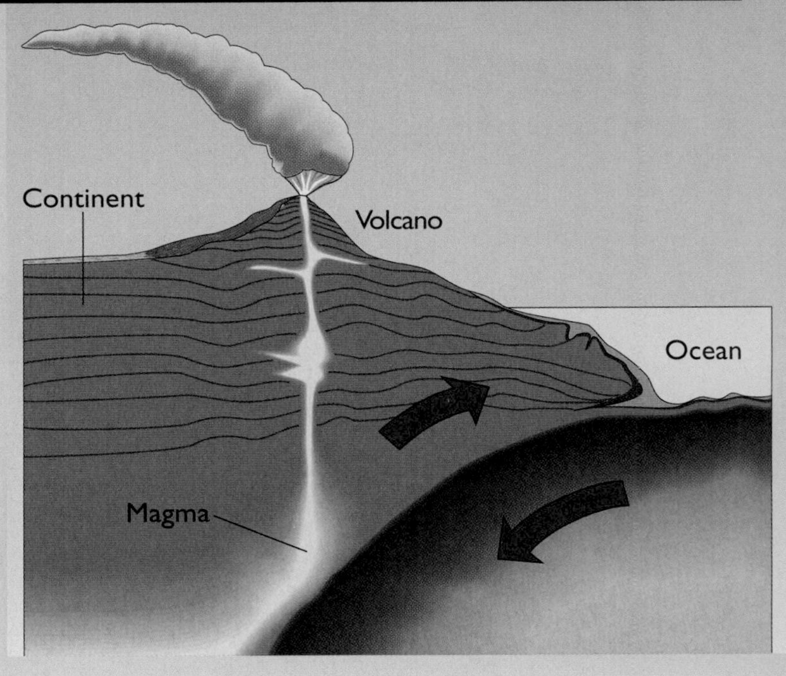

◀▼ The picture on the left shows towering Mount Cook on New Zealand's South Island. Sheep, like these grazing in the hills below Mount Cook, far outnumber New Zealand's human inhabitants. Most of the country's people live in harbor cities, like Auckland on New Zealand's North Island (below).

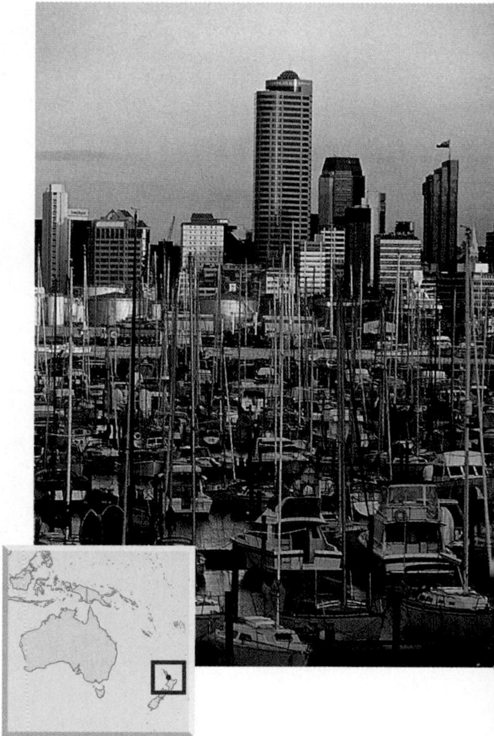

dot the landscape. **Fiords** (fyordz), or narrow inlets, slice the southwest coastline. Here, the mountains reach the sea. To the southeast lies a flat, fertile land called the Canterbury Plain. This is where farmers produce most of New Zealand's crops. Ranchers also raise sheep and cattle here.

Comparing Australia and New Zealand

Although much smaller, New Zealand is like Australia in many ways. In both countries, most of the population lives in cities along the coast. In fact, more than four out of five New Zealanders live in towns and cities. Although their climates are different, both Australia and New Zealand have important natural resources. Both also raise sheep and cattle and grow similar crops.

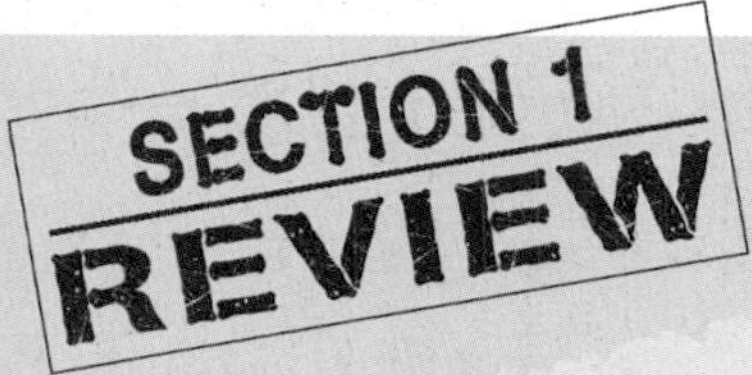

1. **Define** (a) marsupial, (b) tectonic plate, (c) geyser, (d) fiord.
2. **Identify** (a) Great Dividing Range, (b) Outback, (c) North Island, (d) South Island, (e) Canterbury Plain.
3. How did Australia and New Zealand's isolation affect their plant and animal life?
4. How do the landscapes of Australia and New Zealand differ? How are they similar?

Critical Thinking

5. **Recognizing Cause and Effect** How have Australia's geography and climate affected where people live?

Activity

6. **Writing to Learn** Find out more about the unique plants and animals of Australia and New Zealand. Choose one that interests you. Write and illustrate a report about it.

Physical Geography of the Pacific Islands

Reach Into Your Background

Many people dream of living on a tropical island, or at least of visiting one. Do you? Jot down a brief description of your "dream island." Then see how it compares with the real islands in the South Pacific.

Questions to Explore

1. What is the physical geography of the Pacific islands?
2. What is the difference between high islands and low islands?

Key Terms

high island
low island
atoll
coral

Key Places

Melanesia
Micronesia
Polynesia
Papua New Guinea

Luana Bogdan lives in Nauru (nah OO roo), the third-smallest country in the world. Tomorrow, she will be 12 years old. She is very excited, but she is also sad. Luana knows her family may soon have to leave Nauru.

Nauru's economy depended on its phosphate mines. But now the phosphate, used to make fertilizer, is almost gone. Even worse, mining has stripped the tiny island of its trees and vegetation. Nauru's leaders are trying to restore the island's ruined environment. If they fail, the Nauruans will have to find a new homeland.

▼ This picture shows a phosphate mine on Nauru. Phosphate is Nauru's only natural resource.

Melanesia, Micronesia, and Polynesia

The Pacific Ocean covers nearly one third of the Earth's surface. About 25,000 islands similar to Nauru dot the Pacific. The region is divided into three areas. *Melanesia* (mel uh NEE zhuh) means "black islands." *Micronesia* (my kruh NEE zhuh) means "small islands." *Polynesia* (pahl uh NEE zhuh) means "many islands." Any island that falls inside the boundaries of a particular area belongs to that group.

A High Island in Polynesia

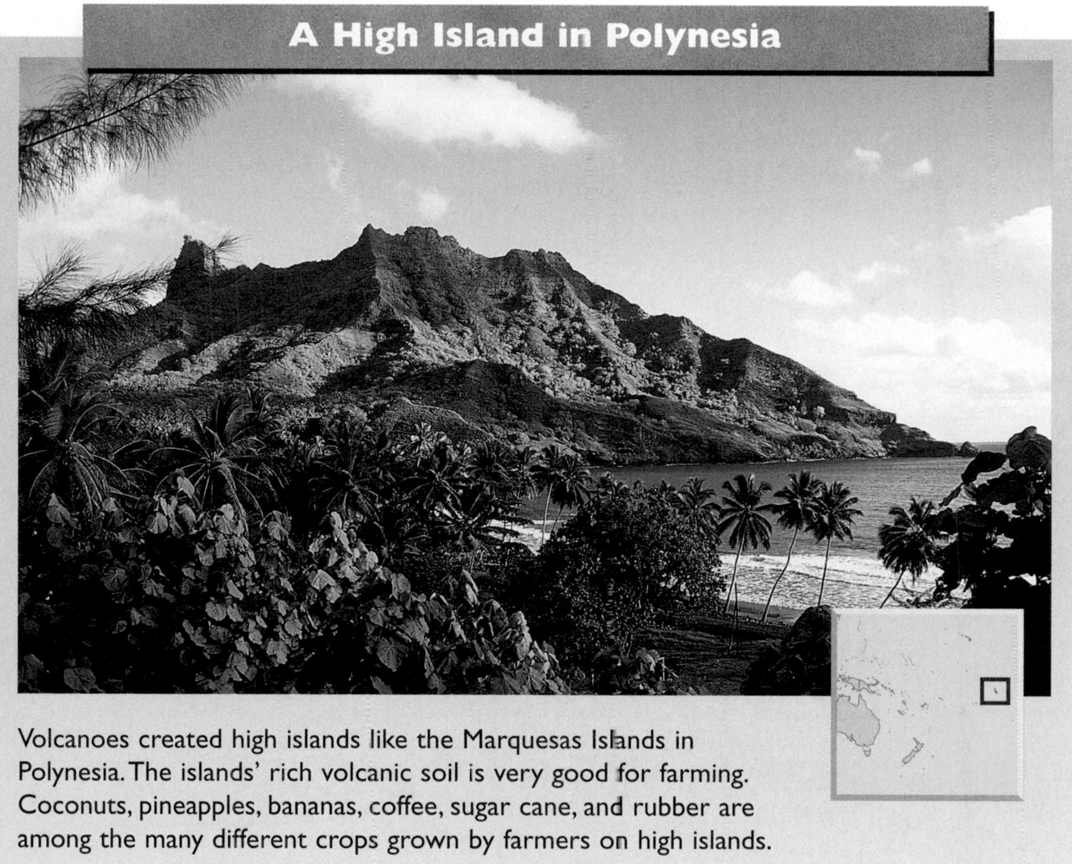

Volcanoes created high islands like the Marquesas Islands in Polynesia. The islands' rich volcanic soil is very good for farming. Coconuts, pineapples, bananas, coffee, sugar cane, and rubber are among the many different crops grown by farmers on high islands.

High Islands and Low Islands Geographers also divide the Pacific islands into high islands and low islands. Volcanoes form **high islands.** They usually have mountains. The soil, which consists of volcanic ash, is very fertile. Because of their size and because people can grow crops here, high islands support more people than low islands.

Low islands are reefs or atolls. An **atoll** (A tawl) is a small coral island in the shape of a ring. The ring encloses a shallow pool of ocean water called a lagoon. Often, the lagoon has at least one opening to the sea. An atoll often rises only a few feet above the Pacific. Low islands have this shape and low elevation because they are built on coral reefs. **Coral** is a rocklike material made up of the skeletons of tiny sea creatures. A reef develops until it nears the surface. Then sand and other debris accumulate on the reef's surface, raising the island above the level of the water.

Far fewer people live on low islands than on high islands. In part, this is because low islands are quite small. Also, low islands have poor, sandy soil and little fresh water, so it is difficult to raise crops. Most low islanders survive by fishing. They may also grow coconuts, yams, and a starchy root called taro.

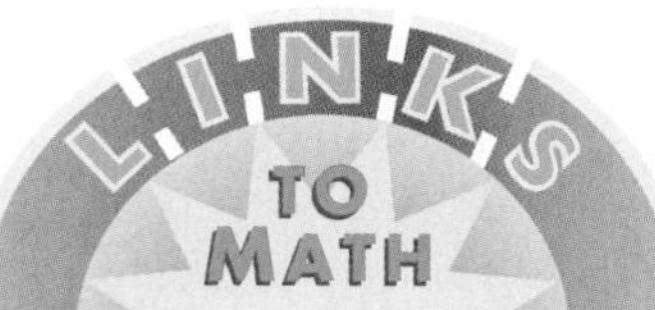

Navigating the Oceans Thousands of years ago, Pacific Islanders navigated hundreds of miles across the open ocean. One of their tools was an "*etak* of sighting." It was the distance a canoe traveled from the time it left an island to the time the island disappeared from the horizon—about 10 miles. They also used an "*etak* of birds." It was the distance between an island and the place where its sea birds usually fed—about 20 miles out to sea.

The Three Regions The island region with the most people is Melanesia, which is north and east of Australia. Most of Melanesia's large islands are high islands. New Guinea, for example, has two ranges of high

A Coral Atoll

Chart Study The diagrams below show how a coral atoll is formed. It begins as a "fringe" of coral around a volcanic island. This coral reef continues to build as the island is worn away. Eventually, only the coral reef is left. This aerial view of Bora Bora (left), near Tahiti, shows the ring structure of a coral atoll. **Critical Thinking** Why do you think coral islands like Bora Bora cannot support much agriculture?

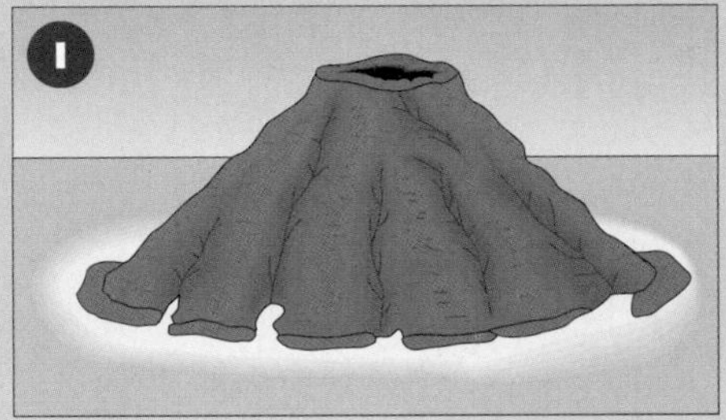

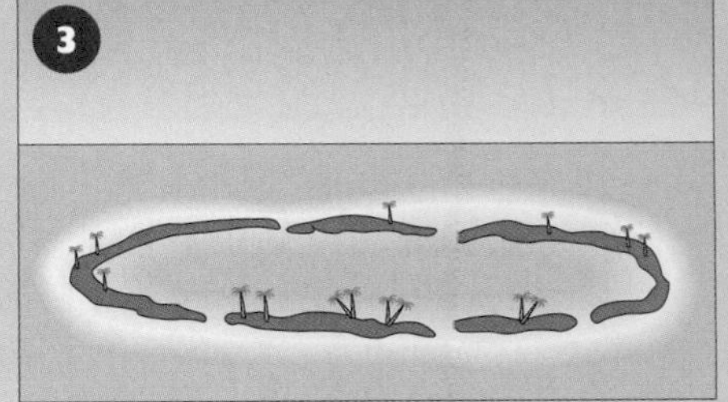

mountains. It is divided into two countries. The western half of the island is called Irian Jaya (IHR ee ahn JAH yuh). It is part of the country of Indonesia. The eastern half is Papua New Guinea (PAP yuh wuh noo GIN ee), the largest and most populated Melanesian country. Some smaller Melanesian islands are Fiji, the Solomon Islands, and New Caledonia.

Most of the islands of Micronesia lie north of the Equator. Made up largely of low islands, Micronesia covers an area of the Pacific as large as the continental United States. Some of Micronesia's 2,000 islands are less than 1 square mile (2.6 sq km) in area. The largest is Guam, which is just 209 square miles (541 sq km). Most of Micronesia's islands are divided into groups. The largest are the Caroline, Gilbert, Marshall, and Mariana islands. Guam is part of the Marianas.

Polynesia is the largest island region in the Pacific. It includes our fiftieth state, Hawaii. Polynesia consists of a great many high islands, such as Tahiti and Samoa. Dense jungles cover their high volcanic mountains. Along the shores are palm-fringed, sandy beaches. The Tuamotus and Tonga are examples of Polynesia's few low islands and atolls.

Climate and Vegetation of the Pacific

The Pacific islands lie in the tropics. Temperatures are hot year-round. Daytime temperatures reach between the 80s and mid-90s in degrees Fahrenheit (around 32°C). Nighttime temperatures average about 75°F

(24°C). The ocean and the winds keep the temperatures from getting too high. The amount of rainfall marks the change from one season to another.

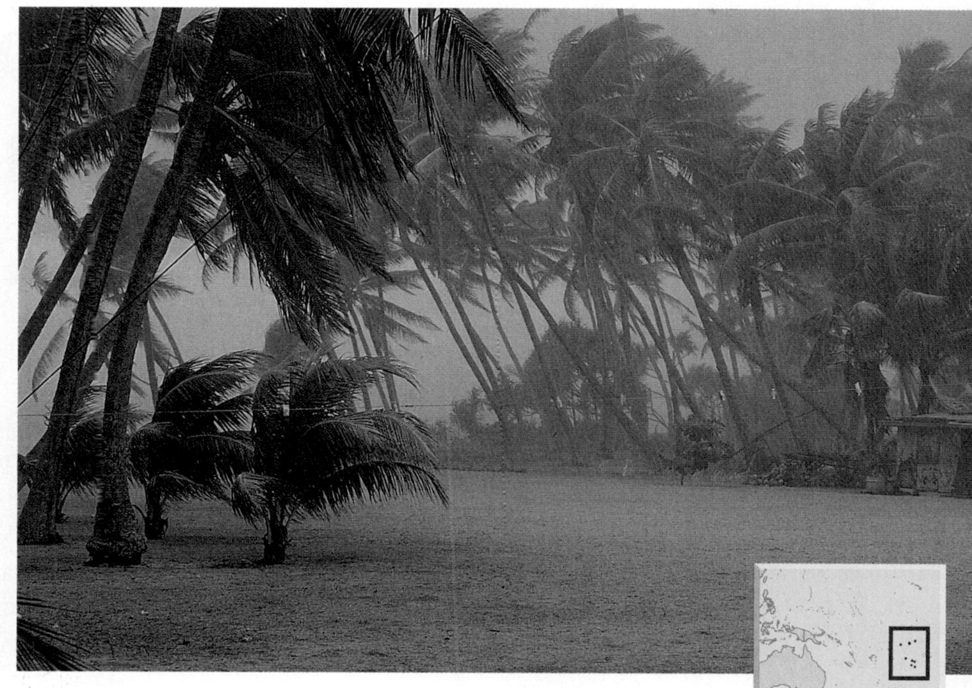

▲ The wet season in the Pacific often brings violent weather. Here, high winds and driving rain bend the coconut palms on Palmerston Atoll in the Cook Islands.

Some Pacific islands have wet and dry seasons. Most islands, however, receive heavy rainfall all year long. In Hawaii, for example, volcanic peaks such as Mauna Kea (MOW nuh KAY uh) receive 100 inches of rain each year. Usually the rain falls in brief, heavy downpours. Some low islands, however, receive only scattered rainfall.

Because of high temperatures, much rainfall, and fertile soil, high islands like Papua New Guinea and the Hawaiian Islands have rich vegetation. Tropical rain forests cover the hills. Savanna grasses grow in the lowlands. Low islands, on the other hand, have little vegetation. The poor soil supports only palm trees, grasses, and small shrubs.

The Pacific island region has few natural resources. The coconut palm is the most important resource. It provides food, clothing, and shelter. Islanders export dried coconut meat, which is used in margarine, cooking oils, and luxury soaps. Some low islands, like Nauru, have phosphate deposits that can be exported. But the Pacific islands' most valuable resource may be their beauty. Tourism is gaining importance in the region and providing a new source of income.

1. Define (a) high island, (b) low island, (c) atoll, (d) coral.

2. Identify (a) Melanesia, (b) Micronesia, (c) Polynesia, (d) Papua New Guinea.

3. Name three large island groups of Micronesia.

4. High islands often have a better standard of living than low islands. Explain why this might be so.

Critical Thinking

5. Drawing Conclusions Most Pacific islands have few natural resources. How might this affect trade between these islands and other, more industrial nations around the world?

Activity

6. Writing to Learn Suppose you have decided to live on one of the Pacific islands. Write a paragraph explaining why you have decided to move. How will you handle the challenges of island life?

Cultures of Australia, New Zealand, and the Pacific Islands

Reach Into Your Background
What if you had to go on a long trip to a place you knew nothing about? How would you get ready? List the things you would take with you. The people who settled in the Pacific island region had to make similar decisions. What do you think they decided to do?

Questions to Explore

1. How did people settle Australia and New Zealand?
2. What groups shaped the cultures of Australia and New Zealand?
3. How have the Pacific island nations been influenced by other cultures?

Key Terms
penal colony
station

Key People and Places
Aborigine
Maori
Easter Island
Auckland

Hundreds of giant stone statues dot the landscape of Easter Island. Made of solid volcanic rock, each statue stands 10 to 40 feet (3 to 12 m) tall. Some weigh more than 50 tons (46 metric tons). A European who saw them in 1722 was astonished:

> "The stone images . . . caused us to be struck with astonishment [amazed us]. We could not comprehend how . . . these people, who have no thick timber for making any machines . . . had been able to erect such images."

Easter Island's statues still impress people. Scientists also wonder how people first came to this faraway island and to the other parts of the Pacific region.

▼ Tourists gaze awestruck at the eyeless giants that dot Easter Island. No one knows for sure how the ancient islanders carved and erected these statues.

Telling the Story of Dreamtime

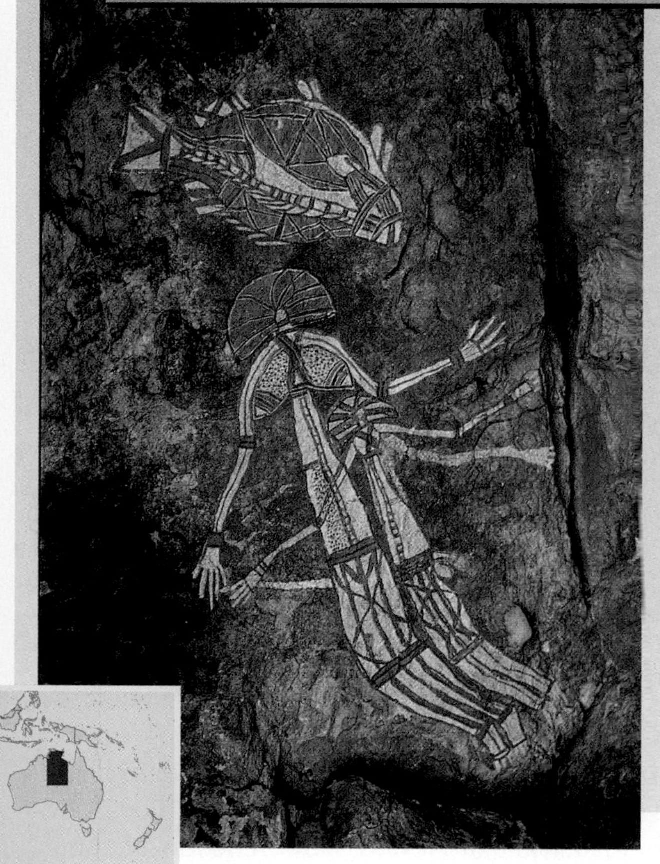

According to Aborigine tradition, in the "Dreamtime" before humans walked the Earth, mythical ancestors formed the world's mountains, rivers, plants, and animals. Aborigines passed their traditions on from generation to generation by word of mouth. Aborigine artists also recorded tales in carvings and rock paintings like this ancient one in northern Australia. Aborigines still use such ancient practices to keep their traditions alive. **Critical Thinking** Why do you think Aborigines used carvings and paintings to pass on their traditions?

Early Settlers in Australia and New Zealand

Scientists think that the Aborigines (ab uh RIJ uh neez), the earliest settlers in Australia, came from Asia about 40,000 years ago. For thousands of years, they hunted and gathered food along the coasts and river valleys. Some learned to live in the harsh Outback.

For thousands of years, the Aboriginal population stayed at a stable, even level. People lived in small family groups that moved from place to place in search of food and water. All had strong religious beliefs about nature and the land. Such beliefs played a key role in their way of life.

The Maori of New Zealand The earliest people in New Zealand were the Maori (MAH oh ree). Their ancestors first traveled from Asia to Polynesia. Then, about 1,000 years ago, the Maori traveled across the ocean to New Zealand. According to Maori legend, seven groups set out in long canoes to find a new homeland. A storm tossed their boats ashore on New Zealand. The Maori quickly adapted to their new home. They settled in villages, making a living as hunters and farmers. But the Maori also prized fighting and conquering their enemies. They often fought other groups of Maori over the possession of land. The Maori used storytelling to pass on their beliefs and tales of their adventures.

Maori Canoes The Maori showed their standing in society by the works of art they owned. For instance, a person might own elaborately carved and painted war canoes. Some were up to 100 feet (30 m) long. Human figures were carved along the hull and into the prow, which is the front part of the boat. The figures often had eyes made of mother-of-pearl. Canoes were painted red and decorated with feather streamers.

A Country With European Roots

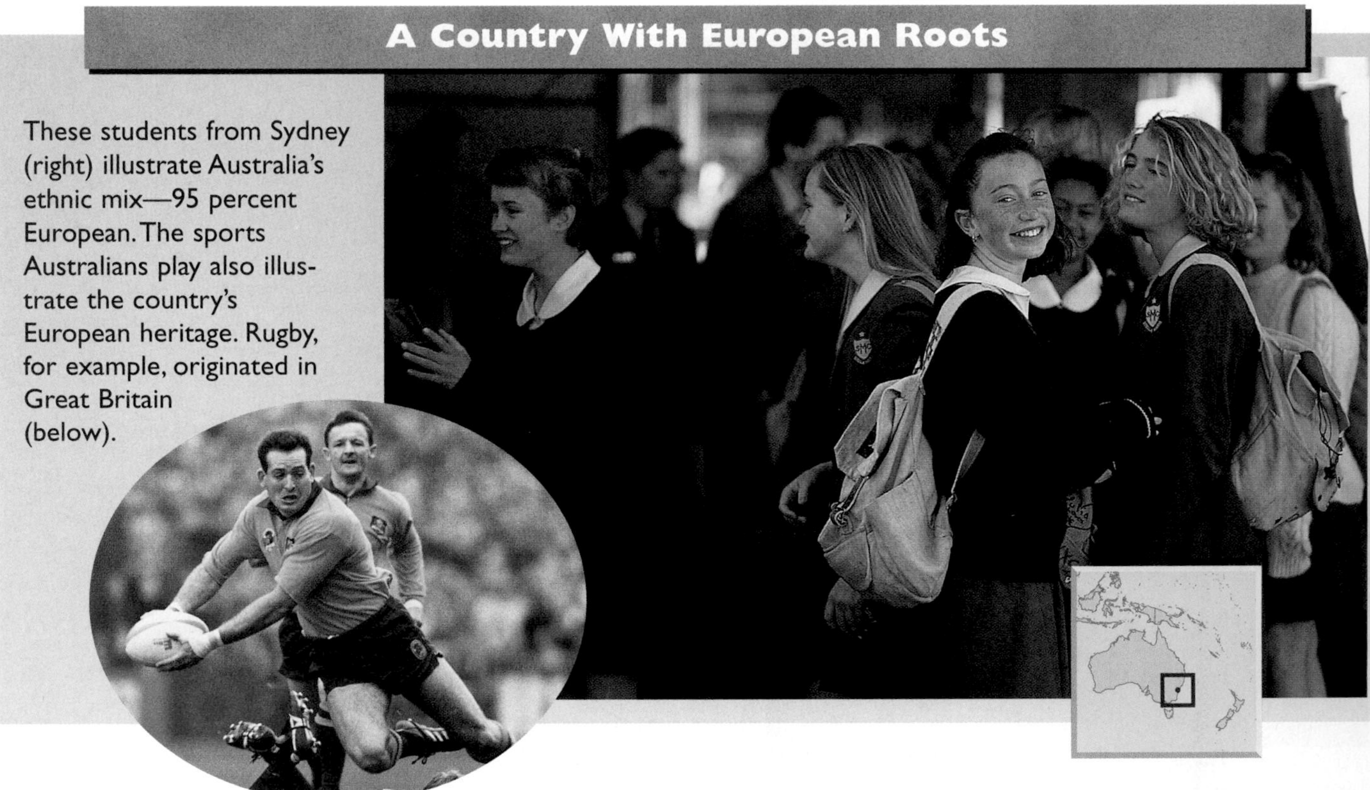

These students from Sydney (right) illustrate Australia's ethnic mix—95 percent European. The sports Australians play also illustrate the country's European heritage. Rugby, for example, originated in Great Britain (below).

READ ACTIVELY

Predict How might the discovery of a resource like gold affect the population of a country?

The Arrival of Europeans European explorers heard about a mysterious continent that lay to the south of Asia. In the 1600s, several ships touched on either Australia or New Zealand. The most famous of these explorers was the Dutch sea captain Abel Janszoon Tasman. The Australian island of Tasmania is named after him. But no one established settlements during Tasman's time. Then, in 1769, British captain James Cook explored New Zealand. The next year, Cook explored the east coast of Australia. He claimed both lands for Britain.

In 1788, the British founded the first colony in Australia as a **penal colony.** This is a place settled by convicts, or prisoners. Soon, other colonists settled in Australia. Some worked for the prison facilities. Others went to find new land. Then, in 1851, gold was discovered. The population soared. Not long after, Britain stopped sending convicts to Australia. Some 50 years later, in 1901, Australia gained independence.

New Zealand was settled by Europeans at about the same time as Australia. In 1840, the British took control of New Zealand. The colony, with its fine harbors and fertile soil, attracted many British settlers. New Zealand gained independence in 1947.

The Cultures of Australia and New Zealand

Today, most Australians and New Zealanders are descendants of British settlers. Some maintain close ties with relatives in Great Britain. They share British culture, holidays, and customs. Most express pride in their British heritage, especially their parliamentary system of government and belief in freedom and democracy.

However, Australia and New Zealand are not exactly alike. Each has its own unique culture. For example, Australians have added many new words to the language. These include *mate,* or "close friend," and *fair go,* or "equal opportunity." New Zealanders are deeply opposed to nuclear warfare. No ships carrying nuclear arms are allowed to use New Zealand harbors.

Most Australians and New Zealanders enjoy a high standard of living. Farming, mining, and manufacturing have made people prosperous. Most families have cars and good housing. Most earn a good income. They spend much of their free time outdoors—camping, on picnics, or relaxing on the beach.

The Aborigines Today Today, about 200,000 Aborigines live in Australia. Since the arrival of Europeans, the Aborigines have suffered great hardships. In the colonial period, settlers forced these native peoples off their lands. Tens of thousands died of European diseases. Others were forced to work on sheep and cattle **stations,** which are extremely large ranches. The settlers demanded that the Aborigines adopt European ways. As a result, they began to lose their own customs and traditions. Recently, however, life for Aborigines has begun to improve a little.

▼ The Asian population in Australia has grown in recent years. Here, dancers perform a dance from the Philippines at a folk fair in Sydney.

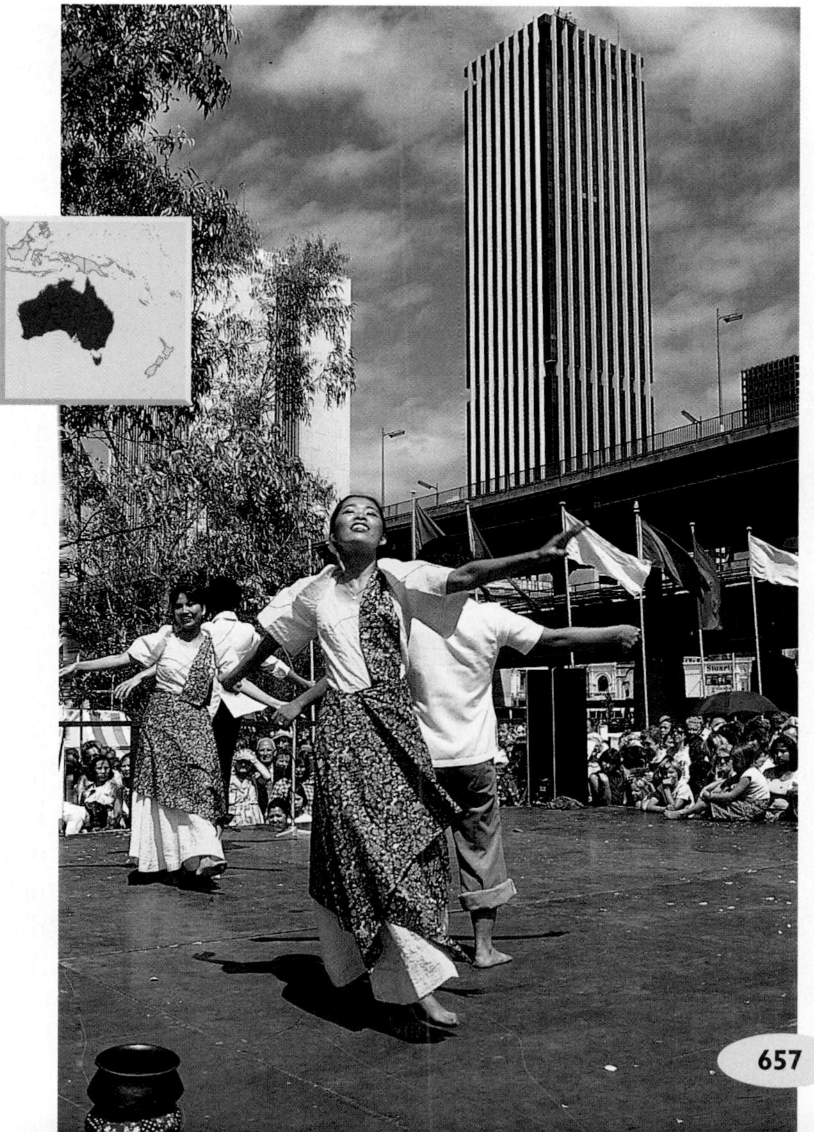

Other Peoples of Australia People other than the British settled in Australia. During the gold rush of the 1850s, many people came, including the Chinese. These immigrants hoped to find riches. Although few succeeded, most remained. Many of Australia's large cities have Chinese communities.

After World War II, many Europeans immigrated to Australia. They came from Italy, Yugoslavia, Greece, and Germany. In the 1970s, people fleeing the war in Vietnam took refuge in Australia. And today, immigrants from all over the world continue to arrive.

The Maori Way of Life When New Zealand became a British colony, Britain promised to protect Maori land. Settlers, however, broke that promise. For many years, the settlers and the Maori clashed violently. The settlers finally defeated the Maori in 1872.

After their defeat, the Maori were forced to adopt English ways. Maori culture seemed in danger of being destroyed. Slowly, however, Maori leaders gained more power. They recovered some traditional lands. New laws now allow the Maori to practice their customs and ceremonies.

Today, there are more than 300,000 Maori in New Zealand. They make up about 9 percent of the country's population. Many Maori now live in cities. They work in businesses, factories, and offices. But they still honor their Maori heritage. Many speak both Maori and English. Thanks to their artists, writers, and singers, Maori culture is an important part of the lives of all New Zealanders.

READ ACTIVELY

Ask Questions What would you like to learn about the culture and history of the Pacific islands?

Other Peoples of New Zealand At the end of World War II, many Europeans migrated to New Zealand. Recently, Vietnamese and Cambodian refugees have looked to New Zealand for safety. And many people from the Polynesian islands have settled here. Today, more Polynesians live in New Zealand's largest city, Auckland, than in any other city in the world.

The Cultures of the Pacific Islands

Scientists believe that the first people to inhabit the Pacific islands came from Southeast Asia more than 30,000 years ago. First, these people settled on New Guinea, Melanesia's largest island. Then, over thousands of years, they traveled across the Pacific by canoe to Micronesia and later Polynesia.

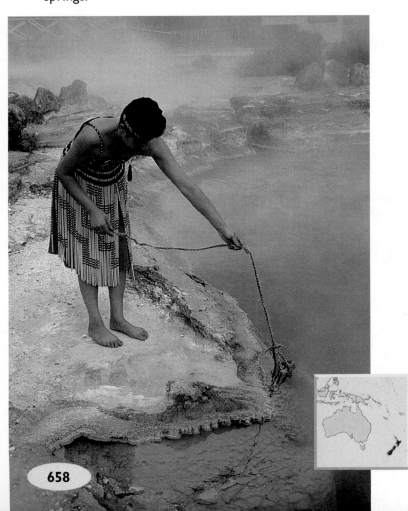

▼ At Rotorua, where many Maori people live, a woman in traditional dress heats her food in the sizzling hot springs.

A Variety of Cultures As people settled the Pacific region, they developed many different cultures. Because of the distances between islands, groups could not communicate with each other. Therefore, each group developed its own language, customs, and religious beliefs. However, the island people did have many things in common. Their ocean environment shaped their lives. It fed them and was their main means of transportation and trade. Most built their lives around their small villages. Many also farmed.

From Colonies to Independence The arrival of Europeans in the 1800s had a great impact on the Pacific islands. Britain, France, and Germany set up trading posts and naval bases on many islands. Japan and the United States soon joined the race for control of the Pacific region. In the late 1800s, these nations turned the islands into colonies. For the next 100 years, foreign nations ruled the people of the Pacific.

Life in the Pacific Islands

Life in the Pacific islands presents vivid contrasts. In cities like Papeete, the capital of Tahiti (left), modern apartment buildings and automobiles are a common sight. In contrast, most of Papua New Guinea's four million residents still farm, fish, and build their houses in the traditional way (below).

After World War II, most Pacific islands gained independence. By then, traditional island cultures had blended with cultures from Europe, America, and other countries. Most governments were democratic. Most churches were Christian. Many Pacific Islanders read and spoke English. Foreign companies operated businesses and large farms here. Since independence, the lives of most island people have improved. But incomes are still low. Many depend on fishing or on growing such crops as taro and yams to make a living.

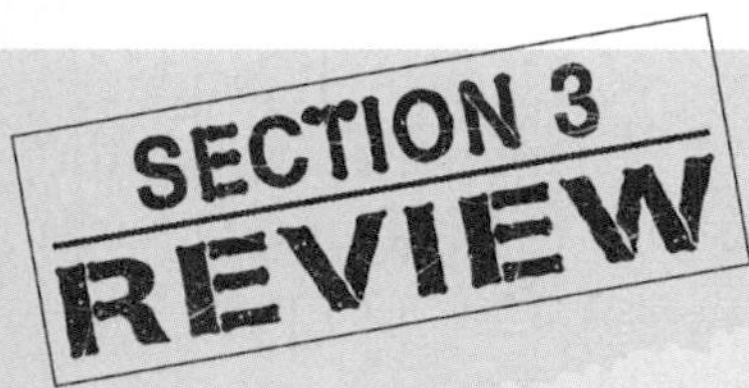

1. **Define** (a) penal colony, (b) station.
2. **Identify** (a) Aborigine, (b) Maori, (c) Easter Island, (d) Auckland.
3. Where do scientists believe the native peoples of Australia, New Zealand, and the Pacific islands come from?
4. What happened to native peoples when Europeans arrived in Australia, New Zealand, and the Pacific islands?

Critical Thinking

5. **Making Comparisons** In what ways are the histories of the Aborigines and the Maori similar? In what ways are they different?
6. **Drawing Conclusions** Why might people who live on an island be able to preserve their culture for a long period without change?

Activity

7. **Writing to Learn** Write 10 brief entries for a time line that shows the history of Australia, New Zealand, and the Pacific islands.

Australia

THREE WAYS OF LIFE

Reach Into Your Background

Think about what you know about American history. When settlers moved west in the United States, what happened to Native American lands and ways of life? European settlers in Australia moved into Aboriginal lands in the 1800s. Make a list of what you think happened to the Aborigines.

Questions to Explore

1. Why is Australia developing close ties with Pacific Rim nations?
2. Why are cattle and sheep ranches important to Australia?
3. How is the Australian government changing the way it deals with Aborigines?

Key Term

artesian well

Key Places

Sydney
Alice Springs

Michael Chang owns a successful trading company in Sydney, Australia's largest city. From his office in a modern glass skyscraper, he sometimes watches Sydney's busy harbor. What interests him most are the large cargo ships.

John Koeyers and his family own a huge cattle ranch in northwest Australia. He uses a Jeep to round up the herds on his ranch. The Koeyers sell most of their cattle to companies that supply fast-food restaurants in Asian nations.

Lyle Sansbury is chairman of the Board of Directors of the Nurungga Farming Company. He is very proud of the farm. It produces barley, wheat, cattle, and sheep. Lyle is full of plans for expanding the company into other activities, such as fish farming. The Nurungga Farm is one of the successful businesses owned and run by Aborigines.

▼ The Sydney Opera House was completed in 1973. The building's white concrete arches look like the sails of a huge ship.

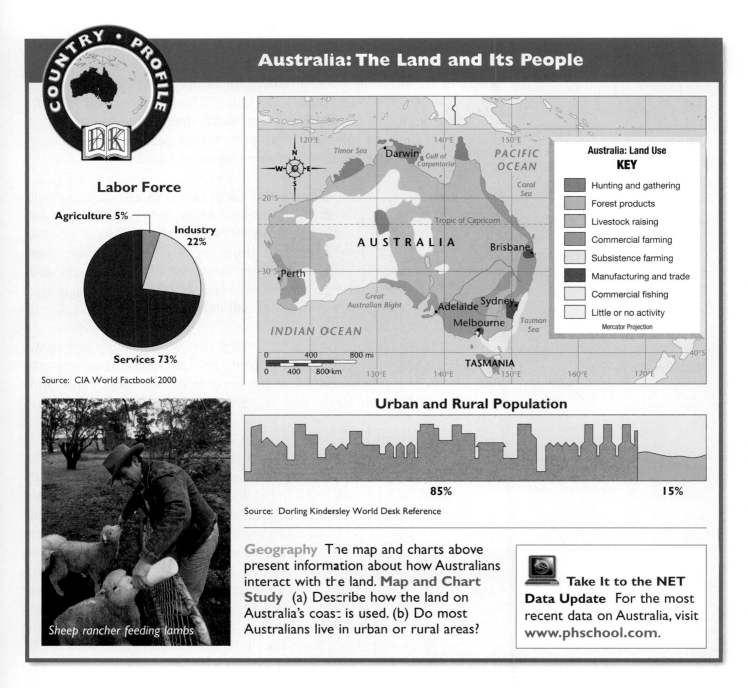

COUNTRY • PROFILE

DK

Australia: The Land and Its People

Labor Force

Agriculture 5%

Industry 22%

Services 73%

Source: CIA World Factbook 2000

Australia: Land Use

Timor Sea
Darwin
Gulf of Carpentaria
PACIFIC OCEAN
Coral Sea
Tropic of Capricorn
AUSTRALIA
Brisbane
Perth
Great Australian Bight
Adelaide
Sydney
Melbourne
Tasman Sea
INDIAN OCEAN
TASMANIA
120°E 130°E 140°E 150°E 160°E 170°E
20°S 30°S 40°S
0 400 800 mi
0 400 800 km

KEY

- Hunting and gathering
- Forest products
- Livestock raising
- Commercial farming
- Subsistence farming
- Manufacturing and trade
- Commercial fishing
- Little or no activity

Mercator Projection

Urban and Rural Population

85%

15%

Source: Dorling Kindersley World Desk Reference

Sheep rancher feeding lambs

Geography The map and charts above present information about how Australians interact with the land. **Map and Chart Study** (a) Describe how the land on Australia's coast is used. (b) Do most Australians live in urban or rural areas?

Take It to the NET
Data Update For the most recent data on Australia, visit **www.phschool.com.**

A Trading Economy

Michael Chang, the Koeyers, and Lyle Sansbury are all Australians. The definition of *Australian* has changed since Australia achieved independence. It is no longer "British." It now reflects the diversity of Australia's people. Today, Australia has close ties with other nations of the Pacific Rim. These nations border the Pacific Ocean. They include Japan, South Korea, China, and Taiwan. The United States is another major Pacific Rim nation. It is one of Australia's key trading partners.

Japan, the United States, and other Pacific Rim nations have invested large amounts of money in Australia's economy. They also have set up banks, insurance companies, and other businesses in Australia. More and more, Australia's economy depends on trade with these Pacific Rim countries.

Predict What do all three people have in common? How do they contribute to Australia's economy?

Michael Chang's trading company is just one of hundreds of companies that do business with Pacific Rim countries. He sends various products to many countries in Asia. John Koeyers is involved in trade, too. Large cargo ships transport his cattle to South Korea and Taiwan. Other cargo ships carry Australian wool, meat, and many other products to foreign markets. And even larger ocean tankers carry Australia's coal, zinc, lead, and other minerals to Japan.

Farming It seems strange that farm products are an important export, because only about 6 percent of Australia's land is good for farming. Most of this land is in southeastern Australia and along the east coast. The country's few rivers are in those areas. Farmers use the river water to irrigate their crops. Australian farmers raise barley, oats, and sugar cane. However, their most valuable crop is wheat. Australia is one of the world's leading wheat growers and exporters.

Visualize Visualize a large sheep or cattle station in the Outback.

Ranching Ranching is another key part of Australia's economy. Australian sheep and cattle provide lamb, mutton, and beef for export. And Australia is the world's leading wool producer. Most cattle and sheep are raised on large stations. Some of the largest are in the Outback.

For example, the Koeyers' ranch is in a hot, dry area in northwest Australia. It covers 680,000 acres (275,196 hectares). Another Outback station, near Alice Springs in the center of Australia, is even larger. It covers 12,000 square miles (31,080 sq km)—about as much as the state of Maryland. Even with this much land, the cattle can barely find enough grass for grazing. Fresh water also is scarce. Rain falls rarely, and the region has only a few small streams. To supply water for their cattle, the Koeyers use underground **artesian wells.** These are drilled deep into the Earth to tap porous rock filled with groundwater.

Cattle Round-Up

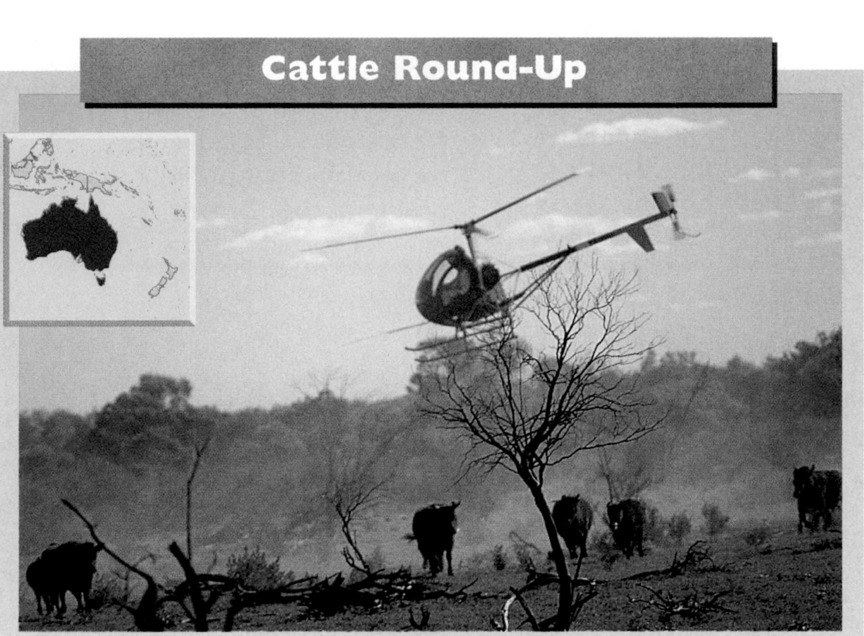

In Australia's hot, dry Outback, ranchers graze sheep and cattle on huge ranches. Some of these ranches, or stations, are bigger than some American states. At round-up time, ranchers often use helicopters to locate stray cattle.

Aborigines: Seeking Respect

Lyle Sansbury is like many young Aborigines. They are working hard to make sure the people and governments of Australia treat them with respect. They are trying to preserve their culture. And they are having a growing role in the economic life of the country.

Aboriginal leaders have worked to improve the lives of their people. Their schools now teach Aboriginal

◀ An Aborigine artist makes a traditional bark painting of a kangaroo, Australia's best-known marsupial.

Early Human Circle Art In northwestern Australia is a giant sandstone rock. At its base, archaeologists discovered circles—thousands of them—carved into it. More were found on boulders nearby. Each circle is about 1.2 inches (3 cm) in diameter. Tests showed that ancient people carved the rings about 75,000 years ago. That is 25,000 years before archaeologists had thought humans migrated to Australia! Everyone's theories had to be revised.

languages. Aborigines again celebrate important events with ancestral songs and dances. And artists have strengthened Aboriginal culture by creating traditional rock paintings and tree bark paintings.

Aborigine leaders like Lyle Sansbury have helped their people in another important way, too. They have influenced the government of Australia. The government has begun to return Aboriginal land to them. The government has built schools and hospitals on their land. It has also set aside some of their sacred places.

Aborigines have gained more rights. But their main goal is to regain their ancestral lands. Australia's courts have helped. However, many ranchers and farmers now live on those lands. These people strongly oppose giving the land back. This struggle may take many years to resolve. But Aborigines believe they will win.

1. **Define** artesian well.
2. **Identify** (a) Sydney, (b) Alice Springs.
3. In what area are Australia's major trading partners located?
4. What are some of the key aspects of Australia's economy?

Critical Thinking

5. **Drawing Conclusions** In American history, Native Americans were forced from their homelands and moved to reservations. For years, Native Americans have been fighting to regain their original homelands. How does this compare with the history and struggle of the Aborigines?

Activity

6. **Writing to Learn** Pretend that you and your family live on the huge cattle station near Alice Springs. Write a description of what you think your life would be like. Include ideas about your special school, your tasks, and your free time.

Drawing Conclusions

Ms. Lee walked into the classroom. Tim looked up at her.

"Uh-oh," he whispered. "Looks like a pop quiz!" Tim flipped open his textbook and started to quickly review the chapter.

Sheila heard Tim. Why did he think there would be a pop quiz?

"How can you tell?" she whispered.

"Look at Ms. Lee!" said Tim, still studying. "Do you see that little yellow notebook in her hand?" Sheila saw it.

"She uses that notebook to write test questions. Whenever she pulls it out, we have a quiz."

That was enough for Sheila. She opened her textbook to review last night's homework. Just then, Ms. Lee said. "Good morning class. Please close your books for a pop quiz!"

Get Ready

Tim was prepared for the pop quiz because he drew a conclusion about Ms. Lee. Drawing conclusions means adding clues, or evidence, that you read or see to what you already know. Drawing conclusions is a skill that will help you get the most out of what you read for school or outside of school.

When you read, you often find information that you already know something about. For example, if you read about a person from Australia, you might remember something you already know—that Australians speak English. You then think to yourself that this Australian person probably speaks English. You have just drawn a conclusion.

Clues
+ What You Already Know

Conclusion

Try It Out

Practice drawing conclusions from the following sentences by answering the questions.

> About 1,000 years ago, the Maori people traveled across the ocean to the large islands of New Zealand.

A. What clues about the Maori are included in this quotation?

B. What do you already know about people who live on islands?

C. What conclusion can you draw about the role of the sea in Maori life?

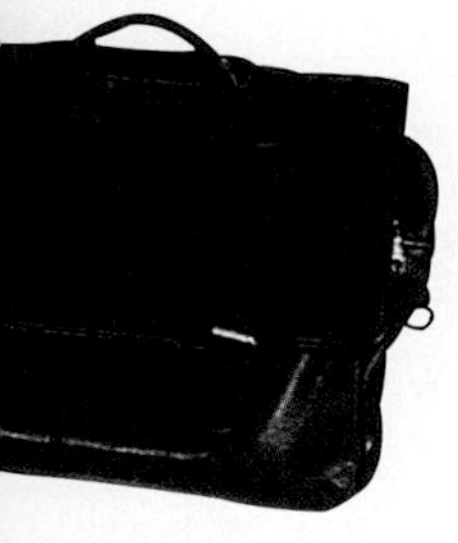

> Pacific Islanders read and speak English.

D. What clue about the people of the Pacific islands is in this quotation?

E. What do you already know about the countries where English is the official language?

F. What conclusion can you draw about the history of the Pacific islands?

Apply the Skill

Practice drawing conclusions by reading the section in this chapter called "Australia: A Continent and a Country." After you first read the paragraph, answer the following questions.

1. What clues about human use of Australian land are in the "Lands of Australia" paragraph?
2. What do you already know about the relationship between geography, climate and human settlement?
3. What conclusions might you draw about where Australians farm and the locations of their cities?

Review and Activities

Reviewing Main Ideas

1. How do scientists explain the unique plant and animal life of Australia and New Zealand?
2. Where do most people in Australia live? Why?
3. How does New Zealand's shape affect its climate?
4. (a) What are two differences between high islands and low islands? (b) What is one similarity?
5. What are the three main groups of Pacific islands?
6. Where do scientists think the first settlers in Australia and New Zealand came from?
7. (a) How did the Europeans' arrival in Australia and New Zealand affect the Aborigines and the Maori? (b) How did it affect the people who lived on the Pacific islands?
8. (a) What rights have Aborigines gained in recent years? (b) What is their chief goal?

Reviewing Key Terms

Match the definitions in Column I with the key terms in Column II.

Column I	**Column II**
1. a ring-shaped coral island surrounding a lagoon	**a. tectonic plate**
2. a rocklike substance made from the skeletons of tiny sea creatures	**b. coral**
	c. fiord
3. a place settled by prisoners	**d. atoll**
4. a large ranch in Australia	**e. penal colony**
5. a narrow valley or inlet from the sea	
6. a large section of the Earth's crust	**f. station**

Critical Thinking

1. **Making Comparisons** European arrival greatly affected the cultures of Australia, New Zealand, and the Pacific islands. Compare the European influences on these places. How were they similar? How were they different? Draw a chart to show similarities and differences.
2. **Drawing Conclusions** Why is British culture so influential in Australia and New Zealand? How might immigration from Asia and other areas affect culture in these two countries? Explain.

Graphic Organizer

Copy the web onto a sheet of paper. Then fill in the empty ovals. Add some ovals to each group of Pacific islands for the names of islands within that group. Fill them in to complete the web.

Polynesia

Pacific islands

Map Activity

Australia and New Zealand

For each place listed below, write the letter from the map that shows its location.

1. New Zealand
2. Sydney
3. Australia
4. Alice Springs

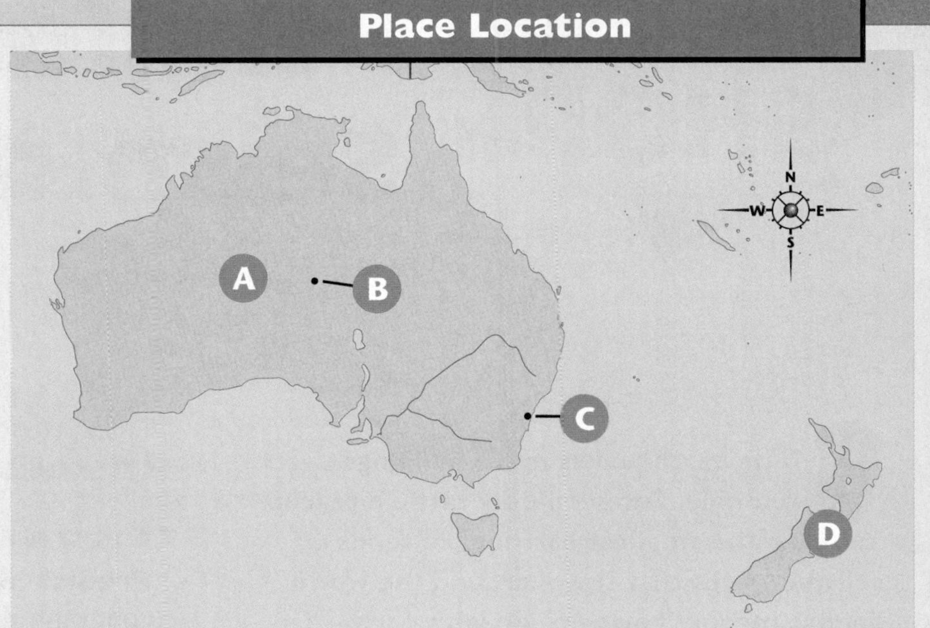

Writing Activity

Writing a Sight-seeing Plan

Choose one country that you read about in this chapter. Then do some research to learn more about it. If you spent a week there, what would you see? Write a list describing the things you would most want to see and do in a week. Then organize your list into a day-by-day plan.

Take It to the NET

Activity Explore several Web sites on the Pacific island nations. How is Australia similar to the other Pacific island nations? How is it different? For help in completing this activity, visit **www.phschool.com.**

Chapter 24 Self-Test To review what you have learned, take the Chapter 24 Self-Test and get instant feedback on your answers. Go to **www.phschool.com** to take the test.

Skills Review

Turn to the Skills Activity.

Review the three-part process of drawing a conclusion. Then answer the following questions: (a) If you conclude that this is the last chapter in your Asia book, what clues tell you so? (b) How can you use what you already know about books?

How Am I Doing?

Answer these questions to help you check your progress.

1. Can I locate Australia, New Zealand, and the Pacific region on a map?
2. Can I describe the history and culture of the region?
3. Do I understand how Europeans affected native cultures in the region?
4. What information from this chapter can I include in my journal?

Building a Seismograph

Some earthquakes make buildings crumble. Others hardly rattle a teacup. Yet even the smallest earthquake sends off seismic waves that travel around the world. *Seismic* means "having to do with earthquakes." To tell an earthquake's strength and size, scientists measure these waves with an instrument called a seismograph.

Purpose

Building a model seismograph can help you understand how scientists measure an earthquake's size. This instrument detects motion and can be built with a few simple materials.

Materials

- two stacks of books, each about 10 inches high
- table or desk
- roll of adding-machine tape
- fine-line marker
- paper cup
- about 30 inches of string
- dozen or so marbles
- ruler
- pencil

Procedure

STEP ONE

Predict what a seismograph does. A seismograph draws lines on a piece of paper to make a seismogram. What do you think a seismogram for a large earthquake might look like? For a small earthquake? Sketch your predictions.

STEP TWO

Begin building your seismograph.

A. Place two stacks of books, each about 10 inches high, on a desk or table. Place the books less than one pencil-length apart.

B. With the pencil, poke a small hole in the center of the bottom of the paper cup. Poke one hole each on two opposite sides of the cup, just under the rim.

C. Slip the fine-line marker, with the point down, through the bottom of the cup. Tie the ends of the string to the holes under the cup's rim.

STEP THREE

Complete your seismograph.

A. Place the ruler across the two stacks of books. Hang the cup from the ruler by the string.

B. As shown in the photo, slide the pencil through the roll of adding machine tape. Place the pencil sideways behind the gap between the stacks of books, so that the tape can be pulled through evenly. Pull the tape through the gap.

C. Fill the cup with marbles, to weight the cup and to hold the marker in place. Now push the marker down until it touches the tape. Adjust the length of string so that the tip of the marker is just touching the paper.

STEP FOUR

Pull the tape through the seismograph. Have two partners stand on opposite sides of the desk. One partner should pull the end of the tape slowly. Notice the line the seismograph makes on your seismogram.

STEP FIVE

Create an earthquake. The second partner shakes the table slowly while the first pulls the adding machine tape under the marker. The moving desk represents the motion of seismic waves inside the Earth. Now shake the desk harder. How does the line change?

Observations

1. How does the motion of the desk change the appearance of the line on your seismogram?
2. How do these lines compare with your predictions in Step 1?

ANALYSIS AND CONCLUSION

1. How do you think scientists measure the size of an earthquake from looking at a seismogram? How might they tell from the seismogram how long an earthquake lasted?
2. Unlike your model, a seismograph can measure seismic waves from earthquakes too far away to be seen or felt. Why might it be useful to have a machine able to measure earthquakes from far away?

ASIA AND THE PACIFIC

PROJECT POSSIBILITIES

As you study Asia and the Pacific, you will be reading and thinking about these important questions.

- **GEOGRAPHY** What are the main physical features of Asia and the Pacific?
- **HISTORY** How have ancient civilizations of Asia and the Pacific influenced the world today?
- **CULTURE** What are the main characteristics of the cultures of Asia and the Pacific?
- **GOVERNMENT** What types of government exist in Asia and the Pacific today?
- **ECONOMICS** How do the people of this region make a living?

What do you know about Asia and the Pacific? It's time to show it!

Project Menu

The chapters in this book hold some answers to these questions. Now you can find your own answers as you do projects on your own or with your classmates. Make your own discoveries about Asia and the Pacific!

Agriculture Center
Build an information center about agriculture in Asia and the Pacific. Draw a large map of the region and hang it on your classroom wall. Then, as you read about different kinds of farming, mark them on the appropriate region of your map. Design a small poster for each major type of agriculture. On your poster, write about the location of this type of agriculture, the land, climate, products, and how the farms work. Find or draw a picture for each poster.

From Questions to Careers

ENGINEER

Many of the countries in Asia export great numbers of electronic, mechanical, and consumer goods. Americans buy many of these products and sell goods to Asian countries as well. American engineers and technicians work on both continents. They design and produce goods such as autos, televisions, and household tools. Engineers use scientific knowledge to design and build these goods. Engineers and some technicians have college degrees, and other technicians learn their skills by working directly with machinery.

People also design and build the factory equipment used to make these products. What is the best way to run a company? How do you make a factory work well? Many Asian and American business managers and engineers share ideas to answer these questions.

▼ American and Japanese engineers plan a new project.

Independence Biography Choose an Asian or Pacific country that was once ruled by colonists from another country. Find a person who played a major role in this country's struggle for independence. Write a biography of this person and his or her part in the end of colonialism. Include a description of some of the problems of the country's struggle for independence, as well as a paragraph or two about its history since independence was gained.

Asian Trade Fair With your class, plan a trade fair for the countries of Asia and the Pacific. As you read this book, choose a country to research. Find out about its major products, factories, and trade partners. Set up a booth to show and tell visitors about trade in your country. Bring books about the country and make posters, pamphlets, and charts for your booth.

Travel Log As you read this book, keep a diary of experiences of a journey through Asia and the Pacific islands. Write an entry for each country you read about. Focus on a part of the country or culture that most interests you. Think about the sights, smells, and sounds of that country. Write about your reaction to things that are new or strange to you. Display your travel log for the class to read.

Reference

TABLE OF CONTENTS

This Map and Globe Handbook is designed to help you develop some of the skills you need to be a world explorer. These can help you whether you explore from the top of an elephant in India or from a computer at school.

You can use the information in this handbook to improve your map and globe skills. But the best way to sharpen your skills is to practice. The more you practice, the better you'll get.

GEO CLEO and GEO LEO

Table of Contents

Five Themes of Geography

Studying the geography of the entire world can be a huge task. You can make that task easier by using the five themes of geography: location, place, human-environment interaction, movement, and regions. The themes are tools you can use to organize information and to answer the where, why, and how of geography.

1 Location answers the question, "Where is it?" You can think of the location of a continent or a country as its address. You might give an absolute location such as "22 South Lake Street" or "40° N and 80° W." You might also use a relative address, telling where one place is by referring to another place. "Between school and the mall" and "eight miles east of Pleasant City" are examples of relative locations.

2 Place identifies the natural and human features that make one place different from every other place. You can identify a specific place by its landforms, climate, plants, animals, people, or cultures. You might even think of place as a geographic signature. Use the signature to help you understand the natural and human features that make one place different from every other place.

1. Location
Chicago, Illinois, occupies one location on the Earth. No other place has exactly the same absolute location.

2. Place
Ancient cultures in Egypt built distinctive pyramids. Use the theme of place to help you remember features that exist only in Egypt.

3 Human-Environment Interaction

Human-Environment Interaction focuses on the relationship between people and the environment. As people live in an area, they often begin to make changes to it, usually to make their lives easier. For example, they might build a dam to control flooding during rainy seasons. Also, the environment can affect how people live, work, dress, travel, and communicate.

4 Movement

Movement answers the question "How do people, goods, and ideas move from place to place?" Remember that, often, what happens in one place can affect what happens in another. Use the theme of movement to help you trace the spread of goods, people, and ideas from one location to the next.

3. Human-Environment Interaction
Peruvians have changed steep mountain slopes into terraces suitable for farming. Think how this environment looked before people made changes.

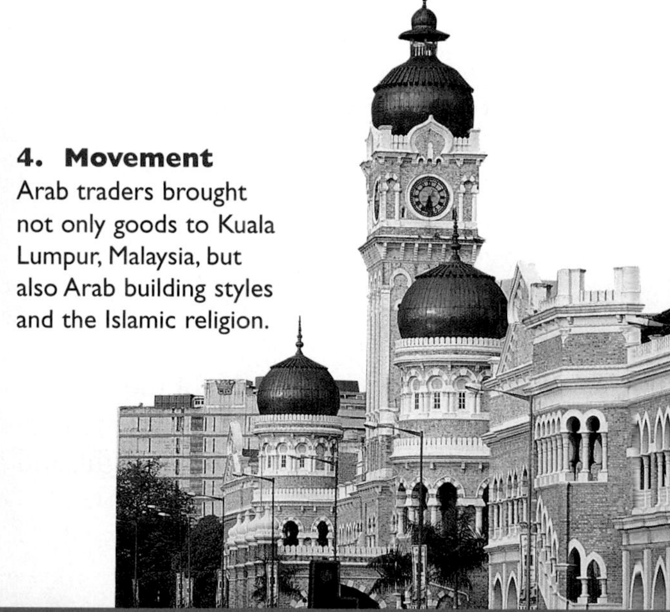

4. Movement
Arab traders brought not only goods to Kuala Lumpur, Malaysia, but also Arab building styles and the Islamic religion.

5 Regions

Regions is the last geographic theme. A region is a group of places that share common features. Geographers divide the world into many types of regions. For example, countries, states, and cities are political regions. The people in these places live under the same type of government. Other features can be used to define regions. Places that have the same climate belong to a particular climate region. Places that share the same culture belong to a cultural region. The same place can be found in more than one region. The state of Hawaii is in the political region of the United States. Because it has a tropical climate, Hawaii is also part of a tropical climate region.

1. What is the absolute location of your school? What is one way to describe its relative location?
2. What might be a "geographic signature" of the town or city you live in?
3. Give an example of human-environment interaction where you live.
4. Name at least one thing that comes into your town or city and one that goes out. How is each moved? Where does it come from? Where does it go?
5. What are several regions you think your town or city belongs in?

5. Regions
Wheat farming is an important activity in Kansas. This means that Kansas is part of a farming region.

Understanding Movements of the Earth

Planet Earth is part of our solar system. The Earth revolves around the sun in a nearly circular path called an orbit. A revolution, or one complete orbit around the sun, takes 365 1/4 days, or a year. As the Earth revolves around the sun, it is also spinning around in space. This movement is called a rotation. The Earth rotates on its axis—an invisible line through the center of the Earth from the North Pole to the South Pole. The Earth makes one full rotation about every 24 hours. As the Earth rotates, it is daytime on the side facing the sun. It is night on the side away from the sun.

The Earth's axis is tilted at an angle. Because of this tilt, sunlight strikes different parts of the Earth at certain points in the year, creating different seasons.

Earth's Revolution and the Seasons

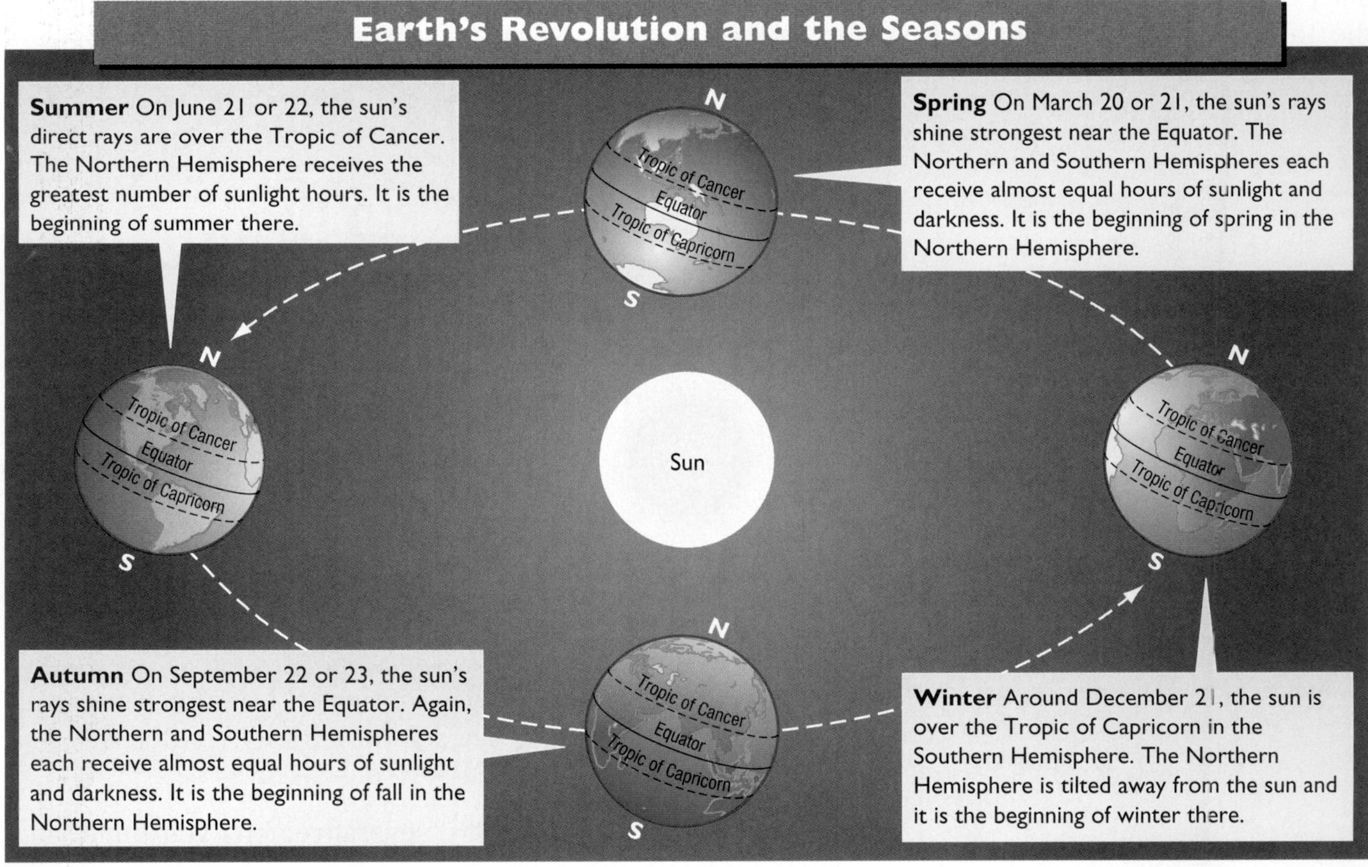

Summer On June 21 or 22, the sun's direct rays are over the Tropic of Cancer. The Northern Hemisphere receives the greatest number of sunlight hours. It is the beginning of summer there.
Spring On March 20 or 21, the sun's rays shine strongest near the Equator. The Northern and Southern Hemispheres each receive almost equal hours of sunlight and darkness. It is the beginning of spring in the Northern Hemisphere.
Autumn On September 22 or 23, the sun's rays shine strongest near the Equator. Again, the Northern and Southern Hemispheres each receive almost equal hours of sunlight and darkness. It is the beginning of fall in the Northern Hemisphere.
Winter Around December 21, the sun is over the Tropic of Capricorn in the Southern Hemisphere. The Northern Hemisphere is tilted away from the sun and it is the beginning of winter there.
Sun
N
S
Tropic of Cancer
Equator
Tropic of Capricorn

▲ **Location** This diagram shows how the Earth's tilt and orbit around the sun combine to create the seasons. Remember, in the Southern Hemisphere the seasons are reversed.

Practice Your World Explorer Skills

1. What causes the seasons in the Northern Hemisphere to be the opposite of those in the Southern Hemisphere?
2. During which two months of the year do the Northern and Southern Hemispheres have about equal hours of daylight and darkness?

Maps and Globes Represent the Earth

Globes

A globe is a scale model of the Earth. It shows the actual shapes, sizes, and locations of all the Earth's landmasses and bodies of water. Features on the surface of the Earth are drawn to scale on a globe. This means a smaller unit of measure on the globe stands for a larger unit of measure on the Earth.

Because a globe is made in the true shape of the Earth, it offers these advantages for studying the Earth.

- The shape of all land and water bodies are accurate.
- Compass directions from one point to any other point are correct.
- The distance from one location to another is always accurately represented.

However, a globe presents some disadvantages for studying the Earth. Because a globe shows the entire Earth, it cannot show small areas in great detail. Also, a globe is not easily folded and carried from one place to another. For these reasons, geographers often use maps to learn about the Earth.

Maps

A map is a drawing or representation, on a flat surface, of a region. A map can show details too small to be seen on a globe. Floor plans, mall directories, and road maps are among the maps we use most often.

While maps solve some of the problems posed by globes, they have some disadvantages of their own. Maps flatten the real round world. Mapmakers cut, stretch, push, and pull some parts of the Earth to get it all flat on paper. As a result, some locations may be distorted. That is, their size, shape, and relative location may not be accurate. For example, on most maps of the entire world, the size and shape of the Antarctic and Arctic regions are not accurate.

PRACTICE YOUR WORLD EXPLORER SKILLS

1. What is the main difference between a globe and a map?
2. What is one advantage of using a globe instead of a map?

Global Gores

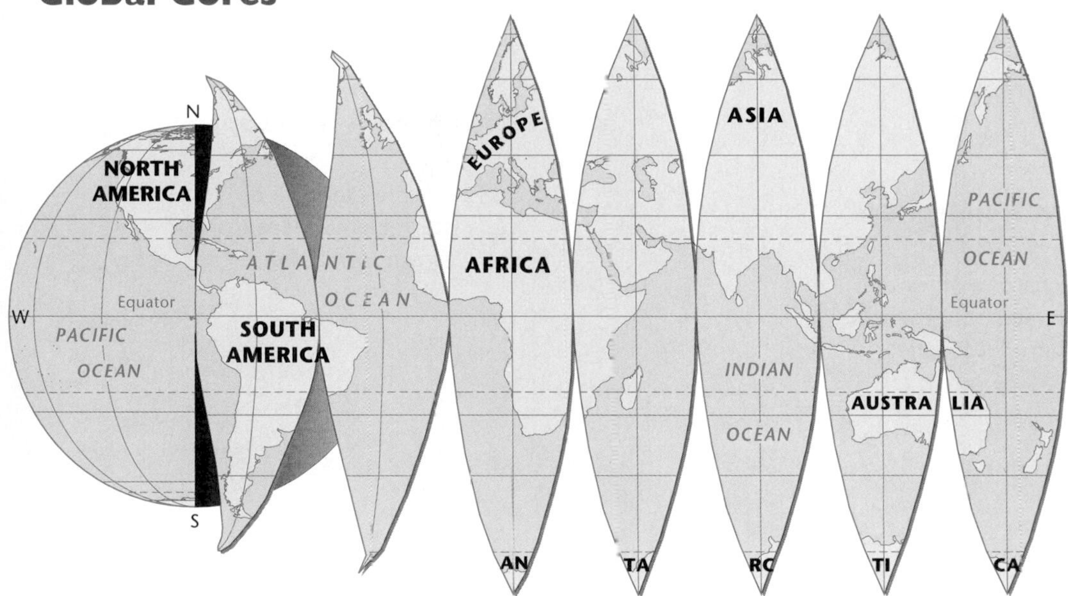

◀ Location When mapmakers flatten the surface of the Earth, curves become straight lines. As a result, size, shape, and distance are distorted.

The Hemispheres

Another name for a round ball like a globe is a sphere. The Equator, an imaginary line halfway between the North and South Poles, divides the globe into two hemispheres. (The prefix *hemi* means "half.") Land and water south of the Equator are in the Southern Hemisphere. Land and water north of the Equator are in the Northern Hemisphere.

Mapmakers sometimes divide the globe along an imaginary line that runs from North Pole to South Pole. This line, called the Prime Meridian, divides the globe into the Eastern and Western Hemispheres.

Northern Hemisphere

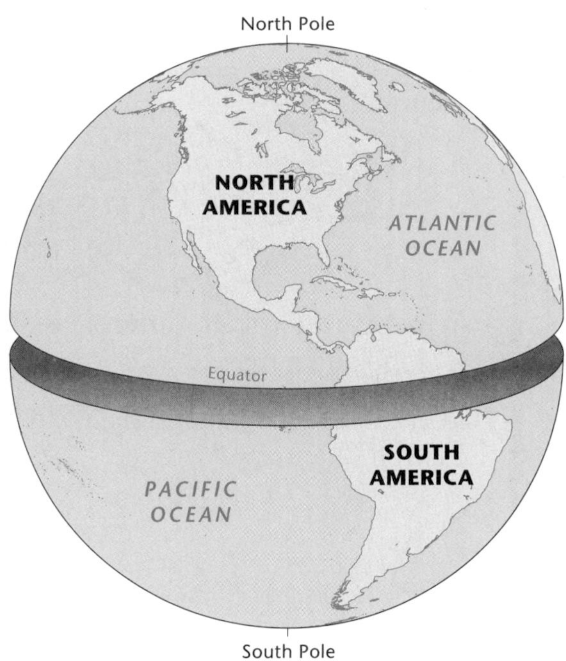

Southern Hemisphere

▲ The Equator divides the Northern Hemisphere from the Southern Hemisphere.

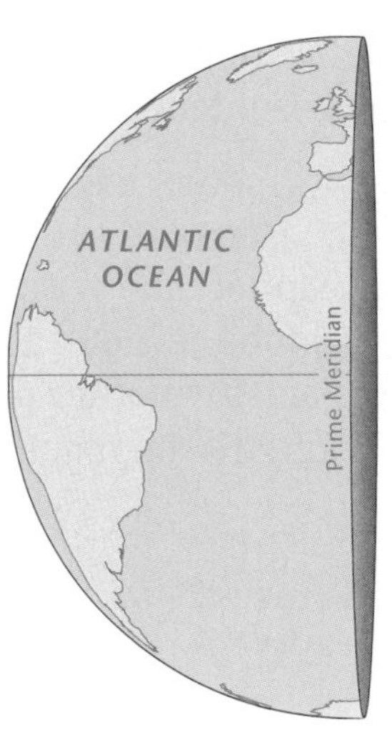

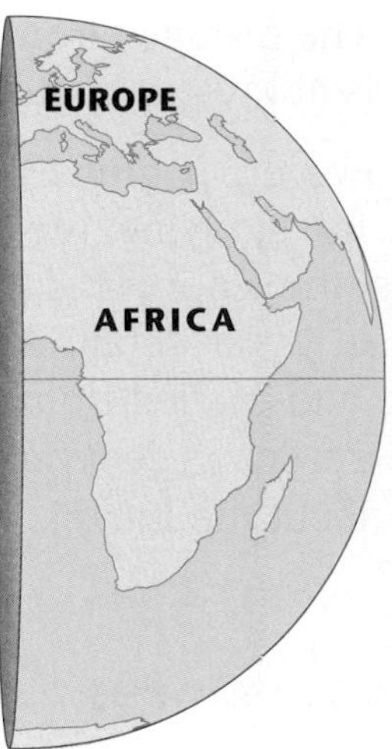

Western Hemisphere **Eastern Hemisphere**

▲ The Prime Meridian divides the Eastern Hemisphere from the Western Hemisphere.

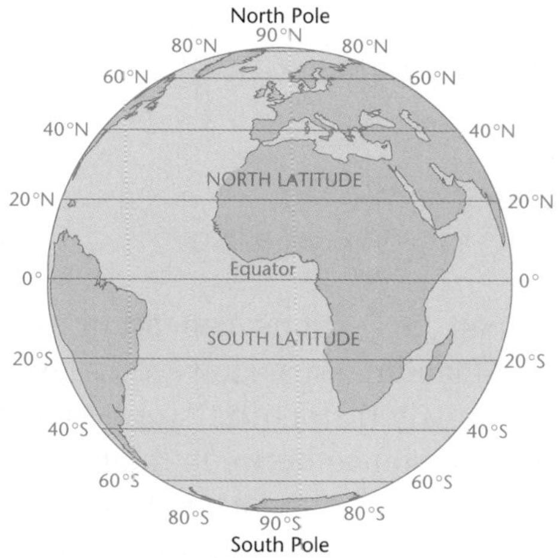

Parallels of Latitude

The Equator, at 0° latitude, is the starting place for measuring latitude or distances north and south. Most globes do not show every parallel of latitude. They may show every 10, 20, or even 30 degrees.

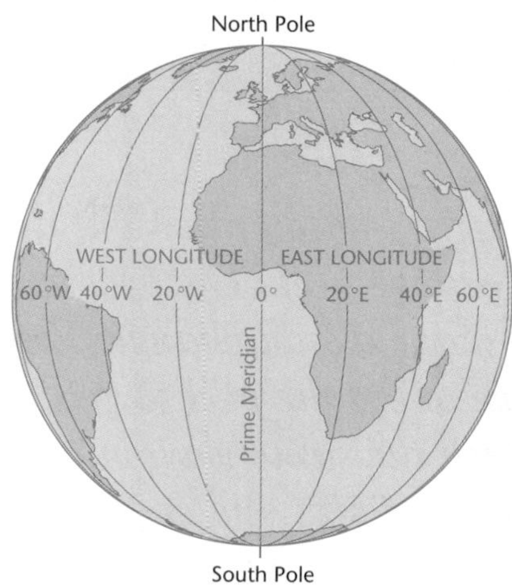

Meridians of Longitude

The Prime Meridian, at 0° longitude, runs from pole to pole through Greenwich, England. It is the starting place for measuring longitude or distances east and west. Each meridian of longitude meets its opposite longitude at the North and South Poles.

The Global Grid

Two sets of lines cover most globes. One set of lines runs parallel to the Equator. These lines, including the Equator, are called *parallels of latitude.* They are measured in degrees (°). One degree of latitude represents a distance of about 70 miles (112 km). The Equator has a location of 0°. The other parallels of latitude tell the direction and distance from the Equator to another location.

The second set of lines runs north and south. These lines are called *meridians of longitude.* Meridians show the degrees of longitude east or west of the Prime Meridian, which is located at 0°. A meridian of longitude tells the direction and distance from the Prime Meridian to another location. Unlike parallels, meridians are not the same distance apart everywhere on the globe.

Together the pattern of parallels of latitude and meridians of longitude is called the global grid. Using the lines of latitude and longitude, you can locate any place on Earth. For example, the location of 30° north latitude and 90° west longitude is usually written as 30°N, 90°W. Only one place on Earth has these coordinates—the city of New Orleans, in the state of Louisiana.

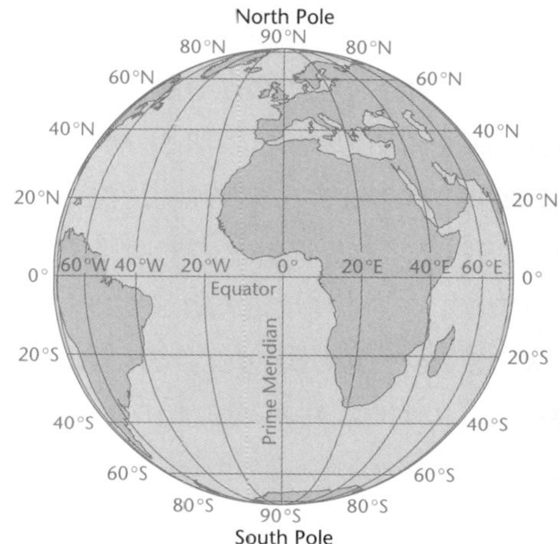

The Global Grid

By using lines of latitude and longitude, you can give the absolute location of any place on the Earth.

1. Which continents lie completely in the Northern Hemisphere? The Western Hemisphere?
2. Is there land or water at 20°S latitude and the Prime Meridian? At the Equator and 60°W longitude?

Map Projections

Imagine trying to flatten out a complete orange peel. The peel would split. The shape would change. You would have to cut the peel to get it to lie flat. In much the same way, maps cannot show the correct size and shape of every landmass or body of water on the Earth's curved surface. Maps shrink some places and stretch others. This shrinking and stretching is called distortion*—a change made to a shape.*

To make up for this disadvantage, mapmakers use different map projections. Each map projection is a way of showing the round Earth on flat paper. Each type of projection has some distortion. No one projection can accurately show the correct area, shape, distance, and direction for the Earth's surface. Mapmakers use the projection that has the least distortion for the information they are studying.

Same-Shape Maps

Some map projections can accurately show the shapes of landmasses. However, these projections often greatly distort the size of landmasses as well as the distance between them.

One of the most common same-shape maps is a Mercator projection, named for the mapmaker who invented it. The Mercator projection accurately shows shape and direction, but it distorts distance and size. In this projection, the northern and southern areas of the globe appear stretched more than areas near the Equator. Because the projection shows true directions, ships' navigators use it to chart a straight line course between two ports.

Mercator Projection

Equal-Area Maps

Some map projections can show the correct size of landmasses. Maps that use these projections are called equal-area maps. In order to show the correct size of landmasses, these maps usually distort shapes. The distortion is usually greater at the edges of the map and less at the center.

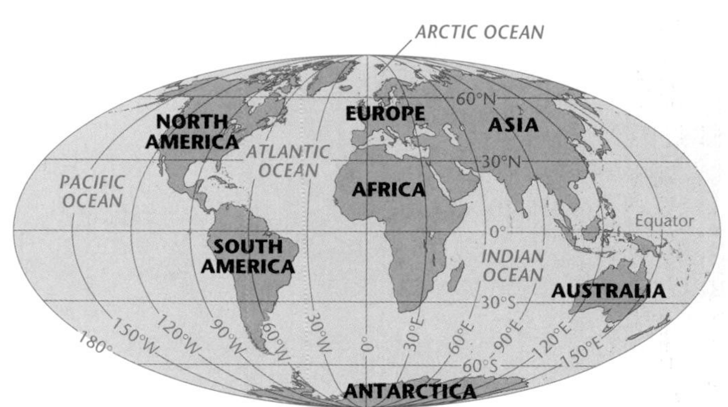

Equal-Area Projection

Robinson Maps

Many of the maps in this book use the Robinson projection. This is a compromise between the Mercator and equal-area projections. It gives a useful overall picture of the world. The Robinson projection keeps the size and shape relationships of most continents and oceans but does distort size of the polar regions.

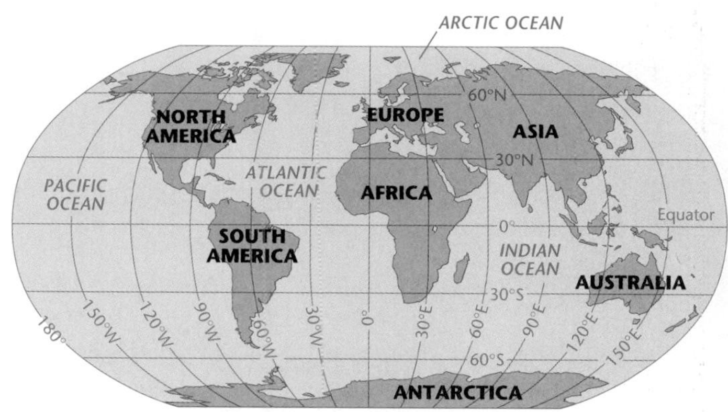

Robinson Projection

Azimuthal Maps

Another kind of projection shows true compass direction. Maps that use this projection are called azimuthal maps. Such maps are easy to recognize—they are usually circular. Azimuthal maps are often used to show the areas of the North and South Poles. However, azimuthal maps distort scale, area, and shape.

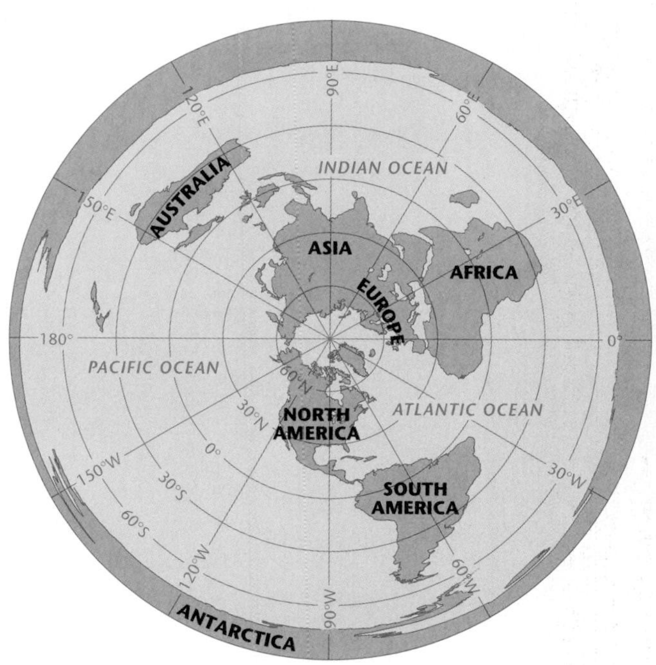

Azimuthal Projection

1. What feature is distorted on an equal-area map?
2. Would you use a Mercator projection to find the exact distance between two locations? Tell why or why not.
3. Which would be a better choice for studying the Antarctic—an azimuthal projection or a Robinson projection? Explain.

Parts of a Map

Mapmakers provide several clues to help you understand the information on a map. As an explorer, it is your job to read and interpret these clues.

Compass
Many maps show north at the top of the map. One way to show direction on a map is to use an arrow that points north. There may be an N shown with the arrow. Many maps give more information about direction by displaying a compass showing the directions, north, east, south, and west. The letters N, E, S, and W are placed to indicate these directions.

Title
The title of a map is the most basic clue. It signals what kinds of information you are likely to find on the map. A map titled *West Africa: Population Density* will be most useful for locating information about where people live in West Africa.

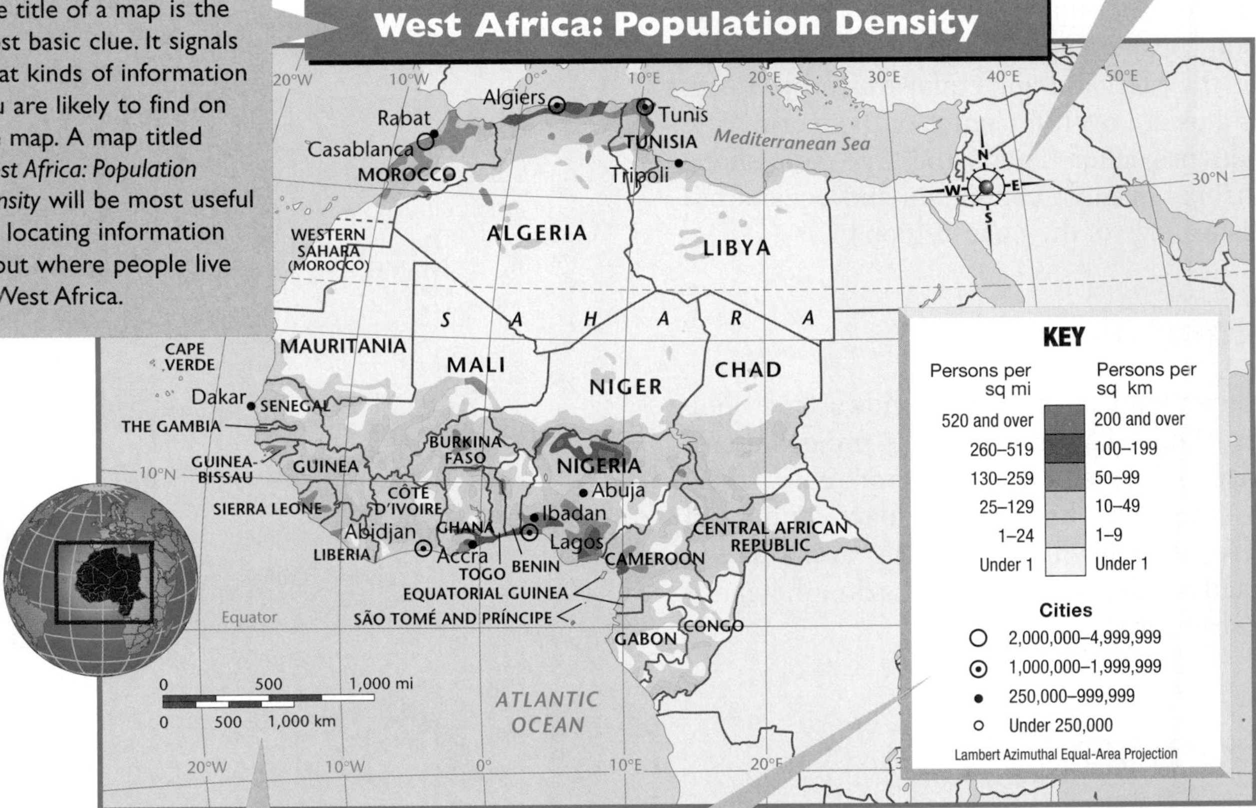

Scale
A map scale helps you find the actual distances between points shown on the map. You can measure the distance between any two points on the map, compare them to the scale, and find out the actual distance between the points. Most map scales show distances in both miles and kilometers.

Key
Often a map has a key, or legend, that shows the symbols used on the map and what each one means. On some maps, color is used as a symbol. On those maps, the key also tells the meaning of each color.

1. What part of a map tells you what the map is about?
2. Where on the map should you look to find out the meaning of this symbol? •
3. What part of the map can you use to find the distance between two cities?

Comparing Maps of Different Scale

Here are three maps drawn to three different scales. The first map shows Moscow's location in the northeastern portion of Russia. This map shows the greatest area—a large section of northern Europe. It has the smallest scale (1 inch = about 900 miles) and shows the fewest details. This map can tell you what direction to travel to reach Moscow from Finland.

Find the red box on Map 1. It shows the whole area covered by Map 2. Study Map 2. It gives a closer look at the city of Moscow. It shows the features around the city, the city's boundary, and the general shape of the city. This map can help you find your way from the airport to the center of town.

Now find the red box on Map 2. This box shows the area shown on Map 3. This map moves you closer into the city. Like the zoom on a computer or camera, Map 3 shows the smallest area but has the greatest detail. This map has the largest scale (1 inch = about 0.8 miles). This is the map to use to explore downtown Moscow.

Map 1

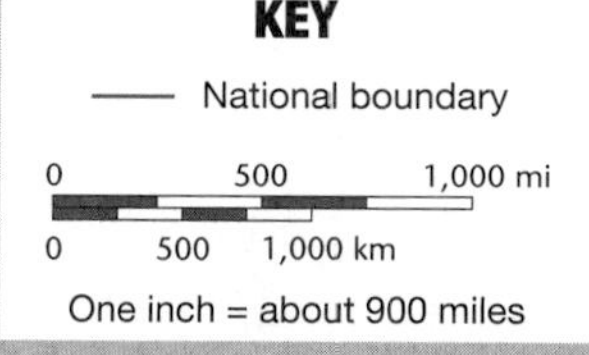

Map 2

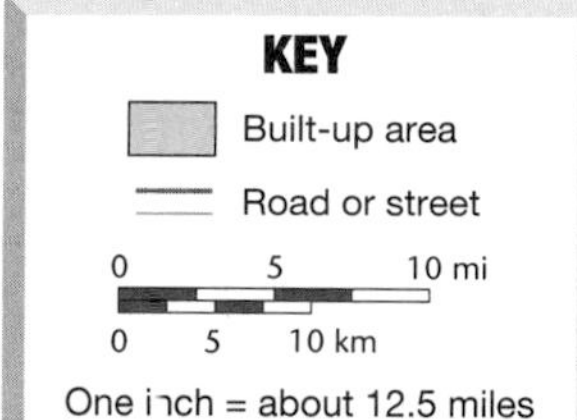

Map 3

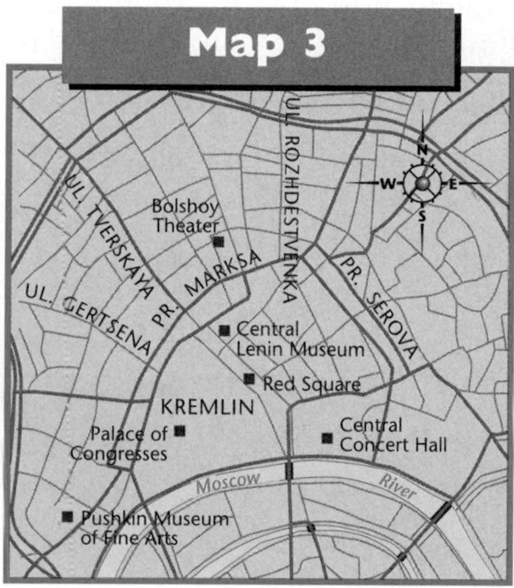

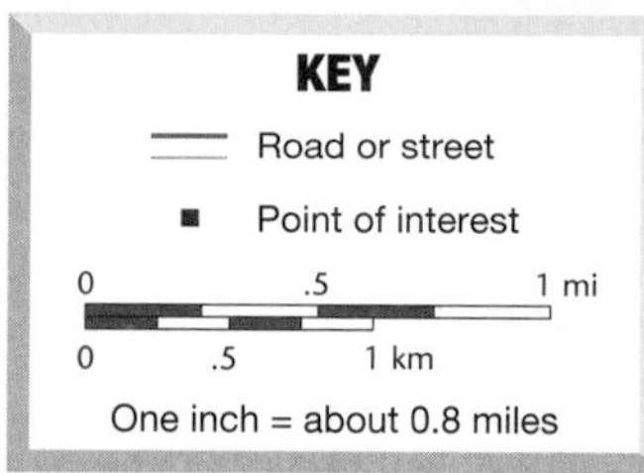

1. Which map would be best for finding the location of Red Square? Why?
2. Which map best shows Moscow's location relative to Poland? Explain.
3. Which map best shows the area immediately surrounding the city?

Political Maps

Mapmakers create maps to show all kinds of information. The kind of information presented affects the way a map looks. One type of map is called a political map. Its main purpose is to show continents, countries, and divisions within countries such as states or provinces. Usually different colors are used to show different countries or divisions within a country. The colors do not have any special meaning. They are used only to make the map easier to read.

Political maps also show where people have built towns and cities. Symbols can help you tell capital cities from other cities and towns. Even though political maps do not give information that shows what the land looks like, they often include some physical features such as oceans, lakes, and rivers.

Political maps usually have many labels. They give country names, and the names of capital and major cities. Bodies of water such as lakes, rivers, oceans, seas, gulfs, and bays are also labeled.

1. What symbol shows the continental boundary?
2. What symbol is used to indicate a capital city? A major city?
3. What kinds of landforms are shown on this map?

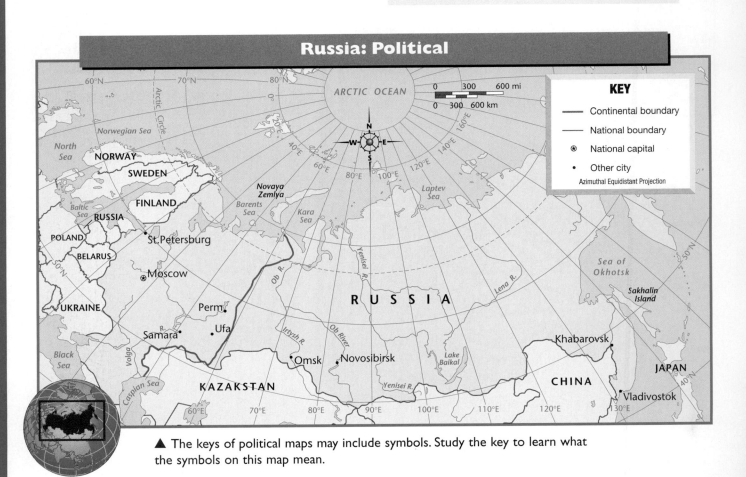

Russia: Political

▲ The keys of political maps may include symbols. Study the key to learn what the symbols on this map mean.

Physical Maps

Like political maps, physical maps show country labels and labels for capital cities. However, physical maps also show what the land of a region looks like by showing the major physical features such as plains, hills, plateaus, or mountains. Labels give the names of features such as mountain peaks, mountains, plateaus, and river basins.

In order to tell one landform from another, physical maps often show elevation and relief. Elevation is the height of the land above sea level. Physical maps in this book use color to show elevation. Browns and oranges show higher lands while blues and greens show lands that are at or below sea level.

Relief shows how quickly the land rises or falls. Hills, mountains, and plateaus are shown on relief maps using shades of gray. Level or nearly level land is shown without shading. Darkly shaded areas indicate steeper lands.

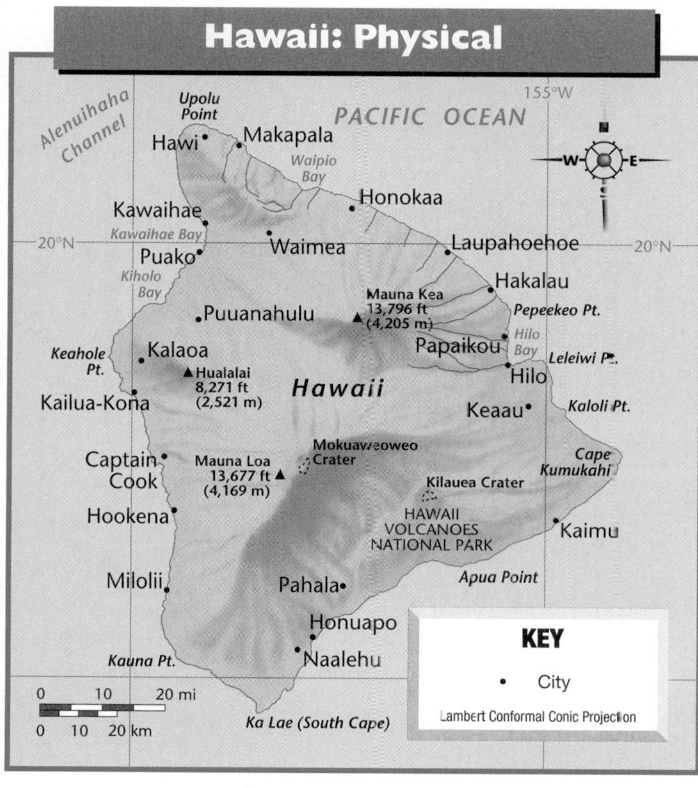

▲ On a physical map, shading is sometimes used to show relief. Use the shading to locate the mountains in Hawaii.

1. How is relief shown on the map to the left?
2. How can you use relief to decide which areas will be the most difficult to climb?
3. What information is given with the name of a mountain peak?

▼ Mauna Kea, an extinct volcano, is the highest peak in the state of Hawaii. Find Mauna Kea on the map.

Special Purpose Maps

As you explore the world, you will encounter many different kinds of special purpose maps. For example, a road map is a special purpose map. The title of each special purpose map tells the purpose and content of the map. Usually a special purpose map highlights only one kind of information. Examples of special purpose maps include land use, population distribution, recreation, transportation, natural resources, or weather.

The key on a special purpose map is very important. Even though a special purpose map shows only one kind of information, it may present many different pieces of data. This data can be shown in symbols, colors, or arrows. In this way, the key acts like a dictionary for the map.

Reading a special purpose map is a skill in itself. Look at the map below. First, try to get an overall sense of what it shows. Then, study the map to identify its main ideas. For example, one main idea of this map is that much of the petroleum production in the region takes place around the Persian Gulf.

1. What part of a special purpose map tells what information is contained on the map?
2. What part of a special purpose map acts like a dictionary for the map?

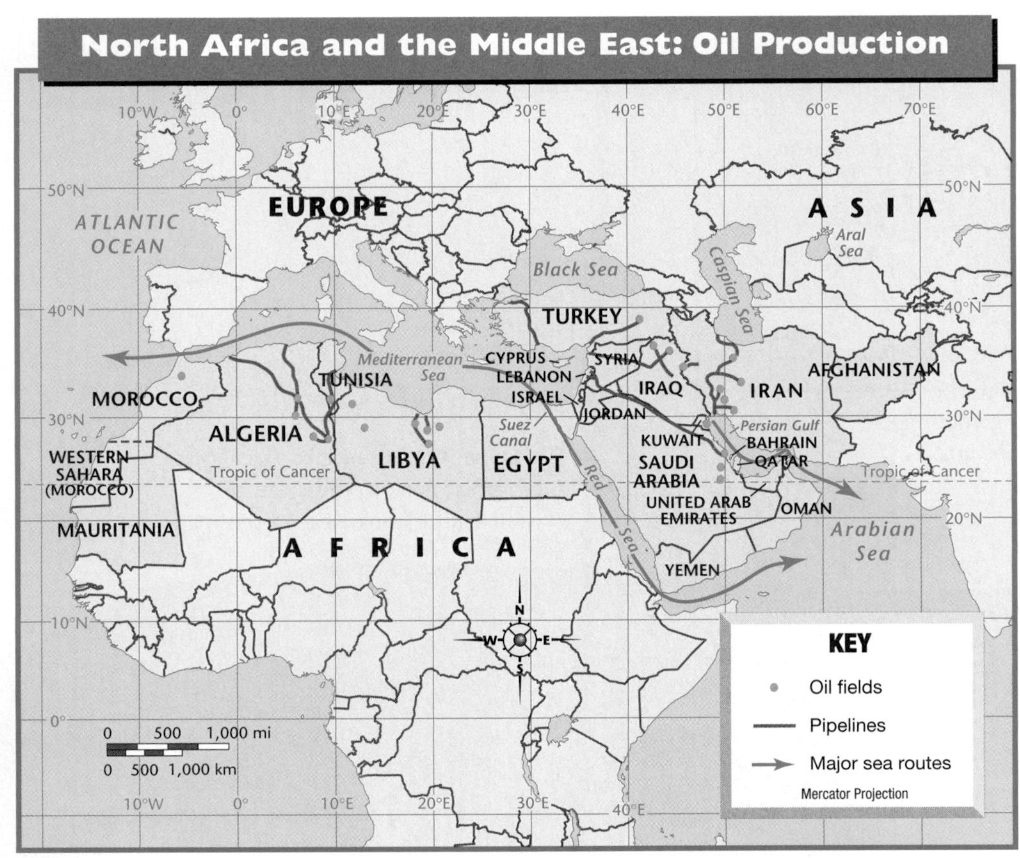

◀ The title on a special purpose map indicates what information can be found on the map. The symbols used on the map are explained in the map's key.

Landforms, Climate Regions, and Natural Vegetation Regions

Maps that show landforms, climate, and vegetation regions are special purpose maps. Unlike the boundary lines on a political map, the boundary lines on these maps do not separate the land into exact divisions. A tropical wet climate gradually changes to a tropical wet and dry climate. A tundra gradually changes to an ice cap. Even though the boundaries between regions may not be exact, the information on these maps can help you understand the region and the lives of people in it.

Landforms

Understanding how people use the land requires an understanding of the shape of the land itself. The four most important landforms are mountains, hills, plateaus, and plains. Human activity in every region in the world is influenced by these landforms.

- **Mountains** are high and steep. Most are wide at the bottom and rise to a narrow peak or ridge. Most geographers classify a mountain as land that rises at least 2,000 feet (610 m) above sea level. A series of mountains is called a mountain range.
- **Hills** rise above surrounding land and have rounded tops. Hills are lower and usually less steep than mountains. The elevation of surrounding land determines whether a landform is called a mountain or a hill.
- A **plateau** is a large, mostly flat area of land that rises above the surrounding land. At least one side of a plateau has a steep slope.
- **Plains** are large areas of flat or gently rolling land. Plains have few changes in elevation. Many plains areas are located along coasts. Others are located in the interior regions of some continents.

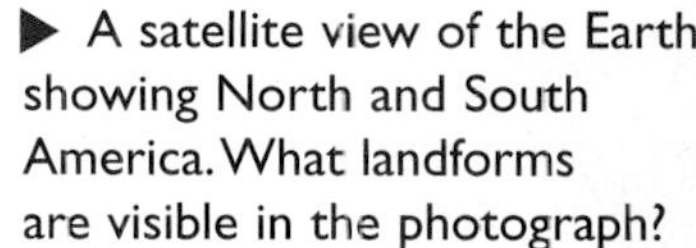

▶ A satellite view of the Earth showing North and South America. What landforms are visible in the photograph?

Climate Regions

Another important influence in the ways people live their lives is the climate of their region. Climate is the weather of a given location over a long period of time. Use the descriptions in the table below to help you visualize the climate regions shown on maps.

Climate	Temperatures	Precipitation
Tropical		
Tropical wet	Hot all year round	Heavy all year round
Tropical wet and dry	Hot all year round	Heavy when sun is overhead, dry other times
Dry		
Semiarid	Hot summers, mild to cold winters	Light
Arid	Hot days, cold nights	Very light
Mild		
Mediterranean	Hot summers, cool winters	Dry summers, wet winters
Humid subtropical	Hot summers, cool winters	Year round, heavier in summer than in winter
Marine west coast	Warm summers, cool winters	Year round, heavier in winter than in summer
Continental		
Humid continental	Hot summers, cold winters	Year round, heavier in summer than in winter
Subarctic	Cool summers, cold winters	Light
Polar		
Tundra	Cool summers, very cold winters	Light
Ice cap	Cold all year round	Light
Highlands	Varies, depending on altitude and direction of prevailing winds	Varies, depending on altitude and direction of prevailing winds

Natural Vegetation Regions

Natural vegetation is the plant life that grows wild without the help of humans. A world vegetation map tells what the vegetation in a place would be if people had not cut down forests or cleared grasslands. The table below provides descriptions of natural vegetation regions shown on maps. Comparing climate and vegetation regions can help you see the close relationship between climate and vegetation.

Vegetation	Description
Tropical rain forest	Tall, close-growing trees forming a canopy over smaller trees, dense growth in general
Deciduous forest	Trees and plants that regularly lose their leaves after each growing season
Mixed forest	Both leaf-losing and cone-bearing trees, no type of tree dominant
Coniferous forest	Cone-bearing trees, evergreen trees and plants
Mediterranean vegetation	Evergreen shrubs and small plants
Tropical savanna	Tall grasses with occasional trees and shrubs
Temperate grassland	Tall grasses with occasional stands of trees
Desert scrub	Low shrubs and bushes, hardy plants
Desert	Little or no vegetation
Tundra	Low shrubs, mosses, lichens; no trees
Ice cap	Little or no vegetation
Highlands	Varies, depending on altitude and direction of prevailing winds

1. How are mountains and hills similar? How are they different?
2. What is the difference between a plateau and a plain?

Europe

Europe and Russia: Political

KEY

- —— National boundary
- ⊛ National capital
- • Other city

Two-Point Equidistant Projection

Background Photo: Eilean Donan Castle, Scotland

GEOFACTS

Europe

Population: 728,646,000

Most Populated City: Moscow, Russia (11.8 million)

Largest Country: Ukraine (223,090 sq mi/ 603,700 sq km)

Smallest Country: Vatican City (0.17 sq mi/ 0.44 sq km)

Highest Point: Mt. Elbrus (18,481 ft/5,633 m)

Lowest Point: Caspian Sea (-92 ft/-28 m)

Longest River: Volga River (2,291mi/3,687 km)

Arc de Triomphe, France

Ben Lomond, Scotland

Northern Europe

Denmark
(DEN mahrk)

Capital: Copenhagen

Area: 16,629 sq mi/43,070 sq km

Population: 5.3 million

Ethnic Groups: Danish, Faeroe, Inuit, Scandinavian

Religions: Evangelical Lutheran, Roman Catholic

Government: constitutional monarchy

Currency: Danish krone, Euro

Exports: machinery and instruments, meat and meat products

Official Language: Danish

Finland
(FIN lund)

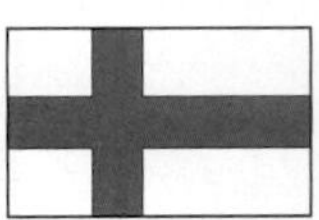

Capital: Helsinki

Area: 117,610 sq mi/304,610 sq km

Population: 5.2 million

Ethnic Groups: Finnish, Sami

Religions: Evangelical Lutheran, Finnish Orthodox, Roman Catholic

Government: republic

Currency: Markka, Euro

Exports: machinery and equipment, chemicals, metals, timber, paper, pulp

Official Languages: Finnish and Swedish

Background Photo: Stockholm Town Hall, Sweden

Iceland
(EYES lund)

Capital: Reykjavik

Area: 38,707 sq mi/100,250 sq km

Population: 279,000

Ethnic Group: Icelanders

Religions: Evangelical Lutheran, Christian

Government: constitutional republic

Currency: Icelandic krona

Exports: fish and fish products, animal products, aluminum, diatomite, ferrosilicon

Official Language: Icelandic

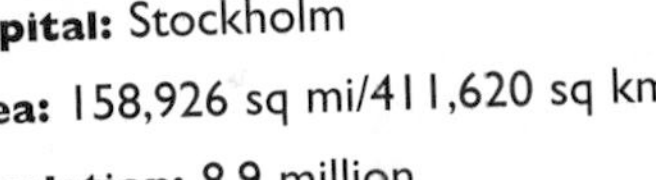

Sweden
(SWEED un)

Capital: Stockholm

Area: 158,926 sq mi/411,620 sq km

Population: 8.9 million

Ethnic Groups: Swedish, Finnish, Sami

Religions: Evangelical Lutheran, Roman Catholic, Russian Orthodox, other Protestant

Government: constitutional monarchy

Currency: Swedish krona, Euro

Exports: machinery, motor vehicles, paper products, pulp, wood

Official Language: Swedish

Ireland
(EYER lund)

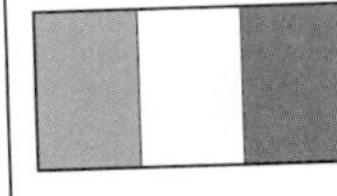

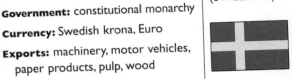

Capital: Dublin

Area: 26,598 sq mi/68,890 sq km

Population: 3.7 million

Ethnic Groups: Celtic, English

Religions: Roman Catholic, Anglican, Jewish

Government: republic

Currency: Punt, Euro

Exports: machinery and equipment, computers, chemicals, pharmaceuticals, live animals, animal products

Official Languages: Irish and English

United Kingdom
(yoo NY tid KING dum)

Capital: London

Area: 93,282 sq mi/241,600 sq km

Population: 58.7 million

Ethnic Groups: English, Scottish, Welsh, Northern Irish

Religions: Anglican, Roman Catholic, Presbyterian, Muslim, Methodist

Government: constitutional monarchy

Exports: manufactured goods, fuels, chemicals, food, beverages

Currency: Pound sterling, Euro

Official Languages: English and Welsh

Norway
(NAWR way)

Capital: Oslo

Area: 118,467 sq mi/306,830 sq km

Population: 4.4 million

Ethnic Groups: Norwegian, Sami

Religions: Evangelical Lutheran, Roman Catholic

Government: constitutional monarchy

Currency: Norwegian krone

Exports: petroleum and petroleum products, machinery and equipment, metals, chemicals, ships, fish

Official Language: Norwegian

Western Europe

Capital: Andorra la Vella

Area: 181 sq mi/468 sq km

Population: 65,000

Ethnic Groups: Spanish, Andorran, Portuguese, French

Religion: Roman Catholic

Government: parliamentary democracy

Currency: French franc and Spanish peseta

Exports: tobacco products, furniture

Official Language: Catalan

Andorra
(an DAWR uh)

Background Photo: Bavaria, Germany

Capital: Vienna

Area: 32,942 sq mi/82,730 sq km

Population: 8.2 million

Ethnic Groups: German, Croat, Slovene, Hungarian

Religions: Roman Catholic, Protestant, Muslim

Government: federal republic

Currency: Austrian schilling, Euro

Exports: machinery and equipment, paper, paperboard, metal goods

Official Language: German

Austria
(AW stree uh)

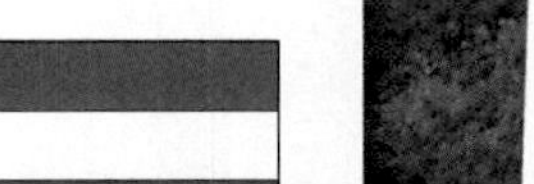

Capital: Paris

Area: 212,394 sq mi/550,100 sq km

Population: 58.9 million

Ethnic Groups: French, North African, German, Breton

Religions: Roman Catholic, Muslim, Protestant, Buddhist, Jewish

Government: republic

Currency: Franc, Euro

Exports: machinery and transportation equipment, chemicals, iron and steel products

Official Language: French

France
(frans)

Capital: Brussels

Area: 12,672 sq mi/32,820 sq km

Population: 10.2 million

Ethnic Groups: Fleming, Walloon, Italian, Moroccan

Religions: Roman Catholic, Muslim

Government: federal monarchy

Currency: Belgian franc, Euro

Exports: machinery and equipment, chemicals, diamonds, metals

Official Languages: Flemish, French, German

Belgium
(BEL jum)

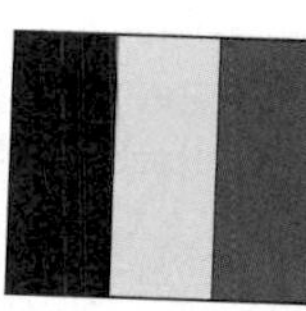

Capital: Berlin

Area: 134,910 sq mi/349,520 sq km

Population: 82.2 million

Ethnic Groups: German, Turkish

Religions: Protestant, Roman Catholic, Muslim

Government: federal republic

Currency: Deutsche Mark, Euro

Exports: machinery, vehicles, chemicals, metals and manufactures, foodstuffs, textiles

Official Language: German

Germany
(JUR muh nee)

Vaduz Castle, Liechtenstein

Liechtenstein
(LIK tun styn)

Capital: Vaduz
Area: 62 sq mi/160 sq km
Population: 31,000
Ethnic Groups: Alemmanic, Italian, Turkish
Religions: Roman Catholic, Protestant
Government: hereditary constitutional monarchy
Currency: Swiss franc
Exports: small specialty machinery, dental products, stamps, hardware
Official Language: German

Luxembourg
(LUK sum burg)

Capital: Luxembourg
Area: 998 sq mi/2,585 sq km
Population: 426,000
Ethnic Groups: Celtic with French and German, Portuguese, Italian
Religions: Roman Catholic, Protestant, Greek Orthodox, Jewish
Government: constitutional monarchy
Currency: Luxembourg franc, Euro
Exports: finished steel products, chemicals, rubber products, glass
Official Languages: French, Letzeburgish, German

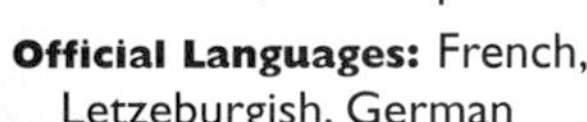

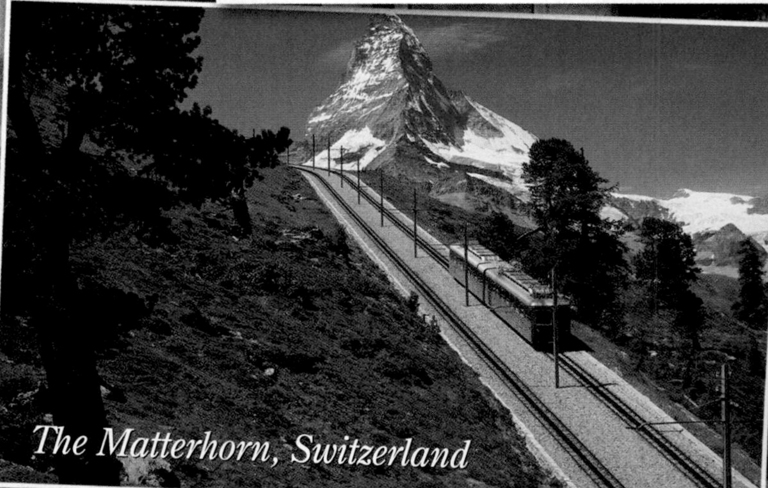

The Matterhorn, Switzerland

Capital: Monaco

Area: 0.75 sq mi/1.95 sq km

Population: 32,000

Ethnic Groups: French, Monegasque, Italian

Religions: Roman Catholic, Protestant

Government: constitutional monarchy

Currency: French franc

Official Language: French

Monaco

(MAHN uh koh)

Monte Carlo, Monaco

Capital: Amsterdam

Area: 13,097 sq mi/33,920 sq km

Population: 15.7 million

Ethnic Groups: Dutch, Moroccan, Turkish

Religions: Roman Catholic, Protestant, Muslim

Government: constitutional monarchy

Currency: Netherlands guilder, Euro

Exports: machinery and equipment, chemicals, fuels, foodstuffs

Official Language: Dutch

Netherlands

(NETH ur lundz)

Capital: Bern

Area: 15,355 sq mi/39,770 sq km

Population: 7.3 million

Ethnic Groups: German, French, Italian, Romansh

Religions: Roman Catholic, Protestant, Muslim

Government: federal republic

Currency: Swiss franc

Exports: machinery, chemicals, vehicles, metals, watches

Official Languages: French, German, Italian

Switzerland

(SWIT sur lund)

Southern Europe

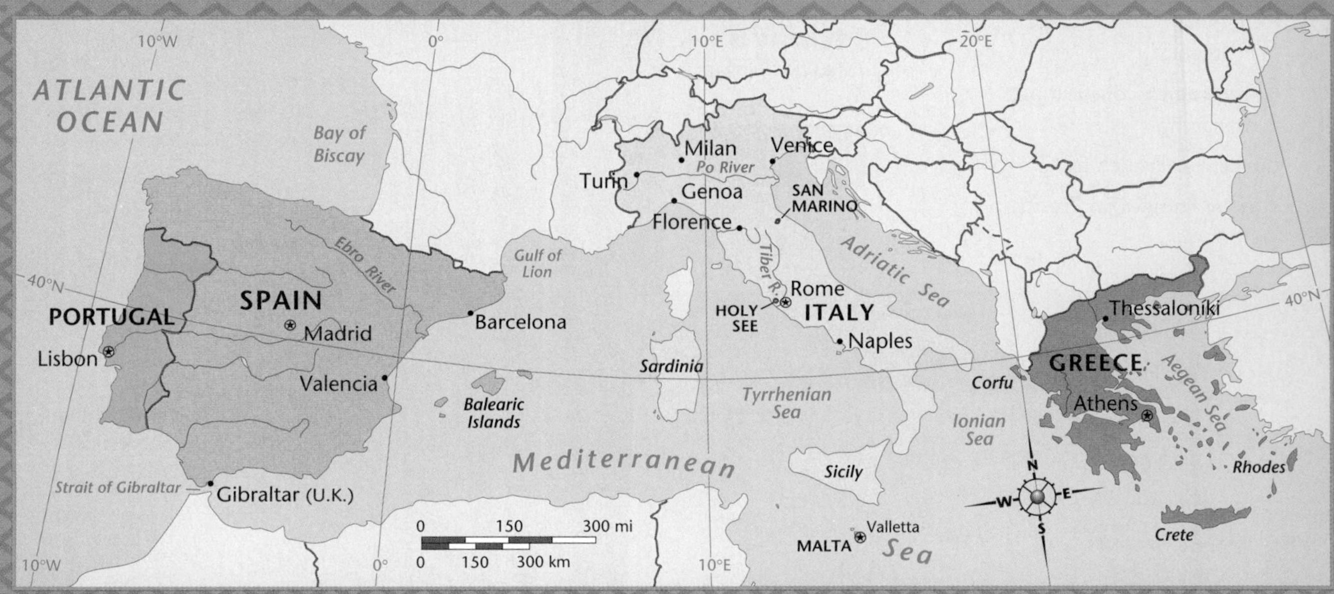

Capital: Athens

Area: 50,521 sq mi/130,850 sq km

Population: 10.6 million

Ethnic Group: Greek

Religions: Greek Orthodox, Muslim

Government: parliamentary republic

Currency: Drachma, Euro

Exports: manufactured goods, food and beverages, fuels

Official Language: Greek

Greece
(grees)

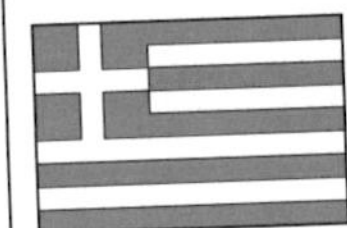

Capital: Vatican City

Area: 0.17 sq mi/0.44 sq km

Population: 1,000

Ethnic Groups: Italian, Swiss

Religion: Roman Catholic

Government: monarchy

Currency: Lira

Exports: none

Official Languages: Italian and Latin

Holy See (Vatican City)
(HO lee see VAT i kun SI tee)

Background Photo: Florence, Italy

Italy
(IT uh lee)

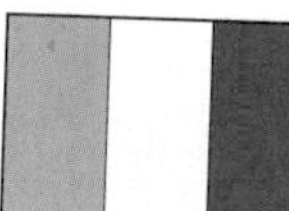

Capital: Rome

Area: 301,270 sq mi/294,060 sq km

Population: 57.3 million

Ethnic Groups: Italian, Sardinian

Religions: Roman Catholic, Protestant, Jewish, Muslim

Government: republic

Currency: Italian lira, Euro

Exports: engineering products, textiles, clothing, production machinery, motor vehicles

Official Language: Italian

San Marino
(san muh REE noh)

Capital: San Marino

Area: 24 sq mi/61 sq km

Population: 26,000

Ethnic Groups: Sammarinese, Italian

Religion: Roman Catholic

Government: republic

Currency: Lira

Exports: building stone, lime, wood, chestnuts, wheat, wine, baked goods, hides, ceramics

Official Language: Italian

Malta
(MAWL tuh)

Capital: Valletta

Area: 124 sq mi/320 sq km

Population: 386,000

Ethnic Groups: Maltese

Religion: Roman Catholic

Government: parliamentary democracy

Currency: Maltese lira

Exports: machinery and transport equipment, manufactures

Official Languages: English, Maltese

Spain
(spayn)

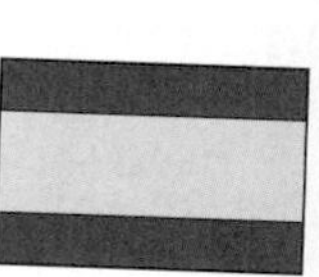

Capital: Madrid

Area: 192,834 sq mi/499,440 sq km

Population: 39.6 million

Ethnic Groups: Castillian Spanish, Catalan, Galician, Basque, Romany

Religion: Roman Catholic

Government: parliamentary monarchy

Currency: Spanish peseta, Euro

Exports: machinery, motor vehicles, foodstuffs, other consumer goods

Official Languages: Spanish, Galician, Basque, Catalan

Portugal
(PAWR chuh gul)

Capital: Lisbon

Area: 35,502 sq mi/91,950 sq km

Population: 9.9 million

Ethnic Groups: Portuguese, African

Religions: Roman Catholic, Protestant

Government: parliamentary democracy

Currency: Portuguese escudo, Euro

Exports: machinery, clothing, footwear, chemicals, cork and paper products, hides

Official Language: Portuguese

REGIONAL • DATABASE

DK

Eastern Europe

Capital: Tirana

Area: 10,579 sq mi/27,400 sq km

Population: 3.1 million

Ethnic Groups: Albanian, Greek, Vlach, Gypsy, Serb, Bulgarian

Religions: Sunni Muslim, Orthodox, Roman Catholic

Government: parliamentary republic

Currency: Lek

Exports: textiles, footwear, asphalt, metals and metallic ores, crude oil

Official Language: Albanian

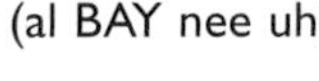

Albania
(al BAY nee uh)

Capital: Minsk

Area: 80,154 sq mi/207,600 sq km

Population: 10.3 million

Ethnic Groups: Belorussian, Russian, Polish, Ukrainian

Religions: Russian Orthodox, Roman Catholic, Muslim, Jewish, Protestant

Government: republic

Currency: Belorussian ruble

Exports: machinery and equipment, chemicals, metals, textiles, foodstuffs

Official Languages: Belorussian, Russian

Belarus
(bel uh ROOS)

Background Photo: Prague, Czech Republic

Bosnia–Herzegovina
(BOZ nee uh hurt suh goh VEE nuh)

Capital: Sarajevo

Area: 19,741 sq mi/51,130 sq km

Population: 3.8 million

Ethnic Groups: Bosniak, Serb, Croat, Yugoslav

Religions: Muslim, Serbian Orthodox, Roman Catholic, Protestant

Government: emerging democracy

Currency: Maraka

Exports: none of significance

Official Language: Serbo-Croat

Croatia
(kroh AY shuh)

Capital: Zagreb

Area: 21,829 sq mi/56,538 sq km

Population: 4.5 million

Ethnic Groups: Croat, Serb, Yugoslav

Religions: Roman Catholic, Orthodox, Muslim

Government: presidential/parliamentary democracy

Currency: Kuna

Exports: textiles, chemicals, foodstuffs, fuels

Official Language: Croatian

Bulgaria
(bul GAYR ee un)

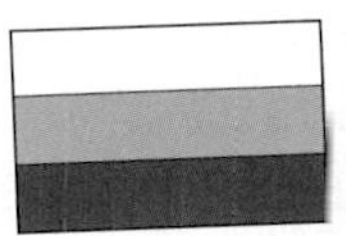

Capital: Sofia

Area: 42,683 sq mi/110,550 sq km

Population: 8.3 million

Ethnic Groups: Bulgarian, Turkish, Macedonian, Romany

Religions: Bulgarian Orthodox, Muslim, Roman Catholic, Jewish

Government: parliamentary democracy

Currency: Lev

Exports: machinery and equipment, metals, minerals, fuels, chemicals

Official Language: Bulgarian

Czech Republic
(chek ri PUB lik)

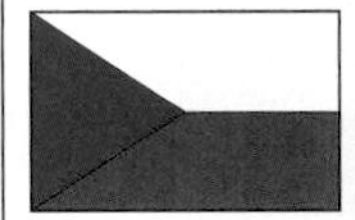

Capital: Prague

Area: 30,449 sq mi/78,864 sq km

Population: 10.3 million

Ethnic Groups: Czech, Moravian, Slovak

Religions: Roman Catholic, Hossites, Protestant

Government: parliamentary democracy

Currency: Czech koruna

Exports: machinery and transport equipment, manufactured goods

Official Language: Czech

Estonia
(e STOH nee uh)

Capital: Tallinn

Area: 17,423 sq mi/45,125 sq km

Population: 1.4 million

Ethnic Groups: Russian, Estonian

Religions: Evangelical Lutheran, Russian Orthodox, Estonian Orthodox

Government: parliamentary democracy

Currency: Kroon

Exports: machinery and appliances, wood products, textiles, food

Official Language: Estonian

Capital: Budapest
Area: 35,652 sq mi/92,340 sq km
Population: 10.1 million
Ethnic Groups: Magyar, German, Romany, Slovak
Religions: Roman Catholic, Calvinist, Lutheran, Greek Orthodox
Government: parliamentary democracy
Currency: Forint
Exports: machinery and equipment, other manufactures, agriculture
Official Language: Hungarian

Hungary
(HUNG guh ree)

Capital: Skopje
Area: 9,929 sq mi/25,715 sq km
Population: 2 million
Ethnic Groups: Macedonian, Albanian, Turkish, Serb, Romany
Religions: Macedonian Orthodox, Muslim
Government: republic
Currency: Macedonian denar
Exports: food, beverages, tobacco, miscellaneous manufactures, iron, steel
Official Language: Macedonian

Macedonia
(mas i DOH nee uh)

Capital: Riga
Area: 24,938 sq mi/ 64,589 sq km
Population: 2.4 million
Ethnic Groups: Latvian, Russian, Belorussian, Ukrainian
Religions: Lutheran, Roman Catholic, Russian Orthodox
Government: parliamentary democracy
Currency: Lat
Exports: wood and wood products, machinery and equipment, metals
Official Language: Latvian

Latvia
(LAT vee uh)

Capital: Vilnius
Area: 25,174 sq mi/65,200 sq km
Population: 3.7 million
Ethnic Groups: Lithuanian, Russian, Polish, Belorussian
Religions: Roman Catholic, Lutheran, Russian Orthodox
Government: parliamentary democracy
Currency: Litas
Exports: machinery and equipment, mineral products, textiles
Official Language: Lithuanian

Lithuania
(lith oo AY nee uh)

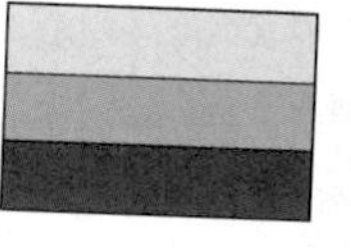

Capital: Chisinau
Area: 13,000 sq mi/33,700 sq km
Population: 4.4 million
Ethnic Groups: Moldovan, Ukrainian, Russian, Gagauz
Religions: Eastern Orthodox, Jewish, Baptist
Government: republic
Currency: Leu
Exports: foodstuffs, wine, tobacco, textiles, footwear, machinery
Official Language: Romanian

Moldova
(mawl DOH vuh)

Poland
(POH lund)

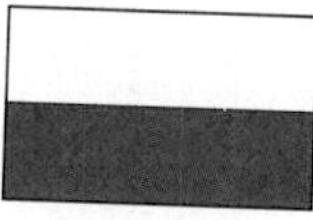

Capital: Warsaw

Area: 117,552 sq mi/304,460 sq km

Population: 38.7 million

Ethnic Groups: Polish, German

Religions: Roman Catholic, Eastern Orthodox

Government: republic

Currency: Zloty

Exports: manufactured goods, chemicals, machinery and equipment, food, live animals, mineral fuels

Official Language: Polish

Slovenia
(sloh VEE nee uh)

Capital: Ljubljana

Area: 7,820 sq mi/20,250 sq km

Population: 2 million

Ethnic Groups: Slovene, Croat, Serb, Bosniak

Religions: Roman Catholic, Orthodox Catholic, Muslim

Government: parliamentary democratic republic

Currency: Tolar

Exports: manufactured goods, machinery, transport equipment

Official Language: Slovene

Romania
(roh MAY nee uh)

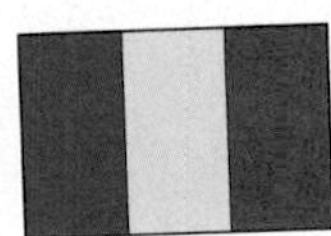

Capital: Bucharest

Area: 88,934 sq mi/230,340 sq km

Population: 22.4 million

Ethnic Groups: Romanian, Magyar, Romany

Religions: Romanian Orthodox, Roman Catholic, Protestant

Government: republic

Currency: Leu

Exports: textiles, footwear, metals and metal products, machinery and equipment, minerals, fuels

Official Language: Romanian

Ukraine
(yoo KRAYN)

Capital: Kiev

Area: 223,090 sq mi/603,700 sq km

Population: 50.7 million

Ethnic Groups: Ukrainian, Russian, Jewish

Religions: Ukrainian Orthodox, Catholic, Protestant, Jewish

Government: republic

Currency: Hryvna

Exports: metals, fuel and petroleum products, machinery

Official Language: Ukrainian

Slovakia
(sloh VAH kee uh)

Capital: Bratislava

Area: 18,933 sq mi/49,036 sq km

Population: 5.4 million

Ethnic Groups: Slovak, Hungarian, Gypsy

Religions: Roman Catholic, Protestant, Orthodox

Government: parliamentary democracy

Currency: Koruna

Exports: machinery and transport equipment, manufactured goods

Official Language: Slovak

Yugoslavia
(yoo goh SLAH vee uh)

Capital: Belgrade

Area: 39,449 sq mi/102,173 sq km

Population: 10.6 million

Ethnic Groups: Serb, Albanian, Montenegrin, Bosniak, Magyar

Religions: Eastern Orthodox, Muslim, Roman Catholic, Protestant

Government: republic

Currency: Yugoslav dinar

Exports: manufactured goods, food, live animals, raw materials

Official Language: Serbo-Croat

Russia

Peterhof Grand Palace, St. Petersburg

Background Photo: St. Basil's Cathedral, Moscow, Russia

Tchesme Church, St. Petersburg

Russian Federation

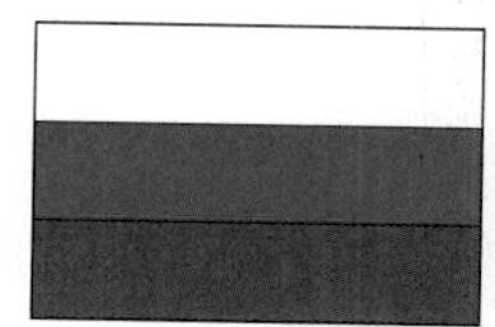

Capital: Moscow

Area: 6,592,812 sq mi/17,075,400 sq km

Population: 147.2 million

Ethnic Groups: Russian, Tatar, Ukrainian, Chuvash

Religions: Russian Orthodox, Muslim

Government: federation

Currency: Ruble

Exports: petroleum and petroleum products, natural gas, wood and wood products, metals, chemicals, civilian and military manufactures

Official Language: Russian

Lake Onega, Russia

Africa

KEY

- National boundary
- ⊛ National capital
- • Other city

Lambert Azimuthal Equal Area Projection

Background photo: Mt. Kilimanjaro, Tanzania

Data compiled from the *Dorling Kindersley World Desk Reference*, the CIA Factbook, and the *Infoplease Internet Encyclopedia*.

GEOFACTS

Africa

Population: 697.3 million

Most Populated City: Cairo, Egypt (6.4 million)

Largest Country: Sudan (917,374 sq mi/ 2,376,000 sq km)

Smallest Country: Seychelles (104 sq mi/ 270 sq km)

Highest Point: Mt. Kilimanjaro (19,341 ft/5,895 m)

Lowest Point: Lac'Assal (-512 ft/-156 m)

Longest River: Nile River (4,160 mi/ 6,695 km)

Uganda

Johannesburg, South Africa

North Africa

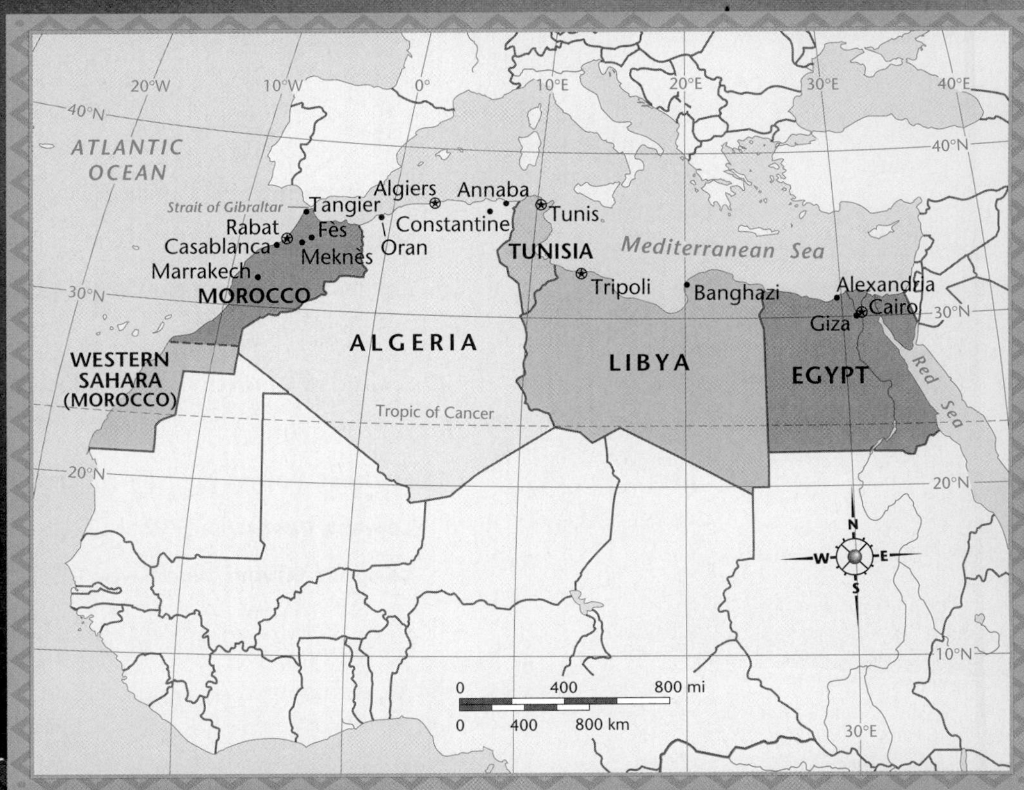

Capital: Algiers

Area: 919,590 sq mi/2,381,740 sq km

Population: 30.8 million

Ethnic Groups: Arab, Berber

Religions: Sunni Muslim, Christian, Jewish

Government: republic

Currency: Algerian dinar

Exports: petroleum, natural gas, petroleum products

Official Language: Arabic

Algeria
(AL jeer ee uh)

Capital: Cairo

Area: 384,343 sq mi/995,450 sq km

Population: 67.2 million

Ethnic Groups: Eastern Hamitic, Nubian, Armenian, Greek

Religions: Muslim (mostly Sunni), Coptic Christian

Government: republic

Currency: Egyptian pound

Exports: crude oil, petroleum products, cotton, textiles

Official Language: Arabic

Egypt
(EE jipt)

Background photo: City of the Dead, Cairo, Egypt

Capital: Tripoli/Benghazi
Area: 679,358 sq mi/1,759,540 sq km
Population: 5.5 million
Ethnic Groups: Arab, Berber
Religions: Sunni Muslim
Government: military dictatorship
Currency: Libyan dinar
Exports: crude oil, refined petroleum products, natural gas
Official Language: Arabic

Libya
(LIB ee uh)

Giza, Egypt

Capital: Rabat
Area: 172,316 sq mi/446,300 sq km
Population: 27.9 million
Ethnic Groups: Arab, Berber, Shluh, Tamazight, French, Spanish
Religions: Muslim, Christian, Jewish
Government: constitutional monarchy
Currency: Moroccan dirham
Exports: phosphates and fertilizers, food and beverages, minerals
Official Language: Arabic

Morocco
(mu ROK oh)

Capital: Tunis
Area: 59,984 sq mi/155,360 sq km
Population: 9.5 million
Ethnic Groups: Arab, Berber, French
Religions: Muslim, Christian, Jewish
Government: republic
Currency: Tunisian dinar
Exports: textiles, mechanical goods, phosphates and chemicals, agricultural products, hydrocarbons
Official Language: Arabic

Tunisia
(too NEE zhuh)

West Africa

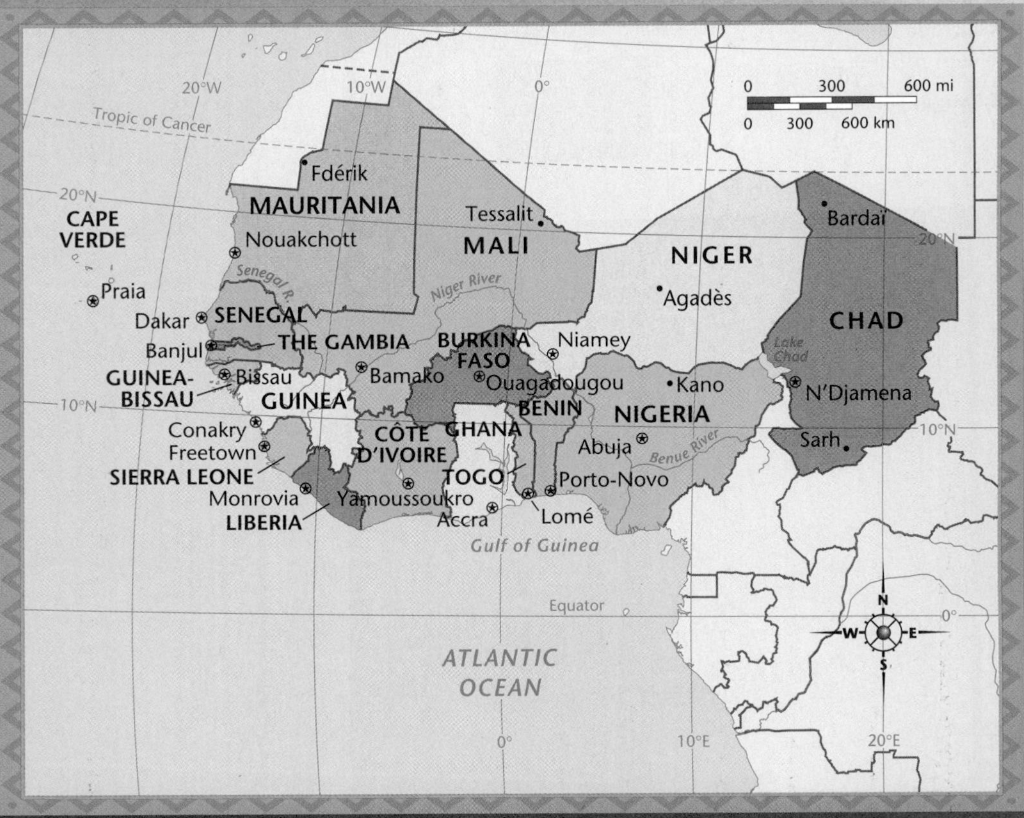

Capital: Porto-Novo

Area: 42,710 sq mi/110,620 sq km

Population: 5.9 million

Ethnic Groups: Fon, Adja, Yoruba, Bariba, Somba, French

Religions: traditional beliefs, Christian, Muslim

Government: republic

Currency: CFA franc

Exports: cotton, crude oil, palm products, cocoa

Official Language: French

Benin
(be NEEN)

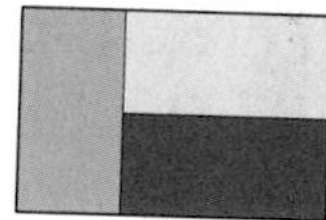

Capital: Ouagadougou

Area: 105,714 sq mi/273,800 sq km

Population: 11.6 million

Ethnic Groups: Mossi, Gurunsi, Senufo, Lobi, Bobo, Mande, Fulani

Religions: traditional beliefs, Muslim, Roman Catholic

Government: parliamentary

Currency: CFA franc

Exports: cotton, animal products, gold

Official Language: French

Burkina Faso
(bur KEE nuh FAH soh)

Background photo: Accra, Ghana

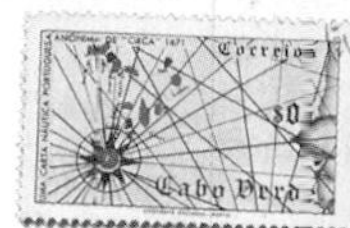

Capital: Praia

Area: 1,556 sq mi/4,030 sq km

Population: 418,000

Ethnic Groups: Mestico, Portuguese Creole, European

Religions: Roman Catholic, Protestant

Government: republic

Currency: Cape Verde escudo

Exports: fuel, shoes, garments, fish, bananas, hides

Official Language: Portuguese

Cape Verde

(kayp vurd)

Capital: Yamoussoukro

Area: 122,780 sq mi/318,000 sq km

Population: 15.9 million

Ethnic Groups: Baoulé, Bete, Senufo, Malinke, Agni

Religions: Muslim, Christian

Government: republic

Currency: CFA franc

Exports: cocoa, coffee, tropical woods, petroleum, cotton, bananas, pineapples, palm oil, cotton, fish

Official Language: French

Cote D'Ivoire

(koht deev WAR)

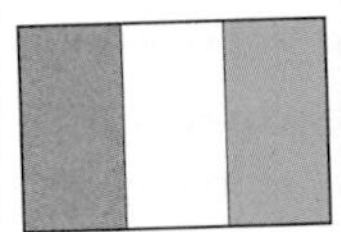

Capital: Banjul

Area: 3,861 sq mi/10,000 sq km

Population: 1.3 million

Ethnic Groups: Mandingo, Fulani, Wolof, Jola, Serahull

Religions: Muslim, Christian, traditional beliefs

Government: republic

Currency: Dalasi

Exports: peanuts and peanut products, fish, cotton lint, palm kernels

Official Language: English

The Gambia

(GAM bee uh)

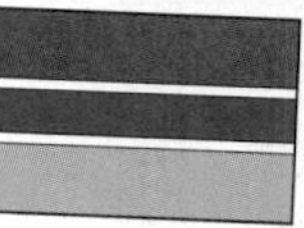

Capital: N'Djamena

Area: 486,177 sq mi/1,259,200 sq km

Population: 7.5 million

Ethnic Groups: Arab, Toubou, Hadjerai, Sara, Ngambaye

Religions: Muslim, traditional beliefs, Christian

Government: republic

Currency: CFA franc

Exports: cotton, cattle, textiles

Official Languages: Arabic and French

Chad

(chad)

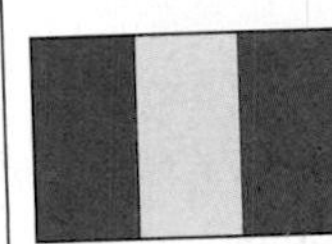

Capital: Accra

Area: 92,100 sq mi/238,540 sq km

Population: 19.7 million

Ethnic Groups: Akan, Mole-Dagbani, Ga-Adangbe, Ewe

Religions: Christian, traditional beliefs, Muslim

Government: constitutional democracy

Currency: Cedi

Exports: gold, cocoa, timber, tuna, bauxite, aluminum, manganese ore

Official Language: English

Ghana

(GAH nuh)

Capital: Conakry

Area: 94,926 sq mi/245,860 sq km

Population: 7.4 million

Ethnic Groups: Fila, Malinke, Soussou, Kissi

Religions: Muslim, Christian, traditional beliefs

Government: republic

Currency: Guinea franc

Exports: bauxite, alumina, gold, diamonds, coffee, fish

Official Language: French

Guinea
(GIN ee)

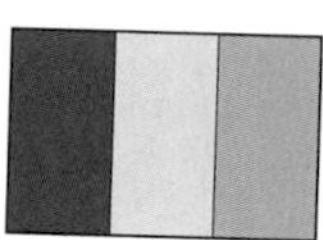

Capital: Monrovia

Area: 37,189 sq mi/96,320 sq km

Population: 2.9 million

Ethnic Groups: indigenous tribes, Americo Liberians

Religions: Christian, traditional beliefs, Muslim

Government: republic

Currency: Liberian dollar

Exports: diamonds, iron ore, rubber, timber, coffee, cocoa

Official Language: English

Liberia
(ly BEER ee uh)

Capital: Bissau

Area: 10,857 sq mi/28,120 sq km

Population: 1.2 million

Ethnic Groups: Balanta, Fula, Manjaca, Mandinga, European

Religions: traditional beliefs, Muslim, Christian

Government: republic

Currency: Guinea peso

Exports: cashew nuts, shrimp, peanuts, palm kernels, sawn lumber

Official Language: Portuguese

Guinea-Bissau
(GIN ee bi SOW)

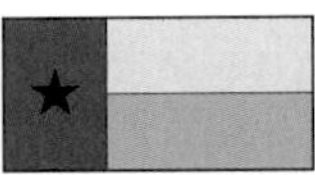

Capital: Bamako

Area: 471,115 sq mi/1,220,190 sq km

Population: 11 million

Ethnic Groups: Mande, Peul, Voltaic, Songhai, Tuareg, Moor

Religions: Sunni Muslim, traditional beliefs, Christian

Government: republic

Currency: CFA franc

Exports: cotton, gold, livestock

Official Language: French

Mali
(MAH lee)

Capital: Nouakchott
Area: 395,953 sq mi/1,025,520 sq km
Population: 2.6 million
Ethnic Groups: Maur, black
Religion: Muslim
Government: republic
Currency: Ouguiya
Exports: fish and fish products, iron ore, gold
Official Languages: Arabic and French

Mauritania
(mawr i TAY nee uh)

Capital: Dakar
Area: 74,336 sq mi/192,530 sq km
Population: 9.2 million
Ethnic Groups: Wolof, Fulani, Serer, Diola, Mandinka
Religions: Muslim, traditional beliefs, Roman Catholic
Government: republic
Currency: CFA franc
Exports: fish, groundnuts (peanuts), petroleum products, phosphates
Official Language: French

Senegal
(sen uh GAWL)

Capital: Niamey
Area: 489,073 sq mi/1,266,700 sq km
Population: 10.4 million
Ethnic Groups: Hausa, Djerma, Songhai
Religions: Muslim, traditional beliefs, Christian
Government: republic
Currency: CFA franc
Exports: uranium ore, livestock products, cowpeas, onions
Official Language: French

Niger
(NYE jur)

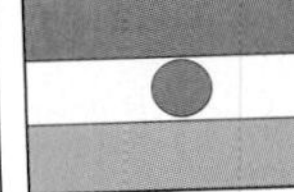

Capital: Freetown
Area: 27,652 sq mi/71,620 sq km
Population: 4.7 million
Ethnic Groups: Temne, Mende, Creole
Religions: Muslim, traditional beliefs, Christian
Government: constitutional democracy
Currency: Leone
Exports: diamonds, rutile, cocoa, coffee, fish
Official Language: English

Sierra Leone
(see ER uh lee OH nee)

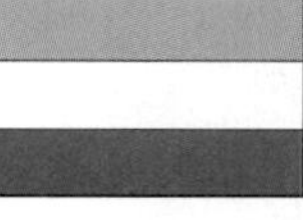

Capital: Abuja
Area: 351,648 sq mi/910,770 sq km
Population: 108 million
Ethnic Groups: Hausa, Fulani, Yoruba, Igbo
Religions: Muslim, Christian, traditional beliefs
Government: republic
Currency: Naira
Exports: petroleum and petroleum products, cocoa, rubber
Official Language: English

Nigeria
(ny JEER ee uh)

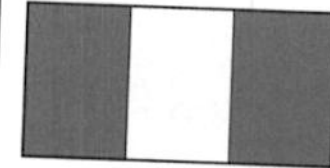

Capital: Lomé
Area: 21,000 sq mi/54,390 sq km
Population: 4.5 million
Ethnic Groups: native African, Ewe, Mina, Kabre
Religions: traditional beliefs, Christian, Muslim
Government: republic
Currency: CFA franc
Exports: cotton, phosphates, coffee, cocoa
Official Language: French

Togo
(TOH goh)

East Africa

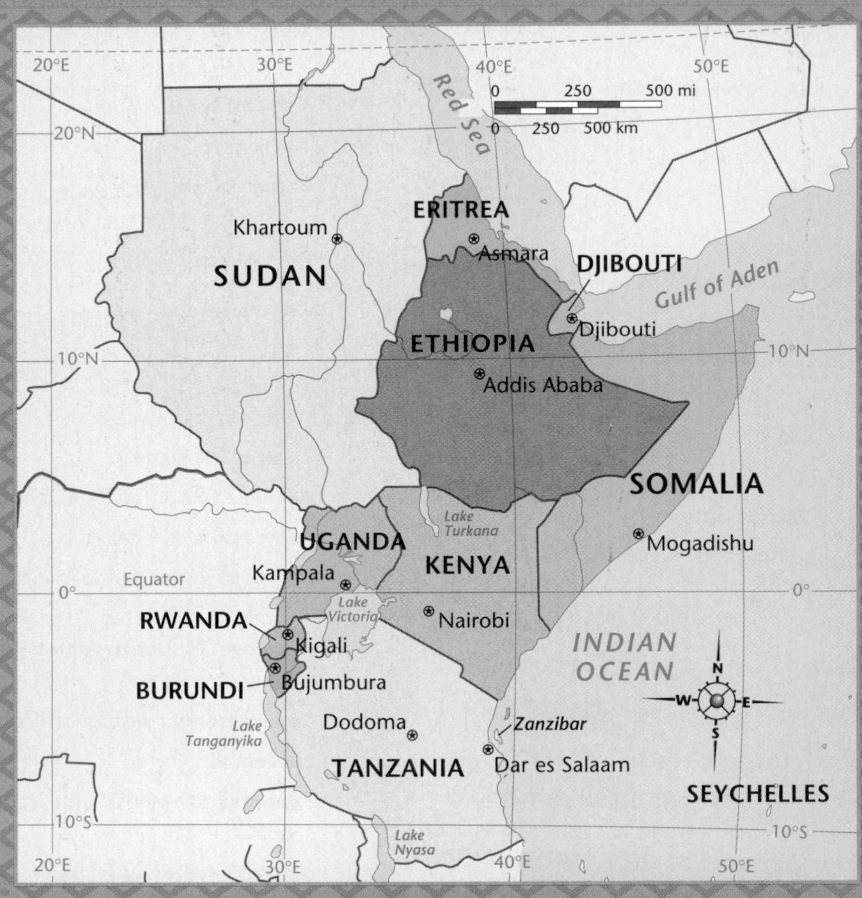

Capital: Bujumbura

Area: 9,903 sq mi/25,650 sq km

Population: 6.6 million

Ethnic Groups: Hutu, Tutsi, Twa

Religions: Roman Catholic, Protestant, traditional beliefs, Muslim

Government: republic

Currency: Burundi franc

Exports: coffee, tea, sugar, cotton, hides

Official Languages: French and Kirundi

Burundi
(boo RUN dee)

Background photo: Shores of Somalia

Djibouti
(ji BOO tee)

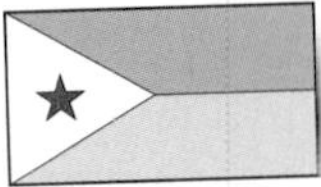

Capital: Djibouti

Area: 8,950 sq mi/23,180 sq km

Population: 629,000

Ethnic Groups: Issa, Afar

Religions: Muslim, Christian

Government: republic

Currency: Djibouti franc

Exports: reexports, hides and skins, coffee

Official Languages: Arabic and French

Ethiopia
(ee thee OH pee uh)

Capital: Addis Ababa

Area: 425,096 sq mi/1,101,000 sq km

Population: 61.1 million

Ethnic Groups: Oromo, Amhara Sidamo, Shankella, Somali, Afar

Religions: Muslim, Ethiopian Orthodox, traditional beliefs

Government: federal republic

Currency: Ethiopian birr

Exports: coffee, gold, leather products, oilseeds

Official Language: Amharic

Eritrea
(ayr uh TREE uh)

Capital: Asmara

Area: 36,170 sq mi/93,680 sq km

Population: 3.7 million

Ethnic Groups: ethnic Tigrinya, Tigre, Kunama, Afar, Saho

Religions: Muslim, Christian

Government: transitional government

Currency: Nakfa

Exports: livestock, sorghum, textiles, food, small manufactures

Official Language: Tigrinya

Kenya
(KEN yuh)

Capital: Nairobi

Area: 218,907 sq mi/566,970 sq km

Population: 29.5 million

Ethnic Groups: Kikuyu, Luhya, Luo, Kalenjin, Kamba, Kisii, Meru

Religions: Protestant, Roman Catholic, traditional beliefs, Muslim

Government: republic

Currency: Kenya shilling

Exports: tea, coffee, horticultural products, petroleum products

Official Languages: Swahili and English

Capital: Kigali

Area: 9,633 sq mi/ 24,950 sq km

Population: 7.2 million

Ethnic Groups: Hutu, Tutsi, Twa

Religions: Roman Catholic, Protestant, Muslim, traditional beliefs

Government: republic

Currency: Rwanda franc

Exports: coffee, tea, hides, tin ore

Official Languages: French and Rwandan

Rwanda

(roo AHN duh)

Capital: Victoria

Area: 104 sq mi/270 sq km

Population: 75,000

Ethnic Group: Seychellois

Religions: Roman Catholic, Anglican, Muslim

Government: republic

Currency: Seychelles rupee

Exports: fish, cinnamon bark, copra, petroleum products (reexports)

Official Language: Seselwa (French Creole)

Seychelles

(say SHELZ)

Capital: Mogadishu

Area: 242,216 sq mi/627,340 sq km

Population: 9.7 million

Ethnic Groups: Somali, Bantu, Arab

Religions: Sunni Muslim, Christian

Government: none

Currency: Somali shilling

Exports: livestock, bananas, hides, fish

Official Languages: Arabic and Somali

Somalia

(soh MAHL yuh)

Victoria, Seychelles

Capital: Khartoum

Area: 917,374 sq mi/2,376,000 sq km

Population: 28.9 million

Ethnic Groups: Arab, Dinka, Nuer, Beja

Religions: Sunni Muslim, traditional beliefs, Christian

Government: transitional

Currency: Sudanese pound or dinar

Exports: cotton, sesame, livestock, groundnuts, oil, gum arabic

Official Language: Arabic

Sudan
(soo DAN)

Capital: Dodoma

Area: 342,100 sq mi/886,040 sq km

Population: 32.8 million

Ethnic Group: Bantu

Religions: Muslim, Christian, traditional beliefs

Government: republic

Currency: Tanzanian shilling

Exports: coffee, manufactured goods, cotton, cashew nuts, minerals, tobacco, sisal

Official Languages: English and Swahili

Tanzania
(tan zuh NEE uh)

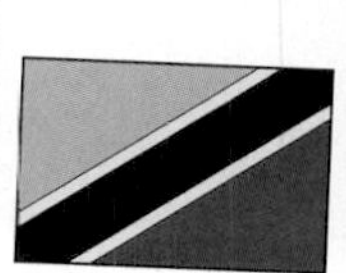

Tanzania

Capital: Kampala

Area: 77,046 sq mi/199,550 sq km

Population: 21.1 million

Ethnic Groups: Baganda, Karamojong

Religions: Roman Catholic, Protestant, traditional beliefs

Government: republic

Currency: New Uganda shilling

Exports: coffee, fish and fish products, tea, electrical products, iron

Official Languages: English and Swahili

Uganda
(yoo GAHN duh)

REGIONAL • DATABASE

Central and Southern Africa

Capital: Luanda

Area: 434,235 sq mi/1,124,670 sq km

Population: 12.5 million

Ethnic Groups: Ovimbundu, Mbundu, Bakongo

Religions: traditional beliefs, Roman Catholic, Protestant

Government: transitional government

Currency: Readjusted kwanza

Exports: crude oil, diamonds, refined petroleum products, gas

Official Language: Portuguese

Angola
(an GOH luh)

Capital: Gaborone

Area: 218,814 sq mi/566,730 sq km

Population: 1.6 million

Ethnic Groups: Tswana

Religions: traditional beliefs, Christian

Government: parliamentary republic

Currency: Pula

Exports: diamonds, vehicles, copper, nickel, meat

Official Language: English

Botswana
(bot SWAH nuh)

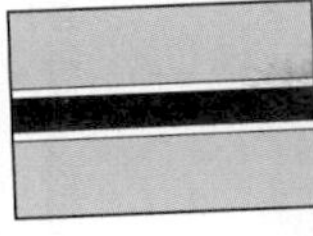

Background photo: Cape Town, South Africa

Cameroon
(KAM uh ROON)

Capital: Yaoundé

Area: 179,691 sq mi/465,400 sq km

Population: 14.7 million

Ethnic Groups: Cameroon Highlanders, Equatorial Bantu

Religions: Roman Catholic, traditional beliefs, Muslim, Protestant

Government: unitary republic

Currency: CFA Franc

Exports: crude oil and petroleum products, lumber, cocoa beans

Official Languages: English and French

Central African Republic
(sen TRAWL AF ri kuhn)

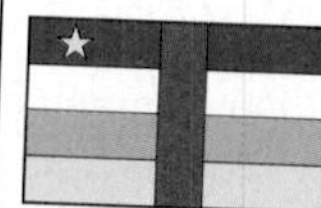

Capital: Bangui

Area: 240,530 sq mi/622,980 sq km

Population: 3.6 million

Ethnic Groups: Baya, Banda, Sara, Mandjia, Mboum, M'Baka, Europeans

Religions: traditional beliefs, Protestant, Roman Catholic, Muslim

Government: republic

Currency: CFA franc

Exports: diamonds, timber, cotton, coffee, tobacco

Official Language: French

Comoros
(KAHM uh ROHZ)

Capital: Moroni

Area: 861 sq mi/2,230 sq km

Population: 676,000

Ethnic Groups: Antalote, Cafre, Makoa, Oimatsaha, Sakalava

Religions: Sunni Muslim, Roman Catholic

Government: independent republic

Currency: Comoros franc

Exports: vanilla, ylang-ylang, cloves, perfume oil, copra

Official Languages: Arabic and French

Congo, Democratic Republic of
(KON goh)

Capital: Kinshasa

Area: 875,520 sq mi/2,267,600 sq km

Population: 50.3 million

Ethnic Groups: Bantu, Hamitic

Religions: traditional beliefs, Roman Catholic, Protestant

Government: dictatorship

Currency: Congolese franc

Exports: diamonds, copper, coffee, cobalt, crude oil

Official Languages: French and English

Congo, Republic of the
(KON goh)

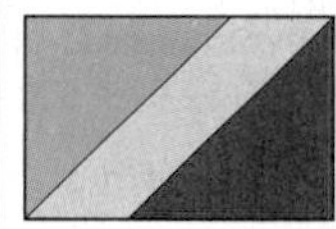

Capital: Brazzaville

Area: 131,853 sq mi/341,500 sq km

Population: 2.9 million

Ethnic Groups: Bakongo, Sangha, Teke, Mbochi

Religions: Christian, traditional beliefs, Muslim

Government: republic

Currency: CFA franc

Exports: petroleum, lumber, plywood, sugar, cocoa, coffee, diamonds

Official Language: French

Equatorial Guinea
(eh kwuh TOHR ee uhl GIN ee)

Capital: Malabo

Area: 10,830 sq mi/28,050 sq km

Population: 442,000

Ethnic Groups: Bioko, Rio Muni

Religions: Roman Catholic

Government: republic

Currency: CFA franc

Exports: petroleum, timber, cocoa

Official Language: Spanish

Gabon
(gah BOHN)

Capital: Libreville

Area: 99,486 sq mi/257,670 sq km

Population: 1.2 million

Ethnic Groups: Fang, Bantu, Eshira, European, African, French

Religions: Christian, Muslim

Government: republic

Currency: CFA franc

Exports: crude oil, timber, manganese, uranium

Official Language: French

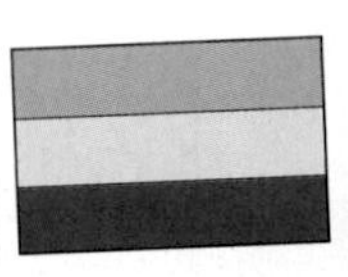

Malawi
(mah LAH wee)

Capital: Lilongwe

Area: 45,745 sq mi/118,480 sq km

Population: 10.6 million

Ethnic Groups: Chewa, Nyanja, Tumbuka, Yao, Lomwe

Religions: Protestant, Roman Catholic, Muslim, traditional beliefs

Government: multiparty democracy

Currency: Malawi kwacha

Exports: tobacco, tea, sugar, cotton, coffee, peanuts, wood products

Official Language: English

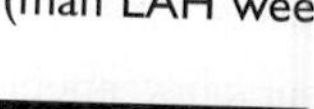

Lesotho
(le SOH thoh)

Capital: Maseru

Area: 11,718 sq mi/30,350 sq km

Population: 2.1 million

Ethnic Groups: Basotho, European

Religions: Christian, traditional beliefs

Government: parliamentary constitutional monarchy

Currency: Loti

Exports: clothing, footwear, road vehicles, wool, mohair, food

Official Languages: English and Sesotho

Mauritius
(maw RISH us)

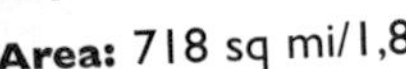

Capital: Port Louis

Area: 718 sq mi/1,860 sq km

Population: 1.2 million

Ethnic Groups: Indo-Mauritian, Creole, Sino-Mauritian

Religions: Hindu, Roman Catholic, Muslim, Protestant

Government: parliamentary democracy

Currency: Mauritian rupee

Exports: clothing, textiles, sugar

Official Language: English

Madagascar
(mad uh GAS kahr)

Capital: Antananarivo

Area: 224,533 sq mi/581,540 sq km

Population: 15.5 million

Ethnic Groups: Malayo-Indonesian, Cotiers, French, Indian, Creole

Religions: traditional beliefs, Christian, Muslim

Government: republic

Currency: Franc malagache

Exports: coffee, vanilla, cloves

Official Languages: French and Malagasy

Mozambique
(moh zahm BEEK)

Capital: Maputo

Area: 302,737 sq mi/784,090 sq km

Population: 19.3 million

Ethnic Groups: Makua Lomwe, Thonga, Malawi, Shona, Yao

Religions: traditional beliefs, Christian, Muslim

Government: republic

Currency: Metical

Exports: prawns, cashews, cotton, sugar, copra, citrus, coconuts, timber

Official Language: Portuguese

Namibia

(nuh MIB ee uh)

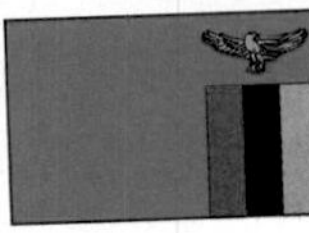

Capital: Windhoek

Area: 318,260 sq mi/824,290 sq km

Population: 1.7 million

Ethnic Groups: Ovambo, Kavango, Herero, Damara

Religions: Christian, traditional beliefs

Government: republic

Currency: Namibian dollar

Exports: diamonds, copper, gold, zinc, lead, uranium, cattle, processed fish, karakul skins

Official Language: English

Swaziland

(SWAH zee land)

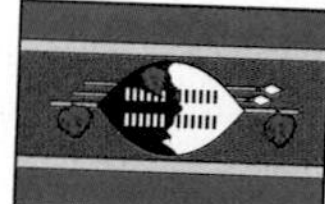

Capital: Mbabane

Area: 6,641 sq mi/17,200 sq km

Population: 980,000

Ethnic Groups: African, European

Religions: Christian, traditional beliefs

Government: monarchy

Currency: Lilangeni

Exports: soft drink concentrates, sugar, wood pulp, cotton yarn, refrigerates, citrus, canned fruit

Official Languages: English, Swazi

São Tomé and Príncipe

(SOU taw ME and PRIN si puh)

Capital: São Tomé

Area: 371 sq mi/960 sq km

Population: 135,000

Ethnic Groups: African, Portuguese, Creole

Religions: Roman Catholic, Evangelical Protestant, Seventh-Day Adventist

Government: republic

Currency: Dobra

Exports: cocoa, copra, coffee, palm oil

Official Language: Portuguese

Zambia

(ZAM bee uh)

Capital: Lusaka

Area: 285,992 sq mi/740,720 sq km

Population: 9 million

Ethnic Groups: African, European

Religions: Christian, traditional beliefs, Muslim, Hindu

Government: republic

Currency: Zambian kwacha

Exports: copper, cobalt, electricity, tobacco

Official Language: English

South Africa

(sowth AF ri kuh)

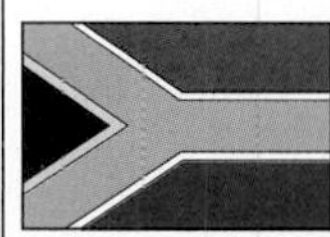

Capital: Pretoria

Area: 471,443 sq mi/1,221,040 sq km

Population: 39.9 million

Ethnic Groups: Zulu, white, mixed, Xhosa

Religions: Dutch Reformed, Roman Catholic, Methodist

Government: republic

Currency: Rand

Exports: gold, diamonds, other metals and minerals, machinery

Official Languages: Afrikaans and English

Zimbabwe

(zim BAH bway)

Capital: Harare

Area: 149,293 sq mi/ 390,580 sq km

Population: 11.5 million

Ethnic Groups: Shona, Ndebele, white, mixed, Asian

Religions: Syncretic, Christian, traditional beliefs, Muslim

Government: parliamentary democracy

Currency: Zimbabwe dollar

Exports: tobacco, gold, ferroalloys, cotton

Official Language: English

Asia

Asia: Political

KEY

— National boundary

⊛ National capital

Two-Point Equidistant Projection

Background photo: Hong Kong, China

Data compiled from the *Dorling Kindersley World Desk Reference*, the CIA Factbook, and the *Infoplease Internet Encyclopedia*.

GEOFACTS

Asia and the Pacific

Population: 3,679,873,000

Most Populated City: Tokyo, Japan (18.1 million)

Largest Country: Asian Russia (13,119,582 sq mi/ 5,065,471 sq km)

Smallest Country: Maldives (116 sq mi/ 300 sq km)

Highest Point: Mt. Everest (29,035 ft/8,850 m)

Lowest Point: Dead Sea (-1,286 ft/-392 m)

Longest River: Yangzi River (3,965 mi/6,380 km)

Hong Kong, China

Taj Mahal, India

East Asia

Capital: Beijing

Area: 3,600,927 sq mi/ 9,326,410 sq km

Population: 1.3 billion

Ethnic Groups: Han, Hui, Zhuang

Religions: traditional beliefs, Buddhist, Muslim

Government: Communist state

Currency: Yuan

Exports: machinery and equipment, textiles and clothing, footwear, toys

Official Language: Mandarin

China
(CHY nuh)

Capital: Tokyo

Area: 145,374 sq mi/376,520 sq km

Population: 126.5 million

Ethnic Groups: Japanese, Korean

Religions: Shinto and Buddhist, Buddhist, Christian

Government: constitutional monarchy

Currency: Yen

Exports: motor vehicles, semiconductors, office machinery, chemicals

Official Language: Japanese

Japan
(juh PAN)

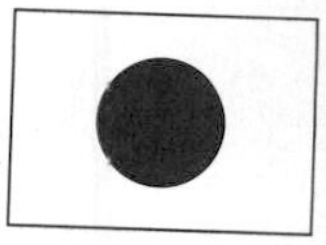

Background photo: Great Wall of China

Capital: Ulan Bator

Area: 604,247 sq mi/1,565,000 sq km

Population: 2.6 million

Ethnic Groups: Mongol, Kazak, Chinese, Russian

Religions: Tibetan Buddhist, Muslim

Government: republic

Currency: Tugrik

Exports: copper, livestock, animal products, cashmere, wool, hides, fluorspar, other nonferrous metals

Official Language: Khalka Mongol

Mongolia
(mong GOH lee uh)

Capital: Seoul

Area: 38,120 sq mi/98,730 sq km

Population: 46.5 million

Ethnic Group: Korean

Religions: Buddhist, Protestant, Roman Catholic, Confucian

Government: republic

Currency: South Korean won

Exports: electronic products, machinery and equipment, motor vehicles, steel, ships, textiles, clothing

Official Language: Korean

South Korea
(sowth kuh REE uh)

Capital: P'yongyang

Area: 46,490 sq mi/120,410 sq km

Population: 23.7 million

Ethnic Group: Korean

Religions: Buddhist, Confucian, Christian, syncretic Chondogyo

Government: authoritarian socialist

Currency: North Korean won

Exports: minerals, metallurgical products, manufactures, agricultural and fishery products

Official Language: Korean

North Korea
(nawrth kuh REE uh)

Capital: Taipei

Area: 12,456 sq mi/32,260 sq km

Population: 21.7 million

Ethnic Groups: indigenous Chinese, mainland Chinese, Aborigine

Religions: Buddhist, Confucian, Taoist, Christian

Government: multiparty democracy

Currency: Taiwan dollar

Exports: electronics, electric and machinery equipment, metals

Official Language: Mandarin

Taiwan
(TEYE wahn)

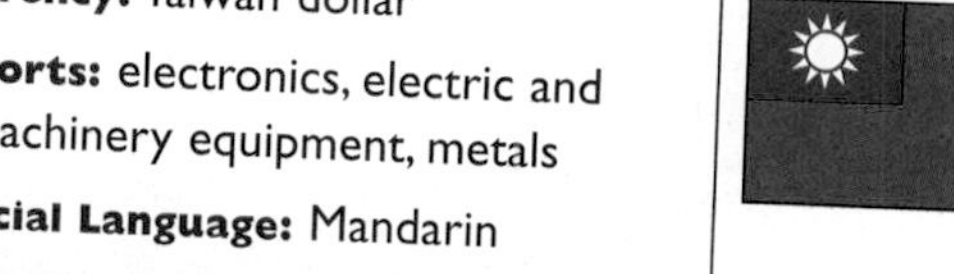

South Asia

Capital: Kabul

Area: 251,770 sq mi/652,090 sq km

Population: 21.9 million

Ethnic Groups: Pashto, Tajik, Hazara

Religions: Sunni Muslim, Shi'a Muslim

Government: administered by factions

Currency: Afghani

Exports: fruits, nuts, hand-woven carpets, wool, cotton, hides, pelts

Official Languages: Dari and Pashtu

Afghanistan
(af GAN i stan)

Capital: Dhaka

Area: 51,703 sq mi/133,910 sq km

Population: 126.9 million

Ethnic Groups: Bengali, Biharis

Religions: Muslim, Hindu

Government: republic

Currency: Taka

Exports: garments, jute and jute goods, leather, frozen fish and seafood

Official Language: Bengali

Bangladesh
(ban gluh DESH)

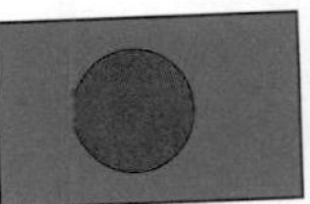

Background photo: Pushker, India

Bhutan
(boo TAHN)

Capital: Thimphu
Area: 18,147 sq mi/47,000 sq km
Population: 2.1 million
Ethnic Groups: Bhote, Nepalese, indigenous tribes
Religions: Mahayana Buddhist, Hindu
Government: monarchy
Currency: Ngultrum
Exports: cardamom, gypsum, timber, handicrafts, cement, fruit, electricity
Official Language: Dzongkha

Nepal
(nuh PAWL)

Capital: Kathmandu
Area: 52,818 sq mi/136,800 sq km
Population: 23.4 million
Ethnic Groups: Newar, Indian, Tibetan, Gurung, Magar, Tamang
Religions: Hindu, Buddhist, Muslim, Christian
Government: parliamentary democracy
Currency: Nepalese rupee
Exports: carpets, clothing, leather
Official Language: Nepali

India
(IN dee uh)

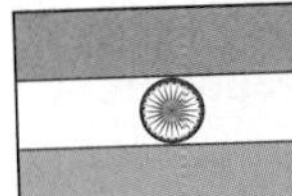

Capital: New Delhi
Area: 1,147,949 sq mi/2,973,190 sq km
Population: 998 million
Ethnic Groups: Indo-Aryan, Dravidian, Mongoloid
Religions: Hindu, Muslim, Christian, Sikh, Buddhist
Government: federal republic
Currency: Indian rupee
Exports: textile goods, gems
Official Languages: Hindi and English

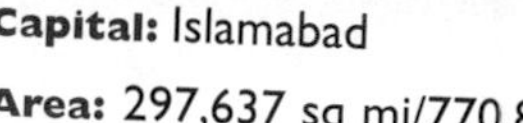

Pakistan
(PAK i stan)

Capital: Islamabad
Area: 297,637 sq mi/770,880 sq km
Population: 152.3 million
Ethnic Groups: Punjabi, Sindhi, Pashtu, Baluch, Muhajir
Religions: Sunni Muslim, Shi'a Muslim, Hindu, Christian
Government: federal republic
Currency: Pakistani rupee
Exports: cotton, fabrics and yarn, rice, other agricultural products
Official Language: Urdu

Maldives
(MAHL dives)

Capital: Male
Area: 116 sq mi/300 sq km
Population: 278,000
Ethnic Groups: South Indian, Sinhalese, Arab
Religions: Sunni Muslim
Government: republic
Currency: Rufiyaa
Exports: fish, clothing
Official Language: Dhivehi

Sri Lanka
(sree LAHN kuh)

Capital: Colombo
Area: 24,996 sq mi/64,740 sq km
Population: 18.6 million
Ethnic Groups: Sinhalese, Tamil, Moor
Religions: Buddhist, Hindu, Christian, Muslim
Government: republic
Currency: Sri Lanka rupee
Exports: textiles and apparel, tea, diamonds, coconut products
Official Languages: Sinhala, Tamil, English

Southeast Asia

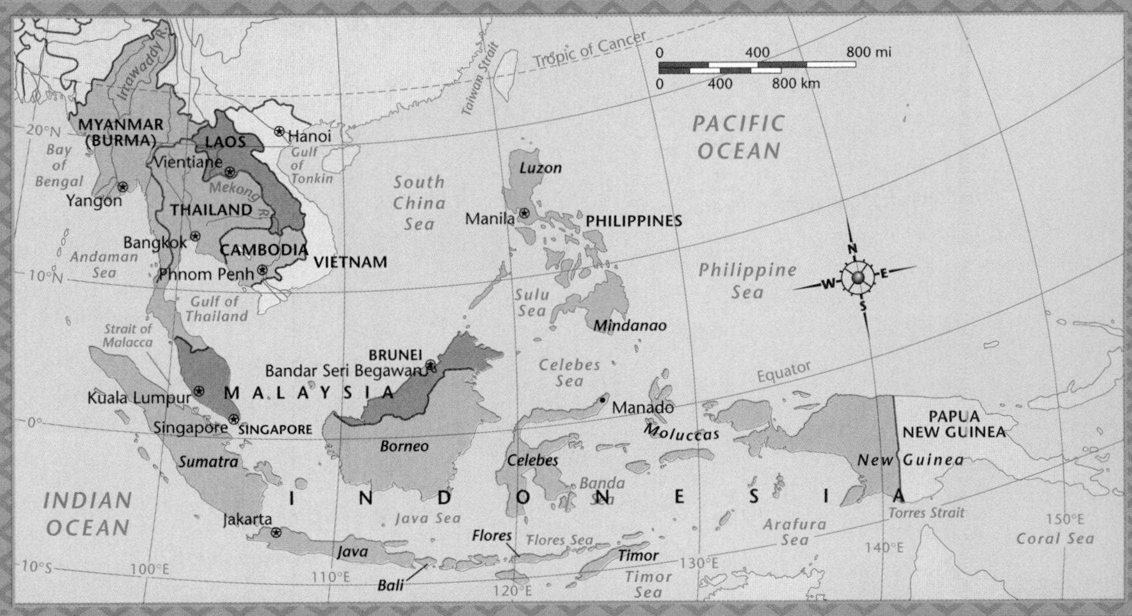

Brunei
(broo NEYE)

Capital: Bandar Seri Begawan
Area: 2,035 sq mi/5,270 sq km
Population: 322,000
Ethnic Groups: Malay, Chinese, indigenous
Religions: Muslim, Buddhist, Christian, traditional beliefs
Government: constitutional sultanate
Currency: Brunei dollar
Exports: crude oil, liquefied natural gas, petroleum products
Official Language: Malay

Indonesia
(in duh NEE zhuh)

Capital: Jakarta
Area: 699,447 sq mi/1,811,570 sq km
Population: 209.3 million
Ethnic Groups: Javanese, Sudanese, Madurese, Coastal Malays
Religions: Muslim, Protestant, Roman Catholic, Hindu, Buddhist
Government: republic
Currency: Rupiah
Exports: oil and gas, plywood
Official Language: Bahasa Indonesia

Cambodia
(kam BOH dee uh)

Capital: Phnom Penh
Area: 68,154 sq mi/176,520 sq km
Population: 10.9 million
Ethnic Groups: Khmer, Chinese, Vietnamese
Religions: Theravada Buddhist
Government: democracy under a constitutional monarchy
Currency: Riel
Exports: timber, garments, rubber, rice, fish
Official Language: Khmer

Laos
(LAY ohs)

Capital: Vientiane
Area: 89,112 sq mi/230,800 sq km
Population: 5.3 million
Ethnic Groups: Lao Loum, Lao Theung, Lao Soung
Religions: Buddhist, Animist
Government: Communist state
Currency: New kip
Exports: wood products, garments, electricity, coffee, tin
Official Language: Laotian

Capital: Kuala Lumpur
Area: 126,853 sq mi/328,550 sq km
Population: 21.8 million
Ethnic Groups: Malay, Chinese, indigenous tribes, Indian
Religions: Muslim, Buddhist, Chinese faiths, Christian, traditional beliefs
Government: constitutional monarchy
Currency: Ringgit
Exports: electronic equipment, petroleum, natural gas, chemicals
Official Languages: English, Bahasa Malay

Malaysia
(muh LAY zhuh)

Capital: Singapore
Area: 236 sq mi/610 sq km
Population: 3.5 million
Ethnic Groups: Chinese, Malay, Indian
Religions: Buddhist, Daoist, Muslim, Christian, Hindu
Government: parliamentary republic
Currency: Singapore dollar
Exports: machinery and equipment, chemicals, mineral fuels
Official Languages: Malay, English, Mandarin Chinese, Tamil

Singapore
(SIN guh pawr)

Capital: Yangon
Area: 253,876 sq mi/657,540 sq km
Population: 45.1 million
Ethnic Groups: Burman, Shan, Karen, Rakhine
Religions: Buddhist, Christian, Muslim, Hindu
Government: military regime
Currency: Kyat
Exports: pulses and beans, prawns, fish, rice, teak
Official Language: Burmese

Myanmar
(myahn mahr)

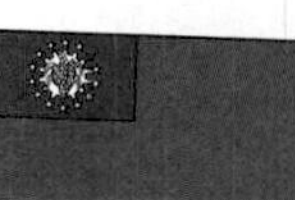

Capital: Bangkok
Area: 197,255 sq mi/510,890 sq km
Population: 60.9 million
Ethnic Groups: Thai, Chinese, Khmer, Malay
Religions: Theravada Buddhist, Muslim, Christian
Government: constitutional monarchy
Currency: Baht
Exports: computers and parts, textiles, rice
Official Language: Thai

Thailand
(TY lund)

Capital: Manila
Area: 115,830 sq mi/300,000 sq km
Population: 74.5 million
Ethnic Groups: Malay, Indonesian and Polynesian, Chinese, Indian
Religions: Roman Catholic, Protestant, Muslim, Buddhist
Government: republic
Currency: Philippine peso
Exports: electronic equipment, machinery, transport equipment
Official Languages: English and Filipino

Philippines
(FIL uh peenz)

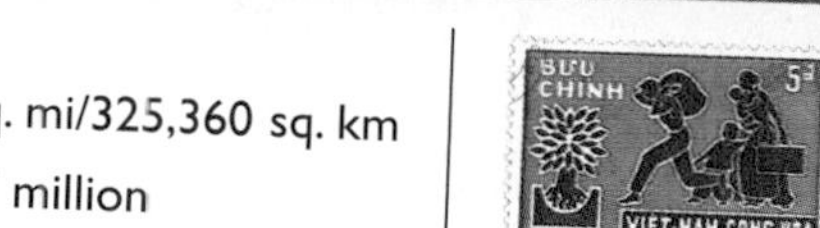

Capital: Hanoi
Area: 125,621 sq. mi/325,360 sq. km
Population: 78.7 million
Ethnic Groups: Vietnamese, Chinese, Thai
Religions: Buddhist, Roman Catholic
Government: Communist state
Currency: Dông
Exports: crude oil, marine products, rice, coffee, rubber, tea, garments
Official Language: Vietnamese

Vietnam
(vee et NAHM)

Background photo: Baracy, Philippines

Southwest and Central Asia

Background photo: Petra, Jordan

Armenia
(ahr MEE nee uh)

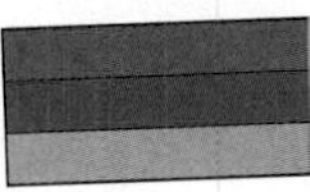

Capital: Yerevan

Area: 11,506 sq mi/29,800 sq km

Population: 3.5 million

Ethnic Groups: Armenian, Azeri, Russian

Religion: Armenian Orthodox

Government: republic

Currency: Dram

Exports: diamonds, scrap metal, machinery and equipment, cognac, copper ore

Official Language: Armenian

Cyprus
(SY prus)

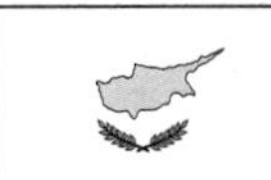

Capital: Nicosia

Area: 3,572 sq mi/9,251 sq km

Population: 778,000

Ethnic Groups: Greek, Turkish

Religions: Greek Orthodox, Muslim, Maronite, Armenian Apostolic

Government: republic

Currency: Cyprus pound

Exports: citrus, potatoes, grapes, wine, cement, clothing, shoes, textiles

Official Languages: Greek and Turkish

Azerbaijan
(a zur by JAHN)

Capital: Baku

Area: 33,436 sq mi/86,600 sq km

Population: 7.7 million

Ethnic Groups: Azeri, Armenian, Russian, Daghestani

Religions: Muslim, Russian Orthodox, Armenian Orthodox

Government: republic

Currency: Manat

Exports: oil, gas, machinery, cotton, foodstuffs

Official Language: Azerbaijani

Georgia
(JAWR ja)

Capital: Tbilisi

Area: 26,911 sq mi/69,700 sq km

Population: 5 million

Ethnic Groups: Georgian, Armenian, Russian, Azeri

Religions: Georgian Orthodox, Muslim, Russian Orthodox

Government: republic

Currency: Lari

Exports: citrus fruits, tea, wine, other agricultural products

Official Language: Georgian

Bahrain
(bah RAYN)

Capital: Manama

Area: 263 sq mi/680 sq km

Population: 606,000

Ethnic Groups: Bahraini, Iranian, Indian, Pakistani, European

Religions: Shi'a Muslim, Sunni Muslim

Government: traditional monarchy

Currency: Bahrain dinar

Exports: petroleum and petroleum products, aluminum

Official Language: Arabic

Iran
(ih RAN)

Capital: Tehran

Area: 3,572 sq mi/9,251 sq km

Population: 66.8 million

Ethnic Groups: Persian, Azeri, Lur and Bakhtiari, Kurd, Arab

Religions: Shi'a Muslim, Sunni Muslim

Government: theocratic republic

Currency: Iranian rial

Exports: petroleum, carpets, fruits, nuts, hides, iron, steel

Official Language: Farsi

Israel
(IZ ree ul)

Capital: Jerusalem

Area: 7,849 sq mi/20,330 sq km

Population: 6.1 million

Ethnic Groups: Jewish, Arab

Religions: Jewish, Sunni Muslim, Druze, Christian

Government: parliamentary democracy

Currency: New Israeli shekel

Exports: machinery, equipment, software, cut diamonds, chemicals

Official Languages: Hebrew and Arabic

Iraq
(ih RAK)

Capital: Baghdad

Area: 168,869 sq mi/437,370 sq km

Population: 22.5 million

Ethnic Groups: Arab, Kurdish, Persian, Turkoman

Religions: Shi'a Ithna Muslim, Sunni Muslim, Christian

Government: republic

Currency: Iraqi dinar

Exports: crude oil

Official Language: Arabic

Jordan
(JAWR dun)

Capital: Amman

Area: 34,336 sq mi/88,930 sq km

Population: 6.5 million

Ethnic Groups: Arab, Armenian, Circassian

Religions: Sunni Muslim, Christian

Government: constitutional monarchy

Currency: Jordanian dinar

Exports: phosphates, fertilizers, potash, agricultural products, manufactures

Official Language: Arabic

Capital: Astana

Area: 1,049,150 sq mi/2,717,300 sq km

Population: 16.3 million

Ethnic Groups: Kazak, Russian, Ukrainian, German, Uzbek, Tatar

Religions: Sunni Muslim, Russian Orthodox, Protestant

Government: republic

Currency: Tenge

Exports: oil, ferrous and nonferrous metals, machinery, chemicals, grain

Official Language: Kazak

Kazakstan
(kah zak STAN)

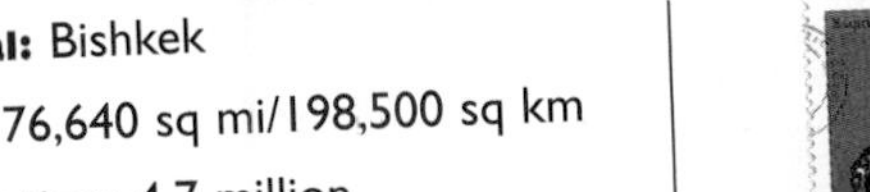

Capital: Bishkek

Area: 76,640 sq mi/198,500 sq km

Population: 4.7 million

Ethnic Groups: Kyrgyz, Russian, Uzbek, Ukrainian, Tatar

Religions: Muslim, Russian Orthodox

Government: republic

Currency: Som

Exports: cotton, wool, meat, tobacco, gold, mercury, uranium

Official Languages: Kyrgyz and Russian

Kyrgyzstan
(kir gi STAN)

Capital: Kuwait City

Area: 6,880 sq mi/17,820 sq km

Population: 1.9 million

Ethnic Groups: Kuwaiti, Arab, South Asian, Iranian

Religions: Muslim, Christian, Hindu, Parsi

Government: nominal constitutional monarchy

Currency: Kuwaiti dinar

Exports: oil and refined products

Official Language: Arabic

Kuwait
(koo WAYT)

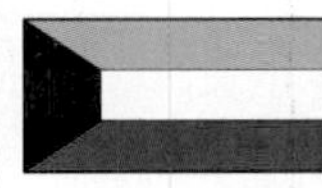

Capital: Beirut

Area: 3950 sq mi/10,230 sq km

Population: 3.2 million

Ethnic Groups: Arab, Armenian

Religions: Muslim, Christian

Government: republic

Currency: Lebanese pound

Exports: foodstuffs and tobacco, textiles, chemicals, metal and metal products, electrical equipment and products, jewelry

Official Language: Arabic

Lebanon
(LEB uh nun)

Capital: Muscat

Area: 82,030 sq mi/212,460 sq km

Population: 2.5 million

Ethnic Groups: Arab, Baluchi, South Asian, African

Religions: Ibadhi Muslim, Sunni Muslim, Shi'a Muslim, Hindu

Government: monarchy

Currency: Omani rial

Exports: petroleum, fish, metals, textiles

Official Language: Arabic

Oman
(oh MAHN)

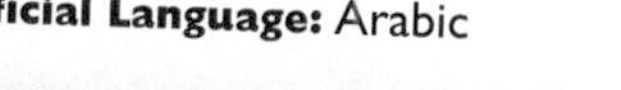

Qatar
(KAH tar)

Capital: Doha

Area: 4,247 sq mi/11,000 sq km

Population: 589,000

Ethnic Groups: Arab, Pakistani, Indian, Iranian

Religion: Muslim

Government: traditional monarchy

Currency: Qatar riyal

Exports: petroleum products, fertilizers, steel

Official Language: Arabic

Syria
(SEER ee uh)

Capital: Damascus

Area: 71,060 sq mi/184,060 sq km

Population: 15.7 million

Ethnic Groups: Arab, Kurdish, Armenian, Turkmen, Circassian

Religions: Sunni Muslim, other Muslim, Christian

Government: republic

Currency: Syrian pound

Exports: petroleum, textiles, manufactured goods, fruits and vegetables

Official Language: Arabic

Saudi Arabia
(SOW dee uh RAY bee uh)

Capital: Riyadh

Area: 829,995 sq mi/2,149,690 sq km

Population: 20.9 million

Ethnic Groups: Arab, Afroasian

Religions: Sunni Muslim, Shi'a Muslim

Government: monarchy

Currency: Saudi riyal

Exports: petroleum, petroleum products

Official Language: Arabic

Tajikistan
(tah ji ki STAN)

Capital: Dushanbe

Area: 55,251 sq mi/143,100 sq km

Population: 6.1 million

Ethnic Groups: Tajik, Uzbek, Russian

Religions: Sunni Muslim, Shi'a Muslim

Government: republic

Currency: Tajik ruble

Exports: aluminum, electricity, cotton, fruits, vegetable oil, textiles

Official Language: Tajik

Turkey
(TUR kee)

Capital: Ankara
Area: 297,154 sq mi/769,630 sq km
Population: 65.5 million
Ethnic Groups: Turkish, Kurdish, Arab
Religion: Muslim
Government: republican parliamentary democracy
Currency: Turkish lira
Exports: apparel, foodstuffs, textiles, metal manufactures
Official Language: Turkish

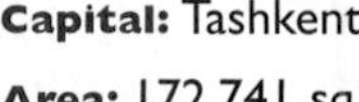

Uzbekistan
(ooz BEH ki stan)

Capital: Tashkent
Area: 172,741 sq mi/447,400 sq km
Population: 23.9 million
Ethnic Groups: Uzbek, Russian, Tajik, Kazak
Religions: Sunni Muslim, Eastern Orthodox
Government: republic
Currency: Som
Exports: cotton, gold, natural gas, mineral fertilizers, ferrous metals
Official Language: Uzbek

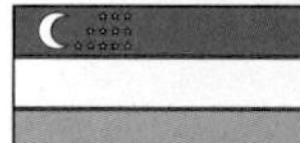

Turkmenistan
(turk MEH nuh stan)

Capital: Ashgabat
Area: 188,445 sq mi/488,100 sq km
Population: 4.4 million
Ethnic Groups: Turkmen, Uzbek, Russian
Religions: Sunni Muslim, Eastern Orthodox
Government: republic
Currency: Manat
Exports: oil, gas, cotton
Official Language: Turkmen

Yemen
(YEM un)

Capital: Sana'a
Area: 203,849 sq mi/527,970 sq km
Population: 17.5 million
Ethnic Groups: Arab, Afro-Arab, Indian, Somali, European
Religions: Shi'a Muslim, Sunni Muslim, Jewish, Christian, Hindu
Government: republic
Currency: Rial and dinar
Exports: crude oil, cotton, coffee, dried and salted fish
Official Language: Arabic

United Arab Emirates
(yoo NEYE tid AYR ub EH muh rayts)

Capital: Abu Dhabi
Area: 32,278 sq mi/83,600 sq km
Population: 2.4 million
Ethnic Groups: Asian, Arab, Emirian
Religion: Muslim
Government: federation
Currency: UAE dirham
Exports: crude oil, natural gas, dried fish, dates
Official Language: Arabic

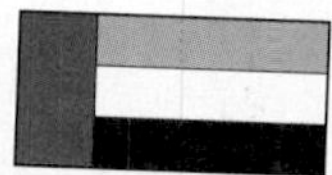

Australia, New Zealand, and the Pacific Islands

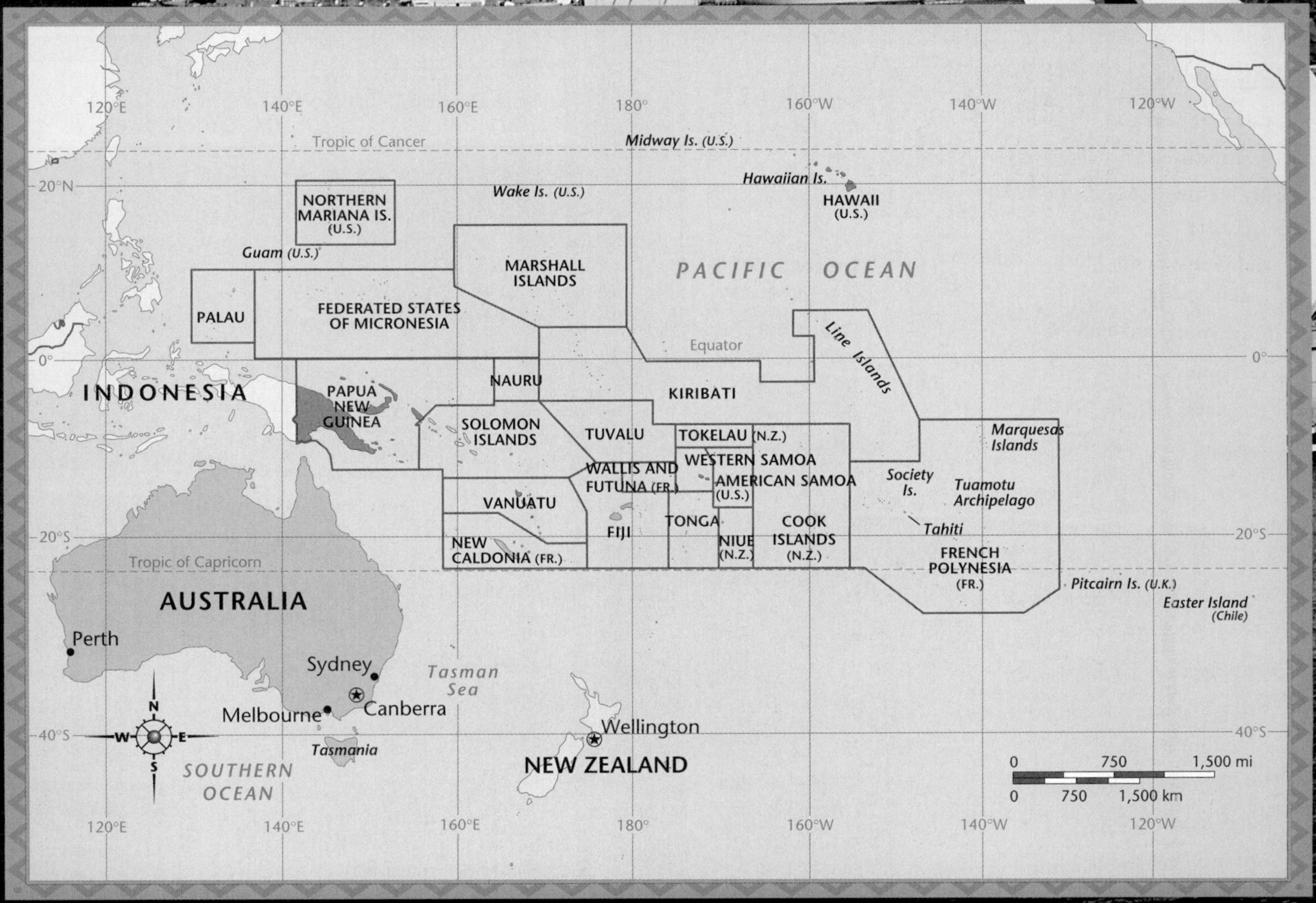

120°E
140°E
160°E
180°
160°W
140°W
120°W
Tropic of Cancer
Midway Is. (U.S.)
20°N
Hawaiian Is.
HAWAII (U.S.)
Wake Is. (U.S.)
NORTHERN MARIANA IS. (U.S.)
Guam (U.S.)
MARSHALL ISLANDS
PACIFIC OCEAN
PALAU
FEDERATED STATES OF MICRONESIA
Equator
Line Islands
0°
INDONESIA
PAPUA NEW GUINEA
NAURU
KIRIBATI
SOLOMON ISLANDS
TUVALU
TOKELAU (N.Z.)
Marquesas Islands
WESTERN SAMOA
WALLIS AND FUTUNA (FR.)
AMERICAN SAMOA (U.S.)
Society Is.
Tuamotu Archipelago
VANUATU
FIJI
TONGA
Tahiti
20°S
NEW CALDONIA (FR.)
NIUE (N.Z.)
COOK ISLANDS (N.Z.)
FRENCH POLYNESIA (FR.)
Tropic of Capricorn
Pitcairn Is. (U.K.)
AUSTRALIA
Easter Island (Chile)
Perth
Sydney
Tasman Sea
Canberra
Melbourne
N
W
E
S
Wellington
40°S
Tasmania
SOUTHERN OCEAN
NEW ZEALAND
0 750 1,500 mi
0 750 1,500 km

Background photo: Sydney, Australia

GEOFACTS

Australia, New Zealand, and the Pacific Islands

Population: 28,658,000

Most Populated City: Sydney, Australia (3.7 million)

Largest Country: Australia (2,941,283 sq mi/ 7,617,930 sq km)

Smallest Country: Nauru (8 sq mi/21 sq km)

Highest Point: Mt. Wilhelm (14,794 ft/4,509 m)

Lowest Point: Dead Sea (-52 ft/-16 m)

Longest River: Darling River (2,330 mi/ 3,750 km)

Australia

Australia and New Zealand

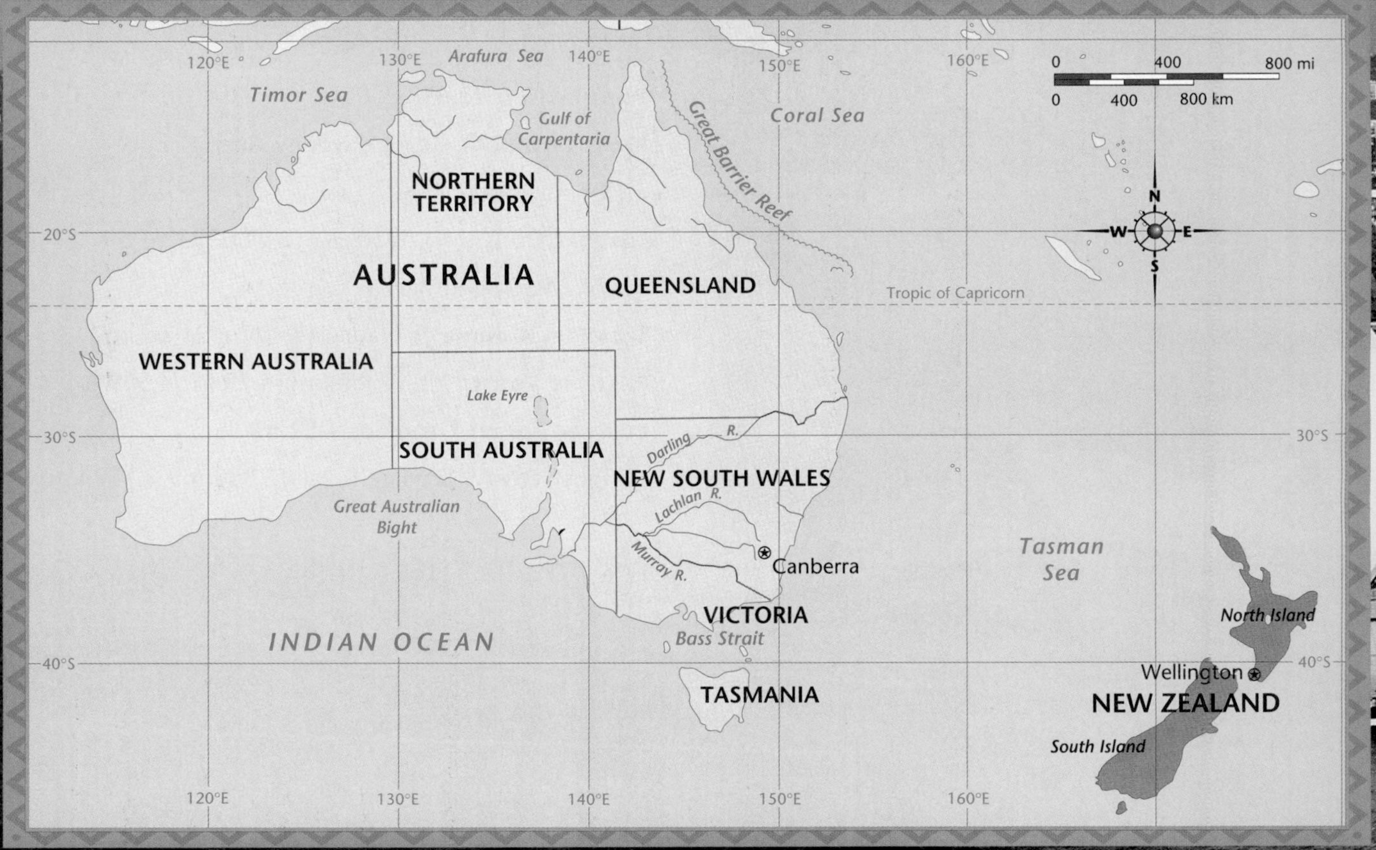

Arafura Sea
Timor Sea
Gulf of Carpentaria
Coral Sea
Great Barrier Reef
NORTHERN TERRITORY
AUSTRALIA
QUEENSLAND
Tropic of Capricorn
WESTERN AUSTRALIA
Lake Eyre
SOUTH AUSTRALIA
Darling R.
NEW SOUTH WALES
Lachlan R.
Murray R.
Great Australian Bight
Canberra
Tasman Sea
VICTORIA
Bass Strait
INDIAN OCEAN
TASMANIA
North Island
Wellington
NEW ZEALAND
South Island
0 400 800 mi
0 400 800 km
N S E W
120°E 130°E 140°E 150°E 160°E
20°S 30°S 40°S

Capital: Canberra

Area: 2,941,283/7,617,930 sq km

Population: 18.7 million

Ethnic Groups: European, Asian, Aboriginal

Religions: Roman Catholic, Anglican, United Church, Protestant

Government: parliamentary democracy

Currency: Australian dollar

Exports: coal, gold, meat, wool, aluminum, iron ore, wheat

Official Language: English

Australia

(aw STRAYL yuh)

Capital: Wellington

Area: 103,733 sq mi/268,670 sq km

Population: 3.8 million

Ethnic Groups: European, Maori, Chinese, Pacific Islander

Religions: Anglican, Presbyterian, Roman Catholic, Methodist

Government: parliamentary democracy

Currency: New Zealand dollar

Exports: dairy products, meat, fish, wool, forestry products

Official Languages: English and Maori

New Zealand

(noo ZEE lund)

Pacific Island Nations

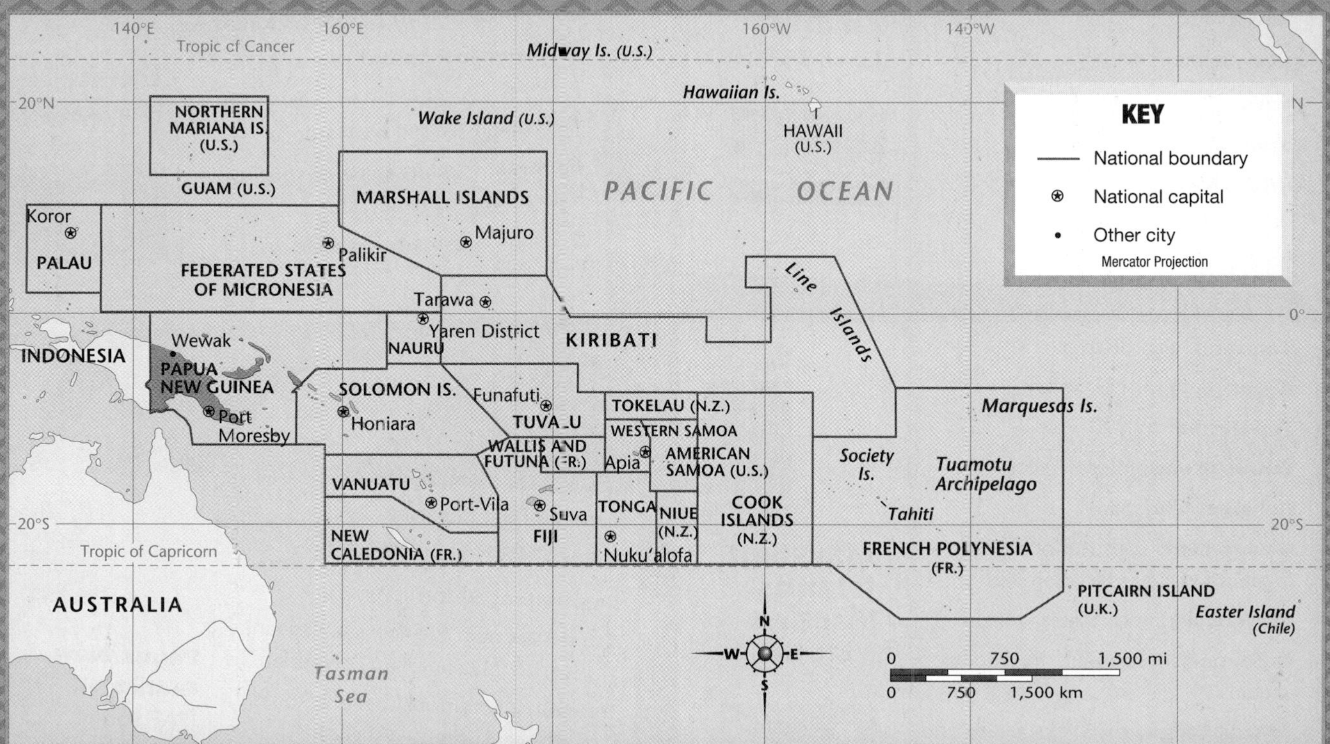

Capital: Palikir

Area: 271 sq mi/702 sq km

Population: 109,000

Ethnic Groups: Micronesian, Polynesian

Religions: Roman Catholic, Protestant

Government: constitutional government

Currency: United States dollar

Exports: fish, garments, bananas, black pepper

Official Language: English

Federated States of Micronesia
(my kroh NEE zha)

Capital: Suva

Area: 7,054 sq mi/18,270 sq km

Population: 806,000

Ethnic Groups: indigenous Fijian, Indian

Religions: Hindu, Methodist, Roman Catholic, Muslim

Government: republic

Currency: Fiji dollar

Exports: sugar, clothing, gold, processed fish, lumber

Official Language: English

Fiji
(FEE jee)

Capital: Bairiki
Area: 274 sq mi/710 sq km
Population: 78,000
Ethnic Groups: Micronesian
Religions: Roman Catholic, Kiribati Protestant
Government: republic
Currency: Australian dollar
Exports: copra, seaweed, fish
Official Language: English

Kiribati
(kir uh BAH tee)

Capital: Koror
Area: 196 sq mi/508 sq km
Population: 18,000
Ethnic Group: Palavans
Religions: Roman Catholic, Modekngei
Government: constitutional government
Currency: United States dollar
Exports: trochus (type of shellfish), tuna, copra, handicrafts
Official Languages: Belauan and English

Palau
(pah LAH oo)

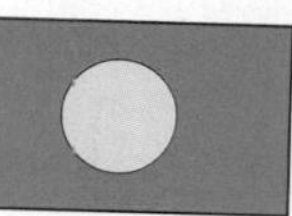

Capital: Delap district
Area: 70 sq mi/181 sq km
Population: 59,000
Ethnic Group: Micronesian
Religion: Christian
Government: constitutional government in free association with the U.S.
Currency: United States dollar
Exports: fish, coconut oil, trochus shells
Official Languages: Marshallese and English

Marshall Islands
(MAHR shul EYE lunds)

Capital: Port Moresby
Area: 174,849 sq mi/452,860
Population: 4.7 million
Ethnic Groups: Melanesian, Papuan, Negrito, Micronesian, Polynesian
Religions: traditional beliefs, Roman Catholic, Lutheran, Anglican
Government: parliamentary democracy
Currency: Kina
Exports: oil, gold, copper ore, logs, palm oil, coffee
Official Language: English

Papua New Guinea
(PAP yoo uh noo GI nee)

Capital: none
Area: 8.2 sq mi/21.2 sq km
Population: 11,000
Ethnic Groups: Nauruan, other Pacific Islanders, Chinese, Vietnamese, European
Religion: Christian
Government: republic
Currency: Australian dollar
Export: phosphates
Official Language: Nauruan

Nauru
(nah OO roo)

Samoa
(suh MOH uh)

Capital: Apia
Area: 1,093 sq mi/2,830 sq km
Population: 177,000
Ethnic Groups: Samoan, Euronesian
Religion: Christian
Government: constitutional monarchy
Currency: Tala
Exports: coconut oil and cream, copra, fish
Official Languages: English and Samoan

Tuvalu
(too vuh LOO)

Capital: Fongafale
Area: 10 sq mi/26 sq km
Population: 10,000
Ethnic Groups: Polynesian
Religions: Church of Tuvalu, Seventh Day Adventist, Baha'i
Government: constitutional monarchy
Currency: Australian dollar and Tuvaluan dollar
Exports: copra
Official Language: English

Solomon Islands
(SAHL uh mun EYE lunds)

Capital: Honiara
Area: 10,639 sq mi/27,556 sq km
Population: 430,000
Ethnic Groups: Melanesian, Polynesian, Micronesian, European
Religions: Anglican, Roman Catholic, South Seas Evangelical
Government: parliamentary democracy
Currency: Solomon Islands dollar
Exports: timber, fish, palm oil
Official Language: English

Vanuatu
(vahn wah TOO)

Capital: Port-Vila
Area: 4,707 sq mi/12,190 sq km
Population: 200,000
Ethnic Groups: Melanesian, French
Religions: Presbyterian, Anglican, Roman Catholic, traditional beliefs
Government: republic
Currency: Vatu
Exports: copra, beef, cocoa, timber
Official Languages: Bislama, English, French

Tonga
(TAHNG guh)

Capital: Nuku'alofa
Area: 278 sq mi/720 sq km
Population: 97,000
Ethnic Groups: Polynesian, other Pacific groups, European
Religions: Free Wesleyan, Roman Catholic
Government: constitutional monarchy
Currency: Pa'anga
Exports: squash, fish, vanilla beans
Official Languages: English and Tongan

Atlas

The World: Political

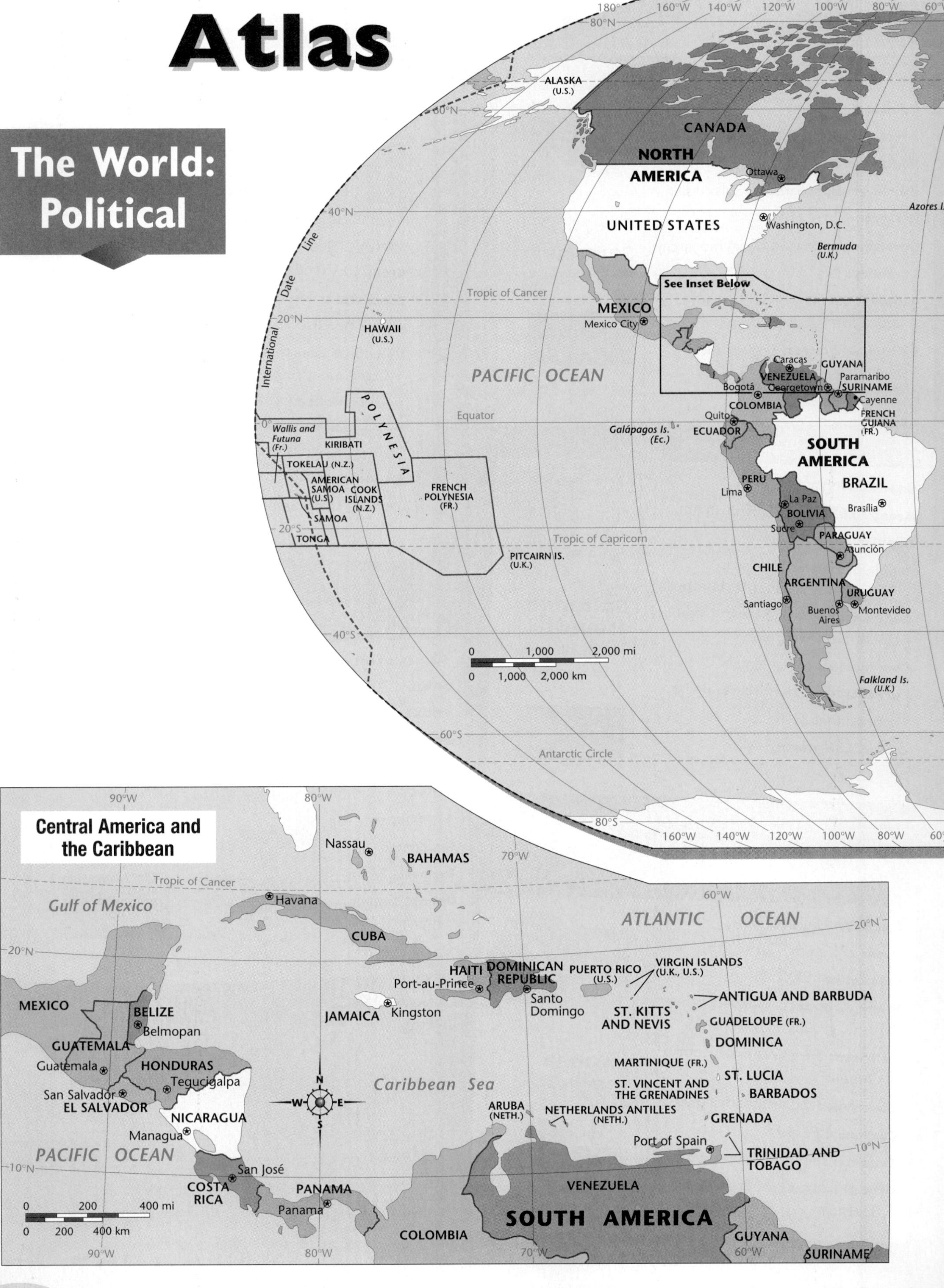

ALASKA (U.S.)
CANADA
NORTH AMERICA
Ottawa
UNITED STATES
Washington, D.C.
Azores Islands (Port.)
Bermuda (U.K.)
See Inset Below
Tropic of Cancer
MEXICO
Mexico City
HAWAII (U.S.)
CAPE VERDE
International Date Line
PACIFIC OCEAN
Caracas
GUYANA
VENEZUELA
Paramaribo
Bogotá
Georgetown
SURINAME
Cayenne
COLOMBIA
FRENCH GUIANA (FR.)
Quito
ECUADOR
Galápagos Is. (Ec.)
Equator
POLYNESIA
Wallis and Futuna (Fr.)
KIRIBATI
TOKELAU (N.Z.)
AMERICAN SAMOA (U.S.)
COOK ISLANDS (N.Z.)
SAMOA
TONGA
FRENCH POLYNESIA (FR.)
SOUTH AMERICA
BRAZIL
PERU
Lima
La Paz
BOLIVIA
Brasília
Sucre
PARAGUAY
Tropic of Capricorn
Asunción
PITCAIRN IS. (U.K.)
CHILE
ARGENTINA
URUGUAY
Santiago
Buenos Aires
Montevideo
0 1,000 2,000 mi
0 1,000 2,000 km
Falkland Is. (U.K.)
Antarctic Circle
180° 160°W 140°W 120°W 100°W 80°W 60°W
80°N 60°N 40°N 20°N 0° 20°S 40°S 60°S 80°S
Central America and the Caribbean
Nassau
BAHAMAS
Tropic of Cancer
Havana
Gulf of Mexico
CUBA
ATLANTIC OCEAN
HAITI
DOMINICAN REPUBLIC
PUERTO RICO (U.S.)
VIRGIN ISLANDS (U.K., U.S.)
Port-au-Prince
Santo Domingo
ANTIGUA AND BARBUDA
MEXICO
BELIZE
Belmopan
JAMAICA
Kingston
ST. KITTS AND NEVIS
GUADELOUPE (FR.)
DOMINICA
GUATEMALA
Guatemala
HONDURAS
Tegucigalpa
MARTINIQUE (FR.)
ST. LUCIA
ST. VINCENT AND THE GRENADINES
BARBADOS
San Salvador
EL SALVADOR
Caribbean Sea
NICARAGUA
Managua
ARUBA (NETH.)
NETHERLANDS ANTILLES (NETH.)
GRENADA
PACIFIC OCEAN
Port of Spain
TRINIDAD AND TOBAGO
San José
COSTA RICA
PANAMA
Panama
VENEZUELA
SOUTH AMERICA
COLOMBIA
GUYANA
SURINAME
0 200 400 mi
0 200 400 km
90°W 80°W 70°W 60°W
20°N 10°N

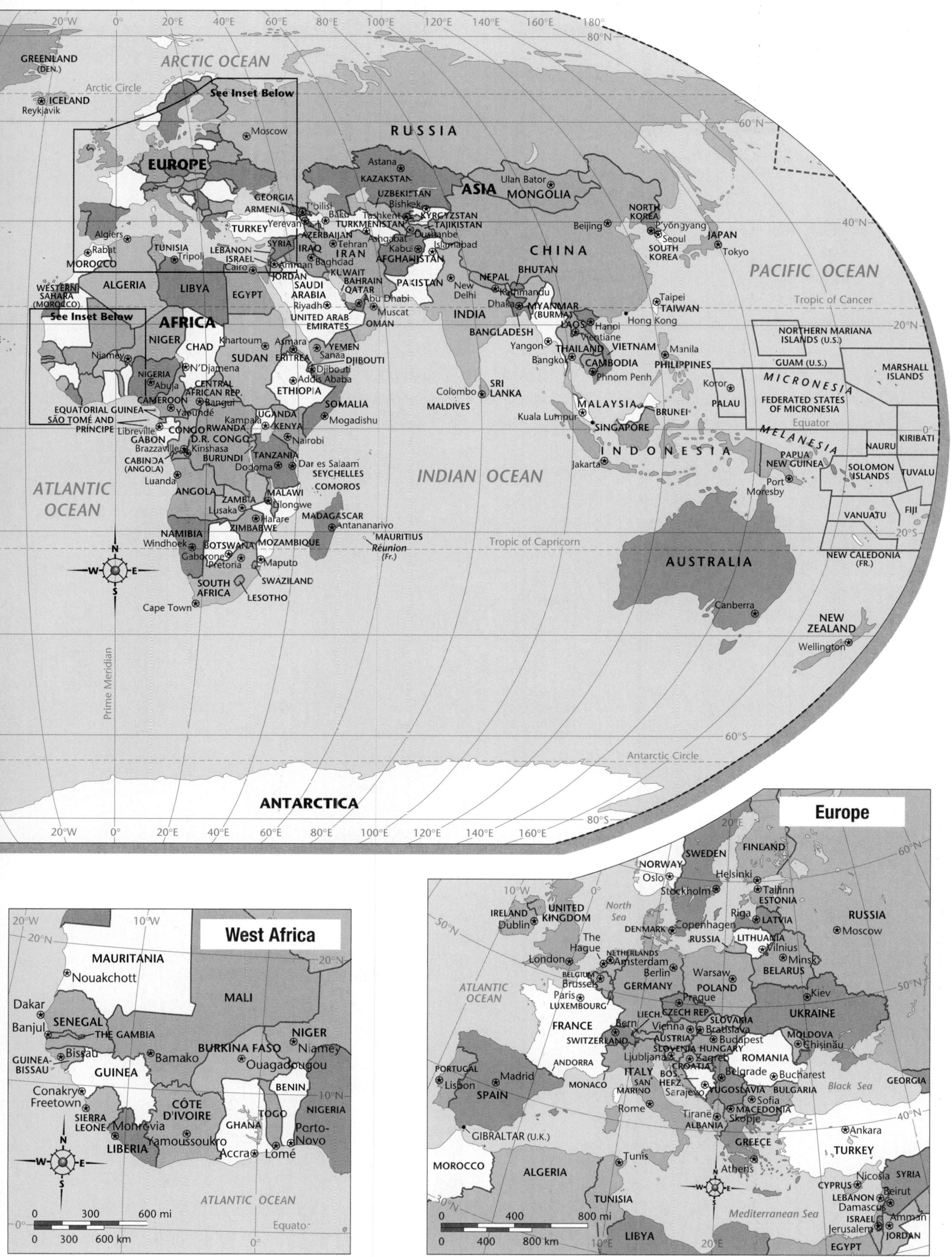

ARCTIC OCEAN
Arctic Circle
GREENLAND (DEN.)
ICELAND
Reykjavik
See Inset Below
Moscow
RUSSIA
EUROPE
Astana
KAZAKSTAN
Ulan Bator
ASIA
MONGOLIA
UZBEKISTAN
Bishkek
GEORGIA
ARMENIA
T'bilisi
Baku
Tashkent
KYRGYZSTAN
TAJIKISTAN
TURKMENISTAN
Dushanbe
NORTH KOREA
P'yŏngyang
Seoul
SOUTH KOREA
JAPAN
Tokyo
Beijing
TURKEY
Yerevan
AZERBAIJAN
Ashgabat
Tehran
IRAN
Kabul
Islamabad
AFGHANISTAN
Algiers
Rabat
MOROCCO
TUNISIA
Tripoli
LEBANON
ISRAEL
SYRIA
IRAQ
Amman
Baghdad
Cairo
JORDAN
KUWAIT
BAHRAIN
QATAR
CHINA
BHUTAN
NEPAL
Kathmandu
PACIFIC OCEAN
WESTERN SAHARA (MOROCCO)
ALGERIA
LIBYA
EGYPT
SAUDI ARABIA
Riyadh
PAKISTAN
New Delhi
Abu Dhabi
Muscat
UNITED ARAB EMIRATES
OMAN
Dhaka
MYANMAR (BURMA)
Taipei
TAIWAN
Tropic of Cancer
Hong Kong
AFRICA
INDIA
NIGER
CHAD
Khartoum
Asmara
YEMEN
Sanaa
BANGLADESH
LAOS
Hanoi
Vientiane
NORTHERN MARIANA ISLANDS (U.S.)
SUDAN
ERITREA
DJIBOUTI
Djibouti
Yangon
THAILAND
VIETNAM
Manila
GUAM (U.S.)
MARSHALL ISLANDS
Niamey
NIGERIA
Abuja
N'Djamena
Addis Ababa
ETHIOPIA
Bangkok
CAMBODIA
Phnom Penh
PHILIPPINES
MICRONESIA
CENTRAL AFRICAN REP.
Bangui
CAMEROON
Yaoundé
SRI LANKA
Colombo
MALDIVES
Koror
PALAU
FEDERATED STATES OF MICRONESIA
SOMALIA
Mogadishu
EQUATORIAL GUINEA
SÃO TOMÉ AND PRÍNCIPE
UGANDA
Kampala
KENYA
Nairobi
RWANDA
Kuala Lumpur
MALAYSIA
BRUNEI
SINGAPORE
Equator
MELANESIA
KIRIBATI
NAURU
Libreville
GABON
CONGO
Brazzaville
Kinshasa
D.R. CONGO
BURUNDI
TANZANIA
Dodoma
Dar es Salaam
SEYCHELLES
COMOROS
INDONESIA
Jakarta
PAPUA NEW GUINEA
Port Moresby
SOLOMON ISLANDS
TUVALU
CABINDA (ANGOLA)
Luanda
ATLANTIC OCEAN
INDIAN OCEAN
ANGOLA
ZAMBIA
Lusaka
MALAWI
Lilongwe
Harare
ZIMBABWE
MADAGASCAR
Antananarivo
VANUATU
FIJI
NAMIBIA
Windhoek
BOTSWANA
Gaborone
Pretoria
MOZAMBIQUE
Maputo
MAURITIUS
Réunion (Fr.)
Tropic of Capricorn
NEW CALEDONIA (FR.)
AUSTRALIA
SOUTH AFRICA
SWAZILAND
LESOTHO
Cape Town
Canberra
NEW ZEALAND
Wellington
Prime Meridian
Antarctic Circle
ANTARCTICA
N
S
E
W
20°W
0°
20°E
40°E
60°E
80°E
100°E
120°E
140°E
160°E
180°
80°N
60°N
40°N
20°N
0°
20°S
60°S
80°S
Europe
SWEDEN
FINLAND
NORWAY
Oslo
Helsinki
Stockholm
Tallinn
ESTONIA
IRELAND
Dublin
UNITED KINGDOM
North Sea
Riga
LATVIA
RUSSIA
Moscow
DENMARK
Copenhagen
LITHUANIA
Vilnius
The Hague
NETHERLANDS
Amsterdam
London
Berlin
Minsk
BELGIUM
Brussels
Warsaw
BELARUS
POLAND
ATLANTIC OCEAN
Paris
LUXEMBOURG
GERMANY
Prague
Kiev
LIECH.
CZECH REP.
SLOVAKIA
UKRAINE
FRANCE
Bern
Vienna
Bratislava
MOLDOVA
SWITZERLAND
AUSTRIA
Budapest
Chişinău
SLOVENIA
HUNGARY
ANDORRA
Ljubljana
Zagreb
ROMANIA
PORTUGAL
CROATIA
Lisbon
Madrid
ITALY
BOS.-HERZ.
Belgrade
Bucharest
SPAIN
MONACO
SAN MARINO
Sarajevo
YUGOSLAVIA
BULGARIA
Black Sea
GEORGIA
Sofia
MACEDONIA
Rome
Skopje
Tiranë
ALBANIA
Ankara
GIBRALTAR (U.K.)
GREECE
TURKEY
MOROCCO
ALGERIA
Tunis
Athens
SYRIA
Nicosia
CYPRUS
Beirut
LEBANON
Damascus
TUNISIA
Mediterranean Sea
ISRAEL
Amman
Jerusalem
JORDAN
LIBYA
EGYPT
0 400 800 mi
0 400 800 km
10°W
0°
10°E
20°E
30°N
40°N
50°N
60°N
West Africa
20°W
10°W
20°N
MAURITANIA
Nouakchott
MALI
Dakar
SENEGAL
Banjul
THE GAMBIA
NIGER
Niamey
GUINEA-BISSAU
Bissau
Bamako
BURKINA FASO
Ouagadougou
GUINEA
BENIN
Conakry
Freetown
10°N
SIERRA LEONE
CÔTE D'IVOIRE
TOGO
NIGERIA
Monrovia
GHANA
Porto-Novo
LIBERIA
Yamoussoukro
Accra
Lomé
ATLANTIC OCEAN
Equator
0 300 600 mi
0 300 600 km
0°

The World: Physical

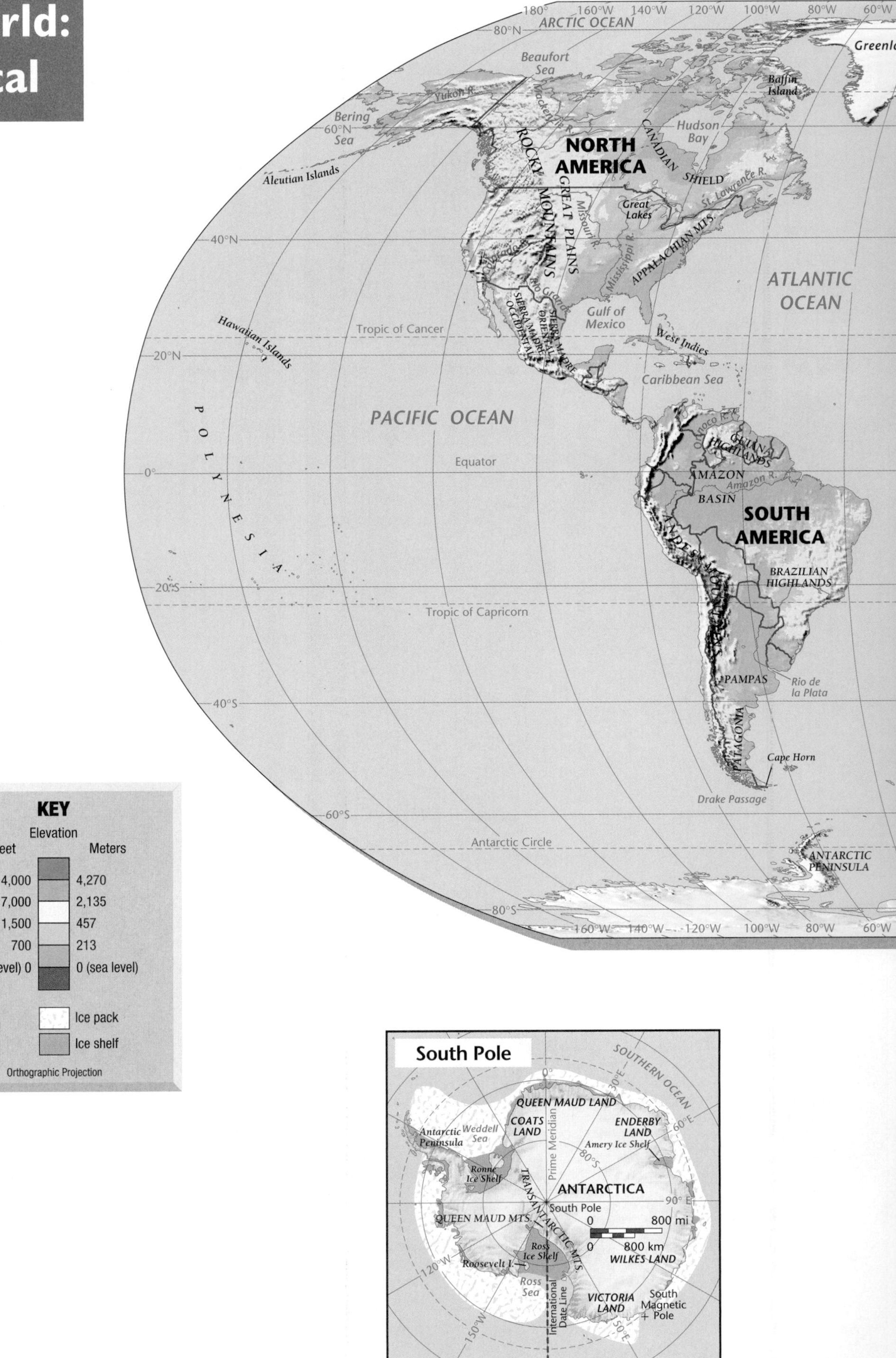

ARCTIC OCEAN
Beaufort Sea
Greenland
Baffin Island
Yukon R.
Bering Sea
Aleutian Islands
Hudson Bay
NORTH AMERICA
ROCKY MOUNTAINS
GREAT PLAINS
CANADIAN SHIELD
St. Lawrence R.
Great Lakes
Missouri R.
Mississippi R.
APPALACHIAN MTS.
Rio Grande
SIERRA MADRE OCCIDENTAL
SIERRA MADRE ORIENTAL
Gulf of Mexico
West Indies
Caribbean Sea
ATLANTIC OCEAN
Hawaiian Islands
Tropic of Cancer
PACIFIC OCEAN
POLYNESIA
Equator
Orinoco R.
GUIANA HIGHLANDS
AMAZON BASIN
Amazon R.
SOUTH AMERICA
ANDES MOUNTAINS
BRAZILIAN HIGHLANDS
Tropic of Capricorn
PAMPAS
Rio de la Plata
PATAGONIA
Cape Horn
Drake Passage
Antarctic Circle
ANTARCTIC PENINSULA
180°
160°W
140°W
120°W
100°W
80°W
60°W
80°N
60°N
40°N
20°N
0°
20°S
40°S
60°S
80°S
KEY
Elevation
Feet
Meters
14,000
4,270
7,000
2,135
1,500
457
700
213
(sea level) 0
0 (sea level)
Ice pack
Ice shelf
Orthographic Projection
South Pole
SOUTHERN OCEAN
QUEEN MAUD LAND
COATS LAND
ENDERBY LAND
Amery Ice Shelf
Antarctic Peninsula
Weddell Sea
Ronne Ice Shelf
Prime Meridian
ANTARCTICA
TRANSANTARCTIC MTS.
South Pole
QUEEN MAUD MTS.
0
800 mi
0
800 km
Ross Ice Shelf
Roosevelt I.
WILKES LAND
Ross Sea
International Date Line
VICTORIA LAND
South Magnetic Pole
0°
30°E
60°E
90°E
120°W
150°W
150°E
80°S

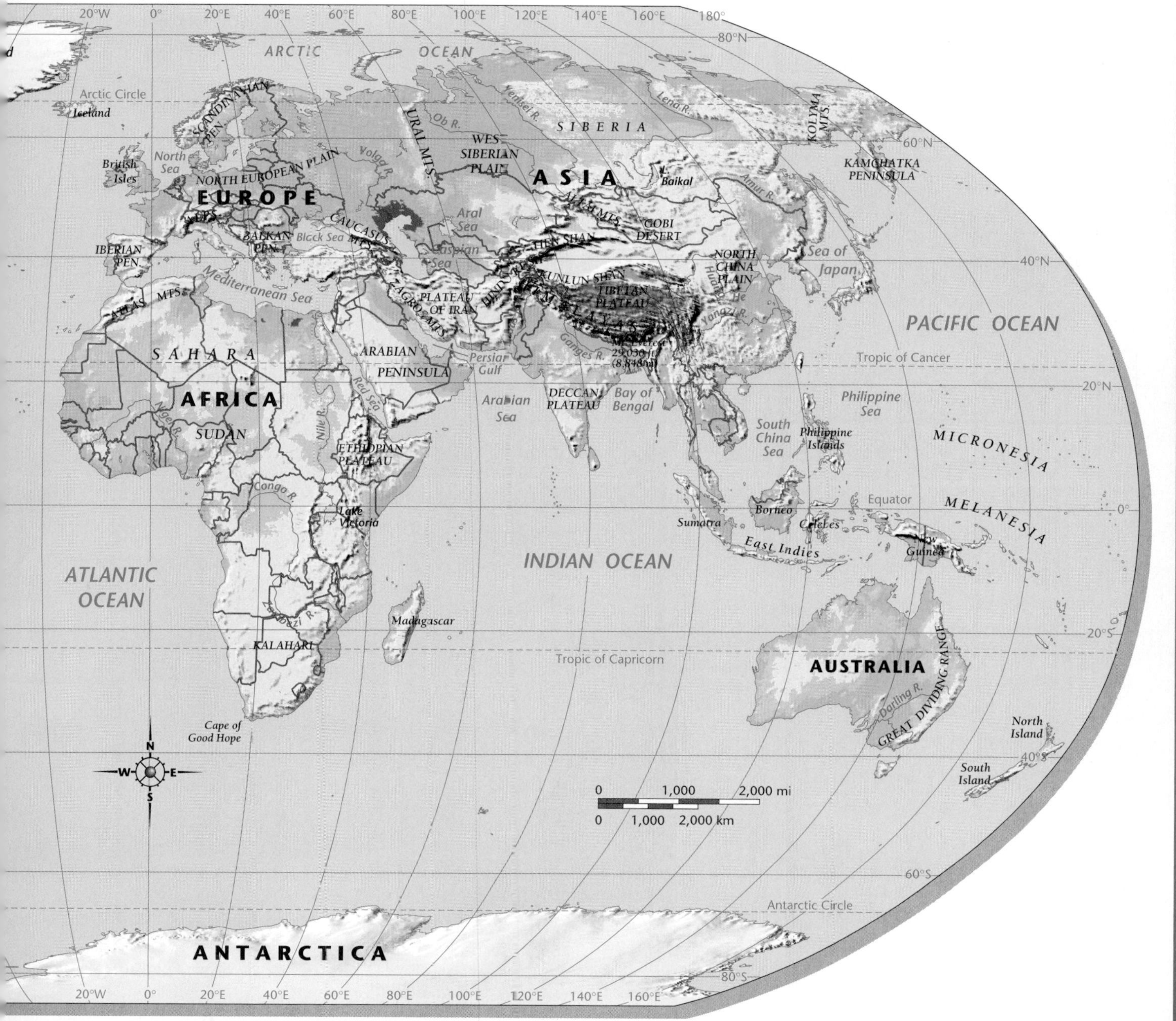

20°W 0° 20°E 40°E 60°E 80°E 100°E 120°E 140°E 160°E 180°

80°N

ARCTIC OCEAN

Arctic Circle

Iceland

SCANDINAVIAN PEN.

URAL MTS.

Ob R.

Yenisei R.

Lena R.

SIBERIA

KOLYMA MTS.

60°N

British Isles

North Sea

NORTH EUROPEAN PLAIN

Volga R.

WEST SIBERIAN PLAIN

ASIA

Baikal

KAMCHATKA PENINSULA

EUROPE

ALPS

Amur R.

Aral Sea

ALTAI MTS.

GOBI DESERT

BALKAN PEN.

Black Sea

CAUCASUS MTS.

TIEN SHAN

IBERIAN PEN.

Caspian Sea

NORTH CHINA PLAIN

Sea of Japan

40°N

Mediterranean Sea

KUNLUN SHAN

Huang He

ATLAS MTS.

PLATEAU OF IRAN

HINDU KUSH

TIBETAN PLATEAU

ZAGROS MTS.

HIMALAYAS

Yangzi R.

PACIFIC OCEAN

SAHARA

ARABIAN PENINSULA

Ganges R.

Mt. Everest 29,035 ft (8,848 m)

Persian Gulf

Tropic of Cancer

20°N

AFRICA

Red Sea

Arabian Sea

DECCAN PLATEAU

Bay of Bengal

Philippine Sea

Niger R.

Nile R.

SUDAN

South China Sea

Philippine Islands

MICRONESIA

ETHIOPIAN PLATEAU

Congo R.

Equator

Lake Victoria

Borneo

Sumatra

Celebes

MELANESIA

0°

East Indies

New Guinea

INDIAN OCEAN

ATLANTIC OCEAN

Zambezi R.

Madagascar

20°S

KALAHARI

Tropic of Capricorn

AUSTRALIA

Darling R.

GREAT DIVIDING RANGE

Cape of Good Hope

North Island

N

W E

S

40°S

0 1,000 2,000 mi

0 1,000 2,000 km

South Island

60°S

Antarctic Circle

ANTARCTICA

80°S

20°W 0° 20°E 40°E 60°E 80°E 100°E 120°E 140°E 160°E

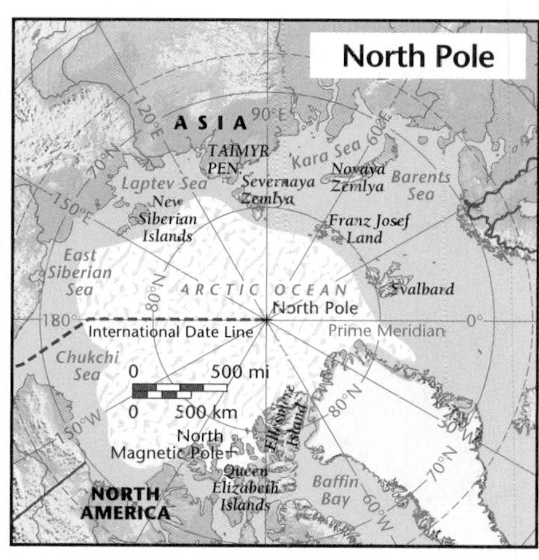

United States: Political

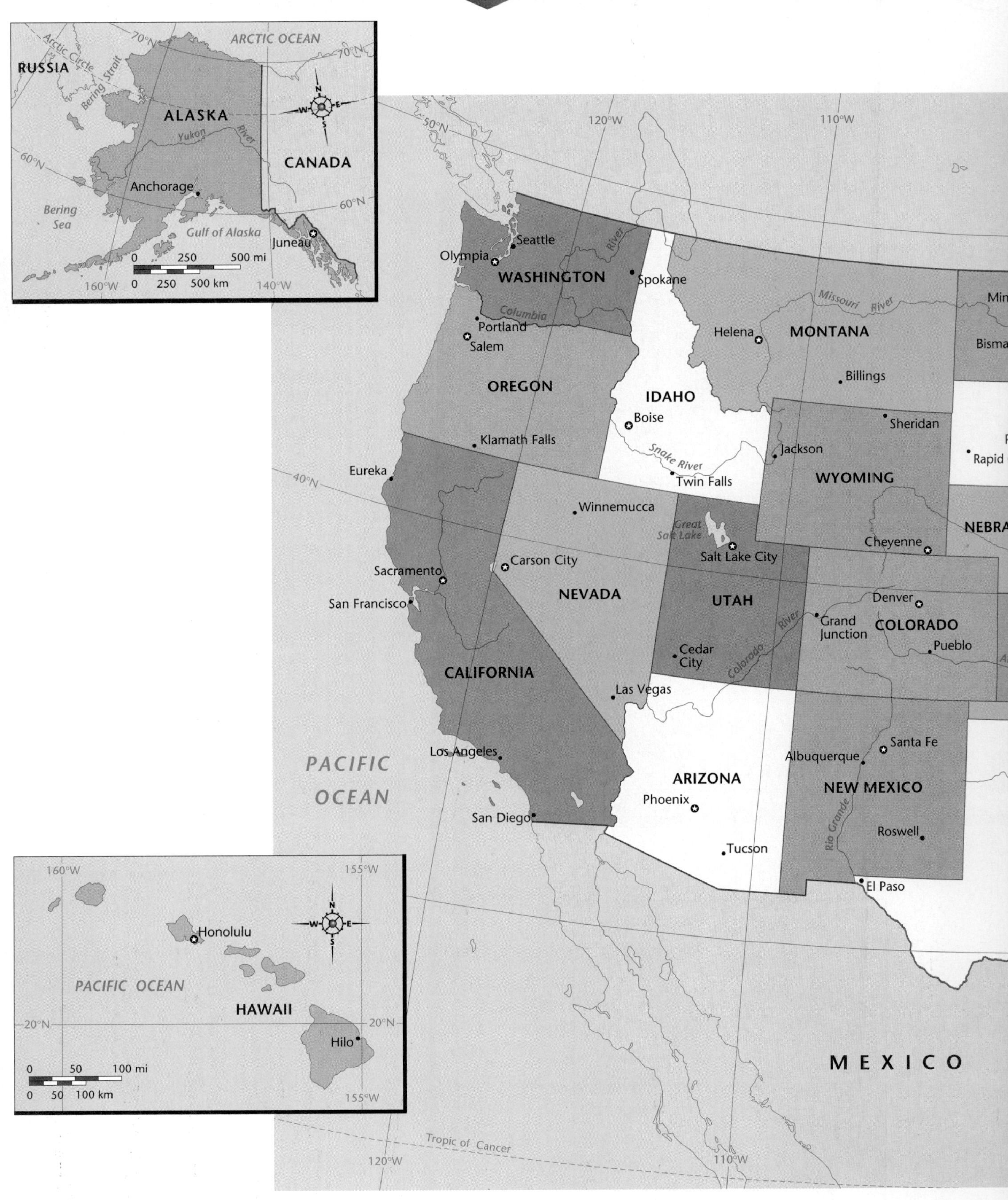

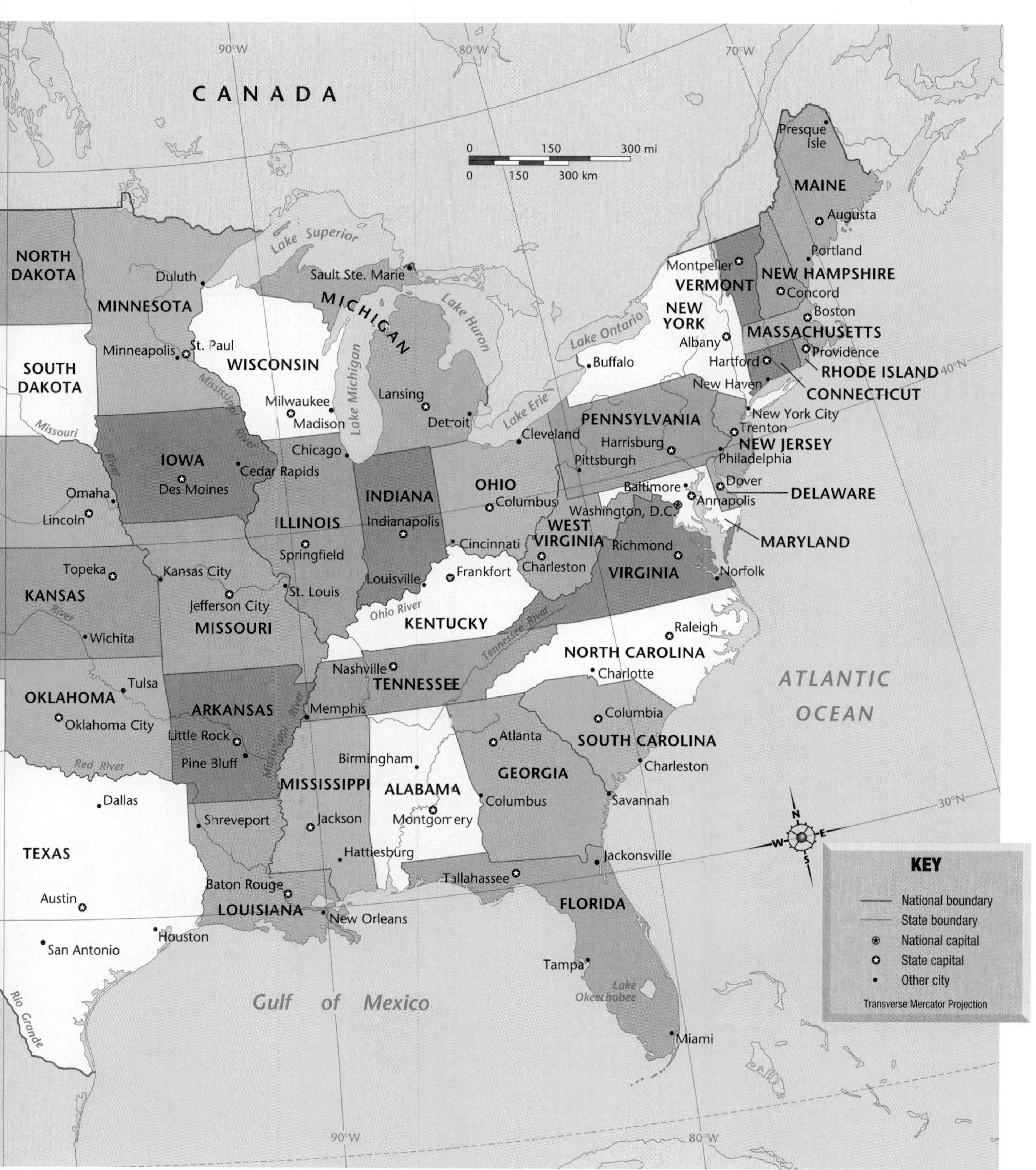
CANADA
90°W
80°W
70°W
0 150 300 mi
0 150 300 km
NORTH DAKOTA
SOUTH DAKOTA
MINNESOTA
WISCONSIN
MICHIGAN
IOWA
ILLINOIS
INDIANA
OHIO
PENNSYLVANIA
NEW YORK
VERMONT
NEW HAMPSHIRE
MAINE
MASSACHUSETTS
RHODE ISLAND
CONNECTICUT
NEW JERSEY
DELAWARE
MARYLAND
WEST VIRGINIA
VIRGINIA
KENTUCKY
TENNESSEE
NORTH CAROLINA
SOUTH CAROLINA
GEORGIA
ALABAMA
MISSISSIPPI
LOUISIANA
ARKANSAS
MISSOURI
KANSAS
OKLAHOMA
TEXAS
FLORIDA
Lake Superior
Lake Michigan
Lake Huron
Lake Ontario
Lake Erie
Mississippi River
Missouri River
Ohio River
Tennessee River
Kansas River
Red River
Rio Grande
Lake Okeechobee
ATLANTIC OCEAN
Gulf of Mexico
Presque Isle
Augusta
Portland
Concord
Boston
Providence
Hartford
New Haven
Montpelier
Albany
Buffalo
New York City
Trenton
Philadelphia
Harrisburg
Pittsburgh
Dover
Baltimore
Annapolis
Washington, D.C.
Richmond
Norfolk
Charleston
Raleigh
Charlotte
Columbia
Charleston
Savannah
Atlanta
Columbus
Jacksonville
Tallahassee
Tampa
Miami
Birmingham
Montgomery
Hattiesburg
Jackson
Nashville
Memphis
Frankfort
Louisville
Cincinnati
Columbus
Cleveland
Detroit
Lansing
Indianapolis
Chicago
Springfield
St. Louis
Milwaukee
Madison
Sault Ste. Marie
Duluth
Minneapolis
St. Paul
Cedar Rapids
Des Moines
Omaha
Lincoln
Topeka
Kansas City
Jefferson City
Wichita
Tulsa
Oklahoma City
Little Rock
Pine Bluff
Dallas
Shreveport
Baton Rouge
New Orleans
Austin
Houston
San Antonio
30°N
40°N
N
S
E
W
KEY
National boundary
State boundary
National capital
State capital
Other city
Transverse Mercator Projection

North and South America: Political

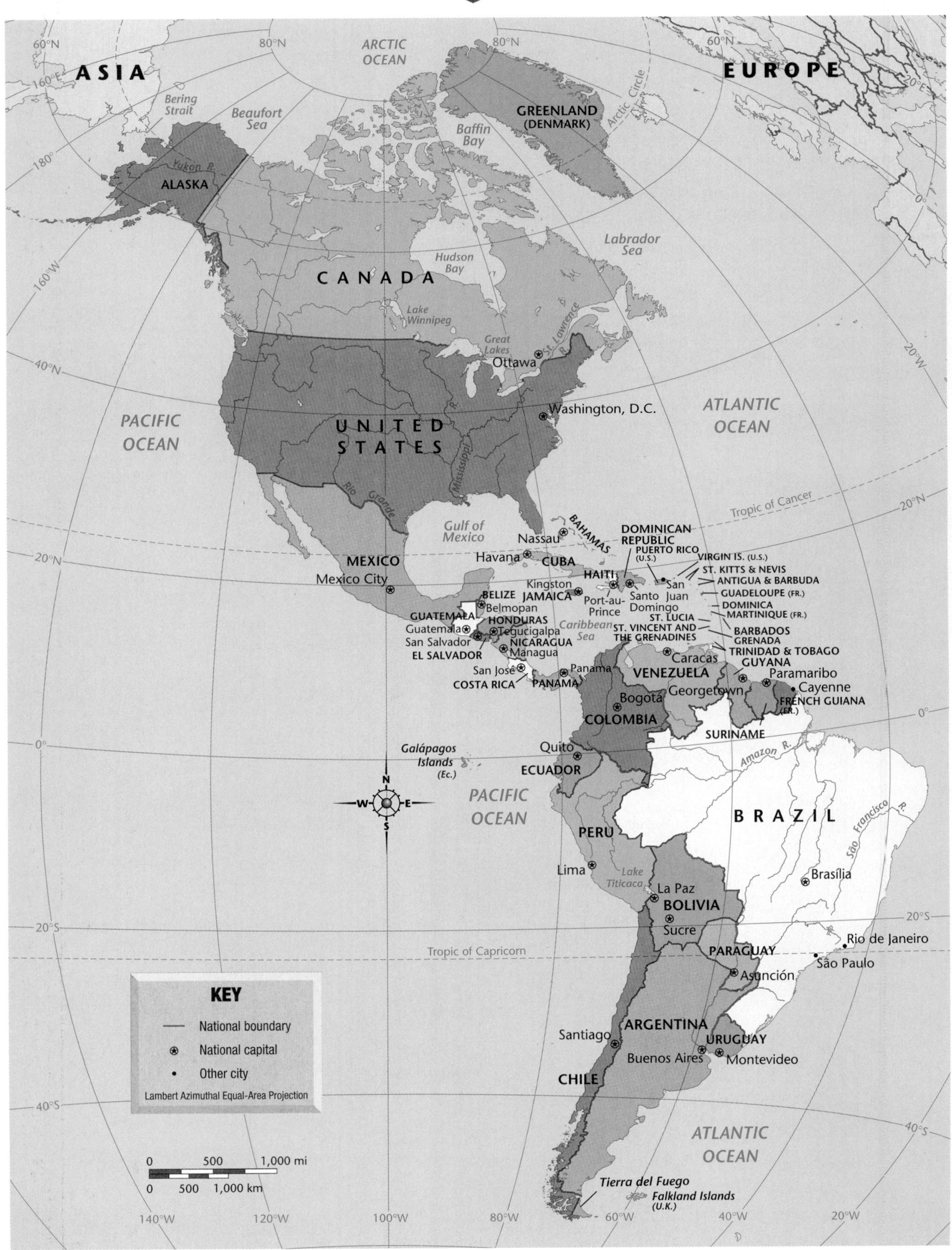

ARCTIC OCEAN
ASIA
EUROPE
Bering Strait
Beaufort Sea
Baffin Bay
GREENLAND (DENMARK)
Arctic Circle
ALASKA
Yukon R.
Labrador Sea
Hudson Bay
CANADA
Lake Winnipeg
Great Lakes
St. Lawrence R.
Ottawa
Washington, D.C.
PACIFIC OCEAN
ATLANTIC OCEAN
UNITED STATES
Mississippi R.
Rio Grande
Tropic of Cancer
Gulf of Mexico
BAHAMAS
Nassau
Havana
CUBA
MEXICO
Mexico City
DOMINICAN REPUBLIC
PUERTO RICO (U.S.)
VIRGIN IS. (U.S.)
ST. KITTS & NEVIS
ANTIGUA & BARBUDA
GUADELOUPE (FR.)
DOMINICA
MARTINIQUE (FR.)
ST. LUCIA
ST. VINCENT AND THE GRENADINES
BARBADOS
GRENADA
TRINIDAD & TOBAGO
HAITI
Kingston
JAMAICA
Port-au-Prince
Santo Domingo
San Juan
BELIZE
Belmopan
GUATEMALA
Guatemala
HONDURAS
Tegucigalpa
San Salvador
EL SALVADOR
NICARAGUA
Managua
Caribbean Sea
San José
COSTA RICA
Panama
PANAMA
Caracas
VENEZUELA
GUYANA
Georgetown
Paramaribo
Cayenne
FRENCH GUIANA (FR.)
SURINAME
Bogotá
COLOMBIA
Quito
ECUADOR
Galápagos Islands (Ec.)
Amazon R.
BRAZIL
São Francisco R.
PERU
Lima
Lake Titicaca
La Paz
BOLIVIA
Sucre
Brasília
Rio de Janeiro
São Paulo
Tropic of Capricorn
PARAGUAY
Asunción
ARGENTINA
Santiago
URUGUAY
Buenos Aires
Montevideo
CHILE
Tierra del Fuego
Falkland Islands (U.K.)
KEY
National boundary
National capital
Other city
Lambert Azimuthal Equal-Area Projection
0 500 1,000 mi
0 500 1,000 km
60°N
80°N
40°N
20°N
0°
20°S
40°S
160°E
180°
160°W
140°W
120°W
100°W
80°W
60°W
40°W
20°W
0°
20°E
N S E W

North and South America: Physical

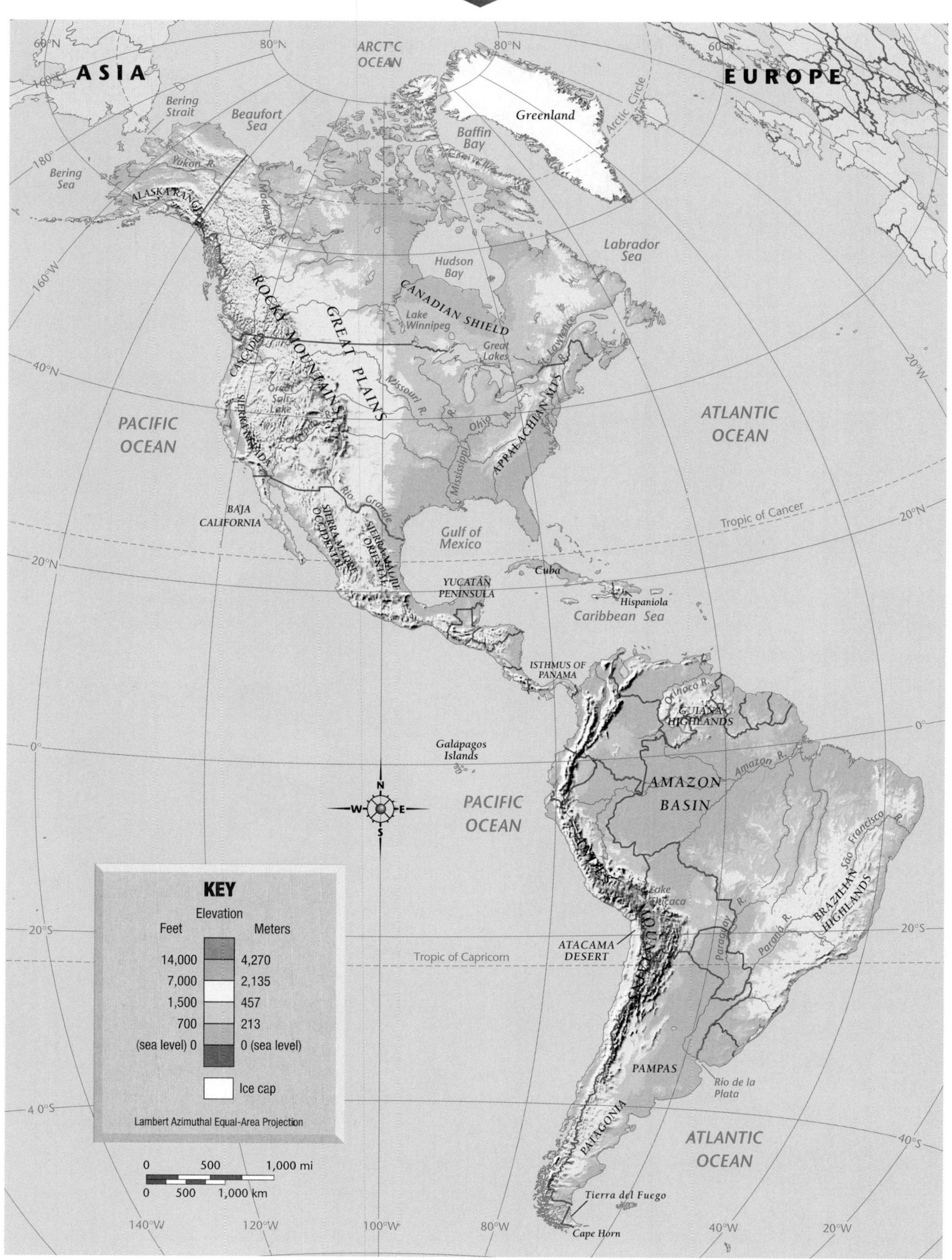
ASIA
EUROPE
ARCTIC OCEAN
Bering Strait
Beaufort Sea
Bering Sea
Greenland
Baffin Bay
Arctic Circle
Yukon R.
ALASKA RANGE
Mackenzie R.
Labrador Sea
Hudson Bay
CANADIAN SHIELD
Lake Winnipeg
ROCKY MOUNTAINS
GREAT PLAINS
CASCADES
Great Lakes
St. Lawrence R.
Great Salt Lake
SIERRA NEVADA
Missouri R.
Ohio R.
APPALACHIAN MTS.
Mississippi R.
PACIFIC OCEAN
ATLANTIC OCEAN
Tropic of Cancer
BAJA CALIFORNIA
Rio Grande
SIERRA MADRE OCCIDENTAL
SIERRA MADRE ORIENTAL
Gulf of Mexico
Cuba
YUCATÁN PENINSULA
Hispaniola
Caribbean Sea
ISTHMUS OF PANAMA
Orinoco R.
GUIANA HIGHLANDS
Galápagos Islands
AMAZON BASIN
Amazon R.
São Francisco R.
BRAZILIAN HIGHLANDS
Lake Titicaca
ANDES
ATACAMA DESERT
Tropic of Capricorn
Paraguay R.
Paraná R.
PAMPAS
Río de la Plata
PATAGONIA
Tierra del Fuego
Cape Horn
60°N
80°N
180°
160°W
140°W
120°W
100°W
80°W
40°W
20°W
40°N
20°N
0°
20°S
40°S
N
S
E
W
KEY
Elevation
Feet
Meters
14,000
4,270
7,000
2,135
1,500
457
700
213
(sea level) 0
0 (sea level)
Ice cap
Lambert Azimuthal Equal-Area Projection
0
500
1,000 mi
0
500
1,000 km

Europe: Political

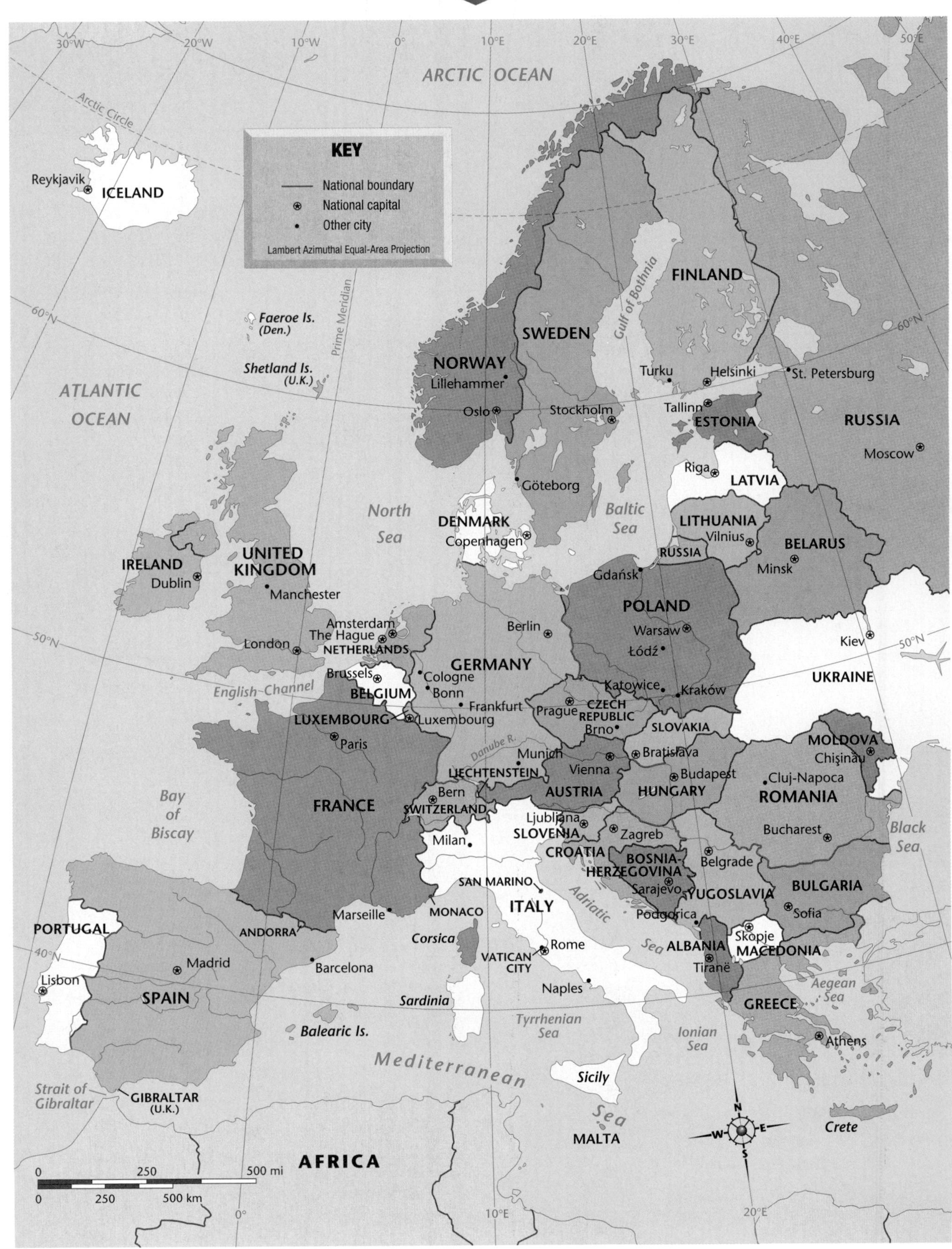

KEY
National boundary
National capital
Other city
Lambert Azimuthal Equal-Area Projection
ARCTIC OCEAN
ATLANTIC OCEAN
Arctic Circle
Prime Meridian
Reykjavik
ICELAND
Faeroe Is. (Den.)
Shetland Is. (U.K.)
NORWAY
Lillehammer
Oslo
SWEDEN
Stockholm
Göteborg
Gulf of Bothnia
FINLAND
Turku
Helsinki
St. Petersburg
Tallinn
ESTONIA
RUSSIA
Moscow
Riga
LATVIA
LITHUANIA
Vilnius
BELARUS
Minsk
RUSSIA
North Sea
Baltic Sea
DENMARK
Copenhagen
IRELAND
Dublin
UNITED KINGDOM
Manchester
London
Amsterdam
The Hague
NETHERLANDS
Brussels
BELGIUM
LUXEMBOURG
Luxembourg
English Channel
GERMANY
Berlin
Cologne
Bonn
Frankfurt
Munich
Danube R.
Gdańsk
POLAND
Warsaw
Łódź
Katowice
Kraków
Kiev
UKRAINE
Prague
CZECH REPUBLIC
Brno
SLOVAKIA
Bratislava
Vienna
AUSTRIA
LIECHTENSTEIN
Budapest
HUNGARY
MOLDOVA
Chişinău
Cluj-Napoca
ROMANIA
Bucharest
Black Sea
Paris
FRANCE
Bay of Biscay
Bern
SWITZERLAND
Ljubljana
SLOVENIA
Zagreb
CROATIA
BOSNIA-HERZEGOVINA
Sarajevo
Belgrade
YUGOSLAVIA
Podgorica
BULGARIA
Sofia
Milan
SAN MARINO
ITALY
MONACO
Marseille
ANDORRA
Corsica
Adriatic Sea
ALBANIA
Tiranë
Skopje
MACEDONIA
PORTUGAL
Lisbon
Madrid
SPAIN
Barcelona
VATICAN CITY
Rome
Naples
Sardinia
Tyrrhenian Sea
Ionian Sea
GREECE
Aegean Sea
Athens
Balearic Is.
Mediterranean Sea
Sicily
MALTA
Crete
Strait of Gibraltar
GIBRALTAR (U.K.)
AFRICA
0
250
500 mi
0
250
500 km
N
E
S
W
30°W
20°W
10°W
0°
10°E
20°E
30°E
40°E
50°E
60°N
50°N
40°N

Europe: Physical

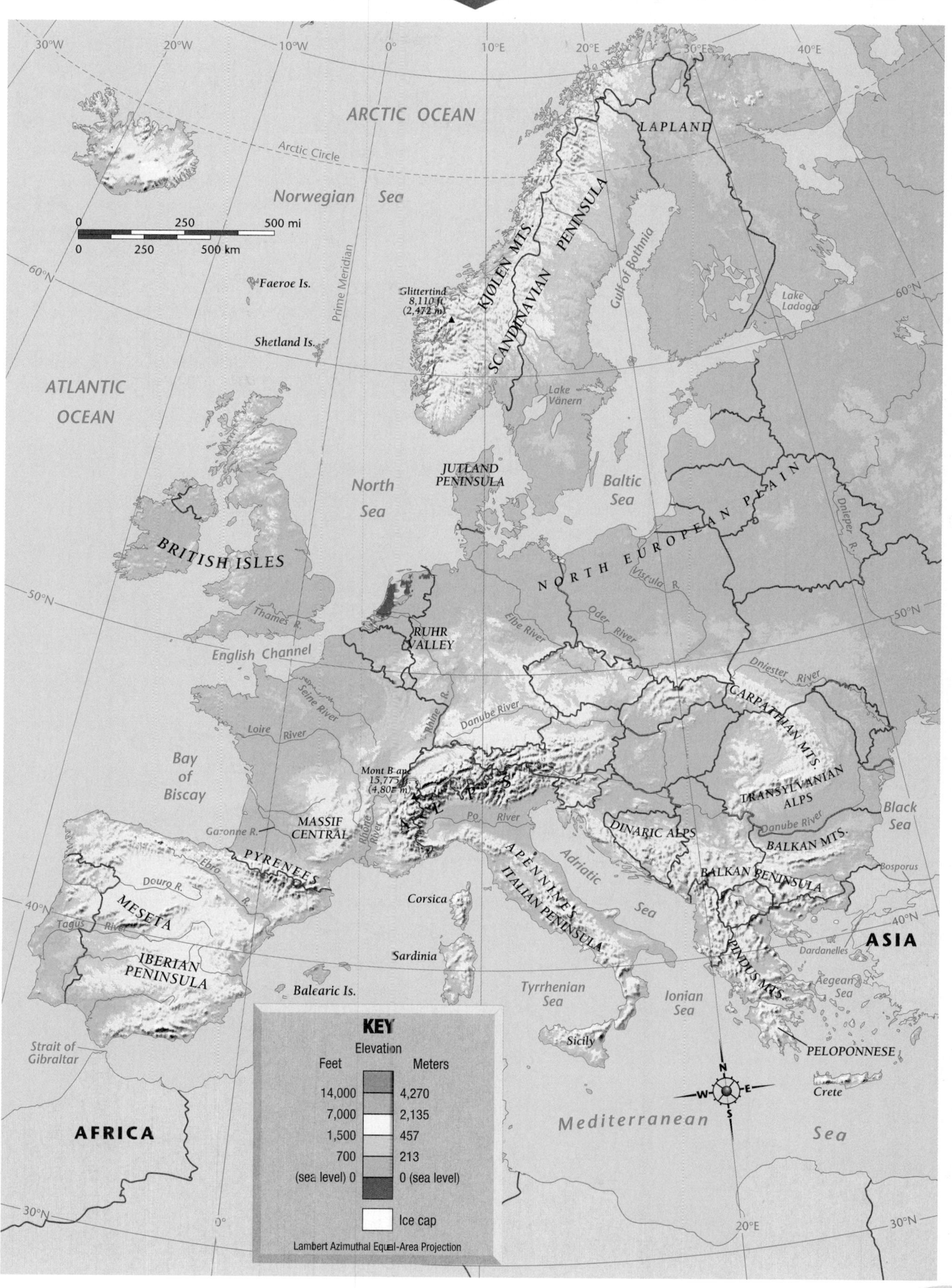

ARCTIC OCEAN
Arctic Circle
Norwegian Sea
ATLANTIC OCEAN
North Sea
Baltic Sea
LAPLAND
KJØLEN MTS.
SCANDINAVIAN PENINSULA
Gulf of Bothnia
Lake Ladoga
Glittertind 8,110 ft (2,472 m)
Faeroe Is.
Shetland Is.
Prime Meridian
Lake Vänern
JUTLAND PENINSULA
BRITISH ISLES
NORTH EUROPEAN PLAIN
Vistula R.
Oder River
Elbe River
Dnieper R.
Thames R.
English Channel
RUHR VALLEY
Dniester River
Seine River
Rhine R.
Danube River
Loire River
CARPATHIAN MTS.
TRANSYLVANIAN ALPS
Bay of Biscay
Mont Blanc 15,775 ft (4,808 m)
MASSIF CENTRAL
Garonne R.
Rhône River
Po River
Black Sea
DINARIC ALPS
Danube River
BALKAN MTS.
PYRENEES
Ebro R.
Douro R.
MESETA
Tagus River
APENNINES
ITALIAN PENINSULA
Adriatic Sea
BALKAN PENINSULA
Bosporus
Corsica
Sardinia
IBERIAN PENINSULA
Balearic Is.
Tyrrhenian Sea
Ionian Sea
PINDUS MTS.
Dardanelles
ASIA
Aegean Sea
Strait of Gibraltar
Sicily
PELOPONNESE
Crete
AFRICA
Mediterranean Sea
0 250 500 mi
0 250 500 km
KEY
Elevation
Feet
Meters
14,000 4,270
7,000 2,135
1,500 457
700 213
(sea level) 0 0 (sea level)
Ice cap
Lambert Azimuthal Equal-Area Projection
30°W 20°W 10°W 0° 10°E 20°E 30°E 40°E
60°N 50°N 40°N 30°N

EUROPE
ASIA
Strait of Gibraltar
Mediterranean Sea
Algiers
Tunis
Rabat
Casablanca
TUNISIA
Tripoli
CANARY ISLANDS (SP.)
MOROCCO
Alexandria
Giza
Cairo
WESTERN SAHARA (MOROCCO)
ALGERIA
LIBYA
EGYPT
Tropic of Cancer
Lake Nasser
Red Sea
MAURITANIA
Nouakchott
CAPE VERDE
Praia
MALI
NIGER
CHAD
Khartoum
ERITREA
Asmara
Dakar
SENEGAL
THE GAMBIA
Banjul
GUINEA-BISSAU
Bissau
GUINEA
Conakry
Freetown
SIERRA LEONE
Monrovia
LIBERIA
Bamako
Ouagadougou
BURKINA FASO
Niamey
Kano
L. Chad
N'Djamena
SUDAN
DJIBOUTI
Djibouti
Gulf of Aden
L. Tana
Addis Ababa
ETHIOPIA
CÔTE D'IVOIRE
Yamoussoukro
Abidjan
GHANA
TOGO
BENIN
Lomé
Accra
Lagos
Porto-Novo
NIGERIA
Abuja
Benue R.
CENTRAL AFRICAN REPUBLIC
Bangui
SOMALIA
Mogadishu
Gulf of Guinea
Malabo
CAMEROON
Yaoundé
EQUATORIAL GUINEA
SÃO TOMÉ AND PRÍNCIPE
São Tomé
Libreville
GABON
CONGO
Congo R.
Kisangani
UGANDA
Kampala
L. Turkana
KENYA
Nairobi
RWANDA
Kigali
Lake Victoria
Equator
DEMOCRATIC REPUBLIC OF CONGO
Bujumbura
BURUNDI
Mombasa
INDIAN OCEAN
ATLANTIC OCEAN
Brazzaville
Kinshasa
CABINDA (ANGOLA)
L. Tanganyika
Dodoma
TANZANIA
Dar es Salaam
SEYCHELLES
Luanda
ANGOLA
Lubumbashi
L. Nyasa
COMOROS
Moroni
MALAWI
Lilongwe
ZAMBIA
Lusaka
Zambezi R.
Harare
ZIMBABWE
MOZAMBIQUE
Mozambique Channel
Antananarivo
MADAGASCAR
MAURITIUS
Port Louis
RÉUNION (FR.)
NAMIBIA
Windhoek
BOTSWANA
Limpopo R.
Gaborone
Pretoria
Johannesburg
Maputo
Mbabane
SWAZILAND
Orange R.
Maseru
Durban
LESOTHO
SOUTH AFRICA
Cape Town
Tropic of Capricorn
KEY
National boundary
National capital
Other city
Lambert Azimuthal Equal-Area Projection
0 400 800 mi
0 400 800 km
N
S
E
W

Africa: Physical

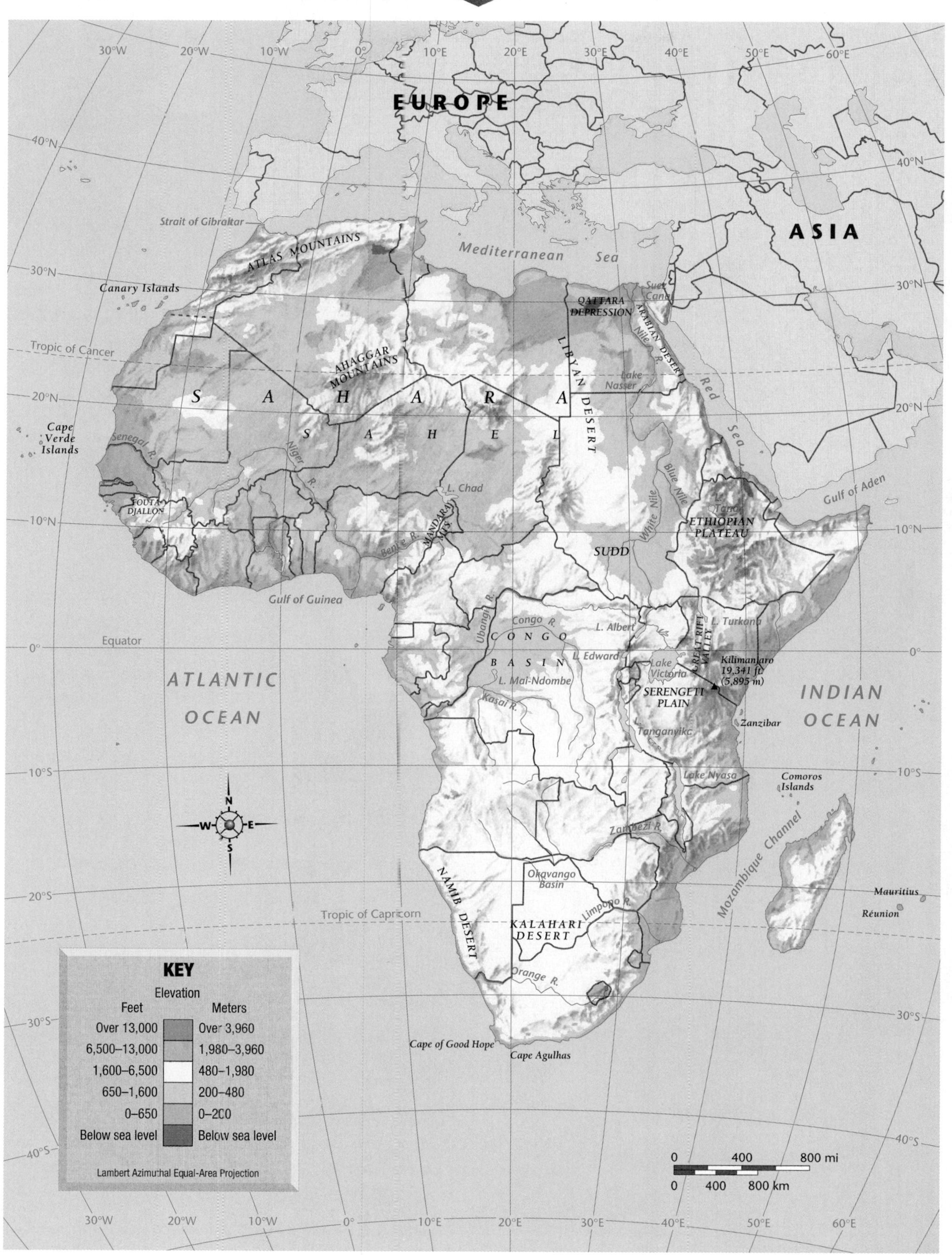

EUROPE
ASIA
Strait of Gibraltar
Mediterranean Sea
ATLAS MOUNTAINS
Canary Islands
Tropic of Cancer
QATTARA DEPRESSION
Suez Canal
ARABIAN DESERT
Nile R.
LIBYAN DESERT
AHAGGAR MOUNTAINS
Lake Nasser
Red Sea
S A H A R A
S A H E L
Cape Verde Islands
Senegal R.
Niger R.
L. Chad
Blue Nile
White Nile
Gulf of Aden
L. Tana
ETHIOPIAN PLATEAU
FOUTA DJALLON
MANDARA MTS.
Benue R.
SUDD
Gulf of Guinea
Ubangi R.
Congo R.
CONGO BASIN
L. Albert
L. Turkana
GREAT RIFT VALLEY
Equator
L. Edward
Lake Victoria
Kilimanjaro 19,341 ft (5,895 m)
ATLANTIC OCEAN
L. Mai-Ndombe
SERENGETI PLAIN
INDIAN OCEAN
Kasai R.
Zanzibar
L. Tanganyika
Lake Nyasa
Comoros Islands
Zambezi R.
Mozambique Channel
NAMIB DESERT
Okavango Basin
Mauritius
Réunion
Tropic of Capricorn
Limpopo R.
KALAHARI DESERT
Orange R.
Cape of Good Hope
Cape Agulhas
KEY
Elevation
Feet / Meters
Over 13,000 / Over 3,960
6,500–13,000 / 1,980–3,960
1,600–6,500 / 480–1,980
650–1,600 / 200–480
0–650 / 0–200
Below sea level / Below sea level
Lambert Azimuthal Equal-Area Projection
0 400 800 mi
0 400 800 km
N
S
E
W
30°W
20°W
10°W
0°
10°E
20°E
30°E
40°E
50°E
60°E
40°N
30°N
20°N
10°N
0°
10°S
20°S
30°S
40°S

Asia: Political

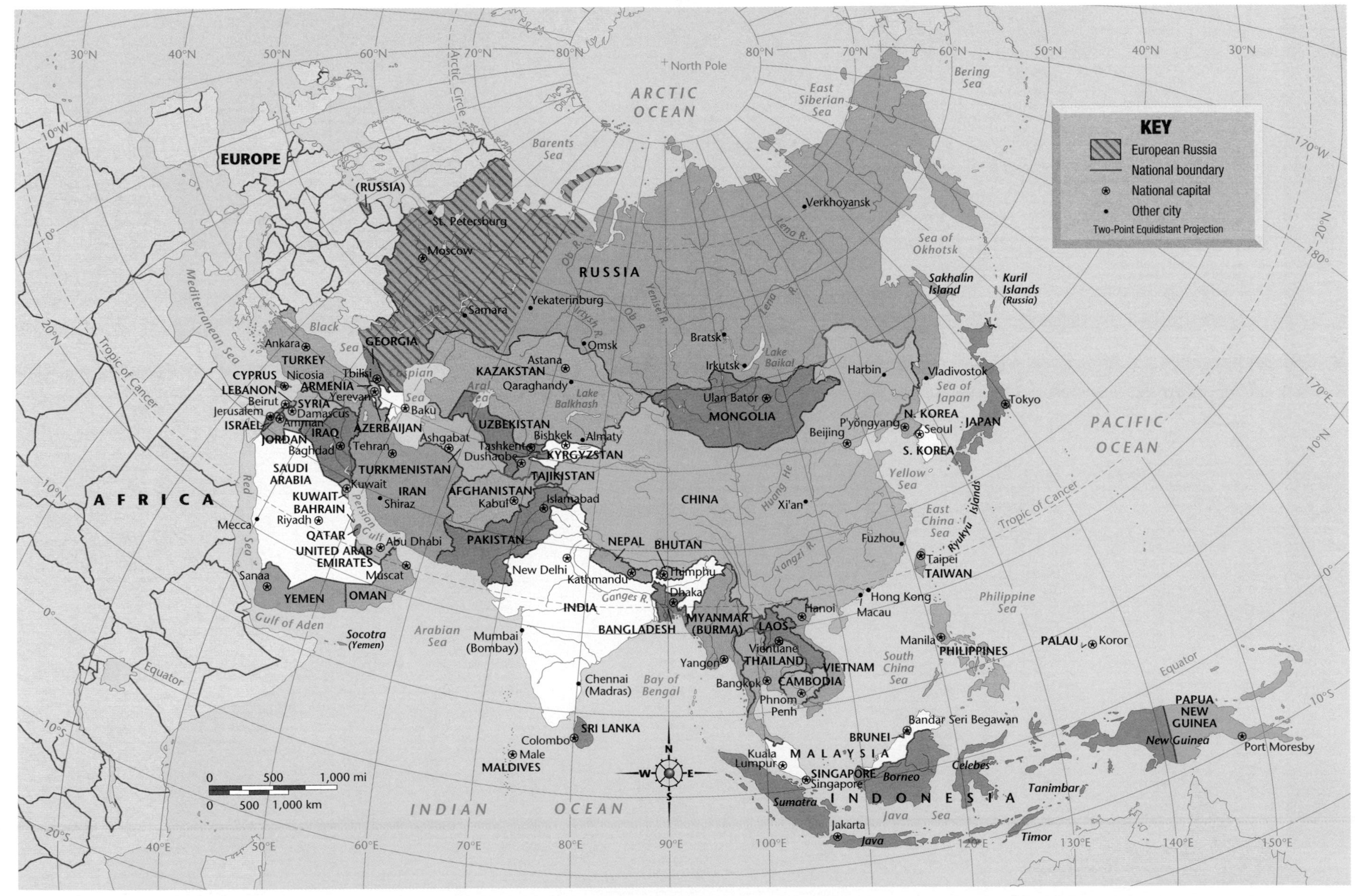

Asia: Physical

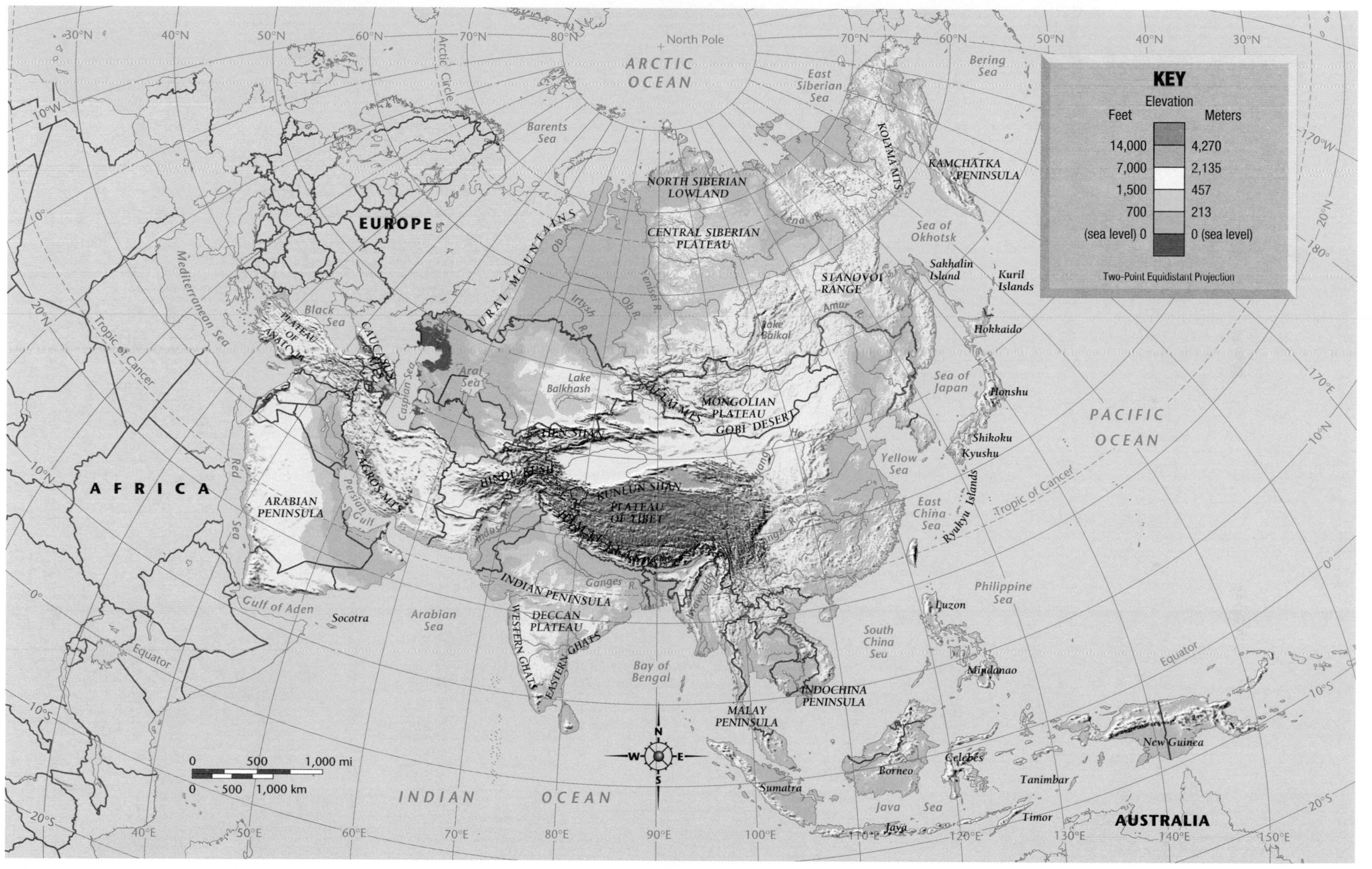

KEY
Elevation
Feet
Meters
14,000
4,270
7,000
2,135
1,500
457
700
213
(sea level) 0
0 (sea level)
Two-Point Equidistant Projection
North Pole
ARCTIC OCEAN
East Siberian Sea
Bering Sea
Barents Sea
Arctic Circle
EUROPE
NORTH SIBERIAN LOWLAND
CENTRAL SIBERIAN PLATEAU
KOLYMA MTS.
KAMCHATKA PENINSULA
Sea of Okhotsk
Sakhalin Island
Kuril Islands
STANOVOI RANGE
Amur R.
Lena R.
URAL MOUNTAINS
Ob R.
Yenisei R.
Irtysh R.
Lake Baikal
Hokkaido
Sea of Japan
Honshu
Shikoku
Kyushu
Mediterranean Sea
Black Sea
PLATEAU OF ANATOLIA
CAUCASUS MTS.
Caspian Sea
Aral Sea
Lake Balkhash
MONGOLIAN PLATEAU
GOBI DESERT
PACIFIC OCEAN
Yellow Sea
East China Sea
Ryukyu Islands
Tropic of Cancer
AFRICA
Red Sea
ARABIAN PENINSULA
Persian Gulf
ZAGROS MTS.
HINDU KUSH
KUNLUN SHAN
PLATEAU OF TIBET
Indus R.
Ganges R.
INDIAN PENINSULA
DECCAN PLATEAU
WESTERN GHATS
EASTERN GHATS
Gulf of Aden
Socotra
Arabian Sea
Bay of Bengal
Philippine Sea
Luzon
South China Sea
Mindanao
Equator
INDOCHINA PENINSULA
MALAY PENINSULA
Borneo
Celebes
Sumatra
Java Sea
Java
Tanimbar
Timor
New Guinea
AUSTRALIA
INDIAN OCEAN
N
S
E
W
0
500
1,000 mi
0
500
1,000 km
30°N
40°N
50°N
60°N
70°N
80°N
10°W
0°
20°N
10°N
10°S
20°S
170°W
180°
170°E
40°E
50°E
60°E
70°E
80°E
90°E
100°E
110°E
120°E
130°E
140°E
150°E

Australia, New Zealand, and the Pacific Islands: Physical–Political

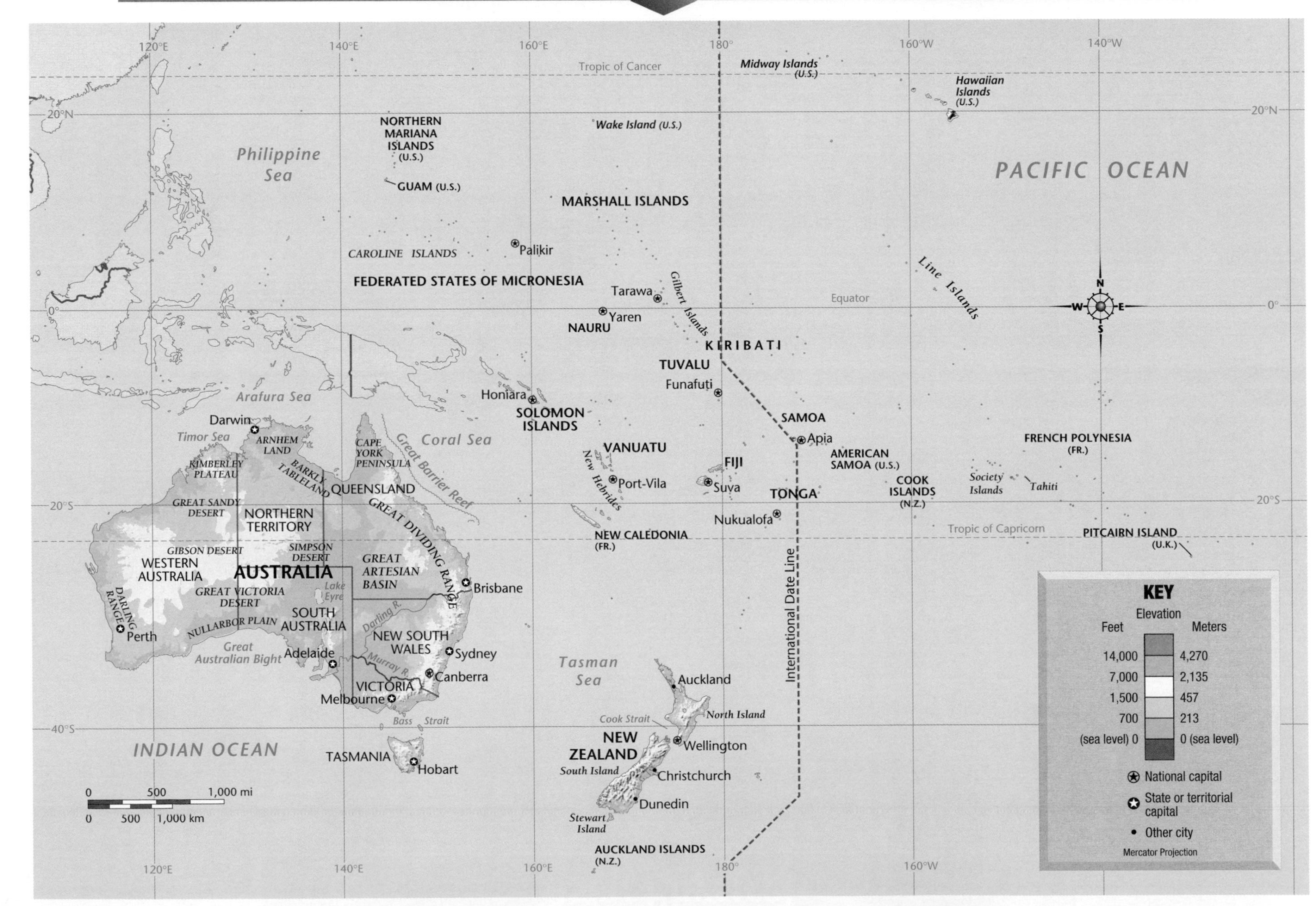

PACIFIC OCEAN
INDIAN OCEAN
Philippine Sea
Arafura Sea
Timor Sea
Coral Sea
Tasman Sea
Great Australian Bight
Bass Strait
Cook Strait
Tropic of Cancer
Equator
Tropic of Capricorn
International Date Line
NORTHERN MARIANA ISLANDS (U.S.)
GUAM (U.S.)
CAROLINE ISLANDS
FEDERATED STATES OF MICRONESIA
Palikir
MARSHALL ISLANDS
Wake Island (U.S.)
Midway Islands (U.S.)
Hawaiian Islands (U.S.)
Line Islands
Gilbert Islands
Tarawa
KIRIBATI
Yaren
NAURU
TUVALU
Funafuti
SOLOMON ISLANDS
Honiara
VANUATU
New Hebrides
Port-Vila
NEW CALEDONIA (FR.)
FIJI
Suva
TONGA
Nukualofa
SAMOA
Apia
AMERICAN SAMOA (U.S.)
COOK ISLANDS (N.Z.)
Society Islands
Tahiti
FRENCH POLYNESIA (FR.)
PITCAIRN ISLAND (U.K.)
AUSTRALIA
Darwin
ARNHEM LAND
KIMBERLEY PLATEAU
BARKLY TABLELAND
CAPE YORK PENINSULA
Great Barrier Reef
QUEENSLAND
GREAT DIVIDING RANGE
NORTHERN TERRITORY
GREAT SANDY DESERT
GIBSON DESERT
SIMPSON DESERT
WESTERN AUSTRALIA
GREAT VICTORIA DESERT
NULLARBOR PLAIN
DARLING RANGE
Perth
GREAT ARTESIAN BASIN
Lake Eyre
Brisbane
SOUTH AUSTRALIA
Darling R.
Murray R.
NEW SOUTH WALES
Sydney
Canberra
Adelaide
VICTORIA
Melbourne
TASMANIA
Hobart
NEW ZEALAND
North Island
South Island
Auckland
Wellington
Christchurch
Dunedin
Stewart Island
AUCKLAND ISLANDS (N.Z.)
120°E
140°E
160°E
180°
160°W
140°W
20°N
0°
20°S
40°S
N
S
E
W
0
500
1,000 mi
0
500
1,000 km
KEY
Elevation
Feet
Meters
14,000
4,270
7,000
2,135
1,500
457
700
213
(sea level) 0
0 (sea level)
National capital
State or territorial capital
Other city
Mercator Projection

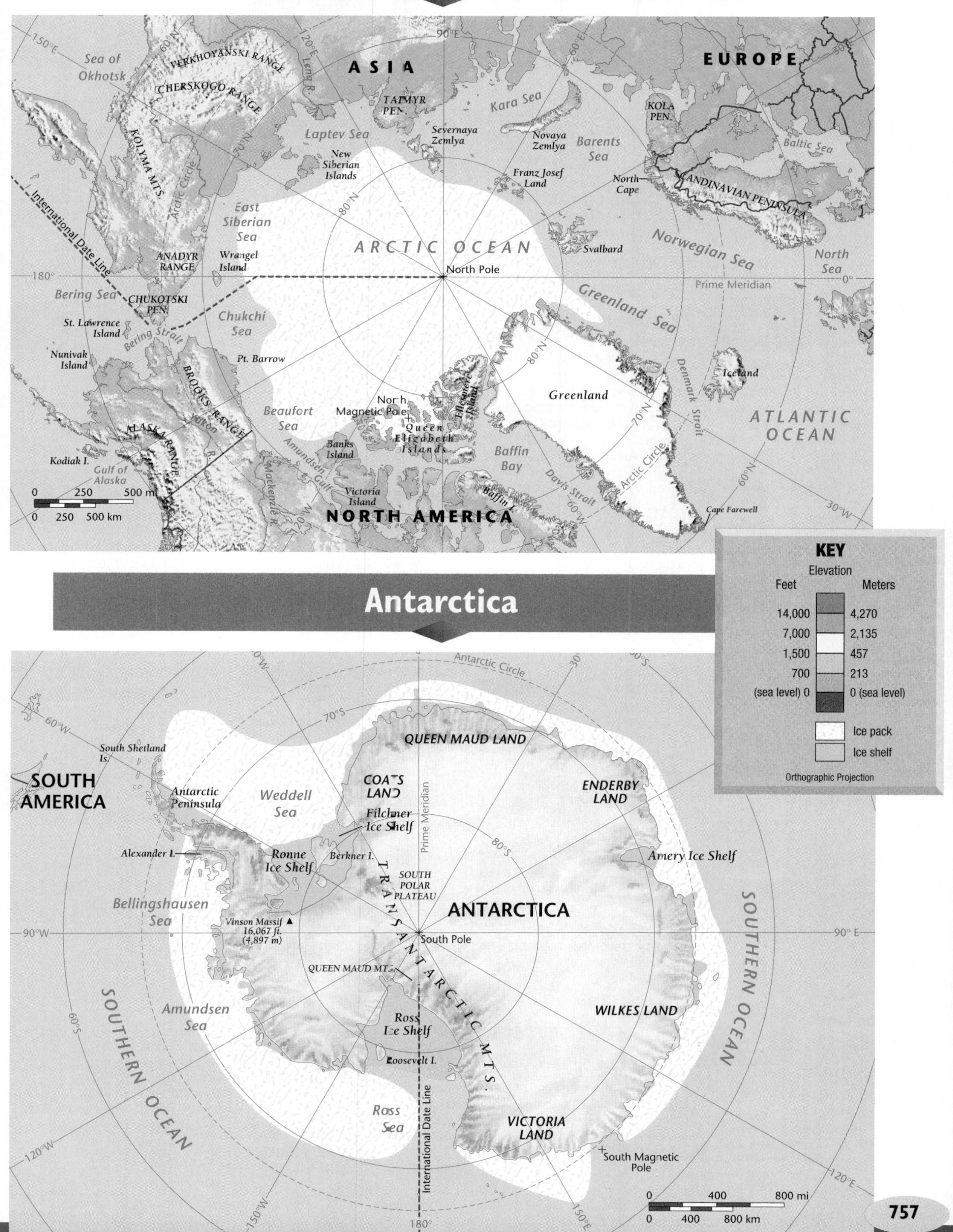
The Arctic
ASIA
EUROPE
NORTH AMERICA
ARCTIC OCEAN
ATLANTIC OCEAN
North Pole
North Magnetic Pole
Sea of Okhotsk
Laptev Sea
Kara Sea
Barents Sea
Baltic Sea
East Siberian Sea
Chukchi Sea
Bering Sea
Beaufort Sea
Norwegian Sea
Greenland Sea
North Sea
Baffin Bay
Gulf of Alaska
VERKHOYANSKI RANGE
CHERSKOGO RANGE
KOLYMA MTS.
ANADYR RANGE
CHUKOTSKI PEN.
BROOKS RANGE
ALASKA RANGE
TAIMYR PEN.
KOLA PEN.
SCANDINAVIAN PENINSULA
Severnaya Zemlya
Novaya Zemlya
Franz Josef Land
New Siberian Islands
Wrangel Island
St. Lawrence Island
Nunivak Island
Kodiak I.
Pt. Barrow
Queen Elizabeth Islands
Ellesmere Island
Banks Island
Victoria Island
Baffin I.
Greenland
Iceland
Svalbard
North Cape
Cape Farewell
Bering Strait
Denmark Strait
Davis Strait
Amundsen Gulf
Lena R.
Yukon R.
Mackenzie R.
International Date Line
Arctic Circle
Prime Meridian
0 250 500 mi
0 250 500 km
Antarctica
KEY
Elevation
Feet Meters
14,000 4,270
7,000 2,135
1,500 457
700 213
(sea level) 0 0 (sea level)
Ice pack
Ice shelf
Orthographic Projection
SOUTH AMERICA
ANTARCTICA
SOUTHERN OCEAN
South Pole
South Magnetic Pole
QUEEN MAUD LAND
COATS LAND
ENDERBY LAND
WILKES LAND
VICTORIA LAND
SOUTH POLAR PLATEAU
TRANSANTARCTIC MTS.
QUEEN MAUD MTS.
South Shetland Is.
Antarctic Peninsula
Alexander I.
Berkner I.
Roosevelt I.
Weddell Sea
Bellingshausen Sea
Amundsen Sea
Ross Sea
Filchner Ice Shelf
Ronne Ice Shelf
Amery Ice Shelf
Ross Ice Shelf
Vinson Massif 16,067 ft. (4,897 m)
Antarctic Circle
Prime Meridian
International Date Line
0 400 800 mi
0 400 800 km

World View

Afghanistan

CAPITAL: Kabul
POPULATION: 21.9 million
OFFICIAL LANGUAGES: Persian and Pashtu
AREA: 251,770 sq mi/652,090 sq km
LEADING EXPORTS: fruits, nuts, hand-woven carpets, wool, and cotton
CONTINENT: Asia

Albania

CAPITAL: Tirana
POPULATION: 3.1 million
OFFICIAL LANGUAGE: Albanian
AREA: 10,579 sq mi/27,400 sq km
LEADING EXPORTS: textiles, footwear, asphalt, metals, and metallic ores
CONTINENT: Europe

Algeria

CAPITAL: Algiers
POPULATION: 30.8 million
OFFICIAL LANGUAGE: Arabic
AREA: 919,590 sq mi/2,381,740 sq km
LEADING EXPORTS: petroleum, natural gas, and petroleum products
CONTINENT: Africa

Andorra

CAPITAL: Andorra la Vella
POPULATION: 65,000
OFFICIAL LANGUAGE: Catalan
AREA: 181 sq mi/468 sq km
LEADING EXPORTS: tobacco products and furniture
CONTINENT: Europe

Angola

CAPITAL: Luanda
POPULATION: 12.5 million
OFFICIAL LANGUAGE: Portuguese
AREA: 434,235 sq mi/1,124,670 sq km
LEADING EXPORTS: crude oil, diamonds, refined petroleum products, gas, and coffee
CONTINENT: Africa

Antigua and Barbuda

CAPITAL: St. John's
POPULATION: 69,000
OFFICIAL LANGUAGE: English
AREA: 170 sq mi/440 sq km
LEADING EXPORTS: petroleum products, manufactures, food, and live animals
LOCATION: Caribbean Sea

Argentina

CAPITAL: Buenos Aires
POPULATION: 36.6 million
OFFICIAL LANGUAGE: Spanish
AREA: 1,056,636 sq mi/2,736,690 sq km
LEADING EXPORTS: edible oils, fuels and energy, cereals, feed, and motor vehicles
CONTINENT: South America

Armenia

CAPITAL: Yerevan
POPULATION: 3.5 million
OFFICIAL LANGUAGE: Armenian
AREA: 11,506 sq mi/29,800 sq km
LEADING EXPORTS: diamonds, scrap metal, machinery and equipment, and cognac
CONTINENT: Asia

Australia

CAPITAL: Canberra
POPULATION: 18.7 million
OFFICIAL LANGUAGE: English
AREA: 2,941,283 sq mi/7,617,930 sq km
LEADING EXPORTS: coal, gold, wool, aluminum, and iron ore
CONTINENT: Australia

Austria

CAPITAL: Vienna
POPULATION: 8.2 million
OFFICIAL LANGUAGE: German
AREA: 32,942 sq mi/82,730 sq km
LEADING EXPORTS: machinery and equipment, paper, and paperboard
CONTINENT: Europe

Azerbaijan

CAPITAL: Baku
POPULATION: 7.7 million
OFFICIAL LANGUAGE: Azerbaijani
AREA: 33,436 sq mi/86,600 sq km
LEADING EXPORTS: oil, gas, machinery, cotton, and foodstuffs
CONTINENT: Asia

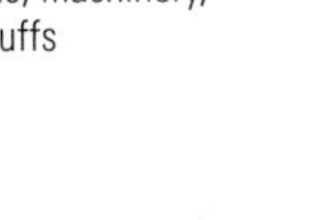

Bahamas

CAPITAL: Nassau
POPULATION: 301,000
OFFICIAL LANGUAGE: English
AREA: 3,864 sq mi/10,010 sq km
LEADING EXPORTS: pharmaceuticals, cement, rum, and crawfish
LOCATION: Caribbean Sea

Bahrain

CAPITAL: Manama
POPULATION: 606,000
OFFICIAL LANGUAGE: Arabic
AREA: 263 sq mi/680 sq km
LEADING EXPORTS: petroleum, petroleum products, and aluminum
CONTINENT: Asia

Bangladesh

CAPITAL: Dhaka
POPULATION: 126.9 million
OFFICIAL LANGUAGE: Bengali
AREA: 51,703 sq mi/133,910 sq km
LEADING EXPORTS: garments, jute and jute goods, leather, frozen fish, and seafood
CONTINENT: Asia

Barbados

CAPITAL: Bridgetown
POPULATION: 269,000
OFFICIAL LANGUAGE: English
AREA: 166 sq mi/430 sq km
LEADING EXPORTS: sugar, molasses, rum, and other foods and beverages
LOCATION: Caribbean Sea

Belarus

CAPITAL: Minsk
POPULATION: 10.3 million
OFFICIAL LANGUAGES: Belorussian, Russian
AREA: 80,154 sq mi/207,600 sq km
LEADING EXPORTS: machinery and equipment, chemicals, metals, and textiles
CONTINENT: Europe

Belgium

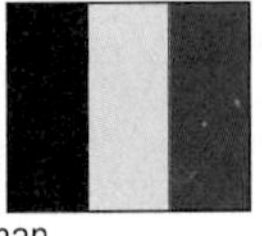

CAPITAL: Brussels
POPULATION: 10.2 million
OFFICIAL LANGUAGES: Flemish, French, German
AREA: 12,672 sq mi/32,820 sq km
LEADING EXPORTS: machinery and equipment, chemicals, and diamonds
CONTINENT: Europe

Belize

CAPITAL: Belmopan
POPULATION: 200,000
OFFICIAL LANGUAGE: English
AREA: 8803 sq mi/22,800 sq km
LEADING EXPORTS: sugar, bananas, citrus fruits, clothing, and fish products
CONTINENT: North America

Benin

CAPITAL: Porto-Novo
POPULATION: 5.9 million
OFFICIAL LANGUAGE: French
AREA: 42,710 sq mi/110,620 sq km
LEADING EXPORTS: cotton, crude oil, palm products, and cocoa
CONTINENT: Africa

Bhutan

CAPITAL: Thimphu
POPULATION: 2.1 million
OFFICIAL LANGUAGE: Dzongkha
AREA: 18,147 sq mi/47,000 sq km
LEADING EXPORTS: cardamom, gypsum, timber, handicrafts, and cement
CONTINENT: Asia

Bolivia

CAPITAL: Sucre
POPULATION: 8.1 million
OFFICIAL LANGUAGES: Spanish, Quechua, and Aymará
AREA: 418,683 sq mi/1,084,390 sq km
LEADING EXPORTS: soybeans, natural gas, zinc, gold, and wood
CONTINENT: South America

Bosnia-Herzegovina

CAPITAL: Sarajevo
POPULATION: 3.8 million
OFFICIAL LANGUAGE: Serbo-Croat
AREA: 19,741 sq mi/51,130 sq km
LEADING EXPORTS: none of significance
CONTINENT: Europe

Botswana

CAPITAL: Gaborone
POPULATION: 1.6 million
OFFICIAL LANGUAGE: English
AREA: 218,814 sq mi/566,730 sq km
LEADING EXPORTS: diamonds, vehicles, copper, nickel, and meat
CONTINENT: Africa

Brazil

CAPITAL: Brasília
POPULATION: 168 million
OFFICIAL LANGUAGE: Portuguese
AREA: 3,265,059 sq mi/8,456,510 sq km
LEADING EXPORTS: manufactures, iron ore, soybeans, footwear, and coffee
CONTINENT: South America

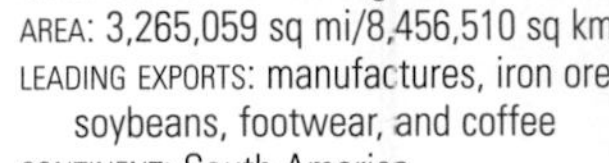

Brunei

CAPITAL: Bandar Seri Begawam
POPULATION: 322,000
OFFICIAL LANGUAGE: Malay
AREA: 2,035 sq mi/5,270 sq km
LEADING EXPORTS: crude oil, liquefied natural gas, and petroleum products
LOCATION: South China Sea

Bulgaria

CAPITAL: Sofia
POPULATION: 8.3 million
OFFICIAL LANGUAGE: Bulgarian
AREA: 42,683 sq mi/110,550 sq km
LEADING EXPORTS: machinery and equipment, metals, minerals, and fuels
CONTINENT: Europe

Burkina Faso

CAPITAL: Ouagadougou
POPULATION: 11.6 million
OFFICIAL LANGUAGE: French
AREA: 105,714 sq mi/273,800 sq km
LEADING EXPORTS: cotton, animal products, and gold
CONTINENT: Africa

Burundi

CAPITAL: Bujumbura
POPULATION: 6.6 million
OFFICIAL LANGUAGES: French and Kirundi
AREA: 9,903 sq mi/25,650 sq km
LEADING EXPORTS: coffee, tea, sugar, cotton, and hides
CONTINENT: Africa

Cambodia

CAPITAL: Phnom Penh
POPULATION: 10.9 million
OFFICIAL LANGUAGE: Khmer
AREA: 68,154 sq mi/176,520 sq km
LEADING EXPORTS: timber, garments, rubber, rice, and fish
CONTINENT: Asia

Cameroon

CAPITAL: Yaoundé
POPULATION: 14.7 million
OFFICIAL LANGUAGES: English and French
AREA: 179,691 sq mi/465,400 sq km
LEADING EXPORTS: crude oil and petroleum products, lumber, and cocoa beans
CONTINENT: Africa

Canada

CAPITAL: Ottawa
POPULATION: 30,750,087
OFFICIAL LANGUAGES: English and French
AREA: 3,851,788 sq mi/9,976,140 sq km
LEADING EXPORTS: motor vehicles and parts, newsprint, wood pulp, and timber
CONTINENT: North America

Cape Verde

CAPITAL: Praia
POPULATION: 418,000
OFFICIAL LANGUAGE: Portuguese
AREA: 1,556 sq mi/4,030 sq km
LEADING EXPORTS: fuel, shoes, garments, fish, and bananas
CONTINENT: Africa

Central African Republic

CAPITAL: Bangui
POPULATION: 3.6 million
OFFICIAL LANGUAGE: French
AREA: 240,530 sq mi/622,980 sq km
LEADING EXPORTS: diamonds, timber, cotton, coffee, and tobacco
CONTINENT: Africa

Chad

CAPITAL: N'Djamena
POPULATION: 7.5 million
OFFICIAL LANGUAGES: Arabic and French
AREA: 486,177 sq mi/1,259,200 sq km
LEADING EXPORTS: cotton, cattle, and textiles
CONTINENT: Africa

Chile

CAPITAL: Santiago
POPULATION: 15 million
OFFICIAL LANGUAGE: Spanish
AREA: 289,112 sq mi/748,800 sq km
LEADING EXPORTS: copper, fish, fruits, paper and pulp, and chemicals
CONTINENT: South America

China

CAPITAL: Beijing
POPULATION: 1.3 billion
OFFICIAL LANGUAGE: Mandarin
AREA: 3,600,927 sq mi/9,326,410 sq km
LEADING EXPORTS: machinery, equipment, textiles, and clothing
CONTINENT: Asia

Colombia

CAPITAL: Bogotá
POPULATION: 41.6 million
OFFICIAL LANGUAGE: Spanish
AREA: 401,042 sq mi/1,038,700 sq km
LEADING EXPORTS: petroleum, coffee, coal, gold, and bananas
CONTINENT: South America

Comoros

CAPITAL: Moroni
POPULATION: 676,000
OFFICIAL LANGUAGES: Arabic and French
AREA: 861 sq mi/2,230 sq km
LEADING EXPORTS: vanilla, ylang-ylang, cloves, perfume oil, and copra
LOCATION: Indian Ocean

Congo (Democratic Republic of)

CAPITAL: Kinshasa
POPULATION: 50.3 million
OFFICIAL LANGUAGES: French and English
AREA: 875,520 sq mi/2,267,600 sq km
LEADING EXPORTS: diamonds, copper, coffee, cobalt, and crude oil
CONTINENT: Africa

Congo (Republic of the)

CAPITAL: Brazzaville
POPULATION: 2.9 million
OFFICIAL LANGUAGE: French
AREA: 131,853 sq mi/341,500 sq km
LEADING EXPORTS: petroleum, lumber, plywood, sugar, and cocoa
CONTINENT: Africa

Costa Rica

CAPITAL: San José
POPULATION: 3.9 million
OFFICIAL LANGUAGE: Spanish
AREA: 19,714 sq mi/51,060 sq km
LEADING EXPORTS: coffee, bananas, sugar, textiles, and electronic components
CONTINENT: North America

Côte d'Ivoire

CAPITAL: Yamoussoukro
POPULATION: 15.9 million
OFFICIAL LANGUAGE: French
AREA: 122,780 sq mi/318,000 sq km
LEADING EXPORTS: cocoa, coffee, tropical woods, petroleum, and cotton
CONTINENT: Africa

Croatia

CAPITAL: Zagreb
POPULATION: 4.5 million
OFFICIAL LANGUAGE: Croatian
AREA: 21,829 sq mi/56,538 sq km
LEADING EXPORTS: textiles, chemicals, foodstuffs, and fuels
CONTINENT: Europe

Cuba

CAPITAL: Havana
POPULATION: 11.2 million
OFFICIAL LANGUAGE: Spanish
AREA: 42,803 sq mi/110,860 sq km
LEADING EXPORTS: sugar, nickel, tobacco, shellfish, and medical products
LOCATION: Caribbean Sea

Cyprus

CAPITAL: Nicosia
POPULATION: 778,000
OFFICIAL LANGUAGES: Greek and Turkish
AREA: 3,572 sq mi/9,251 sq km
LEADING EXPORTS: citrus, potatoes, grapes, wine, and cement
LOCATION: Mediterranean Sea

Czech Republic

CAPITAL: Prague
POPULATION: 10.3 million
OFFICIAL LANGUAGE: Czech
AREA: 30,449 sq mi/78,864 sq km
LEADING EXPORTS: machinery and transport equipment, and other manufactured goods
CONTINENT: Europe

Denmark

CAPITAL: Copenhagen
POPULATION: 5.3 million
OFFICIAL LANGUAGE: Danish
AREA: 16,629 sq mi/43,070 sq km
LEADING EXPORTS: machinery and instruments, meat and meat products
CONTINENT: Europe

Djibouti

CAPITAL: Djibouti
POPULATION: 629,000
OFFICIAL LANGUAGES: Arabic and French
AREA: 8,950 sq mi/23,180 sq km
LEADING EXPORTS: reexports, hides and skins, and coffee
CONTINENT: Africa

Dominica

CAPITAL: Roseau
POPULATION: 74,000
OFFICIAL LANGUAGE: English
AREA: 290 sq mi/750 sq km
LEADING EXPORTS: bananas, soap, bay oil, vegetables, and grapefruit
LOCATION: Caribbean Sea

Dominican Republic

CAPITAL: Santo Domingo
POPULATION: 8.4 million
OFFICIAL LANGUAGE: Spanish
AREA: 18,815 sq mi/48,730 sq km
LEADING EXPORTS: ferronickel, sugar, gold, silver, and coffee
LOCATION: Caribbean Sea

Ecuador

CAPITAL: Quito
POPULATION: 12.4 million
OFFICIAL LANGUAGE: Spanish
AREA: 106,888 sq mi/276,840 sq km
LEADING EXPORTS: petroleum, bananas, shrimp, coffee, and cocoa
CONTINENT: South America

Egypt

CAPITAL: Cairo
POPULATION: 67.2 million
OFFICIAL LANGUAGE: Arabic
AREA: 384,343 sq mi/995,450 sq km
LEADING EXPORTS: crude oil, petroleum products, cotton, textiles, and metal products
CONTINENT: Africa

El Salvador

CAPITAL: San Salvador
POPULATION: 6.2 million
OFFICIAL LANGUAGE: Spanish
AREA: 8,000 sq mi/20,720 sq km
LEADING EXPORTS: offshore assembly exports, coffee, sugar, shrimp, and textiles
CONTINENT: North America

Equatorial Guinea

CAPITAL: Malabo
POPULATION: 442,000
OFFICIAL LANGUAGE: Spanish
AREA: 10,830 sq mi/28,050 sq km
LEADING EXPORTS: petroleum, timber, and cocoa
CONTINENT: Africa

Eritrea

CAPITAL: Asmara
POPULATION: 3.7 million
OFFICIAL LANGUAGE: Tigrinya
AREA: 36,170 sq mi/93,680 sq km
LEADING EXPORTS: livestock, sorghum, textiles, food, and small manufactures
CONTINENT: Africa

Estonia

CAPITAL: Tallinn
POPULATION: 1.4 million
OFFICIAL LANGUAGE: Estonian
AREA: 17,423 sq mi/45,125 sq km
LEADING EXPORTS: machinery and appliances, wood products, and textiles
CONTINENT: Europe

Ethiopia

CAPITAL: Addis Ababa
POPULATION: 61.1 million
OFFICIAL LANGUAGE: Amharic
AREA: 425,096 sq mi/1,101,000 sq km
LEADING EXPORTS: coffee, gold, leather products, and oilseeds
CONTINENT: Africa

Fiji

CAPITAL: Suva
POPULATION: 806,000
OFFICIAL LANGUAGE: English
AREA: 7,054 sq mi/18,270 sq km
LEADING EXPORTS: sugar, clothing, gold, processed fish, and lumber
LOCATION: Pacific Ocean

Finland

CAPITAL: Helsinki
POPULATION: 5.2 million
OFFICIAL LANGUAGES: Finnish and Swedish
AREA: 117,610 sq mi/304,610 sq km
LEADING EXPORTS: machinery and equipment, chemicals, metals, and timber
CONTINENT: Europe

France

CAPITAL: Paris
POPULATION: 58.9 million
OFFICIAL LANGUAGE: French
AREA: 212,394 sq mi/550,100 sq km
LEADING EXPORTS: machinery, transportation equipment, and chemicals
CONTINENT: Europe

French Guiana

CAPITAL: Cayenne
POPULATION: 152,300
OFFICIAL LANGUAGE: French
AREA: 35,100 sq mi/91,000 sq km
LEADING EXPORTS: shrimp, timber, gold, rum, and rosewood essence
CONTINENT: South America

Gabon

CAPITAL: Libreville
POPULATION: 1.2 million
OFFICIAL LANGUAGE: French
AREA: 99,486 sq mi/257,670 sq km
LEADING EXPORTS: crude oil, timber, manganese, and uranium
CONTINENT: Africa

The Gambia

CAPITAL: Banjul
POPULATION: 1.3 million
OFFICIAL LANGUAGE: English
AREA: 3,861 sq mi/10,000 sq km
LEADING EXPORTS: peanuts and peanut products, fish, cotton lint, and palm kernels
CONTINENT: Africa

Georgia

CAPITAL: Tbilisi
POPULATION: 5 million
OFFICIAL LANGUAGE: Georgian
AREA: 26,911 sq mi/69,700 sq km
LEADING EXPORTS: citrus fruits, tea, wine, and other agricultural products
CONTINENT: Asia

Germany

CAPITAL: Berlin
POPULATION: 82.2 million
OFFICIAL LANGUAGE: German
AREA: 134,910 sq mi/349,520 sq km
LEADING EXPORTS: machinery, vehicles, chemicals, and metals and manufactures
CONTINENT: Europe

Ghana

CAPITAL: Accra
POPULATION: 19.7 million
OFFICIAL LANGUAGE: English
AREA: 92,100 sq mi/238,540 sq km
LEADING EXPORTS: gold, cocoa, timber, tuna, and bauxite
CONTINENT: Africa

Greece

CAPITAL: Athens
POPULATION: 10.6 million
OFFICIAL LANGUAGE: Greek
AREA: 50,521 sq mi/130,850 sq km
LEADING EXPORTS: manufactured goods, food and beverages, and fuels
CONTINENT: Europe

Grenada

CAPITAL: St. George's
POPULATION: 98,600
OFFICIAL LANGUAGE: English
AREA: 131 sq mi/340 sq km
LEADING EXPORTS: bananas, cocoa, nutmeg, mace, and citrus
LOCATION: Caribbean Sea

Guatemala

CAPITAL: Guatemala City
POPULATION: 11.1 million
OFFICIAL LANGUAGE: Spanish
AREA: 41,865 sq mi/108,430 sq km
LEADING EXPORTS: fuels, machinery, and transport equipment
CONTINENT: North America

Guinea

CAPITAL: Conakry
POPULATION: 7.4 million
OFFICIAL LANGUAGE: French
AREA: 94,926 sq mi/245,860 sq km
LEADING EXPORTS: bauxite, alumina, gold, diamonds, and coffee
CONTINENT: Africa

Guinea-Bissau

CAPITAL: Bissau
POPULATION: 1.2 million
OFFICIAL LANGUAGE: Portuguese
AREA: 10,857 sq mi/28,120 sq km
LEADING EXPORTS: cashew nuts, shrimp, peanuts, palm kernels, and sawn lumber
CONTINENT: Africa

Guyana

CAPITAL: Georgetown
POPULATION: 855,000
OFFICIAL LANGUAGE: English
AREA: 76,004 sq mi/196,850 sq km
LEADING EXPORTS: sugar, gold, bauxite/alumina, rice, and shrimp
CONTINENT: South America

Haiti

CAPITAL: Port-au-Prince
POPULATION: 8.1 million
OFFICIAL LANGUAGES: French and French Creole
AREA: 10,641 sq mi/27,560 sq km
LEADING EXPORTS: manufactures, coffee, oils, and mangoes
LOCATION: Caribbean Sea

Holy See (Vatican City)

CAPITAL: Vatican City
POPULATION: 1,000
OFFICIAL LANGUAGES: Italian and Latin
AREA: 0.17 sq mi/0.44 sq km
LEADING EXPORTS: none
CONTINENT: Europe

Honduras

CAPITAL: Tegucigalpa
POPULATION: 6.3 million
OFFICIAL LANGUAGE: Spanish
AREA: 43,201 sq mi/111,890 sq km
LEADING EXPORTS: coffee, bananas, shrimp, lobster, and meat
CONTINENT: North America

Hungary

CAPITAL: Budapest
POPULATION: 10.1 million
OFFICIAL LANGUAGE: Hungarian
AREA: 35,652 sq mi/92,340 sq km
LEADING EXPORTS: machinery, equipment, and other manufactures
CONTINENT: Europe

Iceland

CAPITAL: Reykjavik
POPULATION: 279,000
OFFICIAL LANGUAGE: Icelandic
AREA: 38,707 sq mi/100,250 sq km
LEADING EXPORTS: fish and fish products, animal products, aluminum, and diatomite
LOCATION: Atlantic Ocean

India

CAPITAL: New Delhi
POPULATION: 998 million
OFFICIAL LANGUAGES: Hindi and English
AREA: 1,147,949 sq mi/2,973,190 sq km
LEADING EXPORTS: textile goods, gems and jewelry, engineering goods, and chemicals
CONTINENT: Asia

Indonesia

CAPITAL: Jakarta
POPULATION: 209.3 million
OFFICIAL LANGUAGE: Bahasa Indonesia
AREA: 699,447 sq mi/1,811,570 sq km
LEADING EXPORTS: oil and gas, plywood, textiles, and rubber
CONTINENT: Asia

Iran

CAPITAL: Tehran
POPULATION: 66.8 million
OFFICIAL LANGUAGE: Farsi
AREA: 3,572 sq mi/9,251 sq km
LEADING EXPORTS: petroleum, carpets, fruits, nuts, and hides
CONTINENT: Asia

Iraq

CAPITAL: Baghdad
POPULATION: 22.5 million
OFFICIAL LANGUAGE: Arabic
AREA: 168,869 sq mi/437,370 sq km
LEADING EXPORT: crude oil
CONTINENT: Asia

Ireland

CAPITAL: Dublin
POPULATION: 3.7 million
OFFICIAL LANGUAGES: Irish and English
AREA: 26,598 sq mi/68,890 sq km
LEADING EXPORTS: machinery and equipment, computers, and chemicals
CONTINENT: Europe

Israel

CAPITAL: Jerusalem
POPULATION: 6.1 million
OFFICIAL LANGUAGES: Hebrew and Arabic
AREA: 7,849 sq mi/20,330 sq km
LEADING EXPORTS: machinery, equipment, software, cut diamonds, and chemicals
CONTINENT: Asia

Italy

CAPITAL: Rome
POPULATION: 57.3 million
OFFICIAL LANGUAGE: Italian
AREA: 301,270 sq mi/294,060 sq km
LEADING EXPORTS: engineering products, textiles, clothing, and production machinery
CONTINENT: Europe

Jamaica

CAPITAL: Kingston
POPULATION: 2.6 million
OFFICIAL LANGUAGE: English
AREA: 4,181 sq mi/10,830 sq km
LEADING EXPORTS: alumina, bauxite, sugar, bananas, and rum
LOCATION: Caribbean Sea

Japan

CAPITAL: Tokyo
POPULATION: 126.5 million
OFFICIAL LANGUAGE: Japanese
AREA: 145,374 sq mi/376,520 sq km
LEADING EXPORTS: motor vehicles, semiconductors, and office machinery
CONTINENT: Asia

Jordan

CAPITAL: Amman
POPULATION: 6.5 million
OFFICIAL LANGUAGE: Arabic
AREA: 34,336 sq mi/88,930 sq km
LEADING EXPORTS: phosphates, fertilizers, potash, and agricultural products
CONTINENT: Asia

Kazakstan

CAPITAL: Astana
POPULATION: 16.3 million
OFFICIAL LANGUAGE: Kazakh
AREA: 1,049,150 sq mi/2,717,300 sq km
LEADING EXPORTS: oil, ferrous and nonferrous metals, and machinery
CONTINENT: Asia

Kenya

CAPITAL: Nairobi
POPULATION: 29.5 million
OFFICIAL LANGUAGES: Swahili and English
AREA: 218,907 sq mi/566,970 sq km
LEADING EXPORTS: tea, coffee, horticultural products, and petroleum products
CONTINENT: Africa

Kiribati

CAPITAL: Bairiki
POPULATION: 78,000
OFFICIAL LANGUAGE: English
AREA: 274 sq mi/710 sq km
LEADING EXPORTS: copra, seaweed, and fish
LOCATION: Pacific Ocean

Korea, North

CAPITAL: P'yongyang
POPULATION: 23.7 million
OFFICIAL LANGUAGE: Korean
AREA: 46,490 sq mi/120,410 sq km
LEADING EXPORTS: minerals and metallurgical products
CONTINENT: Asia

Korea, South

CAPITAL: Seoul
POPULATION: 46.5 million
OFFICIAL LANGUAGE: Korean
AREA: 38,120 sq mi/98,730 sq km
LEADING EXPORTS: electronic products, machinery and equipment
CONTINENT: Asia

Kuwait

CAPITAL: Kuwait City
POPULATION: 1.9 million
OFFICIAL LANGUAGE: Arabic
AREA: 6,880 sq mi/17,820 sq km
LEADING EXPORTS: oil and refined products, and fertilizers
CONTINENT: Asia

Kyrgyzstan

CAPITAL: Bishkek
POPULATION: 4.7 million
OFFICIAL LANGUAGES: Kyrgyz and Russian
AREA: 76,640 sq mi/198,500 sq km
LEADING EXPORTS: cotton, wool, meat, tobacco, and gold
CONTINENT: Asia

Laos

CAPITAL: Vientiane
POPULATION: 5.3 million
OFFICIAL LANGUAGE: Laotian
AREA: 89,112 sq mi/230,800 sq km
LEADING EXPORTS: wood products, garments, electricity, coffee, and tin
CONTINENT: Asia

Latvia

CAPITAL: Riga
POPULATION: 2.4 million
OFFICIAL LANGUAGE: Latvian
AREA: 24,938 sq mi/ 64,589 sq km
LEADING EXPORTS: wood, wood products, machinery, and equipment
CONTINENT: Europe

Lebanon

CAPITAL: Beirut
POPULATION: 3.2 million
OFFICIAL LANGUAGE: Arabic
AREA: 3,950 sq mi/10,230 sq km
LEADING EXPORTS: foodstuffs, tobacco, textiles, and chemicals
CONTINENT: Asia

Lesotho

CAPITAL: Maseru
POPULATION: 2.1 million
OFFICIAL LANGUAGES: English and Sesotho
AREA: 11,718 sq mi/30,350 sq km
LEADING EXPORTS: clothing, footwear, road vehicles, wool, and mohair
CONTINENT: Africa

Liberia

CAPITAL: Monrovia
POPULATION: 2.9 million
OFFICIAL LANGUAGE: English
AREA: 37,189 sq mi/96,320 sq km
LEADING EXPORTS: diamonds, iron ore, rubber, timber, and coffee
CONTINENT: Africa

Libya

CAPITAL: Tripoli/Benghazi
POPULATION: 5.5 million
OFFICIAL LANGUAGE: Arabic
AREA: 679,358 sq mi/1,759,540 sq km
LEADING EXPORTS: crude oil, refined petroleum products, and natural gas
CONTINENT: Africa

Liechtenstein

CAPITAL: Vaduz
POPULATION: 31,000
OFFICIAL LANGUAGE: German
AREA: 62 sq mi/160 sq km
LEADING EXPORTS: small specialty machinery, dental products, and stamps
CONTINENT: Europe

Lithuania

CAPITAL: Vilnius
POPULATION: 3.7 million
OFFICIAL LANGUAGE: Lithuanian
AREA: 25,174 sq mi/65,200 sq km
LEADING EXPORTS: machinery, equipment, and mineral products
CONTINENT: Europe

Luxembourg

CAPITAL: Luxembourg
POPULATION: 426,000
OFFICIAL LANGUAGES: French, Letzeburgish, German
AREA: 998 sq mi/2,585 sq km
LEADING EXPORTS: finished steel products, chemicals, rubber products, and glass
CONTINENT: Europe

Macedonia

CAPITAL: Skopje
POPULATION: 2 million
OFFICIAL LANGUAGE: Macedonian
AREA: 9,929 sq mi/25,715 sq km
LEADING EXPORTS: food, beverages, tobacco, and miscellaneous manufactures
CONTINENT: Europe

Madagascar

CAPITAL: Antananarivo
POPULATION: 15.5 million
OFFICIAL LANGUAGES: French and Malagasy
AREA: 224,533 sq mi/581,540 sq km
LEADING EXPORTS: coffee, vanilla, cloves, shellfish, and sugar
CONTINENT: Africa

Malawi

CAPITAL: Lilongwe
POPULATION: 10.6 million
OFFICIAL LANGUAGE: English
AREA: 45,745 sq mi/118,480 sq km
LEADING EXPORTS: tobacco, tea, sugar, cotton, and coffee
CONTINENT: Africa

Malaysia

CAPITAL: Kuala Lumpur
POPULATION: 21.8 million
OFFICIAL LANGUAGES: English and Bahasa Malay

AREA: 126,853 sq mi/328,550 sq km
LEADING EXPORTS: electronic equipment, petroleum, and liquefied natural gas
CONTINENT: Asia

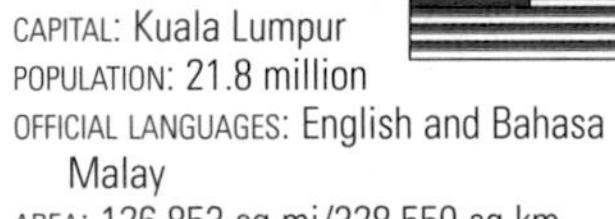

Maldives

CAPITAL: Male
POPULATION: 278,000
OFFICIAL LANGUAGE: Dhivehi
AREA: 116 sq mi/300 sq km
LEADING EXPORTS: fish and clothing
CONTINENT: Asia

Mali

CAPITAL: Bamako
POPULATION: 11 million
OFFICIAL LANGUAGE: French
AREA: 471,115 sq mi/1,220,190 sq km
LEADING EXPORTS: cotton, gold, and livestock
CONTINENT: Africa

Malta

CAPITAL: Valletta
POPULATION: 386,000
OFFICIAL LANGUAGES: English and Maltese
AREA: 124 sq mi/320 sq km
LEADING EXPORTS: machinery, transport equipment, and manufactures
LOCATION: Mediterranean Sea

Marshall Islands

CAPITAL: Delap district
POPULATION: 59,000
OFFICIAL LANGUAGES: Marshallese and English
AREA: 70 sq mi/181 sq km
LEADING EXPORTS: fish, coconut oil, and trochus shells
LOCATION: Pacific Ocean

Mauritania

CAPITAL: Nouakchott
POPULATION: 2.6 million
OFFICIAL LANGUAGES: Arabic and French
AREA: 395,953 sq mi/1,025,520 sq km
LEADING EXPORTS: fish and fish products, iron ore, and gold
CONTINENT: Africa

Mauritius

CAPITAL: Port Louis
POPULATION: 1.2 million
OFFICIAL LANGUAGE: English
AREA: 718 sq mi/1,860 sq km
LEADING EXPORTS: clothing, textiles, sugar, cut flowers, and molasses
LOCATION: Indian Ocean

Mexico

CAPITAL: Mexico City
POPULATION: 97.4 million
OFFICIAL LANGUAGE: Spanish
AREA: 736,945 sq mi/1,908,690 sq km
LEADING EXPORTS: manufactured goods, oil and oil products, silver, coffee, and cotton
CONTINENT: North America

Micronesia

CAPITAL: Palikir
POPULATION: 109,000
OFFICIAL LANGUAGE: English
AREA: 271 sq mi/702 sq km
LEADING EXPORTS: fish, garments, bananas, and black pepper
LOCATION: Pacific Ocean

Moldova

CAPITAL: Chisinau
POPULATION: 4.4 million
OFFICIAL LANGUAGE: Romanian
AREA: 13,000 sq mi/33,700 sq km
LEADING EXPORTS: foodstuffs, wine, tobacco, textiles, and footwear
CONTINENT: Europe

Monaco

CAPITAL: Monaco
POPULATION: 32,000
OFFICIAL LANGUAGE: French
AREA: 0.75 sq mi/1.95 sq km
LEADING EXPORTS: not available
CONTINENT: Europe

Mongolia

CAPITAL: Ulan Bator
POPULATION: 2.6 million
OFFICIAL LANGUAGE: Khalka Mongol
AREA: 604,247 sq mi/1,565,000 sq km
LEADING EXPORTS: copper, livestock, animal products, cashmere, and wool
CONTINENT: Asia

Morocco

CAPITAL: Rabat
POPULATION: 27.9 million
OFFICIAL LANGUAGE: Arabic
AREA: 172,316 sq mi/446,300 sq km
LEADING EXPORTS: phosphates and fertilizers, food and beverages, and minerals
CONTINENT: Africa

Mozambique

CAPITAL: Maputo
POPULATION: 19.3 million
OFFICIAL LANGUAGE: Portuguese
AREA: 302,737 sq mi/784,090 sq km
LEADING EXPORTS: prawns, cashews, cotton, sugar, and copra
CONTINENT: Africa

Myanmar (Burma)

CAPITAL: Yangon
POPULATION: 45.1 million
OFFICIAL LANGUAGE: Burmese
AREA: 253,876 sq mi/657,540 sq km
LEADING EXPORTS: pulses and beans, prawns, fish, rice, and teak
CONTINENT: Asia

Namibia

CAPITAL: Windhoek
POPULATION: 1.7 million
OFFICIAL LANGUAGE: English
AREA: 318,260 sq mi/824,290 sq km
LEADING EXPORTS: diamonds, copper, gold, zinc, and lead
CONTINENT: Africa

Nauru

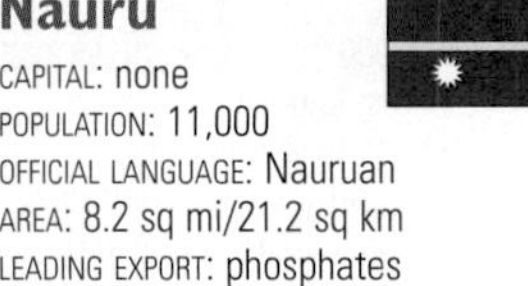

CAPITAL: none
POPULATION: 11,000
OFFICIAL LANGUAGE: Nauruan
AREA: 8.2 sq mi/21.2 sq km
LEADING EXPORT: phosphates
LOCATION: Pacific Ocean

Nepal

CAPITAL: Kathmandu
POPULATION: 23.4 million
OFFICIAL LANGUAGE: Nepali
AREA: 52,818 sq mi/136,800 sq km
LEADING EXPORTS: carpets, clothing, leather goods, jute goods, and grain
CONTINENT: Asia

Netherlands

CAPITAL: Amsterdam
POPULATION: 15.7 million
OFFICIAL LANGUAGE: Dutch
AREA: 13,097 sq mi/33,920 sq km
LEADING EXPORTS: machinery and equipment, chemicals, fuels, and foodstuffs
CONTINENT: Europe

New Zealand

CAPITAL: Wellington
POPULATION: 3.8 million
OFFICIAL LANGUAGES: English and Maori
AREA: 103,733 sq mi/268,670 sq km
LEADING EXPORTS: dairy products, meat, fish, wool, and forestry products
LOCATION: Pacific Ocean

Nicaragua

CAPITAL: Managua
POPULATION: 4.9 million
OFFICIAL LANGUAGE: Spanish
AREA: 45,849 sq mi/118,750 sq km
LEADING EXPORTS: coffee, shrimp and lobster, cotton, tobacco, and beef
CONTINENT: North America

Niger

CAPITAL: Niamey
POPULATION: 10.4 million
OFFICIAL LANGUAGE: French
AREA: 489,073 sq mi/1,266,700 sq km
LEADING EXPORTS: uranium ore, livestock products, cowpeas, and onions
CONTINENT: Africa

Nigeria

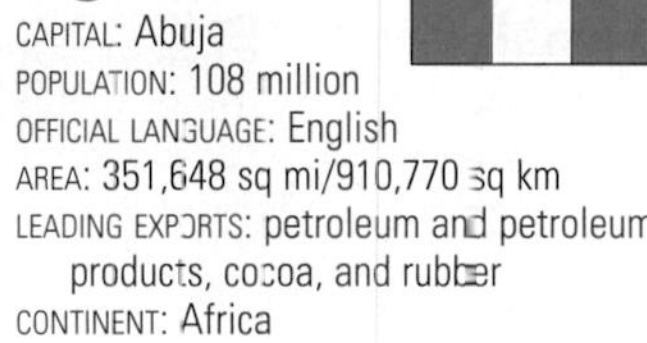

CAPITAL: Abuja
POPULATION: 108 million
OFFICIAL LANGUAGE: English
AREA: 351,648 sq mi/910,770 sq km
LEADING EXPORTS: petroleum and petroleum products, cocoa, and rubber
CONTINENT: Africa

Norway

CAPITAL: Oslo
POPULATION: 4.4 million
OFFICIAL LANGUAGE: Norwegian
AREA: 118,467 sq mi/306,830 sq km
LEADING EXPORTS: petroleum and petroleum products
CONTINENT: Europe

Oman

CAPITAL: Muscat
POPULATION: 2.5 million
OFFICIAL LANGUAGE: Arabic
AREA: 82,030 sq mi/212,460 sq km
LEADING EXPORTS: petroleum, fish, metals, and textiles
CONTINENT: Asia

Pakistan

CAPITAL: Islamabad
POPULATION: 152.3 million
OFFICIAL LANGUAGE: Urdu
AREA: 297,637 sq mi/770,880 sq km
LEADING EXPORTS: cotton, fabrics and yarn, rice, and other agricultural products
CONTINENT: Asia

Palau

CAPITAL: Koror
POPULATION: 18,000
OFFICIAL LANGUAGES: Belauan and English
AREA: 196 sq mi/508 sq km
LEADING EXPORTS: trochus (type of shellfish), tuna, copra, and handicrafts
LOCATION: Pacific Ocean

Panama

CAPITAL: Panama City
POPULATION: 2.8 million
OFFICIAL LANGUAGE: Spanish
AREA: 29,340 sq mi/75,990 sq km
LEADING EXPORTS: bananas, sugar, shrimp, and coffee
CONTINENT: North America

Papua New Guinea

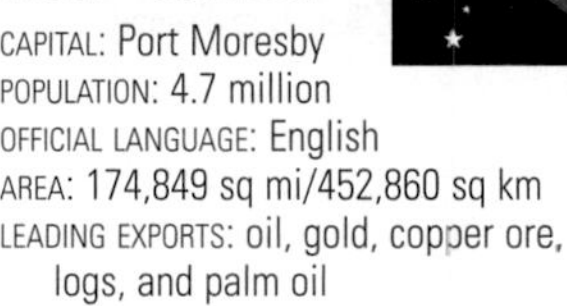

CAPITAL: Port Moresby
POPULATION: 4.7 million
OFFICIAL LANGUAGE: English
AREA: 174,849 sq mi/452,860 sq km
LEADING EXPORTS: oil, gold, copper ore, logs, and palm oil
LOCATION: Pacific Ocean

Paraguay

CAPITAL: Asunción
POPULATION: 5.4 million
OFFICIAL LANGUAGE: Spanish
AREA: 153,398 sq mi/397,300 sq km
LEADING EXPORTS: soybeans, feed, cotton, meat, and edible oils
CONTINENT: South America

Peru

CAPITAL: Lima
POPULATION: 25.2 million
OFFICIAL LANGUAGES: Spanish and Quechua
AREA: 494,208 sq mi/1,280,000 sq km
LEADING EXPORTS: fish and fish products, copper, zinc, and gold
CONTINENT: South America

Philippines

CAPITAL: Manila
POPULATION: 74.5 million
OFFICIAL LANGUAGES: English and Filipino
AREA: 115,830 sq mi/300,000 sq km
LEADING EXPORTS: electronic equipment, machinery, and transport equipment
CONTINENT: Asia

Poland

CAPITAL: Warsaw
POPULATION: 38.7 million
OFFICIAL LANGUAGE: Polish
AREA: 117,552 sq mi/304,460 sq km
LEADING EXPORTS: manufactured goods, chemicals, and machinery and equipment
CONTINENT: Europe

Portugal

CAPITAL: Lisbon
POPULATION: 9.9 million
OFFICIAL LANGUAGE: Portuguese
AREA: 35,502 sq mi/91,950 sq km
LEADING EXPORTS: machinery, clothing, footwear, and chemicals
CONTINENT: Europe

Qatar

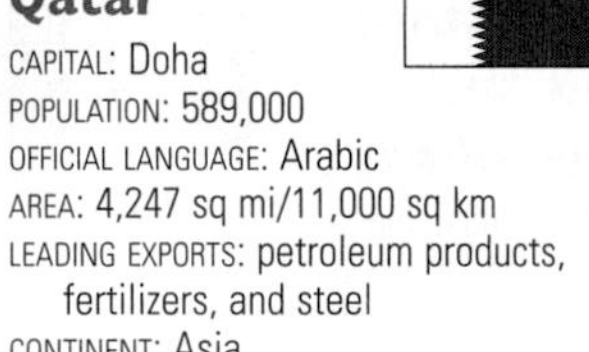

CAPITAL: Doha
POPULATION: 589,000
OFFICIAL LANGUAGE: Arabic
AREA: 4,247 sq mi/11,000 sq km
LEADING EXPORTS: petroleum products, fertilizers, and steel
CONTINENT: Asia

Romania

CAPITAL: Bucharest
POPULATION: 22.4 million
OFFICIAL LANGUAGE: Romanian
AREA: 88,934 sq mi/230,340 sq km
LEADING EXPORTS: textiles, footwear, metals, and metal products
CONTINENT: Europe

Russia

CAPITAL: Moscow
POPULATION: 147.2 million
OFFICIAL LANGUAGE: Russian
AREA: 6,592,812 sq mi/17,075,400 sq km
LEADING EXPORTS: petroleum, petroleum products, and natural gas
CONTINENT: Europe and Asia

Rwanda

CAPITAL: Kigali
POPULATION: 7.2 million
OFFICIAL LANGUAGES: French and Rwandan
AREA: 9,633 sq mi/24,950 sq km
LEADING EXPORTS: coffee, tea, hides, and tin ore
CONTINENT: Africa

Saint Kitts and Nevis

CAPITAL: Basseterre
POPULATION: 41,000
OFFICIAL LANGUAGE: English
AREA: 139 sq mi/360 sq km
LEADING EXPORTS: machinery, food, electronics, beverages, and tobacco
LOCATION: Caribbean Sea

Saint Lucia

CAPITAL: Castries
POPULATION: 152,000
OFFICIAL LANGUAGE: English
AREA: 239 sq mi/620 sq km
LEADING EXPORTS: bananas, clothing, cocoa, vegetables, and fruits
LOCATION: Caribbean Sea

Saint Vincent and the Grenadines

CAPITAL: Kingstown
POPULATION: 111,000
OFFICIAL LANGUAGE: English
AREA: 131 sq mi/340 sq km
LEADING EXPORTS: bananas, eddoes, dasheen, and arrowroot starch
LOCATION: Caribbean Sea

Samoa

CAPITAL: Apia
POPULATION: 177,000
OFFICIAL LANGUAGES: English, Samoan
AREA: 1,093 sq mi/2,830 sq km
LEADING EXPORTS: coconut oil, cream, copra, and fish
LOCATION: Pacific Ocean

San Marino

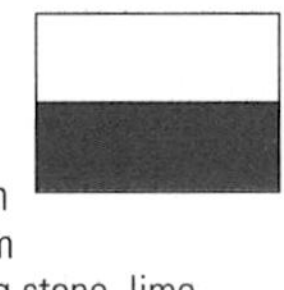

CAPITAL: San Marino
POPULATION: 26,000
OFFICIAL LANGUAGE: Italian
AREA: 24 sq mi/61 sq km
LEADING EXPORTS: building stone, lime, wood, chestnuts, and wheat
CONTINENT: Europe

São Tomé and Príncipe

CAPITAL: São Tomé
POPULATION: 135,000
OFFICIAL LANGUAGE: Portuguese
AREA: 371 sq mi/960 sq km
LEADING EXPORTS: cocoa, copra, coffee, and palm oil
CONTINENT: Africa

Saudi Arabia

CAPITAL: Riyadh
POPULATION: 20.9 million
OFFICIAL LANGUAGE: Arabic
AREA: 829,995 sq mi/2,149,690 sq km
LEADING EXPORTS: petroleum and petroleum products
CONTINENT: Asia

Senegal

CAPITAL: Dakar
POPULATION: 9.2 million
OFFICIAL LANGUAGE: French
AREA: 74,336 sq mi/192,530 sq km
LEADING EXPORTS: fish, groundnuts (peanuts), and petroleum products
CONTINENT: Africa

Seychelles

CAPITAL: Victoria
POPULATION: 75,000
OFFICIAL LANGUAGE: Seselwa (French Creole)
AREA: 104 sq mi/270 sq km
LEADING EXPORTS: fish, cinnamon bark, copra, and petroleum products (reexports)
CONTINENT: Africa

Sierra Leone

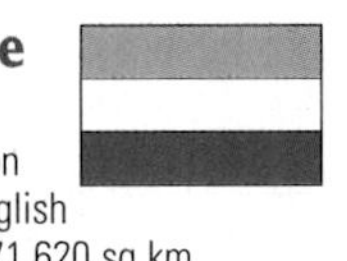

CAPITAL: Freetown
POPULATION: 4.7 million
OFFICIAL LANGUAGE: English
AREA: 27,652 sq mi/71,620 sq km
LEADING EXPORTS: diamonds, rutile, cocoa, coffee, and fish
CONTINENT: Africa

Singapore

CAPITAL: Singapore
POPULATION: 3.5 million
OFFICIAL LANGUAGES: Malay, English, Mandarin Chinese, Tamil
AREA: 236 sq mi/610 sq km
LEADING EXPORTS: machinery and equipment, chemicals, and mineral fuels
CONTINENT: Asia

Slovakia

CAPITAL: Bratislava
POPULATION: 5.4 million
OFFICIAL LANGUAGE: Slovak
AREA: 18,933 sq mi/49,036 sq km
LEADING EXPORTS: machinery, transport equipment, and manufactured goods
CONTINENT: Europe

Slovenia

CAPITAL: Ljubljana
POPULATION: 2 million
OFFICIAL LANGUAGE: Slovene
AREA: 7,820 sq mi/20,250 sq km
LEADING EXPORTS: manufactured goods, machinery, and transport equipment
CONTINENT: Europe

Solomon Islands

CAPITAL: Honiara
POPULATION: 430,000
OFFICIAL LANGUAGE: English
AREA: 10,639 sq mi/27,556 sq km
LEADING EXPORTS: timber, fish, palm oil, cocoa, and copra
LOCATION: Pacific Ocean

Somalia

CAPITAL: Mogadishu
POPULATION: 9.7 million
OFFICIAL LANGUAGES: Arabic and Somali
AREA: 242,216 sq mi/627,340 sq km
LEADING EXPORTS: livestock, bananas, hides, and fish
CONTINENT: Africa

South Africa

CAPITAL: Pretoria
POPULATION: 39.9 million
OFFICIAL LANGUAGES: Afrikaans and English
AREA: 471,443 sq mi/1,221,040 sq km
LEADING EXPORTS: gold, diamonds, other metals, and minerals
CONTINENT: Africa

Spain

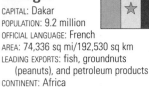

CAPITAL: Madrid
POPULATION: 39.6 million
OFFICIAL LANGUAGES: Spanish, Galician, Basque, Catalan
AREA: 192,834 sq mi/499,440 sq km
LEADING EXPORTS: machinery, motor vehicles, and foodstuffs
CONTINENT: Europe

Sri Lanka

CAPITAL: Colombo
POPULATION: 18.6 million
OFFICIAL LANGUAGES: Sinhala, Tamil, English
AREA: 24,996 sq mi/64,740 sq km
LEADING EXPORTS: textiles and apparel, tea, diamonds, and coconut products
CONTINENT: Asia

Sudan

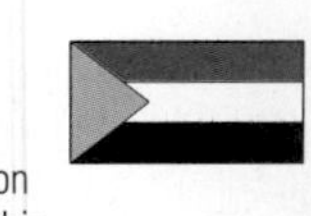

CAPITAL: Khartoum
POPULATION: 28.9 million
OFFICIAL LANGUAGE: Arabic
AREA: 917,374 sq mi/2,376,000 sq km
LEADING EXPORTS: cotton, sesame, livestock, groundnuts, and oil
CONTINENT: Africa

Suriname

CAPITAL: Paramaribo
POPULATION: 415,000
OFFICIAL LANGUAGE: Dutch
AREA: 62,344 sq mi/161,470 sq km
LEADING EXPORTS: alumina, aluminum, crude oil, lumber, shrimp, and fish
CONTINENT: South America

Swaziland

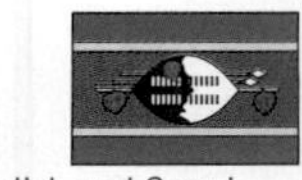

CAPITAL: Mbabane
POPULATION: 980,000
OFFICIAL LANGUAGES: English and Swazi
AREA: 6,641 sq mi/17,200 sq km
LEADING EXPORTS: soft drink concentrates, sugar, wood pulp, and cotton yarn
CONTINENT: Africa

Sweden

CAPITAL: Stockholm
POPULATION: 8.9 million
OFFICIAL LANGUAGE: Swedish
AREA: 158,926 sq mi/411,620 sq km
LEADING EXPORTS: machinery, motor vehicles, paper products, pulp, and wood
CONTINENT: Europe

Switzerland

CAPITAL: Bern
POPULATION: 7.3 million
OFFICIAL LANGUAGES: French, German, Italian
AREA: 15,355 sq mi/39,770 sq km
LEADING EXPORTS: machinery, chemicals, vehicles, metals, and watches
CONTINENT: Europe

Syria

CAPITAL: Damascus
POPULATION: 15.7 million
OFFICIAL LANGUAGE: Arabic
AREA: 71,060 sq mi/184,060 sq km
LEADING EXPORTS: petroleum, textiles, and manufactured goods
CONTINENT: Asia

Taiwan

CAPITAL: Taipei
POPULATION: 21.7 million
OFFICIAL LANGUAGE: Mandarin Chinese
AREA: 12,456 sq mi/32,260 sq km
LEADING EXPORTS: electronics, electric and machinery equipment, metals, and textiles
CONTINENT: Asia

Tajikistan

CAPITAL: Dushanbe
POPULATION: 6.1 million
OFFICIAL LANGUAGE: Tajik
AREA: 55,251 sq mi/143,100 sq km
LEADING EXPORTS: aluminum, electricity, cotton, fruits, and vegetable oil
CONTINENT: Asia

Tanzania

CAPITAL: Dodoma
POPULATION: 32.8 million
OFFICIAL LANGUAGES: English and Swahili
AREA: 342,100 sq mi/886,040 sq km
LEADING EXPORTS: coffee, manufactured goods, cotton, cashew nuts, and minerals
CONTINENT: Africa

Thailand

CAPITAL: Bangkok
POPULATION: 60.9 million
OFFICIAL LANGUAGE: Thai
AREA: 197,255 sq mi/510,890 sq km
LEADING EXPORTS: computers and parts, textiles, and rice
CONTINENT: Asia

Togo

CAPITAL: Lomé
POPULATION: 4.5 million
OFFICIAL LANGUAGE: French
AREA: 21,000 sq mi/54,390 sq km
LEADING EXPORTS: cotton, phosphates, coffee, and cocoa
CONTINENT: Africa

Tonga

CAPITAL: Nuku'alofa
POPULATION: 97,000
OFFICIAL LANGUAGES: English and Tongan
AREA: 278 sq mi/720 sq km
LEADING EXPORTS: squash, fish, and vanilla beans
LOCATION: Pacific Ocean

Trinidad and Tobago

CAPITAL: Port-of-Spain
POPULATION: 1.3 million
OFFICIAL LANGUAGE: English
AREA: 1,981 sq mi/5,130 sq km
LEADING EXPORTS: petroleum, petroleum products, and chemicals
LOCATION: Caribbean Sea

Tunisia

CAPITAL: Tunis
POPULATION: 9.5 million
OFFICIAL LANGUAGE: Arabic
AREA: 59,984 sq mi/155,360 sq km
LEADING EXPORTS: textiles, mechanical goods, phosphates, and chemicals
CONTINENT: Africa

Turkey

CAPITAL: Ankara
POPULATION: 65.5 million
OFFICIAL LANGUAGE: Turkish
AREA: 297,154 sq mi/769,630 sq km
LEADING EXPORTS: apparel, foodstuffs, textiles, and metal manufactures
CONTINENT: Asia

Turkmenistan

CAPITAL: Ashgabat
POPULATION: 4.4 million
OFFICIAL LANGUAGE: Turkmen
AREA: 188,445 sq mi/488,100 sq km
LEADING EXPORTS: oil, gas, and cotton
CONTINENT: Asia

Tuvalu

CAPITAL: Fongafale
POPULATION: 10,000
OFFICIAL LANGUAGE: English
AREA: 10 sq mi/26 sq km
LEADING EXPORT: copra
LOCATION: Pacific Ocean

Uganda

CAPITAL: Kampala
POPULATION: 21.1 million
OFFICIAL LANGUAGES: English and Swahili
AREA: 77,046 sq mi/199,550 sq km
LEADING EXPORTS: coffee, fish and fish products, tea, and electrical products
CONTINENT: Africa

Ukraine

CAPITAL: Kiev
POPULATION: 50.7 million
OFFICIAL LANGUAGE: Ukrainian
AREA: 223,090 sq mi/603,700 sq km
LEADING EXPORTS: metals, fuel, and petroleum products
CONTINENT: Europe

United Arab Emirates

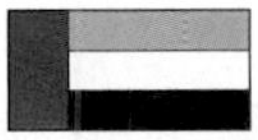

CAPITAL: Abu Dhabi
POPULATION: 2.4 million
OFFICIAL LANGUAGE: Arabic
AREA: 32,278 sq mi/83,600 sq km
LEADING EXPORTS: crude oil, natural gas, dried fish, and dates
CONTINENT: Asia

United Kingdom

CAPITAL: London
POPULATION: 58.7 million
OFFICIAL LANGUAGES: English and Welsh
AREA: 93,282 sq mi/241,600 sq km
LEADING EXPORTS: manufactured goods, fuels, chemicals, and food beverages
CONTINENT: Europe

United States

CAPITAL: Washington, D.C.
POPULATION: 281 million
OFFICIAL LANGUAGE: none
AREA: 3,717,792 sq mi/9,629,091 sq km
LEADING EXPORTS: capital goods and automobiles
CONTINENT: North America

Uruguay

CAPITAL: Montevideo
POPULATION: 3.3 million
OFFICIAL LANGUAGE: Spanish
AREA: 67,494 sq mi/174,810 sq km
LEADING EXPORTS: meat, rice, leather products, vehicles, and dairy products
CONTINENT: South America

Uzbekistan

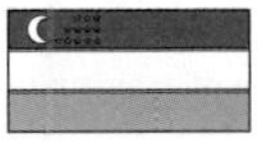

CAPITAL: Tashkent
POPULATION: 23.9 million
OFFICIAL LANGUAGE: Uzbek
AREA: 172,741 sq mi/447,400 sq km
LEADING EXPORTS: cotton, gold, natural gas, mineral fertilizers, and ferrous metals
CONTINENT: Asia

Vanuatu

CAPITAL: Port-Vila
POPULATION: 200,000
OFFICIAL LANGUAGES: Bislama, English, French
AREA: 4,707 sq mi/12,190 sq km
LEADING EXPORTS: copra, beef, cocoa, timber, and coffee
LOCATION: Pacific Ocean

Venezuela

CAPITAL: Caracas
POPULATION: 23.7 million
OFFICIAL LANGUAGES: Spanish and Amerindian languages
AREA: 340,560 sq mi/882,050 sq km
LEADING EXPORTS: petroleum, bauxite and aluminum, steel, and chemicals
CONTINENT: South America

Vietnam

CAPITAL: Hanoi
POPULATION: 78.7 million
OFFICIAL LANGUAGE: Vietnamese
AREA: 125,621 sq mi/325,360 sq km
LEADING EXPORTS: crude oil, marine products, rice, coffee, and rubber
CONTINENT: Asia

Yemen

CAPITAL: Sana'a
POPULATION: 17.5 million
OFFICIAL LANGUAGE: Arabic
AREA: 203,849 sq mi/527,970 sq km
LEADING EXPORTS: crude oil, cotton, coffee, and dried and salted fish
CONTINENT: Asia

Yugoslavia

CAPITAL: Belgrade
POPULATION: 10.6 million
OFFICIAL LANGUAGE: Serbo-Croat
AREA: 39,449 sq mi/102,173 sq km
LEADING EXPORTS: manufactured goods, food, live animals, and raw materials
CONTINENT: Europe

Zambia

CAPITAL: Lusaka
POPULATION: 9 million
OFFICIAL LANGUAGE: English
AREA: 285,992 sq mi/740,720 sq km
LEADING EXPORTS: copper, cobalt, electricity, and tobacco
CONTINENT: Africa

Zimbabwe

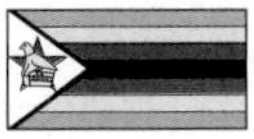

CAPITAL: Harare
POPULATION: 11.5 million
OFFICIAL LANGUAGE: English
AREA: 149,293 sq mi/ 390,580 sq km
LEADING EXPORTS: tobacco, gold, ferroalloys, and cotton
CONTINENT: Africa

Glossary of Geographic Terms

basin
a depression in the surface of the land; some basins are filled with water

bay
a part of a sea or lake that extends into the land

butte
a small raised area of land with steep sides

▲ butte

canyon
a deep, narrow valley with steep sides; often has a stream flowing through it

cataract
a large waterfall; any strong flood or rush of water

◀ cataract

delta
a triangular-shaped plain at the mouth of a river, formed when sediment is deposited by flowing water

flood plain
a broad plain on either side of a river, formed when sediment settles on the riverbanks

glacier
a huge, slow-moving mass of snow and ice

hill
an area that rises above surrounding land and has a rounded top; lower and usually less steep than a mountain

island
an area of land completely surrounded by water

isthmus
a narrow strip of land that connects two larger areas of land

mesa
a high, flat-topped landform with cliff-like sides; larger than a butte

mountain
an area that rises steeply at least 2,000 feet (610 m) above sea level; usually wide at the bottom and rising to a narrow peak or ridge

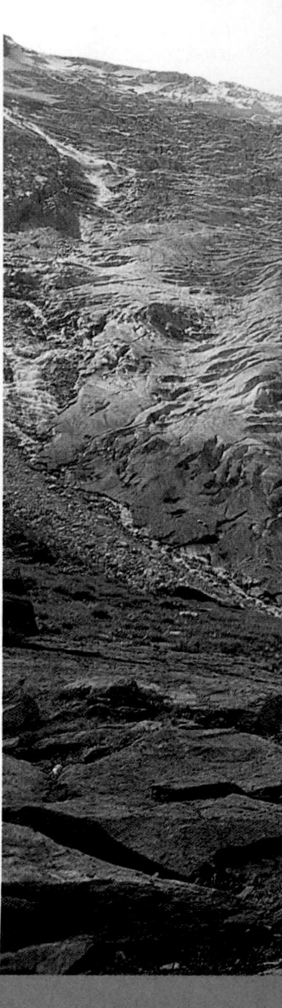

▶ glacier

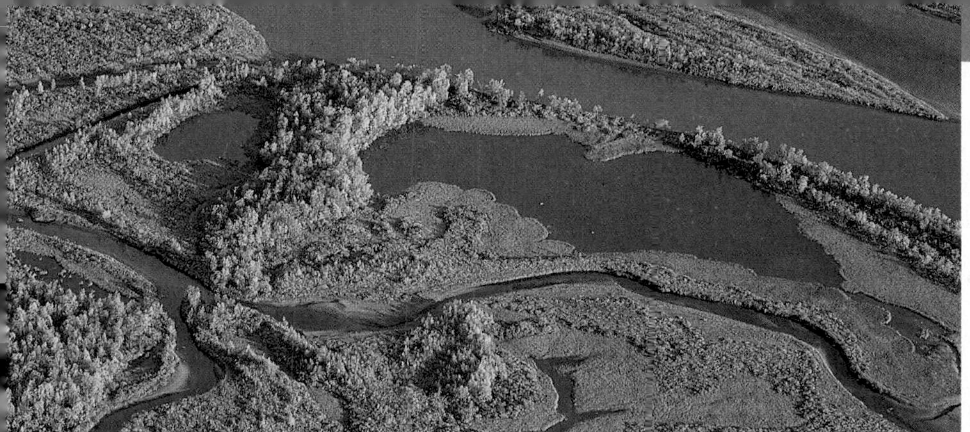

◀ delta

mountain pass
a gap between mountains

peninsula
an area of land almost completely surrounded by water and connected to the mainland by an isthmus

plain
a large area of flat or gently rolling land

plateau
a large, flat area that rises above the surrounding land; at least one side has a steep slope

river mouth
the point where a river enters a lake or sea

strait
a narrow stretch of water that connects two larger bodies of water

tributary
a river or stream that flows into a larger river

volcano
an opening in the Earth's surface through which molten rock, ashes, and gasses from the Earth's interior escape

▶ volcano

Gazetteer

A

Abuja (9°N, 7°E) the federal capital of Nigeria, p. 414

Addis Ababa (9°N, 38°E) the capital city of Ethiopia, p. 443

Adirondack Mountains a mountain range of New York State in eastern North America, p. 118

Africa (10°N, 22°E) world's second-largest continent, surrounded by the Mediterranean Sea, the Atlantic Ocean, and the Red Sea, p. 57

Aix-en-Provence (43.32°N, 5.27°E) a city in southern France, p. 232

Aksum an ancient city in northern Ethiopia, a powerful kingdom and trade center from about A.D. 200 to A.D. 600, p. 339

Alice Springs (23°S, 133°E) a town in Northern Territory, Australia, p. 662

Almaty (43°N, 77°E) the largest city of Kazakstan, a country in Central Asia, p. 607

Alpine Mountain System (46.18°N, 8.42°E) a range of mountains extending through south central Europe; a popular vacation and ski area, includes Mont Blanc and the Matterhorn; also called the Alps, p. 139

Amazon region region of northern South America occupying the drainage basin of the Amazon river, p. 115

Angkor Wat (13°N, 103°E) an archaeological site in present-day Angkor, in northwest Cambodia; the world's largest religious temple complex, p. 569

Antarctic Circle (66°S) line of latitude around Earth near the South Pole, p. 29

Antarctica (80°S, 127°E)the continent located at the South Pole; almost completely covered by an ice sheet, p. 47

Appalachian Mountains a mountain system in eastern North America, p. 35

Aral Sea (45°N, 60°E) an inland saltwater sea in Kazakstan and Uzbekistan, p. 609

Arctic region located at the North Pole, p. 59

Arctic Circle (66°N) line of latitude around Earth near the North Pole, p. 29

Asia (50°N, 100°E) the world's largest continent, surrounded by the Arctic Ocean, the Pacific Ocean, the Indian Ocean, and Europe, pp. 57, 138

Athens (38°N, 23.38°E) the capital city of modern Greece; the world's most powerful cultural center in the 400s B.C., p. 161

Auckland (36°S, 174°E) the largest city in New Zealand, located on North Island, p. 658

Australia (25°S, 135°E) an island continent in the Southern Hemisphere; a country including the continent and Tasmania, p. 57

B

Bali (8°S, 115°E) an island of southern Indonesia, p. 79

Bangladesh (24°N, 90°E) a coastal country in South Asia, officially the People's Republic of Bangladesh, pp. 87, 550

Barcelona (41.25°N, 2.08°E) a city and seaport in northeastern Spain, p. 144

Belgian Congo name for a Belgian colony in central Africa in the early 1900s, officially the Congo Free State; gained independence and became Zaire; now known as the Democratic Republic of Congo, p. 350

Belgrade (44.48°N, 20.32°E) the capital city of Yugoslavia, p. 276

Berlin (51.31°N, 13.28°E) the capital city of Germany; divided into East Berlin and West Berlin between 1949 and 1989, p. 202

Bighorn Mountains a mountain range in Wyoming, in western North America, p. 27

Buckingham Palace (51.3°N, .08°W) the palace in London, England, where the British king or queen resides, p. 228

C

Cairo (30°N, 31°E) the capital of Egypt and most populous city in Africa, p. 370

California Current a southward-flowing oceanic current along the West Coast of North America; flows between 48°N and 23°N, p. 40

Canada (50°N, 100°W) a country in North America, p. 58

Canterbury Plain the lowland area of east-central South Island, New Zealand, p. 649

Cape of Good Hope (34°S, 18°E) a province of the Republic of South Africa; the cape at the southern end of Cape Peninsula, South Africa, p. 346

Cape Town (33°S, 18°E) the legislative capital of the Republic of South Africa; the capital of Cape Province, p. 474

Caribbean Sea (14°N, 75°W) part of the southern Atlantic Ocean, p. 41

Caspian Sea (40°N, 52°E) a salt lake that is below sea level, located between Europe and Asia, p. 142

Central America the part of Latin America between Mexico and South America; includes the seven republics of Guatemala, Honduras, El Salvador, Nicaragua, Costa Rica, Panama, and Belize, p. 65

Central Uplands an area of mountains and plateaus in the center of southern Europe; region of pastureland and mining, p. 139

Chernobyl (51.17°N, 30.14°E) the city in northern Ukraine where a nuclear power station accident occurred in 1986, p. 286

China (36°N, 93°E) a country occupying most of the mainland of East Asia, p. 90

Congo River a river in Central Africa that flows into the Atlantic Ocean, p. 316

Congo, Democratic Republic of (1°S, 22°E) a country in Central Africa, formerly known as Zaire, p. 316

Cuba (22°N, 79°W) the largest island country in the Caribbean Sea, p. 65

Czech Republic (50°N, 15°E) a country in Eastern Europe, p. 212

D

Dar es Salaam (6°S, 39°E) the capital and largest city in Tanzania, an industrial center and major port on the Indian Ocean, p. 383

demilitarized zone (DMZ) a 150-mile-long strip separating North Korea and South Korea, p. 532

Denmark (56°N, 8°E) a country of northern Europe, p. 91

E

Easter Island (26°S, 109°W) an island in the eastern Pacific Ocean, part of Polynesia; known for its giant human head statues, p. 654

Egypt (27°N, 30°E) a country in North Africa, officially the Arab Republic of Egypt, pp. 85, 337

Euphrates River a river that flows south from Turkey through Syria and Iraq; the ancient civilizations of Babylon and Ur were situated near its banks, p. 599

Eurasia the landmass that includes the European and Asian continents, p. 138

Europe (50°N, 15°E) the world's second-smallest continent; a peninsula of the Eurasian landmass bounded by the Arctic Ocean, the Atlantic Ocean, the Mediterranean Sea, and Asia, pp. 57, 138

F

Florida (30°N, 84°W) a state in the southeastern United States that is largely a peninsula, p. 65

G

Galapagos Islands (0.1°S, 87°W) a group of islands located in the eastern Pacific Ocean, part of Ecuador, p. 40

Galilee the northernmost region of ancient Palestine and present-day Israel, p. 628

Ganges River a river in India and Bangladesh flowing from the Himalaya Mountains to the Bay of Bengal; considered by Hindus to be the most holy river in India, p. 545

Germany (51°N, 10°E) a country in Europe, p. 83

Ghana (8°N, 2°W) a country in West Africa, officially the Republic of Ghana, p. 341

Ghat Mountains two mountain ranges forming the eastern and western edges of the Deccan Plateau in India, p. 549

Gorée (16°N, 17°E) an island off the coast of Senegal, p. 345

Grand Bahama Island (26°N, 78°W) one of the Bahama Islands in the Caribbean Sea, p. 18

Great Britain (56°N, 1°W) common name for the United Kingdom, a country in Western Europe including England, Northern Ireland, Scotland, and Wales, p. 83

Great Dividing Range a series of plateaus and mountain ranges in eastern Australia, p. 647

Great Plains (45°N, 104°W) a dry area of short grasses located in North America, stretching from the Rio Grande at the U.S.-Mexico border in the south to the Mackenzie River Delta in the north, and from the Canadian Shield in the east to the Rocky Mountains in the west, also called "The Great American Desert," p. 46

Great Rift Valley the major branch of the East African Rift System, p. 315

Great Wall of China a fortification wall which, with all its extensions, stretched 4,000 miles (6,400 km) through China; under construction from about 600 B.C. to A.D. 1600, p. 512

Greenland (74°N, 40°W) a large, self-governing island in the northern Atlantic Ocean, part of Denmark, p. 16

Greenwich (51°N, 0°) a borough of London, England, and location of the Royal Greenwich Observatory, whose site serves as the basis for longitude and for setting standard time, p. 11

Gulf Stream a warm ocean current in the North Atlantic, flowing northeastward off the North American coast, p. 40

H

Hanoi (21°N, 106°E) capital of Vietnam, p. 9

Himalaya Mountains the Central Asian mountain range extending along the India–Tibet border, through Pakistan, Nepal, and Bhutan, and containing the world's highest peaks, p. 492

Hindu Kush a mountain range in Central Asia, p. 599

Ho Chi Minh City (10°N, 106°E) the largest city in Vietnam, named for the President of North Vietnam; formerly Saigon, p. 586

Huang He the second-longest river in China; it flows across northern China to the Yellow Sea; also known as the Yellow River, p. 493

I

India (23°N, 77°E) a large country occupying most of the Indian subcontinent in South Asia, p. 37

Indian Ocean (10°S, 40°E) the world's third-largest ocean, lying between Africa, Asia, and Australia, p. 9

Indonesia (4°S, 118°E) a country in Southeast Asia consisting of many islands, including Sumatra, Java, Sulawesi (Celebes), Bali, and the western half of New Guinea, p. 68

Indus River a river rising in Tibet and flowing through India and Pakistan into the Arabian Sea, p. 545

Iraq (32°N, 42°E) a country in Southwest Asia, officially the Republic of Iraq, p. 618

Irkutsk (52.16°N, 104°E) a city in east-central Russia, on the Central Siberian Plateau, p. 144

Israel (32°N, 34°E) a country in Southwest Asia, p. 91

Italy (44°N, 11°E) a boot-shaped country in southern Europe, including the islands of Sicily and Sardinia, p. 89

J

Jakarta (6°S, 106°E) the capital and largest city of the Republic of Indonesia, p. 68

Japan (36°N, 133°E) an island country in the Pacific Ocean off the east coast of Asia, consisting of four main islands—Honshu, Hokkaido, Kyushu, and Shikoku, p. 55

Java (8°S, 111°E) the fourth-largest island in the Republic of Indonesia, an archipelago in the Indian and Pacific oceans, p. 556

Jordan River a river in Southwest Asia flowing from Syria to the Dead Sea; Muslims, Jews, and Christians revere the Jordan, in whose waters Jesus was baptized, p. 628

K

Kalahari Desert a desert region in southern Africa, pp. 115, 314

Kano (12°N, 8°E) a city and the capital of Kano state in northern Nigeria; a historic kingdom in northern Nigeria, p. 415

Kashmir (39°N, 75°E) a disputed territory in northwest India, parts of which have been claimed by India, Pakistan, and China since 1947, p. 578

Katanga a southern province in Congo, p. 467

Kazakstan (48°N, 59°E) a country in Central Asia, officially the Republic of Kazakstan, p. 620

Kemerovo (55.31°N, 86.05°E) a city in south-central Russia, p. 290

Kharkov (49.33°N, 35.55°E) a province in eastern Ukraine, p. 288

Kiev (50.27°N, 30.3°E) the capital city of Ukraine, p. 282

Kilwa late tenth-century Islamic city-state located on an island off the coast of present-day Tanzania, p. 343

Kobe (34°N, 135°E) a seaport city in Japan, p. 31

Kuwait (29°N, 48°E) a country in Southwest Asia, officially the Republic of Kuwait, p. 605

L

Lagos (6°N, 3°E) a city and chief Atlantic port of Nigeria; a state in Nigeria, p. 414

Lalibela a town in Ethiopia famous for its stone churches carved in the 1100s, p. 443

Locorotondo (40.45°N, 17.20°E) a city in the "heel" of southern Italy, p. 253

London (51.3°N, .07°W) the capital city of the United Kingdom, p. 202

M

Madrid (40.26°N, 3.42°W) the capital city of Spain, p. 202

Maldives (4°N, 71°E) country consisting of a group of coral islands in the Indian Ocean, formerly known as the Maldive Islands, p. 9

Mali (15°N, 0.15°W) an early African empire; a present-day country in West Africa, officially Republic of Mali, p. 341

Mecca (21°N, 39°E) a city in western Saudi Arabia; birthplace of the prophet Muhammad and most holy city for Islamic people, p. 630

Mediterranean Sea (36.22°N, 13.25°E) the large sea that separates Europe and Africa, pp. 144, 599

Melanesia (13°S, 164°E) the most populous of the three groups of Pacific islands; includes Fiji, Papua New Guinea, and others, p. 650

Mesopotamia a historic region in western Asia between the Tigris and Euphrates rivers; one of the cradles of civilization, p. 615

Mexico (23°N, 104°W) a country in North America, p. 41

Micronesia one of the three groups of Pacific islands; includes Guam, the Marshall Islands, and others, p. 650

Middle Kingdom the name given to China by its Chinese leaders, p. 512

Milan (45.29°N, 9.12°E) a city in northwestern Italy, p. 252

Milky Way a galaxy consisting of several billions of stars, including the sun, p. 27

Minnesota (46°N, 90°W) a state in the north central part of the United States, p. 65

Morocco (32°N, 7°W) a country in northwestern Africa, p. 67

Moscow (55.45°N, 37.37°E) the capital city of modern Russia; the home of the czars, p. 141

Mount Everest (28°N, 87°E) highest point on Earth, located in the Great Himalaya Range in Asia, pp. 47, 497

Mount Fuji (35°N, 138°E) the highest mountain in Japan; a dormant volcano and sacred symbol of Japan, p. 490

Mount Kenya (0.10°S, 37°E) a volcano in central Kenya, p. 450

Myanmar (Burma) (21°N, 95°E) a country in Southeast Asia, p. 9

N

Nairobi (1°S, 36°E) the capital of Kenya, p. 456

Namib Desert a desert extending along the Atlantic Coast of South Africa, p. 314

Negev Desert a triangular, arid region in southwest Israel, touching the Gulf of Aquaba, p. 625

Nepal (28°N, 83°E) a country in South Asia, p. 47

Niger (18°N, 8°E) a country in West Africa, officially the Republic of Niger, p. 357

Niger River the river in West Africa that flows from Guinea into the Gulf of Guinea, p. 315

Nile River the longest river in the world, flows through northeastern Africa into the Mediterranean Sea, p. 315

Nile River valley the fertile land located on both sides of the Nile River in Africa; site of one of the earliest civilizations, p. 59

North America (45°N, 100°W) the world's third-largest continent, consisting of Canada, the United States, Mexico, and many islands, p. 57

North China Plain a large, fertile plain in northeastern China, p. 497

North European Plain a plain extending from the European part of Russia all the way to France, p. 139

North Island (37°S, 173°E) the smaller and more northern of the two islands composing New Zealand, p. 648

North Pole (90°N) northernmost end of Earth's axis located in the Arctic Ocean, p. 29

North Sea (56.09°N, 3.16°E) an arm of the Atlantic Ocean between Great Britain and the European mainland, p. 137

Northwestern Highlands a mountainous timberland in the far north of Europe, p. 139

Norway (63°N, 11°E) country in northwestern Europe occupying the western part of the Scandinavian peninsula, p. 56

Nubia an ancient region in North Africa, p. 337

O

Outback in general, a remote area with few people; specifically, the arid inland region of Australia, p. 647

P

Pakistan (28°N, 67°E) country in South Asia, between India and Afghanistan, officially the Islamic Republic of Pakistan, p. 63

Palestine (31°N, 35°E) a historical region at the east end of the Mediterranean Sea, now divided between Israel and Jordan, p. 618

Pamirs a mountain range in Central Asia, p. 599

Pangaea (pan JEE uh) according to scientific theory, a single landmass that broke apart to form today's separate continents; thought to have existed about 180 million years ago, p. 33

Papua New Guinea (7°S, 142°E) an island country in the southwest Pacific; the eastern half of New Guinea, officially the Independent State of Papua New Guinea, p. 652

Paris (48.51°N, 2.2°E) the capital city of France, p. 202

Peru Current a cold-water current of the southeast Pacific Ocean; flows between 40°S and 4°S, p. 40

Philippines (14°N, 125°E) an island country in Southeast Asia, officially the Republic of the Philippines, p. 570

Polynesia largest of the three groups of Pacific islands, includes New Zealand, Hawaii, Easter, and Tahiti islands, p. 650

R

Republic of South Africa (28°S, 24°E) southernmost country in Africa, p. 385

Rhine River (50.34°N, 7.21°E) a river flowing from Switzerland north through Germany, then west through the Netherlands, and into the North Sea in Holland, p. 142

Ring of Fire a circle of volcanic mountains that surrounds the Pacific Ocean, including those on the islands of Japan and Indonesia, in the Cascades of North America, and in the Andes of South America, pp. 31, 505

Riyadh (24°N, 46°E) the capital of Saudi Arabia, p. 631

Rocky Mountains the major mountain range in western North America, extending south from Alberta, Canada, through the western United States to Mexico, p. 35

Rome (41.52°N, 12.37°E) the capital of modern Italy; one of the world's greatest ancient empires (753 B.C.–A.D. 476), p. 164

Rub al-Khali the largest all-sand desert in the world, located on the Arabian peninsula; the "Empty Quarter," p. 597

Ruhr (51.18°N, 8.17°E) a river along the major industrial region in western Germany, p. 154

Russia (61°N, 60°E) a country in northern Eurasia, p. 138

S

Sahara largest tropical desert in the world, covers almost all of North Africa, pp. 117, 313

Sahel the region in West and Central Africa that forms a changing climate zone between the dry Sahara to the north and humid savannas to the south, p. 323

St. Louis (38°N, 90°W) a city in Missouri, p. 40

St. Petersburg (59.57°N, 30.2°E) the second-largest city in Russia (previous names: Petrograd, Leningrad), located on the Baltic Sea; founded by Peter the Great, p. 219

Samarkand (39°N, 67°E) a city in Uzbekistan, p. 621

San Francisco (37°N, 122°W) a seaport city in California, p. 8

São Paulo (23°S, 46°W) the largest city in Brazil, p. 68

Sarajevo (43.5°N, 18.26°E) the capital city of Bosnia-Herzegovina, p. 274

Semey (50°N, 80°E) a city in Kazakstan, p. 638

Senegal (14°N, 14°W) a country in West Africa, officially Republic of Senegal, p. 345

Seoul (37°N, 127°E) the capital of South Korea, p. 532

Siberia (57°N, 97°E) a resource-rich region of Russia, extending east across northern Asia from the Ural Mountains to the Pacific Coast, p. 141

Silesia (50.58°N, 16.53°E) a historic region located in today's southwestern Poland, p. 155

Silk Road a 4,000-mile-long ancient trade route linking China to the Mediterranean area in the west, p. 621

Slovakia (48.5°N, 20°E) a country in Eastern Europe, p. 211

Songhai an empire and trading state in West Africa founded in the 1400s, p. 342

South America (15°S, 60°W) the world's fourth-largest continent, bounded by the Caribbean Sea, the Atlantic Ocean, and the Pacific Ocean, and linked to North America by the Isthmus of Panama, p. 40

South Island (42°S, 169°E) the larger and more southern of the two islands composing New Zealand, p. 648

South Pole (90°S) southernmost end of Earth's axis, located in Antarctica, p. 29

Sudan (14°N, 28°E) a country in north central Africa, officially the Republic of Sudan, p. 24

Sydney (33°S, 151°E) the capital of New South Wales, on the southeastern coast of Australia, p. 660

T

Taiwan (23°N, 122°E) a large island country off the southeast coast of mainland China, formerly Formosa; since 1949, the Nationalist Republic of China, pp. 9, 525

Thailand (16°N, 101°E) a country in Southeast Asia, officially the Kingdom of Thailand, p. 554

Tigris River a river that flows through Turkey, Iraq, and Iran to the Persian Gulf; the ancient civilizations of Nineveh and Ur were situated near its banks, p. 599

Tokyo (35°N, 139°E) capital and largest city of Japan, p. 55

Tombouctou (16°N, 3°W) city in Mali near the Niger River; in the past an important center of Islamic education and a trans-Saharan caravan stop (also spelled Timbuktu), p. 342

Tropic of Cancer (23.5°N) the northern boundary of the tropics, or the band of Earth that receives the most direct light and heat energy from the sun; such a region lies on both sides of the Equator, p. 29

Tropic of Capricorn (23.5°S) the southern boundary of the tropics; see above, p. 29

Turkey (38°N, 32°E) a country located in southeast Europe and southwest Asia, p. 67

U

Ural Mountains (56.28°N, 58.13°E) a mountain system in northern Eurasia forming part of the border between Europe and Asia, p. 138

V

Vatican (41.54°N, 12.22°E) an independent state situated in Rome; the seat of the Roman Catholic Church and residence of the pope, p. 249

Vietnam (18°N, 107°E) a country located in Southeast Asia, pp. 66, 550

Volga River (47.30°N, 46.20°E) the longest river in Europe, flowing from Russia through Europe to the Caspian Sea, p. 142

W

Wisconsin (44°N, 91°W) a state in the north central United States, p. 65

Y

Yugoslavia an eastern European nation which broke up in 1991; the official name of Serbia and Montenegro; the former Yugoslavia is now the nations of Yugoslavia, Bosnia-Herzegovina, Croatia, Slovenia, and Macedonia, p. 215

Yangzi the longest river in Asia, flowing through China to the East China Sea, p. 493

Z

Zaire former name of the Democratic Republic of Congo, p. 468

Zambezi River a river in Central and Southern Africa that flows into the Indian Ocean, p. 317

Zanzibar (6°S, 39°E) an island in the Indian Ocean off the coast of East Africa, part of Tanzania, p. 444

Zimbabwe (17°S, 29°E) a country in Southern Africa, officially Republic of Zimbabwe, p. 344

Glossary

This glossary lists key terms and other useful terms from the book.

A

absolute location the exact position of a place on Earth, p. 10

absolute monarch a ruler who has complete power over his or her subjects, for example, Louis XIV of France, p. 171

acculturation the process of accepting, borrowing, and exchanging ideas and traits among cultures, p. 95

acid rain rain whose high levels of chemicals can pollute or damage the environment; usually caused by pollutants from the burning of fossil fuels, p. 113

adaptations features plants have that enable them to live in their particular climate, p. 43

agriculture farming; includes growing crops and raising livestock, p. 80

alliance a mutual agreement between countries to protect and defend each other, p. 180

ally a country joined with another for a special reason such as defense, pp. 180, 583

ancestor a parent of one's grandparents, great-grandparents, and so on, p. 513

apartheid the South African system in which racial groups were separated and racial discrimination was legal, p. 474

aquaculture a cultivation of the sea; common crops are shrimp and oysters, p. 501

arable land land that can produce crops, p. 604

archipelago a group of islands, p. 493

arid hot climate that receives very little rain, with little vegetation, p. 44

artesian well a deep well drilled into the Earth to tap groundwater in porous rock, p. 662

artisan a highly trained or skilled worker, p. 587

atmosphere the multilayered band of gases that surrounds Earth, p. 35

atoll an island made of coral and shaped like a ring, p. 651

authoritarian controlled by one person or a small group, p. 468

automotive industry an industry that puts together vehicles, such as cars, vans, pickup trucks, tractors, and motorcycles, p. 581

axis an imaginary line around which a planet turns; Earth turns around its axis which runs between its North and South poles, p. 28

B

barometer an instrument for forecasting changes in the weather; anything that indicates a change, p. 75

basic business an industry that is essential for a nation to function, such as electricity, p. 88

bazaar a traditional open-air market with rows of shops or stalls, p. 401

benefit a free service or payment, p. 243

birthrate the number of live births each year per 1,000 people, p. 61

blizzard a very heavy snowstorm with strong winds, p. 42

bottomlands low land through which a river flows; flood plain, p. 102

boycott a refusal to buy or use certain products or services, pp. 355, 567

C

canal a waterway constructed or modified to improve irrigation or drainage, p. 12

canopy a layer of branches and leaves at the tops of trees in a forest, p. 44

capitalism an economic system in which people and privately owned companies own both basic and nonbasic businesses and industries, p. 89

caravan a group of traders or others traveling together, p. 621

cardinal direction one of the four compass points: north, south, east, and west, p. 19

casbah an old, crowded section of a North African city, p. 407

cash crop a crop that is raised for sale, pp. 327, 555

caste a class of people in India, p. 564

cataract a rock-filled rapid, p. 315

census a count of the people in a country, p. 417

ceremony a formal, set activity usually carried out by a group of people, p. 228

chernozem a rich, black soil found in Ukraine, p. 284

city-state a city that controls much of the land around it and has its own government, pp. 162, 343

civil war a war between groups within a country, p. 190

civilian a person who is not serving in the armed forces, p. 180

civilization a society with cities, a central government, social classes, and usually, writing, art, and architecture, pp. 336, 512

clan a group of families who claim a common ancestor, pp. 376, 513

climate the weather patterns that an area typically experiences over a long period of time, p. 38

cobblestone a round stone used with others to make streets before modern paving was invented, p. 202

Cold War a time of tension between the United States and the former Soviet Union without actual war; it lasted from about 1945 to 1991, p. 191

collective a large farm created and owned by a national government, pp. 284, 522

colonize to settle an area and take over or create a government, p. 350

colony a territory ruled by another nation, p. 171

Colosseum a stadium built in Rome about A.D. 80, p. 160

commercial farming farming that is done by companies; commercial farms are large and use modern technology; also, the raising of crops and livestock for sale in outside markets, pp. 114, 358

commune a community in which land is held in common and where members live and work together, p. 517

communication systems organized ways for people to contact each other, such as mail, telephone, radio, and computers, p. 116

communism a theory of government in which property such as farms and factories is owned by the government for the benefit of all citizens; a political system in which the central government controls all aspects of citizens' lives, pp. 90, 189

communist of or relating to a government that owns a country's large industries, businesses, and most of the land, p. 516

compass rose a map feature that usually shows the four cardinal directions, p. 19

conformal map a flat map of all of Earth that shows correct shapes but not true distances or sizes; also known as a Mercator projection after geographer Gerardus Mercator, p. 16

coniferous cone-bearing; referring to trees that bear cones to produce seeds; most have needles which they keep year-round, p. 46

constitution a set of laws that defines and limits a government's power, p. 91

constitutional monarchy a government in which a king or queen is the head of state but has limited powers, for example, the present government of Great Britain, p. 228

consumer a person who buys goods and services, p. 88

consumer goods the goods that ordinary people buy, such as food, clothing, and cars, p. 192

continental United States the geographical area that includes all states of the United States except Alaska and Hawaii, p. 57

copse a thicket of small trees or shrubs, p. 74

coral a rocklike material made up of the skeletons of tiny sea creatures, p. 651

coup the takeover of a government, often done by military force, p. 423

crust the outer skin of Earth, p. 33

cultural diffusion the movement of customs and ideas from one culture to another, pp. 95, 371

cultural diversity a wide variety of cultures, p. 373

cultural landscape a landscape that has been changed by human beings and that reflects their culture, p. 79

cultural trait a behavioral characteristic of a people, such as a language, skill, or custom, passed from one generation to another, p. 78

culture language, religious beliefs, values, customs, and other ways of life shared by a group of people, p. 78

custom usual way of doing something, p. 212

czar title of Russian emperors before the formation of the Soviet Union, p. 184

D

dam a barrier across a waterway to control the level of water, p. 12

death rate the number of deaths each year per 1,000 people, p. 61

debate argument; discussion with people arguing opposite sides of a question, p. 238

deciduous leaf-shedding; referring to trees that lose their leaves each year, such as maples and birches, pp. 46, 497

deforestation the process of clearing land of forests or trees, usually to make room for farms and homes, p. 118

degree a unit of measure used to determine absolute location; on globes and maps, latitude and longitude are measured in degrees, p. 11

deity a god, p. 617

democracy a type of government in which people rule themselves through elected representatives, pp. 91, 162

demographer a scientist who studies human populations, including their size; growth; density; distribution; and rates of births, marriages, and deaths, p. 56

desalination the removal of salt from water, p. 626

desert a dry region that has extreme temperatures and little vegetation, pp. 12, 492

desertification the changing of fertile land into land that is too dry for crops, p. 427

devastated destroyed; ruined, p. 585

developed country a country that has many industries and a well-developed economy, p. 500

developed nation a country with a modern industrial society and a well-developed economy, p. 113

developing country a country that has low industrial production and little modern technology, p. 500

developing nation a country with relatively low industrial production, often lacking modern technology, p. 113

dialect a version of a language found only in a certain region, pp. 211, 520

dictator a ruler who has complete power over a country, pp. 92, 573

direct democracy a system of government in which the people participate directly in decision making, p. 91

discriminate to treat people unfairly based on race, religion, or gender, p. 474

discrimination unfair treatment, often based on race or gender, p. 531

distortion a misrepresentation of the true shape; each map projection used by a cartographer produces some distortion, p. 15

diversify to add variety; a country can diversify its economy by producing more products, pp. 329, 535, 631

domesticate to adapt wild plants and animals for human use, p. 336

double-cropping growing two crops on the same land in a single year, p. 502

drought a long period of little or no rainfall, pp. 428, 578

dynasty a series of rulers from the same family; Chinese history is described by dynasties, p. 512

E

economic sanctions actions to limit trade with nations that have violated international laws, p. 279

economy a system for producing, distributing, consuming, and owning goods, services, and wealth, pp. 88, 328

ecosystem a community of living things and their environment; the elements of an ecosystem interact with one another, p. 117

elegant graceful and beautiful, p. 219

elevation the height of land above sea level, p. 314

emigrate to move away, or to leave one country to resettle in another, p. 238

emperor a ruler of widespread lands, p. 512

empire a large collection of people and lands ruled by a single government, p. 163

energy usable heat or power; capacity for doing work, p. 108

energy resources resources that can be used to produce energy, such as oil, coal, natural gas, water, and wind, p. 108

environment all of the surroundings and conditions that affect living things, such as water, soil, and air, p. 12

equal area map a map showing the correct size of landmasses but with altered shapes, p. 16

Equator an imaginary line that circles the globe at its widest point (halfway between the North and South poles), dividing Earth into two halves called hemispheres; used as a reference point from which north and south latitudes are measured, p. 11

equinox two days in the year on which the sun is directly over the Equator and the days are almost exactly as long as the nights; known as spring and fall equinoxes, p. 29

erode to wear away slowly, p. 428

erosion a process by which water, wind, or ice wears away landforms and carries the material to another place, p. 35

escarpment a steep cliff about 100 stories high, p. 315

ethics the standards or code of moral behavior that distinguishes between right and wrong for a particular person, religion, group, profession, and so on, p. 85

ethnic group a group of people who share the same ancestors, culture, language, or religion, pp. 211, 338, 521

export something sold to one country by another in trade, p. 500

extended family a family unit that may include parents, children, grandparents, aunts, uncles, cousins, and other relatives, often living with or near each other, pp. 84, 375

F

famine a huge food shortage, p. 535

fate final outcome; what happens, p. 214

fault cracks in Earth's crust caused by Earth's plates pushing against each other and fracturing, p. 34

fellaheen peasants or agricultural workers in an Arab country, p. 401

fertile containing substances that plants need in order to grow well, pp. 316, 493

fertilized caused to be healthy and capable of producing more plants, p. 9

feudalism a kind of society in which people worked and sometimes fought for a local lord in return for protection and the use of land, p. 166

fiord a narrow bay or inlet from the sea bordered by steep cliffs, p. 649

foreign aid economic and military aid to another country, p. 116

foreign debt money owed to foreign countries, p. 448

fossil fuel any one of several nonrenewable resources such as coal, oil, or natural gas, created from the remains of plants and animals, pp. 108, 154

free enterprise an economic system in which people are allowed to choose their own jobs and start private businesses, pp. 268, 525

G

geography the study of Earth's surface and the processes that shape it, the connections between places, and the relationships between people and their environment, p. 10

geyser a hot spring that shoots scalding water into the air, p. 648

glacial from a glacier; rocks left behind by a glacier, p. 102

global village term used for the people of Earth; referring to the way people are connected by modern transportation and communication, p. 96

global warming a slow increase in Earth's temperature due to the increasing amount of carbon dioxide in the atmosphere; if there is too much carbon dioxide in the atmosphere, more heat than normal is trapped and temperatures around the world increase, p. 121

globe a round model of Earth that shows the continents and oceans in their true shapes, p. 15

goods products that are made to be sold; cars, baskets, computers, and paper are all examples of goods, p. 88

government the system that establishes and enforces the laws and institutions of a society; some governments are controlled by a few people, and others are controlled by many, p. 90

Green Revolution changes in agriculture since the 1950s that have greatly increased the world's food supply; the Green Revolution's reliance on costly technologies and dangerous pesticides can be both financially and environmentally damaging to nations, p. 61

griot an African storyteller, p. 377

groundwater water that flows beneath the Earth's surface and is stored in sail and rock, p. 36

habitat the area in which a plant or animal naturally grows or lives, p. 118

hajj the pilgrimage made by Muslims to Mecca, p. 630

harambee the Swahili word for "let's pull together"; the campaign in Kenya begun by President Jomo Kenyatta in 1963, after the country became independent, p. 454

hemlock a pine tree with drooping branches and short needles, p. 74

herder person who takes care of a group of animals such as sheep and cattle, p. 59

heritage the customs and practices passed from one generation to the next, p. 216

high island a Pacific island that has been formed by a volcano and is usually mountainous, p. 651

high latitudes the regions between the Arctic Circle and the North Pole and the Antarctic Circle and the South Pole, p. 29

hill a landform that rises above the surrounding land and that has a rounded top; a hill is lower and usually less steep than a mountain, p. 32

Holocaust the execution of 6 million Jews by German Nazis during World War II, p. 257

homeland South African lands where blacks were forced to live during apartheid; driest and least fertile parts of the country, p. 475

homogeneous having similar members, in reference to a group, p. 521

human characteristics characteristics of a place that are related to people, p. 25

human-environment interaction how people affect the environment and the physical characteristics of their surroundings and how the environment affects them, p. 10

humanism an approach to knowledge that focused on worldly rather than religious values, p. 169

humid continental climate with moderate to hot summers but very cold winters; supporting grasslands and forests, p. 46

hunter-gatherer person who gathers wild food and hunts animals to survive, p. 335

hurricane wind and rain storms that form over the tropics in the Atlantic Ocean and produce huge waves that can destroy towns along the shore, p. 41

hybrid a plant that is a combination of two or more types of the same plant, p. 359

hydroelectric power the power generated by water-driven turbines, p. 153

hydroelectricity electric power that is produced by running water, usually with dams, p. 501

hydroponics a method of growing plants in water and nutrients rather than in soil, p. 61

I

identity a sense of belonging to a certain group or place, p. 254

immigrant a person who moves to a new country in order to settle there, pp. 64, 204

imperialism the control by one country of the political and economic life of another country or region, p. 178

import something bought by one country from another in trade, p. 499

industrial nations countries that have many industries; people in these nations use factory-made goods, consume large amounts of energy and materials, and export goods to other countries, p. 112

Industrial Revolution a period in European history during the early 1800s when products once made by hand in homes began to be made by machines in factories, p. 176

interrupted projection type of map that uses gaps to show the size and shape of land accurately; impossible to use this map to figure distances correctly, p. 16

intricate fancy; complicated; detailed, p. 218

investor a person who spends money on improving a business in hopes of making more money, p. 292

irrigate to supply dry land with water by using ditches or canals, pp. 321, 501

irrigation supplying dry land with water, p. 12

isoline lines drawn on maps to show elevation; also called contour lines, p. 57

K

key the section of a map that explains the symbols for the map features; also called a legend, p. 19

kibbutz a cooperative settlement found in Israel, p. 627

kinship a family relationship, p. 375

L

landform an area of Earth's surface with a definite shape; mountains and hills are examples of landforms, p. 32

landmass a large area of land, p. 16

latitude lines the series of imaginary lines, also called parallels, that circle Earth parallel to the Equator; used to measure a distance north or south of the Equator in degrees, p. 11

leeward side the side of a mountain away from the wind, p. 40

lichen a plant that is a combination of a fungus and alga that grows and spreads over rocks and tree trunks; found in polar climates, p. 46

life expectancy the number of years that a person is expected, on average, to live, pp. 61, 360

lineage a group of families with a common ancestor, p. 376

lingua franca a common language shared by different peoples, p. 446

literacy the ability to read and write, p. 360

loess a brownish-yellow fertile soil, pp. 153, 493

longitude lines the series of imaginary lines, also called meridians, that run north and south from one pole to the other; used to measure a distance east or west of the Prime Meridian in degrees, p. 11

low island a Pacific island that is a reef or small coral island in the shape of a ring, p. 651

low latitudes the region between the Tropic of Cancer and the Tropic of Capricorn, p. 29

M

magma layer of hot, soft rock underneath Earth's plates, p. 33

manor a piece of land owned by a lord in the feudal system, p. 166

manufacturing the process of turning raw materials into a finished product, pp. 112, 252

marine west coast moderate climate occurring in mountainous areas cooled by ocean currents; supports more forests than grasses, p. 45

marsupial an animal, such as the kangaroo or the koala, that carries its young in a body pouch, p. 646

mediterranean moderate climate that receives most of its rain in winter and has hot and dry summers; plants here have leathery leaves that hold water, p. 45

meridian an imaginary line that circles the globe from north to south and runs through both the North and South poles; the lines of longitude on maps or globes are meridians, p. 11

meteorologist scientist who studies the weather, p. 80

Middle Ages the period in European history between ancient and modern times; approximately A.D. 500–1500, p. 162

middle class a group of people that included traders, merchants, and others who were economically between the poor and the very rich, p. 170

middle latitudes the regions between the Tropic of Cancer and the Arctic Circle and the Tropic of Capricorn and the Antarctic Circle, p. 30

migrant worker a person who moves from place to place to find work, p. 386

migrate to move from one place to another, p. 337

migration the movement of people from one country or region to another in order to make a new home, pp. 64, 210, 513

mineral a natural resource that is obtained by mining, such as gold, iron ore, or copper, p. 107

moderate a group of climates found in the middle latitudes; marked by medium rainfall, seasonal changes, but temperatures rarely falling below zero, p. 45

monarch the ruler of a kingdom or empire, such as a king or queen, p. 170

monarchy a system of authoritarian government headed by a monarch—usually a king or queen—who inherits the throne by birth, p. 91

monastery a place where monks or nuns live, work, and study, p. 439

monsoons the winds that blow across East Asia at certain times of the year; in summer, they are very wet; in winter, they are generally dry unless they have crossed warm ocean currents, p. 496

moshavim small farming villages in Israel, p. 627

mosque a Muslim place of worship, p. 407

mountain usually, a landform that rises more than 2,000 ft (610 m) above sea level and is wide at the bottom and narrow at the peak, p. 32

muezzin a leader who summons Muslims to pray by chanting, p. 617

multicultural influenced by many cultures, p. 205

multiethnic containing many ethnic groups, p. 413

multiparty system two or more political parties in one country, p. 448

N

national debt the amount of money a government owes, p. 246

nationalism a feeling of pride in one's country; an elevation of one's own nation above others, p. 179

nationalist a person who is devoted to the interests of his or her country, p. 572

nationalize to put a once-private industry under national control, p. 468

NATO (North Atlantic Treaty Organization) an alliance between the United States, Canada, and other western nations; founded in 1949 to protect the interests of the member nations and to promote international cooperation, p. 215

natural resource any useful material found in the environment, p. 105

navigable wide enough and deep enough for ships to travel through, p. 143

nomad a person who moves around to make a living, usually by herding animals, trading, hunting, or gathering food, pp. 323, 520

nonrenewable resource a resource that cannot be replaced once it is used; nonrenewable resources include fossil fuels such as coal and oil, and minerals such as iron, copper, and gold, pp. 107, 605

nuclear family a family that includes parents and children, pp. 83, 375

oasis a fertile place in a desert where there is water and vegetation, pp. 321, 598

ocean current a fast-moving river-like flow of water in the ocean created by Earth's rotation, p. 40

orbit the path followed by an object in space as it moves around another, such as that of Earth as it moves around the sun, p. 28

Organization of Petroleum Exporting Countries (OPEC) organization of oil-producing countries that agree on how much oil they will sell as well as oil prices, p. 109

outlaw to make something illegal, p. 623

ozone layer the layer of gas in the upper part of the atmosphere that blocks out most of the sun's harmful ultraviolet rays, p. 119

P

Pan-Africanism a movement that stressed unity among all Africans, p. 352

parallel in geography, any of the imaginary lines that circle Earth parallel to the Equator; a latitude line, p. 11

Parliament a group of elected officials in Great Britain who help govern by deciding about taxes and other laws, p. 227

parliament a lawmaking body, p. 577

partition a division, p. 568

Pax Romana Roman peace; a 200-year period of peace that began when Augustus, the first emperor of Rome, took power in 27 B.C., p. 164

penal colony a place settled by convicts or prisoners; the British founded the first colony in Australia as a penal colony, p. 656

peninsula land area nearly surrounded by water, pp. 139, 494

permafrost soil that is permanently frozen, p. 149

petroleum an oily substance found under Earth's crust; the source of gasoline and other fuels; an energy resource, pp. 107, 605

physical characteristics the natural features of Earth, p. 25

pilgrimage a religious journey; for Muslims, the journey to Mecca, p. 342

plain a large area of flat or gently rolling land usually without many trees, p. 13

plantation a large estate, usually in a warm climate, on which crops are grown by workers living there; plantations usually raise a single crop for export, pp. 115, 382

plate in geography, a huge section of Earth's crust, p. 33

plate tectonics the theory that Earth's crust is made of huge, slowly moving slabs of rock called plates, p. 33

plateau a large, mostly flat area that rises above the surrounding land; at least one side has a steep slope, pp. 32, 314, 491

polar climates of the high latitudes that are cold all year with short summers p. 46

polder a new piece of land reclaimed from the sea; in the Netherlands, land created by building dikes and draining water, p. 137

policy one of the methods and plans a government uses to do its work, p. 162

population the people living in a particular region; especially, the total number of people in an area, p. 55

population density the average number of people living in a given area, pp. 58, 494

population distribution how a population is spread over an area, p. 55

prairie an area of grassland, p. 148

precipitation all the forms of water, such as rain, sleet, hail, and snow, that fall to the ground from the atmosphere, p. 38

Prime Meridian an imaginary line of longitude, or meridian, that runs from the North Pole to the South Pole through Greenwich, England; it is designated 0° longitude and is used as a reference point from which east and west lines of longitude are measured, p. 11

producer a person who makes products that are used by other people, p. 88

projection a representation of the Earth's rounded surface on a flat piece of paper, p. 16

propaganda the spread of ideas designed to promote a specific cause, p. 218

province a political division within a country, similar to a state in the United States, p. 277

purdah the practice of secluding women by covering their heads and faces with veils, especially in Islamic and some Hindu countries, p. 577

"push-pull" theory a theory of migration that says people migrate because certain things in their lives "push" them to leave, and certain things in a new place "pull" them, p. 65

Q

quota a certain portion of something, such as jobs, set aside for a group, p. 576

Quran the holy book of the religion of Islam, p. 342

R

radiation poisoning a sickness caused by exposure to radiation as a result of nuclear explosions, nuclear reactor accidents, or other causes, p. 638

radical extreme, p. 524

rain forest a thick forest that receives at least 60 inches (152 cm) of rain a year, p. 550

rain shadow an area on the sheltered side of a mountain that receives little rainfall, p. 146

raw material a resource or material that is still in its natural state, before being processed or manufactured into a useful product, p. 106

recession a period of time when an economy and the businesses that support it slow down, p. 530

recyclable resource a resource that cycles through natural processes in the environment; water, nitrogen, and carbon are recyclable resources, p. 107

recycle to reuse materials to make new products, p. 107

refugee a person who flees his or her country because of war or armed conflict, p. 587

region an area with a unifying characteristic such as climate, land, population, or history, p. 12

relative location the location of a place as described by places near it, p. 10

Renaissance a period of European history that included a rebirth of interest in learning and art, peaking in the 1500s, p. 169

renewable resource a natural resource that the environment continues to supply or replace as it is used; trees, water, and wind are renewable resources, p. 107

representative a person who represents, or stands for, a group of people, usually in government, p. 227

representative democracy a system of government in which the people elect representatives to run the affairs of the country, p. 91

repress to put down, keep from acting, p. 217

republic a type of government run by officials who represent the people being governed, p. 516

reserves the available supplies of something, such as oil or coal, p. 156

reunification the process of becoming unified again, p. 260

revolution a complete change in government, often achieved through violent means, p. 171

revolution one complete orbit of Earth around the sun; Earth completes one revolution every 365 1/4 days, or one year, p. 28

revolutionary relating to or causing the overthrow of a government or other great change, p. 188

ridge underwater mountains formed by the cooling of magma in the oceans, p. 34

rift a deep crack in the Earth's surface, p. 315

robot a computer-driven machine that does tasks once done by humans, p. 527

rotation the spinning motion of Earth, like a top on its axis; Earth takes about 24 hours to rotate one time, p. 28

rural having to do with country areas as opposed to cities, p. 68

rural area an area with low population density, such as a village or the countryside, p. 68

S

sanitation disposal of sewage and waste, p. 62

savanna region of tall grasses, p. 322

scale the size of an area on a map as compared with the area's actual size, p. 15

Scandinavia a historical term for a region of northern Europe that includes Norway, Sweden, and Denmark, p. 264

Scientific Revolution a movement that took place during the 1600s and 1700s, when scientists began to base their study of the world on observable facts rather than on beliefs, p. 172

security safety; freedom from needing or wanting something important, p. 244

semiarid hot, dry climate with little rain; supports only shrubs and grasses, p. 44

serf a person who lived on and farmed a lord's land in feudal times; he or she did not own land and depended on the lord for protection, p. 166

services work done or duties performed for other people, such as the work of a doctor or of a television repair person, p. 88

shrine a holy place, p. 270

silt bits of rock and dirt on river bottoms, p. 316

Slavs a major ethnic group in Eastern Europe whose members share a similar cultural background though not the same religion; there are several subgroups of Slavs, each with their own language, p. 211

smog mixture of dangerous smoke and fog caused by pollution, p. 39

social structure the ways in which people within a culture are organized into smaller groups; each smaller group has its own particular tasks, p. 82

socialism an economic system in which the government owns most basic industries, such as transportation, communications, and banking; nonbasic industries are privately owned, p. 89

souq an open-air marketplace, p. 407

sovereignty political independence, p. 422

standard of living the material quality of life, p. 606

station in Australia, a very large sheep or cattle ranch, p. 657

steppe a mostly treeless plain; in Russia the steppes are grasslands of fertile soil suitable for farming, p. 149

subarctic continental dry climate with cool summers and cold winters; supports short grasses, some areas support large coniferous forests, p. 46

subcontinent a large landmass that is a major part of a continent; for example, the Indian subcontinent, p. 543

subsidize to economically support; some governments subsidize certain industries, p. 529

subsistence farming farming that provides only enough food and animals for the needs of a family or village, pp. 115, 326

summer solstice first day of summer in the Northern Hemisphere, on which the sun shines directly overhead the Tropic of Cancer, p. 29

summit the very top, p. 491

surplus more than is needed, p. 336

Swahili an African language that includes some Arabic words, p. 342

T

taiga an enormous Russian forest, covering more than three million acres, p. 149

tariff a fee or tax that a government charges for goods entering the country, p. 207

technology tools and the skills that people need to use them; the practical use of scientific skills, especially in industry, p. 79

tectonic plate a large piece of the Earth's crust, p. 646

temperature the degree of hotness or coldness of something, such as water or air, usually measured with a thermometer, p. 38

tendril threadlike part of a climbing plant that supports the plant, p. 102

terrace a platform cut into the side of a mountain, used for growing crops in steep places, pp. 405, 502

textile a cloth product, pp. 177, 581

thunderstorm heavy rain storm with lightning and thunder, and sometimes hail, p. 42

tradition a practice or way of doing something passed from one generation to the next, p. 227

transportation systems means by which products are carried from manufacturers to consumers, p. 112

treaty a formal, legal agreement between countries, p. 585

tributary a river or stream that flows into a larger river, pp. 142, 317

tundra a region where temperatures are always cool or cold and where only certain plants, such as low grasses, can grow, pp. 46, 149

typhoon violent storm that develops over the Pacific Ocean, pp. 41, 496

unified brought together as one; united, p. 171

unique one of a kind; having no equal, p. 238

United Nations an organization of countries established in 1945 that works for peace and cooperation around the world, p. 279

urban area an area with a high population density; a city or town, p. 68

urbanization the growth of city populations caused by the movement of people to cities, pp. 68, 204

vegetation the plants in an area, p. 43

verdant green; covered with growth, p. 9

vertical climate the overall weather patterns of a region as influenced by elevation; the higher the elevation, the colder the climate, p. 47

wadi a waterway that fills up in the rainy season but is dry the rest of the year, p. 602

weather the condition of the bottom layer of Earth's atmosphere in one place over a short period of time, p. 37

weathering the breaking down of rocks by wind, rain, or ice, p. 35

welfare government help to people in need, p. 245

welfare state a country in which many services are paid for by the government, p. 243

westernization the adoption of Western culture, as is taking place in Russia and many Eastern European countries, p. 183

wind patterns ways that the wind flows over Earth; affected by the sun, p. 35

windward side side of a mountain from which the wind blows, p. 40

winter solstice first day of winter in the Northern Hemisphere, on which the sun shines directly overhead the Tropic of Capricorn, p. 29

World Bank agency of the United Nations that makes loans to member nations and private investors, encourages foreign trade, and makes investments throughout the world, p. 62

Index

The *italicized* page numbers refer to illustrations. The *m, c, p, t,* or *g* preceding the number refers to maps (*m*), charts (*c*), pictures (*p*), tables (*t*), or graphs (*g*).

A

B

D

F

H

I

J

L

N

O

Q

R

S

T

U

V

Z

Acknowledgments

Cover Design

Bruce Bond, Suzanne Schineller, and Olena Serbyn

Cover Photo

Jon Chomitz

Maps

MapQuest.com, Inc.
Map information sources: Columbia Encyclopedia, Encyclopaedia Britannica, Microsoft® Encarta®, National Geographic Atlas of the World, Rand McNally Commercial Atlas, The Times Atlas of the World.

Staff Credits

The people who made up the ***World Explorer*** team—representing editorial, editorial services, design services, on-line services/multimedia development, product marketing, production services, project office, and publishing processes—are listed below. Bold type denotes core team members.

Joyce Barisano, Margaret Broucek, **Paul Gagnon, Mary Hanisco, Dotti Marshall,** Kirsten Richert, Susan Swan, and Carol Signorino.

Additional Credits

Art and Design: Emily Soltanoff. Editorial: Debra Reardon, Nancy Rogier. Market Research: Marilyn Leitao. Publishing Processes: Wendy Bohannan.

Program Development and Production

Editorial and Project Management: Summer Street Press
Production: Pronk&Associates

Text

9, Excerpt from *Carrying the Fire* by Michael Collins. Copyright © 1974 by Michael Collins. Reprinted by permission from Farrar, Straus & Giroux, Inc. **27,** Excerpt from *North American Indian Mythology* by Cottie Burland, rev. by Marion Wood. Copyright © 1965 by Cottie Burland, Copyright © renewed 1985 by the Estate of Cottie Burland. Reproduced by permission of Reed Books. **31,** Excerpt from "The Kobe Earthquake: A Chance to Serve," by Megumi Fujiwara, *JAMA,* January 3, 1996, volume 275, p. 79. Copyright © 1996, American Medical Association. Reprinted with permission of the American Medical Association. **74,** From *My Side of the Mountain* by Jean Craighead George. Copyright © 1959 by Jean Craighead George, renewed 1987 by Jean Craighead George. Used by permission of Dutton Children's Books, a division of Penguin Books USA Inc. **102,** "Rough Country" copyright © 1991 by Dana Gioia. Reprinted from *The Gods of Winter* with the permission of Graywolf Press, Saint Paul, Minnesota.**196,** From *Pearl in the Egg* by Dorothy Van Woerkom. Copyright © 1980 by Dorothy Van Woerkom. Reprinted by permission of HarperCollins Publishers. **289, 294,** Excerpt from "New Face of Russia a Year After Coup, Ordinary Citizens Adapt to Change," by Howard Witt, *Chicago Tribune,* August 16, 1992. Copyrighted, Chicago Tribune Company. All rights reserved. Used with permission. **300,** From *Zlata's Diary* by Zlata Filipović, Translation copyright © 1994 Editions Robert Laffont/Fixot. Used by permission of Viking Penguin, a division of Penguin Books USA Inc.**323,** From *Sand and Fog: Adventures in Southern Africa,* by Jim Brandenburg. Copyright © 1994 by Jim Brandenburg. Reprinted with permission of Walker Publishing Company, Inc. **325,** From *Cocoa Comes to Mampong,* by Dei Anang. Copyright © 1949. Reprinted with the permission of Methodist Book Depot. **384,** From "African Statesman Still Sowing Seeds for Future," by James C. McKinley, Jr., *New York Times,* September 1, 1996. Copyright © 1996 by *The New York Times.* Reprinted by permission. **391,** From *The Africans,* by David Lamb. Copyright © 1982 by David Lamb. Reprinted with the permission of Random House, Inc. **403,** From "The World in Its Extreme," by William Langewiesche. Copyright © 1991 by William Langewiesche as first published in *The Atlantic Monthly,* November 1991. **421,** From *Ghana in Transition,* by David E. Apter. Copyright © 1955, '63, and '72 by Princeton University Press. Used with permission. **436,** "My Village" from *The Distant Talking Drum.* Text copyright © 1995 by Isaac Olaleye. Reprinted with permission of Wordsong/Boyds Mills Press, Inc. **437,** "Village Weavers" from *The Distant Talking Drum.* Text copyright © 1995 by Isaac Olaleye. Reprinted with permission of Wordsong/Boyds Mills Press, Inc. **445, 447,** From "Three Leaders," by Andrew Meldrum, *Africa Report,* September–October 1994. Copyright © 1994 by *Africa Report.* Reprinted by permission. **454,** From *Baricho - A Village in Kenya,* by Richard Wright. Copyright © 1993 by Warwickshire World Studies Centre. Distributed by DEDU, **457,** Cardigan Road, Leeds, LS6 1LJ, United Kingdom. Reprinted with permission of Warwickshire World Studies Centre. **457,** From "Back to No Man's Land," by George Monbiot, *Geographical Magazine,* July 1994. Copyright © 1994 by *Geographical Magazine.* Reprinted by permission. **460,** From *A Promise to the Sun* by Tololwa M. Mollel. Text Copyright © 1991 by Tololwa M. Mollel; Illustrations Copyright © 1991 by Beatriz Vidal. By permission of Little, Brown and Company. **490,** From *Living Japan* by Donald Keene. Copyright © 1959, published by Doubleday & Company, Inc. **532,** From "South Korea: A Time of Testing," by Kevin Buckley, *Geo* magazine, April 1980. **540,** From *An Introduction to Haiku* by Harold G. Henderson. Copyright © 1958 by Harold G. Henderson. Used by permission of Doubleday, a division of Bantam Doubleday Dell Publishing Group, Inc. **541,** "The Birth of a Stone," by Kwang-kyu Kim, from *Faint Shadows of Love,* translated by Brother Anthony, of Taizé (London: Forest Books, 1991). Original poem copyright © by Kwang-kyu Kim 1983, translation copyright © by Brother Anthony 1991. **584,** From "Vietnam Now," by Stanley Karnow, *Smithsonian Magazine,* January 1996. **592,** Excerpt from *The Clay Marble* by Minfong Ho. Copyright © 1991 by Minfong Ho. Reprinted by permission of Farrar, Straus & Giroux, Inc. **618,** From *Voices from Kurdistan,* edited by Rachel Warner. Copyright © 1991 by the Minority Rights Group. Reprinted with permission of the Minority Rights Group. **633, 634,** From *We Live in Saudi Arabia* by Abdul Latif Al Hoad. Copyright © 1986 by Wayland Publishers, Ltd. Reprinted with permission of Wayland Publishers Ltd. **636, 637,** From "Kazakhstan: Facing the Nightmare," by Mike Edwards, *National Geographic,* March 1993. Copyright © 1993 by the National Geographic Society. Reprinted by permission of the National Geographic Society.

Photos

iv BR, © Radhika Chalasani/Gamma Liaison International, **iv CL,** © British Museum, **iv BL,** © Connie Coleman/Tony Stone Images, **v TR,** © Robert Fox/Impact Visuals, **vi TL,** © SuperStock International, **vi BL,** Michael Rosenfeld/Tony Stone Images, **vii BL,** © J. Highet/Trip Photographic, **vii TR,** © Boyd Norton/Boyd Norton, **viii TL,** © B. Mnguni/Trip Photographic, **viii BL,** © Cary Wolinsky/Tony Stone Images, **ix CR,** Erich Lessing/Art Resource, **ix B,** © Jerry Alexander/Tony Stone Images, **x CL,** Zigy Kaluzny/Tony Stone Images, **x B,** © Matthew Neal McVay/Tony Stone Images, **1 TL,** © Rod Planck/Tom Stack & Associates, **1 TR,** © Paul Chesley/Tony Stone Images, **1 C,** © Jose Carrillo/PhotoEdit, **1 BL,** © Adam Wolfitt/Corbis, **1 BR,** © Dennis MacDonald/PhotoEdit, **1 background,** Artbase Inc., **2 BL,** Peter Carmichael/Tony Stone Images, **2 CL,** © Ken Graham/Tony Stone Images, **3 CR,** Robert Frerck/Odyssey Productions, **3 TR,** © Alan Abromowitz/Tony Stone Images, **4 TL,** © Mark Thayer, Boston, **8 CR,** © Baron Wolman/Tony Stone Images, **9 BR,** © Kevin Kelley/Tony Stone Images, **12 BR,** The Rift Valley—Lake Naivasha, by Edwin Rioba, age 16, Kenya. Courtesy of the International Children's Art Museum, **14 BL,** © British Museum, **15 CL,** © Custom Medical Stock Photo, **15 BL,** © Custom Medical Stock Photo, **15 CR,** © Custom Medical Stock Photo, **15 BR,** © Custom Medical Stock Photo, **20 CR,** © David Young-Wolff/PhotoEdit, **21 BC,** © David Young-Wolff/PhotoEdit, **24 BR,** © Stephen Studd/Tony Stone Images, **24 BL,** © Mike McQueen/Tony Stone Images, **26 CR,** © ESA/TSADD/Tom Stack & Associates, **27 BR,** © Photri, **37 BR,** © David Falconer/Tony Stone Images, **43 BR,** © Rod Planck/Tom Stack & Associates, **46 TL,** © Jonathan Nourok/PhotoEdit, **46 TR,** © John Beatty/Tony Stone Images, **46 BL,** © John Beatty/Tony Stone Images, **47,** no credit available, **49 TR,** © Grant Taylor/Tony Stone Images, **53 TR,** © David Young-Wolff/PhotoEdit, **54 CR,** © Robert Fox/Impact Visuals, **55 CR,** © Paul Chesley/Tony Stone Images, **56 BL,** © Tony Stone Images, **58 TL,** © Connie Coleman/Tony Stone Images, **58 TR,** © Bill Pogue/Tony Stone Images, **58 CR,** SuperStock International, **61 TR,** © Jason Laure'/Laure' Communications, **64 BL,** © Chris Brown/SABA Press Photos, **66 BR,** © Ted Streshinsky/Corbis, **67 T,** © Mariella Furrer/SABA Press Photos, **69 TR,** © Donna DeCesare/Impact Visuals, **70 CR,** © Earth Imaging/Tony Stone Images, **75 TL,** © Carr Clifton/Carr Clifton Photography, **76 CR,** © Lawrence Migdale/Tony Stone Images, **77 BR,** © Paul Conklin/PhotoEdit, **78 B,** © Don Smetzer/Tony Stone Images, **79 TR,** © David Young-Wolff/PhotoEdit, **82 CL,** © Donna DeCesare/Impact Visuals, **83 TL,** © David Young-Wolff/PhotoEdit, **83 TR,** © Inga Spence/Tom Stack & Associates, **83 CL,** © Andrew Errington/Tony Stone Images, **87 BR,** © Julia Vindasius/Vindasius, **88 B,** © Ithaca Money, **89 TL,** © AP/World Wide Photos, **90 BR,** Untitled, by Olga Loceva, age 14, Russia. Courtesy of the International Children's Art Museum, **91 TR,** © Adam Woolfitt/Corbis, **92 TL,** © Hulton Deutsch Collection/Corbis, **93 BR,** © Robert Frerck/Tony Stone Images, **94 TL,** © Felicia Martinez/PhotoEdit, **95 BR,** © The Granger Collection, **97 TR,** © Jose Carrillo/PhotoEdit, **98 B,** © Billy E. Barnes/PhotoEdit, **103 TL,** © Philip & Karen Smith/Tony Stone Images, **103 TR,** Peter Pearson/Tony Stone Images, **103 TC,** © Bruce Hands/Tony Stone Images, **104 CR,** © Manfred Gottschalk/Tom Stack & Associates, **105 BR,** © SuperStock International, **107 BR,** © Larry Tackett/Tom Stack & Associates, **110 TR,** © Dennis MacDonald/PhotoEdit, **112 T,** © Paul Conklin/PhotoEdit, **113 BR,** © Andy Sacks/Tony Stone Images, **115 BR,** © Radhika Chalasani/Gamma Liaison International, **116 TR,** © Jean-Marc Giboux/Gamma Liaison International, **117 BR,** © Mike Bacon/Tom Stack & Associates, **118 BL,** © Rich Frishman/Tony Stone Images, **121 C,** © David M. Dennis/Tom Stack & Associates, **122 TR,** © Jonathan Nourok/PhotoEdit, **123 B,** © Michael Newman/PhotoEdit, **126 BL,** © Mark Thayer, Boston, **127 TR,** © Roger Chester/Trip Photographic, **129 TL,** © Robert Wallis/Sipa Press, **129 TR,** © Superstock International, **129 C,** © Superstock International, **129 CL,** © Superstock International, **129 CR,** © George Steinmetz, **129 background,** Artbase Inc., **133 C,** © Mark Thayer, Boston, **136 CR,** © Julian Calder/Tony Stone Images, **137 BR,** © B. & C. Alexander/Bryan & Cherry Alexander Photography, **138 BL,** © M. Feeney/Trip Photographic, **139 B,** © W. Jacobs/Trip Photographic, **141 TR,** © James Balog/Tony Stone Images, **142 CR,** © Robert Wallis/Sipa Press, **143 TL,** © Adam Woolfitt/Woodfin Camp & Associates, **144 BL,** © D. MacDonald/Trip Photographic, **147 BL,** My Family in Winter, by Helin Tikerpuu, age 12, Estonia. Courtesy of the International Children's Art Museum, **152 BL,** © Arnulf Husmo/Tony Stone Images, **155 CR,** © Eastcott/Momatiuk/Woodfin Camp & Associates, **157 TL,** © Wolfgang Kaehler/Wolfgang Kaehler Photography, **157 TR,** © Wolfgang Kaehler/Wolfgang Kaehler Photography, **160 CR,** © N. Ray/Trip Photographic, **161 BR,** © Matthew Stockman/AllSport USA, **163 TR,** © SuperStock International, **164 TR,** © Scala/Art Resource, **165 C,** © Erich Lessing/Art Resource, **166 BL,** © Marie Ueda/Tony Stone Images, **168 BL,** © The Granger Collection, **169 TR,** © Biblioteca Reale, Turin, Italy/SuperStock International, **169 TL,** © Erich Lessing/Art Resource, **170 BR,** The Granger Collection, **170 BL,** The Granger Collection, **171 TR,** © SuperStock International, **172 CL,** © Explorer, Paris/SuperStock International, **172 TR,** © SuperStock International, **174 B,** © Michael Newman/PhotoEdit, **176 BL,** © North Wind Picture Archives, **177 TL,** © The Granger Collection, **178 TL,** © The Bettmann Archive/Corbis-Bettmann, **178 TR,** © The Bettmann Archive/Corbis-Bettmann, **178 TL,** © Stock Montage, **180 B,** © The Granger Collection, **181 TL,** © AP/Wide World Photos, **182 BL,** © Historical Museum, Moscow, Russia/SuperStock International, **183 BR,** © Bridgeman/Art Resource, **185 BL,** © Charles Lenars/CORBIS/MAGMA, **186 BR,** © Stock Montage, **187 TL,** © SuperStock International, **188 BL,** © Novosti/Corbis-Bettmann, **189 TC,** © SuperStock International, **190 BL,** © The Granger Collection, **191 TC,** © UPI/Corbis-Bettmann, **192 B,** © Reuters/Corbis-Bettmann, **193 TL,** © SuperStock International, **197 BR,** © Giraudon/Art Resource, **198 TR,** © Erich Lessing/Art Resource, **200 CR,** © SuperStock International, **201 BR,** © David Barnes/Stock Market, **202 B,** © Stephen Johnson/Tony Stone Images, **202 CL,** © SuperStock International, **203 TR,** © SuperStock International, **205 BL,** © Joseph Okwesa/Trip Photographic, **206 CR,** © UPI/Corbis-Bettmann, **207 TL,** © Michael Rosenfeld/Tony Stone Images, **209 TL,** © Michael Newman/PhotoEdit, **210 BL,** © North Wind Picture Archives, **212 TR,** © Alain Le Garsmeur/Tony Stone Images, **212 TL,** © Ibrahim/Trip Photographic, **213 BL,** Prague Castle, by Darina Vassova, age 10, Czech Republic. Courtesy of the International Children's Art Museum, **215 TL,** © AP/Wide World Photos, **216 BL,** © SuperStock International, **217 BR,** SuperStock International, **217 BL,** © A. Kuznetsov/Trip Photographic, **218 TR,** © Alexandra Avakian/Woodfin Camp & Associates, **219 CL,** © Joseph Coscia, Jr., Metropolitan Museum of Art, The FORBES Magazine Collection, New York. All rights reserved/Forbes, **220 B,** © Wolfgang Kaehler/Wolfgang Kaehler Photography, **220 CL,** © J. Wiseman/Trip Photographic, **221 TR,** © Sichuv/Sipa Press, **225 BC,** © John Drysdale/Woodfin Camp & Associates, **227 BL,** © AP/Wide World Photos, **227 BR,** © The Bettmann Archive/Corbis-Bettmann, **228 TR,** © SuperStock International, **228 CL,** © Stuart Westmorland/Tony Stone Images, **230 BR,** © John Madere/Stock Market, **232 BL,** © Chad Ehlers/Tony Stone Images, **233 BL,** © Miles Ertman/Masterfile, **234 BR,** © SuperStock International, **236 BR,** © Corbis-Bettmann, **237 TL,** © George Hunter/Tony Stone Images, **237 CR,** © Chad Ehlers/Tony Stone Images, **238 BR,** © AP/Wide World Photos, **238 BL,** © SuperStock International, **239 TR,** © A. M. Bazalik/Trip Photographic, **240 B,** © Michael Newman/PhotoEdit, **242 BL,** © Joseph Nettis/Tony Stone Images, **243 CL,** © Trip/C. Gibson, **244 TR,** © Gary A. Conner, **245 B,** © SuperStock International, **246 TR,** © Raymond Reuter/Sygma, **247 BL,** © Chad Ehlers/Tony Stone Images, **247 BR,** © Lorentz Gullachsen/Tony Stone Images, **248 TR,** © J. Merryweather/Trip Photographic, **249 BR,** © Jean Pragen/Tony Stone Images, **250 CL,** © John Heseltine/Dorling Kindersley, **251 BL,** © Mary Altier/Mary Altier Photography, **252 BL,** © George Steinmetz, **252 BR,** © The Granger Collection, **253 TC,** © SuperStock International, **254 TC,** © Archive Photos, **255 BR,** © AP/Wide World Photos, **256 CL,** © Helga Lade/Peter Arnold, **258 BR,** © AP/Wide World Photos, **258 BL,** © UPI/Corbis-Bettmann, **259 TL,** © AP/Wide

World Photos, **260 TL,** © SuperStock International, **260 TR,** © Corbis-Bettmann, **261 T,** © Owen Franken/Corbis, **264 CR,** © Michael Newman/PhotoEdit, **265 TR,** © David Young-Wolff, **267 BR,** © Momatiuk/Eastcott/Woodfin Camp & Associates, **268 CL,** James P. Blair/National Geographic Image Collection, **269 BL,** © Reuters/Corbis-Bettman, **269 BR,** © SIPA Press, **270 TR,** © Henryk T. Kaiser/Envision, **272 B,** © Bob & Ira Spring/Kirkendahl Spring Photography, **273 TL,** © Tony Stone Images, **274 BL,** © Peter Northall/Black Star Publishing/PictureQuest, **276 B,** Hulton Archive/Getty Images, **278 BR,** © AP/Wide World Photos, **278 BC,** © Ibrahim/Trip Photographic, **279 CR,** © Associated Press/Reuters/Canpress, **282 BL,** © AP Wide World Photos, **283 CL,** Dean Conger/National Geographic Image Collection, **284 BR,** © W. Jacobs/Trip Photographic, **285 T,** © SuperStock International, **286 TR,** © Corbis-Bettmann, **286 CR,** © Wojtek Laski/Sipa Press, **287 BL,** © UPI/Corbis-Bettmann, **287 TR,** © UPI/Corbis-Bettmann, **288 TR,** © SuperStock International, **289 B,** © SIPA Press, **290 CL,** Steven L. Raymer/National Geographic Image Collection, **291 TL,** © Wolfgang Kaehler/Wolfgang Kaehler Photography, **292 B,** © B. & C. Alexander/Bryan & Cherry Alexander Photography, **292 BL,** © B. & C. Alexander/Bryan & Cherry Alexander Photography, **293 TL,** © B. Turner/Trip Photographic, **294 BR,** © SuperStock International, **295 TL,** © Peter Wilson/Private Collection/Bridgman Art Library, **295 TR,** © J. Lee/Tropix Photographic Library, **298 BR,** © Kevin Schafer/Tony Stone Images, **301 TL,** © Paul Lowe/Magnum Photos, **302 BL,** © Mark Thayer, Boston, **303 CR,** © SuperStock International, **305 CL,** Reuters/Corbis-Bettman, **305 TL,** Comstock, **305 C,** © Robert, Frerck/Odyssey Productions, **305 TR,** © Courtsey of Museum of Fine Arts Boston, **305 CR,** © Betty Press/Woodfin Camp & Associates, **305 background,** Artbase Inc., **309 CR,** © Mark Thayer, Boston, **313 BR,** © Paul C. Sereno/Paul C. Sereno, **314 B,** © Robert Frerck/Odyssey Productions, **314 CL,** © Wendy Stone/Odyssey Productions, **315 TR,** © G. Winters/Trip Photographic, **316 TL,** © SuperStock International, **317 CL,** © Comstock, **318 TR,** © Steve McCutcheon/Visuals Unlimited, **319 BR,** © Frans Lanting/Minden Pictures, **321 BR,** © Don W. Fawcett/Visuals Unlimited, **323 TR,** © Nicholas Parfitt/Tony Stone Images, **324 TR,** © Penny Tweedle/Tony Stone Images, **325 BR,** © Victor Englebert/Victor Englebert Photography, **325 BC,** © Cabisco/Visuals Unlimited, **326 BL,** © Victor Englebert/Victor Englebert Photography, **326 BR,** © Wendy Stone/Odyssey Productions, **326 BC,** © Brian Seed/Tony Stone Images, **329 CR,** © Ian Murphy/Tony Stone Images, **330 B,** © David Young-Wolff/PhotoEdit, **335 BR,** © The Granger Collection, **336 C,** © Lee Boltin/Boltin Picture Library, **336 TC,** © Lee Boltin/Boltin Picture Library, **336 TL,** © Lee Boltin/Boltin Picture Library, **337 TL,** © Courtesy of Museum of Fine Arts Boston, **339 BR,** © H. Rogers/Trip Photographic, **341 TC,** © The Granger Collection, **343 C,** © The Granger Collection, **343 TL,** © SuperStock International, **344 TL,** © Jason Laure'/Laure' Communications, **345 BR,** © Erich Lessing/Art Resource, **346 B,** © Robert Frerck/Odyssey Productions, **348 BL,** © The Granger Collection, **348 BR,** © The Granger Collection, **351 BR,** © Jason Laure'/Laure' Communications, **352 BR,** © L. P. Winfrey/Woodfin Camp & Associates, **353 TL,** © UPI/Corbis-Bettmann, **355 BR,** © UPI/Corbis-Bettmann, **356 TR,** © Wolfgang Kaehler/Wolfgang Kaehler Photography, **357 BR,** © W. Jacobs/Trip Photographic, **360 T,** © Jason Laure'/Laure' Communications, **361 TL,** © Marc & Evelyn Bernheim/Woodfin Camp & Associates, **362 B,** © Bill Aron/PhotoEdit, **366 CR,** © M. & E. Bernheim/Woodfin Camp & Associates, **367 BR,** © Glen Allison/Tony Stone Images, **368 B,** © Robert Frerck/Woodfin Camp & Associates, **369 CR,** © Robert Azzi/Woodfin Camp & Associates, **370 TL,** © Bob Smith/Trip Photographic, **370 TR,** © Ben Nakayama/Tony Stone Images, **372 TR,** © Lorne Resnick/Tony Stone Images, **373 BR,** © Jason Laure'/Laure' Communications, **374 BR,** © Wolfgang Kaehler/Wolfgang Kaehler Photography, **375 TL,** © Wolfgang Kaehler/Wolfgang Kaehler Photography, **375 TR,** © M. & V. Birley/Tropix Photographic Library, **376 B,** © Wolfgang Kaehler/Wolfgang Kaehler Photography, **377 TL,** © Betty Press/Woodfin Camp & Associates, **378 TR,** © M. & E. Bernheim/Woodfin Camp & Associates, **379 BR,** © Victor Englebert/Victor Englebert Photography, **380 C,** © Robert Frerck/Odyssey Productions, **381 TL,** © P. Joynson-Hicks/Trip Photographic, **382–383 C,** © D. Saunders/Trip Photographic, **384 TL,** © Boyd Norton/Boyd Norton, **385 BR,** © Jason Laure'/Laure' Communications, **386 CL,** © Jason Laure'/Laure' Communications, **387 TC,** © Jason Laure'/Laure' Communications, **388 BR,** © D. Davis/Tropix Photographic Library, **389 TL,** © Robert Caputo/Aurora & Quanta Productions, **390 BL,** © Betty Press/Woodfin Camp & Associates, **391 CL,** © Michael Newman/PhotoEdit, **394 CR,** © M. & E. Bernheim/Woodfin Camp & Associates, **395 BL,** © Adam Novick/Village Pulse, **397 BR,** © P. Mitchell/Trip Photographic, **398, CL,** © Carmen Redondo/CORBIS/MAGMA, **399 TL,** © Roland & Sabrina Michaud/Woodfin Camp & Associates, **400 B,** © Donna DeCesare/Impact Visuals, **401 TL,** © Israel Talby/Woodfin Camp & Associates, **402 T,** © Don Smetzer/Tony Stone Images, **403 BL,** © Victor Englebert/Victor Englebert Photography, **404 CL,** © Andrea Jemolo/CORBIS/MAGMA, **405 BC,** © Sylvain Grandadam/Tony Stone Images, **406 TL,** © Sean Sprague/Impact Visuals, **407 TR,** © Victor Englebert/Victor Englebert Photography, **407 TL,** © Wendy Stone/Odyssey Productions, **414 CL,** © Paul Almasy/CORBIS/MAGMA, **415 BR,** © Marc & Evelyn Bernheim/Woodfin Camp & Associates, **416 TR,** © Robert Frerck/Odyssey Productions, **417 B,** © J. Highet/Trip Photographic, **417 TR,** © Sylvan Wittwer/Visuals Unlimited, **418 TC,** © Trip/Trip Photographic, **419 BR,** © AP/Wide World Photos, **420 CL,** Milepost 92 1/2/CORBIS/MAGMA, **421 BC,** © Frank Fournier/Woodfin Camp & Associates, **422 TL,** © Tim Beddow/Tony Stone Images, **423 CR,** © AP/Wide World Photos, **424 CL,** © M. & V. Birley/Tropix Photographic Library, **424 CR,** © M. & V. Birley/Tropix Photographic Library, **425 BR,** © M. Jelliffe/Trip Photographic, **427 BL,** © Norman Myers/Bruce Coleman Inc., **428 BC,** © Wolfgang Kaehler/Wolfgang Kaehler Photography, **429 TL,** © Betty Press/Woodfin Camp & Associates, **430 BL,** © Michael Newman/PhotoEdit, **434 BR,** © David Young-Wolff/PhotoEdit, **435 TR,** © David Young-Wolff/PhotoEdit, **436 BC,** © Betty Press/Woodfin Camp & Associates, **437 C,** © Lawrence Manning/Tony Stone Images, **439 BR,** © Robert Caputo/Aurora & Quanta Productions, **441 BR,** © The Granger Collection, **441 BL,** © The Granger Collection, **443 TR,** © R. Ashford/Tropix Photographic Library, **444 BL,** © AP/Wide World Photos, **445 CL,** © Miller Photography/Animals Animals, **446 TR,** © Reuters/Corbis-Bettmann, **447 B,** © M. & V. Birley/Tropix Photographic Library, **448 BR,** © Gerald Cubitt/Gerald Cubitt Photographer, **448 BL,** © Gerald Cubitt/Gerald Cubitt Photographer, **449 T,** © AP/Wide World Photos, **450 BL,** © James P. Rowan/Tony Stone Images, **452 BL,** © M. & E. Bernheim/Woodfin Camp & Associates, **453,** Dorling Kindersley Picture Library, **454 TL,** © Betty Press/Woodfin Camp & Associates, **455 BL,** © Victor Englebert/Victor Englebert Photography, **456 BR,** Matutu Ride, by Ian Kamau, Kenya. Courtesy of the International Children's Art Museum, **461 TR,** © Marc Chamberlain/Tony Stone Images, **462 BL,** © Tim Davis/Tony Stone Images, **465 BL,** © Jason Laure'/Laure' Communications, **466 CL,** Paul Almasy/CORBIS/MAGMA, **467 BR,** © M. Jelliffe/Trip Photographic, **468 BL,** © Betty Press/Woodfin Camp & Associates, **470 BL,** © Michael Newman/PhotoEdit, **472 BL,** © B. Mnguni/Trip Photographic, **473 CL,** © Paul Almasy/CORBIS/MAGMA, **474 BL,** © Jason Laure'/Laure' Communications, **475 TR,** © Paula Bronstein/Impact Visuals, **476 BR,** © African Institute of Art, Funda Art Centre in Soweto, **477 CR,** © Reuters/Corbis-Bettman, **480 BL,** © Mark Thayer, Boston, **481 CR,** © Betty Press/Woodfin Camp & Associates, **483 background,** © Artbase Inc., **483 C** Andrea Booher/Tony Stone Images **487 TR,** © Mark Thayer, Boston, **488 B,** © Art Wolfe/Tony Stone Images, **490 CR,** © Wendy Chan/The Image Bank, **491 BR,** © Scott Fisher/Woodfin Camp & Associates, **494 TR,** © Deke Erh/Woodfin Camp & Associates, **495 BR,** © Dave Bartruff/Artistry International, **497 TR,** © Musee Guimet, Paris, France/Lauros-Giraudon, **498 TR,** © Reuters/Will Burgess/Archive Photos, **499 BR,** © D. E. Cox/Tony Stone Images, **501 BL,** © Ettagale Blauer/Woodfin Camp & Associates, **501 BR,** © Mark Lewis/Tony Stone Images, **502 CR,** © Karen Kasmauski/Woodfin Camp & Associates, **502 B,** © Wolfgang Kaehler/Wolfgang Kaehler Photography, **503 TL,** ©

Baldev/SYGMA, **504 B,** © Michael Newman/PhotoEdit, **505 BR,** © Greg Vaughn/Tony Stone Images, **508 B,** © Howard Sochurek/Woodfin Camp & Associates, **510 CR,** © Mike Surowiak/Tony Stone Images, **511 BR,** © Vanni/Art Resource, **513 CR,** © Lee Boltin/Boltin Picture Library, **517 BR,** © Cary Wolinsky/Tony Stone Images, **518 TR,** © A. Ramey/Woodfin Camp & Associates, **519 B,** © Matthew Neal McVay/Tony Stone Images, **521 TL,** Untitled, by Chen Di, age 12, China. Courtesy of the International Children's Art Museum. **522 BL,** © D. E. Cox/Tony Stone Images, **523 CL,** Ric Ergenbright/CORBIS/MAGMA, **524 BR,** © William Sewell/E.T. Archive, **527 BR,** © Karen Kasmauski/Woodfin Camp & Associates, **528 CL,** Michael S. Yamashita/CORBIS/MAGMA, **529 TL,** © AP/Wide World Photos, **530 B,** © Ettagale Blauer/Laure' Communications, **531 C,** © Cameramann International, Ltd., **532 BL,** © SuperStock International, **534 T,** © Kim Newton/Woodfin Camp & Associates, **536 CR,** © Philadelphia Free Library/SuperStock International, **540 BR,** © Janette Ostier Gallery, Paris France/SuperStock International, **541 TL,** © Corbis-Bettman, **542 CR,** © Photri, **543 BR,** © D. Jenkin/Tropix Photographic Library, **546 CL,** © Chuck O'Rear/Woodfin Camp & Associates, **547 BR,** © Jason Laure'/Laure' Communications, **550 T,** In the Park, by Atima, age 11, India. Courtesy of the International Children's Art Museum, **551 TL,** © Wolfgang Kaehler/Wolfgang Kaehler Photography, **551 TR,** © M. Aukland/Tropix Photographic Library, **552 B,** © Wolfgang Kaehler/Wolfgang Kaehler Photography, **553 BL,** © Charles Preitner/Visuals Unlimited, **553 BR,** © Christopher Arnesen/Tony Stone Images, **554 B,** © Robert Frerck/Woodfin Camp & Associates, **555 TR,** © Robert Frerck/Woodfin Camp & Associates, **557 TL,** © Mickey Gibson/Animals Animals, **562 CR,** © Brian Vikander/CORBIS/MAGMA, **563 BR,** © Dilip Mehta/Woodfin Camp & Associates, **566 BR,** © M.M.N./Dinodia Picture Agency, **566 BL,** © Cameramann International, **567 T,** © Wolfgang Kaehler/Wolfgang Kaehler Photography, **568 TR,** © SuperStock International, **569 B,** © Jerry Alexander/Tony Stone Images, **570 T,** © Mike Yamashita/Woodfin Camp & Associates, **570 B,** © Steve Vidler/Tony Stone Images, **572 BR,** © UPI/Corbis-Bettman, **573 T,** © AP/Wide World Photos, **574 BL,** © Ann & Bury Peerless/Ann & Bury Peerless, **575 CR,** © Eye Ubiqitous/CORBIS/MAGMA, **576 BR,** © Steve Vidler/Tony Stone Images, **576 BL,** © Joel Simon/Tony Stone Images, **577 TC,** © Jason Laure'/Laure' Communications, **578 BL,** © SuperStock International, **579 BL,** Roger Wood/CORBIS/MAGMA, **580 BR,** © Charles Preitner/Visuals Unlimited, **581 TL,** © D Forbert/Photri, **582 TR,** © Photri, **583 BR,** © Natalie Fobes/Tony Stone Images, **584 C,** Bohemian Nomad Picturemakers/CORBIS/MAGMA, **585 top left,** © Arthur R. Hill/Visuals Unlimited, **586 BL,** © Radhika Chalasani/Gamma Liaison International, **587 TL,** © Wolfgang Kaehler/Wolfgang Kaehler Photography, **593 TL,** © Leah Melnick/Impact Visuals, **594 TR,** © SuperStock International, **596 CL,** © Tom Till/Tony Stone Images, **597 BR,** © Tony Howarth/Woodfin Camp & Associates, **599 BL,** © Buddy Mays/Travel Stock, **599 CR,** © Cameramann International, Ltd., **600 TR,** © Zeynep Sumen/Tony Stone Images, **601 BR,** © D. Jenkin/Tropix Photographic Library, **603 TL,** © Wayland Publishers Limited/Wayland Publishers, Ltd., **604 TR,** © Robert Frerck/Woodfin Camp & Associates, **604 TL,** © Adam Woolfitt/Woodfin Camp & Associates, **605 CR,** © Bill Gasperiri/Impact Visuals, **608 TR,** © Buddy Mays/Travel Stock, **610 BR,** © Michael Newman/PhotoEdit, **614 CR,** © The Granger Collection, **616 CL,** © Erich Lessing/Art Resource, **617 BL,** © A. Ramey/Woodfin Camp & Associates, **618 B,** © Max Engel/Woodfin Camp & Associates, **619 TR,** © Al Stephenson/Woodfin Camp & Asscociates, **620 BL,** © Wolfgang Kaehler/Wolfgang Kaehler Photography, **621 TR,** © Serguei Fedorov/Woodfin Camp & Associates, **621 TL,** © J. Lee/Tropix Photographic Library, **622 TR,** © Wolfgang Kaehler/Wolfgang Kaehler Photography, **622 TL,** © Chuck Nacke/Woodfin Camp & Associates, **623 B,** © Ian Murphy/Tony Stone Images, **625 BR,** © A. Ramey/Woodfin Camp & Associates, **626 CL,** © Alistair Duncan/Dorling Kindersley, **627 BL,** © Cameramann International, Ltd., **627 CR,** © ASAP/Israel Talby/Woodfin Camp & Associates, **628 BL,** © Israel Talby/Woodfin Camp & Associates, **629 TL,** © AFP/Corbis-Bettman, **630 BL,** © Nabeel Turner/Tony Stone Images, **631 CL,** Wolfgang Kaehler/CORBIS/MAGMA, **632 BL,** © Barry Iverson/Woodfin Camp & Associates, **632 TR,** © Barry Iverson/Woodfin Camp & Associates, **633 BL,** © Barry Iverson/Woodfin Camp & Associates, **633 CR,** © Jane Lewis/Tony Stone Images, **635 BL,** © Wolfgang Kaehler/Wolfgang Kaehler Photography, **636 C,** Associated Press, AP, **638 BR,** © Eastfoto/Sovfoto, **638 CL,** © Eastfoto/Sovfoto, **639 TL,** © Buddy Mays/Travel Stock, **640 BR,** © Feldman & Associates, **641 T,** Text and artwork copyright © 1996 by YAHOO!, Inc. All rights reserved. YAHOO! and the YAHOO! logo are trademarks of YAHOO!, Inc./Feldman & Associates, **645 BR,** © SuperStock International, **647 B,** © Patrick Ward/Tony Stone Images, **647 CR,** © Tammy Peluso/Tom Stack & Associates, **649 CR,** © Doug Armand/Tony Stone Images, **649 TL,** © Philip & Karen Smith/Tony Stone Images, **650 BL,** B. & C. Alexander/Bryan & Cherry Alexander Photography, **651 TL,** © Wolfgang Kaehler/Wolfgang Kaehler Photography, **652 TL,** © Paul Chesley/Tony Stone Images, **653 TR,** © Wolfgang Kaehler/Wolfgang Kaehler Photography, **654 B,** © Wolfgang Kaehler/Wolfgang Kaehler Photography, **655 T,** © Ahrem Land, Northern Territory, Australia/SuperStock International, **656 TL,** © Reuters/Corbis-Bettman, **656 TR,** © Zigy Kaluzny/Tony Stone Images, **657 BR,** © Robert Frerck/Tony Stone Images, **658 BL,** © Tony Stone Images, **659 CR,** © Wolfgang Kaehler/Wolfgang Kaehler Photography, **659 TL,** © Wolfgang Kaehler/Wolfgang Kaehler Photography, **660 B,** © Randy Wells/Tony Stone Images, **661 CL,** Michael S. Yamashita/CORBIS/MAGMA, **662 BL,** © SuperStock International, **663 TL,** © SuperStock International, **664 BR,** © Michael Newman/PhotoEdit, **668 BC,** © Michael Newman/PhotoEdit, **669 TL,** © Michael Newman/PhotoEdit, **669 TR,** © Michael Newman/PhotoEdit, **670 B,** © Mark Thayer, Boston, **671 CR,** © Charles Gupton/Tony Stone Images, **673 BL,** © Mark Thayer, Boston, **674 CL,** © Steve Leonard/Tony Stone Images, **674 B,** © Robert Frerck/Odyssey Productions, **675 CL,** © Wolfgang Kaehler/Wolfgang Kaehler Photography, **675 BL,** © John Elk/Tony Stone Images, **675 BR,** © Will & Deni McIntyre/Tony Stone Images, **685 B,** © G. Brad Lewis/Tony Stone Images, **687 BR,** © Nigel Press/Tony Stone Images, **690–741,** Flags, The Flag Institute, Chester, **690–691 background,** Artbase Inc., **691 CL,** Artbase Inc., **691 BR,** Artbase Inc., **692–693 background,** Artbase Inc., **694–697 background,** Artbase Inc., **696 TL,** Artbase Inc., **696 BR,** Artbase Inc., **697 TR,** Artbase Inc., **698–699 background,** Artbase Inc., **700–703 background,** Artbase Inc., **704–705 background,** Artbase Inc., **704 BR,** Artbase Inc., **705 TL,** Artbase Inc., **705 BC,** Artbase Inc., **706–707 background,** Artbase Inc., **707 C,** Artbase Inc., **707 BR,** Artbase Inc., **708–709 background,** Artbase Inc., **709 C,** Artbase Inc., **710–711 background,** Artbase Inc., **712–713 background,** Artbase Inc., **714–715 background,** Artbase Inc., **716 BR,** Artbase Inc., **716–717 background,** Artbase Inc., **717 CR,** Artbase Inc., **718–719 background,** Artbase Inc., **720–721 background,** Artbase Inc., **722 background,** Artbase Inc., **723 BR,** Artbase Inc., **723 BL,** Artbase Inc., **724–725 background,** Artbase Inc., **726–727 background,** Artbase Inc., **728–729 background,** Artbase Inc., **730–735 background,** Artbase Inc., **736–741 background,** Artbase Inc., **737 BC,** Artbase Inc., **758–765,** Flags, the Flag Institute, Chester, **766 BL,** © John Beatty/Tony Stone Images, **766 TL,** © A & L Sinibaldi/ Tony Stone Images, **766–767 B,** © Spencer Swanger/Tom Stack & Associates, **767 CR,** © Paul Chesley/Tony Stone Images, **767 TL,** © Hans Strand/Tony Stone Images.